MW01037194

A Limited Edition
of

THE LIFE OF HERBERT HOOVER
Imperfect Visionary, 1918-1928

Presented by the Herbert Hoover
Presidential Library Association, Inc.

To:

Copy Number_____

THE LIFE OF HERBERT HOOVER
Imperfect Visionary
1918–1928

THE LIFE OF
HERBERT HOOVER

★★★★

IMPERFECT VISIONARY

1918–1928

KENDRICK A. CLEMENTS

palgrave
macmillan

First published in 2010 by PALGRAVE MACMILLAN® in the United States—a division of St. Martin's Press LLC, 175 Fifth Avenue, New York, NY 10010.

Where this book is distributed in the UK, Europe, and the rest of the world, this is by Palgrave Macmillan, a division of Macmillan Publishers Limited, registered in England, company number 785998, of Houndmills, Basingstoke, Hampshire RG21 6XS.

Palgrave Macmillan is the global academic imprint of the above companies and has companies and representatives throughout the world.

Palgrave® and Macmillan® are registered trademarks in the United States, the United Kingdom, Europe and other countries.

ISBN: 978-0-230-10308-5

Library of Congress Cataloging-in-Publication Data is available from the Library of Congress.

A catalogue record of the book is available from the British Library.

Design by Scribe Inc.

First edition: June 2010

10 9 8 7 6 5 4 3 2 1

Printed in the United States of America.

For Ryland Alden Clements

Contents

Preface ix

1 Feeding Europe, 1918–1919 1

2 Family Affairs, 1918–1920 27

3 An Economic Program for the Consumer Society 35

4 The Election of 1920 49

5 The European Relief Program, September 1919–1921 71

6 Family and Business, 1921 87

7 The Commerce Department, 1921 101

8 The 1921 Unemployment Conference 131

9 The Russian Famine, 1921–1923 149

10 Hoover and the American Child Health Association 161

11 Family, 1922–1923 181

12 Hoover's Economic Idealism 195

13 The Commerce Department, 1922 209

14 The Commerce Department, 1923 239

15 Alaska and Washington, 1923–1924 265

16   The Commerce Department, 1924   281

17   The Commerce Department, 1925   303

18   Family and Public Service, 1925–1928   325

19   The Commerce Department, 1926–1928   341

20   The Mississippi River and New England Floods of 1927   371

21   The Election of 1928   395

22   Imperfect Visionary   427

Notes   433

Bibliography   571

Index   593

Preface

This fourth volume of *The Life of Herbert Hoover* begins where George Nash's third volume, *Master of Emergencies, 1917–1918* (1996) ended, with the armistice at the end of World War I in November 1918. It carries the story forward to his election to the presidency, in November 1928. I urge readers who would like to know more about Hoover's youth and career prior to 1918 to read Nash's splendid volumes, but I have tried to make this volume sufficiently self-contained so that it can be read separately from Nash's earlier works.

Hoover faced an unprecedented situation in November 1918. The war that had just ended had swept away the imperial trappings of the "long nineteenth century," leaving even the victors more weakened than they initially realized and destroying the Russian, Ottoman, and Austro-Hungarian empires that had dominated Eastern and Central Europe. The Bolshevik Revolution in Russia had unleashed civil war and transformed one of the most backward nations into a laboratory for radical political experimentation. Only the United States had emerged from the war vastly strengthened, economically and militarily.

President Woodrow Wilson welcomed self-determination for the subject peoples of the old empires and proposed to create a new order of democratic states cooperating to keep the peace through a League of Nations. In an unprecedented step, he planned to attend the peace conference in Paris to ensure that the peace treaty really embodied his vision. His task, in the face of the war's devastation, the Allied desires for vengeance on the Germans and Austrians, and the defeated nations' bitterness, would be monumental.

To deal with some of the war's legacies and to create a firm foundation for his new political order, Wilson asked the head of the American Food Administration, forty-four-year-old Herbert Hoover, to expand his wartime relief program for Belgium into a continent-wide relief and rehabilitation plan. The challenge, as Wilson and Hoover saw it, involved not only feeding the hungry but also, especially in Central Europe, where new states had been carved out of the old Russian, Ottoman, and Austro-Hungarian empires, helping to build or rebuild administrative structures, restore agricultural and industrial production, and reconstruct distribution systems interrupted by war and new national boundaries. Hoover thus faced a task no less Herculean than Wilson's, and his success in it would lead to his being identified, ever after, as "the great humanitarian." It would also bring him further relief assignments, in Russia in 1921 to 1923 and in the Mississippi River Valley and New England in 1927.

Following Hoover's return to the United States in September 1919, President Wilson turned to him again, this time to serve in a national conference to seek remedies for the industrial conflicts tearing the economy apart. His work in that role, as well as his humanitarian endeavors, marked him as a potential presidential candidate in 1920, a role that he eventually accepted, albeit reluctantly and halfheartedly. Eliminated as a candidate before the Republican convention, he tried and failed to persuade Warren Harding to support ratification of the Treaty of Versailles. When Harding won the election, he asked Hoover to join his administration as secretary of commerce. Some people wondered at his acceptance of a department whose duties had traditionally been only to "put the fishes to bed and [light] the lamps on the coast," but Hoover asked for and received authority to range widely, well beyond the usual limits of the Commerce Department's authority. Republican conservatives suspected, correctly, that he would push his authority as far as he could. The easygoing Harding did not mind, but Hoover would clash with some of his cabinet colleagues as he poached on their territory and with President Coolidge.[1]

The gusto with which Hoover embraced his new assignment led to him being referred to in Washington as "secretary of commerce and undersecretary of everything else." In addition to reorganizing and expanding the activities of the Commerce Department, he also pushed aggressively to control agricultural marketing, both in the United States and abroad, ventured onto State Department turf by urging the appointment of Commerce Department attachés overseas and by demanding authority to evaluate proposed foreign loans, and trespassed on Treasury Department territory by offering policy recommendations on the repayment of Allied war loans, German reparations, and the Federal Reserve's rediscount rates. He also reached out to bring regulation of radio and aviation under the control of the Commerce Department, and he accepted the chairmanship of an interstate commission to apportion the water of the Colorado River and another to do the same for the Rio Grande, as well as continuing work with the American Relief Administration, the chairmanship of a committee to investigate construction of a waterway from the Great Lakes to the Atlantic, and a number of other official or semiofficial committees. Although he failed to solve some of the problems he tackled and moved to the White House in 1929 with other initiatives still incomplete, he believed that he had improved life for most Americans. Years later, he looked back on the Commerce period as "happy years of constructive work."[2]

Hoover identified his primary goal in the Commerce Department as increasing "material welfare and standards of living for the American people." That meant distributing the fruits of the consumer economy as widely as possible, to elevate Americans' daily lives not only materially but also intellectually and spiritually. To do that, he strove to show labor and management that they shared a common interest in increasing production and making it more efficient. If the costs of production could be reduced and its volume increased, he argued, prices could be cut without reducing profits, and workers' wages would go further in purchasing both necessities and new products to make life easier and more pleasant. Trade associations, responsible labor unions, and shop councils could all foster such cooperation. The government, in Hoover's vision, would encourage and exercise general supervision over the process but would rely primarily on business to govern its own affairs.[3]

In practice, Hoover's dream of economic self-government proved elusive. In some troubled areas of the economy, such as agriculture, coal, and the railroads, little progress was made. In other areas, Commerce Department leadership became more heavy-handed than Hoover originally intended. Philosophically, he believed in limited government and voluntarism, but temperamentally, he inclined to governmental activism and strong leadership. He could never reconcile the two approaches fully.

A comparable ambivalence marked his approach to foreign relations. As Commerce Secretary, he made the expansion of trade and the search for foreign investment opportunities a major part of the department's mission. He not only cultivated new markets and investment opportunities in Asia and Latin America, but he also recognized that improving the economic and political health of America's major trading partners in Europe would make them better customers for American companies. His European relief work aimed not only to alleviate suffering but also to create political and economic stability that would serve American self-interest in the future. The importance of that objective led him to support ratification of the Treaty of Versailles and American membership in the League of Nations and the World Court, despite his belief that the treaty contained injustices that could exacerbate the very instability it tried to prevent. American membership in the World Court, he said in 1923, would not guarantee peace, but would "build . . . a little of the road to peace." As an even more practical step toward that ultimate goal, he also supported sharp reductions in European war debts to the United States, cuts in interest rates, and lengthy extensions in payment periods.[4]

Yet at the same time, he found excuses to support Harding in the 1920 presidential election and rejected outright cancellation of the debts. As secretary of commerce, he endorsed the protective tariff that curtailed the sales of European finished products in the United States while he favored keeping duties low on the raw materials that American companies needed. He warned American companies that they faced cutthroat competition from European firms and urged them to do everything in their power to undersell foreign products. He constantly warned his colleagues in the administration that the European nations sought a closed European economic system that excluded American trade and investments. Foreign monopoly control over raw materials critical to American businesses, such as rubber, loomed in his mind as a dangerous threat. In short, at the same time that he pushed international economic interdependence and political cooperation, Hoover pursued an economic nationalism that saw the United States as struggling to compete rather than as the world's dominant trader and investor.

Contemporary observers often noted that Hoover, although a talented executive and administrator, had none of the skills of a politician. Painfully shy, exceptionally sensitive to attacks, and a poor public speaker, he relied on logic backed by reams of statistics to gain support for his ideas. Some members of Congress, listening to him testify on problems facing the government, felt that he was talking down to them. His range of interests and substantial knowledge about a dazzling number of subjects could make him intimidating to those who knew him casually. Bowled over by the force of his arguments, people sometimes found themselves agreeing to take actions with which they did not fully agree and later regretted. His family and those who knew him well or worked closely with him, however, found him charming and warm. On camping and fishing trips, he relaxed and told fascinating stories about his experiences around the world. Above all, his friends and co-workers found his dedication to public service inspiring. Those who worked with him in the Belgian relief program or the Food Administration remained admirers all his life and happily came to his call whenever he asked.

As an orphan raised on the frontier by his aunt and uncle, Hoover climbed from poverty to wealth and power largely through his own hard work and intelligence. Like many people in such circumstances, he regarded his personal values as the explanation for his success and thought that if individuals and nations followed his path, they too would succeed. Engineering's rational analysis of the world, he believed, showed the way people could control their own destinies and plan their routes to happiness and prosperity. In a decade when the promise of technology seemed unlimited, wealth excited general admiration, and most people looked forward to increasing prosperity, Hoover exemplified success and hence seemed to many people an ideal leader for the times.

From his Quaker background and wartime experience, Hoover drew the lesson that the American people would respond generously to appeals for voluntary commitment to a common cause. If leaders analyzed problems rationally, he became convinced, and presented them to the public as challenges requiring cooperative action, Americans would answer their call. Lacking the habit of introspection and moving rapidly from issue to issue, he rarely looked back to assess which programs had actually succeeded and which failed. President Coolidge, who viewed his endless ideas and recommendations for government action with skepticism, referred to him derisively as "wonder boy."

Yet whatever his limitations, Hoover did enormous good during his public career. His relief work alone saved many millions of lives. "Few men who have ever lived," wrote the journalist Bruce Bliven, "had so good a claim on the world's gratitude." Moreover, as secretary of commerce, Hoover did much to build the transportation, power, communications, and credit networks upon which the consumer economy depended. Amid racial, ethnic, religious, and cultural divisions at home and international instability, he worked hard to help Americans make the transition from nineteenth-century rural isolation to urban-industrial world power. His colleagues' limitations, as well as his own background and experience, shaped and sometimes restricted his ideas, but his extraordinary energy, intelligence, and capacity for hard work made him an outstanding leader during the decade.[5]

Neither Hoover nor his colleagues foresaw the coming economic catastrophe of the Great Depression. Hoover believed that the policies he initiated had largely tamed the business cycle and made crashes unlikely. Obviously, he was wrong, but there is no doubt that his work helped to advance economists' understanding of the way the economy worked and began to familiarize politicians with the possibility that government could take steps to control its fluctuations. I have tried to outline what I think are the strengths and limitations of his approach, but it seems to me that ongoing debates among economists and historians about the causes of the depression should make us cautious in assessing blame.

A biographer dealing with a person who has Hoover's range of activities confronts a problem. On one hand, it makes sense to take up a specific issue—his struggle to rationalize the railroad industry, for example—explain its background, and carry the story of his involvement through to its completion. That approach, however, obscures the degree to which a large number of issues landed on his desk all at once, interacted with each other, and demanded simultaneous consideration. To convey that aspect of his experience, I have followed a generally chronological rather than topical organization. I have tried to minimize the repetition required to remind readers where each issue stands when it comes up a second or third time.

I first began working on Hoover (though not on this book) in the mid-1980s. The indispensable resource for anyone working on Hoover and his era is the Herbert Hoover Presidential Library in West Branch, Iowa, and in my experience, it offers one of the most pleasant places to work within the National Archives and Record Administration. When I began working there, Tom Thalken was its director; when I finished, Tim Walch had assumed the position. Both were invariably supportive and accessible. The staff remained remarkably stable over those years and made the library an easy and happy place to work. Brad Bauer, Jim Detlefson, Kathy Grace, Pam Hinkhouse, Mildred Mather, Scott Nolen, Matt Schaefer, Shirley Sondergard, Robert Wood, Cindy Worrell, and Craig Wright all went beyond the call of duty to make my work pleasant as well as rewarding. Spencer Howard, Dale Mayer, Dwight and Pauline Miller, Lynn Smith, and Pat and Mary Wildenberg deserve special thanks, not only for their willingness to share their deep knowledge of all issues Hooverian but also for their many kindnesses to me both during and after working hours. Jim Norris, a longtime volunteer at the library, offered entertaining asides during working hours and friendly guidance to the sights of the region. Elsewhere, Carol Leadenham at the Hoover Institution and Carol Rudisill at the Stanford University Library, along with many other archivists and librarians, gave me valuable help and guidance. Jennifer Kepler, at Scribe, copyedited the manuscript thoroughly and constructively, steering me away from many small errors, although I fear that some remain despite her best efforts.

The Hoover Presidential Library Association, the sponsor of the biography, provided generous economic and intellectual support for the project without ever hinting that its members wanted to control or influence my interpretation in any way. Pat Forsythe, Ruth Farmer, Kathy Frederick, Cathy Hammel, Pat Hand, and Kelly Lamb made my job easier in many ways, not least by allowing me to stay for extended periods at the house owned by the Association on Main Street and by paying my endless photocopying bills without complaint. The association's trustees all took an interest in the project and treated me with great kindness, but I owe a special debt to Audrey and John Kofoed and Herbert Wilson, who went several extra miles for me.

A number of fellow scholars provided me with valuable advice and encouragement at various times. They include Gary Dean Best, Nicholas Clifford, Lawrence Gelfand, Mark Hall, David Hamilton, Martin Horn, Lee Nash, Geoffrey Smith, David Tyler, Hal Wert, and Silvano Wueschner. Elliot and Carol Rosen offered both stimulating critiques of my conclusions and warm hospitality, both in Iowa City and New Jersey. George Nash's first three volumes of the biography set a high standard for the other authors to aim at, and George himself has been unfailingly generous in sharing his own remarkable knowledge of Hoover. I have noted a few places in the book where his expertise was particularly valuable, but his influence goes far beyond that recognized in the endnotes.

Two distinguished historians of this period, Ellis Hawley and Stephen Schuker, read the penultimate version of the manuscript. Professor Hawley's thorough reading and generous comments both encouraged and guided me as I began revisions. My copy of his comments is covered with my notes and questions as one step led to the next. Professor Schuker gave the manuscript the most meticulous reading I have ever received for my work, and his detailed comments on content and helpful suggestions about where to look for further information were combined with excellent recommendations for improvements in the writing. I am delighted to acknowledge the debt I owe these two scholars for strengthening the book in a variety of ways and to absolve them of any responsibility for remaining weaknesses.

As anyone who had tried to write a book knows, family and friends also play important roles in the process. Don and Nancy Barnby, Dave and Susie Hodges, Tom and Valen Brown, Jon and Deborah Krass, Neal and Ann McNabb, Dick and Ann Rempel, Miriam Spongberg, Wilson Clements, Carole Weaver, James Clements, and as always, my wife, Linda Clements, inspired, encouraged, and sustained me. Our new grandson, Ryland Alden Clements, will surely inspire future projects.

CHAPTER 1

Feeding Europe, 1918–1919

On the evening of November 23, 1918, five Americans and four British officials sat down to dinner at the Ritz Hotel in London. Although the armistice had been signed more than a week before, Londoners still felt suspended between war and peace. Blackout curtains covered the restaurant's windows, and dimmed streetlights outside cast a subdued glow. Piles of sandbags surrounded railroad bridges and building entrances, reminders that German airships had bombed the city only a few weeks before. In Regents Park, captured German airplanes and artillery lined the paths for the pleasure of residents, and small boys climbed over them and took away parts for souvenirs. Despite the chilly, gloomy weather, people smiled at each other in the streets.[1]

The Americans, led by Herbert Hoover, age forty-four, U.S. food administrator, chairman of the U.S. Grain Corporation, head of the Sugar Equalization Board, chairman of the Inter-Allied Food Council, and commissioner for relief in Belgium, represented a still-developing American program to restore Europe's civilian economy and feed those brought to the brink of starvation by the war. The British had requested a meeting with them to inquire whether the Americans could be ready in two or three weeks to begin food shipments. To their astonishment, they heard that the first ships were already on the ocean and that Hoover's men expected to be at work within days, not weeks.[2]

I

On November 25, two days after the London meeting, Hoover left for Paris to start operations there. With him he carried a bleak report from nutritional

1

expert Dr. Alonzo Taylor estimating German and Austrian cereal, potato, and fat resources at roughly half the levels needed to prevent starvation. Taylor's report overstated shortages in Germany, but with winter only weeks away, sustaining other parts of central and Eastern Europe would require Herculean measures. Within days, Hoover's men arrived on the docks in Britain, Belgium, and France, surveying the situation and arranging for the unloading of ships and the transportation of food. Inland, in Belgium and France, they discovered that they would have to replace miles of railroad track blown up by the retreating Germans before shipments could move.[3]

Letters from Hoover's young American assistants revealed no discouragement or pessimism about the monumental problems they faced. One letter writer likened the miles of twisted railroad tracks to "fluted edging on a dress." Finding new rails and laying them would be a nuisance, not an impossibility. Confident that their "chief" would slash through red tape, welcome their doing likewise, and provide the resources they needed to do their jobs, they leaped into the work. Brash, impatient, and irreverent, they epitomized the "can-do" Americanism that both delighted and sometimes outraged Europeans.[4]

Having traveled frequently to Belgium and France during the war, Hoover knew better than anyone in the Wilson administration what physical devastation the conflict had left in much of Europe and, even more serious, how it had destroyed industry and trade, crippled agriculture, slaughtered a generation of young men, and brought whole nations to the brink of destitution and starvation. The war had left behind pessimism, depression, and bitterness as well as physical destruction. Unless the Americans could restore hope, Hoover feared that political extremism would sweep the continent. During the war, Hoover's Commission for Relief in Belgium (CRB) had demonstrated how American food and other aid could sustain a nation even in the midst of catastrophe. As the war neared its end, he recommended to the president that the CRB be continued and expanded for postwar relief. Wilson also saw the danger. On November 7, 1918, he instructed Hoover to create "a single agency" based on an expanded CRB to "coordinate the whole effort of the American people and government, in the furnishing of supplies, machinery, finance, exchange, shipping, trade relations and philanthropic aid." Hoover and his assistants had arrived in Europe to inaugurate the work of the new American Relief Administration (ARA; see Figure 7.1).[5]

Hoover expected the ARA to provide humanitarian aid, but he also meant to protect American interests. He warned the president that Allied leaders still intended, as they had since 1916, to create an organization that would control postwar food distribution and would attempt to exclude American trade and investment from the continent in coming years. Anticipating that the United States would provide more than half of the "export food supplies of the world" for some time after the armistice, he contended that American acceptance of the Allied plan would enable the Europeans to dictate "prices and distribution." Such an arrangement would be economically disadvantageous to the United States, and moreover, it would prevent the American government from using its resources to "maintain justice all around." Hoover proposed to use the leverage created by American aid to maintain an "open door" in Europe—to lay the foundations, in other words, for international economic cooperation comparable to the political cooperation Wilson hoped to foster through the League of Nations.[6]

Before leaving the United States, Hoover arranged to have the army begin shipping food to southern France for distribution in Central Europe and asked the president to request a special appropriation from Congress to fund the relief program. With Wilson's permission, he also authorized the U.S. Grain Corporation to ship to the neutral states of northern Europe, recognizing that some of those shipments would find their way into still-blockaded Germany. Nevertheless, that arrangement left the nations of the former German and Austro-Hungarian empires, still technically defined as enemies, inadequately provided for. But senators with whom Hoover discussed the matter before he sailed to Europe told him that wartime animosity in Congress made passage of direct relief for those states impossible. Hoover shared the hostility to the German government and military, but the hunger of German and Austrian civilians, especially children, seemed different to him.[7]

Many years later, Hoover wrote that the plight of children in postwar Europe had moved him more than any other aspect of the suffering he witnessed. Malnourished, orphaned, diseased, and stunted children, he believed, were "pitiable," but more importantly, their distorted minds would make them "a menace to their nations," and eventually, "a menace to all mankind." Children's welfare would remain a major preoccupation for the rest of his life.[8]

Often noted by contemporaries and historians, Hoover's obsession with children's welfare has never been explained definitively. He himself did not regard it as sufficiently unusual to require explanation. The "love of children," he observed, "is a biological trait common to all races." Historians, insofar as they have dealt with the matter at all, have usually attributed his concern to his being orphaned early and raised in a strongly Quaker community. Since he usually described his childhood as idyllic and rarely talked about his religious views, however, the role of his childhood experiences and religion in his adult psyche must remain speculative.[9] Never introspective, Hoover may not have known the origin of his feelings.

Efficient organization provided the foundations for the success of Hoover's European relief operation. To supplement the minuscule civilian staff he had brought with him or could borrow from Food Administration offices in Europe, he requisitioned officers from the U.S. Army and dispatched them, along with civilian representatives, to survey conditions and begin setting up relief offices in major capitals. Recruiting the soldiers proved a masterstroke. They were physically fit, self-reliant, accustomed to living in Europe and working with Europeans, and since in most cases they continued to draw their army pay, using them saved the relief program money. Best of all, they gave the ARA authority and official status. As General John J. Pershing observed, "Officers in uniform in many places would be able to do more than if they were not in uniform."[10]

The speed and efficiency with which Hoover's men set to work impressed the British and French, but that only made them more determined to control the operation through the Supreme War Council that had been established to coordinate military operations. Hoover and Edward M. House, who had been handling armistice and postarmistice negotiations on behalf of the president, met in Paris shortly after Hoover arrived. They agreed that unless the United States had complete control over relief, the Europeans would bend it to their own interests. House suggested, nevertheless, as a sop to the British and French, that Hoover, as director general of relief, accept the nominal authority of the Supreme War Council. The council would set "united policies," but Hoover would maintain actual control by directing day-to-day operations.[11]

On December 10, Hoover met with Allied leaders in London to discuss the control issue. The Americans, he declared blandly, did not intend relief to be "solely an undertaking by the American Government" and accepted that the Supreme War Council would control "broad policies." Inasmuch as the British had been saying, at least in public, that they only wanted to reassure Europeans about their support of the relief program, this face-saving formula seemed to meet their wishes without weakening American authority. But, of course, as Hoover well understood, the British and French actually wanted joint control for other reasons, primarily "to prevent Germans from getting raw materials to compete against them in markets of the world." As the meeting went on, the Allied leaders shifted their ground adroitly, dropping the proposal of "an Allied administrative board" for relief and raising new issues about the use of German ships to carry relief supplies. They also suggested the creation of an inter-Allied council to control not merely relief shipments but "all raw material, finance, transportation, and food" for the Allies as well as the rest of Europe. That proposal confirmed Hoover's darkest suspicions about British and French intentions. They had not abandoned the goals they had set in 1916. Furious, he exploded to Gordon Auchincloss, House's son-in-law and private secretary, that the United States should simply "start sending food to these peoples irrespective of what the Allies did."[12]

On Saturday, December 14, President Wilson arrived in Paris. Millions of people lined the streets to welcome him, but Hoover's men had little use for such pomp and ceremony. As a great roar signaled the approach of the president on the boulevard, wrote one of them, a "poor scared yellow dog comes lickety split down the center of the broad street, seeking some opening to escape and seeing none short of the end of the avenue a mile away and determined to get there as soon as possible." Then came the open carriages bearing Wilson, President Poincaré, and other dignitaries, and "in a few minutes . . . the great event of Wilson's arrival was accomplished."[13]

Irreverent though his men might be, Hoover found Wilson's presence in Paris helpful. On December 15, he and the president drafted a blunt message to the Allies reaffirming the American insistence on sole control over the relief program. Unwilling to break with the Americans over the issue, the French and British capitulated. On January 11, 1919, Wilson named Hoover director general of relief in Europe, although the appointment did not become official until February 24, after Congress passed an aid bill. Hoover spent long hours over the next months in meetings of the impressively titled Supreme Council of Supply and Relief and its successor (after February 7), the Supreme Economic Council. Those organizations theoretically oversaw shipping, the blockade, transportation, and finances, as well as food, but in practice they exercised little control over the ARA's operations. The council's meetings became so boring and pointless, Hoover recalled in his *Memoirs*, that the Americans "arranged shifts . . . by which one of our members attended the meeting each day and the others carried on their work."[14]

Hoover did not wait for final agreement on the structure of the relief program to start work. As soon as his men submitted reports on conditions in Central and Eastern Europe, he authorized them to set up offices, inviting Allied representatives to join them when they were ready, but making it clear that his people would go ahead regardless of what others might do. Since aid recipients soon realized that the Americans controlled the program, Allied representatives in most cities had little to do. Pending congressional action on the special relief appropriation requested by the president, Hoover got Wilson to order the War Department to continue to ship food to European ports and to transfer $5 million from his National Security and Defense Fund to make initial payments.[15]

On December 1, clergymen across the country read Hoover's appeal to Americans to observe a "food conservation week for world relief" to their congregations. By Christmas, the Paris staff had outgrown their original two rooms in the Hotel Crillon and spread out into ten rooms. Shortly after the first of the year, they moved again, to a fifty-room apartment building at 51 Avenue Montaigne. More to the point, they already had over a hundred ships on the seas headed for ports in the neutral and liberated countries of Europe. Hoover ordered their captains to ignore any blockade that attempted to prevent them from landing their cargoes, and the American Navy assured Hoover that they would make sure no one interfered with the shipments.[16] The Supreme Council might set policy to its heart's content. Hoover would do as he thought best.

In the early days of the program, and to some extent throughout it, the costs of supplying food for relief far outran the money available to pay for supplies. Despite Hoover's December appeal for donations, he never expected to fund the relief program with private charity. Only governments had the resources required to meet Europe's vast needs. The president's $5 million and the provisions secured from the army provided only drops in the ocean of need, however, and Hoover refused to await congressional action. He asked for and received Wilson's permission to have the U.S. Grain Corporation use its borrowing power and administrative resources to buy and ship food, often on the basis of little more than faith that the recipients, Congress, and the Allied governments would pay eventually. Lacking legal authorization for purchases, he sometimes made them on no more than his private word. At one point, he estimated, the Grain Corporation's and his personal obligations exceeded $550 million.[17]

Arranging relief for the former enemy nations proved tougher than controlling the relief program. Hoover had no love for the Central Powers, but he believed that, for humanitarian reasons and the future stability of Europe, Germany and Austria must be assisted. His tolerance had limits, however. When the Germans asked for a meeting with him to discuss relief and proposed to send as their representatives two officers who had been particularly notorious in the occupation of Belgium, he lost his temper and instructed Walter Lyman Brown, director of the Belgian relief program, to "tell the pair personally to go to hell with my compliments." Then, having vented his feelings, he had second thoughts and ordered the message stopped. No one lamented, however, when it leaked to the press. It accurately reflected both Hoover's personal feelings and those of most Americans in the relief organization—but so did his suppression of it. Building the future, not reliving the past, must govern American policy.[18]

II

Before leaving for Europe, Hoover had told the press that, with the war over, the blockade of the enemy states should be relaxed. Germany, he said, did not need charity. The Germans could use their gold reserves to cover short-term needs, but only by reestablishing their economy and trade could they stabilize their economy and pay what they owed to Belgium and France for war damages. The blockade of Germany and Austria no longer had "any military or naval value," he advised Wilson on December 10, adding on December 20 that the relief program should be extended to Germany "not only out of humanity but . . . to prevent anarchy." Bolshevism had already achieved a foothold in many German cities, he warned, and separatist movements in some German states raised the possibility that the government would lose control of its domestic food sources. He argued that the blockade exemplified the sort of governmental barrier to free trade that had helped to cause the war and that could impede American access to European markets in the future.[19]

The Allies rejected Hoover's argument that the blockade no longer had any military purpose. Fighting had stopped, to be sure, but only on the basis of an armistice, not a peace treaty. Until the Germans signed a binding treaty, surrendered their merchant fleet, and agreed to pay reparations, the blockade remained the only effective tool the Allies had to put pressure on them. Cecil

Harmsworth, the acting British director of the postwar blockade, complained that "our American friends do not in the least realize that the blockade is not an arbitrary and vexatious system established by the European Allies for the purposes of obstructing trade, but that it is in fact an implement of war and now a lever for securing the results of war." Hoover persisted, however, and at the meeting of the Supreme Council for Supply and Relief on January 12, three months after the signing of the armistice, he insisted that conditions in Germany verged on starvation and anarchy. The other members of the council disagreed with his assessment, but cognizant of their need for American support, they reluctantly agreed to recommend to the Supreme War Council that if Germany surrendered its passenger and cargo fleet, limited shipments of grain and pork would be permitted to pass the blockade. The Germans, however, refused to hand over their ships unless guaranteed a full supply of food, warning that continuation of the blockade might lead to revolution and economic collapse that would make payment of reparations improbable, a threat that the rise of radical Spartacists in several German cities made plausible. Thus the stalemate continued.[20]

The blockade issue provided a special problem for the French. Not only did they regard its continuation as a valuable deterrent to a new German attack, but they also wanted to be assured that reparations would be the first charge against German gold reserves. Without those payments, they could see no way to finance the tremendous reconstruction costs they faced. Hence, they proposed to let Germany buy food only if the Americans would loan the German government money to pay for the shipments.[21]

Although the British needed reparations less than the French, another dispute between Washington and London prevented them from agreeing on a common policy. The problem related to wartime contracts with the Americans for future pork purchases. During the war, German submarines had largely cut Britain and France off from foreign food sources other than North America. To meet the Allied need for meat, Hoover's Food Administration "undertook large policies of expansion in production" of pork, including "price assurances [to American farmers] . . . at a level necessary to assure the production." The program succeeded, and even though it forced the Allies to pay more for pork than before the war, they accepted it because they had no choice. As long as the war continued, the arrangement satisfied both European purchasers and American producers, but when war ended more suddenly than anyone expected, the British and French, resentful of high wartime prices and finding their economies in shambles, decided to cancel future American pork contracts and buy on the world market.[22]

Although Hoover professed sympathy for the Europeans' situation, he raged privately at the cancellation. Not only would it be ruinous to American farmers who had loyally increased production and now faced a collapse of their market, but if the Europeans only honored their obligations for the next few months, he believed, the peak period of American production would be over, and farmers would have a year to adjust to a smaller market. Moreover, once the relief program got into full operation over the next few months, it seemed certain that every pound of American pork would be wanted, if not in Britain and France, then to feed the hungry peoples of Europe and particularly those of Germany and Austria. In mid-December, Hoover argued that the situation could work out without loss to anyone, provided the Allies would just honor their contracts for the next three months and agree to lift the food blockade on Germany. Instead, early in January, the British and French abruptly canceled commitments to buy both pork and wheat. The wheat could be stored until demand increased, but perishable meat could not. Hoover warned that unless the Allies reversed their decision immediately, the American pork industry would almost certainly default on several hundred million dollars in bank loans, and there would be "a debacle in the American markets."[23]

The best solution to the crisis, Hoover argued, would be for the British and French to honor their contracts (perhaps at a reduced level) and resell the food to the Germans, but arranging that would take time. If the Germans used their gold reserves to buy American pork, the French pointed out, they would have less with which to pay reparations. Pending some arrangement of that and other problems, Hoover suggested stopgaps, including an increase in relief shipments to northern Europe and more pork purchases by the army. Unsympathetic to the French outlook, he continued his efforts to get the food blockade against Germany relaxed and suggested a short-term loan to the British to make it easier for them to honor their contracts and then resell to the Germans.[24]

Secretary of the Treasury Carter Glass objected to any such loan. By enabling the Europeans to buy pork at artificially high prices, the loan would drive up prices for American consumers as well as those in other countries, he argued, and indeed many Americans already blamed Hoover for high food prices. Hoover conceded that restoration of a free market was desirable, but he pointed out that so long as the British and French continued to use "consolidated buying agencies" such as the Allied Purchasing Commission, no free market existed. If those agencies halted their American purchases, the result would be "a total collapse of price, far below its natural level and one that may be [a] complete disaster to the American people." Until collective purchasing could be phased out, the Europeans would remain in the driver's seat.[25]

Hoover also contended to the British that the pork contracts represented more than just legal obligations. They embodied, he declared, a "moral obligation" created when American farmers undertook to produce "far beyond any commercial justification of [the] normal market" to help the Allies. He warned that cancellation would cause "a financial crisis in the United States" and, having overcome Glass's objections, renewed the loan proposal. Privately, he speculated that "certain people in London" intended to "break our market."[26]

In fact, the price collapse in the United States that Hoover feared never took place. When price controls ended on March 1, 1919, domestic pork prices remained high. Hoover had no good explanation for this situation, attributing it improbably to "the law of supply and demand." Of course, by that time, the peak period of pork production had passed and the relief program had taken over as a major purchaser of pork. Obviously Hoover had overestimated the threat.[27]

Hoover's warnings about an economic catastrophe in the United States seemed reasonable in early 1919, however, and many members of the British government acknowledged the "moral obligation" he preached. British leaders also realized that Germany, France, and Italy faced fat shortages and that the French and Italians had threatened to break with the British and resume purchases of American grain and pork. The British tried to hold out for an American loan to pay not only for grain and pork but also for all British purchases in the United States, but Hoover would have nothing to do with that. In the end, the British gave in, accepting Hoover's proposal of an American loan to permit them to honor their pork and wheat contracts in the United States and resell the products to Germany.[28]

The resolution of the "pork battle" cleared the way for a solution of the blockade impasse by creating an incentive for the British to open food sales to Germany. But even so, progress on the issue dragged. The French remained opposed to any arrangement that might draw hard currency out of Germany other than for reparations payments, and the Germans held out stubbornly against surrendering their merchant fleet unless assured they would get all the food they needed. Indeed, the French even opposed lifting the blockade on the neutrals for fear that doing so would permit the Germans to circumvent restrictions on their trade. "No right in the law of God or man" justified that policy, Hoover declared sanctimoniously, although he admitted privately that food would "filter in through the surrounding neutrals" unless the blockade remained in effect.[29]

Early in February 1919 and again at the beginning of March, the Germans, Americans, and Allies held low-level talks at Spa, Belgium, to try to resolve the issue of the German fleet. The Germans and French both remained immovable. Discouraged at the lack of progress during February, Hoover feared the United States would "have to play a lone hand in relief." But by early March, the British, as well as the Americans, began to recognize that trying to isolate Germany was like "living on a volcano." On March 1, Hoover met with the chief British delegate to the Supreme Economic Council, Lord Robert Cecil, to discuss what could be done. Lord Robert, whom Hoover regarded as "a sensible man," agreed that the time had come to force a showdown with the French over the blockade. Following the breakdown of the second set of Spa talks, the council took up the issue on March 7. David Lloyd George, the British prime minister, presented the Anglo-American position forcefully. The British and Americans argued that if the French would agree to permit the Germans to import 270,000 tons of already promised food at once and 370,000 tons a month until September 1, they believed Berlin would agree to surrender their ships, but still the French would not budge. In the end, the council could only agree to pass the buck to the Council of Ten, where the heads of state would have to struggle with it. The council devoted two days of debate to the issue, and on March 8, it proposed a compromise. The blockade would be eased and the Germans permitted to use gold to pay for food but only after they surrendered their ships.[30]

On March 13 and 14, American, British, French, and Italian representatives met with a German delegation in Brussels and informed them the food blockade would be lifted as soon as Germany surrendered its merchant vessels and deposited enough gold to cover the cost of the food being supplied. Tying the surrender of the ships to relaxation of the blockade saved face for the Germans, although the Allies did their best to cover up any appearance of a concession by having the agreement signed in Belgium, so recently occupied by Germany. Hoover attended the ceremony and enjoyed watching Belgian soldiers march the German delegates to the signing table. From his point of view, the outcome represented an acceptable compromise. He had lost the battle for unconditional termination of the blockade but protected American pork producers and assured that the Germans would get the food they needed. After the meeting, he ordered the SS Carnifax, en route to Europe with a load of wheat, to dock at Hamburg. Its cargo, landed on March 25, provided the first installment of about 1.2 million tons of food delivered to Germany during the armistice period (November 1918 to January 1920). The United States provided a little more than half, for which the German government paid $173,645,000 in gold. More than twice as much food went to Germany during this period than to the second-largest recipient, Austria, and together the two former enemy states received 42 percent of all food relief.[31]

In the midst of this stress and conflict, Hoover remained mostly "as fit as a fiddle," although some problems with his teeth required a few unpleasant trips to the dentist. Adapting to European customs, he started his day about 9:30 AM and then worked until about 8:00 in the evening, returning to the "frivolous white-and-gold mansion" he had rented at 19 rue de Lübeck for dinner and conversation with whichever members of the ARA happened to be in town. Then, reported one of them, "at ten of the clock he clutches a blood-and-thunder story and goes off to bed." At the rate he consumed the novels, his friends feared, "there wont [sic] be enough books to see him through the Peace Conference." On Sundays, Hoover and whichever ARA men might be available sometimes drove out into the French and Belgian countryside to see portions of the former front lines or to visit a cathedral.[32]

III

Hoover's central role in every economic issue made him, after Wilson and House, the most important American at Paris and a major figure at the peace conference. As director general of relief, he had great autonomy and ultimately answered to no one but the Big Four, and Wilson in particular. His role as relief director made him far more important than the other seven "technical advisers" to the American Commission to Negotiate Peace, who had a vague assignment to provide expert advice to the commission on such matters as international law, military issues, shipping, and, in Hoover's case, food. Except for House, most of the commissioners (House, Secretary of State Robert Lansing, General Tasker Bliss, and Henry White) became relatively unimportant because Wilson assumed personal control over the peace negotiations. Pushed to the sidelines, some of them resented the fact that Hoover, a mere "technical adviser," seemed to have more access and influence with the president than they did.[33]

Their concerns had some basis. As would be the case throughout his career, Hoover construed his mandate in the broadest possible terms. Relieving hunger required, he believed, not only the delivery of food but also the reconstruction of financial, transportation, and even political systems. The interconnections between food and politics became obvious early in the peace conference, when Italy closed the Adriatic port of Trieste for the transshipment of American aid to Central Europe. On February 12, Hoover sent an angry letter to Wilson recommending that further Treasury loans to Italy be held up until the Italians reopened the railway. Wilson, although initially sympathetic, decided on further reflection that the issue did not justify straining relations with Italy. The mere threat, however, contributed to worsening Italian-American relations during the remainder of the conference.[34]

Hoover's faith in food aid, what Arthur Walworth calls "a sedative for revolutionary ferment," led him not only to resist anything that might impede the flow of aid but also inclined him to support the new governments in Central Europe that adopted American ideas of democracy and to oppose any that did not. Because Wilson realized that it would be difficult if not impossible to use military force to secure American aims, Hoover's conviction that political goals could be achieved through food aid gained general acceptance among American leaders. Governments reported by Hoover's men as cooperative and democratically inclined (e.g., Finland and Poland) or that seemed essential to the free flow of aid—(e.g., the Baltic states) received his support and the benefit of his influence with policy makers. Those that seemed obstructive or radical—Italy, Romania, Hungary, Russia—drew his active opposition and the exercise of his influence on American and Allied leaders to isolate them or even to change their governments. In the case of a proposal by the Allies that the United States accept a mandate over Armenia, Hoover's opinion that the task would require the commitment of 150,000 American troops proved decisive in Wilson's decision to reject the assignment.[35] Although it is unlikely that Hoover's interventions changed the direction of American policy in any major way, the fact that his men provided the most detailed information about conditions in Central Europe, and the lack of any viable alternative to the policies he recommended, gave him influence that went far beyond merely controlling the distribution of relief.

The large size of the American delegation in Paris and the vague lines of responsibility within it produced jealousies and rivalries. Hoover, who often seemed the very stereotype of the self-made man—humorless, brusque, impatient, and tactless—inspired dislike as well as admiration for his blunt single-mindedness. Vance McCormick, for example, who had been Wilson's campaign manager in 1916 and had come to Paris as the chairman of the American War Trade Board, initially suspected Hoover of "attempting to dominate everything" and only gradually came to respect him. Nor were the frictions that attended Hoover's progress felt only among the Americans. Lloyd George, British prime minister, observed that Hoover "has many great qualities, but tact is not one of them." Lloyd George thought that many of the difficulties of dealing with the French over the blockade and other issues could have been avoided if Hoover's "surliness of mien and peremptoriness of speech" had not "provoked a negative answer to any request he made." Accustomed to concealing national self-interest behind a facade of elaborate courtesy, European leaders suspected that Hoover's relief program masked an American plot to dominate postwar Europe economically and politically.[36]

And, of course, they had reasons for their suspicion. Hoover *was* hard-driving, often humorless, sometimes rude, and he *was* determined to protect American economic interests wherever possible. For a moment, his humanitarian commitment to relief aligned perfectly with American self-interest. The fact that European leaders appeared to be scrambling for political and economic advantage while their people poised on the brink of starvation and revolution gave him extraordinary moral and practical advantages. If he had to offend people, break rules, cut corners, or bully and intimidate in order to stop starvation and head off revolution, he could wrap his undiplomatic behavior in the mantle of noble motives. His bulldozer determination won him the undying loyalty of the people who worked for him and shared his passion, and it earned him the gratitude of some of the millions he helped to survive, while at the same time it stabilized the prices of pork and wheat and protected the interests of American packers, shippers, and others in the food industry. Rarely in his later career would there be other situations where virtue and self-interest coincided so neatly, though he would frequently claim such a conjunction.

Hoover's style did not offend everyone. Soon after he arrived in Europe in November 1918, the Belgians organized a grand public celebration to honor him for his wartime assistance. He grumbled about going, and about a week before the event, he suddenly sent word that problems in organizing the relief program made it impossible. The American ambassador, Brand Whitlock, tried frantically to get him to change his mind but ultimately failed. On the appointed day, the celebration went ahead, in pouring rain, without the guest of honor. Instead of being angry, however, Belgian officials said they understood perfectly, and King Albert declared that any time Hoover could come to Brussels, he would be welcome, "even if it was for breakfast." As it turned out, when Hoover made a brief, informal visit to the Belgian capital in February

1919, he and the king enjoyed a cordial conversation over lunch rather than breakfast. To the Belgians, Hoover would always be a hero. The French were far less enthusiastic.[37]

On February 24, 1919, President Wilson signed into law a bill establishing a $100 million revolving fund to finance the relief program and formally appointed Hoover director general to run the operation. Under the so-called Lodge Amendment to the law, the congressional appropriation could not be used to finance aid to former enemy states, so Hoover planned to sell most supplies directly to the Germans in return for gold (in contravention of Germany's primary obligation to use its gold for reparations) and to channel support for a special program to feed German children through the American Friends Service Committee. He also circumvented the law banning aid to Austria by loaning money to the British, French, and Italian governments, who used it to purchase food that they resold to the Austrians on credit. The $100 million congressional appropriation mainly financed shipments to Eastern and Central European countries that had no gold and could only promise to pay sometime in the future. A major problem soon arose, however, when the comptroller of the Treasury ruled that no part of the appropriation could be used to pay for shipping and other overhead costs of the program. To parry this potentially fatal blow, Hoover had to improvise. He did so in large part by having the Grain Corporation borrow from private bankers, trusting that income from sales of relief supplies for slightly more than their actual cost would eventually cover the loans. He thus created a complex and fragile structure that teetered on the brink of insolvency and illegality, but the system worked, and during the armistice period, the ARA delivered 1.7 million tons of food, with a total value of more than $363 million.[38]

One of Hoover's least attractive characteristics was hypersensitivity to criticism triggered by his conviction that everything he did was morally impeccable. Keenly aware that the jury-rigged financial structure of the relief program might be attacked by critics, he suggested to Colonel House a strange scheme to forestall criticism. When the Republican-controlled Congress reconvened in the fall, Hoover predicted, it would "undoubtedly . . . devote itself very largely to investigation of the conduct of the war," mixing together "demagoguery, politics and sincerity of desire to maintain a high standard of administration." The process, he opined, would be "unlikely to reach the truth" but would damage the reputations of the programs and their administrators by focusing on mistakes and failing to illuminate "the successes of a vast number of financial, economic, social and military measures." To forestall a congressional probe, he proposed that the president immediately "appoint a tribunal, composed of independent men of pre-eminent character who have themselves been free from administrative work during the war, who will sit as a commission to investigate the conduct of the war."[39]

The possibility of a hostile congressional investigation was certainly real, but Hoover's idea of having an appointed commission focus on only the program's "successes" was absurd. Everyone in the Food Administration and the ARA, he assured House, would welcome "an entire public illumination at the hands of some just and independent body." But, of course, he really wanted praise, not an impartial review. When House ignored his suggestion, Hoover made a preemptive strike by releasing an avalanche of documents to bury potential critics and by publishing, or arranging to have published, studies of various aspects of the relief program that told the story from his point of view. Although a few members of Congress offered criticism of his record anyway, his method headed off a major investigation.[40]

Dr. Vernon Kellogg, Hoover's old friend, set up the first ARA mission in Warsaw on January 4, 1919. Poland generally enjoyed a positive image in the United States as a symbol of the struggle for liberty, although some people had begun to raise questions about Polish nationalism, anti-Semitism, and territorial ambitions. Hoover had strong personal ties to the Poles. While an undergraduate at Stanford, he had arranged for the great Polish pianist, Ignace Paderewski, to give a lecture at the university. The lecture never took place, but during World War I, Paderewski, then emerging as a Polish political leader, had actively cultivated Hoover, staying several times with the Hoovers at their S Street house.[41]

Two days after arriving in Warsaw, Kellogg reported to Hoover that the Polish situation had become dire. The Germans had carried most of the country's food reserves away, and in some cities, particularly Lemberg, people faced starvation. Conditions for children and the sick had become particularly desperate throughout the country. The Socialist government, headed by General Józef Piłsudski, appeared weak and divided, and the makeshift Polish army thrown together after the Germans, Russians, and Austrians withdrew had few weapons and could not maintain order. Paderewski's return to the country just before the ARA men arrived had led to an attempted coup against Piłsudski. Kellogg reported that he had tried to "keep free from political matters," but he obviously believed Piłsudski incapable of organizing an effective government and much preferred Paderewski, as did Hoover.[42]

Many years later, during the cold war, Hoover recalled that, at Kellogg's recommendation, he had gone to President Wilson in mid-January and that Wilson persuaded the Supreme War Council to inform Piłsudski that unless Paderewski became prime minister with effective control over the Polish government, "American co-operation and aid would be futile." Paderewski, after becoming prime minister, declared that Colonel House had won Wilson's support for him. Other observers, often with little direct involvement or knowledge, told various other stories about how American intervention had brought Paderewski to power. A careful modern study of the period concludes, however, that although American support for Poland undoubtedly helped to secure its interwar independence, internal politics, not Hoover's or anyone else's external interference, explained Paderewski's rise to power.[43]

Financing relief to Poland prior to the passage of the congressional appropriation proved complicated. Hoover could use some money from the $5 million authorized by President Wilson from his emergency funds, and the Jewish Joint Distribution Committee and the Polish National Relief Committee in the United States provided another $2 million. Nevertheless, he sometimes needed sleight of hand to keep the aid flowing. For several weeks, when ships sent by the War Department and Food Administration arrived in Poland with cargoes to be paid for on delivery, the ARA simply "misplaced" the bills. Hoover felt relieved to be able to pay them off after Congress passed the relief appropriation in February.[44]

An even more serious restriction on aid to Poland resulted from transportation problems. The prewar Polish railroad system had been poor, and the war nearly destroyed it, with much of the rolling stock carried off by the occupying powers. To complicate matters still further, most relief shipments were landed at Danzig and then shipped through German territory in what would become the "Polish Corridor" to Poland itself. Understandably, the Germans objected to transshipping food to Poland when the blockade denied them the right to import any for themselves, but Hoover's opposition to the blockade gradually softened their position. The problem of the Allied blockade of the neutrals proved more difficult to resolve. The U.S. Navy prevented interference with food shipments to neutral ports, but the navy declined to protect shipments of raw materials going into Poland or Polish products being exported. That left the Poles with no income to pay for food. Although Hoover branded the blockade unwise and immoral and the ARA warned that it encouraged Bolshevism, the Allies did not agree to lift it until April. To Hoover's great frustration, all these problems, in combination with the disastrous state of the railways, made it impossible for the ARA to provide more than a bare subsistence level of food for the Poles.[45]

Nor did the Poles help their own cause. On April 11, a telegram arrived in the ARA offices in Paris reporting that thirty-seven Jews had been executed at Pinsk on April 5 by a Polish army firing squad. Lewis Strauss, himself a Jew, took the telegram to Hoover. As he read it, Strauss recalled, Hoover's hand shook and his face "seemed to grow suddenly older." He instructed Strauss to telephone the representative of the Polish National Committee in Paris and ask for an explanation. The representative calmly assured him that those shot had all been Communists. All Communists in Poland were Jews, explained the representative, so it followed that all Jews were Communists. This bit of mindless anti-Semitism confirmed a warning that Rabbi Stephen Wise had given to Wilson a month earlier and outraged Hoover. He immediately summoned Paderewski, who happened to be in Paris, to his office and asked him about the report. Paderewski repeated very much the same defense, whereupon Hoover advised him that it would be prudent for him to launch an immediate, impartial investigation. In June, with Congress and public meetings in the United States demanding action, Hoover made clear to Paderewski that he must request an independent American investigating commission. Wilson named General Edgar Jadwin, former Congressman Homer Johnson, and Ambassador Henry Morgenthau to investigate not only the Pinsk massacre but also other anti-Jewish riots and pogroms. The commission's October report greatly understated the seriousness of anti-Semitism in Poland, but it calmed public outrage in the United States, and the episode as a whole may have had some benefit by encouraging the inclusion of clauses in the peace treaty guaranteeing the rights of racial, national, and religious minorities in the states of Central Europe. Unfortunately, the guarantees, like the commission's report, proved ineffective in protecting minority religious rights in the region.[46]

Expansionism also complicated Polish-American relations. Before the war, Poland had been partitioned between Russia and Germany, but the Poles remembered past days of glory when they had ruled much of Central Europe, including most of the Ukraine. Piłsudski, in particular, hoped to exploit Russian weakness to reassert those claims, and the French saw the Poles as possible leaders of a movement to overthrow the Bolsheviks. The British and Americans disagreed, fearing that conflict between the Poles and the Soviets might get out of hand, but they shared the French view that Poland should form part of a cordon sanitaire between Russia and Germany. The United States became the first nation to recognize the independence of Poland, on January 22, 1919, and President Wilson named Hoover's friend Hugh Gibson as the first American minister to Poland. From Hoover's viewpoint, however, Polish attempts to reconquer its eastern empire in 1919 and 1920 became something of an embarrassment because they provided ammunition for his American critics who charged that aid had been used improperly to supply the Polish army. The charge had some merit, since war costs accounted for 62 percent of the Polish budget between mid-1919 and March 1920, leaving very little for reconstruction of the country's infrastructure and support of the civilian population. To escape the charge that the relief program fostered Polish aggression, Hoover had to confine aid only to child feeding. He certainly would have preferred that the Poles abandon their military operations in the east.[47]

Elsewhere in Eastern Europe, the ARA faced variations on the Polish situation. In the Baltic states of Estonia, Latvia, and Lithuania, nationalists battling with Russians and Germans complicated the relief situation. In Czechoslovakia, Yugoslavia, and Romania, problems arising from the breakup of the old empires and the establishment of new governments made more difficult the reestablishment of trade relationships and transportation by rail and river. In Austria, a large urban population suddenly cut off from the rural areas of the old empire and thus facing starvation suffered even more because Austria's role as a German ally blocked direct American aid. Bulgaria and Hungary had also been enemy states, and the rise of a strong Communist movement in Hungary in the immediate postwar period created further problems. To evade the congressional prohibition against using any of the $100 million relief appropriation to assist enemy nations, Hoover channeled aid to them indirectly through private agencies like the Jewish Joint Distribution Committee and through the Allied governments, who faced no such restrictions.[48]

Many of the problems with which the ARA grappled could not be confined within national boundaries. Central Europe's railroad network, for example, had been built during the age of empires. With the system severely damaged by the war and fragmented at the borders of eighteen new postwar states, it became almost impossible to ship anything, including relief supplies, through the region. Hoover tackled the problem by creating a Railway Section in the ARA under Colonel William G. Atwood and sending experienced American railway men into each of the new countries. Using the authority of the ARA, they significantly reduced border delays. When necessary, they improvised freely. One day, Hoover reported, the Paris office received a telegram: "Have arranged [to] sell Galicia ten locomotives for eggs. How many eggs go to a locomotive?" Paris replied, "Does not matter. We have no confidence in the age of either." By the time the ARA began to close down its operations in the summer of 1919, the American railway men had been so successful that the Council of Railway Ministers of the Central European States asked a number of them to stay on as paid advisers.[49]

A rapid and dependable communications system played a crucial role in making the relief operation successful. Again, however, national borders proved a major obstacle. Every state insisted on the right to read and censor messages passing over its telegraph lines, which meant, Hoover recalled, that it could take a week to get a telegram from Paris to Warsaw. The ARA avoided the problem at first by having a navy ship with a radio stationed in every major port. After the navy withdrew its ships, the Army Signal Corps set up a special telegraph system between ports, capitals, and other major points. Hoover allayed most local suspicions by having all messages sent in plain language, but the French refused to cooperate unless they had the right to read and censor any message sent over their wires. With the ARA headquartered in Paris, the French attitude posed a major problem until General Pershing offered the use of American military lines from Paris to the border, where messages could be relayed over ARA lines to their destinations. The system provided quick, reliable service, and the State Department and the other governments represented at the peace conference, as well as the press, demanded access to it. Hoover agreed, but the traffic quickly overburdened the system. Eventually, the ARA set up a telegraph office in Paris for the benefit of the other users and charged them for the service. Fees of up to $5,000 a month helped subsidize the Children's Relief Fund.[50]

The only limitation of the system was the requirement that all messages be sent en clair, to reassure the governments over whose lines messages passed. The requirement could sometimes be a nuisance, but the ever-resourceful ARA men got around it by making use of American slang and private nicknames.

An American diplomat regarded as useless became "The Cocktail Eater"; the Habsburg archduke who briefly ruled Hungary became "Archie."[51]

Europe depended heavily on coal, which not only powered the trains and ships that moved goods but also fueled factories and homes. The war had damaged or closed down many mines, however, and the new national boundaries often created impassable obstacles to coal shipments. As with so much else, General Pershing provided a solution to the problem, sending Hoover Colonel Anson C. Goodyear, whose civilian background included both railroading and coal mining. The gregarious, energetic, and ingenious Goodyear cheerfully accepted Hoover's orders to do anything necessary to get the coal moving. Employing his native charm and his authority to provide or withhold food shipments, he calmed strikes and opened borders. At one point, he got Hoover to send him $25,000 worth of tobacco to distribute among miners. Within a month, his unorthodox methods contributed to doubling coal production in Central Europe.[52]

IV

Russia presented one of the largest and most difficult problems not only for Hoover and the ARA but also for the peace conference in general. Described by Wilson in his Fourteen Points speech as the "acid test" of peacemaking, policy toward Russia aroused bitter disagreement among the conferees at Paris. The British and French remained furious about the Russian withdrawal from the war in 1918, and all of the Western leaders worried about the postwar threat of Communism in Europe. Prior to the beginning of the peace conference, some Allied soldiers had been sent to Russia, where they had been assigned to protect stores of Allied supplies and equipment. The British and French hoped they might become the nucleus of an anti-Bolshevik force, which Wilson opposed. Hoover could see merit on both sides of the issue. He believed that communism posed a military and political threat to Europe, especially the new states of Central Europe. What was more, he argued, "Bolshevik economic conceptions" were killing the Russian people "at the rate of some hundreds of thousands monthly in a country that formerly supplied food to a large part of the world." Yet, like Wilson, he believed that military intervention would drag the United States into "years of police duty and make us a party to reestablishing the reactionary classes in their economic domination over the lower classes."[53]

Although opposed to diplomatic recognition of the "murderous" Bolshevik regime, Hoover suggested that an aid program might offer a way out of the dilemma. He recommended that some neutral individual "of international reputation for probity and ability" organize a relief program for Russia. Such a policy, he argued, would test whether the Bolsheviks were "engrossed upon world domination" and might "at least give a period of rest along the frontiers of Europe and . . . some hope of stabilization."[54]

Hoover's recommendation to Wilson almost certainly drew upon a report on Russian conditions by William Bullitt, a young American diplomat who had just returned from Moscow. Bullitt reported to Colonel House that, at the moment, Russia seemed "orderly but starving" and predicted that "if relations are not reopened with the outside world, anarchy will be prevalent." On the basis of Bullitt's report, House suggested that the moment might be ripe to urge the Russians "to stop fighting on all fronts" and to "leave the boundary lines as they stand today." If denied outside help, he argued, Russia might "link up" with Germany to dominate Europe.[55]

Hoover doubted Bullitt's contention that the Bolsheviks had undergone a change of heart, but he saw in the reports of famine both a duty and an opportunity. That dual imperative led him to write to Wilson on March 28. He argued that a neutral relief commission for Russia would test House and Bullitt's theory about the stabilizing potential of aid without committing the American government to anything.

Finding a neutral executive with the drive and ability to run the proposed Russian aid program proved difficult. The best person Hoover could suggest at short notice was Fridtjof Nansen, a Norwegian explorer and scientist with whom Hoover had become friendly during the war when Nansen came to the United States to purchase food for Norway. Many years later, Hoover wrote that, although Nansen had "great moral and physical courage," he had been "timid and hesitant" in politics. If he knew that when he asked Nansen to come to Paris to talk about a Russian relief program, it is difficult to see why he invited him, but perhaps he had not yet seen that side of the explorer. In any case, if he had not realized Nansen's limitations, he soon discovered them. Presented with the outlines of the proposed program and asked to sign letters to launch it, Nansen balked, saying that he "had never handled such large amounts of food; that he had no experience with such negotiations; that he did not like the Bolsheviks." In the end, he agreed to attempt the task, largely, it appears, because Hoover assured him that the ARA would provide the food, ships, and staff to run the operation. On April 3, Nansen sent a letter (drafted by Hoover) to the president proposing the plan and, after winning the consent of the Big Four, wired the offer to Lenin on April 17.[56]

The result was anticlimax. The French, unwilling to do anything to keep the Bolsheviks in power, never sent Nansen's telegram to Lenin. The offer had to be resent, by radio, on May 3. And when the Russians responded on May 14 (their reply also blocked by the French but picked up by radio in Copenhagen and relayed to Hoover), their refusal to stop fighting until they had achieved their objectives killed the whole project.[57]

On June 21, shortly before Wilson was to leave Paris, Hoover raised the Russian problem once more. He argued that Russia had enough food available to feed its people, but a total breakdown of the currency and the transportation system under the Bolsheviks prevented available supplies from being distributed. Perhaps, he suggested, someone should send in an economic commission under the authority of a single man to sort out the problems of the currency and transportation. He contended that such a mission could be carried out without interfering in Russia's politics, but in any case, he believed the Bolshevik regime would soon collapse. He did not explain how the Russians might be induced to accept his naive plan, although he obviously wanted a chance to attempt it. Wilson gently vetoed his suggestion, telling him that he had concluded that "the Russian people must solve their own problems without outside interference."[58]

If Hoover could not solve Russia's internal problems, he could at least try to resolve the thorny puzzle of Russian prisoners held in Germany. The Treaty of Brest Litovsk between Germany and Russia in March 1918 declared that "the prisoners of war of both parties will be allowed to return home," but for various reasons, only limited exchanges took place before the end of the war. The State Department estimated that at the time of the armistice, up to 3 million prisoners remained in Germany and Austria. In the confusion following the armistice, many of them simply wandered away, and a month later, the German government reported that it held only about 700,000. Since the Germans had inadequate food even for themselves, the prisoners' condition quickly became appalling. Nevertheless, the Germans delayed repatriation because prisoners substituted for German farm workers who had been killed or refused to return to the countryside. On Christmas Day in 1918, Hoover reported that the remaining prisoners faced "the most suffering in Europe today" and were "dying wholesale from neglect." He urged that the Red Cross try to help them.[59]

The task overwhelmed the Red Cross, however, and Hoover concluded that the United States and the Allies must take it on. But with reports arriving from Russia that returning prisoners were being shot or forced into the Bolshevik army, no one wanted to rush repatriation. After some grumbling about how the Germans had not lived up to their obligations, the French eventually agreed to pay for whatever food and clothing Hoover could supply. Initially, the French paid the U.S. Army to replace food given to the prisoners, but in the middle of March, the ARA began direct food shipments.[60] No one, however, took responsibility for a repatriation program.

On July 15, Hoover reminded the Supreme War Council that some 250,000 Russian prisoners still remained in Germany. The ARA's congressional authorization had expired on July 1, and the British Red Cross and the U.S. Army, which had been delivering aid to the prisoners, would leave Germany in August. Were the prisoners to be repatriated, he asked, and if so, how? Thus goaded, the council agreed that the time had finally come to deal with the problem, especially since Hoover assured them that the remaining prisoners were "largely Bolshevik." But nothing happened. Poland objected to having prisoners shipped through its territory because the Poles believed, with good reason, that they would immediately become soldiers in the Bolshevik armies confronting them to the east. General George Harries, the American member of the Inter-Allied Commission on Repatriation of Russian Prisoners of War in Berlin, pointed out that the situation would not change unless the British, French, and American governments insisted that Poland and Lithuania allow the prisoners to pass. Forwarded by Tasker H. Bliss of the American Peace Commission to the State Department, Harries's memorandum at last produced action. The Allies issued passes, and 252,272 prisoners and civilian internees returned to an uncertain fate in Russia.[61]

By the summer of 1919, Hoover's immediate role in European relief neared an end. The ARA expired as a government agency on July 1, and although the ARA European Children's Fund continued as a private organization, the organization's broad responsibility for feeding Europe ended with the fall harvest. Between December 1, 1918, and May 31, 1919, Hoover reported, the ARA had supplied 512 shiploads (2,486,230 tons) of food, with a value of approximately $636,175,000. On June 10, he informed the Supreme Economic Council that he had notified each of the countries receiving relief that the ARA's activities would end and suggested that each prepare an estimate of its future food needs to be submitted to the American government through an international commission empowered to handle collective buying, shipping, and related functions.[62] The parallels between such an organization and the collective Allied purchasing control against which he had fought so hard at Paris did not seem to occur to him, and since the organization was never created, he never had to confront its implications.

The near-conclusion of ARA work freed Hoover to think more broadly about the European situation. Like many others in the American delegation in Paris, he believed that the peace treaty, as it emerged from the pushing and pulling among the negotiators, had become seriously flawed and would foster bitterness, conflict, and might lay the groundwork for another war. In the short term, the injustices of the treaty, he argued, might lead the Germans to refuse to sign it, and if that happened, restoration of the blockade or occupation of Germany would result in "complete chaos." From his point of view, Hoover warned the president, such a situation would force the ARA "to pile up large amounts of foodstuffs in Europe" and would "seriously jeopardize the financial stability of the Food Administration."[63]

Fortunately, the Germans did sign, but Hoover remained convinced that the reparations clauses of the treaty, in combination with the war's destruction, threatened European recovery. In a May 16 letter to Colonel House, he proposed continuation of the American aid program but in a radically altered form. The Allied governments, he recommended, "should be outright forgiven the interest on their obligations for three years, conditional on their doing the same thing amongst themselves." The new countries of Eastern and Central Europe should be provided with credits guaranteed by the War Finance Corporation and the U.S. Grain Corporation to purchase raw materials, necessary finished products, and grain as needed. Congress should appropriate half a billion dollars with which to provide gold to European countries for currency stabilization. And Germany should be authorized to issue bonds to finance reconstruction, payments on which would take priority over reparations payments (except to Belgium).[64]

The origins of Hoover's proposal are obscure. Some European leaders and a few Americans in Paris at the time, including New York Federal Reserve Board Governor Benjamin Strong and Edward Stettinius, then working for J. P. Morgan and Company, had been speculating about policies along the same lines. But the possibility that the United States might assume responsibility as a world economic as well as political leader went far beyond what Wilson had imagined. During the 1920s, Hoover himself espoused a less ambitious international economic policy for the United States, and by World War II, when a comparable vision of America's world role become common among American leaders, he had moved toward economic nationalism. In 1919, it is safe to say, most Americans would have rejected his proposal as entailing too much responsibility for European problems and, by the Allied governments, as threatening the leadership they had exercised before the war and expected to resume in the postwar era. House did not reply to Hoover's letter or forward it to the president. He did ask Strong to outline ideas about American economic leadership, but the discussion seems to have died without ever approaching policymaking levels.[65]

On July 3, when Hoover sent a long statement on the European economic situation to the Supreme Economic Council, he endorsed a much more limited and conventional policy. "The solution . . . of the problem" of European recovery, he wrote, "does not lie in a stream of commodities or credit from the Western Hemisphere, but lies in a . . . realization [by the European nations] that productivity must be instantly increased." Before sailing to the United States on September 6, he recommended that the United States terminate its membership in the Supreme Economic Council and proposed to disband the council entirely. Continued membership, he contended, would bind the United States to accept "a sort of American European board of directors advising how and where we should place our credits and raw materials, and the assumption of a position which is disadvantageous to us and for which there is no reason or obligation for us to accept." He had concluded that economic reconstruction did not require an actual partnership with European governments. As he reflected on his experiences during and after the war, his old suspicions about the British and French had come flooding back. Nor had his recent experience with the new states of Central Europe inspired confidence. He told Lloyd George's personal secretary, Philip Kerr, that doing business with the Germans had proved easier than working with the leaders of the new states, who struck him as incompetent and untrustworthy. If the United States took a role in European reconstruction, it should do so on its own, as it had with relief.[66]

Before he left, Hoover hoped to establish a continuing program to feed the hungry children of central Europe. The general relief program, he told the president, "under the difficulties of distribution in weak governments" had been "more or less a hit or miss as to whether the children, especially of the poor," would receive sufficient nutrition. The ARA had built up some monetary surplus because it had charged a little extra on every shipment of relief supplies to cover possible accidents and losses, and he asked the president for permission to use that surplus to fund a year's program to provide milk and a daily hot meal for children throughout the affected area. Wilson immediately approved the proposal, and the privatized ARA created the European Children's Fund in July 1919 to carry it out. Over the next several years, it cooperated closely with local organizations in fourteen European nations to provide food, clothing, and medicine for 14 to 16 million children.[67]

Hoover worried that the chaos prevalent in Central and Eastern Europe at the end of the war would return. He urged the countries of the region to set up economic councils made up of representatives from government ministries and American advisers supplied by the new, privatized ARA. Poland, Austria, Czechoslovakia, and Yugoslavia accepted the idea, and Hoover arranged to have the salaries and expenses of the American advisers paid out of leftover relief funds held by the ARA in New York. On the whole, the American advisers tried to do their jobs in a neutral fashion, and in Austria, Poland, and Czechoslovakia, they had considerable success in helping the governments adjust to independence and postwar economic conditions. The American advisory mission in Yugoslavia, headed by Colonel William G. Atwood, limped along for only a year. Atwood undermined his impartiality by pushing American economic interests, but the political instability of the Yugoslav government presented an even more serious problem and prevented much of anything being done during the advisory period.[68]

During the summer of 1919, the ARA also reluctantly undertook the containment of a typhus epidemic in Eastern and Central Europe. At the end of March, the British warned that typhus had become pandemic in the Ukraine and Serbia and appeared likely to spread westward unless fought vigorously. The main technique for fighting the disease—delousing to kill off the carriers—was not complex but required many men, large quantities of soap, and supplies of clean clothing, all of which remained in short supply in the area. Hoover suggested that the Red Cross take on the problem, but two months later, the organization reported that it lacked the personnel and resources to do so. In late May, Wilson asked Hoover to deal with the epidemic, and he agreed reluctantly. By that time, the ministers of health in the affected countries estimated that a million people had contracted the disease, with as many as a hundred thousand dying every week. With the help of General Pershing, Hoover rounded up a combined force of military physicians and civilians commanded by Colonel H. L. Gilchrist, and in cooperation with national health departments and local police forces, they went village to village and house to house delousing. They then established a line around affected areas where soldiers stopped travelers to shave heads and delouse clothing. Even

Vernon Kellogg, sent by Hoover to report on the progress of the campaign, was caught by a zealous American sergeant and returned shaven-headed to Paris. The approach worked, however, and what might have become a European epidemic ended within months.[69]

V

The precise impact of Hoover's relief work during the Armistice period is difficult to measure. As director general of relief, he oversaw the delivery of $1.1 billion in aid. Of that, $363 million came directly from the American government through the ARA, and $48 million through the Joint Allied Finance Committee, set up to make American loans to Britain, France, and Italy, with which they purchased relief supplies for Austria and Germany. Hoover also had partial control over $462.6 million from other American organizations, of which the U.S. Liquidation Commission, created by the war department in February 1919 to sell off surplus military supplies in Europe, provided $381.7 million. About $81 million came from private charitable organizations like the American Friends Service Committee, the Joint Distribution for Jewish Relief, and the Commission for Relief in Belgium. Other countries contributed $238.8 million, with the largest single amount ($59.5 million) coming from Great Britain.[70]

By the standards of post–World War II American aid programs, post–World War I aid does not seem generous. What Hoover called "benevolence"—that is, outright gifts—made up only 1.5 percent of total spending. The rest came in the form of either cash sales (37.3 percent) or sales on credit (61.2 percent). Hoover's principal contribution lay less in securing outright charity for the people of Europe than in finding needed supplies, organizing their timely delivery, clearing political and military obstacles to shipments, and rebuilding the transportation, communications, finance, and distribution systems to get supplies to the people who needed them. His work reduced hunger, provided shelter, and combated disease, but his achievement proved more organizational than charitable. Rather than "the great humanitarian," it might have been more accurate to refer to him as "the great manager." Vernon Kellogg later described him as "an organization man" who achieved his goals by mobilizing "every agency that can help" and inspiring them to work as hard as he did toward a common goal. Historian David Burner makes a similar point in a slightly less complimentary way, observing that Hoover managed "the economic reconstruction of Europe with typical cold aggressiveness."[71]

Given that the ARA's European staff, even supplemented with army officers, always seemed far too small to do the work that confronted it and that its work was often impeded by the very governments whose people it tried to help, one of the secrets of Hoover's success lay in his ability and willingness to make extensive use of local volunteers in moving, storing, and distributing relief supplies. The ARA provided the supplies and organization and cut through the tangles of red tape, but it was Hoover's recognition that the victims of disaster could be, as a recent study puts it, "resilient, resourceful, generous, empathic, and brave" that made the whole program work effectively. For the remainder of his career, he would seek ways to evoke the same sort of genuinely participatory democracy in the United States only to find, sadly, that except in moments of crisis, the goal was elusive.[72]

As many European leaders and some Republicans in the United States pointed out, Hoover's recollection of his relief work in Europe as "non-political and humanitarian" distorts reality. His program pursued national self-interest by making sure that American farmers who had expanded production in order to meet Allied needs did not lose thereby, and more broadly, by supporting the establishment of democracy and a liberal capitalist order in Europe that would be open to American trade and investments. He opposed and worked to undermine Communism in Germany, Hungary, and Russia, and argued that food provided the best bulwark against the spread of political radicalism. The same capitalist system that had made him wealthy, he believed, could make Europe prosperous as well.[73]

The crucial point to remember in judging Hoover's relief work is that the American people would not have supported, in 1918 and 1919, an aid program that provided assistance without strings. By putting his program on a businesslike basis and requiring recipients to pay for what they received, he made it acceptable to Americans. And indeed, he was correct in believing that although they did not like it, the Europeans could eventually pay for what they received (although most did not do so). John Maynard Keynes, not a notably charitable observer of American policy, said of the ARA: "It was their efforts, their energy, and the American resources placed by the President at their disposal, often acting in the teeth of European obstruction, which not only saved an immense amount of human suffering, but averted a widespread breakdown of the European system." He was correct that the European governments were often reluctant partners in postwar aid and, even more than Hoover, regarded it as a tool to secure national economic and political advantage. Hoover, wrote Keynes, "was the only man who emerged from the ordeal of Paris with an enhanced reputation."[74]

A heartfelt testimonial to the significance of Hoover's relief work came from the people of Poland. At the end of June, before Wilson returned to the United States, Paderewski invited the president to visit Warsaw to demonstrate American support against the threat of attack from Russia. Exhausted from the work of the peace conference and perhaps cautious about seeming to endorse Polish annexation of a large area claimed by Russians and Ukrainians, Wilson did not go. Instead, he asked Hoover to represent him. On August 12, Hoover and a retinue of military officers intended to impress the Soviets arrived in Warsaw. At the railway station, a huge crowd waving American flags, massed bands playing "The Star Spangled Banner," and a host of Polish officials greeted them. Two days of official tours and meetings followed, and

then the group gathered at a local racetrack where some of the children who
had been fed by the ARA were to come and "pay their respects." The occasion
was informal, and the children came, not by the hundreds, as organizers had
expected, but by the thousands. They came, not in tidy lines, but "romping
by, ten, twenty, thirty abreast . . . , laughing, shouting, capering, waving anything they chanced to hold in their hands . . . , but very often beating loudly
with their little tin or wooden spoons upon their little tin cups or pannekins."
To the delight of the observers, "they ran and skipped and jumped as though
there had been no long months or years when they had actually forgotten
how, but sat day in and day out in a crumpled heap on the floor, too listless to
move." The usually stolid Hoover stood watching, with tears rolling down his
cheeks, until darkness halted the procession.[75]

CHAPTER 2

Family Affairs, 1918–1920

Christmas 1918 found the Hoovers scattered across two continents. Bert remained in Paris, where he had a quiet Christmas with some of his staff members in their rented house at 19 rue de Lübeck. Lou and Herbert (known in the family as "Pete"), who had turned fifteen in August, celebrated the holiday in Palo Alto, California, where they had gone partly so that Lou could supervise planning for the family's new house and partly because doctors had advised them that Herbert's hearing, damaged during a bout of influenza earlier in the fall, might respond to a warm climate. He would attend school in Palo Alto during the spring.[1]

Eleven-year-old Allan, a student at the Sidwell Friends School, stayed in Washington at the family's rented house at 1720 Rhode Island Avenue. He hoped to "welcome back his daddy" soon, but Bert could not tell whether he would "remain in Europe two weeks or two months." In the meantime, Ruth Sampson, a friend of Lou's from the Red Cross, and Dare Stark, the daughter of a mining engineer whom Hoover had met at Stanford and worked with in South Africa, looked after Allan. Dare had become a protégée of the Hoovers after her father's death and had gone to work as Lou's secretary and assistant following her graduation from Stanford in 1918. Laurine Anderson Small, Hoover's secretary and assistant in the Food Administration and a good friend of Lou's, also kept an eye on Allan. She had become the informal manager of the Food Administration Club as well as doing various tasks for the Hoovers.[2]

Lou and her friend Abbie Rickard had started the club after the United States entered the war in 1917. They intended it to house the young women who had flocked into Washington to staff war agencies, including the Food Administration. Located in three rented houses on I Street, the club offered the young women working in the agency a safe place to live and eat their meals. At its busiest, it housed and fed about seventy women, and the income from rents, dues, and meals nearly covered operating costs, with the rest coming from profits at a cafeteria set up by Lou and her friends in the Food Administration. The war did not last long enough, however, for the club's profits to recoup the cost of furniture and equipment that Lou had bought out of her own pocket. In the spring of 1919, as the Food Administration closed down, its cafeteria also closed, and the number of women staying in the houses on I Street dwindled, though the expenses did not. Over the next several months, as the leases on the houses ran out, Laurine sold off its equipment. Lou never complained, but the closing of the club must have relieved her, since by the end it seems to have been costing her nearly $4,000 a month.[3] The club had given her valuable business experience and made a useful contribution to the war effort, but its lessons had been expensive.

As Christmas 1918 drew near, Laurine reported that Allan and Dare had cut down a tree and put it up in the living room, where it teetered precariously and then fell over "like a most irresponsible merry maker." Unfazed by this setback, Allan set to work decorating the rest of the house and cleaning his room in preparation for the coming great event.[4]

Like Allan, Lou did her best to be cheerful in the face of long family separations, but beneath the surface, she frequently worried. She knew that many of Bert's mining investments around the world had been severely damaged by the war. He had shifted some of his money to "gilt-edged securities," but he needed time that never seemed to be available to salvage what he could from other interests and reinvest it. More importantly, she felt that "a certain, definite and very original kind of joy of life was stamped out of him by those war years." The "old sparkling spontaneity," which she had loved, was "now only occasionally glimpsed far below the surface."[5] Perhaps, she feared, the war had cost him more than anyone knew.

I

By early 1919, it had become apparent that Bert would not return to the United States for several months. Lou decided that it would make sense for Allan and Dare to join her and Herbert in California. In January, she terminated the lease on the Washington house and arranged to have their stored furniture shipped to California from London and Washington. She also notified the owner of a summer cottage called "In the Woods" in suburban Maryland where she and the children had escaped Washington's summer heat, that they would no longer need the house. Then Allan and Dare, accompanied by a pregnant black cat disguised as a "noisy basket of lunch," took the train to California.[6]

From Palo Alto, Dare reported a cheerful round of mud-soaked picnics; adventures with various dogs, cats, and other livestock; and "the lady" hard at work "correcting [architect Birge] Clark's plans of the new house every time he draws them." The house, to be built on a hill overlooking the Stanford campus, gradually evolved in an eclectic style with terraces on every flat roof to foster easy outdoor entertaining. Lou had scaffolding built "to see just the effect of the different views from the different elevations." She wanted the house to be large and comfortable enough for family, servants, and lots of visitors, yet unpretentious in appearance and conducive to informality—in sum, what Dare described as "a Hooverish place." Bert, a bit embarrassed by the idea of building a big house during the postwar recession, joked about it as "a 'palace' containing seven rooms and a basement, a kitchen and a garage, all on the university campus," but in fact it was considerably grander, even in its planning stages, although its full size would not become evident until construction began in June.[7] (See Figure 7.2.) Bert had very little influence on its design. It would be "Lou Hoover's house."

In the midst of house planning, Allan broke his arm and Herbert had his tonsils removed in the hope that the operation might improve his hearing. Allan's arm quickly healed, but Herbert's hearing remained poor, a problem that would plague him all his life. Lou struggled at long distance to arrange the delivery of various pieces of Belgian lace that she had commissioned to help support Belgian lace workers during the war. With the war over, the necessity for the program had diminished, but back orders and confusion over deliveries created frequent frustrations.[8]

In July, with work on the house begun, Lou and Allan crossed the continent and sailed for France to join Bert. Traveling with him through Europe, they got a vivid sense of his relief work and the gratitude of its recipients. Then, in September, they returned with him to the United States. Meanwhile, Herbert, still convalescing, spent a month at his uncle Theodore Hoover's Santa Cruz ranch, where he gained fourteen pounds and returned home in better health than he had enjoyed for several years.[9]

Bert, Lou, and Allan arrived in Palo Alto on September 25, 1919, the same day that Woodrow Wilson collapsed after a speech in Pueblo, Colorado, an ominous event of which the Hoovers happily knew nothing. The next day, Hoover attended a Stanford trustees' meeting to discuss the construction of a war memorial on the Stanford campus, a project to which he had promised to contribute $10,000. But business was not foremost in the minds of any of the family. Hoover announced that, for the next month, he did not intend to answer telephone calls, read letters longer than one page, or address any of the groups that importuned him for speeches. Loading the car with fishing gear, the family headed into the mountains. But instead of the planned month, the trip lasted only four days. By the beginning of October, the Hoovers had returned to Stanford, where on October 1 Hoover attended the president's reception and the next day addressed students about the importance of ratifying the Treaty of Versailles. In mid-October, he helped entertain the king and queen of Belgium during their visit to California, and on October 17 he left Palo Alto for the East Coast. How little vacation he actually enjoyed in California may be guessed at from the fact that he spent nearly $500 just to send telegrams during the month.[10]

Lou planned to go east with him, but just before he left, she fell and had to stay in bed for several days. Worried about her, Hoover urged her to join him as soon as possible but warned that an impending coal strike might make rail travel difficult. She recovered quickly from the fall, but decided that overseeing the construction of the house and arranging to store thirty cases of furniture made it prudent for her to stay in California.[11]

In November, Bert looked for an apartment in New York while he raised money for the American Relief Administration (ARA) European Children's Fund. Lou planned to join him, but just before she left California, doctors found that her mother, Florence Henry, had contracted colon cancer. Abandoning plans for the trip east, Lou left immediately for Monterey to be with her parents.[12]

For Bert, an invitation to serve as vice chairman of a conference called by the White House to discuss the nation's troubled economic situation and urgent reports of new food shortages in Europe overshadowed the family crisis. He explained to Lou that he still hoped to get to California for Christmas, but he warned that he felt "duty bound to spend the winter between Washington and New York." Hopes that Lou and Allan might move east for the spring became casualties of her mother's illness.[13]

After a quiet Christmas in Palo Alto, Bert went east on January 2, 1920, for the industrial conference and further fund-raising. Hailed by admirers as the "master of emergencies," he also faced increasing pressure to become a candidate for the 1920 presidential nomination. Lou and Allan accompanied him for a visit, dividing their time between New York, where they took an apartment, and Washington, where they occupied a rented house at 1228 17th Street Northwest.

II

By March, Lou felt she needed to return to California. Not only did her mother's health remain uncertain, but she also hated to leave Herbert alone, and Allan, still with her, had not been in school since before Christmas. What was more, construction of the house in Palo Alto had been going badly. Rising lumber, glass, and hardware prices; shortages of plate glass; a strike in the planing mills that were making the house's trim; and a shortage of carpenters all slowed progress. Lou dealt with the problems as best she could at long distance, but she preferred to supervise the process personally. The house, once dismissed by Hoover as having only seven rooms, had expanded to three stories and fifty-seven rooms, with exterior measurements of 192 feet by 65

feet. Lou even tried—and failed—to purchase the house next door to provide
a site for a planned swimming pool. With a formidable price tag of $170,000,
the modest house had become a mansion.[14]

Built largely of poured concrete to make it fireproof (one of Bert's few
requirements) and with asymmetric cubes rambling along the hillside on several levels, the house had been, in architect Birge Clark's words, "hammered
down" into the site to minimize its size. Lou had its stuccoed exterior painted
a soft cream color and partially disguised by climbing vines. With its flat roofs
and terraces, it had a Southwestern pueblo look, though its Tudor-style leaded
glass windows and terraces opening out from almost every room reflected Lou's
personal taste rather than any specific style. Inside, oak paneling and floors,
eclectic furniture, and fireplaces in almost every room softened the austerity of the concrete structure. On the walls hung paintings the Hoovers had
acquired in their travels, and oriental rugs covered some of the floors.[15]

The house embodied Lou Hoover. As an old friend said, "She has the hospitality of a California patio—that says tie your horse and come in, here is our
garden and the house is yours, without words." It revealed her love of being
outdoors, of "get[ting] to the top of hills and look[ing] over," of having "a sunset with tea, and tea with a sunset." Her "one important rule of protocol" was
that "no-one's feelings must be hurt, ever, no matter what conventions go by
the board." On the terraces and in the yard, visitors encountered dogs, boys,
and interesting guests, "strolling about . . . with a cigar and willing to trade
with you conversationally." Both Lou and Bert read omnivorously, quickly,
and unostentatiously, so she filled the rooms with bookcases and comfortable
chairs for her own and her guests' pleasure. As a hostess, she listened intently
to talkative guests and drew out those who seemed shy. "When I was first
married," she said, "I practised talking to everybody." She remembered her
friends' families and interests, knew when their relatives came to visit, and
invited them for a cup of tea or a meal. She liked clothes and took pains with
hers, but she cared more about texture and line than cost. She refused to wear
jewels because, a friend believed, "she still thinks of them in terms of possible
college educations for youngsters, and trips for convalescents, and pensions
for old servants."[16] The Stanford house, which made all the things she cared
most about easy and natural, showcased her values and personality.

Near the end of March 1920, Lou planned to return with Allan to New
York to find him either a tutor or a private school where he could catch up on
his missed studies. Before they could leave, however, Allan came down with
the mumps, and Bert announced that he would enter the California Republican primary. Of those two afflictions, Lou judged the second by far the worse.
When a family friend gave Allan a cardboard White House with a picture of
his father in one window, Allan told the donor, "Mummy says that she likes to
see Daddy in the window, but she wouldn't like to see him there in real life."
Lou explained to a friend that Bert's election would be a long shot but added

that if he should win, it "would be a very doubtful benefit to the family."[17] She mailed the letter on March 29, her forty-sixth birthday.

Yet despite her uneasiness, Lou did not entirely dislike the prominence that Bert's candidacy brought. It gave her an opportunity to speak out on issues that she thought important, as she did in a speech at Bryn Mawr College on April 10. Although never an extreme feminist, she believed that women ought to enjoy educational and career opportunities comparable to those of men. At Bryn Mawr, she urged the young women to use their new political power to ensure that schools, water supplies, and sewer systems were made adequate for the needs of a modern society, that injustices were righted, and that the world was indeed made safe for democracy. "That we *have* the vote means nothing," she declared. "That we use it in the right way means everything. Our political work has only begun when we have the ballot." Bryn Mawr students must not be merely cultured, she concluded, but must mold the nation's character and lead "its soul's awakening."[18]

In late April, the Hoovers, minus Allan, who stayed in New York, returned to California to vote in the May 4 Republican primary. Lou, who had been fretting over every detail of the nearly completed house, looked forward to showing it off to Bert. The architect, Birge Clark, who accompanied the Hoovers on their tour, reported that Bert seemed to like the house but enjoyed teasing Lou about some of her cherished touches. The ceiling over the stairs, which she had finished with an antiqued glaze, he declared to be no "worse" than "some basements in Belgium," and the cove lighting that she intended to cast a soft, indirect glow over the living room ceiling he described as "kind of like early Pullman." Lou found his comments irritating and later telephoned Clark to say that "Mr. Hoover was merely making a little joke to tease me, and he really thought the living room ceiling was just fine."[19] Still, she must have been disappointed that the house on whose every detail she had lavished so much care and thought seemed to mean no more to him than the succession of houses the family had rented during the twenty years of their married life

Hoover cared little about life's amenities. He liked having a spacious, well-run house where he could invite friends to stay and where he could conduct business meetings over pleasant meals, but he seemed on the whole insensitive to his surroundings. When he traveled, he would leave behind a trail of forgotten shirts and books unless Lou, his friends, and his staff picked up after him. From time to time, he ordered three or four identical blue suits and two dozen removable shirt collars, which he wore interchangeably until they frayed and new ones had to be purchased. His high, stiff collars had already become old-fashioned by the 1920s, but Hoover found them convenient, and his friends could not persuade him to try a more modern style. Frugality interested him more than fashion. Suits nearing the end of their life as business attire became fishing clothes, to squeeze the last bit of usefulness out of them. Houses, clothes, and cars must be of good quality and work well, but otherwise possessions interested him very little.[20]

A late and unenthusiastic entrant into the 1920 presidential contest, Hoover did not bemoan his loss in the California primary. Following the election, life resumed its normal course. Lou found just the right shade of color for the final coat of paint on the house's exterior but deplored delays in finishing the interior because of strikes at the mills. Her mother seemed much better after an operation for her colon cancer. Herbert, now 5 feet 10 inches tall, took great pride in being old enough to drive. On one memorable trip to Monterey, he drove in spite of a sprained knee that forced him to reach down and lift his foot onto the brake pedal whenever he needed to stop.[21]

During the summer and autumn of 1920, Bert and Lou shuttled back and forth across the country as Bert raised money for European relief, pushed Congress to act on the proposals made by the industrial conference, and tried to induce the Republican presidential candidate, Warren Harding, to support American membership in the League of Nations. In October, the American Child Hygiene Association elected him its president, and the work of that organization quickly became one of his main preoccupations. Lou dealt with the last details about the house, which neared completion in mid-September.

III

Being slightly less busy than usual with public issues, the Hoovers used the autumn of 1920 to sort out their personal economic affairs. They transferred Lou's assets, including substantial holdings in wartime Liberty Bonds, to the West Branch Corporation, a holding company created to distance Hoover from business matters. In September, he gave serious consideration to an offer from the Wall Street banker Paul M. Warburg for a business partnership but ultimately decided to continue in public service for the time being. With Harding's victory in November, it seemed likely that the service would take the form of a cabinet appointment, and if that were to materialize, the Hoovers would have to find a place to live in Washington again. They concluded that four years would be a long enough time to make buying more sensible than renting, but until Harding made an announcement about an appointment, they did not want to appear overeager by buying. The West Branch Corporation provided a convenient solution to the dilemma. In December, they purchased a handsome brick house at 2300 S Street, near Dupont Circle, making the purchase through the West Branch Corporation and arranging to put the property up for rent if they did not occupy it themselves. It would become their main home for the next four years.[22]

In December, Bert, along with trusted ARA associates Edgar Rickard, Julius Barnes, Edwin P. Shattuck, and Edward Flesh, set up the Intercontinental Development Company (IDC). The IDC controlled five other companies: the Pejepscot Paper Company in Maine, a pioneer in the use of sustained yield forestry; the Klearflax Linen Rug Company, which was experimenting with making carpets from flax straw; the Park Realty Company in Duluth; the

Caliminn Publishing Company, which held the majority of the stock in the Washington *Herald*; and the Western Cotton Company, which owned a thousand acres of cotton-growing land in the San Joaquin Valley of California.[23] Hoover felt certain that Barnes, his longtime associate in the Grain Corporation and the ARA, would be a strong president of the new company. With his financial affairs again in good order, he looked forward to new challenges.

Those challenges, while hardly profitable, would prove demanding. By mid-December, the new "invisible guest" drive for the ARA Children's Fund had reached a frenzied level, and Hoover found himself attending fund-raising dinners nearly every evening. The ARA urged families across the country to hang an "invisible guest" stocking on their Christmas tree and drop loose coins into it. The Hoovers sent out warm Christmas cards, but they could not be together for the holiday. Bert stayed in New York, while the rest of the family spent the holiday with the Henrys in Monterey. The boys were disappointed not to have their father home for Christmas, but the family looked forward optimistically to the new year. A conference with Harding about the cabinet on December 12 and the closing of the sale on the S Street house on December 23 suggested that 1921, if no less busy, might finally bring the family together as had not been the case since 1918.

CHAPTER 3

███████████████████████████████

An Economic Program for the Consumer Society

For a few days in September 1919, as the *Aquitania* bore Hoover, Lou, and Allan toward New York, Herbert Hoover floated between a completed chapter of his life and the beginning of an unknown future. For the past five years, he had been at the center of a world at war, struggling to save millions of noncombatants from slaughter and famine and working to mobilize the United States for its role in the contest. As he recalled later, during his last eleven months in Paris, he never went to a theater and never visited a museum, gallery, or cathedral. Occasional weekend automobile trips into the country ended at battlefields or cemeteries that emphasized the horrors of war. Most of the time, he worked twelve to eighteen hours a day, including Sundays, even using mealtimes to discuss problems with his staff or foreign officials. When Lou and Allan came to join him a few weeks before his departure for home, he saw them only at meals, if then. He had found it difficult to plan, or even to imagine, a peacetime future.[1]

On shipboard, Hoover recalled thirty years later, he began to "live again," but planning hardly went beyond the immediate moment. Upon arrival in New York, the family would "take the first train for the West, get out the fishing rods, motor into the mountains," and relax at last. He told reporters waiting on the dock when the ship docked on September 13 that "he was glad the work was done and he never cared to see Europe again." Europe's future had ceased to be his responsibility. It had become the obligation of the U.S.

35

government, which must "assist the rest of the world in the restoration of economic conditions" by ratifying the Treaty of Versailles. As to his own future, Hoover would only repeat what he had been telling everyone—he was going to California.[2]

The transatlantic passage, anticipated by the family as a restful interlude between past and future, had provided little respite for relaxation and planning. Before he left Europe, the American Institute of Mining and Metallurgical Engineers (AIMME) had invited him to a welcome-home banquet at which he had to make "some remarks." The first day or two of the trip passed happily, but drafting his speech, in which he summarized his work in Europe and reflected on the Bolshevik threat, "cast a gloom over the rest of the voyage." Having escaped the "seething social and political movements and economic chaos of Europe," he looked ahead and found that "America was not a quiet pool either."[3]

I

Before he could relax, he had to close down the Food Administration without producing chaos in American and world food markets. The agency's authorization to control the production and distribution of food in the United States had expired on June 30, 1919, but wartime disruptions still affected markets, British and French government purchasing agencies still dominated foreign buying, and American farmers remained vulnerable to world forces. At Hoover's recommendation, the president asked Julius Barnes to become chairman of the U.S. Grain Corporation. The company would continue to buy American wheat through the autumn of 1919 at $2.25 a bushel and resell it to foreign purchasers. The guaranteed price, Barnes assured reporters, would stabilize commodity markets but would not raise the cost of living because it approximated the world price.[4]

During the late winter and spring, a debate had taken place within the administration over wheat prices. Secretary of the Treasury Carter Glass, labor leaders, and consumer advocates urged deregulation in the hope of reducing the cost of living in the United States, which had almost doubled since 1914. Hoover, Barnes, and Secretary of Commerce William Redfield, on the other hand, contended that abruptly terminating controls would destabilize prices and ruin American farmers. Redfield endorsed deregulation in principle but proposed that if market prices fell, the Treasury would make up the difference between $2.25 and the market price. That raised an alarming possibility. Estimates indicated that the 1919 crop would be about 1.1 billion bushels. A dollar a bushel drop in the world price could thus cost the Treasury millions of dollars. What, Wilson asked, did Hoover advise?[5]

Hoover sent a soothing reply. A price drop, he argued, seemed less likely than a dramatic rise as world demand revived and shipping shortages ended. Maintaining the guaranteed price in the United States would have a stabilizing effect for the immediate future. As to next year's crop, there would be time enough to decide on policy later when conditions became clearer.[6] Wilson accepted Hoover's argument, appointed Barnes, and extended the price guarantee.

The case of sugar illustrated what could happen if wartime controls ended too abruptly. In 1918, the president had named Hoover chairman of a Sugar Equalization Board, which purchased most of the Cuban sugar crop and allocated it at controlled prices to the Allies and American consumers. Hoover argued that the controls prevented the price spikes in the United States that affected most European countries, but after the war, Secretary Glass and some members of Congress claimed that the arrangement raised prices artificially. Hoover disagreed. He believed that rising world demand and governmental purchasing by the Europeans, not American price controls, created an inflationary pressure that would continue for at least a year until production caught up with demand. In the end, however, Wilson yielded to the public clamor, not canceling controls outright but transferring authority over sugar purchasing to the Justice Department, which abandoned any effort to control prices. Within months, the retail price of sugar doubled, proving Hoover correct, but it was too late to go back to price controls.[7]

II

The United States in September 1919 was a troubled land. During the course of the year, nearly 4 million workers took part in more than three thousand strikes. Emboldened by the growth of labor unions during the war and outraged by rampant inflation and what they saw as excessive corporate profits, workers challenged capital as never before, demanding substantial raises, reduced working hours, and recognition of their unions. Four days before Hoover landed in New York, the Boston police went on strike, opening the city to looting and violence that led the governor of Massachusetts, Calvin Coolidge, to mobilize the National Guard and begin hiring replacements for the striking officers. Coolidge's attitude typified the hardening antilabor stance of employers across the country. Like the governor, corporate executives in the coal and steel industries not only refused to make concessions to strikers but also set out to break the unions.

Rapid and unplanned demobilization compounded the turmoil. By August 1919, only about 40,000 of the original 2 million servicemen remained in uniform. Early in 1919, Congress had cut off funding for the U.S. Employment Service, which matched workers to jobs during the war, leaving veterans with little help in finding civilian employment. An Industrial Board, set up in the Commerce Department in February 1919 to foster continuation of wartime cooperation between business and government, had run into opposition from the Justice Department's antitrust division and also ceased operation before it could influence reconversion. Other wartime economic management agencies, including the Fuel and Food Administrations and the War Industries Board, expired within months after the armistice or shrank to shadows of their former selves. Although most veterans found jobs in 1919, by the end of the year the government retained few tools to manage the economy or deal with the major recession that began a year later.

On September 3, 1919, President Wilson called an industrial conference made up of representatives of industry, labor, and the "public" to meet in early October and consider both the immediate crisis caused by the wave of strikes and the long-term industrial health of the nation. Also on the agenda was the question of what to do with the nationalized railroads and a growing fleet of government-owned merchant vessels. During the war, the government had taken over the railroads when the antiquated private system had collapsed in the face of the challenge of shipping vast quantities of freight and millions of soldiers to the East Coast. As soldiers and freight began to move toward the ports, the administration embarked on a frantic shipbuilding program to transport the men and goods to Europe. With the war over, the public seemed to favor returning the rail lines to the companies and transferring the ships to private ownership, but some farsighted observers also argued that a growing economy would need a better transportation system than the nation had before the war.

Adding to the postwar tension was a Red Scare. It began in February 1919 with a brief general strike in Seattle that seemed to many people a sign that European revolutionary tactics had been imported to the United States. Later in the spring, when the New York post office discovered a series of bombs addressed to prominent people, Attorney General A. Mitchell Palmer launched a massive investigation into alleged foreign radicalism. Several months later, a series of "Palmer raids" rounded up thousands of aliens, deporting hundreds of them without hearings. Hoover frequently said that he thought the danger of communism had largely passed in Europe and had never been serious in the United States, but many Americans thought otherwise. The fear of radicalism combined with labor unrest and rising living costs to create national anxiety by early 1920.

On May 6, 1919, over a million New Yorkers had turned out to cheer as returning veterans of the Seventy-seventh Division paraded up Fifth Avenue, but flag-waving patriotism could shade over into racism and xenophobia, as it had during the war. In August, a series of race riots directed against African Americans swept through more than twenty towns and cities, from Blaine, Arkansas, to Washington and Chicago. More than 120 African Americans died in the riots, and a hundred more were lynched during that murderous year. The Ku Klux Klan, dormant since the 1870s but resurrected in 1915, began to grow outside the South, becoming a major political force by the mid-1920s. Xenophobia influenced the murder trial and appeals of the Italian immigrants Nicola Sacco and Bartolomeo Vanzetti beginning in 1920 and led to the passage of immigration-restriction bills in 1921 and 1924.

To Hoover's chagrin, it seemed likely that American membership in the League of Nations and American leadership in reconstructing Europe would fall victim to the nation's changing mood. The day before the *Aquitania* docked in New York, William Bullitt, an embittered young member of the American peace delegation in Paris, had testified before the Senate Committee on Foreign Relations that he and others in the delegation, including Secretary of State Robert Lansing, regarded the Treaty of Versailles as a disaster. The committee seemed to agree, reporting the treaty to the full Senate with four reservations and forty-five amendments. Its action overshadowed Hoover's September 13 statement to the press as well as President Wilson's speeches in Tacoma and Seattle in support of the treaty.[8]

Yet despite the turmoil, not all signs appeared dark. American farmers had vastly increased their production during the war, and if markets for their surplus could be found, a golden age for commercial agriculture might be at hand. Industries producing consumer goods had expanded, and although advertising, transportation, and consumer credit had not yet caught up with production, the consumer economy was poised for takeoff. Wartime progress in radio and air travel fired the imaginations of the young, and the number of automobiles on the roads had doubled from 2.5 million in 1915 to 5 million in 1919.

The Hoovers quickly embraced the new technology. Soon after returning to the United States, they purchased a phonograph and records and began assembling a small fleet of cars—three in Washington and one in California by early 1920. Both Bert and Lou became enthusiastic motorists. So did young Herbert, who turned sixteen on August 4, 1919, before his parents and brother returned from Europe. He spent the summer tinkering with a car and joined thousands of other young men across the country in discovering the excitement of amateur radio.[9]

His father quickly grasped the opportunities and risks of the postwar situation. The consumer economy could transform ordinary Americans' lives, but it could also be strangled by inadequate transportation, labor-management conflict, agricultural overproduction and farm depression, a loss of world markets, and shortages of the coal and oil needed to power modern industry. Those posed problems with which he had grappled previously, during the Belgian relief, in the Food Administration, and in the postwar relief program, and it seemed to him that their solutions were obvious in theory, if difficult to achieve in practice. Ambitious and vigorous at age forty-five, he quickly shook off the fatigue of the war years and embraced the challenge of helping the economy realize its potential. In the fifteen months after returning to the United States in September 1919, he issued thirty-one press statements, wrote twenty-eight magazine articles, made forty-six speeches, and testified before nine congressional committees on various issues.[10]

III

The outlines of Hoover's ideas about national development began to emerge in his speech to the AIMME on September 16, 1919. Europe had collapsed at the end of the war, he told the engineers that evening, "not only from military and naval defeat" of the Central Powers, but from "total economic exhaustion" of the Allies as well as their enemies. In the resulting chaos, "Bolshevism and anarchy" had threatened to sweep into power. But socialism, instead of relieving the Continent's economic problems, made matters worse by depriving farmers of any incentive to produce and workers of any reason to labor. The immediate threat had been turned back by "the economic strength of the United States and its coordination with the remaining economic strength of Europe," but danger remained. Only the United States, by working with other democratic nations to maintain peace, and by maximizing its own production through cooperation between industry and labor, could both supply the needs of Europe and assure rising living standards at home. For the short term, stabilization required "the provision of credits to those countries whose total exhaustion abolished all hope of normal payment," but as the European countries recovered, American relief programs and loans must be replaced by "payment from those who had gold or commodities."[11]

The three major elements of the foreign policy program for the United States that Hoover set out in the fall of 1919 included membership in the League of Nations to promote political stability, short-term humanitarian aid and economic credits to strengthen European economies, and a return as soon as possible to an international trade system based on the gold standard. He regarded Communism as a fading threat that would soon collapse under the weight of its own failure. Already it had increased poverty in Russia to such an extent that the country had become incapable of feeding its own people.

The elements in Hoover's program for American domestic development emerged during Wilson's Second Industrial Conference in the winter of 1919 to 1920. The first conference, called by the president on September 3 and made up of equal numbers of representatives of capital, labor, and "the public," met thirteen times in October and deadlocked bitterly over the causes and solutions for current strikes. Business representatives insisted on the open shop; the labor group demanded a closed shop; and the public delegates proposed a complex plan to resolve disputes through a series of boards representing both labor and management. Unable to compromise among these radically different approaches, the conference members reported failure and adjourned on October 23. They never got to the problems of the railroads and merchant marine.[12]

A month later, on November 19, the same day the Senate defeated the Treaty of Versailles, the White House called a second industrial conference, this time with all members serving at large and not representing specific interests. The invitation urged conferees to ignore current strikes and focus on finding a labor-management relationship that would encourage the worker "to put forth his best effort," assure the employer "an encouraging profit," and guarantee that "the public will not suffer at the hands of either class." The sixteen people invited to the conference included mostly politicians and businessmen, whom Hoover described flatteringly as "industrialists." American Federation of Labor (AFL) president Samuel Gompers testified at an executive session on January 27, but the conference included no labor representatives. Although Secretary of Labor William B. Wilson served as nominal chairman, Hoover, as vice chairman, presided over meetings, set the agenda, and wrote most of the final report. He also chose most of the conferees, including banker Henry M. Robinson, Sears president Julius Rosenwald, and General Electric director Owen D. Young, all of whom had worked closely with him during the war and would later be associates in major projects during the Commerce years. Several years later, Julius Rosenwald recalled how Hoover had dominated the whole process: "I found the energetic, resourceful Hoover at its head . . . asking for suggestions—tolerant always of the opinions of others—he collected, correlated and coordinated essential facts and data— upon which the Conference could base its conclusions."[13]

Shortly before the conference's first meeting on December 16, Hoover laid out his own ideas about how to deal with the issues facing the country in an article in the *Saturday Evening Post*. The fundamental "object of all national economic policy," he wrote, "must be to maintain and improve the standard of living of the whole population." Achieving that goal required improved cooperation between workers and managers to maximize production; waste elimination; commitment to full effort by all members of the community; protection of the "physical, moral and intellectual welfare of the producer"; and expansion of available capital through increased savings. Workers' rights to unionize and bargain collectively should be guaranteed, Hoover thought, but if unions became so strong that they dominated basic industries such as coal or transportation, then the public's interests must be protected either by compulsory arbitration or reference of disputes to "some independent body" that could "determine the rights and wrongs and give public opinion the opportunity to exert pressure." By the same token, abuses by powerful corporations should be checked by vigorous enforcement of antitrust and antiprofiteering laws and through the authority of the Interstate Commerce Commission. To prevent the concentration of wealth and power in the hands of a few, he endorsed the maintenance of the progressive income tax and the inheritance tax. Above all, every possible method for reinforcing "the joy of craftsmanship and the mutual responsibility between the head managers and the employees that exist in smaller units," such as shop councils and profit-sharing plans, should be explored.[14]

Increasing productivity and the broadest possible distribution of its fruits throughout society, Hoover argued, would lay the foundations of a rising standard of living for everyone. For the most part, that goal could be achieved through voluntary adoption by business of scientific management and through genuine cooperation between management and labor. Government would play a part but "primarily as a coordinator, mediator, and information-dispenser, not as a coercive or restrictive force."[15]

Both in substance and method, the Second Industrial Conference reflected Hoover's ideas about managing the economy. Although his economic emphasis clashed with that of the conservative businessmen who controlled such major industries as steel and coal, he nevertheless assumed that most public spirited "industrialists" would willingly adopt the best academic advice available to shape economic policy. At the conference, as at similar gatherings he had convened during the war, he called on academic experts to marshal evidence before the meeting began. When the conferees arrived, the carefully assembled evidence and the prestige of the experts inclined them to rubber-stamp the ready-made plans that Hoover offered. That approach, which he used consistently during his public career, enabled him to lead without appearing to impose his will. Its long-term effectiveness depended on his ability to persuade those who attended his conferences that their self-interest coincided with his vision of the public welfare—and on his ability to popularize that vision to the public at large. His method, in short, supplemented rather than substituting for traditional political leadership. The results of the industrial conference would underline that point.

A week before Christmas, the conference unanimously adopted a preliminary report that closely followed Hoover's *Saturday Evening Post* proposals. The report recommended the establishment of shop councils (derisively labeled "company unions" by labor) and regional labor-management boards to investigate and propose solutions to conflicts. If the regional boards failed to resolve disputes, a series of additional boards leading to a National Industrial Tribunal appointed by the president would handle appeals. Employees of public utilities and all levels of government would be denied the right to strike (though not to join a union) and would be required to submit all disputes to a special tribunal.[16]

The draft not only reflected Hoover's respect for existing labor unions, particularly the AFL but also his belief that the closed shop was unreasonably coercive and his recognition that the craft-union structure of the AFL had become increasingly anachronistic in assembly-line factories. He proposed to allow the craft unions to continue but to supplement them with shop committees that would unite all workers in a factory, skilled and unskilled, union or nonunion, in a single organization that included managers as well. Shop committees would provide a mechanism for well-paid workers to work with scientifically trained managers in advancing their common goals of increasing production and minimizing waste. The system, he believed, would enable reasonable workers and managers to see that their mutual interest lay in cooperation.[17]

The conference's final report, issued on March 6, 1920, suggested that, in practice, Hoover's assumptions about labor-management cooperation might be overoptimistic. Its most liberal sections urged abolition of child labor, reduced hours for workers, better housing, and the development of plans for old-age pensions but offered no suggestions for concrete action. On the other hand, its plan for shop councils included no labor input, and its rejection of industrial unions reflected the conferees' management bias. Its proposed mechanism for the settlement of labor disputes sounded to union leaders like compulsory arbitration. Labor leaders quickly concluded that the report's main recommendations would "enhance employer control rather than foster genuine cooperation."[18]

The conference report received widespread press coverage and became the centerpiece of a Senate Committee on Education and Labor hearing in mid-May, but none of its recommendations attracted strong support. Unionists condemned the failure to recommend laws to protect the right of unionization and ban the use of injunctions in labor conflicts, while conservative businessmen, feeling they had the unions on the run, had no interest in any program that seemed to legitimate collective bargaining, even in a denatured form. When Hoover defended the report in a speech before the Boston Chamber of Commerce on March 24, 1920, he confessed ruefully that "the applause would not have waked a nervous baby." Despite his subsequent efforts to sell the conference's recommendations, the report quickly disappeared into obscurity.[19]

Years later, Hoover admitted that the conflict-resolution mechanisms in the report had been "overelaborate" and possibly unworkable, but he continued to believe that cooperation between labor and management to maximize production would serve everyone's best interests. As secretary of commerce, he would try to promote that goal indirectly by supporting the growth of economic associations among businessmen, farmers, and labor, which he saw as building common interests across class lines. The industrial conference might have been ahead of its time, he acknowledged, but lack of widespread support for its conclusions did not undermine his confidence in the use of similar conferences to develop policy on issues, nor did it lead him to question his conviction that workers and managers could learn to work together. In his view, improvements in worker productivity could boost corporate profits and justify higher wages, while increased production would make possible a higher standard of living for everyone.

Hoover recognized, however, that finite resources might limit future production increases. In his December 1919 *Saturday Evening Post* article, he argued that labor-management harmony must be combined with waste elimination to ensure national prosperity. Waste reduction, he wrote, offered the only route to "maintenance and increase in the production of commodities and services up to the maximum need of the entire number" of Americans. He defined waste broadly as "the support of nonproducers, oversized armies and navies . . . , extravagance, strikes, lockouts, or lack of skill in either labor or administrators." At other times, he added to this list "failure to conserve properly our national resources . . . , undue intermittent employment in seasonal trades . . . , waste in transportation, waste in unnecessary variety of articles used in manufacture, lack of standardization in commodities . . . , failure to develop our water resources," and a variety of other wastes and inefficiencies.[20] Defined that way, waste elimination represented a huge challenge that would require a commitment from both government and the private sector.

IV

Hoover regarded engineers as uniquely qualified to point the way to waste reduction. In his presidential address to the AIMME on February 17, 1920, he urged his colleagues to take the lead in helping the United States adjust to the changed economic and technical situation created by the war and its aftermath. At home, he argued, the government had been distorted and the economy disrupted by the necessities of war; abroad, "great moral and social forces [had] been stimulated by the war and will not be quieted by the ratification of peace." Engineers, standing "midway between capital and labor," could provide impartial guidance in reconversion and the shaping of postwar society. As they showed America the way to greater efficiency, Hoover argued, engineers would create a more moral economy, because efficiency would produce the highest possible standard of living, including leisure to cultivate "the finer flowers of life."[21] An America shaped by engineering principles would be both materially and morally superior to those European societies dominated by radical theories or hereditary classes.

In June 1920, Hoover led the AIMME in joining with the three other major engineering organizations (the American Society of Civil Engineers, the American Society of Mechanical Engineers, and the American Institute of Electrical Engineers) and seventeen smaller groups to form the Federated American Engineering Societies (FAES). He intended the umbrella organization to provide a forum for engineers in varying fields to discuss common interests and to give the profession as a whole a single voice on public issues. An executive committee, known as the American Engineering Council (AEC), would coordinate and speak for the new organization. It elected Hoover its first president on November 19, 1920.[22]

Even before taking office, Hoover proposed an agenda for the new organization in a speech to the AIMME in Minneapolis on August 26, 1920. "The time has arrived in our national development," he said, "when we must have a definite national program in the development of our great engineering problems." Unplanned, "haphazard" development of resources had given the nation only "a fifty per cent result." A national plan to eliminate waste and inefficiency had become essential. If engineers worked cooperatively to create such a plan, "greater production with less human effort" would be possible without a vast expansion of federal authority.[23]

On November 17, shortly before the AEC's first meeting, Hoover attended a meeting of the AFL's Executive Council to discuss his ideas and to solicit labor support for them. AFL president Samuel Gompers had been offended by a February report in the *New York Times* alleging that he opposed the industrial conference's plan for dealing with labor-management conflicts. Although the article accurately described Gompers's attitude, he expressed irritation that his testimony to the conference had not been kept confidential. Hoover, recognizing that the union leader had been angered less by the leak than by his exclusion from the industrial conference, took the November 17 meeting as an opportunity to rebuild a relationship. Engineers, he told the AFL Council, did not "belong to either class of employer or labor." They recognized that industry was not merely a "matter of processes and machines" but "a human problem." Gompers responded cordially that he was pleased to learn that there had been "a very great change in the mental attitude of the . . . engineering profession toward the labor question and labor problem." As a result, he believed that labor and the engineers had "been drawn very much closer to each other." The interchange seemed, to Hoover, to open the way for labor and engineers to work together, not only to solve the labor-management conflicts that he regarded as a major cause of industrial waste, but also to develop cooperative strategies to attack issues such as seasonal employment, unemployment insurance, and old-age pensions. The next day, Hoover took a young engineer, Robert B. Wolf, who had been studying methods to encourage cooperation between labor and management, to a second meeting with Gompers.[24]

Hoover's conversations with Gompers did not go far enough to reveal a potential flaw in his vision of eliminating class conflict. Gompers wanted to raise workers' wages and benefits. Hoover hoped to maximize production. He assumed that engineers could achieve "greater production with less human effort" in all industries through improved efficiency and reduced waste. In his view, greater production, improved working conditions, and higher wages were all compatible. His model made more sense, however, in capital-intensive industries such as steel and automobiles than in labor-intensive production of shoes, textiles, or cigars. Where labor was the main cost, disputes over pay and benefits could not be engineered away entirely.

In his AEC presidential address on November 19, Hoover reiterated the argument he made to the AFL. The AEC, he alleged, had "no special economic interest for its members" and sought only to "be of service in bringing about cooperation between . . . great economic groups of special interests." He reported that the AFL had asked for the support of engineers "in the development of methods for increasing production," and he recommended that the new organization make reduction of waste resulting from intermittent employment, unemployment, and strikes and lockouts its first order of business. Future prosperity, he concluded, depended upon the nation's success in stimulating "craftsmanship and *the contribution of the worker's intelligence to management.*"[25]

When he made his speech, Hoover had already proposed to the executive board of the AEC the creation of a special committee to study industrial waste. On November 20, the board approved his proposal, and a month later, the Committee on Elimination of Waste in Industry held its first meeting, with Lew Wallace, Jr., as chairman and journalist Edward Eyre Hunt, who had been one of Hoover's assistants in the Belgian relief program, as executive secretary. Initially, Hoover thought the committee would concentrate only on studying how to encourage labor productivity and reduce unemployment, and its budget was set at a modest $2,190, but during the spring of 1921, the scope of the investigation expanded, mutating into an "exhaustive inquiry into elimination of industrial waste as a basis for increased national efficiency, productivity, and thus for both reconstruction and progress." Hoover undertook to raise $50,000 from the member organizations to fund the enlarged study.[26]

When he became secretary of commerce in March 1921, Hoover's positions as president of the AEC and a member of the industrial waste committee created a possible conflict of interest, so he stopped soliciting contributions and on April 16 resigned the presidency of the AEC. His departure dealt a serious blow to the organization, making fund-raising much more difficult and forcing a reduction of the waste committee's budget to about $28,000. Nevertheless, under Hunt's frugal management, the committee persevered, and in May it completed its work. Committee members presented a summary of their findings to the FAES at a meeting in St. Louis on June 3, and the final report was published in the fall.[27]

The nearly four hundred pages of the published report, *Waste in Industry*, opened with twenty-five pages of general discussion of the causes and possible cures for industrial waste. The remainder was divided into two sections. One synthesized reports from field investigations into waste in six industries: construction, men's clothing, shoes, printing, metal fabrication, and textiles. Experts evaluated each industry on its management, use of modern equipment, and treatment of workers. The case studies concluded that seasonal variations in operations, inefficient management, and poor labor relations frequently caused waste.[28]

The second section of the report comprised seven chapters by experts summarizing available information on unemployment, strikes and lockouts, legal machinery for resolving labor conflicts, industrial accidents, workers' health and vision, and purchasing and sales policies. Individual reports sometimes highlighted acute problems—the shortage of reliable unemployment statistics, for example—but these chapters offered more data than recommendations.[29]

From Hoover's standpoint, the most important sections of the report were the two chapters dealing with the causes of waste and recommendations for its reduction. In every industry studied, the report argued, between 50 and 81 percent of the responsibility for waste and inefficiency could be laid at the door of management. Labor, on the other hand, took the blame for less than a quarter of problems. "Other factors" such as demands for style changes or lack of community support for industries played smaller roles.[30]

The report concluded that managers needed to plan better, correlate production with sales, secure and maintain good equipment, adopt better accounting practices, develop "a sense of mutual interest" with workers, and standardize products, materials, and equipment. Labor and the public could help by increasing production and avoiding needless spending. Communities could encourage trade associations and chambers of commerce educate managers, workers, and consumers.[31]

The committee reflected Hoover's influence in its recommendations for an enhanced federal role. A "National Industrial Information Service" should distribute "information on current production, consumption and available stocks of commodities"; a "National Statistical Service" should report on "employment requirements and conditions"; a national system to settle labor disputes should be adopted; "a national policy regarding public health" should be implemented; and federal programs should promote "a nation-wide program of industrial standardization" and encourage year-round production.[32]

The recommendations for federal actions echoed steps that Hoover's Commerce Department had already taken or hoped to take. Businessmen generally applauded such initiatives, but they rejected flatly the report's conclusion that managers were mainly responsible for industrial waste. Almost equally offensive from their point of view was the report's approach to labor relations, which Edward Eyre Hunt touted as a basis for genuine cooperation between labor and management, "instead of the pseudo-cooperation which consists in labor's lying down and playing dead at the will of the employer." Even many of the engineers who Hoover had confidently expected to back his efforts reacted coolly, identifying with management rather than taking the neutral position that Hoover had predicted. Dissatisfaction with the report contributed to the breakup of the FAES in the mid-1920s.[33]

Hoover was proud of the industrial waste report and continued to emphasize its findings throughout the decade. In retrospect, however, neither that report nor the earlier one from the Second Industrial Conference articulated a program for national economic growth that commanded the full support of industry and labor. Even people sympathetic to Hoover, like the journalist Mark Sullivan, did not share his vision of engineered prosperity in a classless, cooperative society. The government, Sullivan told his daughter, "is not entitled to tell the citizen what size screw he can make."[34]

CHAPTER 4

The Election of 1920

In the spring of 1919, with the war over and the end in sight for the peace conference and the relief program, Hoover faced the question of what to do next. Although he felt worn out after five years of unremitting work, he had not yet turned forty-five. After a few weeks in California and a fishing trip, his prodigious energy would demand an outlet. Should he return to business or, despite all its frustrations, look for a new challenge in public service?

Newspaper publishing offered one possibility. The Sacramento *Union* and the Washington *Herald* were both for sale. Perhaps they could provide him with a pulpit from which to influence national affairs. But neither paper had a large circulation. Accustomed to going to the top, to issuing orders and having his plans put into operation at once, Hoover had little patience for the slow process of molding public attitudes. He liked immediate, direct action. In December 1919, he told reporters that he had "put up some money" to help an old friend buy the *Herald*, but he had no intention of "going into the publishing business on any scale whatever." He loaned money to another friend to purchase the *Union*.[1]

I

Inevitably, the White House drew his attention. Theodore Roosevelt died in January 1919, and Wilson was completing his second term and in poor health. With those two giants out of the picture, no obvious front-runners had appeared for 1920. People working with Hoover in Paris saw him as a strong candidate.[2] After all, as John Maynard Keynes had said, he was the only man to emerge from the peace conference with an enhanced reputation. Hoover's assistants, like young Lewis Strauss, believed he could be the man of the hour.

Strauss overestimated the popularity that Hoover's relief work had earned him in the United States, but "the Chief" had some enthusiastic supporters at home. Food Administration and American Relief Administration (ARA) workers, along with professional engineers, formed a core of loyalists, and newly enfranchised women, who had cooperated willingly with the Food Administration, might become political supporters. In California, petroleum engineer Ralph Arnold, Stanford 1898 graduate and a trustee since 1914, offered to organize a state and national Hoover-for-president movement.[3]

Despite Arnold's enthusiasm, however, serious obstacles stood in the way. Experienced politicians had already committed themselves or leaned toward other possible candidates. And the most powerful California politician, Republican Senator Hiram Johnson, also nurtured presidential ambitions.

The Constitution's requirement of fourteen years' continuous residence within the United States prior to election also offered a possible problem. Although a rumor that Hoover had become a British citizen while living and working in London could be squelched fairly easily, the fact remained that he *had* spent most of the last twenty years outside the country. As a precaution, Lewis Strauss asked Edgar Rickard to try to find and photograph Hoover's Iowa birthplace. Hoover prepared a detailed record of his visits to the United States and claimed that he had always maintained a legal residence there.[4] But the question of his status would reappear over and over during Hoover's political career.

His own attitude toward a candidacy seemed ambivalent. He told a New York friend that "the whole idea" of a campaign filled him "with complete revulsion." In the absence of a national emergency, he declared, he saw no reason to sacrifice his personal interests and be dragged down into the "political mud." But then he launched into a detailed discussion of issues that seemed to him important. Although the issues he identified—governmental reorganization and the establishment of a system to allow Cabinet members to sit and speak in Congress—had little to do with the questions agitating Americans in 1919, he certainly had strong political interests.[5] His widely circulated letter left the impression that, although a reluctant candidate, he could be talked into running.

Realists warned that winning a nomination would not be easy. ARA executive Vernon Kellogg in New York and California lawyer Warren Gregory pointed out that, in the absence of a crisis, party loyalty would probably influence candidate choice more than competence. More importantly, whatever Hoover's experience and skills, he had no strong political affiliations to recommend him to the decision makers in either party. At the urging of Edgar Rickard and others, Kellogg agreed to begin putting together a campaign biography, but his doubts were obvious.[6]

En route to New York aboard the *Aquitania*, Hoover told Rickard that he intended to issue "a positive denial and refusal of any possible candidacy for the presidency." His statements on arrival, however, sounded far less categorical. Although declaring that he was "not in politics," he left open the possibility that he might support either the Democrats or the Republicans and perhaps even be available as a candidate, depending on what policies the parties proposed.[7]

Three days after arriving in New York, Hoover made it clear that he did not intend to await the party platforms. Before a cheering audience of members of the American Institute of Mining and Metallurgical Engineers (AIMME) on September 16, he declared that American relief had saved the European economic and political system from imminent collapse. The United States, he proclaimed, must now demonstrate to the world a better system in which "every section of this nation, the farmer, the industrial worker, the professional man, the employer, are all absolutely interdependent . . . in this task of maximum production and the better distribution of its results."[8]

Candidate or not, Hoover confronted national issues. With a Senate vote on the Treaty of Versailles pending and Wilson ill, Hoover abruptly terminated his brief vacation to speak out in favor of ratification. He also found himself in the public spotlight because of his fund-raising for hungry children in Europe and his work as vice chairman of the president's Second Industrial Conference. The nation, it appeared, had made his choice for him—his future would lie in public service. But the question remained, would it be in politics?

Throughout December and January, both Bert and Lou traveled extensively, raising money for the relief program. On December 24, Hoover told reporters that his relief work and the demands of the industrial conference left no time for politics. Refusing to endorse either party, he added that he was "not considering being a candidate for President of the United States." Yet once again, he framed his disavowal of candidacy in a way that left supporters hoping he might change his mind and enemies fearing he would. A Christmas Eve cartoon by John T. McCutcheon in the New York *News* depicted a parade of some thirty potential candidates, with Hoover prominent in the center of the picture.[9]

A curious project launched over Christmas 1919 underlined the amateurism of Hoover's early supporters. Two California Republican friends, Ralph Arnold and Ralph Merritt, joined a Democrat, Sam A. Lindauer, in sending some 20,000 letters proposing a Hoover candidacy to people listed in *Who's Who in America*, members of the AIMME, and Stanford alumni. Encouraged by positive responses to this scattergun approach, Arnold encouraged volunteers in other states to start nonpartisan Hoover-for-president committees and persuaded twenty-five or thirty of Hoover's friends and admirers to form a national Hoover-for-President Club. After handing off the leadership of the new organization to Captain John F. Lucey of Texas, Arnold returned to California to join with Ralph Merritt in organizing Hoover's home state prior to the May primary election.[10]

Arnold's nonpartisan approach broadened Hoover's appeal but made it hopelessly shallow. As the *Literary Digest* pointed out, the "cold bare fact" was that "political conventions, and not the people, select Presidential candidates." Meyer Lissner, Hiram Johnson's Southern California manager, commented happily that the nonpartisan approach made Hoover suspect in both parties. Neither would turn to him unless "they think it is doubtful whether they can win with anyone else." The only risk for Johnson, Lissner thought, lay in pro-League progressives deserting him for Hoover because of Johnson's opposition to the Treaty of Versailles. Johnson himself felt less confident. He knew that his opposition to the treaty had weakened his support among California progressives and that old enemies, sensing weakness, had been plotting to lure pro-League progressives into a Hoover Republican Club.[11]

Hoover could hardly have been unaware of all this, but he offered no comment on Arnold's efforts, continuing to deny his candidacy and refusing to state a party affiliation. Invited by Oregon Democrats to address their Jackson Day banquet in Portland, he declined, saying mysteriously that an endorsement by either party would be "entirely wrongly directed."[12]

As the presidential race intensified in early 1920, Hoover came under increasing pressure to at least declare a party preference. His most obvious affiliation was with the Democrats. He had been a prominent member of the Wilson administration and an outspoken supporter of the treaty, and he enjoyed warm relations with many important Democrats, including Ray Stannard Baker and Franklin Roosevelt. Democrats in Oregon, Massachusetts, and Georgia urged him to run, as did the leading Democratic newspaper, the New York *World*. The Democratic nomination seemed within reach, but as a Philadelphia paper put it, his refusal to identify his loyalties left his followers "up a tree." If "the only people in this country who are boosting Hoover for president are the independents," observed an Iowa editor, "this is equivalent to saying that Hoover boosters are about as scarce as hen's teeth."[13]

Hoover's nonpartisan stance did not shield him from attack. Democratic Senator James A. Reed charged that the ARA had illegally diverted millions of dollars intended for Polish relief to the Polish army to support its campaign against the Bolsheviks. The food reporter of the New York *Globe* alleged that the Food Administration had shipped rotten grain to Belgium. Neither charge stood up to investigation, but mere rumors of Hoover's candidacy had thrust him into public controversy, no matter what he said.[14]

In fact, despite Hoover's nonpartisan pose, he had often referred to himself privately as a Republican. He had declined to state his affiliation only in hopes of influencing the party platforms, but by mid-January, he realized that he had made a mistake, accomplishing nothing except to invite condemnation from all sides. Yet if he now declared himself a Republican, everyone would see that as a declaration of his candidacy, which he had not yet decided to embrace.

Finding no good solution to the dilemma, he asked Julius Barnes to make the announcement for him. In a speech before the National Wholesale Dry-Goods Association in New York on January 14, Barnes declared that Hoover's "affiliations have been with the Progressive-Republicans" and emphasized that his main interest lay in promoting "equality of opportunity in this country" and turning back the challenge of "bankrupt" communism. The speech accomplished its immediate goal, but the "amateurish" device of having it given by a proxy at a business convention convinced professional politicians that Hoover was "not an organization man." Republican Senator Asle Gronna of North Dakota sneered, "We don't take Hoover seriously out our way," and a California Johnsonite mocked him for pretending to be above party. Hoover was "not exactly George Washington," he observed.[15]

For Hoover's California friends, however, Barnes's speech served as a long-awaited signal to start organizing for a primary contest with Hiram Johnson. Hoover must win in the Golden State if he were to be a serious candidate. But the nonpartisan approach weighed heavily on him. A San Francisco group polled Republicans, Democrats, and independents across the state and declared the favorable response a mandate for Hoover. A nonpartisan California Hoover-for-president organization was announced at a meeting at the St. Francis Hotel in San Francisco on January 27.[16]

At that point, a Hoover Republican campaign really existed only in Southern California. Ralph Arnold; Ralph Merritt; Clara Burdette, a former California Food Administration executive and Republican Party activist; and Ida Koverman, assistant to movie executive Louis B. Mayer, had begun organizing, while Harry Chandler's Los Angeles *Times* and Edward Dixon's Los Angeles *Express* publicized the cause in their columns. Northern California, dominated by Hiram Johnson's formidable political machine and home to the hostile Hearst press, remained enemy territory. Hoover's old friend, Stanford president Ray Lyman Wilbur, could muster only a feeble counterattack against Hearst's allegations that Hoover had "British" support by issuing a statement affirming Hoover's love for the United States and emphasizing that, even during his service abroad, he had kept his legal residence in California.[17]

As it turned out, the Californians' efforts were premature. Hoover had still not made up his mind to run. On February 6, he issued a statement reminding everyone that he was working full time on the Industrial Conference and the European children's relief program. He had no time for political activity, and he expected to "vote for the party that stands for the League." At the same time, he seemed to take a swipe at both parties, rejecting both those "who hope to regulate free speech, or free representation, who hope to re-establish control of the government for profit and privilege," as well as those who favored "any form of socialism, whether it be nationalization of industry, or other destruction of individual initiative."[18]

Washington observers cynically interpreted Hoover's statement as "an actual enunciation of his platform," while the Sacramento *Bee* reported dryly that he was "Battl[ing] Bravely to Escape Being President." A flippant letter to Caspar Hodgson denying that he had profited from relief work or that he had applied for British citizenship while working abroad did nothing to improve his reputation. Ralph Arnold soldiered on bravely, but even a warning from former President William Howard Taft that Republicans should avoid throwing the election to the Democrats by endorsing an anti-League candidate did more to damage Johnson than to help Hoover.[19] With the California primary a little over two months away, Hoover had shown little interest in the Republican nomination and less political aptitude.

Yet while he spurned political maneuvering, Hoover continued to speak out about issues. On February 17, he delivered his inaugural address as president of the AIMME. He might have given a nonpartisan speech on professional issues, but instead he focused on broad economic policy. The war, he declared, had left the country with an "over-centralized" government. The time had come to restore "the vitality of production," end "experiments in socialism necessitated by the war," and return the railroads and merchant marine to private control where "the hard school of competition" would bring the best executives to the fore. "Cooperation between employer and employee" could raise living standards for everyone, even if greater efficiency temporarily displaced some workers. They would soon find better jobs in other industries.[20]

Although Hoover's February 17 speech avoided overt partisanship, it sounded like a political manifesto. In Georgia, Democrats proposed him for their party's nomination, while in Michigan state officials responded to petitions by entering his name in both of that state's April 5 primaries. He stopped the process in Georgia, but Michigan law did not permit him to withdraw. In Oregon, impatient Democrats threatened to enter him in their state's primary, whether he liked it or not. And in Ohio, Senator Warren Harding, angling for the nomination himself, hinted that he might endorse Hoover for the vice presidency or a cabinet position in return for the Californian's support. Whether deliberately or not, Hoover had thrust himself into the contest, and the *New Republic* chided him for saying that he would wait for party leaders to declare themselves before choosing which party to support. He must show leadership, wrote the editors, not wait passively to see what "a group of politicians" would offer.[21]

On February 23, Hoover fanned speculation about his intentions by using a speech at Johns Hopkins University, purportedly about education, to again urge the Senate to approve the Treaty of Versailles, which was scheduled for a second vote a few days later. Whereas at Stanford he had contended that American membership in the League would strengthen international order, in Baltimore he emphasized that American self-interest required ratification. The chaos threatening Europe, he argued, endangered the development of democracy, American trade, and European reconstruction. Reasonable men should be able to accept a treaty with mild reservations, leaving time to focus on "pressing domestic issues" in the national campaign.[22]

Another opportunity for Hoover to present his ideas in a nonpartisan context came at the end of February, when the Western Society of Engineers gave him its Washington Award in recognition of his work with the Food Administration and European relief. As at Baltimore, he chose a broad topic for his speech—"the inter-relationship of general industry and food production and distribution." Declaring that those questions involved "not only engineering" but also "social and political issues of the first importance," he argued that some means must be found to make agriculture economically attractive in order to slow the migration from farms to cities and ensure that the United States never needed to import food. The solution to rural decline, he contended, lay in reducing transportation costs between farm and market. Railroads must modernize their equipment, and a waterway from the Great Lakes to the Atlantic by way of the St. Lawrence River should be built to give farmers inexpensive access to world markets. Along with improved transportation, strict regulation of railroads and middlemen and the development of cooperative marketing would gradually solve farm problems. Some attrition in the number of farmers seemed inevitable, he admitted, but agricultural prosperity was within reach.[23]

The Chicago speech did nothing to win Hoover support in farm states. In the Midwest, his wartime record as food administrator outweighed his ideas about future policy. On February 13, an influential farm paper, *Wallace's Farmer*, published a sharp attack on his policies. The editorial "What's the Matter with the Farmer" charged that the Food Administration had kept wartime hog prices unreasonably low and thus deprived Midwestern farmers of legitimate profits. Although Hoover promptly denied the old accusation, the paper continued to repeat the charges.[24]

In California, Hoover's supporters tried briefly to make the best of his ambiguity about party affiliation. They suggested that he planned "to lay back, keep friends with everybody, and then, when the big tangles come in the conventions be in a position to be the emergency candidate and secure one or both nominations by way of the well-known stampede." On March 5, however, Hoover killed the two-party candidacy by stating flatly that he would not enter the California Democratic primary. That narrowed his options drastically. If he lost the Republican primary, even a stalemated convention would be unlikely to turn to him. His supporters warned him that he must commit himself wholeheartedly or forget the nomination.[25]

On March 6, a California delegation, along with Julius Barnes, Robert Taft, and others, met with Hoover in his New York office and urged him to initiate a national campaign. They failed, reporting to Ralph Arnold in California that Hoover was "not satisfied" that a national organization was necessary. He seemed to place naive confidence in "unorganized public sentiment." In another meeting with lawyer Jeremiah Milbank, Hoover reiterated that he had "no desire for the Presidency" and again encouraged "the crystallization of independence [*sic*] sentiment." Milbank dismissed that approach as unrealistic but left feeling that he had made no headway. Hoover's assistant, Lewis Strauss, loyally echoed the chief's position, claiming disingenuously that a circular letter sent out by Arnold on behalf of a "Make Hoover President Club" in Los Angeles probably came from "a spontaneous organization." A St. Louis cartoonist depicted the "Hoover boom" as an unoccupied automobile, floating above the road in violation of the laws of physics, while a Republican elephant and Democratic donkey looked on perplexed. The Louisville *Courier-Journal*'s cartoonist drew Hoover as the Sphinx.[26]

Of course, potential candidates frequently disclaim any desire to run during the early stages of a campaign, but the California primary would take place in less than two months. Hoover had no chance of winning unless he jumped in with both feet. In the absence of his commitment, his supporters struggled to assemble a national organization. J. F. Lucey, chairman of the national Make Hoover President Club, insisted that "a very strong organization" already existed and urged others to get on the bandwagon. Arnold, undeterred by Hoover's standoffishness, released a statement that California Republicans were "more than ever convinced that he is available as a candidate upon the Republican ticket." Gertrude Lane, editor of the *Women's Home Companion*, assured Strauss that women across the country favored Hoover and recommended aggressive organization. Ralph Arnold compiled a list of 190 newspapers that had spoken favorably of Hoover and might offer editorial support. Along with former federal Fuel Administrator Mark Requa, Arnold launched a national drive to "perfect organization" of the Hoover movement. Rose Wilder Lane published a campaign biography, which was serialized in *Sunset* magazine, beginning in April. The March 13 issue of the *Literary Digest* featured a portrait of Hoover on the cover, but its story, titled "The Man Without a Party," highlighted the campaign's persistent problem.[27]

The flurry of Hoover organization in California in early March, which culminated in the founding of a "Hoover Republican Club of California" on March 11, led to reports that he would enter the Republican primary and might run as a Democrat as well. On March 8, Hoover stoked the fires by denouncing both "reactionary" Republicans and "radical" Democrats. He added that although he did not want public office and would not participate "in any organization to that end," he felt an obligation "like any other citizen . . . to be ready for service when really called upon." Everyone read this as a coy declaration of candidacy, although experienced politicos thought he had left it "too late" for an effective primary campaign.[28]

Nevertheless, neither Leonard Wood nor Frank Lowden, the early Republican front-runners, had established a clear lead nationally by mid-March. Hoover trailed Johnson in California but had significant support across the country, especially among women. Despite his late start, if he could win in California, he might vault to the front nationally. Encouraged by that assessment, Ralph Merritt, Hoover's unofficial state campaign manager, launched a petition drive on March 18 to qualify him for the state's Republican primary.

Within a day, 7,500 people signed, more than three times the number required. A few days later, Merritt began setting up local organizations and recruiting primary voters. His success led to the first overt attacks on Hoover by the Johnson and Wood supporters.[29] The attacks delighted Hoover organizers as evidence that their man had become a serious candidate.

Meanwhile, Hoover sounded more and more like a candidate. He again urged ratification of the Treaty of Versailles with reservations and also reached out to isolationists by releasing an April 1919 letter to President Wilson warning against membership in other proposed economic organizations. The League, he wrote, would promote peace, but the Europeans would use the other organizations to perpetuate unjust relationships within Europe and prevent the United States from advancing its own interests.[30]

On March 24, Hoover seized upon another nonpartisan occasion, a speech to the Boston Chamber of Commerce, to discuss labor policy. He described labor relations as nothing less than "the whole problem of the successful development of our democracy." Endorsing worker aspirations for more influence in industry, provided those desires were "turned into helpful and co-operative channels," he acknowledged the importance of unions in protecting against unscrupulous employers. His main focus, however, was on another approach to industrial peace, the shop council. Councils representing both managers and workers within a particular factory, he contended, would restore the "personal contact between employers and employees" that had disappeared as corporations grew. With renewed trust, managers and workers could unite in pursuit of increased productivity and an improved standard of living for all.[31]

Yet despite appearances, Hoover continued to deny any plans to run, telling Edward Keating, editor of *Labor*, that he was "not a candidate for the nomination to the Presidency," although he added again that he could not "prevent any citizen or group of citizens from advocating that [he] undertake public office." His supporters refused to take such half-hearted denials seriously. On March 25, a group of them convoked a Chicago miniconvention to popularize his candidacy, create a national organization, and plan the distribution of campaign materials. Soon the new organization was producing a stream of position papers on issues and a newsletter, the "Hoover National Bulletin." Lewis Strauss declared that organizations already existed in twenty-three states and that rapid progress was being made in most others.[32]

II

The pressure on Hoover had finally become irresistible, and sometime between March 26 and 28 he decided at last to enter the California Republican primary. In announcing his decision on March 30, he said that he was running mainly to offer California Republicans a pro-League alternative to Hiram Johnson. The ideas he had been propounding for months, however, about "the size of our armament, reduction in taxation, and the prevention of agricultural and industrial depression and consequent unemployment" were closely related to the League issue. Domestic progress, he argued, depended on "stability abroad and upon our access to the world's markets." The United States would be at an economic disadvantage so long as it stayed out of the League.[33]

Having been a member of the Wilson administration for almost three years, Hoover had enough political experience to know that his late entry into the race burdened him with a huge handicap. His rivals welcomed him with sharp attacks on his positions, but they obviously discounted him as a threat. A sense of duty, more than ambition, appeared to be the main factor in his decision. Lou Hoover summed it up when she said that she opposed his candidacy personally, but as a public-spirited citizen, she could "not but feel differently inclined."[34]

In fact, Hoover's late entry created virtually insuperable obstacles to a national campaign. His surprising first-place finish in the Michigan Democratic primary and second-place finish in the same state's Republican contest on April 5 led to widespread predictions that he could win if nominated, but it was unclear how that might happen. His amateur organization remained fragmentary, and even if it had been stronger, the filing deadline for most state primaries had passed. California offered his best opportunity, and his supporters had been at work there for some time, but they had taken few practical steps toward setting up a campaign. When they tried to secure billboard space to advertise his candidacy, for example, they discovered that every billboard in the state had already been rented for the duration of the campaign. Indeed, even a win in California, although essential to prevent total disaster, would not make him a viable national candidate. Increasingly, it appeared that his only chance would be as a third-party nominee, which he said he would not consider. The obvious question, then, was why run at all if he had no chance of winning?[35]

On April 7, Hoover released a statement offering an explanation of his viewpoint. Essentially conceding that he could not win enough delegates to secure the nomination, he advised the abandonment of write-in campaigns in Illinois, Nebraska, Ohio, and other states. Instead, he urged his friends to apply their energies to popularizing his ideas among voters and "the delegates already named, with full respect to their prior pledges." Observers, reading between the lines, concluded that he hoped for a deadlocked convention in which he might be nominated as everyone's second choice.[36] No one but his closest associates took seriously the possibility that he really meant what he said and had entered the race primarily to popularize policies he thought important.

In any case, the crucial first step must be taken in California. A defeat there, Ralph Arnold admitted, would be "a terrible setback to our cause." Although the national organization tried to keep Hoover's name and ideas before the voters in preparation for a fall campaign, the main focus during April was on California.[37]

Two days after Hoover's statement abjuring a national write-in campaign, the *New York Times* reminded readers that on November 2, 1918, he had published a letter calling for election of a Congress that would support Wilson's peace program. The *Times*'s article suggested that Hoover, a closet Democrat, had written the letter at the request of Vance McCormick, chairman of the Democratic National Committee. The story caused a minor panic among Hoover's California supporters, who feared the Johnson forces would use it to deadly effect. They breathed a sigh of relief when the Johnsonites did not exploit it. Only later did they discover that the story contained a crucial error. Hoover had written his letter not at the request of McCormick but of Frederic R. Coudert, a New York Republican banker. Coudert believed that Wilson's international program would "immeasurably advance human progress" and "service American interests in the best and truest sense." He had urged Hoover to endorse it on those grounds, and Hoover had agreed. Like the president, Hoover had demonstrated political naiveté in calling for the election of a Wilsonian Congress, but Coudert's explanation showed that he was not secretly a Democrat. To preempt a later attack, the California campaign office flooded the state with Hoover's more recent statements praising the Republican Party.[38]

A rumor that Hoover had failed to employ women in wartime and postwar organizations, or in leadership positions in his campaign, was more easily countered. George Barr Baker compiled a three-page memorandum describing the important roles women had played in the Food Administration. No other wartime agency, Baker claimed, had employed so many women in executive positions. A pamphlet titled "What Herbert Hoover's Election Will Mean to Women" emphasized the close links between women and the Food Administration during the war. It also highlighted Hoover's worldwide service, his support for the League of Nations, his commitment to child welfare, and his promise to reduce the cost of government through implementation of a budget for the nation like those that women used in their homes.[39]

A third attack on Hoover erupted in the last days of the campaign but probably had little effect on the outcome. Johnson supporters charged that Hoover and other foreign directors of a Chinese mining company had colluded in 1900 to cheat the Chinese stockholders. The allegations had been examined by a court in London in 1905 that found Hoover not culpable, but the case was complex, and it seemed likely that *someone* had cheated the Chinese. In April 1920, Hoover's friends were unable to get an affidavit from the presiding judge stating that he had been cleared, but the issue never caught on anyway. The case was simply too old, too complicated, and too foreign to serve as an effective campaign weapon.[40]

The bipartisan support for Hoover demonstrated by the Michigan primaries, plus a statement from former President Taft that "the pro-Germans, the Sinn Feiners, the radical labor men, Nonpartisan leaguers and Socialists" favored Hiram Johnson, gave a lift to the campaign in early April. Then, in the middle of the month, a serious problem developed when Theodore Roosevelt's old ally Gifford Pinchot blasted Hoover's Food Administration as having been "run mainly by and for the packers, canners, millers, and other great middlemen" and staffed by their paid employees. The farmers, Pinchot charged, had been "wholly left out." Hoover had rebutted the charges many times, but Pinchot remained influential among progressive Republicans, and the majority of Californians still lived on farms.[41]

Hoover's supporters quickly launched a counterattack. Ray Wilbur labeled Pinchot "a high priest among those who farm the farmer," and Joseph P. Cotton, a Democratic lawyer who had headed a division in the Food Administration, dismissed the attack as "a particularly nasty bit of mud slinging from a man who knows better." Mark Requa, former director of the Fuel Administration, described Pinchot as an "impractical idealist" who had resigned from the Food Administration because he found that he would not be able to "dictate the policy." On the positive side, George C. Roeding, president of the California State Agricultural Society and former member of the wartime National Agricultural Advisory Board, assured farmers that, as Food Administrator, Hoover had done "everything in his power to see that [farmers] received returns for their food products commensurate with the increased cost of production caused by the War." Charles Collins Teague, president of the California Walnut Growers' Association and vice president of the California Fruit Growers' Association, praised Hoover's concern for the growers' welfare. And an anonymous campaign handout informed grape producers that Hiram Johnson had "helped kill the California Wine Grape industry" by supporting prohibition, leaving readers free to assume (erroneously) that Hoover would favor repeal.[42]

Hoover himself took no direct part in the Pinchot controversy. He had laid out his own views on the farm situation in an article in the *Saturday Evening Post* shortly before Pinchot made his attack. Postwar farm problems, he argued, resulted only partly from wartime programs to stimulate production. As he saw it, expanding worldwide production had depressed prices, and "no easy formulas" could fix the problem. Ultimately, he contended, world population growth and rising living standards would increase demand and boost prices, but in the meantime, farmers needed better transportation to get crops to markets more cheaply and cooperative marketing programs to cut out middlemen. The wartime excess profits tax increased food prices to consumers and should be repealed. Taken together, he assured voters, those measures would both raise farm incomes and reduce food prices.[43]

Throughout the California primary campaign, Hoover continued to play the role of the statesman above the fray. He did not campaign in the state, and most of his speeches and statements addressed national and international rather than local issues. Campaign pamphlets reaffirmed his support for the ratification of the Treaty of Versailles but attempted to distance him from Woodrow Wilson by stressing his support for reservations to the treaty and his argument that "team work" was essential between the president and Congress. He left local issues to his campaign workers, who tried to set up organizations in every county, college, and university across the state; cultivated friendly relations with the press; and organized a blitz of public meetings in northern California during the last days of April and the beginning of May.[44]

Johnson's supporters derided the Hoover organization as amateurish, to which Hoover's men replied that their campaign was being "run along engineering lines," although they never explained what, if anything, that meant. In practice, all the press releases, pamphlets, circulars, posters, and lapel buttons distributed by the Hoover Republican Club could not compensate for the organization's late start in grassroots organizing and its scanty budget. Nowhere did Johnson enjoy a greater advantage than with organized labor. The Hoover men claimed a number of endorsements from individual labor figures, but they could not crack the big unions such as the Building Trades or the American Federation of Labor, where Samuel Gompers favored Hoover privately but declined to endorse him publicly. P. H. McCarthy, president of the Building Trades Union in California and a Johnson supporter, confidently predicted that, except in the southern part of the state, Hoover would not carry more than a quarter of the union vote and that he would lose by 150,000 votes.[45]

An effort to enlist California Democrats to support Hoover in the Republican primary proved a double-edged sword. Elsewhere in the country it raised anew questions about Hoover's party loyalty and gave plausibility to the charge that he had enrolled in a "plan or conspiracy by . . . the Wilson administration . . . to perpetuate its policies." Hoover attempted to square this particular circle by saying that, while he sought only the Republican nomination, he recognized that he probably would not get it. He therefore urged his supporters to concentrate on promoting his policy recommendations "to the country and delegates already named." Those issues, he told the New York *Tribune*, included "some form of a League of Nations," reorganization and economy in the federal government, readjustment of taxation, reduction of the cost of living, suppression of profiteering, support for agriculture, improved relations between capital and labor, a fairer distribution of wealth, an American merchant marine, protection of civil liberties, extension of education, improvement of waterways, and "many other items." Thanking California campaign workers on the eve of the primary, he reiterated many of those points, contending that rejection of the League would force the country to rearm, increase the burden of taxation, and militarize the government dangerously.[46]

How Hoover evaluated his prospects at this point is unclear. He had enjoyed his greatest influence before he identified his affiliation, when each party feared he might support the other. Once he declared himself a Republican, however, he lost all chance of shaping the Democratic program and had influence with the Republicans only in proportion to the number of votes he won. Since he had no chance of winning outright, his only hope was to become a compromise candidate in a deadlocked convention. In that case, he would have little or no control over the party platform. As the *New Republic* pointed out, his only choice would be "to decline the nomination on principle, or accept an unprincipled nomination."[47]

Yet while such arguments suggested that Hoover could not get the Republican nomination on acceptable terms, his California supporters remained optimistic about the state primary. He enjoyed support on the editorial pages of both Republican and Democratic newspapers, and public opinion polls indicated that he remained, by a considerable margin, the first choice among Democrats. Since California permitted cross-over voting, Democratic supporters might yet carry him to victory. Moreover, Johnson's once-dominant standing among Californians had been eroded by his opposition to the League, support of prohibition, equivocal positions on Japanese immigration and labor, and a new eagerness to court wealthy businessmen. On the eve of the primary, Hoover's supporters also took heart from the endorsements of several prominent California labor leaders and former president Taft.[48]

As primary day neared, the campaign devolved into name-calling. The Hearst press published a front-page cartoon showing Hoover bowing deferentially to the British king, and Johnson's Los Angeles manager, Meyer Lissner, derided Hoover as a spoiler, a "Wilson Californian," and a "shameless servitor of corporate intrigues." Hoover's supporters retorted that Johnson had sold out the common people of California by allying himself with San Francisco businessmen W. H. Crocker and M. H. DeYoung. They urged Californians "to defeat Johnson in his home State."[49]

On the evening of May 4, Ralph Arnold jubilantly telegraphed Hoover that "we have carried Southern California," but it became clear over the next several days that his optimism had been premature. The final tally showed 368,952 for Johnson and 201,231 for Hoover, a bigger win than Johnson's supporters had predicted. Even in Los Angeles County, Johnson won a narrow victory. Most experienced observers, including former President Taft, concluded that Hoover's defeat had eliminated him from the race.[50]

Finding it difficult to recognize the inadequacy of his own campaign, Hoover blamed the California outcome on a combination of voter loyalty to Johnson for "his able rescue of the State during his governorship from vicious corporation control," the activities of the Johnson "machine," and a smear campaign by the Hearst press. Had the election been fought only on the issues, he contended, a majority of Californians would have rejected Johnson's "too narrow vision on our international necessities." Despite his defeat, he convinced himself that duty required him to continue in the national race "as a rallying point for those citizens who believe as I believe." Far from withdrawing from the campaign, he telegraphed Lou to send "full data vital to establish residence in United States."[51]

Hoover's supporters welcomed his willingness to continue the fight. "The Hoover movement in California has just begun," proclaimed Ralph Merritt, while in Chicago Harry A. Wheeler proposed to create a national publicity department. From New York, the Hoover National Republican Club solicited contributions and proposed to coordinate "the spontaneous citizens' movements for Mr. Hoover which have sprung up all over the country." Ray Lyman Wilbur insisted that Hoover would "easily carry the country in a long campaign when the issues can be worked out and the lies answered." The Johnson forces, Wilbur alleged, had spread false reports among Protestants that Hoover was a Catholic, and among Irish and German Catholics that he was anti-Catholic. Nevertheless, Wilbur argued that if the "lower levels" of voters had really understood Hoover's economic proposals, they would have ignored slurs against him. His ideas were simply too sophisticated; they needed to have their "bowels jerked out and exposed to view in catch phrases that carry the political and economic argument."[52]

George Barr Baker described Hoover as unaffected by the California defeat, going "cheerfully on his way, doing his enormous job, and saying very little about politics." Lou Hoover, however, wrote bitterly to twelve-year-old Allan that "we can't really say that [Johnson] beat Daddy, for they told so many perfect lies about him in the [San Francisco] *Chronicle* and *Examiner* . . . that the man they were voting against was not really Daddy but a fake gentleman they had made up—like a snow man whom they then fought against." There should be laws, she declared, to punish campaign lies.[53]

In Oregon, the next state to hold a primary, Hoover's backers downplayed the importance of Johnson's victory in California. An old friend, lumberman W. B. Ayer, ridiculed Leonard Wood's call for Republicans to unite behind him, but realists admitted that a victory for Johnson in the state would make him more difficult to stop. From the perspective of the East Coast, however, the situation looked less dire. With almost five hundred votes needed to nominate at the convention, it seemed virtually certain that no one would secure a first-ballot victory. Wood, the front-runner, had only two hundred delegates, Johnson about one hundred, and Illinois Governor Frank Lowden fewer than one hundred, with nearly four hundred delegates uninstructed. Since neither Johnson nor Lowden would concede to Wood, it looked more and more like a "dark horse year," in which hope still lingered that Hoover might emerge as a consensus second choice. "No man has been decided on," reported the authoritative *Whaley-Eaton Newsletter* in mid-May, "nor will one be decided on until the conferences in Chicago begin."[54]

Certainly neither Johnson nor Hoover behaved as if Hoover had been eliminated from the race. They swapped barbs over the League issue, and Meyer Lissner, Johnson's Southern California manager, charged that the Hoover forces' expenditures in the California primary had been "the worst saturnalia of political extravagance that was ever exposed or conducted in Southern California." From New York, John F. Lucey countered that "Tammany Hall in its palmiest days never conducted a political campaign such as the one conducted by Mr. Lissner in Southern California in behalf of Senator Johnson." Hoover himself telegraphed Ray Lyman Wilbur, asking him to investigate rumors of improper spending by the Johnson people. The charges of wild spending and corrupt patronage became so loud that Idaho's William E. Borah introduced a resolution in the U.S. Senate calling for a full investigation.[55]

In the thrust and counterthrust between Johnson and Hoover over the League, the sick man in the White House had disappeared from the front pages. But on May 9, Wilson suddenly reentered the fray. Responding to an inquiry from a Democratic county committee in Oregon, the president rejected any possibility of compromise with Senate Republicans on reservations. Hoover, who had played down the distance between the parties on the treaty issue, expressed shock. In refusing to compromise, he declared, Wilson and Johnson had forged "an alliance of destruction" contrary to "the aspirations of the great majority of our people." The Republican Party must respond to the wishes of most Americans and "support the League with reservations."[56]

Wilson's statement proved a wake-up call for Hoover. Recognizing at last that he had no chance of winning the nomination, he urged his Oregon supporters to suspend their campaign for him and concentrate on influencing the voters to choose only delegates to the convention who were "committed to the League of Nations with Senate reservations." He also resisted appeals from some supporters to make a personal appearance at the convention. In testimony before a Senate committee, he focused on issues he thought important, discussing ways to resolve labor disputes and criticizing the Wilson administration for its handling of sugar prices.[57]

On May 20, the Senate unanimously adopted Senator Borah's resolution calling for an investigation of campaign spending. Hearings began on Monday, May 24. Although each of the campaign organizations professed to have nothing to hide and predicted shocking revelations of its rivals' villainy, the principal loser in the investigation turned out to be the front-runner, Leonard Wood. Wood, the committee discovered, had raised nearly $1.8 million, including a half-million dollar contribution from William C. Procter, president of Procter and Gamble, as well as other large contributions from wealthy businessmen. Frank Lowden, the second biggest spender, had used less than a third as much, about $415,000. Hiram Johnson reported spending just over $194,000, and Hoover just under $174,000, of which about $71,000 had been spent in California and the rest elsewhere. Considering the substantial amounts put into the campaign, Louis Seibold's wry observation that none of the candidates seemed to have gotten "his money's worth in the contest for . . . delegates" was not far off the mark. With only a handful of delegates still to be selected before the beginning of the convention, more than half of the delegates (486) remained uninstructed. Everyone assumed that party leaders would pick the candidate, and many predicted that a "dark horse" would win the nomination. Hoover's name reemerged in the speculation, with a last-minute poll of delegates showing him third behind Wood and Johnson and gaining.[58]

As the convention opened in Chicago on June 8, Hoover's friends expressed guarded optimism. Former Attorney General George Wickersham produced a legal brief arguing that, despite long residences abroad, Hoover had maintained offices and homes in the United States during the last fourteen years and thus qualified for the presidency under the Constitution. Eugene Meyer reported that Johnson's role in pushing the campaign finance investigation had earned him enemies on the Credentials Committee. "Strong indications of [a] blockade on [the] three leaders" might yet clear the way for a Hoover nomination. Hoover, ever optimistic, gave Julius Barnes, C. J. Hepburn, and Royal Victor "absolute power" to act for him at the convention. In public, however, he feigned detachment, assuring reporters during a visit to Philadelphia that he only followed events in Chicago in the newspapers.[59]

From the Chicago convention, Ray Wilbur reported that "the old Food Ad[ministration] crowd is much in evidence" and that "Victor, Barnes, et al." were "working hard and intelligently" to win over some of the "Wood men." Ohio delegate Joseph C. Green claimed progress in building support for Hoover in his delegation. Wilbur urged Hoover to come "a few hours nearer" to Chicago in case a "break" should begin. But Wilbur and Green proved overly optimistic. Henry Cabot Lodge's keynote speech attacking the League served notice that the Old Guard had firm control over the convention, a point underlined when they won support for a platform plank on the League so vague that it would not embarrass even the most ardent League opponent. Belatedly, Hoover flirted with the idea of withdrawing. But it was too late for second thoughts, and on June 10, Judge Nathan Miller of New York nominated Hoover in a speech emphasizing his wartime experience and proclaiming him the only candidate above class and special interests. Henry Brown of Nevada, seconding the nomination, stressed Hoover's Western ties. Following his speech, "a bunch of shouting Irish," recruited by Ralph Arnold and "placed strategically" in the galleries, provided the loudest and longest demonstration for any candidate.[60]

Despite their confident statements, the Hoover forces at the convention had fallen into disarray. The Californians led by Ralph Arnold and the Barnes-Hepburn-Victor group named by Hoover as his agents both expected to control strategy. When the convention deadlocked on the first day of balloting, Arnold seized the initiative, proposing a deal to switch Wood's votes to Hoover. Wood's two hundred delegates would not assure Hoover the nomination, but Arnold reasoned that their switch might start a stampede. But his enthusiasm could not change the reality that he had nothing to offer the Wood people. On the final, climactic ballot, Hoover received just nine and one-half votes, and the convention turned to another dark horse, Warren Harding. Amateurism had doomed their effort, Lewis Strauss admitted, but "those of us who were amateurs on this occasion, will be veterans" in a future campaign.[61]

III

Following the convention fiasco, Hoover reexamined his options. One possibility would be to run as a third-party candidate. That choice, he concluded, would vitiate liberal influence within the Republican Party. "I am convinced," he wrote, "that unity of action among the liberal thinkers of the party, especially if they exert themselves in the current congressional elections, will insure the country against legislative reaction." After breakfasting with Harding in Washington, he issued a press release implying that the two were in agreement on the direction the party should take. More wishful thinking than realism, the statement marked the beginning of what Hoover and his friends regarded as a quiet struggle for the soul of the Republican Party.[62]

Since, according to rumors, Harding stood in awe of the engineer, Hoover felt initial optimism about being able to push the candidate in whatever direction he wanted. On June 26, at Harding's request, Hoover laid out the programs that he believed the candidate should endorse to prove the "constructive ability" of the Republican Party to move beyond the "hymn of hate" that he asserted had been its chief theme in the recent past. Not surprisingly, he recapitulated the programs he had been advocating in recent months: more cooperative labor-management relations, reorganization of government agencies, improvements in rail and water transportation, and taxation of excess profits. He did not discuss the League of Nations, but he enclosed a clipping from the New York *Evening Post*, which reported an interview in which he had advocated ratification of the treaty without Article X of the League Covenant. This new approach, he suggested, might attract those Republicans "who are not satisfied with the expressions in the platform."[63]

Pleased with Harding's request for advice, Hoover apparently told friends that the candidate would support the League after all. He soon learned that he had misread the Senator, who had the veteran politician's skill in making everyone think he agreed with them. But Harding's speech accepting the Republican nomination on July 22 threw supporters of the League into despair. The speech, wrote Warren Gregory from California, amounted to "an unqualified surrender to the Johnson-Borah position."[64]

To Hoover's protest about his apparent abandonment of the League, Harding replied soothingly that he was "confident we can eliminate all doubts and distresses about this difficult matter as the campaign progresses." He intended, he said, "to commit the party to a harmony program and trust to good common-sense and willingness to give and take in order to harmonize our activities as we go along." Members of his staff invited some of Hoover's advisers, including Julius Barnes, Edgar Rickard, and Warren Gregory, to join Harding campaign committees.[65]

Hoover was unimpressed. When Republican National Committee Chairman Will Hays proposed that he, Leonard Wood, Frank Lowden, and Hiram Johnson form a national campaign committee, he declined, unless, as he told

Hays, Harding would publicly "correct the impression given by Senator John-son" that he favored "a separate peace treaty with Germany and the aban-donment of the League." Instead, Hoover embraced George Wickersham's proposal to organize some fifty prominent Republicans to pressure Harding privately on the League issue.[66]

Harding, warned about the Wickersham initiative, invited the former attorney general to meet with him in Marion, Ohio, and also addressed the League issue again in a speech on August 28. The meeting and the speech, which Hoover admitted seemed more positive toward the League than the acceptance speech, temporarily averted a definite break between Harding and the pro-League group.[67]

In mid-September, Hoover finally accepted that Harding had no intention of endorsing the League. Testifying before a Senate committee, he delivered what sounded very much like a campaign speech, urging government reor-ganization, tax reform, a national housing program, improved water and rail transport, and the expansion of the postal savings bank system. And when the Chicago *Daily News* asked for his opinion on the League question, he supplied an extended and vigorous argument in favor of ratification of the treaty with reservations and American membership in the League. Two weeks later, in a letter meant for publication, he asserted that the Republicans, if elected, would implement his ideas. After reading the letter, Harding replied blithely that "if I had been dictating it myself I could not have done it so well." But his subsequent speeches gave no evidence that he had accepted any of Hoover's ideas.[68]

While addressing key issues publicly, Hoover also worked behind the scenes with a group of intellectuals organized by Jacob Gould Schurman on a plan to publish a statement signed by prominent citizens supporting both the Republican ticket and the League. The group wrote a preliminary draft at a dinner meeting in New York on September 18, but they delayed its release in the hope that former Secretary of State Elihu Root would sign. On October 4, however, before Root had reached a decision, Harding made another speech that Hoover, Schurman, and others interpreted as a rejection not only of the League but also of the whole "principle of organized international association for the preservation of peace." Schurman and Hoover immediately warned Will Hays that their group would not endorse the nominee "without further information as to Senator Harding's attitude." Harding again replied sooth-ingly that he had not changed his opinion about the League. And in speeches in Des Moines and Indianapolis, he made a nebulous promise to support "an association of nations for the promotion of international peace" and insisted that he favored "cooperation among nations." By this time, however, Hoover and the other members of the Schurman group had become disillusioned with private assurances and vague public words.[69]

Nevertheless, the Schurman group's statement published on October 20 reflected the ambivalence that had surrounded its composition. After rehears-ing various Republican objections to the League, particularly Article X, it quoted the platform's vague endorsement of "an international association" and Harding's favorable mention of "an Association of Free Nations." It contrasted those positions with the Democrats' frank support of the League but concluded, paradoxically, "that we can most effectively advance the cause of International Cooperation to promote Peace by supporting Mr. Harding for election to the Presidency." Party loyalty had trumped principle, and fifty-five Republicans, including Charles Evans Hughes, Elihu Root, and Hoover, signed the document.[70] The frequently underestimated Harding had outmaneuvered the League supporters. He, not Hoover, would control the party's program and future.

Signing the Schurman statement left Hoover with no excuse to avoid taking part in the campaign. When the Republican Speakers' Bureau asked him to spend two weeks campaigning in the Midwest, he agreed. In a series of tepid and platitudinous speeches, he attacked the Wilson administration for financial mismanagement and blurred his disagreements with Harding. To fellow engineer Morris L. Cooke, he confessed that he really saw no difference in "moral principle . . . between the two parties," but he hoped that the Republicans would take the "most practical" steps toward "organized international action for the preservation of peace." Lou Hoover put the situation more bluntly to one of her correspondents: "Our choice of political paths to follow is so unpromising now that very few can feel that they are going straight to the desired goal. Each one has, like my husband, to work where he feels he can get the most accomplished for the vital good of the Nation." On October 23, Hoover sent one last futile plea to Will Hays. He implored the party chairman to urge Harding to spell out what he would do to promote international organization after he was elected. Then he boarded a train to California to cast his vote.[71]

IV

Hoover's 1920 campaign was a folly of amateurism into which he was pushed against his better judgment by eager supporters from the ARA, the Food Administration, and the engineering societies. A seasoned California Republican summed it up as "initiated too late" and under "amateur management." It also lacked adequate finances and suffered from conflicts among its key personnel. Hoover's frequent assertions that he did not want to run and did so only to promote policies he supported, particularly American membership in the League of Nations, seemed sincere, at least at first. As time went by, he realized that he could not advance those policies without an effective candidacy, but by the time he decided to make a serious commitment, it was too late. Now well infected by the presidential bug, he would have to bide his time before newly kindled ambition could be satisfied.[72]

The war, Hoover believed, had transformed the world, disrupting European political and economic institutions while elevating the political and economic power of the United States. That situation presented both a challenge and an opportunity for the nation—a challenge because America required a stable, prosperous world for its own safety and prosperity, and an opportunity because the development of the national economy to deliver the benefits of the consumer revolution to all would chart the path to future happiness for the rest of the world. Few Republicans yet understood and embraced his full program, which challenged most party leaders' conception of the proper role of government. As the writer Mary Austin put it in a perceptive essay, "The truth is that all the average Hoover booster has seen of Hoover is the streak he makes across the landscape, the meteoric shower of sparks, the thunder and the quiver of his speed." If they really understood his ambitions, she concluded, his admirers would be left "far behind in a state of indignant bewilderment."[73] Outmaneuvered by Harding at every turn in 1920, Hoover had much to learn before he could turn his ambitious ideas into policy.

CHAPTER 5

The European Relief Program, September 1919–1921

On May 7, 1919, a servant awakened Hoover at 4:00 AM to give him the printed draft of the peace treaty that would be presented to the Germans later in the day. He read through the document, seeing it as a whole for the first time, and was "greatly disturbed." Going for a walk through the streets of Paris to organize his thoughts, he ran into General Jan Smuts of South Africa and British economist John Maynard Keynes, whose faces reflected their own concern. They all agreed that if the treaty remained unaltered, it would guarantee future disaster. From the American perspective, Hoover thought, "the economic consequences alone would pull down all Europe and thus injure the United States."[1]

As Hoover, Keynes, and Smuts anticipated, the Germans balked at signing the treaty, but the "Big Three" (Wilson, Lloyd George, and Clemenceau) rejected most changes. Early in June, Hoover met with Wilson to urge modification of some of the draft's economic clauses. He found the president exhausted, defensive, and unreceptive to his advice, but he plunged ahead anyway. The transfer of major German coal-mining regions to France and Poland, plus the requirement that Germany send 25 million tons of coal annually to France, he pointed out, would leave the Germans with barely enough coal to heat their homes and virtually no fuel to power the industries needed to produce income to pay reparations. He argued that the dismantling of the Austro-Hungarian Empire would disrupt the economic unity of the

Danube basin, while a rump state of Austria "would never be self-supporting and in consequence would always be a center of instability." The transfer of large ethnic minorities to the new states of Central and Eastern Europe would foster resentment and conflict.[2]

Hoover recalled that Wilson "flushed angrily" at what he took to be a personal attack on the document over which he had labored for so many months, but he would have done well to listen to Hoover and the others who urged changes on him. The Treaty of Versailles, signed on June 28, 1919, along with the treaties with Austria (September 10, 1919), Bulgaria (November 27, 1919), Hungary (June 4, 1920), and Turkey (August 20, 1920), created a disastrously unstable peace. From Hoover's point of view, its worst economic features could not be separated from its political provisions, which left a bitterly resentful Germany saddled with an indeterminate reparations bill, a truncated and economically unsustainable Austria, and Central Europe so politically chaotic that economic recovery and growth seemed unattainable. The treaty assured that Hoover's relief work would not end in 1919 and that dealing with the German problem would become a central preoccupation of his next decade.[3]

When Hoover sailed for home aboard the *Aquitania* on September 6, 1919, he bore with him the heartfelt gratitude of millions of Europeans. To reporters who surrounded him on the dock at Southampton, he declared his work finished. Seventeen and a half million tons of American food worth some $3 billion had been distributed, he estimated (though he was careful to point out that all but about $10 million worth of that aid had been paid for by the recipients), and now a privately funded program would take over feeding about a million European children during the coming winter. American aid, he declared, had "saved Europe from total chaos."[4]

Privately, he knew better. Not only did the ongoing child-feeding program need to be coordinated and funded, but also European economic recovery remained uncertain. The Continent continued to be plagued with "wabbly [*sic*] governments," marginal transportation systems, and serious coal shortages, and its "class stratification" would always mean that "when there is a food shortage the rich eat and the poor do without." In that class division lay the danger of "disorder and the possibility of a total collapse."[5] Embittered Germans and Austrians would plot to evade their treaty obligations and recover their old power. Nevertheless, Hoover believed that despite the treaty's faults, American ratification would be a vital step toward stability. Benjamin Strong, governor of the New York Federal Reserve Bank who had traveled in Europe in the summer of 1919, described the situation even more urgently. "If America refuses its support to this necessary organized work of reconstruction," said Strong, "she will be regarded as the world's most dangerous and selfish business rival, and all the nations, as soon as the power to do so develops, will be forced to arm themselves with every economic weapon at hand against her." On his arrival in New York, Hoover reiterated, "Until peace is consummated, none of the European countries which have been at war can borrow money; none can reorganize their internal finance; raw materials cannot be obtained; industry cannot be restarted."[6] Economically, even more than politically, ratification of the peace treaty had become fundamental to postwar stability and recovery. All that had been built by the relief program could easily be lost.

Practically speaking, said Hoover, "the food situation" had become "a matter of credits," not American charity. European agriculture would recover gradually, but in the short term, many states would have to borrow to feed their people. Those loans could only come from the United States, which alone had both available capital and surplus food. "The method whereby these credits will be extended," he said, "will have to be worked out here." In Central Europe in particular, privation would continue "until credits are extended so the people may import the materials and foodstuffs necessary to bring about a resumption of normal conditions."[7] Self-interest, in the form of markets for surplus American agricultural production, thus went hand in hand with the benevolent instinct to feed the hungry. Hoover reminded Americans that both required a sustained economic and political commitment to European recovery.

John Maynard Keynes also saw the situation as urgent, and in April 1919, he had proposed a plan to promote recovery. He suggested that the enemy and new states issue bonds, using three-quarters of the revenue to cover reparations payments, 7.6 percent to retire debts to neutral states, and the remainder to buy food and raw materials. The governments involved and the Allies would guarantee the interest on the bonds.[8]

Keynes and Hoover agreed that the plan might be worth a trial, but Washington rejected it out of hand. Treasury Department officials argued that any plan dependent on government loans or guarantees of bond interest would alarm isolationists in Congress and jeopardize ratification of the peace treaty. Nor did Keynes's proposal gain support in the British government, where a number of influential people thought that the simplest and best policy would be outright cancellation of war debts. Thomas W. Lamont and Norman Davis, the Treasury's representatives in Paris, proposed still another plan—cancellation or reduction of interest on wartime loans and the creation of a series of private committees in Europe and the United States to coordinate private loans and credits to the European states. That idea did not attract much support, however, and in May, Hoover suggested yet another plan—a three-year moratorium on inter-Allied debts and an undefined "German bond scheme."[9]

None of the various proposals came to anything. Not only did American leaders oppose any scheme that might involve the American government in financing European reconstruction, but they also suspected every British or French proposal of being a stratagem to exclude or curtail American trade and investments in Europe. Hoover, for all his belief that European recovery would benefit the United States, shared his countrymen's fears. His wartime experience in Europe had convinced him that the British and French hoped to create spheres of influence in Europe and elsewhere from which American traders and investors would be excluded. He favored ratification of the peace treaty in part because he hoped that the international organization created by it would make it more difficult for the Europeans to accomplish those aims.[10]

But if ratification might reduce the threat of European collusion in an anti-American economic policy, it would not necessarily assure the economic recovery that Hoover also thought important to American interests. Since American leaders had ruled out government support of reconstruction, any American participation in the process would have to come through private loans and investments. Prior to the passage of the Edge Act in December 1919 permitting American national banks to charter foreign subsidiaries and make long-term loans to foreign governments, however, no machinery existed to organize the large private loans and credits needed for restoring European economies. Even when the Edge Act passed, it took time to put it into effect. The American Bankers' Association organized a Foreign Trade Financing Conference in Chicago in December 1920, but that only began the process. It would require several years before what Hoover called "the systematic, permanent investment of our surplus production in reproductive works abroad" could have a significant impact on European economies. Much as the Americans, including Hoover, might want to bring short-term aid to an end, Europe's slow recovery seemed certain to make humanitarian assistance necessary for some time to come.[11]

I

Following the war, federal support had enabled the American Relief Administration (ARA) to undertake not only ambitious relief programs but also to assist in some reconstruction projects such as the restoration of Central European railways and coal mines. The termination of government funding for the ARA on June 30, 1919, however, brought that period to an end. The privatized ARA, created by Hoover in the summer of 1919, had only about $15 million with which to work, and it lacked the political clout enjoyed by its official predecessor. Even supplemented by private donations and contributions of food and clothing collected by immigrant groups in America, its limited resources permitted it to do no more than respond to the most serious suffering.[12]

Hoover later estimated that the ARA's European Children's Fund fed about 4 million children over the winter of 1919 to 1920. Lingering popular animosities toward the former enemy countries and the general exhaustion of the American public's generosity made it impossible for him to raise the funds to do more. In December 1919, therefore, he decided to broach the possibility of a new government program to members of the cabinet. Wilson, who had been his main ally previously, had been incapacitated by a stroke, largely paralyzing the government, but Hoover hoped that the cabinet members to whom he talked would support his plan for the creation of a nonpartisan commission to control both private charity and new government assistance.[13]

If Hoover could have acted on his belief that, as he had told Wilson, European recovery depended on American support for the economic unity of the Continent, he might have advocated a more ambitious policy. But he knew that his countrymen had lost their taste for solving Europe's problems. Political realism dictated that he seek support only for humanitarian relief, not reconstruction. "The rehabilitation of Europe is immediately and primarily a European task," he declared. He contended that because the war's physical damage had been relatively limited, modest aid in the form of raw materials, tools, and a small amount of food would restore Europeans' energy and reawaken their desire to produce. Following that pump-priming, private capital could step in to fund reconstruction. The government's role, he assured those to whom he spoke, would be limited in scope and duration and primarily humanitarian in purpose. It would provide the psychological stimulus needed to revive the Europeans' own will to succeed.[14]

As he had feared, even Hoover's carefully framed suggestion ran into opposition spearheaded by Assistant Treasury Secretary Russell C. Leffingwell. Leffingwell's outlook had been colored by his concern about an ambitious plan advanced in the summer of 1919 by J. P. Morgan partner Henry P. Davison and backed by Commerce Secretary William C. Redfield. The Davison plan envisioned federal guarantees of private bonds to be issued by a consortium of bankers and used to finance European reconstruction. In Leffingwell's eyes, Hoover's more modest proposal raised echoes of the Davison plan. Worried that the British and French would see any official role in European relief or reconstruction as an invitation to renegotiate war debts, Leffingwell and Treasury Secretary Carter Glass opposed anything that looked like a move in that direction.[15]

Discouraged by Treasury opposition to federal relief funding, Hoover pressed ahead with private initiatives. Just after Christmas in 1919, he launched an innovative new program. Americans with relatives in Europe, he explained, had found that packing and shipping food and clothing to their relatives was prohibitively expensive, sometimes doubling the cost of the items being sent. If they sent money instead, recipients found it difficult to exchange dollars for local currency at reasonable rates, and in any case, little local food could be found. To solve those problems, he proposed that the ARA establish warehouses in Europe and that American banks sell "food drafts" that could be redeemed by European recipients at the warehouses. By taking advantage of the ARA's bulk purchasing and shipping, American buyers of the drafts could provide food to their relatives at a lower price. At Hoover's urging, the American Bankers' Association endorsed the program, and nearly five thousand local banks agreed to sell the drafts. To keep costs down, the organizers planned standardized packages of dry milk, flour, rice, and either bacon or beans (one for Christian recipients, the other for Muslims and Jews). When bulk shipments arrived at the warehouses in Europe, workers created individual food packets by cutting up and resewing the large sacks in which the shipments arrived. That method saved money on both shipping and packaging. During the first nine months of the program's operation, it sold 178,000 food drafts in the United States and distributed almost $5 million worth of food in Europe.[16]

A movie, *Starvation*, made with the cooperation of the ARA, attempted to dramatize European problems for the American public. Released in New York with a special showing at the Metropolitan Opera House on January 9, 1920, the film opened with scenes of agrarian prosperity in prewar Russia and then shifted to postwar pictures of thousands of emaciated, partially clothed children. Scenes of American ships bringing relief and of ARA kitchens serving long lines of the hungry illustrated what had been done, but new images of want and suffering in Poland, Austria, Belgium, Armenia, Romania, and Germany underlined the continuing crisis. From Vienna, pictures of hungry children being fed by the ARA in the courtyard of the Schönbrunn Castle juxtaposed the shattered glories of the Austro-Hungarian Empire with the present-day reality of privation and suffering.[17]

If Hoover hoped that release of *Starvation* would produce a great flood of contributions to the ARA, he must have been disappointed. Newspaper reports played up the film's shocking scenes and urged Americans to see it, but their articles, like the one in the New York *Tribune* headed "Scenes Show How American Food Has Saved Europe," implied that the hunger problem had already been resolved by American charity and know-how. Most viewers apparently came away feeling that the crisis had ended.[18]

Hoover knew better, though he dared not arouse congressional fears of economic commitments to European recovery. The European situation, he assured reporters, did not warrant "hysteria." The United States did not need to "feed all Europe" nor "restore the commercial prosperity of nations which are not doing what they could and should to help themselves." Europe only needed help in rebuilding fuel and transportation systems so that food could be shipped from places where a surplus existed to areas of scarcity, and modest loans to reestablish production. At most, he estimated, no more than 5 percent of Europeans needed actual relief, and since the major European powers had a strong interest in reestablishing political and economic stability as quickly as possible, he thought they should be willing to assist to the fullest extent of their resources.[19] Americans had a moral duty to relieve suffering but not to provide grants for recovery. Government recovery grants, he added, might lead to permanent European dependence on the American taxpayer.

II

Except in the case of child feeding, Hoover emphasized that relief should be seen as an investment as well as charity. The war had turned the United

States into the world's greatest creditor and vastly expanded its production. In Hoover's opinion, further growth depended in part on finding markets for American products and investment opportunities for surplus capital. Europe, with its large population and relatively high standard of living, attracted both manufacturers and capitalists—but only if British and French efforts to close the continent to American business could be blocked. The area's postwar economic collapse and political disorder thus presented a challenge and opportunity. By succoring the needy, America would win friends and impede British and French ambitions. And moreover, if the United States provided its relief mostly in the form of loans rather than outright gifts, it would create economic leverage to open the door for trade and investment. Although he certainly felt a moral obligation to relieve suffering, Hoover thus envisioned relief as serving long-term American economic interests. He regarded the two goals as compatible and even complementary.

Worn down by Hoover's arguments, on January 10, Treasury Secretary Glass asked Congress to authorize the use of $150 million of the capital appropriated for the U.S. Grain Corporation's wartime operations for short-term European food relief. The situation in Europe, Hoover reassured the House Ways and Means Committee on January 12, had "so far improved itself that practically all Europe, except a small area, will be able or should be able to provision itself without calling upon the American Treasury." The areas most seriously in need of aid included Poland, where the threat of a Soviet army on the border had made it impossible for businesses to secure the foreign capital they needed to restart their operations; Austria, which "now stands as a population based on an empire, with the empire cut off"; Hungary, where Romanian forces that overthrew the Béla Kun government had looted food reserves; and Armenia. He estimated that Finland, Belgium, and possibly Italy might also need small amounts of aid until their economies stabilized, although that was not certain.[20]

The situations in Germany and Austria, Hoover pointed out, had been complicated by political tensions. He believed Germany capable of financing its own food purchases, "if they have the intelligent cooperation of the reparations commission," but British and French resistance to any reduction of reparations had thus far made the problem not "even discussable." The situation in Austria, where a population of some 2 million had been cut off from prewar agricultural resources by the loss of the empire, posed even more serious and perhaps insoluble difficulties. One solution, Hoover suggested, would be to create a Danube economic federation that would restore Vienna's access to the agricultural lands of the old empire; another would be to permit Austria to unite with Germany. But again, the British and French stood in the way. That left the United States little choice, said Hoover, but to try to avert starvation and "give the world a little time to cool off and to realize the forces that have been set in motion." To avoid having aid to Austria become a matter of "perpetual charity," however, the British and French must be made to understand that "those who consider they benefit by maintaining this condition should pay the bill."[21]

Although the $150 million that the administration proposed for new aid to the Europeans seemed modest next to the $2 billion already spent between the armistice and the end of 1919, Hoover feared that Congress would balk at *any* expenditure. Reluctant to ask for an appropriation, Secretary Glass recommended that the $150 million be taken instead from unexpended portions of the $10 billion appropriated during the war for loans to the Allies. Hoover had drawn on those funds, and an additional $100 million appropriation, for the $2 billion he had previously spent on aid. Offered in the form of loans rather than outright grants, all but the $12 million used specifically for child feeding of those earlier expenditures had been covered by short-term notes of the various governments and municipalities where the money was spent. Upon hearing that, the incredulous Texas Representative John Nance Garner exclaimed that Congress "expected you to use that $100,000,000 and . . . never get a cent of it back!" Impressed by Hoover's frugality, no member of the House Ways and Means Committee expressed a word of criticism of the new proposal.[22]

The honeymoon did not last long. Secretary of War Newton Baker and General Tasker Bliss, testifying after Hoover, reported to the committee that the war then going on between Poland and Russia had resulted from a Polish attack on Russia, not the other way around. Baker rashly justified aid to Poland as "a military measure" to sustain the Poles as a bulwark against the expansion of Communism. When the Baltimore *Sun* reported erroneously that Hoover had declared privately that the United States "must stand by Poland for two years" to "protect the world from Bolshevism and militarism," committee members became alarmed. Despite a rare public plea from President Wilson, the committee cut virtually all aid for Poland from the bill, reducing the relief authorization from $150 million to $50 million.[23]

The Allied governments, invited to share in the aid program, responded as reluctantly as Congress. Lou Hoover lamented that they seemed "inclined to let the populations of Poland, Austria and Armenia starve" while they debated "the question of who is really responsible for feeding them." Under the circumstances, Hoover felt that he had no choice but to "go back into the breach" to try to raise $33 million in private donations to fund a temporary program. Among other things, he made a personal appeal for support to the American Institute of Mining and Metallurgical Engineers, and his supporters organized a grand charity ball in Greenwich, Connecticut, and a benefit performance of "Carmen" at the Metropolitan Opera, where the sale of artwork, including a sculpture by Auguste Rodin and a painting by John Singer Sargent, supplemented box office receipts.[24]

Optimistic press reports heralded the success of the fund-raising drive, but contributions came in slowly, and still Congress failed to act even on the reduced appropriation. On February 22, Hoover joined with a long list of religious, charitable, business, and educational leaders to issue a new appeal. They implored Congress, if it would not appropriate relief funds directly, to authorize the Grain Corporation to raise $125 to $150 million by selling abroad about 10 million of the 60 million barrels of surplus flour it had in its warehouses and to use the profits for relief. Exaggerating the crisis, they claimed that "thousands must slowly starve if we hold our surplus." From Belgium, Emile Francqui, Hoover's old colleague in the Commission for Relief, wrote to say that the collapse of the distribution system had compounded short-ages and led to huge price increases. If the United States failed to help, it would not only lose all the credit it had gained during the war for saving Europe but would also "bring European society to anarchy." He warned that "the distance which separates [America] from Europe will not soften the shock."[25]

With the $50 million appropriation still stuck in Congress, Julius Barnes, head of the U.S. Grain Corporation, announced on March 5 that he had authorized the shipment of 5 million barrels of low-grade soft winter wheat flour, valued at $10.75 a barrel, to Central Europe for sale on long-term credit. This particular wheat, Barnes maintained, had proven unsalable in the United States, and he did not "propose to allow it to spoil in warehouses here while people in Europe on the verge of starvation are offering their customs, their art galleries and everything they have as security to obtain this food." Existing law, Barnes contended, permitted him to take his action, but Republicans in Congress, recognizing an opportunity to do well by doing good, rushed through a resolution specifically authorizing the shipment. Hoover praised the step as an "amelioration of the situation" but pointed out that flour sold on credit to European governments (Armenia, Austria, and Poland were not creditworthy and could not participate) would be offered to consumers only for cash. With inflation driving the price of bread "beyond the reach of many," merely ship-ping wheat to Europe would not solve the problem. Nor would it eliminate the continuing shortage of fats in some areas. Additional aid and restructuring of European economies remained essential.[26]

When Hoover transformed the ARA into a private organization in the summer of 1919, everyone assumed that it would continue feeding European children for no more than a year, until the 1920 harvest arrived. By May 1920, however, it had become obvious that because of the slow pace of Eastern and Central European recovery, the program should be extended for another year. In June, Hoover asked the president to authorize the use of leftover Grain Administration money to help fund the relief effort. That summer he met with representatives of nine relief organizations working in Europe and announced on September 22 that they would merge their resources under a new "Euro-pean Relief Council" (ERC). The umbrella organization would attempt to raise $23 million to fund a program for the coming year to feed about 2 to 2.5 million children in Poland, Austria, Czechoslovakia, Serbia, Hungary, Fin-land, Lithuania, Estonia, Latvia, North Russia, and Armenia, plus perhaps a million more children in Germany who had been helped previously through programs run by the American Friends Service Committee.[27]

Through speeches, as well as letters and articles in popular magazines, Hoover carried his appeal to the American people in the autumn of 1920.[28] In Chicago, both Hoovers spoke at a dinner, and Lou made a particularly powerful appeal, urging listeners to join the effort to save European children so that their own children would know that they were living up to the ideals of "their brothers and fathers who made the final sacrifice in the great war." The children who America would save, she said, "are the citizens we are going to make, the future citizens of those countries for whose independence our men fought—and died."[29]

Although children were and remained the main focus of the ARA's concern during the spring of 1920, a large number of appeals for help began to arrive in the United States from Austrian, Hungarian, Czech, and Polish university students and professors, as well as from doctors, scientists, teachers, lawyers, artists and musicians, clergymen, architects, and civil servants, both active and retired—all members of what the ARA referred to as "the intellectual class." Poorly paid even before the war, many of these people now found themselves without regular work and destitute amid rising prices and shortages. Believing that intellectuals represented a vital resource for the future of democracy in the region, Hoover secured two special gifts aggregating $500,000 specifically for their support. The ARA used some of the funds to provide food for university kitchens where they still operated, but the organization employed most of it to distribute supplies through the relief package system. The program assisted about eighteen thousand people, over and above the main child-feeding program.[30]

As the fund-raising campaign swung into high gear in the fall of 1920, the ARA found itself stretched thin, with its small staff taking on heavier and heavier responsibilities and working long hours in cramped, uncomfortable offices in the New York headquarters. Most of the organization's officers, like Hoover, worked for little or no pay, and their attitude, that every possible cent should be spent on relief, led them to keep staff salaries painfully low. By late November, workers had reached the point of rebellion, and on December 1, Hoover met with them to talk about the situation. "We have been calling for a great deal of over-time and extra work," he admitted, but he hoped they would feel, as he did, "that this is a good deal more than a service for pay." The ARA was responsible for the lives and welfare of thousands of children. Everyone in the room had "some share in this responsibility to keep this organization going . . . smoothly . . . with the devotion it deserves." To that end, he proposed that the staff appoint a small committee to meet regularly with a similar committee of the organization's executives to promote "teamwork." With the country sinking into a recession, he pointed out, raising the amount of money that would be needed was "probably the most difficult task that has been undertaken by a charitable operation." Whether the drive succeeded or failed, he declared, would depend "on the enthusiasm and confidence that radiates out from the staff that have to carry out the detail and hard work." "We are not going to call on you for more than we are willing to give ourselves," he assured them, concluding with the announcement that he would leave the next day for several weeks of fund-raising across the country.[31]

Hoover's approach to the ARA's labor problem, the appointment of a shop council, applied the theory of labor-management relations that he had been championing since the industrial conference the year before. It also demonstrated the style of leadership that had served him so well in the Food Administration and during the Belgian and postwar European relief programs: the exhortation to fellow workers to join him in a noble cause. It had inspired great feats of voluntary service among businessmen, engineers, and the military officers he recruited for the ARA's work in Europe, but it worked less well with the office staff. They applauded Hoover for volunteering his time to the program, but they pointed out that few of them could afford to serve as volunteers. They needed their pay to support themselves and their families. Nor was money their only concern. Almost everyone had worked beyond their regular hours, but many who did so "receive[d] no extra pay—and very little extra consideration—for the effort," while others had received overtime pay regularly. Likewise, some recent hires had been paid more for the same work than others who had been with the organization for months. They asked that the staff's pay be regraded to eliminate inequities and that a definite system of overtime pay be introduced. "Those who do not wish to accept payment for overtime work," they concluded dryly, "could donate it to the Children's Fund."[32]

When the ARA Council representing management met a few days later, they quickly agreed to overtime pay for everyone who worked extra hours (though they declined to pay for overtime workers' meals) and to set a "basic wage scale" that would operate "rather in the nature of a guide for setting a minimum wage" rather than standardizing pay for everyone doing similar work. Although those arrangements did not fully meet the staff's complaints, they acquiesced as a "contribution to the relief."[33] There is no further record of friction within the organization. As elsewhere, the shop council seemed to work primarily to the benefit of management, although it also fostered commitment to the organization's goals, as Hoover had maintained it would do.

Certainly no one on the staff could think that Hoover did less than his full share, as a glance at his schedule during mid-December makes clear. On Saturday, December 18, he took the train to Wilmington, Delaware, to appeal to local businessmen. The next morning he returned to New York to join the Reverend Harry Emerson Fosdick, Mrs. August Belmont, and other notables in speaking to an overflow crowd at the Metropolitan Opera House and raising almost $650,000. That evening he attended a private dinner, where he made his appeal to "fifteen or more bankers, probably the richest men in town," and the next morning he went to Springfield, Massachusetts, where a disappointing crowd scattered across the seats of the municipal auditorium.

On Christmas Eve, he worked at the office after everyone else had gone home and then spent Christmas with friends. But on Sunday, December 26, he left again for Yonkers to speak and then continued to Tarrytown for a dinner with potential donors at Mrs. Ogden Reid's home. On Monday, he spoke in Brooklyn, and on Tuesday, December 28, in New Haven.[34]

On Wednesday, December 29, he launched a new program, the "invisible guest" dinners, at a gala gathering for two hundred in New York. Newspaper photographs showed a dour (perhaps just tired) Hoover seated at the head of the table, next to a child's high chair with a candle on its tray to symbolize Europe's hungry children. On the other side of the high chair sat General Pershing, commander of the American Expeditionary Force in Europe, while behind them stood women dressed in white nurses' uniforms. (See Figure 7.3.) The assembled diners paid a thousand dollars apiece for what the newspapers described as "twenty-two cents worth of stew, bread, and cocoa, served on bare plank tables in tin mess kits, which is the ration of 1,200 calories, spared from our abundance to keep these little ones alive." Violinist Fritz Kreisler's playing made the meal a little more savory. Americans, Hoover told the diners, drove nearly 7 million cars and spent "a billion dollars annually maintaining these automobiles, another billion dollars on ice cream, cosmetics and chewing gum, and a few billion more on tobacco and other things" and could well afford to donate to European relief. Although the dinner invitation had promised that no additional appeal would be made beyond the ticket price, the audience voted unanimously to take up a collection, and Hoover made no objection. The collection produced another million dollars, which John D. Rockefeller, Jr., later matched, making the total from this one affair more than $3 million, an excellent start toward the $33 million goal.[35]

Hoover continued his breakneck pace into the new year, delivering at least nineteen speeches in cities throughout the Northeast and Midwest in January alone, not to mention an appearance in John D. Rockefeller's Bible class, a day's testimony before the House Agriculture Committee, and a day working on the docks in New York with volunteers putting labels on bundles of food being loaded for shipment to Europe. For the Baltimore *Sun*, he dashed off a column reiterating the desperate need of the children in Europe and lauding the American volunteers who ran the relief programs. By the middle of the month, he had appeared so often in evening clothes that he had literally worn them out and had to buy a new set. In private, he groused about his schedule, describing the organizer of a meeting in Indianapolis as a "prize boob" and labeling the members of a New York women's club a flock of "old fat hens." The cold weather, incessant travel, and slow pace of donations all depressed him, and he longed to escape to California and the family. In his heart he knew that the relatively modest returns from his grueling schedule hardly justified the effort involved. But he symbolized the campaign, and in every section of the country local volunteers declared that they "could raise at least five times as much with the Chief there to start it as [they] can without him." Out in California, Lou Hoover did her part for the cause, urging on a drive to raise $800,000 in the state with speeches in San Francisco, Berkeley, and at Mills College in Oakland.[36]

In the midst of all this, Hoover took on a battle with Senator James A. Reed of Missouri, who charged that $40 million of relief money previously appropriated by Congress had been illegally diverted by the ARA "to keep the Polish army in the field." "The Venomous Senator Reed," as Hoover's secretary called him, was a gadfly whose unfounded and usually outrageous attacks on the Food Administration during the war had been a frequent irritation to Hoover. But his outburst had to be taken seriously, because it threatened to derail the $100 million appropriation being debated in the Senate. To his intense annoyance, Hoover had to steal several days from the "Invisible Guest" campaign to explain to senators how he had spent previous relief funds in Poland and to secure a statement from William R. Grove, who had been in charge of the Polish relief program, explaining in detail the safeguards the ARA had instituted to make sure that relief supplies went only to civilians.[37]

Reed's attack had no significant effect, and Congress eventually authorized the shipment of almost half a million tons of surplus grain worth nearly $76 million to Europe. But the problem of child feeding in Germany proved more difficult to solve. Hoover had always maintained that "if the world were to have peace, it had to choose one of two alternatives—either destroy the German race or set about the job of strengthening the democratic forces in Germany in the hope that they might develop a nation of peaceable membership in the family of mankind." His assertion that "we have not been fighting with women and children" oversimplified the reality of modern war, but he was correct that a stable, democratic Germany would benefit all of Europe. Americans had not lost their wartime bitterness, however, and Hoover dared not risk an open appeal for funds to feed German children. Accordingly, he arranged to have German relief channeled indirectly through the American Friends Service Committee. The system worked reasonably well, although Hoover sometimes faced attacks for being "pro-German" or, on the other side, for collecting money from German Americans under false pretenses.[38]

Aid for Russia proved only slightly less troublesome. The failure of the Nansen initiative in the spring of 1919 had ended an earlier relief effort, but the continuation of the civil war and the general collapse of the Russian economy led to deteriorating conditions. In February 1921, the American Friends Service Committee, the lone Western charitable organization then operating in Russia, reported that even in Moscow children's needs had outstripped their capabilities. At that point, the ARA had begun feeding some Russian refugees in Warsaw, but no one wanted to venture further into the Russian morass. Within a few months, the issue would become acute.[39]

On February 22, president-elect Warren Harding telephoned Hoover, who was attending a special benefit performance for the relief drive at the Metropolitan Opera, to formally offer him an appointment as secretary of commerce. The performance culminated a busy week during which Lou Hoover had been campaigning extensively for the relief fund in the Greenwich, Connecticut, area, while her husband worked in New York.[40] To have Harding's offer coincide with the Metropolitan Opera gala seemed neat symbolically, but since Hoover and Harding had been discussing a cabinet appointment since December, it hardly came as a surprise. Nevertheless, the offer created a new problem. Hoover wanted to complete his work with the relief program and indeed had made the freedom to do so a condition for his acceptance of the cabinet post. But obviously, he would no longer be able to devote his entire energies to the campaign, as he had been doing for several months. At the beginning of March, the ARA ended its fund drive, having raised a little over $29 million of the planned $33 million. Despite the shortfall, Hoover believed enough had been raised to sustain the program during the spring and summer, and he felt optimistic that the coming harvest would eliminate the need for further relief, except perhaps in Germany, Austria, and Poland. Although he remained the titular ARA chairman, vice-chairman Julius Barnes and members of the Executive Committee assumed supervision of its daily activities after the beginning of March.[41]

III

Hoover's prediction about the adequacy of available funding proved accurate. By the time the ERC formally ended its operations at the end of May 1921, it had spent just under $27 million of the $29 million collected. About $10 million was distributed through the Red Cross, another $2.2 million through the Jewish Joint Distribution Committee, and about $1 million through the American Friends Service Committee. The remainder, except for some small amounts spent by other organizations, paid for the work of the ARA—a total just over $13 million. Just how many children the various programs fed and provided with medicines, clothing, and other benefits is impossible to determine, since children went in and out of the program without anyone trying to keep precise records. Hoover estimated the total at somewhere between 15 and 20 million. Given the various sources of food and money that programs drew on and the vagueness of the period to which he alluded, it is impossible to know whether he was correct.[42]

When the ERC ceased operation, its remaining funds were transferred, with the consent of the members, to the ARA, which incorporated under New York State law on May 27, 1921. The purpose of the new organization, according to its certificate of incorporation, was "to collect, receive and maintain a fund or funds and apply the income and principal thereof to relieve suffering and distress and otherwise to promote the well-being of mankind throughout the world." Throughout the remainder of the 1920s and into the mid-1930s, the organization and various subdivisions would provide funding for benevolent projects dear to Bert and Lou Hoover, including the American Child Health Association, the American Friends Service Committee, the Red

Cross, the Boys Clubs of America, the Boy and Girl Scouts, the National Amateur Athletic Federation, the National Outdoor Recreation Conference, the President's Conference on Home Building and Home Ownership, and the White House Conference on Child Health and Protection, among others.[43]

In an extended interview with the journalist Isaac Marcosson on February 23, 1921, Hoover reviewed the achievements of the postwar relief program and speculated on the future. The program, he pointed out, had not been the first American experience with large-scale relief but the third, the first being the Belgian program and the second the provisioning of the Allies during the war. By the time of the armistice, then, his organization had extensive experience with how to set up and operate an effective program. The key to success, he argued, was "to stimulate self-help," both by arranging that local relief programs would be managed and run by local people with Americans involved only in providing supplies and organizing transportation and by moving as rapidly as possible toward having "local charities and local governments . . . perform the whole task." The ultimate test of success, he said, would be the rebuilding of the "physical, mental and moral health and the economic and social progress" of the nations involved, and more specifically, providing nutrition, health, and education of children, for "the children are the army with which we must march to progress." He firmly believed that, as a result of the relief program, "we have the love and the gratitude of millions of [Europe's] children," who were "growing up with a feeling of faith in America and in Americans." Their love, he declared optimistically but erroneously, would offer "greater protection to the United States than any battleship."[44]

By the harvest of 1921, Hoover predicted, "the end will be nearly in sight." By then, he believed that even Germany would have recovered sufficiently to feed itself, and only Austria, Poland, and Russian refugees in Eastern Europe would continue to need significant assistance. But the unsolved political problems created by the peace treaty precluded full recovery. Poland had suffered extensively in the war, and their conflict with Russia in 1920 had worsened the situation. "Racial prejudices and recollections of former tyranny" had erected barriers to trade between Austria and the new states created from its former empire. If Vienna could reclaim its place as the commercial center of the region, it could prosper. If not, the country would have "an excess population of one million people, who must go hungry." For this bleak situation, he could see no immediate solution, and he concluded that the United States must, until it was resolved, continue to feed Austrian children. The Russian refugees presented a dilemma "for which there is no solution as far as I can see until the Bolshevik Government falls." A million such refugees, scattered from Helsinki to Constantinople (Istanbul), must be kept alive as the "nucleus out of which to build the future Russia."[45]

Yet despite the bleak outlook for Austria and the Russian refugees, Hoover was upbeat about the overall achievements of the relief program. Central Europe, he believed, had been put on the road to economic self-sufficiency and stable democracy. It had turned back the threat of Bolshevism outside of Russia and laid a base for future progress in the sturdy bodies and grateful hearts of millions of healthy children. What was more, at the instance of the Belgian government, the ARA had used unexpended relief funds in Belgium to establish an educational foundation to sponsor an exchange program for Belgian and American university students and professors; to fund economic, scientific, and social research in the two countries; and to help rebuild war-damaged universities in Belgium.[46]

The central goal of all his programs, said Hoover, was to "bridge the gulf between classes" by feeding and educating children "on a wholesale scale," thus helping to end "the eternal bane of Europe—class conflict." He denied any direct link between relief and immediate economic advantages for Americans, but he did not doubt that it would bring long-term benefits, both economic and political. "The sole idea," he said, "has been the social and economic restoration of Europe, and through that regeneration, the economic safety of the rest of the world, including the United States. If Europe is plunged into chaos America, too, will have economic demoralization. My firm belief is that our relief is neutralizing the ferment. In preventing famine and worse on the other side of the Atlantic, we have insured ourselves against disaster on this side." He added, "We have done more, for we have left the mark of the true heart of America upon the world."[47]

Despite his self-congratulatory assessment, it is true that his honest, efficient relief program had triumphed over difficult situations, both in Europe and the United States, and saved many lives. The essential foundation for permanent European stability that Hoover had identified in the autumn of 1919, however, a long-term American economic and political commitment to involvement with the Continent's well-being, had not been achieved. In selling humanitarian relief to the government and the public, he had found it expedient to drop his early support for government involvement in European recovery and to maintain that reconstruction could be achieved entirely through private investments. Had he persuaded himself of the validity of that argument by 1921? Only time would tell.

CHAPTER 6

Family and Business, 1921

The Hoovers had an exceptionally busy time during the first two months of 1921, as they tried to raise funds for European relief, complete the Palo Alto house, and get ready for their new lives in Washington, where Bert would become secretary of commerce in Warren Harding's cabinet. Amid the rush, their twenty-second wedding anniversary on February 10 passed unnoted, with Bert working in the East, and Lou in California.

From Palo Alto, Lou asked old friends Alida Henriques and Ethel Bullard to oversee readying the S Street house for the family. Having seen the place only briefly, she had to trust them to arrange for and supervise any necessary repairs. The most urgent work, she wrote, would be getting the "kitchen regions, servant[s'] sitting rooms," and a few upstairs bedrooms in "sleepable" condition so that the family and guests could stay there during inauguration week. She suggested that "cream or very pale gray walls uniform throughout the downstairs, and furnished with colonial furniture" would suit a house that would frequently serve as a backdrop to official business. To an acquaintance who might gossip about the Hoovers' plans if she knew them, she wrote disingenuously that an unnamed "Investment Trust" had bought the house, and the family had simply rented it with the possibility of subletting.[1]

I

Bert happily left domestic arrangements to Lou. Continuing his crowded schedule as a fund-raiser, he also pressed his fellow engineers in the Federated

American Engineering Society to authorize and pay for a study of industrial waste. He also helped to organize a Foreign Trade Financing Corporation under the recently passed Edge Act, which had created new mechanisms for selling agricultural and industrial surpluses overseas. On October 20, 1920, the American Bankers Association established a committee, with Hoover as a member, to organize an Edge Act corporation for that purpose. The group began assembling $100 million in capital, which it envisioned as the foundation for a billion-dollar stock offering to provide operating funds. They anticipated that the company would pay producers—including farmers—cash for products that they could not afford to sell on credit and then resell those items overseas, on credit if necessary. It would also offer a test case for Hoover's argument that private American investment could help to finance European reconstruction. As purchasers repaid loans, or profits came in from foreign investments, a revolving fund would be created to continue the process. "There is no limit," declared retiring Secretary of Commerce William Redfield, "to the world that opens before us if we have the vision to put American money into American-owned, American-run, American-controlled industries and institutions all around the globe."[2]

As a further aid to the establishment of the Foreign Trade Financing Corporation, Hoover urged Congress to extend temporarily the life of the government-owned War Finance Corporation. Most Americans, he pointed out, found the concept of the Foreign Trade Financing Corporation novel. It would give the public confidence in the new company's stock if the War Finance Corporation backed it, at least for the short term.[3]

Hoover correctly anticipated that American investors would be dubious about the new idea. Although the company filed for incorporation with the Federal Reserve Board in Washington on January 28, 1921, and set up subcommittees in sixty-five cities to solicit subscriptions, only about $12 million of the projected $100 million stock offering had been sold when Hoover resigned from the organizing committee to become secretary of commerce. He and Secretary of the Treasury Andrew Mellon did their best to encourage the project from behind the scenes, but as government officials, they could not endorse it publicly. Several major corporate executives, such as A. C. Bedford of Standard Oil, John J. Raskob of General Motors, Alexander Legge of International Harvester, and Roy Chapin of the Hudson Motor Car Company, joined the organizing committee, but bankers never warmed to the project. With investment lagging, Hoover concluded that the enterprise was hopeless and switched his energies in the late spring of 1921 to new plans for promoting foreign trade through the Commerce Department. In a major speech about export promotion to the National Shoe and Leather Exposition in Boston on July 12, he said nothing about the FTFC, nor did he mention it in his memoirs.[4]

Inauguration Day, March 4, 1921, dawned sunny but cold in Washington. Harding took the oath of office at 1:15 PM and began his inaugural address, speaking seemingly without looking at his notes on the podium in front of him. A loudspeaker system carried every word clearly to the gathered crowd, and lusty cheers greeted his promise of a return to "normalcy." Equally loud applause followed his assurance that the United States would "accept no responsibility except as our own conscience and judgment, in each instance, may determine." Hoover, listening attentively, saw his last flicker of hope for League membership wink out.[5]

II

Bert and Lou, of course, attended all the festivities, but at times their thoughts turned to California, where Allan was having his tonsils removed. The operation went smoothly, and Lou decided that since the family was now officially centered in the capital, it would be well for him to recover in Washington rather than stay with Dare Stark and Herbert in Palo Alto. She planned to have him tutored at home instead of enrolling him in a new high school to finish his freshman year. Lou herself would shuttle back and forth between Washington and Palo Alto to supervise work on the house and look after Herbert and her mother. Allan took to life on S Street enthusiastically, making new friends and excavating a pond in the backyard for various turtles, frogs, and even two baby alligators, which became unpopular when they chewed the tops off the pond's water lilies. "Beauty and the Beast," reported Lou's secretary Philippi Harding, "are not congenial." Turning fourteen on July 17 and with a weekly "salary" of fifty cents (increased after his birthday to a dollar) for ice cream sodas and the use of a rented tennis court nearby, Allan quickly became a personage in the neighborhood.[6]

Herbert remained in California to finish his senior year at Palo Alto High. Lou reported that he had become "frightfully keen over wireless, aeroplanes, and all things mechanical." When he came to Washington for the summer, his father found him unpaid internships, first with the Army Signals Corps and later with the Bureau of Standards of the Commerce Department. Also living on S Street, he happily divided his time between science and the tennis court. He turned eighteen on August 4, and a substantial allowance of $5 a week covered carfare, lunches, and other necessities. On weekends, the boys and their father sometimes went down the Potomac and out onto Chesapeake Bay on a fishing expedition aboard one of the Commerce Department's utility vessels, the USS *Kilkenny*, and occasionally to the theater. Bert even stole time to take the boys and their friends out into the country for a day or two of dam building on some small stream and to lend his engineering expertise to the improvement of the pond in the backyard. Under a strictly enforced agreement, all three Hoover males ate breakfast together every morning, with a rule that anyone who arrived late paid a dollar fine, which went into a tennis ball fund. On July 2, Lou's secretary reported, the commerce secretary himself had to pay for a tardy arrival. In odd moments, Ralph Peacock, an English artist commissioned by Lou, worked on a portrait of Bert, who endured the sittings to please his wife.[7]

For Lou, the spring brought new opportunities for public influence. The League of Women Voters solicited her support, and she contributed a thousand dollars during each of the next several years. Publicity about her earlier work with Bert in translating *De Re Metallica* led the *American Historical Review* to invite her to review a book about German mining, which she declined, and a letter from a student in architectural engineering at Ohio State University asked her opinion about "women engineers." She responded that a woman should be free to enter any field of engineering "that she feels capable of and interested in attempting." Any woman who had "taken correct care of herself" should have no problem with the physical requirements of engineering. The question whether such a profession would make her "unwomanly," she snapped, was "incomprehensible." An "advocate of the education of the sexes on a common footing," as the Washington *Sunday Star* reported, she embraced the "new era" ideal that women as well as men had a right to pursue rewarding professions and take part in public life.[8]

Just as the Hoovers really began to get into the swing of life in Washington, word arrived that Lou's mother, Florence Henry, had a recurrence of her colon cancer. In mid-May, Lou took the train for California. There, despite her anxiety about her mother, who was seeing doctors almost daily and finding it difficult to eat, Lou loved being back in her house on the hill. She slept on the boys' porch, she reported, had her breakfast under the "upstairs pergola," and thoroughly enjoyed her "lovely house." Mornings, afternoons, and even some evenings, she and Dare, and sometimes her sister, Jean Large, worked on "boxes, boxes, boxes being unpacked and sorted out and repacked." Like everyone else in the midst of a move she lamented, "You would never believe we had so many boxes, or things!"[9]

By the third week of July, Lou felt comfortable enough about her mother's condition to return to Washington, leaving the house and her mother under her sister's and Dare's supervision. Behind her she left detailed instructions for the servants Albert Butler and his daughter Carrie about how she wanted the house cleaned and maintained during the summer. With Dare, her sister, and her mother staying there off and on, the place never stood empty, and in the autumn the Hoovers invited an English friend, Francis Hirst, former editor of *The Economist*, to live in it while he lectured at Stanford. Another friend, a Mrs. Franklin, showed up suddenly in late July also expecting to stay at the house—Lou had completely forgotten that she had invited her. The incident, revealing of the Hoovers' casual hospitality, typified their daily life.[10]

The S Street house proved a pleasant surprise when Lou got back to Washington. The furniture and redecoration had turned out well, and she found the house, even in the capital's summer heat, "cool and fresh." Downtown, however, the city steamed, and Lou plotted to get Bert away for a couple of weeks' rest. Abbie and Edgar Rickard had invited them to their summer place in New England, but Lou feared that Bert would become bored unless he had projects to occupy him. If they could take a car and have a loose schedule of visits to friends, she thought, "he might not realize how long he was staying at any one place."[11]

Early in August, she put this benevolent scheme into motion, and the family headed north. Then, while they visited at Cape Cod, a telegram arrived from her father in California. Her mother had taken a sharp turn for the worse, and there seemed little hope of recovery. Taking the first train west, Lou poured out her heart in a letter to Allan. "It will be such a loss to have her go away from us," she wrote, but if her illness should become painful, "it would be very selfish to want to keep her with us." Her job now, she added, was "to be as much of a comfort to Grandpa as I can," and Allan's was "to cheer up Daddy all you can." Sadly, she arrived in California a day too late. Her mother had died peacefully on August 18. After a memorial service at the Stanford chapel, Florence Henry's body was taken to San Francisco for cremation, and her ashes buried in a Palo Alto cemetery.[12]

In the East, the summer flowed along happily. Allan stayed on with the Rickards in New England until nearly the end of August, while Bert, Herbert, and various guests enjoyed weekend fishing trips on the *Kilkenny*. On one trip Bert hooked his thumb on a fishhook and had to have it bandaged for a week, but he recovered fully in time for a final expedition just before Herbert departed for Palo Alto, where he began his Stanford freshman year in early October. The young man had thoroughly enjoyed his summer, working at the Bureau of Standards during most days and putting together a hundred dollars' worth of radio equipment purchased with his graduation money. He and his father purchased one of the new phonographs, a "Brunswick," and the boys consumed hours deciding what records to order. Allan, who spent several unpleasant days at the dentist just before Herbert left, would attend Western High in Washington, though he declared that he would much rather go to "Paly High" in California. Lou's secretary, Philippi Harding, took him to school on September 15 to present his credentials and be admitted officially, and classes began a few days later.[13]

By early September, Lou had settled her mother's affairs and Herbert had moved into the house and declared himself ready to begin classes at Stanford. The time had now come, she decided, to launch an adventure she had been considering ever since she arrived in California. She wanted to drive her father across the country, stopping off along the way to visit various Henry and Hoover relatives. Given the primitive condition of American roads, especially in the West, and the absence of reliable road markings and maps, a transcontinental drive in 1921 entailed risks for anyone. It would be doubly so for a party made up of a woman, her father, her young nephew Del Large, and a single Filipino servant, whose main duty, since Lou did all the driving and cooking, was "to pitch our tent." Only twelve years previously Alice Ramsey had become the first woman make the cross-country trip, taking forty-one days to do it, and Americans still regarded it as something of an assertion of feminist independence.[14]

The Agriculture Department's Bureau of Public Roads published a map in 1921 showing a "national highway system," but it existed only on paper. Despite the efforts of the private Good Roads Movement beginning in the 1890s and the work of various federal agencies after the turn of the century, by that year the United States had only about thirty thousand miles of paved highways in cities and isolated rural segments. The Federal-Aid Highway Act of 1916 had directed the Bureau of Public Roads to assist states in building rural roads to help farmers get their products to market rather than to construct an interstate highway network.[15]

As the reliability of private automobiles improved and their numbers increased rapidly after the war, the attractions of automobile tourism grew. Private cars allowed Americans not only to see the country as they could from the windows of a train but also to experience it more intimately, to choose their own routes, to stop and explore along the way. Many promoters of automobile tourism linked the idea of seeing the country's natural wonders with the promotion of its historical heritage. The Lincoln Highway, the National Old Trails Road, and the National Park to Park Highway all existed more as concepts than roads in 1921, but they popularized the idea that highways should enable Americans to see and learn about their country firsthand rather than just make it easier for farmers to get to town. When Lou began her trip, a bill was pending in Congress to shift some of the federal money authorized by the 1916 act into the construction of interstate highways.[16]

But that remained in the future as Lou and her father set off on September 12 in the Hoovers' Cadillac from Palo Alto on what the magazine *American Motorist* would call "the great American pilgrimage." Although coastal California boasted some of the nation's best roads, travel grew increasingly difficult as the group went east toward the mountains, where highways degenerated into wagon roads. For the next ten days, they made their way through the gold fields of California, over the Sierra Nevada through Donner Pass, and across the desert of Nevada, rarely managing more than a hundred miles a day. Although they followed more or less the projected route of the Lincoln Highway, no highway numbers and few informational signs marked the roads; no national system of highway marking would even be planned until 1925. Occasionally, they found a hotel in which to stay, but mostly they camped. After driving from Carlin to Elko, Nevada, Lou proudly reported they had just covered what was "said to be [the] worst stretch of road between Oceans."[17]

On September 21, they arrived in Salt Lake City, having covered 130 miles that day, the best of the trip so far. A day later, they headed north, turning east at Ogden into the southwest corner of Wyoming and continuing east on what is now U.S. 30 over the Rockies past Fort Bridger and Laramie, then turning south to Fort Collins. After a night camped near Fort Collins, they swung west again, following the Thompson River to Estes Park on the eastern edge of Rocky Mountain National Park. That night they camped in the park, and the next morning drove up the narrow, tortuous, gravel Fall River Road to the Continental Divide at almost twelve thousand feet. They pitched camp that night at over nine thousand feet, and the next morning the chilled car refused to start with either the electric starter or crank until the sun warmed it. Choosing not to attempt the newly opened western extension of the Fall River Road, which dropped down from the Continental Divide along the western side of the park through the Never Summer Mountains, they turned around and returned to Estes Park, then swung south toward Denver. The next night, September 30, they stayed at a hotel in Henderson, Colorado, a few miles northeast of Denver. In eighteen days since leaving Palo Alto, they had covered 1,648 miles. The car had run beautifully, and their log of this portion of the trip records only one flat tire and one minor accident when someone bumped into them in Ogden—an extraordinary record for the time and state of the roads.

East of Denver, they emerged onto the high plains, and the going got easier, but ironically, the car gave them more trouble. On Saturday and Sunday, October 1 and 2, they averaged better than 140 miles a day but had three flat tires and a broken spring. After a brief delay for repairs, they arrived in Omaha on the evening of Tuesday, October 4, and in Waterloo, Iowa, Lou's birthplace, on October 6. There they visited family, but unfortunately some of them contracted food poisoning and spent most of the visit in bed. On October 10, they drove to Iowa City, and the next day to West Branch, where George Hoover showed them the sights around his cousin Bert's boyhood home. That afternoon they crossed the Mississippi and spent the evening in Dixon, Illinois, unaware that they were in the hometown of a future president, Ronald Reagan. The rest of the trip, despite minor inconveniences, proved relatively easy. The roads were much better, and they easily averaged two hundred miles a day, arriving in Washington on the evening of Sunday, October 16, just a little over a month after leaving California. The trip, Lou wrote to a friend, had been "delightful, and the weather was perfect,—giving us just ten minutes of rain during the entire journey."[18]

Lou's trip encapsulated the transformation of America in the early twentieth century. In twenty years, automobiles had progressed from unreliable toys to dependable transportation and would advance still further during the 1920s. Whereas prewar cars had been designed and marketed mainly for male drivers, by the 1920s manufacturers had begun to cater to women as well, although the industry still felt uncertain about what would attract female consumers. The electric starter in the Hoovers' Cadillac proved one of the most successful of the innovations of the period. The roads that Lou and her father traversed in the Sierras and Nevada typified the state of nearly all American roads only a few years before—little more than dirt paths wandering from farm to farm, full of rocks and stumps, and deep in dust in dry weather and even deeper in mud when it rained. By the time the party reached the Midwest, however, they found some all-weather, paved roads, engineered for comfort and safety, and laid out to run from city to city rather than farm to farm. Within a few years, driving coast to coast would become easy and popular.

Hoover intended, as secretary of commerce, to make such trips parts of normal life. The very idea of the trip, as well as the car, roads, telephone, and electricity and other conveniences upon which Lou depended during it, demonstrated the rising American standard of living he wanted to promote. Success, however, depended on rapidly increasing exploitation of natural resources. One form of exploitation, the transformation of wilderness into "scenery," delighted most people and worried only a few, but development also raised a practical problem. The industries that built the cars, the roads they traveled on, and the other amenities of the consumer society all devoured resources at an ever-accelerating rate. Conservationists had been urging caution and restraint in the use of resources for a number of years, and Hoover hoped to build on their work. A planned program of standardization and waste elimination, he argued, could further extend the resources that made possible the consumer economy.[19]

Lou and her father arrived in Washington to discover Bert absorbed in a major unemployment conference, and Allan engrossed in his new school, where he had been admitted as a sophomore and signed up for history, geometry, French, and English, though he declined to take biology. He had found that Western High, like all the Washington public schools, suffered from overcrowding so severe that students could only attend in half-day shifts. Allan, with morning classes, worked in the afternoons on his homework (Lou sometimes worried that he was overly conscientious) or on his stamp collection, a new and passionate hobby, which the family thought might have contributed to eye problems that necessitated several trips to the doctor in early October. Goldfish from the Commerce Department's aquarium had replaced the alligators, now banished to the Washington Zoo, in the backyard pond. Looking ahead to the winter, he tried to figure out how to flood the yard for skating. Inside the house, workmen turned a back room on the ground floor into a study for Bert. Almost every evening he hosted "big men-dinner-parties" as the unemployment conference got into full swing.[20]

Charles Henry stayed with the Hoovers for about two weeks before returning to California. When he left, Lou plunged into a multiyear lobbying campaign to get Congress to increase appropriations for the underfunded Washington school system. She also agreed to serve on the board of trustees of a new settlement house known as Neighborhood House. Bert, for his part, seemed busier than ever with the Commerce Department, the unemployment conference, and then, beginning in November, the Washington Disarmament Conference, for which the Commerce Department provided statistics and background information.

III

Hoover had tried to distance himself from his various business enterprises in the months before he entered the cabinet, but it proved impossible to escape all connection to them. The Sacramento *Union*, purchased with a loan from Hoover by his Food Administration associate, Ben S. Allen, seemed a money pit. Although Allen assured Hoover the paper would eventually return a profit of as much as $50,000 a year, Hoover had to put up an additional $15,000 during 1920 to deal with what Allen brushed off as start-up costs.[21] The Washington *Herald*, in which Hoover transferred his interest to the Intercontinental Development Company in December 1920, remained "his paper" in the eyes of official Washington. If it published an editorial that stepped on someone's toes or a vacancy opened on its staff, he heard about it, no matter how much he might protest that he had no influence.[22]

Although none of the Intercontinental Development Company enterprises proved as successful as the associates hoped, the California farm became a particular headache. Located twenty-four miles northwest of Bakersfield in Kern County near the hamlet of Wasco, the farm comprised just over 1,200 acres. When Hoover acquired it, in 1920, six miles of canals, dug some thirty years previously when flooding remained the main method of irrigation, criss-crossed the property. For several years, the land had lain fallow, however, and it had grown up to weeds. Hoover employed Ralph Merritt, his erstwhile California campaign manager, to manage the property, now called the Poso Land and Products Company. In late 1920, Merritt set about clearing land and drilling five 500-foot wells to replace the inefficient and unpredictable canal irrigation system. He installed thirty horsepower electric pumps to provide a steady flow of irrigation water and built roads to make all parts of the property accessible. On a well-treed, six-acre site near the center of the property, he erected a new house for the resident manager, Harvey Kilburn, and green-roofed, cream-colored cabins for seventy-five farm workers and their families. Ranch employees drove the farm workers' children back and forth to school in Wasco. Construction costs escalated, but the local newspaper gushed that the owners believed "economical operation" would justify the initial investment.[23]

In fact, the Poso operation seemed to gulp money as fast as water. Merritt reported in 1923 that grading had cost $60,000, the wells $40,000, buildings $30,000, equipment another $30,000, and miscellaneous additional expenses some $12,000, not to mention the cost of the land itself—all before anything had been planted. He estimated that raising crops of cotton, corn, wheat, oats, melons, vegetables, and various fruits would cost as much as $78,000 per year, although he admitted that in the depressed agricultural market, the crops would probably not earn more than $80,000 gross. Given the original purchase price of $181,950 ($150 an acre), which had been secured by a mortgage to the Kern County Land Company, the farm seemed unlikely to turn a profit in the foreseeable future.[24]

Nevertheless, in December 1923, Merritt predicted cheerfully that income from cotton and vegetables would cover operating costs. Net returns, he claimed, would be $75 an acre, and he had worked out an arrangement with the mortgage holder to postpone payments on both principal and interest, provided the farm expanded its vineyards and orchards. He told the skeptical partners in the East that he had not sent them detailed plans because he assumed that they only wanted to hear about profits and losses, not details. An article in the *California Cultivator*, apparently based on an interview with Merritt, lauded the operation as a notable success without inquiring into its financial structure.[25]

In a letter to Edgar Rickard in early January 1924, Hoover expressed growing uneasiness about the situation at Poso. The partners had bought the property, he wrote, on his personal assurance that it would provide a good investment, and he felt "obligated to make good any loss that might result from it." He thought he had made the situation clear to Merritt more than a year previously, he added, but obviously that was not the case.[26]

The tension between Hoover and Merritt continued throughout 1924, and by autumn the partners had decided to try to sell out. When a report reached them that a possible purchaser had expressed interest, they instructed Merritt to explore the opportunity. No evidence indicates that he ever did so. Instead, he wrote that, given "the depression in farming and the continuing liquidation of large holdings," no sale would cover what they had invested, still less return a profit. They could, he told them bluntly, either "hold on to the property until the depression is entirely past" or "sell at a sacrifice."[27] The advice, so utterly contradictory to what he had been saying for years, confirmed the partners' worst fears.

Unfortunately, at this point some letters that Hoover, Barnes, and Merritt exchanged appear not to have survived. Indirect evidence suggests, however, that Merritt proposed not a retrenchment or sale of the property but a purchase of additional land or equipment and expansion. Hoover found that too much. In April 1925, he drafted a testy letter to the manager pointing out that the partners had originally intended to invest no more than $250,000 but had been compelled to spend between $650,000 and $690,000. With more than $250,000 in loan payments due over the next four years, and a maximum income of about $50,000 a year, the farm had become a disaster. He proposed that Merritt use any profits to pay the interest and as much of the principal of the mortgage as possible, that he try to refinance the loan balance in 1928, and that he avoid any purchases of new equipment unless the partners specifically authorized them. The partners had evidently decided to wait out the agricultural slump, cutting costs wherever possible and basing management not on Merritt's fanciful predictions but on actual cash flows.[28]

One day in June 1925, when the temperature in the San Joaquin Valley topped a hundred degrees in the shade, Hoover, Allan, and Edgar Rickard paid a visit to the farm. Merritt gave them a personal tour and an excellent lunch, and everyone, from the manager down to a "small 12 year old Chinese boy," expressed confidence that everything was going well. Rickard, however, noticed something that their hosts did not point out: despite unusually heavy rains that spring, the water level in the wells had not risen. Discussion of the probable water shortage must have occupied much of the visitors' three-hour drive back to Palo Alto.[29]

By the autumn of 1925, relations between Merritt and the partners had deteriorated further. When Rickard met with Merritt in mid-October, he barely concealed his annoyance. Whatever Merritt's political skills, Rickard later told San Francisco attorney Warren Gregory, he had proved a poor administrator "when it comes to hard financial problems." Gregory agreed, predicting that Merritt, who had also been organizing a cooperative of raisin producers that would become the Sun-Maid Raisin Company, would fail in the new enterprise, as he had with the Hoover farm. Their pessimism was borne out in mid-December, when Merritt telegraphed the partners that the farm's profits would not cover the mortgage payment due to the Kern County Land Company at the end of the month. They must send an additional $71,000 immediately. Rickard now suspected that Merritt hoped to buy the property himself, but Hoover concluded that there was no choice but to pay. In a brusque letter to Merritt he expressed "shock" at the new demand and pointed out that raising the money had created serious problems for him and Barnes. He all but ordered Merritt to come East in January to sign a reorganization agreement. Without waiting for a reply from the manager, he complained to his friend Thomas Gregory in San Francisco that Merritt had not even "acknowledged" the reorganization plan. He asked Gregory to look into the whole matter.[30]

While Hoover awaited Gregory's report, another shock arrived. Edward Flesh, also an Intercontinental Development Company partner, paid a visit to the farm, where the resident manager, Harvey Kilburn, told him that Merritt, instead of cutting back, proposed to lease two hundred additional acres of land from the Kern County Land Company. The land company had offered to provide the land rent-free, provided Poso would install a well, at an estimated cost of $20,000. No one at Intercontinental had been told of this scheme, and the prospect that they would be asked for an additional $20,000 on top of the $70,000 they had just sent horrified them all.[31]

A few weeks later, Gregory submitted his report. He had visited the farm and conferred with Merritt. Merritt insisted that he had signed the reorganization agreement but had been forced to delay returning it to get someone else's signature. Gregory let that go and focused on the question of the farm's future. With half the property planted in orchards and vineyards that had not yet begun to produce, he doubted the ranch could earn enough to cover the mortgage and interest fully. It seemed unlikely, he added, that the $70,000 Hoover and his associates had sent recently could be refinanced in California as a debt of the ranch. The lawyer advised the partners to hold on until prices stabilized and then sell for whatever they could get.[32]

Whatever Hoover thought of Gregory's recommendations, he had not quite given up on securing a new loan in California to cover the farm's outstanding debts. Early in February 1926, he asked Edward Flesh to make another trip to California to explore possibilities. Although Merritt protested at this usurpation of his management authority, the partners insisted. Hoover did not share Rickard's conviction that Merritt was "not to be trusted," but all the partners felt that someone of greater financial experience than Merritt needed to take charge. Flesh, the former treasurer of the American Relief Administration, seemed the ideal choice. It took him a month of hard work, but with the help of Hoover's friend Henry M. Robinson of the First National Bank in Los Angeles, Flesh arranged a new $240,000 mortgage on the property. He used the money to pay off the remainder of the Kern County Land Company's mortgage, wiping the slate for a new start.[33]

Given their experience, it might have been expected that the fresh start would have included a new manager, but the partners stuck with Merritt, and for a time, things seemed to go smoothly. Then, in 1927, the old problems reappeared. Merritt failed to send reports or provided incomplete information, and once again the partners found themselves in the dark. During the summer of 1927, Hoover paid a personal visit to the ranch and must have laid down the law to the manager. That fall, full monthly reports began to arrive, and Merritt promised to provide a complete annual financial statement, as well as a planting plan at the beginning of each year. He also ordered the replacement of rotting tents that had been housing twenty-four families of farm workers with new two-room houses and communal baths, toilets, and laundry facilities. He expected to cover construction costs by charging each family $30 a month rent.[34]

With Hoover planning a presidential run, the housing improvements at Poso came none too soon. In April 1928, a committee from the Kern County Labor Council visited the ranch and reported enthusiastically that not only were workers well housed and well paid (an average of $3.50 a day) but also—always a sensitive issue in California—a majority of them were white and only a minority black or Mexican. Articles in the press lauded the operation's treatment of its workers, as well as the scientific management principles under which the farm was run. The great engineer, a reporter assured readers of the *New York Times*, had applied "simple scientific principles to the art of growing things." The ranch, he gushed, exemplified "the Ford idea applied to the soil."[35]

Buried deep in one of the published reports about the farm lay a crucial question: "Does a Hooverized ranch pay?" It was, the reporter concluded cautiously, "a bit too early to answer the question with finality," though he added that, even in the "years of plague for American agriculture," the farm had never run "in the red."[36] That, of course, was true only if one excluded the capital investment in the enterprise, but Hoover, who had a vested interest in having people believe that he understood how to make farming profitable, made no attempt to correct the public impression of his farm's success during his election campaign.

An unpublicized incident in the summer of 1928 suggested a different conclusion. When Ralph Merritt informed Julius Barnes that business would take him away from California for a protracted period, the partners sensed an opportunity. Joseph Di Giorgio, who was then assembling the forty thousand acres of the Di Giorgio Fruit Corporation in the San Joaquin Valley, approached Barnes with an offer to take over the management of the Poso Company, assuming all obligations and promising an equal division of any profits. No record of what happened at this point survives, but inasmuch as three years later Hoover could say that he had had "no interest" in the California farm for the last three years, it seems probable that the partners accepted the Di Giorgio offer or one much like it.[37]

Started at a terrible time in American agriculture, the Poso ranch had never been a promising investment. As Hoover's partners contended, a significant part of the problem lay in Ralph Merritt's management. His large capital expenditures and unwise commitment to growing fruit and vegetables in the midst of an arid region would have made achieving profitability difficult even in the best of times. Had Merritt's political loyalty not won him Hoover's affection and gratitude, he would probably have been fired. But Hoover's responsibility for the ranch's failure went beyond misplaced loyalty. Not only was his advocacy of a new agricultural venture in a period of overproduction rash, but also his experience as a mining engineer should have led him to investigate the adequacy of the farm's water supply more carefully prior to the purchase. By the summer of 1928, nine deep wells could not bring up enough water from the depleted aquifer to irrigate the ranch's thirsty crops. Within a few years, reported Scott Turner, director of the Bureau of Mines in Hoover's Commerce Department, the wells had been driven down to as much as four thousand feet, and still "there wasn't enough run to keep [them] replenished."[38]

Perhaps the most surprising aspects of the Poso fiasco were Hoover's willingness, despite his extensive business experience, to believe Merritt's grandiose claims and his slowness to make needed corrections. As far as can be determined, none of the various enterprises controlled by the Intercontinental Development Company proved very successful. Most of them were speculative, and Hoover never had the time to focus on their management, but the partners all knew that when they began. Why, then, did they choose to invest in such risky ventures? More importantly, what does it say about Hoover's business sense that he seemingly misread the agricultural situation so seriously and then poured good money after bad as the Poso venture sank into the desert? Perhaps, despite his general prudence and experience, he, too, had become infected to a certain degree with the speculative atmosphere of the 1920s.

CHAPTER 7

The Commerce
Department, 1921

On November 5, 1920, three days after the election, president-elect Harding invited Hoover to meet with him at Harding's home in Marion, Ohio. Harding admired Hoover as a businessman, humanitarian, wartime administrator, and leader in postwar reconstruction, and he wanted him in his cabinet. But the appointment posed difficulties. Hoover favored American membership in the League of Nations and had frequently said so. He and Hiram Johnson, California's powerful senator, were bitter rivals politically and disliked each other personally. The conservative grandees of the Republican Party— Henry Cabot Lodge, Boies Penrose, Philander C. Knox, Frank Brandegee— distrusted Hoover for his internationalism and his close association with the Wilson administration. Republican progressives like Gifford Pinchot, William Borah, and George Norris had criticized his policies as food administrator and doubted his party loyalty.[1]

Although Hoover had much more foreign experience than any other prominent Republican, Harding rejected him as a possible secretary of state because of his support for the League. The president-elect hoped, however, that he might accept a lesser position at Interior or Commerce. As an engineer, he would be suitable for an Interior Department focused on public works rather than conservation, and his business experience and leadership in Wilson's industrial conference suggested an affinity for the Commerce Department. Even leaders of the American Federation of Labor said they thought he would be acceptable in that post.[2]

When the two men met on December 12, they discussed both cabinet offices, and Hoover said that, although people usually saw Interior as more important, he preferred Commerce because he thought the administration needed to focus on "reconstruction and national development." He told reporters outside the meeting only that he and Harding had discussed "the league of nations, the industrial situation in America, famine, relief and reconstruction in Europe, and the whole gamut of the world's troubles."[3]

Ten days later, Hoover wrote to Harding offering to drop out of cabinet contention because of the "opposition in certain politically-minded quarters" to his appointment. In fact, he had mixed feelings about going into the cabinet. Although the idea of shaping policy appealed to him, neither he nor Lou had found Harding's "hopeless looking" associates impressive. Having recently purchased an interest in the Washington *Herald*, moreover, he was intrigued by the possibility of turning it into a "first-class, well run, utterly honest" paper that would provide reliable political and economic reporting to the capital and the country.[4]

Hoover had accurately assessed his standing among Republican politicians. Charles Evans Hughes, Harding's choice for secretary of state, supported Hoover, but almost no other influential Republican did. Hiram Johnson did everything in his power to block the nomination, and, for once, conservatives agreed with him. In January 1921, Hoover's prospects turned even bleaker when a rumor circulated that he opposed Harding's choice for secretary of agriculture, Henry C. Wallace. Wallace had often criticized Food Administration policy during and after the war and had opposed Hoover during the 1920 campaign, so the report was plausible. Cannily, Hoover assured Harding on January 12 that Wallace was "not only admirably fitted for the work but . . . would render a great sense of teamwork in the real interest of agriculture." He brushed off Wallace's previous attacks as the result of "misinformation" given him by "intriguing persons." Harding, no fool on such matters, probably discounted Hoover's explanation, but he chose to accept it at face value. Nevertheless, Hoover told Lou that "every trend" was "negative owing to opposition," an opinion confirmed in late January by the *New York Times* and other papers, which reported that Harding had dropped him from consideration.[5]

Then, less than a week later, he mysteriously reappeared in the paper's predictions. Luck, it appeared, had taken a hand. Harding's first choice for secretary of the treasury, Chicago banker Charles G. Dawes, had declined, and Pennsylvania Senators Knox and Penrose had suggested Andrew W. Mellon instead. Harding recognized an opportunity in the situation and asked his campaign manager, Harry Daugherty, to suggest to Knox and Penrose that if they would support Hoover for Commerce, he would nominate Mellon for the Treasury. The deal proved tricky and took a while to work out, but on the evening of February 22, the president-elect telephoned Hoover to make the offer official.[6]

The next day, Hoover replied to Harding's offer, laying out a number of conditions for his acceptance. Americans had contributed a large amount of money for European relief, he noted, and he felt an obligation to continue to supervise its expenditure. In terms of his official duties, he asked for authority to reorganize and strengthen the Commerce Department to make it the principal agency for promoting cooperation among domestic industries and harmony between labor and management and foreign trade. Such tasks would require the cooperation of the State and Labor Departments and other agencies, and Hoover asked that he "have a voice" in their policies insofar as they affected business and foreign trade.[7]

As the *New York Times* pointed out, Hoover had in effect asked for "an absolutely free hand" to "make the position just as important as he desired." Unless that happened, said Hoover, he did not feel "warranted in shifting [his] responsibilities for relief work." When the president-elect accepted his conditions, Hoover became, in the cliché of the period, "Secretary of Commerce and under secretary of everything else." Reporters immediately predicted that the commerce secretary's power would produce friction with his cabinet colleagues.[8]

I

The cabinet that Harding announced on March 4, 1921, contained the usual mixture of strong, independent men and political hacks. Charles Evans Hughes at State, Andrew Mellon at the Treasury, Hoover at Commerce, and Henry C. Wallace at Agriculture were the most important members. John W. Weeks at the War Department, Edwin Denby as secretary of the navy, and James J. Davis as secretary of labor were competent administrators but not leaders. Attorney General Harry Daugherty, Postmaster General Will Hays, and Secretary of the Interior Albert B. Fall were frankly political appointments, and of the three, only Hays would escape relatively unscathed from subsequent scandals. In his memoirs, Hoover singles out Hughes, Mellon, Weeks, Denby, and Hays as particular allies, but in fact, he had several clashes with both Hughes and Mellon behind the scenes, although none of them equaled his battles with Henry Wallace.[9] And, although he was unwilling for obvious reasons to say so in his memoirs, he really liked the roguish Albert Fall, who reciprocated the friendly feelings of his fellow westerner.

The tall, bearded, imposing Charles Evans Hughes had the most impressive résumé in the cabinet, having been governor of New York, Supreme Court justice, and Republican presidential candidate in 1916. Hoover thought that the president was "a little afraid of his stiff Secretary of State," but Hoover professed himself unintimidated. Having wrestled figuratively with the leaders of Europe during the war, he respected Hughes even when poaching on his territory as he pushed to expand the Commerce Department's overseas role.

The two men both favored American membership in the League of Nations, but recognizing that was impossible in the current political climate, they concentrated on ameliorating what they agreed were the main flaws of the peace settlement—reparations, debts, boundaries, and disarmament.[10] Both Hoover and Hughes regarded economic and political stability in Europe as important to American self-interest and made the attainment of that goal a centerpiece of their policy.

Secretary of the Treasury Andrew Mellon was as diminutive as Hughes was large, weighing only about a hundred pounds and shy in demeanor. He was shrewd, frugal, and conventional in outlook—"in every instinct a country banker," as Hoover put it many years later. But he was also patriotic, committed to public service, and capable of great generosity to people whose character he respected. Above all, businessmen and the president admired him for his enormous wealth. A major contributor to Harding's campaign, he advocated reducing the size and scope of government activity, cutting taxes, paying down the national debt, and generally leaving business alone. He believed, with some justification, that lowering high wartime tax rates on business would stimulate investment. He and Hoover disagreed about some tax issues and whether the Federal Reserve should move aggressively to curb stock market speculation in the late 1920s, although Mellon had no sympathy for speculators.[11] Sometimes, he allied himself with conservative members of Congress to block Hoover's efforts to manage the economy, and surprisingly, he would prove more internationalist in his outlook than Hoover. When he became president himself in 1928, Hoover kept the Pennsylvanian at Treasury to reassure the business community. But frustrated during the depression by the secretary's belief that no one could control the business cycle, Hoover shipped him off to London in 1932 as American ambassador. Although Hoover professed agreement with Mellon's philosophy of small government and laissez-faire policies for business, as secretary of commerce he often displayed a much more activist conception of the government's role in the economy.

Hoover fought his most public battles during the Commerce period with Secretary of Agriculture Henry C. Wallace. Both men had been born in Iowa, but they had nothing else in common. As the publisher of *Wallace's Farmer*, Wallace had attacked Food Administration policies during the war for denying wheat, corn, and hog farmers the profits to which they were entitled for their patriotic expansion of production. Hoover had denied the charges vigorously, and when farmers slid into chronic depression during the 1920s, the antagonism carried over into the cabinet. Despite Hoover's complimentary letter about Wallace to Harding in January 1921, he not only disagreed with Wallace's belief that the government ought to purchase farm surpluses and dump them overseas, but he also constantly connived to steal control over farm marketing from Agriculture. Wallace gave as good as he got, blocking passage of the Jones-Winslow bill in 1924, which would have given Commerce authority to appoint agricultural attachés overseas. Following Wallace's sudden death later that year, President Coolidge, who concurred with Hoover's opposition to the McNary-Haugen plan to aid farmers, asked Hoover to become secretary of agriculture. But Hoover shrewdly dodged direct responsibility for the intractable agricultural problem. Wallace's successor, William Jardine, cooperated with the Commerce Department, but a fundamental impasse remained between those who, like Hoover and Coolidge, wanted to avoid government responsibility for agricultural incomes, and the McNary-Haugenites in the farm states and Congress.[12]

With the other members of the cabinet, Hoover maintained pleasant but not particularly close relations, with the exception of Secretary of Labor James J. Davis. Born in Wales, Davis immigrated with his parents to the United States, becoming an ironworker and rising to the presidency of the iron and steelworkers' union. A strong advocate of collective bargaining as a method of resolving labor-management conflicts, his position in the conservative wing of the union movement made him attractive to Republicans in the 1920s. In the cabinet, he usually deferred to Hoover, who liked him so well that he kept him on as secretary of labor in his own administration.

II

In January 1918, Joseph Tumulty, Woodrow Wilson's secretary, had begun to sketch the outlines of a postwar liberal reform program. Concerned about what he saw as the increasing dominance of big business, Tumulty wrote that "the mass of the people, underfed and dissatisfied, are clamoring for a fuller recognition of their rights to life and liberty." The Democratic Party, he warned, would "cease to live as a progressive instrumentality" unless it supported policies that would "make life more easy, more comfortable, and more prosperous for the average [man]." The president, engrossed in issues of war and peace, toyed briefly with trying to plan postwar reconversion along the lines Tumulty suggested, but in the end, he rejected the idea. In his annual message to Congress in December 1918, he declared that Americans did not want "to be coached or led. They know their business, are quick and resourceful at every readjustment, definite in purpose, and self-reliant in action." Returning the economy to a peacetime footing, he said, "will not be easy to direct . . . any better than it will direct itself."[13]

Hoover's views fell somewhere between those of Tumulty and Wilson. Like Wilson, he wanted to terminate wartime agencies and free business from government regulations, but he also believed that the government had a continuing role to play in the economy. It should retain its regulatory functions to prevent abuses, he thought, and cuts in taxes and spending ought to be accompanied by a thorough review of the whole tax system, including the tariff, and a reorganization of government agencies to make them more efficient. Active promotion of disarmament and restructuring of European debts could reduce federal expenditures and increase revenue. Like Tumulty, he believed that Americans wanted and deserved a higher standard of living. The government should exercise positive leadership to that end, shaping and stimulating the economy. In the words of historian Joan Hoff Wilson, he wanted to help Americans "cope with the critical transition that was facing the nation—the transition from a chaotic, nineteenth-century semi-industrialized society to a fully rationalized twentieth-century one."[14]

By March 4, 1921, when Hoover was sworn in as secretary of commerce, the clash between the old America and the new, as well as the clamor of ordinary Americans of which Tumulty spoke, had become obvious. The 1920 census had found that slightly more Americans lived in cities than on farms, and neither farmers nor city dwellers were satisfied. Wartime production increases created agricultural surpluses that had been worsened by a drop in foreign demand, thrusting farmers into chronic depression during the 1920s. Urbanites had just endured an epidemic of major strikes, the Red Scare, and race riots that demonstrated how fragile city life could be. Now, as unemployment soared in a severe postwar recession, workers complained about the high cost of living even as prices actually fell. City and country were locked in a cultural struggle over religion, prohibition, sexual morés, race, and consumerism. New technology rushed the country into modernity while making Americans more keenly aware of their differences—and more uncertain about what they wanted to become.

Possibly better than anyone else in the Harding administration, Hoover understood the broad outlines of what was happening to the country in 1921. As secretary of commerce, he intended to foster what he saw as desirable in the economic and cultural revolutions of the day and to harness the voluntary cooperation of Americans to minimize what was dangerous and destructive. He brought to the Harding and Coolidge administrations a unique background of training as an engineer, the most modern of professions, and of international business and diplomatic experience, yet he shared with most leading Republican politicians of the day a small-town childhood and a strong commitment to rural values of hard work and self-reliance. In his own person, he came closer to bridging the chasm between city and country than many Americans, and he believed fervently that it ought to be possible to combine the moral and cultural values of the nineteenth century with the material progress of the twentieth.[15]

The president who appointed Hoover to office, Warren G. Harding, as well as the vice president, Calvin Coolidge, shared his small-town background, but neither had his technical training and international experience. Harding had begun his career as a newspaper publisher in Marion, Ohio, and parlayed the contacts he made that way into a political career. His personal experience shaped his beliefs that maximum freedom for business ensured prosperity and that the Republican Party was perfectly suited to preside over the government. Although limited by his background and given to platitudinous speeches, he was neither stupid nor politically unsophisticated, as his pursuit of the 1920

Republican presidential nomination and deft handling of Hoover and the League of Nations issue during the campaign demonstrated. Whether he fully grasped what Hoover had in mind is difficult to determine, but the two men liked and trusted each other, and of course Hoover willingly accepted the broad authority granted to him by the new president. A few months before Harding's death, Hoover told his friend Mark Sullivan that he admired the president's "real qualities of personality." He said nothing about the more important political qualities of character, intelligence, and leadership.[16]

In late February and early March, Hoover met briefly with outgoing Secretary of Commerce Joshua Alexander and with Alexander's predecessor, William Redfield, both of whom wished him well. Redfield told Hoover and others that he hoped the new secretary would turn the department into "a genuine Department of Commerce" instead of the bureaucratic backwater that it had been. Franklin K. Lane, secretary of the interior during most of the Wilson administration and a fellow Californian and longtime ally in Hoover's relief efforts, sent a warm letter cautioning Hoover to watch out for political appointees—a warning, as it turned out, he might better have sent to Harding.[17]

For the most part, the business world welcomed Hoover's appointment, but the Hearst press charged that he was under the thumb of J. P. Morgan and other New York bankers (a ludicrous charge that Hoover dismissed), and the bellicose populist Senator Tom Watson of Georgia expanded that assertion to include unspecified "international financial interests." The liberal *New Republic* praised him as "easily the most constructive man in American public life."[18] Conservative leaders of the Republican Party, who doubted his party loyalty and suspected him of closet liberalism, remained his most dangerous critics.

III

Hoover gave little sign that he cared what politicians thought. Having taken possession of his unprepossessing office ("especially superheated for summer," he noted) in the eleven-story rented building at Nineteenth Street and Pennsylvania Avenue that served as the Commerce Department's cramped headquarters, he established a schedule that shaped his days whenever he was in Washington. After breakfast at home at 8:00, often with guests with whom he would discuss some current issue, he would drive or be driven to the office, arriving punctually at 9:00, Saturdays included. Thereafter, he broke his day into half-hour segments, during each of which he would meet with people or dictate letters and make phone calls. Normally, he would work until 6:30 PM or so and would often have a dinner or some other evening function to attend. Many days he would stay at the office into the evening, and almost always he took some work home with him, making him probably the hardest working man in the administration. On Saturday mornings he usually met with his bureau chiefs or their designees for an open discussion of policies and issues, at which he encouraged everyone to ask questions or make suggestions. The meetings built departmental morale and kept him abreast of ideas and concerns among his staff. In addition, he maintained close relations with a large number of people in the business, philanthropic, and academic worlds, frequently soliciting their advice and recruiting them to serve on various advisory boards and commissions.[19]

His greatest advantage was that, from the moment he took office, he knew exactly what he wanted to achieve. On March 11, a week after being sworn in, he outlined two major goals in a long press release. The first was to make the Commerce Department "a department of service to the commerce and industry of the country" by fostering "a wider and better organized cooperation with the trade and commercial associations." Reorganization of the department would put it in position to promote a national transportation system, with a strengthened merchant marine, improved domestic waterways, including "the opening of the Great Lakes to ocean-going vessels," reorganized railroads, expanded and integrated electrical systems, and a labor system controlled by "moderate men on both sides." During the war, he argued, a "spirit of spontaneous cooperation" between business and labor; among businesses; and among business, labor, and government had accounted for an extraordinary expansion of production. He meant to revive that spirit. As a *New York Times* reporter put it several months later, Hoover expected to establish links between "fairly intelligent business and intelligently fair government."[20]

His second goal was to "push our foreign commerce." (See Figure 14.1) The department was not a regulatory agency, he emphasized, and would work closely with industry to stimulate productivity and enlarge domestic and foreign markets and investment opportunities. Because the war had damaged European economies and depressed the region's standard of living, he warned, European labor costs would be lower than those in the United States for a number of years to come. Accordingly, European companies would be in a position to undersell their American counterparts. If Americans were to compete successfully, they would have to "work harder . . . , eliminate waste," and "further improve our processes, our labor relationship, and business methods." Above all, he told New York *Globe* editor Bruce Bliven, business must foster "collective co-operation where all the elements in an industry work together for their mutual advantage." The prewar German cartel system, he argued, had given German industry "a powerful advantage in the markets of the world," and while he denied any desire to create anything comparable in the United States, he emphasized his wish to eliminate "waste in our industrial processes wherever that is possible by applying collective intelligence to what is, after all, a collective problem."[21]

Hoover recognized that serious obstacles stood in the way of the sort of growth and prosperity he envisioned. The country had sunk into a severe postwar recession, with "three or four million idle men walking the streets"; the railroads, electrical power system, highways, and waterways were inadequate; there was a serious housing shortage; and both agriculture and industry were producing more than could be absorbed by the domestic market. Although exports had accounted for only a small part of the country's prewar gross national product, Hoover was convinced that expanding foreign trade and investments could solve many current problems. American bankers needed to get together, using the provisions of the 1919 Edge Act, to provide the short-term credits needed by European countries to buy American agricultural and industrial products. And the American government must mobilize its forces to head off European efforts to establish a continent-wide economic organization that could dump their products on the world market while erecting insuperable barriers to American goods.[22]

Beyond the ambitious program laid out in Hoover's March 11 press release lay a still broader if vaguer objective. In May, he told *New York Times* reporter John Corbin that he aspired to nothing less than the creation of "a new economic system, based neither on the capitalism of Adam Smith nor upon the socialism of Karl Marx," a "third alternative that preserves individual initiative, that stimulates it through protection from domination." If he could achieve that, he added immodestly, he would have given "a priceless gift to the twentieth century." Exactly the nature of that "third alternative" remained unclear in the interview. But its outlines were evolving in his mind, and elements of it would emerge gradually over the next year or two, appearing most fully in his little booklet, *American Individualism*, in 1922. It emphasized the elimination of class conflict between capital and labor and the promotion of close cooperation between government and the economic associations within which he believed that American business and agriculture could learn to work together for common ends.[23] Like Marx and Adam Smith, he imagined a harmonious world where national prosperity and happiness would arise naturally from the unfettered operation of the economic system.

IV

In the meantime, work needed to be done, and Hoover plunged into it in his usual whirlwind style. Within his first month in office, he met with the directors of the U.S. Chamber of Commerce to explore ways to develop closer relations between the department and the business community, commenced monthly meetings with the editors of the major business newspapers, began to consider whether commercial aviation should come under civilian or military control, asked the Federal Trade Commission to investigate foreign monopolies over essential goods and foodstuffs, urged the reorganization of the railroad system and the adoption of pay scales for railroad workers, advocated development of a national waterway system, proposed a search for new foreign oil sources, recruited an academic Advisory Committee on Statistics for the department, and began reorganizing the department's bureaus. And, in his spare time, he continued to oversee American Relief Administration (ARA) relief work and the Federated American Engineering Societies study of waste in industry and promoted organization of the Foreign Trade Financing Corporation.

Departmental reorganization constituted Hoover's most important but least publicized work during his first months. Before he took over, Commerce did little more than conduct the decennial census, maintain lighthouses on the coasts, test products purchased by the government, protect fisheries, and inspect steamboat boilers. Of the department's seven bureaus, Foreign and Domestic Commerce, created in 1912 to collect and publish "information relating to commerce for the use and benefit of the manufacturing and commercial interests of the country," rated sixth in size and importance. Hoover saw that as an inversion of priorities. The technical bureaus were important, to be sure, but he believed that Foreign and Domestic Commerce should become the heart of the department's program of service to American business at home and abroad. To that end, he set up an advisory committee of economists to recommend ways to make the bureau's collection and use of statistics more constructive. In June, he brought in Julius Klein, former chief of the department's Latin American division and commercial attaché at Buenos Aires and now professor of Latin American history and economics at Harvard, to head the bureau. Klein quickly became Hoover's right-hand man, and under his direction the Bureau of Foreign and Domestic Commerce emerged as the most important in the department. Over the next eight years, its budget sextupled, and its personnel quintupled. During the whole year of 1921, its staff dealt with some 150,000 letters and inquiries from businesses; in 1928, it responded to ten thousand or more items each day.[24]

To oversee the planned reorganization of the department, Hoover asked his friend Arch Shaw, publisher of the Chicago business papers *System* and *Factory*, to become assistant secretary. Hoover and Shaw had met during the war, when Shaw served as conservation director of the War Industries Board. Hoover credited him with the board's success and believed he would be perfect to oversee the changes he planned at Commerce. The publisher felt he could not afford to take a lengthy absence from his business, but he agreed to become an informal adviser and persuaded his friend Frederick Feiker, vice president of the McGraw Hill Company, to work directly with Hoover. Feiker joined the Commerce Department as Hoover's assistant in May 1921, providing invaluable guidance for reorganization and initiating a departmental publicity program during the next nine months. Also important in the reorganization was E. Dana Durand, who had worked with Hoover in the Food Administration and the ARA. In 1921, Hoover named Durand Chief of the Eastern European Division of the Bureau of Foreign and Domestic Commerce. A professional statistician, in May 1921 Durand strongly recommended the creation of an independent statistical division to gather, analyze, and disseminate facts and figures on domestic and foreign production and distribution, as well as on markets. A month later, in cooperation with the Federal Reserve, departmental statisticians began informally collecting such information. Harvard professor Frank Taussig, editor of the *Quarterly Journal of Economics*, immediately endorsed Durand's efforts, and Hoover agreed. In 1924, he made Durand Chief of a new Division of Statistical Research.[25]

By the end of April, the main outlines of the Commerce Department's reorganization began to emerge. The Bureau of Foreign and Domestic Commerce became the core of the department. Within the bureau, a dozen (eventually fifteen) "commodity sections" would collect information across the country and furnish industries with advice on markets and sources of raw materials. Section heads usually came from experts recommended by advisory groups from the industries concerned. Each section gathered and disseminated information on such things as productive capacity, capacity utilization, sales, and inventory so that companies could plan operations and minimize business cycle fluctuations. Commodity sections ranged from Hides and Leather to Motion Pictures, from Coal and Lumber to Industrial Machinery, and from Foodstuffs to Housing. A Foreign Commerce Division placed agents overseas in major cities to assist businessmen (fifty-one of them by 1928). Technical sections advised companies on such matters as foreign agents and buyers, foreign banking, tariffs, legal questions, and shipping routes and methods. Within a year, the number of people working in Foreign and Domestic Commerce doubled. Hoover also strengthened other bureaus offering technical services such as navigation and tried to bring overlapping agencies from other departments into Commerce. He would eventually create new divisions to oversee radio broadcasting and commercial air service.[26]

The Bureau of Standards, historically only a test laboratory for products purchased by the government, also became an important part of Hoover's Commerce Department through its new Division of Simplified Practice, which championed product standardization and simplification. Beginning in November 1921 with a conference of brick-paving manufacturers, which agreed to reduce sixty-six sizes of brick to eleven (eventually five), the division by 1928 facilitated the adoption of simplified practices in eighty-six different industries, which it claimed saved industry and consumers $600 million a year. Within a year, the once sleepy bureau doubled its personnel.[27]

Some of the new units in the Bureau of Foreign and Domestic Commerce that Hoover proposed required congressional authorization, which was slow in coming. Congress approved a new Housing Division in 1922, but failed to authorize an Aeronautics Division until 1926 and a Radio Division until 1927. Hoover's proposal to transfer as many as sixteen agencies, ranging from the Treasury Department's Bureau of Customs Statistics to the War Department's Panama Canal to the Commerce Department, aroused the alarm and opposition of other departments, and only the Bureau of Mines and the Patent Office were finally moved from Interior to Commerce in 1925. Interdepartmental friction also emerged over some of his other ideas, including a bitter dispute over whether Commerce, Agriculture, or State would control commercial agents in foreign countries. When frustrated in his attempts to seize formal powers from other agencies, Hoover frequently entered their fields anyway by duplicating their work in Commerce.[28]

As Hoover recalled many years later, the Commerce Department in 1921 resembled a confederation of largely independent agencies. Scattered across Washington in fifteen separate buildings, some of the bureaus even omitted from their letterheads the fact that they were part of the Commerce Department. But a serious space shortage impeded consolidation. The new secretary had hardly settled in his office when the department's chief clerk handed him a memorandum detailing the department's space problems and urging construction of a new building. Hoover saw the point immediately, urging the erection of a new building in his 1921 annual report and repeating the recommendation regularly thereafter. Not until 1926, however, did he win administration approval, and he had moved on to the White House before the building at Fifteenth Street and Pennsylvania Avenue finally opened its doors.[29]

Even more urgent than the problem of space was the matter of staff. When he took over, Hoover found much of the department filled with political hacks who had obtained civil service protection during previous administrations but had no real qualifications for their positions. Pay had not increased in years, and many workers with twenty-five or thirty years of service received no more than $60 a month, with no pension when they retired. Morale was rotten, and few people felt any sense of a departmental mission. Recognizing that such conditions would nullify the effect of reorganization, Hoover asked Harding to lift civil service protection for Commerce Department employees and then had the Civil Service Commission administer tests for positions. If incumbents failed the examinations, they were replaced by qualified people and civil service coverage reinstated. The housecleaning, combined with an increase in minimum salaries from $720 to $1,200 a year, a merit raise system, and a promise of pensions on retirement, transformed the atmosphere in the department.[30] From one of the least desirable places to work in Washington, the Commerce Department became one of the best, with a staff fiercely loyal to Hoover and eager to implement the changes he proposed.

Hoover's transformation of the Commerce Department sounded an alarm in an administration that had adopted Secretary Mellon's principle of cutting taxes and forcing departments to reduce spending. At the end of April, Harding circulated a letter expressing concern at the size of the "deficiency appropriations" that various departments had requested. Hoover responded with a detailed justification of his request for an additional $627,000 and promised that his reforms would "result in economies much larger than the additional expenditures asked for." In the face of this aggressive reaction, Harding backed down, and Hoover, mollified, suggested to Congressman James Good of the House Appropriations Committee that Congress authorize new fees for some departmental services and eliminate some "deadwood" services. He estimated those changes would save or raise $1.5 million a year, more than covering the additional $600,000 he had requested. In June, Congress gave Commerce $500,000 with no strings attached.[31]

By that time, the nation's press had begun to recognize that major changes had come to the Commerce Department. An analysis of press coverage prepared for the secretary reported that reporters had been scrutinizing the department "with a vigilance which was formerly accorded only to the State Department and the War Department." Increasingly, the press expected Hoover to solve national economic problems, in particular a threatened coal strike and the deepening agricultural depression. When he failed to provide instant solutions, one editorialist complained that he "hasn't yet Hoovered up to advance notices."[32]

V

Hoover had, of course, long struggled with agricultural problems. As Food Administrator during the war, he had worked to increase farm production to feed the troops and the Allies while holding price increases down for the benefit of American consumers. Although a rising wartime cost of living revealed his incomplete success on the domestic side, he succeeded brilliantly in increasing production and selling the surplus to the Allies. When the war ended suddenly in November 1918, however, triumph turned to disaster. That year, the United States had an exportable grain surplus of about 16 million tons as compared to a prewar surplus of 7 million tons, but the British and French, realizing they could buy grain elsewhere more cheaply, were eager to cancel wartime contracts. Anticipating a potential catastrophe for American producers, Hoover fought to make the Europeans live up to their promises and to lift the blockade on the former enemy nations, even though Germany still resisted implementation of the peace terms. Following his return to the United States a year later, he worked to create a $100 million Foreign Trade Financing Corporation to provide loans to the exporters of both industrial and agricultural products.[33]

Investors showed little interest in the Foreign Trade Financing Corporation, and in January 1921 Hoover went before the House Agriculture Committee to offer a new suggestion. The heart of the farm problem, he said, was "not a question of over-production but one of under-consumption" in Europe. In addition to the export finance corporation, he suggested the creation of "a national marketing board of experts, under the Department of Agriculture," whose function would be to standardize grain exchanges and "secure the extension of public warehouses" where farmers could store surplus grain and receive credit against it. The board, he added, could also "give great assistance to the development of co-operative marketing and other important improvements in our marketing processes."[34] Focused on the wheat question, neither he nor the members of the committee asked what should be done about surpluses of other farm products such as cotton.

In fact, the measures Hoover suggested would have had little effect on the farm problem. During the war, farmers had purchased land and expensive equipment and brought marginal lands into production. After the war, changes in Americans' dietary and clothing preferences, as well as a decline in demand for animal feed as cars and trucks replaced horses, altered and reduced domestic markets for farm products. Deep in debt and facing rising costs, farmers hoped to save themselves with foreign sales, only to find markets flooded as trade and production revived around the world. During 1920, they began to default on loans, bringing down local banks and worsening the situation. Short of massive government intervention, the only solution seemed to be for many farmers to go out of business. Hoover occasionally admitted that, but it was more politically expedient to claim that other measures would solve the problem without so much pain.[35]

By the time Hoover became secretary of commerce in early 1921, the farm problem had become worse. The proposed export-financing corporation had drawn little support, and Congress had rejected Hoover's suggestion for a national marketing board. A sharp disagreement between Hoover and Wallace over how to handle the problem erupted in the early days of the new administration. Hoover emphasized marketing, with financing to come from the private sector; Wallace insisted the government must purchase surpluses and dump them on the world market. The two did not even agree on market prospects in Europe, with conflicting reports coming from the Commerce and Agriculture agents overseas.[36]

In mid-April, Senator Arthur Capper of Kansas, chairman of the Senate agriculture committee, invited Hoover to lay out his ideas about the agricultural problem. In an April 23 letter, Hoover observed that the prices farmers received for their products had scarcely increased over prewar levels, while the costs of building materials, clothing, railroad freight, and even industrial wages had all risen substantially. He argued that some means had to be found to bring the incomes of farmers and other Americans into better balance, but he had little new to propose. He reiterated his argument that an increase in European consumption would solve the problem, urged the provision of private credits to European purchasers, and repeated his recommendations that farmers establish cooperative marketing arrangements and the Agriculture Department create a national marketing board. His only new idea was to reexamine and restructure railroad rates to lower the cost of transporting agricultural products to market, but he admitted that doing that would be complicated because rates must remain high enough to keep the railroads solvent.[37]

At about the same time as the Hoover-Capper exchange, Julius Barnes, Hoover's friend at the head of the Grain Corporation, offered another suggestion: a conference of grain dealers to consider improvements in warehousing and marketing of grain. The conference, held in Washington on June 13 under the auspices of the secretaries of agriculture and commerce, considered a proposal that farmers be guaranteed the right to take their grain to a local elevator, where a certificate of its quality would be issued that could be used as collateral in securing loans for seed and equipment.[38] The plan might have helped farmers in the short run, but it did not explain how to preserve and sell the stored grain or provide any way to deal with multiyear surpluses.

Nebraska Senator George Norris considered the grain storage proposal totally inadequate. In late May, he proposed the creation of a government corporation like the War Finance Corporation (WFC) with a capital of $100 million to purchase surplus farm products and sell them overseas. Hoover much preferred a private export corporation, but his efforts to establish one had failed, and he admitted that "the pressure [was] growing steadily stronger" for some sort of direct governmental intervention. By June, three pending bills in Congress offered schemes for organizing a government export corporation or providing federal guarantees for a private organization.[39]

A month later, Hoover capitulated, at least in part. Although he insisted that having a permanent government agency set up to purchase farm surpluses would put "government into business in its most vicious form," he reluctantly admitted that a temporary compromise might be necessary. In consultation with a number of senators (but not Norris), he helped to draft an Agricultural Credits Act authorizing the WFC to provide credit for farm exports. He did not get everything he wanted in the bill, however. He wanted the corporation to be authorized to loan money directly to European governments to buy American food, and he wanted to expand its board of directors to include himself and Secretary Wallace. The key element of the bill, as he saw it, would be its empowerment of the WFC to help restore the European market for American goods by making loans to European governments.

Eugene Meyer, director of the WFC, disagreed and beat Hoover on both points. At Meyer's recommendation, President Harding informed Hoover that since the WFC had been "functioning so satisfactorily," he thought that enlarging its board would "only make the situation more involved and probably more expensive." Meyer also disagreed with Hoover's contention that, given the failure of the private Foreign Trade Financing Corporation, the WFC should be authorized to make loans to European governments for the purchase of American products. He believed that the Europeans had been shunning American products not because they had no money but because they thought they could supply their needs more cheaply through domestic production. Once they exhausted domestic supplies, he argued, they would resume buying American products. If, instead of lending to the Europeans, the WFC merely provided short-term loans to American banks and cooperatives, they would be able to tide farmers over until the Europeans came back into the market. Although Senator Norris grumbled that the bill would only benefit "the middleman and the banker and the trust company," it passed because neither Norris's idea of having the government purchase and dump surpluses overseas nor Hoover's argument for direct loans to European governments attracted strong support. When Harding signed the bill into law on

August 24, no one felt enthusiastic about it, and subsequent experience proved Meyer wrong. Although the WFC extended some $300 million in loans over the next year, the program did little to solve farmers' problems.[40] It reflected the administration's general caution and conservatism in regard to the agricultural crisis.

Hoover also faced another agricultural crisis in 1921—the crash of the sugar market. During World War I, when European sugar beet production virtually halted, the Food Administration warned that sugar prices could rise uncontrollably for both American and Allied consumers. To prevent that, the president created a Sugar Equalization Board, with Hoover as chairman, to purchase the entire Cuban sugar crop and distribute it at controlled prices. The approach had stabilized prices in the United States, and in July 1919 Hoover recommended that it be continued for a year to prevent a price spike before the Europeans reestablished production. The White House ignored his advice, and in November 1919 it transferred the Sugar Equalization Board's price-control authority to the Justice Department, which terminated the wartime policy.[41]

The lifting of controls, followed by a resurgence of European demand, had exactly the effect Hoover predicted—a rapid rise in retail sugar prices, accompanied by speculation and some profiteering. Opponents unfairly blamed this situation on Hoover during the 1920 presidential campaign, and no amount of explaining seemed to kill the issue. What was more, the inflation of sugar prices in 1920 had a disastrous sequel in 1921. Rising prices drove down demand at the same time that they encouraged overproduction on Cuban cane plantations and American sugar beet farms, resulting in a vast sugar surplus. In the spring of 1921, sugar prices plummeted from a high of twenty-five cents or more a pound to a low of around two cents a pound. Panicky American producers demanded a sharp tariff increase on Cuban sugar, and American banks begged for help to avoid massive loan defaults by producers. Hoover recognized the seriousness of the situation, but he pointed out that raising the tariff would injure American investors in Cuba, and he contended that the sugar glut would solve itself in a few months. Privately, he thought that letting "the price level to fall at so low an ebb as to crowd out high cost producers" would provide the "ultimate method" of resolving the crisis. But since Americans owned much of Cuba's sugar production, no one dared say that aloud, any more than they dared to say that some American farmers should leave farming in order to reduce the grain surplus. Instead, he recommended a couple of essentially cosmetic gestures: having the Federal Reserve urge member banks to avoid foreclosing on sugar loans temporarily and encouraging sugar producers to export as much of the surplus as possible. Whether these palliatives had much effect may be doubted, but in early 1922 the international market had stabilized, and the crisis vanished as quickly as it appeared.[42]

Behind the problems of agriculture and sugar in 1921 loomed the reality that the country faced a serious recession. That economic crisis also greatly complicated two other major problems facing Hoover in 1921—the desperate sickness of the coal and railroad industries. And since those two industries were so intertwined, the problems of each worsened those of the other.

VI

Although by 1921 the United States had begun to move into the oil age, coal still heated most homes, provided power for most industries, and moved people and freight on railroads and ships. Hard, or anthracite, coal came almost exclusively from highly unionized mines owned by eight Pennsylvania companies and sold mostly in the Northeast and Canada. Relatively dust free and even burning, it provided heat for homes in the area and power for the railroads, but its cost led most industries to prefer soft or bituminous coal. Thirty states had soft coal mines, but most lay in the Appalachian region along the mountains from Virginia to Alabama. An area poor in capital and rich in unskilled labor, Appalachia's eight thousand mines were mostly small and unmechanized. Operators resisted unionization and often insisted that miners live in company towns. Too many mines producing more coal than a shrinking national market could absorb had led to cutthroat competition. The companies tried to undersell each other, driving the price of coal and wages down. Most mines operated only part time, and the operators expected miners to supplement their uncertain pay by subsistence farming. The region's poor soil prevented full-time farming from being a viable alternative to mine work, which would have forced the mines to pay higher wages. Neither operators nor miners had much control over demand, prices, or working conditions, and most miners felt lucky if they worked two hundred days a year. Hoover estimated in 1922 that more than a quarter of the mines needed to close in order to make the industry profitable.[43]

Early in 1920, the American Institute of Mining and Metallurgical Engineers, under the leadership of incoming President Hoover, began to consider the problems of the bituminous coal industry. Hoover believed that engineers, standing "midway between capital and labor" and "without prejudice either way," could offer impartial advice on such issues. As he saw it, the industry's difficulties resulted from too many mines with too much equipment and too many miners and, to complicate the matter, lack of coordination among the railroad companies that impeded the efficient transportation of coal from mines to distributors. Although he did not immediately see how to solve these weaknesses, he believed that the industry would be better off if a smaller number of mines and miners were able to work continuously, and the public would benefit from a reliable supply of coal at stable prices. He seemed unaware of how Appalachia's pervasive poverty and shortage of local capital had contributed to the development of the dysfunctional patterns he hoped to rectify and oblivious to the human suffering that closing mines would cause. In November 1920, he presented his thoughts about the bituminous industry to a Committee on the Stabilization of the Coal Industry of the national industrial conference.[44]

Diagnosing the problem proved to be easier than fixing it, particularly given a shortage of accurate information about costs, production, demand, supplies, waste, and distribution. The Federal Trade Commission had attempted to collect such statistics early in 1920, but the National Coal Association won an injunction on the ground that dissemination of the information would reduce competition. As a result, when Hoover became Secretary of Commerce and proposed that his department gather statistics on production and distribution of coal, he found both producers and wholesalers reluctant to cooperate. So recalcitrant were the mine owners that he eventually had to seek specific legislative authorization for what he wanted to do.[45] Aside from concerns about infringing the antitrust laws, profitable companies feared that sharing any information would eliminate their small competitive advantage.

In May, Senator Joseph Frelinghuysen of New Jersey introduced a bill authorizing the Commerce Department to gather and publish information about coal production and distribution, and he also urged the Federal Trade Commission to promote summer reductions in railroad rates on coal shipments to enable consumers to buy early. Hoover strongly favored the bill, but it attracted little support. Even Commerce Department staff complained that it would saddle the department with an enormous amount of new work, strain relations with the coal companies, and yet would give the department too little authority to do anything effective. A meeting on June 7 among Hoover and Secretary of the Interior Fall representing the executive, Senators Frelinghuysen and Calder representing the Senate, and three coal company executives representing the National Coal Association ended in disagreement and misunderstanding. The coal company men left declaring that the Frelinghuysen bill was the first step toward "government control," perhaps even nationalization, of the industry and proceeded to publish their charges in industry journals. Hoover was outraged at what he saw as their willful misrepresentation of his position.[46]

Concerned at the coal companies' lack of cooperation, Hoover tried without much success to increase pressure on them in the summer of 1921. In July, he warned utility companies of an impending shortage of railroad cars and urged them to stock up on coal well in advance of autumn and winter needs, although he despaired of getting mine owners to increase production during the summer. Bituminous coal miners, Hoover reported to the national unemployment conference that met in October, would probably work no more than 168 days during 1921, as opposed to a normal (but inadequate) prewar work year of 213 days.[47]

With labor contracts due to expire in April 1922, Hoover warned of "a greater battle between [miners and operators] than ever before" and predicted that it might "prostrate the entire country." Major operators reluctantly endorsed his proposal that the two parties try to reach agreement prior to

April on as many issues as possible and then submit the remainder to arbitration, but the union spurned the idea as weakening its bargaining position. Neither side, Hoover concluded, really wanted an agreement. He believed that the operators saw a major strike as an "opportunity to deunionize the coal mines," while the union believed that a strike would "paralyze industry," force "great trade associations" to support the strikers, and eventually compel the government to impose "some favorable solution."[48]

By December 1921, momentum was building toward a strike. European markets, which had served as an outlet for the American coal surplus during the early part of the recession, virtually disappeared as European governments, particularly the British, subsidized their producers. American producers even warned that cheap British coal might flood the American market. Their fears were never realized, but the loss of foreign markets led to cuts in production and miners' working hours and further soured relations between miners and operators. Then, in November, the owners persuaded a federal judge to issue an injunction against the "checkoff," a system under which companies collected union dues directly from workers' pay. The injunction lent plausibility to the miners' belief that the owners intended to destroy the union. Hoover had no new ideas to offer. As the year ended, he again urged the passage of a bill to authorize the Commerce Department to collect and publish statistical information about coal and promoted the work of a committee created by the unemployment conference to suggest ways to reduce seasonal unemployment.[49]

Hoover had hoped to help the bituminous coal industry by finding ways to ship coal to market more quickly, efficiently, and less expensively, but the chaos in the national railroad system prevented him from implementing his ideas. After boom times in the late nineteenth century, the railroads had come under heavy state and federal regulation in the Progressive Era. Suspicious about the companies' claims of dwindling income, the regulators denied their repeated requests for rate increases. And without rate hikes, the companies ceased to be profitable enough to attract the investment they needed to modernize their lines and equipment. As a result, when the United States entered the war in 1917, the antiquated railroad system could not meet the demands put on it, and in the winter of 1917 to 1918, it broke down almost completely.[50]

In March 1918, Congress passed the Federal Control Act nationalizing the railroads for the duration of the war and up to twenty-one months afterward. When the war ended, debate began over what to do next. The railroads had functioned adequately under nationalization, and some people favored permanent national control, but most wanted to return them to private operation. The question was when. The railroad brotherhoods hated the no-strike restrictions of the Federal Control Act. Director General of Railroads William Gibbs McAdoo complained that the companies had taken advantage of the system to reap guaranteed profits while blaming every problem on the government. Railroad executives responded that the government had largely ignored maintenance during the war. President Wilson seemed not to care very much about the whole question, and Congress found it difficult to agree on any policy. Eventually, the Esch-Cummins Act provided for the return of the roads to private control on March 1, 1920. The act retained considerable government control, giving the Interstate Commerce Commission (ICC) six months to investigate and set new rates, and creating a Railway Labor Board to handle disputes. For the long term, the act instructed the ICC to promote consolidation of competing lines.[51]

Following the return of the lines to private control in March 1920, the situation went from bad to worse. The Esch-Cummins Act instructed the ICC to allow the roads to set rates high enough to assure them a 6 percent annual profit. To that end, in July 1920, the ICC authorized substantial increases in both passenger and freight rates. But despite the increases, the lines reported profits of less than 4 percent in both 1920 and 1921, partly because of the general recession and partly because the Railroad Labor Board had awarded workers a large wage increase in July 1920. Having rates controlled by one body and wages by a separate one virtually guaranteed that the lines would be whipsawed. In addition, antirailroad senators and congressmen blocked the payment of millions of dollars of claims by the railroads against the Railroad Administration for deferred maintenance that might have alleviated the lines' cash shortage. The railroads, claiming dire financial straits, proposed cutting workers' pay. Wartime cooperation among the lines, which they had promised to continue when they went back to private control, quickly disappeared. In the absence of any national coordinating organization, some areas of the country had no cars to carry waiting shipments, while in other areas trains sometimes ran empty. The ICC worked for months to come up with a plan for regional groupings of railroads but found the companies resistant to their efforts. As the new administration took office in March 1921, the only hope was that Hoover, who had extensive experience in dealing with the lines while serving as Food Administrator, would somehow be able to impose order and save individual companies from bankruptcy and the system from nationalization.[52]

The commerce secretary had no magic wand with which to solve the industry's problems. Believing that the railroads would benefit if shippers could sell more, he urged a temporary reduction of freight rates on coal and West Coast fruits and vegetables to boost sales during the recession. When the railroads rejected his suggestion, the ICC stepped in to force rate reductions on livestock shipments in July, on grain in October, and on other agricultural products in January 1922. The Railroad Labor Board authorized a 12.5 percent cut in workers' pay in July 1921, but the cost reductions did not offset revenue losses, nor did rate reductions eliminate opposition in Congress to payment of the railroads' claims. In desperation, Hoover suggested in July that the WFC buy railroad securities held by the Railroad Administration, which would use the money to make partial payments on the railroads' maintenance claims. Such an approach, he suggested, would give the lines capital with which to "purchase supplies, to undertake betterments, to meet their frozen credits, to repair their rolling stock and employ their usual staff of labor."[53]

Although Harding had doubts about the legality of the partial payment plan, he approved it on July 18. It ameliorated the railroads' desperate need for cash and postponed a financial collapse, but it did nothing to solve the more basic problems: too many competing lines, too little coordination among them, and rate and wage structures determined by political rather than economic forces.[54]

The railroads' delicate financial condition made it impossible for them to do the one thing that Hoover thought essential to pull the country out of the recession—reduce freight rates, particularly on agricultural products. As a result of his continuing pressure, however, on September 21 the Association of Railway Executives convoked a secret meeting of industrial and agricultural representatives in New York to discuss freight rates. Three weeks later, on October 14, the railroads announced a reduction in rates, conditional upon pay cuts to workers. At about the same time, a small item appeared in newspapers across the country stating that Hoover favored big cuts in railroad workers' pay. It is unclear whether this was a deliberate attempt on the part of the railroads to trap the administration into supporting pay cuts in return for rate reductions, but Hoover had certainly not been a party to any such arrangement, and his office immediately sent denials to every paper that published the story. As he well understood, the unions saw "pay cuts" as fighting words, and they immediately threatened to strike if the railroads made the cuts.[55] Neither Hoover nor the unions explained how the struggling companies would afford rate cuts if denied the possibility of reducing their costs.

Alarmed by the prospect of a strike with winter just weeks away, Hoover contacted his Food Administration associates across the country to begin developing an emergency distribution plan for essential commodities. With the support of the War Department, he set up federal, regional, and state distribution committees and encouraged food and fuel suppliers to build up reserve stocks at strategic locations around the country. On October 22, Hoover informed the president that contingency plans were complete. The Railway Labor Board made their implementation unnecessary, however, when it postponed a strike by announcing that it would permit no wage reductions for six months.[56]

Hoover strenuously denied that he had designed his emergency distribution plan to break a railroad strike or that he had developed it in collusion with the railroad companies, but labor leaders regarded it with suspicion. An article describing his arrangements that appeared in *Labor* carried the headline, "Hoover Creates Government Strikebreaking Agency." When the secretary sought a correction, the article's author contended that, whatever his intentions, the effect of creating an emergency distribution system would be to undermine a strike.[57] The incident provided a valuable lesson for Hoover. Believing that both capital and labor would benefit from maximizing cooperation, he had no desire to antagonize the unions. He concluded that a new mechanism for settling conflicts between the railroad companies and their workers had become essential. He turned his attention to that goal in the new year.

The problems of agriculture, coal, and the railroads, along with reorganization of the Commerce Department, consumed much of Hoover's time during his first year in office, but he never lost sight of his broader goal of national development. In pursuit of that objective, he ranged sometimes outside the direct responsibilities of his own department, as was the case with the superpower project and the Colorado River development effort.

VII

The concept of "superpower," meaning the creation of a single electric grid for the East Coast, and particularly the Northeast, was novel in the early 1920s. Installation of the first hydroelectric generating plant at Niagara Falls in 1895 had suggested the possibilities of factory electrification, and the idea caught on quickly. Within a decade, many cities in the Northeast had electrified, usually generating the power with hydroelectric or steam plants, but distribution systems remained small and local. Entrepreneurs such as Samuel Insull saw an opportunity in this situation, and in the years around World War I, they began consolidating small utilities under larger holding companies. By the end of the war, consolidation of the small companies had reduced one obstacle to a regional "superpower" system, but the creation of a grid still presented major technical and political problems. In the spring of 1920, the Geological Survey took the next step toward the creation of such a system by proposing the establishment of a Superpower Advisory Board. Hoover spoke out vigorously in support of the appropriation to fund the panel, estimating that a grid covering the area between Washington and Boston might save as much as $300 million a year for transportation and industry. His enthusiasm earned him a seat on the advisory board.[58]

Hoover did not attend the first meeting of the board, on November 20, 1920, at which a touchy issue arose. E. G. Buckland, president of the New York, New Haven, and Hartford Railway, suggested that, because of the interstate nature of the contemplated superpower project, Congress should create a federally owned corporation to implement it. Hoover made no objection to the concept of a federal corporation at the board's December 1 meeting, only urging inclusion of incentives for the company's managers to do good work. Buckland embraced his criticism, proposing at the January 5, 1921, meeting that the company be permitted to retain a percentage of the profit it could earn by producing and selling electricity more cheaply than private companies. Since Hoover did not attend that or the subsequent meeting of the board, he took no position on Buckland's revised proposal, which would have put the public superpower company into direct competition with private utilities.[59]

By May, the Advisory Board had reached agreement. It would recommend chartering a federal corporation to generate and sell electricity to public utilities on an interstate basis. The company would be incorporated in a state within the region to be served, and it could employ eminent domain to secure sites for generators, substations, and transmission lines. Chairman William S. Murray admitted, however, that private utility companies were "most anxious to avoid a Federal charter," and, as it turned out, so was Hoover. After reviewing the proposed legislation, he wrote that he could not "conceive that the Congress of the United States will ever give such unlimited rights as suggested in the bill proposed." Although he had previously seemed open to the idea of a publicly owned corporation, he now threatened to resign from the commission rather than endorse its recommendation. His opposition, together with objections from private utilities, forced the board to change its direction.[60]

Accepting a renewed appointment to the board in the summer of 1921, Hoover urged that the superpower corporation be privately rather than publicly owned. In September, the board bowed to his wishes, although they recommended that the company retain the power of eminent domain. But sticky questions remained unanswered. How would state utility regulations apply to a company that, by definition, would operate in several states? Could enough private capital be raised to finance such a gigantic undertaking? Could a private company be entrusted with the right of eminent domain? Until those questions were answered, Congress was unlikely to act.[61]

Development of the Colorado River also lay outside Hoover's direct responsibilities as secretary of commerce, although it fitted within his broad goal of encouraging the development of all major river systems for transportation and power. The project appealed to him as an engineer, and as a Californian, he had heard the demands from growers in Southern California's Imperial Valley for protection from the river's floods and access to its water for irrigation. Under the Federal Water Power Act of 1920, the government had the authority to "provide for the improvement of navigation; the development of water power; and the use of public lands in relation thereto," but a vast federal project like controlling the Colorado seemed certain to conflict with the administration's preference for private enterprise.[62]

The 1,700–mile long Colorado River carries the third-greatest water volume among American rivers and flows through or borders seven states. Rising in the Rockies and coursing largely through an arid or semiarid region, its sudden, violent fluctuations in water level often produced devastating floods, as it had in Southern California in 1905. The next year, President Theodore Roosevelt called on Congress to adopt a program for permanent control of the river, but for several years nothing happened, largely because Western water law held that a dam built on the upper river created a preemptive claim to its waters that might preclude use by states farther downstream. After several years' delay, in 1920 Congress passed the Kettner Act authorizing the construction of an "All-American Canal" to channel Colorado River water to the irrigation projects of the Imperial Valley, as well as the Kincaid Act instructing the Reclamation Service to survey the lower Colorado and report on the feasibility of a major dam to control flooding and generate power.[63]

With momentum for the construction of a dam growing, leaders of the seven river basin states realized that they needed a common policy for the river's development. Their representatives met in 1918, 1919, and 1920, and at the last of the meetings, Reclamation Service Director Arthur Powell Davis and Denver lawyer Delphus E. Carpenter proposed a solution to the prior appropriation issue: a regional compact to apportion the river's water and decide the dam's location. In early 1921, all the affected state legislatures approved the idea, and in August Congress authorized creation of an inter-state commission with a neutral chairman to be appointed by the president to negotiate the compact.[64]

The new administration did not immediately embrace the Colorado proj-ect. When Harry Chandler, publisher of the Los Angeles *Times* and a major landowner in the Imperial Valley, went to Washington to lobby for the imme-diate construction of the dam and All-American Canal, Secretary of Agri-culture Wallace dismissed his arguments with the observation that irrigating more farm land would only worsen the country's agricultural surplus. Secre-tary of War Weeks asked whether Chandler had forgotten his New England prudence and "turned into a wild man when he got to living in the deserts." Others in the administration expressed reluctance to involve the federal gov-ernment in a project that seemed certain to require large expenditures. Only Hoover favored the enterprise, and he told Chandler it fell outside his depart-ment's responsibilities.[65]

Congress's approval of the Colorado River Commission in August 1921 altered the administration's position. On September 24, Secretary of the Interior Albert Fall warned Harding that negotiating an interstate compact would be difficult. Failure seemed possible and could be politically embar-rassing. The president, Fall urged, should appoint a chairman "of nation wide reputation if possible, and one whose advice would be respected by the Con-gress and by the people of the different States interested." Although Fall did not mention Hoover, his background as a Western engineer with a particu-lar interest in river development made him an obvious choice for the task. The White House announced his appointment on December 17, but he had already begun organizing the Colorado River Commission by the beginning of November.[66] Negotiating and securing the approval of the seven states to an agreement apportioning the river's water would become a major preoccu-pation for several years.

The question whether power generation and distribution should be con-trolled by the government or by private enterprise complicated the Colorado River project, as it did the superpower proposal. The same issue also proved central to the issue of what the government should do with the Wilson Dam and nitrate plant it had built in 1918 at Muscle Shoals on the Tennessee River in Alabama. When the war ended, public power advocates such as Senator George Norris envisioned the site as the nucleus of a great public development to provide energy, flood control, and fertilizer for the impoverished Tennessee Valley. In July 1921, however, Henry Ford offered to lease the facilities for a hundred years and develop a fertilizer plant as well as electric generating capacity. Hoover applauded the Ford offer, but the situation soon became complicated. Several other companies demanded an opportunity to bid on any contract, and public power advocates objected to private control. Realizing that his endorsement of the Ford bid had been premature, Hoover asked P. M. Downing, vice president in charge of electrical construction and operation for the Pacific Gas and Electric Company, to evaluate the Muscle Shoals site. Downing concluded that Ford's offer was not advantageous to the government. His judgment accorded with Frederick Feiker's analysis of the situation, which suggested that Muscle Shoals could become the nucleus of a superpower development for the whole region. Armed with the two reports, Hoover met with Ford and his advisers on November 18 and outlined substantial changes that he thought Ford needed to make in his proposal. Although no supporter of public power, Hoover insisted that those who profited from the use of public property must provide real benefits in return.[67]

The same principle also shaped his policy toward oil pollution of navigable waters. As oil became an increasingly common fuel, oil spills and the deliberate dumping of waste oil into rivers, harbors, and coastal waters began to have a serious impact on both sport and commercial fishing. A Boston biologist had first reported the problem in 1902, and in 1916 the U.S. Biological Service cited oil pollution as a threat to wildfowl. Yet although Congress authorized the Public Health Service to investigate the problem as early as 1912, it appropriated no money to fund the studies.[68]

As an ardent fisherman, Hoover listened attentively to the complaints of sport and commercial fishermen that pollution was ruining the coastal fisheries, and since the Commerce Department included the Bureau of Fisheries, the problem definitely came under his jurisdiction. In May 1921, he convoked a two-day conference of East and Gulf Coast commercial fishermen at the Commerce Department. Although the meeting mainly focused on ways the department could help with practical problems of catching, preserving, and distributing seafood products, one committee report raised the question of pollution. That apparently caught Hoover's eye. At a second conference in mid-June, he presided in person, and the opening session began with a speech by Senator Joseph S. Frelinghuysen of New Jersey about water pollution. Participants in the subsequent discussion agreed the problem was serious but disagreed whether the dumped oil came mainly from shore-based sources or from ships. In his summary of the discussion, however, Hoover stressed spills and dumping from ships in coastal waters over shore-based sources, perhaps because he thought that the federal government had jurisdiction over the ocean and might not have authority to regulate land-based polluters. His interest had obviously been piqued, but since most delegates regarded the issue as a diversion from their main concerns, he let the matter drop for the time being.[69]

Back in his office, Hoover raised the pollution issue with E. T. Chamberlain of the Bureau of Navigation and departmental solicitor William E. Lamb. Chamberlain pointed out that floating oil had become a problem for other maritime activities as well as fishing. In harbors it posed a fire risk to ships, wharves, and warehouses, and all along the Atlantic Coast it fouled beaches and ruined swimming. Hoover instructed Lamb to look into the matter further and begin developing legislation to deal with the problem.[70]

Others had also begun to think about oil pollution. On June 24, 1921, Representative Theodore F. Appleby of New Jersey. introduced a bill banning all discharge of oil into navigable waters from either ships or shore-based sites. Hoover testified in favor of Appleby's bill before the House Committee on Rivers and Harbors on December 7, 1921, but those hearings revealed two very serious problems with the measure. The first was that there was overwhelming opposition from American businesses to federal regulation of shore-based pollution, and considerable doubt about the government's power to undertake such regulation. The other was that no technology existed to separate oil from bilge water aboard ships. Prohibiting ships from pumping their bilges in coastal waters might well deal a deathblow to the already enfeebled American merchant marine. That seriously concerned Hoover, whose duties included promoting the health and development of the shipping industry. While dropping shore-based pollution from the bill would eliminate the first problem, there was no point in legislating against ship-based pollution until the technical problem was solved. Several years would pass before scientists developed a practical separator.[71]

As 1921 drew to a close, Hoover had established himself as a major figure within the Harding administration. Interested in nearly every issue and a tireless worker, he offered recommendations for dealing with domestic issues ranging from conflict in the coalfields of the Appalachians to floods in California's Imperial Valley. Nor did he confine himself to domestic issues. While continuing to manage the ARA's relief program in Eastern Europe, he also spoke out in support of American membership in the League of Nations and urged the adoption of programs to foster European economic recovery. Aside from a major reorganization of the Commerce Department, most of his ideas remained unrealized at year's end, but he was confident that he would have a leading role in ushering in a new era of prosperity, peace, and progress. In his eyes, the Commerce Department had become the engine of the administration.

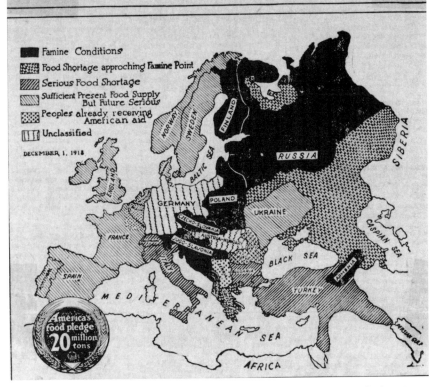

Figure 7.1. "Hunger Draws the Map" dramatized Europe's postwar food crisis as Hoover saw it in 1919.

Figure 7.2. By 1934, Lou Hoover's Palo Alto house had begun to blend into its setting as she hoped it would.

Figure 7.3. At a December 29, 1921, "invisible guest" dinner in New York, Hoover and General John Pershing flanked a high chair with a candle symbolizing a hungry European child.

Figure 7.4. The ARA's August 1921 "Hunger Map of Europe" shows a huge area around the Volga River in Russia affected by famine. The ARA had not yet discovered an equally large famine area to the east around the Dnieper River in the Ukraine.

CHAPTER 8

![black bar]

The 1921 Unemployment Conference

A week after taking office, Hoover issued a press release outlining his ideas for using the Commerce Department to promote national development. Looking forward optimistically, he did not at first realize that the economy had begun to slide rapidly into a serious recession. Only gradually, as the specter of "three or four million idle men walking the streets" loomed before him, did he understand that the economic crisis posed the new administration's most urgent problem.[1]

Over the next several months, Hoover spoke several times about the state of the economy, attempting to put the most positive light on the situation, an approach he described privately as "whistling while passing the economic graveyard so as to keep up public courage." In a speech to the U.S. Chamber of Commerce on April 28, he acknowledged that the country faced "great economic difficulties" but insisted that "we have fundamentally turned the corner." Despite unemployment, falling industrial production, problems with the railroads, "demoralization" in agriculture, and a "stoppage" in construction, the financial system remained sound. There had been no monetary panic, and Americans had adequate clothing and shelter. The root of the problem, Hoover maintained, lay in the war's destruction of Europe's economy, making the downturn "a world situation" and proving that "the shrinkage in our exports thunders at the doors of every home in America the warning that we have no isolation from the problems of the world." The government could

131

and should take action to promote the growth of American exports and over-seas investments, as well as steps at home to assist the railroads and construction industry in their "readjustment" to peacetime conditions.[2] In short, while acknowledging the seriousness of current problems, Hoover hoped to convince his listeners that they were transitory and would resolve themselves with minimal government involvement.

Hoover's emphasis on the worldwide nature of the recession, while partially correct, underestimated the domestic causes of the slump. Rapid, uncontrolled demobilization and reconversion of the economy in the months following the end of the war, along with a continuation of high government spending, reconstruction loans to Europe, and pent-up demand among consumers, had produced a brief boom in 1919 and rapid inflation. In November 1919, the cost of living stood 82.2 percent above the 1914 level; by July 1920, it had shot up to 104.5 percent above the 1914 level. The Federal Reserve reacted slowly to inflation, moving only to raise its rediscount rate from 4.75 percent in late 1919 to 6 percent in early 1920 and to 7 percent in June 1920. At that point, with the economy teetering on the brink of recession, the tightening of credit simply made matters worse. Nor did the Wilson administration, headed by the crippled president, act effectively. Continued high wartime tax rates, combined with reduced military spending, began to produce a federal budget surplus that sucked investment capital out of the economy and contributed to the growing crisis. The proliferation of strikes across the country reflected the fact that wages had not kept up with the rising cost of living, and as incomes fell behind prices, consumer buying slowed dramatically. In the spring of 1920, a rapid decline in agricultural prices presaged a 30 to 40 percent drop in general wholesale prices. Retail prices fell less, but between July 1920 and March 1922, the cost of living declined 24.4 percent. The total gross national product (GNP) dropped by about 16 percent from 1918 to 1921. Deflation forced companies to defer investments and lay off workers, resulting in a jump in unemployment to perhaps 20 percent by early 1921.[3]

Hoover's experience in the Food Administration and in Europe after the war inclined him to overestimate Europe's troubles as a cause of the 1921 recession. A large part of wartime farm prosperity *was* attributable to the growth of export markets that absorbed growing surpluses at good prices, and the rapid shrinkage of those markets after the war hit farmers hard. For most producers of nonfarm products, however, foreign markets had never been very important. Healthy foreign sales would certainly have helped the American economy recover from the recession, but under the circumstances, recovery would depend much more on restoration of domestic markets than on creation of foreign ones.[4]

As Hoover pointed out in his April 28 speech, a serious obstacle to the new administration's efforts to deal with the recession resulted from its lack of accurate information on "the current production and consumption and stocks of every great commodity." If information of that sort were made available to businessmen, he argued, it would help to smooth out the fluctuations of the business cycle. He returned to the theme on May 23, in a speech at a dinner honoring the 125th anniversary of the *New York Commercial*. "There is perhaps no complete cure for booms and slumps," he said, but he was convinced that if the government were free to collect and distribute more information, the "storms would come less often and be of less violence."[5]

As an engineer, Hoover had always measured his achievements numerically, but ordinary Americans in the early twentieth century had little experience in interpreting the state of the economy statistically. The U.S. Bureau of Labor published its first index of wholesale prices in 1902, adding a retail price index in 1907 and a general cost of living index only in 1919. Accurate measurements of national income and unemployment did not yet exist in the early 1920s, nor did reliable figures on foreign trade and investments. The idea that business cycles could be measured statistically, possibly predicted, and perhaps even controlled had been suggested by Wesley Clair Mitchell's pioneering study, *Business Cycles*, in 1913. The book had made a huge impression on economists, but its arguments had not yet reached the general public.[6]

World War I made statistics an indispensable governmental tool. With so much at stake, political leaders needed to know what worked and what did not, to have precise measurements of how many and what kind of weapons and other materials were needed for victory. Inspired by wartime advances, postwar economists carried statistical analysis over into peacetime. In 1920, Mitchell at Columbia University and Edwin F. Gay, dean of the Harvard business school and director of the government's wartime statistical service, founded the National Bureau of Economic Research with a grant from the Russell Sage Foundation. With a heterogeneous board of directors including socialists, businessmen, academics, and representatives of labor, Mitchell predicted that the new organization would produce "exact and impartial investigations" of how the economy worked and how it could be improved. A cool public reaction to the bureau's study of income disparities in the United States showed, however, that ordinary Americans were not yet ready to embrace the statistical approach.[7]

Even among experts, there was often disagreement about complex social phenomena such as the causes or possible cures for the 1921 recession. Some blamed the deflationary, tight-money policy of the Federal Reserve System (which members of the Federal Reserve denied vigorously), while others blamed excessive speculation by businessmen. Hoover himself argued that the absence of stable exchange rates among the world's currencies created a major obstacle to the revival of international trade and suggested "intermittent production due in considerable degree to seasonal fluctuation in demand" might be a contributing factor to the persistence of unemployment at home. Early in July, he asked the National Research Council (established in 1918 to coordinate scientific information) to appoint a committee of engineers "to consider the question of shifting dates under which contracts for highway construction are let" in order to promote year-around construction work. Following the committee's recommendations, he sent a letter to the governors of all the states suggesting that contracts be let in the fall rather than the spring to make possible "employment over the winter in the manufacture of material and equipment and in the placing of material ready for construction early in the spring."[8]

I

None of these measures, or others such as the revival of the War Finance Corporation, seemed to make much impact on unemployment, which remained somewhere between 3.5 and 5.7 million, depending on whose figures one accepted. The truth was, no one really knew how many people were out of work, and the huge variations in the statistics cited by various authorities helped to account for disagreements about the seriousness of the situation and what should be done about it. As time passed, however, precise figures seemed less important than the fact, upon which everyone came to agree, that conditions had not improved. On August 20, Hoover at last admitted that the economy had not rebounded and recommended to the president that a major conference be called to recommend ways to attack the problem.[9]

Harding agreed, and Hoover started at once choosing approximately a hundred conferees (the group included only four women and one African American man) from manufacturing, labor, and the public, with the manufacturing representatives chosen from the most troubled industries: construction, coal mining, and the railroads. Hoover emphasized statistically based approaches to the problem, appointing an advisory committee of twenty economists and statisticians, divided into subcommittees on unemployment statistics, temporary relief measures, and long-term solutions to unemployment, to gather information and prepare the conference's agenda. He worked especially closely with the National Bureau of Economic Research's Edwin Gay; Otto Mallery, author of an experimental public works project in Pennsylvania; and Edward Eyre Hunt, a former socialist who had worked for Hoover with the Commission for Relief in Belgium and as secretary of the Federation of American Engineering Societies (FAES) industrial waste study, who became conference secretary.[10]

It did not follow, however, that the actions of the conference would necessarily be guided by the findings of the experts. When the group convened on September 26, Hoover immediately ruled out any radical approaches the social scientists might suggest. In his opening remarks, he denounced "direct doles to individuals," which had been employed in some European nations. That "most vicious of solutions" would create an "ultimate paternalism" and "undermine our whole political system." Instead, he called upon the conference to mobilize the "fine cooperative action of our manufacturers and employers." Statistics could be used to measure the problem and provide information upon which businessmen might act voluntarily, but the secretary did not envision such analysis as leading to an aggressive government approach to the problem.[11]

Hoover had little to worry about. The conference's twelve labor delegates all came from the conservative American Federation of Labor (AFL) and, except for the obstreperous John L. Lewis of the United Mine Workers, were a pretty docile group. When Lewis threatened to get out of line, Hoover and E. M. Poston, president of the New York Coal Company, took him aside and dissuaded him from publicizing what Poston described as a "very unwise plan." Gompers went along with the program laid down by Hoover and the business members of the conference, describing it to AFL members as "in accord with the expectations of those seeking practical measures." The rest of the delegates, almost without exception conservative businessmen, academics, and local politicians, entirely embraced Hoover's approach. Joseph Defrees, president of the U.S. Chamber of Commerce, stretched truth to the breaking point when he declared that the conference had adopted "extraordinary" proposals "for solving many of the major economic difficulties of the nation and suggested machinery for the immediate relief of the unemployed." In fact, the conference's proposals reflected the traditional ideas of its business members rather than suggestions from its social science advisers.[12]

Typically, the Committee on Emergency Measures in Construction, chaired by Ernest Trigg, vice president of a Philadelphia construction company, recommended only that mayors "organize community action." The Committee on Emergency Measures by Manufacturers, led by National Implement and Vehicle Association President W. H. Stackhouse, suggested an increase in the tariff, reduced federal taxation, and shortened workdays and workweeks, as well as part-time work, during the recession. A minority report by seven members of the committee urged that the government immediately pay all of the railroads' pending claims, abolish the Railway Labor Board, and repeal the Adamson Act, which had established an eight-hour day for railway workers. The three labor members of the committee, including Samuel Gompers, protested mildly against the committee's antilabor bias, but their objections never appeared in its final report. In general, the committees recommended that business do pretty much what it had always done in recessions—defer investments, cut prices to reduce inventories, and minimize labor costs. Only two modest new ideas came out of the gathering: that a national organization should attempt to coordinate local initiatives to create economic activity and relief, and that the broad exchange of information about conditions might promote recovery.[13]

Only one of the conference's experts dissented vocally from the prevailing assumption that limited volunteer action would cure the recession. That was Otto T. Mallery, a member of the Pennsylvania State Industrial Board and secretary of the state's Emergency Public Works commission. Mallery urged the adoption of a countercyclical public works program, under which governments would set aside a percentage—10 to 20 percent—of public works appropriations during prosperous times and add that amount to spending during recessions. He initially suggested guaranteeing every wage earner a federal payment of $10 a week during periods of unemployment, but that conflicted with Hoover's rejection of the dole, so Mallery turned instead to the public works proposal. The Committee on Permanent Public Works endorsed the principle but suggested no way to implement it, so when the conference ended, Mallery struck out on his own, pushing state and local governments to commit as much money as possible to projects. For a moment, it appeared he might succeed at the federal level, where he discovered that some $20 million worth of projects had been authorized for the Reclamation Service but never funded by Congress. By dint of extraordinary effort, he persuaded President Harding to endorse a $20 million appropriation bill in Congress, but it died when Congress adjourned. A series of optimistic press releases from the Committee on Community, Civic and Emergency Measures announced promises by federal and state governments to spend several hundred million dollars on future projects, but no government at any level had created a reserve fund prior to the recession, which meant that Mallery's proposal could not help in the current crisis. California adopted a law in 1921 requiring that public works projects be planned years in advance to anticipate recessions, but the idea gained little support elsewhere. A bill authorizing the application of the countercyclical principle to federal public works that Mallery persuaded Senator William Kenyon of Iowa to introduce failed.[14]

II

The Committee on Community, Civic and Emergency Relief Measures led the implementation of the conference's recommendations. Chaired by Colonel Arthur Woods, a former New York City police commissioner and War Department assistant hired in 1919 to help servicemen reintegrate into civilian life, the committee set out initially to identify "the best forms of community organization." Then, following the adjournment of the main body, it publicized the conference's program of voluntary action and encouraged local governments to adopt it.[15]

The committee's report on September 29 concluded that "cities and towns must be relied upon for the immediate attack upon the emergency created by unemployment." To that end, it offered ten recommendations for the guidance of local mayors. The list abounded in platitudes such as "strengthen and increase the resources of the local family welfare agencies," or "it must always be remembered that an unemployed person needs work," or "we suggest that each city avail itself of the experience of others," but provided little of substance. Cities, it declared, should "provide real work by stimulating industry," but it offered no advice about how to do that. In the end, it provided only a handful of specific suggestions: creation of municipal employment agencies, collection and dissemination of economic statistics, promotion of local improvements, encouragement of part-time employment by businesses, implementation of local "spruce-up" campaigns, and extension of the school year. The committee offered no advice about how cash-strapped cities would pay for even those modest initiatives.[16]

While the conference was precedent setting as even a limited national approach to combating a recession, its emphasis on voluntary efforts at the local level was based on a prevailing myth that wartime mobilization had been achieved through voluntary citizen cooperation rather than through central planning and control. Drawing on that belief, it urged local governments to "use 'four minute men,' movies and community singing and other wartime methods in raising funds" to recreate the sense of a common cause in which all differences would be submerged for the duration of the crisis. "Just as in wartime," said conference secretary Edward Eyre Hunt, Hoover "appealed successfully to the spirit of service in the American people . . . He didn't put his faith in legislation; he put it in the spirit of service."[17]

Not everyone embraced the conference's outlook. The conservative New York *Journal of Commerce* derided its recommendation that unemployment be dealt with entirely at the local level as "lame and impotent." The basic problems, declared the *Journal*, were "national in their scope and call for national treatment." The relief of unemployment, it added, was not a matter of charity, but a problem of "economic maladjustment" that could be solved "only through setting right the underlying economic evils which have contributed to the existence of the difficulty." From the left, William Chenery, in a column in the New York *Globe*, suggested that the *Journal*'s analysis did not go far enough. He argued that although organizers billed the conference as an "unemployment" conference, unemployment was not really its subject. The conferees, like the editors of the *Journal*, viewed unemployment not as an inevitable by-product of capitalism but as a peripheral problem resulting from "economic maladjustment." Focusing on taxes, railroad rates, the disagreement between the railroads and the government, waste in industry, fluctuations in foreign exchange rates, and so on, they never even considered the possibility of a national unemployment insurance program. Taking as his model Lloyd George's national unemployment insurance program in England, Chenery argued that the problem of unemployment would never be solved until those in power accepted that it must be dealt with on a national level, not as a symptom of maladjustment, but as a permanent reality in even a perfectly functioning system.[18]

Such arguments were lost on Hoover and his advisers, as letters to the editor of the *Globe* from Edward Eyre Hunt made clear. Ignoring Chenery's argument that unemployment was an inherent feature of capitalism and blurring the distinction between a "dole" and a national unemployment insurance program, Hunt accused the editor of wanting to nationalize charity and insisted that the problem was only temporary, a question of how "to carry the unemployed over the coming winter." In a later letter to the editor, Hunt dismissed Chenery's criticism that organized labor had little representation and influence on the conference as irrelevant. "The main thing," he wrote, "was to emphasize industrial responsibility and the necessity for action by employers." He stressed that the conference's approach of mobilizing local resources to alleviate unemployment through cleanup campaigns in factories, municipalities, and homes was "industrial action, and not charity." The conference was not "a relief body." Seeing unemployment as exceptional and rejecting permanent structural reforms of the capitalist system, Hunt believed it important that actions taken to relieve the temporary crisis not be regarded as charity but as a form of work that maintained the essential structure of the capitalist order. That meant that the response to unemployment would be controlled by employers, not by workers. A "fifty-fifty representation of labor," Hunt maintained, would not have "been any more effective in framing recommendations than the representation which we had." In his view, the capitalist system would be fine if its employers simply took a few extra steps to live up to their responsibilities.[19]

Given that mind-set, it is not surprising that the conference never considered a national unemployment insurance system similar to the one in Britain. On this, however, the conference was somewhat more conservative than Hoover. Prior to the conference, he had discussed with Senator Joseph Frelinghuysen the possibility of converting a proposed bonus for war veterans into a privately run unemployment insurance program, and after the meeting he explored the idea further with New York insurance executives. In December 1921, he recommended to the president a scheme involving not unemployment insurance but a form of life insurance with a disability pension clause. Harding believed, however, that the public would reject any plan that denied a cash bonus to veterans who preferred it. Unfazed by the rejection, Hoover proposed to a Harvard economist that the bonus might be transformed into a comprehensive insurance program including "unemployment insurance, disability insurance, insurance for dependents and old age pensions." That marked the high point of his engagement with the issue. By January 1923, he had dropped the idea of using the bonus as the foundation of an insurance program, suggesting instead in a speech to an insurance managers' banquet that the companies consider offering private unemployment insurance to be funded by employer and employee contributions. The insurance industry did not respond to the idea, nor did anyone else endorse it when he mentioned it thereafter from time to time during the 1920s.[20] Although intrigued by the ideal of a comprehensive social insurance program, he never made a serious effort to develop a plan.

The autumn of 1921 provided no time to work through the intricacies of unemployment insurance, and in any case, Hoover believed that voluntary efforts could solve the immediate crisis. Voluntary measures would not be effective, however, if they were implemented gradually. The country had to be galvanized as a whole and at once, as it had been in April 1917. Hence Hoover arranged meetings with the presidents of major industries and sent out a barrage of telegrams and letters to state and local government offices, as well as to major publicity outlets such as the motion picture industry, asking them to begin organizing and to report back as quickly as possible what they were doing. To coordinate all this activity, he asked Colonel Woods, the chairman of the Committee on Community, Civic and Emergency Relief Measures, to stay on as a special assistant in the Department of Commerce. He also hired a professional public relations specialist, Lupton A. Wilkinson, to organize a national publicity campaign. Somewhat flippantly, Hoover's assistant, Christian Herter, described the process as "trying to find work for the unemployed by means of tremendous gatherings and pow-wows," "another one of those three ring affairs that the Chief likes to take on which keeps everybody working at high speed."[21]

Herter was not given to joking about matters his "chief" took seriously, so it may be that Hoover too was skeptical about the methods that had been adopted to fight the recession. There is no direct evidence that he had doubts, however, and certainly most Americans did not question the claim that voluntarism had won the war. In any case, ideological and budgetary restrictions made a more forceful federal approach impossible.

Within days of the end of the conference, reports began to come in from the 327 municipalities of 25,000 or more across the country to which Woods sent requests for action. Soon, patterns became obvious. Milwaukee's mayor, for example, created an Emergency Unemployment Committee, which sent an impressive-looking list of thirteen points—until one realized that they were only recommendations that various public and private entities begin or continue projects and that none of the organizations involved had actually promised action. Portland's mayor sent a similar list, with the interesting addition of a promise that the "municipal rockpile" would be available "for the benefit of those who refuse to work." He added helpfully that the city would advertise the rockpile extensively throughout the region "to prevent an influx of men." The District of Columbia promised to create a "register of unemployed," ranked by their willingness to work at any wage. Only those on the list would receive public assistance. The unemployed, obviously, had little input into these plans, which business leaders intended, at least in part, as instruments of social control. The prolabor mayor of Chicago, William H. Thompson, denounced the whole unemployment program as "a capitalistic move with the following objects: a blacklist, a refusal of charity to American union laboring men, a drive against union labor, a conspiracy to lower wages."[22]

While urging on local organizers, Hoover also focused on predicting and controlling future fluctuations in the business cycle. On November 4, he convened the Standing Committee of the Unemployment Conference, which had been set up at his suggestion to investigate basic issues after the conference adjourned. Many of the committee's ten members, including Edward

Eyre Hunt, Julius Barnes, E. M. Poston, and Ernest Trigg, were old Hoover friends, and they quickly agreed on what should be done. They first set up a Committee on the Business Cycle, chaired by Owen D. Young, vice president of General Electric. The conference's Committee on Unemployment and the Business Cycle had made a preliminary study of the matter and recommended a more thorough investigation focusing on the prevention or amelioration of future downturns. The Standing Committee also authorized its chairman (Hoover) to appoint committees to study the construction and bituminous coal industries, as well as any other committees he thought desirable.[23]

At the end of the committee's meeting, Arthur Woods reported that 209 of the targeted cities had already established community organizations, and announced that he had appointed fifteen regional representatives to assist with the process. His optimism notwithstanding, however, organization was proceeding less well than Woods would have liked. In some of the most heavily industrialized states, where unemployment was high, including New York, Pennsylvania, New Jersey, and Ohio, major cities not only remained unorganized but also resisted the whole concept. New York City, for example, with an estimated 343,000 unemployed, refused to cooperate with the national program, although the city's commissioner of public welfare, Bird S. Coler, had served as a delegate to the conference. A committee representative privately branded New York's mayor, John F. Hylan, an "obstinate and brainless jackass." Nor was New York the only such case. The Democratic "jackasses" who controlled many of the large cities were notably cooler to the conference's approach than Republicans, and in cities where one or two industries had furnished most of the jobs, even enthusiastic local organizers could do little. Promoters of the local, voluntary approach had not foreseen such a problem.[24]

Woods tackled uneven progress by creating a list of the cities where organization lagged, by recruiting the Federal Council of Churches of Christ and the Federation of Women's Clubs to take a hand in spurring action and by employing four special agents, Arthur L. Bristol, Fred W. Caswell, Whiting Williams, and the wonderfully named Sherlock Herrick, to visit cities and encourage engagement in the program. The committee drew up a "Blacklist" (quickly relabeled the "Trouble Book") of "cities in which the unemployment situation is especially unsatisfactory" and assigned each of the four agents a region. When he visited a city, the agent told the mayor that he had been sent by Washington to find out what they were doing and then called on "some of the leading citizens, that is one or two big businessmen, one or two of the principal pastors in the town," and the editors of local newspapers to "get their idea of how the situation is." No one proposed meetings with the unemployed or representatives of local unions, and when unemployed workers in Detroit and New York organized their own gatherings, Woods declared their requests for "*government aid*" (his emphasis) unacceptable. "The best way to meet their demand," he said, "was to show that the situation was being handled in better ways."[25]

III

During December 1921 and January and February 1922, Woods's agents energetically crisscrossed the country visiting cities, sometimes more than once. They reported that unemployment rates were very uneven around the country and that most local officials had only the vaguest conception of the labor situation in their cities. As the agents saw it, local officials receptive to guidance from Washington achieved success more often than those who resisted, although an equally plausible explanation of inconsistent results was that public works programs and "cleanup" campaigns worked best where unemployment posed little problem in the first place. In the hardest-hit cities dominated by single industries, the methods suggested by the conference proved ineffective.[26]

Some organizers recognized the limitations of the approach adopted by the unemployment conference. As one put it, "Where a city was in bad condition at first, it shows but slight improvement now. Cities in first-class condition now were never very bad." There was not, his report concluded, "a single instance" in the organization's records of a city's employment situation improving dramatically following "remedial measures . . . taken by the mayor or his committee as a result of the recommendations of this conference." One of Woods's own investigators, Whiting Williams, an independent labor consultant to several large companies, evaluated the program even more negatively. "In certain industrial centers furnishing a population of fully ten million people," wrote Williams in mid-February 1922, "the amount of unemployment is greater and the amount of distress *much* greater than in November."[27]

Amid the frenetic attempts to organize local programs, no one in authority paid much attention to negative reports, and no evidence indicates that any of them percolated upward to Hoover. Impervious to evidence, Woods and Hunt remained true believers in their approach, and Hoover seemed entirely confident that the methods proposed by the conference had succeeded completely. Publicly and privately, he insisted from mid-December onward that "unemployment has been so mitigated as to remove the greater anxieties of the matter for the present." To forestall a new downturn, he urged the president to ask federal departments "to advance any work that they may have available in order to assist unemployment during the winter months."[28]

Most departments promised to do what they could, although budgetary restrictions severely limited their ability to initiate programs. In fact, the recession had largely run its course. By March 1922, a recovery was beginning that would lead on to the boom of the mid-1920s. On March 23, the Commerce Department issued an optimistic press release rejoicing that "the tide of business depression has turned and that the worst is over." A few days later, Hoover confidently predicted that "prosperous conditions are ahead."[29]

By late April and early May, the campaign against unemployment was winding down. Two of Woods's investigators who had been borrowed from the military returned to their units, and he let the other two go. The national publicity campaign run in house by Major R. L. Foster and externally by Lupton Wilkinson in New York quietly expired. In mid-May, Hoover began sending personal notes of thanks to people who had helped with the program and drafted a form letter for the president's use. Harding thanked Hoover personally for "a work quietly and efficiently carried out" in getting the nation through "the winter of the greatest unemployment in the history of our country."[30]

Harding and Hoover greatly overestimated the importance and effect of the unemployment program. The conference focused attention on joblessness and deployed modest palliatives, but it led to no significant legislation, nor did it establish federal responsibility for fixing what had become a national problem. Instead of approaching the recession as a symptom of serious problems in the economy, the conference regarded it as a minor, temporary aberration that should be treated, despite the rhetoric about making work for the jobless, through charity. Responsibility for relief could be left to businessmen and local governments, with the federal government merely coordinating and disseminating information. Workers and the unemployed were expected to be grateful for whatever they received and had no role in setting policy.

The coincidence that the recession ended at the same time the unemployment program went into high gear led Hoover and his advisers to conclude erroneously that the program had caused the outcome. The experience reinforced the prevailing belief that voluntarism had won the war and confirmed faith in the soundness of the country's economic system. In a speech in Englewood, New Jersey, in November of 1922, Hoover laid out what he regarded as the lessons of the experience: "With the vast unemployment there came a great demand that the Government should adopt the patent medicine cure of European countries and give doles to our unemployed from the Public Treasury. Instead of this, the Administration called a great conference of representatives of our manufacturers, municipalities, and public bodies, and drew up a plan for handling the unemployed by voluntary action . . . , and through all these efforts we passed through the greatest winter of unemployment ever known in our history without a single disturbance, without suffering, and without resort to any pauperizing or wasteful expenditure of public money."[31] That was a lesson he would apply in the future.

Others believed that even the limited approaches of the unemployment conference had gone too far. When the Senate debated the Kenyon Bill to set aside funds appropriated for public works to be used in times of recession, several senators opposed it on the ground that business cycles could not be controlled. Senator Harry S. New of Indiana, for example, referred to the plagues of the Old Testament as proof that "these recurring periods of plenty and of famine have been going on for some time"; he doubted that "even . . . the Congress of the United States" could prevent them. Senator George Norris of Nebraska, no admirer of Hoover, made the issue more personal. "I would rather postpone a panic," he declared, "until the time when God brings it on than to have Hoover entrusted with this power, and get the panic a year sooner . . . We had better let God run it as in the past, and not take the power away from Him and give it to Hoover."[32]

IV

The idea, so colorfully expressed by New and Norris, that economic cycles lay beyond human control commonly held sway among businessmen as well as legislators in the 1920s, although economists did not share it. Hoover had been unwilling to make the federal government responsible for helping the unemployed, but he did believe that the government could and should act to head off or moderate the extremes of the business cycle in the future. The boost given by the conference to the argument by professional economists that the collection and analysis of statistical information about the economy would provide tools for controlling the business cycle, as well as the creation of the conference's Business Cycles Committee to undertake an in-depth study of the whole issue, provided perhaps the most important and lasting achievements of the conference.[33]

Soon after the unemployment conference adjourned, Hoover moved to organize the new committee. He asked Owen D. Young of General Electric to chair it and named Joseph H. Defrees, president of the U.S. Chamber of Commerce; Clarence M. Wooley of the American Radiator Company; Matthew Woll of the AFL; and Mary Van Kleeck of the Russell Sage Foundation to serve as members, with Edward Eyre Hunt as secretary. The National Bureau of Economic Research, which had already begun examining the problem under the leadership of Edwin Gay and Wesley Mitchell, set aside its plans for an independent study and agreed to provide the technical expertise for Hoover's committee. The FAES, which had identified intermittent employment as a serious waste in its 1921 report, also offered to cooperate. Hunt estimated optimistically that it would take about six months and cost approximately $50,000 to make a basic assessment of the causes and management of business cycles, and Hoover asked the Carnegie Corporation, the Commonwealth Fund, and corporate leaders to fund the study.[34]

Hoover introduced the committee members to the press at a Commerce Department briefing on February 20, 1922. The committee's experts went quickly to work, and although hampered by unreliable unemployment statistics and spotty information about business conditions, drafted a preliminary report by summer. During the autumn they gathered and distilled further information, presenting their findings to the committee in Chicago on December 28, 1922.[35]

Their report first described the business cycle and attempted to provide more reliable figures than had been available previously about the impact of the 1921 recession. It estimated total unemployment at the worst point of the downturn at about one million, or roughly one-sixth of the workforce, with large companies more severely affected than small ones and joblessness greatest in the areas around such companies. The authors noted that some companies had been experimenting with methods to level out peaks and troughs in their own operations, but they concluded on the basis of careful analysis of the data that, despite a few conspicuous successes, this approach was inadequate to moderate the boom and bust cycle for the economy as a whole.

The report then moved on to examine larger-scale private and public remedies for unemployment. On the private side, those included attempts by labor unions to provide unemployment benefits and efforts by banks to stabilize the economy. As with efforts by individual companies, the authors found such approaches ineffective. On the public side, they took note of the recently adopted British national unemployment insurance system but did not recommend a similar program for the United States. Instead, they recommended countercyclical public works spending, a more active role by the Federal Reserve in controlling inflation and deflation, and the creation of a national system of employment offices. Emphasizing the importance of accurate long-range forecasting of the economic cycle, they urged that the government collect as much information as possible from businesses and trade associations as the foundation of such forecasts. They recognized, however, that the concept of sharing such data was "just beginning to enter into the minds of a considerable number of business men."[36]

After hearing the experts' findings, the committee discussed what to do next. The experts proposed circulating the preliminary report as widely as possible and allowing six months or a year for the business community to respond, but committee members thought that would blur and weaken the report. They decided instead to publish the preliminary report unaltered, and four months later it appeared, at full length as a book by the McGraw-Hill Company and in a condensed form as a Commerce Department pamphlet. Lupton Wilkinson, who had previously worked as a publicist for the unemployment conference, signed on again to disseminate and popularize the committee's recommendations.[37]

The report impressed economists but did not have the widespread impact for which Hoover hoped. He sent a copy to his S Street neighbor, Adolph Miller, at the Federal Reserve Board, but the Federal Reserve did not follow up. Nor did Congress pass either the Kenyon Bill providing for countercyclical public works spending or another to recreate the wartime federal unemployment service. As Hoover noted ruefully, most economists agreed that the business cycle could be controlled, but many businessmen and members of Congress still believed that its fluctuations were inescapable, "that there is an ebb and flow in the demand for commodities and services that cannot from the nature of things be regulated." Even the *New Republic*, basically sympathetic to Hoover's point of view on this issue, commented that the business cycle was "as characteristically human as leprosy . . . , and like leprosy, it looks like an incurable disease." Hoover rejected that defeatism and, throughout his years in office, attempted to fight it but with only limited success [38]

Unfazed by the skeptical reception given the business cycle report, Hoover quickly proposed a second study of a basic problem: seasonal unemployment. In May 1923, he wrote to Robert Brookings, founder of the Institute of Economics that would later bear his name, to propose that its staff undertake the same sort of study of this problem that the National Bureau of Economic Research had done on the business cycle. When the Carnegie Corporation offered $10,000 to fund the study and several companies contributed an additional $4,000, Hoover asked Ernest T. Trigg to chair "a thorough economic investigation . . . into the seasonal industries from the point of view of the industry itself rather than from a point of view wholly of labor."[39]

Finding that a study of seasonal unemployment in industries as diverse as construction, coal mining, the manufacture of agricultural implements, machine tools, textiles, boots and shoes, and transportation lay beyond the capacity of a single committee, Hoover asked the Carnegie foundation in October 1923 to fund separate committees for each of the industries. That required a greater commitment of resources than the foundation's directors thought wise, and the study of *Seasonal Operation in the Construction Industries*, published by the Commerce Department in July 1924, remained unique.[40]

"Custom, not climate, is mainly responsible for seasonal idleness in the construction industries," wrote Hoover in an introduction to the committee's report. He argued that the reason most construction workers were fully employed for only a few months a year was because companies had not exploited "improvements in building materials, the development of new equipment, and innovations in management methods" that made "most types of construction . . . possible . . . the year round in all parts of the United States." Everyone involved in construction—architects, engineers, contractors, suppliers, real estate people, and workers—needed to familiarize themselves with new materials and methods and to join in planning ahead to schedule construction and repair work. If that were done, it would contribute to stabilizing employment in all the other industries that supplied the construction industry and depended upon it. "Conscious planning ahead," Hoover concluded, was all that was needed to smooth out seasonal variations in this basic industry by eliminating the "wastes of seasonal idleness" that dragged down the growth of the whole economy.[41]

Hoover believed that the reports of the business cycle and seasonal employment committees, building on the work of the 1921 conference and the industrial waste report, pointed the way to "practically full time employment in the United States." During the 1924 presidential campaign, he bragged that since 1921 the Republicans had found "the solution of unemployment," turning 4.5 million unemployed men into productive workers. All that was still needed, he told the trustees of the Rockefeller Foundation in a request for a $100,000 grant, was one more study—"of the most promising bases for adjusting [labor-management] disputes without resort to strikes and lockouts" and "emphasizing public participation."[42]

The Rockefeller Foundation proved less than enthusiastic about the proposed new study, offering half or a quarter of the requested funds and making even that offer conditional on Hoover raising the remainder from other sources. That was the arrangement under which the Carnegie foundation had funded the seasonal employment study, and Hoover and Hunt regarded it as "very unsatisfactory." Since Carnegie grants had depended on the investigators raising matching funds, money trickled in unpredictably, and in the end they received less than half of the originally requested $25,000, with the last payment arriving after the study was finished.[43] Rather than undertake the study under those conditions, Hoover and Hunt deferred the project indefinitely.

In the autumn of 1927, Hoover and Hunt applied to the Carnegie Corporation for a grant to make a second study of the business cycle. Armed with Carnegie support, they then turned to the Rockefeller Foundation, and early in 1928 the two foundations promised a total of $75,000 for the new project. Again conducted by Wesley Mitchell and the National Bureau of Economic Research, the result was a two-volume study of *Recent Economic Changes in the United States*, published in 1929 after Hoover had moved on from the Commerce Department to the White House. The report provided much new data, but its conclusions echoed those of the earlier investigations Hoover had sponsored: the possibility of understanding and controlling the business cycle, the elimination of seasonal unemployment through planning, the use of counter cyclical public works spending to stabilize the economy, and voluntary cooperation among economic interests to make the system work.[44]

V

In 1928, when Hoover ran for the presidency, he based his campaign largely on the claim that the Republicans had cured unemployment in 1921 and discovered methods for maintaining permanent prosperity. The mainstream media seldom challenged his argument, but the left-wing *Nation* magazine raised questions about his assertions. In 1921, the magazine pointed out, the unemployment conference's own statisticians had estimated a maximum of 3.5 million out of work, not the 5 to 6 million Hoover claimed in 1928. In 1922, the Bureau of Labor Statistics had estimated that not more than 1.5 million of that 3.5 million had found work as a result of the efforts of the unemployment conference and the general revival of the economy. *The Nation* pointed out correctly that Hoover overstated both the number of unemployed in 1921 and the effect of the unemployment conference's measures on reducing the number. But did his exaggerations really matter? In fact, the United States during the 1920s did enjoy unusual price stability and low unemployment (despite brief increases in 1923–24 and 1926–27). Consumer prices actually fell by about 4 percent between 1921 and 1929, while taxes were reduced for people with lower incomes as well as for the wealthy. It was only natural for a presidential candidate to claim that this happy situation resulted from policies he had championed.[45]

The weakness in Hoover's position in 1928 lay less in his confidence that the Republicans had discovered the keys to prosperity than in his belief that he knew how to cure a recession. On the basis of the 1921 experience, he believed that voluntary cooperation and local initiatives had been sufficient to relieve the needs of the unemployed, while the collection of economic data and its dissemination by the government would enable businesses to avoid future collapses. The pioneering studies of the business cycle he sponsored did greatly advance understanding of the economy, though they did not make possible the degree of control for which he hoped. And his ideas about how to deal with unemployment were completely inadequate. In fact, the reports from Colonel Woods's agents made it clear that the committee's measures had proved ineffective in combating serious unemployment and only marginally helpful in alleviating light to moderate joblessness. No one brought those reports to Hoover's attention, and he seems never to have seen them. Too busy to pay close attention to the details of the unemployment program, he naturally assumed that it had been effective when the recession ended. His mistaken assumption would have serious consequences during his presidency.[46]

For all the absurdity of much of the action generated by the unemployment conference, the meeting had important long-term consequences. Its underlying assumption, that a recession was a national problem requiring a national approach, exemplified a new economic sophistication. As the historian Robert Zieger points out, "The conference illuminated the part played by industrial waste and poor economic coordination in creating joblessness, dispelling the time-honored notion of individual inadequacy as the root cause." And although the conference itself made little use of the expertise of its economic advisers, the subsequent business cycle and seasonal employment investigations were conducted by experts and did much to advance understanding of how the economy worked and how it should be managed. Other by-products of the conference included a boost to the work of the Commerce Department's Division of Simplified Practice in standardizing construction materials and practices; support for the Housing Division's efforts to popularize zoning and construction codes and cooperative enterprises in construction; and in June 1922, the organization of the American Construction Council under Franklin Roosevelt, which sought to promote cooperation among manufacturers, builders, and workers in constructing and marketing low-cost houses for more Americans. As a tool to combat the recession of 1921, the unemployment conference, hobbled by economic and ideological limitations, never fulfilled Hoover's hopes for it, but it suggested opportunities for future action that went far beyond the limited possibilities of the present.[47]

CHAPTER 9

The Russian
Famine, 1921–1923

On July 13, 1921, the Russian writer Maxim Gorky addressed an urgent appeal to the American people. Millions of Russians, wrote Gorky, had been brought to the brink of starvation caused by massive drought that had destroyed the wheat crop. He begged the West to send food and medicines to prevent a catastrophe.[1]

Early in 1921, reports of a terrible drought in the wheat-growing area along the Volga River began to reach Moscow. Coming on top of years of revolution and civil war during which the Bolsheviks had seized all surplus grain in the region and even commandeered seed supplies, it was not difficult to foresee a crisis. The Soviets replaced confiscation with a tax in 1921, but the change came too late. Fury at Bolshevik policies combined with hunger to create an explosive mixture in the villages. Peasant rebels across Russia blew up bridges, cut down telegraph poles, tore up railroad lines, and slaughtered communist officials. Shipments of grain to the cities dwindled to almost nothing, and urban workers went on strike, seriously threatening Bolshevik authority. With most of the Red Army far in the west fighting the Poles, Moscow could do little to restore control. Even the weather seemed to conspire against the Reds. An unusually cold winter followed by drought in many areas ravaged crops and compounded the chaos in the countryside. By summer, the country faced famine, although the government would not admit it officially until July.[2]

I

The Russian disaster came as no surprise to Hoover and his colleagues in the American Relief Administration (ARA). The ARA had been working in Eastern Europe since the end of the war, and during the summer of 1921 its men heard much about the Russian drought. Even prior to Gorky's appeal, Hoover's friends had suggested that he might have to "take on a few more continents."[3] (See Figure 7.4.)

Hoover's personal hostility to Bolshevism, which had been intensified by his postwar experiences with Hungary and Germany, complicated his reaction to Gorky's letter, as did his memory of the Russian rejection of his previous attempt to organize a relief program through Fridtjof Nansen in 1919. Moreover, in 1921 Hoover had become secretary of commerce in an administration committed to nonrecognition of the Soviet Union. He explained his point of view in a press release on March 21, 1921. Under the Bolshevik economic system, "no matter how much they moderate it in name," he said, "there can be no real return to production in Russia, and therefore, Russia will have no considerable commodities to export, and consequently, no great ability to obtain imports." He regarded this as unfortunate, because "Europe cannot recover its economic stability until Russia returns to production." Russia's economic paralysis under the communists thus affected the United States by preventing European recovery. Nevertheless, until the Russians assured "the safety of life . . . , private property, the sanctity of contract, and the rights of free labor," the United States had no "basis for considering trade relations."[4]

Although Gorky's appeal evoked formidable obstacles, some circumstances favored a positive response. On the Russian side, Lenin responded to the crisis by announcing a New Economic Policy, which made concessions to the peasants and restored some elements of capitalism, including greater opportunities for foreign investment. In Washington, some people thought a relief program might provide a way to subvert the Soviet system and encourage the restoration of capitalism. Hoover had no wish to help the Bolsheviks but reacted to reports of starving children. Hearing that the Soviets' program of child feeding, in the cities as well as in the countryside, had "practically broken down" and that, especially in the cities, "children are threatened with extinction," he concluded that he must suppress his aversion to helping the Bolsheviks. Yet even so, he refused to offer unconditional aid. In his July 23 reply to Gorky, he demanded the immediate release of all Americans being held prisoner in Russia. If he launched a relief program, he continued, the ARA must have "full liberty to come and go and move about Russia" and must be able "to organize the necessary local committees and local assistance free from governmental interference." The Russians must provide free transportation, storage, and handling of relief items, and people receiving help from the Americans must remain eligible for any additional supplies distributed by the

Russian government. In return for those assurances, he guaranteed that ARA workers would "engage in no political activities."[5]

In reply to American critics who argued that American aid would prop up the Soviet government, Hoover contended that denying it would give the Soviet leaders an excuse to continue the dictatorship because of the alleged hostility of the Western powers. Provided an aid program remained outside the control of Russian authorities, he argued, it would weaken rather than strengthen the Soviet government. As "an entering wedge" for Western influence, a relief program firmly controlled by Americans would bring home to Russians "that their present economic system is hopeless."[6] ARA men need not engage in overt political activity in Russia; their simply being there would make a powerful political statement.

II

Hoover's promise that the ARA would avoid political interference in Russia would have been more convincing had the organization not taken an active role in the overthrow of Béla Kun's communist government in Hungary in 1919. Kun, a protégé of Lenin, had established a communist regime in Hungary on March 21, 1919. At first, Hoover tolerated the new government, partly because Hungary's location made it an important distribution point for shipments to other areas in Eastern and Southern Europe. When Marshal Foch proposed overthrowing Kun by force, Hoover urged Wilson to resist the idea. But by June, as the Romanians invaded Hungary, strikes paralyzed the country, and government soldiers raided villages to seize produce the peasants refused to sell for worthless money, Kun turned increasingly toward dictatorship. From Hoover's point of view, the chaotic situation was disrupting ARA operations throughout Eastern Europe and Kun's open espousal of communism only made matters worse. Influenced by the ARA representative in Budapest, Captain Thomas T. C. Gregory, Hoover flirted briefly with the idea of encouraging the French to intervene but by mid-July returned to advocating nonintervention. But when Gregory reported that a socialist member of Kun's government, Vilmos Böhm, proposed to stage a coup and replace Kun's regime with a social-democratic government, Hoover relayed the report to the Allied leaders in Paris. They liked the idea and promised to lift the blockade they had imposed if a new government came to power in Hungary. On August 1, Kun fled to Russia.[7]

Following Kun's flight, Romanian forces, which had invaded Hungary, installed the Habsburg Archduke Joseph as the new head of state. Hoover viewed this as a restoration of the military absolutism that the war had been fought to eliminate. "I consider that the American Army fought in vain if the Habsburgs are permitted to retain power," he said, and he told United Press that he would resign if the archduke remained in office. His threat to disrupt the whole American relief effort in Europe brought quick results. The Allied leaders sent word to the archduke through the Food Administration that they would not recognize his government. Captain Gregory took great pleasure in relaying this ultimatum and on August 23 reported cheerily that the archduke had abdicated: "Archie on the carpet 7 p.m. Went through the hoop at 7:05 p.m."[8]

Although there is no doubt that Hoover played a role in overthrowing the Kun government and a more important one in ousting Archduke Joseph, it is a distortion to argue that he simply used food aid for political purposes. Inevitably, Western leaders saw relief, Eastern European stability, and communism as interrelated. Hoover certainly applauded the collapse of the communist government in Hungary, but his policy recommendations had been more cautious than those of Captain Gregory, and he played an important part in blocking French intervention in Hungary and in preventing a postcoup return of the Habsburgs. Recognizing the impossibility of complete neutrality, he sought a course that would leave the Hungarian people politically free to choose their own direction. Whether democracy would survive in the face of hyperinflation remained to be seen.[9]

Unfortunately, many Americans first heard about events in Hungary in a lurid account published by Captain Gregory in June 1921. In his article, Gregory maintained that he and Hoover had, virtually single-handedly, organized the overthrow of the Béla Kun government. This exaggerated tale, repeated in the columns of liberal journals such as the *Nation* and the *New Republic*, provided a foundation for the charge that the Russian government was justified in fearing "that the power of American food will be used politically to undermine its authority." Hoover denied this assertion vigorously, but the damage was done. Then and afterward many liberals asserted confidently that he had used food aid to impose a reactionary regime in Hungary and hoped to do the same in Russia.[10]

III

Hoover regarded protecting a relief program from interference by the Russian government or by other aid organizations as equally important. He had no problem in bringing all American organizations under his authority, but a proposal from the Red Cross in Switzerland to internationalize control of relief reminded him of the Allied pushing and pulling that had complicated his postwar work. In reply, he sent a diplomatically phrased letter suggesting that the scope of the problem exceeded the Red Cross's resources. Only the ARA, with its unique access to American government support, he implied, could undertake so enormous an operation. In case any doubt remained about the American position, he secured a letter from the president virtually ordering that "the distribution in Russia of all charity arising in the United States should be carried on through the one American organization," the ARA. Armed with this order, Hoover immediately cabled his ARA chief in Europe, Walter Lyman Brown, to notify the Red Cross "that their offers to enter Russia without proper agreements will preclude American co-operation and they should at once line up with you."[11] Brown softened Hoover's language but made his position clear, and from that point on, the ARA had sole control over the Russian relief program.

Brown, like Hoover, was a mining engineer. During the war, when he volunteered to work for the Commission for Relief in Belgium, Hoover asked him to take charge of moving food shipments through Rotterdam. Although he had no previous experience with such work and received minimal guidance from the "Chief," Brown was a natural diplomat who did his job so well that he earned Hoover's lasting confidence. Following the war, Hoover made Brown, now based in London, the head of ARA operations in Europe.[12]

Not surprisingly, Hoover asked Brown to handle the demanding task of working out a detailed agreement covering the operations of the relief program with the Russians, though he supervised the process by cable. Brown met with Maxim Litvinov, assistant people's commissar of foreign affairs, at Riga, Latvia, in mid-August, and on August 20 they signed a twenty-seven-point "treaty of Riga" covering in great detail the ARA's authority in Russia.[13] No one thought the agreement would prevent all conflicts, but at least it provided a basis for defending the independence of relief workers.

A week after the signing of the Riga agreement, seven experienced ARA men left Riga for Moscow as an advance party to get a firsthand picture of conditions and appraise local facilities. From Moscow, one part of the group headed east into the area around the central and northern Volga, while a second part turned south toward the mouth of the river at the Black Sea. As they went, they arranged for the first shipments of food into the famine area from Petrograd (St. Petersburg) in the north and Riga in the west.[14]

In the meantime, Colonel William N. Haskell and his staff, appointed by Hoover to run the Russian operation, proceeded to Moscow. Haskell, a professional soldier, had graduated from West Point in 1901 and served in the Philippines as well as in Europe during the war. At the end of the war, Hoover appointed him, through the Allied Supreme Council, to be Allied high commissioner in Armenia, where he controlled all relief operations in the Transcaucasus region, as well as exercising substantial executive authority in the absence of established local government. It is not clear why Hoover chose him rather than an ARA man to head the Russian mission, but it may have been because of his quasidiplomatic experience in dealing with the Allied governments, the American delegation in Paris, and local authorities. He had never run a substantial child-feeding program nor worked with the ARA. Perhaps Hoover chose him in part because, as a forty-three-year-old professional soldier, he projected an air of authority and maturity that many of the younger—and often irreverent—ARA men lacked. Whatever the reason, the appointment seemed initially to have been a mistake. The ARA men, many of them former army volunteers, shared a widespread resentment felt by volunteers during the war against the regulars, whom they saw as pompous, rigid, and class conscious. When Haskell was appointed, even Walter Brown, a Hoover loyalist, muttered rebelliously that the colonel was not "sufficiently one of us" to run a smooth operation in Russia.[15]

Haskell got off to a bad start, bringing a staff of seventeen with him to Moscow and setting up his headquarters on a formal military model. Fortunately, circumstances prevented early friction from becoming a major problem. Hearing that Haskell's hard-drinking chief of staff, Captain Thomas C. Lonergan, sometimes seemed under the influence while on duty, in March 1922 Hoover replaced him with Cyril J. C. Quinn. Quinn had served under Haskell during the war but had also worked with Brown in London and had been Brown's chief deputy during the Riga negotiations. He smoothed relations between Haskell and the ARA men, who in any event greatly outnumbered the regular soldiers in the operation. Given the vast distances and poor transportation in Russia, the ARA men necessarily had enormous autonomy—which suited them perfectly.[16]

Over time, Haskell's diplomatic experience proved valuable. One such case had to do with the Russian-American committees that were supposed to recruit and supervise the Russian employees of the ARA. Given that only 381 Americans represented the ARA in Russia, many thousands of Russians had to be hired to distribute relief supplies and man kitchens. Under the Riga agreement, the Americans had authority to hire anyone they chose for those tasks, but local Bolshevik authorities sometimes arrested ARA employees they regarded as counterrevolutionaries or members of the old regime. After the arrest of some key Russian workers, Haskell negotiated a compromise. It abolished the Russian-American committees, giving the Americans a free hand to choose their own staff, and Haskell warned the Russians that future arrests might jeopardize aid. In return, the ARA promised to submit lists of prospective employees to the Russian authorities in advance of hiring them and generally agreed to honor Russian objections to hiring certain people.[17]

Busy with his duties as secretary of commerce, Hoover took only an occasional part in the routine operations of the ARA in Russia. Selling the relief program to the American people and securing a sizable appropriation from Congress to fund ARA activities comprised his main contributions. To make his case, he needed firsthand reports on the seriousness of the situation in Russia from credible observers.

Reports on the crisis began to come in as soon as the first ARA men entered Russia in August 1921, but those reports, from youthful albeit experienced ARA workers, did not provide the breadth of view and political weight that Hoover needed to popularize his program in the United States. To supplement their reports, he turned to an old friend, Dr. Vernon Kellogg, a Stanford professor of entomology then serving as secretary of the National Research Council in Washington, with whom Hoover had worked closely on Belgian relief, the Food Administration, and the ARA. Kellogg combined experience as a relief administrator with skill as an observer and reporter. His reports, beginning in October, provided the human interest Hoover wanted. "They sit there just waiting to die," Kellogg reported from a village beside the Volga. "I saw one woman with four children all huddling on a single blanket. One of the children died under my own eyes, and there was no help for it. No one had food to give it." Such reports would become depressingly familiar from other famines over coming years, but Americans found them shocking in 1921. They put a human face on Kellogg's grim estimate that starvation imperiled 15 million people and that, without outside aid, probably 5 to 10 million would die in the coming winter.[18]

Another sort of report came from James P. Goodrich, a former Republican governor of Indiana and friend of President Harding. Although Goodrich had no experience with Russia or relief, Hoover sent him to the famine zone because of his standing as an independent Midwesterner with important Republican political connections. His reports, which began to arrive in early November, at one level seemed to contradict what Hoover was hearing from the ARA men and Kellogg. Goodrich concluded that previous reports had overstated the immediate crisis. Cases of acute suffering existed, but most villages along the Volga probably had a four- or five-month supply of grain on hand. But, he added, almost nothing had been planted, so when current stocks ran out, starvation would be general. Moreover, wrote Goodrich, a much larger area had been affected than anyone had previously realized. He believed the ARA must greatly increase the number of children it was prepared to feed and extend its charity to include adults as well.[19] Hoover found his reports, with their unemotional and tough-minded tone, enormously valuable.

In the meantime, the first ARA workers arriving in Russia to set up feeding stations independently confirmed Goodrich's report of a vast problem. Not only did famine threaten the whole Volga valley and an uncertain area to the east, but it also took in the Ukraine south of Minsk, an enormous wheat-growing area. One resident of the area later recalled a truly desperate situation:

> It is now the winter of 1921. The famine has reached such a scale that words fail to describe it. The crop was a total failure, the grain mostly being so sparse that it could not be cut with a machine and had to be harvested painstakingly by hand.
>
> The people go about emaciated and weak, living as they do mostly on all kinds of refuse. Cases of cannibalism are not wanting, parents and children murdering one another. In a window at the headquarters of the Cheka [secret police] in a neighboring city almost daily were posted pictures of people who had been condemned to death for cannibalism, in order to deter others from doing the same thing. But hunger knows no fear of punishment.[20]

ARA workers in Russia disagreed over whether drought or Bolshevik policies contributed most to the famine, but whatever the causes of the disaster, the relief program would need to be far more extensive and costly than anyone had imagined.[21]

In October, Hoover asked Congress to authorize the War Department to give the ARA any surplus medical and food supplies in Europe for transfer to Russia, but that proved only a drop in the bucket. So did a program initiated later in the month to allow private citizens in the United States to send food drafts to friends and relatives in Russia, who could redeem the drafts at ARA warehouses. Early in December, Hoover asked Goodrich and Kellogg to come to Washington to support him in urging the president to include in his annual message a request that Congress authorize a donation of some 15 million bushels of corn and seed grains. Harding was moved, though not to the degree that Hoover hoped, asking instead for only 10 million bushels of corn and a million bushels of seed grain.[22]

On December 10, House Republicans introduced a bill authorizing an appropriation of $10 million for the purchase of corn and seed, but following a dramatic appeal by Hoover on December 13, they doubled the amount to $20 million. The American people, Hoover contended, spent "something like" a billion dollars a year "on tobacco, cosmetics, ice cream, and other non-essentials of that character" and could well afford $20 million to save the lives of children. The agricultural surplus in the United States, he added, had led farmers to feed milk to hogs and burn corn under boilers. The relief program would, at modest cost to taxpayers, convert the surplus to humanitarian use. On December 22, the Senate passed the $20 million relief bill, and President Harding signed it into law the next day.[23]

When the aid bill passed Congress, the ARA issued a press release personally drafted by Hoover guaranteeing Americans that every penny would be used for relief. A special commission, made up of ARA directors and representatives of the farmers, would do all purchasing to assure absolute fairness (it began work on December 23). The ARA would cover, out of its own funds, all administrative costs of the program. Transportation costs within Russia would be borne entirely by the Russian government, which would also contribute $10 million in gold to the program. American ARA officials would control all food distribution.[24]

In Russia, the program expanded rapidly. Beginning in September 1921 with the feeding of only about two hundred children in St. Petersburg, ARA feeding stations served 68,598 in October and by February 1922 were providing meals for more than a million children every month. Fewer than four hundred Americans supervised some eighty thousand local employees who actually ran 15,700 kitchens. In August 1922, the high point of the program, they provided at least one meal a day to 4,173,339 children. In addition, they fed increasing numbers of adults, beginning in November 1921, and peaking in August 1922, when they served 6,317,958 adults as well as the children, for a grand total of more than 10 million people. The program also expanded geographically as the ARA added an area along the Dnieper River in central Ukraine in early 1922 and the Minsk and Crimean regions later that spring. In addition, relief workers distributed more than $10 million worth of food packages paid for by private citizens in the United States and elsewhere. All told, between September 1921 and April 1923 the organization purchased and shipped more than 900,000 tons of food and other supplies, at a total cost of more than $60 million, of which the U.S. government provided slightly less than half, and the Soviet government and various private sources the remainder.[25]

As ARA workers observed conditions in rural Russia, they realized that urgent needs went beyond food. Hence they purchased and distributed nearly $1.5 million worth of clothing, as well as handling more than four hundred tons of clothing donated by private charitable organizations. And, in an effort to improve the health of people who had never had access to modern medicine, the ARA also distributed almost $8 million worth of medicines and medical supplies to more than thirteen thousand hospitals, clinics, schools, and old-age homes and inoculated or vaccinated more than 7 million people against various diseases.[26]

By the late summer of 1922, things were improving in Russia. The drought had broken, and partly as a result of seeds donated by the ARA, the 1922 crop was some 10 million tons larger than that of 1921. Many areas that had produced almost nothing in 1921 were again nearing self-sufficiency. Perhaps more important for the long-run recovery of Russian agriculture was the fact that peasants, who were being driven to the cities by the famine, were able, because of food aid and the adoption of the New Economic Policy, to stay on their land and begin planting again when conditions improved. Without American aid, the disruption of Russian agriculture would have been far greater.[27]

The gradual improvement of conditions in Russia reopened the question of American policy. Hoover addressed the issue in a speech before the International Chamber of Commerce in Washington on May 15, 1922. As a result of the changes during the last year, he noted, some people were once again arguing that diplomatic recognition of the USSR would create great opportunities for trade and investment. But even before the war and the Bolshevik revolution, he pointed out, Russia had taken no more than 1 percent of American exports. The idea that it would now become a large market and a valuable field for investment was an illusion. The Bolsheviks had bankrupted the economy. Mines and factories produced 75 percent less than before the war, the railroads carried less than 7 percent of their prewar freight, agricultural production remained inadequate for domestic consumption, and the Russian government still refused to pay prewar debts to foreign investors. American businessmen would not invest in Russia, he repeated, until assured of "the safety of life, the recognition by firm guarantees of private property, the sanctity of contract, and the rights of free labor." Nothing had changed in the last year, he concluded. Not "moral or political standards" but "hard, cold, economic fact" dictated nonrecognition.[28]

But that did not mean he favored an economic quarantine of the USSR. Like Haskell, James Goodrich, and most of the ARA men in Russia, Hoover favored, when it became politically possible, a limited resumption of trade relations. They all thought, as Goodrich put it, that trade would undercut Soviet leaders' claims that economic ostracism impeded Russia's recovery and believed it would gradually undermine communism. Goodrich even wondered whether President Harding, who had urged American membership in the World Court in the spring of 1923, might take steps toward recognition of the Soviet Union after he returned from his trip to Alaska that summer, but of course, the president's death eliminated that possibility.[29]

In fact, recognition remained unthinkable in 1923. The Red Scare had barely ended, and although Lenin talked about "socialism in one country," many Bolsheviks regarded communism as an "international messianic crusade to liberate the world." In the United States, even the relief program and Hoover's cautious talk about future trade drew criticism. From the left, the *New Republic* charged him with wanting to halt evolutionary change in the Soviet Union and bring about the collapse of the Russian government. More commonly, conservative critics suggested that he secretly hoped to regain his own prewar mining concessions in Russia. Senator Tom Watson of Georgia accused him of taking $10,000 per month for himself from relief funds and of paying large salaries to assistants "who did nothing but ride around in limousines and have a good time." Hoover angrily rejected these and similar charges about the relief program, but he recognized that it had become something of a political liability, and he planned to terminate it as soon as possible. In June 1922, he endorsed a plan by the directors of the U.S. Grain Corporation, a wartime holdover that had done much of the actual purchasing and shipping of relief food, to close down its operations in the expectation that the adult feeding program would end following the autumn harvest. Limited child feeding would continue through the autumn of 1923.[30]

By late 1922, Hoover hoped that his relief obligations were nearly behind him. In Austria, despite continuing problems resulting from the country's limited agricultural resources, the ARA anticipated winding up its operations by November 1. In Poland, an enormous public celebration on October 29 expressed the gratitude of the Polish people to the United States and especially to Hoover. But then new problems arose in Russia.[31]

Although Russian grain production had by no means recovered fully, in November 1922 the Soviet government, desperate for hard currency, proposed to export some $10 to $12 million worth of grain. At the same time, Colonel Haskell reported from Moscow that the number of starving Russians might increase to 8.5 million during the winter. Recognizing that if the Russians started exporting grain, continuation of ARA grain shipments to the country would become politically impossible, Hoover responded to the Russian announcement with a blunt threat to cut off future aid. When the Russians countered with an offer to stop the grain sale in return for a $10 to $12 million American loan, the State Department simply ignored the suggestion.[32] The incident emphasized, if emphasis was needed, that although Hoover had promised to refrain from political intervention in Russia, the Americans could not separate aid completely from politics. How could the ARA meet what they still believed was a huge need in Russia and yet prevent the Soviets from exploiting the program for their own purposes?

Soon after the papers reported that the threat to cut off food relief had not prevented Russian grain sales to Finland, Germany, and Italy, Hoover called a meeting at his S Street house on January 23, 1923. The group included several ARA officials, representatives of the Rockefeller Foundation, and a public relations man, Allen Burns. Burns had planned a national fund-raising campaign for Russian relief, but the group quickly agreed that, with the Russians exporting grain and planning to replace it with American aid, such a campaign would be futile. Nevertheless, Hoover said that despite the exports and the probability of a bumper harvest in Russia that fall, reports from ARA workers on the spot had convinced him that continuation of at least the child-feeding program was essential. It would be impossible, he conceded, to continue feeding adults, but "the problem of children," in his view, was "always separate from all other questions." Given the impossibility of a public appeal, he proposed instead to spend "the resources of the American Relief Administration and of its fully informed supporters on the children of Russia, even in the present situation." The ARA's directors, who did not fully share Hoover's obsession with child welfare, were slow to accept his argument, but more than a month later they authorized him to announce termination of the general relief program and continuation of child feeding.[33]

Constant harassment of the ARA operation by the Russians, including searching ships, delaying or not providing trains, seizing supplies, arresting relief workers, and of course, the foreign grain sales, violated all of their promises in the 1921 Riga agreement. But despite everything, Hoover remained strangely optimistic about the future. Lenin's New Economic Policy, he said in March 1923, had "restored a large measure of individualism and initiative in agriculture, small trades, and small industries" and thus "in some measure restored primary self interest in production." Diplomatic recognition and major foreign investment would be premature prior to the full restoration of capitalism and the transfer of state-owned major industries to private ownership, but in the meantime, continued humanitarian aid to children and medical relief were justified to "lift special groups from utter destitution up to the level of the general poverty and thus to prolong life for the future." Although relief did not guarantee normalization of relations, Hoover viewed it as helping to establish conditions that might transform the Russian government or at least moderate its behavior in the future.[34]

IV

The conclusion of the Russian relief program brought to an end an epoch in Hoover's life. He estimated in 1924 that he had administered, in one fashion or another, the distribution of some $3 billion in American aid to Europe since the commencement of the Belgian relief program in 1914.[35] How many lives his work saved can only be guessed, but certainly 20 million is a modest estimate. In thousands of homes around the world, the descendants of those who survived the aftermath of war and famine because of his relief programs thought of him as the greatest hero of the World War. Not everyone agreed, however. The Soviets accused the ARA of spying and of trying to undermine the communist regime. The French, and others, believed that an American drive to achieve economic and political dominance in the postwar world motivated the relief programs at least as much as humanitarianism.

Hoover's decision to continue child feeding in Russia in 1923 highlights both the major goal of the program and its unintended consequences. From the outset, a principal object of the relief program had been to save a generation of children from starvation and the lingering effects of malnutrition. Rescuing them, Hoover believed, would prevent their "distorted minds" from becoming "a menace to all mankind," and he hoped, moreover, that the "evidence of someone's concern for their children" would lessen the "consuming hates" that burned in the hearts of their parents. As it turned out, the outcome was more ambiguous. The ARA rescued some 9 million children from starvation, but many of their parents did not survive. At the time, some people in the ARA wondered about the ethics of saving children destined to be orphans in a society without resources to care for them. When Colonel Haskell visited Russia in 1925, he saw gangs of those children living on the streets, surviving by begging and stealing. In the Stalinist era, some of them, indoctrinated by the Communist Party, became zealous supporters of the regime.[36] Whether those saved from famine went on to become political zealots, criminals, or valuable members of their societies depended, to a large extent, on what happened to them after the ARA left Russia. For all its virtues, humanitarian relief could only give children the possibility of a brighter future, not guarantee that they would be able to enjoy it and share their good fortune with others.

CHAPTER 10

Hoover and the American Child Health Association

In the years prior to World War I, child health experts became deeply concerned about the high rate of infant mortality in the United States. Since most states did not keep birth records, the figures could only be guesses, but the conservative estimate of the Bureau of the Census in 1911 placed infant deaths at 124 per thousand live births, and many experts believed the figure ran much higher. Virtually all the countries of Western Europe, which did keep accurate statistics, had lower rates. Nor did health problems end with infancy. When the United States entered the war in 1917 and adopted a draft, examining doctors were shocked at the number of draftees who had to be rejected because of physical defects. Apparently, many children who survived infancy had grown up with permanently impaired health.[1]

Concern about infant mortality contributed to the establishment in 1912 of the U.S. Children's Bureau in the Labor Department. Under its first chief, Julia Lathrop, the bureau focused primarily on research and education, but the appointment of the professional social worker Grace Abbott as the bureau's second chief in 1921 gave it a more activist bent. Abbott's appointment coincided with the passage of the Sheppard-Towner Act, which authorized the Children's Bureau to make federal grants to states for prenatal and early infancy care programs, and with rising public concern about the results of the draft physicals. In that context, the Children's Bureau provided a mechanism through which the federal government might take on a greater role in protecting children's health and welfare, but many Americans did not accept that idea. Most Americans took it for granted that parents would look after the health and well-being of their children, even though the evidence suggested that many of them had been doing a poor job. And likewise, most people rejected the idea that government should assume responsibility for child welfare, aside from providing basic education and incarceration for those judged criminal or insane. Insofar as anyone looked after orphaned or grossly neglected children, in most parts of the United States the duty fell to institutions run by churches or charitable groups rather than the state. By the middle of the nineteenth century, most Americans had come to accept protection of public health as a government duty, but few regarded children's health issues as distinct from public health in general. Assuming that everyone wanted children to do well, most reformers merely aspired to teach parents how to do their jobs better and to show local governments how they could help.[2]

I

Hoover's work in feeding and clothing children in Europe naturally brought him to the attention of Americans concerned about child welfare. He accepted the vice presidency of the National Child Welfare Association in 1919, but he felt uncomfortable with that group's emphasis on government welfare programs and the expansion of the powers of the Children's Bureau. The American Child Hygiene Association, which invited him to St. Louis for its annual meeting in October 1920, seemed much more congenial. It had been organized in 1908 by doctors, nurses, and other health professionals and made parental education and the encouragement of local health initiatives its main objectives.[3]

In his speech to the Hygiene Association, Hoover reflected briefly on his relief work in Europe but focused primarily on conditions in the United States and especially on the problems revealed by draft physicals. The examiners, he reminded the audience, had discovered "mental and moral" as well as physical deficiencies in the young men they examined. The "economic and social progress" of the nation, he argued, not only required that basic health care must be available to all children, but it also demanded better schools, safe milk supplies, and elimination of child labor to ensure that every child would have both a "strong physique" and a "sound education and character." Failure to provide adequately for all aspects of children's health constituted "a charge upon the community as a whole and a menace to the community itself."[4]

To improve the situation, Hoover proposed two programs: one for preschool-age children and a second for those between school-entering and adolescence. For preschoolers, he proposed an expansion of community nursing programs and the adoption of compulsory milk sterilization on a national basis. Once children entered school, he recommended that all of them receive at least one nutritious meal a day. Communities should also see to it that, where necessary, parents received professional advice on their children's health and nutrition. In sections of the country where school attendance was not compulsory, it should be made so, and the federal government ought to adopt a constitutional amendment prohibiting child labor. The states that were "so backward in their social development that they will sacrifice their children to industrial advantage," he declared, were "not only unfair to the other States," but were "poisoning the springs of the nation at their source." Newly enfranchised women, he hoped, would push reforms, but he did not believe progress would be quick or automatic. In the end, he said, "child development still rests with parents, and parents need much bringing up." Governments, from the federal down to the local, could do some things, but it would require the "day to day, disinterested, voluntary devotion" of organizations like the Child Hygiene Association to build public support for change.[5]

Hoover's ideas about voluntary organization, action at the local level, and education as the methods for improving child welfare offered an alternative to the federalized approach of the Children's Bureau. Local governments, he argued, should undertake the upgrading of health services and schools, with the help and support of volunteer organizations. The role of government above the local level should be primarily educational. The evil of child labor resulted not from racial discrimination and poverty, he thought, but from mistaken priorities of local leaders and could be corrected mainly by educating them. He applauded the Sheppard-Towner Act's goal of improving prenatal and maternal care but remained dubious about the role to be played by the federal Children's Bureau in administering the program.[6]

Hoover's speech to the Child Hygiene Association received an enthusiastic reception, and the board of directors unanimously invited him to become president-elect of the organization. He accepted, but as he perused the minutes of the executive committee and board of directors meetings, he concluded that the organization exemplified the weaknesses of the child welfare movement in general. As one of about sixty uncoordinated organizations in the field, the Association's 1,720 members had little chance of achieving anything substantive.[7] Hoover's European experience had proved to him the advantages of unified action through a single organization, and he saw a similar situation in the American child welfare problem. The leaders of the Child Hygiene Association were attracted to him by his support of local initiatives and voluntarism, but paradoxically, he would give them a centralized, hierarchical organization to promote those goals.

Hoover's observation of the operations of the association during early 1921 confirmed his judgment about its ineffectiveness. It committed more than half of its annual budget of $63,750 to administrative expenses and spent much of the rest on "field visits" to various organizations by the field director, Harriet Leete. The vague purposes of these visits ("to feel . . . the vital pulse of Child Welfare interests," "to obtain information for the . . . Association," and "to interest new members in the activities of the . . . Association") promised little action. The only tangible recommendations made by Miss Leete in a report to the board of directors in May 1921 were to organize a series of training clinics for community nurses and to consult further with other national organizations "in connection with special group plans."[8]

Impatient with this ineffectual approach, Hoover wrote in June to the well-known Denver reformer, Judge Ben B. Lindsay, about organizing a national child welfare conference. He meant to use the gathering to unite as many child-oriented organizations as possible into an effective and visible national movement. Because of the national economic crisis and the unemployment conference, however, the proposed meeting never took place, and Hoover even found it impossible to attend the Child Hygiene Association convention in November at which he was officially confirmed as president. But that did not mean he had lost interest. Behind the scenes, he approached both the Rockefeller and Commonwealth funds with a proposal to more than double the organization's budget to $150,000 a year. Both foundations responded favorably, but the officers of the Hygiene Association seemed overwhelmed by the opportunity he offered. Dr. Philip Van Ingen, chairman of the executive committee, suggested that they ask for only $100,000, to be paid not all in one year but over the next three years. That approach, Van Ingen argued, would permit the organization to plan and expand its staff and programs gradually.[9]

II

Dismayed by the timidity and lack of imagination of Van Ingen and his associates, Hoover plotted a quiet revolution. If they would not seize the opportunity he offered them, he would find others who could share his vision. He moved the organization's headquarters from Baltimore to Washington and began holding executive committee meetings in his Commerce Department office. At the May 4 meeting, he cut short a tedious report on the program for the next annual meeting and instead opened a discussion of "closer cooperation with other child health organizations." He described the recent formation of the National Child Health Council, a loose confederation of half a dozen organizations, as a good first step, but real progress depended, he argued, on "a closer and more satisfactory arrangement."[10]

As a further step toward the larger and more comprehensive organization he envisioned, Hoover proposed that the Child Hygiene Association merge with the Child Health Organization of America. Since the Child Health Organization stressed health education for school-age children and the Hygiene Association had focused on preschool children, everyone quickly recognized the logic of combination. By the end of June, both were ready to merge. The only resistance came from Sally Lucas Jean, director of the Child Health Organization, who objected to the centralization of authority implied by the merger. Like many of the other social workers and medical professionals involved with children's welfare organizations, Miss Jean, a registered nurse, had been accustomed to setting her own agenda. The prospect that she would be reduced to an employee of an organization where others determined priorities threatened her sense of professionalism and autonomy. Nevertheless, the directors of the two organizations agreed by the beginning of July to proceed. At the annual meeting of the Child Hygiene Association on October 13, Hoover announced that the new organization, to be called the American Child Health Association (ACHA), would receive major support for the next five years from the Commonwealth Fund. He would become its first president.[11]

Hoover explained his plans for the ACHA in a pair of speeches. At the National Conference of Social Work in Providence, Rhode Island, on June 27, he focused on the prohibition of child labor. "The moral and economic results of debilitated, illiterate, and untrained manhood and womanhood that must spring from these cesspools where child labor is encouraged and is legitimate, infect the entire nation," he declared. Legislation having failed to abolish this great evil, Hoover set aside his preference for local and voluntary action and urged the adoption of a federal constitutional amendment.[12]

His presidential address to the ACHA on October 12, 1922, emphasized a second priority. The merger, said Hoover, aimed to ensure "that the enormous activity in America for the welfare of children and mothers shall be directed in a scientific manner and by scientifically trained men and women." To that end, the ACHA would focus on providing expert advice and education to community organizations. He proposed to launch that approach dramatically by having the organization provide $300,000 to each of three American cities—one in the Midwest, one in the West, and one in the South—to develop model programs of "health instruction and help."[13]

Two weeks later, the full dimensions of his plans began to emerge. Not only did he intend to replace individual projects planned and implemented by social workers and doctors with a single, centrally planned national project, but he also envisioned the replacement of current staff members by professional administrators. The American Relief Administration (ARA), now winding up its work in Russia, would "take over the organization and inauguration of a membership campaign for the Child Health." The phrase "take over" would have chilled the hearts of those who controlled the old organization had they heard it. In public, Hoover simply announced that the ARA would put its experience with European relief at the disposal of the new organization. Actually, he intended not only to impose the centralized structure characteristic of the ARA on the ACHA but also to move ARA personnel into direct control in the new organization. The principal agents of his plan were Edgar Rickard, his closest friend and associate in the Food Administration and ARA; George Barr Baker, a journalist and former aide in the postwar relief program; and Frank Page, son of the publisher and former ambassador to Great Britain, Walter Hines Page. Under the guidance of these Hoover lieutenants, the ACHA would become essentially a division of the ARA.[14]

For the doctors, nurses, and social workers who had previously controlled the child welfare organizations, the ARA takeover represented both a loss of personal autonomy and an assault on their status in a nation where prestige increasingly depended on professional credentials. They were as proud of their standing as medical and social work professionals as Hoover was of his as an engineer. Soothing statements from the ARA men that nothing would change except that they would now have more time and resources for their work did not reassure them.[15]

From the ARA's standpoint, the situation proved equally frustrating. Initially, the ARA men thought they would merely conduct the national fundraising and membership drives that Hoover had proposed, but they soon found themselves being pulled in more deeply. They discovered that the ACHA's officers had never run a major fund-raising drive and had no idea of how to set one up, nor did they know how to manage a budget of hundreds of thousands of dollars. The ARA staff, Walter Lyman Brown told Hoover, were "all enthusiastic in regard [to] cooperation" but were reluctant to commit themselves fully unless Hoover intended to "control [the] administration of this association under [the] ARA."[16]

Well aware of the professionals' sensitivities, Hoover preferred not to show his hand directly. Instead, he told Dr. Van Ingen that the Rockefeller Foundation was very interested in providing major funding for the new organization but was concerned that "our [sic] organization is composed entirely of professional people, and that it does not possess a contingent of highly experienced business administrators." Accordingly, said Hoover, he felt compelled "to include in the executive committee some men of an actual business type." He pigeonholed a press release drafted by Van Ingen announcing that new administrative personnel would be hired and new organization implemented "only after experience has shown where improvement can be made."[17] He had no interest in gradualism.

As the date for the merger of the two organizations approached, the leaders of the Child Health Organization began to have misgivings. On December 26, its president, Dr. L. Emmett Holt, telephoned the ARA's George Barr Baker to ask for a meeting the next day at his Washington home. Attendees included Baker, on behalf of Hoover and the ARA; Courtenay Dinwiddie, the general executive of the new ACHA; Holt; and Child Health Organization Director Sally Jean. The meeting might have turned out awkwardly for Baker, but in the event Sally Jean proved an unwitting ally. She so vehemently attacked the new organization's threat to her personal standing that the men present, embarrassed by her outburst, felt that siding with her would make them seem equally insecure and irrational. United in masculine solidarity, they followed Baker and silently acquiesced in the ARA takeover. It proved a crucial moment for Hoover's control of the new organization.[18]

Nevertheless, the struggle continued as the merger proceeded in January 1923. The conflicts turned on budget and organization. Early in January, the Budget Committee met in Edgar Rickard's office, with ARA men Rickard, Edward Flesh, and Frank Page present in addition to four ACHA members (but not Sally Jean). The ARA men temporarily disarmed the others by emphasizing that they intended to leave the definition of mission to the ACHA experts, but they criticized the proposed budget, which they said allotted too much for administration. They predicted that the Rockefeller Foundation would not make a major contribution unless reassured that its money would be used efficiently. The point was obvious: the ARA's control of the money would give it a major voice in future decisions.[19]

Behind the budget issue lurked another touchy question. All the professionals were beginning to realize, at some level, that they were losing power in the new organization. As that reality sank in, minor issues acquired sudden importance, Holt and Van Ingen, former officers of the Child Hygiene Association, warned that "the rather difficult Miss Jean" and other former members of the Child Health organization might control the ACHA if its headquarters was established in New York, perhaps in the old Child Health offices on Seventh Avenue. Frank Page understood perfectly well that neither the Child Hygiene nor the Child Health people were going to control the new organization, and the dispute offered a chance to play them off against each other. He suggested that the ACHA's national headquarters remain in Washington, and that Courtenay Dinwiddie set up an executive office in New York somewhere between the ARA headquarters at 42 Wall Street and the existing Child Hygiene and Child Health offices. That arrangement, Page explained to Hoover, would allow Sally Jean to "run her little show up at 370 7th Ave . . . until she realizes that it is a whole lot better to play in with the family rather than to try to run it on her own hook."[20] Although he did not say it, the same was also true of the Child Health group. By giving everyone a separate office, Page maintained the fiction of autonomy but in practice tightened ARA control over the ACHA.

In February 1923, another phase in the ARA takeover began with a memo from George Barr Baker to ARA leaders. One of the most important projects the new organization could undertake, Baker suggested, would be a national educational campaign, including syndicated columns, articles for magazines and weeklies, and a regular series of "health hints" for daily papers. But such a campaign, Baker thought, was "beyond the capacity" of the existing organization and "so new to them . . . as to be beyond their present vision." For the ARA, on the other hand, the project offered a wonderful challenge, "the greatest and most popular that we have ever attempted."[21] It also provided an opportunity for the ARA to further extend its dominance of the ACHA.

Baker's memorandum made it clear that, despite previous assurances that the ARA would confine itself to raising money to finance projects planned and controlled by the ACHA professionals, the ARA expected to control the organization completely. Two weeks later, in a second memo, Page extended the takeover, setting out a plan for ACHA development far different from the programs previously followed by either the Child Hygiene Association or Child Health Organization and relegating the experts to the status of employees. As Page envisioned it, the ACHA would no longer solicit individual memberships but rather become a confederation of "groups, states, cities, towns and various other national organizations," in which the child welfare experts would become merely "special technical people" to advise other organizations on achieving the goals set by the ACHA's directors. Hoover was even more blunt. In a set of "Organization Principles" he outlined to the ACHA in a meeting early in April, he declared that "all staff members shall be assignable by the General Executive to whatever duties may seem most urgent, unless otherwise specified by the Executive Committee." To forestall rebellions against this policy, Edgar Rickard recommended that Hoover, Baker, Flesh, and he "make it a rule to act in unison" and not respond individually to policy inquiries from staff members.[22]

Fund-raising difficulties got the new organization off to a slow start. Hoover circulated a letter on March 1, 1923, to 150,000 people who had previously contributed to the ARA's relief programs, but the results were disappointing. He estimated the new organization needed $400,000 to finance its program and hoped to raise half of that from major foundation grants, with the rest coming from private contributions. The first month of the public drive, however, brought in $50,000 from the Commonwealth Fund, but only $11,978.25 from the general public. The failure particularly disappointed Hoover because the Rockefeller Foundation had conditioned a $100,000 grant on the ACHA raising $300,000 from other sources. Fortunately, he secured new contributions from the Red Cross and the Commonwealth Fund that offset the lack of private donations. By the beginning of June, the ACHA could count on having a budget of $425,000.[23] Since Hoover had raised most of the funding personally, he further solidified his control over the organization, but the lack of broad public support for a group that emphasized grassroots voluntarism raised serious questions about its future.

By May, the transformation of the ACHA had alienated many of its professionals. The first to depart was Harriet Leete, the field director of the old Child Hygiene Association. Prior to amalgamation, she had served as the organization's public face, traveling extensively to present lectures and demonstrations and to consult with local child welfare organizations. In that role, she had enormous autonomy, but under the new organizational structure, she became merely a "staff member." The ACHA, she wrote in her letter of resignation to Courtenay Dinwiddie, might do great work, but it had no role for her as an independent child welfare professional.[24] What Leete did not say—perhaps did not fully realize—was that the ACHA was adopting a very different role from the old Child Hygiene Association. The CHA's role had been to advise existing local health professionals and organizations. The ACHA was moving toward developing its own program and then creating or recruiting local organizations to carry it out if they did not already exist.

The person chosen to succeed Leete symbolized the new direction. Hoover recommended Amy Pryor Tapping, whom he had met just after the war while she was working for the Young Women's Christian Association in Poland. Although Tapping had no professional training in child welfare or public health, Hoover considered that unimportant. She was, he thought, "an ideal person for the Child Health Association to take on their local organization work." He was "thoroughly disgusted" when the organization failed to hire her immediately and, at an Executive Committee meeting, declared "that there was to be no temporizing in the matter of engaging" her. Dinwiddie was to be "instructed to do so at once." Brought face-to-face with the reality of Hoover's authority, the Executive Committee gave in. Sent to Georgia and Florida, Tapping proved a talented agent of the ACHA's new program, putting together community organizations that worked effectively with public health officials in various child welfare programs—exactly the sort of local organizing that Hoover had envisioned as a major function of the ACHA. When, in 1925, budget pressures led the ACHA to discuss cutting some staff members, Hoover made sure Tapping stayed.[25]

Sally Jean presented greater difficulties. She had not, as Baker hoped, relinquished her offices on Seventh Avenue and subordinated herself to the ACHA. Instead, she maintained her physical distance and fought stubbornly to control the full budget of her Health Education Division, including the power to choose her own staff. Since health education was a primary function of the overall organization, she remained a major thorn in the side of the ARA administrators. Frank Page lamented that she was "altogether too much in the minds of everybody," admitting that "every time we make a move, we wonder what effect it will have on Miss Jean and what effect Miss Jean will have on it."[26]

The matter came to a head in June 1923 when Jean submitted a formal demand to the ACHA executive committee that the Health Education Division be given "a budget necessary for its effective autonomous functioning." Hoover and Rickard muttered that perhaps they should "chuck the whole business and let them worry out their own troubles," but Courtenay Dinwiddie's assistant, Ella Phillips Crandall, found a way out of the dilemma. When Sally Jean left for a vacation, Crandall suggested that the executive committee simply ignore her demand for autonomy and give her division a modest budget for the rest of the year. At the next executive committee meeting, Edgar Rickard secured the adoption of a resolution stating that budgetary uncertainties made it impossible to give any division a fixed budget. Each division would be free to propose new projects, which the executive committee would evaluate within the ACHA's overall goals.[27]

In fact, the issue had become largely moot, because Hoover had decided to take the organization in an entirely different direction. In his inaugural address in October 1922, he had suggested $300,000 grants to each of three cities for studies of child welfare needs. Given the budget constraints and organizational struggles of succeeding months, that idea had been set aside, and the ACHA had gone back to distributing information to local governments and private organizations. In May 1923, however, Frank Page pointed out that no one really knew whether such material was having any impact at the local level. That struck a responsive chord with Hoover. At the June 14 executive committee meeting, he suggested that the time had come to organize a self-study by towns and counties about their situations and to begin offering them guidance on making use of available information.[28] His proposal went far beyond the mere distribution of information and was much more ambitious than anything the Educational Division had hitherto attempted. If adopted, it would require a commitment of the whole organization's resources.

Such a large undertaking seemed, however, beyond the capacity of the ACHA executive officer, Courtenay Dinwiddie, to organize and run—and no one even suggested putting Sally Jean in charge of it. Once again, Hoover and Rickard turned to the ARA for help. Lt. Col. Henry Beeuwkes, an army public health physician, had worked for the ARA in Europe and Russia and seemed an ideal choice to succeed Dinwiddie. But Beeuwkes was still on active duty and had been invited by the Rockefeller Foundation to conduct a study on yellow fever, so he was unavailable for the executive directorship. The War Department agreed, however, to loan him to the ACHA for a few months to study "the whole field of child health work" and suggest future activities. The study, Hoover told Dinwiddie vaguely, would provide "a comprehensive picture of the entire problem and the directions in which effective results can be obtained."[29]

Meanwhile, Hoover and his associates in the ARA quietly transformed that organization from an international aid agency into the ARA Children's Fund. Its new function was to use the leftover funds from European relief ($4.1 million) to "promote the health, education, and well-being of children throughout the world, and particularly in the United States."[30] Although the articles of incorporation theoretically limited how money could be spent, in practice the foundation became Hoover's to use as he thought best. It gave him a reliable source of money through which he could further tighten his control over the ACHA. During 1924, the Children's Fund contributed $230,000 of its total income of $309,000 to the support of the ACHA, accounting for nearly half of that organization's total budget.[31]

After consultations with the ACHA's professional staff, Beeuwkes set out in September 1923 to develop "a scale, by which the status of conditions affecting child health in any community may be measured" and which, after being tried out in "one or two communities," could be applied nationally. The scale, Beeuwkes promised, would furnish the ACHA "with a clear-cut objective" and would lay the basis for "a balanced program of useful work." Although not an avowed goal, his project would also perfect ARA control over the ACHA. A few months earlier, that might have led to a major confrontation with the child welfare professionals, but Beeuwkes shrewdly invited the professionals to participate in designing his study. His vague phrase, "a balanced program of useful work," disguised the extent to which Hoover intended to change the ACHA's role from providing expert advice to existing local health officers to creating a structure that would carry out a program determined by the national organization. Pleased that Beeuwkes solicited their advice on the specifics of the study, the staff overlooked the important change in philosophy that accompanied it. Only Sally Jean objected to the study, and her protests were easily dismissed as sour grapes because her Educational Division was being bypassed.[32]

Despite this impression of unity, Page remained concerned about Courtenay Dinwiddie. Child welfare experts respected him, but he was "extremely weak" as a business manager and seemingly incapable of explaining the technical aspects of the ACHA's work to nonspecialists. If he remained in office, Page predicted, the organization would have trouble carrying out Beeuwkes's proposed program.[33]

In his presidential address to the ACHA meeting in Detroit in October 1923, Hoover focused on the new program for "the systematic determination of the shortcomings in child health protection, community by community, and the demonstration of remedy." He expressed confidence that when problems had been identified scientifically and remedies suggested, Americans would pitch in voluntarily to improve conditions. Government action would play a part in the solutions, but "the local community is the unit of responsibility in American public life." Once the ACHA identified problems and proposed a program to solve them, implementation would be up to public and private agencies at the local level.[34] Having changed the ACHA's loose, decentralized organization into a hierarchical, corporate structure, he now proposed to do much the same thing with the country's public health programs. Like the simplification and standardization program being pushed by the Commerce Department, Hoover's ACHA program was far less empowering to local organizations than he claimed.

Within the ACHA, the question of who would control the organization's agenda had not yet been settled completely. In a last-ditch defense of their authority, the doctors, nurses, and social workers contended that they must control the organization's program because their work was too technical to be understood by laymen. The ARA men dismissed that argument out of hand. The so-called experts, sneered Edgar Rickard, could not even prepare and follow an agenda for a meeting, let alone plan and carry out a national program. By December, Hoover and his ARA lieutenants were bypassing the ACHA staff entirely in planning for the coming year, a tendency that increased when they discovered that the association had overspent its budget in the last months of 1923. Hoover immediately ordered a layoff of office staff, closed the Washington headquarters, and cut the number and activities of the technical staff. Page said pointedly that he could not understand how "the general executive [Dinwiddie] of any organization" could permit such a situation to develop.[35]

In late November, Beeuwkes completed the development of his scale to measure child health in local communities and began testing it in Chattanooga, Tennessee; McKeesport, Pennsylvania; and East Orange, New Jersey. Satisfied with the scale's effectiveness, Hoover proposed to apply it in eighty-six medium-sized cities with populations between forty thousand and seventy thousand. Since another private organization, the American Public Health Association, and a federal agency, the United States Public Health Service, had already undertaken similar work in larger cities, it seemed likely that a reasonably full picture of children's health and the conditions affecting it would soon be available. Secretary of the Treasury Andrew Mellon rejected a last-minute claim from the surgeon general that the Public Health Service should have exclusive jurisdiction over such work when Hoover pointed out that letting the ACHA do it would save the government approximately $300,000.[36]

When, in the spring of 1924, the ACHA's executive committee agreed to implement the Beeuwkes scale in the eighty-six cities, Sally Jean finally realized that any hope of restoring her old authority was gone. The executive committee's announcement of a new rule specifying that "no division shall initiate policies or projects without consultation with the Director and if necessary with the Staff Council" was the last straw. She and several of her associates submitted their resignations, which were accepted at the April 24 meeting.[37]

Everyone in the ACHA and the ARA had found Jean difficult, and probably none of them was sorry to see her go. Her prickly insistence on her autonomy raised sensitive issues about masculine authority as well as questions about policy. But at the same time, she spoke for all the professional staff when she insisted that they, not the outsiders from the ARA, should set the organization's course. When she resigned, the last embers of rebellion within the ACHA flickered out. Henceforth, for better or worse, the organization would follow "Mr. Hoover's program."[38]

Yet, despite his control over the program, Hoover found the day-to-day operations of the organization maddeningly chaotic. He installed his ARA colleague, Edward Flesh, as treasurer to rein in overspending, but Flesh reported that the executive committee continued to authorize expenditures without regard to his advice. Frustrated, Flesh resigned and suggested that Hoover do likewise. When the executive committee asked him to take a second term as president, Hoover drafted a petulant letter declining but then decided not to send it. Instead, he said he would agree to serve, provided the executive committee would give him final authority over programs and budget, leaving the committee with no function other than fund-raising.[39]

On October 30, 1924, the issue of control arose in an executive committee discussion of the budget for the coming year. Committee members instructed Executive Director Dinwiddie to prepare a budget not to exceed $400,000, but he refused. He would prepare a budget on the basis of the needs of the various divisions, he said, and he would expect the executive committee to support it. Behind his position, of course, was the old belief of the professionals that they, not the administrators, should determine the organization's program. Dinwiddie had not yet grasped that the professionals had already lost that issue, and moreover, he stated his argument poorly. The physicians—also professionals—who dominated the committee heard only a challenge to their authority and failed to recognize the broader issue. The staff, they informed Dinwiddie, were "paid employees" who "could not, in the greatest stretch of imagination, consider themselves as dominating the policy of the organization." One committee member added bluntly that if Dinwiddie "had any sense he would offer his resignation to take place, not in a few months from now or even in a few weeks, but immediately."[40]

In December, after the board reaffirmed its determination to set the budget, Dinwiddie did resign. In his place, Hoover named Dr. S. J. Crumbine executive director. A former dean of the medical school at the University of Kansas, Crumbine had served most recently as the principal liaison between the ACHA and public health officers in the eighty-six cities. He quickly understood that "any 'suggestion'" from the Chief was "a positive order." Edward Flesh, who had resigned as treasurer in the fall when expenditures seemed to spin out of control, returned at Hoover's request. When the executive committee threatened to challenge his authority, Hoover ignored the association's bylaws, which required the committee to meet monthly, and stopped calling meetings. Edgar Rickard announced that with the survey of eighty-six cities nearly complete, the organization's operating expenses, which had approached $600,000 by the end of 1924, would be cut back to about $400,000 for 1925, and new projects "limited to objectives which seem[ed] most vital and which [could] be accomplished with a largely reduced expenditure."[41]

The public health survey in the eighty-six cities was completed during the spring of 1925 and published in May. As Hoover had anticipated, it revealed serious deficiencies and unevenness in the nation's health system. Many cities had no facilities for the treatment of tuberculosis, and a surprisingly large number offered no smallpox vaccinations, although that method of prevention had been known since the eighteenth century. Half of the cities had done nothing to eliminate diphtheria. Public water supplies remained unreliable. Almost half had no full-time public health officer or prenatal clinic, and many others had no boards of health and public nursing programs. A fifth of the cities surveyed still did not keep birth records, and less than a quarter of them pasteurized at least 90 percent of their milk. A fifth of eleven-year-olds drank no milk at all. Although conditions had improved since before the war, the study found, and city dwellers were now slightly healthier than their country cousins, the United States still lagged behind many other countries in nearly every category of public health, and programs for children's health were particularly weak.[42]

Hoover hoped that publication of the report would inspire lagging cities to upgrade their services voluntarily, but he did not intend to stand back and leave improvement to local officials. At his request, President Coolidge declared that May Day would be dedicated to calling the public's attention to the situation, and the ACHA set out to organize programs across the country to achieve that goal. It launched national campaigns to promote clean milk, birth registration in all states, the recognition of May Day as "Child Health Day," and a training program for health education teachers. A major two-year survey of school health programs attempted to determine what health education methods worked best. In Georgia, Amy Tapping worked with the state board of health, the state council of social agencies, and the governor's wife to expand a state preschool child care program into every county. Elsewhere, local health programs promoted by the ACHA also seem to have had some success, although evidence is sketchy.[43]

Despite the publication of the eighty-six-city survey and various follow-up activities, the ACHA seemed to suffer a letdown in late 1925. The directors of the Rockefeller Fund, perhaps sensing some loss of direction, provided a small grant but made it clear that they would not commit themselves to long-term support. Hoover secured a $300,000 grant to cover most of the ACHA's 1926 budget from the ARA Children's Fund, but some of that fund's directors were becoming a little restive. Much as they applauded the work of the ACHA, Lou Hoover and Julius Barnes would have liked to have more money available to support the Girl Scouts, whose presidency Lou had assumed in January 1922.[44]

In his annual address to the ACHA national meeting in May 1926 and again a week later in a speech to ten thousand child health professionals gathered at an "American Health Congress" of sixteen organizations, Hoover proposed a new challenge. During the seven years of his wartime and postwar relief work, he said, he had labored to help "subnormal children, the toll of orphanage, famine and destitution," and to "rebuild these children up to an ideal of 'normal.'" Americans must remain committed to "pulling up the sub-normals on a nation-wide scale." But, he continued, the experts had never provided a clear definition of what a "normal child" was, nor explained exactly what communities needed to do to assure that as many children as possible reached that standard. It would be nice to have "perfect children," but that was probably "asking too much." Instead, he challenged the organization's experts to "make it clear to Mrs. Jones and Mrs. Smith how they can make their Mary and their John approximate that normal child." They needed to define "what the factors are which contribute to the development of the healthy body, the healthy mind, the healthy social organism, and we should have those factors stated in positive rather than in negative terms of safeguards." The ideal, he said, should be "not only a child free from disease" but also "a child made free to develop to the utmost his capacity for physical, social and mental health." To that end, the physical needs of children must be guaranteed, and in addition, their "emotional needs" must be met: "the need for wise love and understanding, for protection against such psychic blights as fear, and the abuse of primitive emotions such as anger."[45]

In speaking of a "normal child," Hoover assumed that "normality" could be measured scientifically, a view that reflected the influence of the early twentieth-century eugenics movement in the United States. Coined in 1883 by Charles Darwin's cousin, Sir Francis Galton, the term eugenics referred specifically to "the science of improving stock," which, "in the case of man, takes cognisance of all influences that tend in however remote a degree to give to the more suit-able races or strains of blood a better chance of prevailing speedily over the less suitable." Social eugenicists, like social Darwinists, believed that scientists could control the forces that shaped the intelligence, character, and behavior of humans in ways that would produce what they regarded as superior people. At the extreme, they assumed that "everything from intellect to sexuality to poverty to crime was attributable to heredity" and accordingly advocated the sterilization or even euthanasia of people regarded as defective or inferior in order to improve the race.[46]

Hoover never went nearly that far, but he did draw a distinction between "abnormal" and "subnormal" children. He believed that abnormal children's problems, whether physical or mental, resulted from heredity. Society owed them kindness and help, but they could never become "normal." The prob-lems of the subnormal child, on the other hand, resulted from malnutrition, disease, and poor education. With proper food, medicine, and care, subnor-mal children could be returned to normality, just as he had seen the children of Eastern Europe swing from lethargy to animation under the care of the ARA. "The breeding ground of the gangster," he said in his May 1926 ACHA speech, "is the over-crowded tenement and subnormal childhood. The anti-dotes are light and air, food and organized play. The community nurse and the community safeguard to health will succeed far better than a thousand police-men." Like many members of the American medical profession, Hoover thus identified environmental conditions as causes of subnormality, yet he main-tained that such problems could be eliminated solely by education and vol-untary community activism. Neither he nor the physicians who agreed with him regarded poverty, racism, unemployment, slums, and the exploitation of women in industry as fundamental causes of subnormality that needed to be addressed by the government. He remained entirely confident that, given the sort of information and guidance provided by the ACHA, parents, schools, and local organizations would voluntarily take the steps necessary to lift all subnormal children up to normality. The ACHA, proudly proclaimed a 1927 report, had "pricked public conscience to demand more effective health pro-tection for children."[47]

The insistence by Hoover and other child health advocates on local volun-tarism to carry out their ideas reflected a widespread belief among reformers that the family, not just the child, provided the key to improvement. "Igno-rance on the part of mothers is often at the bottom of the evil," wrote one English child health advocate, and American reformers shared that opinion. It followed, therefore, that community organizations that educated the family provided the surest route to improvement for children. It would require a sea change in attitudes before the idea that government had a direct responsibility for children's welfare became widely accepted.[48]

By 1927, the ACHA had been increasingly absorbed into the ARA Children's Fund, a fact tacitly recognized by the election of three ACHA stalwarts, S. J. Crumbine, Samuel M. Hamill, and Philip Van Ingen, to the board of directors of the Children's Fund, and by Edgar Rickard's frank statement that the financial support of the ACHA "rested almost entirely on the A.R.A. Children's Fund." In recognition of this obligation, at the February 12 annual meeting of the Children's Fund, the members voted to invade capital if income proved inadequate to fund the ACHA's activities.[49]

III

Hoover's personal role in the ACHA dwindled in 1927 and thereafter. His Mississippi River flood relief work kept him away from the organization's May 1927 meeting, and the presidential campaign prevented him from attending the 1928 meeting as well. Without his personal engagement, the ACHA budget for 1927 shrank to $276,000, not all of which was spent, although the organization did spend an extra $62,000 provided by the Children's Fund to complete the school health study. Other projects for that year were a continuation of the "Clean and Safe Milk Campaign," the promotion, on behalf of the Conference of State and Provincial Health Authorities, of a North American program to suppress diphtheria, typhoid fever, and smallpox; the support of the annual "May Day–National Child Health Day"; and writing and placement of articles on child health in newspapers and magazines.[50]

By 1929, although Hoover remained honorary president, his personal connection to the ACHA had largely ended, and active leadership passed to Secretary of the Interior Ray Lyman Wilbur. Under Dr. Wilbur, the organization became mainly an advisory body on issues involving children's and public health—activities not dissimilar, although at a higher professional level, to those of the old Child Hygiene Association prior to its merger with the Child Health Organization to form the ACHA. In 1931, the ARA Children's Fund, which was nearing the end of its resources, provided a final grant of $650,000 to support the organization for three years at its current budget level. At the same time, Hoover, beginning what he realized would be a difficult reelection campaign, decided that the time had at last come to sever his official connection with the ACHA and resigned as honorary president. In 1935, with the depression continuing, the directors recognized that they had little hope of replacing ARA support and voted to terminate the ACHA. "The work was by no means finished," wrote Will Irwin sadly, but there was no way to continue it under the circumstances.[51]

During Hoover's last year as honorary president, the ACHA played a major part in organizing the 1930 White House Conference on Child Health.

Announced by Hoover in July 1929, the conference attempted a comprehensive report on children's health and what needed to be done to improve it. For the next sixteen months, the ACHA led seventeen committees and 140 subcommittees in studying issues ranging from prenatal care to physical and mental handicaps and juvenile delinquency, and in November 1930, more than two thousand people, including child health experts and representatives of state and local governments, gathered in Washington. Many of the committee reports included valuable and important information that eventually appeared in a thirty-volume series, although some committees did not complete their reports in advance of the meeting, and those that did sent them out no more than two weeks in advance. In any case, the sheer volume of material and tight control by the organizers prevented much serious discussion at the meeting.[52]

In his speech opening the conference on November 19, Hoover stated explicitly the assumption that had guided the organizers: "The ill-nourished child is in our country not the product of poverty; it is largely the product of ill-instructed children and ignorant parents." By 1930, many scientists, social workers, and child health experts were questioning that belief, but no hint of their doubts appeared in the committee reports or official statements from the conference. Some delegates tried to gain a hearing for the theory that "great social and economic fundamentals" were major causes of children's problems and required federal action, but Hoover's hand-picked committee chairmen made sure that all such "controversial issues of a disruptive nature" were omitted from the conference report. Following the conference's adjournment, the ACHA undertook follow-up work, including circulation of pamphlets and the preparation of articles for newspapers and magazines. But the assumption of the organizers that, once they made information available, it was the responsibility of local organizations to implement it and their unwillingness to consider any federal responsibility for dealing with such environmental problems as unemployment and inadequate housing, despite the ravages of the depression, limited the conference's long-term influence. In the opinion of one critical observer, the labor of four thousand people had "brought forth a mouse."[53]

The ACHA played an important part, along with many other child welfare organizations, in a dramatic improvement in public health, and children's health in particular, during the 1920s. Infant mortality fell to fifty-eight per thousand births by 1933, tuberculosis and diphtheria were largely eliminated, public health offices were established in all states and many cities, health education became part of most school curriculums, and physicians and public health authorities learned to work together more effectively. Hoover and his colleagues in the ACHA had every reason to be proud of their achievements. But much remained to be done, as the 1930 White House conference made clear, and as Hoover's Commission on Recent Social Trends confirmed in 1933.[54]

Hoover's own role in the ACHA was not only important but also revealing of the limitations of his leadership. Certainly there can be no doubt about his personal commitment to the cause of child welfare. From the beginning of his European relief work to the end of his life, there was no issue to which he devoted a greater part of his energy and thought. In the case of the ACHA, he transformed a well-meaning but largely ineffectual amateur organization into a professionally managed, well-financed, and dynamic body that undertook studies of conditions and launched initiatives to improve them in ways that had national significance.

But there are also aspects of the ACHA story that suggest important but unattractive aspects of Hoover's personality and methods. His ruthless demotion of the health and social work professionals who had previously run the organization, for example, demonstrated considerable insensitivity. He was correct, of course, about their administrative ineptitude. A charitable organization that spends half or more of its budget on administration is badly run, and one that consistently overspends its budget will not survive long. Nor had the Child Hygiene Association had much impact before Hoover took over its presidency. He was right to demand improvements in those areas, but the training and experience of the professionals merited greater respect and attention in regard to programming than he gave them. Although he evinced a mastery of bureaucratic infighting in capturing control of the organization, he also displayed an arrogant disregard for the judgment and advice of the professionals on substance as well as administration. As the case of Sally Jean demonstrated, bringing them into planning as equals would have been difficult, yet when he failed to do so, some of them resigned, and those who stayed on seem to have lost much of their energy and commitment. The rapid decline of the organization after Hoover stepped down from its active leadership was not attributable merely to the effect of the depression. The structure he created was effective, but it depended far too much on his personal involvement and leadership, as was the case with some of his other initiatives in other fields, such as the Commerce Department's standardization campaign.

A contradiction also existed between Hoover's stated goals and the methods he employed to implement them. He intended to secure reform through the work of voluntary organizations and local governments. Within the ACHA, however, he replaced decentralized initiatives with a hierarchical structure and centralized planning, which he dominated personally. Then, with a predetermined program in hand, he dispatched ACHA agents to create local groups that would carry it out. Given those methods, voluntarism and local initiatives existed more in rhetoric than reality.

Hoover's constant talk about voluntarism and local initiatives created a somewhat false impression of the differences between his approach and that espoused by supporters of the Children's Bureau. The difference was less between a decentralized, voluntary, educational campaign to improve child welfare and one mandated by the federal government than between a national program controlled by Hoover through the ACHA and an equally national one controlled by Grace Abbott and her allies through the Children's Bureau. But the conflict between Abbott and Hoover was more than merely personal.

At bottom, it turned on a disagreement over whether childhood problems resulted primarily from the ignorance of parents and local officials or from poverty, racism, and other environmental factors over which families and local governments had little or no control. In 1930, Hoover seemed to have the upper hand. His approach dominated the White House Conference, and he had proposed to Congress that the functions of the Children's Bureau be transferred to the Public Health Service in the name of governmental efficiency. The depression sidetracked his reorganization plans, however, and the Children's Bureau survived to fight another day under very different conditions during the New Deal.[55]

CHAPTER 11

Family, 1922–1923

By 1922, the Hoovers had adjusted to their new life in Washington. Being prominent meant a loss of privacy, but prominence had compensations in their ability to influence policies and move events in directions they thought important. That was particularly true for the secretary of commerce, of course, but Lou Hoover also found that her new position gave her gratifying opportunities to pursue her own political and social goals.

Even obligations could sometimes bring unexpected opportunities. When the Pan American Scientific Congress met in Washington early in 1922, Lou, as the wife of the secretary of commerce, felt she had to accept a membership on its Women's Auxiliary Committee. Her Stanford degree in geology impressed the other committee members, however, and they elected her to the Executive Committee. That in turn provided a forum from which she could publicize her belief that women ought to be free to pursue careers in the sciences and other professions.[1]

I

She also made her presidency of the Girl Scouts a platform from which to encourage the ambitions of young women. Active in the Washington, DC, area council since the Hoovers moved to the city in 1917, she became national vice president in 1921 and president in January 1922. (See Figure 14.2.) In her remarks at that year's national meeting in Savannah, she set as her goals for the organization promoting the "'fun' part of scouting" (hiking and camping);

helping the girls understand how to keep "an orderly household"; and developing scouts' civic consciousness and sense of responsibility for their neighborhoods, local areas, and eventually "national and world activities." As far as she was concerned, domestic and public did not constitute "separate spheres" but blended seamlessly. She told a correspondent that she kept two goals constantly in mind and made "equal efforts . . . to attain them": "They are to make good citizens of the Girl Scouts, and to make good home-makers of them." Setting an example of what she had in mind, she became an extremely active president, visiting scout troops across the country, recruiting new leaders, and working to expand membership, raise money, and put the organization on a business basis—all while running family homes in California and Washington, playing the social role expected of a cabinet member's wife, and keeping a close eye on her sons' progress.[2]

Lou also became an ardent advocate for improving public education in the District of Columbia. Although the Hoovers could have easily afforded a private school for Allan, they believed strongly that "public schools were a better prelude to American life than many private schools," so in September 1922 they enrolled him as a junior at Western High School in Washington. The school tested their commitment to public education. Grossly overcrowded and underfunded, the school had been forced to institute double shifts the year before, and it seemed possible that triple shifts would soon be necessary. It had almost no athletic fields or facilities for extracurricular activities. Although district residents had agreed to a tax increase to fund new schools, as Lou reminded Senator Frank Kellogg, a member of the Senate's District of Columbia committee, nothing could be done without congressional action. Unless improvements came quickly, she warned Bureau of the Budget director Herbert M. Lord, the public schools would soon serve only the poor and middle classes, instead of providing a democratizing experience for children of all classes.[3]

In March, the Hoovers visited California and their Stanford home. Lou's sister, Jean Large, and her three children joined them. As the two families sat talking one afternoon, they suddenly realized that six-year-old Walter had disappeared. A quick search located the child, unconscious at the bottom of the swimming pool in the garden. The Hoovers' good friend, Ray Lyman Wilbur, a physician and president of Stanford, immediately began artificial respiration, and together with another physician, worked for nearly three hours to try to revive the child—but without success.[4]

The family all felt young Walter's death deeply. Hoover canceled two speaking engagements in San Francisco, and the family drew together for the child's funeral. Then Bert took Herbert, now a sophomore at Stanford, east with him when he went back to Washington; and the Larges, Jean, and Lou's father, Charles Henry, returned to Monterey. Alone in Palo Alto, Lou wrote sadly to Allan that she imagined she could still see little Walter "playing all around the house now, with his adorable smile." His "little sun-tanned sweater" still hung "over the foot of my bed," she wrote, "as though he were going to run in to get it soon." Worriedly, Bert telegraphed from Salt Lake City that he and Herbert felt well but were "anxious to know how you are and what your movements are."[5]

Lou, naturally even-tempered, did not remain depressed long. At the beginning of April, she left for Washington, where she announced a drive to raise $35,000 to pay for an extension to a Girl Scout camp at Briarcliff, New York. Soon afterward, she announced plans to reorganize the management of the organization's national funds and in the fall launched the first of a series of fund-raising drives, this one for about $122,000 to carry on and extend scout work for the following year.[6] Like Bert with the American Child Health Association, she envisioned more ambitious projects for the scouts than previous leaders had imagined.

II

In April, Lou's presidency of the Girl Scouts earned her an invitation to participate in the formation of a new organization, the National Amateur Athletic Federation (NAAF). As she recalled later, the idea originated at a small meeting she organized at 2300 South Street in late 1921 or early 1922. At it, army and navy officers representing the secretaries of war and navy discussed their concern about the poor physical condition of wartime draftees, but the conversation soon broadened to the physical condition of all young people, girls as well as boys. Agreeing that all of them needed better physical conditioning, the group drafted a proposal for the creation of a national organization to promote general youth health and fitness. Most of them thought that the new NAAF ought to include "men and women, boys and girls, on an equal footing, with the same standards, same program, same regulations." Lou agreed that the new organization should include both sexes, but she questioned whether the same standards were appropriate for both. Normally, she said, she believed that men and women should have "the same membership and activities in nearly all organizations," but in sports, she argued, "there were such fundamentally differing factors . . . that it would be advisable to have them grouped under separate sub-divisions."[7]

Colonel Henry Breckinridge, who had been assistant secretary of war in the Wilson administration, was chosen as chairman of an organizing committee at the first official NAAF board meeting in New York early in 1922. He invited the Girl Scouts to designate a representative to a general meeting to be held in Washington on May 8 and 9. The meeting elected Lou to be a vice president and member of the Board of Governors in the new NAAF.[8]

Lou's position on the board enabled her to follow up on whether men and women should be assigned to separate divisions. The founders of the rival National Amateur Athletic Union believed that gender equality required opening a full range of competitive athletics to women and, in particular, participation in the Olympics. A vocal faction in the NAAF felt the same way. When the Board of Governors considered membership in the American Olympic Association in November 1922, the board, including Lou, voted unanimously to join, but they were thinking primarily about male athletes. Lou and others expressed concern at the "tendency to exploit young girls in spectacular and undesirable forms of competitive sport." To avoid a split, the board postponed adopting a policy regarding sponsorship and preparation of female Olympians. At its December 29, 1922 meeting, the board created a special committee to study the issue and report in 1924. And early in 1923, Col. Breckinridge asked Lou to organize and chair a special meeting of women's groups to consider the same question.[9]

III

In September 1922, another blow fell on the Hoovers when they learned that Dr. Henry John Minthorn had been diagnosed with terminal cancer. It was, of course, with Dr. Minthorn's family in Oregon that Hoover had spent most of his childhood after the death of his parents. The doctor had been a severe guardian, but Hoover had come to love and respect him, not only for taking in various indigent relatives, including Bert, but also for his charitable work in Oregon and in later years with the natives in Alaska. Hoover later described him as "my second father," but in truth, because his father died so early, Dr. Minthorn influenced Hoover more than his real parent. Among other things, the doctor provided young Bert with a powerful example of service to others and stoic reticence about his personal feelings. Although he could not get to Alaska for Dr. Minthorn's funeral in October, 1922, Hoover made a special effort to visit his widow, Matilda, when he went to Alaska with President Harding in the summer of 1923 and invited her to stay with them at the S Street house when she visited Washington in October 1925.[10]

The Hoover boys, Allan and Herbert, soon recovered from the death of their little cousin. Bert, always interested in the latest technology, purchased a phonograph for the S Street house, and Allan, grown-up at fourteen in his first long trousers, occupied himself with buying records for it. His preference, reported Lou's secretary Philippi Harding, was for "records of the most modern jazzy kind!" Herbert, back in California after a brief visit to Washington, conspired with a fellow Stanford sophomore, Will Irwin, Jr., son of one of Bert's oldest friends, and Charles K. Field, a member of the class of 1896, to create an elaborate hoax. At the annual University Day banquet, a gathering of about a thousand Stanford alumni and friends, Herbert set up his apparatus and announced that his and young Irwin's father would address the gathering by radio from the East Coast. Instead, the two young men impersonated their fathers, made the speeches, and capped the stunt with a "materialization séance" in which they "delivered special messages from the elder Irwin to old-time friends in the audience dealing with intimate details of the scandalous days of long ago." When, at the end, Field explained the joke, the audience roared with applause.[11]

Following the end of classes in May, Herbert decided to avoid the Washington heat and stay on in Palo Alto for the summer. To keep himself productively occupied, he enrolled for the summer quarter at the university, but in August, his health, never robust since his bout with influenza in the autumn of 1918, became worse. Without telling either his parents or university officials, he stopped attending classes. Eventually Dean George Culver discovered what had happened, but instead of simply recording failing grades for the young man's courses, he postdated and entered an official withdrawal.[12] Obviously, there were advantages to being the son of a university trustee.

IV

Hoover had won election to the board of trustees in 1912 in recognition not only of his financial generosity to the university (he had pledged $11,000 toward a $50,000 university union in 1909) but also of his strong support for improving its intellectual quality. In his first years as a trustee, he had played a major part in securing a substantial increase in faculty salaries that began to attract first-class scholars to the campus and an ambitious building program that included a new library, gymnasium, stadium, and several buildings for the medical school. While in Europe during and after the war, he began collecting "fugitive literature" (e.g., pamphlets and newspapers) dealing with the war and European revolutions, as well as gathering the records of the Commission for Relief in Belgium (CRB). Continued and expanded over the coming years, his collection at Stanford came to supplement and in some ways even surpass official archives as a record of the period's international history. Hoover also donated his personal collection of geology, mining, and geography books (between one and two thousand volumes) to the university's Geology Library.[13]

In 1915, Hoover had engineered the appointment of his old friend, Ray Lyman Wilbur, as president of Stanford. He told his fellow trustee Ralph Arnold that, had he not been so occupied with European affairs, he might have been willing to take the job himself, but he happily supported Wilbur, a fellow Westerner and experienced administrator. Following Wilbur's appointment, he told Arnold that, having done all he could for Stanford and being burdened with public responsibilities, he intended to resign from the board. But when Wilbur and other board members urged him to reconsider, he agreed. He would later be glad that he did. When he returned to the campus in 1919, he found the university again in financial trouble. Wartime inflation had badly eroded faculty salaries, and growing student enrollments exceeded dormitory space. Early in 1919, Hoover promised a gift of $100,000 to be paid in installments for the construction of the long-delayed student union, provided other trustees matched the gift, and that autumn he proposed that for the first time

Stanford charge students tuition in order to raise faculty salaries. In October, the board voted to begin charging $40 a quarter, effective January 1, 1920.[14]

The decision to initiate tuition was momentous for an institution that had been created by the Stanford family to offer the best education at no cost to bright but poor students like Hoover. To soften the blow, the trustees created a number of fellowships for graduate students and a tuition loan program for needy undergraduates, to which Hoover contributed $5,000. Hoover also pursued a major grant from the Rockefeller Foundation's General Education Board that could tide the university over until the new tuition fees built up a pool large enough to supplement salaries. At his urging, the board of trustees launched a million-dollar drive to increase the university's endowment. They also approved an ambitious five-year program to build more student housing at a cost of almost $1.5 million and established a Faculty Housing Fund from which professors could borrow up to 90 percent of the cost of new houses and pay the loans back, interest-free, over twenty years. Although some students and alumni objected to the new tuition fees (soon increased to $75 a quarter), the income strengthened and stabilized the faculty and financed a building boom in the 1920s that gave the campus much of its modern shape. In recognition of the importance of his services, the trustees elected Hoover to a second ten-year term on December 14, 1922.[15]

In addition to his concern as a trustee with the general health of the university, Hoover also supported specialized projects. After the trustees accepted his offer in early 1920 of $50,000 to expand and house his collection of books, pamphlets, and other materials on the war, he personally employed two Stanford historians, Frank Lutz and Frank Golder, to canvass Europe for additional items for the collection, expanding it to cover the Russian Revolution as well as the war. As secretary of commerce, he instructed departmental attachés around the world to be on the lookout for relevant newspapers, government documents, and books, and to purchase and ship them to Stanford at his expense. And while all of that was going on, Hoover approached his wartime food adviser, Dr. Alonzo E. Taylor of the University of Pennsylvania, with a proposal to start a Food Research Institute at Stanford to utilize Hoover's own extensive Food Administration and relief files, and to undertake new research on food, diet, and standards of living in general. To finance the institute, he negotiated a grant of $704,000 from the Carnegie Corporation to be paid over ten years. The Food Institute became one of the first university-affiliated research institutes in the United States and established a precedent for other centers for pure and applied research on the campus in the future.[16]

Hoover made the first proposal about funding the Food Institute to a trustee of the Carnegie Corporation at the exclusive, male-only Bohemian Club in July 1920, and four years later he again took advantage of the club's annual "encampment" to approach San Francisco business leaders about creating a business school at Stanford. As a member of the club since 1913, Hoover knew perfectly well that business and politics were supposed to be banned from its annual summer gatherings in the redwoods of northern California, but, like other powerful club members, he often ignored the rule. On the basis of commitments he won from business leaders at the 1924 encampment, the university opened the second graduate-level school of business in the United States in 1925. And in 1925 and 1926, he also used Bohemian Grove conversations to explore the possibility of establishing an institute focused on pure and applied science. Slower than his other initiatives to gain momentum, this one did not come to fruition until 1946, when the Stanford Research Institute was born.[17]

Not surprisingly, Hoover's generosity to Stanford gave him a proprietary feeling about the university. Always confident that he knew best how things should be run, he generally got his way by making sure that his people were put in charge of the institutions he supported, and he could be heavy-handed if they did not do as he thought they should. In 1913, he had suggested to a faculty friend, Dr. E. D. Adams, that the university simply fire unproductive faculty members. When Adams replied that such an attack on the tenure system would drive away able professors and make the university a pariah in the academic world, he backed down, but in 1924, when some faculty members supported the presidential candidacy of Robert La Follette, he returned to the attack. In a heated letter to President Wilbur (which Wilbur wisely ignored), he proclaimed, "I am in favor of academic freedom in truthful statements, honest opinion and to competent men." But he claimed to see no reason why the tenure system required the university "to promote and advance" the "deliberately untruthful" or "incompetent" people supporting La Follette. And, on somewhat solider ground, he urged Wilbur to curb undergraduate drinking (it was, after all, Prohibition) and the ownership of expensive cars. His own sons, he pointed out, were not permitted to own anything but inexpensive used cars; possession of flashy new cars created "a class distinction and a luxury unwarranted to persons who have not earned it for themselves."[18]

Not everyone at Stanford responded as tolerantly as Wilbur did to Hoover's penchant for dictating policy. The university's touchy librarian, George T. Clark, clashed with him over control of the War Library. Clark believed that libraries were for published works and hated dealing with the flood of manuscripts, pamphlets, and foreign-language materials pouring in from Hoover's agents in Europe. From the outset, he conducted a sort of guerilla warfare against Hoover's principal purchasing agents, the Stanford historians Golder and Lutz, denying them space, stalling on paying their expenses, and even delaying mail deliveries to them. Worst of all, he diverted money from the acquisition of new materials to cover the costs of processing and cataloging the items already on campus. Hoover was outraged by this attitude. "There will be a thousand years to catalogue this library but only ten years in which to acquire the most valuable of material," he told Wilbur in 1924.[19]

The rapid growth of the War Library contributed to both its problems and their solution. In 1922, when the Belgian relief organization's trustees liquidated the organization, they turned over most of its remaining funds to a new CRB Educational Foundation, but they also allotted $200,000 to Stanford to provide for the preservation of the CRB records and to acquire additional related materials in the future. The following year, the ARA also gave $250,000 to Stanford for similar purposes. In both cases, Hoover expected that part of the money would go toward protecting and housing the agencies' collections, with any surplus devoted to collection of additional materials, but that the university would assume the cost of administering the library. Wilbur resisted this arrangement, however. He intended the War Library to be a part of the university libraries and under his control. With Hoover and Wilbur seemingly at cross-purposes, Lou Hoover stepped in. Late in September 1923, she met with Wilbur and went over the whole business in detail. In a long letter to Bert, she reassured him that Wilbur "seemed to agree with you throughout the whole subject" and would hold off on any decisions until he and Hoover had a chance to talk in person. Some months later, they agreed on a compromise. The university president would appoint a ten-member board of directors, including Hoover ex officio, the director of the libraries, and representatives of interested departments. The board would submit an annual budget to the president, and the director of libraries would have the power to nominate (but not appoint) all staff members.[20]

The 1924 compromise did not resolve all conflicts over control of the War Library, but those were soon overshadowed by a bigger issue. The collection had outgrown available space, occupying a fifth of the stacks of the main library. In 1925, History Professor E. D. Adams suggested erecting a new building to house the War Library. Hoover, Wilbur, and Edgar Rickard all thought that an excellent idea, and, after the trustees approved the proposal, Rickard launched a campaign to raise $750,000 for the project. Because of his official position, Hoover felt that he should not take an active part in the campaign, and without his involvement, progress was slow. When he launched his presidential candidacy in 1928, the drive had not yet reached its goal. Further delayed by the depression, the Hoover Library finally opened in June 1941, in ceremonies that also commemorated the university's fiftieth anniversary.[21]

Hoover's connection to Stanford also had its humorous side. In the summer of 1922, the grateful Belgians sent to the United States a large bronze statue of the Egyptian goddess Isis, in Egyptian mythology the mother and queen of all gods, the goddess of life and especially of growing grain. Sculpted by Auguste Puttemans, the larger-than-life-size seated goddess had her head and shoulders draped by a veil and held, in her right hand, three flames connoting the past, present, and future, and in her left hand, partly covered by the veil, the key of life. On the base, in French, were the words, "I am that which was and is, and will ever be; and no mortal has yet lifted the veil which covers me." Belgian children had raised the money for the statue in gratitude for Hoover's wartime relief program.

The Belgians apparently expected that the statue would be placed on the grounds of Hoover's birthplace, which they may have imagined as considerably grander than was actually the case. In any event, the Hoovers did not own the West Branch cottage, so the question of where the statue should go presented a considerable problem. Hoover proposed to ship it to Stanford and let President Ray Lyman Wilbur figure out what to do with it. "The proposition," he wrote to Wilbur, "is to dedicate the lady with great formality to her eternal job of sitting for some centuries in front of something, in this very stolid attitude, hanging on to this Lamp—in some place where she will receive constant public regard." And, he added, once the statue was in place, "various important Belgians" would arrive to make "long speeches—delivered no doubt in French," which would have to be answered with other long speeches by local dignitaries, whose choice Hoover left to Wilbur. As for himself, Hoover declared, he intended to be elsewhere during the statue's presentation.[22]

But, of course, he could not escape. The Belgians were determined to honor him, and so, when the Belgian delegation arrived to dedicate the statue on December 4, Hoover fidgeted nearby. As he had predicted, Belgian Senator Albert Lejeune made a long and florid speech conveying the eternal gratitude of the Belgian royal family and people to Hoover and the entire American relief program, while Hoover suffered. When finally forced to the podium, the honoree's speech consisted of just five sentences—mostly devoted to thanking the Californians, and especially the graduates of Stanford and the University of California, who had worked in the relief programs. The man who was so sensitive about his reputation that he would write a personal letter correcting a misrepresentation in an obscure small-town newspaper equally could not bear to be praised in public for his good works. The moment he could decently make his escape, he left for the railroad station and a train to Southern California.[23]

Isis stayed on the Stanford campus until 1939, after Lou Henry Hoover repurchased her husband's West Branch birthplace. That summer, the statue was shipped to Iowa, where it was set up to gaze across Wapsinonoc Creek at the birthplace cottage. The beginning of World War II forced the cancellation of ceremonies planned for its dedication in the new location—probably to Hoover's relief—but there it remains.

V

In the autumn of 1922, the Republicans recruited Hoover and other members of the cabinet to campaign for the party's candidates in the midterm elections. He had to curtail his schedule, however, when he was suddenly taken ill. Although the illness was not serious—perhaps a minor case of food poisoning—the phenomenon of his being sick and taking a few days off to recover merited national newspaper coverage. And indeed, he had hardly ever been ill during his adult life. Possibly the prospect of making campaign speeches, which he hated, had as much to do with his illness as infection. A few days later, recovered in body if not spirit, he departed for the Midwest, where he dutifully spoke in Toledo, Grand Rapids, and Detroit. He was visibly happier speaking in Albuquerque soon after the election about conditions in Europe.[24]

Meanwhile, Lou worked on final details of a campaign to raise $122,000 to cover the Girl Scouts' operating expenses for the coming year. Plans included a parade of six thousand scouts in uniform up Fifth Avenue, the distribution of small gifts by scouts to children in New York hospitals, and simultaneous demonstrations in towns and cities across the country of completed and planned projects. In combination with the demonstrations, adult "captains" would attempt to sell "grownup membership" to as many people as possible at a dollar apiece.[25]

Lou's scout work, in combination with her prominence as a cabinet member's wife, inspired many requests for her support. In addition to her work for the NAAF, Mary Anderson of the Labor Department's Women's Bureau asked her to send a Girl Scout representative to a planned conference on women in January 1923. Mary Austin, a writer whom the Hoovers had known for many years, implored her assistance in opposing a pending bill making it easier for whites to purchase Indian lands. Organizers of a new Women's News Service solicited an article from her as they attempted to find newspaper subscribers for their service. Almost certainly she never wrote the requested article, but she did send them a check for a hundred dollars to purchase two shares of stock in the new enterprise.[26] In addition to her other charitable work, she had obviously acquired a reputation as a supporter of women's causes, and she welcomed the opportunity. Modern houses, she frequently said, had become so easy to take care of that there was no excuse for a woman not to be active outside the home.

On March 2, Lou invited about two hundred women at schools, universities, colleges, and playground and recreational associations across the country to a meeting in Washington on April 6 to discuss ways to promote physical activity for women. The meeting received wide coverage in the press, some of it jocular. "War Department to Aid Women to Become Physical Goddesses," read one headline, while another warned, "Boys, Look Out! Women Train in Athletics with Government Aid." Ziegfield Follies showgirl Gilda Gray suggested bringing a troupe of Follies girls to the meeting to demonstrate that dancing was "the most rational and exhilarating form of recreation in the world and the most beneficial physically."[27]

Apparently, Miss Gray did not receive her invitation. Most of the physical education and hygiene experts who convened in Washington on April 6 approached the topic soberly, although the chairman of the American Folk Dance Society drew headlines by declaring that more exercise for girls would lead to the decline of "spooning." Refusing to be diverted, Lou stressed that the meeting was being held "to promote the health, fitness and morale of every woman and girl in America." The conference, she said, would discuss appropriate standards and tests for women's physical activities, both "'mass' activities, and their effect upon the individual and the community," and competitive athletics. She intended the meeting, she told delegates on April 6, to promote cooperation across the field of women's athletics and recreation.[28]

Substantive discussions among the delegates quickly demonstrated that the experts disagreed about basic questions. How young should girls start athletics? What standards should govern women's sports? Should women be encouraged to compete athletically? A consensus emerged that physical activity was desirable for all women and that highly competitive athletic programs did not benefit the great majority, but disagreement prevailed on other issues. Accordingly, after adopting a series of general resolutions endorsing the principle of women's physical activity, the group elected a committee to organize a Women's Division of the NAAF and to oversee studies of the unresolved issues. Lou Hoover was naturally elected chair of the committee.[29]

In May, a study committee that Lou had named reported on the touchy topic of competitive sports for women. It recommended general participation in physical activities for all girls and women and opposed the "exploitation" of spectator sports and organized school teams. Lou agreed strongly with that point of view, and in later years she urged "play days" for female students instead of competitions. In practice, however, Lou and the Women's Division found themselves bucking a strong trend toward opening competitive athletics to women both nationally and internationally. The NAAF's stubborn resistance to that trend contributed to the organization's slow initial growth and then gradual decline over the following decade. The Women's Division's national meeting in December 1923, however, celebrated the year's achievements and looked ahead optimistically to the future.[30]

The tensions and uncertainties pervading the NAAF did not trouble the Girl Scouts, where Lou dominated policy. With a membership of just over 100,000 girls when Lou became president in 1922, the scouts reached about 160,000 by the end of 1923. Everywhere she went, she preached her vision of scouting as an opportunity for girls of every race and religion "to fit themselves for leadership in the domestic and civic problems of the Republic." Reelected unopposed to the scout presidency in April 1923, she broadcast her message to the nation over radio station KDKA in Pittsburgh the following month. The wholesome, outdoor activities of scouting, enthused the Pittsburgh *Sun*, should remind Americans that not all young girls were flappers, "rouged, powdered, and addicted to cigarets, whose highest ambition is to have a good time, and who regard jazz-dancing, joy-riding and cabaret entertainment as the things in life most worth while."[31]

During the summer of 1923, Lou launched the Girl Scouts on a major new project that would occupy her and the scouts for several years. In June, the Federation of Women's Clubs opened a model house on Sherman Square in Washington near the Treasury Department. Sponsored in part by the Better Homes in America organization, of which Bert was chairman, the exterior of the house emulated the Easthampton, Long Island, home of John Howard Payne, composer of "Home Sweet Home." The interior showcased modern appliances and design features. Open to the public for two weeks, the house drew about three thousand visitors a day, but because it had been erected on government land, it had to be demolished or moved after the demonstration period. In late June, the Federation of Women's Clubs offered the house to the Girl Scouts, provided they would move it to another location.[32]

The scouts, as a volunteer organization with limited resources, were reluctant to accept such a large undertaking. Lou believed, however, that a demonstration house run by the scouts could provide valuable education and publicity. She undertook to find a new site in Washington and to raise the money to move the house. Finding donors proved difficult, and the War Department, on whose land the structure had been built, became impatient. In late October, Lou thought she had finally located both a site near Red Cross headquarters and the necessary money, but the Red Cross, citing legal concerns, backed out in November. At year's end, the fate of the project remained uncertain.[33]

In the summer of 1923, Lou and Bert joined the Hardings and a large official party for a trip along the West Coast to Alaska. Bert used the trip to gather information about the Alaskan fisheries (and to do some fishing of his own), and Lou happily went along. On the way to join the official party in Seattle, she recruited scout leaders along the West Coast. Together, the Hoovers stood vigil when the president fell fatally ill as he traveled through the Northwest at the beginning of August. Upon their return to Washington on August 11, Lou sent an article to the Girl Scout magazine praising Harding as "a good Scout" who had devoted his public life to promoting understanding among his fellow men. She confessed to a friend that she had enjoyed the trip, despite its sad ending. "The coast of that part of the country is beautiful," she wrote, "and [it] makes one want to go back again some time, and explore it with much leisure. The weather was very pleasant, and we really had great fun."[34]

Everyone in the administration found the official ceremonies following the president's death trying, and when they ended, Lou did something uncharacteristic: she decided to skip the annual Girl Scout convention held in Minneapolis in early September. Instead, she took Herbert and Allan camping. It was, she explained to a friend, her only chance to spend some time with them before they went back to college and high school.[35]

Both boys stayed in Palo Alto that September. The Hoovers had at last given up on the public schools in Washington and agreed to let Allan take his senior year at Palo Alto High. He could live at the house on the hill, where his Aunt Jean and her family came to stay for much of the winter, and Lou also arranged for a young man from the university to stay there as a sort of "guardian-tutor" and fellow-mechanic on the car Allan was building in a room on the lowest level of the house. Probably she rejoiced that he seemed to have given up the idea of getting a motorcycle license, which he had contemplated just before leaving Washington for the summer. By late September, he had recovered completely from a severely sprained ankle suffered in a fall in August and was "settling in very well and apparently very happy at the High School."[36]

Herbert, after working all summer on San Francisco's Hetch Hetchy dam project in a job arranged by his father, returned to Stanford just in time to begin his junior year as an engineering major. Still an amateur radio enthusiast, he devoted his free time to setting up a receiver at the football stadium, from which he relayed the scores of other games to the Stanford fans. He got around town in what a family friend described cryptically as a "new nude Ford," which was very likely a stripped-down Model T, since his father did not approve of college students having expensive cars.[37]

Shortly before the boys' classes began, they and Lou went north to join her father at a cabin he had rented in the Siskiyou Mountains of northern California. There they spent a week deer hunting, fishing, and enjoying early autumn in the mountains.[38]

While in California, Lou left the running of the household in Washington in the hands of her secretary, Louisette Losh. The secretary of commerce, Lou warned, paid no attention to the mundane details of daily life. Except for his neckties, he wore identical clothes every day so he never had to think about what to put on. And he gave other domestic matters even less attention. Someone else had to pay the bills and answer invitations, which often meant going through his pockets to see what he had forgotten. Sometimes, Lou said, he simply threw invitations away if he thought they were of no importance, which could be embarrassing. And sometimes, she warned, such things turned up "in coat pockets or books and out-of-the-way places" only months later, if at all. She advised an old friend to never, "ever leave a book with him that you want to see again." When he traveled by himself, she added, "he always returns with about a fourth of his impediments missing. Clothing, shoes, toilet articles and above all, books, get simply scattered by the wayside! So the family moral is never to let him be in possession of anything we should mind him losing."[39]

After getting the boys settled and spending some time sorting through the family's accumulated possessions, many of which were still in boxes after having been shipped from England or Washington, Lou felt the call of duty from Washington. There she served not only as her husband's official hostess and an executive of the NAAF and the Girl Scouts but also with a wide range of other organizations. Much of her work was with charities, such as the Visiting Nurse Society, but she also had an active role in the League of Women Voters and spoke occasionally to women's Republican groups, especially in California. Her work was less directly political, more in the mold of upper-middle-class club women than that of her contemporary, Eleanor Roosevelt, but like many other American women in the first generation after suffrage, she asserted a new independence and claimed the right to a public role.[40]

Lou's self-image was rudely jolted by a sketch of her that appeared in an anonymously authored book called *Boudoir Mirrors of Washington*. "I want to be a background for Bertie," the chapter claimed she had said. She wrote angrily in the margin, "Never said it!" The book's author, Lou suspected, must be her supposed friend, Mary Austin, the Southwestern writer who had met the Hoovers in London and was, according to Lou, the "only person" who called Bert "Bertie." In a series of outraged marginal notes, she pointed out error after error.[41] The book attracted little notice and had no lasting effect, but even years later it still galled her. Although unwilling ever to thrust herself into the spotlight or to brag about her accomplishments, Lou took pride in her work and her independence, and it angered her to be disparaged. Only "a background for Bertie," indeed!

If Mary Austin really wrote *Boudoir Mirrors*, she may have regarded it as payback for a slight that she imagined she had received from the Hoovers. Austin had been a zealous supporter of Indian rights for some time, but in the spring of 1923, she heard a rumor in Phoenix that Hoover had described her as "not reliably informed on the Indian question." Lou, who opened Austin's angry letter in Bert's absence, replied mildly that he could not possibly have said any such thing. Not only had Bert and his family had a long and sympathetic association with Indians, she pointed out, but recently he had recommended Austin to the secretary of the interior for membership on a proposed Indian Advisory Committee. When her friendly correction failed to placate Austin, Lou asked a friend in Phoenix whether there could be any basis for the writer's suspicions and, when assured that they must come from some misunderstanding, simply let the matter drop. Under the circumstances, it was not surprising that when *Boudoir Mirrors* appeared later in the year, Lou concluded that Mary Austin was very likely its author.[42]

By 1923, Bert and Lou had each carved out a place in American public life. They pursued separate projects and were often apart for days or weeks, but their interests also overlapped and reinforced each other, particularly in the area of service to children, in which they both took a passionate interest. Raised in a culture that discouraged public displays of affection, they were both reticent even by the standards of the time. The occasional letters between them that have survived include neither expressions of devotion nor any hint of disagreements, making it nearly impossible to explore their relationship in depth, but all evidence indicates that they had been passionately in love when they married and that twenty-five years of marriage had solidified their mutual respect and commitment. They seized every opportunity to be together, but as a friend said, neither would "mind the other one's business." Both obviously loved their sons deeply, stealing time whenever they could to go fishing or camping with them and taking a genuine interest in their activities. Although they took pains to make sure the boys were safe, they also encouraged them to be independent and pursue their own interests. The family's relationship was unusual, perhaps, but it provided all of them with both support and freedom to follow their own courses.[43]

CHAPTER 12

████████████████████████████████

Hoover's Economic Idealism

In December 1922 the Doubleday, Doran Company published a pamphlet by Herbert Hoover titled *American Individualism*. Within two months, fifteen thousand copies of the booklet had been sold, and during 1923 it was translated into Japanese, Spanish, Italian, Czech, Russian, and Polish. The following year, it appeared in Bulgarian and German. New editions followed regularly in succeeding years, and it remains in print today.

American Individualism distilled the essence of Hoover's economic and social philosophy and outlined, in general terms, his plans for the future course of the American government. It reflected his upbringing in a Quaker family on the frontier, his experience as a mining engineer and businessman around the world, the lessons he learned as the head of an international relief organization and as Food Administrator during World War I, his observations on the flaws that the war had exposed in European governments and societies, his conclusions about the social and industrial conflicts that had swept the United States in 1919, and his aspirations for the country's future. He would continue to develop and apply the basic arguments set forth in *American Individualism* for the remainder of his public life.

Written in fits and starts over a period of years, elements of the booklet's theses had appeared in various speeches and articles, particularly during the election campaign of 1920, but Hoover did not start combining them into a single work until mid-1921. Late that summer, he solicited comments on a rough draft of the pamphlet from several people, including the economist Wesley Mitchell, and his close friend, the journalist Mark Sullivan. Mitchell

195

offered only one minor suggestion, but Sullivan returned the manuscript in
October with recommendations for substantial reorganization, which the journalist underplayed as merely making "the transition from thought to thought
a little easier." Recognizing that Sullivan's suggestions greatly strengthened
his argument, Hoover replied that he was "deeply grateful," but he did not
resume work on the essay until December 1921 and apparently did not complete it until late in the autumn of the following year.[1]

I

Hoover addressed himself in *American Individualism* to one overriding
problem—whether the United States could find a way to combine the protection of citizens' welfare promised by socialism with the growth and prosperity
offered by capitalism. His observations in postwar Europe convinced him that
socialism stultified innovation and growth, but capitalism tended to monopoly
and exploitation of workers. Europe, he had argued in a speech to fellow engineers on his return from Paris in September 1919, had attempted to solve its
problems through socialism. Those experiments, he believed, had resulted
in an "extraordinary lowering of productivity of industrial commodities to a
point that, until the recent realization of this bankruptcy, was below the necessity for continued existence of their millions of people." "I am not a Socialist,"
he had told Herbert Croly in 1918. "I am opposed to the whole theory, root
and branch, and I believe that the worst disaster that could come out of the
war will be any rush of public opinion for some panacea of this kind."[2]

"On the other hand," he continued, "I am not a believer in the use of
property to impose either political or economic power over fellow-men."
He argued that "individualism run riot, with no tempering principles," had
provided a long history of "inequalities . . . , tyrannies, dominations, and
injustices." Rejecting Adam Smith's argument that each man's pursuit of self-
interest would assure prosperity for all, he contended that unrestricted laissez
faire had instead resulted in the rule of "every man for himself and the devil
take the hindmost." Americans, believing "that the foremost are not always
the best nor the hindmost the worst" and, even more fundamentally, that "the
impulse to production can only be maintained at a high pitch if there is a fair
division of the product," had tempered competition with "certain restrictions
on the strong and the dominant." But Hoover went further. The American
commitment, he emphasized, must be that "*while we build our society upon the
attainment of the individual, we shall safeguard to every individual an equality of
opportunity to take that position in the community to which his intelligence, character,
ability, and ambition entitle him.*"[3]

The balance between protecting individual opportunity and liberating the
dynamism of capitalism was, Hoover admitted, difficult to achieve and maintain. One of the major difficulties arose because keeping the two in equilibrium seemed to require a constant expansion of government authority, and

that paradoxically tended to create imbalances and abuses comparable to those of unchecked capitalism. Although he took it for granted that "as a theory" almost everyone opposed the growth of government, in practice government had grown larger and more centralized over time. Conflicts that states had passed to the federal government because they could not resolve them (such as the restriction of child labor) and "public indignation at practices which had grown in our business world" both led to expansion of federal power. But an even more common impetus for centralization came from the very group that deplored it the most, the business community. Some groups of businessmen, believing that they were "suffering from some kind of injustice, and that something ought to be done to save them from difficulties of some sort or other," would appeal to the government for help. Given that pattern, he concluded, unless businessmen could learn to remedy grievances and solve their problems through cooperation, "I see no other situation than the constant pressure in Washington for further and further expansion of Federal activities."[4]

Hoover challenged business to combine cooperation with voluntary self-regulation and to reject the price-fixing, marketing conspiracies and other abuses that the antitrust laws sought to prevent. Relations among businesses, government, and labor during the war had proved that ethical cooperation was possible, he believed, but future progress depended on recognition that "intelligent self-interest" required development of economic associations that would solve conflicts while retaining and fostering competitive opportunities for individuals and small enterprises.[5]

Hoover's "associationalism" paralleled but differed from the European corporatism of the 1920s. Both had their principal impetus in the massive economic mobilization of World War I, which hugely enhanced the power of business and organized labor. To secure maximum production, governments had surrendered or suspended regulatory powers, allowing representatives of business, labor, and agriculture to regulate their own activities. Following the war, European conservatives saw in that erosion of state power an opportunity to reassert older class hierarchies. By the mid-1920s, Mussolini's Italy had already merged corporatism with authoritarianism, and Germany was moving toward what would become the Nazi version of corporatism.[6]

Although the associationalist theory Hoover articulated in *American Individualism* derived partly from his wartime experience and from the corporatist ideas common in Western thought, he saw the war's lessons quite differently from his European contemporaries. In August 1917, before the war transformed business-government relations in the United States, he had urged that mobilization be a "democratic movement" based on voluntary cooperation among economic groups, not on coercion. In that way, democracy would demonstrate its superiority over autocracy. In practice, American mobilization, including Hoover's Food Administration, involved substantial coercion, but the short span of American belligerence allowed the myth of voluntarism to survive largely unchallenged.[7]

Hoover's memory of his wartime experience gave specific form to his associationalism, but the Progressive Era's stress on efficiency and technocracy
within democracy had equal influence on his thought. He did not need to
study Henry Ford's production innovations, Frederick W. Taylor's theory of
scientific management, or Thorstein Veblen's philosophy of producer empowerment to share their common assumption that engineers would lead the way
to a new society of efficiency, productivity, and abundance. Progressive Era
thinkers had already made the argument that democracy and efficiency were
complementary, and the experience of the War Industries Board seemed to
bear that out. Unlike Veblen, who argued that the engineer could revolutionize
a capitalist system that tended "to manufacture waste to preserve hierarchy,"
Hoover saw engineering's role as helping "to eliminate the frictions of a basically superior economic order." From Hoover's perspective as a self-made man,
the unique power of capitalism lay in its ability to liberate individual energy and
creativity. Coercion and regimentation would stifle that creative power.[8]

Hoover admitted frankly the serious dangers inherent in business self-regulation through professional associations. They might "dominate legislators
and intimidate public officials"; they might "develop the practice of dog-eat-
dog between groups"; they might, ultimately, lead the nation "into a vast
syndicalism." Nevertheless, he argued, the nation's industrial transformation
required thought and planning. The task of statesmanship lay in finding the
"identity of interest" among groups and organizing them "to limit the area of
conflict." Business "must learn that progress will not come from crushing the
individual into a shapeless mass, but in giving to him enlarged opportunity.
They must learn to understand each other and not to fight." Management
of competition, improved business practices, technical progress, simplification and standardization, expansion of foreign trade, and more harmonious
labor-management relations, Hoover reiterated endlessly, would make industry more efficient and had the potential to raise everyone's living standards.[9]

In a June 1925 commencement address at a small Quaker college in Iowa,
Hoover reflected on why he believed that Americans could learn to cooperate across class lines and to regulate the economy through voluntary associations. The nature of the economy, he said, had changed during his lifetime.
During his Iowa childhood, "the farm was still a place where we tilled the
soil for the immediate needs of the family," selling only a small part of its
products on the market and buying little as well. By the 1920s, in contrast,
farming had become a business largely dependent on sales in distant markets
over which farmers had little or no control. Likewise, he recalled, when he
first entered engineering, most industries had been small and marketed to
local communities. In those small businesses, personal relationships bound
employer and employee together and enabled each to understand the needs
of the other. But now "the growth of the country and the force of international competition" required mass production by enormous corporations
and "impersonal organization."[10]

That transformation, Hoover argued, had produced numerous and not entirely beneficial results. The size and efficiency of the modern corporation had made possible a higher standard of living for Americans, but the employee's security had diminished because of "greater specialization and the greater liability of unemployment from every passing economic storm." The government had grown "fabulously" to "prevent competitive business from crystalizing [*sic*] into monopolies" and to protect Americans increasingly dependent on imports and exports. Like it or not, America found itself enmeshed in a "great but delicate [international] cobweb on which each radius and spiral must maintain its precise relation to every other one in order that the whole complex structure may hold."[11]

A lesson could be learned from the experience of the pioneers, Hoover argued. Their pursuit of individual opportunity had pushed them west, but they had also understood the importance of cooperation. "Our fathers and grandfathers" had broken the prairie and built the roads, bridges, towns, and schools. They had "combined to fight the Indians" and "worked together to harvest their fields, to raise their barns," and they had "co-operated to build themselves a government without paternal nursing from without [*sic*]." That earlier generation, Hoover emphasized, had seen no incompatibility between "pioneer qualities of independence, of rugged character, of self reliance, of initiative," and "neighborly cooperation and service for mutual advancement."[12]

Hoover's memory glossed over the fact that his father had been less a subsistence farmer than a blacksmith and farm implement dealer firmly connected to the industrial revolution. He also overlooked the fact that the self-sufficient farmers he praised had benefited from federal subsidies for the railroads that carried their products to market and, for that matter, that had transported Hoover himself west into the future after his parents' death. Nor, as the New York *Tribune* pointed out in a review of *American Individualism*, did he explain why the frontier individualism he lauded had not become obsolete with the disappearance of the frontier. The mythologized past evoked in the Penn College speech affirmed and validated Hoover's personal experience and values. He needed to believe that Americans could combine competition and cooperation through "associational activities for the advancement of ideas in national welfare or for the mutual advancement of economic purposes" because he interpreted his own past in those terms. If trade associations could be made "benevolent and just," they would restore the American tradition of self-sufficient farmers coming together for "barn-raising and mutual protection from the Indians, whether savage or in business." As in the past, Americans could blend individualism with community.[13]

Just as Hoover believed that trade associations could create community among industries, so he believed that shop councils could restore the close relationship between managers and employees that had been lost with the rise of giant corporations. "Great areas of mutual interest" existed between employers and employees, he argued; each must recognize that they were "both producers," not "separate 'classes' fighting each other." Shop councils in each factory made up of elected worker representatives and members of management could restore "open and frank relations" between the two groups as well as provide "a renewal of the creative opportunity of the individual workman." Unlike those businessmen who saw shop councils as no more than company unions, Hoover believed that traditional unions and collective bargaining retained an important place in industry. The shop council, he argued, would supplement the union, bridging the artificial divisions between craft unions and emphasizing the common interest of everyone concerned in expanding and making production more efficient.[14]

II

The vulnerable point in Hoover's argument for the associational state lay in his assumption that the new associations, unlike the old trusts, would commit themselves voluntarily to service, efficiency, and ethical behavior. Their leaders would understand that maximizing production through cooperation among business, labor, and agriculture benefited everyone. And the guidance of technical experts would ensure that, unlike government agencies, trade associations would remain flexible, responsive to challenges, and innovative.[15]

Those optimistic assumptions rested partly on Hoover's belief that Americans could be educated to understand that enlightened self-interest required extension of wartime cooperation into the postwar era. But they also depended on his reading of human nature. In addition to the "selfish" instincts of self-preservation, acquisitiveness, fear, and the drives for power and adulation, he believed that people also responded to more altruistic instincts of "kindness, pity, fealty to family and race; the love of liberty; the mystical yearnings for spiritual things; the desire for fuller expression of the creative faculties; the impulses of service to community and nation."[16] Such creative and spiritual aspirations, he believed, could best find their outlet through collective activities.

Hoover never identified the origins of the contradictory instincts he described in *American Individualism*. Traditional Quaker doctrine specifically denied that any principle of "spiritual light, life or holiness" inhered by nature "in the mind or heart of man." His mother, however, who came from a more evangelical wing of the church, had preached that people could be aroused to an awareness of the inner light through an active ministry.[17] It is hard to say how much of his mother's outlook Hoover had absorbed as a child. As an adult, he was not conventionally religious, but his confidence that businessmen, workers, and farmers could be led toward a selfless commitment to the general welfare suggests a lingering sense of the "inner light."

American Individualism offers a meditation on maximizing the altruistic instincts while minimizing or channeling the selfish ones. Hoover argued optimistically that "education, [and] the higher realization of freedom, of justice, of humanity, of service" would gradually triumph over "selfish impulses."

Yet he warned also that "for the next several generations we dare not abandon self-interest as a motive force to leadership and to production, lest we die." In the short term, the "small percentage" of people who fully grasped the potential of cooperation must exercise leadership. Their goal would be the encouragement of democracy's "authorities in morals, religion, and states-manship . . . from its own mass." Like the Marxist state, the associative state would supposedly wither away or recede to a minor status as referee, care-taker, and symbol of unity as the cooperative commonwealth developed.[18] The argument, of course, celebrated Hoover's own leadership style, which included more than a little benevolent authoritarianism.

Hoover envisioned progress as a balance between "spirituality, service, and mutual advancement," on the one hand, and "high and increasing standards of living and comfort," on the other. A higher standard of living required greater invention, greater elimination of waste, greater production, and better distri-bution of commodities and services, and that in turn necessitated large-scale planning, industrial organization, and a closely coordinated economic system. "Spiritual progress," on the other hand, lay with the individual, though he discerned a "vital connection between human happiness, mental and spiritual advancement, and material well being." The higher qualities of human nature, he believed, "flowered when man met a measure of success in his economic struggle." Thus *American Individualism* was intended to be more than simply an economic creed. It proposed a route to self-expression, "not merely eco-nomically, but spiritually as well."[19]

Curiously, although Hoover set a high and rising standard of living for ordinary Americans as the principal goal of the associational state, *Ameri-can Individualism* says almost nothing about the emerging consumer society. Hoover's utopia featured "mental and spiritual advancement," not mate-rial wealth. The main result of a rising living standard, he told the Advisory Council of the National Conference on Outdoor Recreation in 1924, would be "a larger and increasing period of leisure." That leisure must be filled by "increased facilities of recreation and of education," for greater leisure with-out "constructive occupation" would result in "a disastrous train of degenera-tion." Like the economist Simon Patten, whose arguments he echoed perhaps unwittingly, Hoover assumed that people would soon tire of unlimited mate-rial goods and would turn instead to intellectual, moral, and religious pursuits to fill their leisure. He himself lived comfortably rather than luxuriously and used his leisure for simple recreations—camping and fishing—rather than for commercial entertainment, and he anticipated that others would choose to do likewise, if such opportunities were available to them. He focused, both in his public activities and in *American Individualism*, on ways to maximize the pro-duction that would provide people with modest affluence and leisure, not on what they would do with those blessings once they had them.[20]

III

Hoover remained convinced throughout his career that individual opportunity, associational activities, economic growth, and spiritual fulfillment could all be reconciled and would mutually supplement and sustain each other, but implementation raised the vexing problem of how to reconcile trade associations with antitrust law. Hoover had first raised that problem in 1917, when he pointed out that essential wartime cooperation among industries could be subject to prosecution under the antitrust law. President Wilson and Attorney General Thomas Gregory agreed that would be undesirable, and Gregory interpreted the law so as to exempt the cooperation among supposedly competing industries promoted by the Food Administration and other war agencies from antitrust prosecution. But when a Federal Trade Commission (FTC) investigation revealed monopolistic practices in the meatpacking industry, Hoover also supported measures intended to restore competition. Although he favored cooperation within industry, he recognized that cooperation could lead to monopoly and believed the government must prevent that from happening.[21]

In the immediate postwar period, Hoover kept his distance from both a movement to legalize cartels and another to employ the Sherman Act more aggressively against big business. Large size, he said in December 1919, was "economically sound," unless a company grew so big that "bureaucratic administration" made it less efficient than a smaller unit. He assured President-elect Harding that he did not favor restricting or repealing the Sherman Act as some businessmen had proposed.[22]

The Commerce Department's campaign to reduce industrial waste and promote rational management of the economy through associational activities inevitably raised the antitrust issue. Some businessmen seized upon Hoover's call for the collection of statistical information and the promotion of trade associations as a license to promote "open price plans" that easily became price-fixing schemes. Hoover regarded the open price plans as clearly illegal under the Sherman Act, but he hoped that trade associations that did not restrain competition would avoid the problem. Having been questioned by several manufacturers about the formation of a Copper and Brass Publicity Association, he asked Attorney General Harry Daugherty in May 1921 about the application of the antitrust laws to such an organization. Daugherty declined to take a position on the matter because, he argued, the law did not authorize the Justice Department to offer opinions on the legality of private organizations.[23]

Daugherty's cautious reply, in combination with a number of other Justice Department statements about illegal activities by trade associations, created considerable uneasiness among businessmen. Hoover believed that the atmosphere impeded the Commerce Department's efforts to secure statistical information from trade associations upon which to base predictions about the direction of the economy. In July, he invited Nathan B. Williams, Associate

Counsel of the National Association of Manufacturers, to discuss the situation. Hoover emphasized that he would not sanction any association that might be described as a "trade conspiracy" but that he also opposed "regulatory legislation." Williams left reassured that they had laid the foundations for cooperation that would "dignify the work of trade and craft organizations." Perhaps in fulfillment of a promise to Williams, Hoover then scheduled a meeting with Daugherty and his staff to discuss the whole problem further.[24]

The Supreme Court's December 1921 ruling that the Hardwood Manufacturers Association's open price plan restrained trade under the Sherman Act aborted whatever accommodation the Justice and Commerce Departments might have reached on the trade association issue. Under some interpretations of the court's ruling, even Commerce's *Survey of Current Business*, which Hoover had started in July 1921 to collect and publish statistical data from businesses and trade associations, might be construed as contributing to trade restraint. Alarmed, Hoover arranged to confer again with Daugherty and other Justice Department officials. He hoped they could agree that collection and publication of trade statistics, and the promotion of standardization and codes of ethics, were legal trade association activities. Daugherty declined to issue a general statement but agreed to have Justice review a list of eleven specific trade association activities, including adopting a uniform system of cost accounting, providing insurance for members, or collecting statistics on production volumes, wages, and domestic and foreign consumption. In his response, Daugherty agreed that most of the activities seemed legal but warned that the Justice Department would have to review specific applications of each. When Commerce released the exchange to the press in February 1922, antitrust experts disagreed about what, if anything, it meant. Hoover tried to put the best face on the situation, arguing in a speech to the National Federation of Construction Industries and an article in the New York *Evening Post* that many constructive opportunities were now open to trade associations. He also assured five hundred trade association representatives at a Washington conference that the collection and reporting of trade statistics would not violate the law. But many businessmen expressed serious doubts, and Hoover found it difficult to get the information he needed to make the *Survey of Current Business* effective.[25]

In May 1922, Hoover moved to resolve the antitrust problem by asking his special assistant for trade association statistics, David Wing, to work with FTC Chairman Nelson Gaskill and Senator Walter Edge of New Jersey in drafting a bill that would permit a government agency to extend antitrust immunity to a trade association for specific forms of collective activity. But unresolved issues delayed progress. Should the bill be a new law or an amendment to the Sherman or Clayton antitrust laws? Should the power to exempt be entrusted to an existing government agency, or should a new body be established to undertake it? What activities should be exempted, and what limits should be set on exemptions? Discussion dragged on through the autumn of 1922, and whatever support had initially existed among businessmen and members of Congress gradually eroded.[26]

Reports that Hoover wanted to exempt trade associations from the anti-trust laws produced a highly publicized attack on him by the New York lawyer Samuel Untermyer. From 1919 to 1920, Untermyer had served as counsel to a joint committee of the New York legislature set up to investigate allegations of a conspiracy to inflate prices for building materials between labor leaders and building materials manufacturers and dealers. He later acted as a special prosecutor in cases arising out of the investigation. An ardent Democrat and admirer of Louis Brandeis, Untermyer was predisposed to be suspicious of anything supported by the Republicans, and his experience in the building materials investigation intensified his skepticism about all trade associations.[27]

Untermyer pitched into Hoover with gusto. Trade associations, he proclaimed, were "thinly-disguised devices under cover of which prices are fixed." He charged that Hoover had engaged in a "naive bit of special pleading" on behalf of organizations that might do some good but certainly did great harm. Defending such groups, Untermyer contended, was "very much like arguing that a man who picks pockets or robs banks may be a good husband and father or that a receiver of stolen goods may be also doing an honest business on the side."[28] People might smile or boil at Untermyer's excess, but his attacks helped make Congress hesitant about modifying the antitrust laws in any way.

In December 1923, Hoover again exchanged letters with Attorney General Daugherty following a decision in the U.S. District Court for the Southern District of Ohio in the case of *United States v. Tile Manufacturers Credit Association.* The court ruled that the association concerned could gather statistics on production, shipments, stocks on hand, and prices, provided it gave such information only to the government and did not share it with members of the organization. Seeing in this ruling an opportunity to legitimate the department's practices, Hoover asked Daugherty for an interpretation of it. Daugherty agreed that trade associations could properly collect statistical information for the Commerce Department but added that such information could be released only through a government publication, not shared among members of the association directly. Businessmen distrusted Daugherty's narrow interpretation of what was permissible, but Hoover bowed to it and ordered his staff to draw up a detailed set of guidelines for trade associations on what information they could gather and how it should be handled. The experience reinforced the secretary's belief that the antitrust law should be amended, or at least that the Justice Department's interpretation of it should be modified.[29]

The opportunity to change the Justice Department's opinion arose in March 1924 when Harlan F. Stone succeeded Daugherty as Attorney General. After a successful career as a corporate attorney, Stone had become dean of Columbia's law school. A close friend of both Hoover and Coolidge, Stone shared Hoover's ideas about trade associations. His Justice Department

cooperated with Commerce and the U.S. Chamber of Commerce in drafting
legislation to amend the antitrust law and also prepared a "test case" involving
the statistical program of the Maple Flooring Manufacturers' Association that
Stone and Hoover hoped would produce a Supreme Court ruling affirming
the legality of such activities.[30]

Meanwhile, Hoover proposed a new approach to the problem in a May
1924 speech to the annual meeting of the U.S. Chamber of Commerce,
strongly endorsing a proposal from the organization's Business Ethics committee for the adoption of codes of ethics by trade associations. Such codes, he
argued, would benefit both business and the public because they would reduce
the need for government regulations while strengthening the prevention of
abuses by tailoring codes to the specific needs and practices of industries.[31]
The idea fitted well with Hoover's conception of industrial self-government.
Although many people remained skeptical about trade associations, codes of
ethics gave association members a line of defense against criticism.

Hoover also hoped to make the FTC less a policeman and more an adviser
for trade associations. Although Republican appointees to the FTC during
the Harding and Coolidge era were more pro-business than Woodrow Wilson's nominees, the commission lacked the authority to offer prior advice to
businesses about the legality and propriety of proposed courses of action and
had few ways to deal with controversial cases other than through the courts.
Hoover discussed this situation widely, and although not all members of the
administration shared his enthusiasm for trade associations, he persuaded
President Coolidge to include a vague endorsement of less confrontational
methods by the FTC in his December 1923 annual message. The fact that
in 1914 Congress had specifically refused to grant the FTC power to offer
prior clearance to trade associations for their activities made Commerce
Department staff members reluctant to ask for such an amendment to the
law. Instead, in January 1925, Republican Senator James W. Wadsworth of
New York and Representative Arthur B. Williams of Michigan introduced a
bill empowering the commission to attempt resolution of unfair competition
cases through informal hearings before proceeding to formal legal action.[32]

While the Wadsworth-Williams bill hung fire in Congress, the Supreme
Court took up the test case involving the Maple Flooring Manufacturers
Association that had originated under Attorney General Stone's supervision.
Stone, appointed to the court in early 1925 by President Coolidge, not only
failed to recuse himself from the case but wrote the majority opinions in *Maple
Flooring Manufacturers Association v. United States* and *Cement Manufacturers Protective Association v. United States*, which were decided the same day.
According to Stone's opinions, which were endorsed by five other justices, the
pooling of information on market conditions, sources of supply, trade practices, and even prices, did not illegally restrain trade. Hoover applauded the
decisions at a June 4 press conference but emphasized that the court had not
freed businesses "to fix prices or control distribution." The point, he observed,

was that while bricks "can be used to commit murder, it is not necessary to prohibit the construction of brick houses in order to prevent it." Rather, the rulings permitted trade associations to collect and provide to the Commerce Department the statistical evidence upon which so much of the department's work depended while, at the same time, fostering the development of self-government and commitment to the general welfare.[33]

The Supreme Court's ruling by no means stood as the last word on the matter of information gathering and sharing by associations. On the left, the *Nation* warned darkly that American business was moving toward cartelization, while organized business increasingly pressed during the next several years for revision of the antitrust statutes. Hoover continued to believe that it would be desirable to give a federal agency limited authority to exempt trade associations from some antitrust provisions, but he doubted such legislation could pass Congress, and business's enthusiasm for cartelization made him uneasy. In remarks that he drafted (but never delivered) for a meeting of the Academy of Political Science, he warned of the danger that "some may take advantage of these rulings to push across the line which divides the legitimate from the unlawful." He warned that the prosecutions that would "properly and inevitably follow such conduct" would "raise again the feeling of fear in the minds of many whose activities are wholly proper" and impede the Commerce Department's useful activities. The inherent conflict between the need to gather and disseminate the information required to run a modern economy efficiently, and the prevention of activities that would curtail competition and deny individuals opportunity, could not be resolved readily. The problem, Hoover argued in proposing the name of an economist for a vacancy on the FTC in 1926, was "much more economic than legalistic," but many experts, and certainly Hoover's critics, were unwilling to judge the issue on that ground.[34]

Despite Hoover's continuing enthusiasm for business self-regulation in theory, he failed during the Commerce years to find a practical solution to the problem of trade associations and the antitrust laws. As a pamphlet that the department published in 1927 admitted, the collection of statistical information "as to production costs, volume of production, stocks, sales, and selling prices can be conducted in a lawful manner and for a lawful purpose," but it was "equally capable of misuse." Experience showed that "both methods of treatment have been employed." The choice whether use of the information would be legal or illegal, proper or improper, the authors concluded, depended upon "the spirit of the members of the association projected through the agency which they create." That standard, however, was far too vague to provide useful policy guidance. However enthusiastically Hoover might laud "a new merchant spirit, the essence of which is service to the community," in his more realistic moments he conceded that not everyone would necessarily follow ethical principles.[35]

IV

As befitted an evangelist, Hoover did not dwell on government's power to enforce ethical behavior through the antitrust laws. Europe's recent experience with the decay and abandonment of democracy and the rise of autocracy, he believed, served as a warning against "overloading" governments with functions that "should be borne by individual enterprises." The democratization of corporate ownership through widespread stock holding and the rise of the consumer economy in which workers became customers, he argued in *American Individualism*, had made companies "more sensitive to the moral opinions of the people." If corporations behaved unethically and treated workers badly, they would lose investors and customers. The *New Republic* derided this rosy interpretation of business behavior as totally unsubstantiated by experience, but such fact-checking missed Hoover's main point. Whatever the shortfalls and imperfections of the past, he believed, in the future the "organizations for advancement of ideas in the community for mutual cooperation and economic objectives" would provide "a school of public responsibility." Thus, in the end, his promise to combine a rising standard of living, maximum individual opportunity, and corporate morality came down to faith. He believed fervently that "there is developing in our people a new valuation of individuals and of groups and of nations." For all its horrors, the war had opened a new vision of "service to those with whom we come in contact, service to the nation, and service to the world itself." As Ralph Arnold wrote in a form letter promoting the pamphlet, it was indeed "a sermon."[36]

The praise heaped upon *American Individualism* suggests that it stood squarely at the center of what Richard Hofstadter called "the American political tradition." Its optimistic celebration of business reflected not only Hoover's personal experience but also the experience of his generation and, indeed, of the one before his. Ever since the late nineteenth century, the United States had been on an upward trajectory, its corporations growing larger, wealthier, and more dominant around the world. Wages and living standards of Americans in general had risen. In the almost thirty years since the end of the great depression of the 1890s, the country had experienced only two brief recessions, in 1907 and 1921, and neither had seemed to most people to reveal serious flaws in the system. To be sure, the Progressives had criticized unbridled capitalism, but they sought to control, not smother, it. *American Individualism* embraced their warnings and concluded that the system, now nearly perfected, promised even brighter days ahead.[37]

CHAPTER 13

The Commerce Department, 1922

After a year of struggling with the postwar recession and restructuring the Commerce Department to promote American business at home and abroad, Hoover saw the department as poised to make a major impact in 1922. Old problems never seemed to go away, however, and new ones thrust themselves forward, demanding attention.

The agricultural situation proved particularly intractable, and differences about how to handle it hardened, making it less likely that the administration would arrive at any effective policy. By 1922, the bottom seemed to be dropping out of the farm economy, and no one could guess how much worse things would get. In 1919, wheat had sold for $2 a bushel, cotton for thirty cents a pound, and Iowa farm lands for $500 an acre. By mid-1922, wheat and cotton prices had declined by 50 percent, corn by two-thirds, and the value of farm land by almost 40 percent. Farmers who had borrowed heavily to buy land and machinery faced ruinous debts, and the banks that had made loans to them found themselves in equal trouble. In fact, 1922 turned out to be the bottom of the slump, and the farm economy began a slow and uneven recovery in 1923, but the incredible volatility and unpredictability of farm prices over the previous six years left farmers frightened and receptive to unprecedented options.[1]

The issue began to come to a head at a national agricultural conference called by Secretary of Agriculture Henry Wallace in January 1922. President Harding dashed some delegates' hopes at the outset by declaring that the government could do "little more than give the farmer the chance to organize and help himself," but that did not prevent others from urging government action. George N. Peek, a delegate representing the agricultural machinery industry, spoke for the distressed when he introduced a resolution demanding that the government take immediate steps to restore the parity of farm products with manufactured goods. A divided conference endorsed Peek's resolution, but he never presented the full details of the plan that he and his colleague at the Moline Plow Company, Hugh S. Johnson, had worked out. Their plan proposed that the government extend tariff protection on farm products, then charter an export corporation to purchase surplus commodities at parity prices for export. If world prices for some commodities fell below stabilized domestic prices, the export corporation would recover its losses by charging an "equalization fee" to the producers of protected crops whose prices had stayed high because of tariff protection.[2] Caricatured by opponents as a proposal to have the government purchase farm surpluses and dump them overseas, the general theory of the Peek-Johnson plan became widely popular among farmers during the 1920s. Although Harding, Coolidge, and most administration leaders opposed it, Henry Wallace's Agriculture Department eventually sided with the farmers.

Hugh Johnson gave Hoover a copy of the Peek-Johnson plan in January 1922, and the secretary turned it over to his staff for analysis. They concluded it would not work. With the prices of manufactured goods falling, they argued, it would be impossible to calculate a price index that could be used to set a parity relationship between manufactured and agricultural goods. And while higher agricultural prices might help farmers, more expensive food would hurt consumers. Hoover agreed, adding that he believed the plan would drive up prices in general, leaving the farmer no better off. He argued increasingly adamantly that the only feasible solution to the farmer's problems lay in better marketing and curtailing waste in transportation and distribution. Secretary Wallace, who had received the Peek-Johnson plan with interest but had not yet committed himself to support it, resented Hoover's assertive position on the issue. According to Washington rumors, Hoover's meddling in Agriculture's business had driven Wallace to the brink of resignation.[3]

Whatever the strengths or weaknesses of the Peek-Johnson plan, it represented at least a new idea for dealing with the agricultural crisis. Secretary Wallace responded slowly to it but at least seemed willing to consider it. Hoover, having rejected Peek-Johnson, had nothing better to offer farmers. He could only reiterate his previous proposals for stimulating exports and for loaning money to banks and cooperatives in the farm states. By year's end, the agricultural outlook seemed as gloomy as ever. A pessimistic press release from the Commerce Department warned that overproduction would ultimately be solved by farmers moving to the city, where they would compete with urban workers for jobs. Organized labor, it contended, must curtail strikes and cooperate with management to increase production. Doing that would result in higher wages and improved living standards, thus creating new domestic markets for agricultural products.[4]

I

The threat of a catastrophic coal strike looming in the spring of 1922 made the idea of cooperation between labor and management seem utopian. With contracts due to expire on April 1 in both the bituminous (soft) and anthracite (hard) coal mines, the country faced the dismaying possibility that there would be no coal available to heat homes; power railroads, ships, and industry; or generate electricity.[5]

Characteristically, Hoover responded to the threatened strike by setting up an expert committee to gather information and recommend solutions for problems. Securing a $10,000 grant from the Cabot Trust Fund of Boston, in late January he asked a number of prominent union men and operators to serve on a study committee. As with the Unemployment Conference, Edward Eyre Hunt would lead a team of experts in collecting data and drafting recommendations for the committee. The committee never met, however, because the beginning of the strike made it impossible to separate underlying problems from current conflicts. Hunt and Hoover hoped that "when the edge has been taken off the strike," the committee's examination of the industry might show the way to a permanent settlement, but they concluded that the study should be postponed for the time being.[6]

A second initiative, to try to avert the strike by stimulating the export market for coal, proved even less fruitful. In December 1921, Hoover and C. C. McChord, chairman of the Interstate Commerce Commission (ICC), asked the railroads to consider a temporary, dollar-a-ton reduction of freight rates on coal intended for export. The railroads agreed to study the proposal but rejected it early in January. Already squeezed by rising labor costs and rigidly controlled rates, they argued that a special coal rate would lead other industries to demand rate reductions and would not, in any case, make American coal competitive with the British product in the chaotic European market.[7]

In March, Ohio coal companies proposed a series of regional contracts in place of a national labor agreement, arguing that differing costs of production in each coal-producing area made such an approach logical. The United Mine Workers saw that as a divide-and-conquer strategy, however, and would have nothing to do with it. Given the intransigent attitudes of labor and management, the expectation on both sides of quick victory, and the fact that the public had not yet suffered from a coal shortage, Hoover concluded that he could do nothing to avert the impending strike, which began on April 1.[8]

A month after the strike started, Hoover began to sound out reactions to another idea—the possibility of stabilizing the industry by creating a marketing cooperative among producers. The idea paralleled a proposal he had suggested as a solution to the agricultural depression, but, as he admitted, a marketing cooperative sounded much like a "coal trust." Harry Garfield, the former Fuel Administrator in Hoover's Food Administration, warned also that any cooperative plan would surely fail unless coal companies, unions, and the railroads had equal shares in administering it. Since the coal strike would have been averted if those three groups could have cooperated, Hoover's idea never developed beyond speculation.[9]

By mid-May, the country faced a serious coal shortage, and with only non-union mines in production, rising prices and hoarding worsened the situation. Hoover blamed the nonunion producers for "profiteering" and summoned them to Washington for "consultation" during which he lectured them that "far-reaching action by the Government must become inevitable" if prices continued to rise. He also told them that he had suggested to the railroads and public utilities that they form "buying committees" for the purchase of coal, and he planned to advise "other large consuming industries" to use a similar approach to prevent the suppliers from starting bidding wars.[10]

In fact, Hoover was bluffing, and the producers knew it. "Buying committees" would almost certainly have been illegal under the Sherman Act. When prices continued to rise, the Commerce Department fell back on suggesting prices for each of the mining districts according to World War I scales. The department then put pressure on high-price sellers by publicizing the difference between their prices and the scale. As Hoover admitted, however, the system had "no force in law." Even so, the National Retail Coal Merchants Association complained that, when the department proposed a wholesale price for a district, consumers suffered because dealers could not bargain for a lower price. Although irritated by what he saw as the uncooperative attitude of both dealers and some producers, Hoover rejected an offer by Senator William E. Borah to introduce price control legislation. Probably, he thought, the strike would end before the bill passed, but even if it passed in time, controls would be of doubtful constitutionality and would require a large and expensive bureaucracy. Recent price statistics, he contended, showed that voluntary restraints had worked fairly well, and he thought it better to continue that program. On June 8, he issued a press release claiming that the "run away market" had been halted and prices rolled back to pre–May 15 levels, except for a few uncooperative producers.[11]

Despite Hoover's claims, the voluntary price plan had not worked. Not only did a minority of producers refuse to cooperate, but the policy came under attack from other directions as well. John L. Lewis, president of the United Mine Workers, accused the nonunion mines of cheating and profiteering, while the retail dealers insisted that price restraints would bankrupt them. Democratic Senator David Walsh denounced Hoover's efforts as a concealed giveaway to the nonunion operators and threatened an investigation. Hoover vigorously denied all the charges and invited representatives of the National Coal Association and other organizations to a meeting at the Commerce Department on June 15 to discuss ways to bring the uncooperative producers into line. When the meeting produced nothing new, he had to face the reality that the voluntary program had failed. On June 17, he recommended that President Harding summon operators and miners to the White House and press them to begin serious negotiations. The so-called Herrin massacre, in which striking miners killed twenty-one strikebreakers in southern Illinois during late June, underlined the secretary's concerns and demonstrated how explosive the situation had become.[12]

At the White House meeting on July 1, 1922, the president urged the two sides to start talks and to resume production while negotiating. Both sides rejected the restart proposal, but the White House meeting led to substantive bargaining with Secretary of Labor James J. Davis and Hoover mediating. To no one's surprise, the two sides started far apart. The operators insisted on separate contracts for each district and proposed that the president appoint an arbitration board for each, while the union demanded a single contract and spurned arbitration. In the hope of averting a complete breakdown, Hoover proposed lumping the thirty-five existing districts into eight or nine larger ones, but he doubted the union would accept the idea. Finally, on July 5, after four frustrating days, he suggested that everyone take the weekend off and meet again with the president the following week.[13]

Over the weekend, Hoover, Davis, and Harding worked out a new proposal, which the president presented to the contending parties on July 10. Harding stressed the vital importance of settling the strike before winter and proposed the establishment of a committee made up of representatives chosen by each side, and with the power to propose, within a month, a temporary wage scale that would apply until April 1, 1924. In the meantime, miners would return to work at their old wages. If negotiators failed to reach agreement by August 10, the old scale would remain in effect. In either case, Harding promised that after August 10 he would ask Congress to create a coal commission to investigate the industry "exhaustively." He would charge the commission to find ways to eliminate labor conflicts and reduce intermittent operation and to assure the nation a dependable fuel supply.[14]

Neither Hoover nor Harding felt optimistic that the miners and operators would accept the proposal. But, in fact, the issue had become moot. By mid-July, time had run out for the committee approach. A U.S. Geological Survey memo on July 18 warned that the nonunion mines alone, even working at full production, could not supply the country's basic coal needs for winter. All mines, unionized or not, needed to resume full production as soon as possible.[15]

Hoover responded quickly to the new information. On July 19, he forwarded to the president a plan that had been germinating in his mind for some time. In a nutshell, he proposed the formation of regional committees having the authority to assign coal orders from railroads and utilities to operating mines and to allot railroad cars to ship the coal. With a committee of railroad executives and ICC members in Washington setting shipping priorities, the plan would guarantee coal supplies to the most vital customers. Regional committees would apportion contracts and railroad cars among producers who cooperated in holding down prices while denying them to those who refused to cooperate. Hoover believed the plan could be put into effect without specific authorization from Congress. He did not indicate who would serve on the regional committees or how priorities in coal distribution would be determined.[16]

Since the plan raised obvious antitrust issues, Hoover sought opinions from the director general of the Railroad Administration, the secretary of the interior, the attorney general, and the ICC. They all agreed that it would be legal if it merely denied interstate transportation to those producers who failed to comply with fair prices set by the Commerce Department. On July 26, the White House announced the establishment of a Coal Distribution Committee made up of representatives from the departments of Commerce, Interior, and Justice, and from the ICC. The president named Henry C. Spencer, a former vice president of the Southern Railway and the wartime purchasing agent for the Railroad Administration, "federal coal distributor." He announced that an administrative committee made up of representatives of the coal operators, railroads, and "where necessary, the larger consuming groups" would advise and assist the coal distributor. The announcement did not identify "the larger consuming groups," nor indicate when or how they might be consulted. At the regional level, orders and railroad cars were to be assigned by committees made up of mine operators. No labor representatives were included at any level, and not surprisingly, Samuel Gompers strongly suspected the plan of being a barely concealed attack on the unions. Recognizing the danger of labor hostility, Edward Eyre Hunt urged that Hoover or Harding invite Gompers to Washington at once to "talk out all the suspicion and doubt that is in him."[17]

Hoover agreed that Gompers needed reassuring, but he worried even more because the fuel distribution plan did nothing to address the underlying problems of the coal industry. Except in the very best of times, the industry suffered from chronic overproduction, and inefficient transportation, poor storage facilities, and chaotic labor relations exacerbated the problem. Labor conflicts, he believed, would be largely eliminated "if there were less intermittency," and collective bargaining determined "standards of wages and conditions of labor." He preferred to leave to the presidential coal commission the delicate questions of how to reduce overproduction and stabilize the industry permanently. He had been living night and day with coal's endless problems, wrote Lou, until "the very word Coal" had become "quite hateful." Her secretary declared that Hoover had nearly turned into "a Pillar of Coal."[18]

By August, the strike had exhausted both labor and management, and in mid-August, union and operator representatives from about 20 percent of the soft coal fields met in Cleveland and agreed to extend the prestrike contract to April 1, 1923. The group also endorsed the idea of a presidential commission to suggest better ways of resolving future disputes. The Cleveland settlement set a pattern for other regional negotiations, and by early September the strike had come to an end. The soft coal agreements put pressure on the anthracite operators and strikers, and in early September they also reached agreement, extending their contract to August 31, 1923. Given the wild economic fluctuations of the past two years in the economy as a whole, both operators and miners welcomed a deal that restored some stability to the industry. Everyone hoped that a presidential coal commission could find a new approach to negotiating contracts. Although the union undoubtedly took a beating during the strike, its leaders claimed at least a minor victory in an antiunion era.[19]

Hoover kept abreast of the progress of the strike negotiations but took no direct role. By the time negotiators at last reached agreement, he worried that winter would arrive before adequate coal supplies could be mined and distributed. A strike by railroad shopmen, which began on July 1, could make the delicate situation catastrophic. Moreover, the nonunion coal companies, released by the strike settlements from their promises to hold down prices, could now exploit the shortage and jack up prices outrageously. Although in public Hoover continued to maintain that the voluntary cooperation and patriotism of the nonunion operators had carried the country through the crisis, in private he expressed very different views. There were "swine" among the operators, he declared, who had exploited the situation to "plunder the consumer." To prevent that from continuing, he proposed that the administration support legislation making permanent the ICC's authority over coal distribution. In addition, he appealed to the governors of coal-producing states to establish "some sort of voluntary arrangement for establishing fair prices" on intrastate sales of coal. For the longer term, he urged the president to do as the coal companies and union both requested and appoint a federal commission made up of representatives of the miners and operators, with a neutral chairman to be named by Hoover. The commission would investigate "every phase of the industry" and suggest measures to assure continuous production and settle labor conflicts.[20]

On September 12, in a speech to a convention of chemical salesmen, Hoover reiterated his call for a coal commission. The public, he argued, had a right to a reliable supply of coal at reasonable prices, but adversarial labor-management relationships in both the hard and soft coal mines, and the enormous number of small competing mines in the soft coal industry, made that impossible. None of the traditional means for resolving labor issues—collective bargaining, conciliation, or arbitration—had prevented frequent, lengthy strikes. Somehow, a coal commission must find a method of resolving conflicts that would assure "the public [of] a continuous supply of its vital necessities and services upon terms fair to the employer and employee." If, in the process of doing that, private interests conflicted with the public's needs, "then the dominant right is public right." In the soft coal industry, the commission must promote a reorganization that would minimize overproduction, reduce layoffs, rationalize storage and distribution, and perhaps promote cooperative marketing.[21]

For the short term, Hoover hoped to alleviate shortages until the mines caught up with demand by organizing, through the U.S. Chamber of Commerce, a voluntary rationing and distribution system. At the secretary's suggestion, Julius Barnes and Alexander Legge of the Chamber called a meeting of business, railroad, and public utility executives in Washington on September 15. Hoover urged the business leaders to set an example for the country by ordering no more coal than they needed immediately. Overpurchasing, he argued, would lead to rapid price inflation.[22]

Following his signing on September 22 of the bill authorizing federal control over coal distribution, Harding appointed Conrad E. Spens, vice president of the Chicago, Burlington and Quincy Railroad, to succeed Henry C. Spencer as fuel distributor. Spens immediately began setting up machinery to carry out his charge. In fact, however, striking miners went back to work and production increased more quickly than anyone expected, bringing an end to the immediate crisis without Spens needing to invoke the new law. On January 1, 1923, Spens turned over his job to F. R. Wadleigh, who had been one of Hoover's assistants in the Commerce Department. Wadleigh would hold the thankless office during the next phase of the controversy.[23]

The appointment of a presidential coal commission in mid-October fulfilled Hoover's longstanding recommendation for a thorough study of the structure and operations of the industry. Pleased with this step, he informed E. M. Poston, chairman of the private committee he had set up to undertake a similar study, that the committee, its work suspended since the beginning of the strike, could be disbanded. In early 1923, Hoover returned the remainder of the money that had been contributed by the Cabot Foundation for the committee's work.[24]

Encouraged as Hoover was by the creation of the coal commission and the apparent success of his coal distribution plan, he knew that the soft coal agreement would expire on April 1, 1923, and that in the anthracite fields would run out on August 31, 1923. Nothing substantive had been done to resolve the industry's underlying problems or to remedy shortages in transportation, and the 1922 strike had left reserves alarmingly low. A new strike, he warned the president, would be far more dangerous to the nation than the previous one had been.[25]

II

Following the end of the strike, coal prices averaged almost 60 percent higher than before it began. Low supplies and the late season accounted for part of the jump, but Hoover argued that a shortage of railroad cars also contributed significantly to the increase. The mines, he estimated, could increase production by 20 or 30 percent—if the railroads could transport the coal. "Railway cars are the red blood corpuscles of commerce," he said, "and we suffer from commercial anemia every year, because they are starved." Nor was the problem confined to coal. Seasonal demands for scarce cars also drove up shipping costs for farmers and made them less competitive in the world market. Yet what could be done? Uncontrolled operation, regulation, and nationalization of the railroads had all been tried, and the problems had worsened under each approach. Instead, Hoover proposed "positive regulation," by which he meant that the ICC would encourage "voluntary consolidation of the weaker and stronger roads into larger systems" under the guidance of the commission. But, he admitted, although the Transportation Act of 1920 (the Esch-Cummins Act), which had returned the railroads to private control, endorsed such consolidation, neither the railroads nor the commission had pushed for it. Meanwhile, irrational rate structures and an "unsatisfactory" mechanism for resolving labor conflicts further weakened the lines.[26]

No problem Hoover faced as secretary of commerce proved more intransigent than the railroad tangle. As he explained in testimony before the ICC on February 3, 1922, high railroad rates inhibited national economic recovery, but rates were driven up in large part by high labor costs, which in turn resulted partly from the high cost of living, which was influenced by high transportation costs. Each segment of the problem depended on the others, in a closed circle that seemed to offer no point of access. "Great social and economic problems find their solutions slowly and by a process of trial and error," he concluded in his testimony, and in this case that process must begin with the railroads themselves. Rarely did the secretary reveal such uncertainty and lack of direction.[27]

During the spring of 1922, Hoover did his best to promote an evolutionary solution of the railroad problem, pushing regional conferences to address labor issues and suggesting the creation of a National Car Trust that would control the distribution of cars during peak load periods. None of this seemed to go anywhere, however, and in June a frustrated Hoover put the blame on lack of vision among railroad executives. "The impossibility of a hundred railway presidents agreeing on anything," he wrote, resulted in an "almost hopeless" drift toward nationalization. ICC Commissioner Ernest Lewis agreed. When the commission had tried to hold hearings on a proposal to consolidate lines, he told Hoover, it had found railroad executives unprepared even to discuss the matter. He predicted that it would be a year at best before there would be any progress on the issue.[28]

That summer, the Railway Labor Board, yielding to the railroads' lamentations that excessive labor costs were bankrupting them, announced a seven-cents-an-hour pay cut for workers. Lacking authority to permit the lines to fire excess employees protected by union contracts, the board could only cut wages for all workers rather than attacking the underlying problem of "featherbedding." On the first of July, 400,000 railroad shopmen went on strike.

A few days after the strike began, Hoover told the president that he did not expect any serious disruption from it. Whether his optimism resulted from the fact that only the shop craft unions, not operating personnel, had struck, or from the railroads' success in hiring strikebreakers, was unclear, but in any case, he showed little initial concern about the strike. By the end of July, however, the issue had acquired new urgency as a settlement of the coal strike neared. The cabinet divided over what should be done, with Attorney General Daugherty urging strong action against the strikers and Labor Secretary Davis supporting the strikers' claims that they had been treated unfairly by the Railway Labor Board. Harding dithered but eventually agreed to recommend a compromise suggested by Davis, under which strikers would go back to work with their seniority rights protected but at the reduced pay proposed by the Railway Labor Board.[29]

Hoover regarded the proposed arrangement as reasonable and went to New York on August 1 to try to sell it to railroad executives. They rejected it the next day, whereupon Harding sweetened the offer by proposing that restoration of workers' seniority rights be left up to the Railway Labor Board. Before either side responded, however, railroad operating personnel began walking out in Tennessee. If that strike spread, the situation would become much more serious, and the administration came under increasing pressure from the business community to cut it short. Without informing other cabinet members, Attorney General Daugherty persuaded the president that he should seek legal action against the strikers. On September 1, Daugherty appeared before federal judge James H. Wilkerson in Chicago and obtained a sweeping injunction forbidding workers from interfering in any way with the operation of the railroads, or from supporting or encouraging the strike in any manner. Hoover later recalled that both he and Secretary of State Hughes denounced the injunction on both moral and legal grounds at the next cabinet meeting, but Daugherty remembered no such objections. Railroad executives reacted ecstatically to the injunction, while labor leaders expressed fury. Harding, somewhat shocked by the outcry, instructed Daugherty to seek withdrawal of the sections of the injunction that most flagrantly violated workers' civil rights, and on September 16, the attorney general reluctantly complied. Nevertheless, the injunction broke the back of the strike, and gradually, over the next weeks, most local unions reached settlements with the companies.[30]

Hoover denied that he had pressured the railroad executives to accept the president's proposed settlement and also seemed anxious to distance himself from the antiunion tone adopted by the president and from the injunction. He had been working hard, he assured a former member of the ICC, to improve "personal relationships" between railroad executives and labor leaders. His efforts, he thought, had done "some good," though he admitted that much more needed to be done to replace an adversarial relationship with a cooperative one. But when U.S. Chamber of Commerce President Julius Barnes proposed a national transportation conference to seek broader solutions to the railroad problem, Hoover quietly discouraged the idea. Harding, he told Barnes, did not think the time was right for any new railroad legislation. Perhaps, he suggested, a small conference with the minority of "constructive minded railway men" could pinpoint "fundamental problems" and suggest "what could be accomplished amongst transportation people entirely outside the field of legislation."[31]

Hoover never shared the antiunionism expressed by Attorney General Daugherty during the railroad strike. He refused to believe that labor and management would inevitably clash. Finding a way to show both sides that their self-interest lay in cooperation seemed to him one of government's most important tasks. As he put it in a letter to Samuel Gompers, elimination of conflict between labor and management could expand production by 5 to 30 percent, and that in turn would justify increases in both wages and profits.[32]

III

Despite his best efforts, Hoover made little progress toward securing cooperation between labor and capital in the railroads, but he did better with the steel industry. By the 1920s, steel had become one of the last major industries to retain a twelve-hour workday, which they justified as essential to maintain continuous production without excessive labor costs. Efforts to move to a ten- or even eight-hour day had begun before the war, but wartime labor shortages and demand for steel had given the companies excuses not to change. Following the war, the return of the German steel industry to twelve-hour shifts, which had been abolished in 1918, reinforced the American steel makers' argument that they would be at a competitive disadvantage if forced to end the two-shift system.[33]

Nevertheless, both American and German steelmakers faced increasing pressure to abandon the twelve-hour workday. The inclusion of the charter of the International Labor Organization (ILO), with its endorsement of the eight-hour day, as Part XIII of the Treaty of Versailles, set a worldwide goal for labor, and President Wilson had invited the ILO to hold its first meeting in Washington. The Senate's rejection of the Treaty of Versailles during the ILO's Washington meeting cast a dark shadow over the new organization, but its American supporters, including Hoover, hoped that it would become an effective advocate of the eight-hour day anyway. When Albert Thomas, director general of the organization, visited the United States in early 1923, Hoover met with him unofficially, and, at a dinner closed to the press, urged the U.S. Chamber of Commerce to forge a private connection with the ILO, very much as the American Federation of Labor (AFL) had already done under Samuel Gompers's leadership.[34]

Meanwhile, Hoover had been working quietly behind the scenes to advance the idea of the eight-hour day in the steel industry. Early in 1921, the reform engineer Morris L. Cooke had suggested that a scientific study of the twelve-hour shift in "continuous process industries" such as steel might demonstrate its inefficiency. The wealthy Bostonian Philip Cabot, Cooke noted, had recently completed an article on the subject that would be published in a forthcoming issue of the *Atlantic Monthly*. What about asking him to support a study of the issue? Hoover welcomed Cooke's suggestion and approached Cabot about funding a Federated American Engineering Societies (FAES) study committee. When Cabot agreed, the committee organized quickly and published its report that autumn.[35]

Hoover, relatively certain that the committee's report would favor replacing the twelve-hour shift with an eight-hour system, had begun softening up the steel executives in advance of the report. In April, he suggested that the president call a meeting of steel men at the White House to discuss the issue. The conference, he argued, would make a favorable impression on the public and would put "a certain moral pressure" on the steel companies to take action.[36]

Hoover had judged the situation correctly. The steel companies remained dead set against the change. As Elbert H. Gary, chairman of the U.S. Steel Corporation, explained, the company had already reduced the number of men working twelve-hour shifts from 32 percent of the workers to 14 percent, but the necessity of keeping the furnaces running twenty-four hours a day made it difficult to eliminate the long shifts completely. In any case, said Gary, the men themselves wanted "to work longer hours in order to make larger compensation." If one company went to a three-shift system and others stayed with the two-shift system, he contended, all the employees of the three-shift company would immediately go to the two-shift companies in order to make more money.[37]

Gary's insistence that only the workers stood in the way of abolishing the twelve-hour day put the argument rather one-sidedly, but he was correct that all the companies had to adopt the reform at once or those that did not would gain a competitive advantage. The forty-one steel company executives who met with the president, Hoover, Treasury Secretary Mellon, and Secretary of Labor Davis at the White House on the evening of May 18 all contended that the change would be ruinous. With no technological innovations in sight to increase productivity, they contended that going from twelve- to eight-hour shifts for furnace operators would increase their labor costs enough to make American steel uncompetitive on the world market.[38]

That autumn, the FAES committee published its report, with a foreword by President Harding. It challenged the companies' positions on every issue, contending that a change to eight-hour shifts would increase worker efficiency, raise morale, and improve companies' relations with the public. The committee estimated that, because of the small number of men tending the furnaces, the increased cost to the companies of going from two to three shifts without reducing each worker's pay would be no more than 3 to 15 percent, which, they argued, was "less than the variations . . . already experienced by plants competing with one another." Small improvements in efficiency would easily offset the increased costs.[39]

It would be another year before the industry, under public pressure orchestrated in part by Hoover, would move reluctantly toward the eight-hour day. When it came, the change turned out to be something of a pyrrhic victory for workers, for the companies cut costs by replacing most of their twelve-hour shift men with new, lower-paid, black and Latino laborers. In 1924, U.S. Steel estimated that the changeover to the eight-hour day had increased costs by about 10 percent a year. Given strong demand for steel during the decade, the change did not bring the ruin steel executives had predicted, but the industry's experience raised questions about Hoover's argument that labor-management cooperation would necessarily increase productivity and result in higher profits and wages.[40]

For Hoover, the twelve-hour-day issue encompassed more than concern about the welfare of steelworkers. As Columbia University Professor Samuel McCune Lindsay argued, the men who worked twelve-hour days played only a limited role in their families' lives and almost none in community affairs. That situation struck at the heart of Hoover's vision of an America with a rising standard of living in which everyone would share in education, healthful recreation, and participation in public affairs. He hoped not merely for greater prosperity, bigger profits, and higher wages, but stimulating leisure activities for all Americans.[41]

IV

Nothing was more central to that vision than improved housing. A year after the end of the war, a Senate Select Committee on Reconstruction and Production, chaired by Senator William M. Calder of New York, had estimated that the country lacked a million units of housing as a result of a slowdown in building during the war. In testimony before the committee on September 23, 1920, Hoover argued that the war had so disrupted both housing construction and transportation that the federal government needed to take a hand in promoting a revival. He did not mean that the government should take direct responsibility for construction, he explained, nor even, as earlier witnesses had suggested, that the interest income from money loaned out in the form of mortgages should receive a tax exemption, as did the interest on government bonds. He characterized the income tax as "one of the most just and sound taxes ever imposed," and he opposed "the exemption of any additional classes of investments." But he did believe that multiple federal agencies dealing with construction should be consolidated into a single "national commission" charged with promoting cooperation among builders, suppliers, lending agencies, and local governments. Such "active cooperation" would create the public confidence necessary for increased construction.[42]

When he became secretary of commerce, Hoover made housing a major priority. He immediately invited Franklin T. Miller, former secretary of the Calder Committee, to investigate what the department could do to stimulate "voluntary action" in local communities among builders, suppliers, and financial agencies. Miller brought experts on various aspects of construction, zoning, building codes, and finance into the department, and in April 1921 he arranged for the introduction of legislation in Congress to create a "Division of Construction [later Building] and Housing" in the Commerce Department. To head the new division, Hoover named Dr. John M. Gries, a former Harvard economics professor and adviser to the U.S. Shipping Board, who had worked before and during the war on government studies of lumber and transportation costs. The new division, Hoover explained, would promote the voluntary cooperation of the construction industry in eliminating waste, standardizing construction and building codes, encouraging the development of model zoning codes, and increasing access to financing. In Hoover's view, rationalized construction would not only make better housing available to more Americans, but it also would help to transform the construction industry from a frequent victim of the economic cycle to a stabilizing force.[43]

Gries went enthusiastically to work, setting up national committees to draft model zoning and construction codes, surveying real estate boards across the country about conditions in their areas, and establishing committees to study such things as standardizing plumbing fixtures, bricks, and lumber sizes. In addition, the department called more than a hundred local conferences of chambers of commerce, labor organizations, builders, suppliers, and bankers to discuss ways to stimulate construction. Hoover hoped that those steps, while not revolutionary individually, would cumulatively produce "a radical departure in house construction and economics" that would provide a "real solution" to the housing shortage as well as improvement in housing quality. When Senator William H. King of Utah proposed calling a national housing conference, Hoover listed the department's recent activities and argued that his incremental approach was preferable to a national conference, which might bog down in debate over "the prices of materials and wages" and never produce substantive proposals.[44]

Whether as a result of Hoover's initiatives or because of the general upturn in the economy, in March 1922 the Commerce Department predicted "a big year for home builders." Contracts awarded for housing construction in the last three months, a departmental press release reported, had run well ahead of 1921. "The year 1922," the release enthused, "could easily rank ahead of any year since the beginning of the War."[45]

By summer, the Housing Division had become the cheerleader of a national campaign to make affordable houses available to middle-income Americans. The division's "plumbing code committee" drafted a model code for cities and sought reactions from people in the field. A "zoning primer" published by the division explained the purpose of urban zoning and suggested ways to develop local ordinances. John Gries estimated that between fifty and a hundred thousand copies of the "Zoning Primer," published in June, would be distributed to civic and industry organizations by September 1. In New York City, the Russell Sage Foundation went even beyond zoning to fund the development of a "comprehensive plan" for the development of the whole city. And in Chicago, Benjamin J. Rosenthal, founder of the Chicago Mail Order House, pushed the Chicago Housing Association to begin the construction of five hundred low-cost houses for the poor.[46]

The American Construction Council, established in 1922 by Hoover in cooperation with R. C. Marshall representing the Associated General Contractors of America, and with Franklin D. Roosevelt as first president, worked closely with the Housing Division. It set out to make construction a stabilizing force by establishing fair practice codes, reducing cutthroat competition, and gathering information on orders and contracts. The publication of information on "probable conditions for several months ahead" in regard to the demand for labor and materials, Hoover argued, would enable "those contemplating building" to postpone or accelerate their plans in order to avoid or take advantage of shortages or surpluses. "Building fever," Roosevelt explained, "comes in epidemics like the influenza or the grippe." Planning through the council would spread construction out over seasons and years. Unfortunately, whatever the merits of the council idea, it worked poorly in practice. Roosevelt had little luck securing either money or members, and the council never developed an effective program. By early 1928, it could no longer pay its tiny staff, and Roosevelt had largely given up on it. "I am frankly pretty skeptical about the council accomplishing any great things in the next year or two," he wrote in March.[47]

Along with his attempt to enlist builders in self-regulation through the Construction Council, Hoover set out to popularize the ideas being generated in the Housing Division. A way of doing that emerged through a request from Mrs. William Brown Meloney that Hoover serve on the advisory council of a new organization. Kentucky-born Marie Meloney (known to her friends as "Missy") was a journalist and editor with a long record of devotion to social causes. She had begun her journalistic career at sixteen as assistant to a Washington newspaper correspondent, became the first woman reporter admitted to the Senate press gallery, and reported on both Democratic and Republican conventions before she turned eighteen. In 1922, she edited the popular magazine, *The Delineator*, which she left in 1926 to become editor of the *New York Herald Tribune Magazine*. She happened to be present in the autumn of 1921 when President Harding, visiting a model home in Dayton, remarked that he would like to see similar displays in every American city. Inspired by the president's comment, she set out to make it happen by founding Better Homes in America, which attempted to organize an annual "Demonstration Week" in every American city and town during which the latest advances in home building and home economics would be demonstrated and popularized.

Thinking big, she invited a number of prominent people, including Vice President Coolidge, Hoover, Secretary of Agriculture Wallace, Labor Secretary Davis, and John Gries to sit on an Advisory Council for the new organization. Hoover accepted eagerly, recognizing that Meloney's energy made Better Homes in America an ideal tool for popularizing the new ideas bubbling up in the Housing Division. During the next twelve years, he served as president or chairman of the organization and raised $75,000 to $100,000 a year from donors to support its activities. In 1922, Better Homes sponsored exhibits or model homes in 2,500 American towns and cities during its October Demonstration Week.[48]

Hoover always worried that Demonstration Week, which the organization intended merely to showcase advances in home building, would become commercialized and that companies would hijack demonstrations to promote particular products. The Advisory Council issued strict orders that any government employee involved with the program must avoid endorsing or seeming to endorse specific products and must prevent any company involved from capitalizing on the displays. A strong advocate of comparison shopping, Hoover urged that visitors to demonstrations be warned clearly that "the houses offered will not, in all cases, be bargains." The demonstration program, he told an overeager Toledo realtor, would undoubtedly create "an increased desire for home ownership," but it must not "be made an excuse for unwarranted profits in the selling of houses." He explained in a Better Homes in America pamphlet that his goal was not merely to spur the building of more houses but to create homes that would strengthen families and improve Americans' lives.[49] That emphasis on long-term benefits to the society over immediate profits proved difficult to institutionalize. As with other organizations through which he worked, the balance frequently slipped after he gave up active leadership.

V

Occasionally, of course, long-term development harmonized with immediate interests. That seemed the case with proposals to develop an integrated navigation and shipping system in the Mississippi River drainage area and to build a navigable waterway linking the Great Lakes to the Atlantic through the St. Lawrence River. Hoover endorsed both those projects soon after his return to the United States and often spoke out in support of them thereafter. As he saw it, they would assure the prosperity of the Midwest, where waterways would supplement the railroad system to link the region firmly and inexpensively to world commerce. (See Fig. 14.3) But even more, developed waterways would help solve problems in "flood control, reclamation, irrigation, [and] electrical power," and thus contribute to the greater productivity and prosperity of the entire country. The intimate link between national development and waterway development, he contended, justified the direct involvement of the federal government in planning and financing those great projects. Washington should take responsibility for navigational improvements and flood control, encouraging local governments and private interests to participate wherever possible. The federal government must take the lead in planning and promoting the projects, as well as helping to clear local obstacles and parochial resistance.[50]

For those reasons, Hoover had agreed in December 1921 to become the chairman of a commission charged with negotiating an interstate compact among the states bordering the Colorado River. The compact would clear the way for federal construction of a major dam on the river to control floods, generate power, and supply water for irrigation. Representatives of the seven river basin states met in Washington between January 26 and January 30, 1922, and agreed to hold public hearings in the major cities of the Colorado basin later that spring. Hoover discussed the project with California Congressman Phil D. Swing, who, along with Senator Hiram Johnson, would sponsor legislation authorizing federal construction of the Colorado dam. Swing and Hoover agreed that the dam should be located on the Arizona-Nevada border, not far from Las Vegas, and that the federal government should build it, but the Congressman left the meeting thinking that Hoover favored only a low, flood-control dam, not a high dam that would generate significant power as well. But Swing, who suspected that Southern California utilities fearful of competition from publicly generated power had influenced the secretary, may have heard what he expected to hear. Hoover subsequently denied he had ever preferred a low dam. And his consistent support of multiuse development in other river systems makes it improbable that he favored limiting the Colorado project to flood control. In any event, following the publication of a Reclamation Service report in February that strongly endorsed a high dam in Nevada's Boulder Canyon to combine power generation, flood control, and irrigation, the secretary became an outspoken advocate of a high dam.[51]

In March, the commissioners held public hearings in the Colorado basin states. The hearings demonstrated broad public support for the project and brought an additional bonus as well. During the Nevada stopover, Hoover took the opportunity to visit the proposed damsite in Boulder Canyon and, while there, remarked that it looked like a good place for a dam. Back in Washington, his reputation as an engineer converted the casual comment into something much more substantial.[52]

Late in April, Swing and Johnson introduced identical bills in the House and Senate authorizing the construction of a high dam on the Colorado. But despite that auspicious start, things did not go smoothly. Mexico worried that the project would divert water to which it had legal title, and Wyoming asserted the right to much of the water from a major tributary of the Colorado on the basis of "prior appropriation," the legal doctrine that assigned water rights to the first user to claim them regardless of the needs of others, and regardless of the fact that Wyoming had not yet used the water. The Supreme

Court's June 1922 decision upholding Wyoming's position jeopardized all plans for the river's development. In testimony on the Swing-Johnson Bill before the House irrigation subcommittee on June 21, Hoover suggested inserting a provision in the bill that would set aside the prior appropriation doctrine and protect the water rights of all riparian states.[53]

The possibility that Congress might replace prior appropriation with federal dictation of water distribution alarmed practically everyone in the affected states. Over the summer, state leaders discussed the subject, and in the autumn Delph Carpenter, Colorado's commission member, came up with a workable compromise: namely, that the water be divided between the Upper (Colorado, New Mexico, Utah, and Wyoming) and Lower (Arizona, California, and Nevada) Basin states on a fifty-fifty basis. That broke the stalemate, and at a commission meeting in Santa Fe on November 16, the commissioners unanimously endorsed an interstate compact accepting the compromise. Hoover proclaimed triumphantly that "this River system has been freed from a generation of litigation, strikes and arrested development." At the commission's farewell dinner on November 24, he praised the commissioners fulsomely as having been uniquely "honest and straightforward throughout."[54]

Privately, he had less kind feelings for the state representatives. The negotiations had sorely tried his temper, he told Albert Fall. And although he liked the compact and thought that most of the states would welcome it, he feared that Arizona's "Bolshevik governor" might make trouble. Nor was that all. Some Californians had been grumbling that the compact favored the thinly populated Upper Basin states, and Midwestern farm organizations had objected that new irrigated farm lands would worsen the agricultural surplus. If Swing pushed for immediate passage of a large appropriation to build the dam, Hoover warned, it might arouse opposition to the whole project. It might be better, he suggested, to start by building a modest flood-control dam and plan to raise it later.[55]

Hoover's suggestion, intended as an expedient to avert political complications, revived all of Swing's fears. A flood control dam, he complained, would not raise the water level enough to make possible the long-promised All-American Canal to irrigate California's Imperial Valley. Instead, farmers would have to depend on the existing canal, which diverted water from the Colorado south of the Mexican border. Moreover, said Swing, a low dam might silt up quickly, effectively curtailing the Lower Basin's water rights. He recommended that California ratify the compact with a reservation that it would take effect only after Congress authorized a high dam at Boulder Canyon. Hoover protested that the low dam would protect the Imperial Valley from floods until money became available for the high dam, but Californians dismissed his argument.[56] His proposal had been a political blunder, and it was clear that his troubles with the interstate compact had not ended at Santa Fe.

Hoover had accepted the Colorado River Commission chairmanship because river system development occupied a central place in his vision of a rising American standard of living. He advocated tax reform for the same reason. Like most Republicans, he believed that wartime excess profits taxes should be repealed, but he also thought that the wealthy should continue to bear the principal share of the tax burden. At present, he argued, many of the wealthy evaded that responsibility by shifting their investments from taxable stocks and bonds to tax-free government securities. That left the government excessively dependent on corporate taxes, siphoned money out of the market that might otherwise be loaned to businesses and farmers for growth, and increased the tax burden on the "earned incomes" of middle- and working-class Americans. Since there were good arguments for retaining the tax-exempt status of government bonds, he suggested instead raising inheritance taxes on large estates. Doing that, he contended, would help the middle class without reducing incentives for investment and innovation, would protect the borrowing power of local governments, would lower rates of interest to farmers and businesses, and would "tend to redistribute the economic power of large estates." The shift would be justifiable, therefore, on both economic and social grounds to promote stable economic growth and the general welfare.[57]

Treasury Secretary Mellon rejected Hoover's argument for an inheritance tax increase. Although they agreed that wartime tax policy had shifted the burden excessively to the wealthy and the upper-middle class, which curtailed the amount of risk capital available for economic expansion, Hoover and Mellon had sharply different views on how much revenue the government needed. Mellon argued that federal taxes should cover only minimal government expenses and reduction of the national debt, while Hoover had a more expansive conception of the government's role, including such things as river system development. On the whole, that meant he favored somewhat higher taxes than Mellon, but that was only a matter of degree. Their disagreement over the inheritance tax revealed a difference on principle. Hoover emphasized the social function of the tax in limiting the political and social influence of great wealth, while Mellon opposed it on economic grounds because he believed it impeded the "accumulation of capital" upon which progress depended. President Harding admitted that he found the whole business confusing. Usually, in such cases he tried to find a middle ground, but Mellon seemed so certain of his position, and Harding had such respect for Mellon's economic wisdom, that he bowed to the secretary's views. Wishing to avoid confrontation, he tried to let Hoover down gently, telling him that his inheritance tax proposal did not seem like "good tactics . . . at the present time."[58]

Blocked on the question of tax reform, which was arguably not the concern of the Commerce Department anyway, Hoover turned his attention to the promotion of foreign trade and overseas investments, which certainly did fall within his purview. Just as Iowa farmers and Pittsburgh businessmen could no longer detach themselves from distant markets in New York or San Francisco, the United States found itself inextricably caught up in the international economic system and must attempt to make that system work to its advantage.

When Hoover assumed office in March 1921, he found both the domestic economy and foreign trade in a slump. Imports and exports had declined by nearly 50 percent from prewar levels. Although foreign trade accounted for less than 10 percent of the gross national product, Hoover argued that imports improved Americans' living standards, and exports provided "the great balance wheel for our production." For some products such as cotton and wheat, foreign markets accounted for a majority of all sales. "While many of the causes of the present depression lie within our own borders," he argued, "yet there may be no recovery from these hard times for many years to come, if we neglect our economic relations abroad." Nor, he contended, did this imply only a more aggressive effort to push sales of American products abroad. "The recovery of our foreign trade can march only in company with the welfare and prosperity of our customers," he declared.[59] For a short time, as in 1919 and 1920, the Europeans might purchase American goods on short-term credit, but to sustain and develop trade in the future, the United States needed to do what it could to promote the restoration of European economies.

In the spring of 1921, Hoover had hoped that either the private Foreign Trade Finance Corporation or the government's War Trade Finance Corporation would provide a major impetus for American exports. As it became clear by summer that neither would achieve all he hoped, he turned instead to developing the resources of the Commerce Department to attack what he saw as the various components of the problem. Soon after taking office, he had begun meeting with major American producers to see what the department could do to help them with foreign sales. They told him that while the relaxation of antitrust laws prohibiting collaboration among companies on export prices and markets under the 1918 Webb-Pomerene Act had been helpful, they hoped for more direct assistance from the Commerce Department. They wanted the same sort of government support in the development of existing markets that the German and British governments provided to their exporters, and they needed help in finding and developing new markets like China. Hoover intended the reorganization and expansion of the Division of Foreign and Domestic Commerce, as well as the increase in the number and responsibilities of overseas commercial attachés, to meet this request, but he did not stop there.[60]

One area that he believed showed promise for American business was Latin America, which during the 1920s took some 18 percent of American exports—more than either East Asia or Canada. The American Section of the Inter-American High Commission, he thought, offered a tool for further expanding that trade. The High Commission, comprised of the finance ministers of most of the Western Hemisphere states, had been established in 1915 and joined by the United States in 1916 in the hopes of expanding hemispheric trade. During the war, it had lapsed into inactivity, and Secretary of the Treasury Mellon showed little interest in reviving it. Hoover, ever inventive, persuaded Mellon to become "honorary chairman" of the American

Section, while he served as actual chairman. During 1922, he used his position to promote pan-American cooperation on trade law, product standardization, and the stabilization of exchange rates. That summer, he briefly considered but eventually postponed a trip to Latin America to investigate the economic situation personally.[61]

For all his interest in Latin America, Hoover believed that a recovering Europe would provide, as it had before the war, America's most important customers. In the immediate postwar period, he had suggested various schemes for American government involvement in European reconstruction, but by 1922 he had turned away from that idea. The Europeans, he now argued, must finance their own recovery through sacrifice and hard work. American bankers could help by extending short-term loans and credits for the purchase of American food and other products that would lay the foundations of a full recovery, but the region's stability depended ultimately on its commitment to doing whatever was necessary to restore economic normality—in particular, the payment of war debts and the restoration of the gold standard.

VI

Hoover had little sympathy for the common argument that the United States must open its markets to European imports in order to stimulate the Continent's recovery. In fact, he argued, cheap labor, a depressed standard of living, and inflated currencies would make European products artificially cheap for several years during which the United States could expect to face a flood of cheap imports. Rather than further opening their domestic market to such imports, Americans needed to maintain their tariff protection, strengthen the merchant marine, curtail defense spending, and help domestic manufacturers make their products competitive through greater efficiency, scientific research, simplification and standardization, improved transportation on land and water, and the development of electric grids to reduce power costs. Vigorous competition, not easy money from foreign loans, he argued, would encourage the Europeans to make the reforms necessary to full recovery.[62]

Hoover's prediction of a commodity trade deficit served his interests in that it reinforced his domestic campaign to curtail industrial waste and maximize production, but the deficit never materialized. Indeed, his own department's statistics contradicted his claim. In the year ended June 30, 1921, the department estimated, the United States exported products worth about $2.9 billion more than those they imported, and in the following year, the American trade surplus remained $1.2 billion. Modern analyses modify the figures somewhat but confirm that the United States did indeed have a substantial, albeit diminishing, commodity trade surplus every year between 1919 and 1923, for a net total of nearly $10 billion. That surplus would continue, averaging nearly $687 million a year, for the remainder of Hoover's term in the

Commerce Department.[63] Nevertheless, his certainty that the United States had a net balance of payments deficit remained unshaken.

The basis of Hoover's belief was what the department called "invisible exchange"—private loans and investments in foreign countries, tourist spending, money sent abroad by immigrants, overseas expenditures on freight. Although the money spent abroad on such items was offset to some extent by similar spending by foreigners in the United States, the department estimated (guessed might be a better term, since they had no reliable figures) that in 1920 and 1921 Americans had spent between $1.1 and $1.4 billion more in invisible exchange than the country earned from exports and that, in 1921 and 1922, this figure had increased to between $1.4 and $1.5 billion. The department estimated, furthermore, that the deficit would increase in future years.[64]

A number of economists at the time disputed Hoover's belief that invisible exchange turned the American current accounts balance into a deficit, but modern statistics confirm his general point, although the department's figures exaggerated the size of the invisible exchange. The department's guesses about invisible exchange items such as illegally imported alcohol, immigrant remittances, and tourist spending in Europe proved too high, but Hoover was on the right track. The United States' current accounts balance—that is, its commodity trade surplus minus the "invisibles"—was negative every year between 1920 and 1929 except 1920, 1921, 1922, and 1924.[65]

At the end of 1922, Hoover warned that the Europeans had not adopted the policies essential to assure recovery. Agriculture and industry had grown stronger in most countries, he reported, but government budgets remained unbalanced as a result of subsidies to industries and armaments spending. The Eastern European countries and Germany in particular had been supporting irresponsible spending by printing paper money and taking short-term loans, and other European nations had followed somewhat in their steps. At the root of the problem, Hoover contended, lay political rather than economic issues: rearmament and Germany's reparations burden. As long as those issues dominated policy, balanced budgets and a return to peacetime stability would remain elusive. Furthermore, the Allied insistence that Germany must make reparations payments its primary foreign obligation could mean that American suppliers of vital food and other products to Germany would have to stand in line behind British and French creditors and that Germany might be unable to import adequate quantities of items essential to its full recovery.[66]

The reparations issue loomed over the whole problem of European recovery. The Allies had set the total German reparations bill in 1921 at 132 billion gold marks, or roughly $33 billion, but at a conference in London they had divided the total obligation into three bond series. They made Germany immediately responsible for amortization and interest on only two of those series, totaling 50 billion marks, or roughly $12.5 billion dollars. The remainder of the bill would come due only when and if Germany became sufficiently prosperous to handle it, and realistic European leaders doubted that part of the debt would ever be paid. Payments on the portion of the reparations bill for which the Germans had immediate responsibility would have consumed roughly 5.37 percent of Germany's national income in 1921, which compared reasonably with the 5.6 percent of France's annual income required to pay its reparations to Germany after the Franco-Prussian War. Payment would not cripple the German economy, in other words. In practice, however, the Germans regarded the whole reparations obligation as unjust. They had no intention of paying if they could possibly avoid it, and their domestic policy of subsidizing food, paying pensions, and generously compensating companies that had suffered wartime losses, all without tax reform, resulted in large deficits and hyperinflation. Domestic political pressures made it difficult for the German government to come to terms with inflation, but they also found it useful to contend that the economic chaos made paying reparations impossible. The roots of the reparations problem might be more political than economic, but the fact remained that until some resolution of it could be found, Germany, France, and to a lesser degree, Britain, could not recover fully.[67]

Hoover had little sympathy for the unwillingness of the Europeans to make the sacrifices necessary to set their economies in order. Indeed, he suspected that if they did recover, they would then collaborate on policies intended to close the Continent to American trade and investment. His estimate that the United States would face an unfavorable trade balance with the European nations thus provided him with justification for the get-tough policy toward Europe that he favored on economic, ideological, and political grounds. If the United States had a negative current accounts balance, it became much easier to justify raising the tariff, insisting on repayment of European loans, and discouraging new private loans to European governments unless they met American conditions.[68]

Early in 1922, Hoover outlined for the president what he regarded as "the minimum upon which economic stability can be attained in Europe." In return for "a holiday on interest payments" on European war debts to the United States and a possible private American loan to finance reconstruction in Belgium and northern France, he proposed to ask the Europeans to cut armaments by 50 percent; reduce German reparations payments; draw down the Allied occupation army in the Rhineland to 25,000 men; adopt fiscal austerity programs in Germany and France sufficient to enable the mark and franc to become convertible into gold; and promise to assist the states of Eastern and Central Europe in stabilizing their currencies in return for their adoption of programs leading to balanced budgets. Behind the scenes, he worked to develop collaboration between the directors of central banks in Eastern and Central Europe and the Federal Reserve Bank of New York in order to "formulate a plan for financial cooperation" to stabilize currencies, and to assure reliable supplies of raw materials for European industries and promote the adoption of financial policies to strengthen and expand recovery.[69]

Hoover assumed that European opposition to his proposals arose only from wartime bitterness and postwar selfishness. "The great sense of injury that remains from the war, the disbelief of the human animal in the economicly [*sic*] inevitable, [and] the differences in political and social thought both between nations and domestic divisions on these questions" impeded agreement, he feared. He believed his plan would assure prosperity and stability for all. The Europeans saw only immediate economic privation and eventual restoration of German power. A far more meaningful American offer, from their point of view, would have involved the cancellation of war debts. Hoover, however, regarded the debts as the only leverage the United States had to induce the Europeans to make the sacrifices necessary to restore the health of the whole system. Given the gulf separating the two sides in the spring of 1922, Hoover believed it would be unproductive to send an American delegation to a European economic conference to be held at Genoa in March 1922. No general agreement was likely, he thought. It would be more prudent to try to make small steps toward the ultimate goal.[70]

The Europeans themselves disagreed so greatly on the issues likely to come before the conference that its success seemed improbable, and some likely topics posed special perils for the United States. Proposals for collective action to reopen relations with Russia and reduce the German reparations bill, for example, implied a degree of American involvement in European affairs that most Americans opposed. The French, administration leaders suspected, wanted to draw the United States into an anti-German alliance, and the British and French hoped to secure the reduction or forgiveness of their war debts. None of the countries involved showed any disposition to adopt the austerity programs that Hoover believed essential to stabilization. The vague possibility that the conference might make progress in stabilizing the German economy and extending to Europe the system of agreements negotiated at the Washington Conference for East Asia thus did not seem to the Americans to offset the difficulties likely to arise at the conference. Given the improbability of the meeting's serving American interests, Hoover's advice about continuing to follow an independent policy seemed prudent to everyone.[71]

VII

While familiar problems like the state of the European economy and the continuing weakness of major industries like coal, construction, and transportation demanded much of Hoover's attention, issues raised by the new industries of radio and aviation also challenged him. Not only did he welcome their economic and social potential, but he also believed that their uncontrolled growth had created problems that could best be resolved by the federal government.

From the time that Guglielmo Marconi received his patent in 1897, men had been broadcasting words and music, but radio had been slow to catch on with the public. During the war, its military value resulted in rapid technical advances, and in the 1920s it became an international sensation. In the last seven months of 1921 alone, Hoover reported, the number of commercial broadcasters in the United States increased from five to 320, and the number of people with receivers grew from 200,000 to 1.5 million. Among the hordes of ardent amateurs building primitive transmitters and receivers in their basements was young Herbert, who spent hours tinkering with his equipment. Like others, however, Herbert soon found that in the absence of any regulation; a growing number of broadcasters, both amateur and commercial, infringed freely on each other's frequencies; and the resulting interference often made listening impossible.[72]

To cope with this problem, the Commerce Department drafted legislation in March 1921 to create a Radio Division in the Bureau of Standards with authority to license radio stations and assign frequencies. But perplexing problems delayed introduction of the radio bill. The military contended that the military value of radio proved that they ought to control the airwaves, while the owners of pioneer commercial stations insisted that they had acquired vested interests in their wavelengths. Amateur broadcasters interfered and competed freely with both the military and commercial operators. Hoover recognized the importance of radio to the military but insisted that its commercial potential must not be curtailed. Nor was he willing to grant anyone a monopoly over radio frequencies. Stations should be licensed, he argued, and their licenses subject to periodic public review before being renewed.[73]

In February 1922, Hoover convened a meeting of interested parties in Washington to discuss the future of radio. Representatives of the army and navy; the Commerce, Agriculture, and Post Office Departments; and commercial and amateur radio gathered at the Commerce Department on February 27 to discuss their common problems. In his introductory remarks to the conference, Hoover observed that the recent growth of radio had been "one of the most astounding things that has come under [his] observation in American life." Its development, he pointed out, had made the 1912 federal law granting the Commerce Department authority to regulate radiotelegraphy obsolete. Problems had become national, and because even amateur broadcasts could not be prevented from crossing state lines, the federal government seemed the only logical regulator. Accordingly, Hoover proposed a new federal law, to include a number of specific provisions: a ban on amateur broadcasting; limitation of commercial radio to a relatively small number of "central stations" operating under public licenses that would restrict them to specific broadcast wavelengths; restriction of broadcast content to news, education, entertainment, and "the communication of commercial matters as are of importance to large groups of the community at the same time" and the prohibition of "advertising chatter"; and private rather than government ownership of radio stations. He did not explain why businessmen would be willing to spend the money to build and operate radio stations if they could not sell advertising, although he suggested that government bureaus, universities, and the larger newspapers might be interested in the medium for educational and news purposes. And there must have been some tension in the Hoover household over his suggestion that amateur broadcasting should be prohibited. But his basic contention, that broadcasting should be licensed and supervised by the government, would become the cornerstone of the American system.[74]

After lengthy discussion, the Radio Conference issued a report on April 27 recommending that broadcasting should be regulated as a public utility by the federal government and that the authority to do so should be vested in the Commerce Department, not the military. Hoover's proposed ban on amateur broadcasting disappeared, as did his suggestion that the number of commercial stations be limited. The conference recommended that radio frequencies be divided into some twenty categories, ranging from transoceanic to amateur broadcasting, and from military to educational broadcasting, with the Commerce Department to assign each broadcaster a specific frequency within its general group. The conferees also surprisingly endorsed Hoover's recommendation that "direct advertising in radio broadcasting service be not permitted and that indirect advertising be limited to a statement of the call letters of the station and of the name of the concern responsible for the matter broadcasted." With the medium still so new, commercial broadcasters like the Westinghouse Company had not yet realized its advertising potential. The Westinghouse representative at the conference, L. R. Krumm, explained that his company viewed broadcasting mainly as a way to create a market for radio components, not as a medium for selling other products.[75]

The report of the Radio Conference laid out a rational plan for regulating radio broadcasting, but until new legislation passed, Hoover had only authority under the 1912 law to draft toothless regulations and ask broadcasters to cooperate voluntarily. In practice, he told a senator, the department had no choice but to issue broadcast licenses to anyone who applied. Representative Wallace H. White, Jr., of Maine, who had attended the conference, introduced the Commerce Department's radio bill in the House, but it aroused immediate opposition because it placed exclusive power over licensing in the hands of the secretary. Those suspicious of Hoover's political ambitions responded by proposing the creation of an independent regulatory commission instead. With neither side able to command a majority, legislation stalled, and the cacophony on the airwaves grew worse. By autumn, Hoover complained, the situation had become "simply intolerable," but despite his importuning, the House did not even begin hearings on a radio bill until January 1923.[76]

Commercial aviation, although not making as rapid technical progress as radio in the early 1920s, also desperately needed the federal regulation that Congress was slow to authorize. The war had given aviation a tremendous boost, and in the early postwar period, the idea of flying passengers and the mail around the world attracted widespread interest. In 1921, Congress authorized the establishment of a Bureau of Aeronautics in the Navy Department.

Yet despite a recommendation from the National Advisory Committee for Aeronautics, made up of manufacturers and commercial interests, that the legislators create a similar bureau in the Commerce Department to regulate commercial aviation, they failed to act. Their delay meant that flying remained a pastime for daredevils, not a viable business. Hoover was perfectly willing to have his department take on this assignment in addition to regulating radio, but departmental lawyers disagreed about whether the federal government could regulate purely intrastate aviation and whether regulatory powers should be vested in a bureau of the Commerce Department or a separate Department of Aeronautics. Not until mid-June 1923 did department staff, working closely with William P. MacCracken, a former World War I pilot and chairman of the American Bar Association's committee on aviation law, finally complete the draft of a bill. Then, in a rush to get the draft to Congressman Samuel Winslow, chairman of the House Committee on Interstate and Foreign Commerce, who had been complaining about the department's foot-dragging, Hoover forwarded the measure without reading it. Not until several hours later did he discover that it proposed a Department of Air rather than an Aeronautics Bureau under Commerce. Realizing that no political support existed for a new cabinet post, he withdrew the bill and instructed his staff to redraft it. By that time Winslow, who had never cared much about the issue anyway, had lost interest, and the bill languished in committee during 1923 and 1924.[77]

If his sons were swept up in the contemporary enthusiasm for the new technologies of radio, aviation, and automobiles, Hoover reserved his passion was for the more traditional pursuit of fishing. He had a special interest in the Commerce Department's Bureau of Fisheries. Its work enabled him to combine his interest in the application of science and technology to public policy with his desire to have the government serve industry and his private fascination with the art of catching fish.

From his childhood, Hoover had been an ardent fisherman, recalling nostalgically in his memoirs the "rude but highly effective epoch of the willow poles and a butcher-string line and hooks ten for a dime." Because the family always welcomed fresh fish, fishing offered him a sanctioned escape from dreary farm chores. As he grew older, he developed more sophisticated tastes, becoming an expert fly fisherman and sometimes stealing time from official duties to spend a day wading in a swift stream. Fishing, he often said, gave him "repose from the troubles of the soul that this vast complex of civilization imposes on us in our working hours and our restless nights." The "equality of all men before fishes," he declared, restored his faith in "democratic values."[78]

The Bureau of Fisheries gave Hoover an opportunity to transform his interest in fishing into a departmental priority. Through the Bureau, he could help sport fishermen by expanding the development of fish hatcheries and the stocking of streams. Fishermen welcomed his support, electing him for several years honorary president of the Izaak Walton League. He used that forum, as well as his presidency of the National Parks Association, to argue that the people who most needed the refreshment of fishing were those who lived in the cities. As he saw it, that meant the building of good roads to put city dwellers within reach of fishing streams, the reduction of pollution to make the streams usable and appealing, and the expansion of parks and wildlife reserves to assure access to unspoiled nature. Nor did he confine his interest only to recreational fishing. Pollution and overfishing, he pointed out, affected commercial fishermen at least as much as sport fishermen. On the East Coast, he encouraged the states to cooperate in the protection of lit-toral species, and on the West Coast, he urged the president and Congress to protect endangered salmon and halibut. Beginning with recreational fish-ing, he emerged as the major spokesman of conservation in the Harding and Coolidge administrations.[79]

Hoover foreshadowed his plans for the Fisheries Bureau in February 1922 when he gave Commissioner of Fisheries Hugh M. Smith, a physician who had stressed scientific research over practical applications, an "opportunity to resign," and replaced him with a career Fisheries man, Henry O'Malley. O'Malley, an advocate of supplementing natural spawning by the introduction of hatchery-raised fish, worked well with the commercial fishing industry and, like Hoover, emphasized the practical application of science to overfishing, fish propagation, and coastal oil pollution. Some of those issues had already come up in conferences with East Coast commercial fishermen that Hoover had held at the Commerce Department in May and June of 1921. In those meetings, the fishermen had discussed oil pollution at sea and federal regula-tion of the fishing industry, but Hoover did not care much for their suggestion that the federal government take the lead in dealing with those problems. Except for a possible law to ban oceanic oil pollution, on which the depart-ment began work following the conference, Hoover preferred local, volun-tary, and perhaps interstate approaches to fisheries problems. As an example of what he had in mind, he sponsored a meeting in July 1921 between repre-sentatives of Maryland and Virginia to discuss the decline of the crab fisheries in Chesapeake Bay. The experts at the meeting proposed that the states adopt new restrictions on the sex, age, and size of crabs caught and ban certain fish-ing methods. Hoover explained to a congressman that he thought the states should take responsibility for the problem, making federal action "only . . . a last resort." He did not change his mind even when Virginia (which would have been most affected by the new regulations) failed to act on the confer-ence's recommendations.[80]

Of course, as Hoover recognized, only the federal government could act on some issues. One of those was the decline of the halibut catch in the Northern Pacific. Commercial halibut fishing in the Pacific had begun in the 1880s, and catches increased until 1915, after which a rapid decline took place, worsened by the introduction of diesel-powered fishing boats after World War I. Since much of the fishery lay in international waters, and fishermen came from both

Canada and the United States, only an international agreement could address the problem. After polling fishermen on both sides of the border, the Bureau of Fisheries concluded that most of them favored a closed season during the winter to give fish populations a chance to recover. Accordingly, Hoover recommended to Secretary of State Hughes the negotiation of an agreement with Canada to address the problem. The two countries signed a Convention for the Preservation of the Halibut Fishery of the Northern Pacific Ocean in March 1923, and it went into effect in October 1924 after the legislatures of both countries approved it. Although the agreement, which provided for a three-month closed fishing season and set up a binational commission to oversee the fishery, turned out to be inadequate to stop the decline of the halibut population, it represented an important start to addressing the problem and ranks as one of Hoover's successes in fisheries conservation.[81]

The problem of salmon conservation in Alaska proved to be far more complicated and contentious. A precipitous decline in the 1921 catch alarmed everyone involved with the industry, but no consensus emerged about dealing with the problem. Hoover, backed by major commercial fishermen and packers, proposed the creation of reserves on the Alaskan coast where fishing would be heavily restricted or banned completely. President Harding proclaimed the establishment of two such reserves in February and November 1922. Native groups and small fishermen opposed these wholesale measures, which they feared would shut them out of their traditional fishing areas, although the Bureau of Fisheries arranged for some local exceptions. There seemed little basis for compromise between the major firms and the locals, however, particularly because Dan Sutherland, delegate to Congress from Alaska, thrust himself into the issue by claiming to be the spokesman of the natives and small fishermen. Sutherland, born on Cape Breton Island, Nova Scotia, had come to the United States with his parents in 1876 and gone to Alaska in search of gold in 1898, where he became a member of the Alaskan Territorial Senate. A Republican progressive of the Hiram Johnson school, he lost no opportunity to lambaste politicians he considered reactionaries. In this case, he proclaimed that Hoover's reservation plan amounted to "parceling out the fishing grounds of Alaska to a few favored interests." Most of those interests, Sutherland pointed out, had their headquarters in San Francisco, in Hoover's home state of California. Then, having implied that Hoover had sold out to the packers, Sutherland went on to accuse O'Malley and the Bureau of Fisheries of being under the "control of the packing interests."[82]

Hoover restrained himself in his official replies to Sutherland's letters, but privately he was livid at the attacks on his integrity and on the impartiality of the Bureau of Fisheries from someone he suspected of being in the pay of some Alaskan canners. Always thin-skinned about criticism, he struck back indirectly at Sutherland in March 1923, drafting a press release to be issued by Assistant Secretary Claudius Huston. Sutherland's charges, the statement declared, amounted to "the most complete demagogic bunk ever put over."

The "infamous" claim that O'Malley and Fisheries scientist Charles Gilbert were in the pocket of the packers would be "resented by every scientist in America." Since Congress had failed to act on bills to regulate salmon fishing and Sutherland's attacks made rational discussion of the issue impossible, Hoover took obvious pleasure in announcing that he had recommended to the president the creation by proclamation of closed salmon reserves off the coast of Alaska.[83] The Alaska delegate had picked a fight with the wrong man. Instead of winning concessions for his supporters or even promoting a serious discussion of the real issues of native fishing rights and the interests of small fishermen, Sutherland had simply hardened the administration's determination to take the sledgehammer approach of creating closed reserves.

Hoover's mood, as 1922 came to a close, was somber. He had made progress toward "reconstruction of the country from difficulties inherited from the war," but the problems of the railroads, the coal industry, the antagonistic relationship between workers and managers, and the European debts remained unsolved. A sizable agenda would carry over into the coming year, but he had staked out an increasingly important role as the administration's principal spokesman of governmental activism. Not only had he proposed direct federal responsibility for the development of the Colorado, Mississippi, and St. Lawrence waterways, but he also had pushed government intervention in the problems of the coal and railroad industries and direct regulation of radio and commercial aviation. His disagreement with Mellon over tax policy had earned the suspicion of the Treasury secretary, Vice President Coolidge, and other limited-government conservatives who had begun to suspect that the secretary of commerce might prove a threat to their control over policy. Their suspicions would harden into enmity in coming years.[84]

CHAPTER 14

The Commerce Department, 1923

In January 1923, Hoover issued a generally optimistic estimate of economic conditions in the United States and the world for the coming year. At home, he thought that unemployment had "ceased to be a problem," with wages and savings at a high level. Although agriculture still lagged, both housing construction and transportation had revived. Production and commerce in Asia, Africa, Latin America, and Australia had risen above prewar levels. Even in Russia, "a mixture of socialism and individualism" had softened communism, civil war had ended, famine and distress had receded below prewar levels, and production had increased greatly. Elsewhere in Europe, the former neutrals had also increased production and reduced unemployment. Only the former "combatant states" lagged because of political uncertainty, excessive military spending, lowered productivity, and unbalanced budgets. "Disarmament and the constructive settlement of German reparations" remained "the outstanding problems of Europe," but Hoover hoped that an increasing recognition of the "growing menace of these situations" might lead to progress in solving them in the near future.[1]

During the spring, Hoover became somewhat concerned that the pendulum swing in construction from recession to boom might trigger inflation. Shortages of labor and materials, as well as an overtaxed transportation system, he warned the president in March, had driven up prices and wages. He suggested that it was time for the Federal Reserve to tighten credit and for the federal government to cut back its own construction projects to exert a countercyclical pressure on the economy. His suggestion, strongly backed by the findings of the Unemployment Conference's special committee on the business cycle and by the Board of Governors of the American Construction Council, led to postponement of several federal construction projects. But instead of eliciting gratitude from a public presumably saved from inflation, news of Hoover's initiative aroused anxiety and confusion. Real estate and construction interests frequently welcomed the slowdown, but others seemed almost willfully to misunderstand his intentions, like an American Legion post that accused him of wanting to stop *all* government construction. With unusual patience, Hoover sent out letter after letter explaining his point of view, but in that pre-Keynesian era a great many influential bankers and business executives did not believe that the federal government could or should interfere with the business cycle.[2]

In a major speech titled "Holding on to Prosperity" on May 8, 1923, Hoover reiterated and extended his arguments. The 6 percent rise in wholesale prices in the last nine months, he said, while less sharp than the 20 percent rise in the nine months prior to the 1920 collapse, should nevertheless provoke concern about inflation. Although living costs had not yet increased proportionately, and increasing productivity had produced a widespread improvement in living standards, he urged that the federal government and private business unite in restraining inflationary pressures. Beyond those cooperative and voluntary measures, he ventured into much more contentious territory when he hinted that the United States might consider finding ways to transfer some of its surplus gold to the European nations. Privately, he thought that the American economy had reached a point where the Federal Reserve's holdings of commercial paper, rather than the gold reserves, had become "the vital point of protection," but of course, it would not do to question the gold standard in public. Instead, he called attention to the danger that if currency supplies and credit expanded along with the growing mountain of gold in federal vaults, inflation would drive up the prices of American goods and make them uncompetitive in the world market. It would be better, he suggested, to set aside some portion of the gold until such time as increasing imports began drawing gold out of the country. The United States would benefit from a temporary flow of gold to Europe that would stabilize currencies and exchange rates and promote political and economic recovery on the Continent.[3]

I

Hoover's goal of stabilizing Europe economically paralleled his belief that the United States would benefit from taking a role in a Wilsonian international political structure. No one in the administration regarded joining the League of Nations as a possibility, but Hoover thought the country could take smaller steps. He welcomed President Harding's recommendation to the Senate on

February 24, 1923, that the United States join the World Court and took advantage of an invitation to speak to a League of Women Voters convention to endorse the idea. Like Harding, Hoover emphasized that joining the court would further America's desire for peace without committing the nation to League membership or promising to submit all disputes to the court. Even if the United States consented to have a dispute considered by the court, he added, enforcement of any decision would rest "wholly on public opinion and not upon force." The court offered a weak alternative to war, he admitted, but American membership would at least "build . . . a little of the road to peace."[4]

Although Hoover's support of court membership pleased some internationalists, his depiction of the court as essentially harmless drew criticism from both isolationists and internationalists. "We should either make it a court with some power to it—with some effectiveness," declared Senator William E. Borah, "or we should turn our attention exclusively to the questions which are troubling the American taxpayer, the American business man, and the American farmer." Others accused the administration of seeking to divert attention from the central issue of League membership or of playing to pro-League voters in the coming congressional elections. Hamilton Holt, a prominent League supporter, discerned a split within the administration between Hoover, who saw court membership as a first step toward greater American participation in world organization, and the president, for whom joining the court represented fulfillment of a campaign promise and an end in itself. Although Hoover and Harding continued to urge American membership during the spring of 1923, the country and the Senate remained hopelessly divided on the issue at the time of the president's death in August.[5]

The Republican leadership's coolness to American membership in any international organization discouraged Hoover only mildly. Europe's continuing need to borrow money in the United States, he believed, offered an opportunity to exercise both economic and political influence. Because he had, as William McNeil puts it, "the most fully developed theoretical perspective of any of the Republican leaders" on international loans, his views had a major if not determinative influence on administration policy.[6]

Three principles underlay Hoover's approach to the question of foreign loans. The first was that loans ought to contribute to the stability and prosperity of the American economy. That principle led him to advise the president in May 1921 that loans should be discouraged "unless the proceeds are to be used to pay for purchases in this country" and to insist later that the Commerce Department as well as the State Department should have an opportunity to evaluate loans before they were made. Second, the Allies' war debts should not be canceled, because doing so would erode the sanctity of the contract that must undergird a stable international economic system. And third, loans should be treated, within limits, as bargaining chips with which to secure political concessions on disarmament and political stabilization.[7]

Others within the administration also had strong opinions about the debt question. Harding rejected as too restrictive Hoover's recommendation that loan proceeds must be used to purchase American products, and a debate about what terms, if any, should be imposed on new loans took place within the Commerce Department during the spring of 1922. Hoover proposed to require that loans be given only for productive purposes, that any state with a poor record of payment in the last twenty-five years be forced to provide collateral, and that American firms be guaranteed the right to bid on all contracts financed by loans. But Grosvenor Jones, chief of the Finance and Investment Division of the Bureau of Foreign and Domestic Commerce, favored a much looser policy that Benjamin Strong also endorsed. They argued that since international loans often have political purposes, it would be wise to allow lenders greater latitude than in ordinary business and that, in any event, all loans would benefit American exporters either directly or indirectly. Hoover conceded that, for the time being, loans were "the only method by which American exports [could] be promoted," but he insisted nevertheless that the United States should oppose "finance which lends itself directly or indirectly to war or to the maintenance of political and economic instability." When J. P. Morgan asked the State Department about the company taking part in discussions with the Inter-Allied Financial Commission about a new loan to the German government, Hoover told Secretary Hughes that until "a definite, satisfactory reparations settlement had been effected," he would be "forced to announce to the American public that any loan [to Germany] that might be floated to this country was worthless."[8]

The prior approval issue was complicated by disagreement within the government about who should have authority to pass on loans. State, Commerce, Treasury, and the Federal Reserve all had an interest in the matter, and each had a slightly different perspective. Hoover averted a major conflict over the issue by arranging a February 1922 conference with the president, Hughes, Mellon, and banking representatives. After discussion, they agreed that future loan proposals would be submitted to the State Department for an opinion on "political desirability and undesirability," then passed to Commerce for advice on the loan's "security and reproductive character." The State Department would "give advice to the promoters" on those matters but would exercise "no pretense of authority" to sanction or forbid a particular loan, nor would it "assume any responsibility whatever in connection with loan transactions." The agreement produced a partial truce among the various cabinet offices, but the bankers understandably disliked it, and Benjamin Strong conveyed their objections to Hoover vigorously. Hoover continued to believe he was right. Loans should be productive in their effect and should not be used for "military expenditures or in unbalanced budgets, or in bolstering up of inflated currencies." Mellon, feeling that so much intervention in other countries' internal affairs invited trouble, met privately with the president and secured an additional restriction on the loan clearance process. Harding directed that loan reviews must be limited to "passing upon the effect which any particular loan might have directly on our foreign political relations."⁹ The ruling undermined the February compromise and left each of the parties free to assert its point of view on future loan applications.

Complicated as the question of clearing new foreign loans was, however, it proved minor next to the much bigger issue of the European war debts. During and immediately after the war the Allies—chiefly Britain, France, Belgium, and Italy—had borrowed some $10 billion from the American government to finance the war and immediate postwar reconstruction. Desperate for money, the Allied leaders had accepted whatever terms the Americans offered but had assumed that Washington would later scale down or even cancel the debts, which after all had been incurred in a common cause. The Americans did not see it that way. Harding's cabinet discussed the debts at one of its first meetings and agreed unanimously that they must be paid. Failure to require payment would undermine the structure of trust upon which international economic relations rested and would leave American taxpayers, whose bonds had provided the money for the loans, holding the bag. Hoover and Mellon, who took the lead in developing American policy on the issue, recognized, however, that the Allies' depleted economies prevented immediate payment in gold. They hoped to negotiate individual agreements with each debtor, stretching out payments over years and basing interest rates on ability to pay.¹⁰

In May 1921, Hoover and Treasury Secretary Mellon called a White House conference of bankers to discuss "foreign finance." What concerned them, it became clear at the meeting, was the war debt question. Worried about the evident reluctance of the Europeans to pay their obligations, they wanted the bankers to be cautious about making new loans until the borrowers had agreed to pay their current debts. "The whole fabric of international commerce," Hoover reminded the group, depended on the confidence that nations and peoples would live up to their obligations. Gunboats might collect debts in limited cases, but international commerce ultimately required scrupulous and voluntary adherence to commitments. Early in 1922, Secretary of State Hughes instructed Roland Boyden, the American observer on the Reparations Commission, that the United States expected payments on the debts to be the first obligation on any money received from the Germans in the form of reparations. Although the United States had made no reparations claims of its own and officially denied any link between reparations and the debts, the two issues could not be separated.¹¹

Meanwhile, rumors circulating in Congress that Secretary Mellon might be open to cancellation or reduction of the debts led to the passage of a debt funding bill on February 9, 1922. The bill shifted control over debt negotiations from the Treasury Department to a World War Foreign Debt Commission made up of Mellon, Hoover, Hughes, Senator Reed Smoot, and Congressman Theodore Burton. More importantly, it directed the commission to arrange for the payment of all debts in full within twenty-five years, at an interest rate not less than 4.25 percent. In theory, the bill left the commission very little leeway to negotiate individual settlements.[12]

In practice, the three cabinet members who dominated the debt commission agreed that strict adherence to the congressional terms would be impossible. Hoover emphasized the importance of payment to restoration of a stable international economic system. He doubted that the American tariff would, as the Europeans contended, make it impossible for them to earn the money for payments by selling their goods in the United States. Mellon emphasized the problems that would be experienced by the Europeans in paying in gold and saw the tariff as a greater barrier than Hoover did. Hughes focused primarily on European political stability and may have been slightly more willing than the other two to make economic concessions to advance that goal. But all three recognized that their instructions limited their freedom and made it essential that they stick together if, as seemed inevitable, they ended up signing agreements that departed from Congress's orders.[13]

None of the debt commissioners believed that collecting the debts would be a simple matter of telling the deadbeats to pay up. They feared that the congressional restrictions doomed the whole process to failure. Indeed, J. P. Morgan's Thomas Lamont speculated to an English partner that the administration might be secretly hoping that the commission would fail, as a means of making Congress and the public more realistic about debt payment. Europeans, most of whom believed that the United States ought to write off the debts as a contribution to the common war effort and postwar reconstruction, expressed outrage at the American position. The American left, which generally favored cancellation, also thought the congressional action had been a disaster. And even many conservatives felt that it would be a mistake to squeeze the debtor nations too hard if so doing would cause significant hardship.[14]

Early in 1923, members of the British Debt Commission led by Chancellor of the Exchequer Stanley Baldwin arrived in the United States to discuss Britain's debt with the American commissioners. In preparing for the meeting, Hoover, taking it for granted that any agreement would diverge from the congressional instructions, contemplated an audacious idea. Perhaps, he suggested, the commissioners could ignore Congress's orders entirely and conclude an agreement reducing the rate of amortization to 0.5 or 0.75 percent per year, extending the payment period to forty-five or sixty-five years, and lowering interest rates substantially. To win Congress's acceptance of those huge departures from the terms of the Debt Funding Bill, he proposed to demand that the British agree to "substantial disarmament" of about 50 percent. According to a memorandum prepared by Commerce Department staff, such disarmament would stimulate "increased production" and enable London to make its payments "without any increase in taxation." The arrangement, Hoover argued, would reduce Britain's economic burden, promote American security, and strengthen the international economy.[15]

Hoover was not the only person thinking on the eve of the talks about trading debt reductions for political concessions. In London, British economist John Maynard Keynes suggested that since there was "not one chance in a million that a penny [would] be paid in any case," it would make sense for the Americans to use debt forgiveness as a "diplomatic weapon" to extract concessions on other matters.[16]

When the American and British commissions sat down together, however, Baldwin showed no inclination to offer concessions. The debts, he declared, should be considered "the first contribution made by the United States to save civilisation from being engulfed and free peoples being brought under the destructive rule of a military autocracy." Britain, having borne the terrible human and economic sacrifices of the war, would be reduced to "poverty and misery" if forced to pay in full. And in any case, most of the money loaned to Britain had been spent in America, in purchasing American products. The British, Baldwin added in a conciliatory tone, wanted to pay, but they could not at present pay in gold, and until the European allies repaid some of what Britain had lent them during the war, it would be difficult to pay at all. Behind the Chancellor's words lay the unspoken reality that payments by the other Allies to Britain depended upon German reparations payments, and that whole structure had broken down totally. On the same day that Baldwin addressed the American commissioners, the majority on the Reparations Commission declared Germany in default, and the French and Belgians decided to send troops into the Ruhr valley.[17]

Intriguing as Hoover's idea seems in retrospect, it stood no chance of being accepted. The English, like the other Allies, believed that the debts should be forgiven completely and dismissed disarmament on the scale Hoover proposed as totally unrealistic. For his part, Harding thought it essential to placate Congress by securing as much payment as possible. On January 9, the same day Baldwin spoke, the president admitted reluctantly that neither he nor the commissioners expected to be able to reach an agreement in conformity with Congress's instructions. He promised, however, that the American negotiators would try to get as much as they could and would leave it up to Congress to accept or reject an agreement.[18] Given the political pressures on both sides, no one wanted to complicate things still further by broaching the disarmament question.

Harding's implied willingness to accept some debt reduction made real negotiations possible between the British and Americans, and over the next two weeks the talks progressed steadily. Meeting privately and keeping no minutes that could be used to support charges that they had violated their instructions, the negotiators gradually crafted an arrangement. Although its terms substantially reduced British obligations and extended the period of time for payment, Baldwin realized that the agreement would arouse sharp criticism at home. He believed, however, that he had made the best deal he could, and on January 20 the British delegation sailed for home. There, on

January 30 and 31, the cabinet debated the proposal at length. Prime Minister Andrew Bonar Law threatened at one point to resign if the arrangement was accepted, but in the end Baldwin prevailed. On February 2, the American commission made a "recommendation to the president as a basis for settlement which it is understood will be accepted by the British Government." The commission hoped that the proposed agreement, which set interest rates on a sliding scale beginning at 3 and gradually increasing to 3.5 percent over a sixty-two-year payment period, would be approved by Congress as better than nothing. In June, diplomats formalized the arrangement along the lines worked out in February, and Congress, despite grumbling by a few hard-liners, approved it overwhelmingly. The final agreement, which paralleled one with Finland, was signed on August 18, 1925.[19]

Given the circumstances of the British debt negotiations, it is understandable that Hoover did not press his proposal to trade debt reduction for disarmament. Congressional instructions put partial or complete cancellation largely out of reach, and without those concessions—unacceptable also to the president, state, and treasury—the disarmament suggestion remained only a pleasant dream. Hoover reiterated it from time to time in speeches but never made any serious effort to turn it into action. It seems likely that even if he had, the Europeans would have rejected it out of hand.[20]

The administration's policy on the debt question reflected what Melvyn Leffler calls "the ambivalent feelings and contradictory impulses" that dominated Republican policy making throughout the decade. On the one hand, Hoover and other administration leaders recognized that Europe's economic health had become important to the United States. That conviction led them to offer concessions on the debts, encourage cooperation between the Federal Reserve and European central banks, and even participate unofficially in efforts to resolve the reparations problem. On the other hand, they suspected the Europeans—particularly the British and French—of conspiring to minimize American access to European markets and investment opportunities, supported the protective tariff, and continued to reject membership in the League of Nations. Above all, they stressed the primacy of the domestic economy over any foreign policy issue. Given the dramatic growth of American foreign trade and overseas investments during the decade and the absence of any significant military threat to the United States, the internal contradictions of American foreign policy did not seem to matter. Although the slowness of Europe's recovery might threaten the Continent's political stability, it also served American economic interests by fostering the maintenance of an open door for American exports and capital.[21]

Aside from the difficulties in resolving the war debt problem, the continuing weak sales of American agricultural products overseas, and the failure of German recovery, Hoover judged the American foreign trade situation "extremely encouraging" by the autumn of 1923. Trade with Latin America and "tropical countries" had developed particularly well, with a substantial balance in favor of the United States and good prospects for still further expansion. Even the troublesome German reparations issue seemed as if it might yield to reason. Although the United States claimed no direct interest in the issue, Hoover believed that its resolution would promote German economic recovery and halt the runaway inflation that cheapened German goods and enabled them to undersell American products. Accordingly, when the United States received an invitation in the autumn to take part in a conference to revise the reparations bill, Hoover urged Secretary Hughes and the president to send an unofficial American delegation. The group that set out for Europe in November 1923 was headed by Charles G. Dawes and included two of Hoover's friends and former colleagues on the Unemployment Commission, General Electric's Owen D. Young, and the banker Henry Robinson.[22]

II

The nationalist side of Hoover's outlook was reflected not only in his tariff and debt policies but also in his concern with safeguarding supplies of vital raw materials imported from abroad. In that, he followed a pattern set by prewar American leaders who had consistently pursued an open-door policy with regard to raw materials. In the immediate postwar period, Hoover, like other Americans, had become very concerned about a possible shortage of oil. He had urged an aggressive search for foreign oil fields, but his worry abated as production rose from American fields. Throughout the decade, however, he remained extremely concerned about assuring access to other vital raw materials.[23]

The product that brought the issue particularly to his attention was rubber, of which the United States, with its booming automobile production, consumed roughly three-quarters of the world's supply, importing about 95 percent of that from British and Dutch producers in East Asia. Until about 1920, rubber plantations had made reliable profits. Soon thereafter, overproduction, resulting partly from new French plantations in Southeast Asia, forced wholesale prices into sharp decline. The British Growers Association recommended voluntary production cutbacks in the autumn of 1920 and, when those proved ineffective, urged mandatory restrictions on the British government. In October 1921, Colonial Secretary Winston Churchill appointed a special committee, headed by Sir James Stevenson, to examine the issue and make recommendations. The Stevenson Committee proposed an export tax on raw rubber and mandatory export quotas, to go into effect on November 1, 1922.[24]

The possibility that the Stevenson Plan would send rubber prices sky high alarmed American tire manufacturers and the Commerce Department. Tire manufacturer Harvey Firestone began to consider establishing new rubber plantations in Liberia, and Hoover sent Assistant Secretary Claudius Huston to the East Indies to report on the producers' plans. In correspondence with Senator Medill McCormick, Hoover asked for the passage of a $500,000 special appropriation to fund a "study of the world rubber situation" and to investigate possible alternative rubber sources in Latin America and the Philippines. He had no objection to the producers' actions, the secretary told the House Appropriations Committee, provided they aimed only at raising prices to cover production costs, but it appeared that they intended to go much further than that. Export restrictions, he argued, could establish "a price level that would carry disaster to the American consumer" by driving up current rubber prices and discouraging the development of new plantations needed to meet rapidly increasing American demand.[25]

For once, Congress agreed with Hoover about the urgency of an issue, and in March 1923 it passed an emergency appropriation to create a joint Agriculture-Commerce study committee. The investigation turned out to be an idea better in theory than practice. Agriculture Department officials were skeptical about it from the outset, regarding rubber as an agricultural product and suspecting that Hoover secretly hoped to use the joint committee as an excuse to create an "organization of agricultural experts" in the Commerce Department and to further encroach on agricultural marketing in general. That dispute could be papered over, but it soon became obvious that the investigation could not find a solution to the rubber problem. The committee's work would require months at best, and even if it succeeded in finding new locations for rubber plantations, putting them into production would require years. The rubber problem, Hoover became convinced by late 1923, required direct pressure on the British government to lift export restrictions and on producers to lower prices.[26]

III

Despite Hoover's criticisms of the Stevenson Plan, he advocated a similar program to help American farmers. Previously, he had urged farmers to organize to control marketing and production and had considered plans to withhold nonperishable American agricultural products from the world market by storing them in government warehouses pending increases in world prices. Now he proposed a more direct role for the Commerce Department. In addition to conducting a series of special investigations of foreign markets, he urged the creation of a corps of overseas Commerce Department representatives whose duties would include the identification of new markets and the vigorous promotion of agricultural sales. When the Agriculture Department blocked the commercial attaché proposal in Congress, Hoover remarked snidely that Agriculture (meaning Secretary Wallace) did not really care about helping farmers. The political stakes were high, and everyone in the administration wanted to be seen by farmers as committed to effective action.[27]

Frustrated by his failure to bring overseas marketing of agricultural products under Commerce Department control, Hoover cast about for other initiatives. One useful step, he suggested early in 1923, would be "the establishment of a National Agricultural Loan Institution, separate entirely from the Federal Reserve System, for the purpose of providing intermediate credits for the farmer." In cooperation with Senator Irvine Lenroot, Commerce helped to develop the Lenroot-Anderson Bill, which proposed to use $1.2 billion of federal funds to capitalize a new system of Federal Farm Loan Banks authorized to lend to farmers for periods between six months and three years. A competing proposal introduced by Senator Arthur Capper of Kansas would have authorized the Federal Reserve Banks to discount agricultural notes, drafts, and bills. Ultimately, the compromise Agricultural Credits Act of 1923, based mainly on the Lenroot-Anderson model, passed on March 4. It established twelve Federal Intermediate Credit Banks, each with a capital of $5 million and under the oversight of the Federal Farm Loan Board. Although the president, Hoover, Wallace, and the big farm organizations endorsed the new banks, they proved disappointing. They were undercapitalized, their loan procedures were slow and cumbersome, and most importantly, they could not influence the basic cause of the agricultural depression—overproduction.[28] The more the administration grappled with the farm problem, the more elusive a solution seemed to be.

An imbroglio over another agricultural product, sugar, proved equally frustrating. On February 9, 1923, the Commerce Department issued its annual prediction of sugar production and consumption for the coming year. It estimated that world production would be "only 125,000 tons more than in 1922," while demand would be "350,000 tons more than in 1922 and 725,000 tons larger than production." An accompanying table showed that a surplus carried over from 1922 would easily cover the increase in demand and leave a half-million ton surplus at the end of the coming year. At least one press service read the text, however, ignored the table, and predicted a sugar shortage and escalating prices. Panic swept the sugar markets. Although Julius Klein, director of the Bureau of Foreign and Domestic Commerce, hastily issued a correction stating unequivocally that 1923's crop, plus the surplus already on hand, guaranteed there would be no shortage, speculators in New York used the original report to drive up the price. Hoover denied vigorously that the department's statement had caused the panic, and technically he was correct, but the original press release was certainly open to misinterpretation. Before the tumult subsided, the department had to launch an investigation of sugar speculation in Cuba and ask the Justice Department to investigate speculation in New York. Neither investigation revealed a conspiracy, but prices remained high, largely because the rumored shortage stimulated hoarding. In May, Hoover asked housewives to reduce sugar use in order to drive down prices. Since no actual shortage existed, the mere threat of a housewives' boycott soon produced price reductions. In fact, the amount of sugar on hand made Hoover confident that no price spike would last. He urged the boycott not to combat the current situation but to avert a temporary price increase that might mislead sugar producers into expanding excessively and creating a surplus that could result in a catastrophic price slump in 1924. His strategy proved successful, but that did not prevent Robert La Follette, the 1924 Progressive Party presidential candidate, from accusing him of having conspired to drive up the sugar price in the interest of speculators. The charge, echoed during the 1928 campaign, always infuriated Hoover.[29]

IV

As frustrating, but more serious, was the coal problem. Since the 1922 settlement had been only a stopgap, new strikes seemed likely in 1923. Hoover had concluded, after more than a year of thinking about the situation, that a major source of the industry's problems, at least in the soft coal fields, lay in inadequate transportation. At no time did the railroads have enough cars to transport coal during periods of peak demand, and during times of prosperity other industries' shipping needs compounded the shortage. The railroads responded to this situation by rationing scarce cars, sending a few to each producer. The system enabled inefficient, high-cost mines to stay in business while preventing efficient producers from expanding. Every company, whether efficient or not, had to lay off workers whenever transportation became inadequate, and as a result, miners never had enough work to make a decent living. The resulting "discontent, unrest, misery, and difficulty" led inevitably to "strikes and violence." Mine consolidation seemed the only realistic solution to the situation, but the government could only recommend, not compel, any such steps. A strike or threat of a strike, however, offered Hoover an opportunity to address the situation indirectly. In September 1922, Congress had passed the bill he had long advocated, creating a presidential Coal Commission and authorizing the federal coal distributor to apportion railroad cars selectively in the event of another strike. The justification for the apportionment system had been to put pressure on producers who raised their prices excessively, but it occurred to Hoover that the power could be used also to bestow an advantage on efficient producers and drive inefficient mines toward bankruptcy or consolidation.[30]

With labor contracts in the soft coal fields expiring on April 1, 1923, and those in the anthracite fields expiring on August 1, Hoover urged businesses and homeowners to stock up on coal as a protection against strike-caused shortages. A good idea in theory, early buying proved impossible in practice because the previous year's strike had left producers' coal stocks so low that they could not fully satisfy the demand. Although Federal Coal Distributor F. R. Wadleigh pointed out that producers had shipped substantially more anthracite during the first five months of 1923 than in any previous year, a strike in the autumn would almost certainly create shortages and elicit a public demand for government action.[31]

In the bituminous coal fields, the federal coal commission averted a crisis by persuading miners and operators to continue production pending the outcome of labor negotiations, but no such agreement could be reached in the anthracite fields. With the two sides still far apart and the strike deadline fast approaching, a long, bitter clash appeared likely. Hoover urged Coolidge, who had acceded to the presidency just in time to face the coal crisis, to direct the coal commission to try to bring the two sides together. On his own, the secretary warned soft coal producers against attempting to exploit an anthracite strike by raising their prices.[32]

The coal commission, whose verbose and inconclusive report on the causes of labor conflict in the coal fields dribbled out in a series of press releases beginning on September 8, proved as incapable of heading off the anthracite strike as diagnosing the sources of conflict. Its prediction that the industry would eventually solve its own problems seemed ludicrous to anyone who really understood the situation. Hoover did not say so in public, but he must have been deeply disappointed by the commission's ineptitude, particularly when one of his old rivals, Governor Gifford Pinchot of Pennsylvania, intervened in the anthracite talks and brokered a settlement on September 17. The president, who lacked the secretary's enthusiasm for a vigorous government role in managing the economy, accepted the commission's report complacently. He endorsed Hoover's recommendation for the passage of legislation authorizing federal control over coal distribution in the event of a strike in 1924, but otherwise he "was sure the industry would readjust itself if left alone." Hoover observed dryly in his memoirs that it took five years before the boom of 1928 to 1929 brought about that happy event—and then the long-awaited "adjustment" lasted only one year.[33]

Inasmuch as Hoover believed that a large part of the problems facing both coal and agriculture resulted from transportation deficiencies, it made sense for him to put priority on improvements in the railroad system. Armed with estimates from both the Bankers Trust Company in New York and the Interstate Commerce Commission that by the end of 1922 the railroads would be receiving a "fair return" (defined as 5.75 percent per year on their capital investment), Hoover arranged to have the U.S. Chamber of Commerce invite the presidents of the major lines to a meeting in New York. He hoped to promote the adoption of a coordinated national transportation policy that would embrace railroads, truck transport, and waterway development. At the meeting, he spoke bluntly about his frustration that the railroad executives seemed unable to make any progress toward consolidation. He also advanced a new suggestion, proposing the restructuring of freight rates to lower the cost of high-bulk, low-value shipments such as coal and agricultural products. Although shipping rates per ton varied among products, he pointed out, shippers of unrefined products such as coal or some agricultural produce paid a much higher percentage of their value in freight than the shippers of manufactured products such as automobiles and textiles. Thus while shippers of motor vehicles paid $13.58 per ton and shippers of corn only $3.14 per ton, because corn was far less valuable per ton than an automobile, corn shippers actually paid 14 percent of the value of each ton in shipping costs, while automobile and truck shippers paid only 2 percent of the per ton value of their products. A general railroad rate reduction would ruin the lines, he agreed, but it might be possible to help the shippers of agricultural products and raw materials by lowering rates on those items and raising them on high-value manufactured goods.[34]

Like his European disarmament idea, Hoover's railroad rate suggestion had no chance of being adopted. Farmers might like it, but manufacturers hated it, and the railroads saw no advantage in pursuing the idea. Indeed, although almost everyone involved occasionally talked about restructuring rates, the whole subject was so complex that nothing ever got done.

Nor did anyone see any obvious way to implement consolidation among the less efficient lines. Hoover, as usual, proposed the appointment of an expert advisory committee to study the issues and make recommendations. When a proposal to have Congress authorize such a committee fell through, he suggested that the Commerce Department undertake the study on its own. On the basis of findings from departmental experts, he proposed to Senator Albert Cummins, chairman of the Senate Committee on Interstate Commerce, that Congress authorize the creation of a number of federally incorporated "system corporations" (essentially holding companies) that would promote consolidation by the simple device of exchanging shares of their stock for shares of the stock of individual railroads, thus bypassing complex and contentious negotiations among the executives of competing lines. He said nothing about whether the system corporations would be federally owned or somehow financed by private investors. The only difference between his plan and that proposed in the autumn of 1919 by Cummins, Hoover assured the touchy Senator, was that he proposed to allow *individual* shareholders to exchange their shares directly for shares of the new corporations rather than having the *corporations* make the exchange. In November, after further consultation with the president and Cummins, the secretary released a more detailed version of his plan to the press. The plan remained unclear about ownership of the system corporations, however, and Hoover's rejection of Cummins's argument that the government must have the power to *compel* consolidation delayed the introduction of authorizing legislation.[35]

V

Even as he devoted enormous amounts of time and energy to trying to find a way out of the railroad maze, Hoover also looked for alternative methods for getting products to market. As early as 1920, he had argued that waterway improvement, including the Mississippi and all other internal waterways, offered, "the only solution to the economic handling of our bulk material."

During his first two years in office, the energetic lobbying of the Great Lakes–St. Lawrence Tidewater Association had focused his attention on creation of a navigable waterway from the Great Lakes to the Atlantic rather than on the development of the Mississippi. Even before he entered office, the association had courted Hoover through his close friend and Food Administration colleague Julius Barnes, a Duluth grain dealer. In the summer of 1921, Barnes pressed Hoover to join a steamer excursion on the St. Lawrence planned to dramatize the virtues of that route for American and Canadian officials, and to give members of the Great Lakes–Tidewater Association and various Midwestern governors, congressmen, and senators a chance to lobby representatives of the two governments. Hoover initially agreed to join the excursion, at least for a day or two, but when the railroad strike began on July 1, he backed out. Just how enthusiastic he was about this particular jaunt remains uncertain. He favored the project in principle, but doubts in Canada about the waterway's likely cost and the outspoken opposition of New York's Governor Nathan Miller made him cautious. Like Barnes, Hoover believed that a St. Lawrence waterway would give Midwestern farmers inexpensive access to European markets, but he saw no profit in a confrontation with Governor Miller. Instead he encouraged his friend, General Electric's Owen D. Young, to sound out electric power interests in both New York and Ontario, with an eye to finding a plan for development that would win their support.[36] As with other projects, he preferred to have the outlines of a plan agreed upon among the main participants before he ever raised the issue publicly.

If multiple obstacles loomed before the St. Lawrence project in 1923, only a single—albeit serious—impediment prevented the implementation of the Colorado River Compact. Following the signing of the compact in November 1922, legislatures in six of the signatory states ratified the agreement by early 1923, but Arizona refused to act. Its leaders feared that unless California agreed to an allocation of the Lower Basin's water prior to ratification of the compact, the Golden State's larger population and greater development would enable it to grab most of the water. Californians, for their part, fed Arizona's fears by refusing to discuss a bistate agreement until Arizona ratified the compact. Hoover remained an outspoken advocate of the compact, but the inability of California and Arizona to reach agreement outraged the other signatories. By the end of the year, several of them had begun speculating about a new, six-state pact that would simply bypass Arizona.[37] Whether the idea was a sign of desperation or a bluff designed to put pressure on Arizona is unclear, but it appeared unlikely to solve the problem and seemed certain to produce endless litigation as Arizona fought to protect its rights.

Across the country, in the Tennessee River valley, Hoover hoped to make better progress in starting development at Muscle Shoals, Alabama, where the government's dam and wartime nitrate plant continued to sit idle. Farm organizations pressured the administration to get the nitrate plant running for the production of fertilizer, but the question of who would operate it remained unresolved. Public power advocates favored making Muscle Shoals the center of a major public power program, but most members of the administration, including Hoover, preferred private development, at least in theory. The problem was that no private proposal, including that made by Henry Ford, which had broad support across the administration, guaranteed the production of a sufficient quantity of nitrates to meet farmers' needs. Ford, like others who offered to run the facility, understood that major nitrate production consumed large amounts of electric power and provided little assurance of profit, while the direct sale of hydroelectric power generated from the existing facilities could be very profitable. Hence Ford's first proposal stressed power generation and limited nitrate production. Early in 1923, however, he submitted a new proposal, which promised substantially greater nitrate production. Hoover liked the new offer and endorsed it in testimony before the House Appropriations Committee. As in 1921, however, his enthusiasm proved premature. Before the committee could act, Commerce Department scientists studying the proposal concluded that it was economically and technically unrealistic. Their findings forced the secretary to pull back, and in November he recommended to the president that any agreement with a private operator must commit the contractor to the major investment in research and development needed to make substantial nitrate production feasible. Although several bidders, including Ford, continued to profess interest in the project, none of them offered the capital or commitment to make the operation successful. To deflect the farmers' pressure on the administration, Hoover advised the president to propose that Congress create a small, select committee to study the whole matter anew.[38]

VI

Like other issues related to the agricultural crisis, Muscle Shoals generated endless frustration. The Commerce Department's standardization and waste elimination program, on the other hand, proved to be one of Hoover's most gratifying initiatives. He had launched it in 1921 following the publication of the Federated American Engineering Societies' study of waste in industry, and the program reached full stride early in 1922. In each industry identified by Commerce Department staff as a likely candidate for standardization, the department used the same approach. After conferring with industry representatives to identify possibilities, staff members would invite a small group of businessmen (usually selected by a trade association) to Washington to discuss the specific needs of their industry or to devise an industry survey. Using the material thus gathered, Commerce Department staff members would draft a Standardization or Simplified Practice Recommendation and invite industry representatives to Washington for a large conference, where the draft would be adopted—usually without amendments.[39]

A striking feature of the program was the degree to which it was directed and controlled, not by the industries themselves, but by the experts in the Commerce Department. They carried out extensive preliminary research and planning before calling a conference, and they drafted the Simplified Practice Recommendation presented to the conference. Consultations with industry representatives preserved the image of a grassroots movement, but in reality the program fostered not only the standardization of tires and lumber sizes but also the standardization of industrial management practices. It amounted to the application of Frederick Taylor's industrial efficiency principles to whole industries rather than just individual factories.

Perhaps aware of the power the standardization program conveyed over the future of the American economy, Hoover jealously guarded his personal control of it. When Senator William Calder of New York introduced legislation in the spring of 1921 to create a federal Industrial Waste Commission and invited the Commerce Department to comment on the bill, the department buried the request. In January 1922, when Senator Wesley Jones asked a second time for a report on the bill, Hoover replied that since he was already developing a program to reduce industrial waste, creating a new commission merely to study the matter would not be useful. He did not suggest that the committee be empowered to take over the program.[40]

Delighted by the success of its first ventures, the Division of Simplified Practice launched a search for other "worlds to conquer," soliciting opportunities to apply simplification and standardization principles to paving bricks, bed springs, construction hardware, men's suits, rubber boots, tires, seats for farm implements, and other products. During fiscal year 1923, the division held ninety-three conferences related to simplification and standardization, with groups ranging from aircraft manufacturers to wool blanket makers. The monetary value of simplification and standardization, Hoover admitted, was difficult to measure accurately, but he was convinced that it saved "many millions of dollars" and improved the living standards of all Americans.[41]

In no area did simplification and standardization yield more benefits than in housing construction. During 1923, the Commerce Department's Housing Division, in conjunction with the Simplified Practice division, sponsored the publication of standardized house plans drafted by the Architects' Small House Service Bureau of the American Institute of Architects, prepared and promoted a model zoning ordinance and a municipal building code, encouraged the revision and adoption of model plumbing codes, and worked toward the standardization of building materials. Better Homes Week, partially sponsored by the Commerce Department, set up demonstration houses in nearly a thousand towns and cities where the Housing Division's projects and innovations from various industries were displayed. Hundreds of thousands of Americans visited the demonstrations and found encouragement to improve their existing homes or to plan the construction of new, modern suburban houses. During 1923, residential construction, which had accounted for only

22 percent of total construction in 1920, jumped to 44 percent of all building. Home owners, Hoover declared, made better citizens than renters. The home owner, he wrote in the foreword to a Commerce Department pamphlet titled *How to Own Your Own Home*, "works harder outside the home; he spends his leisure more profitably, and he and his family live a finer life and enjoy more of the comforts and cultivating influences of our modern civilization." He viewed high-quality, individually owned houses as a tangible example of what he hoped prosperity would mean for all Americans. Better pay and rising standards of living meant not only more material goods but also the leisure and incentive for families to pursue education and culture in comfortable surroundings.[42]

Much of the Housing Division's outreach to the public continued to be handled by Marie Meloney's Better Homes in America organization, but its very success created problems. Erstwhile supporters, like the Federation of Women, hoped to absorb it, and some companies saw it as an attractive marketing tool. The Butterick Company, publishers of the *Delineator*, had initially donated Meloney's services to run Better Homes and provided much of its financial backing without publicizing its generosity. But as the organization grew, both its expenses and the demands on Meloney's time increased. Butterick president George W. Wilder explained regretfully to Hoover in July 1923 that his company could not afford to continue the relationship.[43]

Wilder's letter came as no surprise either to Hoover or Meloney, who had been discussing ways to avoid having Better Homes hijacked by a volunteer organization like the Federation of Women or by commercial interests. The end of Butterick Company support made it urgent to find a backer that would not appropriate the organization for its own purposes. Meloney suggested seeking formal incorporation for Better Homes, with a corporate structure and a broadly representative board of directors that would make it more resistant to takeovers. Hoover agreed, but thought it essential to arrange solid funding before proceeding with incorporation. In November 1923, he approached the Rockefeller Foundation for $100,000 a year for the next three years to put the organization on an independent footing. The foundation was unwilling to provide the full $300,000, but after some negotiations, it promised $225,000 over the three-year period. Inasmuch as Hoover had estimated that $50,000 a year would cover the organization's needs, the assurance that Better Homes would have $75,000 a year for the next three years must have pleased him greatly. Just before Christmas, Better Homes in America was incorporated under Delaware law.[44]

Better Homes' demonstration houses all featured the latest electrical appliances, which Hoover regarded as playing an indispensable role in improving the residents' living standards. The time had come, he believed, for electricity to power suburban middle-class homes as well as factories. The superpower project to create an interconnected electric grid on the East Coast, which had been stymied in 1921 by a dispute over the proper role of the federal government in ownership and regulation, thus received new life and urgency as the consumer economy and suburbanization developed.[45]

The threat of a coal strike in early 1922 provided the immediate impetus for a renewed attempt to work out the problems in the superpower concept. Engineers estimated that creating a Northeastern regional grid might reduce coal consumption by as much as 50 million tons a year through elimination of duplication in power generation. It could therefore minimize the impact of coal strikes on the region's factories and homes. Hoover explained his ideas at a cabinet meeting on April 7, after which he reopened talks with representatives of private utilities in the region. In a speech delivered over a long-distance telephone line to the National Electric Light convention in Atlantic City on May 19, he argued that the establishment of a superpower system for the Northeast would have an effect comparable to the "Federal Reserve System in stabilizing credit." Yet despite his enthusiasm, nothing happened for a year, in part at least because the governors of New York and Pennsylvania, Al Smith and Gifford Pinchot, supported public ownership of at least some power generation. As GE's Owen Young pointed out, until the state and federal governments agreed on the basic principles of the plan, nothing could be done.[46]

Young's assessment made sense to Hoover, and in August 1923, he urged William S. Murray, chairman of the superpower committee, to sound out utility executives and state public utilities commissioners in New England about a meeting to discuss the concept. When Murray reported a positive response, Hoover issued formal invitations for a meeting in New York on October 13. As usual, he left nothing to chance. Meeting with state utilities commissioners several days before the general session, he told them he wanted to set up a "Northeastern States Superpower Commission" made up of state utilities commission chairmen. He urged them to seek uniform principles and policies for "coordinated State regulation." Once they agreed on regulatory principles, an interstate organization, comparable to the Colorado River Compact, could enforce the regulations. He predicted that, after an initial investment of $1.25 billion to set up the integrated system, the grid would more than pay for itself within three years.[47]

Hoover's ingenious plan for cooperative state regulation of a private superpower corporation provided a possible alternative to a federally owned or chartered company, but it aroused the immediate opposition of public power advocates. The Public Ownership League of America launched a campaign to create "a public superpower system to cover the continent." The Sacramento *Bee* denounced Hoover's plan as a scheme by "private and greedy monopoly to grasp it all, for the enrichment of a few and the exploitation of the many." Nevertheless, the promised benefits of the regional grid were so great that despite their doubts, even Governors Pinchot and Smith agreed in mid-December to send the chairmen of their state public utilities commissions to a meeting to begin planning a superpower system. At the same time, Commerce Department solicitor Stephen B. Davis opened talks with state legal representatives about the complex legal issues involved in the creation of an interstate regulatory system. Hoover began recruiting members for an engineering committee to consider that aspect of the project. He predicted optimistically that if all the groups worked diligently, the legal and technical data needed for further planning could be available early in 1924. Only time would show whether the information would prove so compelling that political opposition would melt away.[48]

VII

The threatened coal strike in the spring of 1923 also drew attention to the possibilities of alternative energy sources. The most obvious was oil, which had already begun to challenge coal in both water and land transportation as well as for heat and electrical generation. But if the coal industry's chaos posed problems, the oil industry faced equal difficulties. In the immediate postwar years, the United States did not seem to have enough oil to seriously threaten coal's dominance. During 1919 and 1920, demand for oil closely paralleled and sometimes exceeded the combination of domestic production and imports. As a result, prices increased dramatically. By mid-1922, however, new fields in California, Texas, and Oklahoma were producing a flood of oil that depressed prices by about 50 percent over 1921 levels. Obviously, if oil were to become a practical alternative to coal, some means had to be found to stabilize prices and production. One possibility was state regulation, but Hoover's friends in the oil business, Ralph Arnold and Mark Requa, warned him that California had tried and failed to control production, demand, and prices. Unless the industry could regulate itself, Requa argued, the public would demand federal action. With the Interior Department increasingly paralyzed by the growing Teapot Dome scandals, Hoover seized the opportunity to stake a claim on the issue for the Commerce Department. In his view, the impact of an oil shortage or a glut on price stability for consumers and industry made it a Commerce Department concern. Besides, the situation seemed tailor-made for the application of his favorite principle of industrial self-regulation.[49]

Initially, Hoover suggested that "the solution of the oil troubles in the United States would be the establishment of a free oil market where sales of crude, fuel, and gas could be made by producers and oil refiners," but an analysis of that idea by the American Petroleum Institute convinced him that it would not work. Instead, the administration began to move in a quite different direction. In the summer of 1924, Henry L. Doherty, a New York oil executive, as well as the Bureau of Mines and the Geologic Survey, all warned President Coolidge that the United States was rapidly depleting its domestic oil reserves. On August 20, Interior Secretary Hubert Work responded to these warnings by recommending to the president the appointment of "a Federal Oil Board to formulate . . . a Federal policy to be substituted for the present disconnected, wasteful methods." Members of the board, Work proposed, should include the secretaries of war, navy, commerce, and interior, along with the chiefs of the Geologic Survey, Bureau of Mines, Bureau of Standards, and other scientists.[50]

Although Work originally intended the Federal Oil Conservation Board to minimize future shortages through conservation, it turned out that it also offered a way to deal with an oil surplus. As the president put it in his December 1924 letter to the officials whom he wanted to serve on the board, the country needed a rational policy agreed on by all parties to regulate drilling and stabilize production and price, in times of surplus as well as shortage. He asked the board "to study the Government's responsibilities and to enlist the full cooperation of representatives of the oil industry in the investigation."[51] His request framed the problem very much as Hoover saw it, but neither man had yet addressed the conundrum of how to implement such a policy without violating the antitrust law's injunctions against collusion and price fixing among allegedly competing businesses.

VIII

Diagnosing the problem in the oil fields was far easier than finding a solution to it, and the same proved to be true with radio. The 1922 Radio Conference had pointed the way toward a regulatory plan, but Congress failed to act. Hoover professed to see no reason for the delay, but everyone else recognized that skepticism about giving him exclusive regulatory power over the industry permeated Congress and prevented passage of any legislation. In hopes of stirring action, he called a second Radio Conference to meet in March 1923. He suggested that, pending the passage of legislation, the conference might "investigate what administrative measures may properly be taken temporarily to lessen the amount of interference in broadcasting." The conferees, however, proved no more enthusiastic than Congress about giving the secretary dictatorial power. They recommended instead that government and university stations broadcasting on frequencies outside those specified for government use by the 1922 conference should move into the approved range but said nothing about commercial and amateur broadcasting. Until Congress finally acted, most broadcasters remained free to use any frequency they chose.[52]

The radio regulation issue displayed a pattern that had become evident in almost every major issue Hoover dealt with in 1923. In virtually every case—controlling the economic cycle, stabilizing European economies, using foreign loans for political purposes, solving the problems of the coal, railroad, oil, and radio industries, developing waterways, promoting standardization and waste elimination in industry, urging the superpower project—he advocated a more vigorous federal role than most others in the administration. In contrast to the rigid, small government philosophy of most of his colleagues, he stood out as a conspicuous exception. For all his genuine commitment to free enterprise, he also believed firmly, as he had said in *American*

Individualism, that individualism "cannot be maintained as the foundation of society if it looks to only legalistic justice based upon contracts, property, and political equality." Government must not only enforce "certain restrictions on the strong and the dominant" but also positively encourage "every individual to take that position in the community to which his intelligence, character, ability, and ambition entitle him."[53]

His views, of course, reflected his temperament as well as his philosophy. Hoover analyzed problems quickly, developed plans for solving them, and never doubted that he would be the best person to implement the plans. Having once reached a conclusion about a course of action, he did not willingly reexamine his assumptions and seldom believed he might have been mistaken. His was not a personality well adapted to service in a limited government.

By the end of the year, Hoover had begun to chafe at what he saw as the timidity and caution of his administration colleagues. In foreign policy, he lamented in a private year-end memorandum, nothing had been done toward "American participation in some world council to eliminate the causes of war," toward calling an international arms limitation conference, or, following Harding's death, to get the United States into the World Court. At home, his recommendations for reorganization of the federal government had failed, Coolidge had opposed what Hoover regarded as "constructive labor legislation," and he had been unable to win support for tax reform that would exchange increased inheritance taxes on the wealthy for reduction of the high brackets of the income tax. Instead, the president seemed committed to Mellon's principle of curtailing revenue to force a reduction in spending and contraction of the government. There had been achievements, to be sure—on waste elimination, housing, countering unemployment, conserving the Alaskan salmon fisheries, and a few other areas—but in almost every case these were initiatives he had launched personally and could control through the Commerce Department. "The main trouble," he complained, "is too much effort to conciliate my political colleagues by giving them ideas which they exploit and usually spoil instead of definitely taking the headship myself." The conclusion was obvious: being secretary of commerce and undersecretary of everything else had become too little. The year 1924 would be a presidential election year, and Hoover's ambition had begun to stir.[54]

Figure 14.1. Maps on the wall behind the commerce secretary's desk suggest his emphasis on developing national and international trade.

Figure 14.2. Lou Henry Hoover served as national president of the Girl Scouts (1922–25) and remained active in the organization until her death in 1944.

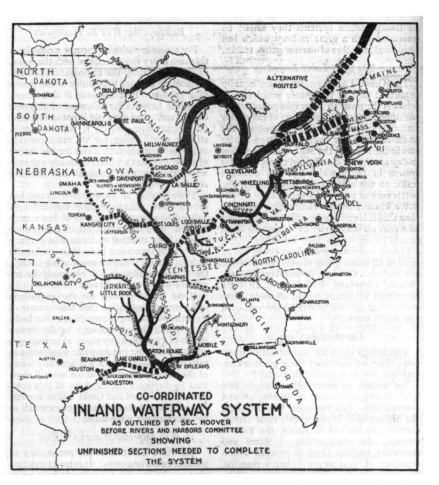

Figure 14.3. This 1926 map illustrates Hoover's vision of a 9,000-mile inland waterway system linking the American Midwest with the Atlantic and the Gulf of Mexico. Coordinated Inland Waterway System map from American Review of Reviews.

The traffic problem in Washington, D. C.

Figure 14.4. "Ding" Darling's April 1927 cartoon, "The Traffic Problem in Washington," offered a humorous view of Hoover's many activities in the mid-1920s.

CHAPTER 15

Alaska and Washington, 1923–1924

On June 20, 1923, President Harding boarded a train west from Washington to begin what he hoped would be a "Voyage of Understanding." Rumors of scandal had begun to circulate in the capitol, and the president's advisers, mindful of the coming presidential election, wanted him out charming the voters. They hoped that contact with the public would recharge his vitality and that a visit to the West Coast and Alaska would distract the reporters from corruption in Washington. The presidential party boarding the train in Washington on that hot, humid afternoon included sixty-five people, of whom the majority were reporters, Secret Service agents, and secretaries, but Florence Harding, Speaker of the House Frederick Gillett, Secretary of Agriculture Wallace, and Secretary of the Interior Hubert Work also joined the party, as did two of Harding's personal physicians. Hoover and his sons had left on June 15 for a brief fishing jaunt in the Sierras, after which Bert and Lou planned to join the group at Tacoma on July 3 for the trip to Alaska, where Hoover would meet with salmon fishermen and canners.[1]

I

Visibly exhausted, Harding nevertheless felt compelled to greet the public at each whistle-stop along the way and to make a number of speeches in major cities. Manfully, he did his best. His recurrent theme was a heartfelt appeal for

world peace, and although he still opposed American entry into the League of
Nations, he reiterated his call for the United States to join the World Court.
Hoover and Secretary of State Hughes welcomed that, but the suggestion
evoked little public enthusiasm, and isolationists viewed it with alarm. Nevertheless, Harding planned another speech on the subject in San Francisco after
he returned from Alaska. When the party reached Tacoma on July 4, where
they were to board the army transport *Henderson* for the trip up the coast to
Alaska, the president still looked gray and troubled. The Hoovers had arrived
the day before, and Lou, president of the Girl Scouts, spent the day meeting
with local Scout leaders.[2]

Aboard ship, Harding attempted to distract himself with endless bridge
games, in which Hoover took a reluctant part. Reports of unfolding scandals
in the Veterans' Bureau and the Justice Department followed the ship like the
coastal fog. At one point, the president called Hoover aside and asked him, "If
you knew of a great scandal in our administration, would you for the good of
the country and the party expose it publicly or would you bury it?" Hoover
immediately replied, "Publish it, and at least get credit for integrity on your
side," but when the secretary asked for more details of the situation, Harding
"abruptly dried up and never raised the question again." As the trip continued,
he grew even more visibly nervous.[3]

By the summer of 1923, Hoover had become Harding's most important
adviser on many aspects of policy, as the president demonstrated during the
western trip by endorsing American membership in the World Court, urging
the end of the twelve-hour day in the steel industry and proposing to expand
the national park system. Hoover grumbled about the endless bridge games
aboard the *Henderson*, but the secretary rejoiced privately in his influence in
the administration, although perhaps feeling a little nervous about the situation in Washington. What Hoover knew or suspected about the scandals that
would be known as the Teapot Dome affair is difficult to say. He had no part
in assigning the oil leases that lay at the heart of the matter or in the affairs of
the Veterans' Bureau, and those directly involved in illegal activities had every
reason to conceal them. The chief culprits in the Teapot Dome leases, Attorney General Harry Daugherty and Secretary of the Interior Albert Fall, had
been cabinet colleagues for two years but were not especially close to Hoover.
Given Hoover's wide-ranging activities and skill at bureaucratic infighting,
however, it seems likely that he knew more than his account of his conversation with the president implied.[4]

Hoover would have preferred to spend the summer in California with his
family, but the Alaskan trip gave him an opportunity to inform himself firsthand about some of the issues that faced the Commerce Department. The
fur seal industry in the Aleutian and Pribilof islands had been studied the
previous year during an expedition led by Assistant Secretary of Commerce
Claudius Huston and seemed to be in satisfactory condition, but incessant
controversy about the salmon fisheries continued. Despite an executive order

closing part of the area around the Aleutians to salmon fishermen, the catch had declined in 1921 and 1922. The Fisheries Bureau needed to decide how to handle the situation, particularly since Alaska's congressional delegate, Dan Sutherland, insisted stridently that no one in Alaska favored any of the conservation measures Hoover had proposed. Regarding Sutherland's statements as totally unreliable, Hoover scheduled a number of hearings in towns along the Alaskan coast to hear for himself what fishermen and canners actually had to say. In the meantime, he told Senator Wesley Jones, "having fitted a lid on the further destruction of the Northwestern Alaskan salmon until Congress acts, I intend to sit on it whether Delegate Sutherland, certain canners, and certain fishermen, or more of the same sort, like it or not."[5]

On July 8, the *Henderson* docked at Metlakatla, a tiny native settlement in Southeast Alaska, where Governor Scott Bone and Delegate Sutherland officially welcomed the party. For Hoover, the highlight of the day came in the chance to see Matilda Minthorn, widow of Hoover's uncle, Dr. Henry John Minthorn, who had taken young Bert into his Oregon home many years before. Dr. Minthorn had died in October of 1922, after several years as a missionary to the natives of Southeast Alaska, but Matilda, his second wife, had continued his work. Bert welcomed this chance to renew one of the last ties to his childhood, while she solicited his influence on behalf of the natives. She joined the party aboard the *Henderson* and traveled with it to Ketchikan. After she went ashore, the ship continued north to Wrangell and Juneau, and then turned northwest to Anchorage, where the party landed to take the recently completed Alaska Railway north to Fairbanks, the northernmost point of the trip. On July 14 and 15, Hoover held hearings about the condition of the northern fisheries in Fairbanks and Nenana, and then presided over further hearings at Seward, Anchorage, and Cordova on July 16, 17, and 19. Between official duties, he and others slipped away in small boats to try the local fishing. When they succeeded, everyone dined royally on fresh seafood, and the evenings passed pleasantly with sing-alongs. A photograph from the trip shows a smiling Hoover holding one end of a rope laden with fish, while behind him another man displays two large salmon. Lou, constrained by propriety from joining the fishermen, delighted in the spectacular coastal scenery and enjoyed exploring the little towns along the shore, where she took part in excursions to see totem poles and gold mines.[6]

Hoover found the hearings very reassuring. Every witness praised the Commerce Department's restrictions on the fisheries, and a number of them roundly condemned Delegate Sutherland for misrepresenting the interests of fishermen and canners. As the trip neared its end, Hoover spoke briefly in Sitka, reaffirming his support for federal fisheries oversight and urging immediate passage of legislation providing "variable and constructive regulation under broad authority" that could be adapted to different conditions in various places.[7]

II

On Thursday, July 26, the *Henderson* docked at Vancouver, where the president delivered two speeches, attended an official luncheon, visited a hospital, and then was driven to a local golf course. Exhausted, he could manage only seven holes before returning to a hotel for an hour's rest before an official dinner, where he had to speak again and then stand in a reception line for half an hour. It was eleven o'clock before he returned to the *Henderson*. That night the ship steamed south toward Seattle, planning to arrive early in the morning, but thick fog and a minor collision with an escorting destroyer delayed the landing. Despite the late start, Harding plunged into his planned itinerary, traveling by car through dense crowds, first to a monument where he spoke briefly, then to a park where he addressed a crowd of children, then on to the University of Washington stadium for a major speech, written largely by Hoover, on Alaskan policy, and finally to the Seattle Press Club, where he made yet another speech, before arriving at about 7:30 in the evening at the special train on which he planned to travel to California. The next day, as the train moved south through Oregon and northern California, the exhausted president asked cabinet members traveling with him to greet the crowds at whistle stops along the way. Hoover and Interior Secretary Work, himself a physician, became increasingly concerned about what appeared to be more than ordinary tiredness, but the president's personal doctor, Dr. Charles E. Sawyer, assured them that the problem was only extreme fatigue, perhaps exacerbated by food poisoning from bad crab aboard the ship.[8]

Originally, the president had planned to visit Yosemite National Park, but concerned about the limited medical facilities there, Hoover and Work proposed that the party proceed to San Francisco instead. They arrived early on Sunday morning, July 29, and Harding was immediately taken to the Palace Hotel. Hoover, in the meantime, had tracked down Dr. Ray Lyman Wilbur in the Sierras and lined up other consulting physicians in case they were needed. After an optimistic report on Harding's condition from Dr. Sawyer, several members of the party accepted Lou Hoover's invitation to spend the day at the Hoovers' house at Stanford.[9]

That evening, Harding took a turn for the worse, and Hoover hastily summoned Dr. Wilbur and the other consultants. After an examination and discussion among the physicians, Wilbur told Hoover that he believed the president had an infected gallbladder, which had exacerbated an underlying cardiac problem. The next morning, however, Harding seemed better, joking with his attendants and getting out of bed to walk to the bathroom. With Florence Harding at his side, he insisted that he would be well enough to deliver his planned speech on American membership in the World Court the next day. However, his condition varied unpredictably over the next two days, and he eventually realized that he could not deliver the speech and must cancel the rest of his California trip. On Wednesday, August 1, his staff released the text of his planned World Court speech to the press. The next morning, August 2, he seemed much better, and everyone began to believe he would recover fully. Hoover felt confident enough to skip his usual 4:00 PM meeting with the doctors and planned to have dinner with the Works and other members of the president's party. Then, suddenly, at about 7:00 PM, a messenger summoned him urgently to the president's suite. There he found the doctors huddled at Harding's bedside. He had, it appeared, suffered a serious relapse, and at 7:32, Wilbur emerged to say that the president had died.[10]

Harding's unexpected death came as a huge shock to Americans. News of the scandals in his administration had not yet spread widely, and his kind personality had made him popular with the public. Dr. Sawyer's diagnosis of food poisoning did not seem adequate to account for the death, and, in fact, it was almost certainly erroneous. Even before the trip, Harding had been suffering from fatigue, shortness of breath, inability to sleep lying down, and high blood pressure—all symptoms of serious cardiac disease—and modern physicians have concluded that he fell victim to a coronary thrombosis. The suddenness and confusion surrounding his death amid increasing reports of scandal, however, set off a torrent of rumors. Suicide, medical incompetence, and even murder were all suggested darkly. Even Hoover, who had done his best to assemble an expert team of consultants, came in for blame. Dr. Wilbur, it was noted, might have been a noted diagnostician at one time, but for many years he had been a college president, not a practicing physician.[11]

If Hoover knew of the rumors, he ignored them, and the Hoovers accompanied Mrs. Harding and the president's body on the train back to Washington. There, on August 7, the coffin was taken to the East Room of the White House, and the next morning to the Rotunda of the Capitol, where Harding lay in state. The next day the casket was again put on the train, back to Marion, Ohio, where the funeral took place on August 10, Hoover's forty-ninth birthday. Florence Harding, reported Lou, had been "perfectly wonderful during the whole ordeal, and never once forgot that her real duty was to take him back to where the Nation might pay him the last honors possible."[12]

The political earthquake of Harding's death was soon followed by a real one on the other side of the world. On September 1, an 8.3-magnitude quake struck Tokyo, killing almost 150,000 people and injuring 800,000. Hoover quickly joined with John Barton Payne, national chairman of the Red Cross, in launching an appeal for aid. Within ten days, it raised over $3.5 million, and over the next month the Commerce Department worked with the Japanese government to buy and ship reconstruction supplies to Japan. For a moment at least, Hoover had returned to his familiar role as the "master of emergencies."[13]

III

Harding's death represented a setback to Hoover's efforts to secure legislation to regulate Alaskan salmon fishing, but the secretary rallied in the autumn of

1923. As previously, Delegate Sutherland and the Hearst press denounced his efforts, charging that proposed restrictions favored the large canners and discriminated against small fishermen and canners. Hoover admitted that the sweeping regulations adopted under the executive orders had been a "stop-gap" and had injured some fishermen and canners. He insisted that fairness would be assured only by passing legislation that would authorize the Fisheries Bureau to tailor regulations to specific locations. When on June 6, 1924, President Coolidge signed into law the new Alaska fisheries act, Hoover could not refrain from gloating quietly at his victory over "strong opposition from various sources."[14]

It is difficult to evaluate the merits of the Hoover-Sutherland conflict. Sutherland expressed an Alaskan frontier spirit and undoubtedly spoke for some small canners and fishermen, while Hoover's sympathies tended to be with business. Yet not a single Alaskan endorsed Sutherland's position during Hoover's 1923 hearings, and some inland Indian tribes, who had suffered from hunger owing to the failure of the salmon runs in the early 1920s, thanked the secretary for restricting fishing. On the other hand, the Fisheries Bureau's claim that, of 129 canneries in Alaska, the "Fish Trust owned only 41" was disingenuous because it said nothing about what percentage of the annual catch those large canneries actually controlled.[15] Conservation often bears most heavily on the small entrepreneur eking out a living by ruthless exploitation of resources. If the personal bitterness of the Hoover-Sutherland conflict can be set aside, the principles at stake between them—that is, the clashes between the individual entrepreneur and the corporation and between local and national control—were the very questions with which Hoover himself struggled throughout his career. Although he did not see it, his own experience as an engineer, successful corporate businessman, and federal official suggested that the values of rural, individualistic America, in which he believed deeply, fell short as guides to policy in the modern world.

The ascendancy that Hoover had gained in the Harding cabinet, which was symbolized by the appointment of his ally Hubert Work as secretary of the interior in the spring of 1923, diminished after Calvin Coolidge moved into the White House. At first, Hoover expressed optimism about relations with the new president. Harding had been a fine person, he told Mark Sullivan, but he was careless about details, and sometimes conflicts developed because he gave several people authority over the same issue. Coolidge, on the other hand, listened closely to reports and quickly grasped the facts. He found that much easier to deal with, said Hoover. In addition, Lou Hoover and Grace Coolidge developed a rapport and remained friends throughout the Washington years. The president's first State of the Union message in December 1923 included a number of projects urged by Hoover, and the two men united in their opposition to the McNary-Haugen farm program. But the honeymoon did not last. Secretary of the Treasury Andrew Mellon, not Hoover, became the dominant figure in the Coolidge cabinet. The new president had little patience with Hoover's restless energy and endless recommendations. Before long, he began referring snidely to the secretary as "Wonder Boy," and near the end of his term he exploded, "That man has offered me unsolicited advice for six years, all of it bad!"[16]

IV

Rumors that Hoover had presidential ambitions for 1924 undoubtedly complicated his relations with Coolidge. Enthusiastic but naive admirers in California broached the idea soon after Harding's death, and despite Hoover's denials, the reports of his interest continued to circulate. Had circumstances been different, there is little doubt that he would have liked to run, and his rivals in California delighted in embarrassing him by publicizing the rumors.

The principal source of the rumors was Hiram Johnson and his followers, who viewed Hoover as a threat to their control of the California Republican Party. Elevated from the statehouse in Sacramento to the U.S. Senate in 1916, Johnson had refused for several months to turn over the governorship to Lieutenant Governor William D. Stephens, who, although a Progressive, had not been Johnson's personal choice for the position. By the time Johnson finally surrendered the governorship in March 1917, the struggle had poisoned his relations with Stephens, and the situation worsened when Johnson tried unsuccessfully to replace Stephens as the gubernatorial candidate in 1918. The clash with Stephens, and Johnson's adamant opposition to the League of Nations, alienated many progressives during the 1920 presidential primary, forcing the senator to turn to conservatives for support. The disillusioned progressives, torn between personal loyalty to Johnson and principle, often sat out the primary or backed Hoover. Johnson retaliated for their disloyalty by supporting the conservative Samuel Shortridge in the 1920 senatorial race and remaining aloof from the 1922 gubernatorial contest, thus enabling the conservative Friend Richardson to win. In 1923, while Johnson traveled in Europe, progressives organized the Progressive Voters League to fight conservative legislation and support a progressive successor to Governor Richardson in 1926. They succeeded in electing Clement C. Young, but the progressive movement had been divided and weakened by the long internecine struggle, and Johnson became convinced that Hoover hoped to seize control of the state party and use it to pursue national political power.[17]

In fact, Hoover's most important California supporters had little in common aside from their support for him. Men like Ralph Arnold, Ralph Merritt, and Mark Requa were middle-of-the-roaders; publisher Harry Chandler and banker Henry M. Robinson were conservatives; journalist Andrew M. Lawrence and Congressman Arthur Free were moderate progressives. Notable progressives such as Fresno publisher Chester Rowell, Governor Young, and Franklin Hichborn remained neutral between Johnson and Hoover, as did conservative businessmen Wallace Alexander, Milton Esberg,

Charles Kendrick, attorney Francis Keesling, and Republican national committeeman William H. Crocker. Mayor James Rolph and Sheriff Thomas
Finn of San Francisco built their own organizations. And divisions between
the northern and southern part of the state, battles over water, labor disputes,
and rural-versus-urban contests cut across and complicated political affiliations. The crosscurrents made state Republican politics unpredictable, and
Hoover had not yet resolved to plunge into the maelstrom.[18]

On January 2, 1924, Johnson announced that he would seek the Republican presidential nomination. Hoover quickly recognized the opportunity
and announced his support of Coolidge. Johnson's defeat in the May primary resulted more from the president's popularity and divisions among state
Republicans than from Hoover's action, but some of his Southern California
friends wanted to believe that he had played a decisive role. At the national
Republican convention, Coolidge indicated no vice presidential preference,
and Idaho Senator William Borah and Illinois Governor Frank Lowden
declined the nomination. Hoover's admirers urged his choice as a candidate
who had the stature and ability to succeed to the presidency, a grim possibility
on everyone's mind after Harding's death. It turned out, however, that only a
minority of the California delegation supported Hoover, and both the Johnsonites and conservatives opposed him. And, it soon became clear, Coolidge
did not want him either. The taciturn president did not explain his reasons,
but personal animosity and a fear that Hoover, as vice president, might overshadow the president undoubtedly played roles. Hoover and former Budget
Director Charles G. Dawes were both nominated, and on the third ballot the
convention chose Dawes, 6,822 to 2,342. Hoover's caution about entering the
presidential contest had been amply justified.[19]

Following the convention, the curious relationship between Coolidge and
Hoover continued. Hoover campaigned extensively for the president, but
he had no assurance Coolidge would reappoint him to the cabinet. When
the invitation came, Hoover accepted it with alacrity. But when Secretary
of Agriculture Henry Wallace died on October 25, and Hoover recommended the Kansas agricultural economist William Jardine as his successor,
Coolidge instead appointed Howard Gore on an interim basis. On January 15, 1925, the president announced publicly that he was asking Hoover
to take over as secretary of agriculture. That made outward sense, because
Hoover, like Coolidge, opposed the McNary-Haugen bill and strongly supported the cooperative marketing program that Coolidge favored as a solution
to the agricultural depression. But it seemed odd that the president would
announce his offer to reporters before talking to Hoover, as became obvious when Hoover announced, also publicly, that he would decline the offer.
In fact, as George Nash has suggested, there may have been more than met
the eye in the exchange. A few days previously, Coolidge had announced that
Frank Kellogg, a former Minnesota senator then serving as American ambassador to Great Britain, would succeed Charles Evans Hughes as secretary of

state. Sixty-nine years old and relatively unknown, Kellogg was an old friend of Coolidge's but not highly regarded either in the senate or among foreign policy experts. Hoover's poaching on State Department turf had soured his relations with that department's staff, but he certainly offered more experience and greater qualifications for the position than Kellogg did. One school of Washington gossip reported that Coolidge had denied Hoover the State Department to prevent him from using it as a stepping stone to the White House. Another, one more charitable to the president, held that Coolidge intended the public offer of the Agriculture Department to mollify Hoover's anger at being passed over for State. The president's handling of the affair suggests that the former interpretation may have been closer to the truth than the latter, but in any case, the outcome further strained relations between the president and the secretary of commerce.[20]

The growing influence of Treasury Secretary Andrew Mellon also exacerbated the tension between Hoover and Coolidge. Allegedly the second richest man in the country, the frail, diminutive Mellon had emerged as the administration's fiercest advocate of limited government. He favored leaving business free to pursue its own interests and usually opposed Hoover's proposals for managing the economy. The secretary of commerce, Mellon thought, not only meddled too much in the operations of the economy but also in the affairs of other departments. When the president sank into a deep depression following the death of Calvin Coolidge, Jr., on July 7, 1924, Mellon's philosophical commitment to passive government fitted perfectly with Coolidge's own loss of interest in daily affairs and reluctance to act. Cabinet members, he made clear, should take care of matters within their jurisdiction and not disturb him with novel initiatives.[21] His attitude dealt Hoover a severe blow.

Woodrow Wilson's death on February 3, 1924, also struck Hoover at least a symbolic blow. As a loyal Republican, the secretary released only a brief statement to the press, vaguely praising "a great leader through a great crisis in our national life," but he could scarcely have failed to see that even before the former president's death, his own hopes for international cooperation and the League of Nations had also gone to the grave.[22] Coolidge preferred to let the Wall Street bankers, with whom Hoover had distant relations, represent the United States overseas, staying well away from any political involvement. Hoover did not alter his conviction that the United States needed peace and economic stability in the world, but for the time being he had been pushed to the side in that arena.

V

Deprived of some of his influence outside the Commerce Department, Hoover redoubled his effort to make the department the driving force to improve living standards for Americans. He believed strongly that prosperity should bring not only material benefits but also greater leisure for middle-class Americans and opportunities to fill that leisure with culture and healthful recreation. Shortened working hours and higher incomes, he had told the National Conference of Social Work in 1922, necessitated enlarging the "opportunity for recreation and intellectual improvement." In December 1923, Assistant Secretary of the Navy Theodore Roosevelt, Jr., suggested a way to implement that broad goal. "The physical vigor, moral strength, and clear simplicity of mind of the American people can be immeasurably furthered by the properly developed opportunities for life in the open afforded by our forests, mountains and waterways," wrote Roosevelt. He proposed a National Conference on Outdoor Recreation to define and expand those opportunities.[23]

Hoover welcomed Roosevelt's idea enthusiastically, and the president, although initially skeptical, went along. According to Leon F. Kneipp, acting executive secretary of the new organization, Coolidge decided "that it would be a good thing to let people know he was human, that he was a nature lover." In April, the president asked the commerce secretary to join with the secretaries of agriculture, interior, labor, war, and Undersecretary of the Navy Roosevelt as members of the president's Committee on Outdoor Recreation. The committee invited 128 organizations ranging from the American Trapshooting Association to the Wild Flower Preservation Society to send delegates to Washington on May 22 to 24, 1924, for an organizational meeting of a National Conference on Outdoor Recreation (NCOR). Arthur Ringland, a Forest Service employee and former member of Hoover's Belgian relief organization, invoked "the Chief's" influence to become the executive secretary of the new organization.[24]

Addressing the conference in December 1924, Hoover pointed out that "we have hitherto directed most of our national activities to the consideration of what we do in the hours of labor and too little to the hours of recreation." He invited the delegates to plan a voluntary, cooperative program to provide healthful recreational opportunities for all Americans. In a second address in January 1926, he talked particularly about the problem of water pollution, noting the legislation already passed to prevent ocean pollution and suggesting that states and local governments establish a triage system for rivers and streams that would abandon efforts to clean up the most polluted but work aggressively to upgrade less contaminated waters.[25]

Taken together, the two speeches reflected Hoover's belief that conservation, like many other aspects of public policy, offered opportunities for both federal initiatives and local, voluntary citizen control. On the one hand, conservation in the broad sense of utilizing resources efficiently for the sustenance of the economy remained, in his view, largely a federal responsibility. That included such matters as waterways development, management of littoral fisheries, and oceanic pollution abatement. The development of the outdoors as an amenity of urban life, a place of refuge and wholesome refreshment for busy city dwellers, on the other hand, should be the responsibility of volunteer organizations like those gathered in the NCOR. Who could better determine the future of outdoor recreation than those who used it? Just as he favored industrial self-regulation through trade associations, so he supported recreational self-government through the voluntary organizations assembled in the NCOR. In both cases, he had faith that the decisions reached by such groups would be wise and beneficial to the nation as a whole.

In 1924, Hoover had an opportunity to apply his ideas directly through the National Parks Association (NPA), which had been organized in 1919 to provide support for the parks and the Park Service. Largely the brainchild of the organization's first executive secretary, Robert Sterling Yard, the organization urged the protection of existing parks and promoted the establishment of new ones that would encompass "consistently great examples [of] the full range of American scenery, flora and fauna," while resisting political pressures to include less distinctive areas within the park system. "The national parks are far more than recreational areas," wrote Yard, "they are . . . the museums of the ages." As the NCOR got under way in 1924, Yard feared that the strict definition of the national parks as including only the most exceptional scenic and natural wonders would be diluted or changed to emphasize recreation. Finding Secretary of the Interior Work not especially concerned about the issue, Yard approached Hoover with the suggestion that he become president of the NPA. To protect the sanctity of the existing parks, Yard wanted Hoover to sponsor the creation of a new "recreational park system in addition to and different in name and type from our 'National Park' group."[26]

Yard seems to have assumed that Hoover shared his preference for the "museum" parks and disdain for the "industrial utilization" of recreational areas. Apparently it did not occur to him that Hoover might think those two values should be reversed, with outdoor recreation taking precedence over the spiritual and scientific emphasis that Yard preferred. Nor did Hoover seem to be aware of possible disagreement. In his February 26, 1924, letter accepting the nomination, he agreed that "the defense and preservation of our national parks is a most worthy effort," adding that "their stimulative, educational, recreational values are, all of them, of vital importance to all of our citizens." And, following Yard's lead, he suggested that the NPA support the creation of "other forms of recreational areas," which were "as necessary to our advancing civilization as are wheat fields and factories."[27]

Delighted by attracting a president with Hoover's prestige and prowess as a fund-raiser, leaders of the association did not realize that they and Hoover understood quite different things by the phrase, "recreational values." NPA members wanted to preserve the parks in a pristine state, largely for the benefit of scientists and upper-class travelers who would admire their unspoiled beauty. Hoover envisioned the parks as playgrounds for a middle class made mobile by railroads and cars and with more plebeian tastes in recreation than those of the NPA's members.

The result was misunderstanding and conflict. Within a year after becoming president of the organization, Hoover proposed merging it with the American

Civic Association, the American Park Society, the American Association of Parks Executives, and the National Conference of State Parks into a new Public Parks Council. The federated body, he argued, would consolidate fund-raising, reduce duplication of effort, and offer savings on staff salaries. Its purpose would be "to bring about coordination among activities of various associations interested in national, state, municipal, and county parks and playgrounds."[28]

Hoover's suggestion horrified Yard and other directors of the NPA. In such an organization, they feared, the museum, scenic, and scientific purposes of the national park system would be lost, and the parks would become *only* playgrounds. After lengthy debate, seventeen of the twenty directors of the association opposed the proposal. In the meantime, Hoover, foreseeing defeat, had already indicated his intention of stepping down from the organization's presidency at the end of the year. To former Secretary of the Interior John Barton Payne, he explained diplomatically that "it seems to me that they are accomplishing a great deal but that better progress might be made by consolidated effort."[29]

The history of the NPA presidency revealed some of Hoover's basic values. He saw the parks primarily as appendages of the consumer society. He had little patience with commercial entertainments and none with what he called "destructive joy," but neither did he sympathize with the elitism implicit in Yard's conception of the parks as cathedrals to be protected from rude hands. It made sense to him as an engineer that all the organizations interested in parks (or other uses of nature) should join forces; to do so would make them all more efficient and thus more effective advocates of their interests. It also made sense from his standpoint for all of the groups who might want to use the parks to unite in determining their future. But he did not regard the issue as vital. When the NPA's trustees rejected his proposal, he simply severed his connection with the organization and moved on.

VI

In the meantime, Lou Hoover pursued her own version of constructive recreational opportunities for Americans through the Girl Scouts and the Women's Division of the National Amateur Athletic Federation (NAAF). Both of the organizations initially supported the National Conference on Outdoor Recreation, although the NAAF, chronically short of money, seems to have dropped away after the first year. Like Bert, Lou found that, despite good intentions, controversy and disagreement sometimes frustrated her efforts.

The Girl Scout "Little House" project, which had occupied much of Lou's time in late 1923, proved equally demanding in 1924. She believed that the house could be a valuable way to demonstrate Girl Scout skills to the public and to secure publicity for the organization—but first she had to find the money to get the building moved off public land and to a new site. The Rockefeller Foundation offered $10,000 for the move, if the Scouts asked for it, but the organization also desperately needed to raise at least $275,000 to purchase a building in New York for their national headquarters. Realistically, Lou reckoned that the foundation would probably not contribute to both projects and so turned to others for the money to move the house. It finally opened to visitors in August of 1924, proving so popular that across the country Scouts developed more than 250 local versions of the project.[30]

The growing visibility of the Girl Scouts under Lou's leadership aroused jealousy among the leaders of the national Boy Scout organization. In March 1924, Boy Scout leaders accused the Girl Scouts of misappropriating "material either originated by, or primarily the property of, the Boy Scouts of America," including the Scout name. What particularly galled them, they indicated, was the danger that the average Boy Scout would "resent the constant reminder that he, a boy, has anything in common with 'mere girls.'" They hinted at the possibility of legal action.[31]

The name controversy ultimately came to nothing. Juliette Low, founder of the Girl Scouts, observed shrewdly that as soon as the current leadership of the Boy Scouts changed, the issue would probably disappear. And so it proved.[32] Lou found the whole controversy ridiculous but annoying. It underlined the reality that despite having the vote, women had still not won full equality in American society. She continued to urge the girls to pursue whatever careers they might want, and she emphasized that the Scouts should not simply train girls in woodcraft and domestic skills but fit them to take active roles as citizens.

Amid her other duties as president of the Scouts, Lou also raised money to buy a building in New York City for the Scouts' national headquarters. She learned in the autumn of 1923 that the building they had been renting was to be torn down and that the only suitable replacement would cost at least $275,000. At her urging, the board of directors voted to seek $500,000 to cover both the construction of a new building on Lexington Avenue and an enhanced national budget. She announced that the Scouts would sell 50,300 bricks at $10 each, but in fact, most of the money came from a handful of major donors, including John D. Rockefeller, Jr., and Julius Rosenwald, who opened the drive with gifts totaling $86,000. By the end of November, nearly four-fifths of the targeted amount had been reached. Lou herself contributed $1,000 to the building fund and another $1,000 to the general budget.[33]

Lou also spent a good deal of time getting the new Women's Division of the NAAF off to a strong start. She launched a membership drive in late 1923 among schools and colleges across the country and encouraged the committees drafting appropriate athletic programs for girls and young women to complete their work. At the organization's convention in Chicago in April 1924, the delegates unanimously reelected Lou as chairman, reaffirmed the organization's endorsement of physical activity for all women, and rejected the idea of competition, including women's participation in the Olympic games.[34]

The NAAF's resolute amateurism attracted few adherents, however, and a fund-raising drive in the spring of 1924 brought disappointingly small returns. Fortunately, the Laura Spelman Rockefeller Memorial gave the organization a grant, and Dr. J. F. Rogers, director of the Division of School Hygiene in the Federal Bureau of Education, endorsed it, but in a decade when spectator sports, including women's sports, were becoming big business, the Women's Division slowly shrank.[35]

If Lou's activities with the Scouts and the NAAF brought her frustration as well as satisfaction, she launched at least one philanthropic enterprise in 1924 that gave her pure pleasure. With her father aging and her sister recently divorced, she sought an investment for the family's money that would both provide support for her relatives and benefit others. By selling family properties in Monterey as well as various securities, she amassed the capital for a trust fund, which she used to build several small houses on the Stanford campus. Rented or sold to young faculty members, the houses provided a steady income to support her father and her sister's family.[36]

George Harrison, a young scientist who had been a sort of big brother to Herbert, Jr., during his undergraduate years at Stanford and had recently returned to teach at his alma mater, purchased one of the houses. Lou sold the remainder to other young faculty members who would otherwise have found it difficult to find suitable housing at affordable prices in the area. By 1941, nearly all of the mortgages had been paid off, and the trust, having served its purpose for both Jean's family and Stanford, was dissolved by Lou, who turned over the remaining funds, about $10,000, to her sister.[37]

The year 1924 brought other happy events for the Hoovers. Both boys lived in Palo Alto during the year, where Allan graduated from Palo Alto High and Herbert entered his senior year at the university in the fall. Allan, now over six feet tall, was on the school track team, learning to play the saxophone, and working on building a car, which he labeled a "knock-out." Kenneth Brown, a university student who was acting as his tutor and companion, described it somewhat more ambiguously as "a unique sort of an affair." In September, after a two-month horseback trip in Yellowstone and the Jackson Hole area of Wyoming, Allan enrolled for his freshman year at Stanford. Herbert's big news was his engagement, announced on June 7, to Margaret (Peggy) Watson, a fellow student at Stanford. The Hoovers were delighted by the match and looked forward to the couple's wedding in June 1925, following their graduation. Later that summer, Herbert went to Maine to spend a month at the Intercontinental Company's Pejepscot paper mill, to see whether he wanted to enter the business. Since he had decided against becoming a mining engineer, his father had been urging him gently to look seriously at other professions.[38]

Traveling incessantly during the spring of 1924, Bert and Lou seldom saw each other and dealt with family business at long distance. They learned, at long distance, that the family dog, a Belgian shepherd named King Tut (King

Tutankhamen's sarcophagus had been opened on February 12 and Egyptology was much in vogue) had bitten a child who climbed over the fence at 2300 S Street. They were relieved to hear, a few days later, that the boy had suffered no lasting harm. Also by long distance, Lou issued orders for alterations to one of Bert's old suits, authorized the installation under the stairs at 2300 of a safe he had purchased, and even ordered books for her husband's bedside table. Together briefly, they both approved the dissolution of the West Branch Corporation, which they had established as a trust to hold Bert's various properties during the war. It had proven useful to conceal their purchase of the S Street house in the weeks before Hoover accepted Harding's invitation to join the cabinet, but as Bert looked ahead to a possible political campaign, they feared it might be seen as a device to conceal his wealth or evade taxes.[39]

Christmas 1924 found the Hoovers still spanning the continent, with the boys in Palo Alto and Bert and Lou in Washington. There the Rickard family joined them for the holidays, and Lou did her best to decorate the house as "Allan would have done it." The Vernon Kelloggs came for Christmas dinner, and the next evening Prince Caetani, the retiring Italian ambassador, a mining engineer and old friend of Hoover's, visited for a festive evening. On the West Coast, the boys had an equally happy time with the Henrys and the Watsons. Both parents and boys would have liked to be together for the holiday, but by this time they were so accustomed to separation that it hardly seemed abnormal.[40]

CHAPTER 16

The Commerce Department, 1924

The economic outlook for the United States in 1924, declared Hoover in a Commerce Department press release in January, looked "bright," and the "world situation . . . hopeful." Americans enjoyed "the highest productivity and movement of commodities since the war, with full employment, high real wages, greatly increased savings, large additions to home building, and the largest increase in railway equipment since the war." Although "acute suffering" remained in "Northwest agricultural areas," even there, "the disparity between agricultural prices as a whole and industrial commodities" was "gradually lessening and the economic balance . . . tending to right itself." Outside the United States, in the Western Hemisphere, Asia, Australia, and Africa, Hoover believed that nearly full recovery from the war had taken place. In Russia, the Baltic states, the Balkans, the Middle East, Italy, and Spain there had also been great progress, but some postwar political, social, and economic difficulties remained. Only in Western Europe did he see major problems, which he believed had been worsened by the French and Belgian occupation of the Ruhr area of Germany in January 1923. The occupation, he argued, had led to runaway inflation in Germany, interruption of reparations payments, the flight of European capital to the United States, and serious damage to the economies of all of Germany's neighbors. Privately, Hoover worried that the Ruhr occupation might lead to the formation of a Franco-German economic bloc that would exclude the United States.[1]

I

As Hoover pointed out, the United States could not avoid the economic effects of the German collapse, but the American government could do nothing officially because it had never ratified the Treaty of Versailles and had only unofficial representation on the Reparations Commission. As early as December 1922, however, Secretary of State Hughes had proposed that an unofficial commission of experts, including Americans, be appointed to recommend modifications to the reparations system. Recognizing reluctantly that the Germans would not or could not pay the full reparations bill and that the economies of Western Europe hung by a thread, in the autumn of 1923 the Reparations Commission accepted Hughes's suggestion and agreed to appoint two committees: one to propose a method to stabilize the German mark and the other to seek ways to draw German capital back into the country. On November 5, 1923, Hoover, Hughes, and Secretary of the Treasury Mellon met and agreed to propose to the Europeans that Chicago banker Charles G. Dawes and Owen Young, chairman of the board of directors of General Electric (GE), serve on the currency stabilization committee and that Los Angeles banker Henry M. Robinson serve on the committee on repatriation of German capital. Hoover's influence was evident not only in the choice of Young and Robinson, with whom he had worked closely during and after the war, but also in the fact that the Commerce Department supplied many of the experts who accompanied the three men to Europe in January 1924.[2]

Dawes was a blunt Midwestern banker and former federal budget director "with a long basset hound face who smoked an underslung Sherlock Holmes–style pipe and peppered his conversation with picturesque swearwords." Owen Young had begun his career as a lawyer for GE and worked his way up to become chairman of the board of GE and a founder of the Radio Corporation of America. His most striking features were his wide-set, deep-socketed dark eyes, which accurately suggested a keen observer and perceptive analyst of the world. Hoover first met him during Wilson's Second Industrial Conference in the autumn of 1919 and, much impressed by his broad knowledge of business, frequently turned to him in later years for advice. The third member of the delegation, Los Angeles banker Henry Robinson, served on the American peace delegation in Paris in 1919 and had been the American representative on the Allied Maritime Council. His square face and white, wavy hair set off by round, dark-framed glasses made him look like a complacent small-town businessman, but he was more than he appeared. Hoover described him as not only "able, energetic and diplomatic" but also "when necessary pugnacious." Like Young, he became a trusted friend to whom Hoover often turned for advice on a variety of topics. All three were wealthy and paid their own expenses on the European trip, which enabled the administration to get around the tricky question of American participation in negotiations on the reparations issue.[3]

The German reparations bill had been set at $33 billion originally but, in practice, was reduced to $12.5 billion at the London conference in May 1921. Now the Dawes group proposed to restate the German obligation by tying it to Germany's actual ability to pay after its domestic economic system had been restructured under foreign supervision and to spread the payments out over an extended but unspecified period. A large international loan, primarily from American banks, would support economic restructuring and help pay the first two years of reparations. On April 24, agreement was reached on what came to be called the Dawes Plan.[4] Its name made manifest what everyone understood but did not say aloud—that although American participation in the conference might be "unofficial," resolution of the issue depended on American money.

The unmentioned elephants in the room with the Dawes Plan negotiators were the American refusal to cancel the war debts, the Allied determination to extract their payments to the Americans from the Germans in the form of reparations, and the German determination not to pay if they could possibly avoid doing so. German promises to reorganize their economy and raise taxes to pay their reparations bill meant little in the face of their rejection of the whole obligation. They would pay, but only if foreign bankers—chiefly the Americans—lent them the money.[5]

The American ambassador in Berlin, Alanson B. Houghton, warned the State Department that the Dawes Plan rested on very weak foundations, but Washington did not want to hear bad news. Secretary Hughes assured the president that the world was on the verge of "a new era," and Hoover described the agreement as a "just and practical settlement" that would help to create "a stable and peaceful world." The Germans, for whom the agreement meant the withdrawal of foreign troops from the Ruhr and at least a breathing space before they had to shoulder the weight of reparations, welcomed it. The British and French were much less enthusiastic.[6]

In July, a conference met in London to try to reconcile the British and French to the agreement. Secretaries Hughes and Mellon both attended, although they insisted that they just happened to be in the city on other business. The key players, however, were the bankers, dominated by Montagu Norman of the Bank of England and Thomas Lamont of J. P. Morgan and Company. They not only would control the $200 million loan to the German government that would set the plan in motion but would also decide on $100 million or more in credit that the French needed desperately to stabilize the franc. Unless the bankers were satisfied with the safety of their investments, the plan could not go into operation. That meant that the French must be "out of the Ruhr bag and baggage," as Norman put it, and that a trustworthy American must be named to oversee reparations and the restructuring of the German economy in the crucial post of agent general. Once those points were cleared up, the British signed on, and the French had no real choice but to go along. The plan officially went into effect on September 1.[7]

Acceptance of the Dawes Plan pleased Hoover, but he did not believe it had solved all of Europe's problems. The greatest remaining weakness, in his view, lay in the French refusal to adopt the austerity measures he believed essential to restore economic stability. They continued to rely on reparations payments and foreign loans to balance their budget while refusing to conclude an agreement with the United States to repay their war debts. When they applied to J. P. Morgan in November for another $100 million loan, he exploded in outrage. Not only would the money not be put to productive purposes, he fulminated, but also a situation might well arise where the American government would have to insist that France make payments on their public debt to the United States, even if that meant they could not pay private American creditors. The mess would only get worse, he declared, until the French put their financial house in order. Left to his own judgment, Hoover might well have disapproved the loan, but Secretary Hughes calmed him down and persuaded him that "perhaps at the present time politically it was desirable for the loan to go through." Hoover gave in, but in the future, he declared, the American government "should take a very strong stand and should refuse any assistance to its foreign debtors . . . unless there had been some satisfactory arrangement concluded to pay what they owed to the United States."[8] From his point of view, the debt and loan questions remained unfinished and urgent business.

II

Equally a matter of concern to the secretary was the dependence of the American economy on foreign raw materials controlled, as he saw it, by "foreign monopolies or combinations" that were restricting the distribution of those items in order to drive up prices and economically weaken the United States. Products that he believed were so controlled included sisal for binding twine, nitrates and iodine, potash, rubber, quinine, tin, mercury, coffee, and quebracho bark for tanning leather. Such monopoly control, of course, raised prices for both American producers and consumers. One solution, he suggested to Senator Arthur Capper, might be to amend the 1918 Webb-Pomerene Act, which exempted export combinations from antitrust laws, to permit purchasers of monopoly-controlled products to set up joint-purchasing agencies that "could hold their own in their dealings with such [foreign] combinations."[9]

Not everyone agreed with Hoover's estimate of the foreign monopoly problem. American as well as foreign critics pointed out that the United States encouraged its own cotton and wheat producers to unite to drive up world prices by keeping portions of their production off the market. Samuel Untermyer, a frequent thorn in Hoover's side, declared that the Commerce Department had done more harm to the American people by fostering domestic combinations than could possibly be done by foreign monopolies (a charge that Hoover denounced publicly as slanderous). And a later congressional investigation concluded that the secretary had considerably overestimated the power of foreign monopolies. American buying consortiums, warned even such Hoover friends as Owen Young, would limit American imports and thus impede European recovery. Like the protective tariff, which Hoover also supported, purchasing combinations subverted his argument that world stability depended upon maximum freedom of international trade. Indeed, throughout the decade, Hoover's domestic priorities frequently clashed with his interest in an open-door international economic system.[10]

An alleged rubber monopoly particularly outraged Hoover. Although no one could say with certainty whether the rise in world rubber prices resulted from the success of Britain's Stevenson Plan or from a huge increase in American demand from the automobile industry, Hoover emphasized only the influence of the British monopoly. His old suspicions that the British intended to restore their prewar economic dominance at the expense of the United States had not diminished. At his orders, the Commerce Department launched a vigorous and well-publicized search for alternative foreign sources of the product, as well as a less successful hunt for rubber substitutes. He was delighted when wholesale rubber prices declined after the creation of an "American pool" of purchasers in 1926, but his nationalistic definition of the problem and aggressive policies did not improve Anglo-American relations.[11]

A dispute with Canada over pulpwood provided a distant echo of the rubber controversy. In the spring of 1923, in an effort to strengthen the Canadian paper industry, the Canadian parliament adopted a bill authorizing the government to embargo the sale of pulpwood to the United States. American newspaper publishers, as well as American manufacturers of newsprint such as the Pejepscot Paper Company, in which Hoover had an interest, demanded retaliation. The Commerce Department began drafting retaliatory legislation involving either an embargo on certain exports to Canada or heavy duties on Canadian products imported into the United States, but before any action was taken, protests from Canadian lumbermen and informal representations by Americans in Canada killed the threat. Early in 1925, Secretary Hughes informed Hoover that he felt confident the embargo would never be implemented. Although in this case the threat to paper manufacturers and publishers had been minor, Hoover's reaction demonstrated that he saw every restriction on American imports of raw materials as serious.[12]

III

Yet while Hoover attacked the Stevenson Plan and the proposed Canadian pulpwood embargo, he also argued that something similar to them would be an effective cure for the American agricultural depression. If American farmers could manage to reduce their wheat production by 20 percent and their pork production by 15 percent, he said, their economic problems would be solved. But even if nothing were done, he predicted that rising living standards would turn the United States into a food-importing country within five to ten years. At that point, "the return to agriculture in proportion to the effort given is going to be larger than that in industry."[13]

Farmers' still-enormous political clout made it impossible for the administration to sit back and wait to see whether Hoover's optimistic prediction would prove correct. His belief that agriculture's woes would correct themselves within a few years, however, led him to prefer modest palliatives to radical solutions. He suggested, for example, the creation of a national board to grade and certify the quality of perishable crops in order to stabilize prices and reduce waste in shipping, and the establishment of a $50 million dollar loan fund to promote crop diversification in the Northwestern wheat-growing region. He proposed a $10 million private fund to supplement War Finance Corporation loans to struggling banks in agricultural areas. He urged that the Commerce Department's foreign representatives be given expanded power to promote the marketing of American agricultural products overseas. And, most important of all, he recommended the authorization and promotion of cooperative marketing organizations for both domestic and foreign sales. None of these offered a panacea, as Hoover would have been the first to admit, but together he believed they would help to tide farmers over until demand caught up with production.[14]

Secretary Wallace dismissed Hoover's proposal for creating federally sponsored agricultural marketing cooperatives as likely only to create an expensive bureaucracy that would not solve the farm problem. Ironically for someone who favored the McNary-Haugen bill, the secretary contended that Hoover's plan would give the federal government too much control over farming—precisely the same argument that Hoover advanced against McNary-Haugen. The two Iowans had come to detest each other, and each believed the other had been plotting to encroach on the powers and prerogatives of his department. Each was right. Hoover wanted control over marketing cooperatives and overseas sales of agricultural products, while Wallace thought that the Agriculture Department should control all agricultural marketing. By the time Wallace died in October 1924, the conflict between the two men had spread through farm organizations and the farm bloc in Congress. It contributed significantly to the paralysis of efforts to assist agriculture during the 1920s.[15]

Not only was the conflict between Hoover and Wallace personal, but it also had a philosophical basis. Would the government manage the economy directly, as McNary-Haugen implied, or would the economy be self-regulating, as Hoover hoped? Any issue that touched on that basic question drew the attention of the two secretaries, even a minor dispute over which department would oversee lumber standardization. Early in 1922, Wallace had suggested calling a national lumber standardization conference, but Hoover responded that Congress had given Commerce, not Agriculture, authority to undertake "a systematic national campaign on the simplification of manufactured products and elimination of waste." In May 1922, Hoover had persuaded the National Lumber Manufacturers' Association to establish a committee to draft voluntary standards for the grades and dimensions of finished lumber, and in December 1923 a meeting of manufacturers, distributors, and consumers approved "standardization rules."[16]

Hoover's seeming triumph in December 1923 did not end the matter, however. During early 1924, the Agriculture Department's Forest Products Laboratory continued to study grading standards for hardwoods and conducted other research into manufacturing and using wood products. In October, shortly before his death, Secretary Wallace sent out an invitation to "organizations and individuals concerned in producing, distributing, and using lumber and other forest products" to attend a conference in Washington in November. He invited Hoover to address the meeting "on the general problems of waste in industry and methods of combating it."[17]

Hoover knew a lumber standardization conference when he saw one and refused to have anything to do with Wallace's proposed meeting. He responded that he greatly appreciated the invitation, but he would be in California to vote at the beginning of November, and official business would detain him in the West until after the conference ended. Commerce Department staff members, he said, would attend the meeting, but he did not offer to share their expertise on waste elimination or standardization.[18]

When Wallace died on October 25, however, Hoover suddenly discovered that his schedule permitted him to return to Washington for the conference on November 19 and 20. But he could not control the meeting, which voted to create a permanent "Central Committee on Lumber Standards" under the Agriculture Department to address standardization, reforestation, fire prevention, insect control, timber surveys, and the direction of forest laboratories. The new committee not only appropriated the name of the Commerce Department committee that had drafted the lumber rules adopted in December 1923, but it also claimed control over future developments in standardization. Hoover, however, rose to the challenge. With every appearance of innocence, he urged the acting Secretary of Agriculture, Howard Gore, to join him in asking the president to restore traditional Agriculture Department functions to the Forest Service while confirming Commerce's control over the "elimination of waste in the manufacture and distribution of wood products."[19]

Petty as the lumber standardization squabble looks in retrospect, Hoover regarded it as a vital matter of principle. Lumber standardization, he told the Southern Forestry Conference in January 1924, would not only reduce marketing costs and benefit consumers but would also contribute to timber conservation. Although standardization represented a practical adjustment to the growing economy, he added, it also embodied a much more fundamental principle. It offered an opportunity to demonstrate that "the abuses that give rise" to the intervention of government in business could "be eliminated by the systematic and voluntary action of commerce and industry itself." The onrushing flood of government regulation could be blocked, he contended, if business itself adopted "restraints which will cure abuse; that will eliminate waste; that will prevent unnecessary hardship in the working of our economic system." Business self-regulation would "preserve that initiative in men which builds up the character, intelligence, and progress in our people." Nothing could be more fundamental to the future of capitalism.[20]

IV

Aside from its broader significance in Hoover's drive to make industry self-governing, lumber standardization had an important and direct role in his plan to help American consumers by improving their housing. Along with the publication by the Better Homes organization of a book of "small house plans" prepared by the Architects' Small House Service Bureau, the year 1924 saw Hoover and the Commerce Department pushing zoning regulations, building codes, and city planning. To make sure that the men who built the houses could also afford to buy them, the secretary urged the construction industry to find ways to extend the building season and avoid strikes and lockouts. He urged tax reforms that would favor the middle class by raising inheritance taxes on the wealthy and eliminating tax shelters in government bonds (to free money to be lent on the mortgage market). All these initiatives aimed to reduce income inequalities and drive down construction costs for houses, thus making it easier for middle-class Americans to purchase reasonably priced and well-built houses in pleasant neighborhoods.[21]

Hoover's promotion of suburban housing bore substantial although sometimes bitter fruit. Suburban houses accounted for 60 percent of the housing units erected during the boom of the 1920s, and the resulting spread of the suburbs transformed the structure and appearance of American cities. As urban populations dispersed to the suburbs, racial and class segregation increased, while low population densities and good roads helped to solidify the dominance of automobiles over public transportation. The construction of highways and parking lots to serve suburban commuters began to disrupt the centers of cities, pushing the working class into crowded apartments in the most polluted areas near the factories where they worked. Hoover's vision of comfortable homes for Americans in close proximity to nature thus brought happiness for some but unintended and far from benign consequences for those left behind.[22]

Hoover saw improved housing as a quality-of-life issue, a part of a broader effort to improve the whole environment for Americans. It was for that reason that he continued to support the National Conference on Outdoor Recreation throughout 1924 and that he did his best to push passage of legislation to control oil pollution in coastal waters. An oil pollution bill drafted in the Commerce Department had passed the Senate in 1923 but bogged down in the House over whether the Commerce or War Department would control enforcement. In January 1924, Hoover testified before the House Committee on Rivers and Harbors that the enforcement issue had been resolved: he and Secretary of War Weeks had agreed that Commerce could do it most economically. But the question of jurisdiction hardly had been settled when a new issue arose. The pending bill applied only to coastal pollution from ships, not to land-based sources, and conservationists such as former New Jersey Senator Joseph Frelinghuysen regarded that as a sellout to big companies. Hoover admitted that land sources also contributed to pollution, but he argued that ships had been the main offenders along the coast, and he warned Frelinghuysen that in refusing to accept a half instead of a whole loaf, he might lose the whole thing.[23]

Hoover himself had a chance to show that he would settle for a half rather than a whole loaf when the House Committee, at the insistence of the Corps of Engineers, restored control over enforcement of the law to the War Department. To his credit, he took his own advice. Congress passed the amended bill with Hoover's support, and the president signed it in June. In combination with new devices to separate oil from ships' bilge water that had been tested and improved in the Commerce Department's Bureau of Standards, the law played an important part in cleaning up harbors and beaches along the Atlantic Coast. Although Hoover subsequently exaggerated his own role in the passage of the antipollution law, for which the National Coast Anti-Pollution League, the Izaak Walton League, and the Audubon Society had lobbied hard and effectively, his advocacy of the legislation helped to publicize the issue and persuade Congress to act.[24]

The oil pollution bill, like his work with standardization and housing, fitted into Hoover's broad objective of making the consumer society function more efficiently and benefit more Americans. No aspect of the ways in which Americans lived, did their business, made their livings, and spent their leisure time escaped his interest. Perhaps no other American leader has ever taken so sweeping a view of the public interest or seemed so confident of his ability to improve life for everyone—and to claim that he could do it not by dictation from above but by inspiring people to improve their own lot. His vision of the future intoxicated the relatively few people who comprehended and shared it but alarmed others who saw him simply as an empire builder. And even those who grasped a part of his vision did not always agree with him or with each other about how to achieve it.

V

The limitations of Hoover's vision became manifest in the struggle to control the Colorado River. Hoover had pushed the seven Colorado basin states into signing an interstate compact to share the river's water in November 1922. He believed the agreement would promote the development of the whole region, but implementation of the plan came to a halt in 1923 when Arizona refused to ratify the pact without a prior agreement with California on the division of the Lower Basin's water allotment.[25]

In the spring of 1924, Hiram Johnson, pursuing the Republican presidential nomination, complicated the situation by accusing Coolidge of opposing construction of a high dam on the Colorado. Actually, Coolidge, at Hoover's urging, had endorsed the project in his annual message in December 1923. Opposition to the Swing-Johnson Bill authorizing construction of the dam arose not in the White House but in the Upper Basin states, where leaders hoped that delay in the bill's passage might push Arizona into ratification of the compact. Johnson knew all of that perfectly well, but the accusation played well in Southern California, where he needed to broaden his support. Coolidge's California campaign manager, Mark Requa, had to scramble to reassure anxious Republicans that the president did indeed support the project.[26] As a result of these various crosscurrents, the Colorado project remained stalled throughout 1924 and looked, by the end of the year, as if it might fail entirely.

Similar difficulties also plagued the long-discussed plan to link the Midwest to the Atlantic by means of a waterway connecting the Great Lakes to the St. Lawrence River. A joint Canadian-American commission to study the proposal had endorsed it in 1922, but opposition in Canada and New York blocked action. At Hoover's request, GE board chairman Owen Young met privately with officials in Albany and Canada during 1923, and his report that they might drop their opposition led Hoover to recommend that Coolidge endorse it in his annual message in December 1923. Early in 1924, the Canadian government formally agreed to the appointment of a new binational commission to investigate the feasibility of a waterway for shipping and power generation, and in March Coolidge asked Hoover to chair the American delegation. In mid-June, the American and Canadian members of the commission joined for a boat tour of the possible route from Niagara Falls to Montreal. Although accompanying engineers visited various sites along the way, the trip, as Hoover declared vaguely, was mainly "for the purpose of familiarizing ourselves with the general situation." Translated, that meant that it publicized and popularized the project. At major stops, the secretary socialized with local officials, talked to reporters, and gave brief speeches lauding the opportunity to unite the two countries in "joint development of the navigation and power projects included in the St. Lawrence program." Then the officials returned to Washington and Ottawa, leaving the engineers to study and report on the practical obstacles that would need to be overcome.[27]

Hoover's success in overseeing the negotiation of the Colorado Compact led President Coolidge to appoint him in 1924 as chairman of a similar commission to negotiate an interstate compact governing the waters of the upper Rio Grande. The task, as Coolidge described it to Hoover, seemed relatively simple: to assist the representatives of Colorado and New Mexico in working out an agreement apportioning their share of the river's water between them. It soon became clear, however, that the situation was anything but simple.[28]

A 1906 treaty had validated Mexico's claim to a share of water from the Rio Grande, and the federal government had built the Elephant Butte Reservoir in New Mexico near the Texas border to store the promised water. Surplus water from the reservoir irrigated lands around El Paso, Texas. Because of Mexico's claims on the river's water, for twenty years the Bureau of Reclamation had regularly denied Colorado's and New Mexico's requests to make new diversions upstream from Elephant Butte. As Hoover realized that what he had initially understood as a simple matter of helping New Mexico and Colorado come to agreement amounted, in fact, to a multisided dispute among the two states, the Reclamation Bureau, the El Paso irrigation districts, and the state of Texas, he felt that he had landed in hot water indeed. Belatedly, he asked to be relieved of the chairmanship of the commission, but Secretary Work declined to rescue him, and Hoover reluctantly soldiered on.[29]

Unable to find the time to travel through the Rio Grande Valley himself during September 1924, as the commissioners from Colorado (Delph Carpenter) and New Mexico (J. O. Seth) hoped he would do, Hoover convoked the first meeting of the commission in Colorado Springs on October 26. By that time he had received a letter from Governor Pat Neff of Texas asking that his state have an opportunity to name a member of the commission, and R. F. Burges of El Paso showed up at the meeting to urge the inclusion of the irrigators around that city. Hoover himself suggested that since the Reclamation Bureau controlled so much of the upper Rio Grande, the agency should also be represented in any talks. And, said the ever-practical Hoover, they needed engineering studies to give them reliable information about river flows.[30]

Following his return to Washington in the late fall of 1924, Hoover asked Elwood Mead, director of the Reclamation Bureau, to undertake a "Reclamation Survey" of the upper Rio Grande Valley. Mead agreed to do so and promised a report by mid-June of 1925, when the commission had scheduled its second meeting. The Texas legislature, however, did not authorize the appointment of a commissioner until late March, and then the governor failed to name anyone to the position. Delph Carpenter suggested that Texas wanted to stall, since an agreement might reduce the amount of water available to the state. Carpenter proposed that the others go ahead without Texas, but Hoover responded diplomatically that he saw no reason to hurry, since the summer heat made a fact-finding visit to the area impractical before fall. Before the commission could act, however, Secretary Work threw a huge monkey wrench into the whole process by authorizing the construction of the Vega Sylvestre Dam on the headwaters of the Rio Grande in Colorado. Since the dam would give Colorado a prior claim to the river's hitherto unappropriated water, the secretary's announcement seemed to make the commission pointless. Those affected protested, but Work defended his decision vigorously, arguing that extended study by Interior Department lawyers had demonstrated that the department's twenty-five-year-old ban on using public lands along the upper river for the diversion and storage of water had no legal basis. Colorado rejoiced at the ruling, but it devastated New Mexico and Texas. New Mexico commissioner J. O. Seth resigned from the commission, and the two states announced they would take their cases to the courts. Hoover found the outcome bittersweet—a release from an increasingly onerous burden but a deeply unsatisfactory resolution to the dispute.[31]

VI

While seeking solutions to the various waterway issues, Hoover also grappled with an even more difficult problem, the American merchant marine. When the United States entered World War I, its merchant fleet had proved totally inadequate to the challenge of moving men, supplies, and equipment to Europe. The administration began an emergency shipbuilding program to secure the needed ships and set up two government agencies, the U.S. Shipping Board and the Emergency Fleet Corporation, to oversee and operate the vessels. Few of the ships went into service before the end of the war, however, and those that did proved slow and expensive to run. The administration planned to sell the fleet to private owners after the war and liquidate the two agencies, but American shippers showed no interest in the ships unless the government promised a substantial annual subsidy to defray their high operating costs and the expense of meeting American wages and safety requirements, which were higher than those of other countries. Pending a sale, both federal agencies continued to function, although the overlap and friction between them made the operation of the fleet even more wasteful and inefficient. With economy-minded Republicans unwilling to support a subsidy and powerful Democratic senators insisting on maintaining inefficient shipping lines based in several Southern cities, the Harding administration found a solution to the problem elusive. By the autumn of 1923, American companies were using American ships for only 30 percent of their exports and 29 percent of their imports. Just five passenger liners flew the American flag in 1923, and during the first six months of that year, only 10 percent of American wheat and chemicals, and no cotton goods, steel, lumber, coal, cement, or vehicles, were shipped in American vessels. In a major speech in November 1923, Hoover described the sorry state of the merchant marine and reminded his listeners that "national pride" and "the protection of our foreign trade" required a strong American merchant fleet, but no one seemed to be listening. Nevertheless, with the Fleet Corporation running a deficit of about $15 million a year, finding some solution to the problem became increasingly critical.[32]

In January 1924, Hoover recommended that the president turn the Shipping Board into a purely regulatory agency, like the Interstate Commerce Commission (ICC), and put the ownership, operation, and sale of the government's fleet exclusively in the hands of the Emergency Fleet Corporation. Separating regulatory and operating responsibilities, he argued, would increase efficiency and cut red tape and costs. Coolidge agreed, and the administration recommended the change to Congress, but given a worldwide surplus of shipping capacity and the inferior quality of the government-owned ships, administrative reform alone would not solve the problem.[33]

On March 12, Coolidge asked Hoover to serve, along with the secretaries of the treasury, war, and navy; the chairman of the Shipping Board (T. V. O'Connor); and the president of the Emergency Fleet Corporation (Admiral Leigh C. Palmer), on a Committee on National Policies with Regard to Shipping to review the whole merchant marine question. O'Connor became chairman of the committee, but Hoover wrote its report, which O'Connor delivered to the president on December 29, 1924. The report reflected Hoover's belief in the importance of private ownership but accepted the necessity of temporary continuation of government ownership. It proposed that a single executive charged with privatizing the fleet replace the Shipping Board, but it failed to explain how one man would solve the problems that had defeated the combined efforts of the Shipping Board and Emergency Fleet Corporation.[34]

In November 1925, in a letter to Representative Wallace White of Maine, chairman of a select House Committee studying the merchant marine question, Hoover amplified his recommendations. Essentially, he told White, about twenty trade routes between American ports and various parts of the world needed to be serviced by American flag vessels on a regular basis in order to safeguard American trade. Ideally, all those routes should be covered by privately owned vessels, which, for a variety of reasons, had proved more economical and efficient than publicly owned ships, but at present, private lines covered only a few of the routes. Other routes, although important to certain sections of the country or potentially valuable in the future, had not yet developed a sufficient volume of trade to support regular private shipping lines. On those routes, it would be necessary to continue to run government-owned ships for some time, although he hoped they could be phased out gradually. In the meantime, he suggested optimistically, local governments might agree to share the costs of government-owned ships with the federal government.[35]

The secretary again recommended, as he had in 1924, that Congress reconstitute the Shipping Board as an independent regulatory agency and transfer operating control of the fleet to the Emergency Fleet Corporation. It would be a mistake, he added, to place the new Shipping Board in the Commerce Department, as some people had suggested, because the board's regulatory functions might well conflict with the department's charge to assist all shippers, both public and private. He suggested that a special advisory board made up of the secretaries of the treasury, war, navy, and commerce; the postmaster general; the president of the Fleet Corporation; and the chairman of the Shipping Board be created to advise the Fleet Corporation on such delicate questions as when to start new routes, abandon existing routes, buy or sell ships, or borrow money from private sources or the Treasury.[36]

Whatever the merits of Hoover's administrative proposals, they did not really address the basic problem that private shippers had no interest in buying the slow, inefficient vessels being peddled by the Fleet Corporation, even to use on profitable trade routes. Given the world's shipping surplus left over from the war, foreign governments' subsidies to their shippers, and the lower cost ships being turned out by Japanese shipyards, the corporation had little hope of selling its ships at any price. Already the government had sold many of its worst vessels at a loss or scrapped them, but even so, by 1926 its eight hundred remaining ships cost about $13 million more every year than they earned. What was worse, the presence of the Emergency Fleet ships on trade routes discouraged private American shippers from building new vessels. Despite the creation by Congress in 1924 of a $25-million revolving construction fund administered by the Shipping Board, slowly but surely American-flag vessels vanished from world ports.[37]

The deplorable situation in the merchant marine paralleled the situation in the railroads. Hoover believed that only if small roads merged into a few national systems would it be possible to make the railroads the foundation of a national transportation system. In 1921, the ICC had developed an elaborate plan for achieving consolidation, which railroad executives endorsed in principle, but they did nothing toward adopting it.[38]

In November 1923, Hoover proposed that the government take a more direct role in promoting consolidation, even considering the possibility of compulsion if the lines could not agree on mergers voluntarily. By the time he laid his plan before the president on November 22, however, he had abandoned the idea of compulsion. "I cannot believe that the owners of our railroads," he wrote, "knowing that public opinion has been crystallized into law, and with appreciation of the complete power of the Government to enforce its determination, will fail to comply with its pronounced policy."[39] The belief that businessmen could be brought to adopt policies voluntarily that would serve both the public interest and their own long-term self-interest underlay Hoover's whole approach to government. He would not espouse a policy based on coercion if any alternative might be available.

In January 1923, Hoover had invited the U.S. Chamber of Commerce to convene a meeting of transportation executives and shippers to draft "a coordinated national transportation policy," but by the time a follow-up conference met a year later, the initiative had obviously failed. The group, dominated by railroad executives, produced a report that reiterated a familiar litany: all consolidation must be voluntary; no radical changes should be made to the 1920 Transportation Act; rate revision must be approached only after full and careful study. The report was so predictable that the *New York Times* buried it on page 19 and filled most of its story with an account of Hoover's speech, which, unlike the report, at least mentioned a national plan for resolving railroad labor conflicts and suggested developing waterways in conjunction with other means of transportation. But in reality there was nothing new in the speech, in the conference, or in an article that Hoover published a month later in the *Saturday Evening Post*.[40] It appeared that the administration had run out of new ideas.

During the remainder of the decade, the ICC continued to press the idea of consolidation, but its proposals conflicted with private plans pushed by a handful of entrepreneurs and also aroused opposition from Western congressmen and senators who feared a return to the railroad monopolies of the late nineteenth century. The Van Sweringen brothers of Cleveland put together a railroad empire with thirty thousand miles of track, but their form of consolidation, utilizing a pyramid of holding companies, brought no new investments to the railroads it controlled. Meanwhile, the federal government continued to provide grants to states for highway construction and began to subsidize airlines and waterways development that competed with the railroads. The ICC, focused on consolidation and railroad rates, did nothing to help the railroads compete effectively with other forms of transportation. Thus perhaps the last, best chance in the twentieth century to develop an integrated national transportation plan based on the railroads gradually slipped away.[41]

For all Hoover worked to rescue the railroads, he seemed not to realize that his advocacy of government support for water and air transport increased the railroads' problems. Thus far, he admitted in an interview published in October 1924, air travel had not become reliable enough to challenge the passenger train, but once planes could go two hundred miles an hour and fly safely at night, the advantages of flying over going by rail would become obvious. Commercial aviation, he declared in the department's 1924 *Annual Report*, "offers much to our economic and social progress, and every encouragement, legislative and otherwise, should be given to its development." Throughout 1923 and 1924, the department worked closely with members of Congress to draft a bill to promote, organize, and regulate civil aviation.[42]

Even more immediately threatening to the dominance of the railroads in American transportation were automobiles and trucks. By 1924, fifteen million cars and trucks moved passengers and freight on a network of highways being built, paved, and maintained by state and local governments. Between 1921 and 1930, automobiles accounted for 80 to 90 percent of all intercity passenger travel, and governments, from the federal down to the local, spent $7.9 billion on highway construction. In the same period, the railroads, which had to buy, build, and maintain their own tracks, fell further and further behind.[43]

Along with the proliferation of motor vehicles on American highways came what Hoover labeled "an alarming increase annually in the number of traffic accidents" (22,600 Americans were killed in 1923). In December 1924, he called the first national highway safety conference to seek remedies to the rising accident rate. Over three days, the conferees discussed a variety of topics, from highway and vehicle engineering to uniform licensing and insurance regulations. The conference dramatized the situation, and within two months after it adjourned, bills designed to remedy some of the problems identified at the meeting had been introduced in thirty-eight state legislatures, and a committee appointed by the conference had drafted a model state motor vehicle code. Seldom had one of Hoover's initiatives borne so much fruit so quickly.[44]

While cars, trucks, and planes transformed national transportation, radio revolutionized communications. After a rapid start in organizing and regulating radio broadcasting in 1922, however, progress had stalled in 1923, despite problems highlighted at the second national radio conference in March.

Conferees at the 1923 meeting had suggested hopefully that the Commerce Department might already have adequate power to assign radio frequencies and monitor broadcasting. They were wrong. A year later, the situation had grown far worse, with 790 unregulated commercial radio stations and some 16,590 amateurs all broadcasting on whatever frequency and at whatever power they chose. Some broadcasters, having established themselves on certain frequencies, claimed a permanent title to them, and the Commerce Department had no power to force them to undergo periodic license reviews, as Hoover believed the national interest required. New applications of the technology, including the transmission of photographs by radio and the use of radio to fix latitude and longitude for ships, made establishing some rational system of regulation all the more urgent. In March 1924, the secretary again implored Congress to pass a law giving the department regulatory power over all aspects of broadcasting.[45]

When Congress, suspicious of the secretary's ambitions, still failed to act on the radio bill, Hoover called a third national radio conference in October 1924. Making a virtue of necessity, he urged the conferees to recommend a system of self-regulation. Broadcasters, he proposed, should get together to assign frequencies, regulate the power of individual stations, and above all, to keep broadcasting "a great agency of public service." Radio must not become a commercial medium. "The reader of the newspaper has an option whether he will read an ad or not," he said, "but if a speech by the President is to be used as the meat in a sandwich of two patent medicines, there will be no radio left." He admitted, however, that he did not know how broadcasting would be financed without advertising. He dismissed as impractical the idea of having listeners pay a subscription fee for the service, as had become common in Europe. At wit's end, he suggested "the establishment of a continuing committee for its further consideration"—a familiar but in this case useless device. Within a few years, despite Hoover, broadcast advertising would become ubiquitous.[46]

The members of the conference may have been skeptical about Hoover's suggestions regarding the financing and regulation of radio, but they welcomed the excuse to avoid such difficult issues. Instead, they talked about practical problems such as minimizing interference, developing radio networks, and regulating amateur broadcasting. Aside from recommending that Congress increase Commerce's appropriation to help it carry out its limited functions in regard to broadcasting, the conference took Hoover at his word that the industry could regulate itself voluntarily. The meeting neither endorsed nor opposed the pending radio bill giving the Commerce Department authority to license broadcasters.[47]

Following the conference, Hoover quickly abandoned the fantasy of self-regulation. In December, he wrote to Congressman White to urge the immediate passage of a law authorizing the Commerce Department to license and regulate every broadcasting station in the United States. Recent changes in broadcasting, he argued, including the advent of radio networks, the introduction of new, high-powered transmitters, and the increasing prevalence of on-air advertising, made regulation essential.[48]

Hoover sounded confident, but the dizzying pace of technological change in radio, as well as the rise of nation-wide networks, left him, like everyone else, uncertain about exactly what should be done. With only a limited number of frequencies available, it seemed evident that some means had to be found to decide what new stations would be permitted to broadcast and to manage the behavior of those already on the air. There seemed little alternative to having the government undertake those duties, but no consensus had yet developed on how it should be done.

The increase in broadcast advertising also deeply troubled Hoover. The medium's educational and public service roles, he feared, might be swamped by commercialized entertainment. Perhaps, he suggested to the Rockefeller Foundation, it might be desirable to create a national educational radio network. Or, he speculated in a more optimistic moment, maybe Americans would just get tired of jazz and advertising on the radio and demand more uplifting fare.[49]

Radio, Hoover recognized, had become "one of the necessary adjuncts" of American life. Nothing else, he told a reporter, could "so effectually weld this country into a unit in thought and action as radio." That power meant that its future development could not be left to chance. As "a great public service," it must be "regulated and conducted in all aspects in the interest of the listener." Whether and how that would happen remained to be seen.[50]

VII

As the middle of the decade approached, Hoover grappled not only with rationalizing the nation's transportation and communications but also with assuring the availability of the enormous amount of electricity needed to power modern houses and industry. The superpower proposal, a bold scheme to interconnect the electric grids of the Northeast states, had gotten off to a strong start in 1920 to 1921 but ran into uncertainty over state versus public ownership and the complexities raised by state regulation of an interstate entity. Nevertheless, the potential economic benefits of such a system appeared so attractive that in the summer of 1923, Hoover, Owen Young, and W. S. Murray attempted to revive it by organizing a committee of Northeastern public utilities commissioners to explore the proposal further. The new committee appointed advisory panels drawn from the public utilities in the region, engineers, and the legal staffs of the Commerce Department and the utilities to advise it on how to surmount legal and technical obstacles.[51]

In mid-April of 1924, the engineers finished their study. They strongly endorsed creation of a regional grid and urged that work on it begin as soon as possible.[52] No one, however, had yet proposed a satisfactory way to organize the corporation that most people assumed would be necessary to run the superpower system. Would it be a holding company, a new multistate private utility, or a publicly owned corporation? Inasmuch as it would obviously be a monopoly, that became a crucial question.

Like many others, Hoover at first assumed that a privately owned regional corporation offered the best option. He argued that existing state public utilities commissions could regulate it, even though it would operate across state lines, but not everyone agreed. Governors Al Smith of New York and Gifford Pinchot of Pennsylvania supported public ownership, as did Pennsylvania's chief delegate to the commission, Morris L. Cooke. In the March 1924 issue of the magazine *Survey Graphic*, a featured interview with Hoover made the case for a private corporation regulated by the states, but articles by Smith, Pinchot, and Cooke contended for public ownership.[53]

In May, in a speech to the convention of the National Electric Light Association in Atlantic City, Hoover offered a new approach to the problem. Superpower, he now argued, did not actually require the creation of an interstate corporation. It involved only "the sale and resale of power from one utility distribution system to another and . . . cooperative action between utilities in the erection of central stations." The utility companies would need some coordination to achieve those practical objectives, but not a separate company to run the system. That amounted to a major shift in his conceptualization of the project, and had Hoover stopped there, his argument might have disarmed the public power advocates, but he did not. He went on to say, "I know of no greater disaster that could come to the workers in this industry than to place their fate in the hands of political jobbery" or to stifle "individual opportunities through the leveling of bureaucracy" that public ownership would involve. His gratuitous attack on public ownership undermined his contention that his new proposal offered a way around the public-private dispute and played into the hands of his critics. In July, the committee released the engineers' report to the press, but they could not agree on any other aspect of the problem. A year later, in a speech in San Francisco, Hoover again tried to refocus the debate by relabeling "Superpower" the "Central Generation and Interconnection of Distribution Systems," but it was too late. The practical work of linking state systems into a national grid would continue, but the superpower project as such was dead.[54] It had proved little more than the generator of innumerable teapot tempests.

The electricity to be distributed over the superpower grid came partly from hydroelectric systems, but increasingly, coal and oil-fired steam turbines had supplanted falling water. That meant that stabilizing the coal industry had become more important than ever. In 1922 and 1923, the administration had struggled with coal strikes, and with a new strike impending in the bituminous coal fields in April 1924, Hoover concluded that the public must have a mechanism to cushion the impact of a stoppage. "No adequate machinery exists in the Government by which we can even give consideration to the facts and merits of this dispute or lend aid in settlement," he reminded the president in November 1923, "nor is there any machinery by which the Government may give any protection to the public in the inevitable profiteering that flows from a cessation of production." His comment amounted to an admission that the system of voluntary price controls, which he had touted as a success in 1922, had actually been a failure. He continued to believe that consolidation of small competing mines into larger units would eventually stabilize production and reduce labor conflicts, but that process would take time. As a temporary substitute for consolidation, he proposed that Congress authorize operators in specified areas to form cooperative selling agencies. Such cooperatives would provide a measure of stability, and the competition among areas would, he believed, keep prices under control.[55]

Privately, Hoover moved to make congressional action unnecessary by attempting to head off a strike. On December 1, 1923, he met secretly in New York with John L. Lewis, president of the United Mine Workers, and Michael Gallagher, chairman of the coal operators' wage scale committee for Western Pennsylvania, Ohio, Indiana, and Illinois (the Central District). At the meeting, the operators offered to forgo a wage cut and to begin collecting union dues through a compulsory checkoff system. In return, Lewis promised to recommend a three-year contract to the union on those terms and to attempt to reach a settlement without a strike. Hoover was delighted by this tentative agreement, and when some operators threatened to press for a wage cut, he issued a strong statement urging them to seize the opportunity "not only to protect the public interest but by the maintenance of continuous production and the building up of mutual responsibility between the employers and employees to recreate that stability in the soft coat industry that has been so sadly lost in the last ten years." A three-year contract on the terms agreed upon at the New York meeting was signed in Jacksonville on February 11, 1924. The miners covered by the contract benefited from it, but its costs made the unionized mines less competitive with nonunion Southern mines in a market already shrinking because of competition from oil and gas.[56]

Not everyone welcomed Hoover's role in the coal negotiations. Mine owners who had hoped for a wage cut accused him of having forced an unfair contract on the operators, and by the autumn of 1925, several suggested repudiating the Jacksonville agreement. Lewis immediately demanded that the Commerce Department enforce it, but Hoover replied that since the department had not been represented at the Jacksonville meeting, it could not be a party to the agreement. He deflected Lewis's demands by recommending to the union that if they felt the agreement had been breached, they should take the issue to court, but the incident underlined how easily government intervention in such a tense confrontation could be misconstrued and distorted. In Hoover's view, the episode highlighted a basic question: "whether the coal industry can work out its own destination or whether it must come under Federal regulation." He might better have asked whether anything could save a rapidly declining industry.[57]

The issue of public versus private control also dominated the Muscle Shoals controversy. Farm organizations had been pressing, ever since the end of the war, for development of fertilizer production at the site on the Tennessee River in Alabama. The administration, including Hoover, strongly favored private as opposed to federal development of the site, but the strongest private development proposal, that from Henry Ford, did not guarantee enough nitrate production to satisfy farmers' needs. In testimony before the Senate Committee on Agriculture and Forestry in May 1924, Hoover frankly admitted the dilemma facing the administration. He believed, he said, that the scientific and practical problems involved in large-scale fertilizer production at Muscle Shoals could "be better solved in the interests of our farmers by private capital and enterprise in cooperation with the Government than by the government attempting it itself," but he recognized that at present, "the problem of the cheap manufacture of synthetic nitrates and their most advantageous combination with other fertilizer elements is unsolved." It would take a large amount of expensive experimental work to develop a process to produce a fertilizer competitive in cost with imported Chilean nitrates. Even Henry Ford would not undertake the enterprise without "some stimulus from the government" in the form of what amounted to a gift of the existing facilities at Muscle Shoals, with the right to use them to generate and sell electricity. Aside from pressure from farmers to activate the Muscle Shoals installation, what mostly kept the Ford bid viable in Hoover's eyes was the fact that he believed Chilean nitrates to be controlled by a monopoly comparable to the British rubber monopoly.[58]

When Commerce Department scrutiny of Ford's offer raised serious questions about whether it involved sufficient investment to solve the fertilizer problem, Ford withdrew it, leaving the only remaining proposal on the table one from the Hooker Electro-Chemical Company, which did not promise to produce any fertilizer at all. Unless the administration could somehow pluck a new offer as good as or better than Ford's out of its hat before Congress returned to session at the end of 1924, it seemed possible that the Senate might pass a bill sponsored by Senator Oscar Underwood of Alabama that essentially endorsed the Hooker proposal.[59]

Unmentioned but certainly affecting all of the administration's deliberations about what to do with Muscle Shoals was the Teapot Dome affair, in which former Interior Secretary Albert Fall had reputedly assigned drilling rights in navy oil reserves to private companies in return for cash payoffs.

Senator Thomas Walsh had begun an investigation of the incident in October 1923, and the stench of scandal hung thickly over the capitol. Hoover issued a public statement in late January 1924 that the cabinet had never considered the oil leases that were at the center of the controversy, and denied that he had known anything about the whole matter, but no one in the administration entirely escaped suspicion. In a presidential election year, Lou Hoover observed, opportunistic politicians in both parties would relish an opportunity to expand the investigation. The Hearst papers, she reported, were speculating on a long list of future targets, including one or two in the Commerce Department.[60] Under the circumstances, everyone in the administration preferred to delay any decision about a lease or sale of Muscle Shoals.

VIII

Equally troublesome in a different way was the question of immigration. Pressure to restrict immigration had been building for many years, and in May 1921 Congress passed a bill setting quotas at 3 percent of each country's nationals living in the United States in 1910. The bill directed that a committee made up of the secretaries of state, commerce, and labor should translate the percentages into actual numbers (adjusted for boundary changes following the war). The act sharply curtailed immigration, especially from Eastern and Southern Europe, and its popularity led to its renewal in 1922 and 1923. Then, in the spring of 1924, an election year, Congress adopted a new law that reduced each country's quota to 2 percent of its representation in the American population in 1890. Census Bureau statisticians duly scrutinized the 1890 records but found that they contained little reliable information about national origins. Nevertheless, the law required a report, and in December 1926, the interdepartmental committee produced one. Privately, Hoover declared that its statistical basis was "entirely inadequate for correct conclusions," and even in its official report, the committee concluded that "the statistical and historical information available from which these computations were made is not entirely satisfactory." In practice, the 1890 figures served as the basis for quotas only in 1927 and 1928. The 1924 law provided that total immigration would be limited to 150,000 after 1927, with national quotas based on the white population in 1920, although problems delayed the new system's implementation until 1929.[61]

Despite Hoover's long experience in Asia and Europe, he voiced no opposition to the immigration restriction movement. Insofar as he took a public position, he supported restriction and particularly the exclusion of Asian immigrants under the 1924 law. During the 1924 campaign, he told Congressman John Raker that "ever since I have been able to think and talk I have strongly supported restriction of Asiatic immigration to the United States." In a draft of a letter to the president that year, he wrote, "There are biological and cultural grounds why there should be no mixture of Oriental and Caucasian blood," although he also expressed "high esteem and appreciation . . . for the greatness of Japan, her civilization, and genuine purpose of world advancement." During the 1928 campaign, he declared even more broadly, "I stand for the immigration laws." He deviated from the standard position of politicians of the period only to urge President Coolidge to seek modifications of the 1924 immigration law that would minimize the disruption of families and permit the admission of people with special skills, regardless of quotas.[62]

IX

By the end of 1924, reorganization of the Commerce Department, begun in 1921 when Hoover took office, had been completed, and the department's personnel had increased so much that they now occupied six buildings scattered across Washington. A new five-year lease had just been signed for the main Commerce building, but its owners indicated they would not renew the lease again. The plea that Hoover had been making for several years for the construction of a new, government-owned building for the department had become imperative. "Good administration," declared Hoover with what he regarded as a clinching argument, required it.[63]

The physical expansion of the Commerce Department accurately reflected its growing importance in the American government. Its largest bureau, Foreign and Domestic Commerce, exercised enormous influence, not only in the support and promotion of business at home and abroad, but also in the shaping of American policy toward trade and investment overseas. Energy, communications, housing, and transportation all fell within Hoover's orbit, and his reach extended to matters well beyond the official purview of Commerce, including waterway development, agriculture, and conservation and environmental issues. Coolidge might be less willing than Harding to grant him a free hand, but the new president had done very little in practice to clip the secretary's wings.

CHAPTER 17

The Commerce Department, 1925

In 1925, the American economy, which had recovered fully from the postwar depression, was in the midst of the great boom of the 1920s. Hoover rejoiced in the general prosperity, but like a handful of bankers and other experts, he also worried somewhat about unbridled stock market speculation. The market's crash in 1929 confirmed his fears, but economic historians have since cast doubt on the belief that stock speculation was a major cause of the Great Depression. A more likely culprit, they believe, was a global economic system made rigid by the gold standard and rife with protectionism, which reflected a proclivity on the part of every major participant in the international economy to view the world from the perspective of its own interests rather than the needs of the system.[1]

Hoover's intransigent position on Allied war debts, as well as his support of tariff protectionism and the gold standard, contributed in some measure to the creation of this unstable situation. At the same time, however, he also worked to establish an orderly, peaceful world with maximum freedom of trade and investment that he believed would benefit the United States both politically and economically. The contradiction between his economic nationalism, on the one hand, and his vision of an open door world, on the other, exemplified the tensions that pervaded Republican foreign policy throughout the 1920s.[2]

I

The Commerce Department's annual economic forecast in January 1925 foresaw no major clouds on the economic horizon. The world's economy, it declared, rested "upon more solid foundations than at any time since the war," as a result of "better balancing of budgets and more stable currency" in European countries. The forecasters dismissed as unimportant the fact that exports from those countries still lagged "some 10 or 12 per cent below pre-war" numbers, that the United States was "unique amongst the large combatant nations in having recovered its foreign trade to a point 15 per cent to 20 per cent above pre-war on a quantity basis," and that the United States continued to run a balance of payments surplus of about a billion dollars a year. They contended that the balance of payments surplus, including the inflow of some $260 million in gold in the past year, had been offset by a negative balance in "invisible exchange" resulting from increased tourism, higher shipping rates, and rising loans and investments abroad. As had been the case throughout the period, the department's experts emphasized the domestic economy, which seemed to them strong, with even agriculture and the railroads doing well. Coal and textiles still lagged, the press release admitted, but everything else seemed fine, without even a threat of inflation on the horizon. Viewed through the lens of the domestic economy, the world looked rosy.[3]

By the autumn of 1925, as the stock market continued to climb, Hoover became less confident about the economic outlook. In November, he drafted a letter that Senator Irvine Lenroot, chairman of the Senate banking committee, sent to the Federal Reserve, suggesting that the board tighten credit to discourage stock speculation. He also expressed his concern about the speculative boom to his S Street neighbor and Federal board member, Adolf Miller. Neither Hoover nor Miller, however, could shake the confidence of the board chairman, David R. Crissinger, a Harding crony from Marion, Ohio, that everything was fine. The board voted unanimously, except for Miller, who abstained, not to raise rates. Miller and Hoover believed that the main influence on the board's policy was New York Federal Reserve Bank Governor Benjamin Strong. Strong, they thought, placed undue emphasis on keeping interest rates low so that European capital would not be attracted to the United States, which might jeopardize the recent restoration of the gold standard in Britain, as well as the stability of other European currencies.[4]

In fact, although Hoover and Miller were correct in thinking that Strong favored keeping rates low, an equally important author of the policy was Secretary of the Treasury Mellon, who had pressured the board to lower rates in 1924. Mellon, like Strong, believed that keeping American interest rates below those in Europe would draw American capital to Europe and reduce the flow of gold to the United States. All of that, he believed, would contribute to the stabilization of the French, British, and German economies, and he hoped stability would encourage the French to sign an agreement to fund their debt to the United States. Mellon was furious at Hoover's meddling in Treasury business, but in practice they shared the goal of getting the French to sign a debt agreement. Their difference over interest rates in the autumn of 1925 proved only temporary.[5]

II

The French economic situation by 1925 was tenuous. The government had devalued the franc, and although the Germans had resumed reparations payments under the Dawes Plan, it would be several years before Germany paid enough to enable the French to rebuild war-damaged areas. To tide them over, the French hoped to borrow money in the United States, but the State Department, prodded by Hoover, opposed new loans unless Paris agreed to a debt-funding plan. Although the French continued to believe that their sacrifices in the war justified the cancellation of all debts to the Americans and British, they gradually realized that the Americans would never make that concession. Facing a loan ban, early in 1925 the French government at last indicated its willingness to discuss a debt agreement, provided Washington would agree to reduce the total obligation substantially. To present their case, the French government appointed as chief negotiator Finance Minister Joseph Caillaux, who had put the French budget on the road to balance and negotiated a deal with the British to reduce France's debt to the British by about 60 percent. But Caillaux also carried a heavy burden of personal and political scandals that weakened his political influence. Selling the French people on an agreement to pay the hated American debt would tax his political skills and raise explosive issues within the shaky French political structure.[6]

In addition to the threat of a loan ban, the issue of the "war stocks" also intensified the pressure on the French to reach a settlement on the debt. In 1919, the French had reluctantly agreed to pay $407 million for military supplies and equipment left behind by the departing American army, and had been paying $20 million a year as interest on the debt. Unless an agreement could be reached with the Americans to fold that loan into the general war debt, its full principal would be payable on August 1, 1929.[7]

The American position, on the eve of Franco-American talks in September 1925, was influenced by the gold standard issue. In the spring of 1924, Benjamin Strong had spent several weeks in England meeting with Montagu Norman of the Bank of England. They agreed that restoration of an international gold standard would contribute greatly to reestablishment of world economic stability, but that was impossible so long as the United States continued to control most of the world's gold as a result of its export surplus and the payment of foreign debts in gold. Hoover recognized the problem as well, and he agreed reluctantly that the way to meet it without canceling the French obligation completely would be to reduce the interest rate on the debt and extend the period of payment to sixty-two years, as had been done with the British. If the British formula were followed, Commerce Department experts calculated, French payments over sixty-two years would total about $9.7 billion, a reduction in the debt and interest owed as of 1925 by about 35 percent.[8]

In theory, then, an agreement similar to the British one seemed possible, but many obstacles faced the negotiators when they sat down in Washington on September 24, 1925. Before the French delegation left Paris, French war veterans had met with the American ambassador, Myron T. Herrick, and presented him with a wooden leg, a military medal, American and French army helmets, and a history of the American Revolution. Bitterly, they asked the ambassador to deliver the items to Senator Borah, the most outspoken congressional advocate of payment in full of the debts: "We attach a medal which one of our comrades received for saving the life of an American officer at the front. He does not want it any longer. He is returning it to Senator Borah: we owe him so much money." The members of the Caillaux delegation stated their view of the situation more diplomatically, but the conviction of the veterans that the United States should forgive the debts in light of French sacrifices shaped their whole approach to the negotiations. For their part, the Americans were quite willing to reduce the total debt bill and extend the payment period, but given congressional sentiment, they could not cancel the whole obligation, even if the commissioners had favored such a course. Under the circumstances, the Americans regarded the first French offer, which proposed paying a total of $4.65 billion over sixty-two years and tied payments explicitly to German reparations, as entirely unacceptable. Hoover suspected that its only purpose was to torpedo the talks and set up a situation where the French could go home and blame the failure on "Uncle Shylock."[9]

Nevertheless, meetings continued, and the outlines of an agreement similar to that with the British gradually emerged. Hoover took a somewhat harder line than Mellon in the talks, emphasizing that Congress would never accept outright cancellation of either the interest or the principal of the debt, but he went along with the Treasury secretary on reducing the total obligation. He also suggested a formula for dealing with the French insistence that their debt payments must be tied to German reparations payments. The Americans could not accept any such connection openly, but everyone understood that any agreement that divorced debt payments from reparations would be politically unacceptable in France. To get around the impasse, Hoover drafted a "safety clause" that promised renegotiation of French payments if they should "exceed the capacity" of the French to pay.[10]

At the beginning of October, the French returned with a second proposal, which promised payments totaling $6.22 billion over sixty-two years, which the Americans might have been able to accept, had it not been for French insistence on an explicit link between reparations and debt payments in the "safety clause." Without waiting to receive the American reply, Caillaux made a serious blunder, telling reporters that agreement had been reached. How he could have imagined the Americans would accept such terms remains a mystery. Not only had they never agreed to the French version of the "safety clause," but also Caillaux's announcement seriously breached protocol because the draft agreement had not yet been submitted to either the president or congressional leaders. When the French announcement appeared in the papers, Senator Borah, who had long contended that the French could and should pay in full, rushed to the White House to protest. He need not have bothered. Coolidge and the debt commissioners all agreed that "no acceptable proposition has been made to the American Commission and none has been submitted to the president for approval or disapproval."[11]

Neither Hoover nor Mellon wanted the talks to fail completely. Failure, they believed, would destabilize France and damage their hopes for European recovery. Hoover told Senator Reed Smoot that a substantial reduction of the debt might be useful at some point "to secure disarmament in Europe." At present, he said, the French had done nothing to justify any such concession, but he also advised the president that Europe had "hates enough" and urged that the United States "show the consideration of a great nation seeking to do the generous and just thing." To avert complete failure, he suggested to Secretary Mellon deferring a final settlement for five years, with the French simply paying $40 million a year on the debt's interest for each of those five years. Mellon passed the proposal along to the French, who, shocked at the disintegration of what they had considered a finished deal and worried about the impending payment for the military stocks, agreed to refer the offer to their government.[12]

III

In addition to his concern about the French debt, Hoover had also become worried about the growing number of loans being made by American banks to cities, states, and private borrowers within Germany. The loans attracted American investors because they carried high interest rates, but as Hoover, Mellon, and Kellogg warned the bankers, high returns resulted from high risks. Although approximately 75 percent of the borrowed foreign money eventually found its way into German businesses, much of it went to enterprises that did not generate the foreign exchange Germany needed to pay its reparations obligations. Instead, borrowed money financed imports, supported social programs, helped to pay reparations, or was reexported in the form of foreign investments rather than being invested in the production of profitable exports. After 1924, nearly 40 percent of all investments in Germany came from abroad, and the whole structure became perilously fragile. Without exports, the Germans could only make reparations payments by further borrowing, which increased their debt load. Lured by large profits, however, American bankers remained remarkably blind to the situation's danger. Hoover's hopes for German stabilization, buoyed in 1924 by the Dawes Plan, gradually eroded, and with them his confidence in European stability in general.[13]

The secretary's distress about the whole debt and loan tangle underlay a memorandum he sent to Coolidge in early November. The ability of the United States to provide capital for European reconstruction, he wrote, "should be welcomed as a good fortune to the entire world." But the Europeans, instead of recognizing that American wealth had been built up since the war "by an effort unparalleled in our economic history," claimed that it had been amassed unscrupulously during the war. And, instead of covering their own government expenditures "by taxation or economies in government," they squandered money on weapons and borrowed to cover ordinary expenses.[14] In its assertion that the United States had made enormous sacrifices during the war and earned no profit from it, the memo distorted history, and Coolidge wisely ignored it, but it provides a valuable insight into Hoover's feelings and thoughts at a moment of frustration and pessimism.

Fortunately, the moment soon passed. Within a few days, Hoover had regained his balance and assured a friend in Spokane that "Europe is making steady and solid progress." Some basis for optimism came with the signing of debt agreements with Belgium, Latvia, Estonia, Romania, and Italy. The Italian agreement, in particular, seemed to offer a possible model for an arrangement with France. As the year ended, new overtures from the French held out hope that agreement might yet be salvaged from the wreckage.[15]

The restoration of the gold standard to make currencies readily convertible provided a key element in Hoover's stabilization plan. He rejoiced at Britain's return to gold in April 1925 and predicted that "between 80 and 90 per cent of the entire international trade of the world" would soon "move on a gold basis." As a result, he declared, "the volume of speculative hazard in international trade" would be greatly reduced "because of the elimination of risks that must be taken with currency of fluctuating value."[16]

The greatest obstacle to the restoration of the gold standard remained, as it had been since 1920, the steady flow of gold from Europe to the United States—some $258 million in 1924, according to Commerce Department estimates. Hoover continued to assert that this was offset by "invisible exchange" so that although the gold might be at Fort Knox, many of the dollars it represented were circulating outside the United States. By his calculations, the United States actually had an unfavorable current account balance in 1924 amounting to about $212 million, which meant there should be no practical obstacle to the European nations' returning to the gold standard.[17]

Hoover, Mellon, Benjamin Strong, and others in the American government who favored restoration of the international gold standard genuinely believed that it would stabilize the international economy, but they interpreted the issue from a limited point of view. Since foreign trade played only a modest part in the overall American economy, the convenience of having all currencies convertible into gold outweighed the possible advantages of a system in which policy makers could manipulate currencies to mitigate economic crises. More importantly, those who argued that restoring the gold standard would help to reestablish international stability did not really know whether it had provided the basis for prewar stability, or whether international stability had been a precondition for the success of an economic system based on gold. And even if, as Hoover and many contemporary experts believed, the gold standard facilitated trade, minimized inflation, and fostered international order, no one could be sure that the prewar system that had maintained world price stability without any "arbitrary human agency," as Benjamin Strong put it, could be recreated.[18]

Like Strong and other major leaders in the Coolidge administration, Hoover worked to promote international economic cooperation among private institutions. The Dawes Plan provided the most obvious example of that effort, but he also believed that close relations among the major central bankers of the United States and Europe, as well as intimate relationships among other bankers and businessmen, all facilitated European recovery through private management and investment channels. The advantages of that approach in promoting American national goals while maintaining political nonentanglement made it particularly attractive to Republican leaders. At bottom, the whole program rested on continuing Anglo-American cooperation and commitment to common principles, of which faith in the gold standard provided a vital element.[19]

IV

Even as Hoover worked to strengthen the structure of international economic cooperation, he also vigorously promoted American economic interests. By 1926, the United States produced 42.2 percent of the world's manufactured goods—as much as the next eight industrialized countries put together—and its foreign investments would grow from $7 billion to $17 billion over the course of the 1920s. Yet despite that economic dominance, Hoover's Commerce Department acted as though the United States occupied an inferior position in relation to foreign competitors. The department constantly warned American manufacturers about the dangers of foreign competition and urged them to modernize production techniques, improve quality and service, and market aggressively to avoid being swamped by foreign rivals. Hoover's suspicions about the intentions of the European powers, honed during the war, remained acute, even as he sought to promote international cooperation and stability.[20]

His approach to the tariff provided a striking example of the contradictions in his thought. The American export surplus could have been reduced, and Europe's return to prosperity expedited, by granting foreign imports easier access to American markets, but in fact, the opposite happened. Beginning in 1921 with an emergency tariff intended particularly to help American farmers faced with a postwar price collapse, the Harding administration moved in 1922 to adopt the Fordney-McCumber Tariff, which expanded the emergency measure's protectionism from farmers to manufacturers. Opponents of the policy hoped that a clause allowing the president to raise or lower rates by as much as 50 percent would offset the protectionist features of the bill, but in the thirty-seven cases where Harding and Coolidge used the power, they raised rates in all but five cases.[21]

Privately, Hoover regarded the Fordney-McCumber Tariff in 1923 as "impossible," with schedules that were "too high," but he never expressed that opinion publicly or even within the administration. Like other Republicans, he bowed to the political importance of farmers in the Republican Party, endorsing tariff protection for agricultural products in 1921 and afterward. But what of the tariff on manufactured products? Since the Fordney-McCumber Tariff left most raw materials on the free list, Hoover presumably thought the schedules on manufactured goods "too high," but instead of proposing reductions, he developed an elaborate rationalization for maintaining them. Beginning with the Commerce Department's 1922 *Annual Report*, he contended that the tariff did not actually affect either imports or exports materially. In fact, he argued, rising American living standards attributable in part to protectionism actually created greater demand for imported products. And exports, he contended, had also increased because "somewhere between one-third and one-half of foreign buying power" for them had been "furnished by invisible exchange." According to this view, the tariff had little effect on trade, and "the ability of Europe to pay interest and capital upon the debts to our government or our citizens, would not be influenced by abolishing the tariff." The continuing increase of both imports and exports throughout the decade discouraged skepticism about this seemingly illogical argument.[22]

A closer look at the Commerce Department's own figures might have cast some doubt on Hoover's comfortable assumption, although even those figures did not tell the whole story. The 1925 *Annual Report* recorded an increase of 12.8 percent in exports over 1924 but only a 7.6 percent increase of imports, and it concluded that "the gain in imports . . . was confined largely to crude materials," which were generally admitted free under the Fordney-McCumber Tariff. By 1928, Julius Klein reported, the percentage of American exports taken by Europe and the Middle East had fallen from 63 percent in 1910 to 1914 to less than 48 percent, while Latin America's share had increased from 14 to 18 percent. Even more striking was the fact that imports from Asia and Latin America—mostly raw materials—had increased by 362 percent since 1913, and moreover, most of those imports now came directly from Asian and Latin American ports to the United States rather than being transshipped through European middlemen. When broken down regionally, in other words, the trade figures did indeed show growth in American imports and exports with all areas of the world, but the growth was greater outside Europe. American businessmen, supported by "the increased activity of the Department of Commerce" overseas, had been competing effectively with their foreign rivals, but the statistics on growing imports and exports did not really sustain the assumption that the tariff had no negative effect on trade with Europe or on the ability of Europeans to repay their debts.[23] The negative impact of the tariff, it seems clear in retrospect, was being masked not only by invisible exchange but also by something the department's analysis did not include—the effect of large American loans to Europe that replaced, temporarily, the buying power that should have been generated by exports.

Hoover's view of the United States as an aspiring rather than a dominant power in international economics not only affected his attitude toward the tariff, the gold standard, and European debts, but also contributed to his near panic about foreign monopoly control over raw materials needed by American industry. During 1925, the Commerce Department conducted a vigorous campaign against alleged foreign monopolies in long-staple cotton, coffee, iodine, sisal, camphor, mercury, nitrates, potash, and other raw materials. In general, not much could be done about those combinations, but Hoover urged opposition to them wherever possible. The government, he suggested, could help by having the State Department discourage American loans to monopolies or to countries that supported them and by sponsoring programs to find substitutes or alternative sources of such products. Private citizens could boycott monopoly products. Congress could authorize "some sort of properly controlled machinery for emergencies which would prevent our many hundreds of buyers from bidding against each other." For many of the products of alleged monopolies, Hoover's alarm seemed out of proportion to the threat. The monopolies often existed only on paper, and many of their products had little significance in the American economy, but in a few cases the matter was more serious.[24]

In Hoover's opinion, the most serious danger to American interests came from British control over rubber under the Stevenson Plan. Recognizing that rubber was critical to the rapidly growing automobile industry, in 1923 the Commerce Department had launched a two-year effort to find alternative sources or substitutes, but the search had revealed no immediate solution. American manufacturers of rubber products remained divided about how to respond to the situation. A minority, led by Harvey Firestone, saw the threat as serious, some of them suggesting that the British government intended to collect "a rubber tax against America sufficient to pay the British war debt to the United States." This group demanded retaliation but had only vague ideas about what to do. The majority of manufacturers, represented by the Rubber Association of America, saw no reason for panic. They pointed out that having a dependable supply of rubber available at stable prices enabled both producers and purchasers to undertake the long-term planning essential for their businesses' success, and they assumed that the common interest between sellers and buyers would enable them to reach agreement in the near future.[25]

Hoover sided with the alarmists, predicting that the rubber monopoly, by discouraging new production, would create a world shortage by 1928 or 1929. A sudden spike in the world price, which nearly doubled within a month from

40 cents a pound in May 1925 to 75 cents a pound in June, seemed to confirm his warning. Although he dismissed the "rubber tax" argument as nonsense because profits from rubber went to the producers or the colonial governments, not to London, he believed nevertheless that the situation threatened American interests and required action. Since Congress had not acted on his earlier suggestion for an American purchasing combination, the best option seemed to be to put direct pressure on the British government to modify or repeal the Stevenson Plan. Hoover normally opposed turning a commercial conflict into a governmental confrontation, but unless the British recognized "the consequences of Government controlled production and price" and abandoned "all such governmental action," he believed that the seriousness of this case justified an exception to his rule.[26]

In late November 1925, Hoover sent the State Department a draft of a note to the British government contending that "the whole fabric of international commerce and even of wholesome international relations will be undermined unless a halt can be called to governmental price fixing of commodities in international trade." The State Department forwarded the note, nearly verbatim, to London, where it received a predictably chilly response. There was "little, if any, possibility," Foreign Secretary Austen Chamberlain declared, "of His Majesty's Government being in a position to enforce upon the colonies concerned the abolition of control." Articles in the British press drew parallels between British rubber controls and the American tariff, American control of gold, and private American "corners" in export commodities.[27]

In private, however, the British were more accommodating than in public. In August, they had already begun to lift restrictions on the amount of rubber that could be exported from Malaya, and in October they raised the export quota again, to 85 percent of the available supply, with a promise that the quota would be eliminated entirely shortly after the beginning of the new year. Colonial rubber producers, startled by the government's abrupt retreat, predicted an imminent and catastrophic drop in the world price.[28]

Meanwhile, mounting evidence suggested that some American manufacturers had exploited the increased wholesale cost of rubber to raise the retail price of tires excessively, and that a group of them had been negotiating secretly with rubber producers to establish a preferential price. These developments, combined with the relaxation of export restrictions, made it difficult if not impossible for Hoover to pursue further action against the British. In late December, he decided not to release a statement he had drafted attacking foreign monopolies in general and the British rubber monopoly in particular. Not a word about the subject appeared in the department's *Annual Report*. Thus what had appeared to Hoover as a major threat to American interests at the beginning of the year had, by year's end, virtually disappeared. To Europeans, the whole business appeared a gross overreaction by the Americans. An anonymous postcard from Paris, where Hoover's attitude toward the debt and his opposition to an alleged potash monopoly had made him unpopular, suggested rudely that his statements on the subject "came through some other hole in your body, not through your nose!"[29] And indeed, the violence of his reaction seems out of proportion to the significance of the threat. In his mind, Britain still loomed as a major competitor capable of blighting the American economy at a whim.

V

One of the ways Hoover hoped to undercut the British rubber monopoly was by restoring the old wild rubber trade from the jungles of Brazil. Little came from that idea, but investments and trade in other Latin American products became increasingly important. Julius Klein reported with satisfaction that in the decade between 1913 and 1923, the United States had tripled its direct investments in Latin America and had drawn even with Britain in supplying imports to the continent. "Every year," he wrote, "the statistics of our own trade and of foreign trade throughout the world emphasize the increasing importance of Latin-America and the economic progress which is being made in that region." Hoover drew the attention of the White House to statistics on the growth of American trade with Latin America, and in both 1925 and 1927, he considered making a personal visit to the region. Although the pressure of other duties prevented him from doing so until after the election in 1928, he consistently maintained that, as Europe recovered from the war and became more competitive, expanding trade with Latin America would be as crucial to future American prosperity as maintaining "high stability in employment" and a rising standard of living.[30]

Latin America also played an important part in Hoover's approach to the farm problem. His interpretation of agricultural overproduction and the farm depression as essentially short-term problems brought him into conflict with those who thought that the agricultural depression could only be alleviated by the adoption of permanent machinery for dumping surpluses overseas. But even though he rejected dumping as impractical, he viewed aggressive overseas marketing as an obvious palliative to agriculture's woes. He ordered Commerce Department commercial agents in Latin America to make special efforts to promote agricultural sales along with other American products.

By the time of his death in 1924, Secretary of Agriculture Wallace had become the principal administration advocate of overseas dumping. Hoover won a battle in that war with the appointment of William Jardine as secretary of agriculture in 1925, but George N. Peek, a bare-knuckle fighter with the same talent for infuriating Hoover as Alaska's congressional delegate, Dan Sutherland, took up Wallace's fallen gage. A wealthy businessman, in 1923 Peek had resigned the presidency of the Moline Plow Company to become head of the American Council of Agriculture, where he lobbied incessantly for the McNary Haugen bill and circulated exaggerated allegations about

Hoover's interference in the Agriculture Department. At one point, Hoover actually contemplated suing him for slander but wisely decided not to do so.[31]

In November 1924, shortly after the election, President Coolidge appointed a nine-member committee of agricultural experts and representatives of conservative farm organizations (not the American Council of Agriculture) to make recommendations on farm policy. When Hoover testified before the committee, he brought with him not only his own considerable prestige as secretary of commerce but also the distinction that the president had recently invited him to take over the Agriculture Department. The committee members, already sympathetic to his point of view, thus listened attentively as he laid out his ideas. Crop diversification, he argued, would reduce the surplus that had to be sold outside the country and would cut down on agricultural imports by increasing domestic production. The government could help by continuing tariff protection, assisting in the organization of marketing cooperatives, and exempting cooperatives from the antitrust laws. Ignoring Peek's arguments for the McNary-Haugen approach, the committee adopted Hoover's recommendations in their report, urging the creation of a new Farm Board made up of agricultural leaders to encourage organization among farmers and promote cooperative marketing. In Congress, however, Hoover's ideas fared less well, and the congressional session expired without new farm legislation.[32]

Equally unsuccessful was a private effort that Hoover had promoted to help wheat farmers. Following a White House conference on Northwestern agriculture and finance in February 1924, Hoover had encouraged the creation of a unique combination of private capitalism and cooperative marketing to be known as the Grain Marketing Corporation. Gray Silver, president of the Farm Bureau Federation, agreed to head the new company, which planned to raise $10 million in capital, roughly half of which would be subscribed by bankers and businessmen and half by farmers themselves. Getting farmers to invest their scarce dollars in the enterprise would require a "camp meeting kind of a drive," said Hoover, and it turned out that Silver lacked the personality for the task. Behind the scenes, Hoover tried to attract the support of Bernard Baruch, J. O. Armour, and other major capitalists, but the company went out of business in July 1925. At the end of the year, the secretary was back where he had started, urging farmers to establish cooperative marketing organizations.[33]

VI

The coal industry, like agriculture, aggravated Hoover endlessly. When the expiration of the contract in the anthracite fields led to a strike in the fall of 1925, the administration left its settlement in the hands of Pennsylvania Governor Gifford Pinchot, who negotiated an agreement in February, 1926. In the soft coal fields, no such easy way out presented itself. Although the contract signed in Jacksonville in February 1924 still had two years to run, owners of the unionized mines had found that the assumption behind the Jacksonville agreement—that mechanized, union-operated mines would be so efficient that they could profitably undersell nonunion producers in the South—had been wrong. Moreover, demand for coal had been declining as oil and gas grew more popular. In 1913, coal had accounted for more than 84 percent of American energy production; by 1924, its share had fallen to 68 percent, while oil and gas had increased from about 12 percent in 1913 to almost 27 percent in 1924. By early 1925, the owners of unionized mines found themselves in serious trouble. They put increasing pressure on the United Mine Workers (UMW) to abandon the Jacksonville contract and accept substantial wage cuts.[34]

President John L. Lewis of the UMW believed that if the union gave in to the operators, it would be destroyed, but he also recognized the danger that unionized coal mines would be bankrupted or that owners would simply break the contract and cut pay, as had begun to happen in a few cases early in 1925. In February, therefore, Lewis went to Washington to meet with Hoover, who had been instrumental in pressuring the operators into the Jacksonville agreement. The meeting proved tense and fruitless. Both men understood the economic situation in the coal fields, but Lewis believed that backing down on the Jacksonville wage scale would ruin the union, and Hoover refused to take responsibility for insisting that the operators stick to the agreement.[35]

By July, the situation had grown desperate, with Lewis threatening a national strike unless the administration prevented the abrogation of the wage agreement. Hoover met with President Coolidge at Swampscott, Massachusetts, on August 9 to discuss the situation and emerged from the meeting to issue an uncompromising statement. A strike, he said, presented no serious threat to national prosperity. Lewis responded equally intransigently. The administration, he declared, must "use its influence to see that contracts made with its assistance are kept." John J. Leary, Jr., a Pulitzer Prize–winning labor reporter for the New York *World*, wrote privately to Hoover that Lewis refused to consider arbitration until a strike had "hurt" the public and created a demand for a settlement.[36]

Lewis's strike threat was really a bluff. A union-organizing drive in West Virginia had been a failure, and Treasury Secretary Mellon's brother, who ran the unionized Pittsburgh Coal Company, had decided to break the Jacksonville contract. Unless the government insisted that the companies honor the wage scale, the UMW could do very little. When Lewis wrote to the president demanding that the government enforce the Jacksonville agreement, Hoover drafted a reply. It rejected completely Lewis's contention that the government had been a party to the Jacksonville agreement, pointed out that the administration had refused a request from the operators to "undertake the revision of the contract downward," and argued that the proper place to seek the enforcement of the contract was in the courts. Privately, Hoover suggested that if the courts rejected the case, the administration might sponsor legislation giving them jurisdiction. He also drafted, but apparently did not issue, a statement praising those operators who had stood by the Jacksonville agreement, despite losses.[37]

The administration's refusal to support the union in the battle over the Jacksonville contract struck the UMW a severe blow. Lewis realized that even if the courts agreed to consider the matter, the companies could tie up the issue for years, until long after the Jacksonville contract had expired, and in the meantime, nothing prevented the operators from doing pretty much as they liked. With organizing stalled in the nonunionized mines, the strength of the UMW in the soft coal fields had begun a downward slide from which it would never recover. Hoover still hoped to find some way to stabilize the situation, but neither he nor anyone else had any new ideas.[38]

By 1925, oil had not only cut into coal's domination of American energy production but had also grown in importance because of the increasing number of automobiles, trucks, and planes in use. The establishment of the Federal Oil Conservation Board in December 1924 offered a first step toward a national oil policy, but the policy's outlines remained unclear. A sudden oil glut had drowned predictions of an impending oil shortage and arguments for conservation. Some experts, including G. C. Riddell, chief of the Minerals Division of the Commerce Department, contended that even if wasteful production quickly exhausted current fields, technical innovations would soon provide large quantities of oil and gas from oil shales and coal.[39]

In this confused situation, Mark Requa, Hoover's old colleague from the Oil Division of the wartime Fuel Administration, was one of very few people with a clear policy vision for the long term. The present oil surplus, Requa warned, had resulted from technological advances and new discoveries and would not last indefinitely. To prepare for the future, he argued, the states should adopt a uniform petroleum law that would encourage consolidation of producers and promote storage of unneeded supplies in the ground. And, in a strikingly modern proposal, he urged that the price of oil be permitted to rise to encourage conservation and promote the development of more fuel-efficient engines. This latter idea was a little too much for Hoover, who warned Requa that a sharp increase in gas prices would bring charges that the government wanted to enrich speculators, to which Requa retorted reasonably that "we will not get conservation until the price of the article makes it worth conserving."[40]

Nevertheless, Requa argued that even if a plan could not "be put into full effect today or tomorrow," one needed to be implemented gradually, "within the next 5, 10 or 15 years." But whatever the merits of his friend's argument, Hoover found it politically unrealistic, and neither the Oil Conservation Board nor the American Petroleum Institute, the principal industry spokesman, showed the slightest interest in an aggressive conservation program. As long as the oil kept gushing out of the ground, conservation seemed unnecessary.[41]

VII

The resolution of the railroad problem looked a little closer in 1925. Little progress toward the mergers that Hoover regarded as the fundamental solution to the industry's troubles had been made, but in December a joint worker-management committee agreed on the outlines of a "Board of Mediation" to replace the Railway Labor Board. Delighted by this unwonted harmony, Hoover recommended to the president that the administration let the parties submit their suggestion to Congress, while the administration stayed entirely out of the matter. In addition, James C. Davis, the director general of railways, reported in December that his agency had at last resolved all claims arising out of the wartime federalization of the lines and submitted his resignation. His departure marked the end of an era, if not a resolution of the problems of the railroad system.[42]

The development of waterways also seemed to be going forward well in 1925. In April, Congress appropriated $275,000 for a year's engineering study of the St. Lawrence waterway in comparison with an enlarged Erie Canal system. Hoover felt confident that the study would demonstrate the superiority of the St. Lawrence route, both because it would be far easier to build a channel for ocean-going ships there and because the river offered considerable potential for water power development. The rapid completion of the St. Lawrence waterway, plus the improvement and expansion of navigation on the Mississippi River system, he declared, would reduce transportation costs for Midwestern farmers and manufacturers and promote the economic health not only of that section but also of the whole country. Waterway development, he proclaimed confidently, exemplified a situation where "expenditure on great reproductive works is neither a waste nor is it a burden on the community." Not all members of the administration, however, shared his enthusiasm for spending millions of dollars on such projects. Coolidge believed that government should "prevent harm," not "do good," and especially not attempt to do good if it would cost a great deal of money. Other members of the administration resented Hoover's cavalier disregard of his department's limitations. Even his friend and ally, Interior Secretary Hubert Work, protested mildly against Hoover's loud advocacy of waterway development. Reporters had been asking him, said Work, whether Hoover was the official spokesman for the administration on the subject. Hoover would have been wise to heed the hint.[43]

In the course of the engineering study of the St. Lawrence waterway route, Hoover learned that the center of Niagara Falls had been eroding at a rate of about five feet a year for several years and that, as more and more water poured through the notch thus formed, the wings of the falls had been gradually drying up. Characteristically, he set out immediately to fix the problem, contacting the Army Engineers in the War Department and urging the State Department to propose a cooperative repair program to the Canadians. At first, Canadian insistence on authorization to divert additional water from the falls seemed to put an agreement out of reach, but in the end that was what saved the deal. Power companies on both sides of the border offered to share the cost of repairs if they were allowed to divert additional water. They showed that, by spreading the water more evenly across the river's channel, they could improve the scenic effect of the falls, reduce erosion, and divert more water for power generation, all at the same time. It took three years of negotiations to reach that happy conclusion, but the final arrangement pleased everyone.[44]

In the case of the interstate compact to develop the Colorado River, pleasing everyone, or indeed pleasing anyone, seemed increasingly difficult. In February 1925, Colorado ratified the compact on condition that its ratification would become effective when five of the other six states also ratified, and New Mexico, Wyoming, Utah, and Nevada indicated their intention of doing likewise. California, however, proposed an additional condition to its ratification, that the federal government must guarantee to build a high dam at Boulder Canyon. The states that had already ratified then threatened to adopt other conditions of their own, and the whole compact appeared to be endangered. Hoover lobbied energetically against the California reservation, both directly and through his friends Mark Requa and Ralph Merritt. But supporters of Hiram Johnson and Congressman Phil Swing, who had long suspected that Hoover intended to give private power companies control over the construction and operation of a dam, succeeded in passing the reservation in the state legislature. Hoover protested that the Reclamation Service had favored a privately financed dam and that he had been instrumental in blocking the plan, but that convinced none of Swing and Johnson's allies.[45]

At the suggestion of Chester Rowell, a California Republican activist who had remained neutral between Hoover and Hiram Johnson, the two men met to see if anything could be salvaged from the wreck. They circled each other like a couple of strange dogs, growling and sniffing, and barely avoided going for each other's throats. He blamed himself, Hoover later told Rowell, for ever mentioning the possibility of building a low flood control dam on the Colorado and thus awakening Johnson's "sense of opportunity for demagogic action." Pessimistically, he predicted that the Upper Basin states would take California's action as a signal to abandon the compact, in which case they would be free to claim virtually the whole flow of the river.[46]

In December, Hoover testified before the Senate Committee on Irrigation and Reclamation in support of the Colorado Compact and the construction of a high dam at Boulder Canyon. But if his plan had been to allay the fears of Johnson, Swing, and their allies, his testimony did just the opposite. Southern Californians, he said, "recognized that the people in the eastern and central parts of the country probably would not care to pledge the Government" to pay the whole cost of building a dam and power system at Boulder Canyon. As an alternative, he proposed that the government partner with "some of the private power companies." Like his previous testimony in favor of a low dam, his endorsement of even partial control of the Colorado project by private utilities amounted to an enormous political blunder. Incensed, Swing, Johnson, and other congressional supporters of public power determined to fight him to the bitter end.[47]

Similar confusion surrounded the future of the Muscle Shoals installation in Alabama. After Henry Ford withdrew his offer to lease and operate the installation in October 1924, the administration faced confusion about even the most basic issues. Could nitrogen be extracted from the air and converted into nitrates for fertilizer at a commercially feasible cost? Would any company even make the attempt, given the huge research costs and uncertain outcome? How much electric power could be generated at the site, and who would control its generation and distribution? The administration favored private operation in principle, but some of its members wanted to sell the facility, while others preferred to lease it. In Congress, Senator Oscar W. Underwood of Alabama emerged as the main champion of private operation, while Nebraska's George Norris favored public ownership and operation. But neither side could muster a clear majority, and after much maneuvering, Congress finally passed a resolution calling for the president to appoint a commission to reexamine the whole issue and recommend a solution.[48]

Predictably, Hoover regarded the idea of an expert commission as excellent, and he immediately asked the American Engineering Council (AEC) to suggest the names of competent engineers unconnected with any of the interests involved. The chemical and electrical engineers they suggested joined with a former senator from South Carolina, a congressman from Illinois, and a representative of the Farm Bureau Federation to form a commission heavily biased in favor of leasing the facility, as opposed to either selling or having the government operate it. Although the commission's report to the president on November 14 provided no conclusive findings on the lease versus sale issue, Hoover, eager to get rid of the problem, urged the president to reject public operation categorically and to endorse a lease arrangement.[49]

Coolidge, however, preferred an outright sale to a lease and suggested in his annual message that Congress appoint a joint committee to auction the facility to the highest bidder. The Snell Resolution, passed by the House, accepted the idea of a joint committee but opted for a lease instead of a sale. In the Senate, the resolution was referred to the Committee on Agriculture and Forestry, chaired by George Norris, who strongly favored public ownership and operation of Muscle Shoals. Deadlocked, Norris and Underwood girded themselves for a new round in 1926.[50]

VIII

The problems of the radio industry also remained unresolved in 1925. Technological progress had improved the quality and reliability of both broadcasting and reception, and at the same time, the profitability of commercial stations supported by advertising attracted new broadcasters onto already crowded airwaves. In November, Hoover called a fourth national Radio Conference to discuss those and other issues. The proliferation of broadcasters and the fact that no broadcast could be contained within state borders, he argued in an opening address, required a federal "traffic policeman in the ether" to assign frequencies, control the power of stations, and prevent interference. The more complicated and sensitive questions of who should be licensed to broadcast, and under what conditions, required a large measure of community input, Hoover believed. That "discretionary or semi-judicial function" should rest with "an independent commission" sensitive to community wishes and standards in the granting and periodic review of broadcast licenses.[51]

As usual, the conference endorsed Hoover's suggestions, recommending that the Commerce Department reject all new applications for broadcast licenses because of overcrowding of existing frequencies and declaring that the "public interest, as represented by service to the listener, should be the basis for the broadcasting privilege." But despite this endorsement of the secretary's approach, not everyone associated with the industry was happy. The curtailment of new licenses displeased latecomers to broadcasting, and even some established interests in the industry protested at what National Association of Broadcasters president Eugene F. McDonald, Jr., called Hoover's attempt to acquire "Napoleonic powers." When Congressman Wallace White introduced a bill to create a National (later Federal) Radio Commission to advise the secretary on licensing, technical issues, international radio agreements, and appeals of Commerce Department rulings, those suspicious of Hoover's intentions began to coalesce. The White Bill, which Hoover had hoped would pass quickly, instead encountered opposition and delay.[52]

The regulation of aviation made more progress during the year. Massachusetts Congressman Samuel Winslow, who, although chairman of the House Committee on Interstate and Foreign Commerce, had little interest in aviation, retired at the end of the 1924 session. With a sigh of relief, Hoover turned instead to Connecticut Senator Hiram Bingham, a World War I pilot, as the sponsor of administration proposals.[53]

By this time, Hoover had also clarified his own ideas about the broad outlines of aviation policy. Just as the government cleared and marked channels, provided charts, reported on the weather, and inspected ships for seaworthiness and safety, so it should provide comparable services for aviation. Although he opposed direct subsidies to airlines and believed that airports should be the responsibility of the local areas they served, he favored indirect support to the industry through airmail contracts. Aviation, he argued, had become important to the nation economically, and the development of planes and the training of pilots were also vital to national defense. Europe, Canada, Australia, Japan, and even Colombia, he warned, had begun developing commercial airlines, and the United States, which thus far had only a handful of routes covered by the Postal Service, risked falling behind. The great distances and absence of national boundaries within the continental United

States, he argued, made it a natural site for rapid aviation development. He urged Congress to act quickly to establish an aviation bureau and set basic regulations for the industry.[54]

In May 1924, Hoover had asked the American Engineering Council (AEC), the aviation industry, and Commerce Department experts to cooperate in studying commercial aviation outside the United States and the opportunities and problems within the country. Financed largely by private donations, the joint AEC–Commerce Department study emphasized the value of a viable commercial air service to national defense and outlined a plan for its development. Hoover also helped to establish two industry organizations to lobby for aviation development: the Aeronautical Chamber of Commerce representing manufacturers and the National Aeronautic Association representing pilots and others interested in aviation. In conjunction with the AEC–Commerce Department study group, these new organizations created a substantial demand for aviation legislation by the fall of 1925.[55]

In September 1925, President Coolidge appointed a President's Aircraft Board, which worked closely with Hoover as well. Chaired by Dwight Morrow and made up of retired military officers, members of Congress, businessmen, and engineers, the nine-member board studied both civil and military aviation. Hoover sent it a long memorandum recommending creation of a federal "Bureau of Civil Aviation" to create and manage airways, provide beacons for night flying, inspect planes and pilots, and in general provide services for aviation "comparable [to] those which the government has over a century given to commercial navigation." The board's report, released at the end of November, followed his recommendations closely. By the end of the year, momentum was building rapidly for congressional action.[56]

IX

Momentum was also building, Hoover believed, behind a movement to assure every American family its own home. Home ownership, he frequently said, provided "an incentive to thrift and . . . a medium for developing the highest type of family." When a correspondent wrote to him that "a family man should have, and is entitled to a home where he can have a porch, and even one in the rear of his house and a large yard to give him room to think, breathe and grow," Hoover wrote emphatically in the margin, "Agreed!" At the end of the war, he reported, "the proportion of home ownership in the United States had been decreasing for some years," and the trend had been accelerated by wartime shortages. As secretary of commerce, Hoover had committed himself to making suburban houses affordable to most middle-class Americans. By 1925, he reported happily, his efforts to popularize building and zoning codes, simplify and standardize building materials, promote year-around construction, and educate the public through "Better Homes in America" had resulted in steady growth in the percentage of home ownership among Americans.[57]

Still not satisfied, however, Hoover next turned his attention to home mortgages. Although an increasing number of building and loan associations offered small loans to their members, most of them lacked the capital to provide long-term mortgages. Banks did offer mortgages, but usually for no more than five years and for no more than half the total cost of the house. That meant that families must save half the cost of a house before they could even consider buying one. Loans to cover the second half of a house's cost existed, but their interest rates of 12 to 25 percent per year made them prohibitive for most people, even if they did not require a 15 to 25 percent commission that had to be paid before the loan was even made. Hoover believed that such secondary mortgages could be offered safely and profitably at much lower rates. He persuaded the philanthropist-businessman Julius Rosenwald to provide a million dollars for an experimental program in Chicago run by the Morris Plan Bank. By 1927, the program, which offered second mortgages at 6 percent to regularly employed borrowers, had begun to show a small but steady profit.[58]

The campaign for standardization and waste elimination, which Hoover regarded as fundamental to affordable housing, had become by 1925 a central feature of Commerce Department policy. R. M. Hudson, director of the Division of Simplified Practice, estimated that the division's work saved American industry $293,400,000 a year. In the spring of 1925, Hoover proposed the establishment of two new organizations specifically dedicated to simplification and standardization—a national committee on wood utilization and a national committee on metals utilization—which he anticipated would find significant new ways to save business and consumers money and conserve natural resources. Taken together, Hoover bragged, the waste elimination campaign had produced "a most astonishing reduction in the cost of living and at the same time an increase in average wages."[59]

The success of the simplification and standardization campaign in economic terms, Hoover suggested, justified its being extended into new fields. Reorganization of the government, he proposed in a speech to the U.S. Chamber of Commerce, would be one such place. Under Republican administrations, he argued, substantial savings had been affected by "slashing federal expenditures" through elimination of "extravagance and unnecessary personnel." Additional savings could be realized by draining "the swamp of bad organization." More than "200 different bureaus, boards and commissions," he estimated, had been "thrown hodge podge into ten different executive departments, under Cabinet officers," and more than forty other agencies answered directly to the president or Congress. That situation resulted in divided authority, duplication and conflict, and excessive complexity of laws and regulations. No less that fourteen bureaus or agencies, he estimated, dealt with public works and were housed in nine different departments or agencies. For conservation, the figures were eight and five; for public health, four and two; and so on. The Teapot Dome scandal, he suggested, provided a cautionary example of what could happen when no single agency exercised responsibility over an important question.[60]

Untangling the governmental mess, Hoover argued, required three main reforms: putting all agencies with the same predominant purpose under a single administrative head; separating semijudicial, semilegislative, and advisory functions from administrative functions, with the first two placed under boards and the third under single heads; and transferring much of the president's direct administrative responsibility to subordinates. But, he admitted, presidents, special commissions, and committees of Congress had studied the situation over the years and had come to many of the same conclusions—without result. Vested interests within and outside the government resisted every change. The only solution, Hoover concluded, would be for Congress to give the president or some board sweeping authority to make changes.[61]

As Hoover, who had been talking about government reorganization for many years, well knew, reform appealed to students of government but seldom attracted the support of practical politicians. His speech brought a good deal of complimentary mail, and Representative Martin L. Davey introduced a bill delegating power to the president to reorganize through executive orders, but it died in committee. In the end, Hoover's only accomplishment in this area was the transfer of the Patent Office and the Bureau of Mines from the Interior Department to Commerce.[62] He would return to the issue periodically for the rest of his life, but he never achieved the fundamental restructuring he believed desirable.

Outside the government, Hoover believed that significant waste elimination could be achieved in trade associations and labor-management relations. On June 1, 1925, the Supreme Court ruled, in *Maple Flooring Manufacturers Association v. United States* and in *Cement Manufacturers Protection Association v. United States*, that trade associations could pool information about market conditions, sources of supply, trade conditions, and even price data, without violating the antitrust laws, provided they did not use the information to fix prices or restrict competition. Hoover, who had been contending for years that sharing such information among large and small producers would actually enhance competition, welcomed the court's rulings. The government must remain vigilant to assure that information sharing did not degenerate into collusion and price fixing, but its main role should be to promote "cooperation in the large sense between groups." Collective action by trade associations, he argued, could reduce business friction and waste, raise quality standards, and contribute to "the upbuilding of our whole business fabric" in "the interest of the consumer as well as of the industry."[63]

He also believed that waste elimination through cooperation could provide a key to solving labor problems. As industry had grown, he told Herbert's graduating class at Stanford, the "intimate relation between employer and employees which took into account the necessities both of the employer and the employee" had been lost in impersonality. To restore that human connection, both sides must recognize that "all these economic groups represent but parts of a cooperative society." Of course, areas of friction between employees and employers existed, but he believed deeply that everyone would gain from replacing conflict with cooperation. Above all, workers and managers shared "an identity of interest in waste elimination," which, in a modern economy, offered the only significant source for increased profits and higher wages.[64]

As 1925 drew to a close, Hoover looked back with some satisfaction at the achievements of the past four years. When he had taken on the job of commerce secretary, an old Washington hand had quipped that his only duties would be to "put the fishes to bed and [light] the lamps on the coast." Instead, Hoover had found himself "working from twelve to fifteen hours a day, with the activities of the department branching out fanlike in many directions." The administration, he believed, had achieved a sound economy with widespread prosperity, although there remained worrisome problems with some industries like agriculture and coal mining, and speculation in the stock market and real estate required caution. Foreign trade continued to expand, and political and economic stability seemed to be improving in Europe and elsewhere around the world, even if the intertwined strands of war debts, reparations, and postwar loans raised difficult questions about the future.[65]

Pride in his achievements, of course, reminded Hoover that another presidential election would take place in 1928. Could his success and celebrity as secretary of commerce carry him to the White House? Much would depend on Coolidge, just entering on his first elected term. It would be suicidal for a cabinet member to challenge the president if he decided to run again, but after the death of his son, Coolidge seemed to have lost much of his zest for the office. Personal relations between the two men had become increasingly tense. Coolidge had seemed to mock Hoover's ambition by announcing publicly that he would not elevate the secretary of commerce to the State Department following Hughes's resignation, and he made increasingly snide comments about the secretary behind his back. They also disagreed on major issues like tax policy. Coolidge wanted to abolish the inheritance tax, while Hoover argued that it was "not only sound economically but sound socially as it tends to secure distribution of large estates and prevents consolidation of economic controls." That suggested a fundamental difference in outlook about the purpose of government. More generally, where Coolidge favored restricting government activities and curtailing spending, Hoover believed that investment in infrastructure and services would "make directly for an increment of national wealth."[66] For all that Hoover preached self-help, industrial self-government, and restraint by the federal government, at bottom he had a much more activist philosophy than Coolidge, Mellon, and the more conservative wing of the Republican party. Given his temperament, he could not be content indefinitely as a subordinate bound to someone else's policy.

CHAPTER 18

Family and Public Service, 1925–1928

On February 16, 1925, six days after their twenty-sixth wedding anniversary, the Hoovers arrived in Miami for a week's fishing trip aboard the Commerce Department's utility vessel, the *Kilkenny*. With them were the Harlan Stones (his appointment to the Supreme Court had just been confirmed by the Senate) and the Mark Sullivans. Left behind in Washington were winter, the threat of a coal strike, controversy over war debts, and a tense relationship with the president. Ahead, as Lou Hoover wrote, lay a week of "drifting down alongside the Everglades and through the Florida Keys," where the water near the shore was like "milky, opaque, bright green jade," and a little farther out "the jade became the glimmery clear jade that you could see right through, and you could see the bottom of the sea as plainly at forty, or they said a hundred, feet as you could at five." Farther still was "the real indigo blue of the Gulf Stream," and in the foreground "little dancy waves,—and they are rather an aquamarine blue with tiny little glinty white caps on their crests."[1]

The splendid fishing provided the trip's main entertainment. Hoover caught the most and the largest fish ("fortunately," Lou observed dryly), the biggest being a four-foot, sixty-two-pound hammerjack. The others caught "lots of little ones,—three feet or less," mostly barracudas. But the idyll soon ended. They landed at Key West on the 23rd, and three days later Hoover returned to Washington. Lou stopped off to visit a relative and returned home on the 28th, just in time to greet houseguests who had arrived for Coolidge's inauguration. The festivities, given the president's personal preferences and his lingering depression over the death of his son in July 1924, were modest. Vice President Charles G. Dawes provided the day's sensation with a speech denouncing the right of filibuster in the Senate. Coolidge's own inaugural address ran longer than his usual speeches at forty-seven minutes and offered the novelty of being broadcast live on a national radio hookup, but its content provided no surprises. A single sentence captured its theme: "We are not without our problems, but our most important problem is not to secure new advantages but to maintain those which we already possess." After the inaugural parade, the president took a nap, emerging about 4:30 PM to receive official delegations and attend dinner with his guests. After dinner, he paid a brief visit to a banquet being given by members of the Massachusetts legislature at a Washington hotel, and by 10 PM he had retired for the evening.[2]

Following the inauguration, life for the Hoovers returned to its usual frantic pace. During the spring, Lou passed the Girl Scout presidency to Dean Sarah Louise Arnold of Simmons College, arranged for the sale of the faculty houses she and her sister had built on the Stanford campus, and presided over the meeting of the Women's Division of the National Amateur Athletic Association in Chicago.[3] Bert, in addition to juggling his usual responsibilities at the Commerce Department, also launched several new projects.

I

In 1924, Hoover had finally persuaded the president to include a new building in the administration's five-year construction program, and serious planning began in 1925. It made sense, Hoover told the Washington *Evening Star*, to erect a building large enough to house all of Commerce's functions under a single roof rather than in a series of separate structures. Initial proposals would have put the building either on the Mall or just south of it in an area fronting Independence Avenue that the Agriculture Department also wanted, but in 1927 the Capitol Architect approved the present site, facing The Ellipse and occupying the entire block between Fourteenth and Fifteenth Streets, and between E Street on the north and Constitution Avenue on the south. Demolition of existing buildings on the site and excavation began in 1928, and departmental bureaus began moving in early in 1932.[4]

Hoover also worked hard during the spring of 1925 raising money for a proposed Smithsonian National Museum of Engineering and Industry. In the summer of 1923, Frederic A. Delano, one of the regents of the Smithsonian, had asked Hoover to serve on a committee to raise $10 million for the museum. He liked the idea but, pleading the heavy demands on his time, agreed to serve only as an honorary member. When the campaign got under way in early 1925, he wrote a brief publicity statement, lauding the work of American engineers as an "inspirational" contribution to industrial progress and to "the comfort and happiness of our daily lives." But the project's timing proved unfortunate. Smithsonian Secretary Charles D. Walcott had launched a separate drive to raise $10 million for the general support of the Smithsonian early in 1925, and that took precedence over the more specialized effort. Walcott's death in February 1927, followed by a year with Charles G. Abbot as acting secretary before his confirmation as secretary in January 1928, put the engineering museum on hold even before the Depression choked off contributions. Ultimately, the National Museum of History and Technology (now the National Museum of American History) and the National Air and Space Museum would include the purposes of the museum that Hoover and his colleagues had envisioned.[5]

Hoover also plunged into a third fund-raising project in the spring of 1925. The Germans had burned the library of the University of Louvain when they invaded Belgium in 1914. Hoover had first seen its ruins when he went to Belgium in 1914, and the sight came to symbolize for him the terrible losses Belgium had suffered during the war. In August 1919, as the Commission for Relief in Belgium (CRB) wound up its work, Hoover arranged to have about two-thirds of its remaining funds distributed among Belgian universities, all of which had suffered heavily during the war. Of the $33 million total, $3.8 million went to Louvain. The amount proved sufficient to rebuild most of the library building but not to restore its collection, which before the war had been one of the greatest in Europe.[6]

Following the war, Nicholas Murray Butler, president of Columbia University, announced a national campaign to collect small donations from school children to complete the library project, but Americans had grown tired of appeals for European causes, and the campaign raised little money. Rather than see the effort fail, Hoover stepped in, personally approaching a number of wealthy men who were, as he put it, "reputed to have a natural sympathy for Louvain." By 1927, he had gathered only a little over half of the amount needed, but he arranged for the CRB Educational Foundation to contribute $422,689.46 for the building and collection, and $233,524 for the endowment and upkeep of the library. The United Engineering Society donated a clock and carillon to complete the project, and the university dedicated the new library—and unveiled a bust of Hoover—in a colorful ceremony on July 4, 1928, at which Edgar Rickard and American Ambassador Hugh Gibson represented Hoover and the CRB.[7]

II

Planning for the exhibition in honor of the 150th anniversary of the signing of the Declaration of Independence to be held at Philadelphia in the summer of 1926 also distracted Hoover from regular business during the spring of 1925. He had promised the Commerce Department's support for the exhibition in 1921 but declined an offer to become the full-time director-general of the event at $50,000 a year. That proved a wise decision, as planning for the event dissolved into political squabbling and allegations of corruption. The project looked increasingly hopeless until early 1925, when the city bailed out the foundering Exhibition Association and appropriated millions of dollars to build an art gallery, stadium, and convention hall. Organizers had to cut back their ambitious plans for international exhibits, although they still counted on the federal government for a major display.[8]

When Congress named the secretaries of commerce and state in March 1925 to serve on a National Sesquicentennial Commission, Hoover found himself nearly trapped. On a copy of the Senate resolution creating the commission, he scribbled, "Kellogg says has no time to bother with this. I to take care of it." But the secretary rose to the challenge. In June, he persuaded George Akerson, Washington correspondent of the Minneapolis *Tribune*, to become the secretary of the national commission at a salary of $5,000 a year. Akerson proved the ideal coordinator, efficient, good-natured, and liked by everyone he met.[9]

Hoover's discovery of Akerson provided one of the few lasting benefits of his experience with the Sesquicentennial Commission. Akerson, a rotund, thirty-eight-year-old journalist and press agent, became Hoover's chief campaign organizer, go-between, and general political facilitator. Outgoing and informal where Hoover often seemed dour and reserved, Akerson worked endless hours for "the Chief," knew everyone, and charmed everyone he met. He seemed equally at home cajoling and joking with reporters or sitting in as Hoover's representative in a policy meeting. As Hoover tried to transform his image from hard-driving administrator to attractive presidential candidate, Akerson became the indispensable man.[10]

But even Akerson could not smooth over all the problems of the Sesquicentennial exhibition. Ground breaking for the exhibition grounds, scheduled for April 14, 1925, had to be postponed for ten days when Pennsylvania Governor Gifford Pinchot delayed signing a $750,000 appropriation bill. Other troubles soon followed. The director-general of the exhibition and the chairman of its executive committee both resigned when Philadelphia Mayor W. Freeland Kendrick refused to back their grandiose plans. In October 1925, the mayor took over direction of the project personally. The whole business, declared one influential backer of the original project, had turned into "a tragic fiasco."[11]

Hoover almost certainly agreed, but he resolved that the federal government at least would play its part promptly and efficiently. Even though the powers granted by Congress to the National Commission did not include preparing detailed cost estimates for federal exhibits, in January he collected estimates from nine agencies and forwarded the total, $536,500, to the Bureau of the Budget. Ultimately, the total federal contribution would come to $2.5 million. In addition, Hoover instructed Commerce Department representatives overseas to publicize the event and solicit participation by foreign governments, even though Julius Klein admitted that he felt "somewhat doubtful" about committing departmental resources to such a troubled project. Privately, Hoover had little good to say about the enterprise. The mayor, he told Edgar Rickard after a visit to Philadelphia, appeared to be "a complete crook" with "deplorably rotten political associates," and the whole operation "full of graft."[12]

Yet despite all odds, construction on the exhibition grounds proceeded rapidly during the spring of 1926. Some exhibits remained incomplete when the gates opened on May 31, but rain stopped just before fifty thousand people packed into the new exposition stadium to enjoy the music of massed bands and choruses, an artillery salute, a flyover by military planes, and welcoming speeches by dignitaries. In his speech, Hoover lauded the fifty years of unparalleled progress in science, art, industry, and political life since the centennial exhibit of 1876. Provided the nation avoided the "submergence of the moral and spiritual by our great material success," he predicted that Americans would travel comfortably on the "road to further advancement" for the next half century as well. The ceremony closed with choral and band music, the singing of "The Star Spangled Banner," and dazzling fireworks. Hoover, however, remained unimpressed. A few days later, he remarked sourly to a friend that although the whole project "would have died several times but for my intervention," the mayor "made no single reference at any time or in any form to this service."[13]

Perhaps Hoover should have been grateful to be omitted from the mayor's list of those supporting the project. By late July, the operation had sunk $3.7 million into the red, with expenses twice as great as gate receipts. Even Pennsylvania's attorney general got into the act, threatening to sue the Exhibition Association for operating rides and other amusements on Sundays. In August, Hoover gamely issued a press release declaring the exhibition "complete, excellent and noble," and insisting that with all exhibits now open, "the Philadelphia people deserve support for having endeavored properly to commemorate the 150th anniversary of Independence." But he was whistling past the graveyard. When Edgar Rickard and his family visited in mid-November, two weeks before the gates closed, they found the fairgrounds "deserted." An effort by organizers to recoup some losses by reopening in 1927 foundered when federal, state, and local governments refused to provide the $6.5 million needed to cover existing obligations and subsidize the coming season. Later that year, the Exhibition Association, deep in debt, passed into receivership.[14]

III

Two weeks after the opening of the ill-fated Sesquicentennial exhibition, the Hoovers boarded the Overland Limited with the Rickards, headed west to California. They welcomed the chance to escape the troubled exhibition, the problems of the Rio Grande Compact, which had necessitated a trip to Texas in mid-May, and all of Hoover's other duties, as well as Lou's Girl Scout obligations. In their house at 2300 S Street, workmen had just begun a $13,000 remodeling project that they hoped fervently would be finished when they returned. Ahead lay the celebrations surrounding Herbert's graduation from Stanford and marriage to his classmate, Peggy Watson, and a long-planned family camping trip into the mountains.[15]

Before leaving, Hoover arranged, at the request of his friend and admirer, the Hollywood producer Louis B. Mayer, to have President Coolidge agree to be filmed while handing a dummy diploma to the actor Ramon Novarro during graduation ceremonies at the Naval Academy. Such film publicity, Hoover recognized, could have enormous value. Although the Commerce Department had begun making educational films of its own soon after Hoover took over, their modest efforts could not compete with Hollywood's productions. He welcomed an opportunity to cultivate a mutually beneficial relationship with the studios that would grow over the years.[16]

That done, Hoover had no other official duties to occupy him, and the two families enjoyed the trip, watching the spectacular mountain scenery from the train windows and playing bridge. Edgar Rickard reported that Hoover played surprisingly well for someone who rarely had time for a game, but Lou ignored bridge conventions, which Rickard found "difficult." The group left the train on the east side of the Bay on June 16 and took the ferry across to San Francisco, where Herbert and Allan picked them up and drove them to Stanford. The Rickards had not visited the campus for ten years, and they were pleased to find it less changed than they expected. The Hoovers' hilltop house, which they had never seen, delighted them.[17]

On Sunday, June 21, Hoover's brother Theodore gave his youngest daughter in marriage in the Stanford chapel, with just the family in attendance, and the next day Herbert and Peggy received their degrees at the university's commencement. Bert delivered the commencement address, repeating his familiar argument that interdependence and cooperation accounted for much of the nation's recent prosperity, and predicting that "associational activities" would assure its future happiness and progress. That afternoon, the Hoovers held a large reception at their house to celebrate the graduation and the coming wedding.[18]

Herbert and Peggy's wedding also took place in the Stanford chapel, on Thursday afternoon, June 25, with Allan serving as his brother's best man. There were only about fifty guests, all family except for the Rickards; their two daughters, Peggy and Elizabeth; and Dare Stark McMullin, Lou's former secretary and a longtime family friend. Peggy's gown, a San Francisco paper reported, featured "ivory white crepe georgette trimmed with Duchesse lace, and instead of the conventional veil she wore a graceful hat of ivory tulle" and carried a bouquet of lilies of the valley. The day was unusually hot, but the terrace at the Hoover house where they held the reception got every passing breeze, and as Dare put it, the whole thing seemed "very 'family' and friendly and gay." Herbert caused a brief uproar by misplacing his car keys, but the cake got cut; the couple changed; Herbert's Dodge roadster, loaded down with camping gear, was brought around to the door; and at about 6:30, the newlyweds "fled under [Lou's] movie camera in a rain of rice" to begin their drive across the continent to Maine, where they would spend the summer, and Boston, where Herbert planned to enter the Harvard Business School in the fall.[19]

The family held a birthday party for Lou's sister, Jean Large, on June 30, and two days later, a week after the wedding, Bert, Lou, and Allan set out for the north fork of the King's River. They had a very long and rough horseback ride in and out of the valley, Lou reported, but once camped, everyone had "a really gorgeous time," although the fishing proved unexciting. But when they returned to Palo Alto on July 10, reality returned abruptly. A message informed Bert that the Belgian debt commission would arrive in Washington sooner than expected. They would have to rush back to the capital.[20]

IV

Another piece of disturbing news also awaited the Hoovers on their return to Palo Alto. In June, *Hearst's International Cosmopolitan* had begun serializing "They Called Me the Most Dangerous Woman in Europe," a memoir by Belle Livingstone, who maintained that she had had affairs with some of the most prominent men in London and Paris during the early 1900s. The July issue of the magazine included an anecdote about an encounter between Mrs. Livingstone and "Herbert Hoover" in 1900, in which Hoover allegedly came to her apartment to discuss a mining property she owned, was captivated by her beauty, but ended up hiding in a closet most of the evening to avoid being seen by another visitor. To anyone who knew Hoover, the story seemed highly improbable, particularly since he had spent all but a few days of that year in China. He admitted visiting London for four days on business, but denied having ever heard of Belle Livingstone. Nevertheless, the story could be damaging politically, and Hoover's friends went all out to get the record corrected. Hoover's denials, plus a report from Bewick, Moreing Company's solicitors that the company had employed a mining engineer in 1900 named Hooper, who acknowledged having discussed a mining property with Mrs. Livingstone, satisfied the editor of the *International Magazine* that the author had misidentified her visitor, but she refused to back down. The year might have been 1901 or 1902 instead of 1900, she admitted, but she knew Hooper, and the man she met at her flat had been Hoover.[21]

Mrs. Livingstone's refusal to recant left Hoover in a dilemma. If he issued a public denial, it would "offer further opportunities for malicious news stories," yet ignoring the story might imply it was true. Hoover scented a politically motivated attack and considered filing a libel suit against the magazine unless it published an immediate retraction. His friends in New York and London, however, counseled against any such step. Since no hard evidence existed to support either of their claims, the matter would come down to "she said–he said." Moreover, although the English engineer Edward Hooper confirmed privately that he was the person mentioned in Livingstone's story (he denied the closet episode), he expressed understandable reluctance to face the embarrassing publicity that might accompany a public admission of his role. Under the circumstances, Hoover had no choice but to content himself with a private letter from Ray Long, editor in chief of the International Magazine Company, stating that, after investigation, he believed that the story was "simply a case of mistaken identity" and that the company regretted having published it. There the matter rested until February 1927, when a book version of Livingstone's memoirs, *The Belle of Bohemia*, appeared in London. The possibility that the book might also be published in the United States occasioned a flurry of transatlantic cables, which ended when Hoover's old London friend, John Agnew, pointed out that the publishers would welcome a libel action as free advertising. Agnew was correct. Deprived of the oxygen of publicity, the book never found an American publisher, and the story disappeared from sight.[22]

The Belle Livingstone episode had no lasting effect, but it illustrated a shift in Hoover's way of looking at events. He had always been hypersensitive about attacks on his policies and his personal integrity, but now Edgar Rickard observed a tendency "to weigh almost all matters from the standpoint of political significance." Although he would doubtless have denied it even to a close friend like Rickard, Hoover had begun to plan his route to the White House.[23]

V

In Washington, the Hoovers found the remodeling project at 2300 incomplete. For a couple of weeks, they had only one usable room on the ground floor, but fortunately the weather remained unseasonably cool, and since most government officials had left town for the summer, no entertaining needed to be done. Allan went to work as a secretary for his father, and after work the family talked about what he would do in the fall. He had not done well academically during his freshman year at Stanford, and his father worried that the university had become a party school, with too much bootleg liquor and too many students concentrating on cars and social events rather than study. Allan was not "wild," but he seems to have found it difficult to live up to the expectations of people at Stanford about the son of a major trustee and prominent political figure. After discussion, the family agreed that it might be easier for him if he transferred to another university for his sophomore year. He liked Princeton, but during a campus visit, he learned that if he transferred, he would have to repeat his freshman year. That decided him against the move, and on September 24 he left Washington to return to Stanford.[24]

Meanwhile, from Maine, where Herbert had a summer job at the Pejepscot Paper mill, came reports of problems. Edgar Rickard, a director of the Intercontinental Corporation, the parent company of the Pejepscot mill, paid a visit in August and observed that Herbert, while "earnest," expected unrealistically to become "a Consulting Paper Mill Engineer" before he had mastered the business. Rickard also thought that the young man's deafness had grown worse since the wedding and had become "a terrible handicap" to his work, even amid the din of the mill. As it turned out, Rickard was right. Doctors who examined Herbert concluded that his tonsils had regrown since their removal early in 1919, and infections had affected his hearing. On September 19, he entered Johns Hopkins Hospital in Baltimore for a second tonsillectomy. The operation seemed successful, but severe hemorrhaging followed, alarming everyone before doctors managed to control it a few days later. A week later, he had improved enough to set up a ham radio set in his hospital room to entertain himself. Lou informed Allan that Herbert and Peggy would stay in Baltimore for the fall and go to Boston after Christmas, where he would start a semester late at Harvard. His hearing, unfortunately, had not improved.[25]

Between visits to Baltimore, Lou and Bert continued their regular activities. Lou launched a major fund-raising drive to build a new Young Women's Christian Association building in Washington and traveled extensively on behalf of the Girl Scouts and the Women's Division of the National Amateur Athletic Federation (NAAF). Bert, of course, had his usual duties at the Commerce Department, and during the autumn he also took the lead in a National Research Council (NRC) campaign to raise money to fund basic scientific research. Chartered by Congress in 1918 to promote scientific research during the war, the NRC had severed its official ties in 1921 and 1922 and reorganized as a private foundation. A $5-million Carnegie Corporation grant had enabled it to build a headquarters in Washington and created a modest endowment. Now its trustees turned to Hoover for help in raising $20 million in operating funds.[26]

In December, Hoover took advantage of an invitation to deliver the Henry Robinson Towne Lecture before the American Society of Mechanical Engineers to make his case. "There must first be a pure science before there can be an application," he reminded the engineers. In recent years, he argued, industry had supported applied research generously, but pure science had been starved both for funding and researchers. He predicted that if America continued to spend "less than one-tenth what we spend on cosmetics" on pure research, applied science would soon wither as well.[27]

The National Academy of Sciences formally announced the inauguration of the fund-raising campaign for the NRC in mid-December. They hoped to raise $2 million a year for the next ten years, using all of it to fund pure research. Hoover agreed to chair a special board of trustees, which also included Andrew Mellon, Elihu Root, Edward M. House, Owen Young, and several other prominent men. Officially blessed by the president, the campaign obtained pledges of $3 million by April 1926, but then progress slowed. A number of executives expressed doubts that they could properly use corporate funds for such a purpose, and major figures like John D. Rockefeller, Jr., and J. P. Morgan withheld their support. The number of people who needed to be educated about the importance of basic research to industry, Hoover complained in October of 1927, demanded more time and effort than he could afford. Nevertheless, he soldiered on until June 1928, when the demands of the presidential campaign finally forced him to resign his chairmanship. He had not yet obtained pledges for the full $20 million, but just a few days before his resignation, Hoover had the pleasure of announcing the first fifty grants to scientists, for a total of $120,660.[28]

VI

During December 1925 and January 1926, the Hoovers attended a series of official and semiofficial social events in Washington, although they managed a quiet Christmas at home at 2300 S Street, where the workmen had finally finished the remodeling. Official business (particularly the antimonopoly campaign) absorbed Bert in the new year, so at the end of January, Lou left for California to see Allan and her family. She found them all well, but she came down with a mild but protracted case of influenza. With memories fresh in everyone's minds of the 1918 to 1919 pandemic and the lingering effects of Herbert's illness, Bert worried a great deal about her until she reported her gradual recovery. To keep herself occupied during her convalescence, she wrote articles proposing a "lone Girl Scout" program to enable girls living in areas too isolated to permit the creation of a local troop to take part in scouting activities. Another short essay, on Grace Coolidge's childhood, written with the First Lady's permission for the Girl Scout magazine, *American Girl*, almost got Lou in trouble that fall when the Scout organization proposed to syndicate it in sixty-five newspapers. The Coolidges objected to what they saw as an invasion of their privacy, and Bert had to scramble to cancel the syndication.[29]

If Allan had spent too much time socializing during his first year at Stanford, he swung to the opposite extreme during his second year. In March, after Lou left, he was hospitalized for twenty-four hours following what his aunt, Jean Large, described as his having gone "to pieces nervously" as the result of obsessive studying for end-of-quarter exams. Although she reported him "absolutely happy and care free" a few days later, her letter must have worried his parents.[30]

Before they could get upset, however, other news crowded out concerns about Allan's problems. On March 17, "St. Patrick's first commission," as Lou put it, was the delivery of a four-pound baby girl to Peggy and Herbert. Although more than two months premature, Margaret Ann Hoover appeared healthy, normal, and even "husky." Lou, in New York on Girl Scout business, immediately dropped everything to go to Boston to see her first grandchild.[31]

On May 1, Allan and his Stanford classmate Allen Campbell, son of former Governor Thomas E. Campbell of Arizona, set sail from New York aboard the *Leviathan* for a three-month tour of Europe. Before they left Washington, Bert had released Allan from a pledge not to drink, and the young man confided to Edgar Rickard that "he proposed to take drinks when offered" during the trip. Alcohol had become, of course, the most obvious symbol of youthful rebellion in Prohibition-era America, but Allan was not a rebellious young man at heart, and there is no evidence that the boys caroused through Europe. To the contrary, they seem to have been serious tourists, visiting their parents' friends and using the trip in part to gain perspective on the future. By the time it ended, Allan's doubts about Stanford had diminished, and he decided that he would return for the coming year.[32]

The boys landed in New York on August 27, and Lou and the Rickards treated them to a week of New York shows before she and they started for California, where they expected to meet Bert, who had been making political speeches as he wended his way west. Hoover found the summer and fall of 1926 a difficult period. With a congressional election coming up in the fall, Republican business groups welcomed him as a speaker in the Midwest and West, but the more he spoke, the less the president seemed to like it. What the speeches, which emphasized the importance of federal support for waterway development, highlighted was a fundamental philosophical difference between Hoover and president. Hoover believed in a moderately activist government, with an important role in helping Americans to achieve prosperity and happiness. Coolidge, as he had said in his address accepting the presidency of the Massachusetts Senate in 1914, believed that "the people cannot look to legislation generally for success." The government might "care for the defective and recognize distinguished merit," but "the normal must care for themselves. Self-government means self-support."[33]

VII

The conflict between the two men came out indirectly in October. In the midst of a three-week trip during which Hoover made one or two speeches every day in Midwestern and Western cities lauding Republican economic policies, Coolidge suddenly sent him a sharp telegram complaining that he had not been campaigning in New England and criticizing him for encroaching on Interior Department territory by talking about waterway development. At the same time, the president stayed aloof from the campaign, refusing even to speak out on behalf of senators who had supported the administration loyally. Not until November 1 did he finally break what *Time* magazine called "his campaign silence" to say that he would go home to Massachusetts the next day to vote for Republican Senator William M. Butler and Governor Alvan T. Fuller.[34]

Hoover found Coolidge's passive-aggressive behavior extremely frustrating. Privately, he complained about the president's lack of interest in urgent issues and refusal to exert leadership, and even talked about the possibility of simply resigning from the cabinet. He had some right to feel resentful. His policies had brought the Republicans broad support in the business community, yet the president expressed no gratitude and indeed went out of his way to embarrass and demean the secretary. If Coolidge really felt that Hoover's proposals conflicted with his own plans, he had been free to deny him reappointment in 1924 or to fire him at any time thereafter. That he did not do so suggests that he found the secretary politically useful, while Hoover's failure to follow through on his threat to resign demonstrates his recognition that remaining in the cabinet provided his best and perhaps only chance for succeeding to the presidency. Although he might grumble in private, in public Hoover expressed complete loyalty to the administration and did everything in his power to support the Republicans. He told Edgar Rickard that he "had a lot to do for the administration before the November elections."[35]

Hoover's 1926 campaign swing through the West followed a time-honored path for potential presidential candidates. His campaign appearances elevated him from a still relatively obscure cabinet role and made him a major spokesman of Republican prosperity, while his willingness to make speeches, meet with local leaders, and support local candidates created obligations to him among Republican activists all across the West. Carefully planned and coordinated by George Akerson, the 1926 campaign provided the prologue for 1928. This time, unlike 1920, Hoover intended to make an early start and avoid amateurism.

Nevertheless, as 1927 began, a real question arose whether Hoover would be able to stay in the administration. In April, a rumor circulated that Secretary of State Kellogg would resign and that Hoover would be named as his successor. Either the president or Kellogg might simply have denied the resignation report, but instead Coolidge issued a statement that Kellogg would continue—and that in any case, Hoover would not be his successor. Hoover, who had been privately hoping for the State Department appointment, felt humiliated. Although Coolidge belatedly assured reporters that Hoover was just too valuable in the Commerce Department to be transferred and invited the secretary to the White House for an intimate breakfast meeting, Washington gossips reported that the president had intended not only to embarrass Hoover but also to rebuke him for his interference over the years in the affairs of other departments. The Hoovers were, as Lou admitted to Herbert and Allan, "perfectly boiling with rage" at Coolidge's "small minded and unappreciative" behavior, and even more at the implication in the press that Hoover had been responsible for political attacks on the president. In her version, Bert was "working *for* the American people even more than *with* the President," but that hardly told the full story. Coolidge knew perfectly well that Hoover's ambition would keep him in the cabinet and force him to swallow whatever the president handed him, and, having a bit of a mean streak, he enjoyed watching the secretary squirm. At the same time, the president recognized and valued Hoover's energy and ability, even if that meant the secretary would sometimes launch initiatives and proceed in directions of which the president disapproved. "How can you like a man who's always trying to get your job?" he asked an associate, and that remark went to the heart of his conflict with Hoover. For all his appearance of passivity, Coolidge intended to control his own administration, and he recognized that Hoover would never really accept a secondary role. Bound together by political necessity, the two men would continue as nominal allies, but neither would ever really like or trust the other.[36]

As it happened, at almost the very moment Lou was writing to her sons about the Coolidge incident, major levees were collapsing along the Mississippi. Within a week, the president would ask Hoover to head the relief and recovery effort in the region, and the whole Hoover-Coolidge imbroglio would disappear from the nation's front pages. Instead of a cabinet member on the verge of dismissal, Hoover would become, once again, the "master of emergencies" and "the great humanitarian."[37]

VIII

While Bert was occupied with low politics on the Potomac and high drama on the Mississippi, Lou helped to organize a League of Women Voters political seminar in Washington, presided over the annual meeting of the American Child Health Association, and negotiated a $75,000 loan from the American Relief Administration Children's Fund to help the *American Girl* serve a burgeoning circulation. In April, members of the Girl Scouts named her as one of the women they most admired. At the organization's national meeting in Milwaukee in May, she declared that modern young women should cultivate "a well-balanced mind developed equally by an early education in citizenship, religion, home making and play" and not be content with "the tedious routine of household duties."[38]

In July, Bert managed to escape his Mississippi relief duties long enough to go west, arriving in Reno on July 24, where Allan and Lou met him with a car. The next day, they drove south along the east flank of the Sierras, fishing at little lakes along the way and staying near Mono Lake. The next day, they climbed the ten-thousand-foot Tioga Pass and drove down into Yosemite National Park, enjoying the spectacular scenery but not the clouds of mosquitoes that descended on them whenever they stopped at the higher altitudes. After a day in Yosemite Valley, they continued to Palo Alto, and Bert and George Akerson went up to join the Bohemian Grove encampment.[39] Although they did not know it at the time, the Sierra holiday would be one of the last the family would enjoy for several years to come.

On August 2, President Coolidge issued his bombshell announcement that he did not "choose to run for president in nineteen twenty-eight." Hoover undoubtedly welcomed the announcement, but like everyone else, he found its terse language puzzling and wondered what Coolidge really intended. He asked the members of his nascent presidential campaign organization to "sit tight," though he authorized them to continue discreet fund-raising. Abandoning plans for an inspection trip through the Mississippi flood zone on his way back to Washington, he hastened directly to the capital to confer with political supporters.[40]

Lou accompanied him, as did Allan and Jean Large's daughter Janet, who planned to enroll that fall in the Elm Lea School in Putney, Vermont, where Lou would pay her expenses. Even before a campaign began officially, the psychic costs to the family of a presidential race were becoming obvious. "We . . . never wanted it," wrote Lou, though she must have known that she was really speaking only for herself. Back in Washington, she had to fend off the "tactless" questions of people who demanded to know whether Bert would run. She must often have wished that she could trade the muggy capital for the cool privacy of the Stanford house. A visit from her granddaughter, Peggy Ann, now just over a year old, delighted her but offered only temporary relief from the growing political pressure. Nor was she the only one to feel the strain. Allan, still not comfortable at Stanford, had been thinking again about transferring—perhaps to Yale—but the prospect of his father's candidacy made it a poor time for him to call attention to himself. Better for him to return to Stanford. When he got back to Palo Alto, Lou wrote praising his management of the Palo Alto household, but her concern about him was evident between the lines. A few months later, when she received a telegram telling her breathlessly that he had "found it at last in aviation," she replied calmly that if he only wanted to fly because he could think of nothing else to do, she hoped he would drop the idea, but if he felt "overwhelmingly thrilled" by the prospect, he should go ahead. She, too, had always wanted to fly, she said. Always reticent in expressing their emotions, the Hoovers nevertheless felt some anxiety at the great undertaking ahead of them.[41]

During the fall of 1927 and the spring of 1928, the family carried on as normally as they could. Bert continued to devote time to the aftermath of the Mississippi flood, and then to a second flood in New England, while old issues of foreign monopolies of raw materials and other departmental business also demanded his attention. Lou traveled extensively on Girl Scout and National Amateur Athletic Federation business. Having surrendered direct control over the two organizations, she found both slipping into economic difficulties as less experienced women took her place. But nothing could be done. The presidential campaign would prevent her from running either organization personally.[42]

On a more intimate level, the year brought beginnings and endings. In June, Lou's aunt, Jennie Mager, died of a heart attack while visiting Lou in Palo Alto. Herbert Hoover III, the Hoovers' second grandchild, was born to Herbert and Peggy on November 5, 1927. A normal, healthy baby weighing seven and a half pounds, little "Pete" provided a welcome addition to the family. In mid-July 1928, Lou heard in Washington that her father had suffered a stroke during a camping trip in the Sierras. Brought down to a "sanatorium" at Placerville, he seemed at first to be recovering, but ten days later took a sudden turn for the worse and died on July 18, just two days short of his eighty-third birthday. As with her mother, whose death she had also missed, Lou regretted that she had been unable to get to California in time to have one last visit with her father before his death. Allan, who turned twenty-two the day before his grandfather's death, was with him when he died and made arrangements to have the body returned to Palo Alto pending Lou's arrival for the funeral.[43]

The juxtaposition of her father's death and the presidential campaign may have triggered an idea for Lou. As a sentimental gesture toward her family, she proposed to buy back Bert's birthplace cottage in West Branch, Iowa, and present it to him as a gift for his fifty-third birthday on August 10. The current owner, Mrs. Jennie Scellars, was the widow of a carpenter who had purchased the property in 1890 and connected it to another house, which he had moved onto the property. In 1928, Mrs. Scellars still made a modest living selling admissions and souvenirs to tourists, and with Hoover about to run for president, she declined to sell. Not until 1935, the year after her death, did Lou succeed in purchasing the property from her estate and begin restoring it as the basis for the present-day historical park and site for the Hoover Presidential Library.[44]

During the presidential campaign Lou chose to stay in the background. Through friends and her secretary, Ruth Fesler, she helped to organize women to support Bert's candidacy, but she did not campaign actively, preferring to keep her activities informal and her public appearances as limited as possible. Despite her long experience of life in the public eye, she still hoped to maintain the family's privacy. That may seem an odd attitude for a woman who had taken such a public leadership role during and after the war, but a presidential campaign differed from anything she had experienced previously in her public life—rougher, nastier, and far less controllable. Although she shared Bert's political views and supported him loyally, she never felt comfortable with overtly partisan politics. In an agonized letter written to Edgar Rickard in the midst of the campaign, she lamented not only the "unscrupulous persons peddling untruths" but also the "worthy and gallant men" who failed to "lift a finger against their circulation." The "loss of my faith in humanity," she wrote, "is very much harder upon me than the possible loss of the Presidency." The pain she experienced on the eve of entering the White House would grow far worse over the next four years.[45]

CHAPTER 19

The Commerce Department, 1926–1928

On April 27, 1927, Iowa cartoonist J. N. "Ding" Darling published a cartoon titled "The Traffic Problem in Washington, D.C." It showed a street scene in the capital, with a long line of irate motorists, their cars labeled "Congress," "Secty. Mellon's car," and other government powers being held back by Officer Coolidge, while a swarm of Hoovers, each wearing a different hat, rushed across the intersection. The first Hoovers in the crowd were labeled "Secretary of Commerce," "radio commissioner," "farm economist," "commercial aviation," "export trade," "labor arbitrator," "foreign debt commissioner," "shipping," "child hygiene," and "unemployment commission." Waiting on the curb ready to enter the crosswalk stood another crowd of Hoovers, holding a sign, "Hoover activities." No American seeing the cartoon would have misunderstood Darling's point: Hoover had become the ubiquitous government official. Nothing, it seemed, happened in Washington in which he did not have a role. (See Figure 14.4.)

The labels on Darling's Hoovers seemed so familiar to newspaper readers because they identified issues that had proved intractable in preceding years. Agriculture, the railroads, the coal industry, and the merchant marine remained economic basket cases. Little progress had been made in developing a national waterways policy, controlling the Colorado's waters, regulating radio and aviation, or settling war debts. Yet despite those persistent problems, the economy overall was booming, and the stock market, after

341

a dip at the beginning of 1926, had headed back up. Sooner or later, the Darling cartoon implied, the ever-industrious Hoover would solve all the remaining difficulties.

I

During 1926, letters pouring into the Commerce Department indicated that farmers did not share the general optimism. Organized farm groups, led by George Peek after the death of Henry C. Wallace, insisted that the McNary-Haugen bill provided the answer to the farmers' problems. Based on the Peek-Johnson Plan that Peek had been urging on farmers and the Agriculture Department since 1922, the McNary-Haugen Bill had been drafted in the Agriculture Department and introduced by Senator Charles McNary and Representative Gilbert Haugen in January 1924. It proposed to divide staple agricultural crops into two categories: those needed to satisfy domestic demand and a surplus to be dumped on the world market. Since the tariff kept domestic prices up, provided no surplus depressed them, the domestic price would normally run higher than the world price, and farmers would prosper as long as supply and demand remained in balance. In years when a surplus existed, the bill provided that a government corporation would purchase it and either store it for later sale or dump it on the world market at prevailing prices. To cover the losses of the corporation resulting from its buying at the higher domestic price and selling at the world price, a small tax or "equalization fee" would be charged to producers of an affected crop, whether their products were sold on the domestic or foreign market. Because the fee would be charged on the whole crop, its amount per unit would be small, and farmers would be better off than if the price of everything they sold had been driven down by surpluses.[1]

Hoover consistently opposed McNary-Haugen, arguing that it would encourage overproduction and anger other nations. He denied that a simple panacea for farmers' problems existed. Instead, they must fight their troubles by curtailing production, diversifying crops, and working to improve marketing and distribution. A smorgasbord of his other suggestions included exempting farm cooperatives from the antitrust laws, providing more ships to carry farm exports, securing new credit sources for farmers, coordinating shipping of agricultural products, encouraging waterway development, promoting agricultural education, urging farmers to move to the cities, and stabilizing the business cycle. He recommended the establishment of regional farm marketing cooperatives not only to improve the sales and distribution of agricultural products but also to teach farmers "to regulate in greater measure the supply to the demand." Eventually, he predicted, rising American living standards and a growing population would bring demand into line with supply.[2]

Hoover's assumption that the farm problem would cure itself eventually enabled him to believe that farmers' difficulties resulted more from poor sales and distribution than overproduction. Neither he nor the McNary-Haugenites recognized that the world agricultural market had changed following the war, as greater grain production elsewhere increased world supplies at the same time that rising living standards reduced the demand for cereals and increased the consumption of meat. Those changes foreshadowed continuing troubles for American grain growers that would be solved only by a transformation of agriculture beyond anything envisioned by either Hoover or the Agriculture Department. Although Hoover often went further than conservative Republicans in advocating government intervention in the economy, he could not accept federal production control. The "value of maintaining the responsibility of groups in the country for the conduct of their own industry overweighs almost every other interest," he warned. Any other policy would lead to "complete disaster."[3]

Hoover's opposition to McNary-Haugen resulted in part from painful personal experiences during and after World War I. Midwestern farm leaders, including Henry Wallace and George Peek, often contended that Hoover had fixed wartime wheat and corn prices at levels that prevented farmers from benefiting from increased demand. It did him little good to repeat ad nauseam that a producers' board, not he as Food Administrator, had set the prices. The attacks wounded him both personally and politically. They provided Robert La Follette with ammunition during the 1924 presidential election, and they gave specious plausibility to a claim by Senator Burton K. Wheeler in the summer of 1926 that Hoover had profited personally from the abortive Grain Marketing Corporation in 1925. Above all, they made Hoover extremely sensitive to the dangers of any program that seemed to involve the government in fixing prices. "I have . . . seen the results of it more vividly than anybody . . . who lives," he said, "and I would not propose price-fixing in any form short of again reentering the trenches in a World War."[4]

Hoover marshaled a strong economic argument against McNary-Haugen, including the contentions that it would increase surpluses, enrich middlemen, raise domestic food prices and promote inflation, encourage foreign retaliation, and make the payment of foreign war debts less likely. President Coolidge agreed with the commerce secretary that McNary-Haugen would not solve farm problems, but neither he nor Secretary of Agriculture William Jardine had anything better to offer farmers than cooperative marketing. As it happened, however, although a drop in cotton prices added Southern to Midwestern support for McNary-Haugen, congressional backing of the bill never developed much depth, and its supporters could not override Coolidge's vetoes in February 1927 and May 1928. Like Hoover, Coolidge and Jardine hoped the problem would cure itself, but it did not. Statistics the Commerce Department put together in 1927 indicated that the disparity between the price indexes for manufactured and agricultural products had exceeded the 1920 level for each of the past six years. Nevertheless, philosophically opposed to mandatory federal production controls, no one in the administration had any new ideas to offer disillusioned farm voters on the eve of the 1928 election.[5]

II

Nor could the administration cure the fundamental weakness of the American railroad system. On May 14, 1926, Congress passed the Railway Labor Act replacing the Railway Labor Board by a new Board of Mediation, designed jointly by the railroads and the unions. Under the new system, labor disputes were to be submitted, first, to collective bargaining, and if that failed, next to arbitration and ultimately to a "board of mediation" appointed by the president. By threatening to invoke this process if the unions called a strike, Hoover found it possible to "stimulate conversations" about wages and working conditions between the lines and the railroad Brotherhoods in December 1926, and railroad peace was preserved until the end of the Coolidge administration. On the more fundamental issue of consolidating the many competing lines, however, the Interstate Commerce Commission (ICC) and Commerce Department made no significant progress. Following the death of Senator Albert Cummins in 1926, legislation to promote consolidation stalled in Congress, and although some railroad executives pursued their own consolidation programs, the results only marginally changed the situation. The ICC continued to urge the railroads to consolidate in conformity with a national plan it had endorsed in 1921, but it lacked authority to compel them to do so. In the absence of support among the lines for the ICC proposal, the consolidation section of the 1920 act remained a dead letter, and Congress finally repealed it in 1940.[6]

In the coal industry events also largely bypassed the administration's efforts at reform. In February 1926, Pennsylvania Governor Gifford Pinchot negotiated a settlement of an anthracite strike. Hoover thought that the contract could serve as a model for a long-term settlement in the bituminous industry as well, but a shrinking market for soft coal meant that producers held the whip hand in negotiations with the United Mine Workers (UMW). With nonunion mines able to satisfy most of the national market, the UMW lost members as miners accepted whatever jobs they could get.[7]

On April 9, 1926, the Supreme Court affirmed the legality of the ICC's regulation of coal distribution during the 1922 strike. Hoover believed, however, that the country needed a more permanent mechanism to avert a strike when the Jacksonville Agreement expired in 1927. At his suggestion, Coolidge recommended to Congress the establishment of an emergency mediation commission, an agency to control distribution of coal in the event of a strike, and enhancement of the Coal Commission's fact-finding powers during a conflict.[8]

During the spring of 1926, members of Congress introduced some fifty-three different bills (forty-five in the House alone) relating to the production and distribution of coal, and in May the House Committee on Interstate and

Foreign Commerce held hearings to try to sort out the issue. Hoover testified on May 14. He described the industry's major problem as "periodic suspension of production with attendant unemployment, famine in coal and consequent profiteering in prices." In the absence of "consolidation of ownership," he argued that consumers needed protection through the passage of legislation setting up the structure the president had proposed, unless the miners and owners agreed on a mediation system on their own. Given the confrontational relationship between labor and management in the coal fields, however, such a voluntary arrangement seemed improbable, particularly since the industry's overall decline had rendered the union increasingly irrelevant.[9]

By December 1926, the parties had made no progress toward the establishment of voluntary settlement machinery. Congress had boiled the various legislative proposals down to one, the Parker Bill, which would have authorized the president to order arbitration or mediation in the event of a strike and to appoint a federal fuel administrator with the power to set distribution priorities and curtail excessive profits. That went further than the administration wished, but the impending expiration of the Jacksonville agreement on April 1, 1927, made the situation urgent, and Hoover endorsed the Parker Bill. In February, however, the House Committee suddenly killed the bill, reportedly as the result of a deal with farm state representatives. Both operators and the union apparently wanted a showdown, and farm state representatives agreed to vote down the Parker Bill in return for the coal state representatives' promise to support McNary-Haugen.[10]

A few days after the defeat of the Parker Bill, the UMW and the operators met in Miami to try to negotiate an extension of the Jacksonville agreement. The union insisted that a new contract maintain wage levels, while the operators insisted that wages must be tied to coal prices. The talks broke down on February 22, and both sides prepared for a strike, which began on April 1, 1927. But no one outside the industry seemed to care. Dealers had plenty of coal on hand when the strike began, and with two-thirds of the mines not unionized and hence not on strike, no coal shortage ever developed. In November, the desperate union appealed to the administration for help getting talks started. Coolidge referred the issue not to Hoover, who had led the Harding administration's response to the 1922 strike, but to Labor Secretary James J. Davis, a much weaker figure. Davis called a meeting in Washington in December, to which the union sent a large delegation, but the biggest operators never bothered to appear. Reduced from half a million members in 1922 to about eighty thousand mostly in Illinois and Iowa, the UMW had become a mere shadow of its former self. The strike gradually collapsed in the spring of 1928, and miners settled for whatever wages and working conditions they could get.[11]

Hoover failed in his attempt to achieve continuous production in the bituminous coal fields, a living wage for miners, and consolidation of small coal companies. Consolidation might once have solved some of the industry's problems, but given the shrinking national market for soft coal, it would probably only have postponed the industry's decline. A boom in 1928 to 1929 brought temporary prosperity to the fields and sustained Coolidge's blithe assumption that the industry's problems had solved themselves. Hoover knew better, although as a presidential candidate he had no incentive to challenge the assertion. But if he did not share Coolidge's unrealistic confidence, the evidence suggests that he never fully recognized the industry's fundamental problem of dwindling markets either.[12]

III

As with coal, the decline of the American merchant marine seems in retrospect almost inevitable. Certainly the experiment with government ownership, begun during World War I, had produced nothing but headaches. In 1926, the Emergency Fleet Corporation, despite having sold or scrapped more than 1,500 of its ships, still lost money at the rate of $13 million a year. The sale of its most profitable assets, the United States Line and the American Merchants' Line, that summer did nothing to help. Nevertheless, Hoover applauded the sale, declaring that "it is impossible for the Government to manage a competing business like shipping with anything like the success of a private individual."[13]

Not everyone in the administration agreed with him, however. In January 1927, when the Shipping Board considered whether it should replace ships removed from service, the War and Navy departments overrode the Commerce Department's objections to doing so. Instead, the armed services pushed through Congress the 1928 Jones-White Act to subsidize the construction of new ships. Hoover conceded that the merchant marine provided an essential resource for national defense, both in ships and men, but he preferred to keep ship ownership and operation private, subsidizing construction only to a limited extent and supporting operations through generous mail contracts. As an indirect way to help the industry, he suggested that all merchant marine sailors and officers be enrolled in the naval reserve, with a portion of their pay covered by the navy. That approach, he argued, would keep the merchant marine under private ownership and operation, while benefiting both shipping companies and the navy.[14]

The secretary's ingenious suggestion found no supporters, and the condition of the merchant marine remained troubled throughout Hoover's term. During 1926 and 1927, the total tonnage of ships registered under the American flag declined by 11 percent, continuing a drop that had been going on since the war. That shrinkage helps to explain the fact that American flag vessels carried only 31 percent of American overseas trade in 1926 to 1927, as compared with 35 percent the year before.[15] If any solution existed to the decline of the American merchant marine, aside from permanent federal subsidies, the Republican administrations had failed to find it.

IV

In contrast to the frustrations he experienced in regard to agriculture, the railroads, the coal industry, and the merchant marine, Hoover had reason to be optimistic about his plans for development of national waterways. Indeed, he argued that completion of a Mississippi River system linking the Great Lakes to the Gulf of Mexico and a St. Lawrence waterway connecting the Great Lakes to the Atlantic would bring immeasurable benefits to twenty states, mitigate the agricultural depression, and help the merchant marine. Two-thirds of the nine-thousand-mile Mississippi system, he estimated in 1926, had been opened to shippers, albeit in disconnected segments that prevented it from having its full economic impact. In addition, the administration would soon need to act on the pending joint Canadian-American engineering study of the St. Lawrence route. The president's endorsement of a $20 million appropriation for those projects, Hoover declared enthusiastically, promised "much relief . . . for our farmers."[16] (See Figure 14.3.)

During the summer of 1926, Hoover made a major speaking trip across the Midwest and West to popularize not merely his plans for the St. Lawrence and Mississippi but also the development of the Tennessee and Arkansas in the Southeast; the Rio Grande in the Southwest; and the Colorado, Columbia, and interior rivers in California. He promised that a national waterways program would provide benefits in navigation, flood control, irrigation, and hydroelectric power, and he urged local governments and private interests to get behind his vision. A properly planned national program, he estimated, would cost the United States approximately $100 million a year, two-thirds of which the government had already committed to uncoordinated projects. A modest increase for an integrated program would bring a "rich harvest in wealth and happiness to all of our people."[17]

Only New York State's proposal to widen and deepen the Erie Canal as a link between the Great Lakes and the Atlantic in preference to the St. Lawrence waterway failed to draw Hoover's support. When local advocates recommended a cross-Florida barge canal, improvement of the Intra-Coastal Waterway on the Atlantic and Gulf coasts, and development of the Cumberland River in Tennessee, he cheerfully added those projects to his list. Secretary of the Interior Hubert Work did not initially share his grand vision, but following a six-hour sales pitch from the secretary of commerce, Work became a convert.[18]

Then, just as Hoover's program seemed to be building unstoppable momentum, a serious obstacle appeared. Up to this point, Coolidge seems to have paid little attention to Hoover's waterways plans, but in late October 1926, he suddenly awoke. To a president who had once estimated that the government wasted $125,000 a year on pencils, the idea of adding $35 million to the annual budget for waterway development seemed horrifying. Moreover, the vast scope of Hoover's proposals would increase the power and patronage of the commerce secretary in virtually every state. On October 25, Coolidge fired off a telegram to Hoover complaining that the secretary was "proposing to make addresses and hold conferences on matters that come under the Interior Department." In icy tones, the president instructed him to "take no action of that kind until you have conferred with Secretary Work and me."[19]

Having specifically discussed his ideas with Secretary Work and made waterway speeches for several months, Hoover professed himself "mystified" by the telegram. So did Work, who speculated that Coolidge had misunderstood Work's "no comment" response to a reporter's question whether Hoover's speeches reflected administration policy. Responding to the president, Hoover evaded the question whether the administration should support waterways development and focused narrowly on the charge that he had encroached on Interior Department turf. That he denied. To Work, he contended that the president had endorsed all of the waterways proposals in annual messages.[20]

Although Coolidge never pressed the issue, Hoover was being disingenuous at best. The president had never approved any such broad plan as the secretary was proposing, nor would he ever do so. Indeed, no one in the administration had even looked at elements of Hoover's grand scheme—the cross-Florida canal, for example. Intoxicated by his vision, Hoover had promised too much. Moreover, he and Coolidge had a fundamental difference in outlook. Whereas Coolidge believed in minimal government and regarded retiring the national debt as "the very largest internal improvement . . . possible," Hoover embraced a more activist concept of the federal role and considered that investment in wisely planned public works would return dividends over time. But, as Coolidge reminded him, he did not control the administration's policy. As long as he remained only a cabinet member, he could not expect to implement his full plan.[21]

Looking to a future where he might be in control, Hoover returned to his theme in an address to the Mississippi Valley Association in November 1926. He proclaimed that "every important river, stream and lake presents some opportunity to increase our natural assets through the development of either navigation, power, reclamation, land protection or flood control—or all of them." Not only the Mississippi but also "practically every important river, stream and lake in our country" bore "possibilities of great wealth." The country could develop those resources "without national burden," and "we shall be negligent of our duty if we fail in their organization and development."[22]

Hoover's aggressive support of a national waterways policy instead of separate, local projects might invite the president's disapproval, but he was prepared to take the risk. With 1928 only two years away, he needed a program that might appeal to areas of the country where his agricultural policies had made him suspect, and he really believed that development of an integrated national transportation system would promote economic growth.

In the midst of Hoover's waterways campaign, the St. Lawrence project, a key element of his plan, met a minor obstruction when the Committee on

Resolutions of the Mississippi Valley Association unanimously endorsed the
Erie Canal route over the international St. Lawrence route. Western New
York State Congressman S. Wallace Dempsey engineered the coup, but his
victory proved fleeting. A few days later, a special board of army engineers
reported that, although the Erie Canal could be deepened and widened, the
project would cost American taxpayers an estimated $506 million, whereas
the St. Lawrence waterway would cost only about $173.5 million, of which
Canada would pay half. The cost disparity largely silenced advocates of the
"All American" route, and Hoover confidently endorsed the St. Lawrence
project to the president.[23]

Hoover continued to push the plan during 1927, but the Canadians, suspecting that the waterway would be expensive and bring few benefits to them,
stalled in negotiations for an enabling treaty. The two countries finally reached
agreement in July 1932, but the treaty fell into the political black hole at the
end of Hoover's presidential term. The Senate rejected it in March 1934.
Twenty years would pass before both governments approved the project.[24]

On the other hand, some of the difficulties that had prevented the passage
of the Swing-Johnson Bill to authorize a high dam on the Colorado disappeared in 1926. The original bill ran into opposition because it proposed to
build the dam through congressional appropriations, which meant that everyone in the country would be taxed to pay for it. In addition, Western utilities
opposed a requirement that electricity generated at the dam would be sold
only to municipalities. Secretary of the Interior Work removed the first objection by proposing to finance the dam with federal bonds to be retired through
the sale of water and power. He solved the second problem by suggesting that
Congress authorize the Interior Department to sell power generated at the
dam to public or private purchasers. Hoover had little enthusiasm for even
this limited application of the idea of public power but accepted it in the interest of finally securing agreement. Senator Johnson rejoiced at what he labeled
a "metamorphosis" in the administration's position.[25]

His elation proved slightly premature. On March 18, Secretary of the Treasury Andrew Mellon stalled work on the bill by announcing that he opposed
the use of federal bonds to finance dam construction. Johnson defied him and
persuaded the Senate irrigation committee to report the bill favorably in late
April, but shortage of time precluded its passage before adjournment. The
delay allowed other problems to crop up. Private power companies still hoped
to control the generation and distribution of power, and California Governor
Friend Richardson could not persuade the legislature to ratify the Colorado
Pact without a prior guarantee that a high dam would be built at Boulder
Canyon. Hoover also failed to reassure the Californians and found himself
obliged to spend much of the autumn trying to persuade the Upper Basin
states not to rescind their own ratifications and to accept California's reservation. He succeeded with most of them, but in February 1927, Utah canceled
its ratification. What was more, Senator Johnson failed to win Senate passage

of the Swing-Johnson Bill. With the whole project teetering on the brink of collapse, the governors of all seven states called an August conference to see what they could salvage.[26]

At the conference, five of the seven states expressed their willingness to proceed, but California and Arizona still disagreed about how to divide their share of the water. By November, Hoover had begun to wonder despairingly whether the federal government should "expend further time and money in connection with the project," and even Johnson feared that the obstacles had become "insuperable."[27]

Yet when Johnson introduced a slightly modified bill in December, the prospects for success had improved. The Mississippi River flood that spring had strengthened support in Congress for a dam on the Colorado to prevent a similar disaster, and that consensus eroded the Upper Basin states' negotiating position. A Boulder Canyon dam to provide flood control, if erected before all seven states ratified the Colorado Compact, might give California a preemptive claim to the stored water. That reality made the other states more willing to accept California's reservation. Johnson still gloomily predicted failure, but by mid-March 1928, he had won committee support and had the bill on the Senate floor.[28]

A week later, the House sweetened the deal for Arizona and Nevada by guaranteeing them a share of revenue from federally generated power in lieu of tax revenue from privately owned generators at the dam. The collapse on March 12 of the St. Francis dam, built by the city of Los Angeles, gave power company lobbyists a moment of hope that sentiment might turn against public power, but the disaster turned out to have little effect on support for the federal dam on the Colorado. Hoover, just beginning his presidential campaign, cautiously distanced himself from the issue by denying that he had personally reviewed and approved the engineering studies for the Boulder Canyon project. Yet President Coolidge, on the same day he declared the pending Mississippi flood control bill too expensive, announced his support for Swing-Johnson. With that endorsement, the House passed the bill on May 25, and Johnson won a guarantee that the Senate would vote on it in December when the congressional session resumed. By December 12, a power company lobbyist lamented that the car had "skidded out of control" and landed "more or less in the ditch." On December 14, the Senate passed the bill. A few days later, the president signed it, and the states fell into line, formally ratifying the seven-state compact during the spring of 1929. On June 25, 1929, Hoover, now president, had the satisfaction of proclaiming the Boulder Canyon Act in force.[29]

The same public-private power dispute that slowed resolution of the Colorado issue also raised tempers over the disposition of the Muscle Shoals facility on the Tennessee River in Alabama. During 1926, Senator George Norris, a fierce advocate of public control over the development of rivers, and Oscar Underwood, on behalf of private development, contended in the Senate for control of the site's future. Norris, raised on "a primitive Ohio farm," insisted that rivers must be harnessed to prevent floods, provide irrigation, and generate electricity to lighten "the drudgery of farms and urban homes, while revolutionizing the factories" for as many people as possible. Privatization of a site like Muscle Shoals, he proclaimed, would enable a privileged few to reap "unconscionable profit" from the "development of property which truly belongs to the American people." Hoover, speaking for private development, responded that "government operation of services for hire or the buying and selling of commodities is wasteful, incompetent, and inseparable from baneful political influences." With public power advocates contending passionately that publicly owned resources must benefit the whole people, and private-ownership supporters asserting equally fervently that public ownership would undermine initiative, free enterprise, competition, and progress, compromise seemed impossible.[30]

The bitter differences between public and private power advocates stalemated any decision on the future of Muscle Shoals before Underwood's retirement on March 4, 1927. During 1926, two new private bids to lease the property—one from the American Cyanamid Company that emphasized fertilizer production and a second from the Associated (Alabama) Power Company that concentrated on electrical power—further complicated the situation. An engineering committee chaired by General Edgar Jadwin of the Corps of Engineers found no objective reason for choosing one over the other. Then, to add to the confusion, two additional bids arrived. One, from the Farmers' Federated Fertilizer Corporation, a subsidiary of the Farm Bureau, stressed fertilizer production but offered to produce power as well. The last, a new offer from Henry Ford, promised only power production. When the Treasury Department's Income Tax Unit attempted to compare the four bids early in 1927, it concluded that the differences among the proposals made the task almost impossible. It reported, nevertheless, that strictly on the basis of value to the government, Associated Power offered the most. The report satisfied no one. Underwood objected to limiting the site to power production. Coolidge thought that it should be sold rather than leased. Norris believed it ought to remain under public control to stimulate regional development. Following Underwood's retirement, Norris pushed through a public power bill, but Coolidge vetoed it.[31]

Hoover did his best to steer clear of the Muscle Shoals imbroglio during 1926 and 1927, but he did not escape it during the 1928 campaign. In a speech at Elizabethton, Tennessee, not far from Muscle Shoals, he affirmed his belief that government should not compete with private business. Nevertheless, he continued, "There are local instances where the government must enter the business field as a byproduct [*sic*] of some great major purpose, such as improvement in navigation, flood control, scientific research, or national defense." Asked by a reporter whether Muscle Shoals counted as such a "local instance," Hoover replied, "You may say that means Muscle Shoals." The statement captured headlines across the country and delighted public power advocates. Hoover quickly announced, however, that the reporter had misunderstood his meaning. Because the government already owned the dams and nitrate factories, he explained, what he had intended to convey was that *after* the administration had fulfilled its promise that the facility would be "dedicated to agriculture for research purposes and development of fertilizers in addition to its national defense reserve," who should distribute "surplus power" would be open to discussion. He refused to say whether he thought the government should lease the site to a private company or create a government corporation for research and production of fertilizer.[32] The explanation, of course, clarified nothing. It did, however, highlight the contradiction between Hoover's belief in government support for the development of river systems and his enthusiasm for private enterprise. And it served a useful political purpose, inviting voters to believe, depending on their personal preferences, either that he supported or opposed public development of Muscle Shoals.

V

Although the Muscle Shoals issue remained unsettled after seven years, in his last years at Commerce, Hoover finally secured the regulatory authority he had long sought over radio and civil aviation. The White Bill, granting the Commerce Department authority to issue and review licenses to radio broadcasters, had bogged down in Congress in the last days of 1925, but in January 1926, Hoover testified before the House Committee on Merchant Marine and Fisheries in an effort to revive it. A slightly modified version of the bill passed the House on March 15. He failed, however, to instill a similar sense of urgency in the Senate, where the bill languished. Then, in mid-April, Judge James H. Wilkerson in Chicago ruled in the "Zenith decision" that the communications law of 1912 did not give the Commerce Department power to assign radio frequencies, even though a federal court in the District of Columbia had previously affirmed its authority under the same law. A few months later, a third federal judge, in Kansas City, further confused the issue by ruling that the terms of federal licenses bound broadcasters who accepted them, although those who did not accept licenses presumably remained free to do as they liked. Baffled by the contradictions among the rulings, Hoover asked Attorney General John G. Sargent for an opinion, only to be confused further. Sargent responded that broadcasters could choose any frequency they liked, except in the range between 600 and 1,600 meters, over which the government had authority. In July, Hoover threw up his hands and announced that the Commerce Department would no longer attempt to assign frequencies and would issue licenses to anyone who applied. The radio industry, he declared, had "grown up into a spoiled child" and had begun "'acting up before company.'"[33]

The evangelist Aimee Semple McPherson, one such "spoiled child," demanded that Hoover prevent his "minions of Satan" from limiting her broadcasts to a single frequency. Eventually, however, she gave in, and Hoover admitted that, despite his apprehensions, the number of new, "pirate" stations beginning operation and the number of stations switching wavelengths fell short of what he had feared. Nevertheless, he strongly urged Congress to give the Commerce Department regulatory powers before the situation spiraled completely out of control. By December, both houses had passed bills, but they disagreed whether the Commerce Department or a new, independent, regulatory agency would exercise the power. Not until February 1927 did both houses finally concur on the bill Hoover wanted. Jubilant, the secretary announced that the new law would make it possible to "clear up the chaos of interference and howls in radio reception." It created a new agency, the Federal Radio Commission (FRC), within the Commerce Department, and gave it power to review existing licenses and assign new licenses to all amateur and commercial broadcasters.[34]

Hoover, declared some overenthusiastic news reports, had won everything for which he had contended and would become the new "radio czar." The secretary, however, rejected the idea that he had received or ever wanted personal authority over radio. Licensing, he declared, was "a discretionary or semi-judicial authority which should not rest in any one person or under the control of any political group." Under the new law, the FRC would become an "entirely independent non-political" body with members chosen by the president from "different sections of the country," who would be instructed to base decisions solely "upon public interest." The commission would be housed within the Commerce Department to save money, but aside from using the department's building and staff, it would have complete independence.[35]

In practice, the new commission, hand-picked by Hoover and following standard Commerce Department practices, evinced less independence than many members of Congress and some broadcasters would have liked. Miffed, congressional leaders responded by delaying confirmation of the president's appointees and the appropriation of funds for the commission. Hoover persuaded the president to bypass Congress by making recess appointments, but the commission found its work cramped by a shortage of money and staff. Nevertheless, within a year, the new agency proved so useful that Congress renewed its authorization for a year in 1928, and then made it permanent in December 1929.[36]

The Radio Act of 1927 proved a milestone in American broadcasting in several ways. It specifically affirmed the right of free speech over the airwaves and denied either to the FRC or the broadcasting stations the power of censorship, except to forbid obscenity or profanity. It also attempted to prevent monopoly control over broadcasting, incorporating Hoover's cherished principle of periodic reviews of broadcast licenses. Yet in some ways, the law was outdated even as it passed. Its authors assumed that radio stations would continue to be, as they had been up to that time, mostly individually owned, with commercial-free, locally determined programming. The law mentioned radio networks ("chain broadcasting") and the sale of time for advertising only briefly and vaguely. The FRC would find that it had uncertain authority to deal with those complex and vexatious topics in coming years.[37]

Creation of the FRC emerged as one of Hoover's most lasting achievements during the Commerce years. It helped to clear up what he called the "chaos of howls" resulting from broadcast interference and established a high technical standard that made the United States a world leader in broadcasting. American dominance of the International Radiotelegraph Conference, which met at the Commerce Department in October 1927 with Hoover as chairman, confirmed that leadership. Yet, if Hoover's system promoted technical excellence, it also tended to favor the rich and powerful. The 1927 law upheld the important principle that the airwaves should be under "public ownership and regulation," but FRC licensing complexities tended to privilege wealthy broadcasters with advanced equipment and sophisticated legal staffs over shoestring operations.[38]

The decision to regulate radio came none too soon. Another, even more powerful, communication medium would soon make its debut. On April 7, 1927, Hoover became the first public official to appear on television, during a brief broadcast from his office transmitted live to a receiver at the American Telephone and Telegraph headquarters in New York. He characterized the event as "one of the most interesting events of this decade." Lou Hoover, who also appeared on camera, found the experience disconcerting. "You knew that a hundred people in New York" were "sitting at the other end of it and looking at you," she told Herbert and Allan, but all the speaker could see was the "squarish opening" of a head-sized box, black inside except for "a light that moved hurriedly about" at its back.[39]

The years 1926 to 1927 also brought the resolution of another issue that Hoover had long pursued—federal regulation of commercial aviation. A report from the president's Aircraft Board (the Morrow Committee) in the autumn of 1925 and another from a joint Commerce Department–American Engineering Council committee early in 1926 had suggested that European nations had pulled ahead of the United States in the development of commercial aviation and outlined the steps needed to catch up. Hoover's ideas strongly influenced both reports, and he attempted to increase the pressure on Congress to act in 1926. At his orders, the Bureau of Standards developed and published an aviation safety code, and he persuaded Daniel Guggenheim to establish a $2.5 million foundation for scientific research on aviation. On May 20, 1926, he succeeded, when Congress passed the Air Commerce Act embodying most of the Hoover-Morrow recommendations.[40]

Hoover moved quickly to take advantage of the new law, nominating William B. MacCracken as assistant secretary of commerce in charge of the new Aviation Division. At age thirty-seven, MacCracken had a distinguished record as an Army Air Corps flight instructor during World War I and, afterward, as chairman of the American Bar Association's Aviation Committee. Hoover might have preferred someone with more experience in aviation manufacturing, but MacCracken's practical knowledge, energy, and enthusiasm made him an obvious choice. Together, he and Hoover plunged zestfully into aviation development, steering mail contracts to airline companies, encouraging cities to develop airports, and pushing the development of radio beacons, lights, landing fields, and weather services for fliers. Within a year, they could point to four thousand miles of lighted and beaconed airways; within three years, that had increased to fourteen thousand miles. Commercial flights carried passengers only a few hundred miles during 1926; by 1929, better planes were flying over 25 million miles a year with far greater safety than previously.[41]

The Air Commerce Act and MacCracken's appointment launched commercial aviation in the United States. In August 1926, Hoover dispatched a Commerce Department official, Ernest Greenwood, on the second annual Ford Reliability Air Tour through ten Western states. Greenwood sent back glowing reports, not only about the Ford Trimotor on which he traveled, but also about the potential for air travel generally. Yet neither Greenwood's reports nor Hoover's aviation boosterism had the impact of two fortuitous events in the spring of 1927. The first of these involved the use of military airplanes to provide timely information for the coordination of rescue work during the Mississippi River flood. The greatest boost for aviation, however, came from Charles Lindbergh's successful solo flight across the Atlantic in May 1927. Always keenly sensitive to the value of publicity, Hoover immediately grasped what Lindbergh could do for commercial aviation in the United States. When President Coolidge asked him to join the war and navy secretaries and the postmaster general in organizing Lindbergh's official welcome in the nation's capital, he accepted eagerly.[42]

On the day of Lindbergh's reception, Hoover was away in Gulfport, Mississippi, dealing with flood relief. He joked to reporters that Lindbergh, used to flying alone, would not miss him. But before leaving for the South, he had arranged for the flier's arrival in Washington to be covered live on a nationwide radio broadcast, and he made sure that reporters understood the links between Lindbergh's flight and the value of airplanes to flood relief. Upon his return to Washington, he arranged for the flier to join him in a well-publicized conference about the future of commercial aviation. He posed for pictures with the aviator and thanked the Guggenheim Foundation for sponsoring a three-month tour that would take Lindbergh and his *Spirit of St. Louis* to all forty-eight states. Lindbergh's achievement, he emphasized in a press release, reflected "something besides courage and daring." Behind his exploit lay "a mastery of the art of aviation." Aviation's commercial future, rather than the romance of flying, preoccupied Hoover. He intended, so far as possible, to eliminate the danger and unpredictability of flying and to make it a routine, dependable, commercial activity. As an engineer and businessman, the technical achievement represented by Lindbergh's plane appealed to him more strongly than the flier's personal heroism.[43]

Highway transportation possessed at least as much economic importance as aviation, yet oddly, Hoover never lavished the same attention on highway development as he did on aviation. In a departure from his usual practice of writing speeches personally, he delegated drafting of his address to the 1924 automobile safety conference, as well as an article on a national highway system for the Hearst newspaper chain, to staff members. The 1924 and 1926 street and highway conferences over which he presided stressed driver safety over highway improvement and focused on such mundane matters as the adoption of uniform motor vehicle and driver licensing codes and standardization of regulations for the operation of motor vehicles among the states. At the March 1926 conference, Hoover stressed the importance of redesigning highways to safely handle the growing number of motor vehicles (he estimated their current number at 20 million). At neither meeting did he emphasize the economic value of highways for moving people and goods in the same way that he had stressed the potential of railroads, waterways, the merchant marine, and even aviation. He argued at the time and in his *Memoirs* that automobile accidents wasted human resources, but highways never became a significant element in his vision of a national transportation network.[44]

VI

Waste elimination, a dominant theme of Hoover's approach to highway safety, of course embodied a major aspect of Commerce Department policy in general. "The American standard of living," he liked to say, "is the product of high wages to producers and low prices to consumers. The road to national progress lies in increasing real wages through proportionately lower prices. The one and only way is to improve methods and processes and to eliminate waste." At every opportunity, Hoover continued to proclaim the department's achievements in promoting standardization and waste elimination, but by the end of 1926, he had begun to worry that the campaign had become "somewhat chaotic and [seemed] in many particulars to be losing rather than gaining ground." A Commerce Department memorandum warned that, because the program's impetus had come from the department rather than from the industries affected, it could lose momentum once Hoover left office. The memo recommended creation of a program that would both evaluate the effectiveness of standards and help businessmen understand that component standardization did not mean that all products with the same function must be identical. The authors also urged closer cooperation with other nations in promoting international standardization. And they warned that the American Engineering Standards Committee might, out of jealousy, attempt to subvert the departmental program.[45]

The engineers' challenge to the Commerce Department's standardization program revealed a major flaw in Hoover's approach to the policy. Although the engineers lauded simplification and standardization in principle, they objected to the government's dominant role in the movement. Hoover thought the criticism absurd. Had he not frequently proclaimed his personal commitment to industrial self-government? Had he not encouraged representatives of the industries concerned to draft their own codes? Dismissing the engineers' opposition as "purely jurisdictional," he proposed to get around them by setting up a businessmen's committee to raise a million dollars over the next five years. Using the fund, a "committee of responsible men" could take over the standardization program in the future.[46]

Alas, the businessmen he approached showed no interest. Not only had he overestimated industry's enthusiasm for his pet program, but he also had missed an opportunity to win the support of the engineers. He had to drop the committee plan. Without "a substantial assurance of money," he admitted, privatizing the simplification and standardization program would "amount to nothing more than the appointment of further committees." Years later, embittered by his 1932 defeat, he blamed opposition to standardization on a "conglomeration of professors and intellectuals tainted with mixed socialist, fascist, and antique ideas." In reality, the opposition came less from radicals than from business. Despite his efforts to foster cooperation between business and government, a substantial number of businessmen saw the simplification and standardization program not as their own but as a government program that they were under pressure to accept. Cooperation with the American Engineering Standards Committee might have offered a way around the dilemma, but Hoover proved unwilling to let the program out of his personal control.[47]

Hoover believed that the Better Homes in America organization, like the simplification and standardization program, represented values that should command broad support among Americans. A "detached house with at least some space around it," he declared, helped "to preserve family unity" and offered an opportunity for "home life on a higher plane which in the past has been possible only for those at least moderately well-to-do." But, as with simplification and standardization, Better Homes did not attract the support he anticipated. By 1926, it was running out of money. The Laura Spelman Rockefeller Fund, which had provided major grants for several years, declined to renew its support on the ground that the organization had failed to define its aims sharply. Hoover wrote a new grant application, laying out a three-year plan and asking for $75,000 for 1927, $50,000 for 1928, and $25,000 for 1929, with an optimistic assurance that the organization would supplement the grants from other sources as the Rockefeller contributions diminished. The Rockefellers went along but offered support for only two years and provided less money than Hoover had requested. Adding to their grants from other sources, most notably the American Relief Administration Children's Fund, Hoover kept the organization going through the Commerce years and his presidency as well, but his success was deceptive. Like the American Child Health Association and the simplification and standardization movement, Better Homes became more and more Hoover's personal project rather than developing the widespread public support and popularity for which he hoped.[48]

In addition to his work with Better Homes, Hoover also became honorary chairman of the National Housing Committee for Congested Areas, organized early in 1927 in New York City by August Heckscher, a retired mining executive and real estate investor known for his philanthropic work for slum children in New York. Heckscher proposed that, in areas where the city had condemned properties for street widening on the Lower East Side, his foundation would lease a portion of the land not needed for improvements and erect apartment buildings on it. The buildings would have "garden apartments" more open and airy than older New York tenements and would be leased to tenants for a modest rent—Heckscher suggested $8 a month. He envisioned finding "500 wealthy and public-spirited citizens in New York to promise a contribution of $100,000 each annually for five years" to fund the project. The idea appealed to Hoover, because it proposed to provide affordable urban housing for the poor and to do it entirely with private funds. Although city voters approved the plan in November 1927, however, Heckscher never found the investors he needed. Two cooperatives and two commercial firms planned buildings in 1928, but at most their projects would have housed less than two thousand families in a city of several million.[49]

VII

Projects such as Heckscher's appeared feasible amid the widespread belief that the good times of the mid-1920s would continue. A brief drop in the stock market in February 1926 seemed to confirm the wisdom of Hoover's warnings the previous autumn about overspeculation, but his optimism rebounded with the market. On the verge of launching his presidential campaign, he assured Americans that "good crops, steady employment at high wages, low commodity prices and stocks, high efficiency in production and transportation, and abundant capital at low rates of interest" signified continuing prosperity.[50]

Privately, he harbored doubts about real estate and stock speculation, overextension of installment buying, foreign monopoly controls over some raw materials, and American banks' investments in risky foreign loans. He realized that, despite improved collection and analysis of economic statistics, much of economic forecasting remained guesswork. The department had no adequate wage index, no confidence in the accuracy of farm price indexes, no certainty where the country stood in the business cycle, and no assurance that measures the administration had taken to moderate the cycle's fluctuations would prove effective.[51]

In March 1927, Hoover appointed a departmental committee to begin studying the interrelated issues of forecasting and economic management. That autumn, he asked the Carnegie and Rockefeller foundations to fund a major study of "the foundation of our prosperity and how to maintain it" that would follow up and extend the work of the Business Cycle Committee of 1923. In January 1928, he announced the formation of a committee of businessmen and economists to conduct the study, with the ubiquitous Edward Eyre Hunt as its secretary and the National Bureau of Economic Research carrying out the detailed research with the support of government agencies. Hoover chaired many of the committee's initial meetings, and when the presidential campaign drew him away, the business publisher Arch Shaw filled in for him. The committee published its two-volume report, *Recent Economic Changes in the United States*, the following year.[52]

Projecting a "tempered optimism," the report concluded that recent prosperity resulted from modestly rising incomes, stable or falling prices, increased worker productivity, improved consumer credit, and mass advertising. The growth of the consumer market and greater worker productivity, in turn, had encouraged business to increase investments and permitted it to raise wages. The report concluded that, for the period of the study (1922–29), a "sensitive contact" had been established between production and consumption that had resulted in an "equilibrium" in the economy. Sources of this balance included cooperation among business leaders and between business and the government, improved education, the rise of trade associations, the cooperation of labor in increasing productivity, and the restriction of immigration. On the whole, the committee believed that economic progress could be sustained, but they warned that doing so would require "hard, persistent, intelligent effort," and "a disposition in the several human parts to work in harmony."[53]

Although the general tone of the committee's report was optimistic, its experts pointed out a number of areas of uncertainty and concern. Several of those were certainly familiar to Hoover, including problems in agriculture, coal, railroads, and textiles, as well as overextension of consumer credit and stock market speculation. He also understood, as the committee noted, that management of the economy depended upon having complete and accurate statistics, but "conspicuous gaps and deficiencies" remained in both the collection and interpretation of such information. What Hoover may not have grasped fully, however, was a point made by the economist Frederick C. Mills, that the decade's combination of declining wholesale prices, increasing productivity, rising wages, and growing profits had "but few precedents in prewar experience." Perpetuating that felicitous and unusual balance would be essential to continuation of the rise in American standards of living on which Hoover was about to stake his political future.[54]

One of Hoover's principal goals as commerce secretary had been to "iron out" the fluctuations of the business cycle. He believed that the department's work in collecting statistical information and making it available to business, as well its fostering of cooperation among businesses, and among business, labor, and government, had gone far to achieve that goal. The eminent economist Wesley Mitchell, who examined the issue for *Recent Economic Changes*, felt less confident. Although he noted that cyclical fluctuations since 1921 had been relatively mild in comparison with prewar periods, Mitchell cautioned that the differences were slight and the current period too short for confident analysis. In the end, he concluded, "we can ascribe the mildness of recent fluctuations only in part to intelligent management."[55]

One tool of "intelligent management" favored by Hoover but never really tried during the 1920s was countercyclical spending on public works. The popularizers of the theory, William T. Foster and Waddill Catchings, proposed that some public works projects be deferred during prosperous times so that they could be used to relieve unemployment and stimulate the economy during a recession. Otto Mallery, an economist who had been championing the idea since the 1921 unemployment conference, dubbed it the "Prosperity Reserve." Bills embodying the proposal were introduced at almost every session of Congress after 1921 but never went anywhere until 1928, when Senator Wesley Jones, chairman of the Senate Commerce Committee, sponsored a measure to double public works expenditures whenever the volume of general construction in the United States fell by 20 percent or more over any three-month period. The Jones Bill soon became the center of a lively debate. Labor groups proposed that a 10 percent drop in construction should initiate countercyclical spending; Hoover argued that the economy could absorb a 10 percent reduction without going into recession.[56]

Supporters of the countercyclical principle also disagreed about what index should trigger spending: should it be construction, general unemployment, or some broader measure of business activity? Wesley Mitchell, in a "prefatory note" to a book by Mallery, endorsed the general concept of the "prosperity reserve" but raised serious questions about who would fund and administer it and, more broadly, whether public works spending alone would be sufficient to combat a depression. With such divisions even among supporters of the plan, the Jones Bill never made it out of the Senate. Hoover remained a supporter of the concept, however, and in November 1928, just after the election, he endorsed a proposal by Governor Ralph O. Brewster of Maine calling for governments at various levels to create a $3 billion reserve to combat unemployment. That nebulous idea also went nowhere.[57]

VIII

Hoover also viewed the conservation of resources as a way to sustain prosperity. It seemed to him, he remarked at an Oil Conservation Board meeting in early 1926, "that the case is much the same in all of our natural resources, all of our materials, that we must, as the population increases and the standard of living rises, secure a better utilization of the materials that we have at our disposal." But it was difficult to persuade the public to worry about distant shortages in a period of oil surplus. The board's report, which Hoover said he had "sat up nights" drafting, contended that, without conservation measures and the introduction of new technologies, proven reserves in the

United States would last no more than six years. It urged cooperation among oil companies to curtail current production. In October 1926, Hoover went so far as to suggest that it might be desirable to suspend the antitrust laws to permit competing companies to establish common drilling policies. But when an entrepreneur pointed out that an efficient way to achieve conservation would be to merge the Union, Texas, and Gulf Oil companies into a single corporation, Hoover quickly backtracked. "Slower steps," he said, would be preferable "in these troublesome times." Secretary Mellon added that, in his opinion, the states, not the federal government, should deal with overproduction.[58]

"The chief cause of overproduction is overcompetition," said Secretary of the Interior Work in regard to oil. Hoover had been saying exactly the same thing for years about agriculture and soft coal, but defining the problem did not lead to a solution. For agriculture, he proposed marketing cooperatives; for coal, consolidation; for oil, collaborative drilling arrangements; but his ideas did not lead to action. The logic of his position seemed to support radical modification of the antitrust laws to permit cartelization, but he remained unwilling to go that far. Instead, he continued to believe that voluntary cooperation among industries, combined with more sophisticated economic analysis by the Justice Department's antitrust division, would suffice to achieve his goals.[59]

IX

Although management and development of the domestic economy dominated Hoover's activities during the Commerce years, he also paid close attention to foreign economic relations, including the war debt question. By 1926, the United States had reached agreements drastically cutting interest rates and extending payment periods on the amounts owed by the European nations from the wartime and postwar period. France remained the last significant holdout. The French reluctantly signed the Mellon-Bérenger agreement on April 29, 1926, but, dissatisfied with the agreement's failure to tie French obligations directly to the payment of German reparations, refused to ratify it. French resistance to settlement kept the debt issue alive in the United States. A few people, like Congressman A. Piatt Andrew of Massachusetts, argued that the United States should cancel all the debts, but Hoover rejected that idea. Since, according to Commerce Department calculations, agreements negotiated through 1926 forgave between 35 and 81 percent of the various European countries' debts to the United States, with France and Italy benefiting the most, Hoover saw no justification for further concessions. He continued to believe that the future stability of the international economic system required the debtors to pay as much as they were able. In any case, the majority in Congress opposed further concessions.[60]

When the congressional authorization for the World War Foreign Debt Commission expired on February 9, 1927, negotiating liberalized debt settlements became even more difficult. The first agreements had departed from congressional instructions, but at least they had the cover of being negotiated by the debt commission. A new agreement, outside that framework, would have been scrutinized minutely by Congress and would have stood a good chance of being nitpicked to death. Facing that reality and the imminent maturation of the $400 million war stocks debt on August 1, 1929, the French reluctantly ratified the Mellon-Bérenger agreement. For better or worse, the debt commission's capacity-to-pay formula controlled American debt policy until the adoption of the Young Plan later in 1929 and President Hoover's debt moratorium in 1931.[61]

From a purely economic point of view, Hoover was correct in arguing that an international system in which nations acknowledged and paid their debts would promote stability and growth. He also asserted justifiably that the debt agreements that he helped to design and negotiate in the 1920s provided terms well within the capacity of the debtors to pay. But, as Owen Young pointed out, the American policy failed to deal with the conundrum of German reparations. Although the Dawes Plan, by clearing the way for a large American loan to Germany, reopened a trickle of reparations payments to the Allies, it failed to resolve the underlying problem—that the Germans did not accept the legitimacy of reparations and that the Allies would only pay the United States if the Germans paid first. Unless someone could propose "a program to fix and liquidate the reparations obligations of Germany," Young argued, European economic stability would remain elusive.[62]

The American government, of course, denied any responsibility for reparations, but it insisted on payment of the Allied war debts, albeit at greatly reduced rates. The British and French, in turn, felt that the American demand justified their insistence on German reparations payments. The Dawes Plan tacitly recognized the link between reparations and debt payments by attempting to restart reparations payments, but it underestimated German opposition to paying. Instead of investing the flood of foreign loans that poured into Germany after 1924 in the production of export products to generate revenue with which to pay reparations, the Germans used the money primarily for current expenses. Their foot-dragging on reparations deprived the British and French of the easy income on which they had counted to make their payments to the Americans. In both cases—debts and reparations—the agreements negotiated in the mid-1920s made payment economically feasible, but domestic public opinion prevented a resolution of the issue. The American public demanded payment of the debts; the British and French publics accepted the debt obligation only if the Germans paid reparations; the Germans rejected the validity of the reparations claims.

Leaders on both sides of the Atlantic realized that the debt-reparations impasse had inhibited the development of a stable international economic and political order, but no one could figure out how to escape the political pressure that prevented a resolution. Instead, they each tried to shift the blame to someone else. The Germans blamed the British and French for imposing an unjust reparations system. The French blamed "Uncle Shylock" for insisting on the payment of war debts that should have been forgiven. The British seized on John Maynard Keynes's dubious "circular flow of paper" theory to contend that American bankers were perpetuating the system by lending the Germans the money with which they allegedly paid reparations that, in turn, enabled the British and French to make debt payments. The Americans blamed the British and French for imposing reparations in the first place and contended virtuously that although they had no part in creating the situation, they had cooperated in trying to resolve it in the Dawes Plan. Each country's policy thus remained the prisoner of its domestic political pressures.[63]

Some Americans, and a number of Europeans, argued that high American tariffs prevented the European nations from earning the money needed to pay reparations and the debts. "I am sincerely troubled," wrote Owen Young, "by our national program, which is demanding amounts from our debtors up to the breaking point, and at the same time excluding their goods from our American markets." Economist James Harvey Rogers, in the chapter of *Recent Economic Changes* dealing with foreign trade, accepted Hoover's argument that foreign purchasers of American goods had sustained their buying power through "the steady growth of our tourists' expenditures," but Rogers doubted that invisible exchange alone accounted for continuing foreign purchases of American goods. Rather, those purchases depended upon foreign borrowing in the United States. Over time, he warned, the "heavy and rapidly increasing payments required of foreigners [as a result of this borrowing], combined with the maintenance our high tariff policy," created a dangerous and potentially unstable situation.[64]

Hoover rejected the charge that protective tariffs barred foreign imports, and the statistics support his position. Even in the recession year 1921, the value of American exports to Britain, France, and Germany exceeded the levels in 1913, and exports held steady throughout the decade, despite the adoption of the Fordney-McCumber Tariff in 1922. The value of imports from France surpassed the 1913 level in 1921 and remained above that level throughout the decade. The value of imports from Britain exceeded the prewar level in 1922 and also stayed above it for the remainder of the period. German exports to the United States took longer to recover from the war, and their value did not exceed the 1913 level until 1926, but thereafter the flow of products from Germany continued to increase throughout the remainder of the decade.[65]

Modern statistics also support Hoover's argument that "invisible exchange" (tourist spending, immigrant remittances, etc.) more than offset the American commodity trade surplus. Between 1921 and 1929, the commodity trade surplus exceeded the invisibles only twice, in 1922 and 1924.[66]

Such statistics do not tell the whole story, however. The Fordney Tariff, which taxed manufactured imports more heavily than raw materials, helped American manufacturers and stimulated the shift in exports from 46 percent

finished and semifinished goods in 1922 to 63 percent finished and semifinished goods by 1929. In the same period, the total American share of world
exports increased from 12.4 to 16.0 percent. Although part of this growth
resulted from expansion of world markets, it also seems clear that the American share of those markets increased at the expense of competitors, including Britain and Germany. Moreover, American companies increasingly scaled
foreign tariff walls by establishing branches of American companies in other
countries. The tariff, plus efficient, low-cost American mass production,
writes historian Frank Costigliola, "forced much of the world to become hew-
ers of wood and drawers of water for the American industrial machine."[67]

Lowering the tariff would have made it slightly easier for the Europeans
to pay debts and reparations, but the near self-sufficiency of the American
economy limited marketing opportunities even in the absence of other barriers. Undoubtedly, the United States could have done more to open its markets
and otherwise make it easier for the Europeans to repay their obligations,
but doing so would have required a revolutionary transformation in the way
Americans, including Hoover, saw the world. Entirely aside from Hoover's
conviction that restoration of international economic stability required the
payment of debts, Americans could see no reason to throw open their domestic market and jeopardize the prosperity that good fortune and hard work had
brought them. As Hoover saw it, America's economic position in the world
remained tenuous. He was uncertain "whether, with a stabilized Europe, we
can continue successfully to hold our own share in the growth of the world's
trade in competitive goods."[68] In the face of that question, he favored aggressive promotion of overseas opportunities but caution about entering into
political or economic cooperation with other nations.

The underdog mentality that suffused Hoover's policy particularly influenced his approach to the question of foreign monopolies over raw materials
important to American industry, of which rubber provided the most salient
example. On December 9, 1925, the price of raw rubber reached a little over
$1.09 per pound on the New York spot market. Although most rubber con-
sumers bought their supplies under long-term contracts where prices had
been set months before and hence never paid anything like $1.09 a pound,
Hoover feared that the spot market betokened a future rise in all prices. On
December 10, therefore, he issued a statement calling on American consumers and producers to conserve and recycle rubber as much as possible. Within
a week, the price per pound had fallen to 90 cents on the spot market, and by
the end of February 1926, it had dropped to 51 cents. Claiming a 25 percent
drop in tire consumption in the six months through April 1926, Hoover confidently declared the conservation policy a success.[69]

Whether his policy actually had any effect on rubber use cannot be determined with certainty, but his aggressive stance definitely aroused enormous
resentment in Britain and some skepticism in the United States. Sir Robert
Horne, a former Chancellor of the Exchequer, argued in an influential *New*

York Times article that the Stevenson Plan had actually benefited American companies in the long run by preventing a collapse of rubber prices that would have resulted in the abandonment of many plantations just as the American demand for rubber was rising. The plan, British Ambassador Sir Esmé Howard agreed, helped American consumers by stabilizing prices. In the United States, the *Nation* and a vice president of the National City Bank of New York made similar arguments. Democratic Congressman Ashton C. Shallenberger of Nebraska, noting the large difference between rubber prices on the spot market and the actual price paid by importers with long-term contracts, accused Hoover of concocting a crisis where none existed in order to benefit rubber speculators. In the State Department, William Castle, although an admirer of Hoover, suggested that the secretary of commerce, seeking power and publicity, had exaggerated the issue "out of all semblance of its proper place in the scheme of things."[70]

Hoover's overreaction to the Stevenson Plan resulted in part from his feeling that rubber policy represented one aspect of a British program to weaken the United States and restore their prewar economic dominance. British loans to the Franco-German potash producers and to the Brazilian government's coffee monopoly, he feared, pointed in the same direction. Made suspicious of British intentions by wartime experiences, he exaggerated the immediate impact of the Stevenson Plan on the American economy and advocated a confrontational response. A British decision in late April to continue controls on sales, which Hoover countered with a call to extend and intensify the conservation program, implied an escalation of Anglo-American conflict. Alarmed at the possibility of a trade war, several American rubber purchasers urged accommodation with the British producers.[71]

Hoover flatly rejected that approach. Representatives of the American rubber companies had negotiated price agreements with the British producers in 1923 and again in late 1925, he told Edgar Rickard, and the British had broken their word both times. Moreover, he argued in testimony before the House Committee on Interstate and Foreign Commerce, the rubber monopoly presented only the most serious example of a much larger problem. Eight countries in addition to England, he alleged, had recently instituted government-controlled monopolies over products the United States did not produce, and up to seventy other countries might do likewise if the British succeeded. Americans would pay $1.2 billion in 1926 for monopoly-controlled products, he estimated, and that cost would be from $500 million to $800 million more than it should be in an open market. The Commerce Department had already instituted a policy of discouraging private loans to those monopolies, launched a search for alternative sources of their products, and fostered campaigns to promote economy in the use of such imported products, he reported, and he recommended that the committee look into further actions. But he warned against official retaliation, which could lead to economic warfare. Informal antimonopoly policies, which the rubber conservation campaign had shown to be effective, would be preferable, he and the committee ultimately agreed.[72]

During 1927, the Commerce Department continued its antimonopoly campaign, and Hoover recommended the passage of an amendment to the Webb-Pomerene Act that would permit the organization of buying consortiums for monopoly-produced foreign goods. The threat proved unnecessary, however. Although the British cut rubber shipments twice during the year, the price of rubber on world markets remained stable or even fell a little. In April 1928, the British government announced that it would terminate the Stevenson Plan on November 1.[73]

The British announcement came at an ideal moment for Hoover's presidential campaign, and he happily took credit for the outcome. But the reality was more complicated. As the baffled General Motors executive John J. Raskob put it in March 1928, "The rubber market seems pretty well shot to pieces and no one seems to understand the cause." Almost certainly, a 50 percent increase in world rubber production resulting from new Dutch plantations in the East Indies and the reluctance of the Dutch producers to accept sales restrictions played greater roles than Hoover's conservation campaign in stabilizing world prices. In addition, the introduction of fabric-belted tires in the United States greatly improved tire mileage and helped to offset increases in the number of vehicles and miles traveled per year. But when Hoover recalled the episode years later, he overlooked the technological advances and remembered the conservation program as more important than the increase of Dutch production.[74] As in other cases during these years, faith in the efficacy of voluntary action was fundamental to his political philosophy.

The great defect of American international economic policy in the 1920s, modern economic historians have suggested, was that American leaders failed to recognize the degree to which the United States had become the dominant economic power in the world system and rejected the role of international balancer and stabilizer that Great Britain had exercised during much of the nineteenth century. An alternative possibility of stabilization through international action vanished with the failure of the World Economic Conference in Geneva in May 1927. Summoned by the League of Nations at the instance of the British and French, the conference aspired to expand trade to ease the problems associated with the return to the gold standard and to draw the Soviet Union into the world economic system. The Americans agreed to participate but, fearful of entanglement in European problems, sent only an unofficial delegation led by Hoover's friend, the Los Angeles banker Henry M. Robinson. In the meetings, all the delegates proved unimaginative and timid. The American delegates resisted European efforts to discuss war debts, reparations, immigration, and the American tariff, and the British, French, and Americans joined forces to reject recognition or loans for the Soviet Union. The Americans won an endorsement of unconditional most-favored-nation tariffs, but no one offered actual reductions, and the meeting adjourned with all the old disagreements and conflicts unresolved.[75]

Hoover shared the defensive, suspicious attitude that defined American policy at Geneva. Even as late as 1928, he argued that when European industries had begun "getting on their feet again" in the early 1920s, they had threatened to squeeze American goods out of European markets and made "serious inroads on American trade everywhere." A nationalist to the core, he designed his policies to protect and expand American interests rather than to strengthen and stabilize the international economic system. Foreign trade, he argued, created an outlet for surplus production and "a wider range of customers" for American businesses, thus providing "greater stability in production and greater security to the workers." His comments greatly understated the degree to which American business's role in the world had been transformed during the decade. Between 1919 and 1929, American businesses had moved into more countries, owned more facilities in those countries, made or extracted more products in their facilities, integrated their overseas operations more completely, and diversified operations on a worldwide basis. Around the world, governments had grown concerned about the "American invasion" and had begun to adopt measures to restrict American ownership and control of their companies. American-controlled multinational enterprises might account for only 7 percent of gross national product—the same percentage as in 1914—but that was 7 percent of a vastly expanded economy. Both industrially and financially, the United States now dominated the world economically. Although far ahead of most members of the Harding and Coolidge administrations in his awareness of the global economic situation, Hoover still found it difficult to see foreign trade and investments as anything more than a useful adjunct to the domestic economy.[76] The possibility that such power might carry a responsibility to manage the international economic system no more occurred to him than it did to his fellow countrymen.

X

On the domestic side, Hoover went along generally with the Republican drive to reduce overall tax rates, eliminate wartime excess profits taxes, and reduce surtaxes on high incomes. Like Secretary of the Treasury Andrew Mellon, he thought that high taxes discouraged private initiative and fostered undesirable government growth. But believing that the government had an important role to play in financing capital improvements to waterways and other elements of the infrastructure, he would have reduced income and corporate tax rates less than Mellon and replaced some of the revenue lost by raising the inheritance tax. That tax, he believed, had an important social function of curtailing the accumulation of money and power in a few hands. On that issue, he was overruled first by Harding and then Coolidge, neither of whom had an equally activist conception of government.[77]

Hoover also failed to moderate the easy-money policy followed by the Federal Reserve during most of the 1920s. But in truth, he felt somewhat ambivalent on this issue. Although, as he argued in 1925, low interest rates fueled stock market speculation, cheap money also enabled businesses to borrow to expand, helped farmers to pay their debts, and made it easier for foreigners to float loans in the United States to buy American products. Indeed, Hoover fought for inclusion of terms in foreign loan contracts requiring the recipients to buy American and employ American firms. Hoover, like Mellon and Benjamin Strong of the New York Federal Reserve Bank, also regarded low interest rates as desirable in order to attract American capital to Europe, thus stabilizing European economies and supporting the gold standard. By 1927, however, Hoover had come to believe that the importance of moderating the stock market boom justified a modest rate increase, even at some sacrifice of other goals.[78]

Benjamin Strong disagreed with him. During most of the 1920s, the Federal Reserve Board had allowed Strong to handle relationships with the European Central banks, which he normally did during summer trips to Europe. In the spring of 1927, however, Strong had been in Colorado for treatment of tuberculosis, and he did not feel well enough to travel to Europe. Instead, he invited the European central bankers—Montagu Norman of the Bank of England, Hjalmar Schacht of the German Reichsbank, and Émile Moreau of the Banque de France—to meet him at the Long Island summer home of Ogden Mills, undersecretary of the treasury. Moreau, who spoke no English, sent his deputy, Charles Rist, in his place.[79]

Like Hoover, Strong worried about stock market speculation, but he felt more concerned about the situation in Europe, where the British had set the exchange rate between the pound and gold much too high, and the French had set the exchange rate between the franc and gold much too low. This situation made French goods unnaturally cheap on the world market and British goods excessively expensive, with the result that the French had accumulated huge credit reserves, and the British faced a serious credit drain. Until a permanent solution to this problem could be found, Strong believed that the United States should keep its interest rates low to push American capital toward Europe. In his view, a recent slowdown in the American economy accompanied by falling prices made such a move safe, although a faction on the Federal Reserve Board led by Hoover's ally, Adolph Miller, disagreed.[80]

During secret meetings at Mills's estate in early July, Montagu Norman emphasized that British gold reserves had fallen so low that the country might have to go off the gold standard. He feared that devaluing the pound, an obvious option, would set off an economic panic that might have catastrophic results internationally. No one had a good solution for the problem, but Strong resolved to at least buy time by cutting American interest rates. A few days after the bankers left the United States, the New York Federal Reserve Bank and eight other reserve banks announced an interest rate reduction from

4 to 3.5 percent. Four other reserve banks, in Chicago, San Francisco, Minneapolis, and Philadelphia, refused to go along, arguing that the rate cut would foster stock speculation.[81]

Hoover, in the South working on flood relief when Strong announced the interest rate cut, submitted an angry memorandum to the Federal Reserve Board following his return to Washington in August. Easy credit would not solve European problems, he wrote, and it could "land us on the shores of depression." Adolph Miller, also out of town when the decision was made, agreed with his neighbor, but neither of them could persuade the Federal Reserve Board to overrule the individual banks that had chosen to reduce rates. Nor would President Coolidge or Secretary Mellon intervene. In 1925, Strong had gambled that an interest rate cut would not set off an uncontrollable stock market climb. He had won that time, but this time he lost. By the end of the year, the market had risen over 20 percent, and the great market bubble of 1928 had begun to grow.[82]

Despite his concern about stock market speculation, Hoover put on a smiling face for the beginning of his presidential campaign. Throughout the economy, he declared in a New Year's Day press release, the "forces of stability" appeared to be "dominant in the business world." Even in agriculture, excellent harvests had brought prices about 39 percent above prewar levels. Elsewhere, unemployment had fallen, inventories were down, and although wholesale prices of manufactured goods had fallen slightly, companies had been able to keep wages up through greater efficiency. Except in the bituminous coal fields, labor and management seemed to be at peace. Outside the United States, he discerned a situation more peaceful than at any time since the end of the war and a general recovery of "economic strength and buying power."[83]

The press release's boilerplate concealed a number of problems that Hoover knew perfectly well had not been solved. Agriculture, coal, the merchant marine, and a number of other areas of the economy remained depressed, and the international situation looked less encouraging on closer inspection than the press release suggested. Yet despite the trouble spots, Hoover felt confident that he had built a solid basis for managing the economy. The Commerce Department's collection and dissemination of statistical information, as well as its close cooperation with trade associations, he believed, had "erected a strong barrier against booms and slumps" by empowering businesses to erect "safeguards against the approach of speculative periods or the approach of depressions." Above all, as he accepted the Republican presidential nomination shortly before his fifty-fourth birthday, Hoover felt the shackles that had prevented him from giving full rein to his energy and ideas for improving American life falling away. No longer limited to being "Secretary of Commerce and undersecretary of everything else," he now had an opportunity to set the agenda and direct policy.[84]

CHAPTER 20

The Mississippi River and New England Floods of 1927

The time had come, Hoover told the annual meeting of the Mississippi Valley Association in St. Louis on November 22, 1926, to approach the development of the Mississippi River and its tributaries in a totally new way. The federal government should stop thinking of "single power sites, single land projects, single navigation improvements, or local flood controls," and instead develop "large interconnected systems of trunk lines from [the] seaboard with great feeders from our lateral rivers." Considered that way, the Mississippi River system could become a nine-thousand-mile transportation network opening the markets of the world to Midwestern farmers and businessmen. For an investment of $20 million a year over the next six years in addition to the $10 million a year already being spent by the federal government, Hoover estimated, the project would bring a "rich harvest of wealth and happiness to all of our people."[1]

I

But long before Congress could consider Hoover's proposal, a biblical deluge began in the Mississippi Valley. In the week before Christmas of 1926, more than seven inches of rain fell in Nashville, and almost nine inches in Johnsonville, Tennessee. By the first of the year, the Cumberland River at Nashville had surged sixteen feet over flood stage. Two days later, the Tennessee River swept by Johnsonville at ten feet over flood stage, and on January 7, the Ohio River at Cairo rose four feet over flood stage. The next day, the Mississippi at New Madrid began to edge above flood level.[2]

Meanwhile, to the south, storms inundated the Arkansas, Red River, and Lower Mississippi valleys. During that tempestuous week before Christmas, more than six and a half inches of rain fell at places as widely separated as Memphis; Little Rock; and Jefferson, Texas. By January 21, the Mississippi had passed flood stage at Arkansas City, Yazoo City, and Vicksburg.[3]

And then things got worse. Between December 18 and April 29, Bowling Green, Kentucky, received almost thirty-one inches of rain; Cairo got more than twenty-nine inches; Cape Girardeau, Missouri, over twenty-seven inches; Yankton, South Dakota, more than ten inches; Danville, Arkansas, almost forty inches; Monroe, Louisiana, almost forty-five inches; Vicksburg thirty-six inches; and New Orleans almost thirty-five inches. As the Mississippi's tributaries rose, the main river did as well, reaching flood stage at New Madrid, just south of the confluence with the Ohio River, on January 8. Thereafter, a series of flood crests began moving south, rising and falling somewhat depending on what happened along the tributaries, but even before the major crest developed, by the beginning of April, the river had reached or passed flood level pretty much all the way from the Kentucky-Tennessee border to New Orleans.[4] In four months, the region had received up to double a year's normal rainfall, often in brief but intense downpours that ran off the saturated ground rather than sinking in.

People along the Mississippi had seen many floods before. New Orleans built its first levee to protect the city in 1717, and in the mid-nineteenth century, the Army Corps of Engineers began planning a levee system all along the lower river. In 1879, Congress created the Mississippi River Commission, which, over the next forty-seven years, spent almost $229 million, mostly on levees. Nevertheless, despite the barriers, which reached as high as forty feet in some places, eight floods inundated the valley between 1882 and 1922. Some dissenters had begun to question the levees-only approach by the 1920s, but the work went forward steadily, and the 1926 report by the chief of engineers, Major General Edgar Jadwin, promised confidently that the levees would "prevent the destructive effects of floods."[5]

On Good Friday, April 15, 1927, the river proved Jadwin wrong, bursting through the levee at Walnut Bend, Missouri, 278 miles below Cairo. The next day, 1,200 feet of levee at Dorena, Missouri, collapsed and almost instantly flooded 175,000 acres of farmland. Three days later, a mile of levee collapsed at New Madrid, inundating a million acres, and on the April 21, another mile-wide "crevasse" opened in the levee at Mounds Landing, Mississippi. A wall of water reported to be one hundred feet high roared through the opening, scouring out a channel nearly a hundred feet deep and spreading out over the surrounding delta for ten days. More than 140 other levee breaks followed over the next month and a half. The Mounds Landing crevasse alone flooded an area a hundred miles long and fifty miles wide, with water up to twenty feet in depth, yet the resulting lake constituted only a small part of the thousand-mile-long, fifty-mile-wide, yellow-brown sea that submerged parts of seven states.[6]

By the third week of April, the river had killed more than two hundred people, flooded over 3 million acres of farmland, and submerged dozens of towns and cities. (See Figure 21.2.) The scope of the disaster overwhelmed state and local resources, and governors and members of Congress implored the president for help. No special federal agency yet existed to cope with such emergencies, and indeed, Americans had only begun to conceive of direct federal disaster relief. Traditionally, private citizens and businesses either survived or died without outside help or with the limited assistance of volunteer organizations and local governments. But the scope of the Mississippi flood, reported daily by newspapers, magazines, radio, and newsreels, galvanized a national demand for action. Coolidge responded on April 22 by appointing a special cabinet-level committee chaired by Hoover to coordinate relief with the Red Cross. He authorized Hoover to command whatever federal agencies or resources he needed to meet the emergency. As the man who had fed Belgium during the war and much of Europe after it, Hoover had unique experience with collecting and distributing resources over huge areas under difficult conditions.[7]

In a more limited disaster, the Red Cross would probably have led the relief effort, but this catastrophe exceeded its resources. Founded by the noted Civil War nurse Clara Barton in 1881 and incorporated by Act of Congress in 1900, the Red Cross had first assisted the victims of Michigan forest fires in 1881 and the Johnstown Flood in 1889. In 1913, Ernest P. Bicknell led its first major relief program, spending some $3 million to assist the survivors of a flood in the Ohio Valley. By the time the United States entered World War I in 1917, the organization had amassed a $2 million endowment and had annual revenues of nearly $500,000. During the war, generous donations and eager volunteers permitted it to provide hospitals for wounded soldiers near the front lines and to help families keep in touch with their overseas sons during the war. At war's end, however, contributions and membership dropped off sharply, and the organization seemed to lose its sense of mission. Members of Congress and the Hearst press charged it with wasteful administrative spending and bureaucratic insensitivity to real need. Former Interior Secretary John Barton Payne assumed the executive directorship in 1922 to make reforms. Red Cross supporters welcomed his administrative improvements, but many opposed his decision to shift resources away from emergency relief to social welfare activities. By September 1926, when a major hurricane killed 327 people and did millions of dollars worth of damage in South Florida, the Red Cross's revenue had fallen even from immediate postwar levels, and membership had also declined. The Florida disaster drained already depleted emergency funds and left the organization weakened just as the next spring's Mississippi flood posed its greatest challenge yet.[8]

When the flood began, Payne was in Europe. The acting chairman of the Red Cross, James L. Fieser, a trained social worker, had gained practical relief experience as coordinator for the city of Columbus during the 1913 Ohio River flood. He had organized the first Red Cross chapter in Columbus in 1917, rose during the war to become national director of civilian relief, and then became vice chairman of domestic operations in 1922. Fieser understood immediately that the Mississippi flood would overtax Red Cross resources. He thought the organization could handle the situation in Illinois, Kentucky, Missouri, and Tennessee, but rescuing, feeding, and housing 300,000 to 500,000 refugees on the lower Mississippi were beyond its capacity. Accordingly, he welcomed federal assistance and immediately formed a close partnership with Hoover. Experienced, practical, energetic, and impatient with red tape, Fieser exemplified exactly the qualities that Hoover had sought in his American Relief Administration workers after the war.[9]

II

When Hoover arrived in Memphis on April 23, he found the main crest of the flood just passing the city. He immediately ordered the navy, coast guard, and lighthouse service to round up every ship capable of navigating the river, load them up with small boats with outboard motors, and dispatch them to Vicksburg for rescue work. When those proved inadequate, he asked sawmills along the river to slap together rough skiffs, rented outboard motors from the manufacturers, and sent that fleet out as well. By the beginning of May, just a week after he began, Hoover commanded an armada of over three hundred towboats and barges, almost five hundred small boats, and twenty-seven airplanes, all linked together by thirty radio sets. The fleet fanned out over the flooded area, rescuing people and livestock from roofs, trees, and patches of high ground and bringing them to rapidly growing refugee camps. The process became so efficient that not only did it rescue more than 300,000 people, but by early May, as the flood crest reached Louisiana and began to surge into the Atchafalaya Basin, the rescuers also could actually reach people before the water arrived and offer them the opportunity to move to preprepared camps.[10]

The Red Cross had begun building camps to house refugees in Arkansas in March, but with seventy thousand people already displaced before the major levee breaks of mid-April, their resources had nearly run out. On the afternoon of April 22, following the cabinet meeting that named Hoover to lead the relief effort, the secretary and other members of the cabinet met with Red Cross leaders. The group quickly agreed to use the Red Cross's fund-raising machinery to appeal for $5 million to fund initial phases of the program. Within a week, as they realized that would not be nearly enough, they doubled the appeal, eventually raising some $17 million. Following the meeting, Hoover, Fieser, and General Jadwin boarded a special Illinois Central train and set out on an overnight trip to Memphis, where Henry Baker, the local Red Cross relief director, had set up a headquarters.[11]

Baker, an able and dedicated man, found himself overwhelmed. Information, requests for help, and supplies were pouring in. Baker, at first, tried to handle it all personally. Hoover immediately began assembling an organization to help him. On April 24, he moved the headquarters from an office building to a nearby Ford assembly plant, which offered room to sort and store supplies. He had representatives of every participating federal agency posted to the headquarters where they could respond instantly to Baker's requests. At Baker's suggestion, local Red Cross chapters undertook to administer relief in their communities, and each appointed a single reporter to gather and forward information to relief headquarters. To transport refugees and supplies, Hoover persuaded the railroads to offer free service or reduced rates, and he asked each governor of an affected state to delegate one man with full authority over state resources to coordinate with Baker. Working closely with Fieser and Baker, and wielding his authority from the president when necessary, Hoover slashed through red tape, and within a few days an efficient organization emerged.[12]

Hoover and Fieser understood from the outset that the success of the relief program required massive publicity to generate national support. Their staff found accommodations for reporters, supplied them with an endless flow of press releases and photographs of relief operations, and arranged full access to the principals. When Hoover traveled in the flood area, as he did almost incessantly during the next three months, he ordered that a special press car be attached to his train. From it flowed a steady stream of complimentary stories to newspapers and magazines across the country. Hoover provided, as Fieser put it, the "magnetic center of publicity," but nearly every picture of Hoover on a ship or inspecting a refugee camp also included the Red Cross chief at his side. They set out to dramatize the relief program by every means possible—and succeeded. The money rolled in to the Red Cross. From Hoover's point of view, the process brought a double benefit. While raising money for the relief program, he was also reminding Americans of his reputation as the "Great Humanitarian." He might be too busy at the moment to plan his 1928 campaign, but he welcomed the opportunity to demonstrate his version of federal activism.[13]

Housing the people displaced by the flood—and their livestock—became the relief organization's immediate priority. At first, people camped anywhere they could find a little dry ground, often on the levees themselves, and conditions could be dreadful. William Faulkner, who witnessed the flood, described a sodden "mushroom city of the forlorn and despairing, where kerosene flares smoked in the drizzle and hurriedly strung electrics glared upon the bayonets of martial policemen and the Red-Cross brassards of doctors and nurses and canteen-workers." Often army-supplied tents ran short, and people "sat or lay, single and by whole families, under what shelter they could find, or sometimes under the rain itself, in the little death of profound exhaustion while the doctors and the nurses and the soldiers stepped over and around and among them." Local Red Cross workers and other volunteers did what they could, bringing in food for the people and fodder for the animals and putting up as many tents as they could get. Local army detachments and National Guard units kept order and directed small armies of prisoners and sharecroppers filling sandbags and dumping them fruitlessly into the crevasses in the levees.[14]

As Hoover's organization developed by early May, camp builders recruited from threatened communities gradually got ahead of the crest of the flood, setting up camps before they were needed. Naval aviators provided crucial information about new breaches in the levees and flood levels. Using their reports, Isaac Cline, the Weather Bureau forecaster at New Orleans, provided amazingly accurate predictions about exactly where the flood would go next and how high the water would rise. Cline, who carried a burden of unnecessary guilt for his inability to warn Galveston of the approach of a devastating hurricane in 1900 that killed six thousand people, now more than redeemed himself. Day after day he informed the relief forces exactly how long it would take flood water to fill a basin or low area after a levee broke, how large an area would flood, when water would reach communities, and, often to the inch, how high the water would rise. For example, a May 17 report read, "At Rayville [a] fall [of] five inches in crevasse waters from Arkansas [River] has cleared side walks. Flow through Bayou Des Glaises crevasses has practically filled basin above Texas and Pacific Railroad west of Melville and water now running over rails many places from point six miles west Melville to beyond Rosa."[15]

Armed with this sort of information, a relief representative, often Hoover himself, would rush to a town in the path of the flood. There, as a 1928 campaign biographer told the story, he would summon the leading citizens and tell them bluntly, "'A couple of thousand refugees are coming. They've got to have accommodations. Huts. Water-mains. Sewers. Streets. Dining-halls. Meals. Doctors. Everything. And you haven't got months to do it in. You haven't got weeks. You've got hours. That's my train.' So you go away and they go ahead and just simply do it." Of course, the process was neither that simple nor dramatic. Hoover's visit would be followed by a train or a fleet of trucks full of the supplies needed, and the relief program would provide detailed plans for laying out the refugee camp (down to the width of streets and the distance between tent platforms) and supervision in building it. Yet the description carried truth. The relief program provided money, supplies, and know-how, and local communities created 154 temporary cities for populations of up to twenty thousand people, a total of 325,554 altogether, although as many again were fed by the Red Cross in their own homes. In the camps, tents with wooden floors lined the streets, water and sewer lines were laid or latrines dug, electric lights installed, communal kitchens and dining halls put up, and even hospitals built. At Opelousas, Louisiana, where a camp deviated from

Red Cross standards, Fieser ordered it torn down and rebuilt elsewhere. Only once, Hoover recalled, did a community fail to complete a camp on time.[16]

In late April, the flood—and the relief program—moved into the Cajun country of Louisiana west of New Orleans along the Atchafalaya River. The Mississippi River Commission had tried to block that shorter and straighter route to the Gulf for fear that the whole river would be diverted permanently, leaving New Orleans an inland city, but as the flood crest approached, a major levee collapsed on April 30, and suddenly much of the Mississippi poured into the Atchafalaya basin. Isaac Cline and the engineers could predict precisely how high the water would rise in the isolated towns near the river, but until the flood arrived, the residents refused to believe the warnings. Red Cross worker Ernest Bicknell had experienced the same problem during the Ohio flood a quarter-century before, and the Cajuns proved even more stubborn than Midwestern farmers. In a few cases, relief workers tried using soldiers to force evacuation, but the troops faced so much resistance that they soon withdrew. Like Bicknell, Hoover found that nothing could be done but wait until the water arrived and then send in boats to pluck stranded people off rooftops and out of trees. That, unfortunately, meant the loss of much live-stock that might have been saved with more time. In mid-May, the Red River broke through a levee at Tilden on Bayou Des Glaises, removing the last barrier between the Red, Mississippi, and Atchafalaya rivers. Levee breaks on the Atchafalaya itself at Melville and McCrae accounted for the last of 246 recorded flood deaths.[17]

In New Orleans, every collapse of an upriver levee swelled the flood of panic. Residents knew all too well that the city occupied a bowl lower than the level of the river even in normal times, and they now envisioned the great flood crest racing toward them. Isaac Cline believed that the levees preventing the Mississippi's diversion into the Atchafalaya would collapse as the flood's crest hit them, thus mitigating the threat to the city, but he did not make that argument forcefully to the city fathers, the army engineers, or Hoover. The levees had not yet collapsed as decisions about protecting the city were being made, and perhaps Cline, remembering the catastrophe at Galveston, feared being wrong again. Panicked, civic leaders demanded that the government dynamite the St. Bernard levee, just downriver from New Orleans, to create a spillway that would lower the water level at the city.[18]

The federal government responded to the pressure. Lou Hoover reported that members of the administration, presumably including her husband, felt "very much frightened about New Orleans." On April 22, the same day Coolidge named Hoover to head flood relief, Secretary of War Dwight Davis told a representative of the New Orleans businessmen that he would look "sympathetically" on a request to dynamite the levee if the governor absolved the federal government of any responsibility for property damage. Residents of St. Bernard and Plaquemines parishes protested in vain about the prospective flooding of their homes and properties. But even shots fired from the St.

Bernard levee at a boat carrying Hoover and General Jadwin on an inspection visit to the proposed breach site at Caernarvon on April 28 did not shake their determination to cut the levee.[19]

Blasting began at Caernarvon on April 29, but the levee, built of heavy blue clay, did not immediately give way. It would take thirty-nine tons of dynamite and ten days of blasting before a substantial breach opened. By that time, the main flood was pouring west through the Atchafalaya basin. A crest four feet above flood stage but below the tops of the city's levees arrived at New Orleans on April 25, and by April 29 the river level had already begun to drop. Cline had been right. But Hoover, who left the city by train the day blasting began, remained unaware that the worst danger had already passed. In a radio fund-raising appeal to the nation from Memphis on April 30, he declared that the levee cut had averted "a monumental catastrophe" to New Orleans.[20] In fact, it had visited a totally unnecessary disaster on the parishes below the city.

In his Memphis broadcast, Hoover estimated that more than 300,000 people had already become flood refugees or clung "to the upper floors of their flooded villages" in states from Illinois to Mississippi. The river threatened thousands more in Louisiana. By the beginning of May, almost 23,000 square miles of Mississippi, Missouri, Arkansas, and Louisiana had been submerged. Helping the people in those areas remained Hoover's first priority, but with the rescue and relief operation working well all along the river, he had begun to turn his attention to recovery and beyond that, to the possibility that recovery measures might include the commercial river development of which he had long dreamed. As a Midwestern businessman put it, Hoover had "during the last eighteen months given to our people a vision of what the improvement and utilization of our inland waters could mean to the business and agricultural interests of the Mississippi Valley and the Central West." The flood experience, the businessman predicted confidently, would "force this vision into actual accomplishment."[21]

III

As the frantic pace during the first days of the rescue mission gradually slowed, a serious controversy about the treatment of African American residents of the flood area began to emerge. Initial rumors that white planters had refused to let black sharecroppers flee the flood proved unfounded, and the press carried heartwarming stories of whites taking great risks to rescue trapped blacks, and vice versa. But once African American refugees reached the relief camps, they faced forcible reminders of their inferior status. By early May, Hoover began to receive reports that white National Guard troops were enforcing segregation at gunpoint, sometimes making black refugees pay for inferior food and shelter, denying them medical attention, and refusing permission to leave the camps. Hoover responded immediately that he thought the people raising the charges were "overalarmed," but he promised he would investigate the charges "vigorously." Any such discrimination, he declared, "would be abhorrent" to both the Red Cross and the federal agencies involved in the relief program. He asked Henry Baker to pass on the charges to Red Cross field-workers and "see that no such activity exists directly or indirectly." On May 21, he began assembling a "Colored Advisory Commission," led by Robert R. Moton, principal of Tuskegee Institute, to investigate charges of racial discrimination in the relief program. He assured reporters, however, that he was confident the commission would find that African Americans in the relief camps were "being splendidly treated and cared for."[22]

Meanwhile, similar reports of abuses had reached the headquarters of the National Association for the Advancement of Colored People (NAACP). In mid-May, Walter White, assistant secretary of the NAACP, decided to go to the flood area to investigate personally. With his light skin and blue eyes, White could travel easily in the South and often gained access where dark-skinned African Americans could not. Arriving in Memphis on May 15, White worked his way down the river through the heart of the delta plantation country. Nine days later, he filed his preliminary report. He confirmed that "the heads of the Red Cross have sought impartially to render aid to those who needed it regardless of race or color." But he also reported that in the delta, most whites regarded blacks "as cows or horses," as he had overheard one white woman say. In the camps he visited, he found that "with certain exceptions . . . the Negro sufferers were being given comfortable, sanitary accommodations; adequately fed; and given careful medical attention," including "vaccination against typhoid fever and small pox." On the other hand, General Curtis T. Green, National Guard commander at Vicksburg, told White unblushingly that he had ordered his soldiers to prevent black refugees from talking to strangers who might offer them jobs, nor would they permit them to leave the camps, except to work without pay on the levees or for local businesses. Once the flood waters receded and the land began to dry out, said Green, each plantation owner would send an agent to "pick out his niggers" and take them back to the plantation. "We do not propose to have [the delta] stripped of labor," he said frankly. To add insult to injury, White reported, once the black sharecroppers returned to the plantations, planters sometimes charged them for the relief and recovery supplies that the Red Cross provided free to landowners for distribution. If sharecroppers objected to this exploitation, they were beaten. The system of peonage, reported NAACP researcher Helen Boardman, who visited the camps at about the same time as White, drove about a quarter of the black residents of the camps into flight. They chose to give up food, shelter, and medicine rather than return to the plantations.[23]

Not all African Americans along the lower Mississippi agreed with the grim picture painted by White and Boardman. Two NAACP leaders in Pine Bluff, Arkansas, reported that they had "never before . . . seen the color line obliterated to the same extent." But General Green's blunt declaration that plantation owners did not intend to permit the delta to be "stripped of labor" expressed a fundamental truth. Over and above the daily humiliations and indignities heaped upon blacks, white landowners had resolved to do whatever was necessary to make sure they did not lose their workers. In a report to Hoover and Fieser in December, the conservative black members of the Moton Commission (the Colored Advisory Commission) confirmed and added detail to the previous reports of gross abuses perpetrated on African Americans in the camps and on the plantations to which many of them returned at gunpoint.[24]

The 1927 flood on the lower Mississippi took place in the midst of a society based on absolute white domination in economics, politics, and social relations. With camps patrolled by local National Guard units and relief administered by Red Cross chapters made up of local white citizens, racism pervaded the operation. But major differences existed among the camps. In a meeting with Hoover and Fieser on June 11, the members of the Moton Commission identified camps at Greenville, Mississippi, and Opelousas and Sicily Island, Louisiana, as the worst. They described others as "almost ideal," although it is unclear what they meant by that phrase. A Red Cross official in Arkansas, for example, denounced reports of mistreatment of black refugees as an "absolute lie" and then went on to say that when a landlord notified camp officials that his land was "workable," the Red Cross would tell tenants that they must return to their homes within a week or lose their rations. Hoover, who visited refugee camps frequently, could hardly have been unaware of such behavior, nor of the casual brutality with which guards treated black camp residents. He excused the situation to Walter White as the result of "the economic system which exists in the South" and pointed out that the Red Cross had no power to "undertake either social or economic reforms." Both statements were true, but he seemed unable or unwilling to recognize the more fundamental problem of institutionalized racism. When he rationalized to a critic that rescue workers might be restricting movements within camps "to prevent over congestion," suggested that planters might be charging refugees for relief because they were providing supplies at their own expense, or told his friend Will Irwin that abuses reflected the actions of "irresponsible" Guardsmen, he surely knew at some level that what he was saying was evasive at best. A prospective presidential candidate hopeful of cracking the "solid South," however, had reasons for avoiding a difficult issue.[25]

Many possible reasons underlay Hoover's failure to confront the race issue directly—his inveterate touchiness about criticism, political ambition, the fear of disrupting national fund-raising for relief, a realistic acceptance of local conditions he could not change, and perhaps even his personal racial prejudice or indifference. Neither most white politicians nor the mainstream press emphasized racial justice during the 1920s, and Hoover could be confident that his public statements, the appointment of the Moton Commission, and the Red Cross's well-publicized orders for fair treatment would defuse criticism from all but African Americans and the Left. In the absence of a strong, national civil rights movement that could force the issue, Hoover, like most white Americans, went along with the prevailing system. Satisfied that he had minimized or eliminated abuses within the reach of the relief program, he found it impractical to emphasize the broader injustices of Southern society.

Yet Hoover's experience in the South may also have opened his eyes to some degree. Prior to 1927, he had little direct contact with African Americans other than servants, and he had never worked directly with educated, sophisticated black leaders, as he did during the flood. His observation of black sharecroppers' living conditions, the way they were treated in the refugee camps, and his relations with the Moton Commission suggested to him that "economic independence" might go far to remove injustices. As he traveled through the South in the weeks after the worst of the flood passed, he began to develop an idea.[26]

On July 8, Hoover met in Washington with the members of the Moton Commission. There he broached the possibility of using some leftover relief funds to purchase idle lands in the delta region that could be sold in small plots to sharecroppers, both black and white. He proposed "a land resettlement corporation with capital of anything from one to two millions," which would purchase abandoned or foreclosed plantations, divide them into twenty-acre farms, erect houses and outbuildings, buy farm animals, and provide a small working capital for sharecroppers wishing to become landowners. A total expenditure of about $2,200, he estimated, would suffice to set up such a farm, and its repayment could be financed with modest mortgages over twenty years. Black peonage in the delta, he told Edgar Rickard, had "made his work difficult" and "demoralized the negroes." He hoped his land program would put "the negro in possession of a small plot and give him [a] chance to make good."[27]

Hoover's idea delighted Dr. Moton. In a speech to the National Negro Business League a few weeks later, Moton hinted that "before it completed its disaster work in the Mississippi Valley the Red Cross fund would doubtless be the instrument for doing something in behalf of the negro more significant than anything which had happened since emancipation." His prediction proved overoptimistic. As James Fieser pointed out, many serious obstacles prevented Red Cross involvement in any such scheme, not the least of which were postflood relief obligations that soon exhausted the organization's remaining funds. Hoover therefore set his plan aside during the autumn of 1927, returning to it only in late December when the members of the Moton Commission came to Washington to discuss their report. No record of the meeting was kept, but Moton understood that the secretary had been offended by the criticisms in the committee's preliminary report and probably would not proceed with the resettlement plan unless the committee considerably softened its final report. Accustomed to placating powerful whites, Moton gave in, and the final report muted criticisms of racism in the relief program. Following the meeting, Moton contacted some wealthy backers of Tuskegee, including William J. Schieffelin, chairman of the college's Board of Trustees, and some of the trustees of the Laura Spelman Rockefeller foundation, to explore whether they would finance a "survey of the land situation in the South" as a first step toward putting Hoover's plan in motion. Schieffelin promised to organize a private meeting of possible donors in New York at the end of February 1928.[28]

Before the meeting, Moton met with Leonard Outhwaite of the Laura Spelman Rockefeller Memorial, and Hoover tackled Edwin Embree, president of the Julius Rosenwald Foundation. Optimistic that one or both of these organizations would fund at least the preliminary study, Moton asked Schieffelin to cancel his meeting. But the Rosenwald and Rockefeller meetings went badly. Rosenwald wished the project well, he said, but he had committed his resources to his school construction program in the South, and in any case, previous projects along the same line, including one near Tuskegee, had failed. The Rockefeller people, perhaps influenced by Rosenwald's doubts, also backed away. Hoover promised Moton that he would "battle along in the other fields," but enmeshed in the presidential campaign, which necessitated courting Southern whites, he never returned to the proposal.[29]

Perhaps the Moton Commission's sharp criticisms of racism in the relief program gave Hoover an excuse to drop a proposal that had little prospect of success amid the racial and economic conditions of the delta. As he had demonstrated in other instances such as the first Ford bid to operate Muscle Shoals or the foreign monopolies issue, Hoover sometimes proposed ideas before he had thought through their ramifications. The resettlement scheme was pie in the sky, benevolently intended but inadequately considered, and in its outcome, a cruel blow to African Americans' dreams. After quietly shelving it, however, Hoover took a series of smaller but more practical steps to assist black Americans. They included the appointment in November 1927 of James A. Jackson as a "Special Agent" for "Negro Affairs" in the Bureau of Foreign and Domestic Commerce, the assignment of Commerce Department staff members to assist the National Negro Business League, and the desegregation of the Census Bureau in March 1928.[30]

IV

The economic recovery of the Mississippi Valley region, not the plight of African Americans, became Hoover's focus once the flood crest passed New Orleans. Even more than disaster relief, recovery and rebuilding raised fundamental questions about the future of federal responsibility in the United States. How much should the federal government do? How much should be left to local governments and private citizens?

Within days after arriving at Memphis in late April, Hoover began scheduling meetings with local officials and businessmen. The flood, he proclaimed to reporters, constituted "a national problem and must be solved nationally and vigorously," but it soon became clear that he thought the proper federal role involved much less than local leaders might hope. Once the rescue aspect of the program ended, he believed that federal responsibility should be confined to constructing "adequate engineering works" to prevent future floods. The Red Cross would provide individual relief and limited help for people to reconstruct their homes and resume their lives, including providing seeds for replanting crops, but the restoration of businesses and the regional economy were primarily tasks for private enterprise, albeit with the encouragement and guidance of the government. At his recommendation, the governors of Louisiana, Mississippi, and Arkansas each appointed an official to coordinate state and federal relief activities, and more importantly, to develop local organizations to plan reconstruction. His own role, as he saw it, was to bring local and national bankers together to form a consortium that could make loans to farmers, businesses, and banks.[31]

In early May, Hoover arranged a meeting between a delegation of Arkansas bankers led by the state's reconstruction coordinator, Harvey C. Couch, president of the Arkansas Power & Light Company, and Treasury officials in Washington, including Secretary Mellon. A week later, a Mississippi delegation led by the state coordinator, lumberman L. O. Crosby, also met with Mellon and Eugene Meyer, head of the Federal Farm Loan Bank, in Washington. On May 10, Arkansas chartered a Farm Credit Corporation to raise $750,000 in local capital for short-term loans to businesses and farmers. Mississippi and Louisiana, where former governor John Parker served as state coordinator, soon followed suit.[32]

Announcement of the private credit organizations reduced pressure on the president to call a special session of Congress to consider making reconstruction a federal responsibility. Believing deeply that "the normal must care for themselves," Coolidge adamantly opposed a federal reconstruction program. Unfortunately, however, announcement of the state programs did not make them effective. The Federal Farm Loan Act of 1916 had created a system of land banks that, by 1927, provided low-cost mortgages to farmers, but in the process, it drew the business away from local banks, leaving them weak and poor. The flood, in an already impoverished section of the country, made the situation worse. Local banks thus had little or no capital to invest in the reconstruction corporations, and farmers and planters had no unmortgaged assets to offer as security for loans in any case. Most of them had already mortgaged their only real asset, their land, before the flood arrived in order to purchase seed, now lost, for the new season.[33]

Hoover asked Federal Farm Loan Board chairman Eugene Meyer to solicit investments in the state corporations from northern banks and corporations. Meyer did his best, and, with Hoover adding his own influence, got commitments of some $2 million from the U.S. Chamber of Commerce and the Investment Bankers Association of America. Even with this capital in hand, however, the reconstruction corporations loaned only about 5 percent of their available funds to farmers and planters because few prospective borrowers had unmortgaged assets to pledge as security for the loans.[34]

Hoover gave no sign that he recognized the gap between his rhetoric about recovery and the reality. On May 15, he issued a modestly optimistic press release, declaring that the flood waters had receded from 75 to 80 percent of the territory north of Mississippi and Louisiana, and reporting that people in those areas had begun returning to their land. "A great rescue fleet, working day and night," remained deployed in western Louisiana, where the crest had not yet arrived and levees might still fail, but he felt confident that "serious loss of life" would be avoided. The Red Cross had begun providing free seeds and, where necessary, work animals for farmers, and "an effective organization for reconstruction" had been created in each state to restore the remainder of the region's economy. Although this "greatest national disaster in peace time" had dealt a severe blow to the region, he concluded, residents could now foresee the end of the ordeal, begin to measure the extent of the destruction, and calculate "the necessities for its remedy."[35]

Across the country, a chorus of praise arose for Hoover's work in the flood area. Articles reminded readers of his long record of relief work in Europe during and after the war, and several suggested that he might make an excellent presidential candidate in 1928. The same articles sometimes offered muted criticisms of President Coolidge—for not going personally to the flood zone to see the destruction and meet with refugees and for blocking a special session of Congress to address relief. Hoover's friend Hugh Gibson, always a source of the latest gossip, described the president as "quite peeved" by the favorable publicity Hoover had been receiving.[36]

By the end of May, the great flood crest had rolled on into the Gulf of Mexico (a lesser, secondary flood would occur in June as the result of new storms). People had begun to return to their homes and farms, but before anyone could think about how to prevent a recurrence of the disaster in the future, a more urgent problem loomed. Contaminated drinking water and mosquito-breeding pools and puddles threatened a major outbreak of disease.

When the Red Cross had admitted refugees to camps, they had inoculated them for typhoid and smallpox. Hoover proposed to supplement this limited program with an antimalaria campaign that would form the foundation for a comprehensive public health system new to the area. On June 1, he proposed to officers of the Rockefeller Foundation that they fund such a program for the lower Mississippi Valley in cooperation with state public health programs in the area. Since the foundation had already been working with local officials toward just that goal, foundation officers assured Hoover within a week that his idea would be approved. At the end of the month, the secretary announced that, for thirty days after the flood waters receded, the Red Cross would sponsor a cleanup campaign in every county in cooperation with state and county health officials and that, for the next eighteen months, the foundation and the

U.S. Health Service would establish programs to combat malaria, typhoid, and other serious diseases. The Red Cross would provide $500,000 to finance the first phase of the program, and the foundation would pick up the second phase at an estimated cost of $1.1 million. The foundation set up a training school at Indianola, Mississippi, and by October 1, nineteen fully staffed units were in operation, with twenty-six other units with one to three people on each staff. The program, Hoover predicted confidently, would eliminate endemic malaria "from the Mississippi bottom lands," just as "General Gorgas cleaned it out of Panama" in preparation for the construction of the canal. Hoover's *Memoirs*, which claimed that the health program transformed the South's health, exaggerated its achievements, but certainly it vastly improved conditions in an isolated and impoverished region.[37]

V

Hoover's allusion to the massive construction involved in building the Panama Canal was not entirely fanciful, given the equally enormous project he envisioned to control the Mississippi. As early as 1922, Hoover had asserted his conviction that "control of the Mississippi River" was "a national responsibility," and the flood merely reinforced that belief. Floodwaters had come from thirty states, he pointed out, and as a commercial artery, the river could serve those same states. But voicing that general theory did not ensure that the president and Congress would see matters the same way, nor did it clarify how, exactly, control might be achieved.[38]

On April 30, a week after assuming direction of the relief program, Hoover and Major General Edgar Jadwin, commander of the Army Corps of Engineers, issued a joint statement about flood control on the Mississippi. Dismissing as unworkable proposals for storage reservoirs on the headwaters of the river and reforestation to control runoff in its watersheds, they declared that higher, stronger levees represented the "one practical, feasible and economic solution." The idea of a massive levee program that might cost $10 to $15 million dollars a year for a decade, as General Jadwin estimated, did not appeal to Coolidge. Still less did he like the possibility of a special session of Congress that might rush through some ill-planned and hugely expensive projects. But political pressure for action had grown intense, so in mid-May the president ordered the army engineers, in cooperation with the Mississippi River Commission, to conduct a study for submission to Congress.[39]

Hoover saw an open-ended study as worse than useless. It would merely postpone practical engineering studies to determine where and how to improve the levee system. Levees offered a "sure flood remedy," he told a reporter. It would be pointless to conduct "protracted investigations" of alternative approaches "known to be ineffective." The longer the study went on, he added, the more "crank" suggestions would come in.[40]

Leaders in the flood states shared Hoover's impatience, but at a flood control conference held in Chicago between June 2 and 4, representatives of twenty-seven states and groups ranging from engineers to the Anti-Saloon League failed to agree on specific steps to be taken. General Jadwin forcefully restated his argument for levees but failed to persuade the delegates. At length, they adopted a resolution urging the president to convene a meeting of "army engineers, civil engineers, conservationists, geologists, financiers, agriculturists, and other experts representing the various interests of our country" to draft a comprehensive plan.[41] Those hoping for swift action left the meeting angry and frustrated.

Nevertheless, by mid-May, Hoover had begun to rethink his support for the levees-only approach. He told a reporter for the St. Louis *Post Dispatch* that levees "must afford the main protection" on the lower Mississippi but that storage reservoirs and reforestation merited further study. In newspaper articles and a July 20 interview with the president, he proposed supplementing levees with spillways that could be opened to relieve flooding on the lower river and with special overflow basins. The most obvious spillway, the Atchafalaya, had served precisely that function in the 1927 flood when the levees collapsed. Overflow basins would be low-lying areas that could be surrounded by dikes and opened during floods but otherwise leased for agricultural use. Both spillways and basins presented, of course, risks of property damage and loss of life—problems that Hoover did not mention. Simply trying to contain floods between high walls, he had become convinced, also presented substantial risks.[42]

By late June, with the flooded area finally drying out and a series of celebrations being held along the river to thank Hoover for his work, people began talking seriously about how to control the river. Hoover and General Jadwin believed the problem should be left to the Army Corps of Engineers in the interest of speed and efficiency, but as the Chicago meeting had demonstrated, a great many other people wanted to influence the process. John F. Stevens, president of the American Society of Civil Engineers, proposed to the president and Secretary of War Dwight Davis the appointment of an independent commission of civil engineers. The president's interest in that idea compelled Hoover to feign sympathy. But as he well knew, others had already moved to preempt planning for river control.[43]

In late May, L. O. Crosby of Mississippi, Harvey Couch of Arkansas, and banker James P. Butler of Louisiana met at Hoover's suggestion to unite the most powerful men in their respective states into the Tri-State Executive Flood Control Committee. Governor John Martineau of Arkansas became chairman, former governor John Parker of Louisiana vice-chairman, and Senator LeRoy Percy of Mississippi secretary. The group meant to shape a flood control plan, draft legislation, and push the bill through Congress quickly. In September, Hoover met with committee members during a visit to the flood zone. At a ceremony in Hot Springs, Arkansas, to honor his work during the flood, he casually endorsed the committee's ideas.[44]

The Tri-State Committee's plans represented a revolutionary approach to flood control on the Mississippi. Previously, states and local governments had been required to share the cost of levee construction with the federal government. If the committee's plan passed, the federal government would assume the whole obligation. Moreover, committee members urged that the bill be rushed through Congress, to prevent the growth of public support for reconstruction aid to flood victims that would make the project prohibitively expensive. Hoover, who had for many years favored federal responsibility for navigation and flood control improvements on the Mississippi, found it easy to accept the committee's recommendation. The proposal presented a unique opportunity to win congressional support for the plan he had long favored. Those who raised the cost-sharing principle could be told that the recent flood had virtually bankrupted state and local governments. Past state and levee-district contributions toward river control should be counted, one committee member suggested, as their share in the new construction.[45]

Hoover assured the Tri-State Committee that the Red Cross had adequate reserves to meet the immediate needs of flood victims, and the U.S. Chamber of Commerce had collected a $2 million fund for later reconstruction. General Jadwin promised to draw on Mississippi River Commission funds to repair existing levees, and the president authorized the use of another $2 million from the current Rivers and Harbors appropriation for the same purpose. Those arrangements not only relieved the group's worry that Congress might get sidetracked into funding reconstruction but, by making an extra session of Congress unnecessary, also appealed to the president.[46]

Arkansas's Governor Martineau, recognizing that his state had suffered from flooding on both the Mississippi and its tributaries, proposed a flood control program for the tributaries as well as the main river. The idea fitted well with Hoover's plan for the development of the Mississippi system, but the Tri-State leaders vetoed it. Extending the program to the tributaries, they pointed out, would likely kill it by making it too expensive. To avoid the appearance that the deep South states were being selfish in proposing a narrow program, the Tri-State group suggested letting the War Department, whose own plan covered only the lower Mississippi, take the blame for the circumscribed proposal. If necessary, the beneficiaries could win additional votes by modest logrolling.[47]

In the autumn of 1927, the War Department announced that it would recommend the appropriation of "such an amount as would be necessary to carry on the work as rapidly as consistent with economy of construction," and the army engineers worked to develop a specific proposal. In his annual message to Congress on December 6, President Coolidge endorsed flood control legislation and argued that it should be "confined to our principal and most pressing problem, the lower Mississippi." That suited Hoover and the

Tri-State Committee perfectly, but their hearts sank when the president added "that those requesting improvements will be charged with some responsibility for their cost." Two days later, when the president sent the "Jadwin Plan" to Congress, he was more specific: the federal government would bear the full cost of navigation improvements, but local governments would have to pay 20 percent of the cost of flood control. That meant that, of an estimated $296,400,000 total cost to be spread over ten years, local governments would be required to pay $37,440,000. Although better than they had at first feared, the president's position jeopardized the hopes of Hoover and the Tri-State Committee for full federal assumption of Mississippi improvements.[48]

The Jadwin Plan abandoned the Mississippi River Commission's long-standing reliance on levees as a single defense. Levees would be rebuilt and reinforced, to be sure, but the plan relied fundamentally on "floodways" that could be opened to relieve the pressure on the main channel—one from near Cairo to New Madrid, Missouri, the second from the Arkansas River through the Tensas Basin to the Red River and then into the Atchafalaya and the Gulf. That route would recreate, in a more controlled way, the path of the 1927 flood. The main channel of the upper river would be deepened and widened, with levees strengthened along the 250 mile stretch of the river between New Madrid and the mouth of the Arkansas. The plan also suggested an emergency spillway at Caernarvon below New Orleans to protect the city but deferred that recommendation pending further consideration. The Mississippi River Commission had presented a similar but more expensive plan to Congress on November 28, but both the president and Congress understandably preferred the more optimistic estimates of the Jadwin Plan.[49]

Representative Frank R. Reid of Illinois, chairman of the House Committee on Flood Control, had begun hearings on the issue on November 7, a month before Congress convened, but instead of speeding up the passage of legislation, the hearings complicated it. They provided a forum for representatives of the Chicago Flood Control Conference, who wanted flood control extended to the tributaries of the Mississippi, and they also opened up the debate about requiring local governments to pay part of the cost. On December 21, Reid introduced a bill calling for the federal government to bear the full cost of flood control on the Mississippi and directing an enlarged Mississippi River Commission to report on the flood danger on tributary watersheds. On the Senate side, Senator Joseph Ransdell of Louisiana introduced a bill calling for the adoption of the Mississippi River Commission's plan, with the federal government to shoulder the full cost, now estimated at $775 million, close to three times that of the Jadwin Plan.[50]

In early January 1928, Hoover met with a member of the Tri-State Committee to discuss how to get around Coolidge's insistence on local cost sharing. They decided to recommend that the president appoint a special commission to investigate how much local communities could "afford" to contribute toward flood control. Coolidge, while maintaining his support of the principle that local governments should contribute, agreed to consider the commission suggestion. The commission, he agreed during a February meeting with Hoover, Jadwin, and senators from Louisiana, Arkansas, and Mississippi, would consider not only "the ability of the different communities to pay" but also the amounts "which the communities or political units affected had already paid for flood control." How the delegation won that concession remains unclear, but it delighted Hoover and the Southern leaders.[51]

On February 24, Hoover testified on flood control before the Senate Commerce Committee, which was considering a bill introduced by Senator Wesley L. Jones of Washington providing $325 million for flood control. Senator Jones described the bill as a compromise because it budgeted more than the original Jadwin proposal but less than the Reid bill and because it left a commission to decide how much, if anything, local governments would have to contribute. In testimony before the committee, Hoover declined to discuss the total amount to be spent, the issue of cost sharing, or the technical details of competing schemes, but he insisted that the heavy human and monetary costs of the 1927 flood, as well as its lingering economic impact, made action vital. Construction spending, he observed, "would be of value in stabilizing the economic fabric" of the region and the country. Perhaps, he suggested delicately, it would be sensible to authorize the project in broad outline and let the plan "be altered in details as the work progresses."[52]

On March 28, the Senate passed the Jones Bill unanimously, dropping the fig leaf of a commission to set local contributions and accepting previous local expenditures in lieu of further contributions—exactly as the Tri-State Committee had desired. Three days later, the House Flood Control Committee approved the Senate measure by a vote of 20 to 1, and everyone assumed that the full House would act soon. But then Coolidge, appalled by the cost of the proposed project, announced that he would veto any bill that did not require local contributions. Given the near-unanimous support for the measure in Congress and the public clamor for passage of a plan to prevent a similar disaster in the future, however, his position was impossible. On May 15, he signed the bill. Thus, a president opposed to government spending approved the greatest expenditure the government had ever adopted for a single project.[53]

The Red Cross estimated that the flood had inundated more than 5 million acres of farmland, drowned 1.2 million livestock and poultry, washed away almost 42,000 houses and farm buildings, and flooded 162,000 more. The flood affected almost 700,000 people, but no one could be sure how many died: the Red Cross estimated 246; the Weather Bureau 313. Many of those drowned were black sharecroppers swept away by levee collapses, and local governments had little idea how many had been lost, moved North, or just disappeared. Hoover's self-serving claim that only three people died after he took over on April 23 seems impossibly low, although his relief operation undoubtedly saved thousands. The Red Cross raised and spent $17 million on rescue and relief work during and immediately after the disaster. Estimates of total economic losses to the region and the nation, which ranged from $246 million to a billion dollars, were largely guesses.[54]

Except among African Americans, Hoover and the Red Cross emerged with shining reputations from the 1927 flood. Within days, they had arranged to feed hundreds of thousands of people on farms cut off by flood waters, assembled a fleet that plucked three hundred thousand more from the waters, arranged to house and feed refugees adequately, launched a substantial public health program throughout the region, and provided the poorest of the survivors with modest aid in the form of seed, equipment, and housing when they returned to their lands. The private rehabilitation program, of which Hoover frequently boasted, fell substantially short of its goals, however, and many African Americans, except for the thousands who fled to the North and West, found themselves worse off after the disaster than before. Nevertheless, until the creation of the Federal Emergency Relief Administration during the New Deal, most white Americans saw the 1927 relief operation as a model of how to deal with a national disaster.

VI

Hoover's success in the Mississippi Valley naturally brought him to everyone's mind when another flood hit New England in November 1927. On November 2, freakish weather conditions diverted an Atlantic storm into the interior of New England, where it dumped more than six inches of rain on northern Vermont, western New Brunswick, and southern Quebec on November 3 and 4. Confined within the region's narrow valleys, rivers rose rapidly to record levels, scouring away farms, roads, and railroads, and then receding almost as quickly as they had risen and leaving behind tangles of wreckage and acres of stinking mud. The floods killed as many as 120 people, left thousands homeless, and severely damaged the region's transportation and power networks. Falling temperatures and the threat of snow threatened to compound the disaster.[55]

On November 5, President Coolidge ordered the First Army Corps, headquartered at Boston, to send troops, planes, and supplies into the area to begin rescue work. Governor John Weeks had already mobilized the Vermont National Guard. Governor Al Smith of New York established a relief center at Albany and ordered all state agencies, including the National Guard, to provide personnel and supplies as needed. In isolated towns, neighbors helped neighbors, and those in towns on higher ground fed and housed people from low-lying villages. On November 7, soldiers and Red Cross workers began fanning out across the flooded region, although below-freezing weather and driving snow complicated their work. The storm also grounded army fliers hoping to survey the extent of the damage even as it made the rescue effort more urgent.[56]

On November 9, Governor Weeks convened a meeting of state officials, military officers, financial executives, and Red Cross representatives to plan relief and rehabilitation. The group put the Red Cross in charge and dispatched an urgent message to the president requesting as much federal aid as possible.[57]

Coolidge showed no more sympathy for the travails of his home state than he had for the Mississippi Valley. Not only did he indicate no desire to visit the flood zone, but he also responded initially to Governor Weeks's appeal for help by saying that the army and the Red Cross were already doing everything that needed be done. That, as it turned out, was true, but upon reflection, Coolidge realized he needed at least to make a public gesture. The obvious thing was to send Hoover. But Hoover was in St. Louis to deliver a speech on the development of Midwestern waterways and planned to address the International Radiotelegraph Conference the following week in Washington. At the president's request, he agreed to leave for Vermont on November 12, although train connections made it impossible for him to get to Montpelier before November 16. By the time he arrived, a week after Governor Weeks's request, the army had taken charge of clearing debris, putting up temporary bridges, handling communications, directing traffic, and preventing looting. The Red Cross had the rescue and relief of survivors well in hand, and the railroads had been working for days repairing and reopening lines as rapidly as possible. Hoover's visit dramatized the president's concern, but the secretary could do little other than support local leaders in developing reconstruction plans[58]

That was familiar ground for Hoover, and he had definite ideas about what should be done next. What he offered was national publicity for the state's needs, not federal money. As in the Mississippi flood, local officials must not expect the federal government to fund reconstruction beyond the necessities of immediate relief. Private, not public, money would pay for rebuilding, except in limited cases. In a letter to Governor Weeks on November 17, Hoover spelled out what he had in mind. The Red Cross would help "those who cannot otherwise provide for themselves," providing individuals and artisans with "necessary household furniture, building repairs, new home construction, cattle, horses, livestock, farm implements, tools, food and clothing for winter." Private financial institutions such as the New England Bankers Association or the New England Council should "assume the responsibility for organizing such measures as will assure credits [i.e., loans] to the worthy industrial and commercial establishments which may be embarrassed by the flood." He assumed that the railroads would restore their own lines without government help. The state government would share with the Federal Highways Bureau the cost of repairing roads and bridges. That, as Hoover outlined it, would constitute the federal government's only monetary contribution to reconstruction. Vermonters, he declared, had grappled with the disaster with "self-reliance and courage," and he clearly expected them to do no less in reconstruction.[59]

The New England Council, made up of financial and agricultural leaders from the six New England states, met with Hoover at Springfield, Massachusetts, on November 17. The group promised to underwrite a million-dollar fund for reconstruction to be administered by a Vermont Flood Credit Corporation. It also directed its Industrial Development Committee to work with local utilities to maximize power production and minimize prices in order to attract new industries. But leaders of the council implored the Red Cross to take over responsibility for helping artisans and small businesses to rebuild. With damages in Vermont alone estimated at between $20 and $30 million, the businessmen obviously felt overwhelmed. And well they might; per capita, Vermont's damage exceeded that in any state affected by the Mississippi flood by three times.[60]

The leaders of the Red Cross also felt overwhelmed. On top of the $17 million for their work during the Mississippi flood, by the spring of 1928, they had spent another million dollars for relief and rehabilitation in New England (of which, it must be noted, Vermonters themselves contributed about $300,000). Although they had kept their coffers full through a series of public appeals, they felt unable to undertake a small business rehabilitation program in Vermont. As in the Mississippi Valley, they offered only to help individuals in need, which in this case meant assisting some 3,400 families. But to New Englanders, where lines blurred between farmers and townsmen, or between businessmen and craftsmen, decisions about who received aid and who did not seemed arbitrary. Red Cross president John Barton Payne angered New Englanders by brusquely informing John S. Lawrence, president of the New England Council, that Red Cross policy did not authorize it to finance business rehabilitation. Not until the spring of 1928 did Payne give Lawrence a full explanation of the organization's position. By that time, the Red Cross's alleged insensitivity to suffering had alienated local leaders, while, on the other side, the insistence of some local chapters on spending their funds without oversight, regardless of the national organization's rules, also strained relations. After a meeting with state officials in June 1928, James Fieser complained that they offered no "expression of appreciation for any of the work of the Red Cross."[61] New Englanders, like their counterparts in the South, hoped for more help with recovery than any private organization could provide. Their experiences would contribute to reshaping Americans' conceptions of the proper responses to disaster.

VII

Taken together, the Mississippi and New England floods reveal important aspects of Hoover's philosophy of government. When he described his experiences during the Mississippi flood in his *Memoirs* many years later, he recalled the whole relief and reconstruction effort as a triumph of local voluntarism in a context of small government. "Those were the days when citizens expected to take care of one another in time of disaster," he wrote. "It had not occurred to them that the Federal Government should do it."[62]

In reality, the story was considerably more complicated. Local volunteers did heroic work, rescuing the stranded, setting up and running refugee camps, and rebuilding their lives and those of their neighbors. But they could hardly have succeeded without federal ships and airplanes; federal supplies of food, tents, and other equipment; soldiers, sailors, coastguardsmen, and aviators; and federal guidance and support in the persons of Hoover and his staff. In large part, the federal government organized and ran the rescue and relief phases of the operation, and its role commanded nearly universal approbation among Americans. Even President Coolidge agreed that the government should commit all necessary resources to relieving the immediate effects of a major disaster.

On the second phase of recovery from the Mississippi flood—long-term flood control—a significant division opened between Coolidge and Hoover. In the speech that Hoover was delivering in St. Louis when the president sent him to Vermont, he described the immediate lesson of the Mississippi flood as "the increasing dangers to a growing population which lurk in our great streams if they be not adequately controlled." Coolidge agreed, provided flood control did not cost too much, and he even went so far as to agree that the federal government would pay the whole cost. But he strongly disagreed with Hoover's contention that the federal government should both dredge all nine thousand miles of the Mississippi system to a depth of six feet and also construct the St. Lawrence waterway. In Coolidge's view, a federal responsibility for flood control did not include creating what Hoover called "a new relationship to different parts of our country and to the world markets as a whole." Hoover might envision the Mississippi and St. Lawrence waterways as "undertakings worthy of the effort of mighty nations"; Coolidge had a more limited conception of what the federal government ought to do.[63]

Yet despite the clash between Hoover and Coolidge over the proper federal role in what an earlier generation called "internal improvements," they agreed completely about the third phase of the Mississippi and New England flood programs—that local governments, private companies, and individuals must undertake the cost and responsibility of reconstruction. In this, Hoover's opinion remained unchanged from his days with the European relief program after the war, when he had contended that outright charity should be provided only to the poorest and most helpless. Otherwise, the United States could provide loans for reconstruction, but the principal responsibility for their own futures remained with local peoples. In dealing with the floods, he agreed that the Red Cross should provide seed, tools, and other assistance (including basic health services) to the poor, and the government might help in organizing private lending organizations, but most people and businesses should undertake the hard work and sacrifice necessary for their own recovery. Not all Europeans had agreed with this philosophy after the war, and not everyone in

HOOVER

the flood zones did either. When the Great Depression struck, many of them would vote for a very different approach.

Looking back from the perspective of the New Deal and after, Hoover's insistence on making reconstruction a local responsibility may seem cold and uncaring, but it grew out of his experience with the way people actually respond to disaster as well as to his economic philosophy. Although the federal government and the Red Cross provided organization, equipment, supplies, and some manpower during the Mississippi and New England floods, the bulk of the work of rescuing, housing, and feeding flood refugees was undertaken joyfully and effectively by their neighbors. Local elites, rather than helping, sometimes impeded the process, as was the case when leaders in New Orleans insisted on dynamiting the levee below the city and thus flooded those parishes, or when white plantation owners in the Delta coerced black sharecroppers into returning to work as the flood receded. By and large, however, people responded generously and effectively during the immediate crisis. Hoover's experience with these "disaster communities" helps to explain his belief that the unity forged during the crisis could carry over into the reconstruction period. Unfortunately, that did not prove to be the case.[64]

From Hoover's point of view, his work in the Mississippi Valley and Vermont had boosted his presidential prospects. Nationally, his work reminded Americans of his reputation as "the Great Humanitarian" and humanized his technocratic image as an engineer and bureaucrat. In Vermont, a small but influential group of Republicans prominent in the recovery program organized a Hoover-for-president organization in the spring of 1928. In the southern Mississippi Valley, his work also gained him ardent supporters, although the complicated politics of that region made it doubtful how much support he could actually expect in the election. In helping others in those disasters, Hoover had also helped himself.[65]

CHAPTER 21

The Election of 1928

Whatever Hoover thought about running for president when he began his 1920 campaign, by the end of it he had entered his name on the list of Republicans who would be potential candidates throughout the decade. Exactly when willingness to serve transformed into outright ambition is difficult to pinpoint. Hiram Johnson believed that Hoover had "been a candidate for President from the very instant he came to Washington as Food Administrator," but the 1920 California contest definitely made him an active politician. Stung by Johnson's personal attacks and encouraged by anti-Johnson Republicans in Southern California in particular, he began building the skeleton of a political organization. In 1922, a few of his admirers suggested that he challenge the senator in that year's California senatorial race.[1]

Nothing came of the 1922 boomlet, but organizing continued, perhaps in anticipation that Harding might not run for reelection in 1924. Johnson's political antennae picked up the activity, and following Harding's death in August 1923, the conflict between the two men broke into the open again, subsiding only after Coolidge (supported by Hoover) defeated Johnson in the 1924 California primary and Hoover failed to win the vice presidential nomination.[2]

The next year his supporters began putting together a statewide organization in California. Mark Requa, former federal fuel administrator and millionaire engineer-businessman, became Hoover's principal California lieutenant, and the two worked together to influence political appointments in the state. Early in 1925, Requa raised $16,000 to fund a "Northern Division of the Republican Women's Federation of California" led by Dorothy Lenroot

Black, daughter of Wisconsin Senator Irvine Lenroot, and began developing a comparable men's organization, which got under way that summer. The groups, Requa said, represented "organization for the future."[3]

Both in his relief work and as secretary of commerce, Hoover always had considered publicity indispensable to his success. The Belgian relief organization, the American Relief Administration (ARA), and the Commerce Department all produced reams of material for reporters, and Hoover actively cultivated relations with them. The Commerce Department had its own Press Bureau and, from time to time, hired outside public relations experts like New Yorker Lupton Wilkinson, who publicized the department's work on housing and industrial standardization, among other things. Friendly journalists such as Isaac Marcosson, Arch Shaw, Paul Wooton, William A. Hard, and Will Irwin, although nominally independent, produced books and articles throughout the decade that might as well have been written within the Commerce Department. Hoover, wrote the hostile journalist Oswald Garrison Villard, had become "a marvelous self-advertiser and publicity expert" who had learned how to direct "gigantic enterprises and [get] all the credit for them." A sudden increase in the number of laudatory articles appearing in newspapers across the country in the fall of 1925 suggested the beginning of a new campaign "to boost the Chief." At year's end, Edgar Rickard speculated unhappily that a tendency "to weigh almost all matters first from the standpoint of political significance" had supplanted his friend's longstanding commitment to pure public service.[4]

I

During 1926, Hoover stepped up political organizing, not only in California, but also across the country, seizing the opportunity presented by the year's congressional elections to launch his first major speaking tour. In his speeches, he not only lauded Republican achievements but also presented proposals of his own for waterways development. His ambitious projects went beyond party commitments and drew a sharp rebuke from Coolidge, but, as Kansas Senator Arthur Capper observed, Hoover's speeches "made him much stronger" in the Midwest and West. Every sign indicated that Hoover regarded himself as the spokesman of Republican prosperity if Coolidge should decide not to run for reelection in 1928.[5]

Yet for all his organization and efforts to make himself known to the American people, others challenged him as the early front-runners for the 1928 Republican nomination. Coolidge's distaste for his ambitious secretary of commerce constituted a serious obstacle within the party. One of Coolidge's closest supporters, Charles Hilles of New York, did not even mention Hoover as a possibility when Edgar Rickard sounded him out. Charles Evans Hughes, former Supreme Court justice, former secretary of state, and Republican candidate in 1916, emerged as an early favorite.

Although Hughes announced that his age, sixty-five, made him too old to run, many Republicans hoped he might reconsider. Senators William E. Borah of Idaho and George Norris of Nebraska appealed to the progressive wing of the party, and Charles Curtis of Kansas and Vice President Charles G. Dawes drew support from conservatives. Senators Frank Willis, James Watson, and Guy Goff had "favorite son" support in their home states. Governor Frank Lowden of Illinois, a perennial candidate since 1920, had a strong record as governor and enjoyed the support of farm groups who favored the McNary-Haugen plan for dumping farm surpluses overseas. In early Republican polls, Hoover appeared well down the list of possible candidates, but no one else commanded broad support within the party either.[6]

Coolidge, of course, posed the principal obstacle to Hoover's candidacy. Although some people argued that the "no third term" tradition should prevent him from running, Coolidge, in fact, had been elected only once, in 1924. Closely identified with prosperity, the president could have the 1928 nomination for the asking. Hoover's supporters continued to organize quietly, but everyone recognized he had no chance if Coolidge decided to run.[7]

In the spring and fall of 1927, the weather altered the political landscape. Massive floods in the Mississippi River Valley and New England thrust Hoover, as the organizer of relief and reconstruction programs, into headlines across the country and reminded Americans of his reputation as "the Great Humanitarian." The political reward for his relief work came at the Republican convention, where both New England and the four lower Mississippi states gave him majorities of their votes. Together, the two regions provided 136 votes—a quarter of the 545 he needed to secure the nomination. Elsewhere in the country, press coverage of the floods combined with publicity from the Commerce Department and meticulous political organization to turn Hoover from just one of many potential candidates into the man to beat for the nomination.[8]

Hoover's moment came on August 2, 1927, when Coolidge emerged from his summer White House in the Black Hills to hand reporters slips of papers that said, "I do not choose to run for president in nineteen twenty-eight." The announcement elated Hoover, but its cryptic wording, and the president's refusal to explain it, made it difficult for him to begin his own campaign. Did Coolidge want or expect to be coaxed to run? And if he did not run himself, would he support someone else, and if so, who? Hoover felt sure that 1928 would be "a Republican year" and admitted to his friends that he had "his heart . . . set on [the] Presidency," but he instructed his supporters to "sit tight" until the president's intentions became clear. For the present, at least he would remain in the cabinet, not appointing a campaign manager or national committee, and not beginning serious fund-raising. Publicly, he would "back Coolidge as long as [there was] any chance of his running," but he would also let his supporters "test out the country and get all the strength lined up for the convention." Two of his admirers, William Hard and Will Irwin, began campaign biographies, and a third friend, Vernon Kellogg, published a long two-part article about him in *The Outlook*.⁹

Despite Hoover's discretion, no one in Washington doubted his intentions. At a tribute to Will Rogers staged by the National Press Club at the Washington Auditorium in August 1927, Hoover received a tremendous ovation when the comedian alluded to his relief work and saluted him as the next president. "When a man is sick he calls for a doctor," said Rogers, "but when the United States of America is sick they call for Herbert Hoover." Henry Ford declared Hoover "the logical Republican candidate," and the famed Kansas editor, William Allen White, praised him as "a hard-boiled idealist."¹⁰

George Akerson, who had become Hoover's principal liaisons with the press and de facto campaign manager, kept a close eye on the national scene. Hughes, he thought, regretted that he had declared himself too old to run, but the New Yorker's half-hearted campaign served only to keep the field open for Hoover. In California, essential to Hoover as his base, Akerson maneuvered to gently sideline the enthusiastic but sometimes indiscreet amateurs Ralph Arnold and Ralph Merritt and replace them with cooler, more professional operators like Thomas T. C. Gregory, Milton Esberg, and Mark Requa. Given the factional divisions among California Republicans, Akerson and Gregory hoped to organize the state as much as possible without naming any specific person to lead the movement. By early spring of 1928, this strategy had succeeded in gaining Hoover the endorsements of Governor C. C. Young and his two predecessors, William D. Stephens and Friend Richardson, as well as the current and former lieutenant governors and the influential mayor of San Francisco, James Rolph, Jr. Hiram Johnson agreed to stay out of the presidential campaign in return for an uncontested renomination to the Senate and Hoover's support for the Colorado River dam. Elsewhere across the country, organization and preliminary fund-raising continued through the fall of 1927.¹¹

On December 6, during a meeting of the Republican National Committee in the East Room of the White House, President Coolidge finally lifted the veil of mystery that had hung over his August statement. In ad-libbed remarks at the end of a lengthy speech about administration accomplishments, he reaffirmed his intention not to run and urged the committee members to "vigorously continue the serious task of selecting another candidate." He did not say categorically that he would refuse a draft, but his statement liberated Hoover to become an open candidate. Republican newspapers across the country agreed that the commerce secretary had become the leader. Influential Republicans like National Committeeman R. B. Creager of Texas and New York Committeeman Charles Hilles, who had been among the strongest Coolidge supporters, endorsed Hoover or moved toward neutrality.¹²

Not a great deal changed outwardly in the Hoover campaign following Coolidge's speech. Hoover told Edgar Rickard in late December that announcing his candidacy and opening a campaign headquarters would only involve "a large money expenditure," be "undignified," and "force him personally to answer every fool question." In fact, he never named a campaign chairman. As in every organization with which he had ever been associated, he expected to run things personally. Insofar as anyone emerged as the public face of the campaign other than Hoover, it would be Secretary of the Interior Hubert Work, who managed the Hoover forces at the Republican convention and became chairman of the Republican National Committee in July 1928. Work, a physician and psychiatrist, had become Hoover's closest friend in the cabinet. At sixty-seven, he lacked the energy to run an intense Hoover-style operation, but after a long career in politics, he knew everyone important in the party, thoroughly understood how the political machinery worked, and had great influence with other cabinet members and with congressmen and senators.[13]

Other Hoover loyalists took over the day-to-day operation of the campaign. Former Iowa Congressman James Good, with his small-town Midwestern background and capacity for hard work, quickly earned Hoover's trust. He, along with former Governor James Goodrich of Indiana, Assistant Secretary of Commerce Walter Brown of Ohio, and former Senator Irvine Lenroot of Wisconsin, became the core of the Hoover campaign in the Midwest, where memories of wartime farm policies and Hoover's opposition to McNary-Haugen made him a hard sell. Mark Requa, Tom Gregory, and conservative businessman Milton Esberg dominated the California campaign. Indiana journalist George B. Lockwood, a former secretary of the Republican National Committee, ran the Washington Hoover-for-president operation from the Willard Hotel. Lockwood's office became the main distribution point for campaign literature and a social center where campaign workers informally courted members of Congress. In New York, Edgar Rickard, Alan Fox, and Ogden Mills took charge of trying to capture their opponent's home state. And, of course, George Akerson had a finger in every pie, including overseeing the candidate's personal security, from Hoover's Washington office.[14]

II

In January 1928, Lou wrote that Bert had advanced "with uncanny rapidity" toward winning the Republican nomination, "practically without any effort on his part," and the *Literary Digest* reported widespread agreement in the press that he had virtually locked up the nomination even before the first primaries. Lou clearly dreaded the prospect but tried to convince herself that, even if he won, the family might be able to "go ahead and live our own lives fairly easily" and not be "quite as imprisoned in a glass cage" as their predecessors had been. From California, Tom Gregory reported triumphantly that in a meeting at Governor C. C. Young's home, representatives of all major factions had agreed to back Hoover, while a Washington newspaper reported (prematurely) that Secretary of the Treasury Andrew Mellon would deliver the large Pennsylvania delegation to Hoover at the convention. Gregory maintained that William Randolph Hearst, a longtime critic of Hoover, had been neutralized by his fear that Al Smith, if nominated by the Democrats, would publicly denounce Hearst's extramarital affair with film star Marion Davies (Hearst eventually contributed $20,048 to the Republican campaign). So confident had Hoover's supporters become that, months before primaries in New Hampshire, Michigan, California, Maryland, New Jersey, and Oregon, they were already claiming all of their delegates, along with those of another dozen states, for a total of 323 of the 545 votes needed for nomination.[15]

By January, Governor Al Smith of New York had also assured himself of the Democratic nomination. Smith's only serious competitor, William Gibbs McAdoo, Woodrow Wilson's treasury secretary and son-in-law, withdrew from the race in December 1927. A son of immigrants and a Catholic, Smith exemplified the changing face of the Democratic Party in the urban United States. If he could unite the ethnic voters of the Northeast and the traditionally Democratic South, he could create a new coalition that might give the Democrats a majority for the first time in many years.[16]

Despite a background in New York City's corrupt Tammany organization, Smith had earned a reputation for integrity. In the election of 1924, New York Republicans rode Coolidge's coattails to capture control of the State Senate, but Smith won the governorship and ran a million votes ahead of the Democratic presidential ticket in the state. Facing a legislature controlled for most of his term by Republicans, he nevertheless secured a reduction in working hours for women and children, a 500 percent increase in education spending, an enormous expansion of the state park system, a $45 million bonus for World War I veterans, $50 million for state hospitals and psychiatric facilities, an extensive public works program, the introduction of an executive budget, and a reform in the cumbersome process for adoption of state constitutional amendments, yet even with all of that, he still managed to balance the state's budget and cut taxes twice. As an administrator, his abilities matched or surpassed those of Hoover, and he had political skills greater than Hoover could even imagine. By 1927, he had become essentially unbeatable in New York politics. He never forgot a name or face, and he had so much personal charm that, as one frustrated Republican said, if everyone in New York State knew him personally, "there would be no votes on the other side." Although his Roman Catholicism and support for the repeal of Prohibition would hurt him in some areas of the country, he would present a formidable challenge to Hoover.[17]

III

Early in February, Hoover announced that he would enter nine (he ultimately entered eleven) of the sixteen Republican primaries to be held that spring. In six of the contests where he faced favorite sons, he ran some risks by entering, but in the others, his entry merely publicized his candidacy. Strong supporters like Robert Taft and Congressman Theodore Burton urged him to challenge Senator Frank Willis in the Ohio primary, however, and Hoover decided that the situation offered an opportunity to clarify Coolidge's intentions. Knowing that Willis had often opposed the president, Hoover asked Coolidge if he would enter the primary himself. "No," said Coolidge. Well, the secretary asked, what did he think about Hoover entering? "Why not?" came the laconic reply.[18]

The Ohio contest started with a clash between Willis and Hoover in Washington. Hearing that Hoover and Coolidge disagreed on who should pay the cost of Mississippi flood control, Willis maneuvered the Senate Commerce Committee (on a 7 to 6 vote) into summoning the secretary to testify on the topic. He hoped that Hoover would recommend payment of the whole cost by the federal government, thus displaying disloyalty to the popular president. But Hoover quickly turned the tables, explaining that Coolidge had agreed that past contributions by the states and local levee boards would count toward their share of the cost. His testimony delighted leaders along the lower Mississippi and embarrassed Willis, but it did nothing to weaken the senator with Ohio voters.[19]

Hoover would almost certainly have lost to Willis in Ohio, but the senator died on March 30, less than a month before the election. Elsewhere, favorite sons Frank Lowden and George Norris beat Hoover handily in Illinois and Nebraska. James Watson and Guy Goff defeated him more narrowly in Indiana and West Virginia, their home states. In Wisconsin, where neither he nor his opponent, George Norris, had the advantage of residency, Norris won overwhelmingly. But Hoover gained credit with party insiders for strong challenges to Goff and Watson in unfriendly states, his close contest with Watson being particularly significant because of Watson's Ku Klux Klan support. In California and New Jersey, he ran unopposed, and he faced only token opposition in Michigan, Maryland, and Oregon. He did not enter the Massachusetts primary but received 85.2 percent of the vote anyway as a write-in candidate.[20]

The strategy behind Hoover's entering even primaries he could not hope to win became clear at the convention. Because he did not campaign personally anywhere, he made no enemies and emerged as the second choice of most of the delegates, even where he lost badly, as in Illinois, Nebraska, and Wisconsin. When the convention met, Hubert Work shrewdly exploited the situation. Circulating among the delegates on the convention floor, Work asked if they would vote for Hoover. If they replied that they planned to go with a favorite son on the first ballot, he would put on a solemn expression and say, "That's bad. Looks as though there won't be but one ballot . . . Your State can't afford to be left out." The message was not lost on his listeners.[21]

Like Theodore Roosevelt and William Howard Taft before him, Hoover understood that Southern Republicans could furnish up to one-third of the number of delegates he needed to win the nomination. Candidates struggled fiercely to win the Southern delegates, but the battle remained hidden from public view because organizers realized that premature announcements of support might alienate Northern Republicans without boosting a candidate's chances in the South during the general election, when the Democrat would probably win anyway. Hoover's representatives—Rush Holland, Bascom Slemp, R. B. Creager, Ben J. Davis, Perry Howard, and Horace Mann—maneuvered among the various shoals with little principle and considerable practical skill.[22]

As always, race occupied a central place in Southern politics. In Mississippi, L. O. Crosby, flood relief director for Mississippi and one of the architects of the Tri-State flood control plan, had become an early leader of Hoover forces in his state. Crosby urged Hoover to support a new, all-white Republican group challenging the established, biracial "black-and-tan" Republicans dominated by Eugene Booze and Perry Howard. George Akerson, however, warned that the campaign should "be very careful" about making any commitments to the white Republicans and should "go along . . . at least on the surface" with Howard and Booze, who had already endorsed Hoover. Despite Crosby's professions of support for Hoover, Akerson heard, the Mississippian secretly intended to purge the state party of African Americans and then deliver the state's votes to Governor Lowden at the convention.[23]

Crosby assured Akerson that he had no desire to exclude all blacks from the party, but he refused to work with Howard and "Boozer," as he called Eugene Booze. Howard had a reputation for corruption, and Crosby warned that supporting him "would be very dangerous" because it would alienate Southern whites, who "might resent any assistance that was given to the negroes." Howard responded angrily that if Hoover sided with Crosby, he would antagonize black Republicans not only in Mississippi but also in Louisiana, Tennessee, and Texas. That might not matter in the general election, where white Democrats would outnumber those African Americans able to vote, but it could matter considerably at the convention. Yet Hoover organizers did not want to alienate Crosby's "lily-white" Republicans either. The Hoover people regarded Crosby's promises with skepticism, but caught in the middle, they found it difficult to decide which side to support.[24]

In mid-May, Hubert Work found a way to resolve the dilemma. Working through his friend Rush Holland, a former assistant attorney general, he channeled a $4,000 contribution to Howard to help him with a court challenge to the lily-whites. Howard agreed to let the convention's Credentials Committee determine whether to seat the black-and-tan or lily-white delegation. Crosby withdrew from any active role in the campaign, and the lily-whites pledged their support to Hoover. The arrangement left the Mississippi Republican party weakened and even more divided than it had been previously, but Hoover's managers had what they wanted—assurance of the state's votes at the convention.[25]

The cynical attitude of Hoover's operatives so obvious in Mississippi also controlled their behavior elsewhere in the South. They hoped that Smith's Catholicism and opposition to Prohibition might turn some white Southern voters away from him in the general election, but their immediate concern was winning the nomination. In Arkansas, for example, where the lily-whites had been in control of the party for several years, an ambitious black lawyer, Scipio Jones, who had worked closely with Hoover during the flood, challenged the white organization. Finding that former Arkansas flood relief director Harvey Couch, who was a leader of the lily-whites, demanded patronage in return for support, Akerson maneuvered to dilute his influence by adding Jones to the Arkansas delegation, thus converting the lily-whites into black and tans, and assuring the organization's support of Hoover.[26]

In Louisiana, on the other hand, the Hoover forces not only supported the lily-white organization but also worked in at least a tacit alliance with the Ku Klux Klan, which aimed to undermine the influence of the black New Orleans customs comptroller Walter Cohen, who led the state's black and tans. Cohen and the black and tans antagonized the Hoover forces by supporting Hoover's rival, Senator Charles Curtis, for the Republican nomination. In Florida and Alabama, a few thousand dollars, channeled to local leaders of the lily-whites by Rush Holland to cover campaign and convention expenses, assured the support of those delegations. But in Georgia, the Hoover organization had a rare breakdown, with Holland backing the black and tans and another Hoover worker, Horace Mann, supporting the lily-whites. Eventually, the black-and-tan Hoover supporters won control of the state's delegation, but the situation remained uncertain right up to the convention.[27]

Although specific details are sometimes unclear, it is apparent that Hoover's representatives distributed several thousand dollars to supporters, both black and white, throughout the South in the preconvention period. Such "walking around money" had long been used by both parties to get out the vote, and the Hoover organizers seem to have been no more guilty of the practice than their opponents. But Hoover himself had righteously denounced campaign corruption, and his strong stand against promising patronage in return for support strengthened his public image. In practice, however, he did nothing to stop his representatives from using money to forward his cause, and despite his claims of support for African Americans, his campaign aligned itself with whomever would promise to vote for him at the convention, whether lily-whites or black and tans. The charge that he deliberately pursued a long-term goal of turning the Republican Party in the South "lily-white" does not stand up to scrutiny, but neither did he try actively to strengthen the position of African Americans. Expediency, not principle, shaped campaign policy.

During the presidential campaign, Hoover won some support in the black press for desegregating the Census Bureau. After a complaint from the National Association for the Advancement of Colored People about the practice, he had indeed asked an assistant, Bradley Nash, to investigate and ordered an end to the policy. But an end to official segregation did not necessarily alter custom in the department. There had been, George Akerson assured a white correspondent in October, "no change whatever in the Department of Commerce since the Wilson Administration regarding treatment of colored people." That meant that most of the "colored employees" in the department remained, as they had always been, "clerks, messengers, etc.," regardless of whether they worked in physically segregated facilities or not. Hoover displayed no overt prejudice and, as he had during the Mississippi flood, treated educated African Americans courteously and tried to respond to their concerns, but he and his colleagues practiced a form of de facto segregation based on low expectations. His sin was not bigotry but insensitivity.[28]

On the equally touchy issue of Prohibition, political expediency also dictated Hoover's position. In Europe during and after the war, friends recalled, he had liked a martini before dinner and occasionally drank a little wine with the meal, but when he became secretary of commerce, he announced that "the laws of this country must be enforced," in his home as elsewhere. Although friends reported that he occasionally stopped in at the Belgian embassy for a cocktail on foreign soil on his way home from work, elsewhere he obeyed the letter of the law. He asked his sons to pledge that they would not drink while in college, and Lou Hoover presided over the first meeting of the "Woman's National Committee for Law Enforcement," which focused on tightening the enforcement of Prohibition. He frequently asserted in speeches during the 1920s that Prohibition had contributed significantly to increased industrial productivity and improved living standards for all Americans (although he could never find statistical evidence to support his argument).[29]

In February 1928, Senator William Borah sent a letter to all of the possible Republican candidates, asking them to respond to four questions about Prohibition: whether the Republican platform should endorse it, what each candidate's attitude toward the law and toward enforcement would be if elected, whether national Prohibition should be replaced by state option, and whether the candidates favored repeal of the Eighteenth Amendment or the Volstead Act. As a leading progressive, popular in the farm states, Borah could be a valuable supporter, so Hoover framed his answers with care. His reply ignored the tricky questions of the party platform and state option but expressed strong support for "efficient, vigorous and sincere enforcement of the laws." The country, he wrote, had "deliberately undertaken a great social and economic experiment, noble in motive and far-reaching in purpose" that "must be worked out constructively." Although the letter never said that Hoover actually believed in prohibition, Borah declared himself satisfied.[30]

V

By late winter, Hoover's managers felt reasonably confident about the West and South, but still uncomfortable about the Midwest and Northeast. The West, except for Arizona, where the unresolved Colorado water division still rankled, seemed solid for Hoover, and the South appeared to be falling into line. Across the country, women's organizations offered particularly strong support. The Northeast remained a problem, however. Andrew Mellon doubted Hoover's commitment to the free market, loathed the commerce secretary's constant meddling in the affairs of other departments, and regarded him as excessively nationalistic in foreign policy. But Mellon could find no one else who might be able to win the nomination, and so he declined to commit himself, or the large Pennsylvania Republican delegation, to anyone. Hoover's supporters believed that Mellon, a political realist, would eventually come around, but for the time being, he remained a question mark.[31]

New York also presented problems. The influential Charles Hilles still clung to the hope that Coolidge would accept a draft, although the hope had begun to fade. Wall Streeters disliked Hoover's attempts to tie loans to European borrowers to concessions on war debts and disarmament, suspecting him of isolationism, in general, and Anglophobia, in particular. His well-known disagreement with Federal Reserve Bank of New York Governor Benjamin Strong over monetary policy, and his criticism of Strong as "a mental annex to Europe" also alienated New York bankers. Among New York Republicans, policy differences kept alive the memory that Hoover had served in a Democratic administration during the war and had urged the election of a Democratic Congress in 1918. Edgar Rickard appealed to former Attorney General George Wickersham for support and asked Wickersham to sound out Charles Evans Hughes, but winning significant backing in the state would obviously be an uphill battle.[32]

The farm states posed an even more formidable problem. There, hog and wheat farmers still blamed Hoover for preventing them from profiting fully from the war, and his subsequent opposition to the McNary-Haugen bills convinced many people that he was indifferent to farm problems. Old friends like Secretary of Agriculture William Jardine, Iowa farm editor Dante Pierce, and Frank Howard, former president of the Farm Bureau Federation, did their best for him, and Akerson suggested playing up Frank Lowden's support of McNary-Haugen as evidence of disloyalty to Coolidge, but there seemed no way to dent Lowden's broad support in the region. Unable to win endorsements from Midwestern Republican organizations, Akerson began to gather information about individual delegates to the convention—their home towns, their businesses, their friends, the degree of their commitment to particular candidates, and so on. Laborious as the process was in a precomputer age, it offered the possibility of chipping away at preconvention commitments and eroding the unity of opposing organizations. In an effort to bypass possibly hostile state Republican organizations, Hoover's publicity office mailed more than 2 million flyers and pamphlets directly to farm families.[33]

Former Governor Henry Allen of Kansas and journalist Edward Anthony ran the "campaign publicity" office that distributed propaganda of various types. Anthony early recognized the potential advantage Hoover had among ethnic voters who recalled his relief work in Europe and among black voters in the South for his work during the Mississippi flood. The publicity office pumped out a steady stream of campaign material in many different languages, of which the most popular, according to Anthony, was a "Picture Life of Herbert Hoover" by the cartoonist Herbert W. Satterfield, which provided a capsule biography of the candidate in 72 drawings and 114 lines of text. Anthony also offered plates of pro-Hoover editorial cartoons to newspapers. In New York, Thomas H. Ormsbee organized a Hoover-for-president Business Paper Editorial Advisory Committee, which produced articles for the business press emphasizing the important work the secretary of commerce had done on behalf of business. From Hollywood came personal endorsements of Hoover from such movie luminaries as Louis B. Mayer, D. W. Griffith, and Cecil B. DeMille. More importantly, the studios also provided valuable footage of Hoover's European and Mississippi relief work that could be used with ethnic and black audiences. All in all, the campaign produced an extraordinarily wide range of materials designed to appeal to virtually every identifiable group in the country who might conceivably support Hoover.[34]

By the end of April, Hoover calculated that he had 476 of the 545 convention votes needed for nomination, despite losses in the North Dakota, Wisconsin, Illinois, and Nebraska primaries. The Midwest remained a battleground, but Lowden, Dawes, and Curtis had developed little support outside that area. The strategy of identifying Hoover as the only candidate of national stature by entering nearly all the primaries, coupled with intensive organization across the country, had begun to pay off.[35]

The Indiana primary on May 7 provided the last real hurdle. No one seriously expected Hoover to win it against Senator James Watson, but former Governor James Goodrich led a vigorous campaign to make the contest as close as possible and succeeded. Watson carried the state with 228,795 votes, but Hoover ran a respectable second, with 203,279. As the Chicago *Tribune* pointed out editorially, the fact that Watson, a gregarious and popular senator with the backing of the Klan and the Anti-Saloon League, could beat Hoover by only twenty-five thousand votes in a farm state provided impressive testimony to Hoover's broad strength.[36]

In mid-May, Hoover, accompanied by Larry Richey, Ray Wilbur, and Mark Sullivan, slipped away from the Commerce Department and the campaign to spend a few days trout fishing at the Ogontz Lodge near Williamsport, Pennsylvania, where enterprising photographers took his picture in the midst of a stream, fly rod in hand. He seemed totally unconcerned that at almost the same moment Pennsylvania's Republican convention delegation had caucused to hear its instructions from party bosses. Andrew Mellon, who had avoided committing himself all spring, told them equivocally that he thought Hoover "seems to come closest to the standard that we have set for the Presidency," but privately he still hoped to draft Coolidge or perhaps Hughes. If neither of them would run, Mellon had decided to hold his nose and support Hoover. Mellon's long delay and public equivocation about the candidates had undermined his influence over his state's Republicans, however. Control of the Pennsylvania delegation had passed subtly to Philadelphia boss William Vare, who favored Hoover. That meant seventy-nine more votes in the Hoover column.[37]

A few days before leaving for his fishing trip, Hoover testified before a special Senate committee on campaign expenditures chaired by Senator Frederick Steiwer of Oregon. The committee summoned candidates and campaign workers to testify how much money they had spent up to that time, where the money had come from, and whether anyone had made promises in return for contributions. Hoover, James Good, and Ferry Heath, treasurer of the Washington Hoover-for-president office, testified, as did other campaign workers. All of them painted a picture of the campaign as a loose confederation of volunteer organizations without central direction or control. According to James Good, those groups had collected and spent only $241,274 up to mid-May, primarily in the Ohio, Indiana, and West Virginia contests. Hoover denied that he or any members of his family had contributed a single cent, and indeed, his testimony left the impression that he knew little about what was being done on his behalf. Edsel Ford's campaign contribution of $5,000, Good declared, had been the largest so far, and only twenty-seven contributions of $1,000 or more had been received.[38]

In fact, although both the Democrats and Republicans ran frugal campaigns by modern standards in 1928, it seems likely that Good was being economical with the truth before the committee. The committee's preliminary report, published after the election, showed that the Republicans had received forty-seven contributions of $25,000 or more. In its final report, published in February 1929, the committee reported that the Republican National Committee had spent a total of $4.1 million, and the Democratic National Committee $3.2 million, to which state party organizations added $4.8 million and $2.4 million respectively. Various other organizations not directly affiliated with the parties spent about $700,000 more on behalf of the Republican candidates, and about $1.7 million more for the Democrats. Altogether, the committee reported that the Republicans raised a total of $10 million and spent $9.4 million, and the Democrats raised $7.2 million and spent almost all of it. Each campaign raised and spent more than twice as much as both parties together raised and spent in the elections of 1924 and 1932. The total spending of 1928 would not be matched until the hotly contested election of 1936.[39]

VI

By the time the Republican convention met in the Auditorium at Kansas City, Missouri, on June 12, Hoover had almost locked up a first-ballot nomination. Conservatives still cherished the dwindling hope that Coolidge might consent to a draft, but when he remained stubbornly silent, they could not agree on anyone in his place. In the week before the convention began, as the Platform Committee hammered out the final details of the platform, reporters in hopes of finding something dramatic to write focused on the Credentials Committee. Making sure that Hoover supporters led by Assistant Attorney General Mabel Walker Willebrandt would control that committee had represented one of Work's greatest preconvention achievements. When both black-and-tan and lily-white delegations from Louisiana, Texas, Florida, Tennessee, Mississippi, and Georgia applied to be seated, the committee seated the Hoover delegation in each case, regardless of race or the merits of the challenges. Its decisions had the effect of confirming black-and-tan control over Republican organizations in Tennessee, Mississippi, and Georgia, but of transferring power in Louisiana, Florida, and Texas from African Americans to whites. The black losers denounced Hoover as a racist and declared angrily that they would leave the Republicans and support Al Smith. It was an ominous event for the future of the Republican Party.[40]

On June 11, the day before the convention opened officially, Hoover's courtship of Senator Borah paid off. In a conversation with a friend in the Idaho delegation, Edgar Rickard learned that Borah had released the delegates from a pledge to vote for him on the first ballot. The news confirmed Borah's support for Hoover, and Rickard celebrated by going to hear Will Rogers.[41]

Outside the auditorium that evening, Kansas City offered a political carnival. A gigantic torchlight parade featured floats with tableaux from previous Republican administrations; twenty-two brass bands; groups of "cowboys," "Indians," and "highwaymen"; antique railroad engines; a miniature ocean liner and an airplane on floats; and long lines of cheering, singing supporters of the candidates. Five thousand Kansas City residents sporting "Ask Me" buttons directed delegates and tourists to the city's attractions.[42]

The next morning, at a minute or two after 11:00, the convention officially opened in the hot, bunting-draped auditorium. The floor swarmed with delegates, and noisy spectators filled three balconies. Klieg lights illuminated the scene for cameras, and the venerable opera star, Ernestine Schumann-Heink, sang "The Star-Spangled Banner." But despite all the hoopla, the certainty of the outcome led reporters to describe the event as "dreary and dull." Such excitement as existed remained behind the scenes, where the Vermont and Massachusetts delegations switched their support from Coolidge to Hoover, and where Philadelphia boss William S. Vare announced he would support Hoover even before Mellon had a chance to speak. In the New York delegation, Charles Hilles held out to the end for Coolidge, but exhausted and ill, he found the delegates slipping away despite all he could do. While the roll was being called and Senator Simeon Fess droned on through a long and tedious keynote speech, the "silent smoothness" of the Hoover organization flattened the last traces of opposition. Everything went his way, even outside the auditorium, where a promised demonstration of one hundred thousand angry farmers produced fewer than a thousand. Prevented from entering the building, the protesters milled around in confusion and then quietly drifted away. Their presence, declared one Hoover lieutenant patronizingly, had aroused interest in what might have been a dull convention.[43]

On Thursday afternoon, June 14, the convention turned to nominations. The permanent chairman, Senator George H. Moses of New Hampshire, called on Alabama, which immediately yielded to California, unleashing "a din that literally shook the rafters of the great hall." San Francisco lawyer John L. McNab, an old Hoover friend and the spokesman for the California delegation, rose to nominate him, but when he mentioned Hoover's name in his third sentence, a twenty-five minute demonstration erupted and drowned out most of the rest of his speech. After McNab sat down, Arizona yielded to Illinois, and Illinois Senator Otis Glenn came to the rostrum, not to nominate Frank Lowden as most delegates expected, but to read a terse statement from the governor saying that because the party platform had rejected the McNary-Haugen approach to the agricultural problem, he was withdrawing his name. The statement, although apparently drafted by Lowden at the last moment, did not surprise insiders who knew he had been saying since May that he would not run if the party rejected McNary-Haugen. The convention having done exactly that by an 806 to 278 vote that morning, he felt he had no choice but to withdraw.[44]

Lowden's withdrawal sucked the last vestige of drama out of the convention. A substantial number of delegates might not like Hoover, but they had nowhere else to turn. Pro forma nominations of Senators James Watson, Charles Curtis, Guy Goff, and George Norris, and finally, President Coolidge, produced hardly a ripple of excitement. On the first ballot, Hoover received 837 votes, Lowden 74, Curtis 64, Watson 45, Norris 24, and Coolidge 17, with nearly all the votes for the losing candidates coming from Midwestern states. Chairman Moses then proposed that the nomination be made unanimous, and despite some grumbling from the floor, ruled that the motion had been adopted. That evening, he telegraphed an official notice of nomination to Hoover.[45]

Of the Hoover family, only Allan actually attended the convention, where he shared a room with the son of Congressman Franklin Fort of New Jersey, who would become an important manager of Hoover's postconvention campaign. The rest of the family gathered at Hoover's office in Washington where, with a few friends and staff members, they listened to the proceedings on the radio. Everyone cheered when the balloting passed the 543 votes needed for nomination—everyone, that is, except Hoover, who, according to Edgar Rickard, was the "only person not visibly affected." That evening, after dinner with a few friends at 2300 S Street, where a lone policeman now stood guard outside, Hoover posed on the front steps for photographers and then went back inside to write a brief acceptance message to the convention. The message, in keeping with the complacent tone set at the convention, declared that the welfare of the nation and the world depended on the continuation of Republican policies of opportunity, prosperity, and peace.[46]

That night and the next morning, party leaders in Kansas City discussed the vice presidential nomination. Eastern leaders preferred former governor Channing Cox of Massachusetts to balance Hoover's California background, but for unknown reasons, Senator Reed Smoot of Utah, chairman of the resolutions committee, vetoed Cox. Charles Dawes, Coolidge's vice president, indicated his willingness to serve again if asked, but his support for McNary-Haugen made him unacceptable to both Coolidge and Hoover. Hoover himself had refused to express a preference until his own nomination became definite. What happened thereafter is unclear. Senator Smoot said that he met with half a dozen of the convention's leaders (including Ogden Mills) in Andrew Mellon's hotel suite, and they decided, perhaps after conferring with Hubert Work, to nominate Charles Curtis of Kansas, the Republican majority leader in the Senate. A second version of the story, as adumbrated in Hoover's *Memoirs*, suggests that Coolidge, perhaps working through Mellon, had indicated a preference for Curtis. The affinity between Coolidge and Curtis, who had been a reliable conservative and party loyalist in the Senate, seems obvious, but it also seems strange that the president, who had so scrupulously avoided involvement in the campaign, should break that rule for the vice presidency. In any event, Hoover appears to have cared little about the decision, and Curtis had the advantage of being popular in the farm states. He had even managed to straddle the McNary-Haugen issue, voting for the bill in the Senate and then to sustain President Coolidge's veto. The convention obediently rubberstamped the party leaders' choice, nominating Curtis on June 15 by a vote of 1,052 to 34.[47]

Curtis brought to the ticket a colorful Midwestern background but a reliably conservative adult political career. Born in North Topeka, Kansas, in 1860, he could claim one-eighth Indian blood, and as a youth, he had worked as a jockey during summer school vacations. After high school, he put all that behind him, clerking for a local lawyer while studying the law. Admitted to the bar at twenty-one, he had a brief but successful career as a criminal lawyer. In 1892, he was elected to the House of Representatives, serving until 1907, when the state legislature chose him to fill an unexpired term in the Senate. Although he lost in 1912, he won again in 1914 and served continuously until 1929, when he became vice president. In the Senate, he gained a reputation for constituent service and total party loyalty, which led to his being made Republican majority leader following Henry Cabot Lodge's death in 1924. No legislation bore his name, but his colleagues praised his ability to work behind the scenes to mold bills and move legislation through the Senate's sometimes tangled structure. In 1928, he had competed with Frank Lowden for the Republican nomination on the strength of his popularity in the farm states, but he remained little known outside his home region. He would become one of the most invisible of all vice presidents.[48]

VII

After the convention adjourned, Hoover spent a day reading and answering messages from well-wishers. One, from the president, plumbed the depths of political hypocrisy, wishing the new candidate "all the success that your heart could desire," and predicting that his "great ability" and "wide experience" would enable him "to serve our party and our country with marked distinction." Hoover responded in kind, thanking Coolidge for seven years of "unremitting friendship" and declaring that the president's devotion to public service would always be an inspiration to him.[49]

Two weeks after the Republican convention, the Democrats met at the Sam Houston Convention Hall in Houston. When it became obvious on the first ballot that Al Smith was within ten votes of the two-thirds majority needed to nominate, states that had favored other candidates raced to put him over the top. The delegates then chose Arkansas Senator Joseph T. Robinson, a Protestant supporter of Prohibition who had drawn Smith's attention when he denounced anti-Catholic bigotry on the Senate floor, as the vice presidential candidate in a classic example of ticket balancing. The convention, on the whole, proved harmonious, with the only real debate over the wording of the Prohibition plank in the platform. The Platform Committee originally reported a plank pledging support for the law but nodding to Governor Smiths "wet" sentiments by pointing out that the people could repeal a Constitutional amendment if they chose to do so. A rebellion on the convention floor substituted a "dry" plank that condemned the Republicans for failing to enforce Prohibition and promised to make "an honest effort" to enforce the Eighteenth Amendment and the Volstead Act. In his acceptance letter, however, Smith said frankly that he disagreed with the platform on this issue and, if elected, would work to change the law.[50]

Hoover began the campaign in a strong position with "General Prosperity" on his side. Between 1922 and 1927, the purchasing power of wages had increased by 10 percent, and consumer products like cosmetics, telephones, radios, and refrigerators filled the stores. The 5 million passenger cars on the streets in 1919 had grown to more than 20 million, and an increasing number of airplanes carried travelers across the country. Even struggling farmers had received a boost when the Agriculture Department announced on July 1 that the farm price index had reached its highest level since 1920. For consumers, conditions seemed better than they had ever been, although the economy had definite weak spots. The great stock market boom depended upon cheap money, and Wall Streeters worried that Hoover might attempt to reduce speculation by tightening credit, as he had proposed in 1925. People in the working class complained about unpredictable layoffs, even in good times, and wages had been lagging behind increasing worker productivity ever since the turn of the century. And although the "new" industries producing consumer products had boomed, the "old" industries such as coal mining and textile and shoe manufacturing had experienced little or no growth and shrinking profits. On the whole, however, Republican prosperity was real, and it seemed unlikely the voters would reject the candidate so closely identified with it.[51]

Nevertheless, Hoover had no intention of leaving anything to chance. Meticulous organization had gained him the nomination, and he meant to apply the same technique to the general election. In place of a formal campaign organization, he preferred to depend on the Republican National Committee, now headed by Hubert Work and with an enlarged staff to handle such tasks as fund-raising; relations with ethnic, African American, women, and labor voters; motion pictures; campaign speakers; and "research" on the opposition. The national committee established offices in the Barr Building, near the White House, while a "Hoover personal headquarters" operated at first out of 2300 S Street and later from a large, rented house on Massachusetts Avenue. Work put each state's national committee members in charge of creating or strengthening party organization at the state, county, and even precinct level. Regional coordinators such as Franklin Fort in the East, James Good in the Midwest, Horace Mann in the South, and Tom Gregory in the West kept them working efficiently. The national committee dealt with the essential but routine work of the campaign, while at the "personal headquarters" the Chief himself met with party leaders and planned broad strategy.[52]

The network of volunteer organizations across the country that had worked so well during the preconvention period remained in place, and Nathan W. MacChesney headed a Hoover-Curtis Organization Bureau that promoted and coordinated their work. The campaign established state and county organizations and Hoover-Curtis Clubs in twenty-eight states, along with special organizations for women, first voters, college students, and business and professional groups. Some three thousand "Hoover hostesses" in all forty-eight states opened their homes on the days of Hoover's radio addresses so that supporters could listen together. Ultimately, Director MacChesney estimated, the bureau enrolled nearly 2 million men and women as active workers in its various activities, at a startlingly low cost to the campaign of about one and a half cents apiece. Other volunteer organizations such as the Hoover-for-president Engineers' National Committee, and its Woman's Branch, functioned independently of the Bureau.[53]

VIII

To some extent, Hoover counted on Republican prosperity and meticulous organization to compensate for his own limitations as a campaigner. Although he made thousands of speeches during his public career, he never became a good speaker. "He has not a single gesture," wrote reporter Henry F. Pringle. "He reads—his chin down against his shirt front—rapidly and quite without expression." In his largely inaudible monotone, added Pringle, he could "utter a striking phrase in so prosaic, so uninspired, and so mumbling a fashion, that it is completely lost on nine out of ten of his auditors." And he could not "pose for a photograph without looking quite silly." Before a small group, where his mastery of his subject often evoked enthusiasm, he could appear commanding, eloquent, even charming, but with a large audience his worst qualities came out. Pringle attributed his shortcomings to his being "abnormally shy, abnormally sensitive, filled with an impassioned pride in his personal integrity, and ever apprehensive that he may be made to appear ridiculous." To compensate for his feelings of insecurity, his speeches arrayed battalions of facts and sometimes left listeners feeling that he regarded them as stupid or at least ignorant. His supporters came to expect little of his speeches. One friend damned him with faint praise for not swallowing his words at the end of sentences, and some admirers lauded a couple of speeches he had given in the summer of 1926 because he had digressed briefly from a prepared text to talk, albeit in dry and impersonal language, about the postwar European relief program. For all his ability to inspire absolute loyalty among those with whom he worked closely, he almost totally lacked what another generation would call "political charisma." In 1928, Americans responded less to him as a man than as a symbol of the energy and competence that they hoped underlay the good times.[54]

With the campaign organization established and running well in Washington, Hoover felt free to head west toward home. He telegraphed the president requesting permission to stop off at the summer White House in Superior, Wisconsin, to discuss the campaign. Ten thousand people lined the streets when the candidate's train arrived on July 16, and a boys' band, with orange and black caps and white suits, led a procession for a mile through town. Then the Hoovers were driven thirty miles to the president's retreat at Cedar Island Lodge. Hoover and Coolidge spent the afternoon fly-fishing on the Brule River, but in separate canoes, and were later photographed sitting silently next to each other in rocking chairs on the resort's porch. Their sparse conversation, Hoover told Akerson, had been pleasant but meaningless. Coolidge acknowledged Hoover's letter of resignation from the cabinet but deferred acceptance of it until the secretary could wind up pending departmental business. He made no promises about helping in the campaign, though he later sent cordial congratulations after Hoover's acceptance speech and waxed, for him, positively effusive in his praises when he officially accepted Hoover's resignation on August 21. At the conclusion of the visit, the president chatted about fishing with reporters while Hoover met with local political leaders. Then, duty done, the party drove to Duluth, where the Hoovers boarded their train.[55] (See Figure 21.4.)

On July 18, the train steamed on into Iowa and Nebraska, but word that Lou's father Charles Henry had died led to the cancellation of planned whistlestops and the postponement of a welcoming ceremony in San Francisco. The Hoovers arrived in Palo Alto on the morning of July 20 and attended the memorial service for Charles Henry that afternoon. They spent the next day at home with the family, but the pressures of the campaign crowded in. California supporters pressed for a welcome-home celebration in San Francisco, and Stanford officials needed to finalize plans for the official notification ceremony, to be held in the university's stadium on August 11. From Mississippi came news that Perry Howard had been indicted on bribery charges, a potential embarrassment that required quick action to distance the campaign from him. A host of other matters, great and small, also clamored for the candidate's personal attention.[56]

The various demands on him made it difficult for Hoover to work on his acceptance speech, so he decided to combine business with pleasure and travel into the northern California mountains for fishing and writing. Of course, solitude is a relative matter for a presidential candidate, and the Hoover party that headed north on July 29 included ten cars and nearly fifty friends, reporters, photographers, staff members, and security guards. They stayed their first night at Milton Esberg's camp on the Klamath River, but finding the fishing poor, they turned south and camped near Mt. Shasta before heading back to San Francisco by train on August 2. Despite their best efforts, the party had caught very few fish, and Hoover repeated a well-worn joke to reporters, saying that he was "definitely committed to the platform of more and bigger trout and less time between bites." Nevertheless, he added, he had seen some beautiful country and thoroughly enjoyed himself. Journalists traveling with the group reported favorably on his physical fitness and good humor.[57] (See Figure 21.3.)

Hoover's acceptance speech, delivered at Stanford the day after his fifty-fourth birthday, would be his first major campaign utterance. To make sure that it reached as many people as possible, he agreed to have it broadcast live on the radio and further disseminated through movie newsreels and the press. On the morning of the speech, he stood patiently at the podium as the moviemakers set up their lights and instructed him on how to hold his head and gesture in the most effective way, and the radio technicians ran sound checks and explained how to use the microphone. This would be the first "modern" campaign, making full use of the mass media and advertising to "sell" the candidate. That afternoon, seventy thousand people packed into the stadium, and promptly at 4:00 PM, Senator George Moses delivered the official notification.[58]

IX

Hoover started his speech with a familiar tactic—asking Americans whether they felt better off after eight years of Republican rule. He felt certain that they did. In fact, he boasted, "We in America today are nearer to the final triumph over poverty than ever before in the history of any land." But, of course, obstacles stood in the way of achieving that goal. They included the depressed state of agriculture, which called for tariff protection, improved transportation (including waterways), a reorganized marketing system, and an expansion of the same cooperative relationship between government and farmers that had worked so well with industry. Successful policies, including immigration restriction, promotion of cooperation between labor and capital, strict enforcement of prohibition, and the support and encouragement of private enterprise should be continued. The effort "to save life and health for our children" must be strengthened, and a foreign policy of "peace" would best serve American national interests. The American people, he said, had decided that the nation could "give the greatest real help" to the promotion of peace by staying out of the League of Nations, but that did not mean the country would reject cooperation with the League in its efforts "to further scientific, economic, and social welfare, and to secure limitation of armament." Above all, continued progress toward the abolition of poverty at home and peace in the world required protecting "equality of opportunity." The "success or failure of this principle is the test of our government," he proclaimed. It provided the key not only to economic prosperity but also to the moral and spiritual growth that would guarantee future happiness.[59]

In the Stanford speech, Hoover paid lip service to the traditional American admiration for small farmers. Ten days later, in a homecoming speech in West Branch, Iowa, he spoke to commercial farmers, admitting that their involvement in world markets had brought some insecurity but insisting that it also assured higher standards of living, less hard work, greater opportunities for leisure and recreation, and more of "the joy of living." With the benevolent assistance of government, he contended, the individualism of the past could be united with the advantages of modern collective organization. The spirit of the frontier could be revived, not only in individual independence, but also in the cooperative spirit of the pioneers who had worked together "to build the roads, bridges, and towns," to "erect their schools, their churches, and to raise their barns and harvest their fields."[60]

In a speech on labor issues at Newark on September 17, Hoover pursued the same theme of cooperation between government and private enterprise. "Full and stable employment," he argued, provided the basis for continued economic progress, and achievement of that goal required "sound policies" and close government cooperation with both labor and business "to promote economic welfare." Those policies, he assured listeners, had tamed the business cycle, restored prosperity after the recession of 1921, and maintained it

throughout the decade. He promised that "the ideal of distributed content-
ment among the whole people" would continue to guide his administration.[61]

Hoover knew that no Republican could carry the South, but on one rainy
October day, he made a token foray into the region, speaking in traditionally
Republican East Tennessee. He argued that a 60 percent growth in manufacturing output and a 30 percent rise in the number of employed workers in
the South had resulted from the same Republican policies that had brought
prosperity to the rest of the country. He hinted that the federal government
might contribute further to the region's growth by developing fertilizer and
power production at Muscle Shoals on the Tennessee River. The South, he
suggested flatteringly, could show the nation how to avoid urban problems by
joining "industry with agriculture to their mutual benefit." Southern newspaper editors, however, remained unimpressed. Aside from the Muscle Shoals
reference, they saw little in the speech to challenge old voting habits.[62]

The Northeast, with its hard-drinking immigrant population and interest in foreign trade, presented a special challenge for a Republican running
on a platform that endorsed Prohibition and the protective tariff. In Boston,
Hoover dodged the Prohibition issue but attacked "the fallacy that the protective tariff ruins our export trade" and gave a twist to the lion's tail by demanding that the Europeans pay their wartime debts to the United States. In New
York, he launched his most direct attack on his opponent, charging that during
the war the Democrats had created an "autocratic . . . socialistic state" and that
they now proposed "state socialism" as a solution to all problems facing the
country. "State socialism," he implied, differed in some sinister way from the
centralization of power in the federal government to which he had contributed while food administrator during the war or from the expanded federal
role in the management of the economy he had promoted while secretary of
commerce. The Democrats would endanger the "very foundations" of "our
American political and economic system," he proclaimed, and he urged his
listeners to rally in defense of "equality of opportunity not alone for ourselves
but to our children."[63]

In evoking "state socialism," Hoover implicitly lumped Al Smith's record
of educational and social reforms in New York under that pejorative heading. He was careful to emphasize, however, that he had no desire to return to
a "free-for-all and devil-take-the hind-most" policy. The government must
prevent "domination by any group or combination" and maintain "stability in
business and stability in employment." That theme—"the constructive side of
government"—dominated his final major speech of the campaign, at St. Louis
on November 2. The government, he argued, must exercise "leadership . . .
to solve many difficult problems," undertaking public works in waterway and
highway construction, flood control, reclamation, and the erection of public buildings. It must foster education, promote public health and scientific
research, develop parks and the conservation of natural resources, and support
agriculture, industry, and foreign trade. And it must encourage "the growing

efforts of our people to cooperation among themselves to useful social and economic ends." Ultimately, he concluded, strong government assured the "sound economic life" that provided the foundations for "those things we call spiritual . . . security, happiness, and peace."[64]

Taken together, Hoover's seven major campaign speeches summarized the middle way that he had tried to follow as secretary of commerce and hoped to continue during his presidency. But voters who wanted to understand his values and the programs he espoused would have had to hear or read all of them. Each explored a different issue, with as little overlap with the others as possible. Being new to the world of mass media, he believed that radio "had made it impossible for presidential candidates to repeat the same speech with small variations." Overestimating the public's attentiveness, he never developed and polished a standard "stump speech" that might have compensated for some of his limitations as a speaker.[65]

A voter, pondering Hoover's speeches, might well have wondered how the long list of activities that he urged the federal government to undertake differed from the "state socialism" he had denounced in New York. As Walter Lippmann put it, "the two platforms contain no difference which would be called an issue." And indeed, in a period of prosperity, the programs offered by Hoover and Smith did not seem very different. Both envisioned a departure from the precedents of the recent Republican past and a return to a more activist role for government like that of the Progressive Era. But there was a fundamental difference. Hoover stressed building and maintaining a prosperous economy in the belief that general prosperity would lead to individual happiness and spiritual growth. Smith's program, growing out of his working-class, urban background, emphasized support and assistance to people in need. Hoover assumed that if government merely maintained equality of economic opportunity, individuals would make their own way. Smith concluded that the obstacles to success required active and continued support for people starting at the bottom. The one focused on the economic system, the other on the needs of the individuals who make up the economy. Their visions of a happy society did not differ radically, but they saw government's role in achieving that happiness very differently. In the absence of anything like national debates to clarify the differences between the two men, the Republicans adopted the very effective strategy of having local leaders pick apart each of Smith's major speeches, thus heightening the impression of major differences between the parties without actually specifying what they might be.[66]

A very obvious but not very substantive difference between the candidates lay in the question of Prohibition. Hoover promised strict enforcement, while Smith frankly advocated repeal, but privately, they thought much alike. A temperance advocate, Smith drew his opposition to Prohibition from his urban background, rather than from a principled commitment to the sanctity of individual rights. Hoover found it expedient to go along with his party's support of Prohibition, but he had no moral objections to alcohol, and he doubted privately that the Volstead Act could be enforced.[67]

The candidates appeared also to differ more on the issue of race than actually proved to be the case. African Americans had traditionally voted Republican, but by 1928, their support had begun to waver. The Hoover campaign's unscrupulous practices during the preconvention period antagonized some Southern blacks, while Northern black leaders asked what the Republicans had actually given them other than rhetoric. The *Chicago Defender*, the country's most important black newspaper, endorsed Smith, suggesting that electing a Catholic to the presidency would strike a blow at every form of bigotry. Smith's fight against the influence of the Ku Klux Klan at the 1924 Democratic convention, plus his private statement to Walter White that, if elected, he did not intend to have his policy dictated by the white South, earned him the support of some black leaders. But then Smith backed down when advisers told him he could not possibly win without the support of the South, and Hoover regained some of his support among African Americans when he rejected segregation in the Census Bureau. In the end, a few African American leaders and newspapers supported Smith, but the majority of black voters stayed with the Republican Party.[68]

Religion, like race, played an important part in the campaign but appeared in neither party's platform. No Roman Catholic had ever run for president. Many rural Americans had never had personal contact with Catholics and associated the religion with Irish and Southern and Eastern European immigrants, and above all, with the idea that Catholics obeyed the orders of a foreign pope. As a Quaker, Hoover did not share those fears and prejudices, and in his acceptance speech he spoke out forcefully for "religious tolerance both in act and in spirit." When a published letter attributed to a Virginia member of the Republican National Committee warned against a "Romanized and rum-ridden" country, he repudiated it in direct and forceful language. But if his statements made it clear that he did not share or approve of attacks on Smith's religion, he failed to stop a whispering campaign and the continuing circulation of bigoted materials by his supporters. It would have taken an exceptional effort to do that, and Hoover did not make the effort. Rather, he seemed deliberately to understate the seriousness of the matter. In an off-the-record statement to reporters on September 21, the day after Smith denounced "bigotry, hatred, intolerance, and un-American secular division" in a major speech at Oklahoma City in the heart of Klan country, Hoover argued that the best way to deal with intolerance was to ignore it, because, he said, "the very ventilation of intolerance in the press at the insistence of bigots tends to fan that flame." And then he went on to give a lengthy list of what he described as lying slurs being spread in a "whispering campaign" about him, thus implying that he was at least as much a victim of prejudice as Smith. In a private letter to Bernard Baruch, Hoover alleged that he had ignored "virulent" attacks on him by Catholics in an effort to defuse the issue.[69]

Some of the most outrageous attacks on Smith came from people embarrassingly close to Hoover. Assistant Attorney General Mabel Walker Willebrandt, who had so efficiently manipulated the Credentials Committee in Hoover's interest at Kansas City, addressed a meeting of 2,500 Methodist ministers at Springfield, Ohio, on September 7. In her speech, Willebrandt urged the ministers to use their pulpits to attack Smith's stand on Prohibition. To many people, her speech crossed the traditional boundary between church and state and invited Protestants to attack Smith as much for his Catholicism as for his opposition to Prohibition. To make matters worse, Willebrandt insisted that the Republican National Committee had cleared her speech, and a tepid statement by Hubert Work against "scurrilous" attacks on *both* candidates a few days later did little to distance the committee from her. In Louisiana, the Hoover operative Horace Mann circulated, albeit without the prior knowledge or approval of the national campaign organization, an editorial from the *Protestant* linking Smith's Catholicism and opposition to Prohibition. Hoover's silence about these and similar incidents, and the connections between his organization and the anti-Catholic campaign, gave bigotry the appearance of official sanction.[70]

Hoover himself did not share the anti-Catholic prejudice that darkened the underside of his campaign. His weak response to it, however, particularly a September statement to reporters in which he listed every petty, malicious rumor being circulated about him and implied that because of their numbers they outweighed the attack on Smith's Catholicism, revealed a strange gap in his judgment. Not only did he show little empathy for Smith as a victim of bigotry, but he also suggested that the Democrat had invited attacks by raising the issue. As for himself, he demonstrated here as many times previously what can only be described as a narcissistic conviction that he never made mistakes and ought to be spared all criticism. His family and associates, it must be noted, reinforced his belief that "the Chief" could do no wrong. Lou Hoover, far from deploring the attacks on Smith, dismissed Democratic outrage at the "whispering campaign" as "a travesty." At very least, Hoover's half-hearted reaction encouraged his supporters to believe he approved their actions.[71]

Ultimately, it is not clear that Hoover could have said or done much to prevent Smith's Catholicism from becoming a major issue in 1928. In the South, where Republican campaigners found the going difficult in the best of times, the fact that the Democratic candidate united Catholicism and opposition to Prohibition presented an almost irresistible temptation. Nor did it require encouragement from national party operatives to arouse many Southern Protestants on the issues of Catholicism and Prohibition. In North Carolina and Alabama, Democratic Senators Furnifold M. Simmons and J. Thomas Heflin cited the Prohibition issue as the reason for their defection from the Democrats, and Heflin added religion as well. Hoover's near win in Alabama and victories in North Carolina, Florida, and Texas demonstrate the salience of such issues in the South (although in most Southern states, party loyalty ultimately outweighed other issues), and the 70 percent national turnout of eligible voters and extraordinarily high level of campaign spending suggest that religion and drink aroused voters all over the country. Managing such issues so they did not become destructive may have been impossible and certainly exceeded the ability of the candidates at that point. As a recent biographer of Smith puts it, "If Al Smith had not been a Catholic, a wet, a representative of immigrants, a New Yorker, 1928 *might have been* a referendum on prosperity, and the Democrats *may* have lost anyway. But we will never know, because Al Smith was, in fact, all of the above, and the election hinged on those issues."[72]

Smith appeared scarcely less alien to Westerners than to Southerners. Kansas Senator Arthur Capper observed that "Tammany in the role of friend of the farmer is a joke all over this section." He predicted that, despite Hoover's alleged responsibility for low wheat prices during the war, he would carry Kansas by 250,000 votes (he actually carried it by more than 300,000) and that he would win in all the states west of the Mississippi (correct, except for Arkansas and Louisiana). James Goodrich made a similar—and correct—prophecy about his own state of Indiana and about Missouri, Ohio, West Virginia, Colorado, Montana, and Minnesota. He argued that the Republicans could also win Nebraska, New Mexico, and Oklahoma, if they worked hard. Wisconsin, with its large "wet" population and with the influence of Senator La Follette, posed difficulties, but in the end, as former Senator Lenroot predicted, Hoover carried it as well. A large German-American population remembered that Hoover had broken the "hunger blockade" against their homeland after the war, and Polish-Americans recalled his strong support for Poland with similar gratitude. Throughout the Midwest, some farm leaders remained cool to Hoover, but Smith's confusing attitude toward the McNary-Haugen bill, and his statement that he would leave the solution of the surplus dilemma to "a commission to be worked out during the winter," appeared even more uncertain than Hoover's program for cooperative marketing. Smith's strange accent, urban background, and alien religion contrasted unfavorably in rural voters' minds with Hoover's Iowa birth, flat speech, and mid-American appearance.[73]

Women constituted a particularly valuable part of Hoover's forces. New, ethnic, women voters swelled the Smith vote in the Northeast, but in conservative areas of the country where suffrage had been slow to catch on, women also turned out to vote in larger numbers in 1928 than ever before. Hoover had begun developing a cordial relationship with women during the Food Administration years. He strengthened that bond with his European relief work and while secretary of commerce by his campaign for child health, opposition to child labor, and strong support for home ownership. Women also admired his "humanitarianism." As early as 1925, Hoover supporters in California had begun assembling a women's Republican organization, and the Republicans established a national Hoover-Curtis Organization Bureau of

Women's Activities in August 1928. It emphasized "the miraculous story of Mr. Hoover's successful efforts to relieve hunger and suffering of the women and children of the nations of the world" to mobilize women voters. Influential Republican supporters like Clara Burdette and Ida Koverman in Southern California and Marie Meloney, Ruth Pratt, and Mabel Willebrandt on the national stage spoke widely and wielded substantial influence within the party. Even Lou Hoover took a behind-the-scenes role as an organizer, although she maintained a relatively apolitical stance in public.[74]

On September 12, Hoover met with a delegation from the small but vociferous National Women's Party, who asked him to endorse the Equal Rights Amendment to the Constitution. Senator Curtis, the vice presidential candidate, had sponsored the amendment in the Senate, and Inez Haynes Irwin, wife of Hoover's old friend and campaign biographer, Will Irwin, was a leader of the Women's Party. The amendment, which would have banned both discrimination against women and special protections for women workers, aroused controversy among women as well as men. Since Smith opposed it, Hoover might easily have evaded the issue, but instead he told the Women's Party delegation that he agreed with the amendment "in principle" and might even endorse it specifically if a means could be found to reconcile it with protective laws for women and children. Pleased by even such equivocal support, the party endorsed him and eventually spent $2,573 from its limited resources on his behalf. Veteran women activists, including Jane Addams, Carrie Chapman Catt, and Margaret Sanger, also supported Hoover.[75]

One group that Hoover hoped would give him significant support in 1928, organized labor, remained passive during the campaign. As secretary of commerce, Hoover had opposed child labor and the twelve-hour workday, and he had consistently endorsed collective bargaining. He had cultivated good relations with leaders of the American Federation of Labor. and with John L. Lewis of the United Mine Workers. He had promoted efforts to level out the fluctuations of the business cycle and worked to stabilize employment in the construction and coal mining industries. Yet his goodwill had failed to stem the decline of union membership during the decade, from 5 million in 1919 to just over 3 million by 1929. In his speech at Newark on September 17, 1928, he declared that "real wages and standards of living of our labor have improved more during the past seven and a half years of Republican rule than during any similar period in the history of this or of any other country." Nevertheless, critics (and later historians) questioned the accuracy of his statistics, contending that the buying power of wages was lower and unemployment greater than he claimed. Union workers also regarded the shop councils that he championed as little more than company unions. By 1929, over 2 million workers had enrolled in such organizations, but they found that the councils benefited managers more than workers, particularly in the largely unorganized mass-production industries that increasingly dominated the industrial economy. Workers in those industries, close to their ethnic roots and opposed to Prohibition, often favored Smith. In late October, the Republicans released a list of a hundred union "leaders" supporting Hoover, but it contained not a single nationally prominent name. As Robert Zieger observes, the unions, shrunken and demoralized, "stood on the sidelines in 1928."[76]

In late August, Hoover, perhaps needlessly worried, asked Coolidge and Borah to speak on his behalf. Borah pitched in wholeheartedly, making a half dozen strong speeches throughout the Midwest. So did Charles Evans Hughes, who spoke several times during October. Even Andrew Mellon swallowed his distaste for Hoover and made speeches in support of the Republicans. Coolidge remained silent through the early autumn. Not until the end of the campaign did he consent to have his photograph taken with the candidate at the White House. He sent a congratulatory telegram after Hoover's St. Louis speech on November 2, but his only significant contribution to the campaign came in a radio speech in support of the ticket on election eve. Neither Coolidge nor his wife felt well that summer, but obviously the chilly relations between the president and the secretary of commerce had not warmed much.[77]

As election day neared, Hoover's managers confidently promised not merely a victory but a landslide. Smith, they contended, could count on only South Carolina, Georgia, Mississippi, and Louisiana. Alabama, Arkansas, Wisconsin, and Utah teetered in the balance, but even Smith's home state of New York seemed likely to be in the Hoover column. They predicted that Hoover would win all the other states—a total of 450 electoral votes—leaving only forty-three electoral votes for Smith. On November 1, as the Hoovers boarded the train for the trip home to California, they had every reason to feel confident.[78]

X

When the Hoovers' train drew into the Palo Alto station on November 5, a crowd of ten thousand, including most of the Stanford student body and many of the faculty, welcomed them. All along the route to their house, cheering crowds lined the street. That evening, Hoover made a final radio address to the nation from his home, urging the record number of registered voters to turn out and "vote seriously and earnestly as conscience and mind direct."[79]

Election day dawned bright and sunny in Palo Alto, and the Hoovers, with their sons and Peggy, made their way at midmorning to their polling place in the Women's Clubhouse of the Stanford Union. (See Figure 21.1.) Returning to their house on San Juan Hill, Bert retreated to his study, while Lou prepared for their friends who would come by later. Herbert and Allan listened to the radio. The guests had hardly begun to arrive when the New York *World* predicted a Hoover victory at about 6:30 West Coast time. It would be almost midnight in Palo Alto before Smith conceded formally. Meanwhile, down on the campus, a band concert led by the venerable John Phillip Sousa drew to a conclusion, and when it did, Sousa led the band and a crowd of students up the hill to the Hoover house. The Hoovers greeted the serenaders at the front door and then returned to the second-floor terrace to join their guests. Radio microphones picked up the band's impromptu concert—"El Capitan," the "Stars and Stripes Forever," "The Star-Spangled Banner"—and then, as Hoover stood with tears in his eyes, the Stanford hymn.[80]

Hoover had won an immense victory: 21,427,123 popular votes to Smith's 15,015,464; 444 electoral votes to Smith's 87; 42 states to Smith's 8. He even made inroads into the "solid South," carrying North Carolina, Florida, Texas, and all the border states. Ethnic voters helped Smith win narrow victories in Massachusetts and Rhode Island, but not in New York or Pennsylvania, and farm discontent in the Midwest prevented him from carrying that region. Whether the outcome meant a rejection of Smith, enthusiasm about Hoover, or, as Coolidge put it in his congratulatory telegram, an "endorsement" of his own administration's policies remained unclear. Hoover could interpret the returns any way he liked; he chose to see them as a great mandate.[81]

Figure 21.1. Herbert, Jr., Margaret Watson Hoover, and Allan stand behind the Hoovers in this 1928 campaign photograph.

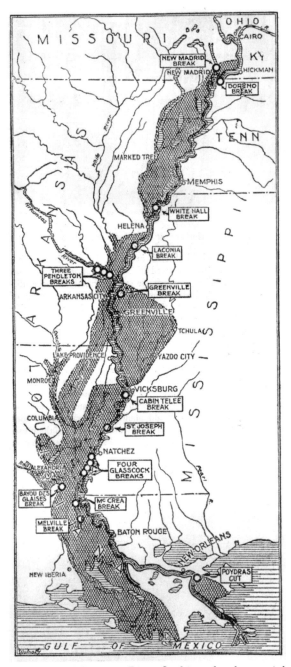

Figure 21.2. The 1927 Mississippi River flood inundated some eighteen thousand square miles—an area almost twice the size of Massachusetts.

Reproduced from a map published in the *New York Times* and *Survey Graphic* magazine in July 1927.

Figure 21.3. Fly-fishing offered Hoover a welcome respite from presidential campaigning.

Figure 21.4. Despite the chilly relations between Hoover and the president, on July 16, 1928, the Hoovers paid a courtesy call on the Coolidges at their vacation retreat in Wisconsin.

CHAPTER 22

Imperfect Visionary

As Hoover approached the end of his eight years as secretary of commerce, he believed that its work had become central to American prosperity. "The obvious purpose of the department," he wrote, "is that its work should express itself ultimately in increased standards of living and material welfare for the American people." To accomplish that, he had attempted to improve "the processes of manufacture and distribution," thus reducing production costs "and therefore the price of the essentials of food, clothing, and housing." When basic needs cost less, he argued, consumers would be left with more disposable income to spend on "education and the growth of understanding." Such general prosperity, he wrote hopefully, would not be "a stimulant to idle and luxurious living."[1]

Active cooperation between government and business, Hoover believed, had laid the foundations of the department's success. Its laboratories had contributed to "the invention of more scientific and economical methods of production." Its statistical services had gathered and disseminated "valuable information which makes for stability and progress in business, and for the elimination of countless wastes." Its "constant conferences and cooperation with industry" had promoted the adoption of "scientifically and economically developed programs of water and rail transportation based upon careful appraisal of business trends and actual needs." Cumulatively, he declared, systematic cooperation between business and government had replaced "hectic irregularities or momentary booms or slumps" with stable employment for workers and orderly commercial and industrial growth.[2]

427

The department, Hoover asserted, had effectively expanded foreign markets for "the 7 to 10 per cent of our production which goes to export," recognizing that such trade enabled American businesses "to use in full our resources and energy," and thus assured "greater stability in production and greater security to the workers." It had also actively encouraged the importation of commodities that contributed to Americans' "standard of living and much of the joy of living" as well. Some sixty Commerce Department agents stationed overseas had helped to make the value of American exports in 1926 to 1927 "more than 2 1/4 times greater than before the war" and the value of imports "more than two and one-half times larger than the pre-war average." In particular, Hoover pointed with pride to 1927 agricultural exports "82 per cent greater than the 1910–1914 average" and to an "appreciable" reduction in the dependence of American industries on imported raw materials such as rubber controlled by foreign monopolies.[3]

The new industries of commercial aviation and radio had become striking success stories during the 1920s, and Hoover happily took credit both for encouraging them and for bringing them under regulation. Likewise, he argued that the department's work, as well of that of its ally, Better Homes in America, had helped Americans to apply "the results of research and investigation to their own individual problems," lightened "the burdens of housework," and "encouraged them to cultivate the worthwhile things in life that come from the home."[4]

Hoover's 1928 summary, tailored for the presidential campaign, claimed more than he had actually achieved. Some projects he had launched remained incomplete; others, notably those involving the problems of the "old industries" (agriculture, coal, the railroads, and the merchant marine), had been failures or near failures. Nevertheless, many years later, after the bitterness of the 1930s, Hoover still looked back on the 1920s as "happy years of constructive work." Perhaps "the final triumph over poverty" that he had glimpsed on the horizon in 1928 had not yet come to pass, but he remained convinced that, in time, "all these advances will be renewed and greatly exceeded."[5]

As befitted a campaign document, Hoover's 1928 survey of Commerce Department policy provided less analysis of existing programs than a vision of future progress. It revealed the degree to which he, more than anyone else in the administration, understood that the United States had been transformed by the rise of the consumer economy. Sustaining that economy, he recognized, would require substantial improvements in the nation's infrastructure, steady employment and adequate incomes for workers, and a stabilized business cycle. Of those goals, the United States had some tradition of federal support for "internal improvements," but railroads and public utilities had generally undertaken to build their networks with private capital, while states and local governments built and maintained highways and water transportation. The federal role in all of these had been minimal, and, except during the war, the government had taken little responsibility for stabilizing employment and the overall economy. Hoover proposed pioneering forays into all of these areas, but he hoped to achieve them through voluntary organization among government, citizens, and businesses rather than through federal control. He believed, in 1928, that he had found a middle way between the laissez-faire policies of the past and socialism.

Although Hoover happily reeled off statistics showing increases in national income, wages, availability of consumer products, quality and quantity of education, savings, home construction, and other measures of material improvements for average Americans, he insisted that "economic advancement is not an end in itself." He regarded prosperity as valuable only insofar as it brought to "the average family a fuller life, a wider outlook, a stirred imagination, and a lift in aspiration." A successful democracy, he insisted, "rests wholly upon the moral and spiritual quality of its people."[6] The man who had done so much to facilitate the growth of the consumer society cared little for its material benefits.

Given the day-to-day emphasis in Commerce Department policy making on tangible economic issues, it is easy to overlook the fundamental assumptions about human nature that underlay Hoover's policies. Although he had a realistic understanding that people could be selfish and dishonest, he continued to believe that they were fundamentally rational and capable of unselfish behavior and that they aspired to intellectual and spiritual growth. As one friend put it, "he had a little more faith than I have in the common sense of the people as a whole." His belief that business could govern itself through trade associations is explicable less as an economic philosophy than a trust that men could be taught to sacrifice immediate gain to long-term progress. The best economic and political system, he believed, was one in which individuals had maximum freedom to pursue their self-interest within a structure of cooperation and self-government.[7]

"Human beings are not equal in these qualities of ability and character," Hoover said in 1920. "But a society that is based upon a constant flux of individuals in the community, upon the basis of ability and character, is a moving virile mass . . . Its inspiration is individual initiative. Its stimulus is competition. Its safeguard is education. Its greatest mentor is free speech and voluntary organization for public good."[8]

As Hoover recognized, however, "voluntary organization for the public good" did not always suffice to prevent antisocial or illegal activity. Where individual morality and associational self-government failed to restrain undesirable activity, he believed that the government must step in. He did not, he said, carry an antipathy to federal action "into extremes that would incline me against Federal action if there is no other way out." Although he talked about modifying federal antitrust law to legitimate collective action by trade associations, he opposed repealing those laws entirely.[9]

Hoover's rhetoric about governing through voluntary cooperation masked the degree to which he practiced a kind of benevolent paternalism. Through his training as an engineer and experience as a businessman, he acquired the habit of analyzing issues, reaching a decision about how to deal with them, and directing others to carry out his plan. Often quicker than others to see to the heart of a problem, he could be brusque and impatient with slower minds. But that pattern of behavior fitted poorly with his belief in cooperative self-government. Hence, he learned to preserve the illusion of collaborative policy making while preparing program proposals so thoroughly that others adopted them without actually realizing they were not their own. The method worked admirably in a series of conferences with industries about simplification and standardization, with the national radio conferences, and with the American Child Health Association. It worked less well with political leaders who had clearly articulated objectives of their own, as in Europe during 1919. The assent of a group to such a policy often eroded if Hoover stepped down from direct leadership. Thus, the Commerce Department's simplification and standardization program seemed to lose its impetus by the late 1920s as Hoover turned to other issues.

Painfully shy and insecure, Hoover never became an effective public speaker, much less a skillful politician, and he could seem impenetrable even to people who worked closely with him. The fear of ridicule or embarrassment sometimes made him more aggressive about asserting his ideas than he really felt. Although those who knew him well found him open to suggestions and willingly collaborative, most people who encountered him in formal circumstances did not have that experience. Intensely loyal to the people he trusted, he found it difficult to see their faults. In the case of his California ranch, for example, he retained Ralph Merritt as manager long after it became obvious to his partners that Merritt was incompetent at best.

By temperament an activist, Hoover served in and shared the philosophy of Republican administrations that believed in minimal government. That fundamental contradiction meant that although his instinct was to use the resources of government to attack problems such as the agricultural depression, the decline of the coal industry and the merchant marine, and the chaos in the railroads, ideology restrained him. The result was an endless round of largely meaningless activity—conferences, study committees, stopgap measures, all in the name of finding solutions from the bottom up rather than imposing them from the top down. "Three ring affairs that the Chief likes to take on which keep everybody working at high speed," as Christian Herter described the 1921 unemployment conference.[10] As with the policies adopted by the unemployment conference, however, Hoover never seemed to realize that the various programs he advocated sometimes had very little effect. Rather, as time passed, he became increasingly insistent that they would work—eventually, if not immediately.

Another contradiction marked his attitude toward Europe. On the one hand, he believed the United States needed a stable, prosperous Europe, while, on the other, he feared and distrusted European leaders and sought to make the United States as self-sufficient as possible. Thus, he favored American membership in the League of Nations and the World Court and recognized that war debts and reparations impeded European economic recovery. He also supported the protective tariff, insisted that the war debts must be paid, and aggressively pursued the expansion of American trade and investments in competition with those of Europe. Despite the pages of statistics produced by the Commerce Department showing the dominance of American commerce around the world, he retained an underdog outlook that emphasized competition with Europeans rather than cooperation. After spending almost a year in Europe feeding the hungry and laboring to stabilize the Continent's new nations, he told reporters on his return to the United States in September 1919 that he "never cared to see Europe again." That conviction that the United States should leave the Europeans to stew in their own juices conflicted with Hoover's recognition of the political and economic importance of Europe to the United States. His extensive international experience, instead of making him more supportive of a policy of cooperation and collaboration to stabilize the international economy, rather reinforced his economic nationalism.[11]

In many ways, Hoover was a strange person to become his era's most notable humanitarian. He spent much of his public career heading massive relief programs—first in Belgium, then in Europe, Russia, and the Mississippi River Valley—and managed them extremely well. He undertook them in each case out of a sense of duty, which was particularly sharp in the case of hungry children, yet he did not see relief primarily in humanitarian terms. Rather, he regarded the disasters that made relief necessary as disruptions of the normal order that should be cleared up as briskly as possible. He believed that aid recipients should pay for assistance if they were able and that they should accept an obligation to repay its cost later if they did not have the money at once. Moreover, once the immediate crisis passed, he thought that disaster sufferers should tax themselves and sacrifice to pay for their own recovery. After succoring the victims of disaster, his aid programs shifted focus almost immediately to restoring the institutions and infrastructure that would permit the victims to rebuild with minimal external assistance. Short-term humanitarianism combined with hard-boiled insistence on having recipients pull themselves up by their own bootstraps make his programs unusual—perhaps unique—among international humanitarian operations.

At the close of his final major campaign speech in St. Louis on November 2, 1928, Hoover repeated words he had used in his telegram to the chairman of the Republican convention when it nominated him for the presidency. "Government," he said, "must contribute to leadership" in solving the problems facing the nation. The president must not only administer the laws but also work in "cooperation with the forces of business and cultural life in city, town, and countryside." That meant, as he had told a *New York Times* reporter in 1921, "a new economic system, based neither on the capitalism of Adam Smith nor upon the socialism of Karl Marx." Under the sheltering wings of the government and business associations dedicated to maximizing production, individual initiative would promote innovation and progress. He believed that he had forged such a cooperative relationship between government and citizens during the previous eight years and that the cooperative principle would strengthen the country during his presidential administration as well. The next four years would sorely test his faith.[12]

Notes

Preface

1. Alfred Pearce Dennis, "Humanizing the Department of Commerce," *Saturday Evening Post*, June 6, 1925, 8.
2. Herbert Hoover, *Memoirs: The Cabinet and the Presidency, 1920–1930* (New York: Macmillan, 1952), 184.
3. Herbert Hoover, "The Larger Purposes of the Department of Commerce," in "Republican National Committee, Brief Review of Activities and Policies of the Federal Executive Departments," Bulletin No. 6, 1928, Herbert Hoover Papers, Campaign and Transition Period, Box 6, "Subject: Republican National Committee," Hoover Presidential Library, West Branch, Iowa.
4. Herbert Hoover, "Responsibility of America for World Peace," address before national convention of National League of Women Voters, Des Moines, Iowa, April 11, 1923, Bible no. 303, Hoover Presidential Library.
5. Bruce Bliven, "Hoover—And the Rest," *Independent*, May 29, 1920, 275.

Chapter 1

1. John W. Hallowell to Arthur (Hallowell?), November 21, 1918, Hoover Papers, Pre-Commerce Period, Hoover Presidential Library, West Branch, Iowa, Box 6, "Hallowell, John W., 1917–1920"; Julius Barnes to Gertrude Barnes, November 27 and December 5, 1918, ibid., Box 2, "Barnes, Julius H., Nov. 27, 1918–Jan. 17, 1919"; Lewis Strauss, "Further Notes for Mr. Irwin," ca. February 1928, Subject File, Lewis L. Strauss Papers, Hoover Presidential Library, West Branch, Iowa, Box 10, "Campaign of 1928: Campaign Literature, Speeches, etc., Press Releases, Speeches, etc., 1928 Feb.–Nov."; Strauss, handwritten notes, December 1, 1918, ibid., Box 76, "Strauss, Lewis L., Diaries, 1917–19."
2. The men who sailed with Hoover to Europe on the *Olympic* on November 18, 1918, were Julius Barnes, Frederick Chatfield, John Hallowell, Lewis Strauss, Robert Taft, and Alonzo Taylor. See Strauss to Bruce Bliven, July 8, 1920, Strauss Papers, Box 36, "Hoover, Herbert, General, 1920."
3. Hoover to Wilson, November 4, 1918, American Relief Administration Documents (hereafter, "ARA Docs."), 1:5–7, Hoover Presidential Library, West Branch, Iowa; Alonzo E. Taylor, "Food Conditions in Germany and Austria-Hungary," November 14, 1918, Hoover Papers, Pre-Commerce Period, Box 15, "Taylor, Alonzo, 1917–1919"; Julius Barnes to Gertrude Barnes, December 3, 1918, ibid., Box 2, "Barnes, Julius H., Nov. 27, 1918–Jan.

17, 1919." The puzzling nutritional imbalance of Hoover's food relief—that is, the exclusive focus on fats and wheat and the complete absence of fruits and vegetables—seems to have resulted not only from storage and shipment limitations but also from the era's scientific emphasis on calories as the measure of nutritional needs. On this, see Nick Cullather, "The Foreign Policy of the Calorie," *American Historical Review* 112 (April 2007): 347–52.

4. Julius Barnes to Gertrude Barnes, December 3, 1918, Hoover Papers, Pre-Commerce Period, Box 2, "Barnes, Julius H., Nov. 27, 1918–Jan. 17, 1919."

5. Wilson to Hoover, November 7, 1918, in Arthur S. Link et al., eds., *The Papers of Woodrow Wilson*, vol. 51, *September 14–November 8, 1918* (Princeton, NJ: Princeton University Press, 1985), 618–20 (hereafter, *PWW*). For the origins of this policy, see Hoover to Wilson, October 21, 26, 1918, ibid., 397–99, 458–59.

6. "Scheme for Relief in Period Immediately after the Conclusion of Hostilities (This originated with the British)," undated, ca. October 30, 1918, ARA Docs., 1:75–77; Hoover to Wilson, November 4, 1918, enclosing (Ambassador William) Sharp to Secretary of State, November 1, 1918, ARA Docs., 1:8–11; Robert Taft to William Howard Taft, December 4, 1918, Hoover Papers, Pre-Commerce Period, Box 15, "Taft, Helen-Robert A., 1920"; draft of dispatch from secretary of state to Joseph Potter Cotton (Food Administration representative in London), enclosed in Hoover to Wilson, November 7, 1918, *PWW*, 51:635; Hoover to Wilson, October 24, 1918, *PWW*, 51: 438; Hoover to Wilson, April 11, 1919, *PWW*, vol. 57, *April 5–22, 1919* (1987), 271–74; Anne Orde, *British Policy and European Reconstruction after the First World War* (Cambridge, UK: Cambridge University Press, 1990), 26–27; Carl P. Parrini, *Heir to Empire: United States Economic Diplomacy, 1916–1923* (Pittsburgh: University of Pittsburgh Press, 1969), 15–22. In his *Memoirs*, Hoover describes his disillusionment with Allied motives as having taken place literally over night, but as George Nash makes clear, he had been a realist about the European situation from at least the beginning of the war. Herbert Hoover, *Memoirs: Years of Adventure, 1874–1920* (New York: Macmillan, 1951), 285–89 (hereafter, *Memoirs* 1); George H. Nash, *The Life of Herbert Hoover: The Humanitarian, 1914–1917* (New York: Norton, 1988); George H. Nash, *The Life of Herbert Hoover: Master of Emergencies, 1917–1918* (New York: Norton, 1996).

7. Hoover to Wilson, November 9, 1918, ARA Docs., 1:25–26; Hoover to Wilson, November 14, 1918, *PWW*, vol. 53, *November 9, 1918–January 11, 1919* (1986), 75–76. For Hoover's desire to move beyond wartime bitterness toward the Germans and his frustration at what he saw as French obstructionism, see Louis P. Lochner, *Herbert Hoover and Germany* (New York: Macmillan, 1960), 29–46. It would be a mistake to see him as pro-German, but he regarded the stability and prosperity of Germany as essential to the future of Europe.

8. Hoover, *Memoirs* 1, 321.

9. Ibid. Among the small number of serious efforts by historians to explore this issue, two stand out: David Burner, "The Quaker Faith of Herbert Hoover," in *Understanding Herbert Hoover: Ten Perspectives*, ed. Lee Nash (Stanford, CA: Hoover Institution, 1987): 53–64; and James P. Johnson, "Herbert Hoover: The Orphan as Children's Friend," *Prologue* 12 (Winter 1980): 193–206.

10. "The Paris Office: An Administrative Summary," no date, Hoover Papers, Pre-Commerce Period, Box 24, "ARA-The Paris Office-An Administrative Summary"; John J. Pershing to Hoover, December 12, 1918, Herbert Hoover Subject Collection, Hoover Institution Archives, Stanford, California, Box 321, "Correspondence: Pershing, John J."; Hoover to Wilson, December 16, 1918, Hoover Papers, Pre-Commerce Period, Box 60, "Relief: Europe, 1914–1920."

11. Edward M. House to Wilson, November 27, 1918, *PWW*, 53:222–25; "Letter of Colonel House to the Allied Governments Transmitting the President's Plan for Director-General of Relief," December 1, 1918, ARA Docs., 1:70–74.

12. Extract from Vance McCormick diary, January 14, 1919, in Suda Lorena Bane and Ralph Haswell Lutz, eds., *The Blockade of Germany After the Armistice, 1918–1919: Selected Documents of the Supreme Economic Council, American Relief Administration, and Other Wartime Organizations* (New York: Howard Fertig, 1972; repr. of 1942 ed.), 39; memorandum of meeting on December 10, 1918, *PWW*, 53:360–61; Hoover to House, December 10, 1918,

ARA Docs., 1:92–95; Edward N. Hurley to Wilson, December 12, 1918, *PWW*, 53:372–75; Sir William Wiseman to Foreign Office, December 15, 1918, ibid., 394–96; Thomas F. Logan to Edward N. Hurley, December 23, 1918, ibid., 480–85; Auchincloss diary, vol. 3, p. 182 (December 14, 1918), Hoover Papers, Pre-Commerce Period, Box 1, "Auchincloss, Gordon, 1919." Bernard Baruch shared Hoover's suspicions about Allied postwar economic ambitions. See Baruch to Ray Stannard Baker, May 22, 1922, ibid., Box 1, "Baker, Ray Stannard, 1919–1920."

13. Julius Barnes to Gertrude Barnes, December 17, 1918, Hoover Papers, Pre-Commerce Period, Box 2, "Barnes, Julius H., Nov. 27, 1918–Jan. 17, 1919."

14. Wilson to House, enclosing note to be delivered to the Allied governments, December 15, 1918, *PWW*, 53:392–93; American Mission in Paris to John W. Davis, January 1, 1919, ibid., 585–86; Wilson to Hoover, January 11, 1919, ibid., 714; Hoover, *Memoirs* 1, 298. The council's minutes, published in Bane and Lutz, *The Blockade of Germany*, confirm Hoover's opinion about the organization's pointlessness.

15. Hoover to Lord Reading, December 16, 1918, ARA Docs., 1:118–20; Wilson to secretary of state for secretary of war, December 16, 1918, and Wilson to secretary of state for secretary of the treasury, December 16, 1918, Strauss Papers, Subject File, Box 2, "American Relief Administration: Special Policy Folder, 1918–19."

16. Hoover, "An Appeal to World Conscience," December 1, 1918, Suda Lorena Bane and Ralph Haswell Lutz, eds., *Organization of American Relief in Europe, 1918–1919: Including Negotiations Leading up to the Establishment of the Office of Director General of Relief at Paris by the Allied and Associated Powers* (Stanford, CA: Stanford University Press, 1943), 66–67; Wilson to secretary of war, December 16, 1918, ibid., 77; Wilson to Carter Glass, January 1, 1919, *PWW*, 53:578–79; Hoover, *Memoirs* 1, 294–95, 299.

17. Hoover to Edgar Rickard, December 16, 1918, in Bane and Lutz, *Organization of American Relief*, 95–96; Hoover to Wilson, December 23, 1918, ibid., 114–15; memorandum by Hoover, January 3, 1919, ibid., 143–45; Frank M. Surface and Raymond L. Bland, *American Food in the World War and Reconstruction Period: Operations of the Organization Under the Direction of Herbert Hoover, 1914 to 1924* (Stanford, CA: Stanford University Press, 1931), 50–51; Hoover, *Memoirs* 1, 333.

18. Hoover to Brown, November 27, 1918, Hoover Papers, Pre-Commerce Period, Box 2, "Brown, Walter Lyman, 1918–1920"; Julius Barnes to Gertrude Barnes, November 29, 1918, ibid., Box 2, "Barnes, Julius H., Nov. 27, 1918–Jan. 17, 1919"; "'Go to Hell,' Hoover Says of Hun Officials," New York *Herald*, ca. December 1, 1918; Hoover to House, ca. November 30, 1918, Hoover Papers, Pre-Commerce Period, Box 8, "House, Edward M., 1915–21 & undated." The cartoonist "Ding" Darling published a cartoon on December 30 showing Hoover writing the famous phrase.

19. "Blockade of Foe Must Be Eased; Hoover," unidentified clipping, November 17, 1918, Hoover Papers, Pre-Commerce Period, Box 70, "June 1918–December 1918"; Hoover to Wilson, December 10, 19, 20, 1918, Strauss Papers, Name & Subject File I: Accretions, Box 53E, "American Relief Administration: Food for Austria and Germany, 1918–19"; Michael J. Hogan, *Informal Entente: The Private Structure of Cooperation in Anglo-American Economic Diplomacy, 1918–1928* (Columbia: University of Missouri Press, 1977), 27–28.

20. Hoover to Wilson, January 12, 1919, enclosing extract from minutes of the meeting of the Supreme Council for Supply and Relief, *PWW*, vol. 54, *January 11–February 7, 1919* (1986), 29–31; Hankey's notes of a meeting of the Supreme War Council, January 13, 1919, ibid., 37–41; Cecil Harmsworth, quoted in Elisabeth Glaser, "The Making of the Economic Peace," in *The Treaty of Versailles: A Reassessment after 75 Years*, ed. Manfred F. Boemeke, Gerald D. Feldman, and Elisabeth Glaser (Washington, DC: German Historical Institute, 1998), 389. Hoover almost certainly knew there was no real danger of starvation in Germany and that the Germans could afford to purchase food if given the chance. His argument for lifting the Allied blockade was that doing so would promote political stability. Likewise, he believed that Allied insistence on taking the German merchant fleet would obstruct economic reconstruction in Germany. See Murray N. Rothbard, "Hoover's 1919 Food

Diplomacy in Retrospect," in *Herbert Hoover: The Great War and Its Aftermath, 1914–23*, ed. Lawrence E. Gelfand (Iowa City: University of Iowa Press, 1979), 93–95.

21. Klaus Schwabe, *Woodrow Wilson, Revolutionary Germany, and Peacemaking, 1918–1919: Missionary Diplomacy and the Realities of Power* (Chapel Hill: University of North Carolina Press, 1985), 193–95.

22. "Draft of a letter to be written by Hoover under authority of the President," January 2, 1919, Hoover Papers, Pre-Commerce Period, Box 40, "Food Problems: Memo, Jan. 2, 1919."

23. Hoover to Wilson, January 8, 1919, *PWW*, 53:687–88; for the secretary of war from the president (quoting a message from Hoover to Wilson), January 9, 1919, Strauss Papers, Subject File, Box 24, "Food Administration: Correspondence & Memoranda, 1919 Jan.–June."

24. Hoover to Capt. Edward L. Snyder, Food Administration, January 13, 1919, Hoover Papers, Pre-Commerce Period, Box 40, "Food Problem: Memo, Jan. 13, 1919"; Hoover to Food Administration, January 21, 1919, ibid., Box 41, "Food Problems: Memo, Jan. 21, 1919, Trade."

25. Hoover to Food Administration for the secretary of the treasury, January 21, 1919, Hoover Papers, Pre-Commerce Period, Box 41, "Food Problems: Memo, Jan. 21, 1919, Trade." Hoover struck back at attacks on the Food Administration by Senator Borah and others in part by writing an article defending his policies: "The Food Future: What Every American Mouthful Means to Europe," *Forum* 61 (February 1919): 210–18. Hoover's fight to protect farmers by preventing a crash in American pork prices was interpreted by American consumer advocates as contributing to the high cost of living.

26. Hoover to L. P. Sheldon, January 2, 1919, Strauss Papers, Subject File, Box 35, "Hogs, 1919 Jan. 1–5"; Hoover to Sir John Beale, January 22, 1919, Hoover Papers, Pre-Commerce Period, Box 41, "Food Problems: Memo, Jan. 22, 1919"; Hoover to the British Food Ministry, January 25, 1919, ibid., Box 41, "Food Problems: Memo, Jan. 25, 1919, British Food Ministry"; unsigned draft of cable to Secretary of Treasury Glass, January 27, 1919, ibid., Box 41, "Food Problems: Memo, Jan. 27, 1919"; Hoover to Food Administration, Washington, January 4, 1919, Strauss Papers, Subject File, Box 35, "Hogs, 1919 Jan.1–5."

27. Hoover to Norman H. Davis, May 17, 1919, Strauss Papers, Subject File, Box 35, "Hogs, 1919 Feb.–May."

28. Hoover to Sir John Beale, January 27, 1919, Hoover Papers, Pre-Commerce Period, Box 41, "Food Problems: Memo, Jan. 27, 1919, British Government"; draft 2, Hoover to Beale, January 29, 1919, ibid., Box 41, "Food Problems: Memo, Jan. 29, 1919"; Hoover to Wilson, February 1, 1919, ibid., Box 706, "Wheat: Wheat and Hogs, 1919–1928"; Hoover, *Memoirs* 1, 332–33; Schwabe, *Woodrow Wilson, Revolutionary Germany*, 198–99.

29. Hoover to Wilson, February 4, 1919, in Bane and Lutz, *The Blockade of Germany*, 76–77; Hoover to Edward M. House, January 4, 1919, Strauss Papers, Subject File, Box 35, "Hogs, 1919 Jan. 1–5."

30. Vance McCormick diary, February 11, March 1, 1919, Hoover Papers, Pre-Commerce Period, Box 48, "McCormick (Vance) Diary, Paris Peace Conference, 1919"; Hoover to the American Peace Commission, February 19, 1919, in Bane and Lutz, *The Blockade of Germany*, 130–31; Vernon Kellogg and Alonzo Taylor to Hoover, February 22, 1919, in ibid., 156–58; Vance McCormick diary, March 1–3, 1919, in ibid., 173–74; "Minutes of Conference between Representative of the Associated Governments and Representatives of the German Government, at Spa, Belgium, on February 6, 7, and 8, 1919, on the Subject of the Supply of Foodstuffs to Germany," and Report on meetings held on March 4 and 5, 1919, in ibid., 95–98, 102–9, 184–88, 190–94; "Supplies for Germany, [Documents] Presented to the Supreme Economic Council at Its Meeting of March 7, 1919," in ibid., 195–97; "Extracts from Minutes of the Meeting of the Supreme War Council . . . ," March 8, 1919, in ibid., 206–7; "Extracts from Minutes of Seventh Meeting of the Supreme Economic Council . . . ," March 10, 1919, in ibid., 224–28; Hoover, *Memoirs* 1, 298.

31. Lewis Strauss, "A Note on the Brussels Conference," March 13, 1919, Strauss Papers, Subject File, Box 27, "Germany: Food Relief Agreement, 1919"; Bane and Lutz, *The Blockade of Germany*, 246–58; Surface and Bland, *American Food*, 194–97, 37.

32. Will Irwin, *Herbert Hoover: A Reminiscent Biography* (New York: Grosset & Dunlap, 1928), 210; Hugh Gibson to Lou Henry Hoover, February 25, 1919, Lou Henry Hoover Papers, Hoover Presidential Library, West Branch, Iowa, Box 2, "Personal Correspondence, 1872–1920: Gibson, Hugh, 1915–20"; R. A. Kleindienst to Edgar Rickard, March 24, 1919, Hoover Papers, Pre-Commerce Period, Box 9, "Kleindienst, R. A., March 1919–June 1920"; W. Parmer Fuller to friends in the United States, September 6, 1919, ibid., Box 33, "European Relief council, 1919–1921."

33. "American Commission to Negotiate Peace: Composition and Functions," May 1, 1919, Hoover Papers, Pre-Commerce Period, Box 57, "Paris Peace Conference, 1919"; Robert Lansing, Henry White, E. M. House, and Tasker H. Bliss to Wilson, December 31, 1918, *PWW*, 53:572–73.

34. Hoover to Wilson, February 12, 1919, and Wilson to Hoover, February 14, 1919, in Francis William O'Brien, ed., *Two Peacemakers in Paris: The Hoover-Wilson Post-Armistice Letters, 1918–1920* (College Station: Texas A&M University Press, 1978), 70, 75; Wilson to Carter Glass, February 19, 1919, *PWW*, vol. 55, *February 8–March 16, 1919* (1986), 208; Arthur Walworth, *Wilson and His Peacemakers: American Diplomacy at the Paris Peace Conference, 1919* (New York: Norton, 1986), 57–58; Margaret MacMillan, *Paris 1919: Six Months That Changed the World* (New York: Random House, 2001), 291–92.

35. Hoover to Wilson, March 31, April 2, 3, 1919, *PWW*, vol. 56, *March 17–April 4, 1919* (1987), 469–70, 547, 574–75; Hoover to Wilson, April 15, 1919, ibid., 57:367–69; Mantoux's notes of a meeting of the Council of Four, April 16, 1919, ibid., 57:391–92; diary of Col. House, April 19, 1919, and Hoover to House, April 19, 1919, enclosing statement on Russia by Hoover, dated April 18, ibid., 57:503–8; Walworth, *Wilson and His Peacemakers*, 90, 102–3, 201–2, 250–53, 260–63, 504–5; MacMillan, *Paris 1919*, 80–81, 133. For further discussion of Hoover and Russia and Hoover and Hungary, see Chapters 5 and 9 of this volume.

36. McCormick diary, January 13, 1919, Hoover Papers, Pre-Commerce Period, Box 48, "McCormick (Vance) Diary: Paris Peace Conference, 1919"; Edgar Rickard to Lou Henry Hoover, February 18, 1919, Lou Hoover Papers, Box 7, "Personal Correspondence, 1872–1920: Rickard, Edgar, 1919"; David Lloyd George, *The Truth about the Peace Treaties* (London: Victor Gollancz, 1938), 1:306–7; MacMillan, *Paris 1919*, 61.

37. E. De Cartier to Robert Lansing, November 21, 1918, Strauss Papers, Subject File, Box 36, "Hoover, Herbert, General, 1918"; Edgar Rickard to Lou Henry Hoover, February 18, 1919, Lou Hoover Papers, Box 7, "Personal Correspondence, 1872–1920: Rickard, Edgar, 1919"; Hugh Gibson to Lou Hoover, ibid., Box 2, "Personal Correspondence, 1872–1920: Gibson, Hugh, 1915–20."

38. "A Joint Resolution Providing for the Relief of Such Populations in Europe and Countries Contiguous Thereto Outside of Germany, German Austria, Hungary, Bulgaria and Turkey, as May Be Determined by the President as Necessary," approved, February 24, 1919, Strauss Papers, Subject File, Box 24, "Food Administration: Correspondence, Memoranda, 1919 Jan.–June"; Wilson, Executive Order No. 3035-B, February 24, 1919, Hoover Papers, Pre-Commerce Period, Box 24, "ARA: Undated to 1921"; "The American Relief Administration: Relief of Enemy States," *ARA Bulletin*, 1st ser., 1, no. 1 (March 17, 1919): 3; Surface and Bland, *American Food*, 35–36, 42–43, 117–20.

39. Hoover to House, March 11, 1919, Hoover Subject Collection, Box 317, "Correspondence: House, Col. E. M."

40. Ibid. For the documents, see Surface and Bland, *American Food*, for example. Hoover's own accounts of the relief program include his *Memoirs*, the first three volumes of *An American Epic* (Chicago: Regnery, 1959–61); and *The Ordeal of Woodrow Wilson* (New York: McGraw-Hill, 1958).

41. Vernon Kellogg to Hoover, January 6, 1919, Hoover Papers, Pre-Commerce Period, Box 9, "Kellogg, Vernon, 1918–1919"; Hoover, *An American Epic*, 3:62–63.

42. Kellogg to Hoover, January 6, 1919, in Bane and Lutz, *Organization of American Relief*, 150–56; Kellogg to A. R. Stuart, January 6, 1919, Hoover Papers, Pre-Commerce Period, Box 9, "Kellogg, Vernon, 1918–1919."

43. Hoover, *Memoirs* 1, 356–57; *American Epic*, 3:66–67; Piotr S. Wandycz, *The United States and Poland* (Cambridge, MA: Harvard University Press, 1980), 127–30. For a variation of the American-influence argument advanced by a Hoover intimate, see H. H. Fisher, *America and the New Poland* (New York: Macmillan, 1928), 120–23.

44. Hoover, *American Epic*, 3:68–69.

45. Vernon Kellogg to Hoover, January 6, 1919, in Bane and Lutz, *Organization of American Relief*, 156–57; James A. Logan, Jr., to Vance McCormick, March 18, 1919, in Bane and Lutz, *Blockade of Germany*, 263–64; Hoover, *American Epic*, 3:72–74.

46. Col. William R. Grove to Hoover, April 10, 1919, Strauss Papers, Subject File, Box 36, "Hoover, Herbert, General, 1919 March"; Hoover to Paderewski, April 15, 1919, ibid.; Lewis Strauss, Jr., "Herbert C. Hoover and the Jews," *The American Hebrew* April 23, 1920, 747, 759; Stephen S. Wise to Wilson, March 2, 1919, enclosing memorandum on the situation of the Jews in Eastern Europe, *PWW*, 55:368–81; Hoover to Wilson, June 2, 1919, *PWW*, vol. 60, *June 1–17, 1919* (1989), 39; Wilson to Robert Lansing, June 16, 1919, ibid., 60:601; Hankey's notes of a meeting of the Council of Four, June 23, 1919, *PWW*, vol. 61, *June 18–July 25, 1919* (1989), 88–92; Wandycz, *United States and Poland*, 165–67; Fisher, *America and the New Poland*, 155–60; Carole Fink, *Defending the Rights of Others: The Great Powers, the Jews, and International Minority Protection, 1878–1938* (Cambridge, UK: Cambridge University Press, 2004), 151–60. For subsequent American attempts to stabilize Poland during the 1920s, see Frank Costigliola, "American Foreign Policy in the 'Nut Cracker': The United States and Poland in the 1920s," *Pacific Historical Review* 48 (February 1979): 85–105.

47. Wandycz, *United States and Poland*, 170–72; George J. Lerski, *Herbert Hoover and Poland: A Documentary History of a Friendship* (Stanford, CA: Hoover Institution, 1977), 9–26; Neal Pease, *Poland, the United States, and the Stabilization of Europe, 1919–1933* (New York: Oxford University Press, 1986), 8–10; Fisher, *America and the New Poland*, 147–55; "Poles' Aggression Caused Big Slash in Aid for Europe," *Washington Star*, February 2, 1920.

48. Hoover, *American Epic*, 3:37–61, 101–55. Space prevents full coverage of the relief program here.

49. Hoover, *Memoirs* 1, 312–16. Hoover's accounts of the practical workings of the relief operation are among the best sections of the *Memoirs* and should be read in full.

50. Ibid., 306–8.

51. Ibid., 307–8.

52. Ibid., 316–19.

53. Hoover to Wilson, March 28, 1919, *PWW*, 56:375–77. The discussions in the peace conference at Paris did not reveal the degree of disagreement within the British government over what to do in Russia. See Richard H. Ullman, *Anglo-Soviet Relations, 1917–1921: Britain and the Russian Civil War, November 1918–February 1920* (Princeton, NJ: Princeton University Press, 1968), 59–98.

54. Hoover to Wilson, March 28, 1919, *PWW*, 56:377–78; from the Gordon Auchincloss diary, March 27, 1919, vol. 4, pp. 474–76, Hoover Papers, Pre-Commerce Period, Box 1, "Auchincloss, Gordon, 1919." George Kennan points out the absurdity of the sort of mission Hoover envisioned. See *Soviet-American Relations, 1917–1920: The Decision to Intervene* (Princeton, NJ: Princeton University Press, 1958), 336–39.

55. From the diary of Col. House, March 25, 26, 1919, *PWW*, 56:279–80, 309; William C. Bullitt, Memorandum for the President and Commissioners Plenipotentiary to Negotiate Peace: Russia, ca. March 29, 1919, ibid., 57:387–91; Inga Floto, *Colonel House in Paris: A Study of American Policy at the Paris Peace Conference of 1919* (Copenhagen: Universitetsforlaget I Aarhus, 1973), 185; Ullman, *Anglo-Soviet Relations*, 144–52, 157–60. Beatrice Farnsworth doubts that House ever fully accepted Bullitt's plan. See *William C. Bullitt and the Soviet Union* (Bloomington: Indiana University Press, 1967), 48–50.

56. Lucy Biddle Lewis to Lydia Rickman, April 26, 1919, Hoover Papers, Pre-Commerce Period, Box 60, "Relief: Russia, 1919–1920," provides a shrewd analysis by a Quaker of the degree to which Hoover expected to run a Nansen relief program from behind the

scenes. See also Hoover, *Memoirs* 1, 414–17; John M. Thompson, *Russia, Bolshevism, and the Versailles Peace* (Princeton, NJ: Princeton University Press, 1966), 247–67.

57. Hoover, *Memoirs* 1, 417–18; Hoover to Wilson, May 16, 1919, enclosing Lenin to Nansen, May 14, 1919, *PWW*, vol. 59, *May 10–31, 1919* (1988), 192–97; summary of R. Cecil to M. P. A. Hankey, May 16, 1919, ibid., 59:300n8.

58. Hoover to Wilson, June 21, 1919, *PWW*, 61:61–63; from the diary of Vance Criswell McCormick, June 23, 1919, ibid., 61:110–11. Currency stabilization was not a Soviet objective. Theorist Nikolai Bukharin described "the revolutionary disintegration of industry" as a historically inevitable stage in the transition to socialism. See Stephen Cohen, *Bukharin and the Bolshevik Revolution: A Political Biography, 1888–1938* (New York: Knopf, 1973), 89.

59. U.S. minister in Switzerland (Pleasant A. Stovall) to Commission to Negotiate Peace, December 11, 1918, Department of State, *Papers Relating to the Foreign Relations of the United States, 1919: The Paris Peace Conference* (Washington, DC: Government Printing Office, 1942), 2: 46–47; acting secretary of state (Frank Polk) to American ambassador in France (William G. Sharp), December 24, 1918, ibid., 477–78; Hoover to Polk, December 25, 1918, ibid., 478; Edward F. Willis, *Herbert Hoover and the Russian Prisoners of World War I: A Study in Diplomacy and Relief, 1918–1919* (Stanford, CA: Stanford University Press, 1951), 11–22; Richard Bessel, *Germany after the First World War* (Oxford, UK: Clarendon, 1993), 200–201.

60. Minutes of the first meeting, Permanent Committee of the Supreme Council of Supply and Relief to assist the director general, January 19, 1919, Bane and Lutz, *Blockade of Germany*, 48–49; minutes of the second meeting of the second session, January 20, 1919, ibid., 50–51; minutes of the first meeting of the third session, February 1, 1919, ibid., 80; minutes of the fifth meeting, February 3, 1919, Document 11, "Russian Prisoners in Germany, Feb. 1, 1919," ibid., 83–84; minutes of the tenth meeting, February 19, 1919, Document 59, "Russian Prisoners of War," ibid., 139–40; Alonzo Taylor to Hoover, February 6, 1919, Bane and Lutz, *Organization of American Relief*, 233–35; Hoover to Pershing, March 5, 1919, ibid., 313–14; Surface and Bland, *American Food*, 608.

61. Hoover, memorandum submitted to Council of Heads of Delegations, July 15, 1919, Bane and Lutz, *Organization of American Relief*, 641–43; Tasker H. Bliss to Assistant Secretary of State Frank Polk, August 15, 1919, ibid., 677; Hoover to the Supreme Economic Council, September 3, 1919, Bane and Lutz, *Blockade of Germany*, 566; Willis, *Hoover and the Russian Prisoners*, 62. Hoover estimated that providing food and clothing to the prisoners between December 1, 1918, and August 31, 1919, had cost the United States, Britain, and France $1,112,350.

62. Memorandum to the Supreme Economic Council from the Director General of Relief, June 10, 1919, *ARA Bulletin*, 1st ser., 1, no. 14 (June 20, 1919): 1–2; report of the director general of relief to the Supreme Economic Council, June 22, 1919, *ARA Bulletin*, 1st ser., 1, no. 16 (July 4, 1919), 1–2.

63. Hoover to Wilson, May 14, 1919, *PWW*, 59:191–92; Vance McCormick diary, May 23, 1919, ibid., 59:448–49; Vance McCormick diary, June 7, 14, 1919, Hoover Papers, Pre-Commerce Period, Box 48, "McCormick, (Vance) Diary: Paris Peace Conference, 1919."

64. Hoover to House, May 16, 1919, Hoover Papers, Pre-Commerce Period, Box 8, "House, Edward M., 1915–21 & undated"; Hogan, *Informal Entente*, 28–29.

65. Hoover seems to have discussed his ideas with visiting New York Federal Reserve Governor Benjamin Strong in Paris on July 30 and may also have talked to Stettinius. See Benjamin Strong journal, July 28, 29, September 10, 1919, Federal Reserve Bank of New York Collection, Benjamin Strong Papers, Hoover Presidential Library, West Branch, Iowa, Box 4, "1000.3 (1), Benjamin Strong Journal, July 21–Sept. 20, 1919"; and Strong to R. C. Leffingwell, August 17, 1919, ibid., Box 4, "Strong's Trip to Europe, July–September 1919"; Lester V. Chandler, *Benjamin Strong, Central Banker* (Washington, DC: Brookings Institution, 1958), 140–47. Strong sent a memorandum outlining a similar plan to Assistant Secretary of the Treasury Russell Leffingwell on August 30 and another to House around September 10. By that time, House had lost all influence with Wilson, so it is unlikely the president ever saw it. See Strong's "Draft Scheme for the Rehabilitation of Economic Life," May 28, 1919,

and his "Memorandum" on a proposal for dealing with Allied debts, undated, ibid. Hoover's plans took nowhere near as concrete shape as those worked out by Thomas Lamont in conversations with Robert Brand and Jean Monnet in May. As details of the Lamont program emerged, it became evident that its main beneficiary would be J. P. Morgan and its allies, at which point the British vetoed it. See Stephen A. Schuker, "Origins of American Stabilization Policy in Europe: The Financial Dimension, 1918–1924," in *Confrontation and Cooperation: Germany and the United States in the Era of World War I, 1900–1924*, ed. Hans-Jürgen Schröder (Providence, RI: Berg, 1993), 385–89.

66. Hoover, "Memorandum on the Economic Situation of Europe," for the Supreme Economic Council, July 3, 1919, Strauss Papers, Subject File, Box 2, "American Relief Administration, Special Folder, 1918–19"; the American Commission to Negotiate Peace to the Secretary of State, September 13, 1919, Department of State, *Papers Relating to the Foreign Relations of the United States, 1919* (Washington, DC: Government Printing Office, 1934), 1:8–9; Walworth, *Wilson and His Peacemakers*, 523n66.

67. Hoover to Wilson, June 6, 1919, *PWW*, 60:230–32; "Future Plans for Children's Relief Work," cablegram from Hoover to ARA office in New York, July 7, 1919, *ARA Bulletin* 1, no. 17 (July 11, 1919); "Memorandum: Organisation and Work, American Relief Administration European Children's Fund," ca. July 12, 1919, Lou Hoover Papers, Box 1, "Subject File: American Relief Administration, Correspondence and Reports, 1919–20"; Hoover, *Memoirs* 1, 321–24.

68. ARA (Paris) to I. J. Paderewski, March 13, 1919, *ARA Bulletin*, 2nd ser., 1, no. 11 (April 1, 1921): 15–17; Hoover to Paderewski, July 12, 1919, and Paderewski to Hoover, July 12, 1919, both in Strauss Papers, Subject File, Box 36, "Hoover, Herbert, General, 1919 July–Dec."; Hoover to Paderewski, August 17, 1919, *ARA Bulletin*, 2nd ser., 1, no. 11 (April 1, 1921): 18–21; memorandum regarding the establishment of an advisory group in Czechoslovakia, June 12, 1919, Strauss Papers, Subject File, Box 36, "Hoover, Herbert, General, 1919 Apr.–June"; Wandycz, *United States and Poland*, 180–81; Gary Dean Best, "Herbert Hoover's Technical Mission to Yugoslavia, 1919–1920," *Annals of Iowa*, 3rd ser., 42 (Fall 1972): 443–59; David Burner, *Herbert Hoover: A Public Life* (New York: Knopf, 1979), 129. On May 20, 1919, Hoover issued a general directive to all ARA personnel affirming that it was essential for recipients of aid to have confidence in the impartiality of all aid workers, who were strictly enjoined not to promote any American or personal business interests and to refrain from involvement "in any local political dispute." See *ARA Bulletin*, 1st ser., 1, no. 19 (May 20, 1919).

69. Hoover, *American Epic*, 1:265–67, 2:440–46. Another major challenge faced by the ARA in the summer of 1919 was Béla Kun's Communist government in Hungary; it is discussed in Chapter 9 of this volume.

70. Surface and Bland, *American Food*, 34–35, 42–43, 49, 54–55, 143.

71. Ibid., 146; Vernon Kellogg, "Herbert Hoover as I Know Him," *The Outlook* 147 (October 26, 1927): 244; Burner, *Hoover*, 116.

72. Rebecca Solnit, *A Paradise Built in Hell: The Extraordinary Communities that Arise in Disaster* (New York: Viking, 2009), 8, 305. This valuable book, based in part on "disaster sociology," appeared too late to have its findings fully integrated into this study.

73. Rothbard, "Hoover's 1919 Food Diplomacy in Retrospect," 107.

74. John Maynard Keynes, *The Economic Consequences of the Peace* (London: Macmillan, 1920), 257, 257n1. Keynes was less fulsome in a private letter to Hoover, saying that Hoover was "the only man in Paris in my judgment who has come through this tragedy without discredit and has accomplished some part at least of his aims. The rest has been all wickedness, greed, meanness, smallness and failure." Keynes to Hoover, June 7, 1919, Strauss Papers, Subject File, Box 36, "Hoover, Herbert, General, 1919 Apr.–June."

75. From a speech by Lou Henry Hoover at Goucher College, in Baltimore, undated, probably, March 11, 1920, Lou Hoover Papers, Box 3, "Subject File: Articles, Addresses, & Statements, 1919–1920: Speech at Goucher College, Towson, Maryland"; Hoover, *Memoirs* 1, 360–61. Lou and Allan came over to Europe in July to join Hoover. I have been unable to confirm absolutely that she was with him in Poland and personally witnessed this scene, but it seems likely she did.

Chapter 2

1. John M. Hallowell to Lou Henry Hoover, January 14, 1919, Lou Henry Hoover Papers, Hoover Presidential Library, West Branch, Iowa, Box 3, "Personal Correspondence, 1872–1920, Hallowell, John M., 1917–19"; Lewis Strauss to Ray Lyman Wilbur, October 9, 1918, Ray Lyman Wilbur Papers, Hoover Institution Archives, Stanford, California, Box 20, "Correspondence: General, 1917–1931."
2. Lou Hoover to A. E. Taylor, January 9, 1919, Lou Hoover Papers, Box 8, "Personal Correspondence, 1872–1920, Taylor, Alonzo, 1919."
3. Laurine Anderson Small to Lou Hoover, April 21, 26, 29, 1919, Lou Hoover Papers, Box 7, "Personal Correspondence, 1872–1920, Small, Laurine Anderson, 1919 March–June"; Lou Hoover to Laurine Small, ca. May 1, 1919, ibid., Box 7 "Small, Laurine Anderson, undated"; Anne Beiser Allen, *An Independent Woman: The Life of Lou Henry Hoover* (Westport, CT: Praeger, 2000), 74–75.
4. Dare Stark McMullin Oral History, Hoover Presidential Library; Laurine Anderson Small to Lou Hoover, December 23, 1918, Lou Hoover Papers, Box 7, "Personal Correspondence, 1872–1920, Small, Laurine Anderson, 1918." For the costs of the Food Administration Club, see Laurine Small to Lou Hoover, April 26, 1919, ibid., Box 7, "Personal Correspondence, 1872–1920, Small, Laurine Anderson, 1919 March–June."
5. Copy of a personal memorandum, ca. July 1932, Lou Hoover Papers, Box 10, "Subject File, Articles & Statements, Undated, Lou Henry Hoover on Herbert Hoover."
6. Edgar Rickard to Lou Hoover, January 6, 1919, Herbert Hoover Papers, Pre-Commerce Period, Hoover Presidential Library, West Branch, Iowa, Box 7, "Hoover, Lou Henry, 1906–1921"; Lou Hoover to John A. Agnew, January 17, 1919, Lou Hoover Papers, Box 1, "Personal Correspondence, 1872–1920, Agnew, John A., 1906–20"; Allan and Dare to Laurine Small, February 4, 1919; Lou Hoover to Herbert Hoover, February 10, 1919; Laurine Small to Lou Hoover, February 17, 1919, all in ibid., Box 7, "Personal Correspondence, 1872–1920, Small, Laurine Anderson, 1919 February"; Lou Hoover to Marian Fairchild, February 25, 1919, ibid., Box 2, "Personal Correspondence, 1872–1920, F Miscellaneous." Because of shipping shortages, the Hoovers' London goods were not shipped until March 1920, when they were sent at a charge of £1033.10. See John A. Agnew to Lou Hoover, March 2, 1920, ibid., Box 1, "Personal Correspondence, 1872–1920, Agnew, John A., 1906–20."
7. Dare Stark to Laurine Small, February 1919, Lou Hoover Papers, Box 6, "Personal Correspondence, 1872–1920, McMullin, Dare Stark, 1919–20 & undated"; Lou Hoover to Edgar Rickard, March 5, 1919, ibid., Box 7, "Personal Correspondence, 1872–1920, Rickard, Edgar, 1919"; statement released to the press by Hoover, September 27, 1919, Lewis L. Strauss Papers, Hoover Presidential Library, West Branch, Iowa, Subject File, Box 22, "European Children's Fund, 1919"; Laurine Small to Lou Hoover, February 17, 1919, and Lou Hoover to Laurine Small, February 27, 1919, both in Lou Hoover Papers, Box 7, "Personal Correspondence, 1872–1920, Small, Laurine Anderson, 1919 February"; Laurine Small to Albert Butler, March 8, 1919, ibid., Box 7, "Personal Correspondence, 1872–1920, Small, Laurine Anderson, 1919 March–June."
8. Lou Hoover to Laurine Small, February 27, March 3, 1919, Lou Hoover Papers, Box 7, "Personal Correspondence, 1872–1920, Small, Laurine Anderson, 1919 March–June"; Lou Hoover to Laurine Small, ca. March 15, 1919, ibid., Box 7, "Personal Correspondence, 1872–1920, Small, Laurine Anderson, undated." For the background of the lace program, see Nancy Beck Young, *Lou Henry Hoover: Activist First Lady* (Lawrence: University Press of Kansas, 2004), 25.
9. Edgar Rickard to Lou Hoover, June 25, 1919, Lou Hoover Papers, Box 7, "Personal Correspondence, 1872–1920, Rickard, Edgar, 1919"; Lou Hoover to Arthur B. Clark, July 12, 1919, reproduced in Birge M. Clark, *Memoirs about Mr. and Mrs. Herbert Hoover, with Particular Emphasis on the Planning and Building of Their Home on San Juan Hill* (Palo Alto, CA: Privately printed, 1969); Lou Hoover to Edgar Rickard, ca. July 12, 1919, and Rickard to

Herbert Hoover, July 23, 1919, both in Hoover Papers, Pre-Commerce Period, Box 7, "Hoover, Lou Henry, 1906–1921"; Dare Stark to Lou Hoover, July 16, 1919, Lou Hoover Papers, Box 6, "Personal Correspondence, 1872–1920, McMullin, Dare Stark, 1919–20 & undated"; Ray Lyman Wilbur to Herbert Hoover, September 4, 1919, ibid., Box 59, "Subject File, Hoover, Herbert Jr., General, 1903–30."

10. Hoover's statement to the press, September 27, 1919, Strauss Papers, Subject File, Box 22, "European Children's Fund, 1919." His schedule for September and early October is in Lou Hoover Papers, Box 112, "Subject File, Trips, Travels and Residences of HH and LHH, 1895–1928"; for the telegraph bill, see Lou Hoover to Edgar Rickard, November 6, 1919, ibid., Box 7, "Personal Correspondence, 1872–1920, Rickard, Edgar, 1919."

11. Edgar Rickard to Lou Hoover, October 17, 1919, and Lou Hoover to Edgar Rickard, November 6, 1919, Lou Hoover Papers, Box 7, "Personal Correspondence, 1872–1920, Rickard, Edgar, 1919"; Herbert Hoover to Lou Hoover, October 27, 1919, and Lou Hoover to Herbert Hoover, October 27, 1919, both in ibid., Box 5, "Personal Correspondence, 1872–1920, Hoover, Herbert, 1917–20 & undated"; Lou Hoover to John A. Agnew, October 28, 1919, ibid., Box 1, "Personal Correspondence, 1872–1920, Agnew, John A., 1906–20."

12. Bert to Lou, November 5, 26, 1919, Lou Hoover Papers, Box 5, "Personal Correspondence, 1872–1920, Hoover, Herbert, 1917–20 & undated"; Lou Hoover to Edgar Rickard, November 6, ca.14, 1919, ibid., Box 7, "Personal Correspondence, 1872–1920, Rickard, Edgar, 1919."

13. Bert to Lou, November 20 and December 9, 1919, Lou Hoover Papers, Box 5, "Personal Correspondence, 1872–1920, Hoover, Herbert, 1917–20 & undated."

14. See the various documents in Lou Hoover Papers, Box 75, "Subject File, Properties and Lots, Stanford House, Correspondence, 1920." For the swimming pool question, see Lou Hoover to Birge Clark, March 4, 1920, in ibid. Lou gave the price of $170,000 in Lou Hoover to Edgar Rickard, March 3, 1925, ibid., Box 111, "Subject File, Taxes for: 1924." Price comparisons between 1920 and the present are difficult. My best guess is that the Hoover house would cost nearly $2 million in today's money.

15. A thorough and fascinating discussion of the house's design, with excellent illustrations, is Paul V. Turner, *Mrs. Hoover's Pueblo Walls: The Primitive and the Modern in the Lou Henry Hoover House* (Stanford, CA: Stanford University Press, 2004), but see also Ruth Dennis, *The Homes of the Hoovers* (West Branch, IA: Hoover Presidential Library Association, 1986), 35–36; George H. Nash, *Herbert Hoover and Stanford University* (Stanford, CA: Hoover Institution, 1988), 57–58. Hoover's concern about fire carried over to his office. In April 1921, he wrote to Senator Miles Poindexter, pointing out that some of the Commerce Department's records, stored in the basement of a wartime building, had recently been destroyed by fire and urging the construction of "a proper fire-proof Archive Building." See Hoover to Poindexter, April 14, 1921, Herbert Hoover Papers, Commerce Period, Hoover Presidential Library, West Branch, Iowa, Box 550, "Senate: Poindexter, Miles, 1921–1923." The proper preservation of the historical record was of great importance to him, as evidenced by his work in collecting materials for the Hoover Institution, his own voluminous records, and his numerous books about the events of his career.

16. "Tell Me What She's Really Like: A Discussion of Mrs. Hoover, by a Friend" (unsigned, but very likely by Dare Stark McMullin), ca. 1932, Lou Hoover Papers, Box 60, "Subject File, Hoover, Lou Henry, Biographical Data."

17. Allan Hoover to George Barr Baker, December 1, 1919, George Barr Baker Papers, Hoover Institution Archives, Stanford, California, Box 3, "Hoover, Herbert C. & Family"; Lou Hoover to Miss (?) Woodward, March 22, 1920, Lou Hoover Papers, Box 8, "Personal Correspondence, 1872–1920, Wi–Wr Miscellaneous"; Lou Hoover to Arthur Clark, March 29, 1920, ibid., Box 16, "Subject File, Campaign of 1920."

18. "A Talk to the Students at Bryn Mawr at Luncheon, April 10, 1920," Lou Hoover Papers, Box 3, "Subject File, Articles, Addresses & Statements, 1920, April 10, Bryn Mawr College Speech, Pennsylvania." For further discussion of this topic, see Kendrick A. Clements, "The

New Era and the New Woman: Lou Henry Hoover and 'Feminism's Awkward Age,'" *Pacific Historical Review* 73 (August 2004): 425–61.

19. Clark, *Memoirs*, 21–22.
20. George Barr Baker to Charles K. Field, November 21, 1931, George Barr Baker Papers, Box 3, "Field, Charles K."
21. Ruby S. Gaunt to Lou Hoover, May 3, (1920), Lou Hoover to Ruby Gaunt, May 4, 1920, both in Lou Hoover Papers, Box 2, "Personal Correspondence, 1872–1920, Gaunt, Ruby S., 1920 & undated"; Lou Hoover to Allan Hoover, May 10, 1920, Allan Hoover Papers, Herbert Hoover Presidential Library, West Branch, Iowa, Box 1, "Correspondence with Lou Henry Hoover, 1920."
22. Lewis Strauss to Paul M. Warburg, September 7, 1920, Strauss Papers, Subject File, Box 36, "Hoover, Herbert, General 1920"; Edgar Rickard to Lou Hoover, September 7, October 7, and December 23, 1920, Lou Hoover Papers, Box 7, "Personal Correspondence, 1872–1920, Rickard, Edgar, 1920 & undated"; Lou Hoover to Edgar Rickard, December 30, 1920, ibid.
23. Julius Barnes, Edgar Rickard, Edwin P. Shattuck, and Edward M. Flesh to William C. Mullendore, December 15, 1920, William C. Mullendore Papers, Herbert Hoover Presidential Library, West Branch, Iowa, Box 15, "Hoover, Herbert, Correspondence, 1918–62"; "Hoover in Combine of Big Enterprises," *New York Times*, January 26, 1921.

Chapter 3

1. Herbert Hoover, *Memoirs: Years of Adventure, 1874–1920* (New York: Macmillan, 1951), 480 (hereafter, *Memoirs* 1); *Memoirs: The Cabinet and the Presidency, 1920–1933* (New York: Macmillan, 1952), 2 (hereafter, *Memoirs* 2). Hoover's recollection, in *Memoirs* 1, 480, that during his residence in Paris, he "saw no cathedrals or 'sights'" and "only twice" took time "for a short motor trip to the countryside" is contradicted by a contemporary letter from W. Parmer Fuller to friends in the United States, September 6, 1919, in Hoover Papers, Pre-Commerce Period, Hoover Presidential Library, West Branch, Iowa, Box 33, "European Relief Council, 1919–1921." Fuller describes in some detail "Mr. Hoover's practice of motoring into the country almost every Sunday" to see various sights, including cathedrals. The point is unimportant—Hoover certainly worked extremely hard during the period—except that it should warn readers that any memoir, written many years after the events described, is likely to have inaccuracies.
2. Hoover, *Memoirs* 2, 2; "Ratify Peace Now, Says Hoover at Pier," *New York Times*, September 14, 1919.
3. Hoover, *Memoirs* 2, 2–3.
4. William Cox Redfield to Wilson, April 4, 1919, in Arthur S. Link et al., eds., *The Papers of Woodrow Wilson*, vol. 56, *March 17–April 4, 1919* (Princeton, NJ: Princeton University Press, 1987), 619–20 (hereafter, *PWW*); Wilson to Julius Barnes, April 15, 1919, *PWW* vol. 57, *April 5–22, 1919* (1987), 375; Barnes to Wilson, April 18, 1919, ibid., 57:475; U.S. Grain Corporation press release, July 17, 1919, Hoover Papers, Pre-Commerce Period, Box 1, "Barnes, Julius H., 1917–1920."
5. Carter Glass to Wilson, February 11, 1919, *PWW*, vol. 55, *February 8–March 16, 1919* (1986), 89–90; Redfield to Wilson, April 4, 1919, *PWW*, 56:619–20; U.S. Industrial Board press release, March 24, 1919, Hoover Papers, Pre-Commerce Period, Box 1, "Barnes, Julius H., 1917—1920"; Wilson to Hoover, April 16, 1919, *PWW*, 57:407.
6. Hoover to Wilson, April 18, 1919, *PWW*, 57:472–74.
7. Hoover to Wilson, February 24, 1919, *PWW*, 55:251–53; Hoover to Julius Barnes, July 23, 1919, Hoover Papers, Pre-Commerce Period, Box 60, "Public Statements, 1917—1920"; Hoover to A. Mitchell Palmer, September 18, 1919, ibid., Box 12, "Palmer, A. Mitchell, 1919—1921"; Hoover, *Memoirs* 2, 16–17; David Burner, *Herbert Hoover: A Public Life* (New York: Knopf, 1978), 110.

8. "The Bullitt 'Bomb'" and "Current Events: Peace Preliminaries," *Literary Digest* September 27, 1919: 12, 65.
9. See the reports on Herbert's summer in Subject File, Hoover Papers, Pre-Commerce Period, Box 100, "Harrison, George, 1919–20."
10. Hoover, *Memoirs 2*, 4–5.
11. "1,200 Applaud Hoover's Name for President," *New York Times*, September 17, 1919.
12. Copies of the records of the First Industrial Conference may be found in Hoover Papers, Pre-Commerce Period, Box 44–45, "Industrial Conference, Second."
13. From the transcript of a radio talk by Rosenwald, October 27, 1928, transcribed by Gary Dean Best, Hoover Papers, Pre-Commerce Period, Box 14, "Rosenwald, Julius, 1920–1926."
14. Herbert Hoover, "Some Notes on Industrial Readjustment," *Saturday Evening Post*, December 27, 1919, 1–2, 145–46. Hoover was intrigued by labor-management innovations pioneered by John D. Rockefeller, Jr., in his Colorado mines and proposed a meeting with Rockefeller to discuss his ideas. Other commitments, however, kept interfering with the meeting. See Ray Lyman Wilbur to Everett Colby, December 9, 16, 1919, Ray Lyman Wilbur Papers, Hoover Institution Archives, Stanford, California, Box 20, "Correspondence: General, 1917–1931."
15. Robert Zieger, "Herbert Hoover, the Wage-Earner, and the 'New Economic System,' 1919–29," in *Herbert Hoover as Secretary of Commerce: Studies in New Era Thought and Practice*, ed. Ellis W. Hawley (Iowa City: University of Iowa Press, 1981), 83.
16. "Preliminary Statement of Industrial Conference Called by the President" (Washington, DC: Government Printing Office, 1919).
17. Zieger, "Hoover, the Wage-Earner, and the 'New Economic System,'" 85–86.
18. "Editor's Introductory Note," ibid., 81; "Report of Industrial Conference Called by the President" (Washington, DC: Government Printing Office, March 6, 1920). At the recommendation of the conference, the White House named a Bituminous Coal Commission on December 19, 1919, charging it to investigate whether higher wages and an increase in the price of coal might end the coal strike. A principal member was Hoover's friend, lawyer, and banker Henry M. Robinson of Los Angeles. The union spurned the commission's report, which called for a substantial wage increase but rejected shortening the workweek. See Edward M. Hurley to Robinson, December 4, 1919, Henry Mauris Robinson Papers, Huntington Library, San Marino, California, Box 3, "Hurley, Edward M."; Woodrow Wilson to Robinson, December 19, 1919, ibid., Box 3, "Wilson, Woodrow"; Robinson to Rembrandt Peale and John White, March 7, 1920, ibid., Box 4, "To Rembrandt Peale & John P. White"; Robinson to Woodrow Wilson, March 8, 1920, ibid., Box 4, "To Woodrow Wilson."
19. *Industrial Conference: Hearing before the Committee on Education and Labor, United States Senate, 55th Congress, 2nd Session, on The Report of the Industrial Commission* (Washington, DC: Government Printing Office, 1920); Felix Frankfurter, "The President's Industrial Conference," *New Republic* April 7, 1920, 179–82; Hoover, *Memoirs 2*, 31; Hoover, "Collier's Strike Cure—and Its Critics," *Collier's* November 27, 1920: 9–10, 16.
20. Hoover, "Some Notes on Industrial Readjustment," 2; *Memoirs 2*, 29.
21. "Mr. Hoover's Inauguration Address to the American Institute of Mining and Metallurgical Engineers, February 17, 1920," Hoover Papers, Commerce Period, Hoover Presidential Library, West Branch, Iowa, Box 193, "Engineers and Engineering, 1918–1922"; Hoover, *American Individualism* (New York: Doubleday, Doran, 1922; repr. West Branch, IA: Hoover Presidential Library), 15; Burner, *Hoover*, 66; Thomas A. Long, "Engineering and Social Equality: Herbert Hoover's Manifesto," *IEEE Technology and Society Magazine* 3 (September 1984): 18.
22. List of member societies of the FAES, ca. June 4, 1920, Hoover Papers, Pre-Commerce Period, Box 33, "FAES—General Corres.—Dec. 1920–March 1921"; Philip N. Moore to Hoover, August 8, 1920; Richard L. Humphrey to Hoover, September 8, 1920; Hoover to Moore, September 13, 1920; draft program for the first meeting of the American Engineering Council on November 18–19, 1920 (September 20, 1920), all in ibid., Box 33, "Federated American Engineering Societies, 1920."

23. "American Institute of Mining Engineers Banquet, Minneapolis, Minnesota, Summary of Address Delivered by Herbert Hoover," August 26, 1920, Hoover Papers, Pre-Commerce Period, Box 60, "Public Statements."
24. AFL Executive Council minutes, November 17, 1920, Hoover Papers, Pre-Commerce Period, Box 6, "Gompers, Samuel, 1917–22."
25. Hoover, "The Engineer's Relation to Our Industrial Problems," presidential speech, *Engineering News-Record* November 25, 1920, 1053–56 (emphasis in original).
26. Hoover to Samuel Gompers, December 6, 1920, Hoover Papers, Pre-Commerce Period, Box 6, "Gompers, Samuel, 1917–22"; Edward Eyre Hunt to Hoover, December 20, 1920, ibid., Box 43, "FAES Industrial Waste Comm.—Meetings"; Hunt to L. W. Wallace, January 4, 1921, ibid., Box 16, "Wallace, L. W., 1920–1921"; "Tentative Budget—American Engineering Council, February 1, 1921, ibid., Box 33, "FAES—General Corres.—Dec. 1920–March 1921"; Hoover, *Memoirs* 2, 31; Hunt to Florence C. Thorne (Gompers's executive secretary), January 15, 1921, Hoover Papers, Pre-Commerce Period, Box 8, "Hunt, E. E., 1921"; "Purpose and Plan of Work of the Committee on Elimination of Waste in Industry Appointed by Herbert Hoover, President of the Federated American Engineering Societies," February 17, 1921, ibid., Box 44, "FAES Industrial Waste Comm.—Policy."
27. Hoover to Max Farrand (Commonwealth Fund), February 25, and Farrand to Hoover, March 2, 1921, Hoover Papers, Pre-Commerce Period, Box 5, "Farrand, Max, 1919–1921" fund-raising circular and tentative budget, ibid., Box 41, "FAES Industrial Waste Comm.—Cir. Ltr., 1921"; "Hoover Quits Post as Engineer Head, Washington *Herald*, 18 April 1921," ibid., Box 23, "American Engineering Council, 1921"; drafts, press releases, and report, November 28, 1921, to members of the AEC Council, ibid., Box 200, "Federated American Engineering Societies, 1921 July–December."
28. American Engineering Council, *Waste in Industry, by the Committee on Elimination of Waste in Industry of the Federated American Engineering Societies* (New York: McGraw-Hill for the Federated American Engineering Societies, 1921), 34–260.
29. Ibid., 261–397.
30. Ibid., 8–23.
31. Ibid., 24–27.
32. Ibid., 30–33.
33. Edward Eyre Hunt, "Industrial Waste," November 13, 1921, Hoover Papers, Commerce Period, Box 649, "Unemployment, Hunt, Edward Eyre, Articles by, 1921"; Burner, *Hoover*, 146.
34. Sydney Sullivan Parker Oral History, Hoover Institution Archives, Stanford, California.

Chapter 4

1. Unidentified clipping, "Hoover Won't Even Designate His Party," December 25, 1919, Herbert Hoover Papers, Pre-Commerce Period, Hoover Presidential Library, West Branch, Iowa, Box 70, "Oct. 1919–Dec.1919."
2. Bernard Baruch believed Hoover wanted to run as a Democrat, but Wilson was unenthusiastic. See Edith Benham diary, April 27, 1919, in Arthur S. Link et al., eds., *The Papers of Woodrow Wilson*, vol. 58, *April 23–May 9, 1919*, (Princeton, NJ: Princeton University Press, 1988), 172 (hereafter, *PWW*).
3. Arnold, "Account of Hoover's Rise to the Presidency: Pioneering in Petroleum and Politics," Ralph Arnold Papers, Huntington Library, San Marino, California, Box 1, "Correspondence, speeches, articles, memorandums, etc., 1920." Initial financing for Arnold's project came from two wealthy Californians, Henry A. Whitley and Edward H. Clark. Another Hoover admirer, Ralph Merritt, was also active in California. See Merritt to Clara Burdette, December 29, 1919, Clara Burdette Papers, Huntington Library, Box 128.
4. Strauss to Rickard, April 8, 1919, Lewis L. Strauss Papers, Herbert Hoover Presidential Library, West Branch, Iowa, Subject File, Box 8, "Campaign of 1920—General, 1920 Jan.–Apr."; draft of letter to Mark Requa, February 21, 1919, George Barr Baker Papers, Hoover

Institution Archives, Stanford, California, Box 6, "Requa, Mark L."; unsigned, undated memorandum in Hoover's handwriting, Hoover Papers, Pre-Commerce Period, Box 27, "Campaign of 1920, Residency of 1874–1920."

5. Hoover to Glasgow, April 12, 1919, Hoover Papers, Pre-Commerce Period, Box 5, "Glasgow, Judge William A., Jr., 1919–1920." A copy of the letter, with Strauss's marginal notes, is in Strauss Papers, Subject File, Box 36, "Hoover, Herbert, General, 1919 Apr.–June."

6. Unsigned, undated letter (probably in Kellogg's handwriting) to Hoover; memorandum to Dr. Kellogg from Edgar Rickard, July 11, 1919, both in Hoover Papers, Pre-Commerce Period, Box 9, "Kellogg, Vernon, 1919–1921" (emphasis in original); Warren Gregory to Hoover, August 26, 1919, ibid., Box 6, "Gregory, Warren, 1916–1920." For the progress of the biography, see a series of letters between Kellogg and Rickard, September 3–October 1, 1919, in ibid., Box 9, "Kellogg, Vernon, 1919–1921."

7. Hoover to Rickard, September 5, 1919, Box 14, "Rickard, Edgar, 1912–1920," ibid.; "Ratify Peace Now, Says Hoover at Pier," *New York Times*, September 14, 1919; draft press statement, September 18, 1919, William Mullendore Papers, Herbert Hoover Presidential Library, West Branch, Iowa, Box 1, "Campaign of 1920."

8. "1200 Applaud Hoover's Name for President," *New York Times*, September 17, 1919.

9. Unidentified clipping, "Hoover Won't Even Designate His Party," December 25, 1919, Hoover Papers, Pre-Commerce Period, Box 70, "October 1919–December 1919"; McCutcheon cartoon, New York *News*, December 24, 1919.

10. Arnold, "Account of Hoover's Rise to the Presidency"; Ralph Merritt to Clara Burdette, January 21, 1920, Hoover Papers, Pre-Commerce Period, Box 128, Clara Burdette Papers; Julius Barnes to (Burdette?), February 26, 1920.

11. "Hoover as President," *Literary Digest*, January 31, 1920, 16; Meyer Lissner to Katherine Phillips Edson, January 5, 1920, Meyer Lissner Papers, Green Library, Rare Books and Special Collections, Stanford University, Stanford, California, Box 11, Folder 216, "Lissner: Corres. Out, January 2–16, 1920"; Lissner to C. K. McClatchy, February 16, 1920, ibid., Box 11, Folder 219, "Lissner: Corres. Out, February 12–28, 1920."

12. "Hoover Refuses White House Race," Portland *Telegram*, ca. Jan. 7, 1920, Hoover Papers, Pre-Commerce Period, Box 70, "January 1920."

13. For Baker, see his letter to the editor in the Springfield, Massachusetts, *Republican* (September 7, 1919); for Franklin D. Roosevelt's famous observation that he wished "we could make him [Hoover] President of the United States. There could not be a better one," see Roosevelt to Hugh Gibson, January 2, 1920, Herbert Hoover Papers, Stanford University, Stanford, California, Box 6, "Gibson, Hugh 1917–21"; John J. Murphy to Hoover, January 13, 1920, Hoover Papers, Pre-Commerce Period, Box 27, "Campaign of 1920: Correspondence 1919–Jan. 1920"; "Georgians Favor Naming of Hoover by the Democrats," New York *World*, February 18, 1920; Philadelphia *Evening Bulletin*, January 15, 1920; Council Bluffs *Nonpareil*, January 15, 19, 29 and February 9, 1920; "Resolution Unanimously Adopted by the Joint Council of Engineers of San Francisco, Jan. 13, 1920," Hoover Papers, Pre-Commerce Period, Box 27, "Campaign of 1920: Correspondence 1919–Jan. 1920"; New York *World*, January 21, 1920; undated clipping from Los Angeles *Times*, January 1920, in Hoover Papers, Pre-Commerce Period, Box 5, "Glasgow, Judge William A., Jr., 1919–1920"; Samuel G. Blythe, "Have the Populi a Vox?" *Saturday Evening Post*, January 14, 1920, 162, 165; "Hoover and the Issues," *New Republic* February 4, 1920, 281–83.

14. "Herbert C. Hoover and the League of Nations, Speech of Senator James A. Reed of Missouri in the Senate of the United States, January 24, 1920," Herbert Hoover Papers, Commerce Period, Herbert Hoover Presidential Library, West Branch, Iowa, Box 512, "Reed, Senator James A., 1921–1924 & undated"; New York *Evening Journal*, January 6, 1920; extracts from Strauss's diary for February 25, 26, 28, 1920, Strauss Papers, Subject File, Box 8, "Campaign of 1920, Strauss Diary"; "To Put Barnes on Grill," Baltimore *Sun*, March 12, 1920; "Grain Probe Is Blow Aimed at Hoover," Sacramento *Union*, March 13, 1920; "The Grain Investigation," Washington *Post*, March 13, 1920; "Promise Speed in U.S. Grain Probe," Washington *Sun*, March 25, 1920. The *Globe* eventually retracted the spoiled

grain story. See Alfred W. McCann, "Scandal Is Laid to Aides of Hoover," New York *Globe*, February 26, 1920; McCann, "McCann Puts the Spotlight on Hoover's Record as Food Administrator," repr. from March 1920 issue of *Reconstruction*, pp. 102–6, in Hoover Papers, Pre-Commerce Period, Box 72, "March 1–4, 1920"; Nathan Straus, Jr., to Lewis Strauss, March 1, July 16, 1920; selections from transcript of January 21, 1919, hearing before Senate Committee on Agriculture and Forestry; Lewis Strauss to Bruce Bliven, July 20, 1920, all in Strauss Papers, Subject File, Box 8, "Campaign of 1920-McCann Smear."

15. "Summary of the Address of Julius H. Barnes, United States Wheat Director, before the National Wholesale Dry-Goods Association, Wednesday Evening, January 14, 1920, Waldorf-Astoria Hotel, New York City," Hoover Papers, Pre-Commerce Period, Box 1, "Barnes, Julius H., 1917–1920"; undated memoir by Barnes, "The 1920 Lightning that Did Not Strike Herbert Hoover," original in the St. Louis County Historical Society, ibid., Box 27, "Campaign of 1920"; General Electric executive Sidney A. Mitchell to Lewis Strauss, February 11, 1920, Strauss Papers, Subject File, Box 8, "Campaign of 1920, General, 1920 Jan.–Apr."; David Lawrence, "Hoover Has Both Parties Up a Tree," Philadelphia *Evening Bulletin*, January 15, 1920; "Perplexed Anew by the Hoover Riddle," Baltimore *Sun*, January 16, 1920; Lewis Strauss to Hoover, January 15, 1920, Strauss Papers, Subject File, Box 8, "Campaign of 1920: General, 1920 Jan.–Apr."; "Comment in Washington on Herbert Hoover for President," Baltimore *Sun*, January 22, 1920; Meyer Lissner to Edgar A. Luce, February 11, 1920, Meyer Lissner Papers, Stanford University, Stanford, California, Box 11, Folder 218, "Lissner: Corres. Out, February 1–11, 1920."

16. "Republicans of S. F. Start Hoover Move," San Francisco *Examiner*, January 22, 1920; Francis Farquhar to Ralph Merritt, January 29, 1920, Hoover Papers, Pre-Commerce Period, Box 27, "Campaign of 1920, Correspondence 1919–Jan. 1920"; press release, "Results of Questionnaire Sent Out January 22, 1920," ca. January 29, 1920, ibid., Box 29, "Campaign of 1920, Hoover Republican Club of California, Organization—Questionnaire Results, 1919–1920"; "The British Envoy Sat in at Famous Gathering," New York *American*, January 24, 1920; "Grey Sat in at Famous Gathering," San Francisco *Examiner*, January 24, 1920; "Statement from Dr. Ray Lyman Wilbur, President Stanford University to Associated Press, January 26, 1920," Hoover Papers, Pre-Commerce Period, Box 17, "Wilbur, Ray Lyman, 1920"; "Hoover Boom Launched at St. Francis," San Francisco *Bulletin*, January 28, 1920.

17. Arnold, "Account of Hoover's Rise to the Presidency"; "Biography of Clara Burdette," *California Life* April 10, 1920, 3, 21; "Republicans of S. F. Start Hoover Move," San Francisco *Examiner*, January 22, 1920; Francis Farquhar to Ralph Merritt, January 29, 1920, Hoover Papers, Pre-Commerce Period, Box 27, "Campaign of 1920, Correspondence 1919–Jan. 1920"; press release, "Results of Questionnaire Sent out January 22, 1920," ca. January 29, 1920, ibid., Box 29, "Campaign of 1920, Hoover Republican Club of California, Organization—Questionnaire Results, 1919–1920"; "The British Envoy Sat in at Famous Gathering," New York *American*, January 24, 1920; "Grey Sat in at Famous Gathering," San Francisco *Examiner*, January 24, 1920; "Statement from Dr. Ray Lyman Wilbur, President Stanford University to Associated Press, January 26, 1920," Hoover Papers, Pre-Commerce Period, Box 17, "Wilbur, Ray Lyman, 1920"; "Hoover Boom Launched at St. Francis," San Francisco *Bulletin*, January 28, 1920. Edgar Rickard and Walter Brown subsequently procured affidavits from London denying that Hoover had ever applied for British citizenship. See John A. Agnew to Edgar Rickard, February 25, 1920, Hoover Papers, Pre-Commerce Period, Box 1, "Agnew, J. A.–J. B., 1905–1921"; Hardee Scott (British Home Office) to "Gentlemen," March 3, 1920, ibid., Box 91, "Citizenship, HH Personal, 1920–1927 & undated."

18. Hoover Papers, Pre-Commerce Period, Box 30, "Campaign of 1920, Speeches & Statements—Hoover Party Politics, Jan.–Oct. 1920." The statement was published in many newspapers on February 8 and 9.

19. "Hoover's Statement Is Discounted Here," *New York Times*, February 9, 1920; "Hoover Battles Bravely to Escape Being President," Sacramento *Bee*, February 13, 1920; Hoover to Hodgson, February 12, 1920, Strauss Papers, Subject File, Box 8, "Campaign of 1920, Campaign Literature and Speeches"; "Hoover Club Launching Marked by War Spirit," Los

Angeles *Times*, February 12, 1920; Arnold to Berkeley Williams, February 18, 1920, Berkeley Williams Collection, Herbert Hoover Presidential Library, West Branch, Iowa, Box 1, "Correspondence, February 18, 1920–May 27, 1931"; summaries of Arnold to A. C. Burrage, Thomas H. Tracy, William Weldin, and David Reger, February 24–25, 1920, Ralph Arnold Papers, Hoover Library, West Branch, Iowa, Box 1, "Correspondence, Speeches, Articles, Memorandums, etc., 1920"; "Mr. Taft's Hoover Warning," New York *World*, February 12, 1920.

20. "Hoover Presents a National Policy," *New York Times*, February 18, 1920.

21. Hoover to secretary of the Democratic Executive Committee of Georgia, February 25, 1920, Hoover Papers, Pre-Commerce Period, Box 30, "Campaign of 1920, Speeches & Statements, Hoover, Declination of Candidacy, 1920"; "Oregon Will Vote on Hoover, Whether He Likes It or Not," Washington *Sunday Star*, February 22, 1920. As it turned out, this was a bluff; Hoover was able to stop the process. For the Harding story, see Frank R. Stewart to George Akerson, June 13, 1930, enclosing copies of Stewart to Harding, February 23, 1920, and Harding to Stewart, February 28, 1920, all in Hoover Papers, Pre-Commerce Period, Box 6, "Harding, Warren G., 1920–1922"; "Mr. Hoover in the Valley of Decision," *New Republic* February 21, 1920, 225.

22. "Mr. Hoover's Address at Johns Hopkins University, February 23, 1920," Strauss Papers, Subject File, Box 8, "Campaign of 1920, Campaign Literature and Speeches."

23. "Mr. Hoover's Address before the Western Society of Engineers at Chicago, February 28, 1920," Strauss Papers, Subject File, Box 8, "Campaign of 1920, Campaign Literature and Speeches."

24. "What's the Matter with the Farmer," *Wallace's Farmer*, February 13, 1920; "Mr. Hoover and the Farmer," *Wallace's Farmer*, March 19, 1920.

25. Hoover to an unnamed correspondent in San Francisco, March 5, 1920, Hoover Papers, Pre-Commerce Period, Box 30, "Campaign of 1920, Speeches & Statements, Hoover—Declination of Candidacy, 1920"; Edward H. Hamilton, "G.O.P. Women Clamor For Hoover; Lay Plans to Capture California," San Francisco *Examiner*, March 3, 1920; Hamilton, "Women Behind Hoover Stir Timorous Men," San Francisco *Examiner*, March 4, 1920.

26. James F. Bell to Ralph Arnold, March 6, 1920, Ralph Arnold Papers, Hoover Presidential Library; Milbank, memorandum of March 5, 1920, meeting, Hoover Papers, Pre-Commerce Period, Box 27, "Campaign of 1920"; Joseph C. Green to George Barr Baker, March 3, 1920, Joseph C. Green Papers, Hoover Institution Archives, Stanford, California, Box 15, "Subject File: Hoover, H., Pol. Cam., 1920, Ohio Com., Corres., Indiv. File, Baker, George Barr"; Joseph M. Price to Strauss, March 3, 1920, and Strauss to Price, March 4, 1920, both in Strauss Papers, Subject File, Box 8, "Campaign of 1920, General, 1920 Jan.–Apr."; Strauss to Berkeley Williams, March 5, 1920, ibid., Box 9, "Campaign of 1920—Virginia"; "How the Papers Size Up the Hoover Boom," *Literary Digest* March 6, 1920, 13–14.

27. Rose Wilder Lane, *The Making of Herbert Hoover* (New York: Century, 1920); J. F. Lucey to Berkeley Williams, March 10, 1920, Berkeley Williams Collection, Box 1, "Correspondence, February 18, 1920–Mary 27, 1931"; press release, March 10, 1920, Ralph Arnold Papers, Hoover Presidential Library, Box 1, "Handwritten and typed notes taken from Ralph Arnold Collection, Huntington Library, 1920"; Gertrude Lane to Lewis Strauss, March 4, 1920, Strauss Papers, Subject File, Box 8, "Campaign of 1920, General, 1920 Jan.–Apr."; Everett S. Brown to Hoover, March 5, 1920, Ralph Arnold Papers, Huntington Library, Box 232, "L. Political Papers: V. Hoover for Presidency"; copy of typed manuscript, "Trip of Ralph Arnold, vice-chairman, Hoover National Republican Club, to California and Return, March 15th to April 11th, 1920," Ralph Arnold Papers, Hoover Presidential Library, Box 1, "Handwritten and typed notes taken from the Ralph Arnold Collection, Huntington Library, 1920"; Jackson E. Reynolds to Ralph Arnold, March 12, 1920, ibid.; undated Hoover telegram to Chester Murphy or O. C. Leiter, ibid.; "Herbert Hoover: The Man Without a Party," *Literary Digest* March 13, 1920, 47–52; In "Fighting for Hoover," *New Republic* March 3, 1920, 4–6, apparently unaware of Hoover's reluctance to commit himself, blamed his supporters for failing to organize effectively.

28. Minutes of organizational meeting for Hoover Republican Club of California, March 11, 1920, Hoover Papers, Pre-Commerce Period, Box 28, "Campaign of 1920—Hoover Republican Club of Calif.—Organization, Initial Meeting (#1), 1920"; Roy V. Bailey, "Hoover Is to Be Placed on G.O.P. Ballot in California," Washington *Sunday Star*, March 7, 1920; Hoover to Arnold, March 8, 1920, Hoover Papers, Pre-Commerce Period, Box 27, "Campaign of 1920, Corres., March 1920"; "Hoover in Race for Nomination as Republican," New York *Sun and Herald*, March 10, 1920; "Hoover Opposed by Old Guard as G.O.P. Nominee," Philadelphia *Public Ledger*, March 10, 1920; James Goodrich to H. E. Barnard, March 10, 1920, James P. Goodrich Papers, Hoover Presidential Library, West Branch, Iowa, Box 1, "Campaign of 1920."

29. "Hoover Sentiment Grows Rapidly over California," New York *World*, March 21, 1920; "Hoover Petitions to Be Circulated Tomorrow," *Daily Palo Alto Times*, March 17, 1920; "7500 Names on Hoover Petitions," San Francisco *Bulletin*, March 18, 1920; form letter from Merritt "to all delegates on the Hoover Republican Ticket, all State Committees and Volunteer Organizers," Hoover Papers, Pre-Commerce Period, Box 28, "Campaign of 1920, Hoover Republican Club of California, Organization—Initial Planning (#1) 1920"; "Johnson Group Fires Shot at Hoover's Camp," San Francisco *Chronicle*, March 21, 1920; "Wood's Boomers Now Fear Hoover May Split G.O.P.," New York *World*, March 24, 1920; "Johnson Expects Big Hoover Fight," New York *World*, March 26, 1920.

30. "Hoover Opposed Our Joining Boards to Enforce Peace," *New York Times*, March 17, 1920; "Ratify the Treaty as It Now Stands, Advice of Hoover," Washington *Evening Star*, March 18, 1920; Hoover to Wilson, April 11, 1919, *PWW*, vol. 57, *April 5–22, 1919* (1987), 271–74.

31. "Mr. Hoover's Address before the Boston Chamber of Commerce, March 24, 1920," Strauss Papers, Subject File, Box 8, "Campaign of 1920, Campaign Literature and Speeches."

32. Hoover to Keating, March 26, 1920, Hoover Papers, Pre-Commerce Period, Box 27, "Campaign of 1920, Correspondence, March 1920"; "Hoover Men Fight for Republican Aid," *New York Times*, March 25, 1920; mimeographed copy of the "Hoover National Bulletin," March 25, 1920, in Subject File, Strauss Papers, Box 8, "Campaign of 1920, Hoover National Republican Club, 1920 Mar.–May and undated"; undated "Skeleton Speech" typescript and printed two-page series of excerpts from Hoover's speeches and articles titled "Hoover's Ideas on Some Public Questions," ibid., Box 8, "Campaign of 1920, Campaign Literature and Speeches"; Strauss to Berkeley Williams, March 26, 1920, ibid., Box 9, "Campaign of 1920, Virginia."

33. Unsigned, "Extract from a Personal Letter," undated, Joseph C. Green Papers, Box 10, "Subject File: Hoover, Herbert; Political Campaign, 1920, Campaign Materials, Information about Herbert Hoover"; Hoover to Warren Gregory, March 30, 1920, Hoover Papers, Pre-Commerce Period, Box 27, "Campaign of 1920, Correspondence, March 1920"; "Hoover Statement Stirs Washington," *New York Times*, March 30, 1920; "Leaders Stunned by Fresh Factor in National Race," New York *World*, March 30, 1920.

34. Lou Henry Hoover to Arthur B. Clark, March 29, 1920, Lou Henry Hoover Papers, Hoover Presidential Library, West Branch, Subject File, Box 75, "Properties and Lots, Stanford House, Correspondence, 1920"; "Hoover Faces Combination of All Rivals," Baltimore *Sun*, March 31, 1920; Lou Hoover, quoted in Hoover Republican Club of California press release no. 79 (ca. April 15, 1920), Hoover Papers, Pre-Commerce Period, Box 28, "Campaign of 1920, Hoover Republican Club of California, Organization, Initial Publicity, 1920 (1)."

35. Harry A. Wheeler to Hoover, telegram, April 1, 1920, Hoover Papers, Pre-Commerce Period, Box 17, "Wheeler, Harry A., 1920"; "Hoover Candidacy Fails to Obtain Congress Support," *New York Times*, April 1, 1920; Francis P. Farquhar to Ralph Merritt, April 3, 1920, Hoover Papers, Pre-Commerce Period, Box 27, "Campaign of 1920, April 1920"; Frederic William Wile, "Vote for Johnson and Hoover Shock to Party Leaders," Philadelphia *Public Ledger*, April 7, 1920; David Lawrence, "Hoover Crowd May Run Him on 3d Ticket," New York *News Leader*, April 1, 1920; press release, April 3, 1920, Hoover Papers, Pre-Commerce Period, Box 30, "Campaign of 1920, Speeches & Statements, Hoover—Declination of Candidacy, 1920"; "Hoover Man Denies Third Party Talk," *New York Times*, April 5, 1920.

36. Hoover's statement and the analysis of it on which this passage is based are found in "Hoover Not in Favor of His Name on Republican Ballots in Any State," Omaha *Daily Bee*, April 8, 1920. Johnson supporter Meyer Lissner argued that Hoover's only chance was as a "'come-to-me' candidate" and concluded that he had largely eliminated that possibility by entering the California Republican primary. See Lissner to C. K. McClatchy, March 27, 1920, Meyer Lissner Papers, Box 11, Folder 222, "Lissner: Corres. Out, March 27–31, 1920." Unfortunately, no clearer explanation of what Hoover was thinking on this important issue seems to have survived.

37. J. F. Essary, "Hoover Faces Combination of All Rivals," Baltimore *Sun*, March 31, 1920; Arnold to Ralph Merritt, April 12, 1920, Ralph Arnold Papers, Hoover Presidential Library, Box 1, "Correspondence, Speeches, Articles, Memorandums, etc., 1920"; "Hoover's Chief Goal Is Now California," *New York Times*, April 2, 1920. In regard to national publicity, see French Strother, "Herbert Hoover," *World's Work* 39 (April 1920): 578–85; T. A. Rickard, "Herbert Hoover: A Sketch," *Mining and Scientific Press*, April 3, 1920, 494–96; John W. Hallowell to Harry A. Wheeler, April 6, 1920, Hoover Papers, Pre-Commerce Period, Box 6, "Hallowell, John W., 1917–1920."

38. "Hoover Handicap Seen by Westerners," *New York Times*, April 1, 1920; Lewis Strauss to Frederick [*sic*] Coudert, April 15, 1920, and Coudert to Hoover, April 19, 1920, Strauss Papers, Subject File, Box 8, "Campaign of 1920, General, 1920 Jan.–Apr." On April 29, the *Times* implied that its April 1 story had originated with the Providence, Rhode Island, *Journal*, which on April 29 retracted the allegation that McCormick had been behind Hoover's 1918 letter. No hint of such a source appeared in the April 1 *Times* article, which indicated that the story had Midwestern sources. For the campaign literature on this topic, see undated "Letter No. 4" to county and local Hoover supporters from the Hoover Republican Club of California, Strauss Papers, Subject File, Box 28, "Campaign of 1920, Hoover Republican Club of California, Organization—Initial Planning, 1920"; pamphlet, "Where Does Hoover Stand?" ibid., Box 8, "Campaign of 1920, General, 1920 May–Oct."; undated typescript, "Herbert Hoover's Views on Party Government," ibid., Box 29, "Campaign of 1920—Hoover Republican Club of California, Press Releases, Campaign Issues, Hoover Statements, Nov. 1918–April 1920." Typical of the somewhat ambivalent attitude toward Hoover among California Republicans was an interview given by lawyer and banker Henry M. Robinson on April 20. Robinson not only expressed his high opinion of Hoover's "work and abilities," but he also spoke positively about Senator Johnson. See Robinson interview, April 20, 1920, Henry M. Robinson Papers, Hoover Institution Archives, Stanford, California, Box 10, "Interview for *NY World*."

39. George Barr Baker to Harold A. Vivian, April 6, 1920, Hoover Papers, Pre-Commerce Period, Box 27, "Campaign of 1920, Correspondence, April 1920"; Baker to Edward Eyre Hunt, April 6, 1920, ibid., Box 8, "Hunt, E. E., 1920"; Hoover National Republican Club pamphlet, "What Herbert Hoover's Election Will Mean to Women," Strauss Papers, Subject File, Box 8, "Campaign of 1920, General, 1920 May–Oct."

40. For the background of this case, known as *Chang Yen-mao v. Bewick, Moreing and Company*, case no. 1905-C-826, see George H. Nash, *The Life of Herbert Hoover: The Engineer, 1874–1914* (New York: Norton, 1983), 204–22; and for its role in the campaign, see Hoover to Ray Lyman Wilbur, April 15, 1920, Ray Lyman Wilbur Papers, Hoover Institution Archives, Stanford, California, Box 20, "Correspondence: General, 1917–1931"; John A. Agnew to Edgar Rickard, April 20, 1920, and George Barr Baker telegram to Ralph Merritt, April 28, 1920, Hoover Papers, Pre-Commerce Period, Box 1, "Agnew, J. A.–J. B., 1915–1921"; undated press release giving Arthur Train's statement, ca. April 29, 1920, ibid., Box 60, "Press Release"; Hoover to Herman Suter (at Washington *Herald*), April 29, 1920, ibid., Box 27, "Campaign of 1920, Correspondence, April 1920."

41. "Vote for Johnson and Hoover Shock to Party Leaders," Philadelphia *Public Ledger*, April 6, 1920; Frederic William Wile, "Hoover Sure Hope of Republicans, Is Michigan Analysis," Philadelphia *Public Ledger*, April 7, 1920; William Howard Taft, "Hoover Regular If Johnson Is, Taft Declares," Philadelphia *Public Ledger*, April 6, 1920; "Hoover Too Autocratic, Says Pinchot," New York *Tribune*, April 17, 1920.

42. Ray Lyman Wilbur to Hoover, April 17, 1920, Hoover Papers, Pre-Commerce Period, Box 17, "Wilbur, Ray Lyman, 1920"; George C. Roeding, "To the Farmers of California," undated (ca. April 16, 1920); Charles Collins Teague, "To my Friends, the Farmers of California," April 16, 1920; campaign handouts, "Johnson Says Prohibition Is a Dead Issue," and "How Johnson Fought the Wine Grape Industry," both undated (ca. April 17, 1920) all in ibid., Box 28, "Campaign of 1920—Hoover Republican Club of California—Organization—Initial Planning (#2), 1920."

43. Herbert Hoover, "Some Notes on Agricultural Readjustment and the High Cost of Living," *Saturday Evening Post*, April 10, 1920. Hoover did not distinguish among American agricultural exports. Different factors affected grain, corn, hogs, cattle, and cotton. In the 1920s, as the European economies recovered, patterns of consumption changed as people ate more meat and less bread. In the middle of the decade, Hoover urged crop diversification to meet the changing market, but within the time frame of his public career, the growth of foreign sales was never sufficient to solve the American farm problem.

44. "Speech of Herbert Hoover at New York Conference, Methodist Episcopal Church, Kingston, N.Y., Apr. 9, 1920," Strauss Papers, Subject File, Box 8, "Campaign of 1920, Campaign Literature and Speeches"; Ray Lyman Wilbur to Hoover, April 8, 1920, Hoover Papers, Pre-Commerce Period, Box 17, "Wilbur, Ray Lyman, 1920"; Hoover, "Armenian Speech, Philadelphia, Apr. 10, 1920," Strauss Papers, Subject File, Box 8, "Campaign of 1920, Campaign Literature and Speeches" (Hoover's support for the Armenians played well with the large Armenian community in the San Joaquin Valley); George Barr Baker to Vernon Kellogg, April 17, 1920, Hoover Papers, Pre-Commerce Period, Box 9, "Kellogg, Vernon, 1919–1921"; Hoover Republican Club of California press release, ca. April 20, 1920; "Herbert Hoover's Views on Party Government," ca. Apr. 20, 1920; "Herbert Hoover's Views on the Relation of Executive to Congress," ca. Apr. 20, 1920, all in ibid., Box 29, "Campaign of 1920, Hoover Republican Club of California, Press Releases, Campaign Issues, Hoover Statements, Nov. 1918–April 1920." For the organizational structure of the Hoover campaign in Ohio, which may have provided a model for the California organization, see draft organizational plan, April 7, 1920, and undated, unsigned outline of campaign organization, Joseph C. Green Papers, Box 11, "Subject File: Hoover, Herbert, Pol. Campaign, 1920, Campaign Plans"; press release of Hoover Republican Club of California, April 26, 1920, Burdette Papers, Box 128.

45. Charles Michelson, "Hoover-Johnson Fight Upsets All California Fences," New York *World*, April 16, 1920, and Michelson, "Hoover Boomers Blaze New Trail out in California," New York *World*, April 22, 1920. For Gompers, see the notes by Lewis Strauss and Felix Frankfurter of a discussion with Gompers in April 1920 in Strauss Papers, Subject File, Box 8, "Campaign of 1920, General, 1920 Jan.–Apr." For examples of materials put out by the Hoover campaign, see Hoover Papers, Pre-Commerce Period, Boxes 28 and 29, "Campaign of 1920, Hoover Republican Club of California, Organization, Initial Planning (#2), 1920"; and Strauss Papers, Subject File, Box 8, "Campaign of 1920, General, 1920 May–Oct."; circular letter, "Ralph Merritt to All County and Local Leaders and Precinct Workers of the Hoover Campaign," April 21, 1920, ibid., Box 28, "Campaign of 1920, Hoover Republican Club of California, Organization, Initial Planning (#2)1920."

46. David Lawrence, "Hoover Letter Serves Notice on Republicans," New York *Journal*, April 29, 1920; "Hoover Will Run Only as Republican," New York *Globe*, April 29, 1920; Hoover, "Important Issues Before Republican Convention": Statement to New York *Tribune*, April 27, 1920 (published April 29), Strauss Papers, Subject File, Box 8, "Campaign of 1920, Campaign Literature and Speeches"; draft of Hoover to Ralph Merritt, April 28, 1920, Hoover Papers, Pre-Commerce Period, Box 11, "Merritt, Ralph P., 1917–1920."

47. "The Politics of the Hoover Boom," *New Republic* April 21, 1920, 238–39.

48. Undated clippings, "Wood and M'Adoo Hold Lead in Poll" and "Wood and M'Adoo Still Lead in Poll," Hoover Papers, Pre-Commerce Period, Box 73, "May 1–2, 1920"; "The 'Hoover Menace,'" *Current Opinion* 68 (May 1920): 589–93; "Johnson Faces Many Enemies in California," *New York Times*, May 1, 1920; press releases nos. 180 and 181, Hoover Republican Club of California, May 1, 1920, Hoover Papers, Pre-Commerce Period, Box

28, "Campaign of 1920, Hoover Republican Club of California, Organization, Miscellaneous Publicity, 1920 (1)."

49. F. Opper cartoon, New York *American*, May 3, 1920; "Fight Grows Hot in Johnson's Home," *New York Times*, May 3, 1920; Meyer Lissner, "Lissner Charges Huge Conspiracy to Beat Johnson," Los Angeles *Examiner*, May 4, 1920.

50. Arnold to Hoover, May 4, 1920, Hoover Papers, Pre-Commerce Period, Box 11, "Merritt, Ralph P., 1917–1920"; "Johnson Wins All but Two Counties," New York *World*, May 5, 1920; "Wood Has 5,393 Lead in Indiana, Hiram Johnson Wins in California, Hoover's Vote More Than 158,000," New York *Evening Post*, May 5, 1920; Taft to James Rogan, May 16, 1920, enclosed in Ernest Walker Sawyer to Hoover, January 24, 1933, Hoover Papers, Pre-Commerce Period, Box 22, "Campaign of 1920, Correspondence, May 1920." Prior to the election, the Johnson campaign predicted a 150,000 vote victory.

51. Press release, May 5, 1920, Strauss Papers, Subject File, Box 8, "Campaign of 1920, General, 1920 May–Oct."; Hoover Republican Club to Robert Stevenson, telegram, May 6, 1920, Hoover Papers, Pre-Commerce Period, Box 27, "Campaign of 1920, Correspondence, May 1920"; Hoover to Lou Hoover, May 10, 1920, ibid., Box 7, "Hoover, Lou Henry, 1906–1921."

52. Press release by Ralph Merritt, May 5, 1920, Hoover Papers, Pre-Commerce Period, Box 28, "Campaign of 1920, Hoover Republican Club of California, Organization, Miscellaneous Publicity, 1920 (1)"; Harry A. Wheeler to Hoover, May 4, 1920, ibid., Box 17, "Wheeler, Harry A., 1920"; Alan Fox to Lewis Strauss, enclosing drafts of form letters, May 5, 1920, Strauss Papers, Subject File, Box 8, "Campaign of 1920, General, 1920 May–Oct."; Wilbur to Hoover, May 5, 11, 1920, Hoover Papers, Pre-Commerce Period, Box 17, "Wilbur, Ray Lyman, 1920." Merritt attributed Johnson's victory to "the power of the press and . . . the State and County machines as well as . . . the combinations made with the Democrats and the kings of the underworld," by which he seems to have meant San Francisco saloonkeepers. See Merritt to Clara Burdette, May 12, 1920, Burdette Papers, Box 128. Burdette agreed about the importance of the Johnson machine and echoed others' complaints about the "lies" told about Hoover. See Burdette to Merritt, May 18, 1920, ibid.

53. Baker quoted in Gary Dean Best, *The Politics of American Individualism: Herbert Hoover in Transition, 1918–1921* (Westport, CT: Greenwood, 1975), 87; Lou Hoover to Allan, ca. May 11, 1920, Allan Hoover Papers, Hoover Presidential Library, West Branch, Iowa, Box 1, "Correspondence with Lou Henry Hoover, 1920." Half-truths, lies, and slanders play a part in almost every political campaign, and there is no evidence that this one was unusually dirty. The attribution of political defeats to such methods was, however, a repeated complaint during Hoover's career. Muted here, it recurred later, culminating in bitter complaints about the "smear books," hostile accounts of Hoover's career published at the time of the 1932 presidential campaign.

54. "Hoover and Lowden Stay in Race Here," Portland *Oregonian*, May 6, 1920; "Hoover Army to Stage Big Final Battle" and "Wood Plan to Beat Johnson Strikes Snag," Oregon *Daily Journal*, May 7, 1920; "Both Big Parties Still at Sea," Baltimore *Evening Sun*, May 6, 1920; Frederic William Wile, "G.O.P. Tangle Likely to Aid Hoover Cause," Washington *Herald*, May 7, 1920; Whaley-Eaton Service, Letter No. 89, May 15, 1920, Hoover Papers, Pre-Commerce Period, Box 27, "Campaign of 1920, Correspondence, May 1920." For the later recalculations of delegate strength, see "Wood Has 205 Delegates Pledged to 98 for Johnson," New York *Tribune*, May 23, 1920.

55. "Hoover Sees No League Defeat in California," New York *Tribune*, May 7, 1920; "Johnson Answers Hoover on League," Philadelphia *Public Ledger*, May 7, 1920; "Johnson Charges Hoover Reversed Views on League," New York *World*, May 8, 1920; "Hoover Declares Johnson Is Evasive," New York *World*, May 9, 1920; Ray Lyman Wilbur to Hoover, May 11, 1920, Hoover Papers, Pre-Commerce Period, Box 17, "Wilbur, Ray Lyman, 1920"; "Borah Demands Inquiry," Philadelphia *Public Ledger*, May 7, 1920; "California Rivals in Countercharges of Huge Expenses," *New York Times*, May 9, 1920.

56. G. E. Hamaker, chairman Multnomah County Democratic Central Committee, to Wilson, May 6, 1920, and Wilson to Hamaker, May 9, 1920, *PWW*, vol. 65, *February 28–July 31*,

1920 (1991), 263–64; Hoover to Chester Murphy and O. C. Leiter, Hoover Republican Club, Portland, Oregon, May 13, 1920, Hoover Papers, Pre-Commerce Period, Box 27, "Campaign of 1920, Correspondence, May 1920." According to the May 15 issue of the usually well-informed *Whaley-Eaton Newsletter*, which Hoover saw only after he sent his own letter, Wilson's letter torpedoed an arrangement worked out between Wilson's closest advisers and Senate Minority Leader Gilbert Hitchcock to resubmit the treaty with mild reservations. See Whaley Eaton Service, Letter No. 89, May 15, 1920, in ibid.

57. Bruce Bliven, "Hoover—and the Rest," *The Independent*, May 29, 1920, 275–76, 297; "Hoover Out of Oregon Primaries," New York *World*, May 15, 1920; Harry A. Wheeler to Hoover, May 22, 1920, Herbert Hoover Papers, Pre-Commerce Period, Box 27, "Campaign of 1920, Correspondence, May 1920"; "Hoover Sees Need of New Labor Code," *New York Times*, May 14, 1920.

58. "Borah Resolution Opens All Phases of Election Costs," New York *World*, May 21, 1920; "Called to Explain Campaign Outlays," New York *World*, May 23, 1920; "$414,984 Spent in Lowden Fight; Johnson $72,000," *New York Times*, May 25, 1920; Francis Farquhar to Ralph Merritt, May 26, 1920, Hoover Papers, Pre-Commerce Period, Box 28, "Campaign of 1920, Hoover Republican Club of California, Organization-Finances, 1920"; "Johnson Spokesmen Attack All Rivals," *New York Times*, May 26, 1920; "Col. Procter Says He Gave $500,000 to Boost General," New York *World*, May 27, 1920; "Wood's Treasurer Is 'Swearing Mad,'" New York *Herald*, May 28, 1920; 66 Cong., 3d sess., Senate, Report No. 823 (February 24, 1921); Louis Seibold, "Delegate Fights Near End without Definite Results," New York *World*, May 24, 1920; "Crane Depended on to Win for Hoover," *New York Times*, May 29, 1920; "Hoover Gaining in Straw Vote," Philadelphia *Public Ledger*, May 30, 1920.

59. Wickersham's brief, June 2, 1920, is in Hoover Papers, Pre-Commerce Period, Box 17, "Wickersham, George, 1920–1921"; Eugene Meyer to Hoover, June 4, 1920, Lou Hoover Papers, Subject File, Box 16, "Campaign of 1920"; Hoover to Julius Barnes, C. J. Hepburn, Royal Victor, June 3, 1920, Hoover Papers, Pre-Commerce Period, Corres., Box 1, "Barnes, Julius H., 1917–1920"; Joseph Swain to Hoover, March 20, 1920, ibid., Box 15, "Swain, Joseph, 1879–1921"; "Hoover Says There Won't Be a Third Party," New York *Tribune*, June 8, 1920.

60. Wilbur to Hoover, June 7, June 8 (9?), 1920, Hoover Papers, Pre-Commerce Period, Box 17, "Wilbur, Ray Lyman, 1920"; Joseph C. Green to James A. Green, June 8, 1920, Joseph C. Green Papers, Box 2, "Correspondence: Green, Mr. & Mrs. James A., 1919–1920"; Louise Lee Schuyler to Nicholas Roosevelt, June 7, 1920, Hoover Papers, Pre-Commerce Period, Box 27, "Campaign of 1920"; Lodge speech, June 8, 1920, ibid., Box 30, "Campaign of 1920, Speeches & Statements, Republican National Convention, Lodge, Henry Cabot"; Julius Barnes to Nathan L. Miller, June 10, 1920, Strauss Papers, Subject File, Box 8, "Campaign of 1920, General, 1920 May–Oct."; nominating speech of Herbert Hoover for Republican candidacy by Judge Nathan L. Miller and speech seconding nomination of Herbert Hoover delivered by Henry Brown of Nevada, both in Hoover Papers, Pre-Commerce Period, Box 30, "Campaign of 1920, Speeches, Statements—Republican National Convention, Nominating Speech of Herbert Hoover, June 1920" and "Campaign of 1920, Speeches, Statements—Republican National Convention, Seconding Speech of Herbert Hoover, June 1920"; Arnold, "Account of Hoover's Rise to the Presidency." Although claiming to be an insider on Hoover strategy, Joseph Green professed "astonishment" at the Hoover demonstration. See Green to James A. Green, June 11, 1920, Joseph C. Green Papers, Box 2, "Correspondence: Green, Mr. & Mrs. James A., 1919–1920."

61. Arnold, "Account of Hoover's Rise to the Presidency"; Strauss to E. L. Roy, June 15, 1920, Strauss Papers, Subject File, Box 8, "Campaign of 1920, General, 1920 May–Oct." George Horace Lorimer, editor of the *Saturday Evening Post*, diagnosed the problems of the Hoover men at Chicago in the same way as Strauss. See "Hoover," *Saturday Evening Post*, July 31, 1920, 20.

62. Arnold, "Account of Hoover's Rise to the Presidency"; Hoover to Robert A. Taft, June 17, 1920, Hoover Papers, Pre-Commerce Period, Box 27, "Campaign of 1920, Correspondence, June–Aug. 1920." The Taft letter is included in Hoover's June 18, 1920, press release,

in ibid., Box 29, "Campaign of 1920—Publicity—Harding Campaign, June–Sept. 1920."
For other pressures on Hoover to stay in the race, see Lewis Strauss to Carol O. Spa-
mer, June 15, 1920, Strauss Papers, Subject File, Box 8, "Campaign of 1920, General, 1920
May–Oct."; Strauss to Berkeley Williams, June 22, 1920, ibid., Box 9, "Campaign of 1920,
Virginia"; James Goodrich to Will Hays, June 16, 1920, James Goodrich Papers, Box 1,
"Campaign of 1920."

63. For Harding's alleged awe of Hoover, see Laura Blackburn to Lou Hoover, June 23, 1931,
Lou Hoover Papers, Subject File, Box 16, "Campaign of 1920." Hoover's letter to Harding,
June 26, 1920, is in Hoover Papers, Pre-Commerce Period, Box 6, "Harding, Warren G.,
1920–1922."

64. Edwin Gay to Hoover, August 4, 1920, Hoover Papers, Pre-Commerce Period, Box 27,
"Campaign of 1920, Correspondence, June–Aug. 1920"; Warren Gregory to Hoover, July
28, 1920, ibid., Box 6, "Gregory, Warren, 1916–1920"; Hiram Johnson to Meyer Lissner,
September 10, 1920, Meyer Lissner Papers, Box 19, Folder 376, "Lissner: Corres. In, Johnson, H., #18 March–April 1917; Jul.–Sept. 1920."

65. Harding to Hoover, August 7, 1920, Hoover Papers, Pre-Commerce Period, Box 6, "Harding, Warren G., 1920–1922"; Warren Gregory to Hoover, August 10, 1920, ibid., Box 6,
"Gregory, Warren, 1916–1920."

66. Hays to Hoover, August 16, 1920, and Hoover to Hays, August 21, 1920, Hoover Papers,
Pre-Commerce Period, Box 27, "Campaign of 1920, Correspondence, June–Aug. 1920";
George Wickersham to Hoover, August 12, 1920 and Hoover to Wickersham, August 21,
1920, both in ibid., Box 6, "Harding, Warren G., July 1, 1920–Feb. 23, 1921, Letter Book";
Hoover to Warren Gregory, August 21, 1920, ibid., Box 6, "Gregory, Warren, 1916–1920";
Julius Barnes to Hoover, August 17, 1920, and Hoover to Barnes, August 21, 1920, ibid.,
Box 1, "Barnes, Julius H., 1917–1920."

67. Hoover to Chester Rowell, September 2, 1920, and Wickersham to Hoover, August 29,
1920, Hoover Papers, Pre-Commerce Period, Box 6, "Harding, Warren G., July 1, 1920–
Feb. 23, 1920, Letter Book."

68. "Mr. Hoover on Reconstruction," *Christian Science Monitor*, September 24, 1920; Hoover,
statement for the Chicago *Daily News*, September 15, 1920, Hoover Papers, Pre-Commerce
Period, Box 60, "Press Release"; Hoover to Mrs. Robert A. Burdette, September 29, 1920,
ibid., Box 3, "Burdette, Clara B., 1920"; Hoover to Harding, October 4, 1920, and Harding
to Hoover, October 12, 1920, both in ibid., Box 6, "Harding, Warren G., July 1, 1920–Feb.
23, 1921, Letter Book."

69. Jacob Gould Schurman to Hoover, September 29, 1920; Christian A. Herter to Schurman, September 30, 1920; Hoover to A. Lawrence Lowell, September 30, 1920; Lowell
to Hoover, October 2, 1920; Paul Cravath to Hoover, October 5, 1920; and Schurman
and Hoover to Will Hays, October 4, 1920, all in Hoover Papers, Pre-Commerce Period,
Box 27, "Campaign of 1920, Correspondence, Sept.–Dec., 1920"; Harding to Schurman,
October 5, 1920, Hoover Papers, Pre-Commerce Period, Box 6, "Harding, Warren G.,
1920–1922"; "Speech of Senator Warren G. Harding in Des Moines, Ia., Oct. 7, 1920,"
ibid.; "Speech of Senator Warren G. Harding in Indianapolis, Oct. 16, 1920," ibid.; George
Barr Baker to Christian Herter, October 14, 1920, ibid., Box 27, "Campaign of 1920, Correspondence, Sept.–Dec. 1920."

70. "Statement in Support of Harding for President by a Group of Advocates of International
Cooperation to Promote Peace," October 20, 1920, Hoover Papers, Pre-Commerce Period,
Box 6, "Harding, Warren G., July 1, 1920–Feb. 23, 1920, Letter Book."

71. James W. Good to Hoover, October 6, 1920, Hoover Papers, Pre-Commerce Period, Box
27, "Campaign of 1920, Correspondence, Sept.–Dec. 1920." For an example of Hoover's
Midwestern speeches, see "Speech by Herbert Hoover before the Columbia Club of Indianapolis, October 9, 1920," ibid., Box 30, "Campaign of 1920, Speeches and Statements,
Hoover—Indianapolis, Columbia Club, Oct. 9, 1920"; Hoover to Cooke, October 20,

1920, ibid., Box 3, "Cooke, Morris L., 1916–1921"; Lou Hoover to Mrs. (Charles Stetson?) Wheeler, October 18, 1920, Lou Hoover Papers, Personal Files, Box 8, "Personal Correspondence, 1872–1920, Wa–Wh Miscellaneous"; Hoover to Hays, October 23, 1920, Hoover Papers, Pre-Commerce Period, Box 6, "Harding, Warren G., July 1, 1920–Feb. 23, 1921, Letter Book."

72. Francis V. Keesling to James B. Reynolds, April 18, 1924, Francis V. Keesling Papers, Green Library, Rare Books and Special Collections, Stanford University, Stanford, California, Box 2, Folder 11, "Polit. Corresp. Out, 1924 Jan.–Apr." Some of Hoover's California supporters hoped that he would run for governor as part of an effort to disrupt the Johnson machine, but Ralph Merritt quickly quashed that possibility. See Merritt to Clara Burdette, November 24, 1920, Clara Burdette Papers, Box 128.

73. Mary Austin, "Hoover and Johnson: West Is West," *Nation*, May 15, 1920, 642.

Chapter 5

1. Herbert Hoover, *Memoirs: Years of Adventure, 1874–1920* (New York: Macmillan, 1951), 461–62 (hereafter, *Memoirs* 1).

2. Ibid., 466–67.

3. Ibid., 473–79; Sally Marks, *The Illusion of Peace: International Relations in Europe, 1918–1933*, 2nd ed. (New York: Palgrave Macmillan, 2003), 20–28.

4. "Hoover Sails, Work in Europe Finished," New York *Sun*, September 7, 1919; Hoover, *Memoirs* 1, 481–82.

5. "Hoover Proclaims Faith in America," *New York Times*, November 16, 1919). Shortly before leaving Europe in September 1919, Hoover reported to the Supreme Economic Council on the coal shortages he foresaw in the coming winter; the report was published as "Herbert Hoover on Europe's Coal Situation," *The Street* 1, no. 18 (November 26, 1919): 1–2, 23.

6. Memorandum, ca. September 10, 1919, Federal Reserve Bank of New York, Benjamin Strong Papers, Hoover Presidential Library, West Branch, Iowa, Box 4, "1000.3 (2) Strong's Trip to Europe, July–September 1919"; "Ratify Peace Now, Says Hoover at Pier," *New York Times*, September 14, 1919.

7. "Herbert Hoover Back, Says Food Saved Europe," New York *Herald Tribune*, September 14, 1919.

8. Donald Markwell, *John Maynard Keynes and International Relations: Economic Paths to War and Peace* (New York: Oxford University Press, 2006), 67.

9. Ibid., 68–72; Michael J. Hogan, *Informal Entente: The Private Structure of Cooperation in Anglo-American Economic Diplomacy, 1918–1928* (Columbia: University of Missouri Press, 1977), 25–29.

10. Elisabeth Glaser-Schmidt, "German and American Concepts to Restore a Liberal World Trading System after World War I," in *Confrontation and Cooperation: Germany and the United States in the Era of World War I, 1900–1924*, ed. Hans-Jürgen Schröder (Providence, RI: Berg, 1993), 356.

11. Carl P. Parrini, *Heir to Empire: United States Economic Diplomacy, 1916–1923* (Pittsburgh: University of Pittsburgh Press, 1969), 80–88. Hoover is quoted on p. 88.

12. Edgar Rickard to Lou Henry Hoover, November 26, 1919, enclosing minutes of ARA Directors' meeting on November 6, Lou Henry Hoover Papers, Hoover Library, West Branch, Iowa, Box 1, "Subject File: American Relief Administration, Correspondence and Reports, 1919–20"; Herbert Hoover, *Memoirs: The Cabinet and the Presidency, 1920–1933* (New York: Macmillan, 1952), 18–19 (hereafter, *Memoirs* 2); Max Farrand to Hoover, October 8, 1919, Herbert Hoover Papers, Pre-Commerce Period, Hoover Presidential Library, West Branch, Iowa, Box 5, "Farrand, Max, 1919–1921"; Hoover to Rufus Jones, November 1, 17, 1919, and Hoover to Wilbur K. Thomas, November 24, 1919, both in ibid., Box 9,

"Jones, Rufus, 1919–1921"; "American of Foreign Descent to Aid Europe," New York *Tribune*, December 19, 1919. During the war, the ARA charged recipients a little more than its costs to cover risks and losses. With the permission of the countries involved, these "profits" funded the new, private ARA. Edge Act corporations loaned approximately $300 to $700 million to foreign borrowers between the armistice and 1923, but the amount was not sufficient to restore the European economy to prewar levels. See David Kennedy, *Over Here: The First World War and American Society* (New York: Oxford University Press, 1980), 338–40.

13. Herbert Hoover, "America's Care of Millions of European Children since the Armistice," *ARA Bulletin*, 2nd ser., 1 (October 4, 1920), and ibid., no. 4 (November 15, 1920); Edgar Rickard to Richard Kleindienst, November 29, 1919, Hoover Papers, Pre-Commerce Period, Box 9, "Kleindienst, R. A., Mar. 4, 1919–June 1919"; Hoover to Rickard, December 4, 1919, ibid., Box 14, "Rickard, Edgar, 1912–1920."

14. Robert H. Van Meter, Jr., "Herbert Hoover and the Economic Reconstruction of Europe, 1918–21," in *Herbert Hoover: The Great War and Its Aftermath, 1918–23*, ed. Lawrence E. Gelfand (Iowa City: University of Iowa Press, 1979), 145, 164–65.

15. Ibid., 166–68; Hogan, *Informal Entente*, 31–32.

16. *ARA Bulletin*, 2nd ser., 1, no. 2 (October 15, 1920): 4–9; "Letter from Mr. Hoover to the Bankers of America," October 14, 1920, *ARA Bulletin*, 2nd ser., 1, no. 4 (November 15, 1920).

17. Helen Pollock, "Hooverized Film at Manhattan," New York *Telegraph*, January 10, 1920. The film, which exaggerated both prewar prosperity in Russia and the current distress in large parts of Europe, was propaganda, not a documentary.

18. Ibid., "'Starvation' Seen in Film," *New York Times*, January 10, 1920; "Film Shows Work of Hoover Abroad," New York *Sun*, January 10, 1920; "Screen Scenes Show How American Food Has Saved Europe," New York *Tribune*, January 10, 1920; "Starvation Scenes Are Shown in a Film," New York *World*, January 10, 1920; "America Feeding Starving Europe Shown on Screen," New York *Herald*, January 10, 1920; George Barr Baker to Hoover, January 13, 1920, George Barr Baker Papers, Hoover Institution Archives, Stanford, California, Box 3, "Hoover, Herbert C. & Family." Archivists at the Hoover Presidential Library have been unable to find a surviving copy of the film.

19. "Mr. Hoover on Hysteria," *New York Times*, January 8, 1920.

20. Statement of Hon. Herbert Hoover, "Relief of European Populations," Committee on Ways and Means, House of Representatives, January 12, 1920, Hoover Papers, Pre-Commerce Period, Box 57, "Pamphlets and Printed Materials, 1917–1920."

21. Ibid.

22. Ibid.

23. "Hoover Plans to Fight for Relief Fund," Baltimore *Sun*, February 4, 1920; "President Pleads for European Loan," *New York Times*, January 28, 1920; "Poles' Aggression Caused Big Slash in Aid For Europe," Washington *Star*, February 2, 1920.

24. Lou Hoover to Sue Dyer, February 17, 1920, Lou Henry Hoover Papers, Box 2, "Personal Correspondence, 1872–1920, D Miscellaneous"; "Works of Art Will Swell Hoover Fund," New York *Post*, February 16, 1920; "Hoover Sure of Fund," New York *World*, February 17, 1920; "State Gets $3,863,907 for the Hoover Fund," *New York Times*, February 17, 1920; "Hoover Fund Nears Goal," *New York Times*, February 20, 1920; "Ball in Greenwich Ends Hoover Drive," New York *Herald*, February 20, 1920.

25. "Urges Food Credit for Starving Cities," *New York Times*, February 23, 1920; E. Francqui to Hoover, March 1, 1920, Hoover Papers, Pre-Commerce Period, Box 5, "Francqui, Emile, 1914–1920." Francqui was right, but distribution problems were not the only cause of shortages and inflation. The widespread printing of fiat money also made peasants reluctant to sell their produce for worthless currency.

26. "Plan to Rush Flour Abroad," New York *Herald*, March 6, 1920); Hoover to Paul M. Warburg, April 19, 1920, Lewis L. Strauss Papers, Hoover Presidential Library, West Branch, Iowa, Subject File, Box 85, "Warburg, Paul M., 1920"; "Do Not Ignore Europe's Plight, Plea by Hoover," New York *Tribune*, May 19, 1920.

27. Hoover to Woodrow Wilson, June 26, 1920, Hoover Papers, Pre-Commerce Period, Box 20, "Wilson, Woodrow, 1920"; minutes of meeting of Executive Committee of ARA European Children's Fund, June 26, 1920, Strauss Papers, Subject File, Box 22, "European Children's Fund, 1920 July–Aug."; Herbert Hoover, "Child Life in Central Europe and the Need of Co-Operation in Relief," September 22, 1920, in *ARA Bulletin*, 2nd ser., 1, no. 1 (October 1, 1920); Hoover, *Memoirs* 2, 19–21.

28. "To the Publishers of *The Literary Digest*," October 19, 1920, Hoover Papers, Pre-Commerce Period, Box 24, "ARA, undated to 1921"; Herbert Hoover, "Three Million Starving Children Crying to America," *Current Opinion*, November 1920, 611–16; Herbert Hoover, "The Appeal of Hungry Children to the American Community Chest," *ARA Bulletin*, 2nd ser., 1, no. 5 (December 1, 1920): 1–5; Hoover, "An Announcement," *Saturday Evening Post*, November 20, 1920, 25; Hoover, "How Much Longer Must We Feed Europe?" *The Forum* 64 (December 1920): 377–79.

29. Lou Hoover, "At the Chicago Dinner," Lou Hoover Papers, ca. November 1920, Box 3, "Subject File, Articles, Addresses & Statements, Children's Relief Address, Chicago, Illinois."

30. A director of the American Relief Administration, "The Situation of the Intellectual Class in Central Europe," *ARA Bulletin*, 2nd ser., 1, no. 3 (November 1, 1920): 36–42.

31. "Transcript of Shorthand Notes of Mr. Hoover's Remarks to the Members of the Staff of the American Relief Administration, at 42 Broadway, New York, on December 1, 1920," December 1, 1920, Hoover Papers, Pre-Commerce Period, Box 24, "ARA-Undated to 1921."

32. "Memorandum Approved by the Members of the General Office Group at Their First Meeting, December 3, 1920," Hoover Papers, Pre-Commerce Period, Box 24, "ARA-Undated to 1921."

33. "A.R.A. Council Meeting," December 6, 1920, marked "Posted Bulletin Board, 12/9/20," Hoover Papers, Pre-Commerce Period, Box 24, "ARA-Undated to 1921."

34. Alice King to Lou Hoover, December 21, 24, 30, 1920, Lou Hoover Papers, Box 1, "Subject File, American Relief Administration, Correspondence & Reports, 1919–20."

35. Unidentified clipping of photographs of December 29 "invisible guest" dinner, Hoover Papers, Pre-Commerce Period, Box 74, "January 7–9, 1921"; Herbert Hoover, "America's Welcome to Its Invisible Guests," December 29, 1920, *ARA Bulletin*, 2nd ser., 1, no. 8 (January 15, 1921); Hoover, *Memoirs* 2, 21.

36. Alice King to Lou Hoover, January 11, 14, 21, 25, 1921, Hoover Papers, Pre-Commerce Period, Box 9, "King, Alice, Dec. 21, 1920–1921; Daily Letters to Mrs. Hoover"; Alice King to Lou Hoover, January 18, 1921, Lou Hoover Papers, Box 16, "Personal Correspondence, 1921–29, King, Alice, 1921"; "Hoover Rests by Loading Food on Ships for Europe," New York *Tribune*, January 22, 1921; Hoover, "Memorandum for the Evening Sun, Baltimore, Md.," January 25, 1921, Hoover Papers, Pre-Commerce Period, Box 26, "*Baltimore Evening Sun*, 1920–1921"; "Hoover's Wife Makes Relief Plea at U.C.," San Francisco *Chronicle*, January 18, 1921; "Mrs. Hoover Is Heard at Big Noon Meeting," San Francisco *Chronicle*, January 21, 1921.

37. "Says Pole Army Got U.S. Funds," New York *Globe*, January 4, 1921; Hoover to Senator Frank B. Kellogg, January 5, 7, 1921, and Kellogg to Hoover, January 6, 1921, both in Hoover Papers, Pre-Commerce Period, Box 9, "Kellogg, Frank B., 1919"; "Denies European Relief Fund Fed Polish Army," Washington *Herald*, January 6, 1921; "Relief Fund Was Not Misused," Sacramento *Union*, January 6, 1921; "Senators in Clash over Hoover Work," *New York Times*, January 7, 1921.

38. Hoover, *Memoirs* 1, 336, 348; minutes of directors' meeting of the ARA European Children's Fund, November 6 and 25, 1919, Strauss Papers, Subject File, Box 22, "European Children's Fund, 1919"; "Cable from a Director of the ARA European Children's Fund on Health of Children in Germany," dated Berlin, April 6, 1920, ibid., Subject File, Box 22, "European Children's Fund, 1920 Mar.–June"; Hoover to the American Friends Service Committee, January 27, 1921, and Rufus Jones and Wilbur K. Thomas to Hoover, January 31, 1921, both in Hoover Papers, Pre-Commerce Period, Box 9, "Jones, Rufus, 1919–1921"; Ruby S. Gaunt to Lou Hoover, March 18, 1921, Lou Hoover Papers, Box 14,

"Personal Correspondence, 1921–28, Gaunt, Ruby S., 1921–22"; Charles Nagel to Christian A. Herter, March 28, 1921, and Herter to Nagel, April 4, 1921, Hoover Papers, Pre-Commerce Period, Box 235, "Germany, 1921 March–September."

39. Clipping from *The Nation*, February 16, 1921, Hoover Papers, Pre-Commerce Period, Box 75, "February 14–18, 1921"; "Relief of Russian Refugees," *ARA Bulletin*, 2nd ser., no. 9 (February 1, 1921): 32–33; John B. Creighton (American Field Service) to Hoover, April 23, 1921, enclosing an "Appeal of the New York Committee for Russian Relief." Christian Herter, Hoover's secretary, replied on April 26 that Hoover was "extremely busy" but that he had "read over the draft of an appeal for Russian relief." Both are in Herbert Hoover Papers, Commerce Period, Hoover Presidential Library, West Branch, Iowa, Box 488, "Quakers 1921." For the 1921 to 1923 Russian relief program, see Chapter 9 in this volume.

40. "Mrs. Hoover to Speak at Dinner," Greenwich *Press*, February 10, 1921; "Mrs. Hoover Opens 'Heart of Gold' for Starving Children of Europe," New York *Evening World*, February 24, 1921; "Proposed Gala Performance at Metropolitan Opera House, on Evening of February 22, 1921, for Benefit European Relief Council Fund," undated, Strauss Papers, Name & Subject File I: Accretions, Box 1E, "American Relief Administration, European Relief Council, 1922"; Harding to Hoover, February 21, 1921, Hoover Papers, Commerce Period, Box 7, "Harding, Correspondence Feb. 1920–1922." In his *Memoirs* 2, 36, Hoover writes that the formal offer was made on February 24.

41. Hoover to Julius Barnes, March 2, 1921, in minutes of the meeting of the Executive Committee of the ARA European Children's Fund, March 10, 1921, Strauss Papers, Subject File, Box 23, "European Children's Fund, 1921"; Alonzo E. Taylor to Hoover, March 8, April 12, 22, 1921, Hoover Papers, Commerce Period, Box 596, "Taylor, Alonzo E., 1921"; "Mr. Hoover Continues to Direct European Children's Relief," *ARA Bulletin*, 2nd ser., 1, no. 11 (April 1, 1921): 1; "The Child Feeding Program for 1921," *ARA Bulletin*, 2nd ser., 1, no 12 (May 1, 1921): 4–6; Alonzo E. Taylor, "American Relief Administration Review of European Conditions," June 15, 1921, Hoover Papers, Commerce Period, Box 596, "Taylor, Alonzo E., 1921."

42. "Interim Report of European Relief Council, Including Statement of Contributions by States and Auditors' Preliminary Report on Accounts," May 31, 1921, Hoover Papers, Pre-Commerce Period, Box 33, "European Relief Council Interim Report, 1921"; Hoover, *Memoirs* 2, 22.

43. Edgar Rickard to all members of the American Relief Administration, April 20, 1921, and "American Relief Administration, Certificate of Incorporation of Unincorporated Association," May 27, 1921, both in Strauss Papers, Subject File, Box 1, "American Relief Administration Incorporation Documents, 1921"; statement of receipts and expenditures, American Children's Fund, Inc., formerly the ARA Children's Fund, Inc., December 1, 1923–June 30, 1937, Lou Hoover Papers, Box 18, "Clubs and Organizations, American Relief Administration, European Children's Fund, 1930–40."

44. Isaac F. Marcosson, "American Relief—And After: An Interview with Herbert Hoover," *Saturday Evening Post*, April 30, 1921, 22, 36.

45. Ibid., 34, 36. Because so many of the ARA men who served in Europe did so without pay or at very low pay, Edgar Rickard worried that the end of the program might leave them stranded in Europe without the means to get home. As far as can be determined, however, that did not happen. See Edgar Rickard to W. L. Brown, December 14, 1922, Herbert Hoover Subject Collection, Hoover Institution Archives, Stanford, California, Box 324, "Correspondence: Rickard, Edgar, 1916–24."

46. Marcosson, "American Relief," 39.

47. Ibid.

Chapter 6

1. Lou Hoover to Edgar Rickard, undated, ca. 1921, Lou Henry Hoover Papers, Hoover Presidential Library, West Branch, Iowa, Box 60, "Subject File: Hoover, Lou Henry, Business & Financial, 1918–27"; Lou Hoover to Alida Henriques, January 10 and undated, 1921, both in ibid., Box 15, "Personal Correspondence, 1921–28, Henriques, Alida, 1921–25"; Lou Hoover to Ethel Bullard, January 10, 1921, ibid., Box 10, "Personal Correspondence, 1921–28, Bullard, Ethel Bagg, 1921–28"; Lou Hoover to D. P. (Daisy Polk) DeBuyer, February 19, 1921, ibid., Box 12, "Personal Correspondence, 1921–28, DeBuyer, Daisy Polk, 1921–28."

2. John McHugh to Hoover, December 14, 1920, and Christian Herter to McHugh, December 18, 1920, both in Herbert Hoover Papers, Pre-Commerce Period, Hoover Presidential Library, West Branch, Iowa, Box 41, "Foreign Trade and Banking, 1920"; "Trade Corporation Conference Begun," *New York Times*, December 11, 1920.

3. Julius Barnes to Sen. Frank B. Kellogg, December 13, 1920, Herbert Hoover Papers, Pre-Commerce Period, Box 9, "Kellogg, Frank B., 1919."

4. A copy of the Articles of Association, January 28, 1921, is in Herbert Hoover Papers, Commerce Period, Hoover Presidential Library, West Branch, Iowa, Box 227, "Foreign Trade—Foreign Trade Financing Corporation, 1921"; "100 Million Trade Board Presidency to W. P. G. Harding," Washington *Herald*, January 20, 1921; William F. Collins to Hoover, February 19, 1921; John McHugh to Hoover, March 10, 23, 1921; Hoover to McHugh, March 12, 1921; Hoover to Paul Warburg, March 16, 1921; Warburg to Hoover, March 22, 25, 1921; Hoover to John McHugh, Paul Warburg, and F. Kent, April 4, 1921, all in Hoover Papers, Pre-Commerce Period, Box 41, "Foreign Trade & Banking, 1921"; Collins to Hoover, March 8, 1921; Hoover Papers, Commerce Period, Box 227, "Foreign Trade—Foreign Trade Financing Corporation, 1921"; "Address of Herbert Hoover before the National Shoe and Leather Exposition," July 12, 1921, ibid., Box 433, "National Shoe and Leather Association Speech 7/12/21."

5. "Harding Inaugurated, Declares against Entanglements; Wilson, Weakened by Illness, Unable to Join in Ceremony; Gen. Pershing Slated to Go to France as Ambassador," *New York Times*, March 5, 1921.

6. Dr. E. C. Sewall to Lou Hoover, March 4, 1921, Allan Hoover Papers, Hoover Presidential Library, West Branch, Iowa, Box 1, "Correspondence with Lou Henry Hoover, 1921 February–June"; Lou Hoover to John Agnew, May 2, 1921, Lou Henry Hoover Papers, Box 9, "Personal Correspondence, 1921–28, Agnew, John & Ellen, 1921–28"; Philippi Harding to Lou Hoover; Lou Hoover to Philippi Harding, ca. May 22, 24, 27, 1921, all in ibid., Box 10, "Personal Correspondence, 1921–28, Butler, Philippi Harding, 1921 March."

7. Lou Hoover to John Agnew, May 2, 1921, Lou Henry Hoover Papers, Box 9, "Personal Correspondence, 1921–28, Agnew, John & Ellen, 1921–28"; Philippi Harding to Lou Hoover, June 2, 23, 28, 1921, ibid., Box 10, "Personal Correspondence, 1921–28, Butler, Philippi Harding, 1921 June"; Philippi Harding to Lou Hoover, July 2, 4, 6, 1921, ibid., Box 10, "Personal Correspondence, 1921–28, Butler, Philippi Harding, 1921 July." The portrait now hangs in the Hoover Institution on the Stanford University campus.

8. Carolina Slade Clary Morisson to Lou Hoover, April 13, 1921, Lou Hoover Papers, Box 31, "Clubs and Organizations, League of Women Voters, Correspondence, 1920–22"; J. Franklin Jameson to Lou Hoover, May 14, 1921, and Lou Hoover to Jameson, May 25, 1921, both in ibid., Box 16, "Personal Correspondence, 1921–28, Ja–Je Miscellaneous"; Zelina Boeshar to Lou Hoover, May 12, 1921, ibid., Box 70, "Subject File, Hoover, Lou Henry, Professions for Women: Views on, 1921–22"; Margaret B. Downing, "Women in the Public Eye: Mrs. Herbert Hoover," *Washington Sunday Star*, June 26, 1921.

9. Lou Hoover to Philippi Harding, May 24, 1921, Lou Hoover Papers, Box 10, "Personal Correspondence, 1921–28, Butler, Philippi Harding, 1921 March–May"; Lou Hoover to the Hoover household in Washington, June 20, 1921, ibid., Box 10, "Personal Correspondence, 1921–28, Butler, Philippi Harding, 1921 June."

10. Lou Hoover to Albert Butler and Carrie Butler, July 21, 1921, Lou Hoover Papers, Box 98, "Subject File, Servants and Aides, Butler, Albert & Carrie, 1921–35"; Lou Hoover to E. D. Adams, July 21, 1921, ibid., Box 9, "Personal Correspondence, 1921–28, Adams, E. D., 1901–25 & undated"; Lou Hoover to Jean Large, July 21, 1921, ibid., Box 17, "Personal Correspondence, 1921–28, Large, Jean Henry, 1921–23."

11. Lou Hoover to Jean Large, July 21, 1921, Lou Hoover Papers, Box 17, "Personal Correspondence, 1921–28, Large, Jean Henry, 1921–23"; Lou Hoover to Edgar Rickard, July 28, 1921, ibid., Box 21, "Personal Correspondence, 1921–28, Rickard, Edgar, 1921–22."

12. Lou Hoover to Allan Hoover, undated, ca. August 17, 1921, Allan Hoover Papers, Box 1, "Correspondence with Lou Henry Hoover, 1921 February–June"; Lou Hoover to Philippi Harding, August 19, 1921, Lou Hoover Papers, Box 10, "Personal Correspondence, 1921–28, Butler, Philippi Harding, 1921 August"; Lou Hoover to Herbert and Allan Hoover, August 21, 1921, Allan Hoover Papers, Box 1, "Correspondence with Lou Henry Hoover, 1921 July–October."

13. Philippi Harding to Lou Hoover, August 22, 25, 1921, Lou Hoover Papers, Box 10, "Personal Correspondence, 1921–28, Butler, Philippi Harding, 1921 August"; same to same, September 5, 10, 1921, ibid., Box 11, "Personal Correspondence, 1921–28, Butler, Philippi Harding, 1921 September–November & undated"; Lou Hoover to Philippi Harding, three letters, undated, ca. August 20–25, 1921, September 11, 1921, ibid.; Lou Hoover to Susan Bristol, September 10, 1921, ibid., Box 10, "Personal Correspondence, 1921–28, Bristol, Susan, 1921–27."

14. Pamphlet, Zoe Beckley, "Mrs. Herbert Hoover: 'American Through and Through'" (reprinted from the Buffalo *Evening News* by the North American Newspaper Alliance, 1928), in Benjamin S. Allen Papers, Hoover Institution Archives, Stanford, California, Box 1, "Correspondence, 1920–1929"; Virginia Scharff, *Taking the Wheel: Women and the Coming of the Motor Age* (New York: Free Press, 1991), 76–88.

15. Bruce E. Seely, *Building the American Highway System: Engineers as Policy Makers* (Philadelphia: Temple University Press, 1987), 11–65.

16. Marguerite S. Shaffer, *See America First: Tourism and National Identity, 1880–1940* (Washington, DC: Smithsonian Institution, 2001), 116–19, 130–55.

17. Shaffer, *See America First*, 161; Lou Hoover's sketchy trip log is in Lou Hoover Papers, Box 112, "Subject File, Trips, Cross Country Drive, 1921."

18. Trip log, Lou Hoover Papers, Box 112, "Subject File, Trips, Cross Country Drive, 1921"; Lou Hoover to Susan Bristol, November 4, 1921, ibid., Box 10, "Personal Correspondence, 1921–28, Bristol, Susan, 1921–27"; Shaffer, *See America First*, 161, 168. Although Lou was an inveterate photographer, no pictures from the trip have been found.

19. For a thoughtful analysis of the way that the rise of the consumer society freed Americans from direct dependence on nature yet increased their use of resources, creating the conditions for the rise of first the conservation movement and later the environmental movement, see Gregory Summers, *Consuming Nature: Environmentalism in the Fox River Valley, 1850–1950* (Lawrence, KS: University Press of Kansas, 2006). On women motorists in the 1920s, see Scharff, *Taking the Wheel*, 135–64.

20. Philippi Harding to Lou Hoover, September 12, 15, 20, 29 and October 3, 6, 1921, Lou Hoover Papers, Box 11, "Personal Correspondence, 1921–28, Butler, Philippi Harding, 1921 September–November & undated."

21. Ben S. Allen to Hoover, December 26, 1919, Lou Hoover Papers, Box 1, "Personal Correspondence, 1872–1920, A Miscellaneous"; Lester J. Hinsdale to Hoover, February 23, 1920, Hoover Papers, Pre-Commerce Period, Box 7, "Hinsdale, Lester J. (Hinsdell, Hinsdile), 1897–1920, 1892–1918, 1897–1899, #2, #3, & #4"; T. T. C. Gregory to Lou Hoover, August 24 and October 1, 1920, Lou Henry Hoover Papers, Box 73, "Subject File, Newspaper Ventures, 1919–1920."

22. See, for example, Senator Reed Smoot to Hoover, June 17, 1921, and Hoover to Smoot, June 20, 1921, Hoover Papers, Commerce Period, Box 551, "Senate: Smoot, Reed, 1921–1923"; or Christian Herter to the editor of the Galveston *News*, November 22, 1921, ibid., Box 448, "Newspapers and Magazines, Washington (DC) *Herald* 1921–1926 & undated";

or Hoover to A. Lawrence Lowell, December 31, 1921, ibid., Box 365, "League of Nations, 1921 July–December"; or Senator Frank B. Kellogg to Hoover, January 11, 1922, and Hoover to Kellogg, January 16, 1922, both in ibid., Box 548, "Senate: Kellogg, Frank B., 1922–1923 & undated."

23. Shafter, California *Progress*, July 28, 1921; typed copy of article from *San Joaquin Power* magazine, undated, Hoover Papers, Commerce Period, Box 269, "Hoover, Herbert, Hoover Farm, 1921–1925."

24. Ralph Merritt to Hoover, ca. September 27, 1923, November 25, 1923 (enclosing Merritt's report to Julius Barnes, November 25, 1923), Hoover Papers, Commerce Period, Box 269, "Hoover, Herbert, Herbert Hoover Farm, 1921–1925"; "Hoover Anecdotes—Hoover Farm," 1928, Hoover Papers, Campaign and Transition Period, Hoover Presidential Library, West Branch, Iowa, Box 75, "Subject: Anecdotes."

25. Ralph Merritt to Julius Barnes, December 11, 1923, Herbert Hoover Papers, Commerce Period, Box 269, "Hoover, Herbert, Hoover Farm, 1926–1928 & undated"; Merritt to Barnes, December 24, 1923, ibid., Box 269, "Hoover, Herbert, Hoover Farm, 1921–1925"; M. A. Jumper, "Hoover Farm," *California Cultivator*, January 26, 1924, 112.

26. Hoover to Rickard, January 17, 1924, Hoover Papers, Commerce Period, Box 269, "Hoover, Herbert, Hoover Farm, 1921–1925."

27. Ralph Merritt to Julius Barnes, October 22, 1924, ibid.

29. Draft of Hoover to Merritt, ca. April 24, 1925, ibid..

29. Edgar Rickard Diaries, Hoover Presidential Library, West Branch, Iowa, June 30, 1925, Box 1, "January–June 1925."

30. Rickard Diaries, October 16, November 25, and December 14, 1925, Box 1, "July–December 1925"; Hoover to Merritt, December 19, 1925, and Hoover to T. T. C. Gregory, December 21, 1925, both in Hoover Papers, Commerce Period, Box 269, "Hoover, Herbert, Hoover Farm, 1921–1925."

31. Edgar Rickard to Hoover, December 23, 1925, Hoover Papers, Commerce Period, Box 269, "Hoover, Herbert, Hoover Farm, 1921–1925."

32. T. T. C. Gregory to Hoover, January 18, 1926, Hoover Papers, Commerce Period, Box 269, "Hoover, Herbert, Hoover Farm, 1926–1928 & undated."

33. Hoover to Ralph Merritt, February 11, 1926, and to T. T. C. Gregory, February 11, 1926, and to Henry M. Robinson, February 11, 1926, all in Hoover Papers, Commerce Period Box 269, "Hoover, Herbert, Hoover Farm, 1926–1928 & undated."; Edgar Rickard Diaries, February 21, 22 and March 30, 1926, Box 1, "1926"; "Big Loan Made on Hoover Farm," Hanford (California) *Sentinel*, May 5, 1926.

34. Hoover to Merritt, February 3, June 15, 1927; Merritt to Hoover, February 3, June 15, and September 9, 1927; Hoover to Edgar Rickard, June 16, 1927; Merritt to Julius Barnes, October 20, 1927, all in Hoover Papers, Commerce Period, Box 269, "Hoover, Herbert, Hoover Farm, 1926–1928 & undated."

35. "Ranching a la Hoover," *Plantation and Outpost Mail*, undated clipping in Hoover Papers, Commerce Period, Box 269, "Hoover, Herbert: Hoover Farm, 1926–1928 & undated" (January 1928): 8–9; Max Stern, "Hoover Ranch Found Model One by Writer," San Francisco *News*, April 17, 1928; Max Stern, "Herbert Hoover Makes His Farm Pay," San Francisco *News*, April 18, 1928. A longer version of this same article was published as "Hoover as a Farmer Makes Ends Meet," *New York Times Magazine*, August 26, 1928, 15, 21. See also a memo on the "Hoover Farm" prepared for the 1928 campaign in Hoover Papers, Campaign and Transition Period, Box 75, "Subject: Anecdotes"; and a campaign pamphlet, "The Hoover Farm," 1928, Hoover Papers, Commerce Period, Box 269, "Hoover, Herbert, Hoover Farm, 1926–1928 & undated."

36. Stern, "Hoover as a Farmer Makes Ends Meet," 21.

37. Rickard Diaries, August 2, 30, 1928, Box 1, "1928"; Lawrence Richey to Pearl Ruschaupt, December 29, 1931, Hoover Papers, Post-Presidential File, Hoover Presidential Library, West Branch, Iowa, Box 153, "Hoover, Herbert, Farm (Wasco, Calif.)." For Joseph (Giuseppe)

Di Giorgio and the Di Giorgio Fruit Corporation, see http://etgdesign.com/family/obje/
DiGiStory.pdf and http://www.weedpatchcamp.com/Reminiscences/family4.htm (both accessed
March 15, 2006).

38. Scott Turner Oral History, Hoover Institution Archives, Stanford University, Stanford, California, p. 37.

Chapter 7

1. Harding to Hoover, November 5, 1920, Herbert Hoover Papers, Commerce Period,
Hoover Presidential Library, West Branch, Iowa, Box 7, "Harding, Correspondence Feb.
1920–1922"; Robert K. Murray, "Herbert Hoover and the Harding Cabinet," in *Herbert
Hoover as Secretary of Commerce: Studies in New Era Thought and Practice*, ed. Ellis W. Hawley
(Iowa City: University of Iowa Press, 1981), 19.

2. Florence Cabot Thorne (executive secretary to Samuel Gompers) to Robert B. Wolf, January 17, 1921, Hoover Papers, Pre-Commerce Period, Hoover Presidential Library, West
Branch, Iowa, Box 15, "Thorne, Florence, 1920–1921."

3. Herbert Hoover, *Memoirs: The Cabinet and the Presidency, 1920–1933* (New York: Macmillan, 1952), 36 (hereafter, *Memoirs* 2); Philip Kinsley, "Hoover Talks to Harding on World
Issues," Chicago *Daily Tribune*, December 13, 1920.

4. Hoover to Harding, December 22, 1920, Herbert Hoover Papers, Pre-Commerce Period,
Box 6, "Harding, Warren G., July 1, 1920–Feb. 27, 1921 (Letter Book)"; Lou Henry Hoover
to Mrs. George T. Gerlinger, February 16, 1942, Lou Henry Hoover Papers, Hoover Presi-
dential Library, West Branch, Iowa, Box 59, "Subject File: Hoover, Herbert, Biographical
Comments by LHH"; Lou Hoover to Thomas T. Gregory, February 23, 1921, ibid., Box
14, "Personal Correspondence, 1921–28, Gregory, Thomas T. and Gertrude, 1921–28."
Hoover's Republican friends were equally doubtful about Harding. See Robert A. Taft to
Joseph C. Green, December 2, 1920, Joseph C. Green Papers, Hoover Institution Archives,
Stanford, California, Box 2, "Correspondence: Taft, Robert A., 1919–1920."

5. Merlo J. Pusey to Hoover, March 11, 1949, and Hoover to Pusey, March 14, 1949, both
in Hoover Papers, Commerce Period, Box 286, "Hughes, Charles Evans, 1925"; Hiram
Johnson to Raymond Robins, January 9, 1921, Hoover Papers, Pre-Commerce Period, Box
14, "Robins, Raymond, 1918–1921"; Hoover to Harding, January 12, 1921, and Harding
to Hoover, January 12, 1921, ibid., Box 6, "Harding, Warren G., July 1, 1920–Feb. 27,
1921 (Letter Book)"; Hoover to Lou Hoover, January 12, 1921, ibid., Box 7, "Hoover, Lou
Henry, 1906–1921"; "No Post for Hoover in Harding Cabinet," *New York Times*, January
28, 1921.

6. "Hoover Is Chosen for Cabinet Post; Hert Also Placed," New York *World*, February 18,
1921; "Hoover Choice Is Blow to Penrose," New York *Evening Post*, February 22, 1921;
"Daugherty Speeds North to Placate Hoover Foes; Denby May Get Navy Post," New York
Tribune, February 23, 1921; Harding to Hoover, February 21, 1921, Hoover Papers, Pre-
Commerce Period, Box 7, "Harding, Correspondence, Feb. 1920–1922."

7. Hoover to Harding, February 23, 1921, Hoover Papers, Pre-Commerce Period, Box 7,
"Harding Correspondence, Feb. 1, 1920–Feb. 23, 1923 (Letter Book)."

8. "Hoover Undecided; Pressed to Accept," *New York Times*, February 24, 1921; Hoover,
"Statement on Acceptance of Secretary of Commerce," February 25, 1921, Hoover Papers,
Bible no. 130, Hoover Presidential Library, West Branch, Iowa; Harold Phelps Stokes,
"Hoover's Strength to Have Early Test," New York *Evening Post* (Feb. 25, 1921).

9. Hoover, *Memoirs* 2, 40.

10. Ibid., 36–37.

11. Ibid., 58; Ronald Allen Goldberg, *America in the Twenties* (Syracuse, NY: Syracuse University Press, 2003), 30–32.

12. Edward L. Schapsmeier and Frederick H. Schapsmeier, "Disharmony in the Harding Cabinet: Hoover-Wallace Conflict," *Ohio History* 75 (Spring–Summer, 1966): 126–36, 188–90;

C. Fred Williams, "William M. Jardine and the Foundations for Republican Farm Policy, 1925–1929," *Agricultural History* 70 (Spring 1996): 216–32.

13. Tumulty quoted in John M. Blum, *Joe Tumulty and the Wilson Era* (Boston: Houghton Mifflin, 1951), 150; Arthur S. Link et al., eds., *The Papers of Woodrow Wilson*, vol. 53, *November 9, 1918–January 11, 1919* (Princeton, NJ: Princeton University Press, 1986), 278, 279 (hereafter *PWW*).

14. For an interesting list of Hoover's priorities, see the July 1921 handwritten memo by James S. Taylor in James Spear Taylor Papers, Hoover Presidential Library, West Branch, Iowa, Subject File, Box 3, "Commerce Dept., 1920–1921"; Joan Hoff Wilson, *Herbert Hoover: Forgotten Progressive* (Boston: Little Brown, 1975), 59.

15. Charming classic introductions to the 1920s include Frederick Lewis Allen, *Only Yesterday: An Informal History of the 1920s* (New York: Blue Ribbon Books, 1931); and Hoover's friend, Mark Sullivan's *Our Times, 1900–1925*, 6 vols. (New York: Charles Scribner's Sons, 1926–1935). Good, recent overviews include John Braeman, Robert H. Bremner, and David Brody, eds., *Change and Continuity in Twentieth-Century America: The 1920s* (Columbus: Ohio State University Press, 1968); Ellis W. Hawley, *The Great War and the Search for a Modern Order: A History of the American People and Their Institutions, 1917–1933* (New York: St. Martin's, 1979); David J. Goldberg, *Discontented America: The United States in the 1920s* (Baltimore: Johns Hopkins University Press, 1999). For the question of progressivism during the 1920s, see Arthur S. Link, "What Happened to the Progressive Movement in the 1920s?" *American Historical Review* 64 (July 1959): 833–51; and Joan Hoff Wilson, *Herbert Hoover*.

16. Sullivan Diary, March 5, 1923, Mark Sullivan Papers, Hoover Institution Archives, Stanford, California, Box 1.

17. "Hoover Looks Over His Department," *New York Times*, February 27, 1921; William C. Redfield to Hoover, March 5, 1921, and W. E. Aughinbaugh to Hoover, March 8, 1921, both in Hoover Papers, Commerce Period, Box 511, "Redfield, William C., 1921–1928"; Franklin K. Lane to Hoover, March 1, 1921, ibid., Box 363, "Lane, Franklin K., 1921–1928."

18. "Hoover Never Met Morgan, He Writes," New York *American*, February 27, 1921; Georgia W. Leffingwell to Hoover, March 8, 1921, Hoover Papers, Pre-Commerce Period, Box 10, "Leffingwell, 1917–21"; "Hoover," *New Republic*, March 9, 1921, 29.

19. The building rented by the Commerce Department was built in 1913 and expanded in 1914 but was inadequate to house all of the department's bureaus by 1921. A fire in the building's basement in January 1921 destroyed part of the department's records and underlined the unsatisfactory situation. Annual rent in 1921 was $65,000. See Department of Commerce, *Ninth Annual Report of the Secretary of Commerce* (Washington, DC: Government Printing Office, 1921), 7–8; Hoover, *Memoirs* 2, 44.

On June 1, 1926, Robert Barry, Washington correspondent for the New York *World*, asked Hoover's assistant, Harold Phelps Stokes, for a copy of Hoover's schedule during a typical day. Stokes sent him a schedule that was packed more tightly than was normal and in which all the "appointments" scheduled were with important people, but examples of actual schedules in the same file illustrate that his imaginary schedule was not too fanciful. See Barry to Stokes, June 1, 1926, with attached documents, in Hoover Papers, Commerce Period, Box 46, "Barrows, H.-Barth, 1921–1928."

20. Press release, March 11, 1921, Hoover Papers, Commerce Period, Box 483, "Press Releases, 1921"; John Corbin, "What Hoover Is Aiming At," *New York Times*, May 29, 1921; Isaac Marcosson, *Caravans of Commerce* (New York: Harper & Brothers, 1926), 31–47.

21. Press release, March 11, 1921; Bruce Bliven, draft of an interview with Hoover, June 14, 1921, Hoover Papers, Commerce Period, Box 444, "Newspaper and Magazines, *New York Globe*, 1921–1923." European companies were underselling American producers less because of depressed living standards than because of depreciated currencies, as Hoover almost certainly knew. Given the almost universal adoption of the eight-hour day in Europe, their unit labor costs were actually relatively high, but Hoover may have thought that an argument about depressed living standards would have more appeal to Americans than a complex explanation of the actual situation. It is also worth noting that his comment about German cartels did not mean that he favored a similar system in the United States. He

frequently said that he believed that competition promoted efficiency. From time to time, however, as we shall see, he acknowledged the value of monopoly.

22. Press release, March 11, 1921. Given Europe's economic problems and the reparations tangle, Hoover was overstating the immediate threat of unified action by European governments.

23. Corbin, "What Hoover Is Aiming At." Hoover's vision of a society in which cooperation would replace conflict was not unique. See, for example, Frank J. Goodnow, *The American Conception of Liberty and Government* (Providence, RI: Standard Printing, 1916), 20–31.

24. Typescript, "The Bureau of Foreign and Domestic Commerce: History," ca. September 24, 1924, Hoover Papers, Commerce Period, Box 514, "Reorganization of Government Depts., Commerce Dept., Foreign and Domestic Commerce"; Hoover to Harding, June 9, 1921, ibid., Box 480; "President Harding, 1921 May–June"; Department of Commerce, *Ninth Annual Report*, 51, 72; Julius Klein, *Frontiers of Trade* (New York: Century, 1929), 198; Joseph Brandes, *Herbert Hoover and Economic Diplomacy: Department of Commerce Policy, 1921–1928* (Pittsburgh: University of Pittsburgh Press, 1962), 4–5.

25. Herbert Hoover, *Memoirs: Years of Adventure, 1874–1920* (New York: Macmillan, 1951), 264 (hereafter, *Memoirs* 1); Arch Shaw to Hoover, March 26, 1921, and Christian Herter to Shaw, April 20, 1921, both in Hoover Papers, Commerce Period, Box 556, "Shaw, Arch W., 1921 March–June"; Frederick M. Feiker to Arch Shaw, May 5, 1921, Frederick M. Feiker Papers, Hoover Presidential Library, West Branch, Iowa, Box 22, "Correspondence Series, 1921"; Frederick M. Feiker, "Nine Months at Hoover's Elbow," Hoover-for-President Business Paper Editorial Advisory Committee, ibid., Box 4, "Subject File: Election of 1928"; Frank Taussig to Hoover, July 14, 1921, and Hoover to Taussig, July 20, 1921, both in Hoover Papers, Commerce Period, Box 595, "Taussig, Prof. F. W., 1921–1927"; Frank M. Surface to F. M. Feiker, July 25, 1921, ibid., Box 433, "National Retail Dry Goods Association, 1921–1927 & undated"; Craig Lloyd, *Aggressive Introvert: A Study of Herbert Hoover and Public Relations Management, 1912–1932* (Columbus: Ohio State University Press, 1972), 62–63.

26. Hoover to Harding, June 9, 1921, Hoover Papers, Commerce Period, Box 674, "United States—Bureau of Efficiency, 1921–1922 & undated"; "Division of Simplified Practice," undated, ibid., Box 1, "Accomplishments of the Department, 1921–28"; Edward Eyre Hunt, "The National Bureau of Standards under Hoover," undated (ca. 1928), Herbert Hoover Subject Collection, Hoover Institution Archives, Stanford, California, Box 14, "National Bureau of Standards"; "Number of Employees in Department of Commerce in the District of Columbia, April 1, 1917, and April 30, 1922," undated, Hoover Papers, Commerce Period, Box 120, "Commerce Department, Miscellaneous, 1922 January–May"; Brandes, *Hoover and Economic Diplomacy*, 6–9.

27. Christian A. Herter to Hugh Humphreys, April 29, 1921, Hoover Papers, Commerce Period, Box 396, "Mississippi Valley Association, 1921"; "Accomplishments of the Department of Commerce, 1921–28," 1928, ibid., Box 1, "Accomplishments of the Department of Commerce (1), 1921–1928"; Robert Brookings to Arch Shaw, May 13, 1921, ibid., Box 60, "Brookings, Robert S., 1921–1927"; Hoover to Elliot E. Goodwin, May 16, 1921, ibid., Box 83, "Chamber of Commerce, United States, 1920–1921 May"; Brandes, *Hoover and Economic Diplomacy*, 6–9.

28. Hoover, *Memoirs* 2, 43; William E. Leuchtenburg, *Herbert Hoover* (New York: Henry Holt, 2009), 56–57. In December 1921, Hoover sent to Representative Walter F. Brown a memorandum listing the sixteen offices and agencies he proposed to have transferred to Commerce. Brown was chairman of the Congressional Joint Committee on the Reorganization of Government Departments. See Brown to Hoover, December 7, 1921, and Hoover to Brown, December 8, 1921, enclosing memorandum, both in Hoover Papers, Commerce Period, Box 674, "United States Bureau of Efficiency, 1921–1922 & undated." On the clash with the State Department, see Christian A. Herter to Assistant Secretary of State Fred M. Dearing, May 3, 1921, ibid., Box 137, "Commerce Department, Foreign and Domestic Commerce, Foreign Service, 1921–1927"; J. Walter Drake to Hoover, October 25, 1921, and Hoover to Drake, October 29, 1921, both in ibid., Box 184, "Drake, John Walter, 1921–1928."

29. Hoover, *Memoirs* 2, 42–43. For the long struggle to get a new Commerce Department building, see the sources cited in note 18 and E. W. Libbey to Hoover, March 10, 1921, Hoover Papers, Commerce Period, Box 126, "Commerce Department: Buildings, Quarters, Etc., 1921–1924"; Department of Commerce, *Thirteenth Annual Report of the Secretary of Commerce, 1924* (Washington, DC: Government Printing Office, 1925), 38; Department of Commerce, *Sixteenth Annual Report of the Secretary of Commerce* (Washington, DC: Government Printing Office, 1928), 2; Department of Commerce, *Seventeenth Annual Report of the Secretary of Commerce* (Washington, DC: Government Printing Office, 1929), 1–2; "Commerce to Get Huge Structure," Washington *Evening Star*, June 3, 1926; "Hoover Approves Site for Building," Washington *Evening Star*, June 8, 1926; memorandums on the new building, July 7, 1926, January 29, 1927, January 27, 1928, all signed by "Grams" (?), Hoover Papers, Commerce Period, Box 126, "Commerce Department: Buildings, Quarter, Etc., 1925–1928 & undated." Several different locations for the building were considered and rejected for one reason or another before the final site was chosen.
30. Hoover, *Memoirs* 2, 42–43.
31. Harding to Hoover, April 30, 1921, Hoover Papers, Commerce Period, Box 480, "President Harding, 1921 April"; Hoover to Harding, May 6, 1921, and Harding to Hoover, May 12, 1921, both in ibid., Box 480, "President Harding, 1921 May–June"; Hoover to James W. Good, May 13, 1921, ibid., Box 278, "House of Representatives, Good, James W., 1921"; Christian Herter to Hugh Gibson, June 13, 1921, ibid., Box 237, "Gibson, Hugh, 1921–1928."
32. Georgia W. Leffingwell, "Statistical and Analytical Report Covering Month of June, 1921," Hoover Papers, Commerce Period, Box 574, "Statistical and Analytical Report, 1921."
33. Herbert Hoover, "Marketing American Surplus Food Products," *Farm and Home* 41 (January 1920): 1, 5, 37; "100 Million Trade Board Presidency to W. P. G. Harding," New York *Herald*, January 20, 1921; William F. Collins to Hoover, February 19, 1921, Hoover Papers, Pre-Commerce Period, Box 41, "Foreign Trade and Banking, 1921"; John McHugh to Hoover, March 10, 23, 1921"; Hoover to Paul M. Warburg, March 16, 1921; Hoover to John McHugh and Paul Warburg, April 4, 1921, all in Hoover Papers, Commerce Period, Box 227, "Foreign Trade: Foreign Trade Financing Corporation, 1921."
34. "Says Credits to Europe Are Essential Aid," Washington *Herald*, January 21, 1921; James H. Shideler, "Herbert Hoover and the Federal Farm Board Project," *Mississippi Valley Historical Review* 42 (March 1956): 710–29.
35. Glen Jeansonne, *Transformation and Reaction: America, 1921–1945* (New York: HarperCollins, 1994), 23.
36. Vernon Kellogg to Hoover, April 5, 1921, Hoover Papers, Commerce Period, Box 433, "National Research Council, 1921."
37. Arthur Capper to Hoover, April 13, 1921, and Hoover to Capper, April 23, 1921 (released to the press on April 28), ibid., Box 544, "Senate: Capper, Arthur, 1920–1922"; Shideler, "Herbert Hoover and the Federal Farm Board Project," 710–13.
38. Hoover to Barnes, April 30, 1921, and Barnes to Herter, May 20, 1921, Hoover Papers, Commerce Period, Box 243, "Grain Dealers Conference, 1921 April–May"; press release, "Secretaries Hoover and Wallace to Confer with Farm and Grain Handling Groups, Improvement in Warehousing Grain, Object," June 6, 1921, and press release, "Regarding the Proposed Plan of Secretaries and Wallace for Improvement in the Warehousing of Grain," ca. June 13, 1921, both in ibid., Box 243, "Grain Dealers Conference, 1921 June 11–21."
39. Norris to Hoover, May 23, 1921, and Hoover to Norris, May 25, 1921, both in Hoover Papers, Commerce Period, Box 549, "Senate: Norris Bill—Data Re, 1921–1924 & undated"; Hoover to Clarence W. Baron, June 29, 1921, ibid., Box 45, "Barron, Clarence W., 1921–1922."
40. Eugene Meyer to Harding, July 23, 1921, Warren Harding Microfilm Papers, Roll 182, Ohio Historical Society; Hoover to Harding, July 25, 1921, and Harding to Hoover, July 26, 1921, Hoover Papers, Commerce Period, Box 480, "President Harding, 1921 July–September"; Extracts from the Agnes E. Meyer Diary, October 30, 1921, Herbert Hoover Papers, Commerce Period, Hoover Presidential Library, Gen. Acq. 692; David Burner, *Herbert*

Hoover: A Public Life (New York: Knopf, 1979), 168; Norris, quoted in Eugene P. Trani and David L. Wilson, *The Presidency of Warren G. Harding* (Lawrence: University Press of Kansas, 1977), 68–69; press release, "Assistance to Agriculture," November 27, 1922, Hoover Papers, Commerce Period, Box 3, "Agriculture, 1919–1922." Hoover's friend, the banker Paul Warburg, had suggested giving similar powers to strengthened federal land banks rather than to the War Finance Corporation, but for some reason that suggestion seems never to have been considered. See Warburg to Hoover, January 9, 1922, ibid., Box 685, "Warburg, Paul M., 1922–1925."

41. A list of the members of the Sugar Equalization Board is in Hoover Papers, Pre-Commerce Period, Box 65, "Sugar-U.S. Equalization Board, 1917–1920"; Hoover to Julius Barnes, July 23, 1919, ibid., Box 60, "Public Statements, 1917–1920."

42. Hoover to Senator Arthur Capper, May 7, 1920, Hoover Papers, Commerce Period, Box 544, "Senate: Capper, Arthur, 1920–1922"; "Hoover Is Blamed for Sugar Crisis," *New York Times*, May 29, 1920; Hoover to W. H. Wallace, June 28, 1921, Hoover Papers, Commerce Period, Box 583, "Sugar: Cuban Sugar, 1918–1921 November"; Hoover to E. G. Crowder, November 15, 1921, ibid., Box 587, "Sugar: Sugar Equalization Board, 1918–1922"; Hoover to H. A. Douglas, December 15, 1921, and Hoover to Harding, December 13, 1921, ibid., Box 583, "Sugar: Cuban Sugar, 1921 December."

43. George Otis Smith, director of the geological survey, provided a long and admirably clear description of the nature and problems of the coal industry in a letter to Senator Walter E. Edge, May 20, 1921, Hoover Papers, Commerce Period, Box 659, "Unemployment, Press Releases, 1920–1921"; Paul Salstrom, *Appalachia's Path to Dependency: Rethinking a Region's Economic History, 1730–1940* (Lexington: University Press of Kentucky, 1994), 39, 72–75, 115; Ellis W. Hawley, "Secretary Hoover and the Bituminous Coal Problem, 1921–1928," *Business History Review* 42 (Autumn 1968): 249–51.

44. Herbert Hoover, "Stabilization of Bituminous Coal Industry," *Mining and Metallurgy*, March 1920, 1–2; Hoover to G. DuBois, October 26, 1920, Hoover Papers, Pre-Commerce Period, Box 62, "Senate Special Committee on Reconstruction & Production-Coal, 1920–Jan. 1921"; minutes of the meeting of the Committee on the Stabilization of the Coal Industry, November 20, 1920, Hoover Papers, Commerce Period, Box 97, "Coal, Miscellaneous, 1920."

45. David L. Wing, Memorandum on the Need of Current and Adequate Information Covering the Coal Industry, undated, Hoover Papers, Commerce Period, Box 97, "Coal, Miscellaneous, 1921 August–November"; George H. Cushing (director of American Wholesale Coal Association) to Hoover, March 25, 1921, ibid., Box 31, "American Wholesale Coal Association, 1921–1922"; Franklin T. Miller, comment on S824, 67 Cong., 1 sess., undated, ibid., Box 184, "Coal: Miller, F. T., 1921."

46. Franklin T. Miller, memorandum to the secretary regarding Senate Bill No. 1807, May 21, 1921, Hoover Papers, Commerce Period, Box 104, "Coal: Miller, F. T., 1921"; unsigned, undated memorandum of meeting on June 7, 1921, ibid., Box 97, "Coal: Miscellaneous, 1921 January–June"; Hoover to Frelinghuysen, June 18, 1921, ibid., Box 108, "Coal: Problems, 1921–1922 & undated"; "An American Coal Journal Staff Correspondent," "Frelinghuysen Bills Opening Wedge for Drastic Legislation on Coal," and "Opposition to Frelinghuysen Control Bill Crystallizes in Coal Industry," *American Coal Journal*, June 25, 1921; W. R. Coyle, president of American Wholesale Coal Association, to Hoover, June 28, 1921, and Hoover to Coyle, July 2, 1921, both in Hoover Papers, Commerce Period, Box 97, "Coal: Miscellaneous, 1921 January–June"; Hawley, "Secretary Hoover and the Bituminous Coal Problem," 254–55. Calder and Frelinghuysen both had personal ties to Hoover, but it seems probable that their support of this bill was because they believed it would benefit consumers in their home states of New York and New Jersey.

47. Hoover to various public utility associations, July 8, 1921, Hoover Papers, Commerce Period, Box 97, "Coal: Miscellaneous, 1921 July"; Hoover to E. M. Poston, July 19, 1921, ibid.; Hoover to Ivy L. Lee, Association of Railway Executives, August 15, 1921, ibid., Box 97, "Coal: Miscellaneous, 1921 August–November"; press release on meeting with coal operators and miners' unions under auspices of Unemployment Conference, October 8, 1921, ibid., Box 659, "Unemployment: Press Releases, 1920–1921"; David L. Wing,

memorandum for Secretary Hoover on coal production and days worked, October 10, 1921, ibid., Box 97, "Coal: Miscellaneous, 1921 August–November."

48. Hoover to Attorney General Harry Daugherty, October 13, 1921, Hoover Papers, Commerce Period, Box 353, "Justice Department: Attorney General Daugherty, 1921 October–December."

49. Hoover to the editor of the *New York Times*, October 15, 1921, Hoover Papers, Commerce Period, Box 97, "Coal: Miscellaneous, 1921 August–November"; W. E. L. (probably Department Solicitor William E. Lamb) to Hoover, November 3, 1921, ibid., Box 110, "Coal: Strikes, 1921"; Rep. Walter E. Newton to Hoover, November 29, 1921, and Hoover to Newton, December 2, 1921, both in ibid., Box 97, "Coal: Miscellaneous, 1921 August–November"; Sanford E. Thompson to Edward Eyre Hunt, December 1, 1921, ibid., Box 102, "Coal: Hunt, E. E., 1921"; press release, "Mr. Hoover's Views in Regard to Export Coal, 1921," December 6, 1921, ibid., Box 97, "Coal: Miscellaneous, 1921 December"; Hoover to Charles C. McChord, December 28, 1921, ibid., Box 297, "Interstate Commerce Commission, 1921 August–December"; Hoover to E. M. Poston, December 31, 1921, ibid., Box 101, "Coal: Coal Committee, 1921–1922." For concerns about whether the British might dump cheap coal in the United States, see the documents in Hoover Papers, Commerce Period, Box 245, "Great Britain, 1912–1921," "Great Britain, 1922 January–March," and "Great Britain, 1922 April–December."

50. Albro Martin, *Enterprise Denied: Origins of the Decline of American Railroads, 1897–1917* (New York: Columbia University Press, 1971), 352–67.

51. Burl Noggle, *Into the Twenties: The United States from Armistice to Normalcy* (Urbana: University of Illinois Press, 1974), 76–83.

52. "Freight Blockade Grows; 235,000 Cars Tied Up; Engineers Vote to Strike," New York *Tribune*, May 13, 1920; letter no. 89, Whaley-Eaton Service, May 15, 1920, Hoover Papers, Pre-Commerce Period, Box 27, "Campaign of 1920, Correspondence, May 1920"; W. W. Jermane, "Hoover to Help Save Railroads," Seattle *Times*, March 11, 1921; Lowell Mellett, "Hoover Expected to Untangle Row over Railroads," Portland (Oregon) *Journal*, March 23, 1921; Robert K. Murray, *The Harding Era: Warren G. Harding and His Administration* (Minneapolis: University of Minnesota Press, 1969), 221–23.

53. Hoover to Daniel Willard (president of Baltimore and Ohio Railroad), April 14, 1921, and Willard to Hoover, April 16, 1921, both in Hoover Papers, Commerce Period, Box 506, "Railroads—Rates—1921 April 5–20"; Willard to Hoover, April 29, 1921, ibid., Box 506, "Railroads—Rates—1921 April 21–30"; Willard to Hoover, May 13, 1921, ibid., Box 506, "Railroads—Rates—1921 May"; Hoover to C. Harold Powell (California Fruit Growers Exchange), June 15, 1921, and Edgar E. Clark (Chairman ICC) to Hoover, June 15, 1921, both in ibid., Box 506, "Railroads—Rates—1921 June 6–26"; Hoover to Andrew Mellon, June 27, 1921, and Hoover to James C. Davis, June 29, 1921, both in ibid., Box 505, "Railroads—Problems—1921 April–June"; Hoover to Harding, July 2, 1921, ibid.; Hoover's remarks to the Association of Railway Executives meeting, July 8, 1921, ibid., Box 505, "Railroads—Problems—1921 July 5–15"; Hoover to Harding, July 11, 1921, ibid., Box 480, "President Harding, 1921 July–September"; Murray, *Harding Era*, 222–23.

54. Hoover to Harding, July 11, 1921; Harding to Hoover, July 15, 1921; Hoover to James C. Davis, enclosing copy of memorandum of agreement between the administration and the Association of Railway Executives, July 18, 1921, all in Hoover Papers, Commerce Period, Box 505, "Railroads—Problems—1921 July 5–15."

55. Hoover to Rep. Sidney Anderson, July 22, 1921, Hoover Papers, Commerce Period, Box 505, "Railroads—Problems—1921 July 16–30"; Hoover to Harding, September 23, 1921, enclosing unsigned memo (September 19, 1921) listing participants in the New York meeting, ibid., Box 506, "Railroads—Rates—1921 July–Sept." Clippings from twelve newspapers about Hoover's alleged support of pay cuts and Christian Herter's correction are in ibid., Box 506, "Railroads—Rates—1921 October–Dec."; Association of Railroad Executives, press statement on rate and pay cuts, October 14, 1921, ibid.

56. Hoover's planning for a strike can be followed in detail in the documents in Hoover Papers, Commerce Period, Boxes 507 and 508, in folders titled "Railroads—Strikes," with various

dates. For Hoover's report to the president, see Hoover to Harding, October 22, 1921, and Harding to Hoover, October 24, 1921, ibid., Box 480, "President Harding, 1921 October–November"; and see also Ellis W. Hawley, "Herbert Hoover and Economic Stabilization, 1921–22," in *Herbert Hoover as Secretary of Commerce*, 59.

57. Hoover to Edward Keating, editor of *Labor*, November 15, December 5, 1921, and draft of an undated article by Charles M. Kelley, Hoover Papers, Commerce Period, Box 579, "Streth-Strikes, 1921–1928."

58. Harold S. Sharlin, *The Making of the Electrical Age: From the Telegraph to Automation* (London: Abelard-Schuman, 1963), 193, 195, 212; Hoover to Senator Frederick Hale, May 13, 1920, Hoover Papers, Pre-Commerce Period, Box 22, "AIMME, Personal Correspondence, May–Aug. 1921." The board's first meeting was on September 24, 1920; Hoover was appointed on September 29. See John Barton Payne to Hoover, September 29, 1920, ibid., Box 12, "Payne, John Barton, 1920–1921." W. S. Murray was chairman of the board; for his views, see "A League for Superpower," *Literary Digest*, November 13, 1920, 30–31.

59. George O. Smith to Hoover, November 20, 1920, Hoover Papers, Pre-Commerce Period, Box 80, "U.S. Geological Survey, Sept. 4, 1920–Nov. 23, 1920"; minutes of advisory board, January 5 and February 18, 1921, ibid., Box 69, "U.S. Geological Survey, November 24, 1920–February 24, 1921"; Interior Department press release about possible publicly owned superpower corporation, February 24, 1921, ibid.

60. Murray to Hoover, enclosing draft of proposed bill, June 7, 1921; Hoover to Murray, June 9,1921; Murray to Hoover, June 29, 1921, all in Hoover Papers, Commerce Period, Box 295, "Interior Department, Advisory Board—Superpower Survey, 1921 May–July."

61. Fall to Hoover, July 20, 1921, Hoover Papers, Commerce Period, Box 590, "Superpower, etc., 1920–1921"; "U.S. Launches Superpower Project to Save Billions," San Francisco *Chronicle*, September 15, 1921.

62. Murray, *Harding Era*, 411–12.

63. Draft of report on Hoover's work with the Colorado River Commission, ca. September 1924, Hoover Papers, Commerce Period, Box 429, "National Conference of Business Paper Editors, 1924"; memorandum on legislative history of the Boulder Canyon Project, May 17, 1933, ibid., Box 429, "Presidential Subject File: Colorado River Commission, Correspondence, 1928–33"; Arthur Powell Davis, "Development of the Colorado River: The Justification of Boulder Dam," *Atlantic* 143 (February 1929): 254–57.

64. Norris Hundley, Jr., *Water and the West: The Colorado River Compact and the Politics of Water in the American West* (Berkeley: University of California Press, 1975), 83–109; Daniel Tyler, *Silver Fox of the Rockies: Delphus E. Carpenter and Western Water Compacts* (Norman: University of Oklahoma Press, 2003), 114–20.

65. "Memorandum on Interview which Dr. Ray Lyman Wilbur Had with Mr. Harry Chandler, in Los Angeles, on October 3, 1938," Herbert Hoover Papers, Post-Presidential File, Hoover Presidential Library, West Branch, Iowa, Box 555, "Wilbur, R. L., Correspondence, 1933–1938."

66. Fall to Harding, September 24 and November 17, 1921, Albert Fall Collection, Huntington Library, San Marino, California, Box 47 (10), "Colorado River Project, Sept. 21, 1921–Feb. 9, 1923"; Hoover to Harding, November 2, 1921, Hoover Papers, Commerce Period, Box 480, "President Harding, 1921 October–November"; Hoover's official commission, December 17, 1921, is in Colorado River Commission Papers, Hoover Presidential Library, West Branch, Iowa, Box 10, "Appointment of Mr. Hoover to Serve in Commission, 1921."

67. Hoover to Secretary of War Weeks, June 22, 1921, Hoover Papers, Commerce Period, Box 422, "Muscle Shoals, Miscellaneous, 1921–1924"; Hoover to Herbert Myrick, July 13, 1921, ibid., Box 396, "Mississippi Valley Association, 1921"; Henry Ford's offer, July 8, 1921, ibid., Box 423, "Muscle Shoals, Henry Ford, 1921"; Department of Commerce press release, "Muscle Shoals Nitrate Plant a Commercial Possibility," July 14, 1921, ibid., Box 483, "Press Releases, 1921"; "Muscle Shoals and Henry Ford," Chicago *Tribune*, July 16, 1921; Hoover to Ralph Merritt, August 16, 1921; P. M. Downing to Hoover, September 1, 14, 1921, all in Hoover Papers, Commerce Period, Box 422, "Muscle Shoals Miscellaneous, 1921–1924"; Downing to Hoover, September 29, 1921, ibid., Box 423, "Muscle Shoals,

Reports, Press Releases, Printed Matter, 1917–1921"; F. M. Feiker to Hoover, September 16, 1921, "Muscle Shoals Plans, 1921–1924," ibid.; Hoover to Secretary of War Weeks, November 19, 1921, "Muscle Shoals, Henry Ford, 1921," ibid.

68. Douglas C. Drake, "Herbert Hoover, Ecologist: The Politics of Oil Pollution Control, 1921–1926," *Mid-America* 55 (July 1973): 208.

69. Minutes of meeting of commercial fishermen at the Commerce Department, May 9–10, 1921, Hoover Papers, Commerce Period, Box 203, "Fish Industry, Conference re: Fish Distribution, 1921 May 9–10"; minutes of conference on Pollution of Waters and Proposed Federal Control of Fisheries, June 16, 1921, ibid., Box 203, "Fish Industry, Conferences of State Fish Commissioners, Anglers and Producers (June 16, 1921), 1921 June 16–November 25." Senator Frelinghuysen, although a conservative Republican, was also, like Hoover, an ardent fisherman and outdoorsman, which may have contributed to his interest in the oil pollution issue. New Jersey also had extensive harbors in the New York City area and popular beaches along the Atlantic coast, all of which were affected by oil pollution.

70. E. T. Chamberlain memorandum, "Pollution of Harbors &c. By Oil-Burning Steamers," June 20, 1921, and Hoover to Lamb, June 23, 1921, Hoover Papers, Commerce Period, Box 472, "Pollution of Waters, 1921."

71. R. L. Fletcher (?) of the American Petroleum Institute to Hoover, February 1, 1922, Hoover Papers, Commerce Period, Box 472, "Pollution of Waters, 1922"; Drake, "Herbert Hoover, Ecologist," 209.

Chapter 8

1. Press release on the Department of Commerce, March 11, 1921, Bible no. 134, Herbert Hoover Papers, Hoover Presidential Library, West Branch, Iowa.

2. Address by Hoover before the U.S. Chamber of Commerce, Atlantic City, April 28, 1921, ibid.; Hoover's private notes on his activities as secretary of commerce in 1922–1923, Herbert Hoover Papers, Commerce Period, Hoover Presidential Library, West Branch, Iowa, Box 268, "Hoover, Herbert, Biography, undated."

3. Robert K. Murray, *The Harding Era: Warren G. Harding and His Administration* (Minneapolis: University of Minnesota Press, 1969), 81–85; Eugene P. Trani and David L. Wilson, *The Presidency of Warren G. Harding* (Lawrence: University Press of Kansas, 1977), 10–14; Anthony S. Campagna, *U.S. National Economic Policy, 1917–1985* (New York: Praeger, 1987), 40–44. All economic statistics for this period must be taken as approximations.

4. Measured in 1929 dollars, the U.S. GNP in 1913 was $39.1 billion, and net exports were $300 million; in 1920, the GNP was $88.9 billion, and net exports were $2.3 billion.

5. Address of Herbert Hoover, secretary of commerce, responding to the toast, "Government and Business," May 23, 1921, Hoover Papers, Commerce Period, Box 444, "Newspapers and Magazines, *New York Commercial*, 1921–1926 & undated"; Wesley Clair Mitchell, *Business Cycles* (Berkeley: University of California Press, 1913); Arthur F. Burns, "Introductory Sketch," in *Wesley Clair Mitchell: The Economic Scientist*, ed. Arthur F. Burns (New York: National Bureau of Economic Research, 1952), 21–26.

6. J. Adam Tooze, *Statistics and the German State, 1900–1945: The Making of Modern Economic Knowledge* (Cambridge, UK: Cambridge University Press, 2001), 7. A major contemporary study of index numbers is Irving Fisher, *The Making of Index Numbers: A Study of Their Varieties, Tests, and Reliability* (New York: Augustus M. Kelley 1967; repr. of 1927 ed., first published in 1922).

7. Dorothy Ross, *The Origins of American Social Science* (New York: Cambridge University Press, 1991), 323–25, 397–98; National Bureau of Economic Research, *Income in the United States: Its Amount and Distribution, 1909–1919*, 2 vols. (New York: National Bureau of Economic Research, 1922).

8. Senator Robert Owen to Hoover, March 31, 1921, and Hoover to Owen, April 2, 1921, Hoover Papers, Commerce Period, Box 550, "Senate: Owen, Robert L., 1921–1926"; Charles H. Hamlin to Adolph Miller, enclosing memorandum on Federal Reserve Board

monetary policy in 1920–1921, July 16, 1924, Federal Reserve System, Board of Governors Collection, Hoover Presidential Library, West Branch, Iowa, Box 1, "Adolph Miller Papers, Charles S. Hamlin File, 1918–1932"; John R. Dunlap to Hoover, June 17, 1921, Hoover to Dunlap, July 26, 1921, and Hoover to Samuel Gompers, undated (ca. July 9, 1921), all in Hoover Papers, Commerce Period, Box 24, "American Federation of Labor: Gompers, Samuel, 1920–1923, & undated"; Hoover to National Research Council, July 9, 1921, ibid., Box 433, "National Research Council, 1921"; Hoover to Henry C. Wallace, July 13, 1921, ibid., Box 11, "Agriculture Department: Secretary of Agriculture Wallace, Henry C., 1921"; Hoover to Gov. William D. Stephens (and to other governors), July 25, 1921, ibid., Box 262, "Highway Construction: Letters to and from Governors, 1921 July."

9. The Department of Labor's best estimate of unemployment in mid-August was 5,735,000, although some experts in the department proposed figures as low as 3,906,450. See Secretary of Labor James J. Davis to Vice President Calvin Coolidge, August 12, 1921, Hoover Papers, Commerce Period, Box 665, "Unemployment Reports, 1921 April–August." A special Economic Advisory Committee appointed to help prepare for the unemployment conference estimated in September that the number of unemployed "was possibly as large as 3,500,000, although more probably somewhat less than that number." See Advance Summary Report of Economic Advisory Committee to the President's Unemployment Conference, September 22, 1921, ibid., Box 665, "Unemployment Reports, 1921 September." A week later, the conference's Committee on Unemployment Statistics (ca. Sept. 29, 1921) estimated unemployment at "not less than 3,700,000 or more than 4,000,000," in ibid., Box 638, "Employment, Committee on Statistics, Correspondence, Minutes, Reports, 1921 September." In a September 22 speech to the unemployment conference, Harding observed that some unemployment was normal even in good times. He referred to this as a "parasite percentage" and estimated it at 1.5 million people. Economists agreed but preferred the more neutral term "natural rate of unemployment." The president's speech was quoted with approval in the Report of the Committee on Emergency Measures in Construction, September 29, 1921, ibid., Box 639, "Unemployment: Committee Reports, 1921 September 27–29."

10. Harding to Hoover, August 24, 1921, Hoover Papers, Commerce Period, Box 658, "Unemployment: President, 1921–1922"; Hoover to Edwin Gay, August 29, 1921, ibid., Box 648, "Unemployment: Gay, Edwin F., 1921–1922"; unsigned "Memo for E. E. Hunt re Unemployment Conference," September 1, 1921, ibid., Box 654, "Unemployment: Methods of Meeting Problems, 1921"; Hoover to Allyn Abbott Young, enclosing list of members of Advisory Committee, September 8, 1921, ibid., Box 718, "Young, Allyn Abbott, 1921–1927"; William S. Rossiter to Hoover, September 8, 1921, ibid., Box 616, "Unemployment: Advisory Committee, Organization, Lists"; press release by Hoover and Secretary of Labor Davis on the conference, September 15, 1921, ibid., Box 483, "Press Releases, 1921"; advance summary of Economic Advisory Committee, September 22, 1921, ibid., Box 616, "Unemployment: Advisory Committee Reports"; David Burner, *Herbert Hoover: A Public Life* (New York: Knopf, 1979), 164; Patrick D. Reagan, "From Depression to Depression: Hooverian National Planning, 1921–1933," in *Business-Government Cooperation, 1917–1932: The Rise of Corporatist Policies*, ed. Robert F. Himmelberg (New York: Garland, 1994), 353.

11. Speech by Hoover, Unemployment Conference, Washington, September 26, 1921, Hoover Papers, Commerce Period, Box 659, "Unemployment: Press Releases, 1920–1921"; John M. Gries to Hoover, September 25, 1921, James Spear Taylor Papers, Subject File, Hoover Presidential Library, West Branch, Iowa, Box 3, "Commerce Department, 1920–21."

12. Directory of the President's Conference on Unemployment, October 10, 1921, Hoover Papers, Commerce Period, Box 644, "Unemployment Conference: Plans and Program, 1921 October"; President Gompers's Report on the Unemployment Conference, November 7, 1921, ibid., Box 616, "Unemployment: American Federation of Labor, 1919–1923 & undated"; Defrees's report to the Board of the Chamber of Commerce, November 13, 1921, ibid., Box 621, "Unemployment: Chamber of Commerce, U.S.A., 1921–1922"; E. M. Poston to Hoover, February 22, 1929, ibid., Box 658, "Unemployment: Poston, E. M., 1921–1923."

13. Minutes of the committee meetings on September 28, 1921, can be found in Hoover Papers, Commerce Period, Box 637. For the final report of the Committee on Emergency Measures in Transportation, October 12, 1921, see ibid., Box 638, "Unemployment: Committee on Emergency Measures in Transportation, 1921 October"; Burns, "Introductory Sketch," 25.

14. Report of the Committee on Permanent Public Works, October 13, 1921, Hoover Papers Commerce Period, Box 637, "Unemployment: Committee on Emergency Measures and Public Works, 1921 and undated"; Mallery to Arthur Woods, October 24, 1921; Mallery to Hoover, Woods, and Edward Eyre Hunt, November 12, 17, 1921; Mallery to Hoover and Woods, November 21, 1921, all in ibid., Box 653, "Unemployment: Mallery, Otto, 1921"; Mallery to Rep. John W. Summers, October 27, 1921, ibid., Box 649, "Unemployment: Interior Dept., Reclamation, 1921"; speech by Edward Eyre Hunt, secretary of the president's Unemployment Conference before the Society of Industrial Engineers, October 26, 1921, ibid., Box 657, "Unemployment: *New York Globe*, 1921 November"; Otto T. Mallery, "Memorandum of the conversation with Under-Secretary of the Treasury Gilbert," December 5, 1921, ibid., Box 653, "Unemployment: Mallery, Otto, 1921." For Committee on Civic and Emergency Measures press releases, dated from November 8 to December 31, 1921, see ibid., Box 615, "Unemployment, 1921 Nov.–Dec"; Edward Eyre Hunt to E. M. Poston, November 23, 1921, and Sen. Frank Willis to Poston, December 15, 1921, both in Box 20, "Unemployment (#2)." Frank Willis Papers, Ohio State Historical Society, Columbus, Ohio; For a copy of the Kenyon Bill (S 2749), see Hoover Papers, Commerce Period, Box 657, "Unemployment: *The Outlook Company*, 1921–1923"; William J. Barber, *From New Era to New Deal: Herbert Hoover, the Economists, and American Economic Policy, 1921–1933* (Cambridge, UK: Cambridge University Press, 1985), 16–19; Alexander Keyssar, *Out of Work: The First Century of Unemployment in Massachusetts* (Cambridge, UK: Cambridge University Press, 1986), 306. In a news conference on February 10, 1931, Hoover credited Mallery and Hunt with the unemployment reserve idea. See his comments on the Unemployment Stabilization Act of 1931 in *Public Papers of the Presidents of the United States: Herbert Hoover; Containing the Public Messages, Speeches, and Statements of the President, January 1 to December 31, 1931* (Washington, DC: Government Printing Office, 1976), 67–68.

15. News release, September 28, 1921, Hoover Papers, Commerce Period, Box 658, "Unemployment: Personnel, 1921."

16. Report of the Committee on Community, Civic and Emergency Measures, September 29, 1921, Hoover Papers, Commerce Period, Box 637, "Unemployment: Committee on Community, Civic and Emergency Measures, 1921–1923."

17. "Four minute men," quoted by Robert Zieger, *Republicans and Labor, 1919–1929* (Lexington: University of Kentucky Press, 1969), 91–92; Edward Eyre Hunt to Harold T. Pulsifer, December 5, 1921, Hoover Papers, Commerce Period, Box 657, "Unemployment: *The Outlook Company*, 1921–1923."

18. "Cart Before the Horse," New York *Journal of Commerce*, October 3, 1921; William L. Chenery, "In What Did Conference On Unemployment Fail?" New York *Globe*, October 17, 1921.

19. Edward Eyre Hunt to William Chenery, October 21, 1921, Hoover Papers, Commerce Period, Box 657, "Unemployment: *New York Globe*, 1921 October"; Hunt to Chenery, December 14, 1921, ibid., Box 657, "Unemployment: *New York Globe*, 1921 December–1922 January."

20. Senator Joseph Frelinghuysen to Hoover, August 9, 1921, enclosing copy of Frelinghuysen to the president of the Penn Mutual Life Insurance Co., July 28, 1921; Hoover to Frelinghuysen, August 15, 18, 1921, all in Hoover Papers, Commerce Period, Box 546, "Senate: Frelinghuysen, J. S., 1921"; editorial, "Second Thoughts on Unemployment," New York *Globe* (ca. October 26, 1921), in ibid., Box 360, "Kohlsaat, H. H., 1921–1923"; Hoover to Darwin P. Kingsley, November 17, December 7, 1921, and Kingsley to Hoover, December 2, 1921, enclosing draft plan to issue insurance based on the veterans' bonus, all in ibid., Box 231, "Frelinghuysen, J. S., 1921–1928"; Hoover to Harding, December 7, 1921, ibid., Box 55, "Bonus for Ex-Soldiers, 1921"; Harding to Hoover, December 10, 1921, ibid., Box 480, "President Harding, 1921 December"; John H. Williams to

Hoover, February 4, 1922, and Hoover to Williams, February 7, 1922, both in ibid., Box 55, "Bonus for Ex-Soldiers, 1922 January–February 15"; Hoover, "Address of Secretary Hoover, Metropolitan Insurance Managers Banquet, January 27, 1923," ibid., Box 615, "Unemployment, 1923–1925"; Hoover to Samuel Gompers, February 19, 1923, ibid., Box 240, "Gompers, Samuel, 1921–1964 & undated"; Haley Fiske to Hoover, March 13, 1924, and Hoover to Fiske, March 29, 1924, both in ibid., Box 672, "Unemployment: Unemployment Insurance, 1923–25 & undated"; "Favor Agreements on Unemployment," *New York Times*, June 2, 1924.

21. Press release on the Emergency Program of the President's Conference on Unemployment, issued by the Chamber of Commerce of the United States, October 1, 1921, Hoover Papers, Commerce Period, Box 621, "Unemployment: Chamber of Commerce U.S.A., 1921–1922"; Hoover to John B. Edgerton, October 1, 1921, and to motion picture theater owners, October 3, 1921, and to state and federal authorities, October 6, 1921, ibid., Box 648, "Unemployment: Hoover, Secretary, 1921–1923"; Edward Eyre Hunt to Lupton A. Wilkinson, October 3, 1921, ibid., Box 673, "Unemployment: Wilkinson, Lupton A., 1921–1922"; Otto T. Mallery to Edward Eyre Hunt, October 3, 1921, ibid., Box 649, "Unemployment: Interior Dept., Reclamation, 1921"; Christian Herter to Hugh Gibson, October 5, 1921, ibid., Box 237, "Gibson, Hugh, 1921–1928."

22. Summary of the recommendations of the Emergency Unemployment Committee established by the mayor of Milwaukee, Wisconsin, October 4, 1921, Hoover Papers, Commerce Period, Box 659, "Unemployment: Press Releases, 1920–1921"; summary of recommendations and plans of Portland, Oregon, mayor's Emergency Unemployment Committee, October 4, 1921, ibid.; summary of organization of Emergency Committee on Unemployment for the District of Columbia, October 5, 1921, ibid.; Hoover to Thompson, November 5, 1921, ibid., Box 615, "Unemployment, 1921 Nov.–Dec."

23. Minutes of the November 4 meeting of the Standing Committee of the President's Conference on Unemployment, November 7, 1921, Hoover Papers, Commerce Period, Box 618, "Unemployment: Business Cycles, 1921"; report of the Committee on Unemployment and Business Cycles of the President's Conference on Unemployment, October 12, 1921, ibid.; press release on appointment of regional directors for President's Conference on Unemployment, November 7, 1921, ibid., Box 657, "Unemployment: *New York Globe*, 1921 November"; press release on Woods's report to the Standing Committee, November 14, 1921, ibid. Young was General Electric's "Vice President in Charge of Policy" at this point; he would become chairman of the board in 1922.

24. Press release on Woods's report to the Standing Committee, November 14, 1921, Hoover Papers, Commerce Period, Box 657; "City Has 343,000 Idle, Survey Finds," *New York Times*, November 7, 1921; Fred W. Caswell to Mayor John F. Hylan, March 28, 1922; Arthur Woods to Bird S. Coler, April 14, 1922; Caswell to Woods, April 21, 1922, all in Hoover Papers, Commerce Period, Box 621, "Unemployment: Caswell, Fred W., 1922 March."

25. Memo, "Cities on Blacklist," November 21, 1921, Hoover Papers, Commerce Period, Box 665, "Unemployment: Reports, 1921 November–December"; Arthur Woods to Major O. G. Palmer, November 29, 1921, memorandum, "Trouble Book," November 29, 1921, ibid., Box 657, "Unemployment: Palmer, O.G."; model interview prepared for use by Special Agent Sherlock Herrick, undated (ca. December 23, 1921), ibid., Box 648, "Unemployment: Herrick, Sherlock, 1921"; minutes of meetings of Committee on Community, Civic and Emergency Relief Measures, December 1, 2, 5, 12, 23, 1921, and January 3, 16, 1922, ibid., Box 654, "Minutes of Col. Woods' Conferences, 1921–1922"; minutes of December 23, 1921, meeting, ibid., Box 648, "Unemployment: Herrick, Sherlock, 1921." For Woods's reaction to the meetings of the unemployed in Detroit and New York, see minutes of December 5 meeting.

26. The agents' reports can be found in Hoover Papers, Commerce Period, Boxes 616, 617, 621, 644, 648, 673, and 712.

27. N. C. Clark to Woods, February 10, 1922, Hoover Papers, Commerce Period, Box 654, "Unemployment: Memorandums, 1923–1926 & undated"; Whiting Williams to Woods,

February 13, 1922, and memo by Williams, "Unemployment—Some General Considerations," ca. March 4, 1922, both in ibid., Box 673, "Unemployment: Williams, Whiting, 1921–1922."

28. For an example of Hunt's enthusiastic evaluation of the situation, see his draft of an article on "The Washington Conference on Unemployment," written for the *International Labor Review*, January 3, 1922, in Hoover Papers, Commerce Period, Box 649, "Unemployment: Hunt, Edward Eyre, Articles by, 1921." For Hoover's personal opinion, see Hoover to Benjamin Strong, December 17, 1921, Federal Reserve Bank of New York Collection, Benjamin Strong Papers, Hoover Presidential Library, West Branch, Iowa, Box 4, "013.1; Hoover, Herbert, Oct. 22, 1917–Dec. 27, 1923"; Commerce Department press release, December 17, 1921, Hoover Papers, Commerce Period, Box 615, "Unemployment: 1921 Nov.–Dec."; Hoover to Harding, January 17, 1922, ibid., Box 480, "President Harding, 1922 January–February"; Harding to the members of the cabinet, January 26, 1922, ibid., Box 615, "Unemployment: 1922 January–March." The amount of government spending affected by Hoover's suggestion would have been far too small to reduce unemployment. At some level, he must have realized that, but his faith in his approach demanded that he regard limited "pump priming" as effective. This is not the only case where the engineer's emphasis on objective facts was warped by ideology.

29. Departmental responses to Harding's January 26, 1922, letter are found in Hoover Papers, Commerce Period, Box 658, "Unemployment: President's Letter of January 26, 1922." All of Woods's investigators reported improvement in their regions during March. See the reports in ibid., Box 617, "Unemployment: Bristol, Arthur, 1922 February–April & undated"; Box 621, "Unemployment: Caswell, Fred W., 1922 March"; Box 648, "Unemployment: Herrick, Sherlock, 1922 March & undated"; and Box 673, "Unemployment: Williams, Whiting, 1921–1922." For the departmental press release and Hoover's letter, see press statement, March 23, 1922, ibid., Box 483, "Press Releases, 1922 March–April"; Hoover to W. T. Rambo, March 27, 1922, ibid., Box 608, "Trips: First Western Trip—Correspondence—1922 March 20–28 & undated."

30. Arthur Woods to Adjutant General, U.S. Army, April 6, 1922, Hoover Papers, Commerce Period, Box 621, "Unemployment: Caswell, Fred W., 1922 April"; Woods to Secretary of the Navy Edwin Denby, April 12, 1922, ibid., Box 617, "Unemployment: Bristol, Arthur, 1922 February–April & undated"; Edward Eyre Hunt to Lupton Wilkinson, April 29, May 5, 1922, ibid., Box 673, "Unemployment: Wilkinson, Lupton A., 1921–1922"; Wilkinson to Hunt, April 28, May 2, 1922, ibid.; R. L. Foster, "Publicity Report," May 8, 1922, ibid., Box 663, "Unemployment: Publicity, Report, 1922 & undated"; Hoover to William H. Allen, May 13, 1922, ibid., Box 20, "Allen, William H., 1921–1927"; Hoover to Harding, May 20, 1922, and Harding to Hoover, May 22, 1922, ibid., Box 615, "Unemployment, 1922 April–November"; Hoover to Edward Eyre Hunt, June 5, 1922, enclosing draft, dated May 27, 1922, of letter to members of the Unemployment Conference, ibid.

31. Excerpt from a speech, November 3, 1922, Hoover Papers, Commerce Period, Box 615, "Unemployment, 1923, April–November."

32. Both senators quoted in Robert Littell, "The Unemployed and a Weather Man," *New Republic*, March 1, 1922, 22.

33. Evan B. Metcalf, "Secretary Hoover and the Emergence of Macroeconomic Management," *Business History Review* 49 (Spring 1975): 60–80; Patrick D. Reagan, "From Depression to Depression: Hooverian National Planning, 1921–1923," *Mid-America* 70 (January 1988): 35–60.

34. Wesley C. Mitchell to Edward Eyre Hunt, October 20, 1921, Hoover Papers, Commerce Period, Box 618, "Unemployment, Business Cycles, 1921"; Edward Eyre Hunt to Joseph H. Defrees, November 5, 1921, Hoover to Edgar Rickard, November 14, 18, 1921, Edgar Rickard to Christian Herter, November 16, 1921, and Hoover to Henry S. Pritchett, November 18, 1921, all in ibid., Box 615, "Unemployment, 1921 Nov.–Dec."; Edward Eyre Hunt, "Plan of Follow-Up Work of the President's Conference on Unemployment," November 2, 1921, ibid., Box 618, "Unemployment, Business Cycles, 1921." On November 30, Hoover approached the trustees of the Cabot Fund in Boston with a proposal for a

study of intermittent employment in the bituminous coal industry, for which he requested $10,000. The grant, which matched one from the coal industry, was made in January 1922, and Hoover asked E. M. Poston, president of the New York Coal Company, to chair the study. See Hoover to the Trustees of the Cabot Fund, November 30, 1921, enclosing a memorandum on "Intermittency in Bituminous Coal Mining," November 28, 1921, ibid., Box 621, "Unemployment, Cabot, Philip, 1921"; Hoover to E. M. Poston, December 31, 1921, ibid., Box 618, "Unemployment, Business Cycles, 1921"; Philip Cabot to Edward Eyre Hunt, December 5, 1921, ibid., Box 621, "Unemployment, Cabot, Philip, 1921"; Edward Eyre Hunt to Hoover, January 7, 1921, ibid. After the appointment of an official president's coal commission in the autumn of 1922, the Poston committee disbanded, and in February 1923, Hoover returned $5,681.97 of the original $10,000 to the Cabot Fund. See Hoover to Philip Cabot, February 17, 1923, ibid., Box 615, "Unemployment, 1923–1925."

35. Press releases, February 20, March 8, 1922, Hoover Papers, Commerce Period, Box 615, "Unemployment Conference, 1922 January–March"; W. I. King to Edward Eyre Hunt, February 27, 1922, ibid., Box 650, "Unemployment, King, Wilford I., 1920–1922 February"; Hoover to secretaries of various chambers of commerce, March 10, 1922, ibid., Box 665, "Unemployment, Reports, 1922–1923"; L. W. Wallace to FAES member organizations, March 29, 1922, ibid., Box 646, "Unemployment, Federated American Engineering Society, 1920 January–April"; minutes of meeting of the Business Cycle Committee, April 13, 1922, ibid., Box 618, "Unemployment, Business Cycles, 1922 January–March"; Wesley Mitchell to Edward Eyre Hunt, July 24, 1922, ibid., Box 655, "Unemployment, National Bureau of Economic Research, 1922 July–December"; same to same, October 13, 1922, ibid., Box 655, "Unemployment, Mitchell, Wesley C., 1922 October–December"; minutes of meeting of the Business Cycle Committee, December 28, 1922, ibid., Box 653, "Unemployment, Manuscripts, 1922."

36. Minutes of meeting of the Business Cycle Committee, December 28, 1922, ibid., Box 653, "Unemployment, Manuscripts, 1922." The quotation is on p. 4.

37. Minutes of meeting of the Business Cycle Committee, December 28, 1922, ibid., Box 653, "Unemployment, Manuscripts, 1922"; press report by the Business in Government League, April 1, 1923, ibid., Box 642, "Unemployment, Hunt, Edward Eyre, Articles by, 1922"; *Business Cycles and Unemployment: Report of a Committee of the President's Conference on Unemployment and an Investigation under the Auspices of the National Bureau of Economic Research* (New York: McGraw-Hill, 1923); *Business Cycles and Unemployment: Report and Recommendations of a Committee of the President's Conference on Unemployment* (Washington, DC: Government Printing Office, 1923); Edward Eyre Hunt to Lupton Wilkinson, March 5, 1923, and Wilkinson to Hunt, March 20, 1923, Hoover Papers, Commerce Period, Box 673, "Unemployment, Wilkinson, Lupton A., 1921–1922."

38. Hoover to Adolph Miller, April 3, 1923, Hoover Papers, Commerce Period, Box 618, "Unemployment, Business Cycles, 1923 April"; drafts of a bill to establish a Federal Unemployment Stabilization Board are in ibid., Box 660, "Unemployment, Public Works—Bills, 1921–1923 & undated"; Hoover's "Introduction" to Lionel D. Edie, ed., *The Stabilization of Business* (New York: Macmillan, 1923), v; "An Open Letter to Mr. Hoover," *New Republic*, May 23, 1923, 334.

39. Hoover to Robert Brookings, May 9, 1923, Hoover Papers, Commerce Period, Box 666, "Unemployment, Seasonal Stabilization, 1923–1924"; Hoover to Ernest T. Trigg, May 28, 1929, ibid., Box 607, "Trigg, Ernest T., 1923–1925."

40. Hoover to Elihu Root, October 9, 1923, Hoover Papers, Commerce Period, Box 529, "Root, Elihu, 1922–1927"; Edward Eyre Hunt to the chairman and members of the Committee on Seasonal Operation in the Construction Industries, March 5, 1924, ibid., Box 638, "Unemployment, Committee on Seasonal Operation in the Construction Industries, 1923–1924"; Hoover to Samuel Gompers, March 27, 1924, ibid., Box 666, "Unemployment, Seasonal Stabilization, 1923–1924"; U.S. Department of Commerce, Elimination of Waste Series, *Seasonal Operation in the Construction Industries: Summary of Report and Recommendations of a Committee of the President's Conference on Unemployment* (Washington, DC: Government Printing Office, 1924).

41. Hoover, foreword to *Seasonal Operation in the Construction Industries*, vii. The report overstated the feasibility of year-round operation in colder parts of the country. Although it was technically possible to work year-round with the aid of gas or electric heaters, such equipment was not available everywhere, and its use increased building costs substantially.
42. Hoover to Arthur Woods, September 26, 1924, Hoover Papers, Commerce Period, Box 715, "Woods, Col. and Mrs. Arthur, 1921–1928"; Edward Eyre Hunt to Hoover, October 28, 1924, and Hoover to Woods, October 28, 1924, and January 13, 1925, all in ibid., Box 617, "Unemployment, Bases of Agreement in Industrial Disputes, 1924–1925"; Hoover to Beardsley Ruml, October 31, 1924, ibid., Box 287, "Hunt, Edward Eyre, 1923–1925"; Hoover to Prof. Allen B. Forsberg, December 1, 1925, ibid., Box 615, "Unemployment, 1923–1925."
43. Edward Eyre Hunt to Hoover, October 28, 1924, and Hoover to Arthur Woods, October 28, 1924, both in Hoover Papers, Commerce Period, Box 617, "Unemployment, Bases of Agreement in Industrial Disputes, 1924–1925."
44. Edward Eyre Hunt to Hoover, September 15, 1927, and Hoover to E. P. Keppel, October 26, 1927, both in Hoover Papers, Commerce Period, Box 618, "Unemployment, Business Cycles, 1924–1928"; Reagan, "From Depression to Depression," 53–57. For more detailed discussion of the 1929 study, see Chapter 19 in this volume.
45. "Mr. Hoover's Misstatements," *The Nation*, October 3, 1928, 310; Campagna, *U.S. National Economic Policy*, 54–58.
46. Carolyn Grin, "The Unemployment Conference of 1921: An Experiment in National Cooperative Planning," in Himmelberg, ed., *Business-Government Cooperation*, 107.
47. Robert Zieger, "Herbert Hoover, the Wage-Earner, and the 'New Economic System,' 1919–29," in *Herbert Hoover as Secretary of Commerce, 1921–1928: Studies in New Era Thought and Practice*, ed. Ellis W. Hawley (Iowa City: University of Iowa Press, 1981), 94; Ellis W. Hawley, "Herbert Hoover and Economic Stabilization, 1921–22," in ibid., 58–61.

Chapter 9

1. *ARA Bulletin*, 2nd ser., 2, no. 16 (September 1, 1921): 2. A group of prominent Russians led by Gorky asked Lenin for permission to make the appeal. A week after sending his letter, Gorky and seventy-three others formed the All-Russian Public Committee to Aid the Hungry (Pomgol). It made appeals at home and abroad for donations to fight the famine. See Orlando Figes, *A People's Tragedy: A History of the Russian Revolution* (New York: Viking, 1996), 779.
2. Benjamin M. Weissman, *Herbert Hoover and Famine Relief to Soviet Russia, 1921–23* (Stanford, CA: Hoover Institution Press, 1974), 1–3; Figes, *People's Tragedy*, 752–64; Orlando Figes, *Peasant Russia, Civil War: The Volga Countryside in Revolution (1917–1921)* (Oxford, UK: Clarendon, 1989), 321–53.
3. Bertrand M. Patenaude, *The Big Show in Bololand: The American Relief Expedition to Soviet Russia in the Famine of 1921* (Stanford, CA: Stanford University Press, 2002), 7–14; Lucy Evelyn Wight to Lou Henry Hoover, undated, Lou Henry Hoover Papers, Hoover Presidential Library, West Branch, Iowa, Box 1, "Personal Correspondence, 1872–1920, Allan (Lucy) Evelyn Wight (Mrs. Mansfield), 1898–1917 & undated."
4. Press release, March 21, 1921, Herbert Hoover Papers, Commerce Period, Hoover Presidential Library, West Branch, Iowa, Box 483, "Press Releases, 1921"; press release, March 25, 1921, James P. Goodrich Papers, Hoover Presidential Library, West Branch, Iowa, Box 25, "Russia: Trade Relations, 1921–23." For the Nansen relief proposal, see Chapter 1 in this volume. Inasmuch as the czarist government had never really guaranteed the right of private property and the sanctity of contract either, Hoover's demands were not entirely reasonable.
5. Hoover to editor, *New York Herald* ("Confidential"), July 27, 1921, Hoover Papers, Commerce Period, Box 444, "Newspapers and Magazines, *New York Herald*, 1921–1926"; Hoover to Gorky, July 23, 1921, *ARA Bulletin* (September 1, 1921): 3–4; "Russia Must Free Captives to Get Aid," *New York Times*, July 25, 1921. Hoover's conditions infuriated Lenin,

but he had no choice other than to swallow his pride and accept them. Living up to them was a different matter, as the ARA would soon discover. Figes, *A People's Tragedy*, 779–80.

6. Christian Herter to Nelson Fell, August 12, 1921, Hoover Papers, Commerce Period, Box 261, "Herter, Christian A., 1921." George Kennan argued, in *Russia and the West under Lenin and Stalin* (Boston: Little, Brown, 1960), 180, that the Soviet government was "importantly aided not just in its economic undertakings, but in its political prestige and capacity for survival" by Hoover's aid program. Hoover might have responded, however, that the myth of "capitalist encirclement" that justified "the maintenance of dictatorial authority" in the USSR was to some extent undermined by the aid program, as Kennan noted in *American Diplomacy, 1900–1950* (Chicago: University of Chicago Press, 1951), 112–13.

7. Thomas T. C. Gregory to Hoover, April 22, June 4, 1919, Thomas T. C. Gregory Papers, Hoover Institution Archives, Stanford, California, Box 1, "Correspondence: Hoover, Herbert"; Gregory to Alonzo Taylor, August 3, 1919, ibid.; Hoover to Robert Lansing, July 1, 1919, Herbert Hoover Subject Collection, Hoover Institution Archives, Stanford, California, Box 318, "Correspondence: Lansing, Robert M."; David Burner, *Herbert Hoover: A Public Life* (New York: Knopf, 1979), 121–24; Herbert Hoover, *Memoirs: Years of Adventure, 1874–1920* (New York: Macmillan, 1951), 398–400 (hereafter, *Memoirs* 1); Rudolf L. Tökés, *Béla Kun and the Hungarian Soviet Republic: The Origins and Role of the Communist Party of Hungary in the Revolutions of 1918–1919* (New York: Praeger, 1967), 192–204; György Borsányi, *The Life of a Communist Revolutionary, Béla Kun*, trans. Mario D. Fenyo (Highland Lakes, NJ: Atlantic Research and Publications, 1993), 174–206.

8. Burner, *Herbert Hoover*, 124–25; Hoover, *Memoirs* 1, 400–404.

9. It is worth noting that two standard works on this period of Hungarian history, Tökés's *Béla Kun*, and Borsányi's *Life of a Communist Revolutionary*, do not even mention a possible American role in the overthrow of the Kun government.

10. T. T. C. Gregory, "Overthrowing a Red Regime," *The World's Work* 42 (June 1921): 153–61; "America and Russia," *New Republic*, August 24, 1921: 342; Unsigned, untitled editorial note on American aid to Russia, *Nation*, August 24, 1921, 187; Hoover to Herbert Croly, September 5, 1921, and Croly to Hoover, October 5, 1921, Hoover Papers, Commerce Period, Box 30, "American Relief Administration, Russia, Miscellaneous, 1921."

11. Hoover to ex-president Ador of Switzerland, August 9, 1921, *ARA Bulletin* (September 1, 1921): 5–7; press release announcing the formation of the European Relief Council (made up of all American private charitable organizations proposing relief to Russia), August 24, 1921, Hoover Papers, Commerce Period, Box 483, "Press Releases, 1921"; Harding to Hoover, August 12, 1921, and Hoover to Walter Lyman Brown, August 12, 1921, both in ibid., Box 534, "Russia: General, 1921 July–August." Hoover sent a more diplomatically phrased version of this message directly to the International Red Cross. See Hoover to President Ador, August 20, 1921, ibid., Box 154, "Conferences, Genoa, 1922, 1921–1922, January."

12. George H. Nash, *The Life of Herbert Hoover: The Humanitarian, 1914–1917* (New York: Norton, 1988), 369.

13. Hoover spelled out the basic outlines of the agreement in a long cable to Brown, August 16, 1921, Hoover Papers, Commerce Period, Box 534, "Russia: General, 1921 July–August." For the Riga agreement, see *ARA Bulletin*, 2nd ser., 2, no. 17 (October 1, 1921): 3–7.

14. *ARA Bulletin*, 2nd ser., 2, no. 17 (October 1, 1921): 8–9.

15. Patenaude, *Big Show in Bololand*, 60–63.

16. Hoover to William N. Haskell, February 16, 1922, Hoover Papers, Commerce Period, Box 255, "Haskell, William N., 1921–1922"; James Goodrich to Walter L. Brown, March 6, 1922, James P. Goodrich Papers, Box 16, "American Relief Administration-Brown, Walter Lyman, 1921–22"; Patenaude, *Big Show in Bololand*, 129–30; Weissman, *Hoover and Famine Relief*, 84.

17. Weissman, *Hoover and Famine Relief*, 85–88.

18. Kellogg, press release, ca. October 15, 1921, Hoover Papers, Commerce Period, Box 355, "Kellogg, Dr. Vernon, 1924–1928 & undated"; talk Given by Dr. Kellogg, ARA Office, October 22, 1921, ibid., Box 355, "Kellogg, Vernon, 1921"; ARA Press Release, October 24, 1921, ibid., Box 355, "Kellogg, Vernon, 1922–23."

19. For Goodrich's reports from his two-week visit to Russia, see James P. Goodrich Papers, Box 24, "Russia-Reports by James P. Goodrich, 1921."
20. William Haskell to Hoover, November 5, 1921, Hoover Papers, Commerce Period, Box 534, "Russia: General, 1921, September–November"; description of Ukrainian famine by Johann Rempel, quoted in David G. Rempel with Cornelia Rempel Carlson, *A Mennonite Family in Tsarist Russia and the Soviet Union, 1789–1823* (Toronto: University of Toronto Press, 2002), 253.
21. Hoover apparently believed that Soviet policies were principally responsible for the situation, but most ARA men in Russia regarded natural causes as primary. See, Patenaude, *Big Show in Bololand*, 127.
22. Hoover to Rep. Julius Kahn, October 15, 1921, Hoover Papers, Commerce Papers, Box 30, "American Relief Administration, Russia, Miscellaneous, 1921"; *ARA Bulletin*, 2nd ser., 2, no. 18 (November 1, 1921): 3–4; Christian Herter to George R. Montgomery, November 10, 1921, Hoover Papers, Commerce Period, Box 35, "Armenia, 1921–1928"; statement given to the president on Russian relief, December 3, 1921, ibid., Box 480, "Notes, Memoranda, Incorporated into Harding's speech of Dec. 6, 1921, 1921–1923 & undated"; James Goodrich to Walter Lyman Brown, December 5, 1921, James P. Goodrich Papers, Box 16, "Russia-American Relief Administration, Brown, Walter Lyman, 1921–22"; Vernon Kellogg to George Barr Baker, December 5, 1921, Hoover Papers, Commerce Period, Box 355, "Kellogg, Vernon, 1921"; from the president's message to Congress, December 6, 1921, *ARA Bulletin*, 2nd ser., 2, no. 20 (January 1922): 1.
23. For Hoover's testimony on December 13, 1921, see *Russian Relief: Hearings before the Committee on Foreign Affairs, House of Representatives, 67th Cong., 2d sess., on HR 9459 and HR 9548* (Washington, DC: Government Printing Office, 1921), 39; *ARA Bulletin*, 2nd ser., 2, no. 20 (January 1922): 2–3. Hoover always felt a special duty to relieve children's suffering. I think his orphan childhood and Quaker background helped shape his outlook, but the question is not one that can be answered decisively. In this case, the fact that the relief program would contribute to reducing the agricultural surplus obviously played a role as well.
24. Press release, "Russian Relief," December 22, 1921, Hoover Papers, Commerce Period, Box 483, "Press Releases, 1921." For Hoover's December 20, 1921, draft of the release, with his handwritten corrections, see ibid., Box 534, "Russia-General, 1921 December."
25. American Relief Administration, "Annual Report of the Executive Committee," April 4, 1923, Hoover Papers, Commerce Period, Box 194, "European Relief, Charitable Donations for 1921–1923," p. 10; Hoover to President Harding, December 16, 1922, ibid., Box 483, "Press Releases, 1922 September–December"; Norman E. Saul, *Friends or Foes? The United States and Soviet Russia, 1921–1941* (Lawrence: University Press of Kansas, 2006), 64–65; Benjamin D. Rhodes, *United States Foreign Policy in the Interwar Period, 1918–1941: The Golden Age of American Diplomatic and Military Complacency* (Westport, CT: Praeger, 2001), 53. The first full reports on famine conditions in the Ukraine were received by the ARA in January 1922. See Lincoln Hutchinson, "Observations in the Ukraine," January 18, 1922, *ARA Bulletin*, 2nd ser., 2, no. 22 (March 1922): 7–13; William R. Grove, "Relief Operations in the Ukraine," *ARA Bulletin*, 2nd ser., 4, no. 31 (December 1922): 13–29. The ARA estimated the total Russian contribution to the relief program at $13,900,850. See "Russian Contributions to Relief in Cooperation with A.R.A., October 1, 1922 to End of Operations," ca. June 30, 1923, Hoover Papers, Commerce Papers, Box 31, "American Relief Administration-Russia, Russian Contributions to Relief in Cooperation with ARA-October 1, 1922 to End of Operation."
26. ARA, "Annual Report of the Executive Committee," April 4, 1923, pp. 8, 9, 12.
27. Ibid., 1; Figes, *A People's Tragedy*, 780.
28. Hoover, "American Relations to Russia: Summary of an address before the International Chamber of Commerce," May 18, 1922, Hoover Papers, Commerce Period, Box 188, "Economic Situation in U.S., 1921–1924."
29. James Goodrich to Hoover, January 30, 1923, and Hoover to Goodrich, February 1, 1923, Hoover Papers, Commerce Period, Box 240, "Goodrich, James P., 1921–1924"; Benjamin D. Rhodes, *James P. Goodrich, Indiana's "Governor Strangelove": A Republican's Infatuation with*

Soviet Russia (Selinsgrove, PA: Susquehanna University Press, 1996), 91–94, 125–26; Saul, *Friends or Foes?* 38–39.

30. Figes, *A People's Tragedy*, 539; "Hoover and Russian Economics," *New Republic*, May 31, 1922, 4–5; Senator Joseph I. France to Hoover, February 4, 1923, and Hoover to France, February 10, 1923, Hoover Papers, Commerce Period, Box 30, "American Relief Administration, Russia, Misc, 1922–1927 & undated"; Hoover to Warren Harding, June 2, 1922, ibid., Box 480, "President Harding, 1922 June–July"; Hoover to Julius Barnes, June 2, 1922, ibid., Box 45, "Barnes, Julius, 1922"; George K. Hyslop to Senator William Calder, ibid., Box 544, "Senate: Calder, William M., 1922"; Hoover to Wilbur K. Thomas, June 15, 1922, ibid., Box 230, "*The Freeman*, 1921–1922"; Hoover to James P. Goodrich, July 20, 1922, ibid., Box 240, "Goodrich, James P., 1921–1924"; Hoover to Edwin P. Shattuck, June 9, 1922; Edward Flesh to Hoover, June 16, 1922; Edwin Shattuck to Hoover, June 16, 1922 (two letters); Hoover to Harding, June 17, 1922, all in ibid., Box 674, "United States Grain Corporation, 1921–1922"; Hoover submitted a report on the role of the Grain Corporation in the relief program to President Harding on July 10, 1922. See Hoover to Harding, July 10, 1922, ibid., Box 480, "President Harding, 1922 June–July." For Russian relief as a political liability, see Alonzo Taylor to Hoover, July 20, 1922, ibid., Box 596, "Taylor, Alonzo E., 1922." ARA plans for 1922 to 1923 are explained in some detail in James Goodrich to "Mr. Hodge," September 10, 1922, James P. Goodrich Papers, Box 15, "Russia-Addresses, Articles, Statements, Correspondence, 1921–23," and Lewis Strauss to Col. William R. Grove, September 12, 1922, Lewis Strauss Papers, Hoover Presidential Library, West Branch, Iowa, Name and Subject File I: Accretions, Box 35E, "Joint Distribution Comm: Russian Relief Program, Grove, William R., 1922." Hoover Presidential Library, West Branch, Iowa. The most recent study of Soviet-American relations in this period concludes that Hoover's attitude toward Russia, while "enigmatic," was not influenced by personal economic interests. See Saul, *Friends or Foes?* 102–3.

31. Julius Barnes to Edgar Rickard, August 25; 1922, Perrin Galpin to Rickard, September 14, 1922; and Edgar Rickard to Hoover, September 26, 1922, all in Hoover Papers, Commerce Period, Box 39, "Austria, 1922"; Hugh Gibson to Christian Herter, October 30, 1922, ibid., Box 237, "Gibson, Hugh, 1921–1928"; Leopold Kotnowsky to Hoover, October 29, 1922; Hoover to Kotnowsky, December 14, 1922; and Hugh Gibson to Secretary of State Charles Evans Hughes, October 30, 1922, all in ibid., Box 471, "Poland, 1922 July–December." Hoover, unmoved by public honors, left it to Christian Herter to draft a four-line acknowledgment of the Polish recognition.

32. Christian Herter to William Mullendore, November 15, 1922, Hoover Papers, Commerce Period, Box 421, "Mullendore, William C., 1922 Jan.–Nov. 15"; Herter to Mullendore, November 18, 1922, ibid., Box 216, "Foreign Debts, H. H. Speeches, 1922 November–December."

33. "Minutes of a Meeting at Secretary Hoover's House," January 23, 1923, and Hoover to Allen T. Burns, January 29, 1923, Hoover Papers, Commerce Period, Box 30, "American Relief Administration, Russia, Misc, 1922–1927 & undated"; press release, March 8, 1923, ibid., Box 483, "Press Releases, 1923 January–July." The quotations come from the letter to Burns. The fact that the ARA controlled the distribution of food within Russia made possible this policy. Had the relief gone directly to the Russian government, there would have been no way to prevent it from being used to feed adults.

34. Public letter from Hoover to C. V. Hibbard, March 23, 1923, Hoover Papers, Commerce Period, Box 483, "Press Releases, 1923 January–July"; "Extract from President Harding's Speech of July 31, 1923," July 31, 1923, ibid., Box 30, "American Relief Administration-Russia, Hoover's Letters to President Harding, February 9, July 10, December 18, 1922." William C. Garner, ARA chief of communications in Russia, provided a more optimistic estimate of the situation after a trip through the famine area along the Volga. See Garner to Hoover, May 24, 1923, ibid., Box 31, "American Relief Administration-Russia, News Releases, 1921–1923." A handwritten note attached to another copy of Garner's report in Box 30, "American Relief Administration, Russia, Misc, 1922–1927 & undated," says "*Not given to Press.*" An even more optimistic assessment, including the assertion that

"Communism is dead and abandoned and Russia is on the road to recovery," was included in William Haskell's final report to Hoover, August 27, 1923, ibid., Box 483, "Press Releases, 1923 August–December."

35. Hoover to President Coolidge, October 23, 1924, ibid., Box 477, "President Coolidge, 1924 October–November."

36. Hoover, *Memoirs* 1, 321–22; Patenaude, *Big Show in Bololand*, 734; Lynne Viola, *The Best Sons of the Fatherland: Workers in the Vanguard of Soviet Collectivization* (New York: Oxford University Press, 1987), 46.

Chapter 10

1. Selection from Albert G. Love and Charles B. Davenport, *Physical Examination of the First Million Draft Recruits: Methods and Results*, U.S. War Department, Office of the Surgeon General (Washington, DC, 1919), and from Emma Duke, *Infant Mortality: Results of a Field Study in Johnstown, Pa.*, United States Children's Bureau Pub. No. 9 (Washington, DC, 1915), both in Robert Bremner, ed., *Children and Youth in America: A Documentary History* (Cambridge, MA: Harvard University Press, 1971), vol. 2, parts 1–6, p. 99, and parts 7–8, pp. 967–68; S. Josephine Baker, *Child Hygiene* (New York: Harper & Bros., 1925), 8–10; Annette K. Vance Dorey, *Better Baby Contests: The Scientific Quest for Perfect Childhood Health in the Early Twentieth Century* (Jefferson, NC: McFarland, 1999), 14–15.

2. Only about 400,000 children were under institutional care across the United States in 1923. See Department of Commerce, Bureau of the Census, *Children Under Institutional Care, 1923: Statistics of Dependent, Neglected, and Delinquent Children in Institutions and under the Supervision of Other Agencies for the Care of Children, with a Section on Adults in Certain Types of Institutions* (Washington, DC: Government Printing Office, 1927), Table 1, p. 14; Lela B. Costin, *Two Sisters for Social Justice: A Biography of Grace and Edith Abbott* (Urbana: University of Illinois Press, 1983), 125–45; Grace Abbott, "Public Protection for Children" (1924), in *The Grace Abbott Reader*, ed. John Sorensen and Judith Sealander (Lincoln: University of Nebraska Press, 2008), 43-52; Baker, Child Hygiene, 14–18, 31–39. On the gradual acceptance of government responsibility for public health, see Barbara Gutmann Rosenkrantz, *Public Health and the State: Changing Views in Massachusetts, 1842–1936* (Cambridge, MA: Harvard University Press, 1972). Congress passed the Sheppard-Towner Act in 1921 but appropriated so little money to implement it that most participating counties received only a few hundred dollars a year. Nevertheless, the program managed to hire about 750 nurses a year, who traveled around the countryside, meeting with mothers and offering child examinations and advice. Many physicians, including the American Medical Association, opposed Sheppard-Towner because they saw the nurses' activities as encroaching on their areas. Other groups objected to federal intervention in what were regarded as local matters. When the act came up for reauthorization in 1929, President Hoover offered no support, and it failed. See Judith Sealander, *The Failed Century of the Child: Governing America's Young in the Twentieth Century* (Cambridge, UK: Cambridge University Press, 2003), 226–31.

3. Richard A. Bolt to Hoover, July 26, 1920; Borden S. Veeder to Hoover, August 6, 1920; Hoover to Veeder, September 15, 1920, all in American Child Health Association Papers (hereafter, "ACHA Papers"), Hoover Presidential Library, West Branch, Iowa, Box 27, "Personnel-Hoover, Herbert-American Child Hygiene Association." Through a mix-up, Hoover accepted an invitation from the St. Louis Republican organization to address a public meeting while he was in the city. Veeder feared that this would give the Child Hygiene meeting a partisan cast, but the concern seems to have been unwarranted.

4. Hoover, "A Program for American Children: An Address Delivered before the American Child Hygiene Association at St. Louis on October 11, 1920," *AR A Bulletin*, 2nd ser., 1, no. 3 (November 1, 1920): 1. Despite all the work of the child health movement during the 1920s and 1930s, more than one in three draftees were again rejected because of physical deficiencies during World War II. See Sealander, *The Failed Century of the Child*, 302.

5. Hoover, "A Program for American Children," 2–6.

6. Hoover to Charles Mitchell, May 26, 1921, Hoover Papers, Commerce Period, Hoover Presidential Library, West Branch, Iowa, Box 448, "Newspapers and Magazines, Washington (DC) *Herald*, 1921–1926 & undated"; James N. Giglio, "Voluntarism and Public Policy between World War I and the New Deal: Herbert Hoover and the American Child Health Association," *Presidential Studies Quarterly* 13 (Summer 1983): 430–31.

7. Philip Van Ingen to Hoover, October 11, 1920; Henry L. K. Shaw to Hoover, October 16, 1920; Hoover to Van Ingen, October 19, 1920; "Minutes of the Annual Meetings of the Executive Committee and Board of Directors of the American Child Hygiene Association, in Connection with the Eleventh Annual Meeting, St. Louis, Mo., October 11–13, 1920," all in ACHA Papers, Box 27, "Personnel: Hoover, Herbert-American Child Hygiene Association"; Baker, *Child Hygiene*, 52–54. Dr. Baker reported that a 1920 list of local child health organizations published by the Children's Bureau included over six hundred organizations.

8. "American Child Hygiene Association: Report of the Director General, January 23, 1921–May 7, 1921," ACHA Papers, Box 27, "Personnel: Hoover, Herbert-American Child Hygiene Association."

9. Judge Ben Lindsay to Hoover, June 25, 1921; Judge Lindsay to Sophie Irene Loeb, June 27, 1921; Loeb to Hoover, July 1, 1921; and Loeb to Hoover, October 29, 1921, all in ACHA Papers, Box 6, "Conferences: National Child Welfare Conference, 1921–1923"; Philip Van Ingen to the members of the Executive Committee, May 16, 1921; Van Ingen to Clarence Stetson, November 29, 1921; Hoover to the Laura Spelman Rockefeller Fund, November 20, 1921; Hoover to Barry C. Smith at the Commonwealth Fund, November 29, 1921; W. S. Richardson of the Rockefeller Fund to Hoover, December 2, 1921; Barry Smith to Hoover, December 2, 1921; and Philip Van Ingen to Hoover, December 8, 1921, all in ibid., Box 1, "American Child Hygiene Association, 1921 November–December."

10. Gertrude B. Knipp to Clarence Stetson, January 9, 1921; Richard A. Bolt to Hoover (two memorandums), March 25, 1922; and "Minutes of Meeting of the Executive Committee, Washington, D.C., May 4, 1922," all in ACHA Papers, Box 1, "American Child Hygiene Association, 1922 January–June."

11. Philip Van Ingen to Hoover, May 23, 1922; Hoover to the members of the Board of Directors of the American Child Hygiene Association, June 1, 1922; informal minutes of a meeting of the special committee of the American Child Hygiene Association to consider consolidation with the Child Health Organization of America, June 12, 1922; Van Ingen to William Mullendore, June 26, 1922; and "Minutes of Special Meeting of Board of Directors [of American Child Hygiene Association], Washington, D.C., June 30, 1922," all in ACHA Papers, Box 1, "American Child Hygiene Association, 1922 January–June"; Richard A. Bolt to the members of the American Child Hygiene Association, September 11, 1922, ibid., "American Child Health Association, 1922–1923"; "Minutes of the Amalgamation Committee Meeting, Held at the Office of the Child Health Organization, Tuesday, October 24, 1922, at 2 P.M.," Hoover Papers, Commerce Period, Box 22, "American Child Health (Hygiene) Assoc., Miscellaneous, 1921"; press release, "Hoover Announces Great Child Health Program," October 11, 1922, ACHA Papers, Box 2, "American Child Hygiene Association, 1922 July–December"; Commerce Department press release, "American Child Hygiene Association," October 13, 1922, Hoover Papers, Commerce Period, Box 483, "Press Releases, 1922 September–December."

12. "National Conference of Social Work: Address of Herbert Hoover at Providence, R.I.," June 27, 1922, ACHA Papers, Box 4, "Child Labor, 1922–27."

13. "Presidential Address by Honorable Herbert Hoover, American Child Hygiene Association Thirteenth Annual Meeting, Washington, D.C., Thursday evening, October 12, 1922," and American Child Hygiene Association press release, October 13, 1922, both in ACHA Papers, Box 2, "American Child Hygiene Association, 1922 July–December."

14. Hoover to Edgar Rickard, October 28, 1922; Hoover statement to press, October 28, 1922; and Hoover to Raymond Fosdick, October 31, 1922, all in ACHA Papers, Box 1, "American Child Health Association, 1922–1923"; Hoover to George Barr Baker, October 31, 1922, Hoover Papers, Commerce Period, Box 42, "Baker, George Barr, 1922–1923"; memo for Edgar Rickard by Frank C. Page, November 24, 1922, ACHA Papers, Box 1,

"Amalgamation of Child Health Organization to form A.C.H.A., 1919–1923 & undated." A handwritten note on the memo says, "The chief has put responsibility of making this thing go on the ARA."

15. George Barr Baker to Florence Wardwell, December 6, 1922, ACHA Papers, Box 1, "Amalgamation of Child Health Organization to form ACHA, 1919–1923 & undated."

16. George Barr Baker to Christian Herter, December 1, 1922, enclosing memorandum, November 28, 1922, on the relationship between the ARA and the ACHA; and Walter Lyman Brown to Hoover, December 1, 1922, both in ACHA Papers, Box 1, "American Child Health Association, 1922–1923."

17. Hoover to Philip Van Ingen, December 12, 1922, ACHA Papers, Box 1, "American Child Health Association, 1922–1923"; press release, "American Child Health Association," ca. December 16, 1922, with handwritten note: "This was written by Dr. Van Ingen for Jany. Health Magazine & held out at request of Mr. Hoover," "Amalgamation of Child Health Organization to form A.C.H.A., 1919–1923 & undated"; and (George Barr Baker?) memorandum, "American Child Health Association," December 27, 1922, all in ibid., Box 22, "Memoranda, 1922–1923."

18. "Memorandum Covering Meeting of G. B. Baker with Dr. Holt, Dr. Van Ingen, Mr. Dinwiddie and Miss Jean at the residence of Dr. Holt from 5:30 to 7 P.M. Wednesday, December 27th," December 28, 1922, ACHA Papers, Box 1, "American Child Health Association, 1922–1923."

19. Edgar Rickard to Christian A. Herter, January 10, 1923, ACHA Papers, Box 1, "Amalgamation of Child Health Organization to form A.C.H.A., 1919–1923."

20. Frank C. Page to Christian A. Herter, January 17, 1923, ACHA Papers, Box 1, "Amalgamation of Child Health Organization to form A.C.H.A., 1919–1923." Marie Meloney, editor of *The Delineator* and organizer of the Better Homes in America organization, worked quietly to reconcile the social work professionals to the new state of affairs. See Marie Meloney to George Barr Baker, January 30, 1923, George Barr Baker Papers, Hoover Institution Archives, Stanford, California, Box 5, "Meloney, Mrs. William Brown."

21. Lupton Wilkinson to Christian Herter, February 26, 1923, enclosing Baker's "Memorandum to Mr. Hoover," February 26, 1923, ACHA Papers, Box 1, "American Child Health Association, 1922–1923."

22. Memorandum by George Barr Baker, March 12, 1923, ACHA Papers, Box 1, "Amalgamation of Child Health Organization to form A.C.H.A., 1919–1923 & undated"; unsigned "Memorandum to Mr. Rickard" (describing Hoover's meeting with the ACHA), April 9, 1923; and unsigned memo, "Two Organization Principles," April 14, 1923, both in ibid., Box 28, "Policy, Miscellaneous"; Edgar Rickard to Edward Flesh and George Barr Baker, April 5, 1923, Herbert Hoover Subject Collection, Hoover Institution Archives, Stanford, California, Box 324, "Correspondence: Rickard, Edgar, 1916–24."

23. Edgar Rickard to Christian Herter, March 17, 1923; undated statement of "American Child Health Welfare Donations, Inception, March 8th, 1923, to April 9th, 1923"; and Edgar Rickard to L. Emmett Holt, enclosing draft of letter to Carnegie Corporation, February 6, 1923, all in ACHA Papers, Box 3, "Appeals-Results"; Frank Page, memorandum, May 31, 1923, ibid., Box 22, "Memoranda, 1922–1923." In October, Hoover had hoped for a major Commonwealth Fund grant for the new organization, but surviving documents do not reveal the precise source of the late-spring infusion of money that supported the proposed budget.

24. Harriet L. Leete to Courtenay Dinwiddie, May 15, 1923, ACHA Papers, Box 28, "Personnel: Leete, Harriet L., 1923."

25. Christian Herter to Edgar Rickard, May 25, 1923; Amy Pryor Tapping to Hoover, June 3, 1923; Herter to Frank Page, June 6, 1923; Page to Herter, November 22, 1923; Courtenay Dinwiddie to Hoover, June 23, 1923; Tapping to Hoover, November 4, 1924; Rickard to Hoover, January 8, 1925; and Hoover to Tapping, January 10, 1925, all in ACHA Papers, Box 28, "Personnel: Tapping, Miss Amy, 1923–1931"; Edgar Rickard to Frank Page, June 15, 1923, Hoover Subject Collection, Box 324, "Correspondence: Rickard, Edgar."

26. Sally Lucas Jean to the Special Committee appointed to consider the work of the Health Education Division of the American Child Health Association, April 28, 1923; "Minutes of meeting of the Special Committee on Organization Problems of the Committee on Administration, held at 4 o'clock on May 2, 1923, at Mrs. Meloney's office"; and Frank Page to Edgar Rickard, May 31, 1923, all in ACHA Papers, Box 28, "Personnel: Jean, Sally Lucas, 1918–1924."

27. Frank Page to William Mullendore, June 8, 1923; Edgar Rickard to Christian Herter, June 8, 1923; and memorandum from Edgar Rickard to E. M. Flesh, Frank Page, and George Barr Baker, June 13, 1923; all in ACHA Papers, Box 12, "Financial: E. M. Flesh Files-Hoover, Herbert, 1923–1926"; "Minutes of a special meeting of the Executive Committee of the American Child Health Association, held at 3 p.m., Thursday, June 14, 1923, Room 1624 Penn Terminal Building, New York City, called by the President at the request of the Health Education Committee," ibid., Box 5, "Committee: Executive, Meetings of, 1923–1924." An unwritten understanding dating from the time of the merger of the two organizations that Miss Jean's division would have a separate budget limited what could be done. See Edgar Rickard to Frank Page, May 18, 1923, Hoover Subject Collection, Box 324, "Correspondence: Rickard, Edgar."

28. Edgar Rickard to Frank Page, May 18, 1923, Hoover Subject Collection, Box 324, "Correspondence: Rickard, Edgar." The paucity of local child welfare agencies and organizations across the country suggests that Page was probably right. See Department of Commerce, Bureau of Census, *Children under Institutional Care*, 14.

29. Edgar Rickard to Hoover, July 26, 1923, ACHA Papers, Box 28, "Personnel: Rickard, Edgar, 1924–1925"; Hoover to Courtenay Dinwiddie, September 14, 1923, ibid., Box 1, "American Child Health Association, 1922–1923."

30. Edgar Rickard to Christian Herter, August 6, 1923; memorandum from Rickard to Hoover, August 6 and September 7, 1923; Hoover to Rickard, September 1, 1923; and Certificate of Incorporation of ARA Children's Fund, Inc., September 17, 1923, all in ACHA Papers, Box 2, "American Relief Administration Children's Funds, 1923." The degree of Hoover's personal control over the new organization is suggested by a letter to Christian Herter from Edward M. Flesh, Children's Fund comptroller, February 19, 1924, in ibid., Box 2, "American Relief Administration Children's Fund, 1924–1928": "The report of the Treasurer . . . shows that funds turned over by the old American Relief Administration have been invested . . . and that the appropriation out of income to the American CHILD HEALTH Association has been cared for. We do not intend to circulate the financial report among the members nor will the report be printed; it will only be held in this office as a matter of record."

31. Edward M. Flesh to Hoover, December 3, 1924, ACHA Papers, Box 2, "American Relief Administration Children's Funds, 1924–1928."

32. Memorandum of "Procedure agreed upon in conference between Colonel Beeuwkes of the American Relief Administration and Dr. George T. Palmer, Dr. S. J. Crumbine and Mr. Courtenay Dinwiddie of the American Child Health Association . . . ," ca. October 3, 1923, ACHA Papers, Box 46, "Survey of Cities, 1923–1926"; Frank Page memorandum for Edgar Rickard, November 19 and 20, 1923, ibid., Box 22, "Memoranda, 1922–1923."

33. Frank Page memorandum for Edgar Rickard, November 19, 1923, ACHA Papers, Box 22, "Memoranda, 1922–1923."

34. Hoover, "The Protection of American Child Health: Address before the First Annual Session of the American Child Health Association, Detroit, Michigan," October 15, 1923, ACHA Papers, Box 21, "Meetings: Annual-Chief's Speech, October 15, 1923." I have altered the order of the quoted passages.

35. Frank Page memorandum for Edgar Rickard, November 19, 1923; Edgar Rickard to Page, November 24, 1923; memorandum of luncheon meeting at the University Club, December 1, 1923; and Frank Page (?) memorandum, "Regarding the American Child Health Association," December 13, 1923, all in ACHA Papers, Box 22, "Memoranda, 1922–1923"; Giglio, "Voluntarism and Public Policy," 436.

36. Henry Beeuwkes to Christian Herter, November 20, 1923, ACHA Papers, Box 46, "Survey of Cities, 1923–1926"; report to ACHA Executive Committee meeting, "Survey and Grading of Medium Sized Cities," December 1, 1923, ibid., Box 5, "Committee: Executive, Meetings of, 1923–1924"; and Hoover to Surgeon General Hugh S. Cumming, December 11, 1923; Cumming to Hoover, December 14, 1923; and Hoover to Andrew Mellon, December 20, 1923, all in ibid., Box 46, "Survey of Cities, 1923–1926." Since Cumming was on the Board of Directors of the ACHA, his protest obviously reflected official duty rather than a genuine objection.

37. Minutes of the Executive Committee, April 24, 1924, ACHA Papers, Box 5, "Committee: Executive, Meetings of, 1923–1924"; Courtenay Dinwiddie to Edgar Rickard, enclosing five "principles of organization and procedure," April 25, 1924, ibid., Box 28, "Policy, Miscellaneous."

38. Unsigned memorandum to Henry Beeuwkes, January 8, 1924, ACHA Papers, Box 22, "Memoranda, 1922–1923." Courtenay Dinwiddie suggested that, in light of Jean's long service, she should be given a month's severance pay, but Edgar Rickard vetoed the idea of spending the organization's limited funds. Instead, he and Hoover (probably out of his own pocket) arranged "a special gift" of $2,100 to cover two months' vacation for Jean and her chief assistant. See Rickard to Dinwiddie, June 18, 1924, and James Berrien to Hoover, June 30, 1924, both in ibid., Box 27, "Personnel: Jean, Sally Lucas, 1918–1924."

39. Edward Flesh to Hoover, September 15, 1924, ACHA Papers, Box 12, "Financial-E. M. Flesh Files-Hoover, Herbert, 1923–1926"; Hoover, memorandum of letter to ACHA Nominating Committee, ca. September 15, 1924, ibid., Box 22, "Memoranda, 1922–1923"; Hoover to Dr. S. McC. Hamill, September 16, 1924, ibid., Box 12, "Financial: E. M. Flesh Files-Hoover, Herbert, 1923–1926"; Aida deAcosta Root to Hoover, September 29, 1924; Courtenay Dinwiddie, George Palmer, Arthur Tomalin, Aida deAcosta Root, Anne Stevens, and Emma Dolfinger to Hoover, October 3, 1924, both in ibid., Box 27, "Personnel: Hoover, Herbert, 1923–1931 & undated"; Hoover to Samuel McC. Hamill, October 8, 1924, ibid., Box 5, "Committee: Executive, Meetings of, 1923–1924"; Edgar Rickard to Edward Flesh, November 6, 1924, Hoover Subject Collection, Box 321, "Correspondence: Rickard, Edgar, 1916–1924." Aida deAcosta Root was divorced from Oren Root in about 1925 and married Henry Breckinridge in 1927.

40. Edgar Rickard to Hoover, October 31, 1924, ACHA Papers, Box 27, "Personnel: Hoover, Herbert, 1923–1931 & undated."

41. Hoover to Edward Flesh, December 23, 1924; and Flesh to Hoover, December 24, 1924, both in ACHA Papers, Box 12, "Financial: E. M. Flesh Files-Hoover, Herbert, 1923–1926"; Edgar Rickard, "Report to A.R.A. Children's Fund, Inc., of the 1924 Activities of the American Child Health Association," March 13, 1925, ibid., Box 2, "American Relief Administration Children's Funds, 1923." For Hoover's view of the results of the survey of eighty-six cities, see his radio address, "Child Health Work," March 30, 1925, Hoover Papers, Commerce Period, Box 87, "Child Health, 1922–1926."

42. The full report was published in a six-hundred-page book, but a convenient summary is in George T. Palmer, et al., "Eighty-Six Cities Studied by Objective Standards," *American Journal of Public Health* 15 (May 1925): 387–93; Herbert Hoover, "May Day-Child Health Day-1925," draft of article for *McClure's Magazine*, May 1925, Hoover Papers, Commerce Period, Box 87, "Child Health, 1922–1926"; Hoover, "Home Training and Citizenship," article draft for *Child-Welfare Magazine*, May 1925, ibid.; Hoover to Edward Flesh, July 13, 1925, ACHA Papers, Box 12, "Financial: E. M. Flesh Files-Hoover, Herbert, 1923–1926."

43. Hoover, "Child Health Needs: An Address Telephoned to New York March 30, 1925, and Broadcast under the Auspices of the Metropolitan Life Insurance Company," March 30, 1925, Hoover Papers, Commerce Period, Box 87, "Child Health, 1922–1926"; Edgar Rickard, "Report to the A.R.A. Children's Fund, Inc., of the 1925 Activities of the American Child Health Association"; "Minutes of the Meeting of the Directors of A.R.A. Children's Fund [held on February 17, 1926]," March 1, 1926; and Edward Flesh to Hoover, February 8, 1926, all in ACHA Papers, Box 2, "American Relief Administration Children's Funds, 1924–1928"; Emma Dolfinger, "Present Status of the School Health Program

Study Compiled from Reports of Staff Members," undated, ibid., Box 45, "School Health, 1924–29"; "Statement as to Progress of School Health Study," June 1, 1926, ibid.; Giglio, "Voluntarism and Public Policy," 438; Dorey, *Better Baby Contests*, 135, 200–201.

44.	Edgar Rickard to Hoover, September 9, 1925, ACHA Papers, Box 27, "Personnel: Hoover, Herbert, 1923–1931 & undated"; "Minutes, Executive Committee, American Child Health Association, October 14, 1925, ibid., Box 5, "Committee: Executive, Meetings of, 1925"; Hoover to Arthur Woods, December 5, 1926, Hoover Papers, Commerce Period, Box 528, "Rockefeller Foundation, 1922–1925"; Edgar Rickard Diaries, Hoover Presidential Library, West Branch, Iowa, February 11, March 12, March 15, 1926, Box 1, "1926"; Rickard to Hoover, April 28, 1926, ACHA Papers, Box 27, "Personnel: Hoover, Herbert, 1923–1931 & undated." A decade later, Barnes threatened to resign from the ARA board because of Hoover's high-handed use of its resources. See Julius Barnes to Hoover, August 18, 1937, enclosing Barnes to Edgar Rickard, August 9, 1937; and a tart reply from Hoover to Barnes, August 25, 1937 (not sent), all in Hoover Subject Collection, Box 313, "Correspondence: Barnes, Julius."

45.	Hoover, "Our Goal—the Normal Child," president's address, ACHA annual meeting, Atlantic City, May 12, 1926, Hoover Papers, Commerce Period, Box 87, "Child Health, 1922–1926"; ACHA press release, May 19, 1926, ibid., Box 484, "Press Releases, 1926 April–October." Hoover later estimated that 35 million of the 45 million American children were "reasonably normal" and that, of the remaining 10 million, only about a million were "abnormal" (crippled, deaf, or blind). See Herbert Hoover, "Forty-Five Million Children," *The Survey* December 15, 1930: 313; Dorey, *Better Baby Contests*, 44–45.

46.	Carl Jay Bajema, ed., "Introduction," in *Eugenics: Then and Now* (Stroudsburg, PA: Dowden, Hutchinson & Ross, 1976), 1, 3 (Galton quoted on p. 1); Nancy Ordover, *American Eugenics: Race, Queer Anatomy, and the Science of Nationalism* (Minneapolis: University of Minnesota Press, 2003), xii. In the 1920s, eugenic arguments contributed to the passage of immigration restriction legislation and to the Supreme Court's decision, in the 1927 case, *Buck v. Bell Superintendent*, that compulsory sterilization of a "feeble-minded" woman was constitutional. In the 1930s, the Nazis would carry eugenic arguments to even uglier extremes. For a more benign application of eugenic theory, see Dorey, *Better Baby Contests*, 23, 71–73.

47.	Giglio, "Voluntarism and Public Policy," 441, 443; Hoover, "Our Goal—the Normal Child," Hoover Papers, Commerce Period, Box 87, "Child Health, 1922–1926"; Herbert Hoover, *Five Years of the American Child Health Association: A Bird's-Eye View* (New York: ACHA, 1927), 8; Wendy Kline, *Building a Better Race: Gender, Sexuality, and Eugenics from the Turn of the Century to the Baby Boom* (Berkeley: University of California Press, 2001), 100–101. For an example of an environmental argument by a leading child health expert of the 1920s, see Baker, *Child Hygiene*, 161–89. The rise of environmental behaviorism in the 1920s and 1930s posed a sharp scientific challenge to eugenics, even in the modified form its advocates espoused in the 1920s. See Aaron Gillette, *Eugenics and the Nature-Nurture Debate in the Twentieth Century* (New York: Palgrave Macmillan, 2007), 121–25.

48.	Susan Pedersen, *Family, Dependence, and the Origins of the Welfare State: Britain and France, 1914–1945* (Cambridge, UK: Cambridge University Press, 1993), 53. Pedersen notes that the introduction of school meals in England was an important first step toward the welfare state, because it was the first time the government acknowledged a right to a benefit for a particular segment of the population that had provided no service to the state and that was not suffering from a contagious disease. Ibid., 54.

49.	Edgar Rickard to Hoover, February 1, 1927; Edgar Rickard, "Report to the A.R.A. Children's Fund, Inc., of the 1926 Activities of the American Child Health Association," ca. February 16, 1927; and "A.R.A. Children's Fund, Inc., Minutes of the Annual Meeting," ca. February 16, 1927; all in ACHA Papers, Box 2, "American Relief Administration Children's Funds, 1924–1928."

50.	R. H. Sawtelle to the members of the ARA Children's Fund, Inc., March 8, 1928, enclosing "A.R.A. Children's Fund, Inc., Minutes of the Annual Meeting," ca. February 23, 1928; and "Report to the A.R.A. Children's Fund, Inc., of the 1927 Activities of the American Child Health Association," undated, all in Lou Henry Hoover Papers, Hoover Presidential

Library, West Branch, Iowak, Box 18, "Clubs and Organizations: American Relief Administration, European Children's Fund 1920–29."

51. Hoover to Edgar Rickard, September 1, 1931 (draft of letter), ACHA Papers, Box 3, "Articles: Mrs. Breckinridge, 'Story of the American Child Health', 1922–1931"; Will Irwin, "Saving the American Child," *Forum and Century* 95 (April 1936): 201–5.

52. Giglio, "Voluntarism and Public Policy," 443–45.

53. J. Prentice Murphy, "When Doctors Disagreed," *The Survey* December 15, 1930: 313, 348–49, 351; "The Gist of It," ibid., 305; Gillette, *Eugenics and the Nature-Nurture Debate*, 125–34. A further split was also apparent at the conference, between social workers who emphasized environmental causes of children's problems and psychologists who focused on and proposed to treat individual children. See Diana Selig, "The Whole Child: Social Science and Race at the White House Conference of 1930," in *When Science Encounters the Child: Education, Parenting, and Child Welfare in 20th Century America*, ed. Barbara Beatty, Emily D. Cahan, and Julia Grant (New York: Teachers College Press, 2006), 137. One of the conference committees, the Committee on Mental Deficiency, recommended not only improved treatment of the mentally deficient but also sterilization. This frankly eugenic approach received little notice in accounts of the conference, and Hoover said nothing about it. See Kline, *Building a Better Race*, 102–3.

54. Lawrence K. Frank, "Childhood and Youth," in Report of the President's Research Committee on Social Trends, *Recent Social Trends in the United States* (New York: McGraw-Hill, 1933), 2:751–800; Giglio, "Voluntarism and Public Policy," 447.

55. Sealander, *The Failed Century of the Child*, 232; Selig, "The Whole Child," 137.

Chapter 11

1. Lou Hoover to Mrs. Charles Evans Hughes, January 5, 1922, Lou Henry Hoover Papers, Hoover Presidential Library, West Branch, Iowa, Box 47, "Clubs and Organizations: Pan-American Scientific Conference, 1916–22"; Ben McKelway, "Women of The Americas to Meet Simultaneously in Own Capitals," Washington *Star*, February 5, 1922.

2. Lou Hoover, Rough draft of remarks to the Savannah Girl Scouts meeting, ca. January 24, 1922, Lou Hoover Papers, Box 3, "Subject File: Articles, Addresses, & Statements, 1922 January; Comments on fun of scout camping, Savannah, Georgia." For surprisingly full press reports of her remarks, see "Mrs. Hoover New Head of Girl Scouts," Rochester (New York) *Post Express*, January 27, 1922; "Mrs. Hoover Elected National President of Girl Scout Order," Niagara Falls (New York) *Gazette*, February 28, 1922; and "Mrs. Hoover Lauds Democratic Training," Toledo *Times*, February 13, 1922; Lou Hoover to Chesley R. Perry, April 28, 1922, Lou Hoover Papers, Box 1, "Girl Scouts, Administrative Correspondence, 1922." For a fuller discussion of where Lou fitted among women with public roles in the 1920s, see Kendrick A. Clements, "The New Era and the New Woman: Lou Henry Hoover and 'Feminism's Awkward Age,'" *Pacific Historical Review* 73 (August 2004): 425–61.

3. Herbert Hoover, *Memoirs: The Cabinet and the Presidency, 1920–1933* (New York: Macmillan, 1952; hereafter, *Memoirs* 2); three drafts of a letter to Senator Frank Kellogg, March 1, 1922, Lou Hoover Papers, Box 16, "Personal Correspondence, 1921–28: Kellogg, Frank B. and Clara, 1921–28 & undated"; Lou Hoover to H. M. Lord, November 4, 1922, ibid., Box 17, "Personal Correspondence, 1921–28-La-Lu Miscellaneous." Although widely believed, the idea that public schools are democratizing institutions is by no means universally accepted. See, for example, George S. Counts, *The Schools Can Teach Democracy* (New York: John Day, 1939); James Bryant Conant, *Education and Liberty: The Role of the Schools in a Modern Democracy* (Cambridge, MA: Harvard University Press, 1953); Lawrence Cremin, *Popular Education and Its Discontents* (New York: Harper & Row, 1989).

4. W. Parmer Fuller, Jr., to Philippi Harding, March 24, 1922, Herbert Hoover Papers, Pre-Commerce Period, Hoover Presidential Library, West Branch, Iowa, Box 33, "European Relief Council, 1919–1921"; "Death Halts Hoover Talk," San Francisco *Call and Post*, March 24, 1922; "Hoover's Nephew Is Drowned in Pool," Pueblo (Colorado) *Chieftain*,

March 24, 1922; Ray Lyman Wilbur to Edgar Rickard, March 25, 1922, Hoover Papers, Commerce Period, Box 709, "Wilbur, Ray Lyman, 1922"; Clara Burdette to Lou Hoover, April 3, 1922, Clara Burdette Papers, Huntington Library, San Marino, California, Box 128.

5. Lou Hoover to Allan Hoover, ca. March 26, 1922, Allan Hoover Papers, Hoover Presidential Library, West Branch, Iowa, Box 1, "Correspondence with Lou Henry Hoover, 1922"; Herbert Hoover to Lou Henry Hoover, March 31, 1922, Hoover Papers, Commerce Period, Box 273, "Hoover, Mrs. Lou Henry."

6. "$35,000 for Girl Scouts," *New York Times*, April 2, 1922; Herbert Hoover to Lou Hoover, April 9 (two telegrams), 1922, Hoover Papers, Commerce Period, Box 273, "Hoover, Mrs. Lou Henry"; Lou Hoover statement, April 22, 1922, Lou Hoover Papers, Box 3, "Subject File: Articles, Addresses, & Statements, 1922 April 22, Dissertation of G.S. Policies, Washington, D.C."; "Girl Scouts to Make Drive for Extension Work Funds," New York *Herald*, October 15, 1922.

7. Edith Harcourt to Miss (?) Hodgkins, May 29, 1939, enclosing undated memorandum by Lou Hoover, Lou Hoover Papers, Box 39, "Clubs and Organizations: National Amateur Athletic Federation, Women's Div., Correspondence, History of Women's Div., 1939–41."

8. Henry Breckinridge to Mrs. J. D. Rippin, April 25, 1922, and Lou Hoover to Henry Breckinridge, May 18, 1922, both in Lou Hoover Papers, Box 32, "Clubs and Organizations: National Amateur Athletic Federation, Men's Division, Breckinridge, Henry, 1922–27."

9. Henry Breckinridge to Lou Hoover, January 15, 1922, Lou Hoover Papers, Box 32, "Clubs and Organizations: National Amateur Athletic Federation' Men's Division, Breckinridge, Henry, 1922–27"; "Information Bulletin concerning the National Amateur Athletic Federation: American Olympic Association developments for the private information of the members of the Board of Governors of the Federation," undated, ca. November 1922, ibid., Box 40, "Clubs and Organizations: National Amateur Athletic Federation' Women's Division, Olympic Participation"; "Minutes of the First Annual Meeting of the Board of Governors of the National Amateur Athletic Federation of America," December 29, 1922, ibid., Box 32, "Clubs and Organizations: National Amateur Athletic Federation, Men's Division, Annual Meeting, 1922."

10. Dr. Henry John Minthorn to Hoover, May 17, 1922; Dr. W. B. Holden and Dr. Karl P. Moran to Hoover, September 21, 1922; Holden to Hoover, September 22, 1922; Hoover, draft of obituary, September 29, 1922; Holden to Hoover, October 11, 1922; Hoover to Mrs. John (Matilda) Minthorn, October 11, 1922, all in Hoover Papers, Commerce Period, Box 396, "Minthorn, Dr. & Mrs. H. John, 1922–1926." Matilda Minthorn (1874–1943) was Dr. Minthorn's second wife; when Hoover lived with the family, the doctor was married to Laura (Miles), who died in 1916. Matilda, who was the same age as Bert, was twenty-eight years younger than her husband.

11. Philippi Harding to Lou Hoover, July 10, 1922, Lou Hoover Papers, Box 11, "Personal Correspondence, 1921–28: Butler, Philippi Harding, 1922 January–July"; "Hoover and Irwin Offspring Hold Seance at Stanford," San Francisco *Chronicle*, May 22, 1922.

12. George Culver to Lou Hoover, September 6, 1922, Lou Hoover Papers, Box 12, "Personal Correspondence, 1921–28: Culver, George, and Sabrina, 1922–23 & undated."

13. George H. Nash, *Herbert Hoover and Stanford University* (Stanford, CA: Hoover Institution Press, 1988), 27–50; Hoover to Ray Lyman Wilbur, Hoover Papers, Pre-Commerce Period, Box 17, "Wilbur, Ray Lyman, 1920."

14. Draft of Hoover to Ray Lyman Wilbur, February 28, 1919, and Hoover to Wilbur, August 28, 1920, both in Hoover Papers, Pre-Commerce Period, Box 64, "Stanford Union, 1919"; Edgar Rickard to Hoover, May 29, 1919, and Rickard to Lou Henry Hoover, June 13, 1919, both in ibid., Box 64, "Stanford-War Memorials, 1919–1922"; Hoover to editor, *Daily Palo Alto*, October 16, 1919, ibid., Box 64, "Stanford-Tuition, 1919"; Hoover to Wilbur, November 13, 1919, ibid., Box 17, "Wilbur, Ray Lyman, 1894–1919"; Wilbur to Hoover, February 23, 1921, Hoover Papers, Commerce Period, Box 709, "Wilbur, Ray Lyman, 1921 January–June"; Nash, *Hoover and Stanford*, 50–63. All quotations come from Nash.

15. Hoover to Ray Lyman Wilbur, January 9, 1920, Hoover Papers, Commerce Period, Box 63, "Stanford: General Education Board, 1918 & 1920"; Wilbur to Hoover, January 20, 1922,

and Hoover to all alumni, January 31, 1922, both in ibid., Box 709, "Wilbur, Ray Lyman, 1922"; secretary of the Board of Trustees to Hoover, December 15, 1922, ibid., Box 569, "Stanford University, 1921–1923"; Nash, *Hoover and Stanford*, 62–67.

16. Alonzo Taylor to Hoover, April 22, 1921, Hoover Papers, Commerce Period, Box 596, "Taylor, Alonzo E., 1921"; Ralph H. Lutz to Edgar Rickard, August 25, 1921, ibid., Box 525, "Rickard, Edgar, 1921–1923"; Nash, *Hoover and Stanford*, 67–70, 75.

17. Unknown to William H. Crocker, July 30, 1924, Hoover Papers, Commerce Period, Box 569, "Stanford University, 1924–1929"; "List of those invited to confer with Mr. Herbert Hoover," undated, ca. July 30, 1924, ibid.; "Hoover Backs Stanford Fund," San Francisco *Examiner*, August 6, 1924; Nash, *Hoover and Stanford*, 74–75.

18. Nash, *Hoover and Stanford*, 39, 72–73. Hoover was never a "dry." In Europe, he usually had a cocktail before dinner and wine with his meal. As commerce secretary, he obeyed the law scrupulously but was reliably reported to stop in at the Belgian embassy on the way home from the office for a cocktail or two on "foreign" soil. See David Burner, *Herbert Hoover: A Public Life* (New York: Knopf, 1979), 218–19.

19. Hoover to Ray Lyman Wilbur, January 16, 1924, Hoover Papers, Commerce Period, Box 709, "Wilbur, Ray Lyman, 1924–1925." Hoover failed to secure one major collection of papers that he wanted—the records of the Washington Naval Conference of 1921 to 1922. Secretary of State Hughes informed him, politely but firmly, that the department would retain those records. See Charles Evans Hughes to Hoover, November 26, 1921, ibid., Box 156, "Conferences, Limitation of Armaments Conference, 1921 November–December."

20. Hoover to Ray Lyman Wilbur, September 1, 1923, Hoover Papers, Commerce Period, Box 709, "Wilbur, Ray Lyman, 1923"; Lou Hoover to Herbert Hoover, September 23, 1923, and Lou Hoover to Ray Lyman Wilbur, September 26 [27?], 1923, enclosing telegram, Hoover to Lou Hoover, September 27, 1923; Wilbur to Hoover, January 26, 1924, all in Lou Hoover Papers, Box 111, "Subject File: Stanford University, Hoover Institution, 1923–24"; Hoover to Wilbur, January 16 and February 6, 1924, Hoover Papers, Commerce Period, Box 709, "Wilbur, Ray Lyman, 1924–1925"; Nash, *Hoover and Stanford*, 77–86.

21. "Report of the Committee on Policy," May 22, 1925, Hoover Papers, Commerce Period, Box 1, "Adams, A.-Frank, 1921–1928"; printed appeal for contributions to the Hoover War Library by Edgar Rickard, October 1, 1925, William C. Mullendore Papers, Hoover Presidential Library, West Branch, Iowa, Box 16, "Hoover Institution, 1924–25"; Edgar Rickard to James Goodrich, February 25, 1926, James P. Goodrich Papers, Hoover Presidential Library, West Branch, Iowa, Box 11, "Hoover Institution, 1926–27"; Nash, *Hoover and Stanford*, 85–89, 107–10.

22. Hoover to Wilbur, July 31, September 27, and October 21, 1922, all in Hoover Papers, Commerce Period, Box 709, "Wilbur, Ray Lyman, 1922." The French inscription reads, "Je suis ce qui a été ce qui est et ce qui sera et nul mortel na encore levé le voile qui me couvre."

23. "Lejeune Presents Gift of Belgians to Hoover," *Daily Palo Alto*, December 4, 1922; typescript of Hoover's response to Senator Lejeune, December 4, 1922, Hoover Papers, Commerce Period, Box 346, "Isis, 1913–1923 & undated."

24. "Cabineteers Soon to Begin Speech-Making Campaign," Washington *Times*, October 15, 1922; "Herbert Hoover Is Entertained at Banquet in the Duke City," Albuquerque *Morning Journal*, November 22, 1922.

25. "Girl Scouts to Make Drive for Extension Work Funds," New York *Herald*, October 15, 1922.

26. Mary Anderson to Lou Hoover, November 22, 1922, Lou Hoover Papers, Box 53, "Clubs and Organizations: United States Department of Labor, Children's Bureau, 1921–27." Perhaps in preparation for this conference, Lou asked Philippi Harding to send her "Steiner's industrial book." Jesse Steiner, a prominent sociologist, had recently published *Education for Social Work* (Chicago: University of Chicago Press, 1921), but it is unclear whether this was the book Lou had in mind. For Mary Austin and the Women's News Service, see Mary Austin to Lou Hoover, November 25, 1922, and Hoover to Austin, December 17, 1922, both in Lou Hoover Papers, Box 9, "Personal Correspondence,1921–28: Austin, Mary, 1922–27"; Ida Clyde Clarke to Lou Hoover, December 18, 1922, and "Secretary Mrs. Hoover" to

treasurer, Women's News Service, June 4, 1923, ibid., Box 58, "Clubs and Organizations: Women's News Service, 1922–24."

27. Form letter from Lou Hoover to various women, March 2, 1923, Lou Hoover Papers, Box 33, "Clubs and Organizations: National Amateur Athletic Federation, Women's Division, Annual Meetings; 1923 Wash., D.C., AGG-Ath"; "Parley on Women's Athletics Planned," *Providence Journal*, March 13, 1923; "War Department to Aid Women to Become Physical Goddesses," New York *World*, March 13, 1923; "Military Training for Women Stirs a Lot of Clashing Views," Washington *Sunday Star*, March 18, 1923; "U.S. Backs Health Drive for Women," Charles City (Iowa) *Intelligencer*, March 19, 1923; "Gilda Lauds Mrs. Hoover," New York *American*, March 18, 1923; "Boys, Look Out! Women Train in Athletics with Government Aid," El Paso (Texas) *Times*, March 25, 1923.

28. "Spooning Stopped by Athletics, Says Woman Physical Expert," Washington *Star*, April 7, 1923; press release, "Women and Girls' Athletics and Physical Recreational Conference Called in Washington by Mrs. Herbert Hoover," ca. April 1, 1923, Lou Hoover Papers, Box 33, "Clubs and Organizations: National Amateur Athletic Federation, Women's Division, Annual Meetings; 1923 Wash., D.C., Bad-Bay"; Lou Hoover, "Opening Remarks," April 6, 1923, ibid., Box 35, "Clubs and Organizations: National Amateur Athletic Federation' Women's Division, Annual Meetings; 1923 Wash., D.C., Opening Address by LHH."

29. "Mrs. Hoover Organizes Athletic Federation," *The Woman Athletic*, clipping in Lou Hoover Papers, Box 32, "Subject File: Clippings, 1923, Clubs and Organizations"; *Resolutions Adopted by the Conference on Athletics and Physical Recreation for Women and Girls, April 6th and 7th, 1923, Washington, D.C.* (New York: National Amateur Athletic Federation of America, 1923). Lou remained chair of the Executive Committee until April 1927, when she became vice chairman and Mrs. Henry A. Strong became chair.

30. "Inter and Intra Institutional Athletic Activities," *School Life*, May 1933, 3; Lou Hoover, "Foreword to 'Play Day—The Spirit of Sport,'" in Women's Division, National Amateur Athletic Federation, *Women and Athletics* (New York: A. S. Barnes, 1930), 67–70; "Women Swimmers Protest A.A.U. Ban," *New York Times*, May 3, 1923; statement by the Women's Division to the Members of the Board of Governors of the A.A.U., ca. September 1923, Lou Hoover Papers, Box 33, "Clubs and Organizations: National Amateur Athletic Federation, Women's Division, Amateur Athletic Union, 1923"; NAAF, "Notice of Annual Meeting," December 3, 1923, and excerpts from Lou Hoover's remarks at the meeting, December 31, 1923, both in ibid., Box 32, "Clubs and Organizations: National Amateur Athletic Federation, Men's Division, Annual Meeting, 1923."

31. Reliable figures on Girl Scout membership are difficult to get. Those cited here come from clippings in Lou Hoover Papers, Box 9, "Girl Scouts: Clippings." One estimate, which put membership at 352,000 in 1923, was so far out of line with others that I did not use it. Dale Mayer, in *Lou Henry Hoover: A Prototype for First Ladies* (New York: Nova Historical Publications, 2004), 208, gives the figures as 7,000 in 1917; 92,000 in 1924; and 167,000 in 1927. See also "Girl Scout Movement Is Booming in U.S.; Many New Troops Formed," Washington *Post*, March 2, 1923; "Girl Scout Chiefs Hear Mrs. Hoover," New York *Herald*, April 26, 1923; copy of Lou Hoover radio address, May 2, 1923, Lou Hoover Papers, Box 3, "Subject File: Articles, Addresses, & Statements, 1923 May 2, Women's Association, Pittsburgh, Pennsylvania"; editorial, "The Girl Scouts," Pittsburgh *Sun*, May 4, 1923.

32. Untitled, History of the "Little House," undated, ca. 1942, Lou Hoover Papers, Box 12, "Girl Scouts, Little House, History, 1942."

33. Herbert Hoover to Col. C. O. Sherrill, October 23, 1923, Hoover Papers, Commerce Period, Box 684, "War Department-Miscellaneous-1923–1928 & undated"; Christian Herter to Lou Hoover, November 14, 1923, ibid., Box 273, "Hoover, Mrs. Lou Henry."

34. "More Girl Scout Leaders Needed, Says Mrs. Hoover," Portland *Morning Oregonian*, July 4, 1923; "Mrs. Hoover Greets Tacoma Girl Scouts," Seattle *Post Intelligencer*, July 6, 1923; Lou Hoover, "The President Is Dead!" typescript, August 3, 1923, Lou Hoover Papers, Box 4, "Subject File: Articles, Addresses, & Statements, 1923 August, President & Mrs. Harding, American Girl"; Lou Hoover to Ethel Bullard, August 15, 1923, ibid., Box 10, "Personal Correspondence, 1921–28: Bullard, Ethel Begg, 1921–28."

35. Lou Hoover to Mrs. (Alice Anne) Winter, September 24, 1923, Lou Hoover Papers, Box 1, "Girl Scouts, Administrative Correspondence, 1923."
36. Frank Richey to (Alida Henriques), February 2, 1923, Allan Hoover Papers, Box 8, "Family Activities, 1910–1926"; Allan Hoover to Lou Hoover, August 7, 1923, ibid., Box 1, "Correspondence with Lou Henry Hoover, 1923"; Lou Hoover to Dean George Culver, August 13, 1923, Lou Hoover Papers, Box 12, "Personal Correspondence, 1921–28: Culver, George & Sabrina, 1922–23 & undated"; Lou Hoover to Herbert Hoover, September 25, 1923, ibid., Box 15, "Personal Correspondence: Hoover, Herbert, 1921–27"; Lou Hoover to (Jeannette C.) Hemphill, November 24, 1923, ibid., Box 15, "Personal Correspondence, 1921–28: He Miscellaneous."
37. Herbert Hoover to M. M. O'Shaughnessy, April 25, May 7, 1923, Hoover Papers, Commerce Period, Box 456, "O'Shaughnessy, M. M., 1921–1923"; Lou Hoover to Herbert Hoover, September 29, 1923, Lou Hoover Papers, Box 15, "Personal Correspondence: Hoover, Herbert, 1921–27"; Lou Hoover to (Jeannette C.) Hemphill, ibid., Box 15, "Personal Correspondence, 1921–28: He Miscellaneous"; Alonzo Taylor to Herbert Hoover, January 12, 1923, Hoover Papers, Commerce Period, Box 596, "Taylor, Alonzo E., 1923."
38. "Siskiyou Reports Many Deer Killed," Sacramento *Bee*, September 13, 1923; "Hoover's Wife, Sons and Father-in-Law in Siskiyou after Deer," Yreka (California) *News*, September 13, 1923.
39. Unsigned "Summer Instructions," June 15, 1923, Lou Hoover Papers, Box 17, "Personal Correspondence, 1921–28: Losh, Louisette (Mrs. William), 1922–23"; Lou Hoover to Louisette Losh, September 16, 1924, ibid., Box 17; Lou Hoover to Mark Requa, August 27, 1924, ibid., Box 17, "Personal Correspondence, 1921–28: Requa, Mark & Florence, 1921–28 & undated"; "National Capital Close-Ups," New York *Telegram*, May 11, 1922.
40. "Mrs. Hoover Supports Summer School for Women," Philadelphia *Inquirer*, February 17, 1923; column, "Dolly Madison's Chats of Capital's Society," Philadelphia *Public Ledger*, March 8, 1923; George Franklin, "Visiting Nurses Campaign for $100,000 Fund," Washington *Times*, April 16, 1923; clipping, "Hays' Own Board Would Bar Arbuckle," no source or date, Lou Hoover Papers, Box 32, "Clubs and Organizations: Motion Picture Industry, 1923"; Second Annual Report of the President, Women's News Service, Inc., August 21, 1923, and Ida Clyde Clarke to Lou Hoover, September 21, 1923, both in ibid., Box 58, "Clubs and Organizations: Women's News Service, 1922–24"; Ralph Arnold to Lou Hoover, November 2, 1923, ibid., Box 9, "Personal Correspondence, 1921–28: Arnold, Ralph, 1923–26"; League of Women Voters resolution calling for American membership in the Permanent Court of International Justice, December 1923, ibid., Box 31, "Clubs and Organizations: League of Women Voters, Correspondence, 1923–28"; League of Women Voters petition, December 1923, ibid., Box 31, Clubs & Organizations, League of Women Voters, Correspondence, 1923–28"; Karen J. Blair, *The Clubwoman as Feminist: True Womanhood Redefined, 1868–1914* (New York: Holmes & Meier, 1980); Lois Scharf, *Eleanor Roosevelt: First Lady of American Liberalism* (Boston: Twayne, 1987), 66–72.
41. See Anon., *Boudoir Mirrors of Washington* (Philadelphia: John C. Winston, 1923), 244–54, in Lou Hoover's copy of the book at the Hoover Presidential Library.
42. Mary Austin to "Dear Friend" (Herbert Hoover), May 25, 1923; Lou Hoover to Mary Austin, June 14, 1923; Mary Austin to "Dear Friend" (Lou Henry Hoover), June 26, 1923, all in Lou Hoover Papers, Box 9, "Personal Correspondence, 1921–28: Austin, Mary, 1922–27"; Lou Hoover to Gayle Campbell, June 14, 1923, and Gayle Campbell to Lou Hoover, July 22, 1923, both in ibid., Box 11, "Personal Correspondence, 1921–28: Campbell, Gayle Allen, 1922–27 & undated." In September, Hoover recommended his sister-in-law, Mildred Brooke Hoover, to the secretary of the interior as a member of the Indian Advisory Committee. See Hoover to Hubert Work, September 28, 1923, ibid., Box 24, "Personal Correspondence, 1921–28; Work, Hubert & Louise, 1923–27."
43. "Tell Me What She's Really Like: A Discussion of Mrs. Hoover, by a Friend," undated, ca. 1932, Lou Hoover Papers, Box 10, "Subject File: Hoover, Lou Henry Biographical Data."

Chapter 12

1. Sullivan to Hoover, October 13, 1921, and Hoover to Sullivan, October 25, 1921, both in Hoover Papers, Commerce Period, Hoover Presidential Library, West Branch, Iowa, Box 589, "Sullivan, Mark, 1921–1925." A page of the galley proofs of *American Individualism* in ibid., Box 24, "*American Individualism*, 1921–1922," has a minor correction proposed by Wesley Mitchell in the margin. Just before Christmas 1921, Hoover asked Everett Colby to return a copy of the manuscript because, he said, it was "the only copy I have," and he wanted to work on it a bit more. See Hoover to Colby, December 22, 1921, ibid., Box 26, "*American Individualism*, Comments on, A-F, 1921–1923 & undated."

2. "Mr. Hoover's Address at the Dinner Given by the American Institute of Mining and Metallurgical Engineers, September 16, 1919," Hoover Papers, Pre-Commerce Period, Hoover Presidential Library, West Branch, Iowa, Box 30, "Campaign of 1920, Speeches & Statements: Hoover, Am. Institute of Mining & Metallurgical Engineering, Sept. 1919–March 1920"; Hoover to Croly, June 11, 1918, Lewis L. Strauss Papers, Hoover Presidential Library, West Branch, Iowa, Subject File, Box 36, "Hoover, Herbert, General, 1918."

3. Hoover to Croly, June 11, 1918, Strauss Papers, Subject File, Box 36, "Hoover, Herbert, General, 1918"; Herbert Hoover, *American Individualism* (New York: Doubleday, Doran, 1922, repr. West Branch, IA, Hoover Presidential Library, n.d.), 4–5 (order of phrases changed; emphasis in original).

4. Hoover, "Growing Tendency toward Centralization of Government in Washington: Speech before American Mining Congress Convention, Washington, Dec. 7, 1926," Hoover Papers, Commerce Period, Box 87, "Child Labor, 1923–1926."

5. Hoover, speech to St. Louis Advertising Club, October 12, 1920, Hoover Papers, Pre-Commerce Period, Box 60, "Public Statements, 1917–1920"; Hoover, "Penn College Commencement Address, Oskaloosa, Iowa, June 12, 1925," Bible no. 496, vol. 20, May–June 1925. The importance of this image to Hoover is suggested by the fact that he repeated the substance of the Penn College speech, omitting his personal recollections, at Herbert's Stanford graduation later that same month (see "Problems of Our Economic Evolution—Address to Stanford University Students," June 22, 1925, Bible no. 499, vol. 20, May–June 1925) and in a campaign speech (with the personal recollections restored) at West Branch on August 21, 1928. See *Public Papers of the Presidents of the United States, Herbert Hoover: Containing the Public Messages, Speeches, and Statements of the President, March 4 to December 31, 1929* (Washington, DC: Government Printing Office, 1974), 521–29.

6. Charles S. Maier, *Recasting Bourgeois Europe: Stabilization in France, Germany, and Italy in the Decade after World War I* (Princeton, NJ: Princeton University Press, 1975), 8–14.

7. From a speech at the Smithsonian Institution, August 28, 1917, in the Hoover Papers, Pre-Commerce Period, Box 60, "Relief Activities, 1900–1919"; Ellis W. Hawley, "Herbert Hoover, the Commerce Secretariat, and the Vision of an 'Associative State,' 1921–1928," *Journal of American History* 41 (June 1974): 117. For the combination of voluntarism and coercion Hoover employed in the Food Administration, see George H. Nash, *The Life of Herbert Hoover: Master of Emergencies, 1917–1918* (New York: Norton, 1996).

8. Charles S. Maier, *In Search of Stability: Explorations in Historical Political Economy* (Cambridge, UK: Cambridge University Press, 1987), 24–29 (quotations from p. 29); David Burner, *Herbert Hoover: A Public Life* (New York: Knopf, 1979), 140–41.

9. Hoover, Penn College speech (the order of phrases has been altered); Commerce Department press release, June 2, 1921, Hoover Papers, Commerce Period, Box 602, "Trade Associations 1921."

10. Hoover, Penn College speech.

11. Ibid.

12. Ibid.

13. "Is Individualism Passing?" New York *Tribune*, December 20, 1922; Hoover, Penn College speech; Nick Cullather, "The Foreign Policy of the Calorie," *American Historical Review* 112 (April 2007): 350–52.
14. Hoover, "Elimination of Industrial Waste in Its Relation to Labor," address to a National Civic Federation conference, April 11, 1925, Hoover Papers, Commerce Period, Box 15, "Subject File—Proposed—Books—Hoover's Philosophy—Trade Associations"; Herbert Hoover, *Memoirs: The Cabinet and the Presidency, 1920–1933* (New York: Macmillan, 1952), 101 (hereafter, *Memoirs* 2); Robert Zieger, "Herbert Hoover, the Wage-Earner, and the 'New Economic System,' 1919–29," in *Herbert Hoover as Secretary of Commerce: Studies in New Era Thought and Practice*, ed. Ellis W. Hawley (Iowa City: University of Iowa Press, 1981), 86–87; Zieger, "Solving the Labor Problem: Herbert Hoover and the American Worker in the 1920s," in *Herbert Hoover Reassessed: Essays Commemorating the Fiftieth Anniversary of the Inauguration of Our Thirty-First President*, comp. Mark O. Hatfield (Washington, DC: Government Printing Office, 1981), 179–80; Burner, *Hoover*, 144–45.
15. Hawley, "Hoover and the 'Associative State,'" 117–18.
16. Hoover, *American Individualism*, 7–8.
17. The quotation comes from the Richmond Declaration of Faith, adopted by ninety-five delegates representing twelve yearly meetings who met in Richmond, Indiana, in 1887. See http://www.quakerinfo.com/rdf.shtml (accessed September 21, 2005). For Hulda Hoover's "call to preach," see George H. Nash, *The Life of Herbert Hoover: The Engineer, 1874–1914* (New York: Norton, 1983), 8–10.
18. Hoover, *American Individualism*, 8, 10–11; Hawley, "Hoover and the 'Associative State,'" 119.
19. Hoover, *American Individualism*, 14–15, 17; Hoover, Penn College speech.
20. Hoover, address to the meeting of the Advisory Council, National Conference on Outdoor Recreation, December 11, 1924, RG 220, National Conference on Outdoor Recreation Papers, National Archives, Washington, DC, Box 5, "Guide: First Conference, Sub-Guide: General Council May '25, Folder: Proceedings of Council, May 1925"; Daniel Horowitz, *The Morality of Spending: Attitudes toward the Consumer Society in America, 1875–1940* (Baltimore: Johns Hopkins University Press, 1985), 75–78; Kendrick A. Clements, *Hoover, Conservation, and Consumerism: Engineering the Good Life* (Lawrence: University Press of Kansas, 2000), 52–55.
21. Ellis W. Hawley, "Herbert Hoover and the Sherman Act, 1921–1933: An Early Phase of a Continuing Issue," *Iowa Law Review* 74 (July 1989): 1068–69.
22. Ibid., 1070.
23. Hoover to Daugherty, May 2, 1921; Daugherty to Hoover, May 16, 1921, both in Hoover Papers, Commerce Period, Box 353, "Justice Department, Attorney General Daugherty, 1921 March–September"; Hawley, "Hoover and the Sherman Act," 1072–73.
24. Nathan B. Williams, "Memorandum of Conversation with Secretary Hoover," July 7, 1921, Hoover Papers, Commerce Period, Box 201, "Feiker, F. M., Correspondence Removed from His Desk, National Association of Manufacturers, 1921"; Hoover to Daugherty, July 27, 1921, ibid., Box 353, "Justice Department, Attorney General Daugherty, 1921 March–September."
25. *American Column & Lumber Co. v. United States*, 257 U.S. 377, 412 (1921); Hoover to Daugherty, February 3, 1922, and Daugherty to Hoover, February 8, 1922, both released to press, February 16, 1922, and both in Hoover Papers, Commerce Period, Box 353, "Justice Department, Attorney General Daugherty, 1922"; Hoover to Sen. Frank B. Willis, February 17, 1922, ibid., Box 602, "Trade Associations, 1922 February 16–28"; Hoover, "National Federation of Construction Industries, Chicago—Address," April 4, 1922, Bible no. 219, vol. 9, "February–May 10, 1922"; Hoover, "Trade Associations Should Stabilize Business," New York *Evening Post*, ca. April 8, 1922, clipping in Hoover Papers, Commerce Period, Box 602, "Trade Associations, 1922 April 1–8"; "Address of Secretary of Commerce to the Trade Association Conference, Apr. 12, 1922," ibid., Box 483, "Press Releases, 1922 March–April"; "Summary of Speech by Herbert Hoover before the National Manufacturers'

Association, New York, May 10, 1922," ibid., Box 427, "National Association of Manufacturers, 1922–1928"; Hawley, "Hoover and the Sherman Act," 1073–77.

26. Hoover to Sen. Walter E. Edge, enclosing proposed amendment to Clayton Act, June 12, 1922, and Edge to Hoover, June 14, 1922, both in Hoover Papers, Commerce Period, Box 545, "Senate: Edge, Walter E., 1921–1923"; memorandum, "The Department's Cooperation for Distribution of Trade Statistics Gathered by Trade Associations," ca. September 14, 1922, ibid., Box 603, "Trade Associations, Undated"; W. C. Mullendore to National Wholesale Lumber Dealers Association, September 14, 1922, ibid., Box 602, "Trade Associations, 1922 June–October"; Department of Commerce, *Tenth Annual Report of the Secretary of Commerce* (Washington, DC: Government Printing Office, 1922), 29–31; Hawley, "Hoover and the Sherman Act," 1077–79.

27. Samuel F. Howard, Jr., "Samuel Untermyer," *Dictionary of American Biography, Supplement 2* (New York: Scribner's, 1958), 675.

28. Samuel Untermyer to Hoover, April 8 and 16, 1922; Hoover to Untermyer, April 11, 1922, both in Hoover Papers, Commerce Period, Box 604, "Trade Associations, Untermyer, Samuel, 1922–1924."

29. *United States v. Tile Manufacturers Credit Association*, Equity No. 201 (S.D. Ohio, final decree filed November 26, 1923); Hoover to Daugherty, December 11, 1923; Daugherty to Hoover, December 19, 1923; and Commerce Department press release, February 16, 1924, all in Hoover Papers, Commerce Period, Box 353, "Justice Department, Attorney General Daugherty, 1923–1924 & undated"; "Cooperative Plan of the Department of Commerce for Distribution of Statistics Gathered by Trade Associations," ca. February 1924, ibid., Box 602, "Trade Associations, 1924"; Hawley, "Hoover and the Sherman Act," 1080–81.

30. Hawley, "Hoover and the Sherman Act," 1082.

31. "Address of Secretary of Commerce Herbert Hoover at the Annual Meeting of the United States Chamber of Commerce, Cleveland, Ohio, Evening of May 7, 1924," Hoover Papers, Commerce Period, Box 120, "Commerce Dept., Achievements, 1924 May–June."

32. Press release, January 20, 1925, Hoover Papers, Commerce Period, Box 199, "Federal Trade Commission, 1925–1928 & undated"; William J. Barber, *From New Era to New Deal: Herbert Hoover, the Economists, and American Economic Policy, 1921–1933* (New York: Cambridge University Press, 1985), 10–11.

33. *Maple Flooring Manufacturers Association*, 268 U.S. (1925); *Cement Manufacturers Association*, 268 U.S. (1925); "The Supreme Court on Restraint of Trade," New York *World*, June 3, 1925; "Statement by Secretary Hoover at Press Conference," June 4, 1925, Hoover Papers, Commerce Period, Box 602, "Trade Associations, 1925"; Hawley, "Hoover and the Sherman Act," 1082–83.

34. George T. Odell, "Herbert Hoover—Super-Business Man," *Nation*, September 23, 1925, 325–27; Samuel McCune Lindsay to Hoover, September 11, 1925; Hoover to Lindsay, September 14, 1925; and rough draft of possible remarks to meeting, undated, all in Hoover Papers, Commerce Period, Box 60, "Brookings, Robert S., 1921–1927"; Hoover to Coolidge, September 22, 1926, ibid., Box 199, "Federal Trade Commission, 1925–1928 & undated."

35. Irving S. Paull, J. W. Millard, and James S. Taylor, *Trade Association Activities*, Domestic Commerce Series No. 20 (Washington, DC: Government Printing Office, 1927), 54; Hoover for President, "Release No. 7 B, Self-Government in Business," undated, ca. 1928, Herbert Hoover Papers, Campaign and Transition Period, Hoover Presidential Library, West Branch, Iowa, Box 158, "Subject: Hoover for President Corres."

36. Hoover to Senator James H. Metcalf, December 9, 1927, Hoover Papers, Commerce Period, Box 548, "Senate, MacL-Morr, 1922–1928"; Hoover, *American Individualism*, 18–19, 13; clipping, Morris R. Cohen, "Mr. Hoover's Individualism," *New Republic* (February 21, 1923), Hoover Papers, Commerce Period, Box 25, "American Individualism, Clippings (2) 1923"; Ralph Arnold, form letter promoting *American Individualism*, December 27, 1922, Ralph Arnold Papers, Huntington Library, San Marino, California, Box 232, "L. Political Papers: V, Hoover for President Miscellany." For a much less sanguine view of the relationship of the corporation and the stockholder, see Adolf A. Berle, Jr., and Gardiner

C. Means, *The Modern Corporation and Private Property* (New York: Macmillan, 1930), 2–9, 119–25, 277–87.

37. Richard Hofstadter, *The American Political Tradition and the Men Who Made It* (New York: Knopf, 1948), 290–95. To a post-1929 generation, *American Individualism* can seem "jejune," its style "chunky," and its assumptions about spiritual values "synthetic." "It is hard to fathom," writes William E. Leuchtenburg, why it "has been taken seriously as a meaningful contribution to social theory." Leuchtenburg, *Herbert Hoover* (New York: Henry Holt, 2009), 66–67.

Chapter 13

1. David E. Hamilton, *From New Day to New Deal: American Farm Policy from Hoover to Roosevelt, 1928–1931* (Chapel Hill: University of North Carolina Press, 1991), 8–11; James H. Shideler, *Farm Crisis, 1919–1923* (Berkeley: University of California Press, 1957), 36–41; Adam D. Sheingate, *The Rise of the Agricultural Welfare State: Institutions and Interest Group Power in the United States, France, and Japan* (Princeton, NJ: Princeton University Press, 2001), 101–2.

2. Shideler, *Farm Crisis*, 202–12.

3. Ibid., 212–16; extract from the diary of Agnes E. Meyer, January 12, 1922, General Acquisition 692, Hoover Presidential Library, West Branch, Iowa.

4. Paul M. Warburg to Hoover, January 9, 1922, Hoover Papers, Commerce Period, Hoover Presidential Library, West Branch, Iowa, Box 685, "Warburg, Paul M., 1922–1925"; Hoover to Gray Silver, February 10, 1922, ibid., Box 559, "Silver, Gray, 1921–1927"; Rep. Martin S. Madden to Hoover, March 6, 1922, and Julius Klein to Hoover, March 7, 1922, both in ibid., Box 280, "House of Representatives: Madden, Martin B., 1922–1926"; Hoover to C. H. Huston, April 1, 1922; Eugene Meyer to Hoover, June 9, 1922, both in ibid., Box 684, "War Finance Corporation, 1922–1926"; E. H. Cunningham to Hoover, July 27, 1922, ibid., Box 675, "United States Grain Growers, Inc., 1921–1922"; Julius Barnes to Hoover, August 4, 15, 1922, and E. G. Montgomery to Christian Herter, August 18, 1922, both in ibid., Box 705, "Wheat, 1922"; Hoover to Sen. Arthur Capper, September 1, 1922, ibid., Box 544, "Senate: Capper, Arthur, 1920–1922"; press release, "Extracts from the Forthcoming Annual Report of the Secretary of Commerce for the Fiscal Year 1921–22," November 27, 1922; press release, "Investigation into various economic problems in pursuance of the organic act," December 4, 1922; E. G. Montgomery to Hoover, December 15, 1922, all in ibid., Box 3, "Agriculture, 1919–1922"; Shideler, *Farm Crisis*, 195–96.

5. For background of the coal problem, see Chapter 7 in this volume and the following: unsigned, undated memorandum, ca. January 1922, giving an evaluation of the coal situation by E. A. Holbrook, acting director of the Bureau of Mines, Hoover Papers, Commerce Period, Box 97, "Coal, Miscellaneous, 1922 January"; "Hoover Says Stage Set for Coal Strike," Buffalo (New York) *Express*, January 20, 1922; "Strike Expected in Coal Industry," Boston *Christian Science Monitor*, January 20, 1922; "Hoover Says Strike of 500,000 Miners April 1 Unavoidable," San Francisco *Journal*, January 20, 1922; Thomas Dublin and Walter Licht, *The Face of Decline: The Pennsylvania Anthracite Region in the Twentieth Century* (Ithaca, New York: Cornell University Press, 2005), 51–52, 54–55.

6. Hoover to J. D. Evans, January 19, 1922, Hoover Papers, Commerce Period, Box 98, "Coal, Miscellaneous 1922 February–March"; Hoover to T. H. Watkins, January 23, 1922, ibid., Box 100, "Coal Committee, 1921–1922"; Edward Eyre Hunt to William Hard, February 14, 1922, ibid., Box 648, "Unemployment, Hunt–Harde, 1920–1922"; Hunt to Philip Cabot, April 7, 1922, ibid., Box 111, "Coal, Strikes–1922 April," ibid.; Hoover to James Couzens, April 18, 1922, ibid.

7. T. N. Collyer to Hoover and C. C. McChord, January 4, 1922, Hoover Papers, Commerce Period, Box 97, "Coal, Miscellaneous, 1922 January."

8. E. M. Poston to Hoover, March 22, 1922, enclosing W. D. McKinney to the Coal Operators of Southern Ohio, March 22, 1922, and W. D. McKinney to Lee Hall, Pres., District 6 of

the United Mine Workers of America, March 21, 1922, Hoover Papers, Commerce Period, Box 474, "Poston, Elias McClellan, 1921–1922"; Hoover to James Couzens, April 18, 1922, ibid., Box 111, "Coal, Strikes, 1922 April."

9. Hoover to H. A. Garfield, May 2, 1922; Garfield to Hoover, May 6, 1922 (telegram and letter); Hoover to William B. Wilson, May 2, 1922; and Wilson to Hoover, 12, 1922, all in Hoover Papers, Commerce Period, Box 106, "Coal, Plans, Mr. Hoover, 1922."

10. Hoover to C. F. Richardson, May 13, 1922, Hoover Papers, Commerce Period, Box 108, "Coal, Prices and Profiteering, 1921–1922 April–May"; press release on coal prices, May 16, 1922; press release, "Call for General Coal Price Conference," May 22, 1922, both in ibid., Box 483, "Press Releases, 1922 May–August"; Hoover to R. H. Ashton, May 23, 1923, ibid., Box 12, "Ashton, R. H., 1922–1927"; press release, "Secretary Hoover's Remarks before Coal Operators, Wednesday, May 31, 1922," ibid., Box 483, "Press Releases, 1922 May–August."

11. "Hoover's Plan Fails to Enthuse Operators," Washington *Star*, June 1, 1923; press release of Hoover's statement on coal prices, June 2, 1922; press release of statement by George Otis Smith, June 3, 1922, both in Hoover Papers, Commerce Period, Box 98, "Coal, Miscellaneous, 1922 May–July"; Hoover to the president of the U.S. Senate, June 5, 1922, ibid., Box 104, "Coal, Legislation, 1921–1922"; Homer D. Jones and Roderick Stephens to Hoover, June 6, 1922; Hoover to Jones, June 8, 1922; Stephens to Hoover, June 9, 1922 (two letters); Hoover to Stephens, June 9, 10, 1922, all in ibid., Box 433, "National Retail Coal Merchants Association, 1921–1922"; William E. Borah to Hoover, June 7, 1922, and Hoover to Borah, June 9, 1922, both in ibid., Box 104, "Coal, Legislation, 1921–1922"; press release on coal prices by Hoover, June 8, 1922, ibid., Box 483, "Press Releases, 1922 May–August."

12. Hoover to John L. Lewis, June 11, 14, 1922, Hoover Papers, Commerce Period, Box 370, "Lewis, John L., 1922–1929 & undated"; Hoover to Frederick Stephens, June 12, 1922; Hoover to C. W. Taylor, June 13, 1922; Hoover to David I. Walsh, June 13, 15, 1922; Walsh to Hoover, June 14, 1922; press release about meeting at Commerce Department, June 15, 1922, all in ibid., Box 108, "Coal, Prices and Profiteering, 1922 June 11–29"; Hoover to Sen. Irvine L. Lenroot, June 13, 1922, ibid., Box 548, "Senate: Lenroot, Irvine L., 1921–1922"; Hoover to Harding, June 17, 1922, ibid., Box 480, "President Harding, 1922 June–July"; James P. Johnson, *The Politics of Soft Coal: The Bituminous Industry from World War I through the New Deal* (Urbana: University of Illinois Press, 1979), 114. At Hoover's request, a committee of the American Institute of Mining and Metallurgical Engineers spent the summer studying the coal situation. It concluded, unhelpfully, that there were too many mines but offered no method for reducing their numbers. See Arthur S. Dwight to Hoover, June 16, 22, July 10 1922; Hoover to Dwight, June 17, 1922; and H. H. Stoek to Edwin Ludlow, July 7, 1922, all in Hoover Papers, Commerce Period, Box 106, "Coal, Plans, Mr. Hoover, 1922."

13. Press release, "Address of the President to representatives of the Coal Operators and Miners, July 1, 1922," Hoover Papers, Commerce Period, Box 480, "President Harding, 1922 June–July"; Hoover to Harding, July 8, 1922, ibid.

14. Press release, "Address of the President to mine operators' and miners' representatives," undated, probably July 8, 1922, Hoover Papers, Commerce Period, Box 481, "President Harding, 1924–1927 & undated."

15. Hoover to Harding, July 14, 1922, and Harding to Hoover, July 15, 1922, both in Hoover Papers, Commerce Period, Box 105, "Coal, Negotiations, 1922"; memorandum on production of nonunion coal companies by the U.S. Geological Survey, July 18, 1922, ibid., Box 480, "President Harding, 1922 June–July."

16. Hoover to Harding, July 19, 1922, enclosing memorandum outlining the coal plan, Hoover Papers, Commerce Period, Box 480, "President Harding, 1922 June–July."

17. James C. Davis to Hoover, July 19, 21, 1922, Hoover Papers, Commerce Period, Box 106, "Coal, Plans, Legal Opinions, 1922 & undated"; Hoover to Albert Fall, July 19, 1922, and Fall to Hoover, July 20, 1922, both in ibid., Box 294, "Interior Department, Secretary Fall, Albert, 1922–1923 & undated"; Hoover to Charles McChord, July 20, 1922, ibid., Box 105, "Coal, Negotiations, 1922"; Hoover to Harry M. Daugherty, July 21, 1922, ibid., Box 353,

"Justice Department, Attorney General Daugherty, 1922"; Edward Eyre Hunt to Hoover, July 24, 1922, ibid., Box 100, "Coal, Coal and Railroads, 1921–1922, August"; Clyde B. Aitcheson to Hoover, July 24, 1922, ibid., Box 105, "Coal, Negotiations, 1922"; Harry M. Daugherty to Hoover, July 24, 1922, ibid., Box 106, "Coal, Plans, Legal Opinions, 1922 & undated"; Commerce Department press release, "A Tentative Plan under Discussion for Distribution of the Current Coal Production and for Restriction of Unfair Prices with Amendments as Agreed to by Operators," July 25, 1922, ibid., Box 483, "Press Releases, 1922 May–August"; Harding to Hoover, July 26, 1922, ibid., Box 480, "President Harding, 1922 June–July"; Commerce Department press release on the appointment of the Coal Distribution Committee and Hoover's telegram to the governors of the states, July 26, 1922, ibid., Box 97, "Coal, 1922 June–July"; press release on the appointment of the coal distributor (erroneously described as "coal administrator"), July 26, 1922, ibid., Box 480, "President Harding, 1922 June–July"; Hoover to the governors of eighteen states, July 28, 1922, ibid., Box 97, "Coal, 1922 June–July"; Commerce Department press release on the operation of the Fuel Distribution Committee, July 30, 1922, ibid., Box 483, "Press Releases, 1922 May–August."

18. Hoover to Julius H. Barnes, July 22, 1922, Hoover Papers, Commerce Period, Box 99, "Coal, Barnes, Julius H., 1922–1924." For a similar analysis of the situation, see Philip Cabot to Edward Eyre Hunt, July 19, 1922, ibid., Box 621, "Unemployment: Cabot, Philip, 1922." It appears from Hunt's July 24 reply that he did not show Cabot's letter to Hoover before Hoover wrote to Barnes. For the comments about Hoover and the coal situation, see Philippi Harding (?) to Ethel Bullard, July 25, 1922, Lou Hoover Papers, Hoover Presidential Library, West Branch, Iowa, Box 10, "Personal Correspondence, 1921–28: Bullard, Ethel Bagg, 1921–28"; Lou Hoover to Hugh Gibson, July 31, 1922, ibid., Box 14, "Personal Correspondence, 1921–28: Gibson, Hugh and Ynes, 1921–28."

19. Melvyn Dubofsky and Warren Van Tine, *John L. Lewis: A Biography* (New York: Quadrangle, 1977), 86–87; A. M. Ogle to Hoover, August 8, 1922, and Hoover to Ogle, August 8, 1922, both in Hoover Papers, Commerce Period, Box 106, "Coal, Plans, Glasgow-Crews Proposal, 1922–23"; Hoover to H. N. Taylor, August 14, 1922, memorandum between Ralph Crews and Wm. A. Glasgow, Jr., August 6, 1922, and Hoover to Wm. A. Glasgow, August 9, 1922, all in ibid., Box 104, "Coal, Material Kept Together by Order of Mr. Hoover (1)"; Robert K. Murray, *The Harding Era: Warren G. Harding and His Administration* (Minneapolis: University of Minnesota Press, 1969), 258–60.

20. Edward Eyre Hunt to Philip Cabot, August 14, 1922, Hoover Papers, Commerce Period, Box 621, "Unemployment: Cabot, Philip, 1922"; Hoover to Sen. William E. Borah, August 18, 1922, ibid., Box 544, "Senate: Borah, William E., 1921–1928" (released to the press on August 19); Hoover to Gov. H. L. Davis (Ohio), August 19, 1922, ibid., Box 483, "Press Releases, 1922 May–August"; Hoover to James Goodrich, August 26, 1922, ibid., Box 101, "Coal: Cooperation, Service, Etc., 1922"; Hoover to Harding, August 23, 1922, ibid., Box 480, "President Harding, 1922 August–September"; Hoover to William W. Potter, August 24, 1922, ibid., Box 483, "Press Releases, 1922 May–August"; Hoover to Sen. Frank B. Kellogg, August 31, 1922, ibid., Box 548, "Senate: Kellogg, Frank B., 1922–1923 & undated"; Hoover to E. M. Poston, August 31, 1922, ibid., Box 474, "Poston, Elias McClellan, 1921–1922"; Ellis W. Hawley, "Secretary Hoover and the Bituminous Coal Problem, 1921–1928," *Business History Review* 42 (Autumn 1968): 258. The railroad strike ended on September 11 and did not materially affect coal distribution.

21. Hoover, "The Public and the Coal Industry," September 12, 1922, Hoover Papers, Commerce Period, Box 648, "Unemployment: Hoover, Secretary, 1921–1923."

22. Press release from the coal distributor about the Washington conference, September 12, 1922, Hoover Papers, Commerce Period, Box 97, "Coal, 1922 September–October"; Hoover to various business leaders, September 13, 1922, ibid., Box 101, "Coal, Conferences, Cooperation of Business and Industrial Organizations, 1922"; Commerce Department press release listing attendees at September 15 conference, ibid., Box 98, "Coal, Miscellaneous, 1922 August–September"; Commerce Department press release on the September 15 conference, "Coal Prices and Distribution," September 16, 1922, ibid., Box 483, "Press

Releases, 1922 September–December"; U.S. Chamber of Commerce press release, September 18, 1922, ibid., Box 100, "Coal: Chamber of Commerce of the U.S., Press Release, 1922 September 18." The railroads, Hoover pointed out in October, were physically incapable of shipping any more coal than they were already carrying. See Hoover to George Barr Baker, October 21, 1922, George Barr Baker Papers, Hoover Institution Archives, Stanford, California, Box 3, "Hoover, Herbert C. & Family."

23. Warren Harding to C. E. Spens, September 22, 1922, Hoover Papers, Commerce Period, Box 483, "Press Releases, 1922 September–December"; Federal Fuel Distributor press release, "Federal Government Action during the Coal Crisis," October 6, 1922, ibid., Box 101, "Federal Fuel Distributor's Office, Press Releases, 1921–1923 & undated"; Hoover to Royal Belge, October 14, 1922, ibid., Box 48, "Bef-Belgian, 1921–1928"; report of Fuel Distributor C. E. Spens, January 1, 1923, ibid., Box 101, "Coal: Federal Fuel Distributor, Reports, 1922"; report of Fuel Distributor H. R. Wadleigh, September 21, 1923, ibid., Box 102, "Coal: Federal Fuel Distributor, Wadleigh, F.R., 1922–1925 & undated."

24. Report of Fuel Distributor H.R. Wadleigh, September 15, 1923, Hoover Papers, Commerce Period, Box 102, "Coal: Federal Fuel Distributor, Wadleigh, F.R., 1922–1925 & undated"; Hoover to E. M. Poston, October 31, 1922, ibid., Box 474, "Poston, Elias McClellan, 1921–1922"; F. R. Wadleigh to Hoover, November 21, 1922, ibid., Box 102, "Coal: Federal Fuel Distributor, Spens, C. E., 1922–1923 & undated"; Edward Eyre Hunt to Hoover, December 30, 1922, ibid., Box 474, "Poston, Elias McClellan, 1921—1922"; Philip Cabot to Edward Eyre Hunt, September 8 and October 6, 1922, Edward Eyre Hunt Papers, Hoover Institution Archives, Stanford, California, Box 2, "Correspondence: Cabot, Philip, 1922–1928."

25. Hoover to Harding, December 22, 1922, Hoover Papers, Commerce Period, Box 480, "President Harding, 1922 October–December."

26. Department of Commerce, *Tenth Annual Report of the Secretary of Commerce* (Washington, DC: Government Printing Office, 1922), 21–25.

27. Hoover, "Economic Factors in Railway Rate Adjustment," statement before the Interstate Commerce Commission, February 3, 1922, Hoover Papers, Commerce Period, Box 502, "Railroads, 1922 Jan.–Feb."

28. Press release on a meeting between Hoover and railroad executives and labor leaders, January 16, 1922; Daniel Willard to Hoover, January 23, 1922, both in Hoover Papers, Commerce Period, Box 505, "Railroads: Railroad Conferences, 1921–1922"; Hoover to Edgar (Ernest) I. Lewis, March 12, 1922, ibid., Box 297, "Interstate Commerce Commission, 1922 February–March"; Hoover to Ernest I. Lewis, June 16, 1922, and Lewis to Hoover, June 19, 1922, both in ibid., Box 502, "Railroads, 1922 March–June."

29. Hoover to Harding, July 6, 1922, Hoover Papers, Commerce Period, Box 508, "Railroads: Strikes, 1922 Feb.–June"; Harding to T. DeWitt Cuyler, July 31, 1922, ibid., Box 508, "Railroads: Strikes, 1922 July 26–31"; Eugene P. Trani and David L. Wilson, *The Presidency of Warren G. Harding* (Lawrence: University Press of Kansas, 1977), 99–100.

30. Summary of a meeting between Hoover and a number of New York bankers and members of the Federal Reserve Board, August 1, 1922, Federal Reserve Bank of New York, Benjamin Strong Papers, Hoover Presidential Library, West Branch, Iowa, Box 4, "013.1, Hoover, Herbert, Oct. 22, 1917–Dec. 27, 1923"; Daniel Willard to Hoover, August 7, 1922, Hoover Papers, Commerce Period, Box 508, "Railroads: Strikes, 1922 August 6–20"; Hoover to Paul Shoup, August 23, 1922, ibid., Box 558, "Shoup, Paul, 1922–1928"; "Eliminate the Compromisers and Give Us a True Harding Policy, Boldly Asserted," New York *Manufacturers Record*, August 17, 1922, 49–50; Herbert Hoover, *Memoirs: The Cabinet and the Presidency, 1920–1933* (New York: Macmillan, 1952), 47–48 (hereafter, *Memoirs 2*); Murray, *The Harding Era*, 255–58, 260–61.

31. W. C. Mullendore to editor, *Manufacturers Record*, August 25, 1922, Hoover Papers, Commerce Period, Box 442, "Newspapers and Magazines: *Manufacturers Record*, 1922–1925,"; Hoover to Robert A. Taft, September 25, 1922, ibid., Box 593, "Taft, Robert A., 1922–1928"; Hoover to G. W. Anderson, September 21, 1922, ibid., Box 32, "Anderson, George W., 1921–1925"; Hoover to Barnes, December 22, 1922, ibid., Box 45, "Barnes, Julius H., 1922."

32. Hoover to Samuel Gompers, October 23, 1920; minutes of American Federation of Labor Executive Council Meeting, November 17, 1920, both in Hoover Papers, Pre-Commerce Period, Hoover Presidential Library, West Branch, Iowa, Box 5, "Gompers, Samuel, 1917–1922"; Robert H. Zieger, "Herbert Hoover, the Wage Earner, and the 'New Economic System,' 1919–1929," in *Herbert Hoover as Secretary of Commerce, 1921–1928: Studies in New Era Thought and Practice*, ed. Ellis W. Hawley (Iowa City: University of Iowa Press, 1981), 82–112.

33. Gerald D. Feldman, *Iron and Steel in the German Inflation, 1916–1923* (Princeton, NJ: Princeton University Press, 1977), 430–44. German steelmakers did not secure repeal of the eight-hour law passed in 1918 until 1923, but American executives were well aware of their campaign.

34. Philip S. Foner, *History of the Labor Movement in the United States*, vol. 7, *Labor and World War I, 1914–1918* (New York: International, 1987), 362–64; David A. Morse, *The Origin and Evolution of the I.L.O. and Its Role in the World Community* (Ithaca, NY: New York State School of Industrial and Labor Relations, Cornell University, 1969), 10–11; Daniel Patrick Moynihan, "Questions for Mr. Hoover," April 1, 1959; Hoover, "Speech at the Dinner of the U.S. Chamber of Commerce, Jan. 12, 1923"; Hoover to Albert Thomas, March 29, 1923, all in Hoover Papers, Commerce Period, Box 296, "International Labor Office, 1921—1927." Hoover discussed the ILO further at a private dinner on June 1, 1923, with Samuel Gompers and U.S. Chamber President Julius Barnes. See Hoover to Barnes, May 29, 1923, ibid., Box 45, "Barnes, Julius, 1923"; Hoover to Barnes, June 7, 1923, ibid., Box 240, "Gompers, Samuel, 1921–1944 & undated." Hoover's January 12 speech was never released publicly, and he apparently kept no copy of it. The copy in his papers is a transcript made by Moynihan from the Thomas papers at ILO headquarters in Geneva, Switzerland.

35. Morris L. Cooke to Edward Eyre Hunt, January 11, 15, 1921, and Hunt to Cooke, January 11, 1921, all in Hoover Papers, Pre-Commerce Period, Box 3, "Cooke, Morris L., 1916–1921"; Philip Cabot, "Judge Gary's Opportunity," *Atlantic Monthly* 127 (May 1921): 599–606; Samuel McCune Lindsay to Hoover, April 8, 1921, Hoover Papers, Commerce Period, Box 371, "Lindsay, Samuel McCune, 1922–1925." The FAES committee included, among others, Morris Cooke, executive secretary of the FAES Lew Wallace, and Robert B. Wolf, a young engineer sympathetic to labor who had previously worked with Hoover and the AFL to explore ways to reduce labor conflicts. Its report was published in November as Committee on Work-Periods in Continuous Industry of the Federated American Engineering Societies, *The Twelve-Hour Shift in Industry* (New York: Dutton, 1922).

36. Hoover to Harding, April 8, May 4, 1922, Hoover Papers, Commerce Period, Box 614, "Twelve-Hour Day, 1921–1922."

37. "Statement by Elbert H. Gary, Chairman United States Steel Corporation, at Annual Meeting," April 17, 1922, pp. 7–8, Hoover Papers, Commerce Period, Box 677, "United States Steel Corporation, 1922–1928 & undated."

38. Samuel McCune Lindsay to Hoover, May 17, 27, 1922, Hoover Papers, Commerce Period, Box 614, "Twelve-Hour Day, 1921–1922"; "White House Dinner to All Steel Heads; President Invites about 40 Executives of Leading Companies to Meet Him Tonight; Labor Main Interest," *New York Times*, May 18, 1922; "Harding Consults Steel Men on End of Twelve Hour Day," *New York Times*, May 19, 1922; "Twelve Hour Day in Steel Industry," editorial, *New York Times*, May 20, 1922; Committee on Work-Periods in Continuous Industry of the FAES, *Twelve-Hour Shift*, ix, 290–93; Zieger, "Herbert Hoover," 95–96.

39. Committee on Work-Periods in Continuous Industry of the FAES, *Twelve-Hour Shift*. For the committee's argument about comparative labor costs, see p. 293.

40. It is difficult to assess the effect of higher labor costs on the steel companies' profits. High domestic demand for steel, especially from the automobile and petroleum pipeline companies, contributed to strong sales through most of the rest of the decade. The companies complained about sharp price competition, especially overseas, but total steel exports remained fairly steady throughout the decade. See William T. Hogan, *Economic History of the Iron and Steel Industry in the United States* (Lexington, MA: Lexington Books, 1971), 3: 874, 895–98, 1090–93.

41. Lindsay to Hoover, May 17, 1922, Hoover Papers, Commerce Period, Box 614, "Twelve-Hour Day, 1921–1922"; Herbert Hoover, *American Individualism* (New York: Doubleday, Doran, 1922, repr. West Branch, IA, Hoover Presidential Library, n.d.), 15.

42. "Summary of Testimony Presented by Herbert Hoover before the Senate Select Committee on Reconstruction and Production," September 23, 1920, Hoover Papers, Pre-Commerce Period, Box 60, "Postal Savings System, 1920"; "Hoover Denounces Federal Bureaus," *New York Times*, September 24, 1920; Hoover to John R. Dunlap, November 18, 1920, Hoover Papers, Pre-Commerce Period, Box 4, "Dunlap, John R., 1920–1921"; report of the Select Committee on Reconstruction and Production, U.S. Senate, March 2, 1921 *Reconstruction and Production* (Washington, DC: Government Printing Office, 1921).

43. Hoover to Harding, March 14, 1921, Hoover Papers, Commerce Period, Box 480, "President Harding, 1921 March"; press release, "The Housing Shortage, A Problem for Community Action," ca. April 1, 1921, ibid., Box 451, "Notes, Memoranda, Etc., 1921–1922 & undated"; F. T. Miller (?) to Henry H. Curran, April 5, 1921, ibid., Box 68, "Building and Housing, Recommendations for Building Committee, 1921"; F. T. Miller to Hoover, April 22, 1921, ibid., Box 67, "Building and Housing: Miller, F. T., Building, 1921 March–April"; "Address of Herbert Hoover before the American Institute of Architects, Washington, D.C., May 12, 1921," ibid., Box 28, "American Institute of Architects, 1921–1926"; Hoover to Ernest T. Trigg, May 16, 1921, ibid., Box 67, "Building and Housing: Miller, F. T., Building, 1921 May–August"; Franklin T. Miller to Hoover, May 19, 1921, ibid., Box 63, "Building and Housing, 1921"; Miller to Hoover, June 7, 1921, ibid., Box 67, "Building and Housing: Miller, F. T., Building, 1921 May–August & undated"; "Address by Herbert Hoover Before the National Association of Real Estate Boards, Chicago, Ill., Friday, July 15, 1921," ibid., Box 428, "National Association of Real Estate Boards, 1921–1926"; Fred A. Bjornstad, "Herbert Hoover, Housing, and Socioeconomic Planning in the 1920s," in *Uncommon Americans: The Lives and Legacies of Herbert and Lou Henry Hoover*, ed. Timothy Walch (Westport, CT: Praeger, 2003), 107–8.

44. Hoover to Joseph H. Defrees, July 28, 1921, Hoover Papers, Commerce Period, Box 68, "Building and Housing, 1921–1922 June"; J. H. Gries to Hoover, August 16, 1921, ibid., Box 67, "Building and Housing: Miller, F. T., Building, 1921 March–April"; Hoover to James H. Angell, September 28, 1921, ibid., Box 63, "Building and Housing, 1921"; John H. Gries to Hoover, December 10, 1921, January 21, 1922, ibid., Box 68, "Building and Housing: Zoning, 1921–1922 June"; Harding to Hoover, February 2, 1922, enclosing King to Harding, January 28, 1922; Hoover to Harding, February 9, 1922, all in ibid., Box 480, "President Harding, 1922 January–February." The department subsequently released Hoover's letter to the press. As president, Hoover did call a national conference on housing. For the work of the department's Division of Simplified Practice in promoting simplification and standardization in construction materials, see F. M. Feiker, "The Trend of Simplification: How the Movement Is Growing, and What the Paving Brick Action Signifies," *Factory* (February 1922): 156–58; Commerce Department press release, "Secretary Hoover's Remarks to Lumbermen," May 22, 1922, Hoover Papers, Commerce Period, Box 483, "Press Releases, 1922 May–August"; Commerce Department press release by William A. Durgin, chief of Division of Simplified Practice, "Simplified Practice: What It Is and What It Offers," July 1, 1922, ibid., Box 145, "Commerce Dept.: Simplified Coml. Practice, 1922, July–Aug."

45. Commerce Department press release, "Big Year for Home Builders Predicted," March 20, 1922, Hoover Papers, Commerce Period, Box 483, "Press Releases, 1922 March–April."

46. Memorandum to Hoover from John Gries, "Zoning Primer," July 6, 1922, Hoover Papers, Commerce Period, Box 68, "Building and Housing: Zoning, 1922 July–1927 & undated"; memorandum to Hoover from Gries, "Plumbing Code Committee," July 7, 1922, ibid., Box 68, "Building and Housing: Sub-Committee on Plumbing, 1921–1922"; Department of Commerce, Advisory Committee on Zoning, *A Zoning Primer* (Washington, DC: Government Printing Office, 1922); Hoover to F. P. Keppel, May 5, 1922; press release on New York plan, May 10, 1922; Russell Sage Foundation, "Plan of New York and Its Environs," May 1922, all in Hoover Papers, Commerce Period, Box 68, "Building and Housing: New York Plan, 1922–1923"; Benjamin J. Rosenthal to Hoover, May 25, 1922, ibid., Box 530,

"Rosenthal, Benjamin J., 1921"; Bjornstad, "Herbert Hoover, Housing, and Socioeconomic Planning," 109.

47. Hoover to Associated General Contractors, April 7, 1923, Hoover Papers, Commerce Period, Box 37, "Associated C-Associated General Contractors, 1921–1927"; Hoover to Roosevelt, June 12, 1923, enclosing draft of Roosevelt to Coolidge, undated; Roosevelt to Hoover, April 18, 1925, both in ibid., Box 22, "American Civil-American Con, 1921–1928"; J. Walter Drake to F. C. McMaph, July 6, 1923; Drake to John W. Staley, July 26, 1923, both in ibid., Box 166, "Construction, 1923 May–December & undated,"; Frank Freidel, *Franklin D. Roosevelt: The Ordeal* (Boston: Little, Brown, 1954), 151–58; Bjornstad, "Herbert Hoover, Housing, and Socioeconomic Planning," 109–10.

48. "Magazine 'This Week' Headed by Prominent Woman Editor," New York *Evening Star*, February 18, 1935; Hoover to George S. Christian, July 12, 1922; Hoover to Marie Meloney, July 24, 1922; Meloney to Hoover, January 8, 1923; Hoover to Harding, February 2, 1923; and press release, "Better Homes in America, Demonstration Week, October 9–14, 1922, Advance General Information," July 31, 1922, all in Hoover Papers, Commerce Period, Box 65, "Building and Housing: Better Homes in America Previous to Incorporation, 1921–1923 June"; Janice Williams Rutherford, *Selling Mrs. Consumer: Christine Frederick and the Rise of Household Efficiency* (Athens: University of Georgia Press, 2003), 112.

49. Hoover to Irving R. Hiett, September 13, 1922, Hoover Papers, Commerce Period, Box 68, "Building and Housing: Own Your Home, 1921–1924"; Hoover, "The Home as an Investment," in Better Homes in America, *Plan Book for Demonstration Week, October 9 to 14, 1922* (New York: The Delineator, 1922), 7–8; Bjornstad, "Herbert Hoover, Housing, and Socioeconomic Planning," 109; Meg Jacobs, *Pocketbook Politics: Economic Citizenship in Twentieth-Century America* (Princeton, NJ: Princeton University Press, 2005), 70.

50. Hoover devoted a full chapter to waterway development in his memoirs, quoting at length from an August 21, 1926, speech on the subject at Seattle. Hoover, *Memoirs* 2, 112–24. See also Hoover to William F. Funsten and to C. L. Niemeir, April 20, 1920, Hoover Papers, Pre-Commerce Period, Box 57, "National Inland Waterways Association, November 1919–July 23, 1920"; Hoover to Franklin K. Lane, May 17, 1921, Hoover Papers, Commerce Period, Box 363, "Lane, Franklin K., 1921–1928"; Charles Craig to Hoover, January 17, 1922, ibid., Box 689, "Waterways: Great Lakes-St. Lawrence, 1922."

51. Report on the Colorado River Commission prepared by order of Hoover for business paper editors, September 29, 1924, Hoover Papers, Commerce Period, Box 429, "National Conference of Business Editors, 1924"; Reclamation Service, "Report on Problems of Imperial Valley and Vicinity Required by Act of Congress approved May 18, 1920," February (28,) 1922, ibid., Box 290, "Imperial Valley and Vicinity, Problems of, 1922"; Beverley Moeller, *Phil Swing and Boulder Dam* (Berkeley: University of California Press, 1971), 30. Although a Stanford graduate, Swing was far closer to Hiram Johnson than to Hoover, whom he regarded as a reactionary.

52. William C. Mullendore to Richard S. Emmet, March 24, 1922, Hoover Papers, Commerce Period, Box 609, "Trips: First Western Trip; Mullendore, W. C., 1922 March 21–April and undated"; Albert Fall to secretary (?), March 24, 1922, Albert Fall Collection, Huntington Library, San Marino, California, Box 47, Folder 10, "Colorado River Project, Sept. 21, 1921–Feb. 9, 1923."

53. Hoover to Secretary of State Hughes, April 20, 1922, Hoover Papers, Commerce Period, Box 571, "State Department: Secretary of State Hughes, Charles E., 1922 April–May"; "Summary of Decision in State of Wyoming vs. State of Colorado," handed down June 5, 1922, Colorado River Commission Papers, Hoover Presidential Library, West Branch, Iowa (hereafter CRCP), Box 24, "Wyoming vs. Colorado"; "Protection and Development of Lower Colorado River Basin," hearings before the Committee on Irrigation of Arid Lands, 67 Cong., 2 Sess., on H.R. 11449 by Mr. Swing, June 15, 16, 21, 1922, ibid., Box 15, "House of Representatives: Hearings re: H.R. 11449, 1922–23," pp. 61–62; *State of Wyoming v. State of Colorado*, 259 U.S. 419 (1922).

54. W. F. McClure to Phil Swing, October 20, 1922; Swing to McClure (two versions), October 28, 1922, all in Phil D. Swing Papers, UCLA Library, Los Angeles, Box 135, "Colorado

River Commission-Compact-Hoover, 1922"; Hoover to Harding, November 16, 1922, Hoover Papers, Commerce Period, Box 480, "President Harding, 1922 October–December"; Hoover to Albert Fall, November 16, 1922, ibid., Box 294, "Interior Department: Secretary Fall, Albert, 1922–1928 & undated"; Clarence Stetson to E. W. Libbey, November 25, 1922, CRCP, Box 22, "Stetson, Clarence C., September–December, 1922"; press release "Colorado River Compact," November 25, 1922, Hoover Papers, Commerce Period, Box 483, "Press Releases, 1922 September–December"; Daniel Tyler, "Delphus Emory Carpenter and the Colorado River Compact of 1922," *University of Denver Water Law Review* 1 (Summer 1998): 228–74.

55. Hoover to Albert Fall, November 27, 1922, CRCP, Box 32, "Interior Department, 1922–24"; Hoover to Herman Kohlsatt [*sic*], November 27, 1922, Hoover Papers, Commerce Period, Box 360, "Kohlsaat, H. H., 1921–1923"; Richard S. Emmet to Philip D. Swing, November 28, 1922, ibid., Box 282, "House of Representatives: Swing, Phil D., 1921–28 & undated." Swing's doubts about the fairness of the compact to the Lower Basin states appear in various documents in the file, "Col. River Commission Compact-Hoover–1922," in Box 135 of the Swing Papers.

56. Swing to Hoover, December 1, 1922, Hoover Papers, Commerce Period, Box 282, "House of Representatives: Swing, Phil D., 1921–28 & undated"; William J. Carr to Swing, December 2, 1922, and Swing to Carr, January 15, 1923, both in Swing Papers, Box 135, "Colo. River Commission-Compact-Hoover1–922"; Hoover to Swing, December 27, 1922, CRCP, Box 34, "Project File: Swing, Phil D., 1922–24, 1926–27."

57. Hoover to Harding, November 28, 1921, Hoover Papers, Commerce Period, Box 480, "President Harding, 1921 October–November."

58. Murray, *Harding Era*, 182–86; Harding to Hoover, December 6, 1921, Hoover Papers, Commerce Period, Box 480, "President Harding, 1921 December"; David Cannadine, *Mellon: An American Life* (New York: Knopf, 2006), 316. The Farm Bloc in the House of Representatives succeeded in postponing the repeal of the excess profits tax for a year in 1921, but the House otherwise followed Mellon's recommendations, increasing the corporate tax, reducing the tax rate on the wealthiest, and increasing exemptions for those with low incomes. Hoover agreed with those changes. Ibid., 287–88.

59. Press release, "Address of Herbert Hoover before National Shoe and Leather Exposition," July 13, 1921, Hoover Papers, Commerce Period, Box 433, "National Shoe and Leather Association Speech, 7/12/21." Carl-Ludwig Holtfrerich argues that the value of American exports to Germany quadrupled between 1919 and 1921, constituting 8.3 percent of all American exports in 1921. For some exports, the German market was even more important, taking 20.8 percent of cotton, 30 percent of copper, 30 percent of meat, and 13 percent of wheat and wheat flour products. Altogether, exports to Germany made up .3 percent of the U.S. GNP in 1921, by Holtfrerich's calculations. See Carl-Ludwig Holtfrerich, *The German Inflation, 1914–1923: Causes and Effects in International Perspective*, trans. Theo Balderson (Berlin: Walter de Gruyter, 1986), 213–14.

60. "Methods for Expanding U.S. Trade Discussed," Washington *Star*, April 5, 1921); "Uncle Sam at Last Has a Crackerjack Sales Manager," Philadelphia *Evening Ledger*, April 9, 1921; press release of a letter from twenty-six prominent businessmen to Hoover, April 29, 1921, Hoover Papers, Commerce Period, Box 483, "Press Releases, 1921"; Elliot F. Jordan (?), resident vice president of the U.S. Chamber of Commerce, to Hoover, June 3, 1921, ibid., Box 83, "Chamber of Commerce, United States, 1921 June–December"; William C. Redfield to Hoover, June 13, 1921, ibid., Box 511, "Redfield, William C., 1921–1928"; memorandum by Christian Herter on the functions and duties of commercial attachés and trade commissioners, and the distinction between their duties and those of the consular service, June 24, 1921, ibid., Box 133, "Commerce Department, Foreign and Domestic Commerce, Commercial Attaches, Duties, 1921."

61. Julius Klein, *Frontiers of Trade* (New York: Century, 1929), 139–40; Christian Herter to Mr. (?) Herring, April 11, 1921; Andrew Mellon to Harding, November 30, 1921; and Hoover to Harding, enclosing a list of proposed members of the American Section, December 7, 1921, all in Hoover Papers, Commerce Period, Box 292, "Inter-American High

Commission, 1921"; press release, "President Harding Names Hoover New Chairman U.S. Section, Inter-American High Commission," December 19, 1921, ibid., Box 292, "Inter-American High Commission"; W. E. Aughinbaugh to Hoover, December 21, 1921, and Hoover to Aughinbaugh, December 23, 1921, both in ibid., Box 444, "Newspapers and Magazines, *New York Commercial*, 1921–1928 & undated"; Hoover to (?) Carter, June 17, 1921, ibid., Box 34, "Argentina, American Chamber of Commerce, 1921 & undated"; press release, "Effect of Exchanges on Inter-American Commerce," January 23, 1922, ibid., Box 293, "Inter-American High Commission, Exchange Situation, 1921–1922"; C. E. McGuire to Hoover, February 28, 1922, ibid., Box 293, "Inter-American High Commission, 1922 February–March"; memorandum for Hoover by L. S. Rowe, April 3, 1922, ibid., Box 293, "Inter-American High Commission, 1922 April."

62. Hoover, unsigned memorandum on economic recovery in Europe, January 10, (1922,) Hoover Papers, Commerce Period, Box 188, "Economic Recovery in Europe, 1921–26 & undated"; "Hoover Insists U.S. Must Give Long Credits to Europe," New York *Journal of Commerce*, January 20, 1921, and Henry M. Robinson to Hoover, December 4, 1920, Box 3, "Correspondence: Hoover, Herbert," Henry M. Robinson Papers, Hoover Institution Archives, Stanford, California. On Commerce's role in clearing overseas loans, see draft of Hoover to Harding, November 30, 1921, Hoover Papers, Commerce Period, Box 480, "President Harding, 1921 October–November"; Hoover to Hughes, December 6, 15, 1921, and Hughes to Hoover, December 13, 16, 1921, both in ibid., Box 286, "Hughes, Charles Evans, 1921"; Hughes to Hoover, December 13, 1921, and Hoover to Hughes, December 13, 30, 1921, ibid., Box 571, "State Department: Secretary of State Hughes, Charles E., 1921 December"; Hoover to Harding, December 31, 1921, ibid., Box 480, "President Harding, 1921 December."

63. Commerce Department press release, "Currents in Foreign Trade," November 6, 1922, Hoover Papers, Commerce Period, Box 659, "Press Releases, 1922 September–December"; Stephen A. Schuker, *American "Reparations" to Germany, 1919–33: Implications for the Third-World Debt Crisis* (Princeton, NJ: International Finance Section, Department of Economics, Princeton University, 1988), 92–94; Hal B. Lary and associates, *The United States in the World Economy: International Transactions of the United States during the Interwar Period* (Washington, DC: Government Printing Office, 1943), Table 1, following p. 216.

64. "Currents in Foreign Trade," November 6, 1922; Department of Commerce, *Tenth Annual Report of the Secretary of Commerce*, 16–19. For a vigorous contemporary defense of the "invisible exchange" concept, see Klein, *Frontiers of Trade*, 176–85. Lary, *United States in the World Economy*, confirms Hoover's general argument, if not the precise figures.

65. Department of Commerce, Bureau of the Census, *Historical Statistics of the United States: Earliest Times to the Present*, Millennial ed. (New York: Cambridge University Press, 2006), vol. 5, part E, "Government and International Relations," Tables Ee7, Ee9, Ee11, p. 455; Table Ee12, pp. 459–460; Schuker, *American "Reparations,"* 92–94, 100. An internal Commerce Department memorandum, prepared in October 1922, concluded that the United States had a favorable balance in merchandise exports, gold and silver, Federal Reserve notes, private interest received, and ocean freights throughout 1919 to 1921 and that this favorable balance was not offset by American government payments, private investments abroad, American securities resold in the United States, immigrant remittances, and tourist expenditures overseas. According to the memo, the balance started to become unfavorable in the first six months of 1922, and a second memo in February 1923 confirmed that trend. See "American Credit Balance Against Europe," October 3, 1922, Hoover Papers, Commerce Period Box 219, "Foreign Debts, World War Foreign Debt Commission, 1920–1922"; "Balance of International Payments of the United States for the Year 1922," February 23, 1923, ibid., Box 136, "Commerce Department, Foreign & Domestic Commerce, Finance & Investments, 1922–1928." By May 1923, the Finance and Investment Division had increased its estimates of tourist spending from $250 million to $350 million and of immigrant remittances from $400 million to $500 million and had added an estimated $50 million expenditure for parcel post shipments as a new item. See Finance and Investment Division to Hoover, "Progress on International Balance of Payments Study,"

May 16, 1923, ibid., Box 227, "Foreign Trade, 1923." Hoover explained the net import of some $246 million in gold in 1922 as the result of the repayment of debts incurred during 1919 and 1920 rather than as a result of a current excess of exports over imports. See press release, "Invisible Exchange," September 17, 1923, ibid., Box 228, "Foreign Trade, Invisible Exchange, 1922–1923." The National City Bank's newsletter pointed out that although American purchases of foreign governments' securities could be considered a debit in the short term, payments of interest and principal would convert it to an asset in the long-term. See Grosvenor Jones to Hoover, October 10, 1923, enclosing National City Bank newsletter for October 1923, ibid., Box 228, "Foreign Trade, Invisible Exchange, 1922–1923." If one includes interest and dividends from foreign investments and payments on European war debts, the United States had a balance of payments surplus in every year from 1920 to 1929. See Schuker, *American "Reparations,"* 92–94.

66. Press release, "Economic Situation in Europe," by Hoover, December 12, 1921, Hoover Papers, Commerce Period, Box 483, "Press Releases, 1921"; Hoover to Theodore Gilman, December 14, 1921, ibid., Box 44, "Banks of Nations, 1921–1922"; Hoover to Paul Warburg, July 2, 6, 1921, and Warburg to Hoover, July 6, 7, 1921, all in ibid., Box 685, "Warburg, Paul, 1918–1922."

67. Schuker, *American "Reparations,"* 14–21; Holtfrerich, *The German Inflation,* 137–55.

68. During the drafting of the Fordney tariff bill in 1921, Hoover said that he had not yet made up his mind about protectionism, except that he definitely favored protection for American farmers. Subsequently, the president of the U.S. Chamber of Commerce, the American Importers and Exporters Association, business paper publisher Arch Shaw, and the banker Paul M. Warburg all urged him to oppose protectionism, often on the ground that it would impede European recovery. He avoided taking a public position prior to the passage of the Fordney Act but argued in the department's annual report in the autumn of 1922 that nearly 60 percent of imports remained free under the new law and that "invisible exchange" subsidized foreign buying power so that 70 to 80 percent of American exports were unaffected. Therefore, he concluded, "it would not seem that the gross volume of exports would be very greatly affected one way or another by the tariff," while "the volume of our imports is likely to be increased by the increasing prosperity at home." See Hoover to James F. Curtis, March 23, 1921, Hoover Papers, Commerce Period, Box 593, "Tariff 1914–1921"; A. B. Farquhar to Hoover, March 21, 1921, ibid., Box 196, "Farquhar, Arthur B., 1921"; "Importers and Exporters Oppose Tariff Plans," New York *Evening Post,* April 13, 1921; Arch Shaw to Hoover, July 21, 1921, Hoover Papers, Commerce Period, Box 556, "Shaw, Arch W., 1921 July–Dec."; Paul M. Warburg to Hoover, July 22, 1921, ibid., Box 685, "Warburg, Paul, 1918–1921"; Department of Commerce, *Tenth Annual Report of the Secretary of Commerce,* 20.

69. Hoover to Harding, January 4, 1922, Hoover Papers, Commerce Period, Box 188, "Economic Recovery in Europe, 1921–22 & undated"; Hoover to Hughes, January 4, 1922, ibid., Box 154, "Conferences, Genoa, 1922, 1921–1922 January"; Harding to Hoover, and Harding to Hughes, January 12, 1921, ibid., Box 222, "Foreign Loans, Armaments and Loans, 1922–25"; Hoover, "No American Loans for Militaristic Purposes," *Manufacturers News,* March 2, 1922, 9–10; Hoover to Benjamin Strong, August 30, 1921; Strong to Hoover, September 1, 1921; Charles Evans Hughes to Hoover, September 1, 1921, all in Hoover Papers, Commerce Period, Box 579, "Strong, Benjamin, 1921–1922." Hoover's proposal was flawed in several significant ways: up to this point, the Germans had paid almost nothing on their reparations bill and seemed unlikely to do better in the future; German properties in the United States had been seized by the Alien Property Custodian during the war and hence were not available as security for bonds; reduction of the occupation force would arguably have reduced any incentive for the Germans to pay; and appreciation of the franc and mark would almost certainly have precipitated deep recessions in both countries that would have delayed or reversed recovery.

70. Draft letter, Hoover to Joseph H. DeFrees, January 11, 1922, Hoover Papers, Commerce Period, Box 188, "Economic Recovery in Europe, 1921–26 & undated"; Hoover to Harding, January 23, 1922, ibid.; "Resentment Against U.S. Sweeping France Since McCormick's

Debts Query" (actually printed as "Resentment Against U.S. McCormick's Debt Query Sweeping France Since"), Oakland *Tribune*, January 29, 1922; press release, "Summary of Address before United States Chamber of Commerce by Herbert Hoover, Tuesday Evening, May 16, 1922," Hoover Papers, Commerce Period, Box 188, "Economic Situation in U.S., 1921–1924"; World War Foreign Debt Commission, *Combined Annual Reports of the World War Foreign Debt Commission, with Additional Information Regarding Foreign Debts Due the United States, Fiscal Years 1922, 1923, 1924, 1925, and 1926* (Washington, DC: Government Printing Office, 1927).

71. Carole Fink, *The Genoa Conference: European Diplomacy, 1921–1922* (Chapel Hill: University of North Carolina Press, 1984), 3–36, 48–49.

72. Department of Commerce, *Tenth Annual Report*, 13–14. For the early development of radio, see Erik Barnouw, *A Tower in Babel: A History of Broadcasting in the United States* (New York: Oxford University Press, 1966), 1:3–64.

73. Rep. Wallace H. White to Hoover, April 12, 1921, Hoover Papers, Commerce Period, Box 283, "House of Representatives: White, Wallace H., 1921–1928 & undated"; Hoover to Sen. Frank Kellogg, April 22, 1921, ibid., Box 501, "Radio: Legislation, 1920–1921"; Hoover to W. D. Terrell, August 29, 1921, ibid., Box 489, "Radio: Radio World's Fair, 1921–1928"; Barnouw, *Tower in Babel*, 64–94; Hugh G. J. Aitken, *The Continuous Wave: Technology and American Radio, 1900–1932* (Princeton, NJ: Princeton University Press, 1985), 348–86.

74. "Hoover to Advise on Radio Control," *New York Times*, February 10, 1922; Hoover to secretaries of agriculture, post office, army, navy, and various private interest groups, February 10, 1922, Hoover Papers, Commerce Period, various boxes (e.g., Box 11, "Agriculture Department: Secretary of Agriculture, Wallace, Henry C., 1922"); Commerce Department press release, "Statement by the Secretary of Commerce at the Opening of the Radio Conference on February 27, 1922," ibid., Box 489, "Radio: Correspondence, Press Releases, Misc., 1922 Jan.–March"; Barnouw, *Tower in Babel*, 94–95; Gleason L. Archer, *History of Radio to 1926* (New York: American Historical Society, 1938), 105–6.

75. Commerce Department press release, "Tentative Report of Department of Commerce Conference of Radio Telephony," ca. April 27, 1922, Hoover Papers, Commerce Period, Box 483, "Press Releases, 1922 March-April"; Archer, *History of Radio*, 249.

76. Hoover to Secretary of Agriculture Henry C. Wallace, March 10, 1922, Hoover Papers, Commerce Period, Box 11, "Agriculture Department: Secretary of Agriculture Wallace, Henry C., 1922"; draft radio bill, April 18, 1922, ibid., Box 489, "Radio: Correspondence, Press Releases, Misc., 1922 April–May"; Hoover to Sen. Charles E. Townsend, April 10, 1922, ibid., Box 551, "Senate: Townsend, Charles E., 1921–1922"; reports on actions regarding S. 3694 and HR 11964, November 24, 1922 to January 2, 1923, ibid., Box 501, "Radio, Legislation, 1922"; Commerce Department press release, "Statement by Secretary on Radio Situation for 'Radio Broadcast,'" ibid., Box 489, "Radio: Correspondence, Press Releases, Misc, 1922 June–December"; Commerce Department press release, "Conference on Radio Standardization," December 2, 1922, ibid., Box 496, "Radio: Conferences (New York, January 13, 1923)."

77. Assistant Secretary of the Navy Theodore Roosevelt, Jr., to Hoover, April 8, 1922; Hoover to Roosevelt, April 11, 1922; William E. Lamb to Richard S. Emmet, April 15, 1922; Hoover to Rep. Samuel E. Winslow, June 12, 13, 19, 1922; Winslow to Hoover, June 14, 1922, all in Hoover Papers, Commerce Period, Box 122, "Commerce Department: Aeronautics, Bureau of, legislation, 1922"; David D. Lee, "Herbert Hoover and the Development of Commercial Aviation, 1921–1926," *Business History Review* 58 (Spring 1984): 90–91.

78. Herbert Hoover, *Memoirs: Years of Adventure, 1874–1920* (New York: Macmillan, 1951), 3; Hoover, "Live—Don't Just Exist" (repr. of Hoover's address to the National Conference on Outdoor Recreation, January 21, 1926), repr. from *Outdoor America*, in Lou Hoover Papers, Box 44, "Clubs and Organizations, National Conference on Outdoor Recreation, 1927–32." For an extended examination of Hoover's relationship to fishing, see Hal Elliott Wert, *Hoover, the Fishing President: Portrait of the Private Man and His Life Outdoors* (Mechanicsburg, PA: Stackpole Books, 2005). For a speculation on the role that fishing may have played in enabling Hoover to escape somewhat from an unhappy childhood, see

Kendrick A. Clements, "Herbert Hoover and the Fish," *Journal of Psychohistory* 10 (Winter 1983): 333–48.

79. Kendrick A. Clements, *Hoover, Conservation, and Consumerism: Engineering the Good Life* (Lawrence: University Press of Kansas, 2000) develops this point in detail.

80. Horace Albright Oral History, Bancroft Library, University of California at Berkeley, pp. 15–16; Joseph E. Taylor III, *Making Salmon: An Environmental History of the Northwest Fisheries Crisis* (Seattle: University of Washington Press, 1999), 221; minutes of conference of Atlantic Coast commercial fishermen at the Commerce Department, May 9–10, 1921, Hoover Papers, Commerce Period, Box 203, "Fish Industry, Conferences Re Fish Distribution, 1921 May 9–10"; program and minutes of Conference on Pollution of Waters and Proposed Federal Control of Fisheries, June 16, 1921, ibid., Box 203, "Fish Industry, Conference of State Fish Commissioners, Anglers and Producers, June 16, 1921, 1921 June 16–November 25"; Christian A. Herter to C. H. Huston, November 28, 1921, ibid., Box 288, "Huston, Claudius H., 1921–1922"; Hoover to Edwin F. Gay, February 13, 1922, ibid., Box 204, "Fisheries, Bureau of Miscellaneous, 1922"; Hoover to Harding, February 7, 1922, ibid., Box 480, "President Harding, 1922 January–February"; Hoover to Gov. E. Lee Trinkle, February 21, 1922, and Hoover to Rep. J. Charles Linthicum, February 24, 1922, both in ibid., Box 203, "Fish Industry, Crab Fisheries, 1921–1922."

81. H. F. Moore to Hoover, April 28, 1922, and Hoover to Charles Evans Hughes, May 1, 1922, both in Hoover Papers, Commerce Period, Box 203, "Fish Industry, Halibut Fisheries on Pacific Coast, 1922"; Commerce Department press release, "Progress in National Fisheries Conservation and Development," June 30, 1924, ibid., Box 166, "Conservation, 1923–28, & undated"; F. Heward Bell, *The Pacific Halibut: The Resource and the Fishery* (Anchorage: Alaska Northwest, 1981), 93–101, 122, 148–51; International Pacific Halibut Commission, *The Pacific Halibut: Biology, Fishery and Management*, Technical Report No. 22 (Seattle: International Pacific Halibut Commission, 1987), 16–17, 24–25.

82. H. F. Moore to Christian Herter, August 22, 1922; Hoover to Sutherland, August 24, December 21, December 30, 1922; and Sutherland to Hoover, December 26, 1922, January 1, 1923, all in Hoover Papers, Commerce Period, Box 282, "House of Representatives: Sutherland, Dan, 1921–1923"; Department of Commerce, *Eleventh Annual Report of the Secretary of Commerce* (Washington, DC: Government Printing Office, 1923), 174–75; Hoover, *Memoirs* 2, 149–51. The huge drop in the Alaska salmon catch in 1921 proved to be unique in the decade, perhaps a result of an El Niño phenomenon.

83. Draft of press release for assistant secretary of commerce, March 3, 1923, Hoover Papers, Commerce Period, Box 282, "House of Representatives: Sutherland, Dan, 1921–1923"; "Fisheries Charges 'Bunk,' Says Huston," Philadelphia *Public Ledger*, March 7, 1923; Hoover's personal notes on achievements of the Commerce Department in 1922 to 1923, undated, Hoover Papers, Commerce Period, Box 268, "Hoover, Herbert, Biography, undated."

84. Unsigned note on "Administration Problems," November 2, 1922, Hoover Papers, Commerce Period, Box 2, "Addison, Wadven, 1921–1928."

Chapter 14

1. Commerce Department press release, "World Economic Situation for 1923 by Secretary of Commerce Herbert Hoover," January 1, 1923, Hoover Papers, Commerce Period, Hoover Presidential Library, West Branch, Iowa, Box 188, "Economic Situation in U.S., 1921–1924."

2. Hoover to Harding, March 2, 17, 1923; Harding to Hoover, March 2, 1923, all in Hoover Papers, Commerce Period, Box 481, "President Harding, 1923 March–May"; Hoover to William Seaver Woods, March 27, 1923; D. Knickerbacker Boyd to Hoover, March 19, 1923; J. W. Cowper to Hoover, March 19, 1923; Richard H. Edmonds to Hoover, March 23, 1923; and unidentified, undated clipping, "Hoover Suggestion Variously Received," all in ibid., Box 166, "Construction, 1923 March–April"; press release from the Business

Cycle Committee of the Unemployment Conference, April 2, 1923, ibid., Box 483, "Press Releases, 1923 January–July"; Hoover to Adolph C. Miller, April 3, 1923, ibid., Box 199, "Federal Reserve Board & Banks, 1923–1924"; Hoover to Associated General Contractors, Chattanooga, April 7, 1923, ibid., Box 37, "Associated General Contractors, 1921–1927"; Hoover to M. E. Cooley, April 9, 1923, ibid., Box 154, "Conferences: Government Construction, 1923 March 8–22"; Richard S. Emmet to A. B. Duncan, April 9, 1923, ibid., Box 28, "American Legion, 1923–1924"; Hoover to Cecil F. Baker, April 12, 1923, ibid., Box 42, "Baker, George, 1922–1923"; Hoover to Ray Yarnell, ibid., Box 291, "Inflation, 1923–1924 & undated"; Hoover to National Association of Credit Men, April 26, 1923, ibid., Box 427, "National Association of Credit Men, 1921–1923"; "Halt in Building Urged on Nation," *New York Times*, May 17, 1923; William Atherton Du Puy, "Booms and Slumps Yield to Control," *New York Times*, December 30, 1923.

3. "Address of Secretary Hoover before the Chamber of Commerce of the United States," May 8, 1923, Hoover Papers, Commerce Period, Box 486, "Prohibition, 1922–1924"; Hoover to George J. Seay, June 9, 1923, ibid., Box 188, "Economic Situation, 1923–1924"; Hoover to J. H. Puelicher, June 13, 1923, ibid., Box 502, "Railroads 1923."

4. President Harding to the Senate, February 24, 1923, Hoover Papers, Commerce Period, Box 465, "Permanent Court of International Justice at the Hague, 1923 Feb.–April"; Hoover to Lewis H. Smith, March 13, 1923, ibid., Box 564, "Smith, Lewis H., 1921–1926"; Hoover to Will Hays, March 30, 1923, ibid., Box 256, "Hays, Will H., 1922–1923" (Hoover asked Hays to read a draft of the speech); Hoover, "Responsibility of America for World Peace: Address before Annual Convention of National League of Women Voters, Des Moines, Iowa," April 11, 1923, Bible no. 303, vol. 13, April 1923 to September 1923.

5. Editorial, "Mr. Borah's Interpolation," Peoria *Journal*, April 13, 1923; editorial, "Must Have Force, Too," Savannah *Press*, April 13, 1923; editorial, "Playing Politics," Wheeling *Register*, April 13, 1923; editorial, "The Fight Is On," Nashville *Tennessean*, April 13, 1923; James R. Nourse, "Hoover's Court Stand Denounced; Borah Cites Folly in Proposal," San Francisco *Examiner*, April 13, 1923; editorial, "A Latter-Day Confusion of Tongues," New York *Globe*, April 13, 1923; editorial, "Hoover vs. Lodge," Grand Rapids *Press*, April 13, 1923; Paul Wooten, "Harding's World Court Idea Splits Ranks Of G.O.P.," New Orleans *Times Picayune*, April 20, 1923; Hoover to Lewis H. Smith, April 25, 1923, and Hamilton Holt to Hoover, April 26, 1923 (Holt released his letter to the press); both in Hoover Papers, Commerce Period, Box 465, "Permanent Court of International Justice at the Hague, 1923 Feb.–April"; Alice Owens Winter to Hoover, May 14, 1923; Bronson Batchelor to Hoover, May 18, 1923; and Samuel Colcord to Hoover, July 4, July 29, August 2, 1923, all in ibid., Box 465, "Permanent Court of International Justice at the Hague, 1923 May–July"; Christian Herter to William Mullendore, July 7, 1923, ibid., Box 19, "Alaska Trip, Mullendore, W. C., 1923"; Hoover (?), "Amendments to President's San Francisco Speech," July 23, 1923, ibid., Box 19, "Alaska Trip, Miscellaneous Drafts, Speeches, etc., 1923"; "To Kill Harding's Speech," Los Angeles *Times*, August 16, 1923.

6. William C. McNeil, *American Money and the Weimar Republic: Economics and Politics on the Eve of the Great Depression* (New York: Columbia University Press, 1986), 36; David Cannadine, *Mellon: An American Life* (New York: Knopf, 2006), 288–89; Joseph Brandes, *Herbert Hoover and Economic Diplomacy: Department of Commerce Policy, 1921–1928* (Pittsburgh: University of Pittsburgh Press, 1962), 27–28.

7. McNeil, *American Money*, 36–47.

8. Thomas W. Lamont to E. C. Grenfell, February 20, 1922, Hoover Papers, Commerce Period, Box 211, "Foreign Debts, 1922 January–February"; C. H. Huston to Morris Brothers Corporation, March 17, 1922; Grosvenor Jones to Hoover, April 1, 5, 1922; Hoover, "Suggestions in connection with Foreign Loans," April 6, 1922; and Grosvenor Jones, "Comments on Mr. Hoover's Suggestions in Connection with Foreign Loans," undated, all in ibid., Box 221, "Foreign Loans, Miscellaneous, 1922"; Charles Evans Hughes to Hoover, April 20, 1922, enclosing copy of undated memo by Benjamin Strong, ibid., Box 571, "State Department: Secretary of State Hughes, Charles E., 1922 April–May"; memorandum by Christian A. Herter, April 22, 1922, ibid., Box 515, "Reparations, General Correspondence,

1922 January–June"; Hoover to Hughes, April 29, 1922, ibid., Box 286, "Hughes, Charles Evans, 1922."

9. Harding to Hoover, and Harding to Hughes, January 12, 1922, Hoover Papers, Commerce Period, Box 222, "Foreign Loans, Armaments and Loans, 1922–1925"; Louis Domeratzky, "Memorandum for the Secretary of Commerce," January 19, 1922, ibid., Box 215, "Foreign Debts, Germany, 1921–1928"; State Department press release, "Flotation of Foreign Loans," March 3, 1922, ibid., Box 221, "Foreign Loans, Miscellaneous, 1922"; Hoover, *Memoirs: The Cabinet and the Presidency, 1920–1933* (New York: Macmillan, 1952), 85–89 (hereafter, *Memoirs* 2); Hoover, "No American Loans for Militaristic Purposes," *Manufacturers' News*, March 2, 1922, 9–10. A table prepared in the Commerce Department in November 1922 estimated that France, Poland, Yugoslavia, Greece, Sweden, Latvia, and Spain were all spending more than 31 percent of their total revenues on arms. See "European Armies, Population and Military Expenditures as a Proportion of Total Expenditures and Total Revenues, Latest Available Estimates," November 2, 1922, Hoover Papers, Commerce Period, Box 211, "Foreign Debts, 1922 November–December."

10. Eugene P. Trani and David L. Wilson, *The Presidency of Warren G. Harding* (Lawrence: University Press of Kansas, 1977), 161.

11. For the May 25, 1921, White House conference, see Hoover Papers, Commerce Period, Box 221, "Foreign Finance Conference, 1921 A-W"; Keith L. Nelson, *Victors Divided: America and the Allies in Germany, 1918–1923* (Berkeley: University of California Press, 1975), 194–95. No transcript of what was said at the bankers' conference seems to have survived, but Hoover provided a lengthy and detailed discussion of what he thought should be done in a speech to the National Shoe and Leather Exposition and Style Show in Boston on July 12, 1921, the substance of which it is safe to assume was the same as what he told the bankers on May 25. For the speech, see Hoover Papers, Commerce Period, Box 433, "National Shoe and Leather Association Speech 7/12/21."

12. Trani and Wilson, *Presidency of Warren Harding*, 161.

13. Ibid., 44–46; Herbert Feis, *The Diplomacy of the Dollar, 1919–1932* (New York: Norton, 1950), 8–10; Cannadine, *Mellon*, 289–90; Michael J. Hogan, *Informal Entente: The Private Structure of Cooperation in Anglo-American Economic Diplomacy, 1918–1928* (Columbia: University of Missouri Press, 1977), 50; World War Foreign Debt Commission, *Combined Annual Reports of the World War Foreign Debt Commission, with Additional Information Regarding Foreign Debts Due the United States, Fiscal Years 1922, 1923, 1924, 1925, and 1926* (Washington, DC: Government Printing Office, 1927).

14. Cannadine, *Mellon*, 282–83; William A. Bird, "Resentment against U.S. Sweeping France Since McCormick's Debt Query," Oakland *Tribune*, January 29, 1922; Thomas W. Lamont to E. C. Grenfell, October 19, 1922, and Lamont to J. P. Morgan, October 6, 1922, both in Hoover Papers, Commerce Period, Box 211, "Foreign Debts, 1922 October"; Hoover to William A. Durgin, July 3, 1922, and "The Repayment of European Debts to Our Government," address of Secretary Hoover at Toledo, Monday night, October 16, 1922, both in ibid., Box 211, "Foreign Debts, 1922 May–September. Professor Jacob H. Hollander, a political economist at Johns Hopkins, strongly endorsed Hoover's argument that the debts could be used to encourage European disarmament: "Towering Allied Debts Restraint Against War," *New York Times*, November 26, 1922.

15. Hoover to Andrew Mellon, January 6, 1923, Hoover Papers, Commerce Period, Box 211, "Foreign Debts, 1923"; staff memorandum for Hoover, January 9, 1923, ibid., Box 215, "Foreign Debts, Great Britain, 1923 January–March"; Hoover to Ivy Lee, January 18, 1923, ibid., Box 216, "Foreign Debts, H.H. Speeches, 1923–1924."

16. Undated copy of a column by Keynes, enclosed in Lewis Strauss to Hoover, January 9, 1923, Hoover Papers, Commerce Period, Box 578, "Strauss, Lewis L., 1923."

17. "Speech by the Right Hon. the Chancellor of the Exchequer at the Opening Meeting of the Anglo-American Debt Commission on Monday 8th January 1923," Hoover Papers, Commerce Period, Box 215, "Foreign Debts, Great Britain, 1923 January–March"; Keith Middlemas and John Barnes, *Baldwin: A Biography* (New York: Macmillan, 1969), 128–39,

149–50; Marc Trachtenberg, *Reparation in World Politics: France and European Economic Diplomacy, 1916–1923* (New York: Columbia University Press, 1980), 291–92.

18. Middlemas and Barnes, *Baldwin*, 139.

19. Eliot Wadsworth to Hoover, February 10, 1923, enclosing of copy of Wadsworth to Sen. Porter J. McCumber, February 10, 1923, and loan proposal, February 2, 1923, both in Hoover Papers, Commerce Period, Box 215, "Foreign Debts, Great Britain, 1923 January–March"; Wadsworth to Hoover, June 26, 1923, ibid., Box 215, "Foreign Debts, Great Britain, 1923 May–Nov."; debt agreement between Finland and the United States, May 1, 1923, ibid., Box 213, "Foreign Debts, Finland, 1923–1924"; Anglo-American debt agreement, August 18, 1925, ibid., Box 212, "Foreign Debts, 1925 August–December"; Middlemas and Barnes, *Baldwin*, 139–47; Trani and Wilson, *The Presidency of Warren G. Harding*, 161–62; Robert Blake, *Unrepentant Tory: The Life and Times of Andrew Bonar Law, 1858–1923, Prime Minister of the United Kingdom* (New York: St. Martin's, 1956), 490–96; Robert C. Self, *Britain, America, and the War Debt Controversy: The Economic Diplomacy of an Unspecial Relationship, 1917–1941* (London: Routledge, 2006), chaps. 2–3. Federal Reserve Governor Strong regarded the initial payments expected under the debt agreement as an excessive burden on the British economy. See Lester V. Chandler, *Benjamin Strong, Central Banker* (Washington, DC: Brookings Institute, 1958), 294–95.

20. Hoover discusses the Allied debts in *Memoirs* 2, 177–79, and quotes speeches in which he argued for linking disarmament to loans on p. 89.

21. Melvyn Leffler, "American Policy-Making and European Stability, 1921–1933," *Pacific Historical Review* 46 (May 1977): 208–9; Leffler, "1921–1932: Expansionist Impulses and Domestic Constraints," in *Economics and World Power: An Assessment of American Diplomacy since 1789*, ed. William H. Becker and Samuel F. Wells, Jr. (New York: Columbia University Press, 1984), 255–56; Stephen A. Schuker, "Origins of American Stabilization Policy in Europe: The Financial Dimension, 1918–1924," in *Confrontation and Cooperation: Germany and the United States in the Era of World War I, 1900–1924*, ed. Hans-Jürgen Schröder (Providence, RI: Berg, 1993), 377–81; Hogan, *Informal Entente*, 20–21.

22. Tables showing American foreign trade in 1922, undated, ca. March 1923, Hoover Papers, Commerce Period, Box 188, "Economic Situation, 1923–1924"; Guillermo A. Sherwell, memorandum for Hoover, July 31, 1923, ibid., Box 293, "Inter-American High Commission, 1923 January–September"; article on economic prospects prepared for U.S. Chamber of Commerce Bulletin, October 19, 1923, ibid., Box 227, "Foreign Trade, 1923"; Alan G. Goldsmith to Hoover, January 31, 1923, ibid., Box 236, "Germany, Reparations, 1921–1926 & undated"; Hoover to Rep. Hamilton Fish, Jr., December 8, 1923, ibid., Box 277, "House of Representatives: Fish, Hamilton, 1923–1926"; Hoover, *Memoirs* 2, 181–82; Elisabeth Glaser-Schmidt, "German and American Concepts to Restore a Liberal World Trading System after World War I," in *Confrontation and Cooperation: Germany and the United States in the Era of World War I, 1900–1924*, ed. Hans-Jürgen Schröder (Providence, RI: Berg, 1993), 362, 364.

23. On the oil question, see a series of articles in the *Saturday Evening Post*, August 28, 1920, pp. 29, 57–58; September 4, 1920, pp. 30, 170, 173–74, 177–78; October 30, 1920, pp. 18, 45–46, 48, by wartime Fuel Administrator Mark Requa; Hoover to Harding, December 13, 1920, Hoover Papers, Pre-Commerce Period, Hoover Presidential Library, West Branch, Iowa, Box 6, "Harding, Warren G."; Hoover to Harding, April 2, 1921, ibid., Box 480, "President Harding: 1921 Oct.–Nov."; Mark Requa to Hoover, enclosing memorandum on dwindling American oil reserves, May 2, 1921, ibid., Box 452, "Oil, 2921 May–December"; Hoover to thirteen oil company executives, May 6, 1921, ibid., Box 454, "Oil: Oil Conference, May 16, 1921"; Charles Evans Hughes to Hoover, December 14, 1921, and Hoover to Hughes, December 22, 1921, both in ibid., Box 571, "State Department: Secretary of State Hughes, Charles E., 1921 December"; Brandes, *Hoover and Economic Diplomacy*, 16–17, 108–9.

24. Silvano A. Wueschner, "Herbert Hoover, Great Britain and the Rubber Crisis, 1923–1926," unpublished paper delivered to the Annual Meeting of the Economic and Business Historical

Society, San Antonio, Texas, April 1999, pp. 4–5 (copy provided to the author by Prof. Wueschner).

25. Stedman Hanks to Christian A. Herter, January 25, 1922; Herter to Hanks, January 30, 1922; Herter to Hanks, January 23, 1923, all in Hoover Papers, Commerce Period, Box 370, "Liberia, 1921–1928"; Sen. Medill McCormick to Hoover, January 30, 1923, and Hoover to McCormick, February 2, 1923, both in ibid., Box 531, "Rubber, 1921–1924"; Quincy Tucker to Hoover, February 1, 1923, ibid.; Hoover to H. M. Lord, February 12, 1923, ibid., Box 209, "Foreign Combinations, Rubber, 1923 February–April"; press release on Hoover's testimony before House Appropriations Committee, February 17, 1923, ibid., Box 483, "Press Releases, 1923 January–July"; transcript of Hoover's testimony before House Appropriations Committee, February 17, 1923, ibid., Box 531, "Rubber, 1921–1924." Isaac Marcosson, *Caravans of Commerce* (New York: Harper & Brothers, 1926), 253–70, provides a popularized interpretation of the rubber issue from Hoover's point of view. The Philippines were well suited for rubber cultivation, but Philippine nationalism prevented foreign companies from controlling large amounts of land.

26. Agriculture Department internal memorandum, "The Crude Rubber Investigation and the Expansion of the Agricultural Work in the Department of Commerce," undated, unsigned, Hoover Papers, Commerce Period, Box 5, "Agriculture, Department of Agriculture & Department of Commerce, Propaganda, etc., undated"; "Suggested Outline for a Report on a World Survey of Rubber," April 9, 1923, ibid., Box 16, "Subject File: Speeches and Articles, 1923"; draft of letter from Hoover to Wallace, April 19, 1923, ibid., Box 209, "Foreign Combinations, Rubber, 1923 February–April"; Hoover to Wallace, April 21, May 28, 1923, ibid. Firestone's experience in Liberia confirmed the committee's conclusions. Firestone acquired rights to a million acres in Liberia in 1924, but political and physical obstacles (including the necessity to build a port), as well as the time needed for young rubber trees to reach maturity, delayed production until the mid-1930s. See James C. Young, *Liberia Rediscovered* (Garden City, NY: Doubleday, Doran, 1934), 21–22, 28, 44–47.

27. Hoover to J. M. Skinner, May 18, 1923, Hoover Papers, Commerce Period, Box 3, "Agriculture, 1923"; Hoover to F. C. Taylor, June 1, 1923, ibid., Box 705, "Wheat, 1923, February–August"; Hoover to Julius Barnes, November 30, 1923, ibid., Box 84, "Chamber of Commerce, United States, 1923 June–November"; untitled Commerce Department press release, March 7, 1923, ibid., Box 7, "Investigation of Foreign Trade in Agricultural Products, 1923–1924 & undated"; telegram from Hoover to James F. Bell, et al., March 6, 1923, ibid.; Commerce Department press release, "Farm Credit Agencies," March 12, 1923, ibid., Box 5, "Agriculture: Credits, Loans, Etc., 1923–1924"; Commerce Department press release, "Commission to Investigate Agricultural Export Problems," March 12, 1923, ibid., Box 596, "Taylor, Alonzo E., 1923"; Commerce Department press release, "Investigation of World Trade in Agricultural Products," ca. March 24, 1923, and Commerce Department press release, "Meeting of Committee to Investigate World Trade in Agriculture," Mar 24, 1923, both in ibid., Box 7, "Agriculture: Investigation of Foreign Trade in Agricultural Products, 1922–1924 & undated"; Hoover to Nicholas A. Doyle, May 18, 1923, ibid., Box 3, "Agriculture, 1923"; Hoover to Bascom C. Slemp, September 22, 1923, ibid., Box 476, "President Coolidge, 1923 August–September"; Commerce Department press release, "Conference on British Market for American Bacon," September 20. 1923, ibid., Box 264, "Hogs & Pork Products, 1919–1925"; Eugene Meyer, Jr., and Frank W. Mondell, *Report to the President on the Wheat Situation* (Washington, DC: Government Printing Office, 1923), 4–5, 14; Julius H. Barnes to Coolidge, December 30, 1923, and Coolidge to Barnes, December 31, 1923, both in Hoover Papers, Commerce Period, Box 476, "President Coolidge, 1924 January"; Marcosson, *Caravans of Commerce*, 19; James H. Shideler, *Farm Crisis, 1919–1923* (Berkeley: University of California Press, 1957), 148–49.

28. Hoover to F. D. McCally, January 5, 1923, Hoover Papers, Commerce Period, Box 5, "Agriculture, Credits, Loans, Etc., 1923–1924"; W. C. Mullendore to Ralph P. Merritt, January 16, 1923, ibid., Box 391, "Merritt, Ralph P., 1921–1923"; Henry C. Wallace to Rep. Sydney Anderson, February 23, 1923, ibid., Box 5, "Agriculture, Credits, Loans, Etc., 1923–1924."

29. Commerce Department press release, "Trend of World Sugar Production and Consumption," February 9, 1923, and Julius Klein, statement to press, February 13, 1923, both in Hoover Papers, Commerce Period, Box 483, "Press Releases, 1923 January–July"; Hoover, memorandum on the sugar situation, released to the press, February 15, 1923, ibid., Box 580, "Sugar, 1923 January–April"; E. G. Montgomery to Julius Klein, March 22, 1923, ibid., Box 585, "Sugar: Interdepartmental Correspondence, 1923 January–April"; Commerce Department press release on "Mr. Manly's Statement," March 22, 1923, and unsigned (possibly Julius Klein) to Paul T. Edwards, March 24, 1923, both in ibid., "Press Releases, 1923 January–July"; E. G. Montgomery to Stephen B. Davis, March 27, 1923, ibid., Box 585, "Sugar: Interdepartmental Correspondence, 1923 January–April"; Stephen B. Davis, memorandum on sugar speculation in Cuba and New York, March 29, 1923, ibid., Box 587, "Sugar: Solicitor's File, 1915–1923 & undated"; (Stephen B. Davis?) memorandum on investigation of possible conspiracy to raise sugar prices, undated, ca. April 3, 1923, ibid., Box 585, "Sugar: Foreign and Domestic Commerce Files (Mr. Richey's Material), 1923 March–April"; Hoover to Henry Snow & Son, April 19, 1923, ibid., Box 584, "Sugar: Flurry 1923 April"; Hoover to D. E. Jordan, May 19, 1923, ibid.; Hoover to Sen. Frederick Hale, April 20, 1923, ibid., Box 547, "Senate: Hale, Frederick, 1921–1927"; Commerce Department press release on "curtailment of consumption of sugar" by American women, May 1, 1923, ibid., Box 584, "Sugar: Flurry, 1923 May"; E. G. Montgomery to Hoover, May 8, 1923, ibid., Box 581, "Sugar: American Interests in Cuba (Mr. Richey's Material), 1923 May–August"; Hoover to Harding, May 23, 1923, ibid., Box 481, "President Harding, 1923 March–May"; draft of Commerce Department press release on sugar situation, March 18, 1924, ibid., Box 580, "Sugar, 1924 January–April"; (Harold P.) Stokes to Hoover, July 29, 1924, ibid., Box 610, "Trips 1924, Western trip, telegrams"; "The Sugar Conspiracy," St. Louis *Post Dispatch*, August 1, 1924; George A. Zabriskie, statement to the press on Hoover's role in setting the price of sugar during and after World War I, July 31, 1928, Hoover Papers, Commerce Period, Box 581, "Sugar: American Interests in Cuba (Mr. Richey's Material), 1925–1928."
30. Hoover, draft of an article on coal for *Industrial Management* magazine, January 5, 1923, Hoover Papers, Commerce Period, Box 605, "Transportation, 1921–1925"; Hoover to Rep. Samuel E. Winslow, January 3, 1923, ibid., Box 104, "Coal: Legislation, 1923–1925."
31. Hoover to R. H. Aishton, February 14, 1923, Hoover Papers, Commerce Period, Box 12, "Aishton, R. H., 1922–1927"; Hoover to Julius H. Barnes, April 19, 1923, ibid., Box 84, "Chamber of Commerce, United States, 1923 January–May"; Hoover to Rep. W. R. Wood, April 19, 1923, ibid., Box 284, "House of Representatives: Wood, William R., 1921–1927"; Hoover to E. M. Poston, May 15, 1923, ibid., Box 474, "Poston, Elias McClellan, 1923–1926"; F. R. Wadleigh, "Memorandum on Anthracite Situation," June 15, 1923, ibid., Box 102, "Coal: Federal Fuel Distributor, Wadleigh, F. R., 1922–1925 & undated"; Wadleigh to B. H. Meyer, June 22, 1923, ibid.
32. F. R. Wadleigh to B. H. Meyer, July 8, 1923, Hoover Papers, Commerce Period, Box 102, "Coal: Federal Fuel Distributor, Wadleigh, F. R., 1922–1925 & undated"; Hoover to Coolidge, August 11, 1923, ibid., Box 476, "President Coolidge, 1923 August–September"; Hoover to F. R. Wadleigh, August 24, 1923, ibid., Box 102, "Coal: Federal Fuel Distributor, Wadleigh, F. R., 1922–1923 & undated."
33. Press release, report of United States Coal Commission, September 8 (and following), 1923, Commerce Period, Box 483, "Press Releases, 1923 August–December"; "Regulate Industry Says Coal Com.," *F.A.E.S. Bulletin* 2, no. 10 (October 1923): 1; Edward Eyre Hunt to Hoover, October 2, 1923, Hoover Papers, Commerce Period, Box 648, "Unemployment, Hoover, Secretary, 1921–1923"; "Pax Pennsylvania," *Time Magazine*, September 17, 1923, http://www.time.com/time/magazine/article/0,9171,727376,00.html (accessed February 20, 1007); Christian A. Herter to C. Bascom Slemp, November 17, 1923, enclosing Hoover to Coolidge, November 17, 1923, Hoover Papers, Commerce Period, Box 106, "Coal, President, 1922–1926." Robert Zieger argues that Pinchot's intervention in the anthracite strike ended up undermining progressive influence in the party and strengthening Coolidge. See Zieger, "Pinchot and Coolidge: The Politics of the 1923 Anthracite Crisis," *Journal of American History* 52 (December 1965): 566–81.

34. Bankers Trust Company of New York, "Analysis of Railroad Earnings for November and the Eleven Months of 1922," January 15, 1923, Strauss Papers, Hoover Presidential Library, West Branch, Iowa, Name & Subject File I: Accretions, Box 43E, "Railroad Earnings Figures, 1923"; Chamber of Commerce press release, "Transportation Needs," February 2, 1923; Hoover to C. H. Markham, February 1, 1923; Markham to Hoover, February 3, 1923; and E. S. Gregg to Hoover, February 19, 1923, enclosing table on "Relation of freight rates to value of products carried," all in Hoover Papers, Commerce Period, Box 505, "Railroads: Railroad Conferences, 1923–1927"; E. J. Lewis to Hoover, February 21, 1923, enclosing report from Interstate Commerce Commission, Bureau of Statistics, "Results of Railroad Operation in 1922," February 16, 1923, ibid., Box 507, "Railroads: Reports, 1922–1923"; Hoover to Charles J. Symington, May 7, 1923, ibid., Box 506, "Railroads: Rates, 1923"; Commerce Department press release on railroad rate revision, September 19, 1923, ibid., Box 502, "Railroads, 1923"; U.S. Chamber of Commerce, draft of committee report on railroad rates, October 26, 1923, ibid., Box 506, "Railroads, Rates, 1923"; Christian A. Herter to Lewis Strauss, November 7, 1923, ibid., Box 502, "Railroads, 1923."

35. Hoover to Harding, February 12, 14, 1923, and Harding to Hoover, February 15, 1923, both in Hoover Papers, Commerce Period, Box 481, "President Harding, 1923 January–February"; Hoover to Sen. Albert Cummins, April 24, 1923, enclosing memorandum on railroad consolidation, and Cummins to Hoover, May 7, 1923, both in ibid., Box 503, "Railroads: Consolidation, 1923 Jan.–Sept.";, Hoover to Cummins, May 22, 1923, ibid., Box 503, "Railroads: Consolidation, 1923 Jan.–Sept."; E. S. Gregg, memo, "Methods of Effective Railway Consolidation," May 16, 1923, ibid., Box 503, "Railroads: Consolidation, 1923, Jan.–Sept."; Hoover to Herbert Quick, September 14, 1923, ibid., Box 502, "Railroads, 1923"; Hoover, press release on "Principles" for railroad consolidation, November 7, 1923, ibid., Box 504, "Railroads: Consolidation, 1923 Nov.–Dec."; Hoover to Coolidge, November 22, 1923, enclosing memorandum outlining a revised version of Hoover's consolidation proposal, November 22, 1923, ibid., Box 476, "President Coolidge, 1923 November"; Department of Commerce, *Eleventh Annual Report of the Secretary of Commerce* (Washington, DC: Government Printing Office, 1923), 27–29. The plan Cummins actually introduced in early 1924 bore little resemblance to Hoover's 1923 idea. See Mark H. Rose, Bruce E. Seely, and Paul F. Barrett, *The Best Transportation System in the World: Railroads, Trucks, Airlines, and American Public Policy in the Twentieth Century* (Columbus: Ohio State University Press, 2006), 23–24.

36. Hoover to William F. Funsten, April 20, 1920, Hoover Papers, Pre-Commerce Period, Box 57, "National Inland Waterways Association, November 1919–July 23, 1920"; Charles P. Craig to Hoover, October 30, 1920, Hoover Papers, Commerce Period, Box 172, "Craig, Charles R.-Crame, 1921–1928"; Hoover to Franklin K. Lane, May 17, 1921, ibid., Box 363, "Lane, Franklin K., 1921–1928"; Julius Barnes to Hoover, June 2, 1921, ibid., Box 45, "Barnes, Julius, 1921"; Christian A. Herter to George Barr Baker, November 3, 1921, ibid., Box 538, "St. Ann's–St. Lawrence, 1921–28"; clipping, "Gov. Miller Assails St. Lawrence Canal," undated, ca. November 17, 1921, no source, ibid., Box 689, "Waterways: Great Lakes-St. Lawrence, 1921"; Charles Craig to Hoover, January 17, 1922, and Christian A. Herter to Lewis Strauss, February 4, 1922, both in ibid., Box 689, "Waterways: Great Lakes–St. Lawrence, 1922";, Julius Barnes to Hoover, October 19, 1922, ibid., Box 45, "Barnes, Julius, 1922"; Owen D. Young to Hoover, April 9, May 10, November 20, 1923, and Hoover to Young, May 17, October 27, 1923, all in ibid., Box 719, "Young, Owen D., 1923." Correspondence regarding Hoover's decision not to attend the July 1921 St. Lawrence excursion is in ibid., Box 689, "Waterways: Great Lakes–St. Lawrence, 1921."

37. In the Colorado River Commission Papers, Hoover Presidential Library, West Branch, Iowa, Box 20, there is a folder for each signatory state illustrating the progress of ratification in each. For Hoover's support of ratification, see Hoover to Secretary of Interior Hubert Work, March 16, 1923, ibid., Box 32, "Project File: Interior Dept., 1922–24 and 1926–28"; Hoover to Work, October 3, 1923, Hoover Papers, Commerce Period, Box 295, "Interior Department: Secretary Work, Hubert, 1923"; Dwight Heard to Hoover, November 15, 30, 1923, and Hoover to Heard, November 22, 1923; W. F. McClure to Gov. J. G. Scrugham of Nevada, with copies to governors of other compact states, Hoover, and others, November

8, 1923; Hoover to McClure, November 21, 1923, all in ibid., Box 257, "Heard, Dwight B., 1923"; Hoover to Bascom Slemp, November 16, 1923, ibid., Box 476, "President Coolidge, 1923 November."

38. "Hoover Favors Ford Offer for Muscle Shoals," *New York Tribune*, February 23, 1923; Gray Silver to Hoover, September 15, 1923, Hoover Papers, Commerce Period, Box 422, "Muscle Shoals, Miscellaneous, 1921–1924"; Mark Sullivan Diary, October 21, 1923, Mark Sullivan Papers, Hoover Institution Archives, Stanford, California; memorandum on the production of nitrates by Harry A. Curtis, chief, Nitrogen Division, Division of Foreign and Domestic Commerce, October 12, 1923; draft of Hoover to Coolidge, November 19, 1923; E(lon) H(untington) H(ooker) to Rep. J. Mayhew Wainwright, February 4, 1924, all in Hoover Papers, Commerce Period, Box 422, "Muscle Shoals, Miscellaneous, 1921–1924."

39. Hoover to William A. Durgin, January 4, 1922, Hoover Papers, Commerce Period, Box 145, "Simplified Coml. Practice, 1921–22 June."

40. Senator Wesley Jones to Hoover, January 13, 1922, and Hoover to Jones, January 19, 1922, both in Hoover Papers, Commerce Period, Box 675, "U.S. Industrial Waste Commission, 1921–22."

41. Press release by William A. Durgin, Division of Simplified Practice, "Simplified Practice: What It Is and What It Offers," Hoover Papers, Commerce Period, Box 145, "Simplified Commercial Practice, 1922, July–Aug."; Division of Simplified Practice memorandum, "Conferences Held by Department Officials during Fiscal Year 1923," ibid., Box 120, "Commerce Dept. Achievements, 1921–23"; Department of Commerce, *Eleventh Annual Report*, 19. One standardization proposal on which Hoover declined to act, citing opposition by "practical manufacturers and the many engineers through the United States," was the replacement of English measurement by the metric system. See Hoover to Warren I. Glover, April 6, 1922, Hoover Papers, Commerce Period, Box 392, "Metric System, 1919–1923."

42. Commerce Department press release, "Federal Activity in Promotion of Better Housing Conditions and Home Ownership," ca. November 1923, Hoover Papers, Commerce Period, Box 484, "Press Releases, 1925 [*sic*] November" (the statistics cited are Commerce Department estimates); Hoover, "Foreword," in *How to Own Your Own Home: A Handbook for Prospective Home Owners*, by Department of Commerce, Housing Division (Washington, DC: Government Printing Office, 1923), v–vi; Janet Hutchison, "Building for Babbitt: The State and the Suburban Home Ideal," *Journal of Policy History* 9, no. 2 (1997): 186–87, 191–97.

43. Edgar Rickard to Hoover, May 16, 1923; Hoover to Mrs. William B. Meloney, May 18, 1923; Marie Meloney, memorandum to Mr. Hoover, June 13, 1923; Hoover to George W. Wilder, June 14, 1923; and Wilder to Hoover, July 30, 1923, all in Hoover Papers, Commerce Period, Box 65, "Building and Housing: Better Homes in America Previous to Incorporation, 1921–1923 June."

44. Hoover to Col. Arthur Woods, September 15, 1923; Woods to Hoover, September 27, 1923; Marie Meloney to Hoover, November 30, 1923; Hoover to Beardsley Ruml, December 15, 1923; and Delaware Certificate of Incorporation of Better Homes in America, Inc., December 22, 1923, all in Hoover Papers, Commerce Period, Box 65, "Building and Housing: Better Homes in America Previous to Incorporation, 1923 July–December & undated."

45. Hoover's vision did not include rural electrification, which did not become common until the 1930s.

46. "Superpower Plan to Offset Coal Strikes," *Boston Globe*, April 8, 1922; Hoover to M. H. Aylesworth, May 16, 1922, Hoover Papers, Commerce Period, Box 41, "Aylesworth, M. H., 1921–1928"; Hoover, "Address to National Electric Light Association Convention—Atlantic City, N.J.," May 19, 1922, ibid., Box 590, "Superpower, Waterpower, etc., 1922"; Owen D. Young to Hoover, March 16, 1923, ibid., Box 719, "Young, Owen D., 1923."

47. Hoover to William D. B. Ainey, October 10, 1923, Hoover Papers, Commerce Period, Box 162, "Conferences, Superpower, 1923 June–October"; "Summary of Statement of Secretary Hoover to the Super Power Conference, New York City, Saturday, October 13, 1923," ibid., Box 590, "Superpower, Waterpower, etc., 1923"; Hoover to Richard T. Wiggins, October 20, 1923, ibid., Box 162, "Conferences, Superpower, 1923 June–October";

editorial, "Support Action With Action," *Electrical World* 82, no. 16 (October 20, 1923): 1; editorial, "Superpower and Economic Statesmanship," *Chemical and Metallurgical Engineering* 29, no. 17 (October 22, 1923): 744; F. M. Feiker to Hoover, October 23, 1923, enclosing article distributed to 550 newspapers in the United States and Canada, "Hoover Would Save $500,000,000 Yearly by Electric Super-Power," and Hoover to Gov. Gifford Pinchot and ten other governors in proposed Superpower consortium, October 23, 1923, both in Hoover Papers, Commerce Period, Box 162, "Conference, Superpower, 1923 June–October."

48. John Lathrop, "Super-Power Plans Growing," New York *Herald*, November 5, 1922); Sacramento *Bee* quoted in *Literary Digest* November 17, 1923,15; Hoover to W. S. Murray, November 23, 1923, Hoover Papers, Commerce Period, Box 422, "Murray, William S., 1921–1927 & undated"; (Solicitor Stephen Davis?) to Richard T. Higgins, November 23, 1923, Hoover to M. H. Aylesworth, December 6, 1923, and Hoover to Morris L. Cooke, December 13, 1923, all in ibid., Box 162, "Conferences, Superpower, 1923 November–December."

49. Ralph Arnold to Hoover, July 1, 1921, memorandum to Petroleum (Fuel) Division from Richard S. Emmet, July 27, 1922, J. K. Towles to (?) Emmett, July 29, 1922, and Claudius Huston to Hoover, September 26, 1923, all in Hoover Papers, Commerce Period, Box 452, "Oil, 1922–1923"; Mark Requa, "Memorandum Dealing with the Possibility of Government Regulation of the Petroleum Industry," September 17, 1923, Mark Requa Papers, University of Wyoming; Rep. John E. Raker to Hoover, January 12, 1924, and Hoover to Raker, January 21, 1924, both in Hoover Papers, Commerce Period, Box 281, "House of Representatives: Raker, John E., 1921–1925"; Homer S. Fox to Richard Emmet, March 13, 1924, ibid., Box 546, "Senate: Gooding, Frank R., 1921–1928 & undated."

50. Hoover to Van H. Manning, November 22, 1923, and Manning to Hoover, January 22, 1924, both in Hoover Papers, Commerce Period, Box 452, "Oil, 1922–1923"; Henry L. Doherty to Coolidge, August 11, 1924; C. B. Slemp to Secretary Work, August 12, 1924; H. Foster Bain to Work, August 19, 1924; George Otis Smith to Work, August 20, 1924; Work to Coolidge, August 20, 1924, all in ibid., Box 477, "President Coolidge, 1924 August."

51. Coolidge to the secretaries of war, navy, interior, and commerce, December 18, 1924, Hoover Papers, Commerce Period, Box 477, "President Coolidge, 1924 December."

52. Unsent draft of Hoover to Sen. Frank B. Kellogg, February 1, 1923, Hoover Papers, Commerce Period, Box 548, "Senate: Kellogg, Frank B., 1922–1923 & undated"; Hoover to Postmaster General Harry S. New and other cabinet members, March 6, 1923, ibid., Box 474, "Post Office Department: Postmaster General New, Harry S., 1923–1925"; Commerce Department press release, March 6, 1923, ibid., Box 489, "Radio: Correspondence, Press Releases, Misc., 1923"; press release, "Statement of the Secretary of Commerce at the Opening of the Radio Conference on March 20, 1923," ibid.; Commerce Department press release, March 24, 1923, "Recommendations of the National Radio Committee," ibid., Box 483, "Press Releases, 1923 January–July"; D. B. Carson to Hoover, March 26, 1923, ibid., Box 496, "Radio: Conferences, National—Second (March 20–24, 1923"; Hoover to Secretary of the Navy Edwin Denby, April 9, 1923, ibid., Box 434, "Navy Department: Secretary Denby, Edwin, 1923–1924." Preparatory work for an international radio conference began in May 1923. The conference was finally held in October 1927, and a treaty was signed on November 25, 1927. See P. E. D. Engle to Hoover, May 21 and 22, 1923, ibid., Box 491, "Radio: Conferences, International Correspondence, 1923–1925 & undated."

53. Hoover, *American Individualism* (West Branch, IA: Hoover Presidential Library Association ed., n.d., repr. of 1922 ed.), 4–5. The order of phrases has been changed.

54. Undated memo listing Commerce Department activities and achievements during 1922 and 1923, Hoover Papers, Commerce Period, Box 268, "Hoover, Herbert, Biography Undated." Hoover rarely expressed his frustrations and ambitions even in private correspondence. This document may be unique.

Chapter 15

1. George Barr Baker to Hugh Gibson, July 2, 1923, George Barr Baker Papers, Hoover Institution Archives, Stanford, California, Box 3, "Gibson, Hugh"; Eugene P. Trani and David L. Wilson, *The Presidency of Warren G. Harding* (Lawrence: University Press of Kansas, 1977), 172–73.

2. Francis Russell, *The Shadow of Blooming Grove: Warren G. Harding and His Times* (New York: McGraw-Hill, 1968), 574–81; "Mrs. Hoover Talks of Aims," Portland *Telegram*, July 3, 1923; Robert D. Accinelli, "Was There a 'New' Harding? Warren G. Harding and the World Court Issue," *Ohio History* 84 (Autumn 1975): 168–81.

3. Herbert Hoover, *Memoirs: The Cabinet and the Presidency, 1920–1933* (New York: Macmillan, 1952), 49 (hereafter, *Memoirs* 2).

4. Hoover to George H. Lorimer, May 26, 1923, Hoover Papers, Commerce Period, Hoover Presidential Library, West Branch, Iowa, Box 374, "Lorimer, Goerge H. and Mrs., 1921–28."

5. Hoover to Secretary of Agriculture Wallace, December 29, 1921, enclosing draft of executive order closing salmon fisheries in the Aleutian Islands, Hoover Papers, Commerce Period, Box 14, "Alaska-Aleutian Islands, 1921"; Commerce Department press release regarding Assistant Secretary Huston's trip to Alaska, March 15, 1922, and statement concerning fishery and fur seal industry of Alaska for use in the governor's annual report, June 21, 1922, both in ibid., Box 13, "Alaska, 1922-May–Dec."; Hoover to Assistant Secretary of Interior Edward C. Finney, October 27, 1922, and Commerce Department press release about presidential proclamation creating fisheries reservation in Alaska, November 5, 1922, both in ibid., Box 13, "Alaska, Alaskan Fisheries, Reservations, etc., 1921–1922"; draft of Hoover to President Harding, December 18, 1922, ibid., Box 480, "President Harding, 1922 Oct.–Dec."; Hoover to Rep. William S. Greene, December 21, 1922, ibid., Box 13, "Alaska, Alaskan Fisheries, Reservations, etc., 1921–22"; Delegate Dan Sutherland to Hoover, December 26, 1922, and Hoover to Sutherland, December 30, 1922, both in ibid., Box 282, "House of Reps.-Sutherland, Dan, 1921–23"; undated, ca. June 1, 1923, Commerce Department press release regarding the president's trip to Alaska, ibid., Box 13, "Alaska, 1924–28 & undated"; Hoover to Senator Wesley L. Jones, March 16, 1923, ibid., Box 13, "Alaska, Alaskan Fisheries, Reservations, etc., 1923 January–March"; "Hoover Here; Is Thankful," Portland *Telegram*, July 3, 1923; "Secretary Hoover Visits Portland," Portland *Morning Oregonian*, July 4, 1923; "Notes for Seattle C[hamber] of C[ommerce] Speech by HH," undated, ca. July 3, 1923, Hoover Papers, Commerce Period, Box 13, "Alaska, Alaskan Fisheries Reservations, etc., 1923 July."

6. Matilda Atkinson Minthorn to Hoover, July 18, 1923, Hoover Papers, Commerce Period, Box 14, "Alaska, Hearings, Cases, Complaints, etc., 1923"; William C. Mullendore to his brother, July 25, 1923, William C. Mullendore Papers, Hoover Presidential Library, West Branch, Iowa, Box 15, "Harding (Warren G.) Alaskan Trip, 1923, Correspondence and Diary"; Lou Hoover to Jennie Weed Mager, August 16, 1923, Lou Henry Hoover Papers, Hoover Presidential Library, West Branch, Iowa, Personal Correspondence, 1921–28, Box 18, "Mager, Jessie, 1921–23"; Hal Elliott Wert, *Hoover, the Fishing President: Portrait of the Private Man and His Life Outdoors* (Mechanicsburg, PA: Stackpole Books, 2005), 119–24.

7. William Mullendore's (unsigned) notes on the hearings, July 16–20, 1923, Hoover Papers, Commerce Period, Box 14, "Alaska, Hearings, Cases, Complaints, etc., 1923"; Hoover's remarks at Sitka, July 22, 1923, ibid., Box 19, "Alaska Trip, Miscellaneous Drafts, Speeches, etc., 1923."

8. Hoover, draft of unpublished article, "President Harding's Last Illness and Death," August 25, 1923, Hoover Papers, Commerce Period, Box 481, "President Harding's Last Illness—Hoover's Unpublished Article, 1923."

9. Ibid.

10. Ibid.; Lou Henry Hoover to Ray Lyman Wilbur, July 28, 1923, and Hoover to Wilbur, July 28, 1923, both in Ray Lyman Wilbur Papers, Hoover Institution Archives, Stanford,

California, Box 19, "Pres. Harding's Death (Publications & Corres. About)." Dr. Wilbur later said that what he had at the time described simply as a "gall bladder infection" was cholecystitis, an inflammation of the gall bladder that can include cholestasis, or stoppage of the flow of bile. See Wilbur to Mark Sullivan, September 23, 1935, ibid.

11. Trani and Wilson, *Presidency of Harding*, 177–78; Mark Sullivan Diary, August 8, 1923, Mark Sullivan Papers, Hoover Institution Archives, Stanford, California, Box 1. A heart attack caused by a blood clot in a coronary artery had first been described by a Chicago physician, Dr. James B. Herrick, in 1910, but his description of the disease had not been widely accepted by other doctors. Almost certainly, Harding's physician, Dr. Charles E. Sawyer, a small-town homeopath, had never heard of it and probably would have dismissed it if he had. For an excellent account of Harding's illness and death, see Robert H. Ferrell, *Ill-Advised: Presidential Health and Public Trust* (Columbia: University of Missouri Press, 1992), 20–27. As Ferrell notes, Mrs. Harding would not authorize the autopsy that could have laid the rumors about the president's death to rest.

12. Trani and Wilson, *Presidency of Harding*, 177–78; Lou Hoover to Ethel Bullard, August 15, 1923, Lou Hoover Papers, Subject File, Box 7, "Harding, Warren G., 1923–31." In 1931, Hoover, then president, delivered the eulogy at the dedication of the elaborate Harding memorial in Marion, Ohio. He praised Harding's kindness, generosity, and patriotism and took a few swipes at the men who had "betrayed" his friendship. Interestingly, he does not date the event in his memoirs but makes a point of saying that Harding's friends had wanted "President Coolidge" to deliver the eulogy, thus encouraging the reader to believe that Coolidge, out of office for almost three years, was still president and had declined merely because appearing at the dedication might be a "political liability." The episode offers cause to suspect the sincerity of the following pages' generally favorable account of Hoover's relations with Coolidge. See Hoover, *Memoirs* 2, 52–53.

13. Red Cross press release, September 10, 1923, Hoover Papers, Commerce Period, Box 483, "Press Releases, 1923 August–December"; "Lumber for Japan: Telegrams to Southern Pine Association," October 1, 3, 1923, ibid., Box 46, "Benton, H.-Berend, 1921–1927."

14. Hoover to Sen. William H. King, November 20, 1923; statement drafted by Herbert Hoover to be issued by Commissioner O'Malley, December 20, 1923, both in Hoover Papers, Commerce Period, Box 14, "Alaska-Alaskan Fisheries, Reservations, etc., 1923 Oct.–Dec."; Dan Sutherland to Sen. Peter Norbeck, January 8, 1924, ibid., Box 15, "Alaska, Hearst Attacks & Other Attacks, 1924 January–February"; Hoover to Rep. Arthur M. [N.] Free, February 7, 1924, ibid., Box 277, "House of Rep.: Free, Arthur N., 1921–26"; Hoover to Rep. William S. Greene, February 7, 1924, ibid., Box 278, "House of Rep.: Green[e], Wm. S."; Commerce Department press releases about Hearst attacks, April 27, 30, May 2, 9, 1924, all in ibid., Box 14, "Alaska, Alaskan Fisheries, Reservations, etc., 1924 April–May"; "Scandal Over Huge Salmon Trust Looms," San Francisco *Examiner*, April 27, 1924; "Monopoly in Nation's Fish Is Accusation," Seattle *Post-Intelligencer*, April 27, 1924; "'Big 4' Control Salmon Catch Says Delegate," Seattle *Post-Intelligencer*, April 28, 1924; Mark Sullivan Diary, May 9, 1924, Sullivan Papers; Hoover to Sen. Simeon D. Fess, May 15, 1924, Hoover Papers, Commerce Period, Box 546, "Senate: Fess, Simeon D., 1922–1926"; "New Alaska Fisheries Regulations," Commerce Department press release, June 25, 1924, Herbert Hoover Papers, Rare Books and Special Collections, Green Library, Stanford University, Stanford, California, Box 11, "Fishing (also Wildlife)."

15. Hoover to Sen. Wesley L. Jones, April 29, 1924, Hoover Papers, Commerce Period, Box 548, "Senate: Jones, Wesley L., 1924"; "Alaskan Salmon," Commerce Department press release, May 28, 1924, ibid., Box 14, "Alaska-Alaskan Fisheries, Reservations, etc., 1924 Apr.–May"; Henry O'Malley to Hoover, enclosing list of "Alaskan Salmon Canneries Operated in 1925," January 6, 1926, ibid., Box 13, "Alaska, 1924–1928 & undated." In the margin of this memo, Hoover calculated that the four big companies controlled less than 30 percent of the total number of canneries, but neither he nor the memo estimated the amount of fish canned by those four companies.

16. Mark Sullivan Diary, August 18, 1923, Sullivan Papers; Box 1; Philippi Harding Butler Papers, Hoover Presidential Library, West Branch, Iowa, p. 25; Coolidge, quoted in Robert

K. Murray, "Herbert Hoover and the Harding Cabinet," in *Herbert Hoover as Secretary of Commerce, 1921–1928: Studies in New Era Thought and Practice*, ed. Ellis W. Hawley (Iowa City: University of Iowa Press, 1981), 37.

17. George E. Mowry, *The California Progressives* (Chicago: Quadrangle ed., 1963), 278–88; Richard Coke Lower, *A Bloc of One: The Political Career of Hiram W. Johnson* (Stanford, CA: Stanford University Press, 1993), 213, 237–39; Jackson K. Putnam, "The Persistence of Progressivism in the 1920s: The Case of California," *Pacific Historical Review* 35 (November 1966): 395–411; Russell M. Posner, "The Progressive Voters League, 1923–1926," *California Historical Society Quarterly* 36 (September 1957): 251–61.

18. Francis V. Keesling to James B. Reynolds, May 17, September 23, 1924; Keesling to William J. Tully, September 24, 1924; Keesling to William M. Butler, October 21, 1924; Keesling to George O. Muhlfield, October 21, 1924, all in Francis V. Keesling Papers, Rare Books and Special Collections, Green Library, Stanford University, Stanford, California, Box 2, Folder 12, "Polit. Corresp. Out, 1924, May–Dec." I have been unable to find any comprehensive, recent analysis of California politics in the 1920s to supplement Mowry, although William Issel and Robert W. Cherny do a good job for the Bay Area in *San Francisco, 1865–1932* (Berkeley: University of California Press, 1986), especially chapter 8.

19. Hoover to Coolidge, April 21, 1924, Hoover Papers, Commerce Period, Box 477, "President Coolidge, 1924 April"; Mark Requa to Hoover, March 29, May 2, 1924, ibid., Box 517, "Requa, Mark L., 1924 Jan.–May"; Hiram Johnson to Hiram Johnson, Jr., June 13, 1924, Hiram Johnson Papers, Bancroft Library, University of California at Berkeley, Part VI, Box 4, "1924 May–Sept."; Francis V. Keesling to George E. Crothers, August 21, 1924, Keesling Papers, Box 2, Folder 12, "Polit. Corresp. Out, 1924, May–Dec."; David Burner, "Election of 1924," in *History of American Presidential Elections, 1789–1968*, ed. Arthur M. Schlesinger, Jr., Fred L. Israel, and William P. Hansen (New York: Chelsea House, 1971), 3: 2463–67. George Nash suggests that in the last moment, Coolidge may have preferred Hoover to Dawes but that the heavy-handed tactics of Coolidge's campaign manager, William M. Butler, aroused so much resentment among the delegates that they chose Dawes instead. See George H. Nash, "The 'Great Enigma' and the 'Great Engineer': The Political Relationship of Calvin Coolidge and Herbert Hoover," in *Calvin Coolidge and the Coolidge Era: Essays on the History of the 1920s*, ed. John Earl Haynes (Washington, DC: Library of Congress, 1998), 154–55.

20. A clipping from the Philadelphia *Public Ledger*, January 17, 1925, describing the Washington rumors is in Hoover Papers, Commerce Period, Box 6, "Agriculture: HH & Secretaryship of Agriculture Department, 1924–1925 & undated"; Nash, "The 'Great Enigma' and the 'Great Engineer,'" 156–57; Robert H. Ferrell, *The Presidency of Calvin Coolidge* (Lawrence: University Press of Kansas, 1998), 28–30.

21. David Cannadine, *Mellon: An American Life* (New York: Knopf, 2006), 362. For the impact of young Calvin's death on the president and his administration, see Robert E. Gilbert, *The Tormented President: Calvin Coolidge, Death, and Clinical Depression* (Westport, CT: Praeger, 2003).

22. "Secretary Hoover's Statement on the Death of Woodrow Wilson," February 4, 1924, Hoover Papers, Commerce Period, Box 482, "President Wilson, Information Re: 1921–1928."

23. "Summary of the Address of Secretary Hoover to the National Conference of Social Work, Providence, R.I., Tuesday, June 27, 1922," Hoover Papers, Commerce Period, Box 483, "Press Releases, 1922 May–August"; Theodore Roosevelt, Jr., to Hoover (and other cabinet secretaries), December 31, 1923, ibid., Box 529, "Roosevelt, Theodore Jr., 2922–1927 & undated."

24. Leon F. Kneipp, "Land Planning and Acquisition, U.S. Forest Service," oral history interview by Amelia R. Fry, Edith Mezirow, and Fern Ingersoll, Bancroft Library, University of California at Berkeley, 1:113; "Outline of Subjects for the National Conference on Outdoor Recreation," Hoover Papers, Commerce Period, Box 157, "Conferences: Natl. Conf. On O. Recreation, 1924"; "Summary of Resolutions Adopted at President's National Conference on Outdoor Recreation, [May 22–24, 1924]," Ray Lyman Wilbur Papers, Hoover

Institution Archives, Box 54, "Natl. Conf. On Outdoor Recreation"; "National Conference on Outdoor Recreation: Financial Contributions from date of organization, May 1924 to Dec. 31, 1928," RG 230, National Conference on Outdoor Recreation Papers, National Archives, Washington, DC, Box 10, "Guide: Conference Administration, Sub-guide: Executive Committee, Correspondence after Closing"; Frank Page to Paul Clapp, April 16, 1924, enclosing Arthur Ringland to Page, April 15, 1924, Hoover Papers, Commerce Period, Box 526, "Ringland, Arthur C., 1922–25 & undated."

25. National Conference on Outdoor Recreation, *Proceedings of the Meeting of the Advisory Council . . . , December 11 and 12, 1924*, Senate Document No. 229, 68 Cong., 2d sess. (Washington, DC: Government Printing Office, 1925), 5; "Address by Secretary Hoover at Dinner of the National Conference on Outdoor Recreation, Washington, D.C.," January 21, 1926, Hoover Papers, Commerce Period, Box 157, "Conferences: Natl. Conf. on O. Recreation, 1926."

26. Robert Sterling Yard to Ray Lyman Wilbur, April 9, 1919, Ray Lyman Wilbur Papers, Hoover Presidential Library, West Branch, Iowa, Box 17, "National Parks, 1917–19"; Yard, *The Book of the National Parks* (New York: Scribner's, 1921), 20–21; Yard to Hoover, February 25, 1924, Hoover Papers, Commerce Period, Box 432, "National Parks Association, 1921–24."

27. Hoover to Charles D. Walcott, February 26, 1924, Hoover Papers, Commerce Period, Box 432, "National Parks Association, 1921–24."

28. "National Parks Association: Minutes of the Trustees Meeting to consider a Proposition for Federation, January 12, 1925," RG 48, Interior Department Records, National Archives, Washington, DC, Genl., Box 1971, File 1200 (Part I), "Parks, Reservations and Antiquities: Parks General; National Parks Association, Sept. 19, 1916 to Apr. 5, 1930"; William S. Gregg to Hoover, January 21, 1925, Hoover Papers, Commerce Period, Box 432, "National Parks Association, 1925"; Robert Sterling Yard to E. K. Burlew, February 17, 1925, RG 48, Interior, Secretary Work, Box 29, "National Park Service, Mar. 5, 1923 to Oct. 8, 1925."

29. Hoover to John Barton Payne, February 27, 1925"; Hoover to Frederick A. Delano, April 3, 1925, enclosing memo outlining proposed Public Parks Council; Robert Sterling Yard to Hoover, April 9, 15, 21, 1925; Hoover to Yard, April 10, 16, 22, 1925; Charles D. Walcott to Hoover, April 20, 1925, all in Hoover Papers, Commerce Period, Box 432, "National Parks Association, 1925.

30. Frank G. Hall to Philippi Harding, January 3, 1924, Lou Hoover Papers, Box 11, "Girl Scouts, Little House, Correspondence, 1924 January–March"; Lou Hoover to Edgar Rickard, January 14, 1924, enclosing draft of Lou Hoover to William Bingham, 2nd, and Bingham to Rickard, February 18, 1924, all in ibid., Box 3, "Girl Scouts: Administrative Correspondence, Rickard, Edgar, 1922–41"; Lou Hoover to Alice Blood, March 13, 1924, ibid., Box 1, "Girl Scouts, Administrative Correspondence, 1924"; Multiple copies of clippings from papers around the country describing the laying of the cornerstone of the Little House by Grace Coolidge on March 25, 1924, are in ibid., Box 4, "Subject File: Articles, Addresses, & Statements, 1924 March 25, Dedication of Girl Scout House"; Louisette Losh to Philippi Harding, May 28, June 26, 1924, and Losh to Lou Hoover, August 15, 1924, all in ibid., Box 17, "Personal Correspondence, 1921–28: Losh, Louisette (Mrs. William), 1924." A February 1925 list of Lou's charitable contributions prepared for income tax purposes indicates that she spent $6,143.47 for various Little House expenses in 1924, but no contribution to moving costs is included. See ibid., Box 111, "Subject File: Taxes for 1924." For the post-1924 history of the project, see the typescript in ibid., Box 12, "Girl Scouts and Other Organizations: Little House, History, 1942."

31. F. N. Cooke, Jr., to (James E.) West, March 21, 1924"; James E. West to Jane Deeter Rippin, April 16, 1924; Rippin to Lou Hoover, May 9, 1924, enclosing a thirty-two-page typed compendium of letters and statements by Boy Scout leaders across the country as to the damage being done to the Boy Scouts by the name confusion, all in Lou Hoover Papers, Box 10, "Girl Scouts, Controversy with Boy Scouts over use of name, 1917–26."

32. Juliette Low to Lou Hoover, September 1, 1926, Lou Hoover Papers, Box 10, "Girl Scouts, Controversy with Boy Scouts over use of name, 1917–26."
33. "To Aid Girl Scout Drive," *New York Times*, August 3, 1924; "Girl Scouts Will Sell $10 Bricks," New York *Sun*, September 29, 1924; "'Bricks' for Sale," Rochester *Democrat and Chronicle*, October 11, 1924; "Big Gifts Help Girl Scouts in National Drive," Aberdeen (Washington) *World*, November 21, 1924; "New York Gives $251,234 to National Girl Scout Drive," Scranton (Pennsylvania) *Times*, November 29, 1924; "John D. Gives Big Sum to Girl Scouts," Ogden (Utah) *Standard Examiner*, November 26, 1924; "Rockefeller Gives Another $25,000 to Girl Scout Fund," New Brunswick (New Jersey) *Home News*, November 29, 1924; "Charity Payments for Income Tax Statement of February 1925," Lou Hoover Papers, Box 111, "Subject File, Taxes for 1924."
34. Lillian Schoedler to Lou Hoover, January 7, 1924, enclosing extracts from the report of the Executive Secretary to the Women's Division, December 31, 1923; "Report of Annual Meeting, Women's Division, National Amateur Athletic Federation, April 1924," both in Lou Hoover Papers, Box 36, "Clubs and Organizations: National Amateur Athletic Federation, Women's Division, Annual Meeting, 1924 Chicago."
35. William Tutherly to Herbert Hoover, April 21, 1924, enclosing a "Personal Information Bulletin to the Members of the Board of Governors Concerning the Second Annual Meeting," Hoover Papers, Commerce Period, Box 427, "National Aeronautics–National Amateur Athletic, 1919–1927"; "Women's Athletic Federation Now Great Power," Boston *Telegram*, April 22, 1924; "Pro, Amateur Line Is Sought," Detroit *Free Press*, December 30, 1924; "Will Try to Clarify the Amateur Rules," *New York Times*, December 30, 1924; Grant application to the Laura Spelman Rockefeller Memorial, June 17, 1924, Lou Hoover Papers, Box 41, "Clubs and Organizations: National Amateur Athletic Federation, Women's Division, Rockefeller (Laura Spellman [*sic*]) Foundation, 1924–28"; "Plan to Guard Girl Athletes," Boston *Traveler*, July 21, 1924; "Outdoor Sports Good for Women; Aid Development," La Crosse (Wisconsin) *Tribune*, August 15, 1924.
36. Lou Hoover to William C. Mullendore, January 18, 1924, and Mullendore to Lou Hoover, March 3, 1924, both in Mullendore Papers, Box 43, "Hoover, Lou Henry (Corresp. Series)"; Mullendore to Lou Hoover, February 21, 1924, Lou Hoover Papers, Box 19, "Personal Correspondence, 1921–28: Mullendore, William C., 1922–28"; Lou Hoover to Herbert Hoover, Jr., and Allan Hoover, April 20, 1924, Allan Hoover Papers, Hoover Presidential Library, West Branch, Iowa, Box 1, "Correspondence with Lou Henry Hoover, 1924 January–July."
37. George Harrison to Lou Hoover, September 26, 1924, and Lou Hoover to Florence Harrison, October 6, 1924, both in Lou Hoover Papers, Box 15, "Personal Correspondence, 1921–28: Harrison, George R. & Florence, 1921–26"; "Mrs. Hoover to Build Three Campus Houses," Palo Alto *Times*, October 26, 1924; "Five Houses Will Be Built by Mrs. Hoover," San Jose *Mercury-Herald*, October 26, 1924; Lou Hoover to Herbert Hoover, December 18, 1941, Mullendore Papers, Box 43, "Hoover, Lou Henry (Corresp. Series)."
38. George Barr Baker to Hugh Gibson, May 12, 1923, George Barr Baker Papers, Box 3, "Gibson, Hugh"; Kenneth Brown to Lou Hoover, February 7, March 3, 23, 1924, and four undated letters, Lou Hoover Papers, Box 10, "Personal Correspondence, 1921–28: Brown, Kenneth, 1923–24"; Julian Scott Bryan to Herbert Hoover, April 1, June 6, 1924, ibid., Box 58, "Subject File: Hoover, Allan, Horseback trip, summer 1924"; Philippi Harding to Julian S. Bryan, June 3, 1924, ibid.; Lou Hoover to Allan Hoover, July 11, 1924, ibid.; Louisette Losh to Herbert Hoover, June 16, 1924; Lou Hoover to Herbert Hoover, May 21, 1924; Herbert Hoover to Lou Hoover, May 26 and June 13, 21, 22, 1924; Herbert Hoover to Herbert Hoover, Jr., and Margaret Watson, June 7, 1924, all in Hoover Papers, Commerce Period, Box 273, "Hoover, Herbert Jr. and Allen [*sic*]"; Herbert Hoover to Edgar Rickard, August 11, 1924, Lou Hoover Papers, Box 21, "Personal Correspondence, 1921–28: Rickard, Edgar, 1923–24"; Lou Hoover to Ethel Bullard, July 30, 1924, ibid., Box 10, "Personal Correspondence, 1921–28: Bullard, Ethel Bagg, 1921–28."
39. Louisette Losh to Lou Hoover, June 7, July 5, 1924, Lou Hoover Papers, Box 17, "Personal Correspondence, 1921–28: Losh, Louisette (Mrs. William), 1924"; Herbert Hoover

to Harold F. Stokes, and Stokes to Hoover, both July 14, 1924, Hoover Papers, Commerce Period, Box 610, "Trips 1924, Western Trip, Telegrams"; Virginia Burks to Louisette Losh, September 29, October 20, 1924, Lou Hoover Papers, Box 17, "Personal Correspondence, 1921–28: Losh, Louisette (Mrs. William), 1924"; Edgar Rickard to Lou Hoover, ibid., Box 21, "Personal Correspondence, 1921–28: Rickard, Edgar, 1923–24"; "Notice of Special Meeting" of stockholders of West Branch Corporation, June 19, 1924, ibid., Box 10, "Personal Correspondence, 1921–28: Burton, R. B., 1921–24"; Lou Hoover to William Mullendore, June 30, 1924, Mullendore Papers, Box 43, "Hoover, Lou Henry (Corresp. Series)." The final termination of the West Branch Corporation took place in December 1925. See Edgar Rickard Diary, Hoover Presidential Library, West Branch, Iowa, December 26, 31, 1925, Box 1, "July–December 1925."

40. Lou Hoover to Allan Hoover, ca. January 8, 1925, Allan Hoover Papers, Box 1, "Correspondence with Lou Henry Hoover, 1925"; Allan Hoover to Herbert Hoover, December 26, 1924, ibid., "Correspondence with Herbert Hoover, 1913–1941 & undated."

Chapter 16

1. Herbert Hoover, "Economic Prospects of 1924," Commerce Department press release, January 1, 1924, Hoover Papers, Commerce Period, Hoover Presidential Library, West Branch, Iowa, Box 188, "Economic Situation in U.S., 1921–1924"; Sally Marks, *The Illusion of Peace: International Relations in Europe, 1918—1933*, 2nd ed. (New York: Palgrave Macmillan, 2003), 56–57; Carl-Ludwig Holtfrerich, *The German Inflation, 1914–1923: Causes and Effects in International Perspective* (Berlin: Walter de Gruyter, 1986), 144–45. Uncertainty in Germany about future reparations obligations, as well as the Ruhr occupation, contributed to the rise of German inflation in 1923, but the occupation was not the initial cause of inflation, and Hoover greatly underestimated German reluctance to pay, regardless of external circumstances.

2. Herbert Hoover, *Memoirs: The Cabinet and the Presidency, 1920–1933* (New York: Macmillan, 1952), 181–82 (hereafter, *Memoirs 2*); Stuart M. Crocker to Gerard Swope, January 26, 1924, Hoover Papers, Commerce Period, Box 178, "Dawes, Charles G., 1921–1928." The two-committee approach was a compromise between the French conviction that Germany had deliberately exported and hidden capital abroad in order to make it appear that the country was unable to pay reparations and the British view that the problems were financial instability, an unbalanced budget, and lack of credit in Germany. The committee dealing with repatriation of capital, on which Robinson served, produced a meaningless report saying that capital would return to Germany when its economy was stabilized. See Peter H. Buckingham, *International Normalcy: The Open Door Peace with the Former Central Powers, 1921–29* (Wilmington, DE: Scholarly Resources, 1983), 138–39; William C. McNeil, *American Money and the Weimar Republic: Economics and Politics on the Eve of the Great Depression* (New York: Columbia University Press, 1986), 25–26.

3. Herbert Hoover, *Memoirs: Years of Adventure, 1874–1920* (New York: Macmillan, 1951), 312, 453 (hereafter, *Memoirs 1*); Hoover, *Memoirs 2*, 181–82; Liaquat Ahamed, *Lords of Finance: The Bankers Who Broke the World* (New York: Penguin, 2009), 198–99.

4. Marks, *Illusion of Peace*, 60.

5. Alan G. Goldsmith to Hoover, May 21, 1924, Hoover Papers, Commerce Period, Box 211, "Foreign Debts, 1924"; James A. Logan, Jr., to Hoover, September 5, 1924, ibid., Box 363, "Lamont, Thomas W., 1921–1927"; Commission on Commerce and Marine of the American Bankers Association, "The Dawes Plan for the Payment of Reparations," ca. May 1924, ibid., Box 516, "Reparations: German Reparations, Dawes Plan, 1924 May–December"; Alan G. Goldsmith, untitled memo on the Dawes Plan, October 16, 1924, ibid., Box 516, "Reparations: General Correspondence."

6. Alan G. Goldsmith to Richard S. Emmet, March 26, 1924, Hoover Papers, Commerce Period, Box 236, "Germany: Reparations, 1921–1926 & undated"; Commerce Department press release, "Secretary Hoover Declared To-day," April 10, 1924, ibid., Box 211,

"Foreign Debts, 1924"; "Hoover Sees No Peril to American Trade," *New York Times*, August 26, 1924; James True, "The Dawes Plan and Prosperity," typescript of article for *Printer's Ink*, ca. September 18, 1924; "Address of Secretary Hoover at Dinner Given to Owen D. Young by the Business Men of New York, Waldorf-Astoria, December 11, 1924," both in Hoover Papers, Commerce Period, Box 516, "Reparations: German Reparations, Dawes Plan, 1924 May–December"; Alan G. Goldsmith to (Edward Eyre) Hunt, December 17, 1924, ibid., Box 287, "Hunt, Edward Eyre, 1923–1925"; McNeil, *American Money and the Weimar Republic*, 31–34; Buckingham, *International Normalcy*, 139–40.

7. Ahamed, *Lords of Finance*, 208–15; Buckingham, *International Normalcy*, 140–45. The bankers would have preferred Dwight Morrow, a Morgan partner, or Owen Young as agent general, but when neither was available, they settled for Parker Gilbert, a former Treasury undersecretary who had worked most recently as a liaison between Morgan and the American government.

8. Grosvenor M. Jones to (Harold Phelps) Stokes, November 14, 1924; Hoover to Stokes, November 15, 1924, both in Hoover Papers, Commerce Period, Box 273, "Foreign Loans: France, 1922–1928 & undated"; Leland Harrison, "Memorandum of Conversation with Mr. Herbert Hoover, Secretary of Commerce, Noon, November 20, Respecting the Proposed Loan of One Hundred Million Dollars by J. P. Morgan and Company to France," November 20, 1924, ibid., Box 223, "Foreign Debts: France, 1922–1928 & undated"; Hoover to Hughes, November 20, 1924, ibid., Box 572, "State Department: Secretary of State Hughes, Charles E., 1924 October–December."

9. Hoover to Sen. Arthur Capper, March 6, 7, 1924, Hoover Papers, Commerce Period, Box 208, "Foreign Combinations, Correspondence, Senator Capper, 1924–1927."

10. "Hoover Nullifies All Antitrust Law, Untermyer Holds," Washington *Post*, March 21, 1924; Hoover to Sen. Arthur Capper, March 21, 1924, Hoover Papers, Commerce Period, Box 208, "Foreign Combinations, Correspondence, Senator Capper, 1924–1927"; "America and Rubber: An Anomalous Attitude," *The Financier*, March 21, 1924; Frank G. Smith, secretary, Rubber Growers' Association, to all rubber-producing companies in the United Kingdom, April 10, 1924, Hoover Papers, Commerce Period, Box 209, "Foreign Combinations, Rubber, 1924"; David Burner, *Herbert Hoover: A Public Life* (New York: Knopf, 1979), 186–87; Melvyn Leffler, "1921–1932: Expansionist Impulses and Domestic Constraints," in *Economics and World Power: An Assessment of American Diplomacy since 1789*, ed. William H. Becker and Samuel F. Wells (New York: Columbia University Press, 1984), 226–27.

11. Memorandum of conference of Hoover with executives of rubber companies at the Lotos Club, New York, May 20, 1924, Hoover Papers, Commerce Period, Box 209, "Foreign Combinations, Material Kept Together by HH: Rubber, General, 1924–1926 & undated"; "Vanishing Rubber Supplies Forecast," New York *Journal of Commerce*, June 13, 1924; Julius Klein, *Frontiers of Trade* (New York: Century, 1929), 96–115, 262–63.

12. Hoover to Axel Oxholm, June 15, 1923; Louis Domeratzky to Hoover, September 13, 1923; Hoover to Secretary Hughes, April 26, 1924, all in Hoover Papers, Commerce Period, Box 459, "Paper and Pulpwood, 1920–1925"; Edgar Rickard to Hoover, June 27, 1923; Hoover to Rickard, June 28, 1923, both in ibid., Box 525, "Rickard, Edgar, 1921–1925"; Hoover to Secretary Hughes, May 22, 1924, ibid., Box 572, "State Department: Secretary of State Hughes, Charles E., 1924 April–May"; Domeratzky to Hoover, April 28, 1924, ibid., Box 75, "Canada, 1923–1924"; Frederic W. Hume to Hoover, May 16, 1924; Hugh J. Chisholm to Hoover, May 21, 1924; resolutions passed at conventions of Canadian Pulp and Paper Association, January 30, 1925, and American Pulp and Paper Association, February 5, 1925; Archibald R. Graustein to Hoover, February 6, 1925, all in ibid., Box 460, "Paper and Pulpwood: Canadian Embargo, 1924–1925 & undated"; Charles Evans Hughes to Hoover, February 7, 1925; draft of "A Bill to Protect the Industries of the United States," undated, both in ibid., Box 460, "Paper and Pulpwood: Embargo, 1924–1925 & undated"; ibid.

13. Hoover to M. L. Dean, March 12, 1924, Hoover Papers, Commerce Period, Box 7, "Agriculture: Idaho Agricultural Production Plan, 1924"; Hoover to E. D. Funk, May 31, 1924, ibid., Box 3, "Agriculture, 1924."

14. Julius Barnes to Hoover, January 10, 1924, Hoover Papers, Commerce Period, Box 10, "Agriculture: Northwestern Agriculture, 1923–1924 January"; "Secretary Hoover's Proposal for Reorganizing Perishable Marketing," January 14, 1924, ibid., Box 152, "Conferences: Cooperative Marketing, 1923–1924 & undated"; "Message from the President of the United States Transmitting Special Recommendations for Legislation by Congress for the Relief of Distress in Agricultural Districts in the United States," January 23, 1924, 66th Cong., 1st sess., House Document No. 167; minutes of the president's conference on Northwestern Agriculture and Finance, February 4, 1924, Hoover Papers, Commerce Period, Box 158, "Conferences: Northwestern Agriculture & Finance, President's Conference, 1924 February"; "Corporation, Having $10,000,000 Capital, Urged for Farmers," Washington *Post*, February 5, 1924; Thomas D. Hammatt to Hoover, March 3, 1924; Julius Klein to Hoover, March 5, 1924, both in Hoover Papers, Commerce Period, Box 3, "Agriculture, 1924"; "Wallace May Quit in Clash With Coolidge," Chicago *Tribune*, March 23, 1924; Frederick E. Murphy to Hoover, March 28, 1924; Hoover to Murphy, April 3, 1924, both in Hoover Papers, Commerce Period, Box 3, "Agriculture: Agriculture Credit Corporation, 1924–1925"; Hoover to Coolidge, March 29, 1924, ibid., Box 477, "President Coolidge, 1924 March"; Hoover to Rep. Arthur B. Williams, March 29, 1924, ibid., Box 4, "Agriculture: Cooperative Marketing, 1924 January–September"; Hoover, memorandum on the farm problem and possible solutions, April 3, 1924, ibid., Box 7, "Agriculture: Legislation, Capper Bill & Williams Bill, 1924"; Hoover to Sen. George H. Moses, April 3, 1924, ibid., Box 549, "Senate: Moses, George H., 1922–1928"; "Advancement of Cooperative Marketing: An Address by Secretary Hoover Before the American Dairy Federation, Milwaukee, Wis., October 1, [1924]," ibid., Box 4, "Agriculture: Cooperative Marketing, 1924 October–December."

15. Henry C. Wallace to Coolidge, April 8, 1924, Hoover Papers, Commerce Period, Box 6, "Agriculture: Federal Marketing Board, 1924"; Henry A. Wallace, "Re-Forming the Battle Lines," *Wallace's Farmer*, July 18, 1924; John W. Blodgett to Coolidge, November 22, 1924, Calvin Coolidge, President's Personal Files, Microfilm, Forbes Library, Reel 6; Hoover to Secretary of Agriculture Howard Gore, November 24, 1924, Hoover Papers, Commerce Period, Box 6, "Agriculture: Department of Agriculture & Department of Commerce, Relations of"; Hoover to Coolidge, December 20, 1924, Coolidge Microfilm, Reel 6; Joan Hoff Wilson, "Herbert Hoover's Agricultural Policies, 1921–1928," in *Herbert Hoover as Secretary of Commerce: Studies in New Era Thought and Practice*, ed. Ellis Hawley (Iowa City: University of Iowa Press, 1981), 119–24.

16. Hoover to Henry C. Wallace, February 8 and March 7, 1922; Richard S. Emmet to W. C. Mullendore, March 23, 1922, all in Hoover Papers, Commerce Period, Box 11, "Agriculture Department: Secretary of Agriculture Wallace, Henry C., 1922"; Commerce Department press release, "Secretary Hoover's Remarks to Lumbermen," May 22, 1922, ibid., Box 483, "Press Releases, 1922 May–August"; "The Hoover Conference," *Retail Lumber Dealer* 2, no. 6 (June 1922): 22; L. W. Wallace to members of the Committee on the Elimination of Waste in Industry, June 24, 1922, Hoover Papers, Commerce Period, Box 646, "Unemployment: Federated American Engineering Societies, 1922 May–June"; Hoover to John W. Blodgett, November 6, 1923, ibid., Box 51, "Standardization Conference, Dec. 1923."

17. William A. Durgin to Hoover, June 12, 1924, Hoover Papers, Commerce Period, Box 49, "Bennett, James D.-Benth, 1921–1928"; Hoover to Wallace, September 19, 1924, ibid., Box 11, "Agriculture Dept.: Secy. of Agriculture Wallace, Henry C., 1924–25"; Wallace to Hoover, October 8, 1924, ibid., Box 163, "Conferences: Wood (Forest) Utilization, 1924–25."

18. Hoover to Wallace, October 11, 1924, Hoover Papers, Commerce Period, Box 163, "Conferences: Wood (Forest) Utilization, 1924–25."

19. John W. Blodgett to Coolidge, November 22, 1924, Hoover Papers, Commerce Period, Box 477, "President Coolidge, 1924 October–November"; Hoover to Gore, November 24, 1924; Coolidge to Blodgett, December 1, 1924, both in ibid., Box 163, "Conferences: Wood (Forest) Utilization, 1924–25."

20. William A. Durgin, memorandum to Secretary Hoover, January 1, 1924, Hoover Papers, Commerce Period, Box 145, "Commerce Department: Simplified Commercial Practice, 1924"; Commerce Department press release, "Address of Secretary of Commerce Herbert Hoover at the Annual Meeting of the United States Chamber of Commerce, Cleveland, Ohio, Evening of May 7, 1924," ibid., Box 120, "Commerce Department: Achievements, 1924 May–June"; Hoover, message to Southern Forestry Congress, Savannah, January 28, 1924, Herbert Hoover Subject Collection, Hoover Institution Archives, Stanford, California, Box 11, "Forest (wood util., etc.)."

21. Hoover to Edwin H. Brown, April 9, 1924, Hoover Papers, Commerce Period, Box 28, "American Institute of Architects, 1921–1926"; Harlean James to Hoover, April 14, 1924, ibid., Box 22, "American Civic Association, 1921–1927"; typescript, "Building and Housing," ca. September 1924, ibid., Box 429, "National Conference of Business Paper Editors: Special Reports on Commerce Department, 1924"; John M. Gries to Leo C. Monahan, October 7, 1924, ibid., Box 66, "Building and Housing, Conferences, 1922–1924"; Harlean James to Leo C. Monahan, May 13, 1924, ibid., Box 22, "American Civic Association, 1921–1927"; Commerce Department press release on extending the building season, July 21, 1924, ibid., Box 483, "Press Releases, 1924 July–October"; Hoover to Arthur Woods, September 26, 1924, ibid., Box 528, "Rockefeller Foundation, 1922–1925"; Hoover to Harding, November 28, 1921, ibid., Box 595, "Taxes 1921–1925"; Hoover to (?) Goldsmith, October 31, 1922, ibid., Box 596, "Tax-Exempt Securities, 1920–1926"; Hoover, draft of memorandum on taxation, January 29, (1923?); Hoover to Stephen B. Davis, March 16, 1923, both in ibid., Box 595, "Taxes 1923"; Hoover to Samuel McCune Lindsay, April 4, 1924, ibid., Box 371, "Lindsay, Samuel McCune, 1922–25."

22. Janet Hutchison, "Building for Babbitt: The State and the Suburban Home Ideal," *Journal of Policy History* 9, no. 2 (1997): 203–5; Daniel Lazare, *America's Undeclared War: What's Killing Our Cities and How We Can Stop It* (New York: Harcourt, 2001), 158–60; Dolores Hayden, *Building Suburbia: Green Fields and Urban Growth, 1820–2000* (New York: Pantheon, 2003), 116–18, 121–22; Kenneth Jackson, *Crabgrass Frontier: The Suburbanization of the United States* (New York: Oxford University Press, 1985). Much of the very large modern literature on the subject takes issue with Hoover's contention that Americans would benefit from suburbanization.

23. *Pollution of Navigable Waters: Hearings on the Subject held before the Committee on Rivers and Harbors, House of Representatives, 68th Congress, 1st sess* (Washington, DC: Government Printing Office, 1924), 9–16; J. S. Frelinghuysen to Hoover, January 30, 31, 1924; Hoover to Frelinghuysen, January 30 and February 6, 1924, all in Hoover Papers, Commerce Period, Box 472, "Pollution of Waters, 1924 Jan.–Feb."

24. H. Taylor to Secretary of War Weeks, February 12, 1924; Hoover Papers, Commerce Period, Box 472, "Pollution of Waters, 1924 Jan.–Feb."; W. R. Snyder to Hoover, June 9, 1924, ibid., Box 472,"Pollution of Waters, 1924 Mar.–Dec."; Commerce Department press release, "Bureau of Standards Increases Its Operations," November 23, 1925, ibid., Box 484, "Press Releases, 1925 November"; Hoover, *Memoirs* 2, 151–52; Douglas C. Drake, "Herbert Hoover, Ecologist: The Politics of Oil Pollution Control, 1921–1926," *Mid-America* 55 (July 1973): 222–23.

25. Dwight B. Heard to Hoover, November 15, 30, 1923; Hoover to Heard, November 22, 1923; W. F. McClure to Hoover, all in Hoover Papers, Commerce Period, Box 257, "Heard, Dwight B., 1923"; "Governor of Arizona States His Stand on Colorado River Situation," *Electrical World*, December 29, 1923, 1322; "Governor Hunt Flays Compact," Tempe *News*, January 24, 1924; Heard to Hoover, February 6 and March 5, 1924, and Hoover to Heard, March 23, 1924, all in Hoover Papers, Commerce Period, Box 257, "Heard, Dwight B., 1924–1928 & undated."

26. Rep. Phil D. Swing to Hoover, March 4, 1924, and Hoover to Swing, March 8, 1924, both in Hoover Papers, Commerce Period, Box 282, "House of Representatives: Swing, Phil D., 1921–1928 & undated"; Mark Requa to Richard Emmet, April 5, 1924, ibid., Box 517, "Requa, Mark L., 1924 Jan.–May"; Rep. Walter F. Lineberger to Hoover, April 17, 1924, enclosing clipping, "Evasive Opposition to Boulder Dam Project," from April 4 issue of La

Mesa *Scout*, ibid., Box 279, "House of Representatives: Lineberger, Walter F., 1921–25"; Hoover to Charles B. Warren, June 10, 1924, ibid., Box 119, "Colorado, 1921–28"; Hoover to C. Bascom Slemp, October 7, 1924, enclosing draft of telegram subsequently sent over Coolidge's name to C. C. Teague in Los Angeles, ibid., Box 477, "President Coolidge, 1924 Oct.–Nov."

27. William H. Smith to Hoover, November 22, 1920, Hoover Papers, Pre-Commerce Period, Hoover Presidential Library, West Branch, Iowa, Box 57, "National Inland Waterways Association, July 24, 1920–Feb. 1921"; "Gov. Miller Assails St. Lawrence Canal," *New York Times*, November 17, 1921; Herter to Lewis Strauss, February 4, 1922, Hoover Papers, Commerce Period, Box 689, "Waterways: Great Lakes–St. Lawrence, 1922"; Julius Barnes to Hoover, October 19, 1922, ibid., Box 45, "Barnes, Julius, 1922"; Owen D. Young to Hoover, April 9, May 10, and November 20, 1923; Hoover to Young, May 17 and October 27, 1923, all in ibid., Box 719, "Young, Owen D., 1923"; Hoover to C. Bascom Slemp, November 16, 1923, enclosing draft passages for president's State of the Union message, ibid., Box 476, "President Coolidge, 1923 November"; Hoover to James P. Goodrich, January 24, 1924; Hoover to Secretary of State Hughes, January 29, 1924, both in ibid., Box 689, "Waterways: Great Lakes–St. Lawrence, 1924 January–March"; Hoover to Hughes, February 6, 1924, ibid., Box 572, "State Department: Secretary of State Hughes, Charles E., 1924 January–March"; Hoover to C. Bascom Slemp, March 10, 1924, enclosing draft of letter naming Hoover as chairman of American delegation to the binational commission, ibid., Box 477, "President Coolidge, 1924 March"; White House press release giving names of American members of St. Lawrence Commission and president's instructions to Hoover, dated March 14, 1924, ibid. Box 689, "Waterways: Great Lakes–St. Lawrence, 1924 January–March"; Hoover to Hughes, May 9, 1924, ibid., Box 572, "State Department: Secretary of State Hughes, Charles E., 1924 April–May"; Commerce Department press release, "Canada's National Advisory Committee on the St. Lawrence Waterway Project," May 17, 1924, ibid., Box 75, "Canada, 1923–1924"; "Itinerary on St. Lawrence Trip, June 13–18, 1924"; transcripts of Hoover's speeches during trip, June 14–16, 1924, all in ibid., Box 700, "Waterways: Great Lakes–St. Lawrence, St. Lawrence Commission, Trip, Niagara Falls–Montreal, Correspondence, 1924 June"; "St. Lawrence Waterway," special Commerce Department report, September 1924, ibid., Box 429, "National Conference of Business Paper Editors, Special Reports on Commerce Department, 1924."

28. William B. Ross to Secretary Hubert Work, September 1, 1923, RG 48, Interior Department Papers, National Archives, Washington, DC, Secretary Work, Box 30, "Bureau of Reclamation, Mar. 5, 1923 to Sept. 30, 1923"; Work to Coolidge, December 14, 1923, ibid., "Bureau of Reclamation, Oct. 1, 1923 to Dec. 31, 1923"; Coolidge to Hoover, December 22, 1923, Hoover Papers, Commerce Period, Box 476, "President Coolidge, 1923 December."

29. Hoover to Sen. Morris Sheppard, December 29, 1923, Hoover Papers, Commerce Period, Box 526, "Rio Grande River Compact, 1923"; Hoover to Secretary Work, March 17, 1924, ibid., "Rio Grande River Compact, 1924 Jan.–Sept."

30. Delph E. Carpenter to Hoover, September 15, 19, and October 9, 1924; J. O. Seth to Hoover, September 18, 1924; Gov. Pat M. Neff to Hoover, September 20, 1924; Hoover to Gov. William E. Sweet, September 26, 1924, all in Hoover Papers, Commerce Period, Box 526, "Rio Grande River Compact, 1924 Jan.–Sept."; Seth to Carpenter, October 15, 1924; minutes of meeting of Rio Grande Commission, Broadmoor Hotel, Colorado Springs, Colorado, October 26, 1924, both in ibid., Box 526, "Rio Grande River Compact, 1924 Oct.–Nov."

31. Elwood Mead to Hoover, February 27, 1925; Clarence E. Gilmore to Hoover, March 30, 1925; Hoover to Delph Carpenter, April 4, 25, 1925; Carpenter to Hoover, April 25, 1925; J. O. Seth to Hoover, April 28, May 9, 15, 1925; Hubert Work to Hoover, May 7, 1925; Delph Carpenter to Hoover, May 9, 1925; Sen. Morris Sheppard to Hoover, May 18, 1925; Interior Department press release on public lands along the Rio Grande in New Mexico and Colorado, May 20, 1925; Hoover to J. O. Seth, June 8, 1925, all in Hoover Papers, Commerce Period, Box 526, "Rio Grande River Compact, 1925"; Delph Carpenter to

Secretary Work, May 28, 1925, RG 48, Interior Department Records, Secretary Work, Box 30, "Bureau of Reclamation, Jan. 1, 1924 to June 30, 1925."

32. For the background of the merchant marine problem, see Hoover Papers, Commerce Period, Boxes 675–77. One of Hoover's first official acts was to warn Harding about the problem, and thereafter he struggled with various aspects of it. See Hoover to Harding, March 17, 1921, ibid., Box 480, "President Harding, 1921 March"; Hoover to Harding, December 6, 1921, ibid., "President Harding, 1921 December"; Hoover to Harding, February 2, 1923, ibid., Box 537, "Ship Subsidy, 1923–1925"; Hoover to Coolidge, August 21, 1923, ibid., Box 476, "President Coolidge, 1923 August–September"; E. S. Gregg to Hoover, October 24, 1923, ibid., Box 390, "Merchant Marine, 1923"; Commerce Department press release, "Address by Herbert Hoover, Secretary of Commerce, before the American Marine Congress, New York City, Thursday, Nov. 8, 1923," ibid.; Hoover, *Memoirs 2*, 135–36; Hal B. Lary and associates, *The United States in the World Economy: The International Transactions of the United States during the Interwar Period* (Washington, DC: Government Printing Office, 1943), 72–73; Eugene P. Trani and David L. Wilson, *The Presidency of Warren G. Harding* (Lawrence: University Press of Kansas, 1977), 75–77.

33. Hoover to Harding, February 2, 1923, Hoover Papers, Commerce Period, Box 390, "Merchant Marine, 1923"; "Address by Herbert Hoover, Secretary of Commerce, before the American Marine Congress, New York City, Thursday, November 8, 1923," ibid., Box 29, "American Marine Congress Report, 1923"; Hoover to Coolidge, and Hoover to Rep. George Edmonds, January 17, 1924; Coolidge to Hoover, January 22, 1924; five-page memorandum by Hoover on proposed changes, January 24, 1924; Edmonds to Hoover, January 24, 1924, all in ibid., Box 390, "Merchant Marine, 1924"; Hoover, *Memoirs 2*, 135.

34. Hoover, *Memoirs 2*, 136; Coolidge to Hoover, March 12, 1924, Hoover Papers, Commerce Period, Box 477, "President Coolidge, 1924 March"; Hoover to Secretary Curtis Wilbur, December 3, 1924, ibid., Box 434, "Navy Department: Secretary Wilbur, Curtis D., 1924–1928."

35. Hoover to Rep. Wallace H. White, November 4, 1925, Hoover Papers, Commerce Period, Box 390, "Merchant Marine, 1925 September–November."

36. Ibid.

37. René De La Pedraja, *The Rise and Decline of U.S. Merchant Shipping in the Twentieth Century* (New York: Twayne, 1992), 59–63; K. Jack Bauer, *A Maritime History of the United States: The Role of America's Seas and Waterways* (Columbia: University of South Carolina Press, 1988), 301–5.

38. Mark H. Rose, Bruce E. Seely, and Paul F. Barrett, *The Best Transportation System in the World: Railroads, Trucks, Airlines, and American Public Policy in the Twentieth Century* (Columbus: Ohio State University Press, 2006), 21–23. The author of the ICC plan was William Z. Ripley, a Harvard professor of economics.

39. Hoover memorandum, "Principles" (and handwritten draft), November 7, 1923, Hoover Papers, Commerce Period, Box 504, "Railroads: Consolidation, 1923 Nov.–Dec."; Hoover to Coolidge, November 22, 1923, ibid., Box 476, "President Coolidge, 1923 November."

40. Press release issued by the committee on transportation and communication of the Chamber of Commerce of the United States, February 2, 1923; Hoover to C. H. Markham, February 1, 1923; Markham to Hoover, February 3, 1923, all in Hoover Papers, Commerce Period, Box 505, "Railroads: Railroad Conferences, 1923–1927"; "Conference Backs Rate-making Clause," *New York Times*, January 10, 1924; "Summary of Address by Secretary Hoover before the Transportation Conference, Held at the Hotel Willard, Washington, D.C., Wednesday morning, January 9, 1924," Hoover Papers, Commerce Period, Box 504, "Railroads: Consolidation, 1921–1925 & undated"; Hoover, "Railroad Consolidation," *Saturday Evening Post*, February 9, 1924, 6–7, 137.

41. Rose, Seely, and Barrett, *The Best Transportation System in the World*, 22–33; Robert H. Ferrell, *The Presidency of Calvin Coolidge* (Lawrence: University Press of Kansas, 1998), 67–69; Geoffrey Perrett, *America in the Twenties: A History* (New York: Simon & Schuster, 1982), 342–43.

42. "Interview published in Boston American, October 13, 1924," Hoover Papers, Commerce Period, Box 39, "Aviation, 1922–1924"; Department of Commerce, *Twelfth Annual Report of the Secretary of Commerce* (Washington, DC: Government Printing Office, 1924), 35; Hoover to Rep. Samuel E. Winslow, June 13, 19, 1922; Winslow to Hoover, June 14, 1922, all in Hoover Papers, Commerce Period, Box 122, "Commerce Department: Aeronautics, Bureau of, Legislation, 1922."

43. Rose, Seely, and Barrett, *The Best Transportation System in the World*, 42–43.

44. Hoover to Elliot H. Goodwin (and others), March 26, 1924; Hoover to C. F. Kettering (and others), April 25, 1924; "Hoover Seeks to Improve Traffic Safety," draft of article for *Nation's Business*, June 10, 1924, all in Hoover Papers, Commerce Period, Box 160, "Conferences: Street and Highway Safety, 1924 March–June"; Commerce Department press release, "Secretary Hoover Calls National Conference on Street and Highway Accidents for December 15th," October 27, 1924, ibid., Box 160, "Conferences: Street and Highway Safety, 1924 September–November"; Commerce Department press release, "Address of Secretary Hoover before the National Conference on Street and Highway Safety at the U.S. Chamber of Commerce Building, Washington, D.C., Monday Morning, December 15, 1924," ibid., Box 160, "Conferences: Street and Highway Safety, 1924 December & undated"; Commerce Department press release, "Findings of National Conference on Street and Highway Safety Receive Nation Wide Consideration," February 24, 1925; National Conference on Street and Highway Safety, "Revised Tentative Draft of a Uniform Vehicle Act," ca. 1925, both in ibid., Box 160, "Conferences: Street and Highway Safety, 1925 Conference, 1924–1925 June."

45. Commerce Department press release, "Statement by Secretary Hoover [on monopoly control of radio frequencies] for Release to Monday Afternoon Papers," March 10, 1924, Hoover Papers, Commerce Period, Box 483, "Press Releases, 1924 January–June"; Commerce Department press release, "Statement by Secretary Hoover at Hearings before the Committee on the Merchant Marine and Fisheries on H.R. 7357, 'To Regulate Radio Communication, and for other Purposes,' Mar. 11, 1924"; Hoover to Norman Hapgood, March 26, 1924, both in ibid., Box 489, "Radio: Correspondence, Press Releases, Misc., 1924 Jan.–March"; ibid. Hoover received a photo transmitted by radio in February 1924, and the department announced in June that it had the ability to determine latitude and longitude by radio. See Hoover to C. Francis Jenkins, February 1, 1924, Hoover Papers, Commerce Period, Box 489, "Radio: Correspondence, Press Releases, Misc., 1924 Jan.–March"; Commerce Department press release on radio location, June 12, 1924, ibid., Box 490, "Radio: Correspondence, Press Releases, Misc., 1924 April–September."

46. Commerce Department press release, "Secretary Hoover Calls Third National Radio Conference," August 26, 1924, Hoover Papers, Commerce Period, Box 490, "Radio: Conferences, Press Releases, Misc., 1924 April–September"; "Interview with Secretary Hoover, by S. R. Winters, published in *Radio News*, Oct. 1924," ibid., Box 490, "Radio: Correspondence, Press Releases, Misc., 1924 October–December"; Commerce Department press release, "Secretary Hoover Addresses Third National Radio Conference," October 7, 1924, ibid., Box 429, "National Conference of Business Paper Editors, Special Reports on Commerce Department, 1924"; Daniel E. Garvey, "Secretary Hoover and the Quest for Broadcast Regulation," in *Business-Government Cooperation, 1917–1932: The Rise of Corporatist Policies*, ed. Robert F. Himmelberg (New York: Garland, 1984), 77.

47. "Report of the Third National Radio Conference," October 10, 1924, Hoover Papers, Commerce Period, Box 496, "Radio: Conferences, National, Third (Oct. 6, 1924), Reports and Press Releases."

48. Hoover to Rep. Wallace H. White, December 4, 1924, Hoover Papers, Commerce Period, Box 490, "Radio: Correspondence, Press Releases, Misc., 1924 October–December."

49. Hoover to Col. Arthur Woods, December 10, 1924, Hoover Papers, Commerce Period, Box 490, "Radio: Correspondence, Press Releases, Misc., 1924 October–December"; "Hoover Sees End of Jazz in Radio," Portland *Oregonian*, December 22, 1924.

50. Commerce Department press release, "Radio and the Public, by Herbert Hoover," January 1, 1925, Hoover Papers, Commerce Period, Box 483, "Press Releases, 1925 January–April";

interview with Hoover for Cleveland *Plain Dealer*, May 28, 1925, ibid., Box 490, "Radio: Correspondence, Press Releases, Misc., 1925 May–September."

51. "U.S. Launches Superpower Project to Save Billions," San Francisco *Chronicle*, September 15, 1921; "Superpower Plan to Offset Coal Strikes," Boston *Globe*, April 8, 1922; Hoover, "Address to the National Electric Light Association Convention, Atlantic City, N.J.," May 19, 1922, Hoover Papers, Commerce Period, Box 590, "Superpower, Waterpower, etc., 1922"; Owen D. Young to Hoover, March 16, 1923, ibid., Box 719, "Young, Owen D., 1923"; Hoover to W. S. Murray, August 22, 1923, and Murray to Hoover, September 30, 1923, both in ibid., Box 590, "Superpower, Waterpower, etc., 1923"; Hoover to William B. Ainey (and other state public service commission chairmen), October 10, 20, 1923, ibid., Box 162, "Conferences: Superpower, 1923 June–October"; Commerce Department press release, "Summary of Statement of Secretary Hoover to the Super Power Conference, New York City, Saturday, October 13, 1923," ibid., Box 590, "Superpower, Waterpower, etc., 1923"; "Support Action with Action," *Electrical World*, October 20, 1923; "Superpower and Economic Statesmanship," *Chemical and Metallurgical Engineering*, October 22, 1923, 744; Hoover to Gifford Pinchot (and other Northeastern governors), October 23, 1923, Hoover Papers, Commerce Period, Box 162, "Conferences: Superpower, 1923 June–October"; John Lathrop, "Super-Power Plans Growing," New York *Herald*, November 5, 1922; Hoover to C. Bascom Slemp, November 18, 1923, Hoover Papers, Commerce Period, Box 476, "President Coolidge, 1923 Nov."; "Hoover Out for the Superpower Plan," *Literary Digest*, November 17, 1923, 14; Hoover to Morris L. Cooke, December 13, 1923, Hoover Papers, Commerce Period, Box 162, "Conferences: Superpower, 1923 November–December."
52. Commerce Department press release, "Northeastern Super Power Committee," April 14, 1924, Hoover Papers, Commerce Period, Box 483, "Press Releases, 1924 July–October."
53. William Hard, "Giant Negotiations for Giant Power," *Survey Graphic* 4 (March 1924):577–80; Morris L. Cooke to Gifford Pinchot, April 10, 1924, Hoover Papers, Commerce Period, Box 162, "Conferences: Superpower, 1924 Jan.–Apr."
54. Commerce Department press release, "Address by Herbert Hoover, Secretary of Commerce, by radio to Convention of National Electric Light Association at Atlantic City, May 21, 1924," Hoover Papers, Commerce Period, Box 162, "Conferences: Superpower, 1924 May–1925 & undated"; Commerce Department press release, "Report of the Engineer Sub-Committee of the Northeastern Superpower Committee, Superpower Report Made Public," July 28, 1924, ibid., Box 483, "Press Releases, 1924 July–October"; Commerce Department press release, "Summary of an Address by Secretary Hoover before the Annual Convention of the National Electric Light Association, San Francisco, June 17, 8:30 P.M.," June 18, 1925, ibid., Box 484, "Press Releases, 1925 May–October."
55. Hoover to Coolidge, November 17, 1923, Hoover Papers, Commerce Period, Box 106, "Coal: President, 1922–1926"; Hoover to Coolidge, November 22, 1923, ibid., Box 476, "President Coolidge, 1923 November."
56. "Just a story from CUSHING SURVEY," unsigned, undated memorandum; John L. Lewis to Hoover, January 5, 28 and February 18, 1924; C. J. Goodyear to Hoover, January 18, 1924, enclosing "Call for Joint Conference of the Operators and Miners of Ohio, Western Pennsylvania, Illinois and Indiana (Central Competitive Field)," signed by Michael Gallagher, January 9, 1924; Hoover to C. J. Goodyear, January 26, 1924 (released to the press on January 30); F. R. Wadleigh to Hoover, February 12, 1924; Hoover to John L. Lewis, February 20, 1924; Hoover to Coolidge, February 20, 1924; F. R. Wadleigh to Hoover, March 9, 1925, all in Hoover Papers, Commerce Period, Box 101, "Coal: Conferences, Jacksonville, 1924 February 11"; James P. Johnson, *The Politics of Soft Coal: The Bituminous Industry from World War I through the New Deal* (Urbana: University of Illinois Press, 1979), 95.
57. Hoover to Joseph Pursglove, February 10, 1925, Hoover Papers, Commerce Period, Box 101, "Coal: Conferences, Jacksonville, 1924 February 11"; Hoover to Everett Sanders, November 23, 1925, ibid., Box 104, "Coal: Lewis, John L., 1922–1928 & undated"; Hoover to Frank F. Tirre, May 22, 1924, ibid., Box 102, "Coal: Government Ownership or Regulation, 1921–1926."

58. Typescript of Hoover's testimony before the Senate Committee on Agriculture and Forestry, May 10, 1924, Hoover Papers, Commerce Period, Box 257, "Hearings, 1920–1925"; Hoover, *Memoirs* 2, 81.
59. Harry M. Blair to Hoover, November 22, 1924, Hoover Papers, Commerce Period, Box 422, "Muscle Shoals: Miscellaneous, 1921–1924"; "New Row Brewing On Muscle Shoals," New York *World*, November 22, 1924.
60. Lou Hoover to Herbert, Jr., and Allan Hoover, ca. February 7, 1924, Allan Hoover Papers, Hoover Presidential Library, West Branch, Iowa, Box 1, "Correspondence with Lou Henry Hoover, 1924 January–July."
61. The 1921 immigration act is in Philip R. Moran, ed., *Warren G. Harding, 1865–1923: Chronology, Documents, Bibliographical Aids* (Dobbs Ferry, New York: Oceana, 1970), 49–51, and its history is covered in Trani and Wilson, *Presidency of Warren G. Harding*, 60–61. For the 1924 act, see Hoover to Coolidge, December 30, 1926, Hoover Papers, Commerce Period, Box 289, "Immigration: National Origins, 1926"; "National Origin Provision of the Immigration Act of 1924," 69 Cong., 2nd sess., Senate Doc. 190; Ferrell, *The Presidency of Calvin Coolidge*, 112–15; David J. Goldberg, *Discontented America: The United States in the 1920s* (Baltimore: Johns Hopkins University Press, 1999), 162–63.
62. There are three drafts of a letter to President Coolidge, April 17, 1924, in the Hoover Papers, but eventually Hoover gave his opinion about Japanese immigration to the president orally: see Hoover Papers, Commerce Period, Box 477, "President Coolidge, 1924 April"; Hoover to Mark Requa, April 21, 1924, ibid., Box 348, "Japan, 1922–1926"; Hoover to Robert A. Taft, April 19, 1928, ibid., Box 289, "Immigration: 1928 & undated"; Hoover to Coolidge, December 23, 1924, ibid., Box 477, "President Coolidge, 1924 December"; Francis V. Keesling to President Coolidge, April 18, 1924, Francis V. Keesling Papers, Rare Books and Special Collections, Green Library, Stanford University, Stanford, California, Box 2, Folder 11, "Polit. Corresp. Out, 1924, Jan.–Apr."; Burner, *Hoover*, 197.
63. Department of Commerce, *Twelfth Annual Report of the Secretary of Commerce*, 30–31.

Chapter 17

1. See Barry Eichengreen, *Golden Fetters: The Gold Standard and the Great Depression, 1919–1939* (New York: Oxford University Press, 1992); Ben S. Bernanke, "The Macroeconomics of the Great Depression: A Comparative Approach," in *Essays on the Great Depression* (Princeton, NJ: Princeton University Press, 2000), 7–8; Harold James, *The End of Globalization: Lessons from the Great Depression* (Cambridge: Harvard University Press, 2001); Liaquat Ahamed, *Lords of Finance: The Bankers Who Broke the World* (New York: Penguin, 2009), 404–6; Stephen A. Schuker, "The Gold-Exchange Standard: A Reinterpretation," in *International Financial History in the Twentieth Century: System and Anarchy*, ed. Marc Flandreau, Carl-Ludwig Holtfrerich, and Harold James (Cambridge, UK: German Historical Institute and Cambridge University Press, 2003), 88–91.
2. Melvyn Leffler, "1921–1932: Expansionist Impulses and Domestic Constraints," in *Economics and World Power: An Assessment of American Diplomacy since 1789*, ed. William H. Becker and Samuel F. Wells, Jr. (New York: Columbia University Press, 1984): 225–75.
3. Commerce Department press release, "Economic Prospects of the New Year," January 1, 1925, Hoover Papers, Commerce Period, Hoover Presidential Library, West Branch, Iowa, Box 188, "Economic Situation, 1925–1927."
4. A letter from Irvine Lenroot to Lawrence Richey, May 3, 1933, in the Herbert Hoover Papers, Post-Presidential File, Hoover Presidential Library, West Branch, Iowa, Box 187, "Richey, Lawrence: Correspondence, January–Sept. 1933," outlines Hoover's influence on this process. I am indebted to George Nash for pointing this document out to me. This file also contains Lenroot's letter, November 23, 1925; Crissinger's reply, December 10, 1925; and Lenroot's reiteration of his concerns in a letter dated December 23, 1925. A letter to Lenroot from Benjamin Strong, drafted on December 30, 1925, and apparently revised on January 6, 1926 (but never sent), explains some of Strong's reasons for opposing interest

increases. See Federal Reserve System, Board of Governors Collection, Hoover Presidential Library, West Branch, Iowa, Box 1, "Adolph Miller Papers, Correspondence, 1925–1926." Brief excerpts from the minutes of the board's meetings on December 10, 1925, and January 13, 1926, recording its votes on Lenroot's recommendation, are in ibid., Box 1, "Adolph Miller Papers, D. R. Crissinger File, 1923–1927." For Strong's concerns about the possible effect of an American interest rate increase on the British gold standard, see the notes of an interview with Adolph Miller, ca. February 1949, by Jameson Parker, Mark Sullivan's research assistant, Hoover Papers, Post-Presidential File, Box 230, "Sullivan, Mark: Misc. Correspondence & Prt. Mat., 1933–49, Found in Supplementary Book Matl., *Memoirs*— Interfiled, 2/11/80." George Nash also drew my attention to this material. See also Lester V. Chandler, *Benjamin Strong, Central Banker* (Washington, DC: Brookings Institution, 1958), 254–55; Ahamed, *Lords of Finance*, 274–77.

5. David Cannadine, *Mellon: An American Life* (New York: Knopf, 2006), 318–21; Chandler, *Strong*, 254–55, 303–7, 321–30; Ahamed, *Lords of Finance*, 276–79. Federal Reserve banks did gradually increase interest rates during 1925, although they were kept below European rates. As it turned out, the speculative stock market bubble that Hoover and Miller worried about proved to be unimportant. Prices fell by about 10 percent in early 1926 before resuming a gradual rise.

6. Hoover to Don Livingston, January 8, 1925, Hoover Papers, Commerce Period, Box 236, "Germany, 1925–1927"; S. H. Cross to Hoover, March 30, 1925, ibid., Box 214, "Foreign Debts: France, 1925 January–August"; Denise Artaud, "Reparations and War Debts: The Restoration of French Financial Power, 1919–1929," in *French Foreign and Defence Policy, 1918–1940: The Decline and Fall of a Great Power*, ed. Robert Boyce (Routledge: London, 1998), 93–103; Stephen A. Schuker, *The End of French Predominance in Europe: The Financial Crisis of 1924 and the Adoption of the Dawes Plan* (Chapel Hill: University of North Carolina Press, 1976), 155–60; Ahamed, *Lords of Finance*, 248–50.

7. Benjamin F. Rhodes, "Reassessing 'Uncle Shylock': The United States and the French War Debt, 1917–1929," *Journal of American History* 55 (March 1969): 788, 797, 802; Artaud, "Reparations and War Debts," 103.

8. Unsigned memorandum, "Historical Note on the French Debt to the United States," undated, Hoover Papers, Commerce Period, Box 179, "Debts: French (1), Items 1–12, 1925"; Hoover, *Memoirs: The Cabinet and the Presidency, 1920–1933* (New York: Macmillan, 1952), 177–79 (hereafter, *Memoirs* 2); Schuker, *End of French Predominance*, 160–68.

9. Stephane Lauzanne, "A Poker Party at Washington," ca. December 1925 (a report by the editor of *Le Matin* translated from the French), Hoover Papers, Commerce Period, Box 212, "Foreign Debts, 1925 October–December"; unsigned (Hoover) memorandum, September 24, 1925, ibid., Box 179, "Debts: French (1), Items 13–24, 1925"; Benjamin D. Rhodes, *United States Foreign Policy in the Interwar Period, 1918–1941: The Golden Age of American Diplomatic and Military Complacency* (Westport, CT: Praeger, 2001), 67; Rhodes, "Reassessing 'Uncle Shylock,'" 796–97.

10. Lauzanne, "A Poker Party," 10–13.

11. Ibid., 15–16; Claudius O. Johnson, *Borah of Idaho* (Seattle: University of Washington Press, 1936), 275–76.

12. Unsigned (Hoover) memorandum, September 30, 1925, Hoover Papers, Commerce Period, Box 179, "Debts: French (2), Items 25–37C, 1925"; Lauzanne, "A Poker Party," 15–16; typescript with handwritten heading, "Caillaux Final Reply Oct. 1"; unsigned (Hoover) memorandum, "Conclusions," ca. October 2, 1925; draft of statement to be read by president at press conference, October 2, 1925, all in Hoover Papers, Commerce Period, Box 179, "Debts: French (2), Items 38–44, 1925"; Edgar Rickard Diary, October 1, 13, 1925, Hoover Presidential Library, West Branch, Iowa, Box 1, "July–December 1925."

13. Speyer and Company to Secretary Kellogg, September 28, 1925; Hoover to Kellogg, October 2, 1925; Kellogg to Speyer and Company, October 9, 1925; Hoover to Henry Robinson, October 12, 23, 1925; Robinson to Hoover, October 16, 1925; Leland Harrison to Hoover, October 19, 1925; Hoover to Kellogg, October 30, 1925, all in Hoover Papers, Commerce Period, Box 223, "Foreign Loans: Germany, General Policy, Etc., 1925

October–November"; Rickard Diary, October 13, 1925, Box 1, "July–December 1925"; Derek H. Aldcroft, *From Versailles to Wall Street, 1919–1929* (Berkeley: University of California Press, 1977), 255–57.

14. Hoover to Coolidge, November 6, 1925, Hoover Papers, Commerce Period, Box 478, "President Coolidge, 1925 November."

15. Hoover to Charles Hebbard, November 24, 1925, Hoover Papers, Commerce Period, Box 366, "League of Nations, 1925"; F. E. Blair to Hoover, December 2, 1925, ibid., Box 179, "Debts: French (2), Items 38–44, 1925"; Alex Legge to Hoover, December 4, 1925, ibid., Box 367, "Legge, Alex, 1924–1928 & undated."

16. Commerce Department press release, "Hoover Sees Stability of Trade in Gold Pound," April 30, 1925, Hoover Papers, Commerce Period, Box 483, "Press Releases, 1925 January–August"; Stephen A. Schuker, "Origins of American Stabilization Policy in Europe: The Financial Dimension, 1918–1924," in *Confrontation and Cooperation: Germany and the United States in the Era of World War I, 1900–1924*, ed. Hans-Jürgen Schröder (Providence, RI: Berg, 1993), 394.

17. Commerce Department press release, "Invisible Trade in 1924," Hoover Papers, Commerce Period, Box 484, "Press Releases, 1925 May–October"; unsigned memorandum, "Total Values of Imports and Exports of Merchandise by Grand Division and Principal Countries," ca. April 1925, ibid., Box 194, "Reports 1924–1928 & undated"; Commerce Department Finance and Investment Division memorandum to Harold P. Stokes, August 6, 1925, "Information Desired by the Hon. James Hamilton Lewis, re Foreign Loans," August 5, 1925, ibid., Box 221, "Foreign Loans, Miscellaneous, 1925"; Grosvenor M. Jones to Sen. Theodore E. Burton, November 19, 1925, ibid., Box 218, "Foreign Debts: Materials Assembled by Mr. Clapp, 1926." For a fuller discussion of the "invisible exchange" question, see Chapter 13 in this volume and the tables in Stephen A. Schuker, *American "Reparations" to Germany, 1919–33: Implications for the Third-World Debt Crisis* (Princeton, NJ: Department of Economics, Princeton University, 1988), 92–93.

18. Eichengreen, *Golden Fetters*, xi–xii, 161–62; Robert W. D. Boyce, *British Capitalism at the Crossroads, 1919–1932: A Study in Politics, Economics, and International Relations* (Cambridge, UK: Cambridge University Press, 1987), 66–78. Strong's May 27, 1924, letter to Andrew Mellon is quoted in Stephen V. O. Clarke, *Central Bank Cooperation: 1924–31* (New York: Federal Reserve Bank of New York, 1967), 28.

19. Michael Hogan, *Informal Entente: The Private Structure of Cooperation in Anglo-American Economic Diplomacy, 1918–1928* (Columbia: University of Missouri Press, 1977), 71–72; Frank Costigliola, *Awkward Dominion: American Political, Economic, and Cultural Relations with Europe, 1919–1933* (Ithaca, NY: Cornell University Press, 1984), 111–13; Ahamed, *Lords of Finance*, 7.

20. Julius Klein, "The Coming Conflict in Foreign Trade," speech to the American Manufacturers Export Association, March 25, 1925, Hoover Papers, Commerce Period, Box 483, "Press Releases, 1925 January–April"; Klein, "International Trade Rivalries," speech to the National Association of Farm Equipment Manufacturers, October 30, 1925, ibid., Box 483, "Press Releases, 1925 May–October"; David Lake, "International Economic Structures and American Foreign Economic Policy, 1887–1934," *World Politics* 35 (July 1987): 533–37; Stephen A. Schuker, "American Foreign Policy: The European Dimension, 1921–1929," in *Calvin Coolidge and the Coolidge Era: Essays on the History of the 1920s*, ed. John Earl Haynes (Washington, DC: Library of Congress, 1998), 297–98; Andrew Wyatt-Walter, "The United States and Western Europe: The Theory of Hegemonic Stability," in *Explaining International Relations since 1945*, ed. Ngaire Woods (Oxford, UK: Oxford University Press, 1996), 126–32.

21. Eugene P. Trani and David L. Wilson, *The Presidency of Warren G. Harding* (Lawrence: University Press of Kansas, 1977), 61, 73–74.

22. Hoover, private memorandum on policies and opinions, ca. December 1923, Hoover Papers, Commerce Period, Box 268, "Commerce Personal: Hoover, Herbert, Biography, undated"; Hoover to James F. Curtis, March 23, 1921, ibid., Box 593, "Tariff, 1914–1921"; A. B. Farquhar to Hoover, March 21, 1921, ibid., Box 196, "Farquhar, Arthur B., 1921";

Hoover to Joseph W. Fordney, May 10, 1921, ibid., Box 283, "House of Representatives: Ways and Means Committee, 1921–1922"; Hoover to Rep. Ernest R. Ackerman, July 19, 1921, ibid., Box 274, "House of Representatives: Ackerman, Ernest R., 1921–1926"; Paul M. Warburg to Hoover, July 22, 1921, ibid., Box 685, "Warburg, Paul, 1918–1921"; Rep. Richard Yates to Hoover, July 26, 1921, ibid., Box 277, "House of Representatives: Fordney Tariff Bill, 1921"; draft (marked "not sent") of Hoover to Sen. Boies Penrose, ca. August 1, 1921, ibid., Box 550, "Senate: Penrose, Boies, 1921"; Department of Commerce, *Tenth Annual Report of the Secretary of Commerce* (Washington, DC: Government Printing Office, 1922), 20; unsigned memorandum on the tariff and foreign debts, January 12, 1928, Hoover Papers, Commerce Period, Box 594, "Tariff 1928"; campaign pamphlet, "The Protective Policy: Extracts from the Speeches and Writings of Herbert Hoover," 1928, ibid., Box 593, "Tariff 1924–1925."

23. Department of Commerce, *Thirteenth Annual Report of the Secretary of Commerce* (Washington, DC: Government Printing Office, 1925), 38–39; Julius Klein, *Frontiers of Trade* (New York: Century, 1929), 138–39. By 1926, war debt agreements had reduced the debt burden to manageable levels for all of the European states. In addition to its limitations on trade, the American tariff provided a convenient excuse for them to drag their feet on paying obligations they did not really acknowledge as legitimate.

24. Unsigned memorandum, "United States Imports Capable of Monopolistic Control by Foreign Countries of Origin," no date, Hoover Papers, Commerce Period, Box 208, "Foreign Combinations: Miscellaneous, 1926"; Hoover to Secretary Kellogg, November 13, 1925, ibid., Box 208, "Foreign Combinations: Correspondence, Secretary of State, 1925–1926"; Hoover, "Foreign Combinations Now Fixing Prices of Raw Materials Imported Into the United States," speech before the Chamber of Commerce of Erie, Pennsylvania, October 31, 1925, pamphlet in ibid., Box 209, "Foreign Combinations: Rubber, 1925 June–October"; Hoover to Sen. Arthur Capper, December 10, 1925, ibid., Box 77, "Capper, Senator Arthur, 1924–1928." More than 90 percent of the potash used in the United States in 1925 for fertilizer—primarily for cotton, tobacco, and "truck" gardening—was imported, primarily from the Alsace-Lorraine region of Germany and France and was controlled by two companies, one German and the other French. The companies increased their prices slightly in 1925, but not enough, according to the Commerce Department, to stimulate serious efforts to produce potash in the United States. See A. T. Coons, *Potash in 1925* (Washington, DC: Government Printing Office, 1927), and Coons, *Potash in 1926* (Washington, DC: Government Printing Office, 1927). A 1926 Agriculture Department assessment of the situation, however, concluded that "a French-German monopoly" had been established, and that "there is little that can be interpreted as promising cheaper potash, or in fact the continuance of cheap potash." See J. W. Turrentine, *Potash: A Review, Estimate and Forecast* (New York: Wiley, 1926), 44.

25. Unsigned memorandum, "United States Imports Capable of Monopolistic Control by Foreign Countries of Origin," no date, Hoover Papers, Commerce Period, Box 208, "Foreign Combinations: Miscellaneous, 1926"; E. G. Holt, "Analysis of the Present Crude Rubber Situation," ca. July 1925, ibid., Box 209, "Foreign Combinations: Rubber, 1925 March–May."

26. E. G. Holt, "Analysis of the Present Crude Rubber Situation," ca. July 1925, Hoover Papers, Commerce Period, Box 209, "Foreign Combinations: Rubber, 1925 March–May"; "Statement by Secretary Hoover at Press Conference," June 2, 1925, ibid., Box 209, "Foreign Combinations: Reports, Press Releases, Articles, etc., 1923–1928 & undated"; Harold Phelps Stokes to the editor of the *New York Times*, June 10, 1925; E. G. Holt to (?) Yelverton, June 17, 1925, both in ibid., Box 444, "Newspapers and Magazines: *New York Times*, 1925–1926"; P. L. Palmerston to Harold Phelps Stokes, August 3, 1925, ibid., Box 216, "Foreign Debts: Great Britain, 1925 April–December"; Hoover to Secretary Kellogg, September 25, 1925, ibid., Box 572, "State Department: Secretary of State Kellogg, Frank B., 1925 June–September"; Hoover, "Foreign Combinations Now Fixing Prices of Raw Materials Imported into the United States," speech before the Erie, Pennsylvania, Chamber of Commerce, October 31, 1925, pamphlet in ibid., Box 209, "Foreign Combinations: Rubber,

1925 June–October"; Commerce Department press release, letter from Hoover to Sen. Arthur Capper, December 16, 1925, ibid., Box 208, "Foreign Combinations: Miscellaneous, 1925"; Hoover to Capper, December 19, 1925, ibid., Box 545, "Senate: Capper, Arthur, 1925–1926."

27. Hoover to Kellogg, November 28, 1925, Hoover Papers, Commerce Period, Box 572, "State Department: Secretary of State Kellogg, Frank B., 1925 October–December"; Kellogg to Hoover, December 2, 1925, enclosing copy of instructions to Ambassador Alanson Houghton in London, December 1, 1925; copy of Sir Austen Chamberlain to Sir Esme Howard, December 3, 1925; Kellogg to Hoover, December 4, 1925, enclosing copy of report from Houghton, December 4, 1925, all in ibid., Box 208, "Foreign Combinations: Correspondence, Secretary of State, 1925–1926"; Julius Klein to Harold Phelps Stokes, December 1, 1925, enclosing copy of article from *British Outlook*, November 7, 1925, ibid., Box 208, "Foreign Combinations: Miscellaneous, 1925."

28. Sir Austen Chamberlain to Alanson B. Houghton, August 15, 1925, Hoover Papers, Commerce Period, Box 208, "Foreign Combinations: Correspondence, Secretary of State, 1925–1926"; copy of article from *British Outlook*, November 7, 1925, enclosed in Julius Klein to Harold Phelps Stokes, December 1, 1925, ibid., Box 208, "Foreign Combinations: Miscellaneous, 1925"; copy of Ambassador Houghton to State Department, December 4, 1925, enclosed in Kellogg to Hoover, December 4, 1925, ibid., Box 208, "Foreign Combinations: Correspondence, Secretary of State, 1925–1926"; Harvey S. Firestone to Hoover, December 12, 1925, ibid., Box 210, "Foreign Combinations: Rubber, 1925 December."

29. Harvey Firestone to Hoover, December 12, 1925, and Hoover to Firestone, December 14, 1925, both in Hoover Papers, Commerce Period, Box 210, "Foreign Combinations: Rubber, 1925 December"; "Rubber Criticism Surprises London," *New York Times*, December 16, 1925; Edgar Rickard to Hoover, December 18, 1925, enclosing translations from Belgian press reports on American policy regarding rubber, Hoover Papers, Commerce Period, Box 208, "Foreign Combinations: Miscellaneous, 1925"; "To Be Frank About It," London *Morning Post*, December 23, 1925; Sydney Brooks, "Rubber: What America Pays; A £140,000,000 Bill," London *Sunday Times*, December 27, 1925; P. L. Palmerston to Hoover, December 19, 1925, Hoover Papers, Commerce Period, Box 209, "Foreign Combinations: Material Kept Together by HH, Rubber-Confidential, 1925 & undated"; Secretary Kellogg to Hoover, December 23, 1925, enclosing copy of report from Ambassador Houghton, November 25, 1925, ibid., Box 208, "Foreign Combinations: Correspondence, Secretary of State, 1925–1926"; "Statement by Secretary Hoover," December 23, 1926, marked "Not given out," ibid., Box 209, "Foreign Combinations: Rubber, 1925 June–October"; unsigned postcard to Secretary of Commerce Hoover, December 30, 1925, ibid., Box 210, "Foreign Combinations: Rubber, Comments, 1925–1926."

30. Julius Klein, "The Coming Conflict in Foreign Trade," speech to American Manufacturers Export Association, March 25, 1925, Hoover Papers, Commerce Period, Box 483, "Press Releases, 1925 January–April"; Klein to John Barrett, March 14, 1925, and Hoover to Barrett, March 19, 1925, both in ibid., Box 45, "Barrett, John, 1921–1927"; Harold Phelps Stokes to F. Stuart Crawford, March 17, 1926, ibid., Box 478, "President Coolidge, 1926 January–March"; Guillermo A. Sherwell to Hoover, January 5, 1925, and Hoover to Sherwell, January 7, 1925, ibid., Box 293, "Inter-American High Commission, 1925"; John Matthews, Jr., to Hoover, May 17, 1927, enclosing Matthews to Secretary Kellogg, May 17, 1927, ibid., Box 293, "Inter-American High Commission, 1927–1928"; Harold Phelps Stokes to Isaac Marcosson, December 23, 1925, ibid., Box 385, "Marcosson, Isaac F., 1925."

31. See Chapter 13 in this volume for discussion of the Peek-Johnson agricultural plan.

32. "Statement by Secretary Hoover to the President's Agricultural Committee," January 19, 1925, Hoover Papers, Commerce Period, Box 11, "Agriculture: President's Agricultural Conference, Agricultural Inquiry Commission, Press Releases and Reports, 1925 January."

33. Hoover to Gray Silver, January 24, 1925; Silver to Hoover, March 31, 1925, both in Hoover Papers, Commerce Period, Box 559, "Silver, Gray, 1921–1937"; Hoover to Bernard Baruch, April 17, 1925, ibid., Box 244, "Grain Marketing Corporation, 1925 January–April"; Hoover to David H. Jennings, May 13, 1925; Hoover to James M. Bell and Alexander

P. Legge, May 26, 1925; Legge to Hoover, May 27, 1925, all in ibid., Box 244, "Grain Marketing Corporation, 1925 May–September"; James G. Mitchell, "Discord Prevailed in Grain Marketing Corporation," *Iowa Homestead*, August 27, 1925, 5; Mitchell, "In The Last Days of the Grain Marketing Corporation," *Iowa Homestead*, September 3, 1925, 12; "Address of Secretary Hoover before the National Council of Cooperative Marketing," January 7, 1925, Hoover Papers, Commerce Period, Box 3, "Agriculture: Addresses by Mr. Hoover, 1924–1925"; Hoover to Everett Sanders, November 16, 1925, ibid., Box 478, "President Coolidge, 1925 November."

34. "The Economic Tragedy in the Coal Trade," *Standard Daily Trade Service*, May 18, 1925, 137–48; James P. Johnson, *The Politics of Soft Coal: The Bituminous Industry from World War I through the New Deal* (Urbana: University of Illinois Press, 1979), 118–19; Harold K. Kanarek, "Disaster for Hard Coal: The Anthracite Strike of 1925–1926," *Labor History* 15 (January 1974): 46–62.

35. C. P. White to Hoover, February 26, 1925, Hoover Papers, Commerce Period, Box 104, "Coal: Lewis, John L., 1923–1925 & undated"; "Jacksonville Scale Repudiated," *Cushing's Survey*, February 19, 1925.

36. Harold Phelps Stokes to Hoover, July 22, 24, 1925, Hoover Papers, Commerce Period, Box 98, "Coal: Miscellaneous, 1925 July"; "Statement of Secretary Hoover at Swampscott, Massachusetts, after visit to President Coolidge, August 9, 1925," ibid., Box 98, "Coal: Miscellaneous, 1925 August–September"; John J. Leary, Jr., to Hoover, August 12, 1925, ibid., Box 104, "Coal: Lewis, John L., 1922–1925 & undated."

37. Hoover to Everett Sanders, November 23, 1925, enclosing draft of letter from the president to Lewis; Hoover to Coolidge, November 25, 1925, both in Hoover Papers, Commerce Period, Box 478, "President Coolidge, 1925 November"; undated draft of statement regarding the coal operators and the Jacksonville agreement, ibid., Box 104, "Coal: Materials Kept Together by Order of Mr. Hoover (2)."

38. Melvyn Dubofsky and Warren Van Tine, *John L. Lewis: A Biography* (New York: Quadrangle, 1977), 141–42; Ellis W. Hawley, "Secretary Hoover and the Bituminous Coal Problem, 1921–1928," *Business History Review* 42 (Autumn 1968), 266–67.

39. G. C. Riddell to E. S. Rochester, January 13, 1925, Hoover Papers, Commerce Period, Box 453, "Oil: Federal Oil Conservation Board, 1925." Riddell was a member of the Technical Advisory Board of the Federal Oil Conservation Board.

40. Mark Requa to Hoover, January 6, 1925, Hoover Papers, Commerce Period, Box 517, "Requa, Mark L., 1925 Jan.–Feb."; M. L. Requa, *American Petroleum: Supply and Demand* (n.p., 1925), a pamphlet in the Mark Requa Papers, University of Wyoming, Rare Books and Special Collections, Laramie, Wyoming; Hoover to Requa, August 28, 1925, Hoover Papers, Commerce Period, Box 466, "Petroleum, 1921–26 & undated"; Requa to Hoover, September 6, 1925, ibid., Box 517, "Requa, Mark L., 1925 June–Dec."

41. Mark Requa to Hoover, September 8, 1925, Hoover Papers, Commerce Period, Box 517, "Requa, Mark L., 1925 June–Dec."; Requa, memorandum on the policy of the American Petroleum Institute, December 18, 1925, Requa Papers.

42. Hoover to Everett Sanders, December 12, 1925, Hoover Papers, Commerce Period, Box 505, "Railroads: Legislation, 1921–1926 & undated"; James C. Davis to President Coolidge, December 14, 1925, Calvin Coolidge, President's Personal Files, Microfilm, Forbes Library, Reel 38.

43. Commerce Department press release on joint Canadian-American engineering investigations on the St. Lawrence and Erie Canal waterways, April 23, 1925; Hoover to Brown McCrary, December 8, 1925, both in Hoover Papers, Commerce Period, Box 690, "Waterways: Great Lakes–St. Lawrence, 1925"; Hoover, "A National System of Waterways," December 9, 1925, in *Proceedings of the Twenty-First Convention, National Rivers and Harbors Conference* (Washington, DC: Ransdell, 1925), 16–24; Hubert Work to Hoover, October 28, 1925, Coolidge, President's Personal Files, Microfilm, Reel 6; George H. Nash, "The 'Great Enigma' and the 'Great Engineer': The Political Relationship of Calvin Coolidge and Herbert Hoover," in *Calvin Coolidge and the Coolidge Era: Essays on the History of the 1920s*, ed. John Earl Haynes (Washington, DC: Library of Congress, 1998), 152.

44. Hoover to Secretary of State Kellogg, August 22, 1925; Secretary of War Dwight Davis to Kellogg, October 23, 1925, both in Hoover Papers, Commerce Period, Box 695, "Waterways: Great Lakes–St. Lawrence, Niagara Falls, 1925"; Ambassador Sir Esme Howard to Kellogg, January 18, 1926; Hoover to Kellogg, February 9, 1926; Edward C. Randall to Hoover, April 17, 1925, ibid., Box 695, "Waterways: Great Lakes–St. Lawrence, Niagara Falls, 1926 Jan.–May"; Secretary Dwight Davis to Kellogg, ca. September 9, 1927, ibid., Box 695, "Waterways: Great Lakes–St. Lawrence, Niagara Falls, 1927"; State Department press release, "Summary of the Interim Report of the Special International Niagara Falls Board," January 20, 1928; Special International Niagara Board of Control to the secretary of state and the secretary of the interior, May 3, 1928, ibid., Box 695, "Waterways: Great Lakes–St. Lawrence, Niagara Falls, 1928 & undated."

45. Hoover to Mark Requa, February 14, 1925, Hoover Papers, Commerce Period, Box 517, "Requa, Mark L., 1925 Jan.–Feb."; Requa to Hoover, March 3, 1925, ibid., Box 517, "Requa, Mark, 1925 March"; Hoover to Gov. Friend W. Richardson, March 3, 1925, ibid., Box 524, "Richardson, Friend W., 1923–1926"; Requa to Hoover, March 10, 1925, ibid., Box 517, "Requa, Mark L., 1925 March"; Hoover to Secretary of Interior Hubert Work, March 28, 1925, ibid., Box 295, "Interior Department: Secretary Work, Hubert, 1925"; Ralph Merritt to Hoover, March 30, 1925, ibid., Box 391, "Merritt, Ralph P., 1924–1925"; Hoover to Requa, March 30, 31, 1925; Requa to Hoover, April 3, 1925 (two telegrams and a letter), all in Colorado River Commission Papers, Hoover Presidential Library, West Branch, Iowa, Box 34, "Project File, Requa Pamphlet, 1925."

46. Hoover to Chester Rowell, April 11, 1925, with a penciled note by Rowell, dated 1941, relating what happened at the meeting, Chester Rowell Papers, Bancroft Library, University of California at Berkley, Box 16, "Hoover, Herbert Clark"; Hoover to Mark Requa, September 9, 1925, Hoover Papers, Commerce Period, Box 517, "Requa, Mark L., 1925 Sept.–Dec."; Hoover to Henry M. Robinson, October 23, 1925, ibid., Box 527, "Robinson, Henry M., 1925."

47. Commerce Department press release, "Abstract of Secretary Hoover's Statement on the Colorado River before the Senate Committee on Irrigation and Reclamation," December 10, 1925, Hoover Papers, Commerce Period, Box 257, "Hearings, 1920–1925."

48. "An Act for Making Further and More Effectual Provision for the National Defense, and for Other Purposes, Public No. 85—64th Congress, H.R. 12766," ca. February 26, 1925, Hoover Papers, Commerce Period, Box 423, "Muscle Shoals: Legislation, Hearings, Etc., 1925–1927, HRes.457, 68 Cong. 2 Sess."; Evans C. Johnson, *Oscar W. Underwood: A Bourbon from Birmingham* (Baton Rouge: Louisiana State University Press, 1980), 355–65.

49. Hoover to Coolidge, March 9, 14, 1925; American Engineering Council to Hoover, March 13, 1925, both in Hoover Papers, Commerce Period, Box 422, "Muscle Shoals Commission, 1925–26";, Everett Sanders to Hoover, March 26, 1925, ibid., Box 477, "President Coolidge, 1925 March"; Russell F. Bower to Hoover, November 6, 1925, ibid., Box 422, "Muscle Shoals Commission, 1925–1926"; Hoover's draft of possible statement on Muscle Shoals to be inserted in the president's annual message, November 6, 1925, ibid., Box 422, "Muscle Shoals: Miscellaneous, 1925."

50. Johnson, *Underwood*, 366.

51. Commerce Department press release, "Hoover Calls Radio Conference," October 7, 1925, Hoover Papers, Commerce Period, Box 490, "Radio: Correspondence, Press Releases, Misc., 1925 October–December"; Commerce Department press release, "A Statement by Secretary Hoover on Radio Progress and Problems," November 9, 1925, ibid., Box 484, "Press Releases, 1925 November"; Commerce Department press release, "Statement by Secretary Hoover," December 26, 1925, ibid., Box 444, "Newspapers and Magazines: *New York World*, 1921–1927."

52. Philip T. Rosen, *The Modern Stentors: Radio Broadcasters and the Federal Government, 1920–1934* (Westport, CT: Greenwood, 1980), 77–82.

53. Hoover to Sen. Hiram Bingham, September 23, 1925; Stephen B. Davis to Harold Phelps Stokes, undated, but attached to copy of Hoover to Bingham, September 23, 1925, both in Hoover Papers, Commerce Period, Box 122, "Commerce Department: Aeronautics,

Bureau of, Legislation, 1925–1926"; David D. Lee, "Herbert Hoover and the Development of Commercial Aviation, 1921–1926," *Business History Review* 58 (Spring 1984): 91, 100.

54. Commerce Department press release, "Statement of Secretary Hoover on Commercial Aviation," September 24, 1925, Hoover Papers, Commerce Period, Box 484, "Press Releases, 1925 May–October."

55. E. S. Gregg to J. Walter Drake, September 19, 1925, Hoover Papers, Commerce Period, Box 122, "Commerce Department: Aeronautics, Bureau of, Legislation, 1925–1926"; Commerce Department press release, "Statement of Secretary Hoover on Commercial Aviation," September 24, 1925, ibid., Box 484, "Press Releases, 1925 May–October"; Hoover, foreword to "A report by the Joint Committee on Civil Aviation of the U.S. Department of Commerce and the American Engineering Council," November 5, 1925, ibid., Box 40, "Aviation, 1928 & undated"; Commerce Department press release, "Summary of the Report of the Committee on Civil Aviation Organized Last June by the Department of Commerce and the American Engineering Council," November 5, 1925, ibid., Box 484, "Press Releases, 1925 November"; Lee, "Hoover and the Development of Commercial Aviation," 93–94.

56. *Report of President's Aircraft Board* (Washington, DC: Government Printing Office, 1925); Sen. James W. Wadsworth to Hoover, November 27, 1925, and Hoover to Wadsworth, December 2, 1925, both in Hoover Papers, Commerce Period, Box 41, "Aviation: President's Aircraft Board, 1925 & undated"; Hoover to Sen. W. L. Jones, December 9, 1925, ibid., Box 122, "Commerce Department: Aeronautics, Bureau of, Legislation, 1925–1926." Hoover's recollection, in his *Memoirs* 2, 133, that he proposed the appointment of the Aircraft Board, appears to be erroneous; in his letter creating the board, Coolidge said that he had been discussing the appointment of such a body with several people since the spring of 1925, and Dwight Morrow, chairman of the board, confirmed his statement. But on the more important point, that the board closely followed his recommendations, Hoover was certainly correct.

57. Hoover to Elizabeth Mary Shoemaker, January 13, 1925, Hoover Papers, Commerce Period, Box 68, "Building and Housing: Own Your Own Home, 1925–1928 & undated"; "Statement by Secretary Hoover for Christian Science Monitor," April 16 1925; William L. Moore to Hoover, May 6, 1925, both in ibid., Box 64, "Building and Housing, 1925."

58. Hoover to Wilbur (Willoughby) Walling, March 5, 14, 1925, and Walling to Hoover, March 10, 16, 1925, all in Hoover Papers, Commerce Period, Box 67, "Building and Housing: Home Financing, 1921–1928"; Glenn Griswold, "Interesting Experiment in Second Mortgage Financing to Be Started in Chicago," *Chicago Journal of Commerce*, January 30, 1926; Julius Rosenwald to Hoover, on pamphlet, "Why We Are Making Second Mortgages, and How," by the Morris Plan Bank, August 1, 1926, Hoover Papers, Commerce Period, Box 530, "Rosenwald, Julius, 1921–1928 & undated"; Wilbur Walling to Rosenwald, January 6, 1927, ibid., Box 67, "Building and Housing: Home Financing, 1921–1928"; Hoover, *Memoirs* 2, 95.

59. R. M. Hudson to Hoover, May 4, 1925, Hoover Papers, Commerce Period, Box 145, "Commerce Department: Simplified Coml. Practice, 1925–25"; Hoover to President Coolidge, March 16, 1925 (not sent; delivered orally), ibid., Box 477, "President Coolidge, 1925 March"; Hoover to Raymond B. Fosdick, March 28 and May 19, 1925, ibid., Box 528, "Rockefeller Foundation, 1922–1925"; Hoover to Coolidge, April 21, 1925, ibid., Box 477, "President Coolidge, 1925 April–May"; Commerce Department press release on formation of National Committee on Wood Utilization, May 2, 1925, ibid., Box 484, "Press Releases, 1925 May–October"; Hoover to Edgar Rickard, November 20, 1925, ibid., Box 191, "Elimination of Waste in Industry, 1925 Mar.–Dec."

60. Hoover, "Waste in Government: Address of Secretary of Commerce Hoover before a General Session of the Thirteenth Annual Meeting of the Chamber of Commerce of the United States, Thursday Evening, May 21, 1925," Hoover Papers, Commerce Period, Box 514, "Reorg. of Govt. Depts., 1925."

61. Ibid.

62. Hoover and Secretary of Interior Hubert Work to President Coolidge, March 12, 1925, Coolidge, President's Personal Files, Microfilm, Reel 6; Hoover to Work, June 3, 1925, Hoover Papers, Commerce Period, Box 295, "Interior Department: Secy. Work, 1925";

Rep. Martin L. Davey to Hoover, November 11, 1925, ibid., Box 514, "Reorganization of Government Depts., 1925."

63. "The Supreme Court on Restraint of Trade," *New York World*, June 3, 1925; Hoover to V. P. Hovey, June 4, 1925, Hoover Papers, Commerce Period, Box 602, "Trade Associations, 1925"; "Statement by Secretary Hoover at Press Conference," June 4, 1925, ibid., Box 484, "Press Releases, 1925 May–October"; Hoover, "Problems of Our Economic Evolution: Address to Stanford University Seniors," June 22, 1925, Bible no. 499, Hoover Presidential Library, West Branch, Iowa; draft (not sent) of Hoover to Samuel McCune Lindsay, undated, ca. September 13, 1925, Hoover Papers, Commerce Period, Box 60, "Brookings, Robert, 1921–1927."

64. Hoover, "Problems of Our Economic Evolution: Address to Stanford University Seniors," June 22, 1925, Bible no. 499; Hoover, "Elimination of Industrial Waste in its Relation to Labor," address to a conference sponsored by National Civic Federation, New York, April 11, 1925, Frederick M. Feiker Papers, Hoover Presidential Library, West Branch, Iowa, Box 15, "Subject File: Proposed Books—Hoover's Philosophy—Trade Associations."

65. Alfred Pearce Dennis, "Humanizing the Department of Commerce," *Saturday Evening Post*, June 6, 1925, 8; Commerce Department press release, Hoover, "Economic Prospects for 1926," December 31, 1925, Hoover Papers, Commerce Period, Box 188, "Economic Situation in U.S., 1925–1928."

66. Edgar Rickard Diary, January 11, 1925, Box 1, "January–June 1925"; "Coolidge Would End Inheritance Taxes; Calls It State Field," *New York Times*, February 20, 1925; Hoover, "Memorandum," undated, Hoover Papers, Commerce Period, Box 596, "Taxes: Inheritance Taxes, 1923–1925 & undated"; "Secretary Hoover Tells Engineers of Enormous Returns through Moderate Expenditures," *Power*, January 27, 1925, 160.

Chapter 18

1. Lou Henry Hoover to Herbert and Allan Hoover, February 22, 1925, Allan Hoover Papers, Hoover Presidential Library, West Branch, Iowa, Box 2, "Correspondence with Lou Henry Hoover, 1925."

2. Ibid.; Lou Hoover to Virginia Burks, ca. February 23, 1925, Lou Henry Hoover Papers, Hoover Library, West Branch, Iowa, Box 10, "Personal Correspondence, 1921–28: Burks, Virginia, 1924–26 & undated"; Claude M. Fuess, *Calvin Coolidge: The Man from Vermont* (Westport, CT: Greenwood Press, 1968; orig. pub. 1939), 360–62.

3. Lou Hoover to (John W.?) Hallowell, undated, ca. February 1925; Harry Chandler to Lou Hoover, February 16, 1925; Sarah Louise Arnold to Jeffrey Brackett, July 13, 1925, all in Lou Hoover Papers, Box 9, "Personal Correspondence, 1921–28: Arnold, Sarah Louise, 1921–26"; Jean Henry Large to Lou Hoover, March 17, 1925, ibid., Box 17, "Personal Correspondence, 1921–28: Large, Jean Henry, 1925–27"; Elizabeth Kemper Adams to Lou Hoover, March 27, 1925, ibid., Box 1, "Girl Scouts, Administrative Correspondence: Adams, Elizabeth Kemper, 1925–34"; Lou Hoover to Mrs. Lyman Delano, no date, ca. March 1925, ibid., Box 4, "Subject File: Articles, Addresses, & Statements, 1925 May 20, Eleventh Annual Girl Scout Conv., Boston, Massachusetts"; "Sports Making Girls Taller, Says Athletic Woman," *Chicago Post*, April 6, 1925; "All Girls Athletes Aim of Federation," *Boston Morning Globe*, April 7, 1925.

4. "Hoover Would Put All His Bureaus Under One Roof," Washington *Evening Star*, March 31, 1925; "Commerce to Get Huge Structure," Washington *Evening Star*, June 3, 1926; "Hoover Approves Site for Building," Washington *Evening Star*, June 8, 1926; (?) Grams to Hoover, July 7, 1926; J. Walter Drake to Hoover, July 7, 1926; S. S. Cline to Hoover, September 11, 1926; Hoover to U.S. Grant, 3rd, November 19, 1926; (?) Grams to Hoover, January 29, 1927; same to same, January 27, 1928, all in Herbert Hoover Papers, Commerce Period, Hoover Presidential Library, West Branch, Iowa, Box 126, "Commerce Department: Buildings, Quarters, Etc., 1925–1928 & undated"; Louis Ayers to Hoover, January 12, 1928, ibid., Box 41, "Ayr-Az, 1921–1928 & undated"; "Memorandum Regarding Editorial

Criticism Published in the Chicago Journal of Commerce," undated, ca. 1932, Frederick M. Feiker Papers, Hoover Presidential Library, West Branch, Iowa, Box 4, "Subject File: Criticism of Department of Commerce."

5. Frederic A. Delano to Hoover, August 8, 1923, Hoover Papers, Commerce Period, Box 431, "National Museum of Engineering and Industry, 1923–1924"; H. F. J. Porter to Hoover, January 9, July 3, 1925, ibid., Box 432, "National Museum of Engineering and Industry, 1925–1928 & undated"; Paul H. Oehser, *Sons of Science: The Story of the Smithsonian Institution and Its Leaders* (New York: Greenwood, 1968), 159–60, 174–75; Ellis L. Yochelson, *Smithsonian Institution Secretary, Charles Doolittle Walcott* (Kent, OH: Kent State University Press, 2001), 420, 496–502, 528–29, 531. Ironically, Hoover declined Walcott's request that he chair the general endowment campaign because of his commitment to the more specialized drive. See Hoover to Charles D. Walcott, November 14, 1925, Hoover Papers, Commerce Period, Box 565, "Smithsonian Institute, 1921–1928."

6. Hoover to M. Delacroix, August 28, 1919, Herbert Hoover Papers, Pre-Commerce Period, Hoover Presidential Library, West Branch, Iowa, Box 5, "Francqui, Emile, 1914–1920"; Hoover, *Memoirs: Years of Adventure, 1874–1920* (New York: Macmillan, 1951), 159, 198, 229 (hereafter, *Memoirs* 1).

7. Hoover to George Barr Baker, May 6, 1925; Harold Phelps Stokes to Baker, December 11, 12, 1925, all in Hoover Papers, Commerce Period, Box 42, "Baker, George Barr, 1924–1925"; Edgar Rickard Diaries, Hoover Presidential Library, West Branch, Iowa, August 19 and December 1, 1925, Box 1, "July–December 1925"; Hoover to Martin Maloney, December 10, 1925, Hoover Papers, Commerce Period, Box 384, "Maloney-Mamm, 1921–1928"; Hoover to Edward Dean Adams, November 5, 1927, ibid., Box 1, "Adams, A.-Frank, 1921–1928"; Rickard Diaries, July 4, 1928, Box 1, "1928"; *C.R.B. Bulletin*, October 22, 1930, 5. In his *Memoirs*, Hoover is critical of Butler and attributes the successful fund-raising campaign simply to "the C.R.B." *Memoirs* 1, 230.

8. Hoover, "Sesqui-Centennial Celebration of American Independence: Address by Mr. Herbert Hoover at Luncheon Given by Mr. John Wanamaker in the Bellevue-Stratford, Philadelphia," December 17, 1921, Bible no. 190, Hoover Presidential Library, West Branch, Iowa; "Hoover Declines $50,000 Offer; Will Not Leave Cabinet to Head Philadelphia Sesqui-Centennial Exhibition," *New York Times*, March 12, 1922; James M. Beck to Hoover, October 16, 1923, Hoover Papers, Commerce Period, Box 553, "Sesquicentennial, HHP, 1923"; Beck to Hoover, January 25, 1925, ibid., "Sesquicentennial, 1925 Jan.–Feb."

9. Copy of SJ 187, March 3, 1925, Hoover Papers, Commerce Period, Box 553, "Sesquicentennial, 1925 Jan.–Feb."; Hoover to Kellogg, June 10, 1925, ibid., Box 553, "Sesquicentennial: Akerson, George, 1925–1926."

10. For a perceptive sketch of Akerson, see "Human Dynamo Is Akerson, Herbert Hoover's Secretary," New York *World*, November 16, 1928.

11. Ernest T. Trigg to Hoover, April 10, 1925; Hoover to W. Freeland Kendrick, April 16, 1925, both in Hoover Papers, Commerce Period, Box 553, "Sesquicentennial, 1925 March–May"; Hoover to Coolidge, April 27, 1925, Calvin Coolidge, President's Personal Files, Microfilm, Reel 6; W. Freeland Kendrick to Hoover, October 31, 1925; James M. Beck to Hoover, November 16, 1925, both in Hoover Papers, Commerce Period, Box 553, "Sesquicentennial, 1925 June–Dec."

12. Commerce Department press release, January 26, 1926, Hoover Papers, Commerce Period, Box 484, "Press Releases, 1926 January–February"; Julius Klein to Hoover, February 12, 1926, ibid., Box 553, "Sesquicentennial, 1926 Jan.–May"; Rickard Diaries, April 15, 1926, Box 1, "1926."

13. W. Freeland Kendrick to Hoover, March 19 and April 6, 1926, Hoover Papers, Commerce Period, Box 553, "Sesquicentennial, 1926 Jan.–May"; "Sesquicentennial Opens As Sun Shines; 100,000 Pass Gates," *New York Times*, June 1, 1926; Hoover to Ernest T. Trigg, June 5, 1926, Hoover Papers, Commerce Period, Box 553, "Sesquicentennial, 1926 June–Aug."

14. H. O. Stickney to Hoover, July 28, 1926, Hoover Papers, Commerce Period, Box 354, "Sesquicentennial: Financing, 1926–1927"; "Sesqui Seeks $3,700,000 to Settle Debts," Philadelphia *Ledger*, July 27, 1926; Commerce Department press release, August 10, 1926,

Hoover Papers, Commerce Period, Box 484, "Press Releases, 1926 April–August"; George Akerson to W. Freeland Kendrick, August 18, 1926, ibid., Box 553, "Sesquicentennial, 1926 Jan.–Aug."; Rickard Diaries, November 13, 1926, Box 1, "1926"; "Report of Committee on Continuance of Exposition in 1927," November 19, 1926, Hoover Papers, Commerce Period, Box 555, "Sesquicentennial: Question of Opening in 1927."

15. Lou Hoover to Abbie Rickard, April 21, 1925, Lou Hoover Papers, Box 21, "Personal Correspondence, 1921–28: Rickard, Abbie, 1924–26"; Lou Hoover to Alida Henriques, May 1, 4, 1925, ibid., Box 15, "Personal Correspondence, 1921–28: Henriques, Alida, 1921–25"; Lou Hoover to Virginia Burks, May 4, 1925, ibid., Box 10, "Personal Correspondence, 1921–28: Burks, Virginia, 1924–26 & undated"; Lou Hoover to Edgar Rickard, March 12, 1926, ibid., Box 111, "Subject File, Taxes for: 1925."

16. Louis B. Mayer to Hoover, June 1, 1925, and Hoover to Mayer, June 2, 1925, both in Hoover Papers, Commerce Period, Box 420, "Motion Pictures, 1925"; Christian A. Herter to William A. Brady, August 10, 1921, ibid., Box 420, "Motion Pictures, 1921"; M. F. Leopold to T. R. Taylor, April 10, 1922; Julius Klein to M. F. Leopold, September 13, 1923, both in ibid., Box 420, "Motion Pictures, 1922–1923"; Department of Commerce, Bureau of Mines, "Descriptive List of Motion-Picture Films and Plan of Distribution," July 1926, ibid., Box 420, "Motion Pictures, 1926"; Scott Turner to Hoover, March 2, 1927; Hoover to Hanford MacNider, June 23, 1927, both in ibid., Box 420, "Motion Pictures, 1927–1928 & undated"; Mayer's film was *The Flying Fleet* (1929).

17. Rickard Diaries, June 14, 16, 1925, Box 1, "January–June 1925."

18. Rickard Diaries, June 21, 22, 1925, Box 1, "January–June 1925"; Hoover, "Problems of Our Economic Evolution: Address to Stanford University Seniors," June 22, 1925, Bible no. 499; "Hoover Calls for Good Will as Way to Meet Problems," unidentified clipping, June 23, 1925, Lou Hoover Papers, Box 34, "Subject File: Clippings, 1925, Hoover Family."

19. Rickard Diaries, June 25, 1925, Box 1, "January–June 1925"; Lady Teazle, "Old California Families United by Wedding Ceremony at Palo Alto," unidentified clipping, June 26, 1925, Lou Hoover Papers, Box 34, "Subject File: Clippings, 1925, Hoover Family"; Dare Stark McMullin to Philippi Harding, ca. September 1925, ibid., Box 59, "Subject File: Hoover, Herbert Jr., General, 1903–30."

20. Rickard Diaries, July 2, 10, 1925, Box 1, "July–December 1925"; Lou Hoover to Jessie Jones, July 13, 1925, Lou Hoover Papers, Box 16, "Personal Correspondence, 1921–28: Jones, Edward L., and Jessie Weed, 1921–28 & undated"; Lou Hoover to Jennie Mager, July 13, 1928, ibid., Box 18, "Personal Correspondence, 1921–28: Mager, Jennie Weed, 1924–27"; Lou Hoover to Charles Henry, July 13, 1928, ibid., Box 15, "Personal Correspondence, 1921–28: Henry, Charles and Florence, 1921–28."

21. Belle Livingstone, "The Story of My Life: The Autobiography of the Woman They Called 'The Most Dangerous Woman in Europe,'" *Hearst's International-Cosmopolitan* 42 (July 1925): 217–18; Rickard Diaries, June 24, 1925, Box 1, "January–June 1925"; Edgar Rickard to George Barr Baker, undated, ca. June 15, 1925, June 18; Rickard to "Lingulina" (London cable address of solicitor James Bradwood Birkbeck), June 16, 1925; Baker to Rickard, June 19, 23, 1925; Ray Long to George Barr Baker, June 24, 1925, all in Hoover Papers, Commerce Period, Box 372, "Livingston [sic], Belle, 1925 June."

22. Hoover to George Barr Baker, ca. June 25, 1925 (two telegrams); Baker to Edgar Rickard, June 26, 29, 1925; Mildred Temple to George Barr Baker, June 27, 1925, enclosing copy of undated cable from William C. Lengel; William C. Lengel to Ray Long, June 30, 1925, all in Hoover Papers, Commerce Period, Box 372, "Livingston [sic], Belle, 1925 June"; John A. Agnew to Edgar Rickard, July 3, 6 and September 3, 20, 1925; Baker to Rickard, July 3, 1925; Baker to Hoover, July 8, 1925; Rickard to Agnew, July 31, August 25, and October 20, 1925, all in ibid., Box 372, "Livingston [sic], Belle, 1925 July–October"; Ray Long to Hoover, July 8, 1925, Herbert Hoover Papers, Pre-Commerce Period, Box 10, "Livingston [sic], Belle, 1925: Autobiography"; Rickard to "Lingulina" (James Bradwood Birkbeck), February 4, 1927; John A. Agnew to Rickard, February 8, 1927; notarized statement of facts of case by James Bradwood Birkbeck, February 16, 1927, all in Hoover Papers, Commerce

Period, Box 372, "Livingston [*sic*], Belle, 1927." The book was Belle Livingstone, *The Belle of Bohemia* (London: J. Hamilton, 1927).

23. Rickard Diaries, December 31, 1925, Box 1, "July–December 1925."

24. Lou Hoover to Charles Henry, August 5, 1925, Lou Hoover Papers, Box 15, "Personal Correspondence, 1921–28: Henry, Charles D. and Florence, 1921–28"; clipping from Washington *Times*, August 12, 1925, reporting Allan working for his father, Hoover Papers, Commerce Period, Box 94, "Clippings 1925–1929 & undated"; Rickard Diaries, August 19 and September 28, 1925, Box 1, "July–December 1925"; Ray Lyman Wilbur to H. Alexander Smith, November 17, 1925, Hoover Papers, Commerce Period, Box 709, "Wilbur, Ray Lyman, 1924–1925." In November 1924, Hoover wrote an unusually intemperate letter to Ray Lyman Wilbur (Hoover Papers, Commerce Period, Box 709, "Wilbur, Ray Lyman, 1924–1925") complaining about the prevalence of flashy student cars on campus and alcohol being served in fraternities. The intensity of emotion in the letter suggests that this was a very personal issue with him, and indeed, he said directly that because of the situation, he was "hesitant about leaving Allan" at the university.

25. Rickard Diaries, August 14, 26 and September 22, 23, 24, 27, 1925, Box 1, "July–December, 1925"; Lou Hoover to Allan Hoover, September 30, 1925, Allan Hoover Papers, Box 2, "Correspondence with Lou Henry Hoover, 1925."

26. "Y.W.C.A. to Open Drive for $700,000 for New Building," Washington *Post*, November 8, 1925; "Final Drive Begun for Y.W.C.A. Fund," Washington *Star*, December 6, 1925; "Washington 'Y.W.' Seeking $300,000," New York *World*, March 21, 1926; Lou Hoover talk to Girl Scout leaders, November 16, 1925, Lou Hoover Papers, Box 4, "Subject File: Articles, Addresses, & Statements, 1925 November 16, Girl Scouts, New York City"; "Organization of the National Research Council," no date, Hoover Papers, Pre-Commerce Period, Box 57, "National Research Council, 1919–1921"; National Research Council, *Organization and Members, 1921–1922* (Washington, DC: National Research Council, 1922), Hoover to Julius Rosenwald, November 6, 1925, Hoover Papers, Commerce Period, Box 425, "National Academy of Science: National Research Endowment, General, 1925"; Hoover to Rosenwald, undated, ca. November 15, 1925, ibid., Box 530, "Rosenwald, Julius, 1921–1928 & undated"; George E. Hale to Hoover, November 18, 1925; Vernon Kellogg to Hoover, November 23, 1925, ibid., Box 425, "National Academy of Science, National Research Endowment, General, 1925";both in ibid. Hoover was elected to membership in the Section of Engineering of the National Academy of Sciences in April 1922 and formally inducted at the 1923 spring meeting. See Charles G. Abbot to Hoover, May 4, 1922, ibid., Box 1, "Aa-Abbott, C. J., 1921–1928 & undated," and J. J. Carty to Hoover, October 28, 1922, ibid., Box 425, "National Academy of Sciences, General, 1921–1922."

27. Hoover, "The Vital Need for Greater Financial Support to Pure Science Research," December 1, 1925, Hoover Papers, Commerce Period, Box 541, "Science, Scientific, 1921–1927 & undated."

28. Hoover to W. Cameron Forbes and others, December 5, 1925; Hoover to Coolidge, November 10, 1925, both in Hoover Papers, Commerce Period, Box 425, "National Academy of Science, National Research Endowment, General, 1925";, "Seeks Endowment in Science Research," *New York Times*, December 17, 1925; Gano Dunn to Hoover, January 6, 1926, Hoover Papers, Commerce Period, Box 425, "National Academy of Science, National Research Endowment, General, 1925 "; Hoover, Elihu Root, and Charles Evans Hughes to John D. Rockefeller, Jr., January 16, 1926, ibid., Box 425, "National Academy of Science, National Research Endowment, General, 1926 January"; Elihu Root to Hoover, April 12, 1926, ibid.; Hoover to Gano Dunn, April 30, 1926; Hoover to George E. Hale, April 30, 1926, all in Box 425, "National Academy of Science National Research Endowment, General, 1926 April"; Hoover to Hale, October 2, 1926; Hoover, "The Nation and Science: An Address by Herbert Hoover, Secretary of Commerce, Before the American Association for the Advancement of Science, Auditorium of Drexel Institute, Philadelphia, PA," December 28, 1926, both in ibid., Box 425, "National Academy of Science, National Research Endowment, General, 1926 June–Dec."; R. A. Millikan to Hoover, January 8, 1927; Hoover to Elihu Root, October 10, 1927, both in ibid., Box 425, "National Academy

of Science, National Research Endowment, General, 1927";, press release from the Trustees of the National Research Fund of the National Academy of Sciences, June 18, 1928; Hoover to T. H. Morgan, June 23, 1928, both in ibid., Box 426, "National Academy of Sciences, National Research Endowment, General, 1928 & undated." Obviously, given the small size of these initial grants (averaging about $2,500 apiece), they were intended to provide only supplementary support for research projects.

29. Hoover to Ray Lyman Wilbur, February 6, 1926, Hoover Papers, Commerce Period, Box 709, "Wilbur, Ray Lyman, 1926"; Lou Hoover to Laurine Anderson (Small), ibid., Box 562, "Small, Mrs. Laurine A., 1927–1928"; Lou Hoover, manuscripts of articles on "The Lone Girl Scout" for the *Farmer's Wife*, Lou Hoover Papers, Box 4, "Subject File: Articles, Addresses & Statements, 1926 March, 'The Lone Girl Scout,' The Farmer's Wife"; Hoover to Lou Hoover, October 14, 1926, ibid., Box 2, "Girl Scouts: Administrative Correspondence, Coolidge, Grace (Mrs. Calvin), 1925–26." Lou's innocuous article, "When Mrs. Coolidge Was a Girl," appeared in the November 1926 issue of *American Girl*.

30. Jean Large to Lou Hoover, ca. March 14, 1926, Lou Hoover Papers, Box 17, "Personal Correspondence, 1921–28: Large, Jean Henry, 1925–27."

31. Lou Hoover to Sarah Louise Arnold, ca. March 17, 1926, Lou Hoover Papers, Box 9, "Personal Correspondence, 1921–28: Arnold, Sarah Louise, 1921–26"; Lou Hoover to Allan Hoover, March 18, 1926, Allan Hoover Papers, Box 2, "Correspondence with Lou Henry Hoover, 1926 February–March"; Rickard Diaries, March 17, 1926, Box 1, "1926."

32. Rickard Diaries, April 30, 1926, Box 1, "1926"; Lou Hoover to Allan Hoover, May 25, 1926, Allan Hoover Papers, Box 2, "Correspondence with Lou Henry Hoover, 1926 April–June"; Lou Hoover to Allan Hoover, ca. July 17, 1926, ibid., Box 2, "Correspondence with Lou Henry Hoover, 1926 July–December"; Lou Hoover to Arthur Bullard, August 25, 1926, Lou Hoover Papers, Box 10, "Personal Correspondence, 1921–28: Bullard, Arthur, 1926–28."

33. Coolidge quoted in Donald R. McCoy, *Calvin Coolidge: The Quiet President* (New York: Macmillan, 1967), 54.

34. George Akerson to Walter H. Newton, August 2, 1926, George Edwards Akerson Papers, Hoover Presidential Library, West Branch, Iowa, Box 2, "Campaign of 1926"; Hoover itinerary, August 12–23, 1926, Hoover Papers, Commerce Period, Box 611, "Trips 1926: Western Trip, Correspondence, 1926 November–December & undated"; George Akerson to O. J. Larson, October 1, 7, 1926; Akerson to H. Lindley Hosford, October 6, 1926; Walter H. Newton to Hoover, October 6, 1926; Hoover to T. T. C. Gregory, October 8, 1926; E. T. Franks to Walter H. Newton, October 11, 1926; Akerson to Newton, October 13, 1926; Newton to Akerson, October 14, 1926, all in ibid., Box 611, "Trips 1926: Western Trip, Correspondence, 1926 October 1–15"; Hoover itinerary, October 15–30, 1926, ibid., Box 612, "Trips 1926: Western & Political, Miscellaneous, Cables, letters of thanks, schedules, etc., 1926 October"; Rickard Diaries, October 16, 1926, Box 1, "1926"; "Speech of Honorable Herbert Hoover, Secretary of Commerce, before the National Republican Club, Republican County Committee, and Republican Women's Club, at New York City," October 16, 1926, Hoover Papers, Commerce Period, Box 487, "Prosperity, 1923–1928 & undated"; Akerson to Newton, October 18, 1926, ibid., Box 611, "Trips 1926: Western Trip, Correspondence, 1926 October 16–31"; Hoover to Coolidge, October 19, 1926, ibid., Box 478, "President Coolidge, 1926 August–November"; Hoover to Lawrence Richey, October 22, 1926, ibid., Box 611, "Trips 1926: Western Trip, Correspondence, 1926 October 16–31"; Coolidge to Hoover, October 25, 1926, and Hoover to Coolidge, November 2, 1926, both in ibid., Box 478, "President Coolidge, 1926 August–November"; Akerson to Richey, October 28, 1926, ibid., Box 612, "Trips 1926: Western & Political, Miscellaneous, Cables, Letters of Thanks, Schedules, etc., 1926 October"; Hoover, "Republican Policies and Necessity for Support of Republican Candidates for Election, Radio Address, Los Angeles," October 30, 1926, Bible no. 668 (and see also nos. 652–67 for similar speeches elsewhere); Akerson to Newton, November 2, 1926, Hoover Papers, Commerce Period, Box 611, "Trips 1926: Western Trip, Correspondence, 1926 November–December & undated"; "The Presidency," *Time*, November 1, 1926, 9.

35. Rickard Diaries, June 29, 1926, Box 1, "1926"; Chester Rowell to Hoover, September 27, 1926, and Hoover to Rowell, October 2, 1926, both in Hoover Papers, Commerce Period, Box 366, "League of Nations, 1926–1928 & undated."
36. Rickard Diaries, April 15, 16, 1927, Box 1, "1927"; "President Bars Hoover from Kellogg's Job," Baltimore *Sun*, April 16, 1927; "Capital Scents Presidential Slur at Hoover," Chicago *Sunday Tribune*, April 17, 1927; "Coolidge Breakfast in Hoover's Honor Intended to Quiet Unfavorable Gossip," Washington *Star*, April 17, 1927; David Lawrence, "Hoover Held in High Esteem," ibid.; "Mr. Coolidge Shows His Human Side," Newark (New Jersey) *News*, April 17, 1927; "Coolidge Finds Hoover Best as Commerce Head," Washington *Herald*, April 17, 1927; "Breakfast to Hoover Fails to Quiet Rumors," Washington *Post*, April 18, 1927; "Coolidge Clears View to Appease Hoover's Friends," Springfield *Republican*, April 17, 1927; "Coolidge Breakfast to Hoover Silent on White House Rebuke," Baltimore *Sun*, April 18, 1927; "Coolidge Deepens Hoover Mystery," New York *World*, April 18, 1927; "White House Lauds Hoover's Ability," *New York Times*, April 20, 1927; unsigned, undated memorandum on the affair, Hoover Papers, Commerce Period, Box 710, "Wilbur, Ray Lyman, 1927–1928 & undated"; Lou Hoover to Herbert and Allan Hoover, ca. April 16, 1927, Allan Hoover Papers, Box 2, "Correspondence with Lou Henry Hoover, 1927 March–September"; George H. Nash, "The 'Great Enigma' and the 'Great Engineer': The Political Relationship of Calvin Coolidge and Herbert Hoover," in *Calvin Coolidge and the Coolidge Era: Essays on the History of the 1920s*, ed. John Earl Haynes (Washington, DC: Library of Congress, 1998), 170.
37. For the Mississippi River flood, see Chapter 20 in this volume.
38. "Capital Women Set Up School for Politics," Boston *Transcript*, March 14, 1927; S. J. Crumbine to Lou Hoover, March 18, 29, 1927; Lou Hoover to Crumbine, March 23, 1927, all in Lou Hoover Papers, Box 16, "Clubs and Organizations: American Child Health Assoc., Correspondence, 1923–30"; Lou Hoover to Ralph Peacock, March 24, 1927, ibid., Box 1, "Girl Scouts: Administrative Correspondence, 1927 January–June"; Lou Hoover to Edgar Rickard, April 30, 1927, American Child Health Association Papers, Hoover Presidential Library, West Branch, Iowa, Box 2, "American Relief Administration Children's Fund, 1924–1928"; "Minutes of the Special Meeting of the Directors A.R.A. Children's Fund, Inc.," April 6, 1927, ibid.; "Girl Scouts Name Women They Most Admire," Lima (Ohio) *Star*, April 20, 1927; "Girl Scouts Will Hear Mrs. Hoover Talk to Council," Racine (Wisconsin) *Times Call*, May 19, 1927.
39. Lou Hoover to Edgar Rickard, July 30, 1927, Lou Hoover Papers, Box 21, "Personal Correspondence, 1921–28: Rickard, Edgar, 1925–27"; Lou Hoover to Charles Henry, July 30, 1927, ibid., Box 15, "Personal Correspondence, 1921–28: Henry, Charles D. and Florence, 1921–28"; Lou Hoover to Gayle Campbell, July 30, 1927, ibid., Box 11, "Personal Correspondence, 1921–28: Campbell, Gayle Allen, 1922–27 & undated."
40. Rickard Diaries, August 2, 3, 1927, Box 1, "1927."
41. Lou Hoover to Charles Henry, August 29, 1927, Lou Hoover Papers, Box 15, "Personal Correspondence, 1921–28: Henry, Charles D. and Florence, 1921–28"; Lou Hoover to Herbert and Allan Hoover, ca. April 16, 1927, Allan Hoover Papers, Box 2, "Correspondence with Lou Henry Hoover, 1927 March–September"; Lou Hoover to Will (Henry) and Mary Paul (Henry?), September 8, 1927, Lou Hoover Papers, Box 15, "Personal Correspondence, 1921–28: Henry, William D., 1924–28"; Rickard Diaries, September 22, 1927, Box 1, "1927"; Lou Hoover to Allan Hoover, undated, ca. October 1927, November 8, 1927, Allan Hoover Papers, Box 2, "Correspondence with Lou Henry Hoover, 1927 October–November"; Allan Hoover to Lou Hoover, March 5, 1928, and Lou Hoover to Allan Hoover, March 6, 1928, both in ibid., Box 3, "Correspondence with Lou Henry Hoover, 1928 March–April"; Rickard Diaries, August 25, 29, 1928, Box 1, "1928." Lou paid tuition, board, and incidental expenses for Janet during the 1927 to 1928 school year at Elm Lea School. For details, see Lou Hoover Papers, Box 72, "Subject File: Large, Janet, General, 1927–29."
42. "Green Uniform Replaces Khaki of Girl Scouts," New York *Herald Tribune*, September 30, 1927; "Scouts: Girl Leaders Meet," *Time*, October 10, 1927, 10; Lou Hoover to Abbie

Rickard, March 28, 1928, Lou Hoover Papers, Box 21, "Personal Correspondence, 1921–28: Rickard, Abbie, 1927–28"; Aida de Acosta Breckenridge to Lou Hoover, April 17 and October 30, 1928; Lou Hoover, "Democratic Athletics" (introduction to a NAAF Women's Division pamphlet on "play days"), ca. November 12, 1928, all in ibid., Box 37, "Clubs and Organizations, National Amateur Athletic Federation: Women's Division, Breckenridge, Aida de Acosta, 1924–29"; Ethel Perrin to Lou Hoover, May 11, 1928, ibid., Box 40, "Clubs and Organizations, National Amateur Athletic Federation: Women's Division, Olympic Participation, 1922–28"; "Report of the Fifth Annual Meeting, Women's Division, N.A.A.F., New York City," January 3–5, 1929, ibid., Box 36, "Clubs and Organizations, National Amateur Athletic Federation: Women's Division, Annual Meetings, 1929 New York." The financial statement attached to this report indicated a balance in the treasury of only $762.41.

43. Lou Hoover to Will (Henry) and Mary Paul (Henry?), September 8, 1927, Lou Hoover Papers, Box 15, "Personal Correspondence, 1921–28: Henry, William D., 1924–28"; Lou Hoover to Allan Hoover, November 8, 1927, Allan Hoover Papers, Box 2, "Correspondence with Lou Henry Hoover, 1927 October–November"; Lou Hoover to Allan Hoover, July 5, 18, 1928, ibid., Box 3, "Correspondence with Lou Henry Hoover, 1928 July–November"; Lou Hoover to W. D. Henry, July 18, 1928, ibid., Box 8, "Death of Charles Henry, 1928."

44. "Mrs. Hoover Attempts to Purchase Birthplace of Husband in West Branch," *Iowa City Press-Citizen*, August 14, 1928; Dale C. Mayer, *Lou Henry Hoover: A Prototype for First Ladies* (New York: Nova Historical, 2004), 326–27.

45. Lou Hoover to Edgar Rickard, October 4, 1928, Lou Hoover Papers, Box 21, "Personal Correspondence: Rickard, Edgar, 1928"; Nancy Beck Young, *Lou Henry Hoover: Activist First Lady* (Lawrence: University Press of Kansas, 2004), 37, 43–49.

Chapter 19

1. The clearest explanation of the "equalization fee" I have been able to find is in Robert H. Ferrell, *The Presidency of Calvin Coolidge* (Lawrence: University Press of Kansas, 1998), 88–89.

2. For farmers' concerns in 1926 and Hoover's ideas, see the letters in Herbert Hoover Papers, Commerce Period, Hoover Presidential Library, West Branch, Iowa, Box 3; Hoover to Secretary of Agriculture Jardine, April 1, 1926, ibid., Box 5, "Agriculture: Correspondence, 1917–1926"; Hoover to T. D. Hammatt, March 20, 1926, ibid., Box 7, "Agriculture: Legislation, Miscellaneous, 1926"; Hoover to Coolidge, April 6, 1926, ibid., Box 478, "President Coolidge, 1926 April–May"; Hoover to Rep. Charles Brand, June 2, 1926, ibid., Box 275, "House of Representatives: Brand, Charles, 1923–1927"; draft of letter, Hoover to "Mr. . . . ," June 25, 1926, ibid., Box 5, "Agriculture: Corn Belt, Des Moines Meeting, Answer to Peek, etc., 1926–1928"; E. G. Montgomery to Julius Klein, June 26, 1926, ibid., Box 5, "Agriculture: Department Agriculture & Department Commerce, Propaganda, etc., 1926"; Hoover to President Coolidge, March 15, 1926, enclosing memorandum on agricultural price index by Frank Surface, ca. March 15, 1926, Calvin Coolidge, President's Personal Files, Microfilm, Forbes Library, Reel 6, and Hoover Papers, Commerce Period, Box 11, "Agriculture: Prices, 1923–1927 & undated"; U.S. Shipping Board press release, June 29, 1926, ibid., Box 45, "Barnes, Julius, 1924–1928 & undated"; A. F. Lever to Hoover, August 23, 1926, and Hoover to Lever, September 21, 1926, both in ibid., Box 5, "Agriculture: Credits, Loans, Etc., 1926 & undated"; Joan Hoff Wilson, "Hoover's Agricultural Policies, 1921–1928," *Agricultural History* 51 (April 1977): 353–54.

3. Transcript of Hoover's testimony before the Business Men's Conference on Agriculture, April 15, 1927, Hoover Papers, Commerce Period, Box 4, "Agriculture: Business Men's Conference on Agriculture, Correspondence and Reports, 1927–29 (1)," pp. 3853, 3857–58, 3860–64, 3835, 3876.

4. Hoover to Alexander Legge, February 6, 1926, Hoover Papers, Commerce Period, Box 463, "Peek, George N., 1926–1927"; advertising brochure for book by Frank Surface, *American Pork Production in the World War*, ca. June 1926, ibid., Box 264, "Hogs & Pork Products,

1926"; Hoover, draft of press releases, "What the Haugen Bill Will Cost," undated, ca. June 1926, ibid., Box 8, "Agriculture: Legislation, McNary-Haugen Bill, Annotated Copies of Bill by HH, 1921–1926 & undated"; memorandum by Wheeler McMillan, July 19, 1988, attached to p. 29, typed memorandum on the McNary-Haugen Bill, undated, ibid., Box 8, "Agriculture: Legislation, McNary-Haugen Bill, Miscellaneous, Undated (2)"; "Quiz of 2 Cabinet Members Sought," Philadelphia *Ledger*, July 1, 1926; press release, Hoover to Sen. Simeon Fess, July 1, 1926, Hoover Papers, Commerce Period, Box 546, "Senate: Fess, Simeon D., 1922–1926"; Frank M. Surface to Henry A. Wallace, October 26, 1926, enclosing copy of Hoover to H. C. Stuart, October 24, 1918, and Wallace to Surface, November 1, 1926, all in ibid., Box 264, "Hogs & Pork Products, 1926"; transcript of Hoover's testimony before the Business Men's Conference on Agriculture, April 15, 1927, ibid., Box 4, "Agriculture: Business Men's Conference on Agriculture, Correspondence and Reports, 1927–29 (1)," p. 3852.

5. Ferrell, *Presidency of Calvin Coolidge*, 92–93; Hoff Wilson, "Hoover's Agricultural Policies," 343–45; typed list of "non agriculture" versus agriculture price indexes, 1913–1927, with Hoover's handwritten notes, undated, Hoover Papers, Commerce Period, Box 3, "Agriculture, 1927, July–December."

6. Hoover, "Draft for President Statement on signing the Railway Labor Bill," May 15, 1926, Hoover Papers, Commerce Period, Box 478, "President Coolidge, 1926 April–May"; Hoover to Coolidge, December 30, 1926, Calvin Coolidge, President's Personal Files, Microfilm, Reel 6; Hoover to Everett Sanders, March 9, 1927, Hoover Papers, Commerce Period, Box 479, "President Coolidge, 1927 March–May"; Hoover, draft of passage on railroad consolidation for Coolidge's annual message, ca. November 12, 1927, ibid., Box 502, "Railroads, 1927–1928 & undated"; Mark H. Rose, Bruce E. Seely, and Paul F. Barrett, *The Best Transportation System in the World: Railroads, Trucks, Airlines, and American Public Policy in the Twentieth Century* (Columbus: Ohio State University Press, 2006), 21–27.

7. Ellis W. Hawley, "Secretary Hoover and the Bituminous Coal Problems, 1921–1928," *Business History Review* 42 (Autumn 1968): 267.

8. Blackburn Esterline to Hoover, April 15, 1926, Hoover Papers, Commerce Period, Box 353, "Justice Department: Miscellaneous, 1921–1928 & undated"; C. P. White to Hoover, April 19, 1926, ibid., Box 104, "Coal: Legislation, 1926"; Hoover to Sen. Lawrence C. Phipps, April 23, 1926, ibid., Box 550, "Senate: Phipps, Lawrence C., 1921–1927."

9. "Statement by Secretary Hoover before the House Committee on Interstate and Foreign Commerce," May 14, 1926, Hoover Papers, Commerce Period, Box 97, "Coal: HH Personal, 1922–1928 & undated"; Commerce Department press release by Scott Turner, director of Bureau of Mines, ca. May 15, 1926, ibid., Box 104, "Coal: Legislation, 1926"; Hoover to T. L. Lewis, May 27, 1926, ibid.; Hoover to Southwestern Interstate Coal Operators' Association, July 12, 1926, ibid., Box 98, "Coal: Miscellaneous, 1926"; Hoover to Sen. Simeon D. Fess, August 3, 1926, ibid., Box 546, "Senate: Fess, Simeon D., 1922–1926."

10. Hoover, draft of statement on coal legislation for Coolidge's annual message, ca. November 20, 1926, Hoover Papers, Commerce Period, Box 478, "President Coolidge, 1926 August–November"; Norman W. Baxter, "Coal Strike Power for President Held Gone This Session," Washington *Post*, December 15, 1926; "A United Press Item from Washington by Alfred P. Reck, January 22, 1927, noticed in the Rochester Times-Union, 22d," Hoover Papers, Commerce Period, Box 97, "Coal: HH Personal, 1922–1928"; article by Paul Wooton, Washington reporter for *Coal Age*, February 11, 1927, ibid., Box 716, "Wooton, Paul, 1927 January–April."

11. Draft of article by Paul Wooton, June 17, 1927, Hoover Papers, Commerce Period, Box 716, "Wooton, Paul, 1927 May–December & undated"; Melvyn Dubofsky and Warren Van Tine, *John L. Lewis: A Biography* (New York: Quadrangle, 1977), 144–48.

12. Herbert Hoover, *Memoirs: The Cabinet and the Presidency, 1920–1933* (New York: Macmillan, 1952), 71 (hereafter, *Memoirs 2*).

13. Hoover, "Statement at Press Conference," July 8, 1926, Hoover Papers, Commerce Period, Box 390, "Merchant Marine, 1926."

14. Hoover to Coolidge, January 3, 1927, Coolidge, President's Personal Files, Microfilm, Reel 6; Hoover to Coolidge, November 21, 1927, Hoover Papers, Commerce Period, Box 390, "Merchant Marine, 1927"; typed list of Shipping Board recommendations, undated, ca. February 1928, ibid., "Merchant Marine, 1928."

15. Department of Commerce, *Fifteenth Annual Report of the Secretary of Commerce* (Washington, DC: Government Printing Office, 1927), xvii.

16. Hoover, "The Waterways Outlet from the Middle West," speech delivered before the annual banquet of the John Ericsson Republican League of Illinois, March 9, 1926, Hoover Papers, Commerce Period, Box 687, "Waterways, 1926 March."

17. Hoover, "A National Policy in Development of Water Resources," speech delivered before the Columbia River Basin League, Seattle, August 21, 1926, Hoover Papers, Commerce Period, Box 193, "Engineers and Engineering, 1926–1928 & undated"; "Secretary Hoover in the Middle West," *Waterway Bulletin* of the Illinois River Division of the Mississippi Valley Association, August 23, 1926.

18. W. J. Shuman to Hoover, August 24, 1926, and Hoover to Shuman, September 20, 1926, both in Hoover Papers, Commerce Period, Box 688, "Waterways, 1926 Aug."; unidentified clipping, "Aid Pledged after Study of Program," October 8, 1926, in ibid., Box 688, "Waterways, 1926 October."

19. Coolidge to Hoover, October 25, 1926, Hoover Papers, Commerce Period, Box 478, "President Coolidge, 1926 Aug.–Nov."; Ferrell, *The Presidency of Calvin Coolidge*, 168.

20. Hoover to Coolidge, October 25, 1926, Coolidge, President's Personal Files, Microfilm, Reel 6; Hoover to Work, October 25, 1926, Hoover Papers, Commerce Period, Box 478, "President Coolidge, 1926 Aug.–Nov."; Work to Hoover, October 28, 1926, and Hoover to Work, October 29, 1926, both in Coolidge, President's Personal Files, Microfilm, Reel 6.

21. Ferrell, *The Presidency of Calvin Coolidge*, 168.

22. Commerce Department press release, "Address by Honorable Herbert Hoover, Secretary of Commerce, before the Mississippi Valley Association at St. Louis, Missouri," November 22, 1926, Hoover Papers, Commerce Period, Box 688, "Waterways, 1926 November"; Hoover, "Why Inland Waterways Should Be Developed," *American Review of Reviews* 74 (December 1926): 595–98; "A Vision of What Waterway Development Would Accomplish," *Daily Bulletin* of the *Manufacturers Record*, December 23, 1926.

23. H. C. Gardner to Hoover, November 24, 1926, Hoover Papers, Commerce Period, Box 690, "Waterways: Great Lakes–St. Lawrence, All American Waterway, 1926"; S. Wallace Dempsey to Hoover, November 26, 1926, and Hoover to Dempsey, November 29, 1926, both in ibid.; Committee on Rivers and Harbors, House of Representatives, "Waterway from the Great Lakes to the Hudson River: Letter from the Chief of Engineers, United States Army," 69 Cong., 2d sess., December 6, 1926, Document No. 7; Hoover to Arthur Brisbane, December 13, 1926, Hoover Papers, Commerce Period, Box 688, "Waterways, 1926 December"; Hoover to James Goodrich, December 21, 1926, ibid., Box 241, "Goodrich, James P., 1926–1927 & undated"; Hoover to Coolidge, December 27, 1927, ibid., Box 696, "Waterways: Great Lakes–St. Lawrence, Recommendations to the President, 1926 Dec."

24. "Get Waterway Built, Hoover Tells Chicago," Chicago *Sunday Tribune*, April 10, 1927; "St. Lawrence Improvement," Ottawa *Citizen*, September 29, 1927; Hoover to Coolidge, November 12, 1927, Hoover Papers, Commerce Period, Box 479, "President Coolidge, 1927 Nov.–Dec."; Richard N. Kottman, "Herbert Hoover and the St. Lawrence Seaway Treaty of 1932," *New York History* 56 (July 1975): 314–46.

25. Hiram Johnson, "The Boulder Canyon Project," *Annals of the American Academy of Political and Social Science* 135 (January 1923): 155; Interior Department press releases, January 12 and February 11, 1926, Colorado River Commission Papers, Hoover Presidential Library, West Branch, Iowa, Box 32, "Project File: Interior Dept., 1922–24 and 1926–27"; Hiram Johnson to Hiram Johnson, Jr., and Archibald Johnson, January 16, 1926, Hiram Johnson Papers, Bancroft Library, University of California at Berkeley, Part VI, Box 4, "1926 Jan.–Feb."; "Abstract of Secretary Hoover's Statement on the Colorado River before the House Committee on Irrigation and Reclamation," March 3, 1926, Hoover Papers, Commerce Period, Box 257, "Hearings, 1926."

26. Chester Rowell to Hoover, February 18, 1926, Chester Rowell Papers, Bancroft Library, University of California at Berkeley, Box 6, "1926 Jan.–Feb."; Edgar Rickard Diaries, Hoover Presidential Library, West Branch, Iowa, February 19, 1926, Box 1, "1926"; Hoover to Chester Rowell, February 15, 1926, Rowell Papers, Box 16, "Hoover, Herbert Clark"; Hiram Johnson to Hiram Johnson, Jr., April 26, 1926, Johnson Papers, Part VI, Box 4, "1926 Mar.–Apr."; Chester Rowell to C. C. Young, April 30, 1926, Rowell Papers, Box 6, "1926 Mar.–Apr."; Hoover to Henry M. Robinson, October 14, 18, 1926, Hoover Papers, Commerce Period, Box 528, "Robinson, Henry M., 1926"; Hiram Johnson to Hiram Johnson, Jr., December 3, 1926, Johnson Papers, Part VI, Box 4, "1926 Nov.–Dec."; Phil Swing to Delph Carpenter, December 27, 1926, Phil D. Swing Papers, University of California at Los Angeles, Box 134, "Carpenter, Delph"; Hoover to Phil Swing, January 13, 1927, Hoover Papers, Commerce Period, Box 282, "House of Rep.: Swing, Phil D., 1921–28 & undated"; Commerce Department press release, "Mr. Hoover's Statement apropos of the Debate on Swing-Johnson Bill," January 27, 1927, Herbert Hoover Papers, Campaign and Transition Period, Hoover Presidential Library, West Branch, Iowa, Box 81, "Subject: Boulder Dam"; Hiram Johnson to Hiram Johnson, Jr., March 11, 1927, Johnson Papers, Part VI, Box 5, "1927 Jan.–July."
27. William Mullendore to Stephen Davis, July 25, 1927, William C. Mullendore Papers, Hoover Presidential Library, West Branch, Iowa, Box 1, "Colorado River Commission/Hoover Dam Correspondence, 1927"; Mullendore to Davis, August 30, 1927, ibid.; Hoover to Coolidge, November 12, 1927, Hoover Papers, Commerce Period, Box 479, "President Coolidge, 1927 November–December"; Hiram Johnson to Hiram Johnson, Jr., and Archibald Johnson, December 24, 1927, Johnson Papers, Part VI, Box 5, "1927 Aug.–Dec."; Delph Carpenter to Hoover, December 31, 1927, Hoover Papers, Commerce Period, Box 78, "Carpenter, Delph E., 1921–1927 & undated."
28. Johnson to Hiram Johnson, Jr., and Archibald Johnson, March 2, 17, 1928, Johnson Papers, Part VI, Box 5, "1928 Mar.–Apr."
29. Reports from Southern California Edison lobbyist William Mullendore, March 22, 23, 27, 29; April 5, 22, 29; May 4, 7, 10, 12; November 20; and December 12, 14, 15, 1928, all in Mullendore Papers, Box 11, "Colorado River Comm./Hoover Dam, Diary of Mullendore, 1927–28"; Hiram Johnson to Hiram Johnson, Jr., and Archibald Johnson, April 30, 1928, Johnson Papers, Part VI, Box 5, "1928 Mar.–Apr."; "Coolidge Opposes Revamped Flood Bill; Veto Is Likely for It and Farm Measure," *New York Times*, May 5, 1928; Johnson to Hiram Johnson, Jr., and Archibald Johnson, May 8, 31, 1928, Johnson Papers, Part VI, Box 5, "1928 May–June"; Johnson to Hiram Johnson, Jr., and Archibald Johnson, December 15, 18, 1928, ibid., Box 5, "1928 July–Dec."; Ray Lyman Wilbur and Northcutt Ely, *The Hoover Dam Power and Water Contracts and Related Data* (Washington, DC: Government Printing Office, 1930), 420, 429.
30. George Norris, *Fighting Liberal* (Lincoln: University of Nebraska Press, 1972; orig. pub. 1945), 247–48; Hoover, *Memoirs* 2, 304; draft of paragraph on Muscle Shoals for the president's annual message, November 6, 1925, Hoover Papers, Commerce Period, Box 422, "Muscle Shoals, Miscellaneous, 1925."
31. C. C. Concannon to Hoover, January 7, 1926, Hoover Papers, Commerce Period, Box 423, "Muscle Shoals, Legislation, Hearings, Etc., 1925–1927"; Paul Clapp to Hoover, October 16, 1926, ibid., Box 422, "Muscle Shoals, Miscellaneous, 1926"; unsigned "Memorandum—Present Worth of Muscle Shoals Bids," February 15, 1927, ibid., Box 422, "Muscle Shoals, Miscellaneous, 1927 Jan.–June"; Evans C. Johnson, *Oscar W. Underwood: A Political Biography* (Baton Rouge: Louisiana State University Press, 1980), 366–70.
32. *Public Papers of the Presidents of the United States: Herbert Hoover; Containing the Public Messages, Speeches, and Statements of the President, 1929* (Washington, DC: Government Printing Office, 1974), 554; press release, "Statement by Herbert Hoover Regarding His Muscle Shoals Statement, Printed in the Knoxville News-Sentinel," October 9, 1928, Hoover Papers, Campaign and Transition Period, Box 153, "Subject: Muscle Shoals"; "Hoover and the Scripps-Howard Press," *Nation*, October 24, 1928, 415.

33. "Statement of Herbert Hoover, Secretary of Commerce, before the Committee on Merchant Marine and Fisheries, on H.R. 5589," January 6, 1926, Hoover Papers, Commerce Period, Box 257, "Hearings, 1926"; "Statement by Secretary Hoover," April 20, 1926; Commerce Department press release on assignment of radio frequencies, July 9, 1926, both in ibid., Box 484, "Press Releases, 1926 April–August"; "Federal Court Rules Hoover Can Regulate Broadcasting; Enjoins Conflicting Stations," New York *World*, July 20, 1926; "Radio, New Spoiled Child, Is 'Acting Up,' Says Hoover," typed copy of story from Philadelphia *Public Ledger*, April 16, 1926, Hoover Papers, Commerce Period, Box 490, "Radio: Correspondence, Press Releases, Misc., 1927 Jan.–Apr."; Philip T. Rosen, *The Modern Stentors: Radio Broadcasters and the Federal Government, 1920–1934* (Westport, CT: Greenwood, 1980), 93–95.

34. Matthew Avery Sutton, *Aimee Semple McPherson and the Resurrection of Christian America* (Cambridge, MA: Harvard University Press, 2007), 81–82; Hoover to Everett Sanders, July 27, 1926, Hoover Papers, Commerce Period, Box 478, "President Coolidge, 1926 June–July"; Hoover to Sen. James Wadsworth, August 3, 1926, ibid., Box 490, "Radio: Correspondence, Press Releases, Misc., 1926 May–December"; Stephen Davis to Hoover, September 1, 1926, ibid., Box 611, "Trips 1926: Western Trip, Correspondence, 1926 September 1–9"; Hoover to Coolidge, November 20, 1926, ibid., Box 478, "President Coolidge, 1926 August–November"; Arthur Sears Henning, "Senate-House Radio Conferees Fail to Agree," Chicago *Tribune*, December 22, 1926; Commerce Department press release, February 24, 1927, Hoover Papers, Commerce Period, Box 484, "Press Releases, 1927–1928"; Erik Barnouw, *A Tower in Babel: A History of Broadcasting in the United States* (New York: Oxford University Press, 1966), 195–201.

35. James L. Wright, "Radio Czar's Crown Intact Despite Dill," Buffalo *Evening News*, March 8, 1927; Commerce Department press release, "Statement by Secretary of Commerce Herbert Hoover," March 6, 1927, Hoover Papers, Commerce Period, Box 501, "Radio: Federal Radio Commission, Clippings & Press Releases, 1926–1928 & undated"; Commerce Department press release, "New Radio Division Formed in Commerce Department," March 8, 1927, ibid., Box 144, "Commerce Department: Radio Division, 1925–1932"; Hoover to Harvey Ingham, March 11, 1927, ibid., Box 291, "Ingham, Harvey, 1927 & undated"; Commerce Department press release, "Federal Radio Commission, Washington: Organization of Commission," March 15, 1927, ibid., Box 501, "Radio: Federal Radio Commission, Clippings & Press Releases, 1920–1928 & undated."

36. Rosen, *Modern Stentors*, 107–12, 123–32.

37. Barnouw, *A Tower in Babel*, 197–200.

38. Commerce Department press release, "Statement by Secretary of Commerce Herbert Hoover," March 6, 1927, Hoover Papers, Commerce Period, Box 501, "Radio: Federal Radio Commission, Clippings & Press Releases, 1926–1928 & undated"; commission issued by President Coolidge naming Hoover as a delegate to the International Radiotelegraph Conference, June 13, 1927, ibid., Box 479, "President Coolidge, 1927 June–July"; Hoover to Secretary of State Kellogg, April 20, 1927, ibid., Box 490, "Radio: Correspondence, Press Releases, Misc., 1927 Jan.–Apr."; Commerce Department press release, "An Address by Herbert Hoover, Secretary of Commerce, before the International Radiotelegraph Conference, U.S. Chamber of Commerce Building, Washington," October 4, 1927, ibid., Box 490, "Radio: Correspondence, Press Releases, Misc., 1928–1964 & undated"; Hoover, *Memoirs* 2, 142–48.

39. Arthur W. Page to Hoover, April 4, 1927, Hoover Papers, Commerce Period, Box 598, "Television, 1926–1927"; Lou Hoover to Herbert and Allan Hoover, April 10, 1927, Allan Hoover Papers, Hoover Presidential Library, West Branch, Iowa, Box 2, "Correspondence with Lou Henry Hoover, 1927 October–November."

40. Commerce Department press release on Guggenheim foundation, January 18, 1926, Hoover Papers, Commerce Period, Box 40, "Aviation: Daniel Guggenheim, 1926 & undated"; Commerce Department press release, "Extracts from Civil Aviation Report by Joint Committee of the Commerce Department & American Engineering Council," January 24, 1926, ibid., Box 40, "Aviation, 1926"; David D. Lee, "Herbert Hoover and the Development

of Commercial Aviation, 1921–1926," *Business History Review* 58 (Spring 1984): 95–100. For the background of the President's Aviation Board (the Morrow committee) and the joint American Engineering Council–Commerce Department study, see Chapter 17 in this volume.

41. Hoover to Coolidge, August 3, 1926, Hoover Papers, Commerce Period, Box 478, "President Coolidge, 1926 August–November"; "MacCracken Made Hoover's Air Aid," *New York Times*, August 10, 1926; Hoover, *Memoirs* 2, 133–34.

42. For Greenwood's reports (August 7–21, 1926), see Hoover Papers, Commerce Period, Box 246, "Greenwood, Ernest, 1926 & undated"; Commerce Department press release, Hoover, "Speech before San Francisco Chamber of Commerce," September 2, 1926, ibid., Box 40, "Aviation, 1926"; Commerce Department press release, "Hoover Here [Chicago] Sees Big Aviation Gain," from Chicago *News*, April 9, 1927, Bible no. 720, Hoover Presidential Library, West Branch, Iowa; clipping from Washington *Post* announcing Hoover's appointment to welcome committee for Lindbergh, June 1, 1927, Hoover Papers, Commerce Period, Box 371, "Lindbergh, Col. Charles A., 1927 June."

43. Lawrence Richey to M. H. Aylesworth, June 6, 1927, Hoover Papers, Commerce Period, Box 371, "Lindbergh, Col. Charles A., 1927 June"; unidentified, undated clipping, "Hoover Believes Future Awaits Mississippi Coast," ibid., Box 397, "Miss. Valley Flood: Relief Work, Miscellaneous, 1927 June 11–30"; Hoover to Lindbergh, June 16, 1927, ibid., Box 371, "Lindbergh, Col. Charles A., 1927 June"; "Sees Aviation as Stable," *New York Times*, June 18, 1927; "Good Word for Aviation," Danville (Illinois) *Commercial News*, June 26, 1927; Commerce Department press release on conference between Hoover and Lindbergh, June 24, 1927, Hoover Papers, Commerce Period, Box 371, "Lindbergh, Col. Charles A., 1927 June"; L. C. Speers, "Hoover Foresees a Greater Air Service," Bible no. 755; Commerce Department press release, "Lindbergh Tour Great Boost to Commercial Aeronautics," July 13, 1927, Hoover Papers, Commerce Period, Box 371, "Lindbergh, Col. Charles A., 1927 July–December"; Hoover, "Aeronautical Conference Opening Remarks," December 5, 1927, Bible no. 803; Commerce Department press release, "Statement by Secretary Hoover," December 14, 1927, Hoover Papers, Commerce Period, Box 371, "Lindbergh, Col. Charles A., 1927 July–December"; Hoover, "Progress in Commercial Aviation," undated, ca. late 1927 or early 1928, ibid., Box 40, "Aviation, 1928 & undated"; Hoover, "Development of Commercial Aviation: Radio Address from Washington, D.C. Made in Connection with Lighting of California Airway Beacons," April 15, 1928, Bible no. 850. For a thoughtful essay on the differing ways Americans interpreted Lindbergh's flight, see John William Ward, "The Meaning of Lindbergh's Flight," in *Studies in American Culture: Dominant Ideas and Images*, ed. Joseph J. Kwiat and Mary C. Turpie (Minneapolis: University of Minnesota Press, 1960), 27–40.

44. Hoover to Ernest Greenwood, November 26, 1924, Hoover Papers, Commerce Period, Box 160, "Conferences: Street and Highway Safety, 1924 September–November"; Commerce Department press release, "National Conference on Street and Highway Safety Press Service," March 23, 1926, ibid., Box 163, "Conferences: Street and Highway Safety, 1926 Conference, 1926 March"; "Traffic Program Urged by Hoover," New York *World*, March 26, 1926; Hoover, *Memoirs* 2, 74–75.

45. Hoover, "The Department of Commerce," June 30, 1926, Hoover Papers, Commerce Period, Box 615, "Uncle Sam's History of United States, 1926 & undated"; "Uses of Waste," *Engineering and Mining Journal*, November 13, 1926, 763; "Secretary Hoover Shows Progress in Elimination of Waste as a Factor in American Prosperity," *Daily Bulletin* of the *Manufacturers Record*, November 19, 1926; Hoover to E. M. Herr, December 15, 1926; W. C. Wetherill to Hoover, December 27, 1926, both in Hoover Papers, Commerce Period, Box 160, "Conferences: Simplification and Standardization, 1923–1927 & undated."

46. W. C. Wetherill to Hoover, December 27, 1926; Hoover to C. E. Skinner, March 14, 1927, both in Hoover Papers, Commerce Period, Box 160, "Conferences: Simplification and Standardization, 1923–1927 & undated"; Hoover to John W. Lieb, March 15, 1927, ibid., Box 370, "Lieb, John William, 1921–1928."

47. Hoover to J. H. Gibboney, March 21, 1927, Hoover Papers, Commerce Period, Box 160, "Conferences: Simplification and Standardization, 1923–1927 & undated"; Hoover, *Memoirs* 2, 77.

48. Hoover to Marie Meloney, January 26, 1926; Meloney to Hoover, February 12, 1926, both in Hoover Papers, Commerce Period, Box 65, "Building and Housing: Better Homes in America, Inc., 1926"; Hoover to Meloney, March 12, 1926, ibid., Box 180, "Delineator, 1925–1926 & undated"; Hoover, "The Home and the Nation," *Child Welfare Magazine* 20 (April 1926): 450; Hoover, "Statement for Liberty Magazine," May 11, 1926, Hoover Papers, Commerce Period, Box 64, "Building and Housing, 1926"; Hoover, "Ohio Building Association League: Speech before 'Billion Dollar Convention,' Columbus," October 21, 1926, Bible no. 654; Hoover to John D. Rockefeller, Jr., December 18, 1926, Hoover Papers, Commerce Period, Box 528, "Rockefeller Foundation, 1926–1928"; Meloney to Hoover, January 21, 1927, ibid., Box 389, "Meloney, Mrs. Marie M., 1922–1928 & undated"; Hoover to Edgar Rickard, November 12, 1927, American Child Health Association Papers, Hoover Presidential Library, West Branch, Iowa, Box 2, "American Relief Administration Children's Funds, 1924–1928."

49. Ralph Arnold to Hoover, April 2, 1927, Hoover Papers, Commerce Period, Box 36, "Arnold, Ralph, 1926–1928"; Lawrence Veiller to Hoover, April 27, 1927, and Hoover to Veiller, June 18, 1927, both in ibid., Box 68, "Building and Housing: National Housing Committee for Congested Areas (August Heckscher)"; pamphlet, "The Housing Problem Up to Date," July 26, 1927 (New York: Heckscher Foundation for Children, 1927); August Heckscher to Hoover, August 9 and September 19, 1927; Charles Gray Shaw to Hoover, November 21, 1927, all in Hoover Papers, Commerce Period, Box 68, "Building and Housing: National Housing Committee for Congested Areas (August Heckscher), 1927"; Walter Trattner, "August Heckscher," in *Dictionary of American Biography, Supplement 3, 1941–1945* (New York: Scribner's, 1973), 348–49; Mel Scott, *American City Planning Since 1890: A History Commemorating the Fiftieth Anniversary of the American Institute of Planners* (Berkeley: University of California Press, 1969), 256–57.

50. "Excerpt from Washington Dispatch in New York Times of March 5, 1926," Hoover Papers, Commerce Period, Box 577, "Stock Market, 1921–1927"; Commerce Department press release on the economic outlook for 1927, January 1, 1927; Commerce Department press release on the economic outlook, August 24, 1927; Hoover to Richard Haughton, December 29, 1927, all in ibid., Box 188, "Economic Situation in U.S., 1925–1928."

51. Hoover to Rep. Hatton W. Sumners, January 4, 1926, Hoover Papers, Commerce Period, Box 282, "House of Representatives: Sumners, Hatton W., 1923–1926"; E. Dana Durand to Edward Eyre Hunt, January 5, 1926"; Hoover to Coolidge, March 15, 1926, ibid., Box 488, "Purchasing Power of Dollar, 1923–1927"; Adolf Miller to Hoover, November 29, 1926, ibid., Box 44, "Banks and Banking, 1924–1927"; Commerce Department press release on the economic outlook, January 1, 1927, ibid., Box 188, "Economic Situation in the U.S., 1925–1928." Some economists, such as William Z. Ripley, William Foster, and Waddill Catchings, were even more skeptical about the continuation of prosperity. See David Greenberg, *Calvin Coolidge* (New York: Times Books/Henry Holt, 2006), 144.

52. Committee on Recent Economic Changes of the President's Conference on Unemployment, *Recent Economic Changes in the United States*, 2 vols. (New York: McGraw-Hill, 1929), 1:v. Committee members included Hoover as chairman, Walter F. Brown, Renick W. Dunlap, William Green, Julius Klein, John S. Lawrence, Max Mason, George McFadden, Adolph C. Miller, Lewis E. Pierson, John J. Raskob, A. W. Shaw, Louis J. Taber, Daniel Willard, Clarence M. Woolley, Owen D. Young, and Edward Eyre Hunt, secretary.

53. Ibid., 1:xix–xxii, 512–13, 632–33; Hoover, memorandum for Messrs. Gries, Durand, Grosvenor Jones, Surface, Lane, Klein, Steuart, and Tryon, March 17, 1927, Hoover Papers, Commerce Period, Box 71, "Business Cycles and Situation, 1923–1928"; Thomas W. Lamont to Hoover, May 5, 1927, ibid., Box 363, "Lamont, Thomas W., 1921–1927"; Hoover to F. P. Keppel, October 26, 1927, ibid., Box 71, "Business Cycles and Situation, 1923–1928"; Hoover to Arthur Woods, December 23, 1927; Commerce Department press release, "To Study Economic Currents of United States," January 26, 1928, both in ibid.,

Box 149, "Committees: Economic Study, 1927–1928"; Caro M. Rhind to Hoover, January 28, 1928, Edward Eyre Hunt Papers, Hoover Institution Archives, Stanford, California, Box 2, "Correspondence: The Rockefeller Foundation, 1927–1943"; Guy Alchon, *The Invisible Hand of Planning: Capitalism, Social Science, and the State in the 1920s* (Princeton, NJ: Princeton University Press, 1985), 145–51.

54. Committee on Recent Economic Changes, *Recent Economic Changes*, 1:x, xii, xxiii–xxv, 603.

55. Wesley C. Mitchell, "A Review," in *Recent Economic Changes* 2:890–909. The quotation is on p. 909.

56. William Trufant Foster and Waddill Catchings, *The Road to Plenty* (Boston: Houghton Mifflin, 1928); Otto Mallery to Hoover, February 10, May 10, and December 30, 1926; February 23 and June 6, 1927, all in Hoover Papers, Commerce Period, Box 384, "Mallery, Otto T., 1921–1928"; Otto T. Mallery, "How Can This Prosperity Be Continued?" Philadelphia Chamber of Commerce pamphlet, January 1928, ibid., Box 659, "Unemployment: Prosperity Reserve, 1921–1932"; Meg Jacobs, *Pocketbook Politics: Economic Citizenship in Twentieth-Century America* (Princeton, NJ: Princeton University Press, 2005), 91.

57. Mallery to Hoover, February 7, 1928: John B. Andrews to Hoover, April 27, 1928; Hoover to Coolidge, April 28, 1928; Wesley C. Mitchell, "Prefatory Note" (for Otto T. Mallery, *Public Works to Stabilize Employment and Industry* [n.p., 1931]), ca. 1930, all in Hoover Papers, Commerce Period, Box 659, "Unemployment Prosperity Reserve, 1921–1932"; William J. Barber, *From New Era to New Deal: Herbert Hoover, the Economists, and American Economic Policy, 1921–1933* (New York: Cambridge University Press, 1985), 21–22. Mitchell did not mention the "prosperity reserve" in his essay in *Recent Economic Changes*.

58. "Federal Oil Conservation Board, Complete Record of Public Hearings, February 10 and 11, 1926," RG 48, Interior Department Records, National Archives, Washington, DC, General, File 1-242, "Oil Situation: Federal Oil Conservation Board," p. 130; Hoover to Interior Secretary Work, July 24, 1926, Hoover Papers, Commerce Period, Box 295, "Interior Department: Secretary Work, Hubert, 1926"; "Preliminary Report of the Federal Oil Conservation Board to the President of the United States, September 1926, Part I," ibid., Box 453, "Oil: Federal Oil Conservation Board, Reports, 1926 September"; "Modify Anti-Trust Law Says Hoover," October 25, 1926; Amos R. Beaty to Hoover, December 16, 1926, enclosing A. D. Sumner to Beaty, November 26, 1926; Hoover to Beaty, January 13, 1927, all in ibid., Box 452, "Oil, 1926"; news ticker report (?) on Secretary Mellon's statement that control of overproduction was a state responsibility, undated, ibid., Box 452, "Oil, 1927 January–June."

59. Interior Department press release, "Address of Hubert Work, Secretary of the Interior, and Chairman of the Federal Oil Conservation Board, before the Annual Meeting of the Mineral Law Section, American Bar Association, at Buffalo, New York," August 20, 1927, Hoover Papers, Commerce Period, Box 452, "Oil, 1927 August"; Ellis W. Hawley, "Herbert Hoover and the Sherman Act, 1921–1933: An Early Phase of a Continuing Issue," *Iowa Law Review* 74 (July 1989): 1085–86.

60. For Andrew's position, see "Our Prearmistice Loans," speech in the House of Representatives, January 13, 1926 (Washington, DC: Government Printing Office, 1926), and press release, "Capacity to Pay: A Reply; A Letter to the Editor of the *Atlantic Monthly*," January 30, 1926, Hoover Papers, Commerce Period, Box 214, "Foreign Debts: France, 1926 January–February." Rather than arguing Andrew's points, Hoover simply said that the Debt Commission was bound by its congressional instructions. See Hoover to Andrew, January 7, 1926, ibid., Box 275, "House of Representatives: Andrew, A. Piatt, 1922–1928 & undated"; and Grosvenor Jones to Harold Phelps Stokes, March 20, 1926, ibid., Box 261, "Herter, Christian A., 1926–1927 & undated." For Commerce Department debt figures, see "Memorandum on War Debt Settlement," no author or date, ca. March 1927, Box 212, "Foreign Debts, 1927 January–March." According to these figures, the reductions, with original interest reckoned at 5 percent, for the four major West European debtors were Britain, 35.06 percent; France, 64.81 percent; Italy, 81.47 percent; and Belgium, 63.27 percent.

61. Hoover to Secretary of State Frank Kellogg, July 28, 1926, Hoover Papers, Commerce Period, Box 572, "State Department: Secretary of State Kellogg, F. B., 1926 May–July";

"Debt Commission Ends by Limitation" and "France's Debt Pact Stands as Board Expires," *New York Times*, February 9, 1927; Melvyn P. Leffler, *The Elusive Quest: America's Pursuit of European Stability and French Security, 1919–1933* (Chapel Hill: University of North Carolina Press, 1979), 214–15.

62. Owen Young to Basil Miles, January 9, 1928, Hoover Papers, Commerce Period, Box 719, "Young, Owen D., 1927–1928 & undated."

63. For a persuasive critique of the "circular flow of paper" theory, see Stephen A. Schuker, *American "Reparations" to Germany, 1919–33: Implications for the Third-World Debt Crisis* (Princeton, NJ: Department of Economics of Princeton University, 1988), 90–97. As a table on p. 263 of Bruce Kent, *The Spoils of War: The Politics, Economics, and Diplomacy of Reparations, 1918–1932* (Oxford, UK: Clarendon, 1989), shows, Germany ran a negative balance of payments in every year between 1924 and 1929 except 1926. Although it is true that taxation and foreign borrowing could have offset this enough to cover reparations payments, doing so would have required the Germans to tax themselves heavily and use much of what they borrowed to cover reparations, which, of course, they did not do. For a brief summary of the "circular flow" theory, see Denise Artaud, "Reparations and War Debts: The Restoration of French Financial Power, 1919–1929," in *French Foreign and Defence Policy, 1918–1940: The Decline and Fall of a Great Power*, ed. Robert Boyce (London: Routledge, 1998), 102.

64. Owen Young to Hoover, January 5, 1926, Hoover Papers, Commerce Period, Box 719, "Young, Owen D., 1925–1926"; James Harvey Rogers, "Foreign Markets and Foreign Credits," in *Recent Economic Changes*, 2:752, 754. For a modern version of the same argument, see Robert Boyce, "Business as Usual: The Limits of French Economic Diplomacy, 1926–1933," in Boyce, *French Foreign and Defence Policy*, 111–12; Kent, *Spoils of War*, 264–65.

65. Department of Commerce, Bureau of the Census, *Historical Statistics of the United States, Earliest Times to the Present*, ed. Susan B. Carter et al., Millennial ed. (New York: Cambridge University Press, 2006), vol. 5: Tables Ee 541–43, Ee 559–61. A 1943 Commerce Department study characterizes accurate measurement of the effect of the tariff on imports as "a difficult and uncertain undertaking," but concludes that "the wide fluctuations in domestic economic activity and world prices were of much greater consequence in [determining the level of imports] than were upward or downward revisions of the tariff." See Hal B. Lary and associates, *The United States in the World Economy: International Transactions of the United States during the Interwar Period* (Washington, DC: Government Printing Office, 1943), 53–54.

66. Schuker, *American "Reparations" to Germany*, 92–95.

67. Lary and associates, *The United States in the World Economy*, 29; Frank Costigliola, *Awkward Dominion: American Political, Economic, and Cultural Relations with Europe, 1919–1933* (Ithaca, NY: Cornell University Press, 1984), 142–43; James Harvey Rogers, "Foreign Markets and Foreign Credits," in *Recent Economic Changes*, 2:751–56.

68. Hoover, *The Future of Our Foreign Trade: An Address Given at a Dinner in New York City under the Auspices of the Export Managers' Club of New York*, March 16, 1926 (Washington, DC: Government Printing Office, 1926), 7, 12–13; Julius Klein to Sen. Frank B. Willis, December 10, 1927, Frank Willis Papers, Ohio Historical Society, Columbus, Box 15, "Klein, Julius (#33)"; Hoover to Charles G. Dawes, March 1, 1927, Hoover Papers, Commerce Period, Box 11, "Agriculture: Senate Resolution 337, Promotion of Exports, Manufactures & Agricultural Products, 1927"; Department of Commerce, *Fifteenth Annual Report of the Secretary of Commerce* (Washington, DC: Government Printing Office, 1927), xxi–xxvi. The effects of the American tariff were also offset, to some extent, by the net outflow of long-term capital investments from the United States in these years. A 1943 Commerce Department study concludes that the United States' international economic position during the 1920s "would have been much sounder" if investments had been handled more cautiously and if its balance of payments "had consisted somewhat less of capital funds and more of payments for goods and services." Lary and associates, *The United States in the World Economy*, 168.

69. Commerce Department press release, "Statement by Secretary Hoover," January 26, 1926, Hoover Papers, Commerce Period, Box 210, "Foreign Combinations, Rubber, 1926

January"; Commerce Department press release, "Increase in Use of Reclaimed Rubber," February 15, 1926, ibid., Box 484, "Press Releases, 1926 January–February"; Commerce Department Memorandum, "New York Closing Rubber Prices," 1926, ca. November 1, 1926, ibid., Box 531, "Rubber, 1926 March–June"; Commerce Department, "Memorandum Concerning the Results of the Rubber Conservation Movement in the United States," April 27, 1926, ibid., Box 210, "Foreign Combinations, Rubber, Reduction in Price Through Efforts of HH, 1926–1927 & undated."

70. Philip Blair to William Castle, January 6, 1926, Box 3, "Countries Correspondence File: England, Jan.–March 1926," William Richards Castle, Jr., Papers, Hoover Presidential Library, West Branch, Iowa; Castle to Alanson B. Houghton, January 7, 1927, ibid.; "Ridicules Hoover's Plaint on Rubber," *New York Times*, January 12, 1926; "Sir Robert Horne Answers U.S. Roar on Rubber Prices," *New York Times*, January 17, 1926; "Rubber and Mr. Hoover," *Nation*, January 20, 1926, 50; "Howard Defends Britain on Rubber," *New York Times*, January 24, 1926; Sydney Brooks, "Rubber: What America Pays," London *Times*, January 28, 1926; Rep. A. C. Shallenberger to Hoover, January 30, 1926, Hoover Papers, Commerce Period, Box 210, "Foreign Combinations, Rubber, 1926 January"; George E. Roberts to Grosvenor M. Jones, October 18, 1926, ibid., Box 210, "Foreign Combinations, Rubber, 1926, February–December."

71. Henry Chalmers to Hoover, January 6, 1926, Hoover to Howard Gessner, January 12, 1926, both in Hoover Papers, Commerce Period, Box 210, "Foreign Combinations, Rubber, Comments, 1926 January"; "Rubber Restriction," *Economist* (London), January 30, 1926; press release by A. L. Viles, General Manager of the Rubber Association of America, on the rubber situation, February 24, 1926, Hoover Papers, Commerce Period, Box 210, "Foreign Combinations, Statement by A. L. Viles, 1926"; Hoover to Amb. Alanson B. Houghton, May 1, 1926, ibid., Box 572, "State Department: Secretary of State Kellogg, Frank B., 1926 January–April"; Julius Klein to Hoover, May 18, 1926; George E. Roberts to Grosvenor M. Jones, October 18, 1926; E. G. Holt to Hoover, December 31, 1926, all in ibid., Box 210, "Foreign Combinations, Rubber, 1926 February–December"; Costigliola, *Awkward Dominion*, 144–45. The value of crude rubber imports built rapidly from an index of about 76 in 1924 to an index of about 210 in 1926 and then declined even more precipitously in 1926 to 1928, leveled briefly in 1928 to 1929, and then dropped again. See Lary and associates, *The United States in the World Economy*, 44, Chart 8-A.

72. Rickard Diaries, January 4, 19, 1926, Box 1, "1926"; Hoover, "Statement for the *New York Times*," January 4, 1926; "Statement by Secretary Hoover Regarding Foreign Monopolies," January 4, 1926; "Foreign Combinations to Control Prices of Raw Materials; Statements by Herbert Hoover, and Other Officers of the Department of Commerce," January 6, 1926, all in Hoover Papers, Commerce Period, Box 208, "Foreign Combinations, Miscellaneous, 1926"; draft of report of the House Committee on Interstate and Foreign Commerce on crude rubber, January (?), 1926, ibid., Box 210, "Foreign Combinations, Rubber, 1926 January"; Julius Klein, "Striking Back at Foreign Monopolies," *Country Gentleman*, May 1926, 12–13, 94. Hoover's definition of "economic warfare" is elusive. Apparently, he did not regard controlling the market price of hogs and wheat during and after the war, or pressuring American bankers to deny loans to countries of whose policies he disapproved, as economic warfare.

73. "British Surrender to Rubber Buyers," New York *World*, January 19, 1927; "Rubber Shipments Reduced to 60%," New York *Journal of Commerce*, May 2, 1927; E. G. Holt to Hoover, July 19, 1927, Hoover Papers, Commerce Period, Box 208, "Foreign Combinations, Correspondence, Senator Capper, 1924–1927"; "Hoover Urges Plan for Import Buying," *New York Times*, December 9, 1927; John J. Raskob to Hoover, January 7, 1928, Hoover Papers, Commerce Period, Box 509, "Raskob, John J., 1921–1927"; Walter H. Newton to "My dear Friends," January 23, 1928, Walter H. Newton Papers, Hoover Presidential Library, West Branch, Iowa, Box 1, "Herbert Hoover, Correspondence with or Concerning, 1927–1931"; Commerce Department press release, "American Rubber Situation," undated, ca. 1928, Hoover Papers, Commerce Period, Box 208, "Foreign Combinations, Combined Buying, 1925–1928 & undated"; E. G. Holt, "Five Years of Restriction," *India Rubber World*,

February 1, 1928: 55–57; Rep. L. C. Dyer to Hoover, February 8, 1928, Hoover Papers, Commerce Period, Box 208, "Foreign Combinations, Combined Buying, 1925–1928 & undated"; John J. Raskob to Rep. George S. Graham, March 16, 1928; Commerce Department press release, "Rubber Restriction Reported Removed," April 4, 1928, both in ibid., Box 209, "Foreign Combinations, Reports, Press Releases, Articles, Etc., 1923–1928 & undated."

74. "Rubber Restriction," *New York Times*, June 28, 1927; "Hoover," Whaley-Eaton Newsletter, undated, ca. 1928, Hoover Papers, Commerce Period, Box 210, "Foreign Combinations, Rubber, Comments, 1926 February–1928 & undated"; E. G. Holt to Julius Klein, February 27, 1928, ibid., Box 532, "Rubber, 1928"; John J. Raskob to Hoover, March 6, 1928, ibid., Box 509, "Raskob, John J., 1921–1927"; Hoover, *Memoirs 2*, 83.

75. Thomas Walker Page to Hoover, December 7, 1926; Norman H. Davis to Hoover, January 14, 1927; Hoover to Davis, January 15, 1927; Chester H. Rowell to Hoover, January 15, 1927; Hoover to Rowell, January 20, 1927, all in Hoover Papers, Commerce Period, Box 366, "League of Nations, 1926–1928 & undated"; Christian A. Herter to Allyn A. Young, January 14, 1927; Young to Hoover, February 14, 1927, both in ibid., Box 718, "Young, Allyn Abbott, 1921–1922"; Chester H. Rowell to Hoover, January 25, 1927, ibid., Box 528, "Robinson, Henry M., 1927–1928"; Boyce, "Business as Usual," 110–11; Costigliola, *Awkward Dominion*, 192–96.

76. Unsigned, undated, memorandum, ca. 1928, "Reorganization of the Government's Foreign Trade Service under Hoover," Hoover Papers, Campaign and Transition Period, Box 157, "Subject: Foreign Trade"; Hoover, *The Future of Our Foreign Trade*, 1. For the defensive orientation of Hoover's economic diplomacy, see the unsigned memorandum, "Reorganization of the Government's Foreign Trade Service under Hoover," April 4, 1928, Hoover Papers, Commerce Period, Box 227, "Foreign Trade, 1928 & undated"; Mira Wilkins, *The Maturing of Multinational Enterprise: American Business Abroad from 1914 to 1970* (Cambridge, MA: Harvard University Press, 1974), 138–63; Joseph Brandes, "Herbert Hoover's Economic Diplomacy," in *Herbert Hoover Reassessed: Essays Commemorating the Fiftieth Anniversary of the Inauguration of Our Thirty-First President*, comp. Mark Hatfield (Washington, DC: Government Printing Office, 1981), 380–89. For a description of the role played by "a single country that assumes responsibility for the system" (sometimes referred to as a "stabilizer" or "hegemonic leader") and the American role in the 1920s, see Charles P. Kindleberger, *The World in Depression, 1929–1939: Revised and Enlarged Edition* (Berkeley: University of California Press, 1986), 288–97; David A. Lake, *Power, Protection, and Free Trade: International Sources of U.S. Commercial Strategy, 1887–1939* (Ithaca, NY: Cornell University Press, 1988), 163–83.

77. Hoover to Harding, November 28, 1921, Hoover Papers, Commerce Period, Box 595, "Taxes, 1921–1922"; Hoover to Stephen B. Davis, March 16, 1923, ibid., "Taxes 1923"; Hoover to Samuel McCune Lindsey, April 4, 1924, ibid., Box 371, "Lindsey, Samuel McCune, 1922–25"; "Coolidge Would End Inheritance Taxes; Calls It State Field," *New York Times*, February 20, 1925; unsigned, undated memorandum (probably by Hoover), "Memorandum," Hoover Papers, Commerce Period, Box 596, "Taxes: Inheritance Taxes, 1923–1925 & undated"; Hoover to James C. Darnall, February 8, 1926, ibid., Box 516, "Tax-Exempt Securities, 1922–1926."

78. Hoover, memorandum proposing establishment of a Commerce Department Committee on the Present Business Cycle, March 17, 1927, Hoover Papers, Commerce Period, Box 615, "Unemployment, 1926–1928"; Federal Reserve Board press release, February 5, 1929, Hoover Papers, Campaign and Transition Period, Box 81, "Subject: Banking"; Anthony S. Campagna, *U.S. National Economic Policy, 1917–1985* (Westport, CT: Praeger, 1987), 60–76.

79. Liaquat Ahamed, *Lords of Finance: The Bankers Who Broke the World* (New York: Penguin, 2009), 292–95.

80. Ibid., 293–94.

81. Ibid., 297–99.

82. Ibid., 299–300. For a somewhat more sympathetic treatment of the Long Island conference and Strong's role in these events, see Lester V. Chandler, *Benjamin Strong, Central Banker* (Washington, DC: Brookings Institute, 1958), 374–80.
83. Commerce Department press release, "Statement issued on request of newspapers by Herbert Hoover, Secretary of Commerce," Jan. 1, 1928, Hoover Papers, Commerce Period, Box 188, "Economic Situation in U.S., 1925–1928."
84. Hoover to David Lawrence, December 29, 1927, ibid., Box 123, "Commerce Department, American Business Man and the Department, 1927."

Chapter 20

1. "Address of Honorable Herbert Hoover, Secretary of Commerce, before the Mississippi Valley Association at St. Louis, Missouri," November 22, 1926, Herbert Hoover Papers, Commerce Period, Hoover Presidential Library, West Branch, Iowa, Box 688, "Waterways, 1926 November."
2. Department of Agriculture, *Monthly Weather Review*, suppl. 29, *The Floods of 1927 in the Mississippi Basin* (Washington, DC: Government Printing Office, 1927), 17, 18.
3. Ibid.
4. Ibid., 17–19, 29.
5. "A Brief Chronology of What Congress Has Done since 1824 to Control the Floods of the Mississippi," *Congressional Digest* 7 (February 1928): 44–45; W. M. Black, "The Problem of the Mississippi," *North American Review* 224 (December 1927): 630–40. Jadwin's report is quoted in Pete Daniel, *Deep'n As It Come: The 1927 Mississippi River Flood* (New York: Oxford University Press, 1977), 6.
6. John M. Barry, *Rising Tide: The Great Mississippi Flood of 1927 and How It Changed America* (New York: Simon & Schuster, 1997), 194–209.
7. Gov. Dennis Murphree (Miss.), Rep. J. L. Collier, et al., to Coolidge, April 21, 1927; Hoover to Edward C. Clark, April 23, 1927, both in Calvin Coolidge, President's Personal Files, Microfilm, Forbes Library, Reel 6; press release, "Hoover's Statement," April 22, 1927, Hoover Papers, Commerce Period, Box 402, "Miss. Valley Flood Relief Work: Hoover, Herbert, Material from the President's File, General, 1927 Jan.–May."
8. Ernest P. Bicknell, *Pioneering with the Red Cross: Recollections of an Old Red Crosser* (New York: Macmillan, 1935), 163–75; Foster Rhea Dulles, *The American Red Cross: A History* (New York: Harper & Bros., 1950), 81, 111, 220–44, 265–66. Bicknell's memoir sometimes conflates his experiences during the 1912 Mississippi flood, the 1913 flood on the Ohio, and the 1927 flood. His memoir is useful, however, for its picture of the growth of Red Cross aid in large-scale floods. According to Bicknell, he had only $120,000 for relief during the 1912 disaster.
9. Undated memorandum, "American National Red Cross Mississippi Valley Flood Relief: Department of Agriculture Report: Acres of Flooded Land Planted Last Year (1926) and Acres of Flooded Area Expected to be Planted This Year (1927)," Hoover Papers, Commerce Period, Box 397, "Miss. Valley Flood-Relief Work, Agriculture, 1927 April–June"; Dulles, *American Red Cross*, 237–38.
10. Hoover to Secretary of Navy Curtis Wilbur, April 23, 1927; Acting Commissioner of Lighthouses Bowerman to lighthouse superintendent, New Orleans, April 23, 1923, both in Hoover Papers, Commerce Period, Box 396, "Mississippi Valley Flood-Relief Work, Miscellaneous, 1927 April"; George R. Spalding, Corps of Engineers director of transport, "Memorandum of Boats, Airplanes and Radio Sets in Use This Date," May 5, 1927, ibid., Box 398, "Miss. Valley Flood: Relief Work, Boat Service, 1927 May 5–15"; Hoover, *Memoirs: The Cabinet and the Presidency, 1920–1933* (New York: Macmillan, 1952), 125–26 (hereafter, *Memoirs* 2).
11. "Cabinet Members Ask for $5,000,000 for Flood Relief," Washington *Post*, April 23, 1927; Dulles, *American Red Cross*, 270; Barry, *Rising Tide*, 240, 272–73.
12. Barry, *Rising Tide*, 273–75.

13. George Akerson to manager, Peabody Hotel, Memphis, ca. April 24, 1923, Hoover Papers, Commerce Period, Box 612, "Trips 1927: Mississippi Valley Trips, 1927 April–July"; Ned McIntosh to George Akerson, May 4, 1927; Akerson to McIntosh, May 4, 1927, both in ibid., Box 396, "Miss. Valley Flood: Relief Work, Miscellaneous, 1927 May 1–5"; James L. Fieser to Henry M. Baker, May 5, 1927, ibid., Box 408, "Mississippi Valley Flood Relief Work: Red Cross, Misc., 1927 May 1–15"; Lawrence Richey to George Akerson, May 9, 1927, ibid., Box 396, "Miss. Valley Flood Relief Work, Miscellaneous, 1927 May 6–10"; Hoover to Mrs. M. Butler, May 10, 1927, ibid., Box 389, "Meloney, Mrs. Marie M., 1922–1928 & undated"; Barry, *Rising Tide*, 273; Craig Lloyd, *Aggressive Introvert: A Study of Herbert Hoover and Public Relations Management, 1912–1932* (Columbus: Ohio State University Press, 1972), 75, 84–85. On May 10, 1927, Hoover's staff produced a five-page memo on "The Mississippi Flood and Mr. Hoover's Part in Relief" as it had been reported in the press. See Hoover Papers, Commerce Period, Box 399, "Mississippi Valley Flood: Relief Work, Clippings, Press Analysis, 1927, May."
14. William Faulkner, "Old Man," in *The Portable Faulkner*, ed. Malcolm Cowley (New York: Viking, 1946), 561. This 1927 story provides an unforgettably vivid picture of what the flood was like to those trapped by it.
15. Cline to Hoover, May 17, 1927, Hoover Papers, Commerce Period, Box 401, "Miss. Valley Flood Relief Work: Gauge Readings, 1927 April–May." Many of Cline's reports may be found in this file. For Cline and the Galveston hurricane, see Erik Larson, *Isaac's Storm: A Man, A Time, and the Deadliest Hurricane in History* (New York: Random House, 1999).
16. James L. Fieser to Hoover, November 8, 1928, enclosing press release, "Red Cross Issues Summary Report on Mississippi Valley Flood Relief Work," Hoover Papers, Campaign and Transition Period, Hoover Presidential Library, West Branch, Iowa, Box 25, "General Corres.: Fieser, James"; William A. Hard, *Who's Hoover?* (New York: Dodd, Mead, 1928), 193; "Address by Herbert Hoover, Secretary of Commerce, Delivered by Radio," May 28, 1927, Hoover Papers, Commerce Period, Box 411, "Miss. Valley Flood Relief Work: Reports, Statements, etc., 1927 May 26–31"; Hoover to (?) Porter, May 21, 23, 1927; James Fieser to Leonard Coop, May 21, 1927, both in ibid., Box 410, "Mississippi Valley Flood Relief Work: Rehabilitation, Louisiana, 1927 May 21–25"; Hoover, *Memoirs* 2, 126. It is unclear who did the construction work in the camps. Hoover implied the workers were local volunteers, but since gangs of black sharecroppers were impressed to sandbag the levees under the direction of Guardsmen, it seems probable that a similar method provided labor to build the camps.
17. Hoover press release at Baton Rouge, May 7, 1927, Hoover Papers, Commerce Period, Box 411, "Mississippi Valley Flood: Relief Work, Reports, Statements, Press Releases, Herbert Hoover, 1927 May 1–25"; Isaac Cline, "Special Flood Bulletin, U.S. Department of Agriculture, Weather Bureau, New Orleans, LA, May 15, 1927, 11:00 A.M.," ibid., Box 415, "Miss. Valley Flood: Relief Work, Weather Bureau Reports, Dr. Cline, 1927 April–May"; Hoover to Cline, May 20, 1927, and Hoover to John M. Parker, May 20, 1927, both in ibid., Box 410, "Mississippi Valley Flood Relief Work: Rehabilitation, Louisiana, 1927 May 16–20"; Edgar Rickard Diaries, Hoover Presidential Library, West Branch, Iowa, June 1, 1927, Box 1, "1927"; Hoover, *Memoirs* 2, 127–30; Barry, *Rising Tide*, 284–85; Bicknell, *Pioneering with the Red Cross*, 165–66.
18. Barry, *Rising Tide*, 240–56.
19. Lou Hoover to Allan Hoover, April 26, 1927, Allan Hoover Papers, Hoover Presidential Library, West Branch, Iowa, Box 2, "Correspondence with Lou Henry Hoover, 1927 March–September"; "New Orleans Waits Levee Blast as Last Effort to Stem Flood," Washington *Times*, April 29, 1927.
20. *Monthly Weather Review*, 17; "New Orleans Waits Levee Blast as Last Effort to Stem Flood," Washington *Times*, April 29, 1927; Hoover, "An Appeal to the American People for Support [of the] Mississippi Flood Sufferers," April 30, 1927, Hoover Papers, Commerce Period, Box 402, "Miss. Valley Flood Relief Work: Hoover, Herbert, Material from the President's File, General, 1927 Jan.–May"; Barry, *Rising Tide*, 257–58. Cline issued a "Special Flood Bulletin" on May 10 reporting that the "highest stage" had already been recorded at New

Orleans and that the river level had been falling for several days as a result of diversion into the Atchafalaya basin. See "Special Flood Bulletin, U.S. Department of Agriculture Weather Bureau, New Orleans, LA., May 10, 1927, 11:00 A.M.," Hoover Papers, Commerce Period, Box 415, "Miss. Valley Flood: Relief Work, Weather Bureau Reports, Dr. Cline, 1927 April–May."

21. Hoover press release, "Secretary Hoover Says," ca. April 29, 1927, Hoover Papers, Commerce Period, Box 416, "Mississippi and Vermont, Flood Relief, 1927–1928"; Hoover, "An Appeal to the American People for Support [of the] Mississippi Flood Sufferers," April 30, 1927, ibid., Box 402, "Miss. Valley Flood Relief Work: Hoover, Herbert, Material from the President's File, General, 1927 Jan.–May"; Hoover to Rep. William E. Hull, May 4, 1927, ibid., Box 396, "Miss. Valley Flood: Relief Work, Miscellaneous, 1927 April"; "Hoover, Jadwin Urge Stronger Levees On River," New Orleans *Times-Picayune*, May 1, 1927; memorandum on flooded area from Commerce Department Domestic Commerce Division, May 7, 1927, Hoover Papers, Commerce Period, Box 396, "Miss. Valley Flood: Relief Work, Miscellaneous, 1927 May 6–10"; businessman quoted in Whaley-Eaton newsletter no. 453, May 7, 1927, ibid., Box 216, "Foreign Debts, Great Britain, 1926–1927 & undated."

22. Pilgrim Baptist Church of St. Paul, Minnesota, to Hoover, May 2, 1927; Hoover to Pilgrim Baptist Church, May 3, 1927; Sen. Arthur Capper to Hoover, May 10, 1927; Hoover to Capper, May 13, 1927; Lawrence Richey to George Akerson, May 12, 1927; Hoover to Henry M. Baker, May 13, 1921; Baker to Hoover, May 13, 1921; Margaret Butler to James Fieser, May 14, 1927; Hoover to Robert E. Bondy, May 21, 1927; Robert R. Moton to Hoover, May 26, 1927; Hoover to Moton, May 28, 1927, all in Hoover Papers, Commerce Period, Box 404, "Mississippi Valley Flood: Relief Work, Negroes, 1927 May." Announced on the same day that Hoover made a major radio address about the flood relief program, news of the appointment of the Moton Commission was shoved to the bottom of p. 10 in the *New York Times*. See "Flood Envelops Two More Towns," *New York Times*, May 29, 1927.

23. Walter White, preliminary report on conditions in the flood zone, May 24, 1927; Helen Boardman, "Vicksburg: A Victory for the South," May 23, 1927, both in NAACP Microfilm Records, Part 10, Reel 13. White's report was widely covered in the northern press (e.g., see "Charge Flood Zone Abuses," *New York Times*, May 28, 1927), and a slightly condensed version of it was published as "The Negro and the Flood," *Nation*, June 22, 1927, 688–89.

24. Mrs. L. M. Moon to James Weldon Johnson, May 14, 1927; R. E. Malone to Johnson, May 19, 1927, both in NAACP Records, Part 10, Reel 13; R. R. Moton to Hoover, ca. December 12, 1927, Hoover Papers, Commerce Period, Box 404, "Miss. Valley Flood Relief Work: Negroes, 1927 August–December." Ironically, the Moton Commission subsequently received reports that Jefferson County, Arkansas, of which Pine Bluff was the county seat, was one of the places where rehabilitation aid was entirely in the hands of plantation owners who were charging tenants for it. See Hoover to Fieser, enclosing undated, unsigned memorandum on the situation, June 20, 1927, and Fieser to Moton, June 22, 1927, both in ibid., Box 404, "Miss. Valley Flood Relief Work: Negroes, 1927 June 16–30."

25. Henry M. Baker to James L. Fieser, May 14, 1927; J. W. Richardson to James L. Fieser, May 18, 1927, both in Hoover Papers, Commerce Period, Box 404, "Mississippi Valley Flood: Relief Work, Negroes, 1927 May"; Hoover to Sen. Arthur Capper, May 13, 1927, ibid., Box 77, "Capper, Senator Arthur, 1924–1928"; Hoover to Walter White, June 21, 1927, ibid., Box 404, "Miss. Valley Flood Relief Work: Negroes, 1927 June 1–15"; Will Irwin to Walter White, June 11, 1927, NAACP Records, Part 10, Reel 13. See also the unsigned memorandum, "Red Cross Replies to N.A.A.C.P. Charges of Peonage," ca. July 3, 1927, ibid. Irwin wrote to Hoover that White was a "fanatic" and urged that conservative black leaders be encouraged "to placate or squelch him." See Lawrence Richey to George Akerson, June 9, 1927, Hoover Papers, Commerce Period, Box 404, "Miss. Valley Flood Relief Work: Negroes, 1927 June 1–15." The *Final Report of the Colored Advisory Commission: Mississippi Valley Flood Disaster, 1927* (Washington, DC: American Red Cross, 1927), released in December 1927, omitted charges of abuses and emphasized recommendations for policy changes in the camps that were, by that time, largely moot.

26. Donald J. Lisio, *Hoover, Blacks, and Lily-Whites: A Study of Southern Strategies* (Chapel Hill: University of North Carolina Press, 1985), 29.

27. Hoover to H. C. Couch and L. O. Crosby, July 8, 1927, Hoover Papers, Commerce Period, Box 404, "Miss. Valley Flood Relief Work: Negroes, 1927 July"; Hoover, "Memorandum," July 9, 1927, ibid., Box 414, "Mississippi Valley Flood Relief Work: Rockefeller Foundation, 1927"; Rickard Diaries, July 11, 1927, Box 1, "1927."

28. James L. Fieser to Hoover, August 27, 1927, Hoover Papers, Commerce Period, Box 404, "Miss. Valley Flood Relief Work: Negroes, 1927 August–December"; R. R. Moton to Hoover, January 4, 1928, ibid., Box 435, "Negroes: Survey of Land Situation in South, 1928"; William Jay Schieffelin to Hoover, January 9 and February 6, 1928; Hoover to Schieffelin, January 12 and February 3, 1928; Moton to Hoover, January 18 and February 27, 1928, all in ibid., Box 435, "Negroes: Plan to Make Good Farm Land in South Avail., 1927–1928."

29. R. R. Moton to Leonard Outhwaite, February 27, 1928; Edwin R. Embree to Hoover, March 1, 1928; Embree to Vernon Kellogg, March 1, 1928; Kellogg to Embree, March 3, 1928; Kellogg to Hoover, March 5, 1928; Hoover to Embree, March 6, 1928; Hoover to Moton, March 11, 1928, all in Hoover Papers, Commerce Period, Box 435, "Negroes: Plan to Make Good Land in South Available, 1927–1928."

30. Lisio, *Hoover, Blacks, and Lily-Whites,* 29–30. Barry, *Rising Tide,* 389–95, offers a more critical interpretation of this episode and Hoover's relationship to African Americans in general. The Commerce Department, initially reluctant even to publicize Jackson's appointment, gradually gave him greater support, but little about him appears in the official record. For a thorough account of how he came to be appointed and how his career unfolded, see Robert E. Weems, Jr., and Lewis A. Randolph, "'The Right Man': James A. Jackson and the Origins of U.S. Government Interest in Black Business," *Enterprise and Society* 6 (June 2005): 254–77.

31. Rep. W. M. Whittington to Hoover, April 28, 1927, Hoover Papers, Commerce Period, Box 396, "Miss. Valley Flood: Relief Work, Miscellaneous, 1927 April"; Hoover press release, "Secretary Hoover Says," April 29, 1927, ibid., Box 416, "Mississippi and Vermont Flood Relief, 1927"; Hoover, radio broadcast, "An Appeal to the American People for Support [for the] Mississippi Flood Sufferers," April 30, 1927; Hoover, "Report to the President's Special Mississippi Flood Committee," May 2, 1927, both in ibid., Box 402, "Miss. Valley Flood Relief Work: Hoover, Herbert, Material from the President's File, General, 1927 Jan.–May"; James L. Fieser to James K. McClintock, May 9, 1927, ibid., Box 408, "Mississippi Valley Flood Relief Work: Red Cross, Misc., 1927 May 1–15"; Hoover and Fieser, "Memorandum on Principles of Organization, Mississippi Flood Disaster," ca. May 13, 1927, ibid., Box 407, "Mississippi Valley Flood Relief Work: President, 1927–1928"; Hoover and Fieser, "Memorandum of Instructions to County Committees for Carrying Out Reconstruction Measures," May 19, 1927, ibid., Box 396, "Miss. Valley Flood Relief Work: Miscellaneous, 1927 May 16–20"; Fletcher Chenault, "Arkansas to Care for Own Refugees," Little Rock *Arkansas Gazette,* April 30, 1927; "Hoover, Jadwin Urge Stronger Levees on River," New Orleans *Times Picayune,* May 1, 1927.

32. H. C. Couch to Hoover, May 3, 4, 1927; Hoover to Couch, May 3, 4, 1927; L. O. Crosby to Hoover, May 3, 1927, all in Hoover Papers, Commerce Period, Box 396, "Mississippi Valley Flood: Relief Work, Miscellaneous, 1927 May 1–5"; Hoover to Coolidge, May 6, 1927, Coolidge, President's Personal Files, Microfilm, Reel 6; George E. Scott to James L. Fieser, May 8, 1927; Hoover to Eugene Meyer, May 8, 1927; H. C. Couch to Hoover, May 9, 11, 1927; Hoover to Couch, May 9, 26, 1927, all in Hoover Papers, Commerce Period, Box 409, "Mississippi Valley Flood Relief Work: Rehabilitation, Arkansas, 1927 April–May"; press release, "Mississippi Rehabilitation Corporation: Plans for Making Crop Production Loans," undated, ca. May 6, 1927, ibid., Box 412, "Miss. Valley Flood Relief Work: Reports Miscellaneous, 1928 & undated"; Hoover to Coolidge, May 10, 1927, ibid., Box 407, "Mississippi Valley Flood Relief Work: President, 1927–1928."

33. Coolidge, President's Personal Files, Microfilm, Reel 129, has a number of appeals from members of Congress for a special session of Congress. See also Hoover to S. R. Bertron, May 31, 1927, Hoover Papers, Commerce Period, Box 50, "Bertron, Samuel R.,

1923–1927"; Donald R. McCoy, *Calvin Coolidge: The Quiet President* (New York: Macmillan, 1967), 54; Robert H. Ferrell, *The Presidency of Calvin Coolidge* (Lawrence: University Press of Kansas, 1998), 85.

34. For the difficulties of the private credit operations, see Hoover to Eugene Meyer, May 8, 9 (two telegrams), 10, 25, 1927; Meyer to Hoover, May 8, 9, 10, 1927; Hoover to Louis Pearson (Lewis Pierson), May 26, 1927 (two telegrams), all in Hoover Papers, Commerce Period, Box 400, "Miss. Valley Flood Relief Work: Financial Collections, Commitments, etc., 1927"; "Flood Rehabilitation Planned by U.S. Chamber," Washington *Post*, May 24, 1927; "Hoover Returns to Form Flood Finance Organization," Washington *Star*, May 31, 1927; Alden H. Little to Hoover, May 24, 1927, Hoover Papers, Commerce Period, Box 396, "Miss. Valley Flood Relief Work, Miscellaneous, 1927 May 21–25"; Barry, *Rising Tide*, 377.

35. Press release, "Secretary Hoover's Statement on May 15, 1927," Hoover Papers, Commerce Period, Box 402, "Miss. Valley Flood Relief Work: Hoover, Herbert, Material from the President's File, General, 1927 Jan.–May."

36. Rickard Diaries, June 3, 1927, Box 1, "1927"; Raymond P. Brandt, "Hoover, Directing Flood Relief, Follows Method He Evolved in China, Belgium and Russia," St. Louis *Post Dispatch*, May 1, 1927; "More Help for Flood Refugees," Columbus *Ohio State Journal*, May 4, 1927; unidentified clipping, Charles P. Stewart, "Hoover's Flood Activities Create Talk of Presidency," May 6, 1923, Hoover Papers, Commerce Period, Box 398, "Miss. Valley Flood Relief Work: Clippings, 1927 May"; Vernon Kellogg, "Hoover: First Aid to the Distressed," Washington *Sunday Star*, May 8, 1927; R. M. Gates, "Nation Turns to Hoover in Time of National Disaster," Memphis *Commercial Appeal*, May 9, 1927; "Give, Don't Lend to the South," *Christian Science Monitor*, May 12, 1927; "President Coolidge and the Mississippi Valley Overflow," Baltimore *Manufacturers Record*, May 12, 1927; "Will Coolidge Shatter the Third-Term Tradition," *Literary Digest* May 14, 1927, 5–7; "Again Hoover Does an Emergency Job," *New York Times Magazine*, May 15, 1927; "Calls on Coolidge for Flood Action," *New York Times*, May 19, 1927. The May 19 article, which cited Franklin Roosevelt's call for a federal relief appropriation to supplement private efforts, was a forecast of differences between Hoover and Roosevelt during the Depression. The most strident dissent from the chorus of praise was "Two Louisiana Disasters—The Flood and Hoover," *Daily Worker*, May 10, 1927. Hoover's staff in Washington carefully compiled summaries of what was being said in the press about his work. See memorandum, "The Mississippi Flood and Mr. Hoover's Part in Relief," May 10, 14, 17, 20, 23, 25, 27, 1927, Hoover Papers, Commerce Period, Box 399, "Mississippi Valley Flood Relief Work: Clippings, Press Analysis, 1927 May," and June 1, 4, 1927, in ibid., Box 399, "Mississippi Valley Flood Relief Work: Clippings, Press Analysis, 1927 June."

37. George E. Vincent to Hoover, June 1, 1927, Hoover Papers, Commerce Period, Box 414, "Mississippi Valley Flood Relief Work: Rockefeller Foundation, 1927"; James L. Fieser to Hoover, June 2, 1927, ibid., Box 400, "Miss. Valley Flood Relief Work: Financial, 1927 April–June"; George E. Vincent to Hoover, June 9, 1927, ibid., Box 396, "Miss. Valley Flood Relief Work: Miscellaneous, 1927 June 1–10"; "The Flood Situation," New York *Medical Journal Record*, June 15, 1927; press release, "Statement by Secretary Hoover," June 21, 1927, Hoover Papers, Commerce Period, Box 412, "Miss. Valley Flood Relief Work: Reports, Statements, Press Releases, Herbert Hoover, 1927 June"; Commerce Department press release, "Address Delivered by Herbert Hoover at Little Rock, Arkansas," June 25, 1927, ibid.; J. H. O'Neill, "Relief Measures During and Following the Mississippi Valley Flood," *American Journal of Public Health* 18 (February 1928): 159; Hoover, *Memoirs* 2, 130–31.

38. John M. Parker to Hoover, June 2, 1922, and Hoover to Parker, June 9, 1922, both in Hoover Papers, Commerce Period, Box 460, "Parker, John M., 1921–1927"; "River Efficiency Vital in 25 Years, Hoover Declares," St. Louis *Times*, November 22, 1926; press release, "Secretary Hoover Says," April 29, 1927, Hoover Papers, Commerce Period, Box 416, "Mississippi and Vermont, Flood Relief, 1927–1928."

39. "Hoover, Jadwin Urge Stronger Levees on River," New Orleans *Times Picayune*, May 1, 1927; "President Coolidge and the Mississippi River Overflow," *Manufacturers Record*, May

12, 1927; "Calls on Coolidge for Flood Action," *New York Times*, May 19, 1927; "Hoover Takes Steps to Mend Broken Dikes," *New York Times*, May 19, 1927; "The Fight to Prevent Another Mississippi Flood," *Literary Digest*, May 21, 1927, 8–9. Coolidge held federal expenditures to about $3.1 billion (with revenues of about $3.8 billion) every year during his administration. See Ferrell, *Presidency of Calvin Coolidge*, 26.

40. Rex Collier, "Hoover Opposes Delay in Sure Flood Remedy," Washington *Star*, May 29, 1927.

41. "Resolutions Unanimously Adopted at the Flood Control Conference Held in Chicago, Ill.," June 2–4, 1927, Hoover Papers, Commerce Period, Box 399, "Mississippi Valley Flood Relief Work: Conferences, Chicago, 1927"; "Address of Maj. General Edgar Jadwin, Chief of Engineers, U.S.A., 'Mississippi River Flood Control,' Delivered at Flood Control Conference, Chicago, Ill.," June 3, 1927, ibid., Box 402, "Miss. Valley Flood Relief Work: Hoover, Herbert, Materials from the President's File, General, 1927 June–July"; W. A. S. Douglas, "27 States Join in Conference to End Floods," Baltimore *Sun*, June 3, 1927.

42. "The Fight to Prevent Another Mississippi Flood," 8; Hoover, "Hoover Outlines Plan to Bridle Mississippi," Los Angeles *Times*, June 12, 1927; "Hoover Says Flood Losses May Total as Much as $400,000,000," New York *World*, June 20, 1927; "Coolidge Receives Hoover Flood Plans," *New York Times*, July 21, 1927. As might have been expected, Coolidge was hesitant about approving any expensive program. See "Coolidge Cautious on Flood Control," Philadelphia *Public Ledger*, July 22, 1927.

43. Edgar Jadwin to Secretary of War Dwight Davis, June 17, 1927; Hoover to Davis, June 22, 1927, both in Coolidge, President's Personal Files, Microfilm, Reel 6;, J. R. Fordyce to Hoover, May 26, 1927, Hoover Papers, Commerce Period, Box 396, "Miss. Valley Flood Relief Work: Miscellaneous, 1927 May 26–31"; Coolidge to Hoover, June 20, 1927 (telegram and letter), June 25 and July 1, 1927; Hoover to Coolidge, June 22 and July 5, 1927, all in ibid., Box 479, "President Coolidge, 1927 June–July"; ibid. For the public recognition of Hoover's service in the flood area, see, for example, "Vision of Greater South Sketched by Mr. Hoover," Little Rock *Arkansas Gazette*, June 26, 1927; "Great Ovation Is Given Mr. Hoover," Little Rock *Arkansas Gazette*, June 26, 1927; "Negroes Award Loving Cup to Hoover," Pine Bluff (Arkansas) *Commonweal*, June 27, 1927.

44. L. O. Crosby to Hoover, May 30, 1927, Hoover Papers, Commerce Period, Box 410, "Mississippi Valley Flood Relief Work: Rehabilitation, Louisiana, 1927 May 26–31"; letterhead sheet for Tri-State Executive Flood Control Committee, ibid., Box 404, "Miss. Valley Flood Relief Work: Personnel"; George Akerson to Col. W. H. Sullivan, August 30, 1927, enclosing itinerary for Hoover's trip, ibid., Box 612, "Trips 1927: New Orleans Trip, 1927 August–September & undated"; Maurice Moore, "Hot Springs Citizens Honored Herbert Hoover in 1927 for His Work as Flood Administrator," Hot Springs *Sentinel-Record*, June 7, 1959.

45. Barry, *Rising Tide*, 401–2.

46. Lawrence Richey to George Akerson, July 27, 1927, Hoover Papers, Commerce Period, Box 400, "Miss. Valley Flood Relief Work: Financial, 1927 July–Dec."; Hoover to Everett Sanders, July 22, 1927, Coolidge, President's Personal Files, Microfilm, Reel 6; Lawrence Richey to George Akerson, August 2, 1927, and Akerson to Richey, July 2, 1927, both in Hoover Papers, Commerce Period, Box 400, "Miss. Valley Flood Relief Work: Federal Government, 1926–1928"; H. M. Lord to Coolidge, August 24, 1927; Coolidge to Secretary Edwin Weeks, August 29, 1927; Rep. Martin B. Madden to Coolidge, September 15, 1927, all in Coolidge, President's Personal Files, Microfilm, Reel 36; Hoover, "Address on Mississippi Flood Situation, Baton Rouge," September 9, 1927, Hoover Papers, Commerce Period, Box 412, "Miss. Valley Flood Relief Work: Reports, Statements, Press Releases, Herbert Hoover, 1927 Aug.–Dec."; Hoover to Coolidge, September 15, 1927, ibid., Box 407, "Mississippi Valley Flood Relief Work: President, 1927–1928"; "Funds Ample for All Needs Now Foreseen," Washington *Herald*, September 16, 1927; H. C. Couch, L. O. Crosby, and W. H. Sullivan to the President (draft), ca. October 10, 1927, Hoover Papers, Commerce Period, Box 407, "Mississippi Valley Flood Relief Work: President, 1927–1928."

47. Barry, *Rising Tide*, 402–3; William MacDonald, "Plans for National Flood Relief and Control," *Current History* 27 (November 1927): 269. The Commerce Department carefully

dissociated itself from any specific planning for flood control. See Reuben B. Sleight to Fred G. Frost, October 13, 1927, Hoover Papers, Commerce Period, Box 397, "Miss. Valley Flood Relief Work: Miscellaneous, 1927 Sept.–Dec."

48. "President Coolidge's Analysis of Mississippi Flood Control Problem," *Congressional Digest* 7 (February 1928): 46; "The President Transmits to Congress Flood Control Plan of Army Engineers," *Congressional Digest* 7 (February 1928): 47.

49. Edgar Jadwin, "The Plan for Flood Control of the Mississippi River in Its Alluvial Valley," *Annals of the American Academy of Political and Social Science* 135 (January 1928): 35–36; press release of the League of Women Voters, "Address of Major General Edgar Jadwin, Chief of Engineers, U.S. Army, Given Thursday Night, January 31, in the Radio 'Voters' Service' Program Devoted to 'Flood Control,'" January 31, 1928, Hoover Papers, Commerce Period, Box 431, "National League of Women Voters, 1928"; "A Summary of the Mississippi River Commission's Recommendations for the Control of Floods," *Congressional Digest* 7 (February 1928): 49, 70.

50. Sen. Joseph E. Ransdell to Hoover, November 21, 1927, Hoover Papers, Commerce Period, Box 550, "Senate: Ransdell, Joseph E., 1921–1928 & undated"; L. O. Crosby to Hoover, January 3, 1928, and Hoover to Crosby, January 6, 1928, both in ibid., Box 407, "Mississippi Valley Flood Relief Work: President, 1927–1928"; "Congress Takes Up Flood Control Program," *Congressional Digest* 7 (February 1928): 47–48.

51. Hoover to L. O. Crosby, January 6, 1928, Hoover Papers, Commerce Period, Box 407, "Mississippi Valley Flood Relief Work: President, 1927–1928"; "May Revise Flood Program," *New York Times*, January 4, 1928; "Coolidge Unmoved on Flood Control," Washington *Post*, February 18, 1928; "Local Contributions for Flood Relief Still Favored by President," *U.S. Daily*, February 18, 1928; "Coolidge View on Flood Plans Is Made Clear," New York *Sun*, February 27, 1928; "Coolidge Holds to Position on Flood Control," New York *Sun* (February 27, 1928.

52. "Nothing Done Yet for Flood Control," *Literary Digest*, March 10, 1928, 10–11; "Congress Takes Up Flood Control Program," *Congressional Digest* 7 (February 1928): 47–48; Hoover, "Testimony before Senate Commerce Committee," February 24, 1928, Hoover Papers, Commerce Period, Box 401, "Miss. Valley Flood Relief Work: Hearings, 1928"; "A Compromise on Flood Control," *Outlook* 148 (March 14, 1928): 411.

53. "Floods and the Jones Measure," *American Review of Reviews* 77 (May 1928): 454; "The President's Victory on Flood Control," *Literary Digest* 97 (May 19, 1928): 9–10; "The Fight with the Rampageous Father of Waters," *Literary Digest* 97 (November 3, 1928): 21–22; Barry, *Rising Tide*, 405–6.

54. James L. Fieser to Hoover, November 6, 1928, enclosing press release, "Red Cross Issues Summary Report on Mississippi Valley Flood Relief Work," Hoover Papers, Campaign and Transition Period, Box 25, "General Corres.: Fieser, James"; "The Mississippi Valley Flood of 1927: A Second Preliminary Summary Report by the American National Red Cross," January 1928, Hoover Papers, Commerce Period, Box 416, "Mississippi Valley Flood Relief Work: Weather Bureau Reports, Dr. Cline, 1928 & undated"; Hoover to W. D. Boies, March 12, 1928, ibid., Box 412, "Miss. Valley Flood Relief Work: Reports, Statements, Press Releases, Herbert Hoover, 1928 & undated"; Barry, *Rising Tide*, 285–86. Pete Daniel, who examined with some care Hoover's claim that only a few people died after he took over the relief program, concludes that the actual death count in that period was probably nearer two hundred. See Daniel, *Deep'n As It Come*, 88, 90.

55. Deborah Pickman Clifford and Nicholas R. Clifford, *"The Troubled Roar of the Water": Vermont in Flood and Recovery, 1927–1931* (Durham: University of New Hampshire Press, 2007), 2–32; Charles T. Walter, "Lights and Shadows of the Flood of 1927: Vermont at Its Worst, Vermonters at Their Best," St. Johnsbury (Vermont) *St. Johnsbury Republican*, 1928; "Rising Floods Ravage New England; 212 Reported Lost in Montpelier; 18 Dead Elsewhere; Damage Heavy," *New York Times*, November 5, 1927; "20-Degree Drop in Temperature Due Today; Snow Falls Up-State, While West Thaws Out," *New York Times*, November 4, 1927; "Seek Vainly to Reach Montpelier,"; "Towns Isolated in Granite State"; "Rutland Cut Off By Road"; "Connecticut Suffers $1,000,000 Flood Loss"; "Big Power Systems Are Hit by

Floods"; "New Haven Railroad Hard Hit," all in *New York Times*, November 5, 1927; "New England Flood Deaths Near 100; Heaviest Damage in Vermont Towns; Massachusetts Now Facing Crisis"; "Situation in the Flood Stricken States as Told in Late But Incomplete Reports"; "Coolidge Neighbor Is Victim of Floods," all in *New York Times*, November 6, 1927.

56. "Cold Increases Misery as Flood Waters Recede; Army Aids New England," *New York Times*, November 8, 1927; "Vermont Organizes Flood Relief Work; Whole Area Eased," *New York Times*, November 9, 1927; Red Cross press release, "Red Cross Makes $75,000 Initial Appropriation to Meet Immediate Needs in New England Flood Area," Hoover Papers, Commerce Period, Box 680, "Vermont Flood Relief Work: Reports, Press Releases, etc., 1927"; Clifford and Clifford, *"The Troubled Roar,"* 64–71.

57. "Vermont Appeals to Coolidge for Aid," *New York Times*, November 10, 1927; Clifford and Clifford, *"The Troubled Roar,"* 72–76.

58. "President Directs Flood Relief Study," *New York Times*, November 11, 1927; "Hoover and Sargent Going to Vermont," *New York Times*, November 13, 1927; Red Cross press release, "Red Cross Official to Confer with Hoover and Sargent in New England Flood Area," November 12, 1927, Hoover Papers, Commerce Period, Box 680, "Vermont Flood Relief Work: Reports, Press Releases, etc., 1927"; Bradley Nash to George Akerson, November 12, 1927, ibid., Box 562, "Sleight, Reuben B., 1926–1927"; Hoover to Thomas W. Lamont, November 12, 1927, ibid., Box 363, "Lamont, Thomas W., 1921–1927"; Hoover to Gov. John E. Weeks, November 12, 1927, ibid., Box 679, "Vermont Flood Relief Work: General, 1927–1928"; "Vermont Speeds Up Its Reconstruction," *New York Times*, November 15, 1927; Col. F. E. Hopkins memorandum, "Flood Relief Situation from Point of View of Military Authorities," November 15, 1927, Hoover Papers, Commerce Period, Box 679, "Vermont Flood Relief Work: General, 1927–1928"; unsigned memorandum, "Railroad Transportation Report," November 15, 1927, ibid.; Red Cross press release, "Red Cross Vice Chairman Says New England Flood Reconstruction May Continue into Spring Months," November 19, 1927, ibid., Box 680, "Vermont Flood Relief Work: Reports, Press Releases, etc., 1927." One of Hoover's young assistants, Reuben Sleight, died in an airplane crash while surveying flood damage on November 14 in preparation for Hoover's arrival. See Lawrence Richey to George Akerson, November 14, 1927; Hoover to Mrs. Reuben Sleight, ca. November 14, 1927; Hoover to Adj. Gen. Herbert T. Johnson, November 28, 1927, all in Hoover Papers, Commerce Period, Box 562, "Sleight, Reuben B., Death and Funeral Arrangements, 1927–1928."

59. Hoover to Gov. John E. Weeks, November 17, 1927, Hoover Papers, Commerce Period, Box 679, "Vermont Flood Relief Work: General, 1927–1928"; "Hoover Traverses Flood Swept Area," *New York Times*, November 17, 1927; Clifford and Clifford, *"The Troubled Roar,"* 122–23. In May 1928, Coolidge signed a bill appropriating $2,654,000 for road repairs in Vermont.

60. "New England Plans Flood Aid Credits," *New York Times*, November 18, 1927; "Forms Flood Board to Aid New England," *New York Times*, November 19, 1927; "Secretary Hoover Tells His Plan for Restoring Vermont's Flood Damage," Springfield *Republican*, November 19, 1927; John S. Lawrence to John Barton Payne, November 18, 21, 1927, Hoover Papers, Commerce Period, Box 679, "New England Flood Relief Work: New England Council, 1927"; Clifford and Clifford, *"The Troubled Roar,"* 41.

61. John Barton Payne to Lawrence, November 19, 22, 1927, Hoover Papers, Commerce Period, Box 679, "New England Flood Relief Work: New England Council, 1927"; W. T. (J.?) Rossiter to Hoover, January 13, 1928; Payne to Lawrence, April 24, 1928; James L. Fieser to Hoover, June 6, 1928, all in ibid., Box 679, "Vermont Flood Relief Work: Financial, 1927–1928"; Red Cross Report No. 2, "New England Flood Relief: Statement of Chapter Allotments and Including Cash Grants as of May 17, 1928," ibid., Box 680, "Vermont Flood Relief Work: Red Cross, 1928"; Clifford and Clifford, *"The Troubled Roar,"* 96–106.

62. Hoover, *Memoirs* 2, 126.

63. Hoover, "Improvement of Our Mid West Waterways: Address before Ninth Annual Convention of Mississippi Valley Association, St. Louis," November 14, 1927, Bible no. 791, Hoover Presidential Library, West Branch, Iowa.
64. Rebecca Solnit, *A Paradise Built in Hell: The Extraordinary Communities that Arise in Disaster* (New York: Viking, 2009), explores this phenomenon.
65. Barry, *Rising Tide*, 412–15; Clifford and Clifford, *"The Troubled Roar,"* 129.

Chapter 21

1. Hiram Johnson to Meyer Lissner, January 24, 1920, Hiram Johnson Papers, Bancroft Library, University of California at Berkeley, Part VI, Box 2, "1920 Jan.–Feb."; Christian A. Herter to Ralph Merritt, October 3, 1921, Hoover Papers, Commerce Period, Hoover Presidential Library, West Branch, Iowa, Box 537, "Sacramento and San Joaquin: Sacramento Flood Control, 1921–26," Budd Frankenfield to Ray Lyman Wilbur, ibid., Box 709, "Wilbur, Ray Lyman, 1922"; Politicus, "Hoover Seeks Johnson Seat in U.S. Senate," undated, unidentified clipping, ibid., Box 552, "Senatorship, 1922"; Hiram Johnson to Hiram Johnson, Jr., June 12, 1922, Johnson Papers, Part VI, Box 3, "1922 June"; Johnson to Hiram Johnson, Jr., and Archibald J. Johnson, June 23, 1922, ibid.; Johnson to C. K. McClatchy, September 15, 1922, ibid., Box 3, "1922 Aug.–Sept."; Mark Requa to Hoover, September 15 and October 4, 1922, both in Hoover Papers, Commerce Period, Box 516, "Requa, Mark L., 1921–1923."
2. "Hoover Not Seeking Senatorship Now," San Francisco *Call*, March 17, 1922; "Hiram Johnson Admits Weakness," San Francisco *Journal*, August 12, 1923; James R. Nourse, "Senator Charges Plot to Block Him in '24 Convention," Seattle *Post-Intelligencer*, August 24, 1923; "Hi Johnson and Herbert Hoover in a Real Feud," unidentified clipping, August 24, 1923, Hoover Papers, Commerce Period, Box 547, "Senate: Johnson, Hiram, Letter to McClatchy, 1923"; Hiram Johnson to Hiram Johnson, Jr., June 13, 1924, Johnson Papers, Part VI, Box 4, "1924 May–Sept."
3. Hoover to Harlan Stone, December 30, 1924, Hoover Papers, Commerce Period, Box 353, "Justice Department: Attorney General Stone, Harlan, 1924–1926 & undated"; Mark Requa to Hoover, March 29, 1924, ibid., Box 517, "Requa, Mark L., 1924 Jan.–Mar."; Requa to Hoover, January 5 and February 12, 19, 1925, ibid., Box 517, "Requa, Mark L., 1925 Jan.–Feb."; Hoover to C. Bascom Slemp, January 26, 1925, Calvin Coolidge, President's Personal Files, Microfilm, Forbes Library, Reel 6; Hoover to Requa, March 17, 1925, and Requa to Hoover, March 18, 1925, both in Hoover Papers, Commerce Period, Box 517, "Requa, Mark L., 1925 March"; Requa, "Memorandum #11," August 25, 1925, ibid., Box 517, "1925 April–August"; Edgar Rickard Diaries, Hoover Presidential Library, West Branch, Iowa, August 19, 1925, Box 1, "July-December 1925."
4. Oswald Garrison Villard, "Presidential Possibilities, IV: Herbert C. Hoover," *Nation* February 29, 1928, 235; Rickard Diaries, September 22 and December 31, 1925, Box 1, "July–December 1925"; Craig Lloyd, *Aggressive Introvert: A Study of Herbert Hoover and Public Relations Management, 1912–1932* (Columbus: Ohio State University Press, 1972), 123–42.
5. Hoover to Henry M. Robinson, January 9, 1926, Hoover Papers, Commerce Period, Box 528, "Robinson, Henry M., 1926"; Rickard Diaries, March 16; June 6, 8; December 2, 15, 16, 1926, Box 1, "1926"; Hoover to Ray Lyman Wilbur, April 24 and August 6, 1926, both in Hoover Papers, Commerce Period, Box 709, "Wilbur, Ray Lyman, 1926"; Mark Requa to Hoover, June 30, 1926, ibid., Box 517, "Requa, Mark L., 1926 Jan.–June"; Frank C. Page to Harold Phelps Stokes, June 10, 1926, ibid., Box 458, "Page, Frank C., 1921–1928"; Paul S. Clapp to Etta Goodwin, August 24, 1926, ibid., Box 92, "Clapp, Paul S., 1926"; "Hoover Boosted Again As Leader," New York *World*, August 18, 1926; Thomas S. Rockwell to F. M. Feiker, December 3, 1926, Frederick M. Feiker Papers, Hoover Presidential Library, West Branch, Iowa, Box 15, "Subject File: Proposed Books, Hoover's Philosophy-Trade Associations"; Arthur Capper to Henry P. Fletcher, October 24, 1927, Hoover Papers,

Commerce Period, Box 479, "President Coolidge, 1927 August–October." For more complete discussion of Hoover's role in the 1926 campaign, see Chapter 19 in this volume.

6. Rickard Diaries, February 13, 1927, Box 1, "1927"; Roy V. Peel and Thomas C. Donnelly, *The 1928 Campaign: An Analysis* (New York: Arno, 1974; orig. pub. 1931), 7–9, 14.

7. Lou Hoover to Herbert Hoover, Jr., and Allan Hoover, ca. April 16, 1927, Allan Hoover Papers, Hoover Presidential Library, West Branch, Iowa, Box 2, "Correspondence with Lou Henry Hoover, 1927 March–September"; "Coolidge Will Be Candidate for Re-Election Says Solon on Visit Here; Lauds Harbor," San Diego *Tribune*, May 30, 1927; "Third Term Issue to Face Congress," *New York Times*, June 26, 1927.

8. Peel and Donnelly, *The 1928 Campaign*, 18. For Hoover's role in these two floods, see Chapter 20 in this volume.

9. Rickard Diaries, August 2, 3, 28, 29, 1927, Box 1, "1927"; James P. Goodrich to Otto F. Karbe, August 4, 1927, James P. Goodrich Papers, Hoover Presidential Library, West Branch, Iowa, Box 1, "Campaign of 1928"; Walter H. Newton to George Akerson, August 5, 1927, George Edwards Akerson Papers, Hoover Presidential Library, West Branch, Iowa, Box 11, "Newton, Walter H., 1927–1928"; Whaley-Eaton Newsletters, No. 468 (August 20, 1927), No. 469 (August 27, 1927), both in Berkeley Williams Collection, Hoover Presidential Library, West Branch, Iowa, Scrapbook, Box 1, "Correspondence, February 11, 1920–May 27, 1931"; T. T. C. Gregory to George Akerson, August 22, 26, 1927, Akerson Papers, Box 8, "Gregory, Thomas T. C., 1927"; C. A. Jones to Marshall Sheppey, August 24, 1927, Frank Willis Papers, Ohio Historical Society, Columbus, Box 27, "Presidential Possibilities (#21)"; George Barr Baker to Christian A. Herter, September 29, 1927, George Barr Baker Papers, Hoover Institution Archives, Stanford, California, Box 3, "Herter, Christian A."; William Hard, *Who's Hoover?* (New York: Dodd, Mead, 1928); Will Irwin, *Herbert Hoover: A Reminiscent Biography* (New York: Grosset & Dunlap, 1928); Vernon Kellogg, "Herbert Hoover As I Know Him," *The Outlook*, October 19, 1927, 203–6, and *The Outlook* October 26, 1927, 239–41, 244. George Akerson arranged to have a copy of the Irwin biography given to every delegate to the Republican national convention. See Akerson memo, May 19, 1928, Akerson Papers, Box 10, "Irwin, Will, 1927–1928 & undated."

10. George Akerson to T. T. C. Gregory, August 30, 1927, Akerson Papers, Box 8, "Gregory, Thomas T. C., 1927"; transcript of article from the *New York Times*, August 5, 1927, Hoover Papers, Commerce Period, Box 273, "Hoover, Herbert, Presidency 1923–1928 & undated"; William Allen White to George Akerson, enclosing editorial, "Hoover and the West," September 6, 1927, Akerson Papers, Box 14, "White, William Allen, 1927." Rogers had expressed his support for Hoover as early as April. See "Rogers on the Snyder Trial; Mr. Hoover and Other Topics," unidentified clipping, April 30, 1927, Hoover Papers, Commerce Period, Box 529, "Rogers, Will-Roland, P., 1921–1928"; Samuel Crowther, "Why I Am for Hoover: An Interview with Henry Ford," *Saturday Evening Post*, April 21, 1928, 6–7, 124.

11. George Akerson to T. T. C. Gregory, September 16, 1927, Akerson Papers, Box 3, "Gregory, Thomas T. C., 1927"; Akerson to Charles K. Field, October 7, 1927, and Field to Akerson, November 4, 1927, both in ibid., Box 8, "Field, Charles K., 1927–1928"; Akerson to William Allen White, October 10, 1927, and White to Akerson, October 12, 1927, both in ibid., Box 14, "White, William Allen, 1927"; M. Stinson to Lewis Strauss, October 11, 1927, and Julius Rosenwald to Strauss, October 12, 1927, both in Lewis L. Strauss Papers, Hoover Presidential Library, West Branch, Iowa; Box 29E, Name & Subject File I: Accretions, "Hoover, Herbert, 1927"; Julean S. Mason to Mark Sullivan, October 12, 1927, Akerson Papers, Box 13, "Sullivan, Mark, 1927–1928"; William Mullendore to Lawrence Richey, October 17, 1927, and Richey to Mullendore, October 24, 1927, both in William Mullendore Papers, Hoover Presidential Library, West Branch, Iowa, Box 1, "Campaign of 1928, Correspondence"; Rep. Royal C. Johnson to George Akerson, October 22, 1927, Akerson Papers, Box 10, "Johnson, Royal C. 1927"; Benjamin H. Namm to Lewis Strauss, October 26, 1927, Strauss Papers, Name & Subject File I: Accretions, Box 29E, "Hoover, Herbert, 1927"; H. Keith Weeks to George Akerson, October 28 and December 7, 1927, and Akerson to Weeks, December 14, 1927, all in Akerson Papers, Box 14, "Weeks, H. Keith,

1927–1928"; T. T. C. Gregory to Akerson, December 7, 9, 1927, ibid., Box 8, "Gregory, Thomas T. C., 1927"; Akerson to Gregory, December 15, 1927, Box 95, "Political: Misc. corr., 1921–1927," Ray Lyman Wilbur Papers, Hoover Institution Archives, Stanford, California; J. L. Matthews to Washington Hoover for President Headquarters, April 4, 1928, Akerson Papers, Box 13, "Washington Headquarters, 1928 April"; George West, "California Is for Hoover," *Nation*, October 10, 1928 339–40; Richard Coke Lower, *A Bloc of One: The Political Career of Hiram W. Johnson* (Stanford, CA: Stanford University Press, 1993), 239–43. The risk in Akerson's California strategy was that some potential allies might feel excluded. See, for example, Francis Keesling to E. P. Farmer, February 23, 1928; Keesling to Milton H. Esberg, March 17, 1928; and Keesling to Nicholas Murray Butler, April 19, 1928, all in Francis V. Keesling Papers, Rare Books and Special Collections, Green Library, Stanford University, Stanford, California, Box 2, "Folder 13: Polit. Corresp. Out 1925–1928."

12. "Coolidge Eliminates Self from '28 Race; Tells Party to Select Another Candidate as Decision Must Stand; Annual Message Read," *New York Times*, December 7, 1927; J. F. Lucey to Lewis Strauss, December 16, 1927; Strauss memorandum for Hoover, December 19, 1927, both in Strauss Papers, Name & Subject File I: Accretions, Box 29E, "Hoover, Herbert, 1927." For editorials on the subject from Republican newspapers, see Strauss Papers, Name & Subject File I: Accretions, Box 29E, "Hoover, Herbert, Editorials on Presidential Candidacy, 1927 December."

13. Rickard Diaries, December 30, 1927, Box 1, "1927"; E. S. Rochester, *Coolidge-Hoover-Work: An Intimate Review of An Epochal National Campaign for the Presidency of the United States* (Washington, DC: Terminal, 1929), 10–18, 20–22, 27, 31; Eugene Trani, "Hubert Work," *Dictionary of American Biography, Supplement Three, 1941–1945* (New York: Scribner's, 1973), 845–46; "Hoover's Politician," *Collier's*, May 11, 1929, 66.

14. "Squaring Hoover with the Farmers," Literary Digest, November 12, 1927, 11; Herbert Hoover, Memoirs: The Cabinet and the Presidency, 1920–1933 (New York: Macmillan, 1952), 11 (hereafter, Memoirs 2); George Akerson to James W. Good, October 25, 1928, Hoover Papers, Campaign and Transition Period, Hoover Presidential Library, West Branch, Iowa, Box 29, "Genl. Corres.: Good, James W."; David Burner, *Herbert Hoover: A Public Life* (New York: Knopf, 1979), 197–98; Donald J. Lisio, *Hoover, Blacks, and Lily-Whites: A Study of Southern Strategies* (Chapel Hill: University of North Carolina Press, 1985), 35.

15. Lou Hoover to Herbert Hoover, Jr., and Allan Hoover, ca. January 15, 1928; Lou Hoover to Allan Hoover, ca. February 12, 1928, all in Allan Hoover Papers, Box 2, "Correspondence with Lou Henry Hoover, 1928 January–February"; T. T. C. Gregory to George Akerson, January 9, 1928 (two letters), Akerson Papers, Box 8, "Gregory, Thomas T. C., 1928"; "Hoover Is Mellon's Choice for GOP Standard Bearer," Washington *News*, January 14, 1928; "Hoover Men Count 323 Votes at Start; Expect 250 More," *New York Times*, January 23, 1928; "Hoover's Chances," *Literary Digest*, February 4, 1928, 5–7. Mellon regarded Hoover as deplorably isolationist but concluded in late May 1928 that there was "no other place to go but to Hoover." Quoted in Stephen A. Schuker, "American Foreign Policy: The European Dimension, 1921–1929," in *Calvin Coolidge and the Coolidge Era: Essays on the History of the 1920s*, ed. John Earl Haynes (Washington, DC: Library of Congress, 1998), 304.

16. Samuel Lubell first argued that the 1928 election began the realignment of American politics and laid the foundations for the "New Deal coalition," but Allan J. Lichtman has shown that the forces at play in 1928 were far more complex than merely the creation of a Northeast-Solid South coalition. See Lubell, *The Future of American Politics*, 3rd ed. (New York: Harper & Row, 1965), 49–50; Lichtman, *Prejudice and the Old Politics: The Presidential Election of 1928* (Chapel Hill: University of North Carolina Press, 1979).

17. Lawrence H. Fuchs, "Election of 1928," in *History of American Presidential Elections, 1789–1968*, ed. Arthur M. Schlesinger, Jr., Fred L. Israel, and William P. Hansen (New York: Chelsea House, 1971), 3: 2594–95; Christopher M. Finan, *Alfred E. Smith: The Happy Warrior* (New York: Hill and Wang, 2002), 188–91; Donn C. Neal, *The World Beyond the Hudson: Alfred E. Smith and National Politics, 1918–1928* (New York: Garland, 1983), 42–43;

Oscar Handlin, *Al Smith and His America* (Boston: Little, Brown, 1958), 125–27; Lichtman, *Prejudice and the Old Politics*, 11–14.

18. "Hoover Resolves to Seek Delegates in Nine Primaries," *New York Times*, February 6, 1928; James W. Davis, *Presidential Primaries: Road to the White House* (Westport, CT: Greenwood, 1980), 295–97; Hoover, *Memoirs 2*, 190–91. Coolidge's remark—if he made it—certainly did not mean he wanted Hoover to be president, but it is also noteworthy that the president did nothing to block Hoover's nomination. On this, see Donald R. McCoy, *Calvin Coolidge: The Quiet President* (New York: Macmillan, 1967), 390–91.

19. Typescripts of two articles for the New Orleans *Times Picayune*, February 14, 24, 1928, Akerson Papers, Box 14, "Wooton, Paul, 1927–1928."

20. Davis, *Presidential Primaries*, 45, 161–62, 295–98. Some Hoover supporters saw Watson's candidacy in Indiana as part of a complex Klan plot to seize control of the federal government and begged Hoover to enter the primary to foil it. The idea that he did so seems farfetched, but it is not otherwise clear why he chose to enter this primary. See Thomas H. Adams to J. S. Cullinan, February 14, 16, 1928; Cullinan to Lewis Strauss, February 22, 1928; and John W. Hill to Cullinan, March 17, 1928, all in Strauss Papers, Subject File, Box 13, "Campaign of 1928-Indiana." Hoover's managers, knowing how popular George Norris was in Wisconsin, had no intention of entering that race until Lowden entered, at which point they reasoned that a second-place finish for Hoover, even if he received relatively few votes (9.4 percent of the total, as it turned out), would make him the delegates' second choice at the convention. See George B. Lockwood to Hubert Work, February 18, 1928, Akerson Papers, Box 14, "Washington Headquarters, 1928 January–March."

21. Rochester, *Coolidge-Hoover-Work*, 39–40.

22. For a shrewd analysis of the difficulties attendant on organizing in the South, see Henry W. Anderson to Lewis Strauss, April 2, 1928, Strauss Papers, Subject File, Box 9, "Campaign of 1928: Anderson, Henry M. [*sic*]"; Peel and Donnelly, *The 1928 Campaign*, 4.

23. Eugene P. Booze to George Akerson, January 16, 1928, enclosing Booze to Hubert Work, January 16, 1928, Akerson Papers, Box 7, "Booze, Eugene P."; L. O. Crosby to Akerson, February 6, 9, 1928; Akerson to Crosby, February 13, 1928, all in ibid., Box 7, "Crosby, L. O., 1927–1928."

24. Crosby to E. E. Hindman, February 14, 1928; Crosby to Akerson, March 14 and April 10, 1928; Akerson to Crosby, April 16, 1928, all in Akerson Papers, Box 7, "Crosby, L. O., 1927–1928"; Lisio, *Hoover, Blacks, and Lily-Whites*, 47–48.

25. Lisio, *Hoover, Blacks, and Lily-Whites*, 39, 48–49.

26. Fletcher Chenault to Akerson, January 18, 1928, Akerson Papers, Box 7, "Chenault, Fletcher, 1927–1928 & undated"; Akerson to Col. Thad Brown, March 19, 1928, ibid., Box 6, "Brown, Thaddeus H., 1928"; Lisio, *Hoover, Blacks, and Lily-Whites*, 39.

27. Lisio, *Hoover, Blacks, and Lily-Whites*, 38–42, 49.

28. B. D. Nash to Hoover, March 13, 1928, Hoover Papers, Commerce Period, Box 427, "National Association for the Advancement of Colored People, 1921–1928"; draft of Hoover to Sen. H. D. Stephens, April 11, 1928, ibid., Box 550, "Senate: San-Sum, 1921–1928"; George Akerson to Julius Klein, April 16, 1928; "Annual Statement to the Country by the National Negro Press Association," ca. April 1928, both in Akerson Papers, Box 7, "Colored People, 1928 April–May & undated"; John J. Byrd to Hoover, May 16, 1928, Hoover Papers, Commerce Period, Box 543, "Senate: Bar-Bra, 1922–1928"; George Akerson to K. C. Barnard, October 20, 1928, Hoover Papers, Campaign and Transition Period, Box 164, "Subject: Segregation"; William H. Mulqueen to Lewis Strauss, October 29, 1928, Strauss Papers, Subject File, Box 10, "Campaign of 1928: Campaign Literature, Speeches, etc.—Press Releases, Speeches, etc., 1928 Feb.–Nov." Like other potential candidates, both Democratic and Republican, Hoover ignored a questionnaire sent to him by the Associated Negro Press seeking a commitment to support civil rights. See Associated Negro Press release, April 18, 1928, Akerson Papers, Box 7, "Colored People, 1928 April–May & undated."

29. Adaline (Mrs. W. Parmer) Fuller, Jr., Oral History, pp. 11–16, Hoover Presidential Library, West Branch, Iowa; Hoover to Clinton D. Keeler; Hoover to H. A. Shuder, December

31, 1923, both in Hoover Papers, Commerce Period, Box 486, "Prohibition, 1922–1924"; "Women Start Movement to Enforce Law," Washington *Herald*, March 9, 1924; Lou Hoover to Helen Swett Artieda, July 27, 1925, Lou Hoover Papers, Hoover Presidential Library, West Branch, Iowa, Box 74, "Subject File: Prohibition, 1918–33 & undated"; Hoover, "The Mission of the Y.M.C.A.," October 26, 1925, Hoover Papers, Commerce Period, Box 486, "Prohibition, 1925 August–October."

30. Borah to Hoover, February 9, 1928, Hoover Papers, Commerce Period, Box 486, "Prohibition, 1928 & undated"; Rickard Diaries, February 11, 1928, Box 1, "1928"; Hoover to Borah, February 23, 1928, Hoover Papers, Commerce Period, Box 85, "Herbert Hoover Public Statements, Bible Nos. 831-845A, Folder 836: Prohibition Question; Letter to Senator Borah, February 23, 1928"; Rickard Diaries, May 14, 15, 1930, Box 1, "1930"; "Hoover's Stand for Prohibition," *Literary Digest*, March 10, 1928, 7–9.

31. David Cannadine, *Mellon: An American Life* (New York: Knopf, 2006), 362–63; Schuker, "American Foreign Policy," 304.

32. Finan, *Alfred E. Smith*, 202–3; Lester V. Chandler, *Benjamin Strong: Central Banker* (Washington, DC: Brookings Institution, 1958), 254–55; William E. Leuchtenburg, *Herbert Hoover* (New York: Henry Holt, 2009), 71–72; Burner, *Hoover*, 198–99; Rickard Diaries, March 29, 1928, Box 1, "1928."

33. George Akerson to T. T. C. Gregory, February 16, 1928, Akerson Papers, Box 8, "Gregory, Thomas T. C., 1928"; Dante M. Pierce to Akerson, March 7, 1928, ibid., Box 12, "Pierce, Dante M., 1927–1928"; press release on Hoover farm policies from Hoover-for-President New York State Committee, March 1928, Strauss Papers, Subject File, Box 10, "Campaign of 1928: Campaign Literature, Speeches, etc.-Press Releases, Speeches, etc., 1928 Feb.–Nov."; Akerson to Harry B. Hunt, April 7, 1928, Akerson Papers, Box 10, "Hunt, Harry B., 1927–1928"; George B. Lockwood to Akerson, March 12, 1928, ibid., Box 14, "Washington Headquarters, 1928 January–March"; Ballard Dunn to Akerson, March 15, 1928, ibid., Box 8, "Dunn, Ballard, 1927–1928"; list of members of "Women's Committee," ca. March 24, 1928, ibid., Box 14, "Women's Organizations, 1928 & undated"; statement given out by Mrs. Thomas G. Winter, former president of the General Federation of Women's Clubs, undated, ibid., Box 14, "Winter, Mrs. Thomas G., 1928 & undated"; Edward Anthony, press release from the New York Hoover-for-President Committee, March 26, 1928, Edward Anthony Collection, Hoover Presidential Library, West Branch, Iowa, Box 4, "Washington Correspondence by Edward Anthony, Feb. 29–May 14, 1928"; Akerson to Dante Pierce, March 28, 1928, Akerson Papers, Box 12, "Pierce, Dante M., 1927–1928"; W. S. Norviel to Hoover, March 29, 1928, James P. Goodrich Papers, Hoover Presidential Library, West Branch, Iowa, Box 1, "Campaign of 1928"; Edward Anthony, press release, "Jardine Talks for Agriculture," April 16, 1928, Anthony Collection, Box 4, "Washington Correspondence by Edward Anthony, Feb. 29–May 14, 1928"; C. C. Hamlin to Akerson, April 18, 1928, Akerson Papers, Box 9, "Hamlin, Clarence, 1927–1928"; "Demand That Hilles Abandon His Policy," *New York Times*, April 22, 1928; *National Republic* magazine to J. W. Rhine, April 27, 1928; J. W. Rhine to Akerson, April 27, 1928, both in Akerson Papers, Box 14, "Washington Headquarters, 1928 April."

34. Edward Anthony to Franz G. Lassner, July 13, 1965, Anthony Collection, Box 1, "The Boloney Knife, n/d"; unsigned, undated memorandum about groups to be targeted by campaign, Hoover Papers, Campaign and Transition Period, Box 162, "Subject: Republican Campaign Strategy, 1928"; materials from the Hoover-for-President Business Paper Editorial Advisory Committee, undated, ca. 1928, Akerson Papers, Box 11, "Ormsbee, Thomas H., 1928"; William Shafroth to "Dear Governor" (James Goodrich?), ca. April 1928, Goodrich Papers, Box 1, "Campaign of 1928"; Lupton Wilkinson memorandum for James W. Good, April 9, 1928, Akerson Papers, Box 14, "Wilkinson, Lupton A., 1928"; Akerson to Anthony, April 9, 1928, ibid., Box 5, "Anthony, Edward, 1928 April"; Edward Anthony press release on the use of films in the campaign, ca. May 8, 1928, Anthony Collection, Box 3, "Press Releases, May 1928."

35. James Goodrich to Hubert Work, April 10, 1928, Goodrich Papers, Box 1, "Campaign of 1928"; Richard B. Scandrett, Jr., "Hoover vs. the Politicians," April 12, 1928, Strauss

Papers, Subject File, Box 14, "Campaign of 1928: Scandrett Statement"; Morton R. Hunter to J. W. Rhine, April 12, 1928, Akerson Papers, Box 14, "Washington Headquarters, 1928 April"; Ivy Lee, memorandum, April 23, 1928, George Barr Baker Papers; Box 4, "Lee, Ivy L."; Rickard Diaries, April 27, 1928, Box 1, "1928"; Edward Anthony to Akerson, April 28, 1928, Akerson Papers, Box 5, "Anthony, Edward, 1928 April"; James Goodrich to Thomas A. Marlow, May 7, 1928, Goodrich Papers, Box 1, "Campaign of 1928."

36. Edward Anthony to Akerson, Apr. 28, 1928, Akerson Papers, Box 5, "Anthony, Edward, 1928 April"; David Hinshaw to Lewis Strauss, April 28, 1928, Strauss Papers, Subject File, Box 13, "Campaign of 1928: Hinshaw, David"; James Goodrich to Hoover, May 5, 1928, Goodrich Papers, Box 11, "Hoover, Herbert, 1920–1928"; Goodrich to H. C. Baldridge, May 9, 1928, ibid., Box 1, "Campaign of 1928"; Harry New to Goodrich, May 10, 1928; Goodrich to New, May 14, 1928, both in ibid., Box 15, "New, Harry S., 1911–28 "Hoover and Others in the Indiana Voting," Chicago *Tribune*, May 11, 1928.

37. Rickard Diaries, May 13, 28, 1928, Box 1, "1928"; Edward Anthony, press release, ca. May 14, 1928, Anthony Collection, Box 4, "Washington Correspondence by Edward Anthony, Feb. 29–May 14, 1928"; Hal Elliott Wert, *Hoover, the Fishing President: Portrait of the Private Man and His Life Outdoors* (Mechanicsburg, PA: Stackpole, 2005), 151–52; Cannadine, *Mellon*, 363.

38. "Presidential Campaign Expenditures," *Hearings before a Special Committee Investigating Presidential Campaign Expenditures, United States Senate*, 70th Cong., 1st sess., May 7–14, 15–16, 1928 (Washington, DC: Government Printing Office, 1928), 45–66, 112–81. Good's estimate of total expenditures is on p. 161, and his figures on individual contributions on pp. 115–16.

39. *Presidential Campaign Expenditures*, Senate Report 2024, 70th Cong., 2d sess., pp. 26–31. Only one Republican contributor, New York fire insurance executive Edwin C. Jameson, gave more than $100,000 ($172,000). The next three largest contributions came from Ogden Mills, Julius Rosenwald, and Herbert N. Straus; each gave $50,000. By comparison, among fewer total donors, the Democrats had three contributions of more than $100,000 and five of $50,000 or more. See ibid., 27–31, for lists of all donors of $5,000 or more. Department of Commerce, Bureau of the Census, *Historical Statistics of the United States, Earliest Times to the Present* (Washington, DC: Government Printing Office, 1975), 2:1081, estimates spending by the two national committees at $6.3 million and $5.3 million, respectively. Republican campaign managers met in Washington on August 22 and 23 and prepared a budget estimating overall spending at $3.9 million; it can be found in Hoover Papers, Campaign and Transition Period, Box 162, "Subject: Republican National Committee."

40. Rickard Diaries, March 29, April 23, June 8, 10, 1928, Box 1, "1928"; "A Negro Protest Here," Kansas City *Post*, June 9, 1928; "Negroes Fight Hoover Faction," Kansas City *Journal*, June 9, 1928; Lisio, *Hoover, Blacks, and Lily-Whites*, 58–61. Hoover intervened personally to have Walter Cohen seated with the Louisiana delegation, but that did not change the effect on the black-and-tan organization in Louisiana.

41. Rickard Diaries, June 11, 1928, Box 1, "1928."

42. "Holiday Hosts Converge Here," Kansas City *Post*, June 11, 1928; "Await the Gavel," Kansas City *Post*, June 11, 1928; "Parade Torches Will Light City," Kansas City *Post*, June 11, 1928.

43. Rickard Diaries, June 12, 1928, Box 1, "1928"; "Big Show Is On," Kansas City *Star*, June 12, 1928; Lawrence Sullivan, "Rush to Hoover Bewilders Politicians," Kansas City *Post*, June 12, 1928; "March, Sing and Crowd," Kansas City *Post*, June 13, 1928; "Farm Bolt Fizzles," Kansas City *Journal*, June 13, 1928; "Slemp Grateful to Farmers for Stirring Interest," Kansas City *Post*, June 13, 1928; Rochester, *Coolidge-Hoover-Work*, 44–46; Peel and Donnelly, *The 1928 Campaign*, 23.

44. "Roar for Hoover," Kansas City *Times*, June 14, 1928; "Speech by John L. McNab, Kansas City, June 14, 1928," in Schlesinger et al., eds., *History of American Presidential Elections*, 3: 2668–71; William T. Hutchinson, *Lowden of Illinois: The Life of Frank O. Lowden* (Chicago: University of Chicago Press, 1957), 2:594–601.

45. Rochester, *Coolidge-Hoover-Work*, 48; "National Conventions of 1928: The Republican National Convention of 1928," in *World Almanac and Book of Facts for 1929* (New York: New York *World*, 1929), 847; George H. Moses to Hoover, June 14, 1928, Hoover Papers, Campaign and Transition Period, Box 162, "Subject: Republican National Committee."

46. Lou Hoover to Allan Hoover, May 25, 1928 (two telegrams), Allan Hoover Papers, Box 3, "Correspondence with Lou Henry Hoover, 1928 May–June"; Rickard Diaries, June 14, 1928, Box 1, "1928"; Hoover to George H. Moses, June 14, 1928, Hoover Papers, Campaign and Transition Period, Box 162, "Subject: Republican National Convention."

47. The most incisive account of Curtis' selection, which relies on the Smoot diary, is by Robert H. Ferrell, "The Republican Ascendancy: Calvin Coolidge, Charles Dawes, and Charles Curtis as Vice Presidents," in *At the President's Side: The Vice Presidency in the Twentieth Century*, ed. Timothy Walch (Columbia: University of Missouri Press, 1997), 37–39. Aside from one cryptic note in Edgar Rickard's diary, Box 1, "1928" (June 14, 1928), which indicates that Hoover did not want "to interfere" in the vice presidential selection process until his own nomination was "assured," the Hoover papers are generally silent on the subject. Hoover tells the story about Coolidge's intervention in his *Memoirs* 2, 194, where he attributes it to Curtis. E. S. Rochester, in *Coolidge-Hoover-Work*, 51–52, attributes strong if not decisive influence on the decision to Hubert Work and Ogden Mills, but there is no evidence that either man consulted with Hoover, although they could have done so by telephone. No full biography of Curtis exists. The account of the nomination in a short biographical study by Marvin Ewy, *Charles Curtis of Kansas: Vice President of the United States, 1929–1933* (Emporia: Kansas State Teachers College, 1961), 40–41, is based entirely on a memoir by Curtis's half-sister, Permelia ("Dolly") Gann. See also, Burner, *Hoover*, 200; Hoover to Curtis, August 18, 1928, Hoover Papers, Campaign and Transition Period, Box 19, "Genl. Corres.: Curtis, Charles."

48. Ewy, *Charles Curtis of Kansas*; Ferrell, "The Republican Ascendancy," 37–38; James C. Malin, "Charles Curtis, 1860–1936," in *Dictionary of American Biography*, supp. 2 (New York: Scribner's, 1958), 136–37; Peel and Donnelly, *The 1928 Campaign*, 29–30.

49. Rickard Diaries, June 15, 1928, Box 1, "1928"; Coolidge to Hoover, June 15, 1928; Hoover to Coolidge, June 15, 1928, both in Hoover Papers, Campaign and Transition Period, Box 17, "Genl. Corres.: Coolidge, Calvin."

50. "National Conventions of 1928: The Democratic National Convention of 1928," *World Almanac and Book of Facts for 1929*, 851; "Law Enforcement," in the Democratic Platform of 1928, in Schlesinger et al., eds., *History of American Presidential Elections*, 3:2621; Fuchs, "Election of 1928," in ibid., 3:2595; Robert A. Slayton, *Empire Statesman: The Rise and Redemption of Al Smith* (New York: Free Press, 2001), 246.

51. "How the Nation Sizes Up the Hoover Ticket," *Literary Digest*, June 23, 1928, 6–8; Whaley-Eaton Newsletter no. 511, June 16, 1928, Strauss Papers, Subject File, Box 15, "Campaign of 1928: Whaley-Eaton Reports"; Hoover, *Memoirs* 2, 198; Fuchs, "Election of 1928," in Schlesinger et al., eds., *History of American Presidential Elections* 3:2586; Burner, *Hoover*, 199–200; Robert S. Lynd and Helen Merrell Lynd, *Middletown: A Study in American Culture* (New York: Harcourt, Brace & World, 1956; orig. pub. 1929), 56–59; Gene Smiley, *Rethinking the Great Depression* (Chicago: Ivan R. Dee, 2002), 7–8; Maury Klein, *Rainbow's End: The Crash of 1929* (New York: Oxford University Press, 2001), 123–35; Meg Jacobs, *Pocketbook Politics: Economic Citizenship in Twentieth-Century America* (Princeton, NJ: Princeton University Press, 2005), 88, 90.

52. Hoover to Hubert Work, July 14, 1928, Hoover Papers, Campaign and Transition Period, Box 63, "Genl. Corres.: Slade, Mrs. F. Louis (Caroline)"; Ferry Heath to Lewis Strauss, August 4, 1928, Strauss Papers, Subject File, Box 11, "Campaign of 1928: Contributions and Finance; Heath, Ferry K."; Rochester, *Coolidge-Hoover-Work*, 56–61; "National Republican Committee: Department Heads," undated, ca. June 1928, Hoover Papers, Campaign and Transition Period, Box 27, "Genl. Corres.: Fort, Franklin"; "James M. Good," undated, June–November 1928, ibid., Box 29, "Genl. Corres.: Good, James W." See also the folder of correspondence on organizational matters in ibid., Box 73, "Genl. Corres.: Work, Hubert S." Not everyone understood that the campaign's decentralization was more apparent than

real, with Hoover, Akerson, and Work actually exercising tight control over it. See Edgar Rickard's memorandum, August 1, 1928, Rickard Diaries, Box 1, "1928."

53. Nathan William MacChesney to Hoover, November 7, 1928, Hoover Papers, Campaign and Transition Period, Box 163, "Subject: Report of Hoover-Curtis Organization Bureau, Republican National Committee"; Lillian M. Gilbreth to Lou Hoover, November 10, 1928, Lou Hoover Papers, Box 16, "Subject File: Campaign of 1928, General, October–November."

54. Henry F. Pringle, "Hoover: An Enigma Easily Misunderstood," *World's Work* 56 (June 1928): 131–32, 134; Herbert Croly, "How Is Hoover?" *New Republic,* June 27, 1928, 138–40; Katherine Dayton, "What's the Matter With Hoover?" *Saturday Evening Post,* August 11, 1928, 102; "The Engineer as a Molder of Public Opinion," *Engineering and Mining Journal,* June 30, 1928, 1041. For an August 20, 1926, speech in which Hoover talked about relief, see Bible no. 621.

55. Hoover to Coolidge, July 5, 1928, Coolidge, President's Personal Files, Microfilm, Reel 6; James L. Wright, "Hoover Confers With President," Buffalo *Evening News,* July 16, 1928; James L. Wright, "Hoover's Party Visits Duluth," Buffalo *Evening News,* July 17, 1928; Akerson to Hubert Work, July 17, 1928, Hoover Papers, Campaign and Transition Period, Box 73, "Genl. Corres.: Work, Hubert S."; J. Russell Young, "Coolidge Praises Hoover's Speech," Washington *Evening Star,* August 14, 1928; Coolidge to Hoover, August 21, 1928, Lou Hoover Papers, Box 51, "Subject File: Coolidge, Calvin, 1923–33"; Wert, *Hoover, the Fishing President,* 157–61.

56. T. T. C. Gregory to Akerson, June 25, 1928; Akerson to Gregory, June 26, 1928, both in Akerson Papers, Box 8, "Gregory, Thomas T. C., 1928"; Ray Lyman Wilbur to Hoover, June 27, 1928; Akerson to Wilbur, June 28, 1928; Wilbur to Hoover, June 28, 1928, all in Hoover Papers, Campaign and Transition Period, Box 72, "Genl. Corres.: Wilbur, Ray Lyman"; Hoover to Hubert Work, July 18, 1928, ibid., Box 73, "Genl. Corres.: Work, Hubert S."; Akerson to Gregory, July 18, 1928 (two telegrams), ibid., Box 30, "Genl. Corres.: Gregory, T. T. C."; William Hard, "Mrs. Hoover's Modesty Routs Gloom Aboard Special Train," Buffalo *Evening News,* July 19, 1928; James L. Wright, "Hoover, Quiet Pilot, Fast Falling into Political Role," Buffalo *Evening News,* July 20, 1928; William Randolph Hearst to Hoover, July 20, 1928, Hoover Papers, Campaign and Transition Period, Box 33, "Genl. Corres.: Hearst, Wm. Randolph"; Hubert Work to Hoover, July 21, 30, 1928, ibid., Box 73, "Genl. Corres.: Work, Hubert S."; Marie M. Meloney to Hoover, July 23 (two letters), 24, 1928, ibid., Box 38, "Genl. Corres.: Meloney, Marie M. (Mrs. Wm. B.)"; Hoover to Larry Richey, ca. July 24, 1928, ibid., Box 58, "Genl. Corres.: Richey, Lawrence"; James. L. Wright, "Hoover Is Given First Big Rally by Alma Mater," Buffalo *Evening News,* July 24, 1928; Inez Haynes Irwin to Hoover, July 26, 1928, Hoover Papers, Campaign and Transition Period, Box 38, "Irwin, Will, Mr. & Mrs. (Inez Haynes)"; Lewis Strauss to Hoover, July 30, 1928, ibid., Box 66, "Genl. Corres.: Strauss, Lewis."

57. James L. Wright, "Chinese Cook, Busy at Fire, Lets Hoover Handshake Wait," Buffalo *Evening News,* July 31, 1928; Wright, "Hoover Seeks More Trout on Last Day of His Vacation," Buffalo *Evening News,* August 1, 1928; Wright, "Hoover Party Gets One Trout, But Cameraman Can't Find It," Buffalo *Evening News,* August 2, 1928; Wright, "Points of Hoover's Character Are Disclosed on Fishing Trip," Buffalo *Evening News,* August 6, 1928; Wright, "Correspondents with Hoover Learn to Live Strenuous Life," Buffalo *Evening News,* August 11, 1928.

58. James L. Wright, "Movie-Tones and Engineers Keep Hoover Busy Rehearsing," Buffalo *Evening News,* August 10, 1928.

59. Speech at Stanford, California, August 11, 1928, *Public Papers of the Presidents of the United States: Herbert Hoover: Containing the Public Messages, Speeches, and Statements of the President, March 4 to December 31, 1929* (Washington, DC: Government Printing Office, 1974), 499–520.

60. Speech at West Branch, Iowa, August 21, 1928, ibid., 521–29. Much of the West Branch speech repeated, almost verbatim, speeches Hoover made in 1925 at Penn College and at Herbert's Stanford commencement.

61. Speech at Newark, New Jersey, September 17, 1928, ibid., 529–43.
62. Speech at Elizabethton, Tennessee, October 6, 1928, *ibid.*, 543–57; "Hoover's Attempt to Melt the 'Solid South,'" *Literary Digest* 99 (October 20, 1928): 5–7. For further discussion of the Muscle Shoals reference in the speech, see Chapter 19 in this volume.
63. Speeches at Boston, October 15, 1928, and at New York City, October 22, 1928, *Public Papers of the Presidents*, 557–91.
64. Speech at St. Louis, November 2, 1928, *ibid.*, 591–608.
65. Hoover, *Memoirs* 2, 199.
66. Lippmann quoted in Burner, *Hoover*, 200; George B. Lockwood to George (James) Goodrich, October 16, 1928, Goodrich Papers, Box 13, "Lockwood, George B., 1912–32 & undated"; Hubert Work to Lillian T. Martin (and other "key workers"), September 13, 1928, Hoover Papers, Campaing and Transition Period, Box 73, "Genl. Corres.: Work, Hubert S"; Lichtman, *Prejudice and the Old Politics*, 12. For the platforms, see Schlesinger et al., eds., *Presidential Elections*, 3:2611–40.
67. Lichtman, *Prejudice and the Old Politics*, 12; Edmund A. Moore, *A Catholic Runs for President: The Campaign of 1928* (Gloucester, MA: Peter Smith, 1968), 39–40. In an interview with Kathleen Norris, which, at Hoover's request, was never published, he reflected on the difficulties of enforcing the Volstead Act effectively. See Hoover to Norris (marked "Never Sent"), September 26, 1928, and the draft of the interview, Hoover Papers, Campaign and Transition Period, Box 52, "Genl. Corres.: Norris, Kathleen." Ruth Silva's statistical analysis of the 1928 election concludes that "the so-called liquor, religious, and metropolitan issues had no significant relations to Smith's electoral strength." See Ruth C. Silva, *Rum, Religion, and Votes: 1928 Re-Examined* (University Park: Pennsylvania State University Press, 1962), vii. Allan Lichtman disagrees, arguing that "prohibition was a major if not a transcendent influence on the voting for president in 1928," although he also notes that it is almost impossible to separate the prohibition issue from religion. See *Prejudice and the Old Politics*, 77. It seems impossible to resolve the issue conclusively.
68. Finan, *Alfred E. Smith*, 220; Lisio, *Hoover, Blacks, and Lily-Whites*, 62, 93–94, 100, 110–14; Lichtman, *Prejudice and the Old Politics*, 147. In some southern states, black or black-and-tan Republicans found themselves in a curious de facto alliance with the Klan, whose members feared Smith's Catholicism. See Mississippi Republican National Committee Woman Mary C. Booze to Mrs. Alvin T. Hert, August 27, 1928, Hoover Papers, Campaign and Transition Period, Box 10, "Genl. Corres.: Booze, Eugene P. & Mary."
69. Hoover, speech at Stanford, August 11, 1928, *Public Papers of the President*, 515; "Hoover and the Religious Issue," *The Independent*, October 13, 1928, 341; Smith, speech at Oklahoma City, September 20, 1928, *Campaign Addresses of Governor Alfred E. Smith, Democratic Candidate for President, 1928* (Washington, DC: Democratic National Committee, 1929), 51; Hoover, text of statement at press conference, September 21, 1928, Hoover Papers, Campaign and Transition Period, Box 161, "Subject: Press Statements, Herbert Hoover"; Hoover to Baruch, October 19, 1928, ibid., Box 159, "Subject: Intolerance."
70. "Mrs. Willebrandt to Go on Speaking," New York *World*, September 10, 1928); "Work Denounces 'Whisper' Attacks," New York *Evening Post*, September 1, 1928; Hoover, acceptance speech at Stanford, August 11, 1928, *Public Papers of the President*, 515; "Raskob Charges Republicans Aid Anti-Catholic War," *New York Times*, November 1, 1928; Slayton, *Empire Statesman*, 306–8; Lichtman, *Prejudice and the Old Politics*, 64–66; Moore, *A Catholic Runs for President*, 175; Burner, *Hoover*, 205–6. Critics on the left were convinced that Hoover's response to Willebrandt was hypocritical. See Heywood Broun, "It Seems to Heywood Broun," *Nation*, October 3, 1928, 313. For Smith's own retrospectively moderate and thoughtful treatment of the issue, see *Up To Now: An Autobiography* (New York: Viking, 1929), 395–96, 412–16.
71. Lou Hoover to Edgar Rickard, October 4, 1928, Lou Hoover Papers, Box 16, "Subject: Campaign of 1928, General, October–November"; Lichtman, *Prejudice and the Old Politics*, 66–67. Hoover never changed his mind about the episode. See *Memoirs* 2, 208–9. There are suggestive parallels between these events and Richard Nixon's conviction, during his 1972 reelection campaign, that malevolent "enemies" were targeting him.

72. Henry Allen to George Akerson, September 26, 1928, enclosing editorial from the August 1928 issue of the *Protestant*, "Smith Shows His Hand," Hoover Papers, Campaign and Transition Period, Box 3, "Genl. Corres.: Allen, Henry J. (2), 9/26/28–1/28/29"; "Simmons Assails Smith's Wet Views," *New York Times*, October 13, 1928; "Three Bolting Senators Face Party Wrath; Simmons, Heflin and Blaine [John J. Blaine, R, WI] Are Problems," *New York Times*, October 22, 1928; Barbara C. Wingo, "The 1928 Presidential Election in Louisiana," *Louisiana History* 18 (Fall 1977): 405–29; Slayton, *Empire Statesman*, 324 (emphasis in original). Lichtman, *Prejudice and the Old Politics*, 231–32, stresses the centrality of the religious issue to the election's outcome. Gilchrist Stockton, a Democrat who had worked under Hoover in the ARA and was supporting him in 1928, denied that religion had anything to do with his strength in Florida. See Stockton to Hoover, October 26, 1928, Hoover Papers, Campaign and Transition Period, Box 65, "Genl. Corres.: Stockton, Gilchrist," but by contrast, see Herbert J. Doherty, Jr., "Florida and the Presidential Election of 1928," *Florida Historical Quarterly* 26 (October 1947): 174–86. For other interpretations of the election's outcome, see Silva, *Rum, Religion, and Votes*; Peel and Donnelly, *The 1928 Campaign*, 114–16; Burner, *Hoover*, 207–8.

73. James Goodrich to Hoover, August 18 and September 14, 18, 20, 24, 25, 1928, Goodrich Papers, Box 11, "Hoover, Herbert, 1920–1928"; Arthur Capper, press release, August 20, 1928, Hoover Papers, Campaign and Transition Period, Box 14, "Genl. Corres.: Capper, Arthur"; Smith, speech at Omaha, September 18, 1928, *Campaign Addresses*, 39–40; Irvine Lenroot to Hoover, September 15, 1928, Hoover Papers, Campaign and Transition Period, Box 43, "Genl. Corres.: Lenroot, Irvine L."; Harry S. New to James Goodrich, September 24, 1928, and Goodrich to New, September 27, 1928, both in Goodrich Papers, Box 13, "Hoover, Herbert, 1911–28"; Louis P. Lochner, *Herbert Hoover and Germany* (New York: Macmillan, 1960), 69–70. Paul Carter, "The Campaign of 1928 Re-Examined: A Study in Political Folklore," *Wisconsin Magazine of History* 46 (Summer 1963): 263–72, argues that the rural-urban split provides the best explanation for Smith's defeat in general, but Carter's evidence is drawn largely from the Midwest, where the issue seems to have had a greater effect than it did elsewhere.

74. New York Hoover-for-President State Committee, press release on women for Hoover, undated, ca. May 8, 1928, Anthony Collection, Box 3, "Press Releases, May 1928"; James W. Good to Mrs. Edmund H. Brown, May 28, 1928, Hoover Papers, Campaign and Transition Period, Box 158, "Subject: Hoover for President Corres."; Marie M. Meloney to Hoover, July 23, 1928, ibid., Box 48, "Genl. Corres.: Meloney, Marie M. (Mrs. Wm. B.)"; "To Mrs. Herbert Hoover: The Hoover-Curtis Organization Bureau Women's Activities, Republican National Committee, 1928," Lou Hoover Papers, Box 25, "Subject File: Notebook, 'Report of Women's Activities, 1928'"; press release, "Report of the Publicity Department of the Women's National Committee for Hoover," undated, post-November 3, 1928, Anthony Collection, Box 4, "Women's Page Service, No. 1–8, 1928"; Lou Hoover to Caroline (Mrs. F. Louis) Slade, August 27, 1928, Lou Hoover Papers, Box 25, "Subject File: Campaign of 1928, Women's National Committee for Hoover"; Hoover to Mrs. F. Louis (Caroline) Slade, August 29, 1928, and Slade to Hoover, August 29, 1928, both in Hoover Papers, Campaign and Transition Period, Box 63, "Genl. Corres.: Slade, Mrs. F. Louis (Caroline)"; Clara Burdette to Hoover, October 1, 1928, ibid., Box 13, "Genl. Corres.: Burdette, Robert J., Mrs. (Clara B)"; Nancy Beck Young, *Lou Henry Hoover: Activist First Lady* (Lawrence: University Press of Kansas, 2004), 43–49; Dale C. Mayer, *Lou Henry Hoover: A Prototype for First Ladies* (New York: Nova Historical, 2004), 240–41.

75. Inez Haynes Irwin to Hoover, July 26, 1928, Hoover Papers, Campaign and Transition Period, Box 38, "Genl. Corres.: Irwin, Will, Mr. & Mrs. (Inez Haynes)"; "Statement of Mr. Hoover to National Woman's Party Delegation Which Asked His Support of Equal Rights Amendment," September 12, 1928, ibid., Box 51, "Genl. Corres.: National Women's Party"; National Women's Party press release, September 12, 1928, ibid.; *Presidential Campaign Expenditures*, Senate Report 2024, 70th Cong., 2d sess., p.26; Slayton, *Empire Statesman*, 294–95. The *Nation* declared editorially that the Women's Party had sold out to Hoover. See "The Woman's Party and Mr. Hoover," *Nation*, October 3, 1928, 312.

76. Hoover, address at Newark, September 17, 1928, *Public Papers of the President*, 529; John L. Lewis to Hoover, September 17, 1928, Hoover Papers, Campaign and Transition Period, Box 160, "Subject: Labor"; "Hoover on Labor," *New Republic*, September 26, 1928, 138–41; "Hoover's Appeal to the Workers," *Literary Digest*, October 6, 1928,10–11; Vaughn Davis Bornet, *Labor Politics in a Democratic Republic: Moderation, Division, and Disruption in the Presidential Election of 1928* (Washington, DC: Spartan Books, 1964), 237–38; Robert H. Zieger, *Republicans and Labor, 1919–1929* (Lexington: University of Kentucky Press, 1969), 249–50; Zieger, "Solving the Labor Problem: Herbert Hoover and the American Worker in the 1920s," in *Herbert Hoover Reassessed: Essays Commemorating the Fiftieth Anniversary of the Inauguration of Our Thirty First President*, comp. Mark Hatfield (Washington, DC: Government Printing Office, 1981), 177–86. The quotation is on p. 177.
77. Hoover to Coolidge, August 29, 1928, Hoover Papers, Campaign and Transition Period, Box 17, "Genl. Corres.: Coolidge, Calvin"; Hoover to Borah, August 29, 1928; Walter H. Newton to Hoover, October 2, 1928; Hoover to Borah, October 2, 1928, all in ibid., Box 11, "Genl. Corres.: Borah, William E."; Hoover to James W. Good, September 11, 1928, ibid., Box 29, "Genl. Corres.: Good, James W."; John Q. Tilson to Hoover, September 25, 1928, ibid., Box 37, "Genl. Corres.: Hughes, Charles Evans"; "Mellon Pleads for Prosperity Under Hoover," New York *Herald Tribune*, October 12, 1928; Coolidge to Hoover, November 2, 1928, Hoover Papers, Campaign and Transition Period, Box 17, "Genl. Corres.: Coolidge, Calvin"; Claude M. Fuess, *Calvin Coolidge: The Man from Vermont* (Westport, CT: Greenwood, 1968; orig. pub. 1939), 430.
78. Campaign press release, "Statistics Point to Hoover Victory by Record Plurality of 8,058,150," undated, ca. November 1, 1928, Anthony Collection, Box 1, "Articles Pertaining to HH & Campaign, February–May 1928"; James W. Good to Hoover, November 3, 1928, Hoover Papers, Campaign and Transition Period, Box 29, "Genl. Corres.: Good, James W."; George Akerson to Lawrence Richey, November 4, 1928, ibid., Box 58, "Genl. Corres.: Richey, Lawrence R."
79. Hoover, radio address to the Nation, November 5, 1928, *Public Papers of the President*, 608–11; George H. Nash, *Herbert Hoover and Stanford University* (Stanford, CA: Hoover Institution Press, 1988), 91.
80. Rickard Diaries, November 6, 1928, Box 1, "1928"; Nash, *Hoover and Stanford*, 91–92; Helen B. Pryor, *Lou Henry Hoover: Gallant First Lady* (New York: Dodd, Mead, 1969), 156–57.
81. Coolidge to Hoover, November 7, 1928, and Hoover to Coolidge, November 7, 1928, both in Hoover Papers, Campaign and Transition Period, Box 17, "Genl. Corres.: Coolidge, Calvin"; David Leip, "1928 Presidential Election Data: National, by State," http://www.uselectionatlas.org/USPRESIDENT/data.php?year=1928&datatype=national&def=1&f=1 (accessed May 18, 2005).

Chapter 22

1. Hoover, "The Larger Purposes of the Department of Commerce," in Republican National Committee, *Brief Review of Activities and Policies of Federal Executive Departments*, Bulletin No. 6, 1928, Hoover Papers, Campaign and Transition Period, Hoover Presidential Library, West Branch, Iowa, Box 162, "Subject: Republican National Committee: Bulletins."
2. Ibid.
3. Ibid.
4. Ibid.
5. Herbert Hoover, *Memoirs: The Cabinet and the Presidency, 1920–1933* (New York: Macmillan, 1952), 184 (hereafter, *Memoirs 2*).
6. Hoover, Acceptance speech, August 11, 1928, *Public Papers of the Presidents of the United States: Herbert Hoover: Containing the Public Messages, Speeches of the President, March 4 to December 31, 1929* (Washington, DC: Government Printing Office, 1974), 503.
7. William C. Mullendore oral history, Part I, pp. 19–20, Hoover Presidential Library, West Branch, Iowa.

8. "Speech of Herbert Hoover at New York Conference, Methodist Episcopal Church, Kingston, N.Y., April 9, 1920," Hoover Papers, Pre-Commerce Period, Hoover Presidential Library, West Branch, Iowa, Box 60, "Public Statements, 1917–1920."
9. Hoover to Paul Harvey, February 20, 1924, Hoover Papers, Commerce Period, Box 590, "Superpower, Waterpower, etc., 1924 January–March."
10. Christian Herter to Hugh Gibson, October 5, 1921, Hoover Papers, Commerce Period, Box 237, "Gibson, Hugh, 1921–1928."
11. "Ratify Peace Now, Says Hoover at Pier," *New York Times*, September 14, 1919.
12. Hoover, speech at St. Louis, November 2, 1928, *Public Papers of the Presidents*, 608; John Corbin, "What Hoover Is Aiming At," *New York Times*, May 29, 1921.

Bibliography

Herbert Hoover Presidential Library, West Branch, Iowa

Papers

Herbert Hoover Papers, Pre-Commerce Period
Herbert Hoover Papers, Commerce Period
Herbert Hoover Papers, Campaign and Transition Period
Herbert Hoover Papers, Post-Presidential File
The "Bible" (typed copies of Hoover's articles, addresses, and public statements, 1892–1964)
George Edwards Akerson Papers
American Child Health Association Papers
American Relief Administration Bulletins
American Relief Administration Documents
Edward Anthony Collection
Ralph Arnold Papers
Philippi Harding Butler Papers
Mildred Hall Campbell Papers
William Richards Castle, Jr., Papers
Colorado River Commission Papers
Edward Dana Durand Papers
Federal Reserve Bank of New York Collection, Benjamin Strong Papers
Federal Reserve System, Board of Governors Collection
Frederick M. Feiker Papers
Hugh Gibson Collection
Theodore G. Joslin Papers
James P. Goodrich Papers
Allan Hoover Papers
Lou Henry Hoover Papers
William P. MacCracken, Jr., Papers
Agnes E. Meyer Diary, General Acquisition 692
William C. Mullendore Papers
Bradley DeLamater Nash Papers
Walter H. Newton Papers
Lawrence Richey Papers
Edgar Rickard Diaries

Lewis L. Strauss Papers
Edgar French Strother Papers
James Spear Taylor Papers
Ray Lyman Wilbur Papers
Berkeley Williams Collection

Oral Histories

George E. Akerson, Jr.
Philippi Harding Butler
Mildred Hall Campbell
Birge M. Clark
Allan and Margaret Hoover
Marguerite Rickard Hoyt
Dare Stark McMullin
Ralph Palmer Merritt
William C. Mullendore
Bradley D. Nash
Lewis L. Strauss
Dwight L. Wilbur
Ray Lyman Wilbur

Hoover Institution Archives, Stanford, California

Papers

Benjamin S. Allen Papers
George Barr Baker Papers
Joseph C. Green Papers
Thomas T. C. Gregory Papers
Herbert Hoover Subject Collection
Edward Eyre Hunt Papers
Henry M. Robinson Papers
Mark Sullivan Papers
Ray Lyman Wilbur Papers

Oral Histories

Sydney Sullivan Parker
Scott Turner

Huntington Library, San Marino, California

Ralph Arnold Papers
Clara Burdette Papers
Albert Fall Collection
Henry Mauris Robinson Papers

Green Library, Rare Books and Special Collections, Stanford University, Stanford, California

Herbert Hoover Papers
Francis V. Keesling Papers
Meyer Lissner Papers

Stanford University Archives

Ray Lyman Wilbur Papers

National Archives, Washington, DC

RG 40, Commerce Department Records
RG 48, Interior Department Records
RG 220, National Conference on Outdoor Recreation Papers
RG 79, National Parks Association and National Park Service

Ohio Historical Society, Columbus, Ohio

Walter F. Brown Papers
Simeon Fess Papers
Frank Willis Papers

Bancroft Library, University of California at Berkeley

Papers

Hiram Johnson Papers
Chester Rowell Papers

Oral Histories

Horace Albright Oral History
Leon F. Kneipp Oral History

University of California at Los Angeles

Phil D. Swing Papers

University of Wyoming, Rare Books and Special Collections

Mark Requa Papers

Other

Warren Harding Microfilm Papers (Ohio Historical Society)
Calvin Coolidge, President's Personal Files, Microfilm (Forbes Library)
National Association for the Advancement of Colored People Microfilm Records, Part 10, *Peonage, Labor and the New Deal, 1913–1939* (Lanham, MD: University Publications of America)

Published Documents

American Engineering Council. *Waste in Industry, by the Committee on Elimination of Waste in Industry of the Federated American Engineering Societies.* New York: McGraw-Hill for the Federated American Engineering Societies, 1921.

American Red Cross. *The Mississippi Valley Flood Disaster of 1927: Official Report of the Relief Operations.* Washington, DC: American National Red Cross, 1929.

Bane, Suda Lorena, and Ralph Haswell Lutz, eds. *The Blockade of Germany after the Armistice, 1918–1919: Selected Documents of the Supreme Economic Council, American Relief Administration, and Other Wartime Organizations.* New York: Howard Fertig, 1972. Reprint of 1942 ed.

———, eds. *Organization of American Relief in Europe, 1918–1919: Including Negotiations Leading up to the Establishment of the Office of Director General of Relief at Paris by the Allied and Associated Powers.* Stanford, CA: Stanford University Press, 1943.

Better Homes in America. *Plan Book for Demonstration Week, October 9 to 14, 1922.* New York: The Delineator, 1922.

Business Cycles and Unemployment: Report of a Committee of the President's Conference on Unemployment and an Investigation under the Auspices of the National Bureau of Economic Research. New York: McGraw-Hill, 1923.

Business Cycles and Unemployment: Report and Recommendations of a Committee of the President's Conference on Unemployment. Washington, DC: Government Printing Office, 1923.

Committee on Recent Economic Changes of the President's Conference on Unemployment. *Recent Economic Changes in the United States.* 2 vols. New York: McGraw-Hill, 1929.

Committee on Rivers and Harbors, House of Representatives. *Pollution of Navigable Waters: Hearings on the Subject held before the Committee on Rivers and Harbors, House of Representatives, 68th Cong., 1st sess.* Washington, DC: Government Printing Office, 1924.

———. "Waterway from the Great Lakes to the Hudson River: Letter from the Chief of Engineers, United States Army." 69th Cong., 2d sess., December 6, 1926, Document No. 7.

Committee on Work-Periods in Continuous Industry of the Federated American Engineering Societies. *The Twelve-Hour Shift in Industry.* New York: E. P. Dutton, 1922.

Conference on Athletics and Physical Recreation for Women and Girls. *Resolutions Adopted by the Conference on Athletics and Physical Recreation for Women and Girls, April 6th and 7th, 1923, Washington, D.C.* New York: National Amateur Athletic Federation of America, 1923.

Coons, A. T. *Potash in 1925.* Washington, DC: Government Printing Office, 1927.

———. *Potash in 1926.* Washington, DC: Government Printing Office, 1927.

Department of Agriculture. *Monthly Weather Review*, suppl. 29, *The Floods of 1927 in the Mississippi Basin.* Washington, DC: Government Printing Office, 1927.

Department of Commerce. *Ninth Annual Report of the Secretary of Commerce.* Washington, DC: Government Printing Office, 1921.

———. *Tenth Annual Report of the Secretary of Commerce.* Washington, DC: Government Printing Office, 1922.

———. *Eleventh Annual Report of the Secretary of Commerce.* Washington, DC: Government Printing Office, 1923.

———. *Twelfth Annual Report of the Secretary of Commerce.* Washington, DC: Government Printing Office, 1924.

———. *Thirteenth Annual Report of the Secretary of Commerce.* Washington, DC: Government Printing Office, 1925.

———. *Fourteenth Annual Report of the Secretary of Commerce.* Washington, DC: Government Printing Office, 1926.

———. *Fifteenth Annual Report of the Secretary of Commerce.* Washington, DC: Government Printing Office, 1927.

———. *Sixteenth Annual Report of the Secretary of Commerce.* Washington, DC: Government Printing Office, 1928.

———. *Seventeenth Annual Report of the Secretary of Commerce.* Washington, DC: Government Printing Office, 1929.

Department of Commerce, Advisory Committee on Zoning. *A Zoning Primer*. Washington, DC: Government Printing Office, 1922.

Department of Commerce, Bureau of the Census. *Children Under Institutional Care, 1923: Statistics of Dependent, Neglected, and Delinquent Children in Institutions and under the Supervision of Other Agencies for the Care of Children, with a Section on Adults in Certain Types of Institutions.* Washington, DC: Government Printing Office, 1927.

———. *Historical Statistics of the United States: Earliest Times to the Present*. Washington, DC: Government Printing Office, 1975.

———. *Historical Statistics of the United States: Earliest Times to the Present*, Millennial ed. Edited by Susan B. Carter et al. New York: Cambridge University Press, 2006.

Department of Commerce, Elimination of Waste Series. *Seasonal Operation in the Construction Industries: Summary of Report and Recommendations of a Committee of the President's Conference on Unemployment*. Washington, DC: Government Printing Office, 1924.

Department of Commerce, Housing Division. *How to Own Your Own Home: A Handbook for Prospective Home Owners*. Washington, DC: Government Printing Office, 1923.

Department of State. *Papers Relating to the Foreign Relations of the United States, 1919*. Washington, DC: Government Printing Office, 1934.

Department of State. *Papers Relating to the Foreign Relations of the United States, 1919: The Paris Peace Conference*. Washington, DC: Government Printing Office, 1942.

Final Report of the Colored Advisory Commission: Mississippi Valley Flood Disaster, 1927. Washington, DC: American Red Cross, 1927.

Hoover, Herbert. *The Future of Our Foreign Trade: An Address Given at a Dinner in New York City under the Auspices of the Export Managers' Club of New York*, March 16, 1926. Washington, DC: Government Printing Office, 1926.

House Committee on Foreign Affairs. *Russian Relief: Hearings before the Committee on Foreign Affairs, House of Representatives, 67th Cong., 2d sess., on HR 9459 and HR 9548*. Washington, DC: Government Printing Office, 1921.

International Pacific Halibut Commission. *The Pacific Halibut: Biology, Fishery and Management*. Technical Report No. 22. Seattle: International Pacific Halibut Commission, 1987.

Lary, Hal B., and associates. *The United States in the World Economy: International Transactions of the United States during the Interwar Period*. Washington, DC: Government Printing Office, 1943.

Link, Arthur S., ed. *The Papers of Woodrow Wilson*. 69 vols. Princeton, NJ: Princeton University Press, 1966–94.

"Message from the President of the United States Transmitting Special Recommendations for Legislation by Congress for the Relief of Distress in Agricultural Districts in the United States." 66th Cong., 1st sess., January 23, 1924, House Document No. 167.

Meyer, Eugene, Jr., and Frank W. Mondell. *Report to the President on the Wheat Situation*. Washington, DC: Government Printing Office, 1923.

Moran, Philip R., ed. *Warren G. Harding, 1865–1923: Chronology, Documents, Bibliographical Aids*. Dobbs Ferry, New York: Oceana, 1970.

National Archives and Records Administration. *Public Papers of the Presidents of the United States, Herbert Hoover: Containing the Public Messages, Speeches, and Statements of the President, March 4 to December 31, 1929*. Washington, DC: Government Printing Office, 1974.

National Bureau of Economic Research. *Income in the United States: Its Amount and Distribution, 1909–1919*. 2 vols. New York: National Bureau of Economic Research, 1922.

National Conference on Outdoor Recreation. *Proceedings of the Meeting of the Advisory Council . . . , December 11 and 12, 1924*. Senate Document No. 229, 68 Cong., 2d sess. Washington, DC: Government Printing Office, 1925.

National Industrial Conference. *Preliminary Statement of Industrial Conference Called by the President*. Washington, DC: Government Printing Office, 1919."National Origin Provision of the Immigration Act of 1924." 69th Cong., 2d sess., Senate Document No. 190.

———. *Report of Industrial Conference Called by the President*. Washington, DC: Government Printing Office, March 6, 1920.

National Research Council. *Organization and Members, 1921–1922*. Washington, DC: National Research Council, 1922.

O'Brien, Francis William, ed. *Two Peacemakers in Paris: The Hoover-Wilson Post-Armistice Letters, 1918–1920*. College Station: Texas A&M University Press, 1978.

Paull, Irving S., J. W. Millard, and James S. Taylor. *Trade Association Activities*. Domestic Commerce Series No. 20. Washington, DC: Government Printing Office, 1927.

President's Aircraft Board. *Report of President's Aircraft Board*. Washington, DC: Government Printing Office, 1925.

President's Research Committee on Social Trends. *Report of the President's Research Committee on Social Trends:. Recent Social Trends in the United States*. New York: McGraw-Hill, 1933.

Select Committee on Reconstruction and Production, United States Senate. *Reconstruction and Production*. Washington, DC: Government Printing Office, 1921.

Senate Committee on Education and Labor. *Industrial Conference: Hearing before the Committee on Education and Labor, United States Senate, 55th Congress, 2nd Session, on The Report of the Industrial Commission*. Washington, DC: Government Printing Office, 1920.

Smith, Alfred E. *Campaign Addresses of Governor Alfred E. Smith, Democratic Candidate for President, 1928*. Washington, DC: Democratic National Committee, 1929.

Special Senate Committee Investigating Presidential Campaign Expenditures. "Presidential Campaign Expenditures." *Hearings before a Special Committee Investigating Presidential Campaign Expenditures, United States Senate*, 70th Cong., 1st sess., May 7–14, 15–16, 1928. Washington, DC: Government Printing Office, 1928.

U.S. Senate. *Presidential Campaign Expenditures*. Senate Report 2024, 70th Cong., 2d sess.

U.S. Senate. *Reconstruction and Production*. Report of the Select Committee on Reconstruction and Production, March 2, 1921. Washington, DC: Government Printing Office, 1921.

Wilbur, Ray Lyman, and Northcutt Ely. *The Hoover Dam Power and Water Contracts and Related Data*. Washington, DC: Government Printing Office, 1930.

World Foreign Debt Commission. *Combined Annual Reports of the World War Foreign Debt Commission, with Additional Information Regarding Foreign Debts Due the United States, Fiscal Years 1922, 1923, 1924, 1925, and 1926*. Washington, DC: Government Printing Office, 1927.

Articles, Book Chapters, and Papers

Abbott, Grace. "Public Protection for Children." In *The Grace Abbott Reader*, edited by John Sorensen and Judith Sealander, 43–52. Lincoln: University of Nebraska Press, 2008.

Accinelli, Robert D. "Was There a 'New' Harding? Warren G. Harding and the World Court Issue," *Ohio History* 84 (Autumn 1975): 168–81.

"America and Russia" *New Republic* August 24, 1921, 342.

Artaud, Denise. "Reparations and War Debts: The Restoration of French Financial Power, 1919–1929." In *French Foreign and Defense Policy, 1918–1940: The Decline and Fall of a Great Power*, edited by Robert Boyce, 89–106. London: Routledge, 1998.

Bernanke, Ben S. "The Macroeconomics of the Great Depression: A Comparative Approach." In *Essays on the Great Depression*, 4–40. Princeton, NJ: Princeton University Press, 2000.

Best, Gary Dean. "Food Relief as Price Support: Hoover and American Pork, January–March 1919." *Agricultural History* 45 (April 1971): 79–84.

———. "Herbert Hoover's Technical Mission to Yugoslavia, 1919–1920." *Annals of Iowa*, 3rd ser., 42 (Fall 1972): 443–59.

———. "The Hoover for President Boom of 1920." *Mid-America* 53 (October 1971): 227–44.

"Biography of Clara Burdette." *California Life*, April 10, 1920, 3, 21

Bjornstad, Fred A. "Herbert Hoover, Housing, and Socioeconomic Planning in the 1920s." In *Uncommon Americans: The Lives and Legacies of Herbert and Lou Henry Hoover*, edited by Timothy Walch, 107–12. Westport, CT: Praeger, 2003.

Black, W. M. "The Problem of the Mississippi." *North American Review* 224 (December 1927): 630–40.

Bliven, Bruce. "Hoover—And the Rest." *Independent*, May 29, 1920, 275–76, 279.

Boyce, Robert. "Business as Usual: The Limits of French Economic Diplomacy, 1926–1933." In *French Foreign and Defence Policy, 1918–1940: The Decline and Fall of a Great Power*, edited by Robert Boyce, 107–31. Routledge: London, 1998.

Brandes, Joseph. "Herbert Hoover's Economic Diplomacy." In *Herbert Hoover Reassessed: Essays Commemorating the Fiftieth Anniversary of the Inauguration of Our Thirty-First President*, compiled by Mark Hatfield, 380–89. Washington, DC: Government Printing Office, 1981.

"A Brief Chronology of What Congress Has Done since 1824 to Control the Floods of the Mississippi." *Congressional Digest* 7 (February 1928): 44–45.

Broun, Heywood. "It Seems to Heywood Broun." *Nation*, October 3, 1928, 313.

"The Bullitt 'Bomb'" *Literary Digest* September 27, 1919: 12.

Burner, David. "Election of 1924." In *History of American Presidential Elections, 1789–1968*, edited by Arthur M. Schlesinger, Jr., Fred L. Israel, and William P. Hansen, vol. 3, 2459–90. New York: Chelsea House, 1971.

———. "The Quaker Faith of Herbert Hoover." In *Understanding Herbert Hoover: Ten Perspectives*, edited by Lee Nash, 53–64. Stanford, CA: Hoover Institution, 1987.

Burns, Arthur F. "Introductory Sketch." In *Wesley Clair Mitchell: The Economic Scientist*, edited by Arthur F. Burns, 3–54. New York: National Bureau of Economic Research, 1952.

Cabot, Philip. "Judge Gary's Opportunity." *Atlantic Monthly* 127 (May 1921): 599–606.

"California Is for Hoover." *Nation*, October 10, 1928, 339–40.

Carter, Paul. "The Campaign of 1928 Re-Examined: A Study in Political Folklore." *Wisconsin Magazine of History* 46 (Summer 1963): 263–72.

Clements, Kendrick A. "Herbert Hoover and the Fish." *Journal of Psychohistory* 10 (Winter 1983): 333–48.

———. "The New Era and the New Woman: Lou Henry Hoover and 'Feminism's Awkward Age.'" *Pacific Historical Review* 73 (August 2004): 425–61.

"A Compromise on Flood Control." *Outlook*, March 14, 1928, 411.

"Congress Takes Up Flood Control Program." *Congressional Digest* 7 (February 1928): 47–48.

Costigliola, Frank. "American Foreign Policy in the *Nut Cracker*: The United States and Poland in the 1920s." *Pacific Historical Review* 48 (February 1979): 85–105.

———. "The United States and the Reconstruction of Germany in the 1920s." *Business History Review* 50 (Winter 1976): 477–522.

Croly, Herbert. "How Is Hoover?" *New Republic*, June 27, 1928, 138–40.

Cullather, Nick. "The Foreign Policy of the Calorie." *American Historical Review* 112 (April 2007): 337–64.

"Current Events: Peace Preliminaries" *Literary Digest* September 27, 1919: 65.

Davis, Arthur Powell. "Development of the Colorado River: The Justification of Boulder Dam." *Atlantic* 143 (February 1929): 254–57.

Dayton, Katherine. "What's the Matter With Hoover?" *Saturday Evening Post*, August 11, 1928, 102.

Dennis, Alfred Pearce. "Humanizing the Department of Commerce." *Saturday Evening Post*, June 6, 1925.

Doherty, Herbert J., Jr. "Florida and the Presidential Election of 1928." *Florida Historical Quarterly* 26 (October 1947): 174–86.

Drake, Douglas C. "Herbert Hoover, Ecologist: The Politics of Oil Pollution Control, 1921–1926." *Mid-America* 55 (July 1973): 207–28.

"The Engineer as a Molder of Public Opinion." *Engineering and Mining Journal*, June 30, 1928, 1041.

Feiker, F. M. "The Trend of Simplification: How the Movement is Growing, and What the Paving Brick Action Signifies." *Factory* (February 1922): 156–58.

Ferrell, Robert. "The Republican Ascendancy: Calvin Coolidge, Charles Dawes, and Charles Curtis as Vice Presidents." In *At the President's Side: The Vice Presidency in the Twentieth Century*, edited by Timothy Walch, 24–41. Columbia: University of Missouri Press, 1997.

"The Fight to Prevent Another Mississippi Flood." *Literary Digest*, May 21, 1927, 8–9.

"The Fight with the Rampageous Father of Waters." *Literary Digest*, November 3, 1928, 21–22.

"Floods and the Jones Measure." *American Review of Reviews* 77 (May 1928): 454.

Frank, Lawrence K. "Childhood and Youth." In "Childhood and Youth," in Report of the President's Research Committee on Social Trends, *Recent Social Trends in the United States*, vol. 2, 751–800. New York: McGraw-Hill, 1933.

Frankfurter, Felix. "The President's Industrial Conference." *New Republic*, April 7, 1920, 179–82.

"Frelinghuysen Bills Opening Wedge for Drastic Legislation on Coal." *American Coal Journal*, June 25, 1921, 1.

Fuchs, Lawrence H. "Election of 1928." In *History of American Presidential Elections, 1789–1968*, edited by Arthur M. Schlesinger, Jr., and Fred L. Israel, vol. 3, 2585–2609. New York: Chelsea House, 1971.

Garvey, Daniel E. "Secretary Hoover and the Quest for Broadcast Regulation." In *Business-Government Cooperation, 1917–1932: The Rise of Corporatist Policies*, edited by Robert F. Himmelberg, 76–81. New York: Garland, 1984.

Giglio, James N. "Voluntarism and Public Policy between World War I and the New Deal: Herbert Hoover and the American Child Health Association." *Presidential Studies Quarterly* 13 (Summer 1983): 430–52.

"The Gist of It." *Survey*, December 15, 1930, 305.

Glaser, Elisabeth. "The Making of the Economic Peace." In *The Treaty of Versailles: A Reassessment after 75 Years*, edited by Manfred F. Boemeke, Gerald D. Feldman, and Elisabeth Glaser, 371–99. Washington, DC: German Historical Institute, 1998.

Glaser-Schmidt, Elisabeth. "German and American Concepts to Restore a Liberal World Trading System after World War I." In *Confrontation and Cooperation: Germany and the United States in the Era of World War I, 1900–1924*, edited by Hans-Jürgen Schröder, 353–76. (Providence, RI: Berg, 1993).

"Governor of Arizona States His Stand on Colorado River Situation." *Electrical World*, December 29, 1923, 1322.

Gregory, T. T. C. "Overthrowing a Red Regime." *The World's Work* 42 (June 1921): 153–64.

Grin, Carolyn. "The Unemployment Conference of 1921: An Experiment in National Cooperative Planning." In *Business-Government Cooperation, 1917–1932: The Rise of Corporatist Policies*, edited by Robert F. Himmelberg, 83–107. New York: Garland, 1994.

Hard, William. "Giant Negotiations for Giant Power." *Survey Graphic* 4 (March 1924): 577–80.

Hawley, Ellis W. "Herbert Hoover, the Commerce Secretariat, and the Vision of an 'Associative State,' 1921–1928." *Journal of American History* 41 (June 1974): 116–40.

———. "Herbert Hoover and Economic Stabilization, 1921–22." In *Herbert Hoover as Secretary of Commerce, 1921–1928: Studies in New Era Thought and Practice*, edited by Ellis W. Hawley, 44–77. Iowa City: University of Iowa Press, 1981.

———. "Herbert Hoover and the Sherman Act, 1921–1933: An Early Phase of a Continuing Issue." *Iowa Law Review* 74 (July 1989): 1067–1103.

———. "Secretary Hoover and the Bituminous Coal Problem, 1921–1928." *Business History Review* 42 (Autumn 1968): 247–70.

"Herbert Hoover: The Man Without a Party." *Literary Digest*, March 13, 1920, 47–52.

Holt, E. G. "Five Years of Restriction." *India Rubber World*, February 1, 1928, 55–57.

Hoover, Herbert. "Collier's Strike Cure—and Its Critics." *Collier's* November 27, 1920, 9–10, 16.

———. "The Engineer's Relation to Our Industrial Problems." *Engineering News-Record*, November 25, 1920, 1053–55.

———. "The Food Future: What Every American Mouthful Means to Europe." *The Forum* 61 (February 1919): 210–18.

———. "Forty-Five Million Children." *The Survey* Dec. 15, 1930, 313.

———. "The Home and the Nation." *Child Welfare Magazine* 20 (April 1926): 450.

———. "The Home as an Investment." In *Better Homes in America, Plan Book for Demonstration Week, October 9 to 14, 1922* (New York: The Delineator, 1922), 7–8

———. "How Much Longer Must We Feed Europe?" *The Forum* 64 (December 1920): 377–79.

———. "In Praise of Izaak Walton." *Atlantic* 149 (June 1927): 813–19.

———. "Marketing American Surplus Food Products." *Farm and Home* 41 (January 1920): 1, 5, 37.

———. "A National System of Waterways." December 9, 1925, in *Proceedings of the Twenty-First Convention, National Rivers and Harbors Conference*, 16–24. Washington, DC: Ransdell, 1925.

———. "Railroad Consolidation." *Saturday Evening Post*, February 9, 1924.

———. "Some Notes on Agricultural Readjustment and the High Cost of Living." *Saturday Evening Post*, April 10, 1920, 3–4

———. "Some Notes on Industrial Readjustment." *Saturday Evening Post*, December 27, 1919.

———. "Stabilization of Bituminous Coal Industry." *Mining and Metallurgy* 4 (March 1920): 1–2.

———. "Why Inland Waterways Should Be Developed." *American Review of Reviews* 74 (December 1926): 595–98.

"Hoover." *New Republic*, March 9, 1921, 29.

"Hoover and the Issues." *New Republic*, February 4, 1920, 281–83.

"Hoover and the Religious Issue." *Independent*, October 13, 1928, 341.

"Hoover and Russian Economics." *New Republic*, May 31, 1922, 4–5.

"Hoover and the Scripps-Howard Press." *Nation*, October 24, 1922, 4–5.

"Hoover as President." *Literary Digest*, January 31, 1920, 16.

"The Hoover Conference." *Retail Lumber Dealer* 2, no. 6 (June 1922): 22.

"The 'Hoover Menace.'" *Current Opinion* 68 (May 1920): 589–93.

"Hoover on Labor." *New Republic* September 26, 1928, 138–41.

"Hoover Out for the Superpower Plan." *Literary Digest*, November 17, 1923, 14.

"Hoover's Appeal to the Workers." *Literary Digest* October 6, 1928, 10–11.

"Hoover's Chances." *Literary Digest*, February 4, 1928, 5–7.

"Hoover's Politician." *Collier's*, May 11, 1929, 66.

"Hoover's Stand for Prohibition." *Literary Digest*, March 10, 1928, 7–9.

"How the Nation Sizes Up the Hoover Ticket." *Literary Digest*, June 23, 1928, 6–8.

"How the Papers Size Up the Hoover Boom." *Literary Digest*, March 6, 1920, 13–14.

Howard, Samuel F., Jr. "Samuel Untermyer." In *Dictionary of American Biography*, suppl. 2, 674–76. New York: Scribner's, 1958.

Hutchison, Janet. "Building for Babbitt: The State and the Suburban Home Ideal." *Journal of Policy History* 9, no. 2 (1997): 184–210.

"Inter and Intra Institutional Athletic Activities." *School Life*, May 1933, 3.

Irwin, Will. "Saving the American Child." *Forum and Century* 95 (April 1936): 201–5.

Jadwin, Edgar. "The Plan for Flood Control of the Mississippi River in Its Alluvial Valley." *Annals of the American Academy of Political and Social Science* 135 (January 1928): 35–36.

Johnson, Hiram. "The Boulder Canyon Project." *Annals of the American Academy of Political and Social Science* 135 (January 1923): 155.

Johnson. James P. "Herbert Hoover and David Copperfield: A Tale of Two Childhoods." *Journal of Psychohistory* 7 (Spring 1980): 467–75.

———. "Herbert Hoover: The Orphan as Children's Friend." *Prologue* 12 (Winter 1980): 193–206.

Kanarek, Harold K. "Disaster for Hard Coal: The Anthracite Strike of 1925–1926." *Labor History* 15 (January 1974): 46–62.

Kellogg, Vernon. "Herbert Hoover as I Know Him." *The Outlook*, October 19, 1927, 203–6, and October 26, 1927, 239–41, 244.

Kindleberger, Charles. "U.S. Foreign Economic Policy, 1776–1976." *Foreign Affairs* 55 (January 1977): 395–17.

Kottman, Richard N. "Herbert Hoover and the St. Lawrence Seaway Treaty of 1932." *New York History* 56 (July 1975): 314–46.

Lake, David. "International Economic Structures and American Foreign Economic Policy, 1887–1934." *World Politics* 35 (July 1987): 517–43.

Lee, David D. "Herbert Hoover and the Development of Commercial Aviation, 1921–1926." *Business History Review* 58 (Spring 1984): 78–102.

Leffler, Melvyn. "American Policy-Making and European Stability, 1921–1933." *Pacific Historical Review* 46 (May 1977): 207–28.

———. "1921–1932: Expansionist Impulses and Domestic Constraints." In *Economics and World Power: An Assessment of American Diplomacy since 1789*, edited by William H. Becker and Samuel F. Wells, Jr., 225–75. New York: Columbia University Press, 1984.

———. "The Origins of Republican War Debt Policy, 1921–1923." *Journal of American History* 59 (December 1972): 585–601.

Link, Arthur S. "What Happened to the Progressive Movement in the 1920s?" *American Historical Review* 64 (July 1959): 833–51.

Littell, Robert. "The Unemployed and a Weather Man." *New Republic*, March 1, 1922, 22.

Livingstone, Belle. "The Story of My Life: The Autobiography of the Woman They Called 'The Most Dangerous Woman in Europe.'" *Hearst's International-Cosmopolitan* 42 (July 1925): 217–18.

Lohof, Bruce A. "Herbert Hoover, Spokesman of Humane Efficiency: The Mississippi Flood of 1927." *American Quarterly* 22 (Fall 1970): 690–700.

Long, Thomas A. "Engineering and Social Equality: Herbert Hoover's Manifesto." *IEEE Technology and Society Magazine* 3 (September 1984): 18.

Lorimer, George Horace. "Hoover." *Saturday Evening Post*, July 31, 1920, 20.

MacDonald, William. "Plans for National Flood Relief and Control." *Current History* 27 (November 1927): 268–69.

Malin, James C. "Charles Curtis, 1860–1936." In *Dictionary of American Biography*, suppl. 2, 136–37. New York: Scribner's, 1958.

Mayer, Dale. "An Uncommon Woman: The Quiet Leadership of Lou Henry Hoover." *Presidential Studies Quarterly* 20 (Fall 1990): 685–98.

Metcalf, Evan B. "Secretary Hoover and the Emergence of Macroeconomic Management." *Business History Review* 49 (Spring 1975): 60–80.

"Mr. Hoover and The Farmer." *Wallace's Farmer*, March 19, 1920.

"Mr. Hoover in the Valley of Decision" *New Republic* February 21, 1920, 225.

"Mr. Hoover's Misstatements" *Nation* October 3, 1928, 310.

Mitchell, Wesley C. "A Review" In Committee on Recent Economic Changes of the President's Conference on Unemployment. *Recent Economic Changes in the United States*. 2 vols. New York: McGraw-Hill, 1929 2:890–909.

Murray, Robert K. "Herbert Hoover and the Harding Cabinet." In *Herbert Hoover as Secretary of Commerce, 1921–1928: Studies in New Era Thought and Practice*, edited by Ellis W. Hawley, 19–40. Iowa City: University of Iowa Press, 1981.

Murphy, J. Prentice. "When Doctors Disagreed." *The Survey*, December 15, 1930, 311–15, 348–49, 351.

Nash, George H. "The 'Great Enigma' and the 'Great Engineer': The Political Relationship of Calvin Coolidge and Herbert Hoover." In *Calvin Coolidge and the Coolidge Era: Essays on the History of the 1920s*, edited by John Earl Haynes, 149–90. Washington, DC: Library of Congress, 1998.

"Nothing Done Yet for Flood Control." *Literary Digest*, March 10, 1928, 10–11.

Odell, George T. "Herbert Hoover—Super-Business Man." *Nation* September 23, 1925, 325–27.

O'Neill, J. H. "Relief Measures During and Following the Mississippi Valley Flood." *American Journal of Public Health* 18 (February 1928): 154–60.

"An Open Letter to Mr. Hoover" *New Republic* May 23, 1923, 334.

"Opposition to Frelinghuysen Control Bill Crystallizes in Coal Industry." *American Coal Journal*, June 25, 1921, 1.

Palmer, George T., "Eighty-Six Cities Studied by Objective Standards." *American Journal of Public Health* 15 (May 1925): 387–93.

"The Politics of the Hoover Boom." *New Republic*, April 21, 1920, 238–39.

Posner, Russell M. "The Progressive Voters League, 1923–1926." *California Historical Society Quarterly* 36 (September 1957): 251–61.

"President Coolidge's Analysis of Mississippi Flood Control Problem." *Congressional Digest* 7 (February 1928): 46.

"The President Transmits to Congress Flood Control Plan of Army Engineers." *Congressional Digest* 7 (February 1928): 47.

"The President's Victory on Flood Control." *Literary Digest*, May 19, 1928, 9–10.

Pringle, Henry F. "Hoover: An Enigma Easily Misunderstood" *World's Work* 56 (June 1928): 131–32, 134.

Putnam, Jackson K. "The Persistence of Progressivism in the 1920s: The Case of California." *Pacific Historical Review* 35 (November 1966): 395–411.

Reagan, Patrick D. "From Depression to Depression: Hooverian National Planning, 1921–1923." *Mid-America* 70 (January 1988): 35–60. Also reprinted in *Business-Government Cooperation, 1917–1932: The Rise of Corporatist Policies*, edited by Robert F. Himmelberg, 341–66. New York: Garland, 1994.

Rhodes, Benjamin F. "Reassessing 'Uncle Shylock': The United States and the French War Debt, 1917–1929." *Journal of American History* 55 (March 1969): 787–803.

Rickard, T. A. "Herbert Hoover: A Sketch." *Mining and Scientific Press*, April 3, 1920, 494–96.

Rogers, James Harvey. "Foreign Markets and Foreign Credits" In Committee on Recent Economic Changes of the President's Conference on Unemployment. *Recent Economic Changes in the United States*. 2 vols. New York: McGraw-Hill, 1929 2:752–54.

Rothbard, Murray N. "Hoover's 1919 Food Diplomacy in Retrospect." In *Herbert Hoover: The Great War and Its Aftermath, 1914–23*, edited by Lawrence E. Gelfand, 89–110. Iowa City: University of Iowa Press, 1979.

"Rubber and Mr. Hoover." *Nation*, January 20, 1926, 50.

Schapsmeier, Edward L., and Frederick H. Schapsmeier. "Disharmony in the Harding Cabinet: •Hoover-Wallace Conflict." *Ohio History* 75 (Spring–Summer 1966): 126–36, 188–90.

Schuker, Stephen A. "American Foreign Policy: The European Dimension, 1921–1929." In *Calvin Coolidge and the Coolidge Era: Essays on the History of the 1920s*, edited by John Earl Haynes, 289–308. Washington, DC: Library of Congress, 1998.

———. "The Gold-Exchange Standard: A Reinterpretation." In *International Financial History in the Twentieth Century: System and Anarchy*, edited by Marc Flandreau, Carl-Ludwig Holtfr-erich, and Harold James, 77–93. Cambridge, UK: German Historical Institute and Cambridge University Press, 2003.

———. "Origins of American Stabilization Policy in Europe: The Financial Dimension, 1918–1924." In *Confrontation and Cooperation: Germany and the United States in the Era of World War I, 1900–1924*, edited by Hans-Jürgen Schröder, 377–407. Providence, RI: Berg, 1993.

Selig, Diana. "The Whole Child: Social Science and Race at the White House Conference of 1930." In *When Science Encounters the Child: Education, Parenting, and Child Welfare in 20th Century America*, edited by Barbara Beatty, Emily D. Cahan, and Julia Grant, 136–56. New York: Teachers College Press, 2006.

Shideler, James H. "Herbert Hoover and the Federal Farm Board Project, 1921–1925." *Mississippi Valley Historical Review* 42 (March 1956): 710–29.

Soule, George. "Herbert Hoover: Practical Man." *New Republic* 53 (December 28, 1927): 161.

"Squaring Hoover with the Farmers." *Literary Digest*, November 12, 1927, 11.

Strauss, Lewis, Jr. "Herbert C. Hoover and the Jews." *The American Hebrew*, April 23, 1920, 747, 759.

"A Summary of the Mississippi River Commission's Recommendations for the Control of Floods." *Congressional Digest* 7 (February 1928): 49, 70.

"Superpower and Economic Statesmanship." *Chemical and Metallurgical Engineering*, October 22, 1923, 744.

Strother, French. "Herbert Hoover." *World's Work* 39 (April 1920): 578–85.

Trani, Eugene. "Hubert Work." In *Dictionary of American Biography*, suppl. 3, *1941–1945*, 845–46. New York: Scribner's, 1973.

Trattner, Walter. "August Heckscher." In *Dictionary of American Biography*, suppl. 3, *1941–1945*, 348–49. New York: Scribner's, 1973.

Tyler, Daniel. "Delphus Emory Carpenter and the Colorado River Compact of 1922." *University of Denver Water Law Review* 1 (Summer 1998): 228–74.

Unsigned, untitled editorial on aid to Russia. *Nation*, August 24, 1921, 187.

"Uses of Waste." *Engineering and Mining Journal*, November 13, 1926, 763.

Van Meter, Robert H., Jr. "Herbert Hoover and the Economic Reconstruction of Europe, 1918–21." In *Herbert Hoover: The Great War and Its Aftermath, 1918–23*, edited by Lawrence E. Gelfand, 145–81. Iowa City: University of Iowa Press, 1979.

Villard, Oswald Garrison. "Presidential Possibilities, IV: Herbert C. Hoover." *Nation* 126 (February 29, 1928): 234–37.

Wallace, Henry A. "Re-Forming The Battle Lines." *Wallace's Farmer*, July 18, 1924.

Ward, John William. "The Meaning of Lindbergh's Flight." In *Studies in American Culture: Dominant Ideas and Images*, edited by Joseph J. Kwiat and Mary C. Turpie, 27–40. Minneapolis: University of Minnesota Press, 1960.

"What's the Matter with the Farmer." *Wallace's Farmer*, February 13, 1920.

Weems, Robert E., Jr., and Lewis A. Randolph. "'The Right Man': James A. Jackson and the Origins of U.S. Government Interest in Black Business." *Enterprise and Society* 6 (June 2005): 254–77.

White, Walter. "The Negro and the Flood." *Nation*, June 22, 1927, 688–89.

"Will Coolidge Shatter the Third-Term Tradition." *Literary Digest*, May 14, 1927, 5–7.

Williams, C. Fred. "William M. Jardine and the Foundations for Republican Farm Policy, 1925–1929." *Agricultural History* 70 (Spring 1996): 216–32.

Wilson, Joan Hoff. "Herbert Hoover's Agricultural Policies, 1921–1928." In *Herbert Hoover as Secretary of Commerce: Studies in New Era Thought and Practice*, edited by Ellis Hawley, 116–44. Iowa City: University of Iowa Press, 1981.

———. "Hoover's Agricultural Policies, 1921–1928." *Agricultural History* 51 (April 1977): 335–61.

Wingo, Barbara C. "The 1928 Presidential Election in Louisiana." *Louisiana History* 18 (Fall 1977): 405–35.

"The Woman's Party and Mr. Hoover." *Nation*, October 3, 1928, 312.

Wueschner, Silvano A. "Herbert Hoover, Great Britain and the Rubber Crisis, 1923–1926." Unpublished paper presented at the Annual Meeting of the Economic and Business Historical Society, San Antonio, Texas, April 1999.

Wyatt-Walter, Andrew. "The United States and Western Europe: The Theory of Hegemonic Stability." In *Explaining International Relations since 1945*, edited by Ngaire Woods, 126–53. Oxford, UK: Oxford University Press, 1996.

Zieger, Robert H. "Herbert Hoover, the Wage Earner, and the 'New Economic System,' 1919–1929." In *Herbert Hoover as Secretary of Commerce, 1921–1928: Studies in New Era Thought and Practice*, edited by Ellis W. Hawley, 82–112. Iowa City: University of Iowa Press, 1981.

———. "Pinchot and Coolidge: The Politics of the 1923 Anthracite Crisis." *Journal of American History* 52 (December 1965): 566–81.

———. "Solving the Labor Problem: Herbert Hoover and the American Worker in the 1920s." In *Herbert Hoover Reassessed: Essays Commemorating the Fiftieth Anniversary of the Inauguration of Our Thirty-First President*, compiled by Mark O. Hatfield, 177–87. Washington, DC: Government Printing Office, 1981.

Books

Ahamed, Liaquat. *Lords of Finance: The Bankers Who Broke the World*. New York: Penguin, 2009.

Aitken, Hugh G. J. *The Continuous Wave: Technology and American Radio, 1900–1932*. Princeton, NJ: Princeton University Press, 1985.

Alchon, Guy. *The Invisible Hand of Planning: Capitalism, Social Science, and the State in the 1920s*. Princeton, NJ: Princeton University Press, 1985.

Aldcroft, Derek H. *From Versailles to Wall Street, 1919–1929*. Berkeley: University of California Press, 1977.

Allen, Anne Beiser. *An Independent Woman: The Life of Lou Henry Hoover*. Westport, CT: Praeger, 2000.

Allen, Frederick Lewis. *Only Yesterday: An Informal History of the 1920s*. New York: Blue Ribbon Books, 1931.

American Child Heath Association. *Five Years of the American Child Health Association: A Bird's-Eye View*. New York: American Child Health Association, 1927.

Anon. *Boudoir Mirrors of Washington*. Philadelphia: John C. Winston, 1923.

Archer, Gleason L. *History of Radio to 1926*. New York: American Historical Society, 1938.

Ascoli, Peter M. *Julius Rosenwald: The Man Who Built Sears, Roebuck and Advanced the Cause of Black Education in the American South*. Bloomington: Indiana University Press, 2006.

Bajema, Carl Jay, ed. *Eugenics: Then and Now*. Stroudsburg, PA: Dowden, Hutchinson & Ross, 1976.

Baker, S. Josephine. *Child Hygiene*. New York: Harper & Bros., 1925.

Barber, William J. *From New Era to New Deal: Herbert Hoover, the Economists, and American Economic Policy, 1921–1933*. New York: Cambridge University Press, 1985.

Barnouw, Erik. *A Tower in Babel: A History of Broadcasting in the United States*. Vol. 1, *To 1933*. New York: Oxford University Press, 1966.

Barry, John M. *Rising Tide: The Great Mississippi Flood of 1927 and How It Changed America*. New York: Simon & Schuster, 1997.

Bauer, K. Jack. *A Maritime History of the United States: The Role of America's Seas and Waterways*. Columbia: University of South Carolina Press, 1988.

Beatty, Barbara, Emily D. Cahan, and Julia Grant, eds. *When Science Encounters the Child: Education, Parenting, and Child Welfare in 20th Century America*. New York: Teachers College Press, 2006.

Becker, William H., and Samuel F. Wells, Jr., eds. *Economics and World Power: An Assessment of American Diplomacy since 1789*. New York: Columbia University Press, 1984.

Bell, F. Heward. *The Pacific Halibut: The Resource and the Fishery*. Anchorage: Alaska Northwest, 1981.

Berle, Adolf A., Jr., and Gardiner C. Means. *The Modern Corporation and Private Property*. New York: Macmillan, 1930.

Bernanke, Ben S. *Essays on the Great Depression*. Princeton, NJ: Princeton University Press, 2000.

Bessel, Richard. *Germany after the First World War*. Oxford, UK: Clarendon, 1993.

Best, Gary Dean. *The Politics of American Individualism: Herbert Hoover in Transition, 1918–1921*. Westport, CT: Greenwood, 1975.

Bicknell, Ernest P. *Pioneering with the Red Cross: Recollections of an Old Red Crosser*. New York: Macmillan, 1935.

Blair, Karen J. *The Clubwoman as Feminist: True Womanhood Redefined, 1868–1914*. New York: Holmes & Meier, 1980.

Blake, Robert. *Unrepentant Tory: The Life and Times of Andrew Bonar Law, 1858–1923, Prime Minister of the United Kingdom*. New York: St. Martin's, 1956.

Blum, John M. *Joe Tumulty and the Wilson Era*. Boston: Houghton Mifflin, 1951.

Boemeke, Manfred F., Gerald D. Feldman, and Elisabeth Glaser, eds. *The Treaty of Versailles: A Reassessment after 75 Years*. Washington, DC: German Historical Institute, 1998.

Bornet, Vaughn Davis. *Labor Politics in a Democratic Republic: Moderation, Division, and Disruption in the Presidential Election of 1928*. Washington, DC: Spartan Books, 1964.

Borsányi, György. *The Life of a Communist Revolutionary, Béla Kun*. Translated by Mario D. Fenyo. Highland Lakes, NJ: Atlantic Research and Publications, 1993.

Boyce, Robert W. D. *British Capitalism at the Crossroads, 1919–1932: A Study in Politics, Economics, and International Relations*. Cambridge, UK: Cambridge University Press, 1987.

———, ed. *French Foreign and Defence Policy, 1918–1940: The Decline and Fall of a Great Power*. Routledge: London, 1998.

Braeman, John, Robert H. Bremner, and David Brody, eds. *Change and Continuity in Twentieth-Century America: The 1920s*. Columbus: Ohio State University Press, 1968.

Brandes, Joseph. *Herbert Hoover and Economic Diplomacy: Department of Commerce Policy, 1921–1928*. Pittsburgh: University of Pittsburgh Press, 1962.

Bremner, Robert, ed. *Children and Youth in America: A Documentary History*. Vol. 2. Cambridge, MA: Harvard University Press, 1971.

Brown, Dorothy M. *Mabel Walker Willebrandt: A Study of Power, Loyalty, and Law*. Knoxville: University of Tennessee Press, 1984.

Buckingham, Peter H. *International Normalcy: The Open Door Peace with the Former Central Powers, 1921–29*. Wilmington, DE: Scholarly Resources, 1983.

Burner, David. *Herbert Hoover: A Public Life*. New York: Knopf, 1979.

Burns, Arthur F., ed. *Wesley Clair Mitchell: The Economic Scientist*. New York: National Bureau of Economic Research, 1952.

Campagna, Anthony S. *U.S. National Economic Policy, 1917–1985*. New York: Praeger, 1987.

Cannadine, David. *Mellon: An American Life*. New York: Knopf, 2006.

Chandler, Lester V. *Benjamin Strong: Central Banker*. Washington, DC: Brookings Institution, 1958.

Clark, Birge M. *Memoirs about Mr. and Mrs. Herbert Hoover, with Particular Emphasis on the Planning and Building of Their Home on San Juan Hill*. Palo Alto, CA: Privately printed, 1969.

Clarke, Stephen V. O. *Central Bank Cooperation: 1924–31*. New York: Federal Reserve Bank of New York, 1967.

Clements, Kendrick A. *Hoover, Conservation, and Consumerism: Engineering the Good Life*. Lawrence: University Press of Kansas, 2000.

Clifford, Deborah Pickman, and Nicholas R. Clifford. *"The Troubled Roar of the Water": Vermont in Flood and Recovery, 1927–1931*. Durham: University of New Hampshire Press, 2007.

Cohen, Stephen. *Bukharin and the Bolshevik Revolution: A Political Biography, 1888–1938*. New York: Knopf, 1973.

Cohrs, Patrick O. *The Unfinished Peace after World War I: America, Britain and the Stabilisation of Europe, 1919–1932*. Cambridge, England: Cambridge University Press, 2006.

Conant, James Bryant. *Education and Liberty: The Role of the Schools in a Modern Democracy*. Cambridge, MA: Harvard University Press, 1953.

Costigliola, Frank. *Awkward Dominion: American Political, Economic, and Cultural Relations with Europe, 1919–1933*. Ithaca, NY: Cornell University Press, 1984.

Costin, Lela B. *Two Sisters for Social Justice: A Biography of Grace and Edith Abbott*. Urbana: University of Illinois Press, 1983.

Counts, George S. *The Schools Can Teach Democracy*. New York: John Day, 1939.

Cowley, Malcolm, ed. *The Portable Faulkner*. New York: Viking, 1946.

Cremin, Lawrence. *Popular Education and Its Discontents*. New York: Harper & Row, 1989.

Daniel, Pete. *Deep'n As It Come: The 1927 Mississippi River Flood*. New York: Oxford University Press, 1977.

Davis, James W. *Presidential Primaries: Road to the White House*. Westport, CT: Greenwood, 1980.

De La Pedraja, René. *The Rise and Decline of U.S. Merchant Shipping in the Twentieth Century*. New York: Twayne, 1992.

Dennis, Ruth. *The Homes of the Hoovers*. West Branch, IA: Hoover Presidential Library Association, 1986.

Dorey, Annette K. Vance. *Better Baby Contests: The Scientific Quest for Perfect Childhood Health in the Early Twentieth Century*. Jefferson, NC: McFarland, 1999.

Dublin, Thomas, and Walter Licht. *The Face of Decline: The Pennsylvania Anthracite Region in the Twentieth Century*. Ithaca, NY: Cornell University Press, 2005.

Dubofsky, Melvyn, and Warren Van Tine. *John L. Lewis: A Biography*. New York: Quadrangle, 1977.

Dulles, Foster Rhea. *The American Red Cross: A History*. New York: Harper & Bros., 1950.

Edie, Lionel D., ed. *The Stabilization of Business*. New York: Macmillan, 1923.

Eichengreen, Barry. *Golden Fetters: The Gold Standard and the Great Depression, 1919–1939*. New York: Oxford University Press, 1992.

Ewy, Marvin. *Charles Curtis of Kansas: Vice President of the United States, 1929–1933*. Emporia: Kansas State Teachers College, 1961.

Farnsworth, Beatrice. *William C. Bullitt and the Soviet Union*. Bloomington: Indiana University Press, 1967.

Feis, Herbert. *The Diplomacy of the Dollar, 1919–1932*. New York: Norton, 1950.

Feldman, Gerald D. *Iron and Steel in the German Inflation, 1916–1923*. Princeton, NJ: Princeton University Press, 1977.

Ferrell, Robert H. *Ill-Advised: Presidential Health and Public Trust*. Columbia: University of Missouri Press, 1992.

———. *The Presidency of Calvin Coolidge*. Lawrence: University Press of Kansas, 1998.

Figes, Orlando. *Peasant Russia, Civil War: The Volga Countryside in Revolution (1917–1921)*. Oxford, UK: Clarendon, 1989.

———. *A People's Tragedy: A History of the Russian Revolution*. New York: Viking, 1996.

Finan, Christopher M. *Alfred E. Smith: The Happy Warrior*. New York: Hill and Wang, 2002.

Fink, Carole. *Defending the Rights of Others: The Great Powers, the Jews, and International Minority Protection, 1878–1938*. Cambridge, UK: Cambridge University Press, 2004.

———. *The Genoa Conference: European Diplomacy, 1921–1922*. Chapel Hill: University of North Carolina Press, 1984.

Fisher, H. H. *America and the New Poland*. New York: Macmillan, 1928.

———. *The Famine in Soviet Russia, 1919–1923: The Operations of the American Relief Administration*. New York: Macmillan, 1927.

Fisher, Irving. *The Making of Index Numbers: A Study of Their Varieties, Tests, and Reliability*. New York: Augustus M. Kelley 1967. Reprint of 1927 ed., first published in 1922.

Flandreau, Marc, Carl-Ludwig Holtfrerich, and Harold James, eds. *International Financial History in the Twentieth Century: System and Anarchy*. Cambridge, UK: German Historical Institute and Cambridge University Press, 2003.

Floto, Inga. *Colonel House in Paris: A Study of American Policy at the Paris Peace Conference of 1919*. Copenhagen: Universitetsforlaget I Aarhus, 1973.

Foner, Philip S. *History of the Labor Movement in the United States*. Vol. 7, *Labor and World War I, 1914–1918*. New York: International, 1987.

Foster, William Trufant, and Waddill Catchings. *The Road to Plenty*. Boston: Houghton Mifflin, 1928.

Freidel, Frank. *Franklin D. Roosevelt: The Ordeal*. Boston: Little, Brown, 1954.

Fuess, Claude M. *Calvin Coolidge: The Man from Vermont*. Westport, CT: Greenwood, 1968. (Orig. pub. 1939.)

Gelfand, Lawrence E., ed. *Herbert Hoover: The Great War and Its Aftermath, 1914–23*. Iowa City: University of Iowa Press, 1979.

Gilbert, Robert E. *The Tormented President: Calvin Coolidge, Death, and Clinical Depression*. Westport, CT: Praeger, 2003.

Gillette, Aaron. *Eugenics and the Nature-Nurture Debate in the Twentieth Century*. New York: Palgrave Macmillan, 2007.

Goldberg, David J. *Discontented America: The United States in the 1920s*. Baltimore:, Johns Hopkins University Press, 1999.

Goldberg, Ronald Allen. *America in the Twenties*. Syracuse, NY: Syracuse University Press, 2003.

Goodnow, Frank J. *The American Conception of Liberty and Government*. Providence, RI: Standard Printing, 1916.

Greenberg, David. *Calvin Coolidge*. New York: Times Books/Henry Holt, 2006.

Hamilton, David E. *From New Day to New Deal: American Farm Policy from Hoover to Roosevelt, 1928–1931*. Chapel Hill: University of North Carolina Press, 1991.

Handlin, Oscar. *Al Smith and His America*. Boston: Little, Brown, 1958.

Hard, William A. *Who's Hoover?* New York: Dodd, Mead, 1928.

Hatfield, Mark O., comp. *Herbert Hoover Reassessed: Essays Commemorating the Fiftieth Anniversary of the Inauguration of Our Thirty-First President*. Washington, DC: Government Printing Office, 1981.

Hawley, Ellis W. *The Great War and the Search for a Modern Order: A History of the American People and Their Institutions, 1917–1933*. New York: St. Martin's, 1979.

———, ed. *Herbert Hoover as Secretary of Commerce, 1921–1928: Studies in New Era Thought and Practice*. Iowa City: University of Iowa Press, 1981.

Hayden, Dolores. *Building Suburbia: Green Fields and Urban Growth, 1820–2000*. New York: Pantheon, 2003.

Haynes, John Earl, ed. *Calvin Coolidge and the Coolidge Era: Essays on the History of the 1920s*. Washington, DC: Library of Congress, 1998.

Himmelberg, Robert F., ed. *Business-Government Cooperation, 1917–1932: The Rise of Corporatist Policies.* New York: Garland, 1994.

Hofstadter, Richard. *The American Political Tradition and the Men Who Made It.* New York: Knopf, 1948.

Hogan, Michael J. *Informal Entente: The Private Structure of Cooperation in Anglo-American Economic Diplomacy, 1918–1928.* Columbia: University of Missouri Press, 1977.

Hogan, William T. *Economic History of the Iron and Steel Industry in the United States.* Vol. 3. Lexington, MA: Lexington Books, 1971.

Holtfrerich, Carl-Ludwig. *The German Inflation, 1914–1923: Causes and Effects in International Perspective.* Translated by Theo Balderson. Berlin: Walter de Gruyter, 1986.

Hoover, Herbert. *An American Epic.* 4 vols. Chicago: Regnery, 1959–1964.

———. *American Individualism.* New York: Doubleday, Doran, 1922. Reprint, West Branch, IA: Hoover Presidential Library Association, n.d.

———. *Memoirs: The Cabinet and the Presidency, 1920–1933.* New York: Macmillan, 1952.

———. *Memoirs: Years of Adventure, 1874–1920.* New York: Macmillan, 1951.

———. *The Ordeal of Woodrow Wilson.* New York: McGraw-Hill, 1958.

Horowitz, Daniel. *The Morality of Spending: Attitudes toward the Consumer Society in America, 1875–1940.* Baltimore: Johns Hopkins University Press, 1985.

Hundley, Norris, Jr. *Water and the West: The Colorado River Compact and the Politics of Water in the American West.* Berkeley: University of California Press, 1975.

Hutchinson, William T. *Lowden of Illinois: The Life of Frank O. Lowden.* Chicago: University of Chicago Press, 1957.

Irwin, Will. *Herbert Hoover: A Reminiscent Biography.* New York: Grosset & Dunlap, 1928.

Issel, William, and Robert W. Cherny. *San Francisco, 1865–1932.* Berkeley: University of California Press, 1986.

Jackson, Kenneth. *Crabgrass Frontier: The Suburbanization of the United States.* New York: Oxford University Press, 1985.

Jacobs, Meg. *Pocketbook Politics: Economic Citizenship in Twentieth-Century America.* Princeton, NJ: Princeton University Press, 2005.

James, Harold. *The End of Globalization: Lessons from the Great Depression.* Cambridge: Harvard University Press, 2001.

Jeansonne, Glen. *Transformation and Reaction: America, 1921–1945.* New York: HarperCollins, 1994.

Jenkins, Roy. *Churchill: A Biography.* New York: Farrar, Straus and Giroux, 2001.

Johnson, Claudius O. *Borah of Idaho.* Seattle: University of Washington Press, 1936.

Johnson, Evans C. *Oscar W. Underwood: A Bourbon from Birmingham.* Baton Rouge: Louisiana State University Press, 1980.

Johnson, James P. *The Politics of Soft Coal: The Bituminous Industry from World War I through the New Deal.* Urbana: University of Illinois Press, 1979.

Kennan, George F. *American Diplomacy, 1900–1950.* Chicago: University of Chicago Press, 1951.

———. *Russia and the West under Lenin and Stalin.* Boston: Little, Brown, 1960.

———. *Soviet-American Relations, 1917–1920: The Decision to Intervene.* Princeton, NJ: Princeton University Press, 1958.

Kennedy, David. *Over Here: The First World War and American Society.* New York: Oxford University Press, 1980.

Kent, Bruce. *The Spoils of War: The Politics, Economics, and Diplomacy of Reparations, 1918–1932.* Oxford, UK: Clarendon, 1989.

Keynes, John Maynard. *The Economic Consequences of the Peace.* London: Macmillan, 1920.

Keyssar, Alexander. *Out of Work: The First Century of Unemployment in Massachusetts.* Cambridge, UK: Cambridge University Press, 1986.

Kindleberger, Charles P. *The World in Depression, 1929–1939: Revised and Enlarged Edition.* Berkeley: University of California Press, 1986.

Klein, Julius. *Frontiers of Trade.* New York: Century, 1929.

Klein, Maury. *Rainbow's End: The Crash of 1929.* New York: Oxford University Press, 2001.

Kline, Wendy. *Building a Better Race: Gender, Sexuality, and Eugenics from the Turn of the Century to the Baby Boom.* Berkeley: University of California Press, 2001.

Kwiat, Joseph J., and Mary C. Turpie, eds. *Studies in American Culture: Dominant Ideas and Images.* Minneapolis: University of Minnesota Press, 1960.

Lake, David A. *Power, Protection, and Free Trade: International Sources of U.S. Commercial Strategy, 1887–1939.* Ithaca, NY: Cornell University Press, 1988.

Lane, Rose Wilder. *The Making of Herbert Hoover.* New York: Century, 1920.

Larson, Erik. *Isaac's Storm: A Man, A Time, and the Deadliest Hurricane in History.* New York: Random House, 1999.

Lazare, Daniel. *America's Undeclared War: What's Killing Our Cities and How We Can Stop It.* New York: Harcourt, 2001.

Leffler, Melvyn P. *The Elusive Quest: America's Pursuit of European Stability and French Security, 1919–1933.* Chapel Hill: University of North Carolina Press, 1979.

Lerski, George J. *Herbert Hoover and Poland: A Documentary History of a Friendship.* Stanford, CA: Hoover Institution, 1977.

Leuchtenburg, William E. *Herbert Hoover.* New York: Henry Holt, 2009.

Lichtman, Allan J. *Prejudice and the Old Politics: The Presidential Election of 1928.* Chapel Hill: University of North Carolina Press, 1979.

Lisio, Donald J. *Hoover, Blacks, and Lily-Whites: A Study of Southern Strategies.* Chapel Hill: University of North Carolina Press, 1985.

Livingstone, Belle. *The Belle of Bohemia.* London: J. Hamilton, 1927.

Lloyd, Craig. *Aggressive Introvert: A Study of Herbert Hoover and Public Relations Management, 1912–1932.* Columbus: Ohio State University Press, 1972.

Lloyd George, David. *The Truth about the Peace Treaties.* London: Victor Gollancz, 1938.

Lochner, Louis P. *Herbert Hoover and Germany.* New York: Macmillan, 1960.

Lower, Richard Coke. *A Bloc of One: The Political Career of Hiram W. Johnson.* Stanford, CA: Stanford University Press, 1993.

Lowitt, Richard. *George W. Norris: The Persistence of a Progressive, 1913–1933.* Urbana: University of Illinois Press, 1971.

Lubell, Samuel. *The Future of American Politics,* 3rd ed. New York: Harper & Row, 1965.

Lyman, Robert Hunt, ed. *World Almanac and Book of Facts for 1929.* New York: New York World, 1929.

Lynd, Robert S., and Helen Merrell Lynd. *Middletown: A Study in American Culture.* New York: Harcourt, Brace & World, 1956. (Orig. pub. 1929.)

MacMillan, Margaret. *Paris 1919: Six Months That Changed the World.* New York: Random House, 2001.

Maier, Charles S. *In Search of Stability: Explorations in Historical Political Economy.* Cambridge, UK: Cambridge University Press, 1987.

———. *Recasting Bourgeois Europe: Stabilization in France, Germany, and Italy in the Decade after World War I.* Princeton, NJ: Princeton University Press, 1975.

Mallery, Otto T. *Public Works to Stabilize Employment and Industry: A Program Financial and Administrative, for States and Cities.* N.p., 1931.

Marcosson, Isaac. *Caravans of Commerce.* New York: Harper & Brothers, 1926.

Marks, Sally. *The Illusion of Peace: International Relations in Europe, 1918–1933,* 2nd ed. New York: Palgrave Macmillan, 2003.

Markwell, Donald. *John Maynard Keynes and International Relations: Economic Paths to War and Peace.* New York: Oxford University Press, 2006.

Martin, Albro. *Enterprise Denied: Origins of the Decline of American Railroads, 1897–1917.* New York: Columbia University Press, 1971.

Mayer, Dale. *Lou Henry Hoover: A Prototype for First Ladies.* New York: Nova Historical, 2004.

———. *Lou Henry Hoover: Essays on a Busy Life.* Worland, WY: High Plains, 1994.

McCoy, Donald R. *Calvin Coolidge: The Quiet President.* New York: Macmillan, 1967.

McMillen, Neil. *Dark Journey: Black Mississippians in the Age of Jim Crow.* Urbana: University of Illinois Press, 1989.

McNeil, William C. *American Money and the Weimar Republic: Economics and Politics on the Eve of the Great Depression*. New York: Columbia University Press, 1986.

Middlemas, Keith, and John Barnes. *Baldwin: A Biography*. New York: Macmillan, 1969.

Mitchell, Wesley Clair. *Business Cycles*. Berkeley: University of California Press, 1913.

Moeller, Beverley. *Phil Swing and Boulder Dam*. Berkeley: University of California Press, 1971.

Moore, Edmund A. *A Catholic Runs for President: The Campaign of 1928*. Gloucester, MA: Peter Smith, 1968.

Morse, David A. *The Origin and Evolution of the I.L.O. and Its Role in the World Community*. Ithaca, NY: New York State School of Industrial and Labor Relations, Cornell University, 1969.

Mowry, George E. *The California Progressives*. Chicago: Quadrangle ed., 1963.

Murray, Robert K. *The Harding Era: Warren G. Harding and His Administration*. Minneapolis: University of Minnesota Press, 1969.

Nash, George H. *Herbert Hoover and Stanford University*. Stanford, CA: Hoover Institution Press, 1988.

————. *The Life of Herbert Hoover: The Engineer, 1874–1914*. New York: Norton, 1983.

————. *The Life of Herbert Hoover: The Humanitarian, 1914–1917*. New York: Norton, 1988.

————. *The Life of Herbert Hoover: Master of Emergencies, 1917–1918*. New York: Norton, 1996.

————, ed. *Understanding Herbert Hoover: Ten Perspectives*. Stanford, CA: Hoover Institution, 1987.

Neal, Donn C. *The World Beyond the Hudson: Alfred E. Smith and National Politics, 1918–1928*. New York: Garland, 1983.

Nelson, Keith L. *Victors Divided: America and the Allies in Germany, 1918–1923*. Berkeley: University of California Press, 1975.

Noggle, Burl. *Into the Twenties: The United States from Armistice to Normalcy*. Urbana: University of Illinois Press, 1974.

Norris, George. *Fighting Liberal*. Lincoln: University of Nebraska Press, 1972. (Orig. pub. 1945.)

Oehser, Paul H. *Sons of Science: The Story of the Smithsonian Institution and Its Leaders*. New York: Greenwood, 1968.

Orde, Anne. *British Policy and European Reconstruction after the First World War*. Cambridge, UK: Cambridge University Press, 1990.

Ordover, Nancy. *American Eugenics: Race, Queer Anatomy, and the Science of Nationalism*. Minneapolis: University of Minnesota Press, 2003.

Parrini, Carl P. *Heir to Empire: United States Economic Diplomacy, 1916–1923*. Pittsburgh: University of Pittsburgh Press, 1969.

Patenaude, Bertrand M. *The Big Show in Bololand: The American Relief Expedition to Soviet Russia in the Famine of 1921*. Stanford, CA: Stanford University Press, 2002.

Pease, Neal. *Poland, the United States, and the Stabilization of Europe, 1919–1933*. New York: Oxford University Press, 1986.

Pedersen, Susan. *Family, Dependence, and the Origins of the Welfare State: Britain and France, 1914–1945*. Cambridge, UK: Cambridge University Press, 1993.

Peel, Roy V., and Thomas C. Donnelly. *The 1928 Campaign: An Analysis*. New York: Arno, 1974. (Orig. pub. 1931.)

Perrett, Geoffrey. *America in the Twenties: A History*. New York: Simon & Schuster, 1982.

Pryor, Helen B. *Lou Henry Hoover: Gallant First Lady*. New York: Dodd, Mead, 1969.

Rempel, David G., with Cornelia Rempel Carlson. *A Mennonite Family in Tsarist Russia and the Soviet Union, 1789–1823*. Toronto: University of Toronto Press, 2002.

Requa, M. L. *American Petroleum: Supply and Demand*. N.p., 1925.

Rhodes, Benjamin D. *James P. Goodrich, Indiana's "Governor Strangelove": A Republican's Infatuation with Soviet Russia*. Selinsgrove, PA: Susquehanna University Press, 1996.

————. *United States Foreign Policy in the Interwar Period, 1918–1941: The Golden Age of American Diplomatic and Military Complacency*. Westport, CT: Praeger, 2001.

Rochester, E. S. *Coolidge-Hoover-Work: An Intimate Review of An Epochal National Campaign for the Presidency of the United States*. Washington, DC: Terminal, 1929.

Rose, Mark H., Bruce E. Seely, and Paul F. Barrett. *The Best Transportation System in the World: Railroads, Trucks, Airlines, and American Public Policy in the Twentieth Century*. Columbus: Ohio State University Press, 2006.

Rosen, Philip T. *The Modern Stentors: Radio Broadcasters and the Federal Government, 1920–1934*. Westport, CT: Greenwood, 1980.

Rosenkrantz, Barbara Gutmann. *Public Health and the State: Changing Views in Massachusetts, 1842–1936*. Cambridge, MA: Harvard University Press, 1972.

Ross, Dorothy. *The Origins of American Social Science*. New York: Cambridge University Press, 1991.

Russell, Francis. *The Shadow of Blooming Grove: Warren G. Harding and His Times*. New York: McGraw-Hill, 1968.

Rutherford, Janice Williams. *Selling Mrs. Consumer: Christine Frederick and the Rise of Household Efficiency*. Athens: University of Georgia Press, 2003.

Salstrom, Paul. *Appalachia's Path to Dependency: Rethinking a Region's Economic History, 1730–1940*. Lexington: University Press of Kentucky, 1994.

Saul, Norman E. *Friends or Foes? The United States and Soviet Russia, 1921–1941*. Lawrence: University Press of Kansas, 2006.

Scharf, Lois. *Eleanor Roosevelt: First Lady of American Liberalism*. Boston: Twayne, 1987.

Scharff, Virginia. *Taking the Wheel: Women and the Coming of the Motor Age*. New York: Free Press, 1991.

Schlesinger, Arthur M., Jr., Fred L. Israel, and William P. Hansen, eds. *History of American Presidential Elections, 1789–1968*. Vol. 3. New York: Chelsea House, 1971.

Schröder, Hans-Jürgen, ed. *Confrontation and Cooperation: Germany and the United States in the Era of World War I, 1900–1924*. Providence, RI: Berg, 1993.

Schuker, Stephen A. *American "Reparations" to Germany, 1919–33: Implications for the Third-World Debt Crisis*. Princeton, NJ: International Finance Section, Department of Economics, Princeton University, 1988.

———.*The End of French Predominance in Europe: The Financial Crisis of 1924 and the Adoption of the Dawes Plan*. Chapel Hill: University of North Carolina Press, 1976.

Schwabe, Klaus. *Woodrow Wilson, Revolutionary Germany, and Peacemaking, 1918–1919: Missionary Diplomacy and the Realities of Power*. Chapel Hill: University of North Carolina Press, 1985.

Scott, Mel. *American City Planning Since 1890: A History Commemorating the Fiftieth Anniversary of the American Institute of Planners*. Berkeley: University of California Press, 1969.

Sealander, Judith. *The Failed Century of the Child: Governing America's Young in the Twentieth Century*. Cambridge, UK: Cambridge University Press, 2003.

Seely, Bruce E. *Building the American Highway System: Engineers as Policy Makers*. Philadelphia: Temple University Press, 1987.

Self, Robert C. *Britain, America, and the War Debt Controversy: The Economic Diplomacy of an Unspecial Relationship, 1917–1941*. London: Routledge, 2006.

Shaffer, Marguerite S. *See America First: Tourism and National Identity, 1880–1940*. Washington, DC: Smithsonian Institution, 2001.

Sharlin, Harold S. *The Making of the Electrical Age: From the Telegraph to Automation*. London: Abelard-Schuman, 1963.

Sheingate, Adam D. *The Rise of the Agricultural Welfare State: Institutions and Interest Group Power in the United States, France, and Japan*. Princeton, NJ: Princeton University Press, 2001.

Shideler, James H. *Farm Crisis, 1919–1923*. Berkeley: University of California Press, 1957.

Silva, Ruth C. *Rum, Religion, and Votes: 1928 Re-Examined*. University Park: Pennsylvania State University Press, 1962.

Slayton, Robert A. *Empire Statesman: The Rise and Redemption of Al Smith*. New York: Free Press, 2001.

Smiley, Gene. *Rethinking the Great Depression*. Chicago: Ivan R. Dee, 2002.

Smith, Alfred E. *Up To Now: An Autobiography*. New York: Viking, 1929.

Solnit, Rebecca *A Paradise Built in Hell: The Extraordinary Communities that Arise in Disaster* New York: Viking, 2009

Sorensen, John, and Judith Sealander, eds. *The Grace Abbott Reader*. Lincoln: University of Nebraska Press, 2008.

Steiner, Jesse. *Education for Social Work*. Chicago: University of Chicago Press, 1921.

Sullivan, Mark. *Our Times, 1900–1925*, 6 vols. New York: Charles Scribner's Sons, 1926–35.

Summers, Gregory. *Consuming Nature: Environmentalism in the Fox River Valley, 1850–1950*. Lawrence, KS: University Press of Kansas, 2006.

Surface, Frank M., and Raymond L. Bland. *American Food in the World War and Reconstruction Period: Operations of the Organization under the Direction of Herbert Hoover, 1914 to 1924*. Stanford, CA: Stanford University Press, 1931.

Sutton, Matthew Avery. *Aimee Semple McPherson and the Resurrection of Christian America*. Cambridge, MA: Harvard University Press, 2007.

Taylor, Joseph E., III. *Making Salmon: An Environmental History of the Northwest Fisheries Crisis*. Seattle: University of Washington Press, 1999.

Thompson, John M. *Russia, Bolshevism, and the Versailles Peace*. Princeton, NJ: Princeton University Press, 1966.

Tökés, Rudolf L. *Béla Kun and the Hungarian Soviet Republic: The Origins and Role of the Communist Party of Hungary in the Revolutions of 1918–1919*. New York: Praeger, 1967.

Tooze, J. Adam. *Statistics and the German State, 1900–1945: The Making of Modern Economic Knowledge*. Cambridge, UK: Cambridge University Press, 2001.

Trachtenberg, Marc. *Reparation in World Politics: France and European Economic Diplomacy, 1916–1923*. New York: Columbia University Press, 1980.

Trani, Eugene P., and David L. Wilson. *The Presidency of Warren G. Harding*. Lawrence: University Press of Kansas, 1977.

Turner, Paul V. *Mrs. Hoover's Pueblo Walls: The Primitive and the Modern in the Lou Henry Hoover House*. Stanford, CA: Stanford University Press, 2004.

Turrentine, J. W. *Potash: A Review, Estimate and Forecast*. New York: Wiley, 1926.

Tyler, Daniel. *Silver Fox of the Rockies: Delphus E. Carpenter and Western Water Compacts*. Norman: University of Oklahoma Press, 2003.

Ullman, Richard H. *Anglo-Soviet Relations, 1917–1921: Britain and the Russian Civil War, November 1918–February 1920*. Princeton, NJ: Princeton University Press, 1968.

Viola, Lynne. *The Best Sons of the Fatherland: Workers in the Vanguard of Soviet Collectivization*. New York: Oxford University Press, 1987.

Walch, Timothy, ed. *At the President's Side: The Vice Presidency in the Twentieth Century*. Columbia: University of Missouri Press, 1997.

———, ed. *Uncommon Americans: The Lives and Legacies of Herbert and Lou Henry Hoover*. Westport, CT: Praeger, 2003.

Walworth, Arthur. *Wilson and His Peacemakers: American Diplomacy at the Paris Peace Conference, 1919*. New York: Norton, 1986.

Wandycz, Piotr S. *The United States and Poland*. Cambridge, MA: Harvard University Press, 1980.

Weissman, Benjamin M. *Herbert Hoover and Famine Relief to Soviet Russia, 1921–23*. Stanford, CA: Hoover Institution Press, 1974.

Wert, Hal Elliott, *Hoover, the Fishing President: Portrait of the Private Man and His Life Outdoors* (Mechanicsburg, PA: Stackpole Books, 2005)

Wilkins, Mira. *The Maturing of Multinational Enterprise: American Business Abroad from 1914 to 1970*. Cambridge, MA: Harvard University Press, 1974.

Willis, Edward F. *Herbert Hoover and the Russian Prisoners of World War I: A Study in Diplomacy and Relief, 1918–1919*. Stanford, CA: Stanford University Press, 1951.

Wilson, Joan Hoff. *Herbert Hoover: Forgotten Progressive*. Boston: Little, Brown, 1975.

Women's Division, National Amateur Athletic Federation. *Women and Athletics*. New York: A. S. Barnes, 1930.

Woods, Ngaire, ed. *Explaining International Relations since 1945*. Oxford, UK: Oxford University Press, 1996.

Wueschner, Silvano A. *Charting Twentieth-Century Monetary Policy: Herbert Hoover and Benjamin Strong, 1917–1927*. Westport, CT: Greenwood, 1999.

Yard, Robert Sterling. *The Book of the National Parks*. New York: Scribner's, 1921.

Yochelson, Ellis L. *Smithsonian Institution Secretary, Charles Doolittle Walcott*. Kent, OH: Kent State University Press, 2001.
Young, James C. *Liberia Rediscovered*. Garden City, NY: Doubleday, Doran, 1934.
Young, Nancy Beck. *Lou Henry Hoover: Activist First Lady*. Lawrence: University Press of Kansas, 2004.
Zieger, Robert. *Republicans and Labor, 1919–1929*. Lexington: University of Kentucky Press, 1969.

Dissertations

Arbuckle, Roger Mark. "Herbert Hoover's National Radio Conferences and the Origins of Public Interest Content Regulation of U.S. Broadcasting, 1922–1925. PhD diss., Southern Illinois University, 2002.
Berman, Richard Dale. "The Road to the Presidency: Hoover, Johnson, and the California Republican Party, 1920–1924." PhD diss., University of Southern California, 1965.
Miller, Dorothy Grace. "'Within the Bounds of Propriety': Clara Burdette and the Women's Movement." PhD diss., University of California at Riverside, 1984.
Morrison, Glenda E. "Women's Participation in the 1928 Presidential Election." PhD diss., University of Kansas, 1978.

Index

Abbott, Charles G., 327
Abbott, Grace, 161, 178
Adams, E. D., 187, 188
Addams, Jane, 421
African Americans, 378–82
  Colored Advisory Commission (Moton
    Commission), 379–82
  in election of 1928, 402–4, 408
  and National Guard in 1927 Mississippi
    River flood, 378, 379–80
agriculture, xi, 108, 113–16, 209–11, 285–88,
  313–14, 428
  Agricultural Credits Act (1921), 115–16
  crop diversification, Hoover urges, 314
  McNary-Haugen Bill, 270, 272, 313–14,
    342–44, 397
Akerson, George, 328–29, 336, 398, 399, 402,
  403, 405, 413
Alaska, 184
  fisheries hearings (1923), 267
  fur seal industry, 266
  Harding's visit (1923), 265–67
  salmon, 237–38, 267, 269–70
Alexander, Joshua, 107
Alexander, Wallace, 271
Allen, Ben S., 95
Allen, Henry, 406
Allied Purchasing Commission, 8
Allied war debts. *See* European war debts *and
  specific countries*
American Child Health Association (ACHA),
  84, 161–79, 357
  accomplishments, 177

American Relief Administration, relations
    with, 165–68
  birth registration, 174
  childhood diseases, campaign against, 176
  education of parents and local organiza-
    tions, stress on, 175–76
  and eugenics, 174–75
  health educators, training for, 174
  "May Day-National Child Health Day,"
    173–74, 176
  milk sterilization campaign, 174, 176
  model programs, plans for, 165, 169–74
  proposed by Hoover, 165
  scientifically based programs, emphasis
    on, 165
  White House Conference on Child
    Health, 176–77
American Child Hygiene Association, 33,
  162, 164, 167–68
American Commission to Negotiate Peace, 11
American Construction Council, 147, 223,
  240
American Cyanamid Company, 351
American Engineering Council, 44, 319.
  See also Federated American Engineering
  Societies (FAES)
American Engineering Standards Committee,
  356–57
American Food Administration. *See* Food
  Administration
American Friends Service Committee, 13,
  24, 79
  famine in Russia, warns of, 83
  food relief to German children, 83–84

American Individualism, 109, 195–201, 207
American Institute of Electrical Engineers.
    See Federated American Engineering
    Societies (FAES)
American Institute of Mining and Metallurgi-
    cal Engineers (AIMME), 36, 40, 51, 78.
    See also Federated American Engineering
    Societies (FAES)
    coal investigation (1920), 117
American Relief Administration (ARA), x, 1,
    2, 109, 127 fig. 7.1
    American Child Health Association, rela-
        tionship with, 165–68, 170, 176
    Belgian educational foundation, created,
        86
    and Better Homes in America, 357–58
    Children's Fund, 170, 176, 357–58
    coal, 18
    economic advice in postwar Central
        Europe, 23
    European Children's Fund, 17, 21, 23, 74
    European "intellectual class," relief for, 80
    European Relief Council, 79
    expenditures in 1920–21, 84
    famine relief, scope of in Russia, 156–57
    food drafts, 75–76, 156
    funding, 5–6, 13, 15
    Germany and Austria, relief to, 10, 13
    "invisible guest" campaign, 34, 82
    postwar relief (1918–19), value of, 21,
        24–25, 72
    privatization, 74, 84
    Railway Section, 17
    Russian famine (1921–23), 150–60
    staff, conflict with, 80–81
    Starvation, 76
    typhus epidemic, 23–24
American Society of Civil Engineers, 386.
    See also Federated American Engineering
    Societies (FAES)
American Society of Mechanical Engineers,
    333. *See also* Federated American Engineer-
    ing Societies (FAES)
Andrew, Rep. A. Piatt (R-MA), 361
Anthony, Edward, 406
Appleby, Rep. Theodore F. (R-NJ), 126
Armenia, 11, 77, 79
Armour, J. Ogden, 314
Army Signal Corps, 17
Arnold, Ralph, 185, 258, 271
    and election of 1920, 50, 51–52, 53, 54,
        55–56, 58, 62, 65
    and election of 1928, 398
Associated (Alabama) Power Company, 351
Atchafalaya River Basin, 374, 377, 386, 388

Atwood, Col. William G., 17, 23
Auchincloss, Gordon, 4
Austin, Mary, 69, 194
Austria, x, 16, 71–72, 77, 79, 158
aviation. *See* civil aviation
Ayer, W. B., 63

Baker, George Barr, 59, 63, 165, 166, 167, 168
Baker, Henry, 375, 379
Baker, Newton D., 78
Baker, Ray Stannard, 52
Baldwin, Stanley, 244, 245, 246
Barnes, Julius, 33–34, 36–37, 53, 55, 65, 66,
    79, 84, 96, 99, 114, 140, 174, 216, 218, 253
Barton, Clara, 373
Baruch, Bernard, 314, 418
Bedford, A. C., 88
Beeuwkes, Lt. Colonel, Henry, 170–72
Belgium, ix, 12–13, 30, 77, 308
Belle of Bohemia, The, 332
Belmont, Eleanor Robson (Mrs. August
    Belmont), 81
Better Homes in America, 223–24, 321, 428.
    See also housing; Meloney, Marie
    Demonstration Week, 224, 255
    incorporated, 256
    problems, 357–58
Bicknell, Ernest P., 373, 377
Bingham, Sen. Hiram (R-CT), 320
Black, Dorothy Lenroot, 395–96
"black and tan" Republicans, 402, 408
Bliss, General Tasker H., 11, 20
Bliven, Bruce, 108
blockade, 3, 6–8, 9–10, 15, 113, 151, 435n20
Boardman, Helen, 379
Bohemian Club, 186–87
Böhm, Vilmos, 151
Bonar Law, Andrew, 246
Bone, Scott, 267
Booze, Eugene, 402
Borah, Sen. William E. (R-ID), 64, 101, 212,
    241, 272, 306, 307
    in election of 1928, 397, 404, 408, 422
Boyden, Roland, 243
Boys Clubs of America, 85
Boy Scouts of America, 85
Brandegee, Sen. Frank (R-CT), 101
Breckinridge, Colonel Henry, 183–84
Brest Litovsk, Treaty of, 20
Brewster, Ralph O., 360
Bristol, Arthur L., 140
British Debt Commission, 244–46
Brookings, Robert, 145
Brown, Henry, 65

Brown, Kenneth, 278
Brown, Walter Folger, 399
Brown, Walter Lyman, 6, 152–53, 154, 166
Buckland, E. G., 122
Bulgaria, 16, 72
Bullard, Ethel, 87
Bullitt, William, 19, 39
Burdette, Clara, 53, 421
Bureau of Foreign and Domestic Commerce.
  See Commerce Department
Burges, Richard Fenner, 291
Burner, David, 24
Burton, Rep. Theodore E. (R-OH), 243, 401
Business Cycles, 133
Butler, Albert, 90
Butler, James P., 386
Butler, Nicholas Murray, 327
Butler, Sen. William M. (R-MA), 335

Cabot Trust Fund, 211, 216, 220
Caillaux, Joseph, 305, 306–7
Calder, Sen. William M. (R-NY), 118, 221,
  255
Campbell, Allen, 334–35
Campbell, Thomas E., 334
Canada, 237, 253, 285, 290, 317–18, 347, 349
Capper, Sen. Arthur (R-KS), 114, 249, 284,
  396, 420
Carnegie Corporation, 143, 145, 146, 186,
  333, 358
Carpenter, Delphus E., 124, 226, 291
Castle, William, 365
Caswell, Fred W., 140
Catchings, Waddill, 360
Catt, Carrie Chapman, 421
Cecil, Lord Robert, 9
*Cement Manufacturers Protective Association v.
  United States*, 205, 323
Central Europe. *See specific countries*
Chamberlain, Austen, 312
Chamberlain, Eugene T., 126
Chandler, Harry, 51, 124, 271
Chapin, Roy, 88
Chenery, William, 137–38
Child Health Organization of America, 164,
  166–68
Churchill, Winston, 247
civil aviation, x, 234–35, 320–21, 428
  Air Commerce Act (1926), 354–55
  airplanes, during Mississippi River flood,
    355
  American Engineering Council-Com-
    merce Department committee, 321, 354
  MacCracken, William, 235, 354–55

President's Aircraft Board (Morrow Com-
    mittee), 321, 354
Clark, Birge, 31, 32
Clark, George T., 187
Clemenceau, Georges, 71
Cline, Isaac, 376
coal, xi, 117–19, 250–51, 314–16, 344–46, 428
  Coal Distribution Committee, 214
  distribution control, Hoover's plan for,
    213–15
  federal coal commission and distribution
    program, 216, 250–51
  Jacksonville Agreement (1924), 299–300,
    314–16, 345
  oil, losing competition with, 315–16
  Parker Bill, 345
  price control, voluntary program, 212–13
  and railroads, 216–17
  study committee, 211, 216
  United Mine Workers, declining by mid-
    1920s, 315–16, 344–45
  White House meeting (July 1, 1922), 213
Cohen, Walter, 403
Coler, Bird S., 140
Colorado River Commission, x, 123–24, 225–26
  Arizona-California conflict, 226, 253, 289
  Carpenter, Delphus E., 124, 226, 291
  Compact (1922), 226
  "prior appropriation," 225–26
  Swing-Johnson Bill, 225–26, 290, 349–50
Commerce Department, x
  accomplishments under Hoover, 427–29
  Aeronautics, Bureau of, 111
  building, 112, 302, 326
  commodity sections, 111
  desegregation, of Census Bureau, 382,
    404
  films, 330
  Fisheries, Bureau of, 125, 235–38
  Foreign and Domestic Commerce, Bureau
    of, 110, 111, 228, 302
  Foreign Commerce, Division of (Bureau
    of Foreign and Domestic Commerce),
    111, 147
  Housing, Division of (Bureau of Foreign
    and Domestic Commerce), 111, 147,
    222–23, 255, 288
  Lamb, Solicitor William E., 126
  Minerals, Division of (Bureau of Foreign
    and Domestic Commerce), 316
  Mines, Bureau of, 111, 323
  National Negro Business League, 382
  Navigation, Bureau of, 126
  overseas attachés, proposed, 248
  Patent Office, 111, 323

Commerce Department (*continued*)
  Radio, Division of (Bureau of Standards),
    111, 233
  reorganization, 110–12
  Simplified Practice, Division of (Bureau of
    Standards), 111, 322
  special agent for Negro Affairs, 382
  staff, 112
  standardization and waste elimination,
    44–47, 110, 111, 254–55, 286–88,
    322–24, 356–57, 430
  Standards, Bureau of, 111, 289, 354
  Survey of Current Business, 203
  Waste in Industry, 46–47
  water pollution, 125–26
Commission for Relief in Belgium (CRB), xii,
  1, 2, 79
  Louvain, University of, 327
  and Stanford University, 185–88
Committee on National Policies with Regard
  to Shipping, 293
Commonwealth Fund, 143, 164, 168
Cooke, Morris L., 68, 219, 298
Coolidge, Calvin, x, 37, 173–74, 204, 224,
  251, 270
  agriculture, offers to appoint Hoover
    secretary, 273
  announces decision not to run in 1928,
    337–38, 397, 398
  coal, believes problems will solve them-
    selves, 345–46
  coal strike, not worried by (1925), 315–16
  depression after son's death, 273
  disaster relief, favors, 393
  in election of 1928, 396–97, 398, 401, 405,
    407, 409, 410, 411, 413–14, 422, 423,
    426 fig. 21.4
  Hoover, relations with, 270–71, 302, 324,
    335–37, 411
  inauguration (1924), 325–26
  interest rates, declines to recommend
    increase, 369
  McNary-Haugen Bill, opposes, 272, 343
  Mississippi River flood of 1927, role in,
    373, 384, 386–89
  Muscle Shoals, disposition of, 319, 351
  New England flood of 1927, role in, 390
  State Department, refuses to appoint
    Hoover to, 272–73, 336
  Swing-Johnson Bill, endorses, 290
  waterway development, attitude toward
    Hoover's proposals, 317, 347–48
Coolidge, Calvin, Jr., 273
Corbin, John, 109
Costigliola, Frank, 364

Cotton, Joseph P., 60
Couch, Harvey C., 381, 403
Coudert, Frederic R., 59
Council of Railway Ministers of the Central
  European States, 17
Council of Ten, 10
Cox, Channing, 410
Crandall, Ella Phillips, 169
Creager, Rentfro Banton, 398, 402
Crissinger, David R., 304
Crocker, William H., 62, 272
Croly, Herbert, 196
Crosby, L. O., 383, 386, 402–3
Crouch, Harvey, 386
Crumbine, Samuel J., 173, 176
Cummins, Sen. Albert B. (R-IA), 252, 344
Curtis, Sen. Charles (R-KS), 397, 403, 406,
  409, 410–11
Czechoslovakia, 16, 79

Daugherty, Harry, 102, 103, 202, 203, 204,
  218, 219, 266
Davey, Rep. Martin L. (D-OH), 323
Davies, Marion, 400
Davis, Arthur Powell, 124
Davis, Dwight F., 377, 386
Davis, James J., 103, 105, 213, 218, 220, 224,
  345
Davis, Norman, 73
Davis, Stephen B., 257–58
Davison, Henry P., 75
Dawes, Charles G., 102, 247, 272, 282–84,
  326, 397, 406, 410
Dawes Plan. *See* reparations
Defrees, Joseph, 135, 143
DeMille, Cecil B., 406
Denby, Edwin, 103
DeYoung, M. H., 62
Di Giorgio, Joseph (Di Giorgio Fruit Corpo-
  ration), 99
Dinwiddie, Courtenay, 166, 167, 168, 169,
  170, 171, 172–73
Dixon, Edward, 51
Doherty, Henry L., 258
Downing, P. M., 125
draft physicals, 161
Durand, E. Dana, 110

Eastern Europe. *See specific countries*
Edge, Sen. Walter (R-NJ), 203
Edge Act (1919), 74, 88, 109
election of 1920, x, 31–32, 49–69
  campaign expenditures, 64
  Chinese stock fraud case (1905), 59

labor, role of, 61
Republican convention, 65
election of 1922, 189–90
Senate, supporters suggest Hoover run for, 395
election of 1924
Hoover, rumored eager to run, 271, 395
election of 1926, 335, 336
as rehearsal for 1928, 396
election of 1928, 395–423
African Americans, 402–4, 418
campaign expenditures, 407, 564n39
Coolidge, Hoover visits in Wisconsin, 413–14, 426 fig. 21.4
Coolidge withdraws as possible candidate, 337–38, 397, 398
Credentials Committee, 402, 408
Democratic convention, 411
early favorites, 396–97
East in, 405, 412, 416–17
ethnic voters, 416, 420
floods in Mississippi Valley and New England benefit Hoover, 397
foreign policy in, 416
Hoover, campaign speeches, 351–52, 415–17
Hoover, limitations as campaigner, 413, 417
Hoover and Smith, views compared, 417
Hoover-for-president Engineers' National Committee, 412
labor in, 421–22
Midwest in, 405–6, 412, 415–16, 420
notification ceremony at Stanford, 414
primary elections, 400–401, 406, 562n20
prohibition in, 404, 411, 416, 417–18
prosperity, 411–12
publicity, 406, 412
religion in, 411, 418–20
Republican campaign organization, 412–13
Republican convention, 408–11
results, 422–23
South in, 402–3, 405, 408, 412, 416, 419
vice presidential selection, Republican, 410–11
West in, 405, 412, 420
women in, 420–21
Embree, Edwin, 382
Emergency Fleet Corporation, 292–93, 346
Equal Rights Amendment (to U.S. Constitution), 421
Esberg, Milton, 271, 398, 399, 414
Esch-Cummins Act. *See* railroads: Esch-Cummins Act

Estonia, 16, 79, 308
European Relief Council. *See* American Relief Administration (ARA)
European war debts, xi, 21–22, 73, 231–32
British debt negotiations, 243–46
differences within administration about policy, 242
French debt negotiations, 305–7
Mellon-Bérenger agreement, 361
reparations, linked to, 362
war stocks, 305, 307
World War Foreign Debt Commission, 243–44, 361–62
Young Plan, 362

Fall, Albert B., 103, 118, 124, 226, 266, 300–301
Farmers' Federated Fertilizer Corporation, 351
Federal Council of Churches of Christ, 140
Federal Farm Loan Bank, 383
Federal Highways Bureau, 391
Federal Intermediate Credit Banks, 249
Federal Radio Commission, 353
Federal Reserve Bank of New York, 231, 405
and European stabilization, 231, 368–69
Federal Reserve system, x, 88, 133, 144, 239, 240, 249, 368–69
Federal Trade Commission, 109, 118, 202, 205
Federal Water Power Act (1920), 123
Federated American Engineering Societies (FAES), 44, 109, 143, 254
American Engineering Council, 44
twelve-hour workday in steel mills, report on, 220–21
Federation of Women's Clubs, 140
Feiker, Frederick, 110, 125
Fesler, Ruth, 339
Fess, Sen. Simeon (R-OH), 409
Fieser, James L., 374–75, 380, 381, 392
Finland, 11, 77, 79, 159, 246
Finn, Thomas, 272
Flesh, Edward, 33, 97, 98
American Child Health Association, 167, 168, 172–73
Foch, Marshal Ferdinand, 151
Food Administration, x, xii, 28, 36, 38, 59, 202
Food Administration Club, 27–28
food drafts, 75–76
Food Research Institute (at Stanford), 186
Ford, Edsel, 407

Ford, Henry, 125, 198, 254, 300, 319, 351, 398
Fordney-McCumber Tariff, 309–11, 363–64
Ford Reliability Air Tour, 355
foreign monopolies on raw materials, xii, 247–48, 284–85, 300, 311–13, 364–66, 428. *See also* rubber
Foreign Trade Financing Corporation, 88, 110, 113, 228
Fort, Rep. Franklin W. (R-NJ), 409, 412
Fosdick, Harry Emerson, 81
Foster, R. L., 142
Foster, William T., 360
Fox, Alan, 399
Francqui, Emile, 79
Free, Rep. Arthur M. (R-CA), 271
Frelinghuysen, Sen. Joseph S. (R-NJ), 118, 125, 138, 289
Fuller, Alvan T., 335

Gallagher, Michael, 299
Garfield, Harry, 212
Garner, Rep. John Nance (D-TX), 78
Gary, Elbert H., 220
Gaskill, Nelson, 203
Gay, Edwin F., 133, 134, 143
Genoa Conference (1922), 232
Germany, 6–7, 71, 79, 159, 230–31, 307, 362. *See also* reparations
Gibson, Hugh, 16, 327, 384
Gilbert, Charles, 238
Gilchrist, Colonel H. L., 23
Gillett, Rep. Frederick (R-MA), 265
Girl Scouts of America, 85, 181–82, 183, 190, 191–92, 262 fig. 14.2, 276–77, 326
Glass, Carter, 8, 36, 75, 77, 78
Glenn, Sen. Otis F. (R-IL), 409
Goff, Sen. Guy D. (R-WV), 397, 401, 409
Golder, Frank, 186, 187
gold standard, 21–22, 40, 240, 304–5, 308–9
   British, 308
Gompers, Samuel, 41, 44, 61, 135, 214, 219
Good, Rep. James (R-IA), 112, 399, 407, 412
Goodrich, James P., 155, 157, 399, 406, 420
Goodyear, Colonel Anson C., 18
Gore, Howard, 272, 287
Gorky, Maxim, 149, 150
Grain Marketing Corporation, 314, 343
Green, General Curtis T., 379–80
Green, Joseph C., 65
Greenwood, Ernest, 355
Gregory, Thomas T. C., 97–98, 151–52, 398, 388, 412
Gregory, Thomas Watt, 202

Gregory, Warren, 50, 66, 97
Gries, John M., 223–24
Griffith, David Wark, 406
Gronna, Sen. Asle J. (R-ND), 53
Grove, William R., 83
Guggenheim, Daniel, 354, 355

Habsburg, Archduke Charles Francis Joseph, 151–52
halibut, 236–37
Hamill, Samuel M., 176
Hard, William A., 396, 397
Harding, Florence (Mrs. Warren Harding), 265, 269
Harding, Philippi (Butler), 89, 91, 184
Harding, Warren, x, 33
   Alaska trip (1923), 265–68
   background, 106–7
   cabinet evaluated, 103–5
   and coal strike of 1922, 213
   Commerce Department, offers to Hoover, 83, 101–2
   election of 1920 in, 54, 65–68
   European war debts and, 242, 245
   illness and death, 265–66, 268–69, 514n11
   scandals, 266
   World Court, urges American member-
      ship, 158, 241, 266, 268–69
Harmsworth, Cecil, 6–7
Harries, General George, 20
Harrison, George, 278
Haskell, Colonel William N., 153–54, 157, 158
Haugen, Rep. Gilbert N. (R-IA), 342
Hays, Will, 66–67, 68, 103
Hearst newspapers, 53, 62, 301, 373
   Hearst, William Randolph, 400
Heath, Ferry, 407
Heckscher, August, 358
Heflin, Sen. J. Thomas (D-AL), 419
Henriques, Alida, 87
Henry, Charles, 91–94, 338–39, 414
Henry, Florence (Mrs. Charles Henry), 30, 90–91
Hepburn, C. J., 65
Herald (Washington, DC), 34, 49, 95, 102
Herrick, Myron T., 306
Herrick, Sherlock, 140
Herrin massacre, 213
Herter, Christian A., 139, 430
Hichborn, Franklin, 271
Hilles, Charles, 396, 398, 405, 408–9
Hirst, Francis, 90
Hodgson, Caspar, 54

Holland, Rush, 402, 403
Holt, Hamilton, 241
Holt, L. Emmett, 166, 167
Hooker Electro-Chemical Company, 300
Hooper, Edward, 332
Hoover, Allan, 27, 89, 91, 94, 96, 184, 192–93, 278, 330, 338, 339, 409, 422
   Stanford, 332, 334, 338, 537n24
   trip to Europe, 334–35
Hoover, Herbert, ix, 264 fig. 14.4
   absent-mindedness, 193
   achievements, xiii, 126, 324, 427–32
   African Americans and, 380–82, 402–4
   agriculture and, x, 55, 60, 108, 113–16, 198–99, 248–50, 285–86, 313–14, 342–44, 415, 428, 451n43
   Alaska, trip to (1923), 265–67
   ambition, 260, 324
   American Child Health Association, 165–79, 430
   American Child Hygiene Association, 33, 162, 163
   American Individualism, 109, 195–201, 207
   ARA expenditures during 1920s, controlled by Hoover, 84
   archives, urges construction of, 442n15
   Austria and Russia, pessimistic about future of, 85
   aviation, x, 234–35, 295, 320, 354–55, 428 (*see also* civil aviation)
   Better Homes in America and, 224, 255, 321
   birthplace in West Branch, Iowa, 189
   Britain and France, blames for continued Austrian dependence on U.S. aid, 77–78
   business ability, 99
   business and government, cooperation between, 108, 109, 427, 432
   business cycles, organizes study of, 143–44
   cabinet, considers resigning from, 336
   cabinet colleagues, friction with, x, 104–5, 111–12, 114, 210, 248, 286–88, 305
   childhood, xii, 199
   child labor, opposes, 163, 165
   children, concern about, 3, 22–23, 177–78, 415
   citizenship, questioned, 50, 65
   clothes, 32, 193
   coal, xi, 117–19, 211–16, 250–51, 299–300, 344–46, 428
   Colorado River Commission, x, 123, 124, 225–26, 253, 289–90, 318–19, 349–50
   Commerce Department, goals for, xi, 105–6, 108–9

Commerce Department overseas attachés, proposed appointment of, 248
Commission for Relief in Belgium (CRB), xii, 1, 79
communism, attitude toward, 25, 38, 40, 150, 157–58, 159
conservation, 43–44, 360–61
consumer economy, 39–40, 41–42, 94, 201, 221, 273–74, 415–16, 427, 428–29
Coolidge, relations with, xiii, 270, 302, 324, 335–37, 347–48, 393, 411, 413–14, 426 fig. 21.4, 514n12
daily schedule, 107–8
Dawes Plan, 282–84, 307
"dole," opposes, 134
economic nationalism, xii, 2–3, 309, 364, 367, 405, 416, 430
economic philosophy, 109, 195–208
elected president, 422–23
election of 1924, role in, 271–72
election of 1926, role in, 335–36
election of 1928, role in, 337–38, 351–52, 394, 395–423
Engineering and Industry, Smithsonian Museum of, 326–27
engineers, opinion of role, xii, 44, 45
Equal Rights Amendment to Constitution, favors, 421
European and Russian relief programs, determined to control, 4–5, 152–55
European instability, warns about (September 1919), 73
European relief, director general of, 5, 10–11, 24–25
European relief, as foundation for peace and democracy, 83, 85–86
European relief, as investment in future markets, 76–77, 86
European war debts, x, 21–22, 73, 231–32, 241, 243–46, 305–7, 361–62, 416, 431
European war debts and disarmament, proposes linking, 231, 244–45
family portrait, 424 fig. 21.1
federal farm loan banks, proposed, 249
"final triumph over poverty," predicts, 415
fishing, 29, 89, 91, 235–38, 325, 331, 337, 406, 413, 414, 426 fig. 21.3
foreign monopolies on raw materials, xii, 247–48, 284–85, 300, 311–13, 364–66, 428
foreign relief work, expects to end by 1923, 158
foreign trade and investment, xi, xii, 88, 108, 227–31, 241–43, 246–47, 261 fig. 14.1, 284, 307–11, 363–64, 428, 430–31, 463–64n21, 548n68

Hoover, Herbert (*continued*)
  gold standard, attitude toward, 304–5,
    308–9, 368–69
  grandchildren, 334, 338
  "great humanitarian," x, 24–25, 431
  Harding, relations with, 66, 107
  health, 10, 91, 189
  highway safety, 295–96, 356
  housing, policies on, 108, 221–24, 288,
    321–22, 357–58
  Hungary, overthrow of Béla Kun govern-
    ment in, 151–52
  immigration, 301–2, 415
  industrial conference (1919), x, 38, 40–43,
    51
  inflation, concerned about (1923), 239–40
  "invisible exchange," 231, 308, 363
  "invisible guest" campaign, 34, 82, 128
    fig. 7.3
  Isis, statue of, 188–89
  labor, xi, 41–43, 44–45, 57, 323–24, 415
  Latin America, considers trip to, 229, 313
  leadership, xii, 42, 52–53, 68, 356–58
  League of Nations, x, 29–30, 36, 40, 51,
    54, 57, 59, 60, 64, 66, 68, 71–72, 89,
    240, 415, 431
  limited government, xi, 196–97, 238,
    259–60, 392–94, 416–17, 429–30,
    431–32
  Lou Hoover, relationship with, 194
  merchant marine, 38, 108, 292–94, 346,
    428
  Mississippi Valley flood relief, x, 337, 338,
    371–90, 392–94, 425 fig. 21.2
  Muscle Shoals, 125, 253–54, 300–301,
    318–19, 350–52, 416
  National Academy of Science, 333
  National Conference on Outdoor Recre-
    ation, 274–75, 288
  National Parks Association, president,
    275–76
  National Research Council, 333–34
  New England flood relief, x, 338, 391–94
  "normal child," 174–76
  oil, conservation of, 258–59, 316
  party affiliation, ambiguous about, 50–53
  peace conference, importance at, 10–12
  personality and values, xii, 10, 12, 13, 32,
    39, 178, 187, 193, 200–201, 276, 330,
    392–94, 413, 417, 428–30
  pork contracts, conflict with Allies over,
    7–9
  portrait painted, 89–90
  postwar European recovery, 21–22, 40, 73,
    75, 229–32, 308

  presidential campaign (1920) (*see* election
    of 1920)
  presidential campaign (1928) (*see* election
    of 1928)
  prohibition, 404, 416, 417–18
  pro-Wilson Congress, urges election of in
    1918, 59
  publicity, role in career, 375, 396
  Quakerism, xii, 3, 200, 418
  radio, x, 232–34, 259, 295–97, 319–20,
    352–54, 428
  railroad rates, suggests restructuring,
    251–52
  railroads, xi, 55, 119–22, 216–19, 251–52,
    294–95, 344, 428
  *Recent Economic Changes in the United
    States*, 359–60
  relief (*see specific programs*)
  relief, campaign to raise $33 million for,
    78, 84
  relief, recommends new appropriation for
    European, 78
  relief activities, overview of, 159–60, 431
  relief in Russia (1919–23), x, 18–19,
    150–60
  reorganization of commerce department,
    108, 110–12
  reorganization of government, 322–23
  Rio Grande River, x, 290–92, 329
  Russia, conditions for ARA aid to, 150–51
  Russia (1919), proposes aid instead of
    intervention in, 18–19
  Russian prisoners of war (1919), 20–21
  salmon conservation, 266–67, 269–70
  Secretary of Commerce, appointed as, x,
    34, 83–84, 101–3
  Secretary of Commerce, resigns as,
    413–14
  Sesquicentennial (of Declaration of Inde-
    pendence), 327–29
  sharecroppers, proposal to distribute land
    to, 381–82
  socialism, attacks Smith's alleged support
    of, 416
  soldiers, recruited to work for ARA, 3–4
  standardization and waste elimination, 43,
    45–47, 108, 254–55, 286–88, 322–24,
    356–57, 430, 511n41
  Stanford University, 29, 185
  statistics, xii, 109, 110–11, 134
  stock market, concerned about speculation
    in, 304, 358, 368
  "Superpower," 122–23, 256–58, 297–98
  suspicion of Europeans, xii, 4, 12, 22, 35,
    57, 73–74, 77, 285, 309, 313, 430–31

tariff, xi, 285, 309–11, 363–64, 415, 416, 431

taxation, 227, 260, 367

Teapot Dome and other scandals, 266

television, 354

trade associations, xi, 43, 197–201, 323–24, 429–30

Treaty of Versailles (*see* Hoover, Herbert: League of Nations)

twelve-hour workday in steel, 219–21, 497n40

unemployment, claims that Republicans had cured, 146, 415

unemployment conference (1921), 131–47

unemployment insurance and old age pension plan, 138

vice presidency, loses bid for in 1924, 272

voluntary methods, to deal with unemployment, 138–39, 142

water pollution, 125–26, 236, 288–89

waterway development, x, 55, 108, 224–25, 252–53, 263 fig. 14.3, 290, 317–18, 347–52, 387–89, 415

World Court, xi, 240–41, 260, 431

World War Foreign Debt Commission, 243–44

Hoover, Herbert, Jr. ("Pete"), 27, 89, 278, 332–33, 422–23

    daughter (Margaret Ann Hoover), 334, 338

    deafness, 29, 333

    engaged to Margaret (Peggy) Watson, 278

    son (Herbert Hoover III), 338

    Stanford, student years, 91, 184–85, 193, 330

    wedding, 330–31

Hoover, Lou Henry (Mrs. Herbert Hoover), 27, 58

    Alaska trip and Harding's death, 192, 266, 267, 268–69

    Bert, relationship with, 28, 194

    builds faculty houses on Stanford campus, 278

    California primary, bitter about results of (1920), 63

    Coolidge, Grace, 270, 334

    cross-country drive, 91–94

    election of 1928, role in, 338, 339, 399, 419, 421, 422–23

    Girl Scouts, 174, 181–82, 183, 190, 191–92, 262 fig. 14.2, 276–77, 326, 329–30, 333, 334, 337, 338

    Harding, dubious about, 68

    health, 30, 334

    National Amateur Athletic Federation (NAAF), 183–84, 190–91, 276, 277–78, 326, 333, 338

    nephew's drowning, 182–83

    Palo Alto house, 29, 30–31, 32, 128 fig. 7.2, 422–23

    personality and values, 31, 193–94, 330

    public issues, 32, 90, 94, 181, 190

    public schools in Washington, DC, funding for, 94, 182

    relief, fund raising, 78, 80, 82–84

    television, 354

    War Library, mediates between Hoover and Wilbur over, 188

    West Branch cottage, purchase of, 339

    Women's Committee for Law Enforcement, 404

Hoover, Theodore, 29, 330

Hoover-Curtis Organization Bureau of Women's Activities, 420–21

Hoover family pets, 28, 89, 278–79

Hoover farm, 95–99

    Western Cotton Company, 34

Horne, Sir Robert, 364–65

Houghton, Alanson B., 283

House, Edward M., 11, 13, 14, 19, 21–22, 333

housing, 221–24, 255–56, 288, 321–22, 428

    Division of Building and Housing, 222–23

    effect on social and physical makeup of nation, 288

    influence on economy, 288

    mortgages, 322

    National Housing Committee for Congested Areas, 358

    Senate Select Committee on Reconstruction and Production (Calder Committee), 221–22

Howard, Sir Esmé, 365

Howard, Frank, 405

Howard, Perry, 402

Hudson, R. M., 322

Hughes, Charles Evans, 68, 102, 103–4, 237, 266, 272, 285, 324

    Dawes Plan, 282, 283

    election of 1928, 396–97, 398, 405, 407, 422

    European debt policy, 242–44

Hungary, 11, 16, 72, 77, 79

    Béla Kun government, 151–52

Hunt, Edward Eyre, 46, 47, 134, 137–38, 140, 141, 211, 214

Huston, Claudius, 237, 247, 266

Hylan, John F., 140

immigration, 301–2
Imperial Valley (CA), 123–24, 226
industrial conferences (1919), x, 38, 40–43, 51
  Committee on the Stabilization of the
    Coal Industry, 117–18
Institute of Economics, 145
Inter-Allied Commission on Repatriation of
  Russian Prisoners of War, 21
Inter-Allied Food Council, 1
Inter-American High Commission, 228–29
Intercontinental Development Corporation,
  33
International Labor Organization (ILO), 219
International Radiotelegraph Conference, 354
Interstate Commerce Commission (ICC), 41,
  211, 214, 251, 292, 295, 344
Investment Bankers Association of America,
  383
invisible guest campaign. *See* American Relief
  Administration (ARA)
Irwin, Inez Haynes (Mrs. Will Irwin), 421
Irwin, Will, 176, 380, 396, 397
Isis, 188–89
Italy, 11, 77, 159, 308
Izaak Walton League, 235, 289

Jackson, James A., 382
Jadwin, General Edgar, 16, 351, 372, 375,
  385–86, 387–89
Jardine, William, 105, 272, 343, 405
Jean, Sally Lucas, 164–65, 166–67, 169, 171,
  172
Jewish Joint Distribution Committee, 15, 17,
  24
Johnson, Sen. Hiram (R-CA), 398
  California politics, in, 271
  candidate for presidency in 1924, 272
  election of 1920, 50, 52, 53, 56, 57, 59–60,
    62
  Hoover, 101, 102, 395
  Swing-Johnson Bill, 225–26, 318–19,
    349–50
Johnson, Homer, 16
Johnson, Hugh S., 210
Jones, Grosvenor, 242
Jones, Scipio, 403
Jones, Sen. Wesley L. (R-WA), 255, 360,
  389–90
Jones-White Act (1928), 346

Keesling, Francis, 272
Kellogg, Frank, 272–73, 307, 328, 336
Kellogg, Vernon, 14, 24, 50, 154–55
Kendrick, Charles, 272

Kendrick, W. Freeland, 328
Kenyon, Sen. William S. (R-IA), 136, 144
Kern County Labor Council, 98
Kern County Land Company, 95, 97, 98
Kerr, Philip, 22
Kettner Act (1920), 123
Keynes, John Maynard, 25, 50, 71, 73, 245,
  363
Kilburn, Harvey, 95, 97
Kincaid Act (1920), 123
King, Sen. William H. (D-UT), 222
King Tut, 278–79
Klearflax Linen Rug Company, 33
Klein, Julius, 110, 249, 310, 328–29
Kneipp, Leon F., 274
Knox, Sen. Philander C. (R-PA), 101, 102
Koverman, Ida, 53, 421
Kreisler, Fritz, 82
Krumm, L. R., 234
Ku Klux Klan, 38, 401, 403, 406, 418
Kun, Béla, 77

labor, xi, 323–24
  child labor, 43
  election of 1920, 61
  election of 1928, 421–22
  labor unions, xi, 41, 42, 44, 135, 219, 421
  shop councils, xi, 42–43, 81, 199–200, 421
  strikes (1919), 37–38
La Follette, Robert, 187, 250, 343, 420
Lamb, William E., 126
Lamont, Thomas W., 73, 244, 283
Lane, Franklin K., 107
Lane, Gertrude, 56
Lane, Rose Wilder, 56
Lansing, Robert, 11, 39
Large, Janet, 338
Large, Jean Henry (Mrs. Guthrie Large), 90,
  182, 278, 331, 334, 338
Lathrop, Julia, 161
Latin America, xi, 228–29, 313
Latvia, 16, 79, 308
Lawrence, Andrew M., 271
Lawrence, John S., 392
League of Nations, ix, x, 33, 39, 51, 246, 273,
  366, 415
Leete, Harriet, 163, 168–69
Leffingwell, Russell C., 75
Leffler, Melvyn, 246
Legge, Alexander, 88
Lenin, Vladimir Ilyich, 19, 150, 158, 159
Lenroot, Sen. Irvine L. (R-WI), 249, 396,
  399, 420
Lewis, Ernest, 217

Lewis, John L., 135, 212, 299, 315, 421
"lily-white" Republicans, 402–3, 408
Lindauer, Sam A., 51
Lindbergh, Charles, 355
Lindsay, Ben B., 164
Lindsay, Samuel McCune, 221
Lippmann, Walter, 417
Lissner, Meyer, 52, 63
Lithuania, 16, 21, 79
Litvinov, Maxim, 153
Livingstone, Belle, 331–32
Lloyd George, David, 9, 12, 22, 71, 137
Lockwood, George B., 399
Lodge, Sen. Henry Cabot (R-MA), 65, 101, 410
    Lodge Amendment (to 1919 relief appropriation), 13
Lonergan, Captain Thomas C., 154
Long, Ray, 332
Louvain, University of. *See* Commission for Relief in Belgium (CRB)
Low, Juliette, 277
Lowden, Frank, 56, 63, 66, 272, 397, 401, 402, 405, 406, 409, 411
Lucey, John F., 51, 56, 63–64
Lutz, Frank, 186, 187

MacChesney, Nathan W., 412
MacCracken, William P., Jr., 235, 354–55
Mager, Jennie, 338
Mallery, Otto, 134
    countercyclical public works proposal, 135–36, 360
Mann, Horace, 402, 403, 412, 419
Maple Flooring Manufacturers Association v. United States, 205, 323
Marconi, Guglielmo, 232
Marcosson, Isaac, 85, 396
Marshall, R. C., 223
Martineau, John, 386, 387
Mayer, Louis B., 53, 330, 406
McAdoo, William Gibbs, 119, 400
McCarthy, P. H., 61
McChord, C. C., 211
McCormick, Sen. J. Medill (R-IL), 248
McCormick, Vance, 12, 59
McDonald, Eugene F., Jr., 320
McNab, John L., 409
McNary, Sen. Charles L. (R-OR), 342
McNary-Haugen Bill, 270, 272, 313–14, 342–44, 397, 405, 409, 410, 420
McNeil, William H., 241
McPherson, Aimee Semple, 352–53

Mellon, Andrew, 88, 102, 103, 172, 220, 315, 324, 333, 349, 383
    Coolidge cabinet, domination of, 270, 273
    Dawes Plan, 282, 283
    election of 1928, 399–400, 405, 407, 408, 410, 422
    European debt policy, 242–44, 306–7
    gold standard, attitude toward, 308, 368
    interest rates, attitude toward, 304–5, 368–69
    oil conservation, 361
    tax policy, disagreement with Hoover over, 227
Meloney, Marie (Mrs. William Brown Meloney), 223–24, 256, 421
merchant marine, 38, 108, 292–94, 346, 428
Merritt, Ralph, 51, 52, 56–57, 63, 95–99, 271, 318, 398
Meyer, Eugene, 65, 115, 383
Milbank, Jeremiah, 55
Miller, Adolph, 144, 304, 368–69
Miller, Franklin T., 222
Miller, Nathan, 65, 253
Mills, Frederick C., 359
Mills, Ogden, 368, 399, 410
Minthorn, Henry John, 184
Minthorn, Matilda (Mrs. Henry John Minthorn), 184, 267
Mississippi River Commission, 372, 377, 385, 388
Mississippi Valley Association, 349, 371
Mississippi Valley flood (1927), x, 337, 350, 355, 371–90, 392–94, 425 fig. 21.2. *See also* African Americans
    boosts Hoover's reputation, 390
    Colored Advisory Commission (Moton Committee), 379–82
    costs, 389–90
    deaths, 389
    health concerns, 384–85
    plans for flood control, 385–89
    reconstruction, 383–90
    refugee camps, 374, 375–77
    role of National Guard, 378, 379–80
Mitchell, Wesley Clair, 133, 143, 146, 195–96, 359–60
Moreau, Émile, 368
Morgan, J. P. and Company, 22, 75, 107, 242, 283–84, 334
Morgenthau, Henry, 16
Morrow, Dwight, 321
Moses, Sen. George H. (R-NH), 409, 414
Moton, Robert R., 379, 381–82
    Moton Commission (*see* African Americans)

Murray, William S., 123, 257, 297
Muscle Shoals, 124–25, 253–54, 300–301, 319, 350–52

Nansen, Fridtjof, 19, 150
Nash, Bradley, 404
Nash, George, ix, 272
National Amateur Athletic Federation (NAAF), 85, 183–84, 190–91, 276, 277–78
National Association for the Advancement of Colored People (NAACP), 379–80
National Association of Broadcasters, 320
National Association of Manufacturers, 203
National Bureau of Economic Research, 133, 143
National Child Health Council, 164
National Child Welfare Association, 162
National Coal Association, 118
National Conference on Outdoor Recreation, 85, 201, 274–75
National Housing Committee for Congested Areas, 358
National Parks Association, 236, 275–76
National Research Council, 133
National Security and Defense Fund, 5
National Women's Party, 421
Neff, Pat M., 291
New, Sen. Harry S. (R-IN), 141
New Economic Policy, 150, 157, 159
New England Bankers Association, 391
New England Council, 391–92
New England flood (1927), x, 338, 390–94
    costs, 392
    deaths, 390
    reconstruction, 391–92
    Red Cross, conflict with, 392
New Orleans, 377–78
Niagara Falls, 317–18
Norman, Montagu, 283, 305, 368
Norris, Sen. George (R-NE), 101, 115, 142–43
    election of 1928, 397, 401, 409
    Muscle Shoals, 125, 319, 350–51
Novarro, Ramon, 330

O'Connor, T. V., 293
oil, 258–59
    antitrust law, problem of, 259
    Federal Oil Conservation Board, 259, 316, 360–61
    Requa, Mark, 258
    Teapot Dome, 258
oil pollution of coastal waters, 125–26
O'Malley, Henry, 236, 237, 238

Ormsbee, Thomas H., 406
Outhwaite, Leonard, 382

Paderewski, Ignace, 14, 15–16
Page, Frank, 165, 167, 169, 170, 171
Palmer, A. Mitchell, 38
Palmer, Leigh C., 293
Parker, John, 383, 386
Park Realty Company, 33
Patten, Simon, 201
Payne, John Barton, 269, 276, 373, 374, 392
Peacock, Ralph, 89–90
Peek, George N., 210, 313–14, 343
Pejepscot Paper Company, 33, 278, 285, 332–33
Penrose, Sen. Boies (R-PA), 101, 102
Percy, Sen. Le Roy (D-MS), 386
Pershing, General John Joseph, 4, 17, 18, 23, 82, 128 fig. 7.3
Pierce, Dante, 405
Piłsudski, Józef, 14, 16
Pinchot, Gifford, 60, 101, 251, 257, 298, 328, 344
Poincaré, Henri, 4
Poland, 11, 14–16, 20, 77, 79, 158
    anti-Semitism, 15–16
    expansionism, 16, 78, 83
    gratitude to Hoover, 25–26
    Polish National Committee, 15
Polish Corridor, 15
Polish National Relief Committee, 15
Poso Land and Products Company. *See* Hoover farm
Poston, E. M., 135, 140, 216
Pratt, Ruth, 421
President's Conference on Home Building and Home Ownership, 85
Pringle, Henry F., 413
prohibition, 404
protectionism. *See* tariff

Quinn, Cyril J. C., 154

radio, x, 232–34, 259, 296–97, 319–20, 428
    advertising, 233, 296
    conference (1922), 233–34
    conference (1923), 259
    conference (1924), 296–97
    conference (1925), 320
    federal regulation, 233–34, 296, 320, 352–54
    growth, during 1920s, 233
    innovation, during World War I, 233
    Radio Act of 1927, 353–54

railroads, xi, 38, 119–22, 317, 326, 428
  consolidation proposals, 217, 252, 294–95,
    344
  Esch-Cummins Act (Transportation Act of
    1920), 120, 217, 294
  Federal Control Act (1918), 119
  labor and strikes, 120, 121–22, 215,
    217–18, 317, 344
  Railroad Administration, 214
  Railway Labor Act (1926), 344
  rate restructuring, Hoover proposes,
    251–52
Railway Labor Board, 120, 121, 135, 217,
  218, 317, 344
  Board of Mediation, 344
Raker, Rep. John E. (D-CA), 301
Ramsey, Alice, 91
Ransdell, Sen. Joseph E. (D-LA), 388
Raskob, John J., 88, 366
Recent Economic Changes in the United States,
  146, 177, 359–60, 363
recession of 1921, 108
Reclamation Service (Bureau), 124, 136, 291
Red Cross, 20, 23, 84–85, 168, 192, 269
  and Mississippi River flood of 1927,
    373–77, 379–81, 383–85, 387, 390,
    393–94
  and New England flood of 1927, 390–92,
    393–94
Redfield, William C., 36, 75, 88, 107
Red Scare, 38
Reed, Sen. James A. (D-MO), 52, 83
Reid, Rep. Frank R. (R-IL), 388–89
Reid, Helen Rogers (Mrs. Ogden Reid), 82
relief. *See* American Relief Administration
  (ARA); Commission for Relief in Belgium
  (CRB); Mississippi Valley flood; New Eng-
  land flood; Russia
reparations, x, 7, 22, 71–73, 77, 230–31, 243,
  247, 306–7. *See also* Germany
  Dawes Plan, 282–84, 305, 307, 362, 363
Requa, Mark, 56, 60, 258, 271, 290, 316, 318
  in election of 1928, 395, 398
Richardson, Friend W., 271, 398
Richey, Larry, 406
Rickard, Abbie (Mrs. Edgar Rickard), 27,
  90–91, 329, 330
Rickard, Edgar, 33, 50, 66, 96–97, 98, 188,
  327, 329, 330, 332–33, 339, 365, 381
  American Child Health Association, 165,
    167, 168, 169, 171, 173, 176
  election of 1928, 396, 398, 399, 405, 408,
    410
Riddell, G. C., 316
Ringland, Arthur, 274

Rio Grande River, x, 290–92, 329, 347
Rist, Charles, 368
Robinson, Henry M., 41, 98, 247, 271, 282,
  366
Robinson, Sen. Joseph T. (D-AR), 411
Rockefeller, John D., 82
Rockefeller, John D., Jr., 82, 277, 333
Rockefeller Foundation, 145, 146, 164, 166,
  167, 168, 174, 186, 256, 276, 297, 358,
  384–85
  Laura Spelman Rockefeller Fund, 357,
    382
Roeding, George C., 60
Rogers, James Harvey, 363
Rogers, Will, 398, 408
Rolph, James, Jr., 272, 398
Romania, 11, 16, 308
Roosevelt, Franklin Delano, 52, 147, 223
Roosevelt, Theodore, 49, 123, 402
Roosevelt, Theodore, Jr., 274
Root, Elihu, 67, 68, 333
Rosenthal, Benjamin J., 223
Rosenwald, Julius, 41, 277, 322, 382
Rowell, Chester, 271, 318
rubber, 247–48
  Agriculture-Commerce study committee,
    248
  Firestone, Harvey, 247, 311
  Liberia, 247
  Stevenson Plan, 247–48, 311–13, 364–66
Russia, ix, 11, 18, 79
  famine, 129 fig. 7.4, 149–60
  economic advice, Hoover's proposal,
    19–20
  Nansen, relief proposal, 19
  prisoners, in Germany, 20–21
  refugees, 85
  "treaty of Riga," 153

Sacco, Nicola, and Bartolomeo Vanzetti, 38
salmon, 237–38
Sampson, Ruth, 27
Sanger, Margaret, 421
Sargent, John G., 352
Satterfield, Herbert W., 406
Sawyer, Charles E., 268, 269
Scellars, Jennie, 339
Schacht, Hjalmar, 368
Schieffelin, William J., 382
Schumann-Heink, Ernestine, 408
Schurman, Jacob Gould, 67
Serbia, 23, 79
Sesquicentennial (of Declaration of Indepen-
  dence), 327–29

Seth, J. O., 291–92
Shallenberger, Rep. Ashton C. (D-NE), 365
Shattuck, Edwin P., 33
Shaw, Arch W., 110, 396
Sheppard-Towner Act (1921), 161, 163, 479n2
shop councils. *See* labor
Silver, Gray, 314
Simmons, Sen. Furnifold M. (D-NC), 419
Slemp, Bascom, 402
Small, Laurine Anderson, 27, 28
Smith, Alfred (Al) E., Jr., 257, 298, 390
    in election of 1928, 400, 408, 411, 416, 417–20
Smith, Hugh M., 236
Smithsonian Institution, 326–27
Smoot, Sen. Reed (R-UT), 243, 307, 410
Smuts, General Jan, 71
Snell Resolution, 319
Sousa, John Philip, 422–23
Soviet Union. *See* Russia
Spa, Belgium, 9
Spencer, Henry C., 214
Spens, Conrad E., 216
S Street house (Washington, DC), 33, 87, 89, 90, 330, 332, 334, 412
Stackhouse, W. H., 135
standardization and waste elimination. *See* Commerce Department: standardization and waste elimination
Stanford Business School, 186–87
Stanford Research Institute, 187
Stark, Dare (McMullin), 27, 89, 90, 330
Starvation, 76
statistics, xii, 109, 110–11, 133
Steiwer, Sen. Frederick (R-OR), 407
Stephens, William D., 271, 398
Stettinius, Edward, 22
Stevens, John F., 386
Stevenson, Sir James, 247–48
St. Lawrence waterway, x, 224, 253, 290, 317–18, 347, 348–49
Stone, Harlan F., 204, 325
Strauss, Lewis, 15, 50, 56, 57, 65
Strong, Benjamin, 22, 72, 242, 304, 305, 308–9, 368, 405
sugar, 1, 116, 249–50
    Sugar Equalization Board, 1, 37
Sullivan, Mark, 47, 107, 195–96, 270, 325, 406
"Superpower," 122–23, 256–58
Supreme Council of Supply and Relief. *See* Supreme Economic Council
Supreme Economic Council, 5, 7, 21, 22
Supreme War Council, 4, 7, 20

Sutherland, Delegate Daniel A. (R-AK), 237–38, 267, 270, 313
Swing, Rep. Philip (Phil) D. (R-CA), 225–26, 318–19
    Swing-Johnson Bill, 225–26

Taft, Robert A., 55, 401
Taft, William Howard, 54, 59, 62, 402
Tapping, Amy Pryor, 169, 174
tariff, xi, 285, 309–11, 363–64
Taussig, Frank, 111
Taylor, Alonzo, 2, 186
Taylor, Frederick W., 198, 255
Teague, Charles Collins, 60
Teapot Dome, 258, 300–301
television, 354
Thomas, Albert, 219
Thompson, William H., 139
Tokyo earthquake (1923), 269
trade associations, xi, 108, 197–201
    and anti-trust laws, 202–7
Treaty of Versailles. *See* League of Nations
Trieste, 11
Trigg, Ernest T., 140, 145
Tri-State Executive Flood Control Committee, 386–89
Tumulty, Joseph, 105
Turkey, 72
Turner, Scott, 99
typhus, 24

Ukraine, 23
Underwood, Sen. Oscar W. (D-AL), 300, 319, 350–51
unemployment conference (1921), 131–47
    causes of recession, 132
    Committee on Community, Civic and Emergency Measures, 136
    Committee on Emergency Measures in Construction, 135
    Committee on Permanent Public Works, 136
    Committee on Unemployment and the Business Cycle, 140, 143–44, 240
    evaluated, 146–47
    Seasonal Operation in the Construction Industries, 145
    Standing Committee, 139–40
Union (Sacramento, CA), 49, 95
United Engineering Society, 327
United Mine Workers, 211, 421
United States Steel, 220, 221
United States v. Tile Manufacturers Credit Association, 204

Untermyer, Samuel, 204, 284
U.S. Army Corps of Engineers, 351, 372, 386
U.S. Chamber of Commerce, 135, 205, 219, 251, 294–95, 383
U.S. Children's Bureau, 161, 162, 163, 178–79
U.S. Employment Service, 37
U.S. Grain Corporation, 1, 3, 6, 13, 21, 36–37, 77, 79, 158
U.S. Liquidation Commission, 24
U.S. Public Health Service, 384–85
U.S. Shipping Board, 292–93, 346

Van Ingen, Philip, 164, 166, 167, 176
Van Kleeck, Mary, 143
Van Sweringen, Oris Paxton and Mantis James, 295
Vare, William, 407, 408
Veblen, Thorstein, 198
Vermont Flood Credit Corporation, 392
Victor, Royal, 65
Villard, Oswald Garrison, 396

Wadleigh, F. R., 216, 250
Walcott, Charles D., 327
Wallace, Henry Cantwell, 102, 104–5, 124, 209–10, 224, 265, 272, 313, 343
    lumber standardization, conflict with Hoover over, 286–88
    McNary-Haugen Bill, 286
Wallace, Lew, Jr., 46
Walsh, Sen. Thomas J. (D-MT), 301
Walworth, Arthur, 11
Warburg, Paul M., 33
war debts. *See* European war debts
War Finance Corporation, 21, 88, 115–16, 120–21, 134
war stocks. *See* European war debts
War Trade Board, 11
Washington Disarmament Conference, 94
Watson, Sen. James E. (R-IN), 397, 401, 406, 409
Watson, Sen. Tom (D-GA), 107, 158
Webb-Pomerene Act (1918), 228, 284, 366
Weeks, John W., 124, 288, 390–91
West Branch Corporation, 33, 279
Western Cotton Company. *See* Hoover farm
Western Society of Engineers, 55
Westinghouse Company, 234
Wheeler, Sen. Burton K. (D-MT), 343

Wheeler, Harry A., 63
White, Henry, 11
White, Rep. Wallace H., Jr. (R-ME), 234, 293, 297, 320, 352
White, Walter, 379–80, 418
White, William Allen, 398
White House Conference on Child Health and Protection, 85, 176–77
Whitlock, Brand, 12
Wickersham, George, 65, 67, 405
Wilbur, Ray Lyman, 53, 60, 63, 65, 176, 182, 406
    and Harding's illness and death, 268–69
    president of Stanford, 185, 187, 188
Wilkerson, James H., 218, 352
Wilkinson, Lupton A., 139, 142, 144, 396
Willebrandt, Mabel Walker, 408, 419, 421
Williams, Rep. Arthur B. (R-MI), 205
Williams, Nathan B., 202
Williams, Whiting, 140, 141
Willis, Sen. Frank B. (R-OH), 401
Wilson, Joan Hoff, 106
Wilson, William B., 41
Wilson, Woodrow, ix, 4–5, 13, 14, 18–19, 20, 29, 71–72, 105, 202, 273
    and election of 1920, 49, 57, 60, 64
Wing, David, 203
Winslow, Rep. Samuel E. (R-MA), 235, 320
Woll, Matthew, 143
Wood, Leonard, 56, 57, 63, 66
Woods, Arthur, 136, 139, 140, 141, 147
Wooley, Clarence M., 141
Wooton, Paul, 396
Work, Hubert, 258, 265, 268, 270, 291, 317, 347–48, 349, 361
    election of 1928, 399, 401, 402, 410, 412, 419
World Court, xi, 158, 241, 266, 268–69
World Economic Conference (Geneva, 1927), 366–67
World War Foreign Debt Commission. *See* European war debts

Yard, Robert Sterling, 275–76
Young, Clement C., 271, 398, 399
Young, Owen D., 41, 140, 143, 247, 253, 257, 282, 285, 290, 333, 362
Yugoslavia, 16

"Zenith decision," 352
Zieger, Robert, 147, 422